Nineteenth-Century Literature Criticism

Guide to Gale Literary Criticism Series

For criticism on	Consult these Gale series
Authors now living or who died after December 31, 1999	*CONTEMPORARY LITERARY CRITICISM (CLC)*
Authors who died between 1900 and 1999	*TWENTIETH-CENTURY LITERARY CRITICISM (TCLC)*
Authors who died between 1800 and 1899	*NINETEENTH-CENTURY LITERATURE CRITICISM (NCLC)*
Authors who died between 1400 and 1799	*LITERATURE CRITICISM FROM 1400 TO 1800 (LC)* *SHAKESPEAREAN CRITICISM (SC)*
Authors who died before 1400	*CLASSICAL AND MEDIEVAL LITERATURE CRITICISM (CMLC)*
Authors of books for children and young adults	*CHILDREN'S LITERATURE REVIEW (CLR)*
Dramatists	*DRAMA CRITICISM (DC)*
Poets	*POETRY CRITICISM (PC)*
Short story writers	*SHORT STORY CRITICISM (SSC)*
Literary topics and movements	*HARLEM RENAISSANCE: A GALE CRITICAL COMPANION (HR)* *THE BEAT GENERATION: A GALE CRITICAL COMPANION (BG)*
Asian American writers of the last two hundred years	*ASIAN AMERICAN LITERATURE (AAL)*
Black writers of the past two hundred years	*BLACK LITERATURE CRITICISM (BLC)* *BLACK LITERATURE CRITICISM SUPPLEMENT (BLCS)*
Hispanic writers of the late nineteenth and twentieth centuries	*HISPANIC LITERATURE CRITICISM (HLC)* *HISPANIC LITERATURE CRITICISM SUPPLEMENT (HLCS)*
Native North American writers and orators of the eighteenth, nineteenth, and twentieth centuries	*NATIVE NORTH AMERICAN LITERATURE (NNAL)*
Major authors from the Renaissance to the present	*WORLD LITERATURE CRITICISM, 1500 TO THE PRESENT (WLC)* *WORLD LITERATURE CRITICISM SUPPLEMENT (WLCS)*

ISSN 0732-1864

Volume 161

Nineteenth-Century Literature Criticism

Criticism of the
Works of Novelists, Philosophers, and Other
Creative Writers Who Died between 1800
and 1899, from the First Published Critical
Appraisals to Current Evaluations

Jessica Bomarito
Russel Whitaker
Project Editors

THOMSON
GALE

Detroit • New York • San Francisco • San Diego • New Haven, Conn. • Waterville, Maine • London • Munich

Nineteenth-Century Literature Criticism, Vol. 161

Project Editors
Jessica Bomarito and Russel Whitaker

Editorial
Kathy D. Darrow, Jeffrey W. Hunter, Jelena O. Krstović, Michelle Lee, Rachelle Mucha, Thomas J. Schoenberg, Noah Schusterbauer, Lawrence J. Trudeau

Data Capture
Francis Monroe, Gwen Tucker

Indexing Services
Laurie Andriot

Rights and Acquisitions
Shalice Shah-Caldwell, Kim Smilay, Andrew Specht

Imaging and Multimedia
Dean Dauphinais, Robert Duncan, Leitha Etheridge-Sims, Lezlie Light, Michael Logusz, Dan Newell, Kelly A. Quin, Denay Wilding

Composition and Electronic Capture
Kathy Sauer

Manufacturing
Rhonda Dover

Associate Product Manager
Marc Cormier

LIBRARY OF CONGRESS CATALOG CARD NUMBER 84-643008

ISBN 0-7876-8645-X
ISSN 0732-1864

Printed in the United States of America
10 9 8 7 6 5 4 3 2 1

Contents

Preface

Since its inception in 1981, *Nineteeth-Century Literature Criticism* (*NCLC*) has been a valuable resource for students and librarians seeking critical commentary on writers of this transitional period in world history. Designated an "Outstanding Reference Source" by the American Library Association with the publication of is first volume, *NCLC* has since been purchased by over 6,000 school, public, and university libraries. The series has covered more than 450 authors representing 33 nationalities and over 17,000 titles. No other reference source has surveyed the critical reaction to nineteenth-century authors and literature as thoroughly as *NCLC*.

Scope of the Series

NCLC is designed to introduce students and advanced readers to the authors of the nineteenth century and to the most significant interpretations of these authors' works. The great poets, novelists, short story writers, playwrights, and philosophers of this period are frequently studied in high school and college literature courses. By organizing and reprinting commentary written on these authors, *NCLC* helps students develop valuable insight into literary history, promotes a better understanding of the texts, and sparks ideas for papers and assignments. Each entry in *NCLC* presents a comprehensive survey of an author's career or an individual work of literature and provides the user with a multiplicity of interpretations and assessments. Such variety allows students to pursue their own interests; furthermore, it fosters an awareness that literature is dynamic and responsive to many different opinions.

Every fourth volume of *NCLC* is devoted to literary topics that cannot be covered under the author approach used in the rest of the series. Such topics include literary movements, prominent themes in nineteenth-century literature, literary reaction to political and historical events, significant eras in literary history, prominent literary anniversaries, and the literatures of cultures that are often overlooked by English-speaking readers.

NCLC continues the survey of criticism of world literature begun by Thomson Gale's *Contemporary Literary Criticism* (*CLC*) and *Twentieth-Century Literary Criticism* (*TCLC*).

Organization of the Book

An *NCLC* entry consists of the following elements:

■ The **Author Heading** cites the name under which the author most commonly wrote, followed by birth and death dates. Also located here are any name variations under which an author wrote, including transliterated forms for authors whose native languages use nonroman alphabets. If the author wrote consistently under a pseudonym, the pseudonym will be listed in the author heading and the author's actual name given in parenthesis on the first line of the biographical and critical information. Uncertain birth or death dates are indicated by question marks. Single-work entries are preceded by a heading that consists of the most common form of the title in English translation (if applicable) and the original date of composition.

■ The **Introduction** contains background information that introduces the reader to the author, work, or topic that is the subject of the entry.

■ A **Portrait of the Author** is included when available.

■ The list of **Principal Works** is ordered chronologically by date of first publication and lists the most important works by the author. The genre and publication date of each work is given. In the case of foreign authors whose works have been translated into English, the list will focus primarily on twentieth-century translations, selecting those works most commonly considered the best by critics. Unless otherwise indicated, dramas are dated by first performance, not first publication. Lists of **Representative Works** by different authors appear with topic entries.

- Reprinted **Criticism** is arranged chronologically in each entry to provide a useful perspective on changes in critical evaluation over time. The critic's name and the date of composition or publication of the critical work are given at the beginning of each piece of criticism. Unsigned criticism is preceded by the title of the source in which it appeared. All titles by the author featured in the text are printed in boldface type. Footnotes are reprinted at the end of each essay or excerpt. In the case of excerpted criticism, only those footnotes that pertain to the excerpted texts are included. Criticism in topic entries is arranged chronologically under a variety of subheadings to facilitate the study of different aspects of the topic.

- A complete **Bibliographical Citation** of the original essay or book precedes each piece of criticism.

- Critical essays are prefaced by brief **Annotations** explicating each piece.

- An annotated bibliography of **Further Reading** appears at the end of each entry and suggests resources for additional study. In some cases, significant essays for which the editors could not obtain reprint rights are included here. Boxed material following the further reading list provides references to other biographical and critical sources on the author in series published by Thomson Gale.

Indexes

Each volume of *NCLC* contains a **Cumulative Author Index** listing all authors who have appeared in a wide variety of reference sources published by Thomson Gale, including *NCLC*. A complete list of these sources is found facing the first page of the Author Index. The index also includes birth and death dates and cross references between pseudonyms and actual names.

A **Cumulative Nationality Index** lists all authors featured in *NCLC* by nationality, followed by the number of the *NCLC* volume in which their entry appears.

A **Cumulative Topic Index** lists the literary themes and topics treated in the series as well as in *Classical and Medieval Literature Criticism, Literature Criticism from 1400 to 1800, Twentieth-Century Literary Criticism,* and the *Contemporary Literary Criticism* Yearbook, which was discontinued in 1998.

An alphabetical **Title Index** accompanies each volume of *NCLC*, with the exception of the Topics volumes. Listings of titles by authors covered in the given volume are followed by the author's name and the corresponding page numbers where the titles are discussed. English translations of foreign titles and variations of titles are cross-referenced to the title under which a work was originally published. Titles of novels, dramas, nonfiction books, and poetry, short story, or essay collections are printed in italics, while individual poems, short stories, and essays are printed in roman type within quotation marks.

In response to numerous suggestions from librarians, Thomson Gale also produces an annual paperbound edition of the *NCLC* cumulative title index. This annual cumulation, which alphabetically lists all titles reviewed in the series, is available to all customers. Additional copies of this index are available upon request. Librarians and patrons will welcome this separate index; it saves shelf space, is easy to use, and is recyclable upon receipt of the next edition.

Citing *Nineteenth-Century Literature Criticism*

When citing criticism reprinted in the Literary Criticism Series, students should provide complete bibliographic information so that the cited essay can be located in the original print or electronic source. Students who quote directly from reprinted criticism may use any accepted bibliographic format, such as University of Chicago Press style or Modern Language Association style.

The examples below follow recommendations for preparing a bibliography set forth in *The Chicago Manual of Style,* 14th ed. (Chicago: The University of Chicago Press, 1993); the first example pertains to material drawn from periodicals, the second to material reprinted from books:

Guerard, Albert J. "On the Composition of Dostoevsky's *The Idiot.*" *Mosaic: A Journal for the Interdisciplinary Study of Literature* 8, no. 1 (fall 1974): 201-15. Reprinted in *Nineteenth-Century Literature Criticism.* Vol. 119, edited by Lynn M. Zott, 81-104. Detroit: Gale, 2003.

Berstein, Carol L. "Subjectivity as Critique and the Critique of Subjectivity in Keats's *Hyperion.*" In *After the Future: Postmodern Times and Places,* edited by Gary Shapiro, 41-52. Albany, N. Y.: State University of New York Press, 1990. Reprinted in *Nineteeth-Century Literature Criticism.* Vol. 121, edited by Lynn M. Zott, 155-60. Detroit: Gale, 2003.

The examples below follow recommendations for preparing a works cited list set forth in the *MLA Handbook for Writers of Research Papers,* 5th ed. (New York: The Modern Language Association of America, 1999); the first example pertains to material drawn from periodicals, the second to material reprinted from books:

Guerard, Albert J. "On the Composition of Dostoevsky's *The Idiot.*" *Mosaic: A Journal for the Interdisciplinary Study of Literature* 8. 1 (fall 1974): 201-15. Reprinted in *Nineteenth-Century Literature Criticism.* Ed. Lynn M. Zott. Vol. 119. Detroit: Gale, 2003. 81-104.

Berstein, Carol L. "Subjectivity as Critique and the Critique of Subjectivity in Keats's *Hyperion.*" *After the Future: Postmodern Times and Places.* Ed. Gary Shapiro. Albany, N. Y.: State University of New York Press, 1990. 41-52. Reprinted in *Nineteeth-Century Literature Criticism.* Ed. Lynn M. Zott. Vol. 121. Detroit: Gale, 2003. 155-60.

Suggestions are Welcome

Readers who wish to suggest new features, topics, or authors to appear in future volumes, or who have other suggestions or comments are cordially invited to call, write, or fax the Associate Product Manager:

Associate Product Manager, Literary Criticism Series
Thomson Gale
27500 Drake Road
Farmington Hills, MI 48331-3535
1-800-347-4253 (GALE)
Fax: 248-699-8054

Acknowledgments.

The editors wish to thank the copyright holders of the criticism included in this volume and the permissions managers of many book and magazine publishing companies for assisting us in securing reproduction rights. We are also grateful to the staffs of the Detroit Public Library, the Library of Congress, the University of Detroit Mercy Library, Wayne State University Purdy/Kresge Library Complex, and the University of Michigan Libraries for making their resources available to us. Following is a list of the copyright holders who have granted us permission to reproduce material in this volume of *NCLC*. Every effort has been made to trace copyright, but if omissions have been made, please let us know.

COPYRIGHTED MATERIAL IN *NCLC*, VOLUME 161, WAS REPRODUCED FROM THE FOLLOWING PERIODICALS:

COPYRIGHTED MATERIAL IN *NCLC*, VOLUME 161, WAS REPRODUCED FROM THE FOLLOWING BOOKS:

PHOTOGRAPHS AND ILLUSTRATIONS APPEARING IN *NCLC*, VOLUME 161, WERE RECEIVED FROM THE FOLLOWING SOURCES:

Thomson Gale Literature Product Advisory Board

The members of the Thomson Gale Literature Product Advisory Board—reference librarians from public and academic library systems—represent a cross-section of our customer base and offer a variety of informed perspectives on both the presentation and content of our literature products. Advisory board members assess and define such quality issues as the relevance, currency, and usefulness of the author coverage, critical content, and literary topics included in our series; evaluate the layout, presentation, and general quality of our printed volumes; provide feedback on the criteria used for selecting authors and topics covered in our series; provide suggestions for potential enhancements to our series; identify any gaps in our coverage of authors or literary topics, recommending authors or topics for inclusion; analyze the appropriateness of our content and presentation for various user audiences, such as high school students, undergraduates, graduate students, librarians, and educators; and offer feedback on any proposed changes/enhancements to our series. We wish to thank the following advisors for their advice throughout the year.

The Personal History of David Copperfield

Charles Dickens

The following entry presents criticism of Dickens's novel *The Personal History of David Copperfield* (1850). For discussion of Dickens's complete career, see *NCLC*, Volume 3; for discussion of the novel *Bleak House*, see *NCLC*, Volume 8; for discussion of the novel *Great Expectations*, see *NCLC*, Volume 26; for discussion of the novel *Oliver Twist*, see *NCLC*, Volume 37; for discussion of the novel *Hard Times for These Times*, see *NCLC*, Volume 50; for discussion of the novel *A Tale of Two Cities*, see *NCLC*, Volume 86; for discussion of the novel *Our Mutual Friend* see *NCLC*, Volume 105; for discussion of the novel *Little Dorrit*, see *NCLC*, Volume 113.

INTRODUCTION

The eighth novel published by Charles Dickens, and one of his most enduringly popular, *The Personal History of David Copperfield* (1850) is regarded, in part, as its renowned Victorian author's fictional autobiography. Viewed as a moving study of maturation and recollection, *David Copperfield* is usually categorized as a *Bildungsroman* centered on the personal development of its titular protagonist. It features a sustained, first-person narrative by Copperfield as he relates his imaginative recollection of the past, from his idyllic youth, struggles in early childhood, schooling, maturation, tragic first marriage, budding career as a novelist, and eventual union with the serene Agnes Wickfield. In addition to its narrative core based upon Dickens's personal childhood experiences, the work is said to share certain thematic affinities with his earlier novel *Oliver Twist* (1838) and to prefigure the author's renowned *Great Expectations* (1861), both of which likewise trace the lives of sympathetic boy heroes.

BIOGRAPHICAL INFORMATION

Dickens was the son of John Dickens, a minor government official who persistently lived beyond his financial means and was eventually sent to debtor's prison. As a boy, Dickens was forced to work in Warren's Blacking Factory, pasting labels on bottles of boot-black for meager wages until his father was released. Humiliated and demoralized by this labor, Dickens remained deeply troubled by it over the course of his life, and additionally so by his mother's suggestion that he continue at the factory even after his father's debts were repaid. Following his employment as a law clerk in his late teens, Dickens worked as a journalist and began to compose a series of short stories and sketches that were published in various London periodicals, and later collected to form his first book, *Sketches by Boz* (1836). The appearance of his first novel, *Posthumous Papers of the Pickwick Club* (1837), established a popular and critical recognition of Dickens that would grow over the ensuing decades to a degree rarely equaled in English letters. Dickens's *David Copperfield,* was, like all of his novels, published in a series of monthly installments, and first appeared between May 1849 and November 1850. Usually regarded as Dickens's most autobiographical work, *David Copperfield* was his earliest novel narrated entirely in the first person. As popular as his previous publications, it is viewed as a transitional work in Dickens's oeuvre, completed prior to his so-called "dark period" of the 1850s and 1860s, during which he produced pessimistic social critiques, such as those of *Bleak House* (1853), *Hard Times for These Times* (1854), and *Our Mutual Friend* (1865).

PLOT AND MAJOR CHARACTERS

Critics have pointed to numerous parallels between the early portions of *David Copperfield* and events in Dickens's own life. Like his creator, the young Copperfield is forced as a child to work gluing labels to bottles, and later finds employment as a law clerk. He also eventually becomes a novelist, and in so doing lays out the course of his past life in reminiscing the events of *David Copperfield*. The novel opens with Copperfield's thought: "Whether I shall turn out to be the hero of my own life, or whether that station will be held by anybody else, these pages must show." Looking back to his childhood, he recalls the death of his father, and his early happiness with his mother, Clara, and nurse Peggotty. The remarriage of Clara to the cruel Mr. Murdstone, however, torments the young Copperfield. After being beaten by Murdstone, Copperfield bites his foster father on the hand and is sent away to school as punishment. Meanwhile, Peggotty accompanies Copperfield to Yarmouth and introduces him to her brother, Mr. Peggotty, along with the man's adopted children, Ham and Little Em'ly. Once at Mr. Creakle's school, Copperfield meets the downtrodden Tom Traddles and the wealthy, self-absorbed James Steerforth. Befriending both, an adulatory Copperfield fails to realize that the charismatic Steerforth seeks nothing more than to use this naive boy for his own purposes, and thinks nothing of betraying him. The death of Copperfield's mother prompts the youth's return home to one of the most degrading experiences of his early years: at the age of ten, he begins to work at Murdstone and Grinby's dreary warehouse, washing and affixing labels to wine bottles. Through the ordeal, and throughout the novel, Copperfield maintains the qualities that define his character, proving himself to be generous, loyal, diligent, trusting, and above all, earnest. In London, he secures lodging with the magnanimous but perpetually insolvent Mr. Micawber. Eventually hounded by his creditors, Micawber forsakes the city, and Copperfield goes in search of his aunt, Miss Betsey Trotwood. Miss Betsey secures Copperfield lodging with Mr. Wickfield and a position at the school of Mr. Strong. Over time, Copperfield and Wickfield's daughter Agnes become as close as brother and sister. Meanwhile, Dickens introduces the villainous Uriah Heep, Wickfield's clerk. After a visit to Yarmouth, in which James Steerforth reappears and becomes acquainted with Peggotty and his family, Copperfield returns to London and begins work in the law office of Spenlow and Jorkins. Soon, he meets Mr. Spenlow's daughter Dora and is love-struck. Trouble brews in Yarmouth, where Little Em'ly has broken her engagement with Ham, choosing Steerforth instead in the vain hope of bettering her social station. Back in London, the death of Mr. Spenlow, who found Copperfield a poor match for his daughter, allows Copperfield and Dora to marry. Their union is felicitous for a time, despite Dora's complete inability to run a household. Uriah Heep, meanwhile, causes tension between Mr. Strong and his wife Annie, claiming an affair, but the couple is soon reconciled, and the lie disproved. Events are less fortuitous for Little Em'ly. Steerforth has forsaken her, and she too disappears. Copperfield and Mr. Peggotty begin a search and eventually find her. The Micawbers discover that Uriah Heep has been cheating his business partner Mr. Wickfield, and Heep is sent to prison. Afterwards, the Micawbers, along with Mr. Peggotty and Little Em'ly, depart for Australia to make a new start. Back in Yarmouth, Steerforth reappears. Sailing in a torrential storm, he is shipwrecked. Not knowing who the sailor is, Ham rushes to rescue him, but both perish. Thereafter, Copperfield's young wife Dora grows ill and dies as well. Devastated, Copperfield discovers the comfort of Agnes, and the two eventually marry. Copperfield at last finds true happiness with his new wife and family and with his growing literary prospects as a young novelist.

MAJOR THEMES

The conventional thematic interpretation of *David Copperfield* considers the novel an example of the Victorian *Bildungsroman,* which traces the arc of Copperfield's emotional maturation, worldly education, and eventual conformity to the positive moral values of his society. In a complementary view, the work can be seen as a *Künstlerroman,* with a parallel thematic orientation more principally focused on Copperfield's development as an artist. A standard, twentieth-century thematic understanding of *David Copperfield* was first articulated by Gwendolyn B. Needham in 1954, and identifies Copperfield's efforts to discipline his "undisciplined heart," or more specifically to balance his trusting, affective nature by cultivating emotional control and obtaining both maturity and wisdom of the world. Commentators also view *David Copperfield* as a novel chiefly concerned with memory. Exemplified by Copperfield's narrative recollection and reconstruction of his life, this theme highlights a tension between his innocent, childhood observations and mature, reflective understanding of past events. Issues of family and social class also figure prominently in the novel. In an effort to locate partial surrogates for his lost father and mother in his transition from neglected child to loving husband, Copperfield looks to Peggotty, the Micawbers, his Aunt Betsey, Dora, and finally Agnes, with whom he can establish his idyllic vision of domestic bliss. The question of social class in the novel involves not only Copperfield's search for personal identity, but also the stories of James Steerforth, Little Em'ly, and Uriah Heep, whose actions question the relationship between an individual's moral worth and his or her place within the Victorian social hierarchy. *David Copperfield* is also thought to be informed by elements of spiritual allegory focused on the idealized figure of Agnes, whose perfection Copperfield learns to accept and cherish as a kind of secular transcendence of his past mistakes.

CRITICAL RECEPTION

Dickens once referred to *David Copperfield* as his "favourite child"; Victorian audiences tended to concur, making the novel one of his most well-received works. In the view of contemporary critics, the high level of esteem accorded the novel in its own day was justified, and the work continues to elicit considerable interest from modern scholars. For many such commentators, the close relationship between Dickens's own childhood and the narrative foundation of *David Copperfield* has encouraged the interpretation of autobiographical reflections within its pages, although most have been quick to acknowledge the work as characteristically imaginative, Dickensian fiction. As such, it features a host of comic, eccentric, and grotesque characters from the amusing Mr. Micawber (said to be based upon Dickens's own father) to the venomous Uriah Heep. Scholars have speculated as to the function of these and other ancillary characters in the novel, concluding that, while they bear little significance to the main plot of Copperfield's growth, they provide the necessary humor, pathos, and schematic conflict to make the novel come alive. Other characters of vital importance to a critical understanding of the story include James Steerforth, the focus of Copperfield's youthful hero-worship who is nevertheless seen as a foil to the narrator's gentle, trusting, and respectful nature. Copperfield's eventual wife, Agnes Wickfield, while frequently admired by nineteenth-century readers as the embodiment of Victorian domestic ideals of womanhood, has more generally troubled contemporary critics. Characterized as a lifeless saint or impossibly good, Agnes has been assessed by some modern commentators as a principal example of Dickens's infamously flat, unrealistic characters. Other critics have emphasized Agnes's symbolic function by observing that she represents exactly the qualities missing from the emotionally unruly Copperfield. In addition to the role of character in the novel, numerous critics have studied the narrative strategies employed by Dickens in *David Copperfield*. Recognizing

multiple levels of narrative discourse, such as those of Copperfield's childhood perception, the narrative commentary of the adult Copperfield, and Dickens's own authorial presence, critics have suggested the brilliant narrative complexity of the work, locating within it focused elements of satire, irony, social critique, and psychological suppression. Modern commentators have also begun to question the work's seemingly tidy closure strategies, which would appear to reiterate the norms of Victorian social economy. Ironies of appearance and value, deceptive narrative dissonance, and even hints of repressed sexuality thus predominate in many postmodern interpretations of Dickens's seemingly sentimental tale of maturation and middle-class success.

PRINCIPAL WORKS

Sketches by Boz, Illustrative of Every-Day Life and Every-Day People [as Boz] (sketches and short stories) 1836

*Posthumous Papers of the Pickwick Club [as Boz] (novel) 1837

*Oliver Twist (novel) 1838

*The Life and Adventures of Nicholas Nickleby (novel) 1839

*Barnaby Rudge (novel) 1841

*The Old Curiosity Shop (novel) 1841

American Notes for General Circulation (travel essay) 1842

A Christmas Carol in Prose (short story) 1843

The Chimes (short story) 1844

*The Life and Adventures of Martin Chuzzlewit (novel) 1844

The Cricket on the Hearth (short story) 1845

Pictures from Italy (travel essay) 1846

*Dealings with the Firm of Dombey and Son (novel) 1848

The Haunted Man, and The Ghost's Bargain (short stories) 1848

*The Personal History of David Copperfield (novel) 1850

*Bleak House (novel) 1853

*Hard Times for These Times (novel) 1854

*Little Dorrit (novel) 1857

*A Tale of Two Cities (novel) 1859

*Great Expectations (novel) 1861

The Uncommercial Traveller (sketches and short stories) 1861

*Our Mutual Friend (novel) 1865

No Thoroughfare [with Wilkie Collins] (play) 1867

The Mystery of Edwin Drood (unfinished novel) 1870

*All of Dickens's novels were originally published serially in magazines, usually over periods of one to two years.

CRITICISM

Gwendolyn B. Needham (essay date September 1954)

SOURCE: Needham, Gwendolyn B. "The Undisciplined Heart of David Copperfield." *Nineteenth-Century Fiction* 9, no. 2 (September 1954): 81-107.

[*In the following essay, Needham discusses* David Copperfield *as a complex study of maturation, suggesting that the innate goodness of Dickens's protagonist reaches full thematic development only when Copperfield learns the virtue of emotional discipline.*]

Author, critic, and public have distinguished *The Personal History and Experience of David Copperfield the Younger* by proclaiming it their favorite of all Dickens's works. Much has been written to explain this unusual triple accord, much on the novel's merits and defects. Among many valuable discussions it is surprising that the contribution of the theme of the undisciplined heart to the novel's power has not been more thoroughly appreciated. Study of the part played by theme reveals its importance: it emphasizes and illumines the character of David, showing that his function is far greater than that of narrator; it works within the novel's frame of retrospection to shape the structure; it gives deeper significance to and closer integration of minor episodes with the novel's larger unity; thus it contributes largely to the novel's total effect and pervading tone.

The theme of the undisciplined heart, implicit from the beginning, Dickens does not state explicitly until about three-fourths through the story. In the emotion-charged climax of the Strong episode, the young wife summarizes her history in three memorable phrases which ring forever in David's mind and heart: "The first mistaken impulse of an undisciplined heart." "There can be no disparity in marriage like unsuitability of mind and purpose." "My love was founded on a rock."[1] The highly dramatic presentation is characteristic, but few have noted the significance of Dickens's long and careful preparation for it. Study of the Strong episode in relation to the whole novel demonstrates that from its inception the episode's *raison d'être* is statement and illustration of the theme, and that for maximum effect Dickens planned the episode's development to coincide

at the right moment with the emotional development of his hero. The extended dramatized statement of theme, involving five separately placed chapters, thus helps shape the order and treatment of material in the middle half of the novel.[2] How thereafter the theme's further development affects the arrangement of material is easily perceptible. Only with the entire story in mind, however, can one clearly perceive its implicit presence in the first part and then appreciate the full contribution the theme makes to the novel.

Although David declares his concern is with his personal life, not his writings, since "They express themselves, and I leave them to themselves" (p. 727; p. 889), his own story, ironically enough, has not always been left to express itself. Because Dickens included some authentic autobiographical data, many studies of the novel focus attention on Dickens's character rather than on David's, whose importance to the novel is accordingly minimized and the theme of his undisciplined heart neglected. George Gissing declares David is "decidedly not the hero of his own story";[3] Stephen Leacock dismisses him as "merely the looking-glass in which we see the other characters, the voice through which they speak. He himself has no more character than a spiritualist medium."[4] Ernest Baker believes David "emerges a real man" but leaves only "a pleasant but not very memorable impression." He comes near the truth when he says the story relates "how the boy's character was tried, his mind shaped, and his imagination fed, by all the different things that befell him,"[5] but with Dickens in mind rather than David, Baker unfortunately misses the significant last step—and *his heart disciplined*. Percy Lubbock rightly points out that "the far stretch of the past" makes the shape of the book; that the lesser dramas instead of controlling the novel "sink into the level of retrospect"; that the story is a "clear case for narration in person"; but mistakenly concludes, "Nothing was lost, because the sole need is for the reader to see what David sees; it matters little how his mind works, or what the effect of it all may be upon himself. . . . [He] offers a pair of eyes and a memory, nothing further is demanded of him."[6] Lubbock accounts for the overall form, but not for the novel's power. He fails to consider the importance of feeling and consequently underestimates the importance of David's character and overlooks the fact that within the frame of retrospection, the theme helps shape the selection and arrangement of material.

Those who regard David as only a pair of eyes and ears forget that what they see and hear is colored and heightened by David's feeling. As G. K. Chesterton observes, the novel's characters are romantically felt; "they are not exaggerated as personalities are exaggerated by an artist; they are exaggerated as personalities are exaggerated by their own friends and enemies. The strong souls are seen through the glorious haze of the emotions that strong souls really create."[7] It is David who provides this "glorious haze." We do not see his person so distinctly because we are so often within him and both feel his vibrant personality and feel through it. David's capacity for feeling, his sensitivity to the emotional tone of personal relationships, as well as his remarkable powers of observation, make his story live. Just as David's feeling pervades, colors, and gives significance to the story, so the story in turn reveals David's character and traces his emotional growth. Dickens has David as older narrator continually comment on his feeling *then* and *now,* thus skilfully indicating the varying intensity, importance, and permanence of the experiences in his emotional development while at the same time rendering their account more vivid, poignant, or humorous. The reader may recall numerous examples besides the following:

> As I recall our being opposed thus, face to face, I seem again to hear my heart beat fast and high. . . . God help me, I might have been improved for my whole life, I might have been made another creature perhaps, for life, by a kind word at that season (pp. 48-49). I admired and loved him, and his approval was return enough. It was so precious to me, that I look back on these trifles now with an aching heart (p. 98). I now approach a period of my life which I can never lose the remembrance of while I remember anything, and the recollection of which has often, without my invocation, come before me like a ghost, and haunted happier times (p. 159). There is no doubt whatever that I was a lackadaisical young spooney; but there was a purity of heart in all this still, that prevents my having quite a contemptuous recollection of it, let me laugh as I may (p. 414). I now approach an event in my life, so indelible, so awful, so bound by an infinite variety of ties to all that has preceded it, in these pages, that, from the beginning of my narrative, I have seen it growing larger and larger as I advanced, like a great tower in a plain, and throwing its forecast shadow even on the incidents of my childish days. For years after it occurred I dreamed of it often.

(p. 826)

Study in their context shows how fully and variously Dickens used such comments. They complete the characterization of the hero by revealing the kind of man the boy David has become. They clarify the characterization of other personages by enabling us to feel their personalities as David does and also perceive those qualities which his later judgment discerns. They serve to guide, summarize, or forecast the action and to connect various narrative links. But above all, these comments help to prepare and arouse the reader emotionally.

All the events and people in David's written memory are bathed in his emotions—saturated, steeped in feeling as David was steeped in Dora. This fact impresses us forcibly when we hold this novel of retrospection in our own retrospect. We can see that just as "the knots and networks of action" sink into the level of retrospect, the feeling proportionately rises and pervades the whole with its radiating light and warmth. And it is the feeling evoked by the "wonderful show" that goes straight to our heart and remains. Dickens's basic belief that "real love and truth are stronger in the end than any evil and misfortune in the world" is the foundation for the novel's prevailing tone—a melodic blend of bright humor, tender sorrow, and firm hope. A paraphrase of Dickens's words can best describe the novel's lasting effect: "Of all [the novels] that Time has in his grip, there is none that in one retrospection I can smile at half so much, and think of half so tenderly" (p. 514). Perhaps the chief artistic virtue, shining above other merits and overshadowing the defects, of that long retrospection, *David Copperfield,* is that it evokes so perfectly the emotion natural to retrospection—the mingled tears and laughter which most men feel as they review their past.

When we realize the preëminence of feeling, the importance in the novel of hero and theme becomes manifest; David is feeling's main source, the theme its guiding channel. David appropriately has traits typical of the man of sensibility—innocence, simplicity, gullibility, benevolence, tenderness. If tears be an index of sensibility, David supplies an overflow; they accompany almost every emotion—joy, grief, shame, rapture, indignation, pity—and serve to relieve and refresh, soothe and exalt. Spiritually akin to Goldsmith and Sterne in his tender humanity,[8] Dickens, had he written in the eighteenth century, might well have called David's story, "The History of a Man of Feeling." He does not represent his hero as perfect, for the model of his history is Fielding's *Tom Jones.* A domestic occurrence records the literary fact. At the time when Dickens's mind was "running like a high sea" on plans for *Copperfield,* his sixth son was born (January 16, 1849), and Dickens wrote John Forster that he had changed the child's name from the intended "Oliver Goldsmith" to "Henry Fielding," as "a kind of homage to the style of work he was now bent on beginning."[9]

The example of Fielding probably influenced also Dickens's choice of theme. Fielding, concerned with his hero's way in the world, directly warns that Tom's innate goodness is not enough; he must learn prudence:

> Let this, my young readers, be your constant maxim, that no man can be good enough to enable him to neglect the rules of prudence; nor will Virtue herself look beautiful unless she be bedecked with the outward ornaments of decency and decorum. And this precept, my worthy disciples, if you read with due attention, you will, I hope, find sufficiently enforced by examples in the following pages.

(p. 96)

Dickens's theme of the undisciplined heart encompasses this truth and goes further; natural goodness plus prudence may win affectionate respect, but one must learn a higher wisdom of the heart if he would achieve inner strength and peace. The good heart must have no "alloy of self," must love humanity as well as persons. It must be self-reliant and possess constancy and fortitude in order to be strengthened, not conquered or merely softened, by adversity and sorrow. The good heart must learn the nature of "real truth and love" in order to overcome "evil and misfortune in this world." This is the discipline which David and every good man must achieve.

By use of David as narrator Dickens cannot make, as Fielding does, an early specific statement of his theme. He must present his details and enforcing examples implicitly until David's emotional development reaches the point where David himself can perceive his mistaken impulses and can realize his heart's need for discipline. To use this method effectively, Dickens must sufficiently characterize and soundly motivate his narrator-hero so that David's revelation to the reader of his character and of the developing theme and the fact of his own continued blindness are both rendered convincing. A brief survey of the story up to the explicit statement will show how well Dickens accomplished this task.

When we analyze David's character (and do not unconsciously deprive him, as is too often done, of those traits in which he most resembles his author-father), we find that although easily classifiable as a man of feeling, he emerges a real individual, lovable as boy, youth, and man. He is sensitively alive to the world about him and throws himself with romantic fervor into whatever he does or feels. He possesses honesty, loyalty, generosity, and modesty but lacks active courage. Delicate as a child, he was soon hurt bodily or mentally. Naturally timid, he has a passive fortitude, suffers without complaint (exemplified by his childhood London experience), but exhibits courage only when driven by desperation. He uses his native talents with earnest, persevering industry to win economic success and literary fame. The pervading sensibility of his loving heart wins affection but proves his own greatest weakness. His disposition is too pliant, too easily influenced. At times his loyalty is misplaced, his feeling misdirected or mistaken; his modesty often sinks into lack of self-confidence, his judgment into self-distrust. We must remember, above all, that he is very young. He does not reach twenty-one until the story is two-thirds over, is between twenty-six and twenty-seven at its close, and is thirty-seven when he narrates his history.

Both heredity and environment play their part in forming David's character. Through Aunt Betsey we learn how much he resembles his father and mother, from both of whom he derives his sensibility, earnest heart, and too pliant disposition. Copperfield, Sr., had "a deli-

cate constitution," a dreamy romantic nature without judgment, and a predilection for "wax dolls"; his mother is "a simple affectionate Baby," who becomes an "unhappy, misdirected Baby," a "poor little fool" for trusting Murdstone. Although sure of David's principles (he follows her advice: "Never be mean in anything; never be false; never be cruel") and confident of his powers (he achieves an excellent scholastic record), Aunt Betsey fears his lack of firmness. She urges him to be "A fine firm fellow, with a will of your own . . . with strength of character that is not to be influenced, except on good reason, by anybody, or by anything. . . . That's what your father and mother might both have been, Heaven knows, and been the better for it" (p. 289).

Aunt Betsey herself is the first example we meet of an undisciplined heart, but we do not recognize her as such until Dickens gives his purposely postponed explanation. In the opening chapter we learn enough of her oddities to prepare us for her abrupt departure, never to return, when "niece Betsey" arrives a little David. Knowledge of this formidable eccentric adds to the boy's suspense (also the reader's) in his desperate journey to Dover. Later we find her harsh rigidity hides a good heart that has been closed to the world since her younger husband's deceitful villainy. Embittered by the "first mistaken impulse of her undisciplined heart," Aunt Betsey renounced mankind (save simple Mr. Dick), developed a fixation against marriage, and became an eccentric recluse. Care and responsibility for the orphaned child opens her heart first to love for David, then for mankind; thus she achieves the disciplined heart and proves it by extending the charitable love to Dora that she had denied to Mrs. Copperfield (pp. 366, 672).

Easily recognizable is the example of the undisciplined heart presented by Mrs. Copperfield, who cannot "live under coldness or unkindness" and cannot bear either responsibility or discomfort. The disastrous results of his mother's weakness are clearly revealed in David's account of his childhood sufferings, although even as older narrator he expresses love and pity for her, never criticism. Incapable of understanding the child's unhappy bewilderment when he finds her remarried, she upbraids him and Peggotty for making her unhappy, "when one has the most right to expect [the world] to be as agreeable as possible." The little boy soon perceives Mr. Murdstone's overpowering influence: "I knew as well that he could mould her pliant nature into any form he chose, as I know, now, that he did it" (p. 47). Instead of expecting comfort from his mother, the child tries to help by staying out of the Murdstones' way: "I had perception enough to know that my mother was the victim always; that she was afraid to speak to me, or be kind to me, . . . that she was not only ceaselessly afraid of her own offending, but of my offending, and uneasily watched their looks if I only moved" (p. 125). Such conditions undoubtedly increased David's timidity and deepened that distrust of himself which he later observes, "has often beset me in life on small occasions, when it would be better away." Recall how often his lack of self-assertion makes him an easy victim to the tyranny of waiters, coachmen, and landladies.

What he unconsciously misses in his mother and sorely needs, the child finds in Peggotty—a love "founded on a rock," a trust and constancy on which he can rely. When she refuses to believe he has "bad passions," David observes, "there grew up in my breast a feeling for Peggotty which I cannot very well define. She did not replace by mother—no one could do that; but she came into a vacancy in my heart, which closed upon her, and I felt towards her something I have never felt for any other human being" (p. 64). What the child sensed, the reader can fully perceive—Peggotty has the disciplined heart; his mother's childish nature prevents her loving heart from ever achieving discipline. Fortunately for David's memory of her, his mother with death "winged her way back to her calm, untroubled youth, and cancelled all the rest." Dickens clearly makes the example of Mrs. Copperfield prophetic of David's experience with Dora, another "simple, affectionate Baby."

His school experiences first reveal weaknesses in David's own character. Although the boy cannot perceive Steerforth's faults nor Traddles' merits, his detailed account exposes them, and his comments as narrator plainly intimate the course of future events. David's erroneous valuation of his two friends, so long held, is the first example of his heart's "mistaken impulses." This error, understandable in the boy, not easily excusable in the young man, is destined to bring grief to David and grave trouble to others—sorrow for which David feels partly responsible. Critics who designate the whole Steerforth episode as extraneous, an "artistic blot" on the story, have not realized fully its purpose and use.[10] Both Steerforth and Traddles, absolute foils to each other, serve as foils to David. The stories of each friend's fate are intertwined and integrated with David's own story and with his emotional growth; their parts in the novel both illustrate and develop the theme. The child's self-distrust and need for loving approval—increased by his unhappiness at home—help explain his blind hero-worship of the older Steerforth. His champion's magnetic personality long represents what he himself would like to be but is not. The comic Traddles arouses David's affection but also his laughter—"I never think of that boy but with a strange disposition to laugh, and with tears in my eyes"—and he inevitably feels superior.

Misled by appearances, David long fails to appreciate Traddles' worth, honor, and honest friendship. Years afterwards, when Traddles frees the Wickfields from Heep's net, David confesses that "this was the first occasion on which I really did justice to the clear head, and plain, patient, practical good sense of my old schoolfellow" (p. 798). Further illustrating the theme, Dickens contrasts the love of Traddles and Sophy ("the dearest girl—one in ten, you know") to that of David and Dora. Traddles and Sophy have unselfish hearts, "suitability of mind and purpose," and love "founded on a rock." David finds comparison impossible between their patient love and his and Dora's ecstasy. He cannot comprehend their unselfish consideration for Sophy's preposterous family; his impatient ardor rejects their motto, "Wait and hope." Only when the finally disciplined David returns from Europe does he appreciate how rich in happiness such a marriage as theirs will prove.

When David and Steerforth meet later, the overtures of the jaded young man, attracted by "Daisy's" fresh innocence, indicate true friendship to David's trusting heart: "As he had treated me at school differently from all the rest, I joyfully believed that he treated me in life unlike any other friend he had. I believed that I was nearer to his heart than any other friend, and my own heart warmed with attachment to him" (p. 316). Nourished by sensibility, this warmth inevitably blazes into a bright glorification of *friendship* in Steerforth that blinds David to realities. When Agnes warns of his "bad angel," Steerforth's image is so cemented in David's heart by all his "romantic feelings of fidelity and friendship" that he feels ashamed of entertaining even a momentary doubt. When Steerforth proclaims his philosophy of riding roughshod or smooth-shod over all obstacles to win a race, David merely wishes his friend had a race worthy of his great powers. Equally blinded by innocent love for Emily, David has no suspicion of the impending Yarmouth catastrophe. His shock and grief, therefore, are great when he learns of their elopement and witnesses the widespread disaster resulting from his friend's "roughshod" victory.

From this experience David could have learned much about the real nature of love, truth, and the disciplined heart, for the entire episode teaches this important lesson. In varying ways and degrees, all the principal characters, including himself, provide enforcing examples of the theme. Steerforth, Mrs. Steerforth, and Rosa Dartle, each marred by the "alloy of self," exemplify the misery to which the undisciplined heart can doom itself and bring innocent victims. David does perceive that mother and son are "alike in their moral constitution" and that her misguided mother-love has helped ruin the son. Her proud refusal to be reconciled except on her own terms perpetuates the tragedy which her son's passion has begun. Selfish in their love, she and Rosa Dartle are embittered, not softened, by grief and feel no compassion for others; they are doomed to wear out their desolate years in conflict and misery. Dickens sympathetically depicts some inner conflict in Steerforth, who passionately cries to David, "I wish to God I had had a judicious father these last twenty years! . . . I wish with all my soul I had been better guided! I wish with all my soul I could guide myself better!" (p. 338). He demonstrably lacks the discipline to deny his desires.

The Yarmouth folk all have honest hearts, but only Peggotty and Ham have completely disciplined love. Little Emily, desiring to be a lady and to shower fortune on her family, misjudges the nature of true love and follows her heart's "mistaken impulse." Through suffering and remorse she learns her lesson and thereafter devotes her life in unselfish goodness to others. Her generous uncle, rugged embodiment of simple virtue, yet has to learn pity for society's outcasts. He admits, "The time was when I thowt this girl Martha a'most like the dirt underneath my Em'ly's feet. God forgive me, there's a difference now!" and humbly cries to Martha, "God forbid as I should judge you!" (pp. 713; 720). He expresses compassion and gratitude by taking Martha with them to Australia. The calamity befalling the Yarmouth household also disciplines Mrs. Gummidge, hitherto selfishly engrossed in her own misfortunes. Aroused by others' sorrow, that "lone lorn creetur" ceases moaning about "everythink going contrairy," feels herself needed, and becomes a cheerful prop to Mr. Peggotty in his affliction.

Although David observes, "I could not meditate enough upon the lesson that I read in Mrs. Gummidge, and the new experience she unfolded to me," he is in no condition to apply the truths presented by the Yarmouth happenings. His friend's unworthiness elicits more tenderness than wisdom. He regrets the waste of qualities "that might have made him a man of a noble nature and a great name," and declares

> I am not afraid to write that I never had loved Steerforth better than when the ties that bound me to him were broken. . . . Deeply as I felt my own unconscious part in his pollution of an honest home, I believed that if I had been brought face to face with him, I could not have uttered one reproach. . . . I should have held in so much tenderness the memory of my affection for him.
>
> (p. 478)

This last sentiment, so unmistakably that of a "man of feeling," reveals David's present inability to see and correct the weaknesses of his undisciplined heart. Dickens makes his hero's failure to learn from life's harsh lesson more plausible and also more excusable by showing him already entrapped in an intoxicating new emotion. How can David, "as enraptured a young noodle as ever was carried out of his five wits by love," profit by one mistake when his whole being is absorbed in a sec-

ond? So dazzling is idealized love that even the shattered dream of friendship cannot darken it or cast a doubt on its reality. David confides,

> All this time I had gone on loving Dora harder than ever. Her idea was my refuge in disappointment and distress, and made some amends to me even for the loss of my friend. The more I pitied myself, or pitied others, the more I sought for consolation in the image of Dora. The greater the accumulation of deceit and trouble in the world, the brighter and purer shone the star of Dora high above the world. . . . I should have scouted the notion of her being simply human, like any other young lady, with indignation and contempt.
>
> If I may so express it, I was steeped in Dora. I was not merely over head and ears in love with her, but I was saturated through and through.
>
> (pp. 497-498)

This "very ecstasy of love" also prevents the young man (as age and inexperience had formerly prevented the boy) from reading correctly the lessons that life presents in the characters and fates of his Canterbury-London acquaintants: the Wickfields, the Heeps, the Strongs. Dickens links the stories of these people with each other (also "turns up" the Micawbers and brings in Traddles) and integrates them all with the story of David's developing character and life. Again we find Dickens using the principal characters to develop or illustrate some aspect of the theme. Heep, as villain, provides the contrast of the bad heart, the evil hypocrisy of which is only intensified by discipline. His fate proves that greed and cunning overreach themselves to fall before real truth and good. Agnes obviously demonstrates "the influence for all good" that can come from the disciplined heart; her father as clearly demonstrates the ruin to itself and the suffering to others that the undisciplined heart may bring. Through care for her father, Agnes learned as a child the responsibility of love and early arrived at emotional maturity. She realizes the causes of her father's warped love and its sad consequences, hides her own suffering, and strives for his restoration. Enslaved by alcohol, entrapped by Heep, Mr. Wickfield is shocked into the realization that he, rather than Uriah, is ultimately responsible for the ruin which has culminated in the villain's ignominious scheme to marry Agnes. He analyzes for David and the reader the lesson his life presents:

> "Weak indulgence has ruined me. Indulgence in remembrance, and indulgence in forgetfulness. My natural grief for my child's mother turned to disease; my natural love for my child turned to disease. . . . I have brought misery on what I dearly love, I know—*you* know! I thought it possible that I could truly love one creature in the world, and not love the rest; . . . that I could truly mourn for one creature gone out of the world, and not have some part in the grief of all who mourned. Thus the lessons of my life have been perverted. I have preyed on my own morbid, coward heart, and it has preyed on me. Sordid in my grief, sordid in my love, sordid in my miserable escape from the darker side of both, oh, see the ruin I am, and hate me, shun me!"
>
> (p. 608)

One might deduce from Dickens's wholesale use of orphans (David, Emily, Ham, Traddles, Rosa Dartle; Steerforth, Uriah, Agnes, Annie, Dora are half-orphans) that he sought by this fact partially to extenuate their weaknesses. But in his characterization of parents, Dickens stresses how often parental love itself urgently requires discipline. Not one of them—Mrs. Copperfield, Mrs. Steerforth, Mr. Wickfield, Mr. Spenlow, Mrs. Markleham, or Mrs. Heep—is wise in love's expression; each unintentionally contributes to the child's troubles or unhappiness. These examples of misguided parents imply, of course, that wise training would help; but Dickens makes clear by David's own story that every individual has to learn for himself his need and to accept responsibility for disciplining his heart. Life's teachings prove instructive to David only when he can recognize his need and can apply them correctly to himself. Dickens uses the Strong episode to present this truth. Analysis in their context of its five chapters—Numbers 16, 19, 36, 42, and 45—shows how carefully Dickens integrated its development with David's emotional growth while dramatizing the theme's explicit statement.

In Chapter Sixteen the schoolboy David meets the Strongs, first supposes Annie to be the Doctor's daughter, then observes the household of benevolent sage, pretty wife, her "Old Soldier" mother, and her virile young cousin. Although the innocent child records with equal emphasis trivial and significant details, the knowing reader detects a probable "triangle" situation. At the scene's close, the sensitive boy is puzzled by the feeling look which Annie gives her husband; the older narrator signifies its importance:

> I cannot even say of what it is expressive to me now, rising again before my older judgment. Penitence, humiliation, shame, pride, love, and trustfulness, I see them all; and in them all, I see that horror of I don't know what. . . . It made a great impression on me, and I remembered it a long time afterwards, as I shall have occasion to narrate when the time comes.
>
> (p. 260)

By Chapter Nineteen, David has finished school, is seventeen and ready to brave the world. Experienced in adolescent loves, he can now deduce why Mr. Wickfield distrusts Annie and disapproves of her intimacy with Agnes: "And now, I must confess, the recollection of what I had seen on that night when Mr. Maldon went away, first began to return upon me with a meaning it had never had, and to trouble me." He is haunted by the "impending shadow of a great affliction" that has "no distinct form in it yet" and feels "as if the tranquil sanctuary of my boyhood had been sacked before my face, and its peace and honour given to the winds" (pp. 296-297).

Two years pass before David again meets the Strongs. He has suffered from the Yarmouth happenings and has fallen in love with Dora. His aunt's loss of fortune has made work imperative. David is mature enough to profit by the economic experience but not by the emotional ones. With unusual care, Dickens provides a sound psychological basis for David's emotional state, which he pictures in detail. Neither Aunt Betsey's leading questions about Dora—"Not silly?" "Not light-headed?"—nor her intimated doubts can penetrate David's infatuation. Fearing that like his father, David has run after a "wax doll," and that like his mother, he has poured his soul into ill-judged love, his aunt urges him to seek deep earnestness. The nineteen-year old lover can neither apply the warning of his mother's mistake nor conceive his love of "unfathomable profundity" as a boy-girl attachment. At Aunt Betsey's sad reiteration of "Blind, blind, blind!" David does observe, "And without knowing why, I felt a vague, unhappy loss or want of something overshadow me like a cloud." He has no suspicion that the "want" may lie within himself or Dora. Although love's proverbial blindness is excuse enough, Dickens makes David's infatuation still more probable by having the bewitching doll an almost exact replica of the lad's mother—prettily pettish, innocently vain, truly fond, charmingly childish.

As Peggotty once filled the "vacancy" left by his mother, so does Agnes now supply the "want" David vaguely feels; as the child on his nurse, the unthinking youth depends on Agnes' love, trust, and guidance. Dickens satisfactorily accounts for David's unawareness of the real nature of his love. When the two first meet as children, the boy immediately senses Agnes' greater maturity and feels her "quiet, good, calm spirit." He associates her "tranquil brightness" then and ever after with soft light shining through a church's stained-glass window. His imagination thus colors their relationship with a religious aura that causes him to venerate her goodness and to elevate her effectually beyond his reach. Their years in the same household with Agnes as listener, helper, and adviser lead him to regard her as a sister. Poor Agnes! Revered as an angel, beloved as a sister, she is the victim of David's romantic sensibility; he has etherealized her into a superior being, a removed spirit whose rays warm his heart and guide his path.

While the youth remains blind to the real nature of his love for both Dora and Agnes, his comments as older narrator reveal the actual state and intimate the eventual course of his two loves. For example, when writing Agnes of his secret engagement to Dora, the image of his "good angel" so calms his turbulent spirit that he is "soothed into tears" and fancies that in her "sacred" presence, "Dora and I must be happier than anywhere; as if, in love, joy, sorrow, hope, or disappointment—in all emotions—my heart turned naturally there, and found its refuge and best friend" (p. 515). Another time, he declares that she so directed "the wandering ardour and unsettled purpose within me, that all the little good

I have done, and all the harm I have forborne, I solemnly believe I may refer to her. . . . Oh, Agnes, sister of my boyhood, if I had known then, what I knew long afterwards!—" (p. 546). To highlight this significant hint, Dickens contrives a typical theatrical coincidence. As David gazes at Agnes' window, thinking of her "calm, seraphic eyes," a street beggar wanders by muttering, "Blind! blind! blind!"

His "good angel" advises David of Dr. Strong's need for a secretary; the "star" of his universe inspires him to a frenzy of work; "Great is the labour; priceless the reward. . . . Dora must be won." Thus, in Chapter Thirty-six an eager worker and ardent lover enters the Strong menage and surveys the developing domestic situation. The omnipresent cousin, Jack Maldon, appears no longer a glamorous figure but a lazy dependent on the Doctor's bounty. The young worker's "ferocious virtue" condemns any man not "cutting down trees in the forest of difficulty"; the lover feels the emotional tension of a triangle. Aided by "Old Soldier's" mistaken insistence that Annie have entertainment, Maldon seems an increasing threat to the Doctor's peace and honor. With comic irony Dickens has the youth, so blind yet so sure in his knowledge of love, now wonder how the innocent old Doctor "could be so blind to what was so obvious." But David remains puzzled by Annie: "She did not look very happy, I thought; but it was a good face, or a very false one." David is filled with fears for the Strongs' future; the reader remains in suspense as to the true situation.

In the months intervening between Chapters Thirty-six and Forty-two, David's economic progress is steady but love's progress is not so smooth. Mr. Spenlow's disapproval, then his death, separate David from Dora. David's confession of a "lurking jealousy of Death" which pushes him out of Dora's thoughts shows the instinctive selfishness of undisciplined love. His very loyalty, fidelity, and earnestness help keep David an unconscious victim of his romantic imagination and mistaken impulses. His failure to make Dora understand that one cannot hew his way through a forest of difficulty with a guitar does not open his eyes to any "disparity of mind and purpose" or to the unsuitability of their union. If he occasionally wonders at Agnes' effect on him, his two fixed concepts of angel and sister satisfactorily explain it; his fascination with Dora prevents any suspicion of possible romantic love. The same reasons preclude his sensing Agnes' love for him. David's appeal to Agnes for advice in effecting his betrothal to Dora thus has a dramatic irony which Dickens makes both comic and pathetic. The youth's unconscious conflict of feelings lies beneath his conscious perplexity about himself. He thinks he is earnest, patient, and persevering, but "I get so miserable and worried, and am so unsteady and irresolute in my power of assuring myself, that I know I must want—shall I call it—reliance, of some kind? . . .

When I have come to you, at last (as I have always done), I have come to peace and happiness" (pp. 596-597). Overpowered by feeling, he bursts into tears but knows not what they mean. When Agnes tactfully suggests that he rely on Dora, his dismayed excuses also fail to enlighten. He begs that Agnes will never marry Heep out of a sacrificial sense of duty: "Say you have no such thought, dear Agnes!—much more than sister! Think of the priceless gift of such a heart as yours, of such a love as yours!" The devastating irony pierces her calmness, as well it might, and David never forgets the momentary dimming of her "bright tranquillity." Relieved by her promise, David follows her advice "to do what is right," becomes officially betrothed to Dora, and believes he is supremely happy.

Thus in Chapter Forty-two Dickens presents a decided contrast between David's bright future and that of the Strongs. It grows steadily blacker. The despicable Heep, fearful that Mrs. Strong may injure his suit by putting "my Agnes up to higher sort of game," decides to interfere. To the unsuspicious Doctor, Uriah takes "the liberty of umbly mentioning . . . the goings-on" of Annie and her cousin, who are "too sweet on one another," and contrives to strengthen his case by cunningly forcing Mr. Wickfield and David to admit their fear that the young wife had married for "worldly considerations only." The aged husband's simple trust in his wife's integrity and fidelity remains unshaken, but he is crushed by the conviction of her marital unhappiness. Although he tries to hide his sorrow, Annie feels a change, and unaware of its cause, becomes silent and sad. As the weeks pass, their daily lives grow farther and farther separate. Their friends can only stand helpless and hopeless before the dark picture of increasing domestic unhappiness.

In the months that pass before the climax in Chapter Forty-five, several significant changes occur both in David and to him. Now twenty-one, he has come "legally to man's estate" and has enough physical and mental maturity to deserve the rank. He has successfully cut down "economic" trees and launched his writing career. Young David has achieved discipline of the body and mind; his heart remains undisciplined, unselfreliant. Marriage soon teaches the boyish husband that there are trees other than economic, ones far more difficult to fell, in life's forest of difficulty. His glorification of love makes adjustment to the actualities of marriage more perplexing and makes more acute his sense of loss on the discovery that love is not all of life. He finds "all the romance of our engagement put away upon a shelf, to rust—no one to please but one another—one another to please for life," a sobering thought indeed. The poignant emotion of David's secret unhappy bewilderment lies underneath the exquisitely humorous record of love's joys and vexations in Chapter Forty-four, "Our Housekeeping." Dismayed by their scrambled household and by futile efforts to reason with his pretty wife, David asks Aunt Betsey to advise Dora. Her refusal and sane counsel make him realize what marriage means, that he and Dora alone must work out their future. Their many abortive attempts end with Dora remaining a child-wife and him bearing all the burdens. David sums up his secret feelings:

> I am far from sure, now, that it was right to do this, but I did it for my child-wife's sake. . . . The old unhappy loss or want of something had, I am conscious, some place in my heart; but not to the embitterment of my life. When I walked alone in the fine weather, and thought of the summer days when all the air had been filled with my boyish enchantment, I did miss something of the realization of my dreams; but I thought it was a softened glory of the past, which nothing could have thrown upon the present time. I did feel, sometimes, for a little while, that I could have wished my wife had been my counsellor; had had more character and purpose to sustain me, and improve me by; had been endowed with power to fill up the void which somewhere seemed to be about me. But I felt as if this were an unearthly consummation of my happiness, that never had been meant to be, and never could have been.

> (p. 681)

David here reveals both his secret unhappiness and his present inability to analyze its true causes. This inability is suggestive of an unconscious refusal to face facts too painful to bear, an unconscious desire to preserve at all costs some golden remnants of his dream while acknowledging its imperfect round. He has not yet realized that every individual ultimately must supply himself the inner strength and purpose he needs. Dickens makes clear that David is rationalizing his loss as an ideal unattainable in this life, is trying to keep the feeling submerged and indefinable.

At this appropriate point in David's emotional development, Dickens presents the climactic resolution of the Strongs' domestic unhappiness. His integration of minor incident, major interest, character, theme, humor, and emotional tone gives the scene a powerful two-fold dramatic effect. Until now David could not have felt the full impact of the emotions he witnesses and the truths he hears. Knowing David's secret unhappiness, the reader feels both the drama of the Strongs and David's own inner drama, realizes even more clearly than the dazed youth the poignant applicability of the phrases uttered by Annie's anguished heart. Dickens solves the emotional impasse of the Strong estrangement by pure feeling, uncomplicated by intellect. Simple Mr. Dick with "the mind of the heart" can do what no one else dares—he effects an éclaircissement. Disclaiming any part in her mother's exploitation of the Doctor, Annie courageously lays bare the history of her heart. She publicly avows her gratitude to the Doctor for saving her from a girlish attraction to Maldon, a "first mistaken impulse"; her deep appreciation of their marriage;

her unwavering love and fidelity. Taken alone, this scene might well be termed melodramatic; placed in the context of the novel its high dramatic tone is justified by its direct statement of theme, by its resolution of the tense Strong episode, by its marking the climax of the hero's emotional development. Annie's words have defined David's vague unhappiness; he will have to face the knowledge that his heart is undisciplined, many of its impulses mistaken. At the scene's close, Dickens signifies with a nice poetic touch its effect on David, who walks home surrounded by happy chatter:

> I was thinking of all that had been said. My mind was still running on some of the expressions used. "There can be no disparity in marriage like unsuitability of mind and purpose." "The first mistaken impulse of an undisciplined heart." "My love was founded on a rock." But we were at home; and the trodden leaves were lying under-foot, and the autumn wind was blowing.

> (pp. 700-701)

The symbols of "trodden leaves" and "autumn wind" mark the end of exuberant youth and the beginning of man's graver responsibilities, suggest the successive shocks Death is to bring to David, and foreshadow the long gloomy night of despair David undergoes before he emerges with spirit strengthened and cleansed. The novel's dominant tone of bright cheer softens for a time to harmonize with the autumn wind blowing in David's heart and with the sad events he has to relate. Unable to rationalize away his "old unhappy feeling," David very humanly first acknowledges a lack in Dora rather than in himself: "But that it would have been better for me if my wife could have helped me more, and shared the many thoughts in which I had no partner—and that this might have been—I knew" (p. 734). He knows that they must accept responsibility for their appalling household and for encouraging the delinquency of their servants but fails to make Dora understand. To effect "a perfect sympathy," he vainly tries to form Dora's mind; all he effects is a separating shadow. Forced to analyze the shadow, he finally acknowledges his own undisciplined heart, accepts responsibility for it and for making their marriage as happy as possible:

> "The first mistaken impulse of an undisciplined heart." These words of Mrs. Strong's were constantly recurring to me at this time—were almost always present to my mind. I awoke with them, often, in the night; I remember to have even read them, in dreams, inscribed upon the walls of houses. For I knew now that my own heart was undisciplined when it first loved Dora; and that if it had been disciplined, it never could have felt, when we were married, what it had felt in its secret experience.

> "There can be no disparity in marriage, like unsuitability of mind and purpose." Those words I remembered too. I had endeavoured to adapt Dora to myself, and found it impracticable. It remained for me to adapt myself to Dora; to share with her what I could, and be

happy; to bear on my own shoulders what I must, and
be happy still. This was the discipline to which I tried
to bring my heart, when I began to think. It made my
second year much happier than my first; and, what was
better still, made Dora's life all sunshine.

(p. 735)

In dying Dora achieves an understanding denied her in
life. She tells David that she was not fit to be a wife,
would not have improved, that as the years passed, he
would have wearied of his child-wife and could not
have loved her so well, that "it is better as it is." The
only plausible explanation for her perception is Dickens's phrase "mind of the heart"; Dora's love has sensed
Agnes' love for David, his for Agnes, and probably also
those changes in his feeling for herself that he thought
safely hidden. David's "undisciplined heart is chastened
heavily"; weeping, he thinks "with a blind remorse of
all those secret feelings I have nourished since my marriage. I think of every little trifle between me and Dora,
and feel the truth, that trifles make the sum of life. . . .
Would it, indeed, have been better if we had loved each
other as a boy and girl, and forgotten it? Undisciplined
heart, reply!" (p. 810).

Culminating events prevent David's experiencing the
full effect of grief, and the deaths of Ham and Steerforth augment his load of sorrow before he goes abroad.
Chapter Fifty-eight, "Absence," is one long introspec-
tion in which Dickens has his hero undergo a period of
despair and searching somewhat comparable to Carlyle's "Everlasting Nay" and "Everlasting Yea" in *Sar-
tor Resartus*. Sorrow exposes the weakness of David's
undisciplined heart as love has exhibited its mistaken
ardor:

> The desolate feeling with which I went abroad deep-
> ened and widened hourly. At first it was a heavy sense
> of loss and sorrow . . . By imperceptible degrees it be-
> came a hopeless consciousness of all that I had lost—
> love, friendship, interest; of all that had been shat-
> tered—my first trust, my first affection, the whole airy
> castle of my life; of all that remained—a ruined blank
> and waste, lying wide around me, unbroken, to the
> dark horizon.
>
> If my grief were selfish, I did not know it to be so. . . .
> From the accumulated sadness into which I fell, I had
> at length no hope of ever issuing again. . . . When
> this despondency was at its worst, I believed that I
> should die. . . . Listlessness to everything but brood-
> ing sorrow was the night that fell on my undisciplined
> heart.

(pp. 857-858)

David wanders for months with "no purpose, no sustaining soul within me anywhere" and without the fortitude to write his friends. At last he awakens to some
faint sense of beauty in nature and feels its softening

influence (typical of the "man of sensibility"). A letter
from Agnes stating the lesson of the disciplined heart
lightens his night of despair. Agnes trusts that David
would "turn affliction to good," would be exalted by
trial, that in him "sorrow could not be weakness, but
must be strength," that his purpose would gain from
grief a "firmer and higher tendency," that he would labor on, and that as he had been taught by calamities
and grief, so would he teach others. David understands
the lesson, feels the night "passing from my mind," realizes his true love for Agnes, and knows, "I was not,
and never had been, what she thought me; but that she
inspired me to be that, and I would try" (p. 860).
Through Nature's influence, restored interest in his fellow man, and his writing, David gradually wins his
way back to health—to joy in working and pleasure in
living.

The discipline his heart has gained enables him to analyze more objectively his past and present emotions:

> I cannot so completely penetrate the mystery of my
> own heart as to know when I began to think that I
> might have set its earliest and brightest hopes on Agnes.
> I cannot say at what stage of my grief it first became
> associated with the reflection that, in my wayward boy-
> hood, I have thrown away the treasure of her love. I
> believe I may have heard some whisper of that distant
> thought, in the old unhappy loss or want of something
> never to be realized, of which I had been sensible. But
> the thought came into my mind as a new reproach and
> a new regret, when I was left so sad and lonely in the
> world.
>
> If, at that time, I had been much with her, I should, in
> the weakness of my desolation, have betrayed this. . . .
> I could not have borne to lose the smallest portion of
> her sisterly affection; yet, in that betrayal, I should
> have set a constraint between us hitherto unknown.
>
> I could not forget that the feeling with which she now
> regarded me had grown up in my own free choice and
> course; that if she had ever loved me with another
> love—and I sometimes thought the time was when she
> might have done so—I had cast it away. It was noth-
> ing, now, that I had accustomed myself to think of her,
> when we were both mere children, as one who was far
> removed from my wild fancies. I had bestowed my
> passionate tenderness upon another object, and what I
> might have done I had not done; and what Agnes was
> to me, I and her own noble heart had made her.

(pp. 861-862)

David first hopes that he might "cancel the mistaken
past" and after "some indefinite probation" marry
Agnes, but suffering decides that "in right and honour" he must not turn "to the dear girl in the withering
of my hopes, from whom I had frivolously turned when
they were bright and fresh. . . . I made no effort to
conceal from myself now that I loved her—that I was
devoted to her; but I brought the assurance home to
myself that it was now too late, and that our long-
subsisting relation must be undisturbed" (p. 862).

David recalls what Dora had said might happen to their marriage, mentally lives through those future years, and admits the truth of her prediction. He resolves to be corrected by that visioned future as if it had been a reality and determines to convert what might have been between him and Agnes into a means "of making me more self-denying, more resolved, more conscious of myself, and my defects and errors." After three years' absence, David is ready to return home, confident that he "could think of the past now, gravely, but not bitterly, and could contemplate the future in a brave spirit" (p. 874). He has learned that real love has no "alloy of self," that sorrow should strengthen, and—his final step toward emotional maturity—that one must himself develop the firmness, fortitude, and courage to guide his life in the right path. Knowledge, however, is not enough; the discipline his heart has learned must be tested by trial and proved by action.

Dickens skilfully contrives a test which, plausibly motivated by his hero's character, dramatizes the novel's last bit of action. David's romantic nature has led him from the perception that unselfish love is capable of renunciation to the mistaken conclusion that for him renunciation is inevitable; his sensibility deepens the belief that he deserves thus to expiate his past mistakes; his conviction of her superiority and his modest deprecation of his own powers of attraction quench any hope of winning Agnes. A confident man of action would have unhesitatingly tried his fortune. But Aunt Betsey's well-meaning ambiguous hints only confirm David's conviction that Agnes loves another; he feels intensely his duty to act the part of brother and friend, to make her feel free to confide as he had confided his past loves to her. His awkward efforts only torture them both. When his suffering finally senses hers, his feverish sensibility promptly concludes that she has discovered his love and hesitates to confide her secret for fear of paining him! Crushed by failure in his "brother" role, he nerves himself to the sacrificial test:

> "For Heaven's sake, Agnes, let us not mistake each other after all these years, and all that has come and gone with them! I must speak plainly. If you have any lingering thought that I could envy the happiness you will confer; . . . that I could not, from my removed place, be a contented witness of your joy—dismiss it, for I don't deserve it! I have not suffered quite in vain. You have not taught me quite in vain. There is no alloy of self in what I feel for you."
>
> (p. 906)

Having thus proved his hero's disciplined heart, Dickens rewards him with Agnes' hand and life-long love.

The theme's illumination of his "Personal History" shows David to be, while not a "heroic" figure, a very human hero who struggles with "many opportunities wasted, many erratic and perverted feelings constantly at war within his breast" (p. 638), and shows the story of his development to be paramount. In his conclusion Dickens demonstrates in the fates accorded the characters that "real love and truth are in the end stronger than evil and misfortune in this world." This affirmation cannot be dismissed as mere shallow optimism; his theme qualifies that only the disciplined heart can discern the nature of real love and truth, thus gaining power to conquer, and that such discipline is difficult and painful to achieve. Discipline alone is not enough; natural goodness, while essential, alone is not enough. Dickens shows by his villains that discipline intensifies the evil in their hearts, and shows by many examples that the undisciplined heart also can cause misery and trouble. Although delineated tenderly, Dora and Mrs. Copperfield exemplify that no matter how loving the heart, if mind and character are weak, discipline cannot be learned. Incapable of responsibility in the world, such people must be treated, loved, and protected as children. Dickens sympathetically allows them to die young—perhaps the kindest fate Life can provide for them and theirs. The theme helps control Dickens's use of poetic justice, making it more discriminating than is usual with him. The noble Ham and erring Steerforth meet the same fate. The good, including David, must earn their reward, the highest of which is not material gain but inner peace and strength; the bad are not all punished "to fit the crime." Creakle becomes a magistrate Heep and Littimer are incarcerated, not "pulverized." Dickens's humor also salts the saccharinity and lightens the solemnity of poetic justice. The two arch-villains make captivity comfortable by duping Creakle with their expert rendition of his own hypocritical pose of Christian virtue. Rewarded by a judgeship and prosperity, Traddles and Sophy remain squeezed by their preposterously overcrowded household. That inimitable comic pair, the elastic Micawbers, whose falls, springs, and leaps have given such delight, are rewarded for their great "Spring of no common magnitude" to Australia. The land of the kangaroo appropriately proves their natural habitat; Micawber's final spring into public prominence as a magistrate is superbly extolled by his own magniloquent pen.

Dickens's study of emotional maturity deals with simple fundamentals; a more complex and profound study could hardly be expected from a man who apparently never learned to discipline his heart. Whether he realized the fact or to what extent his hero's achievement expresses a conscious or unconscious wish-fulfillment of his own are questions for his biographers to decide and a subject for another essay. Considering the novel in and by itself, we see that Dickens's use of theme helps shape the novel's inner structure, shows David the hero, and gives closer integration and deeper significance to his colorful and moving history. Understanding of the theme deepens our appreciation of *David Copperfield.*

Notes

1. A survey of Dickens criticism reveals that many enthusiastic admirers have loved him well, but not always wisely. I wish to give credit to a wise lover, my colleague, Mrs. Elizabeth R. Homann, for first suggesting the significance of these phrases to me.

2. The edition of the novel used in this discussion is the Modern Library edition (New York, n. d.). Of the novel's 64 chapters and 923 pages, the five chapters spaced between Chapters 15 and 46 (Numbers 16, 19, 36, 42, and 45) begin on page 237 and end on page 701. Of the book's initial 20 installments, the episode's development extends from the 6th to the 16th installment.

3. *Charles Dickens* (London, 1898), p. 101.

4. *Charles Dickens* (New York, 1936), p. 144; see also Bruce McCullough, *Representative English Novelists: Defoe to Conrad* (New York, 1946), pp. 142-143.

5. *History of the English Novel* (New York, 1936), VII, 288; 308; 239.

6. *The Craft of Fiction* (New York, 1929), p. 130.

7. *Charles Dickens* (London, 1910), pp. 194-195.

8. Gissing, p. 29; p. 182.

9. *The Life of Dickens,* edited by J. W. T. Ley (New York, 1928), p. 524.

10. Baker, p. 283; Leacock, p. 147.

James R. Kincaid (essay date March 1968)

SOURCE: Kincaid, James R. "Dickens's Subversive Humor: *David Copperfield.*" *Nineteenth-Century Fiction* 22, no. 4 (March 1968): 313-29.

[*In the following essay, Kincaid argues that much of the humor of* David Copperfield *is intentionally ironic, and that instead of offering only traditional comic situations in the novel, Dickens renders a sophisticated and deceptive comedy of character informed by the work's tragic themes.*]

Dickens once said that humorous invention was "the easiest thing in the world" for him and that he had constantly to restrain his "preposterous sense of the ridiculous."[1] He had contact with such an overflowing source of fun that, when forced to reduce the material in a number, he habitually made his cuts into the comic scenes.[2] The humor that remained was still ample; John Forster called it "his leading quality, . . . his highest faculty."[3] This judgment has not, however, remained unqualified; A. O. J. Cockshut alters Forster's labels significantly. The biographer's "leading" and "highest" become "best-loved" and "most influential" for the contemporary critic.[4]

This alteration is, no doubt, explained in part by a shift in critical tendency away from the subjective toward the objective and measurable, but the main cause has to be in the new view of the "dark" Dickens. Seeing the novelist as a bitter and ironic artist, we tend to be hesitant and suspicious about the giggles and the horse-laughs. R. J. Cruikshank, trying to combat this tendency with his anthology of the high points of Dickens's humor, says, "A notion has grown up that the humour of Dickens is a regrettable lapse on the part of an eminent economist—as though John Stuart Mill had been caught making a pun."[5]

Perhaps nothing could be so regrettable as a myth identifying Dickens with the sober Mill. This, however, is not an entirely accurate description of the current attitude. Rather than treating the humor as a lapse, most critics indicate their knowledge of its importance and then suggest that everything has been said on the subject. Edmund Wilson says, for example, "In praise of Dickens' humor, there is hardly anything new to say,"[6] and Lord David Cecil is even more conclusive: "He is perhaps the greatest humorist that England has ever produced. All sane critics have felt it, and most have said it; to expatiate at any length on Dickens' humor is unnecessary."[7] Cecil sidesteps the issue very nicely by testily inserting "*sane* critics," but, aside from the sneer, there is little of value in his statement. That critics have "felt" Dickens's humor and "said" it is great does not mean that there is nothing more to say; one wonders if Cecil's decision not to "expatiate at any length" on the subject is really not an evasion.

From the earlier critics come no such exhaustive analyses as Wilson and Cecil would have us believe exist. The best general statements are by Chesterton: "A Dickens character hits you first on the nose and then in the waistcoat, and then in the eye and then in the waistcoat again, with the blinding rapidity of some battering engine."[8] To my mind this is a very helpful comment, but its nature is certainly more evocative than analytical. Chesterton's general position seems to be that while the humor of Dickens is far from being self-explanatory, it is so overwhelming that it dwarfs his own powers of description. This honesty is at least more attractive than the apparent side-stepping now so prevalent.

One is no more satisfied by most of the comments on the humor in *David Copperfield,* which Forster called "the perfection of English mirth."[9] We too often find a solemn warning in place of real analysis.[10] Cockshut has pointed out the major obstacle in coming to grips with this aspect of the novel: "It follows that any detailed critical discussion of *David Copperfield* will tend to be unbalanced because it is impossible to give appropriate space to Micawber."[11] It is the purpose of this article to combat this tendency by examining not only the character of Micawber but also some other typically humorous aspects of the novel.

In the first place, one should notice that, in order to provide relief. Dickens strongly insisted on the use of humor as a contrast to melodrama or tragedy. He consistently urged contributors to his periodicals to "take the taste [of disagreeable characters or incidents] out of the reader's mouth" with some comedy,[12] and he consciously employed the same method himself. In the notes for Number X, for example, he wrote, "First chapter funny—Then on *to Em'ly*."[13] The first chapter of this number (XXVIII) concerns Mr. Micawber's hilarious management of David's dinner party, and the last (XXXI) relates the abduction of Em'ly. Thus Dickens tempers to some extent the shock and distaste of Steerforth's act by juxtaposing it against a scene of wild comedy. The comedy is not, of course, so uncontrolled as to mar the serious effect. One could, in fact, argue that the effect is all the more serious for being set off in bold relief by the preceding humor. If Dickens had really wished to dull the effect of Em'ly's action, he would have arranged matters so that the number ended rather than began with comedy.[14] Consistently, however, he ends each number with a climactic note of seriousness, not of fun.

Even more important than this pattern, however, is the subversive nature of the humor itself. Dorothy Van Ghent points out that much of the humor in Dickens comes from a form of noncommunication in which "speech is speech *to* nobody and where human encounter is mere collision."[15] Admitting that the resultant isolation contains an essential ingredient of humor, aloneness, she says that it "suggests," at the same time, "a world of isolated integers, terrifyingly alone and unrelated."[16] It has been further suggested that Dickens's "gregarious and hearty happiness" represents "a revulsion from the abysses of evil, a strenuous and ardent *wish* to achieve happiness, rather than the realization of it."[17]

While these explanations seem to me perceptive and valid, they do, I think, leave Dickens a little too much the victim of inner conflict and compulsion. I submit that much of the humor in *David Copperfield* is deliberately ironic. Normally comic situations are established and subtly subverted, and comic characters are developed along traditional lines, only to be expanded beyond these limited roles.

The "traditional," in this case, will be assumed to be defined by the criteria established by Henri Bergson for the laughable. Though Bergson's theories might be too narrow to deserve this term,[18] they do, I think, fit Dickens's practices quite well and can, therefore, be used without qualification, at least in this instance, for the purpose of showing Dickens's brilliant and subtle deviation from the purely comic, his expansion of otherwise flat, comic characters into fully developed people, involved in serious issues. This is not to say, of course, that there is nothing funny in *David Copperfield.* Bergson's perceptions are not being applied to squelch our laughter, but to show how it is seriously qualified by the recognition of the complexity of the situations and characters that may be the object of our laughter.

HUMOR OF SITUATION

Though Dickens's extensive work with amateur theatricals shows that he was not unfamiliar with the traditional comic situations, he very seldom employed them in his novels. He ignored, for the most part, the time-worn episodes involving mistaken identity, spying, disguises, and the like.[19] He even dropped the early fondness he had shown in *Pickwick Papers* for the equivocal situation.

In *David Copperfield,* however, there are countless situations which at first appear to be modeled on the traditional. The most striking of these involves David's married life with Dora. There is certainly a kind of stock humor in the young couple's farcical mismanagement of their domestic affairs. The chapter on the dinner party for Traddles at which Dora serves the unopened oysters (XLIV) presents a form of humor derived from dreamy impracticality. Bergson argues that this form of impracticality is rooted in the basis for all humor—rigidity—"something mechanical encrusted on the living."[20] Dora acts as if there were no practicality; she feeds Jip his mutton chop and blots the account book, fondles "Doady," and plays the guitar. The humor of this situation comes, according to Bergson, not from the actions themselves but from the mechanical insistence and continuity of the actor; life demands plasticity, but Dora responds to each situation with the same dreamy evasiveness. Similarly, David persists just as mechanically and unrealistically in his attempts to "form Dora's mind" (XLVIII). reading Shakespeare to her without the slightest effect. Basically, then, Dickens sets up a formally comic situation: two characters relentlessly pursuing a course without regard to reality.

This situation is, however, delicately but definitely expanded in several ways. First of all, both Dora and David extend their rigidity beyond the point Bergson sets for the humorous. Dora's demand that Jip have mutton chops is, in the face of their economic condition, selfishly cruel, and David's insistence on Dora's cultural improvement leads to tears and frustration. Second, David admits to an "old unhappy loss or want of something" after his marriage, and Dora is pushed finally to the point of admitting she was not "fit to be a wife" (LIII). David's dissatisfaction and Dora's pathetic self-abasement violate what Bergson terms an a priori condition of laughter—our emotional aloofness. He says, ". . . laughter is incompatible with emotion. Depict some fault, however trifling, in such a way as to arouse sympathy, fear, or pity; the mischief is done, it is impossible for us to laugh."[21] What happens in this case is that Dora becomes progressively more real. Beginning as a fantastic caricature of impracticality at whom we can easily laugh, she becomes more and more conscious of her own inability to please her husband and more and more hurt by this condition. As she increases in self-consciousness, we become increasingly involved with her problems, losing gradually the detachment Bergson terms necessary for laughter. Dickens finally reverses the originally comic situation completely by letting Dora die. The effect on the reader of such deception is highly complex. Without question, our reaction to the pathos in Dora's death is intensified by the guilt we feel at having once laughed at her.[22] At the same time, we are inclined to feel some hostility toward the author for arousing our guilt and to be more and more hesitant about laughing so easily.

Dickens's process of deception in situation comedy is not always one so closely bordering on trickery. He occasionally juxtaposes violently an ordinarily comic situation with an insistently tragic one. For example, the undertaker Mr. Omer operates his business rather as if it were a confectioner's shop. He and his family exude cheerfulness and whistle to the happy rat-tat-tat of the hammer on the coffin. Here again the situation is one from traditional comedy: Omer's family operates mechanically and rigidly in a totally unrealistic way. But again Dickens extends this situation beyond the Bergsonian limits and utilizes the unwariness produced by our laughter to make more emphatic his serious point. David is met by Mr. Omer on his way home from school at the time of his mother's death (IX). The undertaker takes David to his shop to measure him for mourning clothes and to check up on the progress of Mrs. Copperfield's coffin and the love-making of his daughter Minnie and his partner Joram. The last idyllic affair causes him to double over, "laughing till he choked." The three bustle David into a chaise and boisterously roll off with Mr. Omer chuckling, while Joram steals kisses from Minnie. Of this whole affair, David says, "I do not think I have ever experienced so strange a feeling in my life. . . ."

The reader's feelings are also bound to be at least "strange." Dickens has introduced a comic situation and brilliantly pushed it to a point of grotesqueness; the lively jollity of the undertaker and his group has become unfeeling and monstrous heartlessness, and the total effect of the scene is to underline the loneliness of the young boy. David says he felt "as if I were cast among creatures with whom I had no community of nature." Any tendency we have to laugh, then, is finally checked by the appellation "creatures." Dickens has again employed a normally funny situation to intensify the ultimately serious effect. David is not only given cause for sorrow, but is shown that the world has no sympathy for grief, that he is finally and totally alone. The aloofness and fantasy common to all traditionally humorous situations are thus exploited to show with great power the unspeakable cruelty of laughter. It is an exploitation involving artistic deception of the highest order.

There is, however, at least one situation in which the deceptive nature of the humor is almost totally submerged: the confrontation of Betsey Trotwood and the Murdstones, and the good lady's "triumph" over them (XIV). The refinement and reserve of the comedy of this scene induces the kind of "humor of the mind" advocated by George Meredith.[23] Meredith sees the true Comic Spirit as "a most subtle delicacy" (3) employed in a truly cultivated way. Its function is calmly to expose Folly, to pour the light of common sense over the overblown, the disproportionate, and the self-important (48). Miss Betsey's comments to the pompous Jane Murdstone provide just this kind of polite deflation:

> "I so far agree with what Miss Trotwood has remarked," observed Miss Murdstone, bridling, "that I consider our lamented Clara to have been, in all essential respects, a mere child."
>
> "It is a comfort to you and me, ma'am," said my aunt, "who are getting on in life, and are not likely to be made unhappy by our personal attractions, that nobody can say the same of us."

Jane Murdstone is, at the end of the interview, left sputtering and angry, and her exposure seems complete. But what of Mr. Murdstone? Meredith says the Comic Spirit pursues Folly to the end, "never fretting, never tiring, sure of having her" (33). But, in this case, one wonders if all the Folly is really captured and defeated.[24]

Our suspicions are first aroused by Aunt Betsey's departure from the refined politeness of the Comic Spirit. By the end of the interview, she too has become angry and, in addition, rather coarse: "Let me see you ride a donkey over *my* green again, and as sure as you have a head upon your shoulders, I'll knock your bonnet off, and tread upon it!" There are, of course, good reasons for her anger: the Murdstones are terrible and vicious people. Aunt Betsey cannot long act the part of the humane Comic Spirit, for we cannot look at the Murdstones dispassionately. We feel for them a real contempt, and, as Meredith says, "Contempt is a sentiment that cannot be entertained by comic intelligence" (33). The "laughter of the mind" is thus expanded and our generous feelings cut short; we are relieved to see the Murdstones leave, but we cannot be certain that their departure has not been an escape.

Far from being defeated, in fact, Jane Murdstone does reappear as Dora Spenlow's companion to harass David, and Mr. Murdstone is left to pursue his wicked ways, unencumbered by the maintenance of a child. Aunt Betsey's "victory" has thus produced a disturbingly ironic result: Mr. Murdstone is relieved of a boy whom he had already thwarted to his satisfaction anyway and who could now be nothing but a hindrance. He is left free to expand his malevolent actions to other weak mothers and helpless boys (see Chap. LIX). The originally benign scene thus becomes, by the end of the novel, a very dark one. The Comic Spirit which had seemed at the time so effective is rendered finally impotent, and our civilized laughter is shown to be incomplete and imperceptive.

HUMOR OF CHARACTER

It was admittedly not in the manipulation of comic situation but in the creation of comic characters that Dickens excelled, and though he passed over many traditional comic situations, he utilized virtually the whole stock of comic character. The difference between the great comic characters of Dickens, however, and those of tradition is in the tremendous importance the novelist placed on his characters' language rather than on their actions or gestures. Douglas Bush says that this great gift of language comes from "an overflowing, irrepressible imagination."[25] This imagination is the source of attraction of Dickens's early comic masterpiece, Sam Weller. Though entrapped in a role which is rather a tight fit in terms of sentimental conception—he is, above all, true to Mr. Pickwick—he breaks out in brilliant and expansive language: "'Yes, I have a pair of eyes,' replied Sam, 'and that's just it. If they was a pair o' patent double million magnifyin' gas microscopes of hextra power, p'raps I might be able to see through a flight o' stairs and a deal door; but bein' only eyes, you see, my wision's limited'" (XXXIV).

Language which moves far beyond the situation or character is also employed in *David Copperfield,* but with a vital difference. Julia Mills, for instance, is a character from traditional comedy; she plays the role of the pretended recluse, jolted by an enormous disappointment in life and now acting as a carrier of sage wisdom to other lovers. She is forever singing "about the slumbering echoes in the caverns of Memory, as if she were a hundred years old" (XXXIII), and writing in a journal, which she shows to David, such things as, "Are tears the dewdrops of the heart?" and "Must not D. C. confine himself to the broad pinions of Time?" (XXXVIII) Thus Julia seems to be a comic character drawn directly from the excesses of the sentimental novel. Her appeal

to laughter comes, in Bergson's terms, from the rigidity with which she pursues these excesses. Again, however, Miss Mills transcends the limits Bergson sets for laughter: she carries her rigidity so far that she makes us hate her. Even David suspects that Julia enjoys herself most when real trouble hits the affair: ". . . though she mingled her tears with mine, . . . she had a dreadful luxury in our afflictions. She petted them, as I may say, and made the most of them." He admits, "She made me much more wretched than I was before" (XXXVIII). Not content with this damning remark, Dickens inserts in the last chapter of the novel a picture of Julia as a wealthy woman, "peevish and fine," who thinks of nothing but money and spends her time in the company of the villain Jack Maldon. The guilt, even though by association, is established irrevocably.

It should be noted that this technique is similar to the one Dickens employed in depicting David's married life with Dora. In these instances, the comic situation is established and then subtly deranged; the reader is drawn into the author's presence to laugh heartily with him, not noticing that he is being pushed gently toward the exit, and then suddenly he finds himself out in the street facing a locked door. More often, however, the reader is presented with a door so contrived as to seem both open and shut at the same time. He is given an ambiguous invitation, expressing either hospitality or contempt, and he likely stands outside unable to decide what to do.

For instance, Dickens uses the catch-phrase technique for characters here perhaps as often as in any other novel.[26] This linguistic expression of the mechanical is a clear inducement to laugh. When Miss Mowcher says, for the tenth time, "Ain't I volatile," the tendency is to overlook the falseness and hypocrisy she encourages by her trade and to laugh at her. In addition, we are likely to laugh at her simply because she is so very much like a thing rather than a person.[27] David describes his view of her hopping away in the rain under a gigantic umbrella as that of "an immense bird" (XXXII).

On the other hand, we are presented with concurrent reasons *not* to laugh at Miss Mowcher but to feel sorry for her. Her physical deformity, in the first place, is not one derived from a kind of obstinacy of body—like a big mouth or flapping ears. According to Bergson, *"A deformity that may become comic is a deformity that a normally built person could successfully imitate"* (75).[28] While one might imitate many facial expressions, or even the distortion of a hunchback, it is not hard to recognize that a dwarf is outside the realm of imitation. Miss Mowcher is made small not by physical obstinacy but by the workings of external, unjust forces. The question of injustice immediately calls up our pity and tends to block our laughter.

The only outlet for our laughter, then, forces us to ignore her humanity and look upon her completely as a thing—as a monkey imitating man. This outlet is barred by Miss Mowcher herself, however, when she accuses David of mistrusting her because she is small: ". . . you know you wouldn't mistrust me, if I was a full-sized woman." At the end of the interview, she asks him to trust her as he would a regular woman—no more but no less (XXXII). Her insistence on her femininity is her insistence that she is *not* a thing. Bergson emphasizes the necessity of a comic character's unselfconsciousness; he is "comic in proportion to his ignorance of himself" (71). Miss Mowcher's self-consciousness is deep enough to perceive the effect she has on others, and, thus, the automaton is given both humanity and feelings. Our laughter is embarrassed and hesitant; it partakes of injustice and cruelty.

The same confusion is attendant on most of the other comic characters in the novel. The two clearest examples are Tommy Traddles and Dr. Strong. Traddles is comic in his rather inflexible humility, ignorance, and good nature, but he does, at the same time, make a strong appeal for our pity in his role as the chief victim of Creakle's rod and in his upbraiding of Steerforth for the latter's treatment of Mr. Mell. In this last case (VII), Traddles is the only boy with insight enough to see how shabby and mean Steerforth is, and his insight causes him to be caned. In his sympathy for the virtuous Mell, then, he is alienated from his classmates and retires to his corner to draw skeletons on his slate. This sublimation of the dark, suicidal tendency in Traddles comes up later in the novel when he admits to drawing skeletons still—perhaps because he is still being imposed upon by Mr. Micawber's borrowing, Sophy Crewler's family, and "his old unlucky fortune" (XXVII).[29]

Similarly, Dr. Strong is a combination of the light and the dark, the comic and the tragic. His quixotic devotion to a dictionary he can never hope to finish and his general dreamy detachment constitute a classic comic trait: absentmindedness.[30] At the same time, this very absentmindedness involves him in an extremely unpleasant domestic dilemma, which, in turn, reflects on the sad qualities of David's marriage to Dora. Unable to see that his wife is unhappy with him, Dr. Strong blindly increases her pain and guilt with unflinching kindness. Tortured by her husband's relentless encouragement of her friendship with Jack Maldon, Annie is finally forced to humiliate herself at her husband's feet (XLV), and it is this expression of marital incompatibility that seems to David so striking a parallel to his own.

All these characters—Miss Mowcher, Tommy Traddles, Dr. Strong—have their flat goodness and comicality expanded with an insistent note of seriousness and darkness. Dickens thus uses our initial laughter at these characters as a brilliantly controlled artistic device to make more startling and effective the important and tragic implications of the novel with which they are involved. He consistently uses a similar technique even with villains. With this class, he takes the basic evil and painfulness and injects, as Robert Morse has observed, "a wry surface levity, a playfulness of language, that makes the horror of his subject both more ghastly and more supportable."[31] Actually, the horror is not only more supportable, it verges on the brink of the laughable. Thus the villains produce an ambiguous effect: they are neither totally repulsive nor totally funny, but something of both.

Even the blackest of the villains is partially redeemed by language or situation. For example, even Mr. Creakle has some comic effect; it is contained in his humorous inability to talk above a whisper[32] and in his language: "I'm a Tartar.[33] . . . When I say I'll do a thing, I do it . . . and when I say I will have a thing done, I will have it done" (VI). Creakle's association of firm determination with the Tartars is one which eludes the furthest extension of logic, and it is precisely this flight from the confines of rationality which is usually a trait of funny characters, not of unspeakably brutal sadists. Similarly, Mr. Murdstone is unexpectedly endowed with a wild and comic imagination: "If I go to a cheesemonger's shop, and buy five thousand double-Gloucester cheeses at four-pence-halfpenny each present payment—. . ." (IV). This would be the beginning of a comic speech suitable for Sam Weller, were it not for the fact that David is cruelly punished when he fails to solve the problem posed. The language and the fertile imagination are similar in Murdstone and in Sam, but benevolent impulses are replaced by sardonic ones. Just the same, Murdstone's wit makes a definite appeal to laughter.

The greatest appeals to laughter in the novel, however, are not made by the villains, or even by the benevolent characters, but by characters who escape easy classification: the Micawbers. Virtually every commentator has noticed that the breadth and expansiveness of these characters raise them far above the rest of the characters in the novel. However, the basic ambiguity which we have found in the other comedy in *David Copperfield* is not absent here. Just as the Micawbers are the most impressive characters,[34] so is their treatment the most subtle and the most ultimately deceptive. The complexity of this treatment causes Cockshut to give up: "Everybody can appreciate Mr. Micawber, but what can the critic say about him?"[35]

There are, I think, several things which may be said without incurring the tedium derived from explaining a joke. First of all, it is clear that Mr. Micawber is, in one sense, as firmly rigid and mechanical as any of Dickens's characters. He is inevitably optimistic, waiting for "something to turn up," even when it is perfectly clear that there is nothing whatever to turn up.[36] The relentless pursuit of fancy is, according to Bergson, the essence of comicality.

Even Micawber's speech patterns partake of the mechanical. He is, of course, habitually elegant, but he also has the habit of halting his rapturous flights with an "in short," followed by a clarification.[37] Douglas Bush says that this habit represents "a sort of concession to the requirements of everyday intercourse."[38] The concession is, however, reluctant and, more significantly, partial. Mr. Micawber sometimes adds the "in short" and fakes the concession. A comparison with an earlier instance of this same technique should make this point clearer.

In *The Old Curiosity Shop* Dickens had used the mechanical clarification to great effect in Dick Swiveller. At one point Dick says,

> "May the present moment," said Dick, sticking his fork into a large carbuncular potato, "be the worst of our lives! I like this plan of sending 'em with the peel on; there's a charm in drawing a potato from its native element (if I may so express it) to which the rich and powerful are strangers. Ah! 'Man wants but little here below, nor wants that little long!' How true that is!—after dinner."

(VIII)

The afterthought, "How true that is!—after dinner," abruptly recalls us from the fantasy world and makes us laugh by reminding us how fragile and unrealistic Swiveller's intoxication with language is. At one point, Dickens allows Swiveller the same pattern he later used with Micawber:

> "Why, instead of my friend's bursting into tears when he knew who Fred was, embracing him kindly, and telling him that he was his grandfather, or his grandmother in disguise (which we fully expected), he flew into a tremendous passion; called him all manner of names; said it was in a great measure his fault that little Nell and the old gentleman had ever been brought to poverty; didn't hint at our taking anything to drink; and—and in short rather turned us out than otherwise."

(L)

Again, Dick reminds us himself of his inflexible pursuit of the unrealistic. Micawber's speech occasionally fits the same comic formula:

> "Under the impression," said Mr. Micawber, "that your peregrinations in this metropolis have not as yet been extensive, and that you might have some difficulty in penetrating the arcana of the modern Babylon in the direction of the City Road—in short, . . . that you might lose yourself—. . . ."

(XI)

There are many times, however, when this formula is strongly altered. For instance, Micawber's description of his wife's pregnancy contains a much different kind of tag:

> "You may, perhaps, be prepared to hear that Mrs. Micawber is in a state of health which renders it not wholly improbable that an addition may be ultimately made to those pledges of affection which—in short, to the infantine group."

(XXVII)

While Swiveller's tags are invariably flat, Micawber's additions are occasionally as exalted as the language preceding them. "The infantine group" is neither flat and common nor prosaic. The reader never knows for certain whether or not Micawber's bursts will continue past the intended clarification. When they do, the framework of predictable action on which the comedy of this character is built is overturned.

There are rules of Bergsonian comedy violated other than the one of rigidity; Micawber demands a strong emotional response from us. This response is not only strong but necessarily complex, for there is a definite dark side to Micawber. Edmund Wilson points out that his "vagaries . . . always left somebody out of pocket,"[39] and while we do not much mind his cheating the milkman, we do mind his working on Traddles. He is, further, a very bad provider, and there can be no question that his family suffers from his otherwise comic traits.[40] Finally, we are bound to be disturbed by Micawber's agreement to become an accomplice of Uriah Heep,[41] and even his eventual reformation can hardly take the taste of his treachery out of our mouths. George Orwell responded to this complexity in Micawber by declaring that, in the end, he is "a cadging scoundrel,"[42] and while this extreme view has not been generally accepted, it is possible that it does not go very far beyond the truth.

At any rate, the important point is that one should not have anything like these intense feelings about a character who is *purely* laughable. Bruce McCullough says of Micawber, "There is no depth in him and no sensibility."[43] If this were true, we could properly call him flatly comic, but it is fortunately far from the truth. We have not only strong negative feelings about Micawber, but a strong attraction to him as well. His relation to David is warm and generous, and his feelings toward his wife betray a deeper self-consciousness and pathos than are possible in a purely comic character:

> "But he [Mrs. Micawber's father] applied that maxim [Procrastination is the thief of time] to our marriage, my dear; and that was so far prematurely entered into, in consequence, that I never recovered the expense."
>
> Mr. Micawber looked aside at Mrs. Micawber, and added: "Not that I am sorry for it. Quite the contrary, my love." After which he was grave for a minute or so.

(XII)[44]

Dickens thus pushes Micawber far beyond the narrow limits of the flat role he at first seemed to be playing, and thereby emphasizes not only his character's complex humanity, but also his curious mixture of attraction and repulsion, of open honesty and ugly selfishness.

The case with Mrs. Micawber is similar in its complexity. In McCullough's words, she rigidly moves "to make appraisals of his [her husband's] situation and prospects in which the lucidity of her manner is equalled only by the fantasticality of her material,"[45] and she is forever vowing never to leave her husband. E. M. Forster illustrated his famous distinction between round and flat characters by using Mrs. Micawber: "There is Mrs. Micawber—she says she won't desert Mr. Micawber, she doesn't, and there she is."[46] It takes, however, very little investigation to show how incomplete this description is. David tells of watching the Micawbers loading their coach prior to leaving London:

> I think, as Mrs. Micawber sat at the back of the coach, with the children, and I stood in the road looking wistfully at them, a mist cleared from her eyes, and she saw what a little creature I really was, I think so, because she beckoned to me to climb up, with quite a new and motherly expression in her face, and put her arm round my neck, and gave me just such a kiss as she might have given to her own boy.
>
> (XII)

The fact that the "mist cleared from her eyes" gives her much more depth than Forster's description allows and, at the same time, makes her much more than a purely laughable character. In her role as a mother to David she breaks the bonds of unconsciousness and makes a strong claim on our deepest feelings.

It must be said, then, that the humor in *David Copperfield* is deceptive; it is used not only for laughter, but as a foundation out of which serious and tragic incidents grow. Almost no pure mirth is present and few ordinarily comic situations or characters are allowed to stay within the bounds of the purely entertaining. The reasons for this condition are many, but they include the fact that the comedy which does exist is always wildest when the characters involved in it are on the brink of chaos: the Micawbers are always about to be ruined; Tommy Traddles faces continual beatings; Mr. Dick is forever on the run from his threatening family. Bergson says that laughter is truly a corrective, that we laugh to provoke action (73), and, if this is so, it may well be that the laughter this novel provokes is often on the verge of hysteria. The action our laughter demands is always rather hopeless and, at the same time, desperately needed, for the threats to the established order are strong.

The nature of this "established order" is, of course, not very attractive. Those who are really established are the cruel Murdstones, the cheating Spenlow, and the cowardly Wickfield. Our inclination to laugh, therefore, is further reduced; for laughter is, above all, "a social gesture,"[47] demanding our identification with society. And the society at large in *David Copperfield* is extremely hard to identify with.

Finally, it might be said that the humor in the novel is subverted by the very nature of the tragic themes introduced. As has already been noted, the Bergsonian essence of a comic character is to be found in his rigidity, his unconsciousness, and his unrealistic impracticality. The inability of the major character in *David Copperfield* to escape from unconsciousness into reality, however, is the major block to his fulfillment.[48] Thus the normal traits of comedy are undercut by a serious exposition of their practical failings. The novel not only upsets individual instances of comic situation or character, then, but plays ironically throughout on the very nature of the laughable. It is not so much that we are placed on the slippery banana peel ourselves, but that we are forced to watch someone we know very well take a pratfall. And before the laugh is out of our throats, the knowledge is forced on us that he is hurt seriously and permanently.

Notes

1. Walter Dexter, ed., *The Letters of Charles Dickens,* I, 782; John Forster, August 30, 1846.

2. See John Butt and Kathleen Tillotson, *Dickens at Work* (London, 1957), p. 22.

3. *The Life of Charles Dickens* (London, n.d.), p. 558.

4. *The Imagination of Charles Dickens* (Boston, 1961), p. 16.

5. *The Humour of Dickens* (London, 1952), p. vi.

6. "Dickens: The Two Scrooges," *The Wound and the Bow* (Cambridge, Massachusetts, 1941), p. 13.

7. *Victorian Novelists: Essays in Revaluation* (Chicago, 1958), p. 41.

8. *Appreciations and Criticisms of the Works of Charles Dickens* (London, 1911), p. 203.

9. *The Life of Charles Dickens,* p. 428.

10. K. J. Fielding (*Charles Dickens: A Critical Introduction* [London, 1958], p. 115) says, "The richness and variety of the comedy in *David Copperfield* ought not to be taken for granted." Similarly, George Ford warns, in his introduction to the Riverside edition of the novel (p. v), "The fun to be enjoyed in *David Copperfield* could be overlooked only by a studied variety of solemnity or dulness."

11. *The Imagination of Charles Dickens,* p. 114.

12. *Nonesuch Letters,* III, 393; Percy Fitzgerald, July 27, 1864.

13. See Butt and Tillotson, *Dickens at Work,* p. 144.

14. The facts of serial publication and the necessity of maintaining the reader's attention are reasons

against this pattern, of course, but I think we regard serialization too seriously when we allow it no other form than that of "The Perils of Pauline."

15. "Great Expectations," in *The English Novel: Form and Function* (New York, 1953), p. 127.

16. *The English Novel,* pp. 126-127.

17. Humphry House, *All in Due Time* (London, 1955), p. 187.

18. Because he separates sympathy from laughter (see n. 21), Bergson has been accused of failing to account for the greatest of English comic characters. It seems to me, however, that his statements are very helpful in explaining the most difficult part of our reaction to the admittedly great comic figure in this novel, Micawber. See pp. 325-328 in this article.

19. This same point is made by Cockshut, *The Imagination of Charles Dickens,* p. 17.

20. See his essay, "Laughter," in *Comedy* (Garden City, New York, 1956), pp. 59-190.

21. *Comedy,* p. 150. This statement is felt by many to be extreme. In this case, however (as in the others in this novel), I think the situation supports his argument, however extreme it may be in general.

22. Bergson points out that laughter is a form of revenge by society on those who would deviate from its norms. He shows that there is in laughter "a degree of egoism and, behind this . . . something less spontaneous and more bitter . . ." (p. 189).

23. "An Essay on Comedy," in *Comedy,* pp. 3-57.

24. Critics generally have felt that Miss Betsey's triumph *is* complete. For example, E. K. Brown, "*David Copperfield,*" YR [*The Yale Review*], XXXVII (1948), 660, says, "What a relief! The Murdstones were only stage villains, after all; the sawdust seems to be coursing out of their legs as they hurry out of sight." This reading may describe the reader's immediate reaction, but it fails to account for subsequent events.

25. "A Note on Dickens's Humor," *From Jane Austen to Joseph Conrad,* ed. Robert C. Rathburn and Martin Steinmann, Jr. (Minneapolis, 1958), p. 85. This aspect is also emphasized by K. J. Fielding, *A Critical Introduction,* pp. 116-117, and F. R. Leavis, *The Great Tradition* (New York, 1949), p. 246. Leavis says that in "command of word, phrase, rhythm and image: in ease and range there is surely no greater master of English except Shakespeare."

26. Earle Davis (*The Flint and the Flame: The Artistry of Charles Dickens* [Columbia, Missouri,

1963], p. 43) says, "For most readers, the catch phrase reached fruition in *David Copperfield,* since a host of characters have tags in that novel."

27. Bergson says, *"We laugh every time a person gives us the impression of being a thing"* (p. 97).

28. Interestingly, Mark Spilka, though likewise dealing with Bergson's terminology, treats Miss Mowcher as a comic character because she is mechanical (*Dickens and Kafka* [Bloomington, 1963], p. 81). I think, however, that he ignores both the nature of her deformity and her self-consciousness.

29. The sum of these factors might tend to show that Traddles is not a comic character at all. In treating the humor in *David Copperfield,* however, Cruikshank includes a scene (pp. 13-25) involving Traddles, calling it "The Comfort of Skeletons."

30. Bergson says, "Absentmindedness, indeed, is not perhaps the actual fountain-head of the comic, but surely it is contiguous to a certain stream of facts and fancies which flows straight from the fountainhead. It is situated, so to say, on one of the great natural watersheds of laughter" (p. 68).

31. Robert Morse, "*Our Mutual Friend,*" PR [*Partisan Review*], XVI (March, 1949), 287.

32. He employs a double, Tungay, to repeat his words. This deformity, unlike Miss Mowcher's, is both mechanical and imitable and is expressive of a ridiculousness which should be comically reassuring. That is, we should be less afraid of Creakle because he is so much less a man than any of us.

33. This phrase is also associated with humor by K. J. Fielding, *A Critical Introduction,* p. 117.

34. J. B. Priestley, *The English Comic Characters* (London, 1928 [first published, 1925]), p. 243, says Mr. Micawber is, with the exception of Falstaff, "the greatest comic figure in the whole range of English literature."

35. *The Imagination of Charles Dickens,* p. 114.

36. Jared Wenger, "Character-types of Scott, Balzac, Dickens, Zola," *PMLA,* LXII (March, 1947), 213-232, calls this mechanical aspect to our attention but greatly overemphasizes it. He says that once the idea that something would turn up was there, Micawber "writes his own ticket" (p. 217).

37. Though we might be tempted to say that the humor here is one of contrasts, derived from the juxtaposition of poetic effusion against flat prose, Bergson continually warns against this "contrast theory," saying that the cause of laughter is not the shock of contrast but the habitual rigidity which brings that contrast into being. In this case,

we laugh not at Micawber's using the two styles, but at the inflexibility which makes necessary the flat prose.

38. *From Jane Austen to Joseph Conrad,* p. 89.

39. *The Wound and the Bow,* p. 51.

40. Leonard F. Manheim, "The Personal History of David Copperfield: A Study in Psychoanalytic Criticism," *AI* [*American Imago*], IX (April, 1952), 24-25, says that Micawber represents an attempt "to pillory the father image" and that his "picture is no more flattering than is that of Murdstone."

41. Chesterton was so disturbed he refused to believe that it happened (*Charles Dickens: The Last of the Great Men* [New York, 1942], p. 107).

42. *Dickens, Dali and Others* (New York, 1946), p. 67.

43. *Representative English Novelists* (New York, 1957), p. 149.

44. This illustration and the following one involving Mrs. Micawber are also cited by Douglas Bush (*From Jane Austen to Joseph Conrad,* p. 88) in refuting Forster's discussion of the flatness of Dickens's characters (see n. 46).

45. *Representative English Novelists,* p. 150.

46. *Aspects of the Novel* (New York, 1927), p. 68.

47. Bergson, p. 73.

48. According to this view, David's childhood experiences are so black that they force him into a world of fantasy and escape. Ironically, the "rescue" which Aunt Betsey plans for him forces him further into the delusory world of the Strongs and the Wickfields, and finally into the arms of Agnes, a clear substitute for his childhood nurse and a representation of ultimate unreality. See my article, "The Darkness of *David Copperfield,*" *Dickens Studies,* I, 65-75.

Felicity Hughes (essay date spring 1974)

SOURCE: Hughes, Felicity. "Narrative Complexity in *David Copperfield.*" *ELH* 41, no. 1 (spring 1974): 89-105.

[*In the following essay, Hughes analyzes three levels of narrative construction in* David Copperfield: *David's youthful and naive narrative, the adult perspective presented by the mature Copperfield, and Dickens's implicit commentary on the narrator's interpretation of his past life.*]

David Copperfield is written in a peculiarly complicated way. The reader has not only Charles Dickens to attend to, but the narrator, David Copperfield (himself also a novelist), and his remembered self, young David the protagonist. In fact, from these three sources, three different interpretations of people and events are offered to the reader simultaneously. Whereas it is now universally acknowledged that Charles Dickens must not be identified with David Copperfield, that the book is not autobiographical, it is not sufficiently taken into account that young David is not identical with adult David. Nor is sufficient notice taken of the fact that adult David is a novelist. When these two factors are taken into account the complexities of the method can be seen not as mere virtuosity, but as a significant contribution to the whole meaning of the book. This paper will attempt to investigate the consequences of the method by separating out the three different interpretations of people and events offered in the book.

At the same time, it is proper to keep in mind the relationship between the three interpreters since it influences the status of their interpretations. It will be argued that young David offers a naive, unphilosophical view of his own experience; that adult David offers, at the same time, a systematic interpretation of that experience behind young David's back as it were; and that Charles Dickens simultaneously suggests a critique of that systematic interpretation offered by adult Copperfield, behind *his* back.

In the book young David reports his experiences and gives us his reactions to them in great detail up to his departure for the Continent. His mood at that time is one of depression and bewilderment. Life has afforded him a series of unaccountable deprivations, leaving him with a pervading sense of perplexity and loss. His meditations in Europe are not given to the reader in detail, yet at the end of his wanderings we are asked to accept that he has solved his problems and reached some sort of insight that enables him to return. In other words, he has become that adult David Copperfield who writes the book. For the reader, lacking knowledge of the crucial meditations, the narrator's insight must be conveyed elsewhere in the narrative or we should leave the book feeling cheated. And in fact the narrator does make his interpretation of experience available to the careful reader.

David Copperfield, adult novelist, records a development toward an insight into the human condition, with particular emphasis on the knowledge of good and evil. According to the Christian tradition, people acquire understanding of good only at the cost of the knowledge of evil, and it will be shown that David Copperfield is, in this sense, a traditional thinker. Young David is presented by him as typical in this respect. His appreciation of the nature of goodness is derived from a painfully acquired understanding of evil experienced as personal hurts and shocks which he gradually learns to interpret. Where young David presents his experience as personal and particular, adult David suggests that it is universal and general. As a novelist, he conveys its universal significance by various literary means which will be discussed later. Young David is presented as at best only partially aware of this significance. He is allowed to see it in glimpses, momentary insights, fantasies, dreams and so on without being conscious of the connections between these aperçus. But the material for adult Copperfield's general interpretation is all there so that both young David (in his European meditations) and the reader (in the course of the book) can piece it together. Thus the narrator gives us all we need to know to grasp his interpretation and leave the book satisfied.

But whilst adult David shows up the limitations of young David by offering a comprehensive and (to him) satisfactory interpretation of experience, so in turn does Charles Dickens cast doubt upon the adequacy of that interpretation. Just as David Copperfield, novelist, communicates with the reader so too does Charles Dickens, novelist, offering a comment on the interpretation given by his narrator which is profoundly disquieting. Since the differences between the two novelists focus most sharply on their views of the efficacy of the agents of good and evil, discussion of their contributions will center on that point. And since evil is primary in both cases, the figures of Murdstone, Steerforth and Heep will be looked at in detail. First, consider the contribution of young David.

I

Young David's view of the world is colored by his preoccupation with the problem of finding and maintaining a secure and permanent home. His early experiences dispose him to see threats in terms of intrusion and dispossession. Though David is fatherless, his early home is nevertheless secure and is detailed lovingly among his earliest memories in Chapter II. Its topography is given clearly so that we can follow the intrusion of Murdstone through its stages. First, there is the ringing of the doorbell and David finding there his mother with "a gentleman with beautiful black hair and whiskers." David repels Murdstone "on the threshold," pushing away his hand; so Murdstone gains no entry but, "I see him turn round in the garden, and give us a last look with his ill-omened black eyes, before the door was shut. Peggotty . . . secured the fastenings instantly, and we all went into the parlour" (19).[1] At the second meeting, "there he was, in church, and he walked home with us afterwards. *He came in, too . . .*" (21). He comes in not once but many times before David goes off for the fateful holiday.

It touches me nearly now, although I tell it lightly, to recollect how eager I was to leave my happy home; to think how little I suspected what I did leave for ever.

(26)

As the cart plods off, David's thoughts turn to a fairy tale. He wonders whether, "if Peggotty were employed to lose me like the boy in the fairy tale, I should be able to track my way home again by the buttons she would shed." And with this oblique reference to expulsion from the home by a jealous step-parent the chapter closes.

David's first impression of the barge at Yarmouth is that it is patently not a home but a boat. This superficial difference leads him to the realization that it fulfills the essential function of a home in giving shelter. He returns to his home more aware of its nature, "it was my nest, and . . . my mother was my comforter and friend" (41). But of course he finds Murdstone on the hearth and the big black dog in the kennel. There is no need to recount the process by which David finds himself a prisoner in the house, yet shut out from the home. Nor how he comes to be packed off to school, wondering, when he seems to have missed a connection, "if I started off at once, and tried to walk back home, how could I ever find my way, how could I ever hope to walk so far, how could I make sure of any one but Peggotty, even if I got back?" (73). So when David's mother dies, the calamity does not touch him because she had been lost to him in her important home-making aspect some time before. He says ". . . my thoughts were idle; not intent on the calamity . . . but idly loitering near it. I thought of our house shut up and hushed" (123). When David is sent to the wine-merchant's he becomes a lodger, in the house of the Micawbers. To speak of *the* house of the Micawbers is to wonder which one, because the Micawbers are nomads and their house is perpetually prey to intruders who come at all hours to abuse and threaten. Yet, unlike David who feels his homelessness acutely, the Micawbers are not annihilated. Their resilience astounds David. To him it indicates a deficiency of sensibility to be cheered by mere breaded lamb chops and warm ale. "Mr. Micawber's difficulties were an addition to the distressed state of my mind" (162). Yet they provide him with more of a home than he realizes until he has to find other lodgings, and it is this which finally decides him to run away—not from his situation but *to* Aunt Betsey. Whatever may have been the case in Dickens' own life, it is indubitably the flight to Dover that is the crucial distressing experience of young David, rather than the spell in the ware-house. This unrelieved nightmare begins with the young man with the donkey cart and does not end until David is inside his aunt's cottage hearing Janet being ordered outside to repel trespassing donkeys. The aunt is strong enough to repel intruders and that means safety. As David goes off to sleep he re-

David Copperfield in Finsbury Square, London, being shown the way to his new lodgings by Mr. Micawber. The illustration was done by Fred Barnard for an edition, circa 1850, of David Copperfield.

members all the solitary places under the night sky where he had slept. "I prayed that I never might be houseless any more, and never might forget the houseless" (199). Thus David's early experience teaches him the value and vulnerability of a home and teaches him to fear and hate intruders.

Two further homes are presented to him, the Wickfields' and the Strongs'. Both have already within them an element which threatens their destruction. Arriving at the Wickfields', David surveys the house with pleasure; then, "when the pony-chaise stopped at the door, and my eyes were intent upon the house, I saw a cadaverous face appear at a small window on the ground floor (in a little round tower that formed one side of the house), and quickly disappear" (218). It is Uriah, who is, David soon discovers, very much inclined to see David as a competing intruder, as a competitor for a partnership in the firm. Similarly, the first David hears of the Strong household is a conversation about Jack Maldon of which the burden is "At home or abroad." Maldon appears in person soon afterwards begging pardon for intruding. David has been taught to look for danger from outside. He perceives Dr. Strong's vulner-

ability in this regard. "Outside his own domain, and unprotected, he was a very sheep for the shearers" (238). But slowly he learns that there are dangers *inside.* The first mention of Aunt Betsey's vulnerability comes from Mr. Dick: "who's that man that hides near our house and frightens her?" An inexplicable sense of fear and exposure grows on David throughout his adolescent years until he leaves Canterbury disturbed and anxious:

> I seemed to have left the Doctor's roof with a dark cloud lowering on it. . . . It was as if the tranquil sanctuary of my boyhood had been sacked before my face, and its peace and honour given to the winds.
>
> (282)

Now comes the re-entry of Steerforth and David's fateful introduction of him into the Yarmouth community. One small but significant preliminary is that when they arrive there, Steerforth toys with the notion of going straight into Peggotty's house and, by announcing himself as David grown up, claiming her welcome; whereas in the event David himself knocks at the door and allows her to take him for a stranger at first. But it is the entry into the boat that is crucial and the scene is described in detail as they enter—described as a picture that is instantaneously dissolved by their entrance. When Mr. Peggotty narrates what has gone before, his story comes to this climax:

> 'All of a sudden, one evening—as it might be to-night—comes little Em'ly from her work, and him with her! There ain't so much in *that,* you'll say. No, because he takes care on her, like a brother, arter dark, and indeed afore dark, and at all times. But this tarpaulin chap, he takes hold of her hand, and he cries out to me, joyful, "Look here! This is to be my little wife!" And she says, half bold and half shy, and half a-laughing and half a-crying, "Yes, Uncle! If you please."—If I please!' cried Mr. Peggotty, rolling his head in an ecstasy at the idea; 'Lord, as if I should do anything else!—"If you please, I am steadier now, and I have thought better of it, and I'll be as good a little wife as I can to him, for he's a dear, good fellow!" Then Missis Gummidge, she claps her hands like a play, and you come in. *Theer! The murder's out!'* said Mr. Peggotty—'*You come in! . . .*'
>
> (314-15)

The whole Yarmouth story is developed with reference to "the pollution of an honest home." Mr. Peggotty speaks of the candle in the window as saying "Theer's home." He won't sit down at Mrs. Steerforth's because it is "too evil a house." And David feels responsible because he introduced Steerforth into Peggotty's house, involving himself in the guilt up to the time when Steerforth lies dead on the beach "among the ruins of the home he had wronged" (795).

Meanwhile, David himself finds marriage and homemaking very difficult. David and Dora's courtship and marriage with its housekeeping failure are contrasted with Traddles' patient courtship of Sophy—the pagoda kennel and guitar case against the cherished flower pot and stand. David makes a great fuss about the business of penetrating Spenlow's house, comparing his own behaviour with that of the moon in the old riddle, going "round and round the house, without ever touching the house" (474). Inhibited by his anxiety, David expends a great deal of inappropriate effort struggling through the "forests of difficulty," then the door falls down at a touch with the fortunate death of Mr. Spenlow. But that is where David's troubles begin, for, having walked in and carried off Dora, he finds himself continually in the false position of the ferocious intruder or heartless gaoler. He feels like "a Bandit," who has "carried desolation into the bosom of our joys" (539) or like the "Monster who had got into a Fairy's bower" (543). Dora's words echo those of his poor mother, "I am very affectionate" (604). He finds himself advocating firmness—setting little tests like Murdstone's Double Gloucester cheeses. She calls him "Bluebeard"! Appalled at finding himself in the role he had always feared and hated, David weakens and they are tyrannized by servants. He acknowledges that their failure affects more than themselves. "We are positively corrupting people" (694) he says worriedly to her. Her death merely completes his paralysis and he is a passive spectator at the denouement of the Wickfield-Heep affair. His final step is to exile himself to Europe, becoming a homeless wanderer once more. *Why can he never find a home?*

David's mood is one of depression and bewilderment at this time because he is unable to make sense of what has happened to him. He has never formulated a general theory to account for human behaviour but has instead tried to manipulate the world to fulfil his own driving need for a secure place in it. His attempts to manipulate the world and find security fail because they are based on an imperfect, subjective, incoherent view of it. He never manages to absorb the significance of one experience before the next has taken him by surprise. Consequently, the shocks and disappointments find him perpetually off-balance. So it is, that up to the time of his departure for Europe, he remains naive, in the sense that experience has not taught him how to cope with life, and unphilosophical in the sense that he has no general theory to account for what has taken place.

II

David Copperfield, adult novelist, has however a different end in view. He communicates his interpretation of the same people and events in a variety of ways. If we have been sensitive to his hints and suggestions we know that the answer to David's question has already been presented and needs only to be fully realized. He has traced a development of insight on the part of his protagonist which is presented as a progress.

He begins with David's first experience of dispossession and the imaginative device he uses to cope with it. David's great resource in consoling himself for the damage done to him by Murdstone was fiction. "I believe I should have been almost stupified but for one circumstance" (55). That circumstance is imaginative literature. David's reading and his imagination save him from complete breakdown and are to have enormous influence on his future understanding of life. He interprets Murdstone as the ogre of the fairy story or the bad step-parent of the folk tale.

> It is curious to me how I could ever have consoled myself under my small troubles (which were great troubles to me), by impersonating my favourite characters in them—as I did—and by putting Mr. and Miss Murdstone into all the bad ones—which I did too.
>
> (56)

What the adult narrator finds "curious" about this phenomenon is the effectiveness of the device, not its mode of operation: he knows very well *how* it worked. The important feature of the folk hero, as of Captain Somebody of the British Navy, was that he won in the end, of course. By identifying with the children turned out into the forest, David persuades himself that he will find fame, fortune and the way back home. So this is how he reads Murdstone as not invincible, thinking that it is only a matter of getting through the enemy lines or into fairy godmother's cottage: a less literate boy might not have run away. And Aunt Betsey plays her role very well, even having a magical power to change people's names and nature: Richard Babley, poor simpleton in danger of being locked up, becomes Mr. Dick, a man of unfathomed powers of mind; David becomes Trotwood, a firm self-reliant fellow. Even on leaving Dr. Strong's, David feels that life is "more like a great fairy story, which I was about to begin to read" (273). Steerforth seems to David heroic, the perfect knight, just the sort to rescue ladies in distress. Steerforth knows differently, remarking of Ham, "Upon my soul, he's a true knight. He never leaves her!" (325). Similarly, folk and fairy tales inform David's attitude to Dora. "All was over in a moment. I had fulfilled my destiny. I was a captive and a slave. I loved Dora Spenlow to distraction! . . . She was more than human to me. She was a Fairy, a Sylph . . ." (30). But the ensuing stories of Steerforth and Emily, David and Dora, turn out to be not "great fairy stories" but tragic episodes from the book of real life. Faced with such tragic realities David finally recognizes that the consolations of romance and fairy tale are inadequate because they are illusory.

But meanwhile a different theme has been established in connection with the Wickfield-Heep story. The contrasts between the two are expressed through imagery. The contrast between Dora as Fairy and Agnes as Angel for instance, is often stressed. Agnes, when she speaks of Dora, seems to "shed glimpses of her own pure light" around that fairy-figure (519). Shortly afterwards, David is thinking of Agnes' "calm, seraphic eyes" when he is startled by the street beggar "Blind! Blind! Blind" echoing his Aunt's words. Agnes seems to David "one of the elements of my natural home" (491). The image he cherishes of her is that of the stained glass window. All this vaguely religious imagery surrounding Agnes has a bearing on the imagery surrounding Uriah Heep. This imagery is drawn from the Bible.

The first impression centers around the two ideas of death—he is cadaverous and has a skeleton hand—and reptilian hairlessness. The latter is elaborated. Uriah always "writhes" and is seen by David as "mean" and "fawning." "What? Uriah? That mean, fawning fellow, worm himself into such promotion!" (369). In Aunt Betsey's view he is "galvanic."

> 'If you're an eel, sir, conduct yourself like one. If you're a man, control your limbs, sir! Good God!' said my aunt, with great indignation, 'I am not going to be serpentined and corkscrewed out of my senses!'
>
> (517)

Uriah's eyes are usually red but on one occasion green, and lidless. He writhes like a conger eel on the occasion when David finds him instilling his poison into the of Dr. Strong.

The idea of death is developed in association with that of the serpent. Heep moves into Wickfield's house, into David's old room "polluting it." He brings his mother with her "evil eye." She looks like an "ill-looking enchantress" and the two are like "two great bats hanging over the whole house, and darkening it with their ugly forms" (572). When Uriah forces David to walk with him in the moonlight, David realizes that:

> . . . he was resolved to recompense himself by using his power. I had never doubted his meanness, his craft and malice; but I fully comprehended now, for the first time, what a base, unrelenting, and revengeful spirit, must have been engendered by this early and this long suppression.
>
> (575)

David feels when Uriah stays the night, as if he had "some meaner quality of devil" as his guest, and when he finally hits Uriah, after the scene at Strongs', he tells him to "go to the devil." Micawber's language is high-flown at the best of times but his description of Heep as "diabolical" does not seem out of step with these insights of David's. Nor with Traddles', who has neither a tendency to dramatize nor a personal interest. In describing Uriah after his exposure, Traddles says:

> He is such an incarnate hypocrite, that whatever object he pursues, he must pursue crookedly. It's his only compensation for the outward restraints he puts upon

himself. *Always creeping along the ground* to some small end or other, he will always magnify every object in the way; and consequently will hate and suspect everybody that comes, in the most innocent manner, between him and it. So the crooked courses will become crookeder, at any moment, for the least reason, or for none.

> (778)

The gradual development of biblical imagery centers round the expulsion from the garden of Eden, that most celebrated story of intrusion into a home followed by its pollution and destruction and the dispossession of the inhabitants. I hope it is not too fanciful to note that Uriah writhes like a conger eel before his exposure and creeps along the ground after it.

Thus David Copperfield, novelist, conveys to the reader a development in the perceptions of young David. The change is involved in the way that Murdstone is seen as an ogre, then Steerforth eventually understood as a fallible human being, and Heep finally revealed as the devil. This is presented as a progress from fairy tale and folk lore (romance) through the experience of life (reality) to the higher truths of religion (allegory). To Copperfield they are all versions of the same story and only the last interpretation is correct. The final consummatory insight reveals part of the answer to David's question for whereas ogres are always annihilated and giants fall with a mighty crash, the devil is never destroyed and his intrusion into Eden, though foiled in the major aim, succeeds in the minor: not death but corruption. Innocence is not the human condition: the fallible human will, the undisciplined human heart deprive us of the right to expect security on earth.

Such is the interpretation of evil suggested by David Copperfield, traditional thinker. But the same tradition holds out hope also. Through the knowledge of evil we learn the nature and extent of grace. This constitutes the completion of the answer to young David's question offered by Copperfield. The heavenly battalions are veiled not only by allegory, but by comedy. Mr. Micawber, for instance, appears to be cast in the role of the avenging angel! That, of course is the way he plays the scene, pointing his ruler "like a ghostly truncheon" at Uriah whilst reading the list of his crimes. When Uriah makes a grab for it, "Mr. Micawber, *with a perfect miracle* of dexterity or luck, caught his advancing knuckles with the ruler, and disabled his right hand" (750). In the final scene, Micawber, Traddles, Aunt Betsey and Mr. Dick operate as a group to defeat Uriah Heep. In realistic terms this is implausible and funny; in terms of traditional allegory it is appropriate and consistent. Micawber and Traddles are complementary. Micawber, beaming over a bowl of punch while the bailiffs beat the door in downstairs, is usually taken as a portrait in improvidence. Improvidence may be contrasted with human providence—prudence, or with Divine Providence, in which Mr. Micawber has *faith* in strong measure. That is why he (and we) can enjoy the punch. And he is right. In the end something does "turn up"; his faith is rewarded. Traddles, on the other hand, has *patience* and *constancy*. He is perpetually compared to the pilgrim toiling uphill. It is, in fact "a pull." But again he is not mistaken: though the working and waiting is long and tedious, he finally reaches his goal and his home with Sophy is described in detail at the close of the book. Mr. Dick seems, even before he effects the reconciliation, to surround Dr. Strong and Annie with his simple love "like a building settled into its foundations." And Aunt Betsey, who repels not only the Murdstones but the redoubtable Mrs. Crupp, offers the best kind of security—she protects and shelters. Faith, constancy, love and strength thus come together to save for David the shadowy figure of Agnes, described in the last words of the book as his "soul," pointing upwards toward a promised heavenly home.[2]

III

The readers who have followed David Copperfield, traditional novelist, can go away from the book with their traditional consolations. But what of the readers of Charles Dickens? For them the book is disquieting rather than consoling. This I suggest, is because Dickens does not share his narrator's confidence in the traditional promise of grace and redemption, and that he deliberately plants his doubts in the book. The differences between the two novelists can be seen most clearly in the treatment of the three main agents of evil—Murdstone, Steerforth and Heep. On Copperfield's traditional reading, Murdstone is finally placed as a figure of romance and Heep as an allegorical type. For this reason, neither should feel to us "real." Certainly, Murdstone should seem no more real than Clara, Heep than Agnes. Only Steerforth should emerge as a real character—and even then no more real than Emily. But, in fact, in each case we react quite differently. Murdstone, Steerforth and Heep *all* strike the reader as more real than the characters surrounding them, more real than their place in the Copperfield scheme would warrant. In consequence, their efficacy is more credible than that of characters whose moral force we are asked to believe will finally triumph. And this discrepancy can not be explained away on the grounds of Dickens' notorious inability to draw convincing female characters nor on the grounds of his celebrated ability to create characters with "a life of their own." I shall show that he deliberately set out to convince the reader of the reality of their evil, and that in order to achieve that end, he drew upon the most scientific psychology he knew. Furthermore, I shall argue that he used that material in full awareness that it was associated with a world view very different from that of Copperfield.

First, consider the common elements in the following descriptions of the behaviour of Murdstone, Steerforth and Heep and its effects.

David's reactions to Murdstone are important to the book and they are at times ambivalent. He is fascinated and frightened by his stepfather, unable to sit in front of him on the horse "without turning my head sometimes, and looking up in his face" (22). When they confront each other alone for the first time after the marriage, David reports ". . . he shut the door, and sitting on a chair, and holding me standing before him, looked steadily into my eyes. I felt my own attracted, no less steadily, to his" (46). At that encounter David does as he is bidden but he afterwards comments:

> God help me, I might have been improved for my whole life, I might have been made another creature perhaps, for life, by a kind word at that season. A word of encouragement and explanation, of pity for my childish ignorance, of welcome home, of reassurance to me that it *was* home, might have made me dutiful to him in my heart henceforth, instead of in my hypocritical outside, and might have made me respect instead of hate him.
>
> (46-47, author's italics)

". . . the influence of the Murdstones upon me," David says "was like the fascination of two snakes on a wretched young bird" (55). They make him powerless to act or move, unable to protect or be protected by, his mother; they paralyze his will.

Steerforth fascinates and dazzles David. He appears first in a romantic light. Sitting in the dark, "thinking of his nice voice, and his fine face, and his easy manner, and his curling hair" (87). David finds it easy to understand Miss Creakle's falling in love with Steerforth. "He was a person of great power in my eyes" (88). Mr. Mell is aware of what is going on. Speaking of the power Steerforth can establish "over any mind here," he lays his hand on David's head. David himself offers this analysis of Steerforth's charm in the context of first introducing him to Mr. Peggotty:

> There was an ease in his manner—a gay and light manner it was, but not swaggering—which I still believe to have borne a kind of enchantment with it. I still believe him, in virtue of this carriage, his animal spirits, his delightful voice, his handsome face and figure, and, for aught I know, of some inborn power of attraction besides (which I think a few people possess), to have carried a spell with him to which it was a natural weakness to yield, and which not many persons could withstand.
>
> (104)

When they remeet on the brink of adulthood, Steerforth immediately reasserts his ascendancy. David spends a week at Steerforth's home in a condition he describes as "entranced." Then he takes his friend to Yarmouth where they interrupt the celebration of the betrothal of Emily and Ham. On that occasion Steerforth deplores making a gap in the fireside, and exerting all his skill, brings them "by degrees, into a charmed circle" (316). He even cheers up Mrs. Gummidge, who declares next day that she must have been "bewitched." And the zenith of Steerforth's influence is in the glorious drunk scene, when David declares, "Steerforth, you're the guiding star of my existence" (360).

Uriah Heep repels and horrifies David. After seeing the cadaverous face at the window and at closer quarters outside, David catches a glimpse of him "breathing into the pony's nostrils, and immediately covering them with his hand, as if he were putting some spell upon him" (219). In spite of David's physical repulsion the same fascination recurs.

> Though his face was towards me, I thought, for some time, the writing being between us, that he could not see me; but looking that way more attentively, it made me uncomfortable to observe that, every now and then, his sleepless eyes would come below the writing, like two red suns, and stealthily stare at me for I dare say a whole minute at a time, during which his pen went, or pretended to go, as cleverly as ever. I made several attempts to get out of their way—such as standing on a chair to look at a map on the other side of the room, and poring over the columns of a Kentish newspaper— but they always attracted me back again; and whenever I looked towards those two red suns, I was sure to find them, either just rising or just setting.
>
> (221)

Although David finds Uriah repulsive and hates contact with him, he feels as unable to conceal things from Uriah and his mother as he does from Steerforth's servant Littimer. "They did just what they liked with me; and wormed things out of me that I had no desire to tell . . ." (255). In dreams he muddles Uriah and Steerforth. It is at the height of Steerforth's influence, just after the drunk scene, that David hears of Uriah getting the partnership. Uriah hints at his intentions and David is seized with "an unsteadiness of hand, a sudden sense of being no match for him . . ." (379). When Uriah breaks the news of his love of Agnes, David feels giddy at:

> . . . the image of Agnes, outraged by so much as a thought of this red-headed animal's. . . . He seemed to swell and grow before my eyes; the room seemed full of the echoes of his voice; and the strange feeling (to which, perhaps, no-one is quite a stranger) that all this had occurred before, at some indefinite time, and that I knew what he was going to say next, took possession of me.
>
> (381)

Uriah spends the night by David's fire and David "attracted to him in very repulsion" cannot help going continually to look at him. And he can still compel

David against his will, forcing him to walk in the moonlight where David perceives for the first time "that he was determined to use his power."

What these three have in common is a mysterious power and influence over David which makes him unable to resist them. Although he fears Murdstone, loves Steerforth and hates Uriah Heep, this ability to impose their will on him is common to all three and consistent in its effects. David acknowledges feelings of helplessness and subjection in their company amounting to paralysis, even in situations where there is no overt intimidation. He simply cannot resist their powerful influence.

This influence is presented in terms drawn from hypnotism—magnetism, as Dickens called it. He became interested in the work of Elliotson in the early forties and discovered that he could himself hypnotize, experimenting on Kate. Elliotson became Dickens' family doctor and friend and Dickens continued to practice hypnotism and recommend Elliotson even after he was deprived of his chair by the Council of University College. It was while writing *Copperfield* that Dickens hypnotized Leech, who had been knocked out by a big wave at Broadstairs, and jocularly suggested setting himself up as a magnetist. He also brought Elliotson in at that time to treat his dying sister Fanny who was having difficulty sleeping. Through Elliotson and Chauncy Hare Townshend, Dickens certainly knew a lot of the psychological and physical theory surrounding the phenomenon of "magnetism." Both Elliotson (in the early work) and Townshend, in *Facts in Mesmerism* (1840) supported Mesmer's original theory of a universal force producing tides in the atmosphere and related to the forces of magnetism, gravity and electrical phenomena. The tides of the air are related to the tides of the sea and are higher at the new and full moons. The force was strong in some people, weak in others and, according to Townshend, was transmitted by the imposition of the mesmerizer's will on that of the subject. The management of scenes involving the influence of Murdstone, Steerforth and Heep clearly owes a great deal to what Dickens had observed and read of mesmeric trances: Murdstone sitting in a chair and holding David standing before him then staring into his eyes is behaving in exact accordance with the instructions of contemporary textbooks on mesmerism; Steerforth's "animal spirits" and "inborn power of attraction" are described in terms used by popularists of mesmerism; and the way David becomes giddy when Uriah seems to "swell and grow" before his eyes, accompanied by a feeling of déjà vu, corresponds with contemporary reports of the experience of being mesmerized. The connection is made most clearly with Steerforth, and this often-quoted scene, in which he exerts himself to influence Rosa Dartle, seems to me unmistakably a case of mesmerism:

During the whole of this day, but especially from this period of it, Steerforth *exerted himself with his utmost skill,* and that was with his utmost ease, to charm this singular creature into a pleasant and pleased companion. That he should succeed, was no matter of surprise to me. That she should struggle against *the fascinating influence of his delightful art*—delightful nature I thought it then—did not surprise me either; for I knew that she was sometimes jaundiced and perverse. I saw her features and her manner slowly change; I saw her look at him with growing admiration; I saw her try, more and more faintly, but always angrily, as if she condemned a weakness in herself, to resist the captivating power that he possessed; and finally, I saw her sharp glance soften, and her smile become quite gentle, and I ceased to be afraid of her as I had really been all day, and we all sat about the fire, talking and laughing together, with as little reserve as if we had been children.

(434-35)

Shortly afterwards, Steerforth persuades Rosa to play the harp for him in the following manner:

'. . . Sing us an Irish song, Rosa! and let me sit and listen as I used to do.'

He did not touch her, or the chair from which she had risen, but sat himself near the harp. She stood beside it for some little while, in a curious way, going through the motion of playing it with her right hand, but not sounding it. At length she sat down, and drew it to her with one sudden action, and played and sang.

I don't know what it was, in her touch or voice, that made that song the most unearthly I have ever heard in my life, or can imagine. There was something fearful in the reality of it. It was as if it had never been written, or set to music, but sprung out of the passion within her; which found imperfect utterance in the low sounds of her voice, and crouched again when all was still. I was dumb when she leaned beside the harp again, playing it, but not sounding it, with her right hand.

A minute more, and this had *roused me from my trance:*—Steerforth had left his seat, and gone to her, and had put his arm laughingly about her, and had said, 'Come, Rosa, for the future we will love each other very much!' And she had struck him, and had thrown him off with the fury of a wild cat, and had burst out of the room.

(435)

The connection of the whole Yarmouth-Steerforth plot with tides, the way David's imagination is related to his susceptibility, the importance of his dreams, and the whole memory procedure of the book are all topics touched on by the theories of the mesmerists that I have not space to develop here. The crucial topic for this discussion is the freedom of the will.

One of the objections raised against the physical theory of magnetism was that it precluded free will. Elliotson, as a progressive psychologist, was inclined to accept that consequence, but the Rev. Chauncy Hare Townshend tried to meet the objection. He could only argue, however, that the art itself was neutral—good in good hands, evil in evil hands. In evil hands it could be used to corrupt the will. "But in mesmerism, it is not only the manifestation but the very function of the will which is dominated. It cannot, if it would, rise to freedom; it is under a more than moral restraint."[3] But since it was thought to be a physical force, strong in some people, weak in others, it had to be shown that it was stronger in *good* people for a belief in Divine Providence to be maintained. But in *David Copperfield,* Dickens makes it strongest in *evil* people. Dickens' use of the theory makes it difficult to believe that merely allegorical forces of good will be able to overthrow forces of evil as mechanical and irresistible as the tides. Uriah's writhings are as galvanic as they are Satanic, and by them, he corrupts Wickfield's will. This makes it difficult to be consoled by Copperfield's assurances.

Copperfield could count on the support of people like the Rev. H. Meneile whose sermon, "Mesmerism a Satanic Agency" sold, according to a bitter contributor to *The Zoist,* over 3,000 copies. But Dickens, who practised mesmerism whilst writing *David Copperfield,* can hardly have been of that opinion unless he counted himself, like Steerforth, one of the damned. Perhaps he did. Or perhaps he was moving toward the determinist position of Elliotson. Clearly he had moved away from the traditional beliefs of his narrator, and gives enough evidence, one might almost call it scientific evidence, to throw doubt on those beliefs.

Dickens always held *David Copperfield* in special affection. One reason might be that it was his last farewell to a long and secure tradition: that in writing it he faced the fact that he was *not* David Copperfield. David Copperfield might feel assured of finding a home: Charles Dickens was left with a bleak house to live in.

Notes

1. All references are to the New Oxford Illustrated edition and except where otherwise stated, italics are mine.

2. David Copperfield is no mean novelist. The development is very subtle and carried out with discretion. David speaks of himself "wandering in a garden of Eden all the while with Dora," but this is embedded in references to fairy tales, and Aunt Betsey points to the grim fulfilment of childish fancy by likening them to the tragic Babes in the wood. In the illustrations to Chapter 41, in which Traddles and David are interviewed by Dora's aunts, the titles of pictures and books in the room support the ironies of the writing. Together with pictures called "Arcadia" and "The Last Appeal," there is a copy of *Paradise Regained,* not only ty-

ing together the marriage with David's childhood, but reminding us of Milton and the whole Christian myth. Similarly, the fairy tale imagery persists and is only gradually displaced by religious imagery. As late as p. 747 Uriah is described as an "ugly and rebellious genie watching a good spirit"—a nice combination of Genesis and *The Arabian Nights.*

3. *Facts in Mesmerism* (New York, 1843), p. 135.

Robert M. DeGraaff (essay date fall 1984)

SOURCE: DeGraaff, Robert M. "Self-Articulating Characters in *David Copperfield.*" *The Journal of Narrative Technique* 14, no. 3 (fall 1984): 214-22.

[*In the following essay, DeGraaff examines Dickens's methods of characterization in* David Copperfield, *and comments on the psychological depth of such characters as Mrs. Gummidge, Mr. Dick, Dora, and especially Aunt Betsey.*]

Ever since Forster asserted that Dickens ought to be bad because his characters are flat, but that he is nevertheless "one of our big writers,"[1] critics have been accepting the implied challenge and seeking to explain the mystery of Dickens's effective characterization. One trend has been to accept the view that Dickens's eccentrics are indeed caricatures and explain their power as coming, somehow, directly from Dickens—perhaps via the dramatic power or rhetorical force of his style. The characters are seen as mere puppets, seeming real because they are so vigorously manipulated by their creator. A more recent trend has been to regard Dickens's characters not as representations of people at all, but as symbolic counters—fragments, whose definition is determined by their place in a symbolic structure.

While these approaches can be interesting and productive, Dickens himself consistently claimed and believed that he was creating convincing representations of real people, as, for example, in his "Preface to the Cheap Edition, 1847," of *Pickwick Papers*:

It has been observed of Mr. Pickwick, that there is a decided change in his character, as these pages proceed, and that he becomes more good and more sensible. I do not think this change will appear forced or unnatural to my readers, if they will reflect that in real life the peculiarities and oddities of a man who has anything whimsical about him, generally impress us first, and that it is not until we are better acquainted with him that we usually begin to look below these superficial traits, and to know the better part of him.

It seems to me that Dickens deserves a further hearing on his own terms, and that many of his unforgettable characters, whatever symbolic functions they may be seen to serve, are unforgettable chiefly because of their vividly realized individual personalities.

Many of these characters reveal an inner life, or at least some degree of self-awareness. The problem is that Dickens's dramatic mode usually proscribes direct narrative analysis of personality or motivation. Readers expecting this sort of internal focus are thus bound to be disappointed; as Alfred Harbage notes,

Charges of lack of subtlety, or psychological truth, come from those who prefer a more literal kind of portraiture, but a greater show of accuracy does not always mean a greater impression of genuineness. There is a flaw in the "realistic" method. We do not come to know actual people by reading transcripts of thoughts passing through their minds, or analytical passages on their psyches. . . . We must observe and piece together surface clues to sub-surface characteristics.[2]

When the Dickens reader responds intelligently to his method of dramatic character presentation, he will find that many of the "drolls," who seemed initially to be summed up in a tag line or gesture, take on much greater human depth.

The psychological richness of the Micawbers has already been critically explored. William Hall aptly demonstrates that Mr. Micawber, for example, becomes more than a magnificently absurd rhetorician in being aware of his own absurdity:

His "rhetoric" is one of the means by which he attempts to preserve his "original form" against the inner and outer forces (of which he is clearly aware) which threaten to crush that form out of existence.[3]

Douglas Bush and James Kincaid[4] examine some of the moments of real feeling that humanize this odd couple, such as the moment when Mrs. Micawber, leaving London, suddenly seems to realize how small and defenseless young David really is and embraces him. It might be added that even Mrs. Micawber's tag line, which Forster took as a sign and seal of flatness, takes on a deeper human meaning when the tensions connected with moving to Canterbury lead to several repetitions of "I will never leave Mr. Micawber," to which Micawber responds "a little impatiently, 'I am not conscious that you are expected to do anything of the sort'" (Chapter XXXVI).[5] Touches like these add some human complexity to these "drolls," and convince us of their human reality. There is one special technique, however, which Dickens uses extensively in *David Copperfield,* to give his eccentric characters depth, and which has not received much critical notice—the moment of self-articulation.

Almost every character in *Copperfield,* at some point in the story, explains him or herself. In so doing the character reveals a level of awareness beneath the external eccentricity, and to the extent that this self-articulation seems natural and convincing, becomes more realistically human for us. A look at two of the minor figures in the novel, Mrs. Gummidge and Mr. Dick, and two of the more important ones, Dora and Aunt Betsey, should help to show how and how well Dickens's method works.

At her introduction in Chapter III, Mrs. Gummidge is shown to be a rather peevish, complaining old widow, for whom "everythink goes contrary," and who claims to feel her miseries more than other people do. In Chapter X she dampens the festive mood after the wedding of Peggotty and Barkis by bursting into tears after throwing the old shoe after the honeymoon chaise-cart, and then "sinking subdued into the arms of Ham, with the declaration that she knowed she was a burden, and had better be carried to the House at once." Although young David remarks that this seemed such a good idea "that Ham might have acted on it," the reader may here sense, behind the Gummidge tag line, some of the psychological difficulty in accepting continuous charity from so wonderfully benign a personage as Mr. Peggotty.

In our next brief glimpse of Mrs. Gummidge, we find her so happy at the announcement of Emily's engagement to Ham that she has at last forgotten herself, "clapping her hands like a madwoman" (Chapter XXI). We are now set up for the moment of self-articulation, which occurs in Chapter XXXI when the news of Emily's elopement with Steerforth reaches the Peggotty boat-house. With her benefactor struck down, offering wildly to rush off at once into the night and seek his niece throughout the world, Mrs. Gummidge steps forward to hold the household together, significantly transferring her personal epithets of "lone" and "lorn" to him. While some of her articulation may seem almost too articulate and David's subsequent insistence on her transformation into a cheerful and helpful person may seem rather too insistent, her evolution strikes us as psychologically sound, and therefore convincing.

A similarly effective process of characterization occurs with Aunt Betsey's mentally deranged ward, Mr. Dick.[6] Initially he is part of young David's Dover Road nightmare—a frightening apparition at an upstairs window of the Trotwood cottage when the battered boy first arrives there (though not nearly so daft as he had been described in Dickens's original draft).[7] In his first appearances he is continually scratching his head feebly or threatening to stand on one leg, but he becomes more comfortable with David over time, and we come to see that in dealing with people, as opposed to practical affairs, he is both intelligent and sensitive in his own way. He may be crazy, but he is not stupid. Thus we can accept as credible his self-analysis when he suggests to David that he is probably in a better position than anyone else to clear up the misunderstanding in the Strongs' marriage:

> "A poor fellow with a craze, sir," said Mr. Dick, "A simpleton, a weak-minded person—present company,

you know!" striking himself again, "may do what wonderful people may not do. I'll bring them together, boy. I'll try. They'll not blame *me*. They'll not object to *me*. They'll not mind what *I* do, if it's wrong. I'm only Mr. Dick. And who minds Dick? Dick's nobody! Whoo!" He blew a slight, contemptuous breath, as if he blew himself away.

(Chapter XLV)

Of course, in the subsequent scene Mr. Dick's direct and good-hearted simplicity does effect a strong reconciliation. Interestingly, the heavy melodrama of that scene may well shift the locus of interest for most modern readers from the Strongs to a Mr. Dick who has moved a step beyond mere background eccentricity.

A more important character in the novel, and one that has generated a great range of reader response, is Dora Spenlow. It is difficult for us to accept the sex role stereotyping in a character like Dora, but I think the critical objection to her as a fictional character is directly related to Dickens's technique of character self-articulation, and that critics who reject her would subscribe to some version of Professor Cockshut's critique of Edith Dombey—that her self-articulation is not credible because it would require "exceptional qualities of detachment and self-analysis" which the character, as created, does not seem to possess:

> [Dickens] is guilty here of a failing very common in novelists of strong convictions—he is making a character do the author's work for him by commenting (as if from above) upon her own personality.[8]

In other words, when Dora describes herself, just before her death, as too young and silly to have been a good wife for David (Chapter LIII), she reveals a self-awareness that a young and silly person would not have; and when she tries to arrange the subsequent marriage of David to Agnes, she reveals a quality of self-sacrifice not in keeping with her silly, vain and selfish personality.

Of course, the emotional power of these pathetic final scenes between David and Dora comes partly from the irony of Dora's revealing the very self-awareness that might have made her capable of a deeper human relationship in the future, just at the point of her death. Whether or not this pathos is felt to be justly earned or extorted must depend on whether or not the reader believes that there has been any real development of her character from the point of our introduction to her as a pouty, vain, feather-headed child, through the trials of her marriage and illness, to those final deathbed scenes. Certainly readers who believe in Dora can cite evidence of such development. When, for example, she begs David to regard her as his child-wife, she is clearly revealing an awareness of her own deficiencies (no matter that she may at the same time be attempting to escape or rationalize them).[9] And during her illness she is capable of a new sort of empathy, asking David, for example, whether he is very lonely when he goes downstairs.

While some readers may find Dora's self-articulation questionable, concerning the character of Aunt Betsey Trotwood, I believe there is no ambiguity: she is one of the most successful and satisfactory characters Dickens ever created. Perhaps better than any other Dickens character she justifies his argument in the preface to **Pickwick** that a person's eccentricities are bound to strike us first, our familiarity with the better part of him developing later.

Aunt Betsey first appears, in Chapter I of the novel, as a rigid figure coming up the garden walk and as a nose pressed against the window glass so vigorously that "it became perfectly flat and white in a moment." Her eyes survey the room mechanically from one side to the other "like a Saracen's Head in a Dutch clock," and the ensuing scene in which she assumes the child will be a girl because she wants to be godmother to a namesake-niece, awaits the issue impatiently popping jewellers' cotton in and out of her ears to the great discomfiture of attending Dr. Chillip, and finally aims a blow at the doctor with her bonnet and storms out of the house upon being told that it's a boy—all this emphasizes a mechanical rigidity in Aunt Betsey's character which reduces the scene to farce, and narrator-David concludes the episode by emphasizing her lack of human reality:

> She vanished like a discontented fairy; or like one of those supernatural beings [ghosts or spirits] whom it was popularly supposed I [having been born on a Friday late at night] was entitled to see.

But though her comic eccentricity is the delightful focus of this opening chapter, Dickens provides one suggestion of human feeling when David's childish mother, dissolved in sobs, "had a fancy that she felt Miss Betsey touch her hair, and that with no ungentle hand. . . ."

Aunt Betsey now drops out of the story altogether until Chapter XIII, when the young boy David, with the recklessness bred of hopeless misery and despair at Murdstone and Grinby's, carries out a "great resolution" and seeks her out at Dover. His first sight of her recalls the rigid mechanical qualities of her initial appearance, as she comes stalking out of her cottage "exactly as my poor mother had so often described her stalking up our garden at Blunderstone Rookery." And to this is added a formidable hostility, as she is carrying a great knife which she waves in the air saying, "Go along! No boys here!" But desperate David utters the magic word, "Aunt," transforming the ogre-witch into family:

"'Lord!' said my aunt. And sat flat down in the garden-path." What follows in the rest of this chapter and the next is one of the prime examples in Dickens's work of his potent blend of near-farcical comedy and human drama. The drama results from our sympathetic identification with the suffering child and our hope that he will at last be provided for, and it is intensified by the comic relief of Aunt Betsey's various extravagant actions—in dosing David with sips of everything in her kitchen cabinet ("I am sure I tasted aniseed water, anchovy sauce, and salad dressing"), in consulting the apparently mad Mr. Dick as to what should be done with David, and in punctuating everything with abrupt attacks on donkeys and donkey boys invading her spot of green:

> In whatever occupation she was engaged, however interesting to her the conversation in which she was taking part, a donkey turned the current of her ideas in a moment, and she was upon him straight.

These donkey skirmishes illustrate how Dickens builds up the tension between Aunt Betsey's external comic eccentricity and the internal humanity we hope she will reveal; as David puts it:

> I thoroughly believe that but for those unfortunate donkeys, we should have come to a good understanding; for my aunt had laid her hand on my shoulder, and the impulse was upon me, thus emboldened, to embrace her and beseech her protection.

Nevertheless, the signs of a real humanity beneath Aunt Betsey's crusty exterior become clearer the longer David is with her. When he wakes from his first sleep it is "with the impression that my aunt had come and bent over me, and had put my hair away from my face, and laid my head more comfortably, and had then stood looking at me"—a passage that recalls Aunt Betsey's treatment of David's mother in Chapter I.[10] As David becomes aware (in Chapter XIV) of his aunt's kind treatment of Mr. Dick, his own hopes brighten:

> . . . I must say that the generosity of her championship of poor harmless Mr. Dick, not only inspired my young breast with some selfish hope for myself, but warmed it unselfishly towards her. I believe that I began to know that there was something about my aunt, notwithstanding her may eccentricities and odd humours to be honoured and trusted in.

Dickens skillfully interweaves the farcical and the humane dimensions of Aunt Betsey in the wonderful climax of this episode when she has it out with the Murdstones and formally becomes David's protectress (insisting on Mr. Dick as her co-guardian). On the one hand she shows herself capable of inferring the nature of Murdstone's relations with David and his mother with some psychological subtlety, as when she asserts that Murdstone now finds the sight of David odious because of his guilty feelings about how he had tormented the mother through the son; on the other hand, she is also capable of concluding the interview by turning suddenly upon despicable and metallic Jane Murdstone with: "'Let me see you ride a donkey over *my* green again, and as sure as you have a head upon your shoulders, I'll knock your bonnet off, and tread upon it!'"

From this point in the story on, we share David's developing understanding of the warm personality beneath Aunt Betsey's bluff exterior, but it is not until much later that we get her moment of self-articulation—which comes in two stages. The first occurs in Chapter XXIII, when David questions the appropriateness of her paying a thousand pounds to article him as a proctor:

> "It's in vain, Trot, to recall the past, unless it works some influence upon the present. Perhaps I might have been better friends with your poor father. Perhaps I might have been better friends with that poor child your mother, even after your sister Betsey Trotwood disappointed me [i.e., in being born a boy—David]. When you came to me, a little runaway boy, all dusty and way-worn, perhaps I thought so. From that time until now, Trot, you have ever been a credit to me and a pride and a pleasure. I have no other claim upon my means. . . . Only be a loving child to me in my age, and bear with my whims and fancies; and you will do more for an old woman whose prime of life was not so happy or conciliating as it might have been, than ever that old woman did for you."

The second passage occurs in Chapter XLIV, after David has asked her to help him in his first marriage by advising and counselling Dora a little:

> "Trot," returned my aunt, with some emotion, "no! Don't ask me such a thing."
>
> Her tone was so very earnest that I raised my eyes in surprise.
>
> "I look back on my life, child," said my aunt, "and I think of some who are in their graves, with whom I might have been on kinder terms. If I judged harshly of other people's mistakes in marriage, it may have been because I had bitter reason to judge harshly of my own. Let that pass. I have been a grumpy, frumpy, wayward sort of a woman, a good many years. I am still, and I always shall be. But you and I have done one another some good, Trot—at all events, you have done me good, my dear; and division must not come between us, at this time of day."

What these passages effectively do is fill in, retroactively, the gaps in David's youthful perceptions of his aunt and of their life together by expressing Aunt Betsey's side of the emotional relationship and what it has meant to her. This stimulates the reader to go back over the ground already covered by David's narrative, but from a slightly different point of view; Aunt Betsey is not simply the ogre or fairy godmother perceivable by a child. Despite all the comic eccentricity recorded in the scene of David's birth, we can now give credence to the touch of a sympathetic hand which David's mother thought she felt, and to the expressions of sympathy David overheard while recuperating from his pilgrimage to Dover. As for the behavior that appeared cruel and arbitrary in the beginning, her disappointment in marriage is the explanation she offers.

Given this degree of self-consciousness in Aunt Betsey, and the personality it implies, we can retrospectively imagine something of what her real feelings were when she realized what desperate shape little David was in when he arrived at her house and she decided to adopt him, and then faced down the Murdstones to accomplish it. We may even become convinced that her treatment of Mr. Dick, which Leonard Manheim describes as sound psychotherapy,[11] is consciously practiced psychotherapy. Contained in her self-articulation is an explanation and apology for her early conduct to David's parents, but also an indication of how years of bringing up such a young child as David was have enriched her emotional life and humanized her personality.[12] By stimulating his readers to work backward from Aunt Betsey's moments of self-articulation, Dickens engages them in a collaborative process of filling in the depth of character which he has suggested but not directly expressed; the result in the case of Aunt Betsey is a convincing personality, comically eccentric, but humane. As Sylvere Monod has written:

> The presence of Betsey Trotwood in **David Copperfield** is the supreme achievement of Dickens' art. . . . Miss Betsey is an entirely imaginary creation, yet she is fully as convincing, as lively, and as real as the characters painted from identifiable originals.[13]

The main reason is that her self-description establishes for us a conscious personality beneath the external eccentricities, and stimulates us to supply, by a process of sympathetic imagination, the gaps in human understanding which young David has left in his narrative.

Dickens's technique of character self-articulation, at its worst, can seem contrived, as though the author is manipulating the character from above. But at its best, as in the case of Betsey Trotwood, it becomes an important strategy for giving human depth to characters who may seem initially to be mere caricatures.

Notes

1. E. M. Forster, *Aspects of the Novel* (New York: Harcourt, Brace, and Company, 1927), p. 109.

2. *A Kind of Power* (Philadelphia: American Philosophical Society, 1975), pp. 39-40.

3. "Caricature in Dickens and James," *University of Toronto Quarterly,* XXXIX (1970), 246. A diametrically opposed view of Micawber is taken by Garrett Stewart in *Dickens and the Trials of Imagi-*

nation (Cambridge, Mass.: Harvard University Press, 1974): Professor Stewart regards Micawber's rhetorical circumlocution as "escape artistry" (p. 143).

4. Douglas Bush, "A Note on Dickens' Humor," in *From Jane Austen to Joseph Conrad,* eds. Robert C. Rathburn and Martin Steinmann, Jr. (Minneapolis: University of Minnesota Press, 1958), pp. 82-91, and James R. Kincaid, *Dickens and the Rhetoric of Laughter* (London: Oxford University Press, 1971), especially pp. 180-181.

5. Dickens's reintroduction of the tag line "Barkis is willin'" in the Barkis death scene probably strikes most readers as more contrived and much less successful.

6. Professor Stanley Tick's ingenious case for Mr. Dick as a type of Dickens-as-writer ("The Memorializing of Mr. Dick," *Nineteenth-Century Fiction,* XXIV [1969], 142-53), related in some central way to the core of the novel, is a prime example of the sort of distortion that can occur when symbolic interpretation preempts realistic character analysis.

7. John Butt and Kathleen Tillotson, *Dickens at Work* (London: Methuen and Co., Ltd., 1957), p. 130. See also the commentary on Mr. Dick on pp. 134-35.

8. A. O. J. Cockshut, *The Imagination of Charles Dickens* (London: Collins, 1961), p. 105.

9. Compare Michael Black's contradictory view of this scene in *The Literature of Fidelity* (New York: Harper & Row, 1975), p. 98.

10. Aunt Betsey's sympathy for people, expressed when she thinks them asleep, is a sort of motif in the novel. It recurs in Chapter XXXV when she joins David in his London rooms after her apparent financial ruin. Here David, lying quietly as if asleep, observes her come into his room, sit down near him, and whisper "Poor boy!" to herself several times.

11. "Dickens' Fools and Madmen," in *Dickens Studies Annual,* II, ed. Robert Partlow (Carbondale: Southern Illinois University Press, 1972), p. 88.

12. Q. D. Leavis has an excellent analysis of Aunt Betsey in *Dickens the Novelist* (London: Chatto & Windus, 1970), pp. 61-64. She sees Betsey's development as a humanization of the purely rational.

13. *Dickens the Novelist* (Norman: University of Oklahoma Press, 1968), p. 335.

Iain Crawford (essay date winter 1986)

SOURCE: Crawford, Iain. "Sex and Seriousness in *David Copperfield." The Journal of Narrative Technique* 16, no. 1 (winter 1986): 41-54.

[*In the following essay, Crawford centers on the tension between Dickens's depiction of a Victorian earnestness in David, and the character's submerged feelings of sexual love in* David Copperfield.]

If David's struggle between his wayward emotions and the endeavor to discipline his heart has become a commonplace of *Copperfield* criticism, much recent writing on the novel has focused on those aspects of its narrative which go beyond the limitations of this basic dichotomy.[1] Despite this, the stance which David the narrator adopts towards the materials out of which he constructs his "written memory" has remained problematic, and this has led to wide divergencies of opinion on the ultimate state of his erstwhile undisciplined heart and, consequently, on the nature of his activities as editor of his life's story. I would argue here that, while overtly describing his progress through life in terms of those characteristically Victorian orthodoxies of earnestness and self-help, David in fact adopts such cultural desiderata as an acceptable and, for him, essential alternative to the sublimated sexual emotions which appear as a continual sub-text in his narrative. This strategy is principally evident in the contrast which emerges between the recurrent patterns of narrative motif into which he, apparently unwittingly, organizes his perceptions of the key figures in his life and the more overt account he gives of the parallel discoveries of his love for Agnes and vocation as a writer. It is this contrast between willed idea and insistent desire which surely offers the truest image of David's emotional development, and the unresolved discrepancy between the two that remains with him argues against suggestions that his narrative is a successful act of purgation or that, as Jerome Buckley has put it, he "transcends his miseries and bears few lasting scars."[2]

That David is engaged in a reconstruction of his past through memory has been frequently argued, most effectively by Robin Gilmour,[3] though it is also to be noted that he himself gives some indication of being aware of this process. One instance of this tendency is to be seen in the references he makes to eighteenth-century picaresque fiction, a love of which he shares with his creator. While the influence of this genre is apparent throughout the novels of Dickens's early career, none of them refer to it so frequently or directly as does *David Copperfield,* and on a number of occasions David himself likens some event in his story to an incident in *Roderick Random* or *Robinson Crusoe* (see, for example, 54, 382, 423).[4] Just as he had drawn comfort from his collection of books in the period after his mother's remarriage (48-9), so too in later life they offer him an imaginative alternative to some unpleasant event in the real world. Perhaps the most revealing instance of this is to be seen during his visit to Micawber in the King's Bench. In contrast to the excitement his contemporary, Pendennis, shows on a similar occasion, David responds with characteristic mildness and reduces the impact of what he sees by likening it to Roderick Random's imprisonment (142), thus making the suffering appear less immediate and, by association with the happy outcome of Roderick's story, suggesting the hope of eventual release. David himself is well aware on this occasion of his tendency to fictionalize:

> I set down this remembrance here, because it is an instance to myself of the manner in which I fitted my old books to my altered life, and made stories for myself, out of the streets, and out of men and women; and how some main points in the character I shall unconsciously develop, I suppose, in writing my life, were gradually forming all this while . . . When my thoughts go back, now, to that slow agony of my youth, I wonder how much of the histories I invented for such people hangs like a mist of fancy over well-remembered facts! When I tread the old ground, I do not wonder that I seem to see and pity, going on before me, an innocent romantic boy, making his imaginative world out of such strange experiences and sordid things!
>
> (144-45)

What he is perhaps less conscious of is the possibility of this becoming a habit throughout his narration, and it is precisely the subjective patterns into which he unwittingly organizes his account that give the deepest insight into his nature and which reveal most about his motivations in the retelling of his personal history.

Nowhere is this more the case than in his description of the ways he perceives the people who come into his life. As is Dickens's usual practice, the characters of *David Copperfield* are delineated in terms of a restricted range of their physical features, hands, hair and eyes being the most important—a selection which may owe as much to Dickens's interest it its theatrical potential as it does to Victorian prohibitions against description of the human, and especially the female, body. What is innovatory in *Copperfield,* however, is the extent to which such apparently formulaic description is itself revealing of the perceiving and narrating consciousness which records it. David's inner emotional life is revealed through such description, and it can be observed that his subjects divide into two broad groups: dark, powerful figures who will their dominance upon him; and charming but pliable characters to whom he is attracted.

Although we are given very few details of David's own appearance, what we do know casts significant light upon his relationships with the other characters in his account. He is chubby (77), small for his age as a child (138), and as a young man, retains a certain fresh innocence (246). This latter quality is particularly important, for it is part of a softness and even a pliability which frequently allow other people to dominate him, something true not only of his encounters with his social inferiors (the waiter at the Golden Cross [243-44] or Littimer [278, 291], for example), but also of the major relationships in his life. As Sylvere Monod has appropriately suggested, there is a certain femininity to David,[5] something also evident in certain of Browne's illustrations, most notably Plate XVIII, "I Fall into Captivity." However, we should neither laugh off this soft weakness as David appears to do nor should we allow it to conceal from us the fact that, from very early in life, his physical responses to others are both complex and clearly discriminating.

All of his relationships, for instance, are strongly defined by physical contact. Through touch David expresses much of that personal warmth which is one of his most attractive features. Both during his childhood and later, he and Peggotty frequently embrace (54, 119, 262), a detail which is given an appropriately comic tone by the repeated references to her explosive buttons. A similar expressiveness marks his relationships with Steerforth (245) and Betsy Trotwood (587-88), as well as those with such other characters as Wickfield and Dr. Strong, and it may well be the case that no other Dickensian hero is so defined by touch as is David. The importance of this motif in Dickens's conception of his hero is indicated by his care to include it when David parts from Steerforth for the last time, "Never more, oh God forgive you, Steerforth! to touch that passive hand in love and friendship. Never, never more!" (373), a detail deliberately prepared for in the number plan (765). This emphasis, and the striking parallel it coincidentally finds in Tennyson's recollections of his great lost friendship, may well be indicative of the cultural value touch held for the Victorians, but it is also to have a particular meaning within the novel.

For David similarly reveals his feelings of animosity through motifs of physical contact, most notably with Murdstone and Uriah Heep. From his first childhood meeting with Murdstone, David expresses hostility and reveals his fear of being replaced in his mother's affections: "He patted me on the head; but somehow, I didn't like him or his deep voice, and I was jealous that his hand should touch my mother's in touching me—which it did. I put it away, as roughly as I could" (15-16). As is the case with his fictionalizing of his experience, David reveals far more awareness of his emotional life when recollecting events from his childhood; as the narrative approaches closer to the point from which he writes, he becomes less able to distinguish perception and motivation. Such is certainly the case in his description of Uriah where he reveals a rather more complex set of responses than he had shown in the fairly simple opposition of acceptance and rejection that characterizes his depiction of Murdstone.[6] Few characters in all Dickens are so insistently and repetitively described as is Uriah Heep, and references to his hands make up an important part of David's response. Not only are they clammy and fishlike (202, 519), but they never stop moving, whether it be to rub his chin or, in a superbly grotesque detail, to cover the pony's nostrils after apparently breathing into them (187-88). David can resist neither the fascination these hands have for him nor Uriah's power to dominate him manually (325, 441, 489) and, through his repeated references to this and other aspects of Uriah's appearance, he gives ample evidence of the way he is "attracted to him in very repulsion" (328). Moreover, it is a measure of the complexity of response that *Copperfield* calls for that, where every reader will sympathize with David's biting of Murdstone's hand (50), his striking of Uriah (579) evokes only the feeling of shame and faint self-disgust he himself experiences.

The sexual undercurrent in David's description is even more evident in his observation of hair and eyes. He tends to see people in highly pictorial terms, frequently associating them with one particular image which he retains in his memory like a snapshot, a habit which is especially true of those images of his mother which he stores away and draws upon in times of trouble. One of the most important of these pictures is saved from that single peaceful holiday afternoon:

> I crept close to my mother's side according to our old custom, broken now a long time, and sat with my arms embracing her waist, and my little red cheek on her shoulder, and once more felt her beautiful hair drooping over me—like an angel's wing as I used to think, I recollect—and was very happy indeed.
>
> (96)

The security and protection he thus gains are essential to him and surely make up part of that "fanciful picture" of his mother which sustains him on the road to Dover (160). However, she also offers him another kind of femininity in the sexual attractiveness of her hair, something which she takes pride in and of which he is well aware, even as a child:

> When my mother is out of breath and rests herself in an elbow-chair, I watch her winding her bright curls round her fingers, and straitening her waist, and nobody knows better than I do that she likes to look so well, and is proud of being so pretty.
>
> (13)

Curls are also to be an important part of his later description of Dora's girlish charm (460) and, as has often been remarked, in her David rediscovers aspects of his mother and comes to a temporary solution of his Oedipal conflicts. There are, however, certain key differences, for where his mother had offered him security as well as sexual attraction, Dora fulfills only the latter need. Both women, though, fall victim to his tendency to see people in static terms: when Mrs. Copperfield's sexuality becomes more than the latent attractiveness he had appreciated, and she actually remarries, their relationship loses its idyllic quality and they can only recapture it, fleetingly, on that one holiday occasion. Dora has even more to complain of, since, as far as David is concerned, she so far fails to evolve that he can only solve his emotional needs by transferring his affections to Agnes.

During his childhood, David is also offered a dominating masculine ideal which contrasts strongly with both his mother's delicate femininity and the gentleness of his own character. Murdstone is, as even David admits, an attractive man and he brings the best out of Mrs. Copperfield (16). Although he may in both appearance and activity resemble the Captain Murderer figure of fairy-tale,[7] there is no denying his sexual vitality:

> Several times when I glanced at him, I observed that appearance with a sort of awe, and wondered what he was thinking about so closely. His hair and whiskers were blacker and thicker, looked at so near, than even I had given them credit for being. A squareness about the lower part of his face, and the dotted indication of the strong black beard he shaved close every day, reminded me of the waxwork that had travelled into our neighbourhood some half-a-year before. This, his regular eyebrows, and the rich white, and black, and brown, of his complexion—confound his complexion, and his memory!—made me think him, in spite of my misgivings, a very handsome man. I have no doubt that my poor dear mother thought him so too.
>
> (19)

How engaged such writing is when set beside the stilted tones of his later descriptions of Agnes! For David's reaction here is made up of fascination and resentment, both at the knowledge of the threat of being displaced in his mother's affections and the knowledge of being unable to do anything about it. Even years later when he and Murdstone meet again in London he cannot prevent himself noticing the older man's still imposing masculinity (407), and it is evident that he never fully escapes from Murdstone's hold. That such details of physical description are integral to their relationship is apparent, and Dickens's own conscious awareness of this as a narrative strategy is perhaps indicated by the various references to Murdstone's appearance which are to be found in the number plans as well as in the running title later added to chapter two of the Charles Dickens edition, "The Gentleman with Black Whiskers."

The sexual connotations of hair are also apparent in other less than entirely benign characters. Steerforth's curls (75), together with his nice voice, fine face and easy manner, suggest that luxuriant sensuality which is central to his personality. Uriah's cadaverously cropped head and lack of facial hair (187) are essential details in David's communication of the sense of horror his would-be rival creates in him. It is to be noted, however, that Uriah's desire for Agnes is by far the most vivid rendering of lust in the novel, if not in all Dickens. Beside it even the Steerforth-Emily elopement has very little force. Uriah's feelings for Agnes are far more powerfully urgent than David's and, although such lust lacking quality is typical of the Dickensian hero, the discord between David's statements of feeling and his actual displayed emotion and the further contrast with the equal temper of Uriah's unheroic heart create serious confusion among the novel's scale of sexual values. While it is probably true, as Ross Dabney has said, that "Dickens makes sexual relationships real only when they are horrible to contemplate,"[8] the result is a major dilemma within the novel, the implications of which become further apparent in David's observations of people's eyes.

The contrast between dominated and dominating characters which David first reveals in his patterns of reference to touch and hands is substantially developed through ocular detail, for eyes, as Dickens remarks in **Bleak House,** are the window to the soul, and there is little question but that they offer one of the sharpest insights into David's emotional world. A particularly revealing instance of this is to be found in color coding; it soon becomes apparent that David has a special partiality for things blue. Both Emily and Dora are blue-eyed (121; 549) and this is a detail to which David habitually refers when describing them (632, 552, 609, 655). He is easily captivated by them both and they share a certain delicate beauty and light charm, something which is emphasized by further instances of this formulaic color tagging. Just as Dora will be nicknamed "Little Blossom" by Betsey Trotwood, so too Emily is described by Mr. Omer as "a little piece of blue-eyed blossom" (376). Dora is often seen in or associated with blue ribbons (337, 467, 538); Emily ties a blue ribbon round Minnie Joram's neck on the night of her elopement (392—the color is specified in the running title added for the Charles Dickens edition), and the association of the color with sexuality is later to be reiterated by her poignant recollections of the blue Mediterranean waters (498, 576).[9] Emily's set of blue beads (27) is matched by the ring of blue forget-me-nots David later buys Dora (417), a detail which offers a finely delicate insight into the complexity of David's feelings for her, since he also records the pang he feels when seeing a similar ring on his daughter's finger years later (418). Such parallels serve to bring out delicately the links between the two girls in David's mind, and also, perhaps, through the greater frequency and precision of reference to Dora, which of them matters most to him. Other references to the color blue rein-

force its significance to David as an emblem of his romantic fantasy and also help cement that link between the character and his creator, for blue was also Dickens's own favorite tone.[10] After the blue-eyed charms of Miss Larkins have smitten him in schoolboy days (229-32), for example, he is to be drawn to yet another charmer in the person of the Steerforths' pretty maid with her blue ribbons (367). The narrative pattern of reference revealed through David's descriptive habits thus extends to become a significantly unconscious mode by which he reveals much about his responsiveness to sexual attraction.

A contrasting pattern is, however, revealed through his account of a group of characters who exercise a very different kind of hold over him, almost hypnotically capturing and subduing his personality by the sheer force of their own, and it is perhaps no surprise that his portrayal of their ocular power parallels his observations of their hands and hair. Thus Murdstone, for example, fascinates the young David with eyes from which the boy can hardly tear his gaze during that ride to Yarmouth:

> He had that kind of shallow black eye—I want a better word to express an eye that has no depth in it to be looked into—which, when it is abstracted, seems from some peculiarity of light to be disfigured, for a moment at a time, by a cast. Several times when I glanced at him, I observed that appearance with a sort of awe, and wondered what he was thinking about so closely."
>
> (19)

We are hardly surprised when, a little later, David testifies to the mesmeric hold his step-father has over him (39). As Fred Kaplan has argued, the relationship between mesmeric operator and passive subject is a recurrent one in Dickens's fiction and is invariably associated with sexuality,[11] which is clearly the case with David. For, just as Murdstone's hypnotic eyes haunt him, so too do Uriah's red suns of orbs (190) and, even more revealingly, Rosa Dartle's:

> So surely as I looked towards her, did I see that eager visage, with its gaunt black eyes and searching brow, intent on mine; or passing suddenly from mine to Steerforth's; or comprehending both of us at once. In this lynx-like scrutiny she was so far from faltering when she saw I observed it, that at such a time she only fixed her piercing look upon me with a more intent expression still. Blameless as I was, and knew that I was, in reference to any wrong she could possibly suspect me of, I shrunk before her strange eyes, quite unable to endure their hungry lustre.
>
> (368)

Like Murdstone's black eyes, these fix him helplessly and no other woman in the novel exercises such a hold over him. Even by his susceptible standards, his first reaction to her is unusually intense, "I felt myself falling a little in love with her. I could not help thinking, several times in the course of the evening, and particularly when I walked home at night, what delightful company she would be in Buckingham Street" (304). It is perhaps just as well that he does not see too much of her, since in both this curious comment and in his later reaction when she brings forward Littimer, "The air of wicked grace: of triumph, in which, strange to say, there was yet something feminine and alluring: with which she reclined upon the seat between us, and looked at me, was worthy of a cruel Princess in a Legend" (569), she evokes responses in him that he would find difficult to reconcile with his feelings for either Dora or Agnes.

Agnes provides the one exception to this broad dichotomy of response revealed through David's recording of motifs of physical depiction. She is given almost no physical presence in the novel at all: when she and David touch (312, 718), there is nothing at all sexual in the contact and it is curiously lacking in life beside his other encounters; the one descriptive detail that he does insist upon—that of her "clear calm eyes" (419)—has a similarly neutral effect; and, as Michael Steig has shown,[12] even Browne's illustrations give her very little substance in the text. In this, of course, she is to be contrasted with most of the other women in David's story, but, if he is so alive to the physical attractiveness of almost every woman he encounters, why does he so ignore this aspect of femininity whenever he mentions Agnes? Indeed, it is remarkable that, while almost every woman in the novel reciprocates his attention and frequently displays almost maternal protectiveness towards him—Peggotty, Betsey Trotwood, Mrs. Micawber, and the publican's wife in London (138-9) are all instances of this phenomenon—Agnes's feelings for him remain consistently vague, undefined, and almost vapid.

She can perhaps best be understood if she is seen as a variation upon a type of femininity that Dickens idealizes throughout his fiction, that of the earnest heroine, although I would argue that David's use of the ideal of earnestness constitutes an essential narrative strategem in his resolution of the dilemmas posed by that emotional nature which is revealed through his patterns of physical observation. The earnest heroine, who has much in common with the bride from heaven Alexander Welsh has described,[13] is the single most important feminine stereotype in Dickens, first appearing in the form of little Nell and present as late as ***Our Mutual Friend*** in the person of Lizzie Hexam. Typically, she is meek, devoted, self-sacrificing and largely sexless, and she is frequently subjected to both threats from the villain of the plot and a dilemma of choice between a more or less inadequate father and the new claims of the youthful hero. Her essential moral quality is that Victorian seriousness of purpose, dedication and rectitude cov-

ered under the term earnestness, which is also a characteristic to which the heroes of Dickens's later novel become increasingly responsive and which they themselves display more and more.

Agnes is clearly the example par excellence of this type, and she finds it quite impossible to be anything other than earnest in all she does. Her embodiment of the quality overshadows all other physical and emotional characteristics:

> There was always something in her modest voice that seemed to touch a chord within me, answering to that sound alone. It was always earnest; but when it was very earnest, as it was now, there was a thrill in it that quite subdued me. I sat looking at her as she cast her eyes down on her work; I sat seeming still to listen to her; and Steerforth, in spite of all my attachment to him, darkened in that tone.
>
> (313)

Whenever Dickens falls back from description of speech to that of voice it can usually be said that this is *faute de mieux* and Agnes is no exception. Moreover, the writing here is over-insistent and has none of the convincing delicacy David evinces with almost every other major character he describes—even Uriah Heep is rendered with a complexity of response that originates from a highly delicate sensibility. Throughout his depiction of Agnes, in fact, David insists upon her earnestness to an extent which renders it largely unpalatable and, unlike, for example, Florence Dombey or Amy Dorrit, she does not embody the quality in herself as much as she depends upon his perceiving it in her. In part, this stems from the fact that she has very little to do in the plot other than to sit and wait for him, but it is also related to her role as his spiritual mentor:

> She filled my heart with such good resolutions, strengthened my weakness so, by her example, so directed—I know not how, she was too modest and gentle to advise me in many words—the wandering ardor and unsettled purpose within me, that all the little good I have done, and all the harm I have foreborne, I solemnly believe I may refer to her.
>
> (443)

Though one's hackles may justifiably rise at such a misplaced anticipation of Sidney Carton, what is more important here is to note the extent to which Agnes's earnestness is not defined as an independent quality but takes its sole meaning and value from its significance for David himself:

> Whatever contradictions and inconsistencies there were within me, as there are within so many of us; whatever might have been so different, and so much better; whatever I had done, in which I had perversely wandered away from the voice of my own heart; I knew nothing of. I only knew that I was fervently in earnest, when I felt the rest and peace of having Agnes near me.
>
> (484)

Read in isolation, this might well lead one to assume that David has been guilty of grave moral transgression. He seems, indeed, to be casting himself in the role of the reformed picaresque hero so prominent in eighteenth-century fiction and in such Dickensian characters as Martin Chuzzlewit.

Whatever the limitations of Agnes's presentation, and however much we may question the narrative strategies by which David depicts both her and his life before it came under her influence, there is no doubting the fact that Dickens means us to take it all entirely seriously and, while his Victorian readers may have demurred at the actual presentation of Agnes's character, they certainly found little to object to in her idealized nature. Within the context of David's presentation of his emotional life, however, this stress upon earnestness takes on a specific meaning and has a vital function to perform. For earnestness, or rather the lack thereof, is the criterion by which he exorcises from his life the two characters who touch most deeply upon his deepest emotional being, Steerforth and Dora. Steerforth, while cast by the plot in the conventional and rather peripheral role of villainous seducer, is central to the emotional tides of the novel and exerts considerably more sway over its hero than do either of the heroines. David's very real but largely unacknowledged sexuality finds its principal outlet in his attraction to and vicarious identification with his Byronic doppelganger, and this does much to explain his inability to voice outright condemnation of the seduction of Emily. In startling contrast to this, however, the woman on whom his choice eventually falls has no difficulty in rejecting Steerforth unreservedly and in terms which are astonishingly powerful under the circumstances—a brief glimpse across a theatre (312-14). Agnes's outburst is surely a case of moral over-kill, for not only is it based upon the most superficial of encounters but also, at this stage of the plot, Steerforth has done nothing to merit such reprobation. Even if his purposelessness and lack of moral ballast, together with the attraction he holds for David, do make him a dangerous character and afford some justification for his being cast into the outer darkness, this does not account for Agnes's reaction here.

With Dora, though, the case is far more complex, since not only is it David who rejects the unsuitable character but also he does so through a subtly sustained presentation of her lack of the very quality he most prizes in his future partner. Thus, although Dickens may at first sight appear to be dealing with an issue he had faced in *Dombey and Son,* namely that of the difficulty of reconciling unworldly earnestness with depiction of the heroine as a woman capable of sexual response, what he is also doing is making this opposition central to his characterization of the two heroines, building it into the very structure of the novel. For Dora is anything but

earnest in the way Agnes is and in the way upon which David comes to place an increasing amount of stress as his narrative progresses. She is entirely girlish and her light charm is aptly caught in her nickname of Little Blossom. This, however, is not to say that she is anything other than utterly serious in her love for David and, while one would hardly wish to make any great claims for her personality, it is clear that she gives him all that is in her power to give. Moreover, and as Michael Slater has effectively argued,[14] Dora manages to reconcile within herself the limitations of her conventional upbringing and an instinctive emotional understanding that David clearly lacks. He, however, consciously measures her against a standard of earnestness by which she will inevitably be found wanting:

> I did feel, sometimes, for a little while, that I could have wished my wife had been my counsellor; had had more character and purpose, to sustain me and improve me by; had been endowed with power to fill up the void which somewhere seemed to be about me; but I felt as if this were an unearthly consummation of my happiness, that never had been meant to be, and never could have been.
>
> (552)

Not only does David seem quite unaware of the self-pitying quality of his halting prose and of his evading any responsibility for creating the situation in which he finds himself, but he also reveals an entirely characteristic need to depend upon somebody else for support—though he may use the language of self-help, his self, he appears to feel, is best helped by the efforts of others. Neither he nor Dickens seems aware of the inadequacies of his response to his wife or the horrifying convenience of her dying to make way for Agnes, but Dora at least has some revenge in one of her last remarks to her husband: "I loved you far too well, to say a reproachful word to you, in earnest—it was all the merit I had, except being pretty—or you thought me so" (657). Whether David could affirm a similar fidelity in his love for her seems questionable.[15]

Nevertheless, both he and Dickens seem quite confident that Dora was an unfortunate mistake and, while it was good to have loved, it was even better to have loved and lost. David's presentation of her inadequacies is, moreover, given further and considerable support by his subsequent treatment of the theme of earnestness and the role he accords it in the development of both his character and his career as a novelist. Thus, on a number of occasions he is called upon to supply a certain want in his character:

> "Some one that I know, Trot," my aunt pursued, after a pause, "though of a very pliant disposition, has an earnestness of affection in him that reminds me of poor Baby. Earnestness is what that Somebody must look for, to sustain him and improve him Trot. Deep, down-right, faithful earnestness."

"If you only knew the earnestness of Dora, aunt!" I cried.

"Oh, Trot!" she said again; "blind, blind!" and without knowing why, I felt a vague unhappy loss or want of something overshadow me like a cloud.

(430)

The fact that such an apparently blameless piece of morality emanates from an entirely attractive, if rather eccentric character only helps to authenticate it and to obscure the extraordinary quality of her "blind, blind!" Yet although David appears to be candidly admitting a failing in himself, what he is surely also doing is subtly preparing his defenses for that later depiction of Dora's inadequacies as a wife. For it may be seen that while, here, "earnestness of affection" is cited to his credit, Dora is soon to be reproved for her lack of a more general kind of earnestness. A little over a hundred pages later (552) and when Dora has become his wife, David will closely echo his aunt's use of the language of self-improvement but will also omit any compensatory reference to Dora's earnestness of affection in his repetition of Betsey's emphasis on his need for sustaining help. Poor Dora thus loses out on both occasions and it is hard not to feel that she has become the victim of David's shifting criteria, while the reader, unaware of the change in emphasis, is lulled into unconscious acquiescence with the nature of David's argument.

David himself has no doubt of his own redemption through earnestness and he attributes all his worldly success to the quality:

> The man who reviews his own life, as I do mine, in going on here, from page to page, had need to have been a good man indeed, if he would be spared the sharp consciousness of many talents neglected, many opportunities wasted, many erratic and perverted feelings constantly at war within his breast, and defeating him. I do not hold one natural gift, I dare say, that I have not abused. My meaning simply is, that whatever I have tried to do in life, I have tried with all my heart to do well; that whatever I have devoted myself to, I have devoted myself to completely; that, in great aims and in small, I have always been thoroughly in earnest. I have never believed it possible that any natural or improved ability can claim immunity from the companionship of the steady, plain, hard-working qualities, and hope to gain its end. There is no such thing as such fulfilment on this earth. Some happy talent, and some fortunate opportunity, may form the two sides of the ladder on which some men mount, but the rounds of that ladder must be made of stuff to stand wear and tear; and there is no substitute for thorough-going, ardent, and sincere earnestness. Never to put one hand to anything, on which I could throw my whole self; and never to affect depreciation of my work, whatever it was; I find, now, to have been my golden rules.

(518)

The moving and dignified character of such writing and the fact that it is, to a real degree, a superb testimony to an in many ways admirable ideal which lies at the heart of Victorian culture should not blind us to its implications for David's personality and narration. For he clearly does believe that there is such a thing as fulfilment on this earth, only its name is Agnes and not Dora—to whom he certainly did not devote himself completely. Nevertheless, it is evident that he comes to make the concept of earnestness his most important criterion in judging both himself and others and uses it, above all, to justify transferring his affections from Dora to Agnes.

The often-discussed question of David's credibility as a novelist is relevant here, since it is closely related to the issue of his imaginative life, and through it, to his attitude to the two heroines. David is clearly highly imaginative; even as a child he constructs fictions that enable him to cope with the miseries of his existence. Whatever we may come to feel about the uses to which he puts his imaginativeness in that re-ordering of his life which the narrative constitutes, it is abundantly clear that such a capacity is essential to his whole being as a novelist, and it is Dora who, more than anyone else, most appreciates this aspect of David, paying tribute to it by describing him as "full of silent fancies" (553). By contrast with such delicate sensitivity, Agnes can only call his writing work and emphasize its value to society (698, 721-22), thus aligning herself with David's own comments upon the linked values of earnestness and work. However, if Dora realizes the importance of David's imaginative life, this is not to say that she possesses anything of the quality herself, and, had he made the point, this would have been a far more effective line of attack for Dickens than his condemnation of her inability to have the meals cooked on time. Unfortunately, such criticism would also have drawn attention to Agnes's even greater lack of silent fancy and to the deficiencies of David's (and, in this novel at least, Dickens's) whole conception of women.

This implicit opposition of the values of earnestness and sexual love is not confined to David's presentation of the twin heroines, for he also applies it in his consideration of Emily's elopement. Steerforth is not an earnest character, although he does express a curious "dark kind of earnestness" (275) as his thoughts wander amidst images in the fire—almost as if, once again, he offers an inverted model of David's ideals. So too, Emily herself, despite looking so "extraordinarily earnest and pretty" (123) as an innocent child, "wants heart" when she grows up and is easily tempted away from the earnest and hard-working Ham (227, 287, 629) by Steerforth's charm and the chance to become a lady without any need to ascend upon David's ladder of earnest endeavor. Mr. Peggotty's sole ambition from this point on is his earnest commitment to bring her home (620) and, while there may be something faintly disturbing in such devotion to his niece, there can be no doubting that David is making an equation between earnestness and the values of the family and domesticity, with the corollary that these are disrupted by the undisciplined sexuality of the eloping couple. His refraining from expressing overt condemnation of them may be thus accounted for, since he passes tacit judgement upon their actions by suggesting their aberration from such fundamental norms of the Victorian social world and yet also remains free to voice his own more personal feelings of sadness and loss.

The whole question of the discipline that is involved in the ideal of earnestness is one which raises fresh problems and carries implications that David again fails to appreciate. Not only is his insistence upon the undisciplined nature of his youthful heart subject to the limitations we have already seen, but it also brings him into rather unfortunate parallel with his much-resented stepfather. Just as both he and Murdstone court their future wives with a delicacy and charm emblemized by symmetrical references to geraniums (18, 338),[16] so too both come to find fault with their want of firmness once they are married and both are relieved of their inadequate spouses by illnesses and death—and illnesses, incidentally, which in both cases have their origins in pregnancy. It is as if, in both cases, some monstrous revenge is being wreaked upon the delicate femininity of these women who, not proving able to satisfy their husbands' criteria of personal strength, are punished through that uniquely female capacity, the gift of life. However, where there is no question of Murdstone's own personal strength, David is in many ways a weak character and there is something decidedly inconsistent in his complaining of a lack of resolution in others. If he does indeed discipline himself by the later stages of the novel and thus make himself worthy of Agnes, we may well feel that he has achieved this strength at the expense of many of the less controlled, more spontaneous emotional qualities he possesses and at the price of sacrificing much of his memory of Dora to an ideal which seems seriously deficient in humanity. Earnestness, as it is presented in *David Copperfield,* is a narrowing, exclusive quality which has none of the human warmth or spiritual depth it usually bears in Dickens's novels and we should surely resist David's (and Dickens's) attempts to persuade us to accept it as an unquestioned ideal by which the relative worth of the various figures in his story is to be measured.

There is much in *Copperfield* which lies outside this dichotomy into which David structures his emotional life, and it is part of the novel's greatness that it contains characters and values quite inimical to the orthodox beliefs its hero comes to voice and which he uses so subtly in his direction of the reader's response to the course of his life. Indeed, that same retrospective mode of narration which David uses to re-align certain events in his past with the priorities of his later life also allows and, in fact, obliges him to present that past in truthful immediacy. As Robin Gilmour has aptly put it, there is "a discrepancy between the attitude to the past required by David's attempt to discipline his undisciplined heart and the reality of the past as it is re-experienced in his memory,"[17] and it is this distinction which leads David to give weight to comic and imaginative values that find little place in his and Agnes's scheme of earnestness but which do enrich the narrative immeasurably. The outstanding individual example of this tendency would be Wilkins Micawber, but, more generally, the novel is colored by emotions which, though recollected in the tranquillity of life with Agnes, go far beyond the limitations of her view of the world and humankind.

It is perhaps no wonder that Freud so liked *David Copperfield*: "Every child at play," he wrote, "behaves like an imaginative writer, in that he creates a world of his own or, more truly, he rearranges the things of his world and orders it in a new way that pleases him better . . ."[18] David, of course, does precisely this throughout his narrative, re-ordering the events of his past life so that they and the emotions associated with them may be either excluded from the present or only revived in a controlled form. But if, as Matthew Arnold thought, the novel is an all-containing treasure-house of English middle-class civilization,"[19] this is not to say that it is simply "the epitome of Victorian bourgeois morality."[20] For no fiction is perfect, the treasure-box turns out to be Pandora's and, in opening it, David and Dickens indicate limitations in the very ideals they mean to champion. Like the speaker of the dramatic monologue, David betrays a deeply imaginative insight into those fundamental cultural norms of Victorian society which his life's story claims to uncritically embody. Whether Dickens himself was aware of how much he had given away is debatable, but that he had not finally resolved the issues raised in *Copperfield* is evident from his returning to many of them throughout the 1850s and, above all, from his re-working of many of David's themes in what is perhaps his finest novel, *Great Expectations.*

Notes

1. See, for example, Stanley Friedman, "Dickens' Mid-Victorian Theodicy," *Dickens Studies Annual,* 7 (1978), 128-50, or Gordon D. Hirsch, "A Psychoanalytic Reading of *David Copperfield,*" *The Victorian Newsletter,* 58 (Fall 1980), 1-5.

2. *Season of Youth* (Cambridge, Mass.: Harvard University Press; 1974), pp. 17-18.

3. "Memory in *David Copperfield,*" *The Dickensian,* 71 (1975), 30-42.

4. All references are to the Clarendon edition of the novel, ed. Nina Burgis (Oxford, 1981), and will be included in the text.

5. *Dickens the Novelist* (Norman, Oklahoma: University of Oklahoma Press, 1968), p. 323.

6. Uriah is usefully discussed by Michael Irwin in his *Picturing: Description and Illusion in the Nineteenth Century Novel* (London: George Allen and Unwin, 1979), pp. 78-81.

7. See Gillian M. V. Thomas, "The Miser in Dickens's Novels and Nineteenth Century Urban Folklore," Diss. University of London 1972, p. 27.

8. *Love and Property in the Novel of Dickens* (London: Chatto and Windus, 1972), p. 69.

9. Dickens's own proximity to the characters of this novel is again evident in his comment to Maclise: "If you ever have occasion to paint the Mediterranean, let it be exactly that colour. It lies before me now, as deeply and intensely blue." Quoted in Forster, *The Life of Charles Dickens*, ed. J. W. T. Ley (London: Cecil Palmer, 1928), p. 331.

10. See both the previous note and also Michael Slater, "David to Dora: A New Dickens Letter," *The Dickensian*, 68 (1972), p. 162.

11. *Dickens and Mesmerism: The Hidden Springs of Fiction* (Princeton: Princeton University Press, 1975), p. 188.

12. *Dickens and Phiz* (Bloomington and London: Indiana University Press, 1978), p. 130.

13. *The City of Dickens* (Oxford: Clarendon Press, 1970), Part III.

14. *Dickens and Women* (London: J. M. Dent & Sons Ltd., 1983), p. 248.

15. Rebecca Rodolf, "What David Copperfield Remembers of Dora's Death," *The Dickensian*, 77 (1981), 32-40, reads this scene perceptively, though from a point of view more sympathetic to David than mine.

16. Also, of course, Dickens's favorite flower. See, for instance, Mamie Dickens's *Charles Dickens, by His Eldest Daughter* (London, 1885), p. 103.

17. Gilmour, p. 36.

18. Quoted by Vereen M. Bell, "The Emotional Matrix of *David Copperfield*," *Studies in English Literature*, 8 (1968), 633-49.

19. *Irish Essays* (1882); reprinted in Philip Collins ed., *Dickens: The Critical Heritage* (London: Routledge and Kegan Paul, 1971), p. 269.

20. Angus Wilson, *The World of Charles Dickens* (1970); paperback edition, Harmondsworth: Penguin Books, 1972), p. 216.

Chris R. Vanden Bossche (essay date 1986)

SOURCE: Vanden Bossche, Chris R. "Cookery, not Rookery: Family and Class in *David Copperfield*." *Dickens Studies Annual* 15 (1986): 87-109.

[*In the following essay, Vanden Bossche interprets* David Copperfield *as "David's quest to regain social legiti-*macy *through the discovery of a family" defined according to the precepts of middle-class domesticity.*]

> "Why Rookery?" said Miss Betsey. "Cookery would have been more to the purpose, if you had any practical idea of life, either of you."
>
> (*David Copperfield,* chapter 1, p. 5)

Aunt Betsey's question about the name of the Copperfield home creates a division between two sets of values. Mr. Copperfield had tried to set himself up as a country gentleman by calling his home Blunderstone Rookery; to Aunt Betsey, this idea is as empty as the rooks' nests out in the yard. To the rookery, she opposes her own practical middle-class domesticity, represented by cookery. The rhyming conjunction of rookery and cookery never occurs again in the novel, but the two words do re-appear. Coming as it does, on the eve of David's birth, Betsey's comment directs the search for social legitimacy that constitutes the course of his career. Cast out of the Rookery, losing his family, he seeks to re-establish his identity by finding a new family and a new meaning for rookery. Like his father, he seeks the legitimacy of the country gentleman, and, in the subtitle of his autobiography, claims the title "David Copperfield the Younger of Blunderstone Rookery." But, by the time he completes his search for family and identity, the meaning of rookery has changed a great deal because he has accepted the values of cookery.

Dickens' novels always demonstrate the linkage between class and family, and *David Copperfield* can be read as a story of the triumph of the middle-class family.[1] Like so many novels, *David Copperfield* depicts a search for a family, but the family finally discovered sets this novel apart from eighteenth-century novels and even from an earlier Dickens novel like *Oliver Twist.* In *Twist,* as in *Tom Jones* or *Humphrey Clinker,* the orphan discovers his social identity, his place in the world, by discovering his familial origin.[2] Only within the notion of the aristocratic family does origin matter because this family defines itself in terms of lineage.[3] Oliver's notoriously correct English accent is his patrimony. Even so, when he discovers his parentage, his social origin, he also recovers his birthright and, most importantly, a complex of family relationships that reveal that Rose Maylie is his aunt: "A father, sister, and mother, were gained, and lost, in that one moment."[4] Even though the novel insists upon Oliver's basic human value, it finally affirms that that value rests upon his social origin; Jack Dawkins and Charley Bates, for whom no such discovery is possible, cannot escape from the den of thieves into middle-class respectability. *Great Expectations* returns to the same issues, but has Pip discover that his origins are criminal, that the basis for his status as gentleman is not owing to his natal origin (the motif of misidentification at birth), but to crime and money. It carries out what *David Copperfield* commences, an analysis of the naturalization and legitimation of social status.

David Copperfield establishes an intermediate position between these two novels. Whereas Oliver moves with naive certainty from his childhood in the workhouse into the middle-class world of the Brownlows, David Copperfield, though born and raised in a gentleman's home, never feels certain that he belongs among gentlemen as we are constantly reminded by his fears that servants and other social inferiors can see through his pretenses to that estate. Discovery of social position in family origin has become just as impossible as it is to be in *Great Expectations.* David already knows where he was born and who his parents were, but this is of little use to him in his future life. Nor does the novel reveal an original family or crime; it is not a novel of origin but of destination. In this regard it may be considered every bit as devastating in its critique of society as *Great Expectations.* While the substitution of social destination for social origin still aims to naturalize social status, legitimizing middle-class self-making, this novel also provides us with reasons to doubt that David has always been destined by providence to achieve this end.

David Copperfield begins with an initiatory loss of family and status, and its plot portrays David's quest to regain social legitimacy through the discovery of a family. In the process, he discovers three types of families, which while presented as alternatives, define a complex structure of class relations in which no single one could exist without the others. Only his journey through the first two makes it possible to enter the family he discovers at the novel's end. These three family types correspond to the three major loves in his life: Emily, Dora, and Agnes.

I

The novel's retrospective narration, the story told from David's destination as middle-class novelist and contented family man, reinforces the notion that *David Copperfield* is a novel of destination. This provides us with a way of understanding why the happy ending of *David Copperfield* differs from many other Dickens novels in that the family resides in London, not in a pastoral setting. For, in a significant way, the pastoral, though not depicted, makes the final scene of domestic bliss possible. In order to explain why, we must go back to the domestic and pastoral idylls of Blunderstone and Yarmouth presented in the beginning of the novel.

Blunderstone, before Murdstone arrives, is a self-enclosed community composed of David, his mother, and Peggotty. The idyllic nature of his childhood there is largely retrospective; indeed, it is already so in his childhood. The opening chapters, though presented as comedy, portray a series of childhood anxieties: Aunt Betsey's frightening arrival on the night of his birth, his fears of the ghost of his father, even a tyrannical Peg-

gotty.[5] And already in chapter two Murdstone intrudes upon the scene. The most idyllic scene occurs only after he has been sent away to school (chapter eight), a brief moment that David describes as a last taste of his idyllic childhood, but this former life is already a creative memory, the product of his resistance to Murdstone and Creakle.

His idyllic representation of this moment places it in the same space as Yarmouth. David presents his first visit to Yarmouth as an extension of the early childhood idyll into a timeless dimension. He gives it special force precisely because his visit means the end of that life; he has been sent there to be out of the way while Murdstone usurps his place. The idyll of Blunderstone is limited to the domestic sphere, but Yarmouth is full-blown pastoral, a lively pre-industrial community that, as Peggotty says, is "the finest place in the universe" (*DC,* 3, 25). David describes it as Edenic: timeless, classless, and innocent of the knowledge of good and (future) evil. The immediacy of the sea—the Peggottys live in a boat that has often sailed on it and that now lies on the sands close by it—makes this place seem a part of nature. Dickens' representation makes us want to call it a village rather than a city in order to emphasize what seems to be its natural order; the model is not the industrial midlands, but the agricultural village, its principal activity, fishing, like farming, being the provision of food. Furthermore, it does seem to be classless; the fishermen have no masters, and we see neither boat-owners nor the merchants who take the fish to market. Finally, both the boat-house and the town possess that element of neatness and busy snugness, that elementary but unfussy order, that so often characterizes idyllic spaces in Dickens. The very smallness of the boat-house makes it a child's paradise, as does the ingenuity and simplicity of its conversion to that purpose. And the town, crammed full of "gas-works, rope-walks, boat-builders' yards, ship-wrights' yards, ship-breakers' yards, caulkers' yards, riggers' lofts, [and] smith's forges" would seem to be the Wooden Midshipman of *Dombey and Son* unpacked into its more lively pastoral origins (*DC,* 3, 25).

Yarmouth represents David's first desperate attempt to find a family, the loss of which is symbolized by his displacement by Murdstone. When he first enters the boat-house, which becomes his fundamental emblem of the domestic idyll, "the perfect abode" (*DC,* 3, 26), he sees a family that does not really exist. In an ironic reversal of the discovery of father, mother, brother, and sister that closes novels like *Oliver Twist,* David finds that the occupants of the boat-house whom he sees as husband, wife, son, and daughter do not fit his preconceived categories. Yet he continues to identify them as a family precisely because their solidarity comes from the communal relationships that motivate Mr. Peggotty to gather this group together under his roof, not simply from the fact that they share the same dwelling or name.

By falling in love with little Emily, David expresses his desire to enter into this family that, because it remains outside of time, will remain an essential stage in his search for family. Even when he begins to feel his class difference and can no longer desire Emily herself, she and her family represent one aspect of the family he would ultimately create for himself.

But in making Yarmouth an idyll, he blots out all the problematic elements of the place: the sea, representative of its naturalness, also signifies death, and has "drowndead" two fathers and a husband in this group alone. (Later, we will be introduced to Yarmouth's other principal family, that of Omer and Joram the undertakers.) David's sense of equality is illusory for he is treated with deference, and Emily wants to be a lady, demonstrating her own recognition that Yarmouth exists in a class-bound society. David's failure to recognize these problems only emphasizes the fact that he wants to make Yarmouth an idyll. He never wants the real Yarmouth life, but a life that would fulfill his desires. It represents something that he desires and remains always as a representation, for he already expresses his distance from Yarmouth when he complains of its dreary flatness upon first arriving there (*DC*, 3, 24). In fact, his experiences there make him conscious for the first time of his own social position and, as much as anything, cause him to resist the loss of social status incumbent upon being sent to the bottle factory.

This new awareness of social status, more than Murdstone's shove down the social scale, makes David feel he has been deprived of any secure and legitimate social position. David's anxiety has a real social basis, for social mobility runs in both directions: even as many were arriving in the middle and upper classes others were being proletarianized, their position as lower gentry threatened by the changing structure of economic relations. David does not mind the work so much as the degrading company it forces him to keep, and the passage in which he describes the "secret agony of [his] soul" as he "sunk into this companionship," with its disparaging comparison between Mick Walker and Mealy Potatoes on the one hand and Traddles and Steerforth on the other, betrays a well-developed class consciousness (*DC*, 11, 133). Indeed, the passage shows such emphatic disregard for his fellow workers that, taken from their point of view and not that of the boy suffering the angst of social displacement, it comes as a shocking display of class violence. Yet he never recognizes the similarity between his alienation from the Peggottys and from these boys, and continues to idealize the Peggottys' condition even as he deplores the warehouse.

II

London represents David's exile from home, the city being the antithesis of the pastoral idyll. There he iden-

tifies not with his fellow mistreated workers, but with the Micawbers, who feel, like David, that they have been displaced from their proper social station. Just as David has lost his family, Mrs. Micawber claims to have lost hers. The Micawbers are a comic version of the aristocratic family David idealizes, the Steerforths. Mrs. Micawber constantly refers to her "family" in order to insist upon her pretension to gentility in the face of their actual situation (*DC*, 11, 136; 12, 146; 17, 222-223; 57, 689-691). But the Micawbers are never able to ally themselves with her always absent and therefore functionally fictitious family. We believe so much in their social status that we readily accept that Mr. Micawber's attempts to enter commerce as a corn factor and a coal seller are inappropriate. His (great) expectations that "something will turn up" are a parody of the plot in which the orphan's true identity finally returns him to his proper place in society. This adult orphan still awaits the return to social origins no longer possible in this novel, and, in the meantime, remains a bankrupt. Resisting a decline, whether real or imagined, into the status of middle-class tradespeople or the working class, the Micawbers insist that they belong to and are destined for the gentry just as David clings to the images of Blunderstone and his upper-class school chum, Steerforth.

When, after he has completed his schooling in Canterbury, he takes a journey to "look about" for a profession, he soon encounters the image of his desire, Steerforth, who introduces him to a new family that represents social legitimacy, the next family that David seeks to enter. The Steerforths, like the Peggottys, are fragmented, a bachelor, widow, and orphan, but here the fragmentation divides the family, as every member fights against the others. Nonetheless, whereas Mr. Peggotty immediately disabuses David of his vision of a family, the Steerforths insist that they are one. Family here does not represent communal values, but social status. Rosa speaks for her family when she asks if it is true that the Peggottys, because they are mere rustics, have no feelings (*DC*, 20, 251), and Mrs. Steerforth speaks from this point of view when she insists that it would be impossible for her son to marry Emily (*DC*, 32, 400). Most significantly, Rosa insists that only a real family, one that lays claim to that title through its legitimate lineage, can have a home; to her, only the Steerforth home, not the Peggotty home, is laid waste by the elopement of Emily and Steerforth (*DC*, 50, 614-615). These attitudes, along with their style of living, cause us, like David, to associate them with the aristocracy even though they apparently possess no titles. This family merely asserts its social status by claiming to be a special kind of family. David always seems shocked by their attitude, but he never rejects the Steerforths or submits them to the comic satire with which he represents the same pretensions of the Micawbers. He seems unaware that his sense of the Peggottys as unselfconscious country folk lies very close to the Steerforths' view of them as simply insensitive.

Although he takes the Steerforths as his model, he does not fall in love with Rosa Dartle, though he considers the possibility, but with another apparent representative of the gentry, Dora Spenlow. Aware that his social situation locks him out of the Steerforth world, he nonetheless aspires to it and accepts a career at Doctors' Commons upon Steerforth's assurance that they "plume themselves on their gentility there" (*DC,* 23, 293). Mr. Spenlow lives up to this characterization, claiming that "it [is] the genteelist profession in the world" (*DC,* 26, 331), and David's determination to fall in love with his daughter before he has ever met her indicates that he desires the social legitimacy of gentility as much as Dora's charms. Indeed, Dora's charms themselves simply signify her social status: flirtatiousness, silliness, guitar playing, even curls, all mark her class identity. Almost immediately, David fantasizes living with her in Highgate, the neighborhood where the Steerforths reside, and which he associates, therefore, with gentility.

David's representation of this stage of his career satirizes the aristocratic economy that he had embraced in order to signify his allegiance to that class. His amorous exploits are marked by these aspirations, and, like Steerforth, who can afford to buy a boat and take jaunts whenever he wishes, he becomes wasteful in his pursuit of Dora. Entertaining extravagantly, which incurs Agnes's disapproval, he spends a large portion of his allowance to become a dandy, buying shoes that are, like Dora's housekeeping, uncomfortable. He wastes time seeking a chance encounter with Dora, and when he is not doing that he is pursuing a career in Doctors' Commons where the principle of gentility is allied to the most wasteful of legal operations. With Aunt Betsey's bankruptcy, he undergoes a major transformation. Still motivated, as before, by the goal of attaining Dora, he embraces a totally different economy as a means of attaining her, replacing the show of indolence with dreams of industry. The time he had spent wandering the streets in search of Dora, he now spends as Doctor Strong's secretary, in his spare time working at shorthand to produce a surplus of literal and symbolic capital for his future.

But how can we explain this sudden abandonment of gentility in favor of what would seem to be the more mundane claims of the middle class? When he had previously been threatened with social displacement, it was precisely the aristocratic model that had motivated his escape. When he decided to flee London and the warehouse, he turned to Peggotty only for a loan, feeling that she could do no more than this for him. Betsey Trotwood, his father's aunt, had been his only hope for restoring his social status.

Though he feels he has succeeded, Dover and Canterbury do not represent gentility but the middle class. David encounters all the virtues of middle-class life there: Aunt Betsey's common sense and prudence, Dr. Strong and Annie's companionability, and, above all, the domestic virtues of Agnes Wickfield. He encounters tradespeople and professionals—teachers, lawyers, clerks, butchers—not gentry. Corresponding to the chance meeting with Steerforth that led him to choose Doctors' Commons, his chance encounter with Traddles now provides another model for his new means of attaining Dora. Although David always regards him with condescension, Traddles's steady accumulation of furniture and other capital—each step in his professional progress is a "pull"—in order to marry his Sophy parallels David's more melodramatic visions of self-improvement. Whereas, earlier, David had prided himself on Dora's accomplishments relative to Sophy's, he now seems to wish she had more of Sophy's household experience. Dora, for her part, almost instinctively fears both Traddles and Betsey Trotwood as representatives of an alien way of life (*DC,* 41, 513-514). In Mr. Spenlow he comes to see economic failure caused by the attempt to emulate gentility. Indeed, the middle-class economy defines itself as a rejection of the style of living that it considers a wasteful economy. But this sets up a comic conflict between David and Dora, the occasion of their first dispute in their courtship, and, as he himself points out, their first marital discord. The conflict arises when David announces to Dora that he has become poor, and asks her if she would try to learn about accounts and read a cookery book. We can recognize that in making this suggestion he is drawing on what he learned at Dover, because cookery was first introduced into the novel by Aunt Betsey.

Considering his objectives, David would undoubtedly have given Dora one of the many cookbooks aimed at "the middle class of society."[6] Eliza Acton's *Modern Cookery in All Its Branches,* considered the first cookbook especially designed for the middle class, appeared in 1845 and remained the most popular cookbook until the appearance of *Beeton* in 1861. Alexis Soyer's popular *The Modern Housewife or, Ménagère* (1849), published the same year as **Copperfield,** specifically claimed to aim at the "moderate scale" of the middle class, "leaving the aristocratic style entirely to its proper sphere."[7] Along with the cookery books came a panoply of domestic manuals. The title of the most famous of the nineteenth-century cookbooks, Isabella Beeton's *Book of Household Management* (1861), expresses the claims of cookery books themselves to provide much more than mere recipes. This book, which combined features found in many earlier ones, sold more copies than any Dickens novel. Other manuals—corresponding to our popular "how-to" books—offered specific domestic advice on the "servant problem," health, child-rearing, budget management, accounting, and all aspects of housekeeping, as well as the more edifying moral economy laid out in Sarah Ellis's tetralogy, also aimed at the middle class, *The Women, The Daughters, The Wives,* and *The Mothers of England* (1839, 1842, 1843, 1845).

While the contents vary widely, all of these books align themselves with what their authors prefer to call "domestic economy," the science of creating a "comfortable" home.[8] Nearly all of the domestic manuals instruct wives on how to budget their income and how to keep accounts of what they spend so that they can stay within their budget. Micawber understands the middle-class rule of domestic economy well. His famous advice, "Annual income twenty pounds, annual expenditure nineteen and six, result happiness. Annual income twenty pounds, annual expenditure twenty pounds ought and six, result misery" (*DC,* 12, 150) merely repeats a commonplace of the manuals regarding the basic budgetary process.[9] But Micawber finds this "advice so far worth taking" that he "has never taken it himself" (*DC,* 12, 149) because he lives within the aristocratic economy, and like Dora, cannot really comprehend this middle class one.[10]

The principle of economy extends far beyond income and expenditure. Even the style of cooking comes under this heading since the menus and recipes usually eschewed a complex style, beyond the capabilities of the serving staff of a middle-class household, in favor of fresh ingredients, simply and sensibly prepared. Beeton standardized measurements and provided precise information on how many people each recipe would serve and how much it would cost to prepare. Class distinction can even be found in the basic rules of cooking: "The object, then, is not only to *live,* but to live economically, agreeably, tastefully, and well" (p. 39). Beeton distinguishes her middle-class audience from the working class by awarding them a diet that goes beyond mere subsistence while at the same time proscribing excess; no scrap of food, right down to the drippings, can be wasted.[11] As Soyer's Mrs. B. insists, "I managed my kitchen and housekeeping at a moderate . . . expense compared with some of my neighbors, who lived expensively, but not so well as we did" (*The Modern Housewife,* p. 1).

If the novel represents Yarmouth as the scene of the tragic fall (both in terms of nostalgia for the lost pastoral realm and its destined effacement through the seduction of Emily, linked together by David's class awareness and his complicity with Steerforth), David's courtship of and marriage to Dora belongs to its comic-satiric strand. Writing from the point of view of his final allegiance to the middle class, David makes himself as well as Dora and the Micawbers the object of gentle but insistent satire. Yet he does not satirize their ambitions or their desire for a special social position, only

what he now deems to be a wasteful and irrational economics. From the time of his "conversion," when he rejects the aristocratic economy, the center of the comic scenes shifts from his own antics to Dora's inability to comprehend domestic economy, presenting the comedy of her "irrational" and "impractical" response to housekeeping (*DC,* 37, 461; 41, 516).

Dora's failure can be keyed precisely to a lack of understanding of domestic economy. As the domestic manuals demonstrate, this economy is not only monetary, but spatial, temporal, emotional, and moral. In fact, Dora does not make extravagant purchases, except perhaps the pagoda, and her housekeeping never seems to endanger their overall budget. Rather, David feels "uncomfortable" because she is so inefficient. The pagoda bothers him, not because of its expense, but because it wastes the very limited space of their cottage, as does the rest of the dining room clutter. Because "nothing ha[s] a place of its own," Traddles must squeeze himself in at the table amidst Dora's flower-painting, the guitar case, and the irrepressible Jip. Contrast this with the tranquility of the Wickfield drawing room, or with the Wooden Midshipman where each navigational instrument has its own box perfectly fitted to it, the ultimate expression of the adage "a place for everything and everything in its place" (see Warren, p. 45). Similarly, Dora wastes time because she cannot command her servants to get dinner ready on time, not because she is simply indolent. And, although she does not get into debt, she does waste money because she does not know how to market, choosing lobsters that are all water and unrecognizable joints of mutton, and buying a "beautiful little barrel" of unopened oysters, making her choice on aesthetic rather than economic grounds (*DC,* 44, 548). Because she does not know enough about cooking, her roasts turn out burnt or underdone; because she does not keep her accounts, tradespeople overcharge her for butter and pepper and servants charge cordials to her; and because she does not keep the pantry locked, the servants steal from her. Had she been able to endure the cookery book, it would have advised her on all of these matters.

If David finds Dora impractical and irrational, she finds his insistence on early rising and hard work "nonsensical" and "ridiculous" (*DC,* 37, 464). Since Dora's sense of economy is so totally foreign to his, it is only appropriate that the cookery book makes her head ache and ends up a play thing for Jip. In it she would have found the same complaints made by David without his mitigating charms. When he decides that she is already "formed" and simply will never comprehend his understanding of economy, he gives in to their warnings that the education of daughters is crucial to their future abilities as wives and housekeepers, crucial precisely because it will form their attitudes towards home and family.

Dora's absolute incomprehension of David's pride in his poverty comes from a completely different code of behavior corresponding to an aristocratic economy. These economic codes do not correspond, however, to actual economic differences between classes. This representation of the different economies originates from middle-class sources and a view of the national economy in which the symbolic, political, and economic capital of the aristocracy was felt to be steadily declining as that of the middle class was just as surely accumulating. Dora's code demands her total ignorance of money, while David would impose one that makes the housewife the keeper of the account book. From David's point of view, Dora lives within an open-ended economy that has driven her father to bankruptcy, an economy that employs leisure talents, like guitar playing and flower-painting, to represent its success by displaying the extent to which one can appear not to have to economize. For Dora, allegiance to this code is absolutely necessary if she is to marry, as her father had obviously planned, into the gentry. Whenever she endeavors to act the role of the middle-class housekeeper, however, she soon becomes weary, bored, and frustrated. Her most serious attempt at housekeeping is simply "make-belief . . . as if we had been keeping a baby-house for a joke" (*DC*, 44, 553). This childish and playful attitude towards housekeeping is entirely in keeping with her training and her other talents. She cannot work hard because her identity is formed by a notion of delicacy and ornamentation and her ability to charm with these talents.

The writers of the domestic manuals would have blamed all the problems of Dora's household on her, and on her parents for failing to make her better able to cope with them. Sending a daughter to school was itself suspect since the daughter would likely fail to learn household skills, and might furthermore learn values that would make her unwilling to do so. They argued that education should prepare young women for the role of housewife, both through training in domestic skills and by inculcating the sense of self-effacement necessary to motivate them to always consider the comfort of others.[12] Manuals like *Economy for the Single and Married,* for those like Dora and David whose income ranged between £50 and £500, complain that the education of women "in the middle classes" is "simply *ornamental,*" rendering them "indolent, useless, and a disgrace to their connexions."[13] Nor was this attitude limited to these manuals; Ruskin criticized the middle class for bringing up their girls "as if they were meant for sideboard ornaments."[14] So we should not be surprised when David complains of Dora that she "seemed by one consent to be regarded like a pretty toy or plaything" (*DC,* 41, 515-516).

Because female education had for some time focussed on the "refined accomplishments" identified with leisure activities (drawing, playing the piano, and French conversation), it is criticized for failing to prepare young women for their role as middle-class wives. Sarah Ellis bluntly charges that this sort of education is meant to reinforce the values of the aristocracy, its products learning, "for the future guidance of their future lives, the exact rules by which the outward conduct of a *lady* ought to be regulated" but not conduct appropriate to their own station in life (*Wives,* pp. 164-165). Ellis does not object because she regards this sort of education as pretentious social-climbing but because she believes in the moral superiority of middle-class life. While arguing that the schools fail to prepare young women for domestic duties, she and her fellow writers seem more concerned with the bad moral economy of a system in which these girls lose "the influence of household life and know as little how to cook a dinner as to cure a cold."[15] Consequently, Catherine Beecher, in a *Treatise on Domestic Economy,* suggests that less time be spent at school and more in domestic employments (p. 26), an argument undoubtedly welcome to those who could hardly afford to send their girls away to school anyway (Branca, pp. 45-46). The ideal, of course, is the wife who combines housekeeping efficiency with more refined accomplishments; after all, part of her role of creating a comfortable environment is aesthetic, and Soyer's Mr. B. is proud of his wife who was "first acquainted with the keys of the store-room before those of the piano" (p. 4).[16]

For the purposes of defining one's class status, the moral economy outweighs the economic one. David never complains about the actual economic consequences of Dora's housekeeping; despite the examples of the Micawbers and Mr. Spenlow, he seems confident that his industry will keep them ahead of their creditors. In portraying the comic "Ordeal of Servants," David stresses his public humiliation rather than the financial cost. On their comfortable income (already when they get married he is apparently making £350 which would put them at the top of the middle-class income level),[17] he is not as concerned with the loss of money itself as with the public display of wastefulness. He is ashamed, a feeling that he expresses obliquely when he complains that their housekeeping "is not *comfortable*" (*DC,* 44, 544, emphasis added). The domestic manuals, like David, are much concerned with comfort, whether it be comfort of shoes or the home; through the notion of comfort, the more mundane aspects of domestic economy are transferred to the moral sphere. In *How I Managed My Home,* Mrs. Allison's friend Bertha insists on finding a way to dispose of stale bread because she is concerned with the moral, not the negligible monetary, significance of wasting it. At this point, domestic economy becomes socially significant as well because one's commitment to its morality signifies one's values and class loyalty. David does not care about the physical discomforts of Dora's housekeeping so much as the "something wanting" that pervades his life, the emptiness of that signifier, "David Copperfield the Younger of Blunderstone Rookery," which was to have been filled up by his marriage to Dora, but persists throughout it (48, 594). He learns that Dora's gentility is only another empty signifier, and this ultimately generates his desire for the home-maker, the woman designated upon her first appearance in the book, when still a child, as a "housekeeper" (*DC,* 15, 191).[18]

III

The cookery books and household manuals that would only have hurt and baffled Dora would tell Agnes what she already knew. If she read them, she would not go to them for information but for reinforcement of her identity in a world that had always based social legitimacy upon values other than her own. By implicitly telling women that they should educate their daughters to be home-makers, not idle and decorative, these books created an opposition to the aristocracy that helped define the new realm of the domestic.

The domestic manuals also dealt with the "servant problem," and David and Dora's "Ordeal of the Servants" must be understood in the context of books like *Home Difficulties; or Whose Fault Is It? A Few Words on the Servant Question* (1866).[19] The solution of the manuals is that good wives must start out by being good servants (Warren, pp. iv-vi, 52-55, 67). Agnes, who has dedicated herself to maintaining the comforts of her father's home since childhood, is the ideal woman to replace Dora.

The basket of keys is the sign of the housekeeper's household authority, and Agnes, like Esther Summerson, wields them with confidence and skill. The keys are symbolic scepters of their sovereignty, yet their subjects, the servants, are seldom permitted on stage. Although she must have them, Agnes seems to have no servants in her house, and there is no mention of them in the household described at the end of the book. She has no servant problem because she is herself a housekeeper. She and Esther wave their keys like magic wands that produce order and comfort through selfless devotion alone. (When Aunt Betsey moves into David's quarters after her financial failure, Agnes noiselessly transforms his rooms so they resemble her Dover home [*DC,* 35, 440].) In her attempt to be domestic, Dora takes charge of the keys, but for her the magic does not work; although she goes "jingling about the house," the places to which the keys belong are left unlocked—an invitation to the servants to steal—and the keys become, like the cookery book, a plaything for Jip. Murdstone had forced David's mother, who was equally incompetent, to hand her keys over to Jane Murdstone (*DC,* 4, 42). In effect, when David transfers his affections from Dora to Agnes, and already when he feels that emptiness in his life that only Agnes can fill, he does the same thing.[20]

Out of the creation of the domestic idyll, David hopes to erect his new social identity. In turning the home into an idyll, in marrying the angel in the house, he seems to find an alternative to both the working-class family and the aristocratic family, but, at the same time, the identity of the middle class depends on his belief in these other family forms against which he defines the superiority of his own. His narrative creates an entire mythology of the family, a history and a geography, through which one can distinguish family forms. It accounts for the creation of the middle class by distinguishing between past and present forms of both the gentry and the working class.

The aristocracy represents social legitimacy because it had once deserved its powerful position. To come from a "good family" means that you belong to the ruling class, but also suggests ethical superiority. But the aristocracy's moral and literal bankruptcy—represented by the financial failure of Spenlow and the moral one of Steerforth—forces it to relinquish this position. The world of the Micawbers and Doctors' Commons gives way to that of Betsey Trotwood, Tommy Traddles, and David Copperfield.

Similarly, he splits the working class between Yarmouth and London, a geographic distinction that corresponds to the historical realities of urbanization. But, while urbanization and industrialization are historical facts, nineteenth-century representations of these social phenomena create a history that does more to justify and legitimate the middle class than explain the condition of the working class. Just as the middle class finds the basis for its power in the precedent of the aristocracy, it finds the model for the home in the pastoral image of the rural working class—the Peggottys—while distinguishing itself from the nearby urban proletariat—the rookeries inhabited by the likes of Mealy Potatoes and Mick Walker. Like David's depiction of Yarmouth, these depictions of the communal family, extremely common in the nineteenth century, usually present it as a lost pastoral idyll. The notion of the communal values of the extended family forms the basis for the values of domesticity, and sets the middle class family apart from the urban working class with which it co-existed.[21]

Embracing the home and the *work* ethic, David attempts to reproduce the communal values represented by the older working class while asserting his difference from the new one. His family performs the communal function that the Peggottys, driven apart by the course of events, can no longer perform. In order to claim this realm for the middle class, Gaskell and others depict the pastoral ideal as something that is passing away if not altogether vanished. David, of course, spatializes this by representing the passing order of things in terms of rural Yarmouth, the future as his own London. But he also deals with it temporally, and Dickens himself seems to have preferred things that are "old-fashioned rather than old."[22] While he frequently satirizes affection for "the good old days," he sentimentalizes "old-fashioned" Paul Dombey, and makes old-fashioned furnishings a part of the charm of Bleak House. Old-fashionedness does not belong to the past, to be exhibited in museums; it belongs to the present, an anachronistic transcendence of history. This old-fashionedness sets apart both the Peggotty family, as part of the passing rural era, and the home of the Wickfields, with its "quaint" diamond panes, its "wonderful old staircase," "old oak seats," and "old nooks and crannies" filled with "queer" furnishings (*DC,* 15, 190-191). When David Copperfield senses a distance between himself and Emily, he suggests that the Yarmouth order of life is no longer viable in the modern world he inhabits, but also asserts that it can be recovered in middle-class domesticity.

The middle class absorbs the pastoral, the family as communal unit of production. While the homeless contemporary working class must constantly struggle to survive, the middle-class domestic sphere reconstitutes the lost sense of community. Agnes with her brood of children, gathered around David, reproduces Mr. Peggotty's generosity in gathering in orphans and widows in his boat-house.

Consequently, the conclusion of *David Copperfield* does not require a pastoral setting. The home becomes the urban version of pastoral, a bit of the country within the city.[23] Esther's room in old-fashioned Bleak House represents its own idyllic nature in pastoral scenes of "ladies haymaking, in short waists, and large hats tied under the chin" (p. 116). As the title of Ruskin's "Of Queens' Gardens" suggests, the middle-class family specifically associates itself with the pastoral ideal embedded in this representation of the family; the home "is the place of Peace; the shelter, not only from all injury, but from all terror, doubt, and division" and in "so far as the anxieties of the outer life penetrate into it, and the . . . hostile society of the outer world is allowed . . . to cross the threshold, it ceases to be home" (p. 122, emphasis added).[24] It is a garden of Eden kept by a queen, a refuge for those kings who, as the companion essay's title ("Of Kings' Treasuries") suggests, spend their days in the counting house.

The home, as pastoral refuge of communal labor, depends on the selfless devotion of the housekeeper. The warlike economic forces that threaten the family pervade the male domain outside the home, and the threshold between inside and outside is a place of social transformation. Just as David refuses to see the Peggottys as part of the modern working class, allied to Mealy Potatoes and Mick Walker, he seeks to evade the problematics of this division between domestic and commercial worlds that even affects the form of his narrative. David

needs the city even as he idealizes the country, and this produces a tension between the commercial act of writing his history and the domestic realm that he records through that act.

IV

If the family and its domestic milieu enables the middle class to define a neat structure of classes and social relationships, of upper and lower, inside and outside, these structures themselves cannot entirely enclose society, and they are not able to put everything neatly into place. After defining the roles of men and women through the opposition of home and workplace, Ruskin runs into difficulties, his argument self-destructing in the nearly indecipherable tangle of metaphor that concludes his essay.[25] Both the division into private and public domains, and the even more fundamental division of urban and pastoral upon which it depends, produces disturbing contradictions that may make us feel less than content with the final vision that David offers us.

The home as an enclosed and protective space can also be stifling. The boat-house appeals to young David because its scale is closer to his, its rooms are so neat and snug, its curving walls resembling the womb. And if one of the prime functions of the home is to isolate one from the outside world, what better means than the self-contained boat at sea? Even on land, it lies on the shore apart from the town, giving it a suburban aspect transferable to a cozy cottage in Highgate. The appeal of the ship as home certainly has much in common with our fascination with life on spaceships and space stations. But, as Fredric Jameson has pointed out, this pleasure runs against the almost certain monotony of sensory deprivation, isolation, and the limited society of a small space crew.[26] In transforming his pastoral idyll into a domestic one, David builds his home around one of those women whom Alexander Welsh calls "angels of death," a woman who reminds David of a saint in a stained glass window.[27]

The division between the private home, peaceful sphere of the angelic woman, and the public world, sphere of conflict and the economic activity of the man, also betrays fundamental contradictions and discontinuities. The problem of gender, dividing the world into masculine and feminine spheres, becomes a problem of the binary division itself that creates an ambiguous threshold between the two domains, the necessity of crossing this threshold constantly threatening the division itself. Ultimately, we find that the realms are interdependent and implicated within one another: try as Wemmick (of *Great Expectations*) may to rigidly separate Walworth from the City, the walls around his castle possess an all too ominous resemblance to those of the Newgate prison. Recent analyses of the family have argued persuasively that by accepting this separation of home and commerce we fail to see the way in which they reinforce one another.[28] Beneath this opposition of home and commercial world lies their basic identity: the desired reconstitution of the home as idyllic unit of production.

The notion of "domestic economy" itself should remind us that the home is a site of commercial activity, but, at the same time, it also implies its distinctness from the non-domestic economy. The idyllic portrayal of the home implies the concept of unalienated labor, a labor of love rather than necessity. For the nineteenth century, labor, which is always alienated and performed within the warlike conditions of the marketplace, must take place outside of the home if the home is to maintain its idyllic status. Women's work within the home has wrongly been considered non-work simply because child-rearing and housekeeping, which have important economic functions, are not remunerated with wages. But if we consider the ideological necessity that the home remain unpolluted by the alienated labor of the marketplace, we can begin to see an underlying reason for this attitude.

The notion of unalienated labor suggests that work is not really work because one's relationship to it is fundamentally different than that of the factory worker. This accounts for how the domestic manuals treat housework. Their insistence on self-sacrifice and consideration for others suggests that women perform their work out of love, without any motive of profit (see Ellis, *Women,* II, chapters 1-4). This also accounts for why the actual work of housekeeping is disguised by descriptions of the basket of keys, descriptions that conceal the real work. Ellis proscribes bustling about in a manner that makes your housekeeping obtrusive, and Eliza Warren advises the wife to conceal all signs of her labor before her husband returns from work.[29] Not only do Agnes's servants remain invisible, so does the scrubbing, dusting, and mending that she or they must perform.

This desire to find an unalienated form of labor that does not participate in the violence of the marketplace and can resume its place within the home defined as unit of production produces further discontinuities when the husband crosses the threshold. In *Dombey and Son,* Dickens had presented the problematics of the separation of home and work in the separation between Dombey's house and his "firm." David attempts to reunite them when he rejects the work assigned to him by that advocate of "firmness," Edward Murdstone, in favor of writing, a more genteel profession that seemingly enables him to regain control of the means of production as an author who can work at home. Traddles too combines work and home, in the reverse direction, when he "unprofessionally" moves his family into his law office.

The work ethic, that David embraces so fervently, evokes the pastoral ideal embodied in Caleb Garth of *Middlemarch* and the beehive of activity in the village of Yarmouth, but not washing bottles in London.[30] The difference between washing bottles and writing novels is not just the wages, but where one works, the warehouse or home. Working as a secretary he earns about four times as much (£70) as he did in the warehouse, but the symbolic payoff is much greater than if he had earned the same amount at a menial occupation. For, at the same time that he believes he will find his place through hard work, he believes that only the elect can reach it. Although this paradox employs the theological language of Calvinism, which urges hard work yet insists that salvation cannot be earned, the problem need not be considered in the theological terms it borrows; it belongs to economics, and extends to the nature of domestic economy.[31] In secular terms, domestic economy legitimizes the middle class: the work ethic displays its superiority to the wasteful aristocracy while the theory of the elect, translated as unalienated labor, distinguishes their labor from that of the factory operative. This legitimation is essential in a world in which unrestricted self-making—the ability of just anyone to achieve "respectability"—would destroy the class structure that the middle class only wishes to re-arrange.

The paradox of the work ethic, however, produces discontinuities within the role of the writer. Even as the writer himself enters the home, writers are represented in terms of the woman who crosses into the marketplace: the philanthropist and the prostitute. In "Of Queens' Gardens," Ruskin argues that the only appropriate activity outside the home for middle-class women is philanthropy, as an extension into the public realm of their domestic duties of securing "order, comfort, and loveliness" (p. 136). Philanthropic endeavors, like the home, are non-profit organizations, motivated by selfless regard for others. Women who profit by their economic activity prostitute themselves. In contrast to Agnes and Esther, we have Nancy (of *Oliver Twist*) and Martha Endell. Or Edith Dombey, whose marriage of convenience is clearly marked as prostitution.

Dickens, and David, would like to think that authors too are philanthropists. Dickens works at producing the excess of language that will give joy to his readers as Sleary's circus does, and he attacks social misery with the same aims as the philanthropists. While completing *David Copperfield* he started his weekly *Household Words,* with its obvious allusion to hearth and home, as a vehicle for social reform. During this time he was also helping Angela Burdett-Coutts establish an institution for "fallen women," advising that these women should be trained in home-making.[32] His instinct that these women must yearn for a home suggests that he identifies with them as well in their role as "street-walkers." Significantly, David does most of his street-walking during his extravagant courtship of Dora, and only walks through London when led there by a street-walker (he apparently also walks to think about his writing, like Dickens, but sticks to the suburbs). Martha, whose last name, Endell, suggests the end of life in the dell, has left the rural idyll of Yarmouth to become an urban street-walker in London. Writers, whatever their intentions, must sell their work, and it, like the banknote, is mere paper.

These divisions of pastoral/urban and private/public also produce discontinuities between David Copperfield and Charles Dickens, between the world of the novel's domestic fiction of wedded bliss and its excluded domestic frictions. We find in this novel a clue to some of Dickens' desires: his desire for social legitimacy and his distaste for Catherine Dickens' reported indolence. But, whereas David Copperfield achieves the comfortable home with surprising ease once he sets his mind to it (compared to Traddles for example), Dickens found himself at this time distressed by an apparently loveless marriage (Johnson, p. 494). His home was not comfortable, yet what would he have done with an Agnes even if she were able to bear up to being constantly pregnant while managing the household better than Catherine Dickens did? (Perhaps Dickens did acknowledge the impossibility of his desire by associating Dora's fatal illness, which causes her to remain inactive, with childbirth.)

Dickens was always most at home when he was at work. His compassionate portrayal of prostitutes, as well as his interest in philanthropic endeavors to aid them, suggest his strong identification with the symbolic anti-domestic impulse that they represent. Rather than bringing his work into the home, he constantly fled to Broadstairs and Brighton, even to the Continent, more at home in the streets where he gathered material for writing and worked through its problems, and where he could carouse with friends in a most undomestic way. "Nurses, wet and dry; apothecaries; mothers-in-law; these, my countrymen, are hard to leave," he wrote in tongue-in-cheek response to an invitation from Stanfield, Maclise, and Forster in 1844: "But you have called me forth, and I will come" (Johnson, p. 494).

Because the author works for joy and not merely to accumulate capital, he paradoxically produces an excess within the literary work that defies domestic economy. The parsimony of Dickens' miserly characters must be contrasted with his own extravagance with words and

with David's ability to produce both comedy and melodrama. Yet, though David Copperfield returns his work to the home, he does not bring the rest of the family into the workforce as Mr. Peggotty had done; Agnes's role is to take care of the house, and Dora's assistance with the pens—a parody of the family as unit of production—comes only as compensation for her inability to keep house. Furthermore, the form of David's autobiography reinforces the division of the world into public and private realms, constraining the autobiography within the realm of the domestic and private (he never meant it to be published on any account) while excluding his writing activity and its unwritten *Kunstlerroman*. The excess involved in artistic production might endanger the household economy; to discuss his writings would be to bring his commercial activity into the home. If Dickens' fictional autobiography, representing his progress towards achieving middle-class status, reduplicates the cookery books, his novels would seem to belong to another realm.[33]

Notes

1. My discussion of the Victorian family is indebted to a number of sources. In addition to the social history of the family to be found in the works of Aries, Goode, Laslett and others (see below), I am especially indebted to those who have studied the family as an idea or ideology. Among the latter are Leonore Davidoff, Jean L'Esperance, and Howard Newby, "Landscape with Figures: Home and Community in English Society," in *The Rights and Wrongs of Women,* edited by Juliet Mitchell and Ann Oakley (Harmondsworth: Penguin, 1976); Jeffrey Kirk, "The Family as Utopian Retreat from the City: The Nineteenth-Century Contribution," *Soundings: An Interdisciplinary Journal,* 55 (1972), 21-41; and Patricia Branca, *Silent Sisterhood: Middle Class Women in the Victorian Home* (Pittsburgh: Carnegie-Mellon University Press, 1975). On the developing history of the word family, see Raymond Williams, *Keywords* (London: Croom Helm, 1976), pp. 108-111, and Jean-Louis Flandrin, *Familles, parenté, maison, sexualité dans l'ancienne société* (Paris: Hachette, 1976), pp. 10-15. Finally, on the sociology of cookery, see Jack Goody, *Cooking, Cuisine, and Class: A Study in Comparative Sociology* (Cambridge: Cambridge University Press, 1982).

2. As one of the most familiar plots of romance, this plot precedes the novel by centuries. But this only further reaffirms the argument that this form of discovery of family is linked to the aristocracy, for whom romances were initially written.

3. The history of the word "family" demonstrates this. Its earliest meaning indicated household, but

by the Renaissance, it was defined in terms of lineage and descent, as in the term "the royal family." See Williams and Flandrin above.

4. *Oliver Twist,* edited by Peter Fairclough, (Harmondsworth: Penguin, 1966), p. 463.

5. *David Copperfield,* edited by Nina Burgis (Oxford: Clarendon Press, 1981), chapter 2, pp. 13-14. Chapter and page will hereafter be cited in the text.

6. *The Housewife's Guide; Or, a Complete System of Modern Cookery* (1838). Cited in Eric Quayle, *Old Cook Books: An Illustrated History* (New York: Dutton, 1978), p. 164. These books often were specific about their audience, and others were implicitly designed for the middle class. They first began to appear around the turn of the century. See Maria Rundell's *A New System of Domestic Cookery; Formed upon Principles of Economy, and Adapted to the Use of Private Families* (1806), which she claimed was unlike anything available in her early years.

7. I cite the first American edition (New York: D. Appleton & Company, 1850), p. 6. Soyer also wrote *The Gastronomic Regenerator* (1846), aimed at his Reform Club Clientele, and a *Shilling Cookery for the People Embracing an Entirely New System of Plain Cooking and Domestic Economy* (1854).

8. See Isabella Beeton, *The Book of Household Management* (1861; facs. rpt. New York: Farrar, Straus, and Giroux, 1969), pp. iii, 17.

9. See, for example, Beeton, who cites Judge Haliburton as writing: "'No man is rich whose expenditure exceeds his means, and no one is poor whose incomings exceed his outgoings'" (p. 6). See also Soyer, pp. 1-6, and Catherine Beecher, *A Treatise on Domestic Economy* (1841; facs. rpt. New York: Schocken, 1977), pp. 41, 176. Beecher's American version of domestic economy, despite its emphasis on the needs of American women, follows the English manuals in its basic principles.

10. On the more positive side, his exuberance and wasteful extravagance demonstrate his adherence to the economics of unlimited expense. This is what endears him to us, of course, and is clearly allied to the comic excess that makes him so important in James Kincaid's reading of the novel in *Dickens and the Rhetoric of Laughter* (Oxford: Clarendon Press, 1971), pp. 162-191.

11. See Mrs. Eliza Warren, *How I Managed My House on Two Hundred Pounds a Year* (London: Houlston and Wright, 1864). p. 50.

12. See Ellis, *Wives,* vol. 2, chapters 1-4, on "Domestic Habits."

13. By "One who 'makes ends meet'" (London: C. Mitchell, 1845), p. 44. See also Soyer, who uses almost exactly the same language (p. 338).

14. "Of Queens Gardens," in *The Works of John Ruskin,* edited by E. T. Cook and Alexander Wedderburn (London: George Allen, 1905), 18, 132.

15. *The Hand-Book of Woman's Work,* edited by L. M. H. (London, 1876), pp. 6-7, cited in Branca, p. 24.

16. Consequently, the manuals don't positively discourage education. Ellis even argues for it rather vigorously. Mrs. Allison, of *How I Manage on £200 a Year,* sees with chagrin that her heroic friend Bertha has managed the perfect combination while she has let her own skills in music slip away.

17. I presume that "when I tell my income on my left hand, I pass the third finger and take the fourth to the middle joint" (*DC,* 43, 535) means that he is making £350, a reasonable, though extremely fortunate, increase from the £70 per annum with which he began as Dr. Strong's secretary (*DC,* 36, 446). Branca argues that the middle-class income ranged between £100 and £300.

18. The fact that Agnes and her housekeeping double, Esther Summerson, take up their duties when so young corresponds to the need for early formation of character, since household economy comes about not merely through mathematical calculation but as a result of identification with the values of domestic economy.

19. See N. N. Feltes's excellent essay, "'The Greatest Plague of Life': Dickens, Masters, and Servants," *Literature and History,* 8 (1978), 197-213; Branca, pp. 30-35; and Leonore Davidoff, "Mastered for Life: Servant and Wife in Victorian and Edwardian England," *Journal of Social History,* 7 (1974), 406-428.

20. The comparison between Dora and Clara has been noted frequently, but one must also make distinctions. Murdstone marries Clara in order to "form" her (*DC,* 4, 100); David is confused about why Dora is formed in such a way to make housekeeping impossible. Jane Murdstone is the frugal housekeeper carried to the negative extreme, always suspecting the servants of plots and keeping a parsimonious eye on all goods, in contrast to the benign talents of Agnes and Sophy Traddles. At the same time, this depiction is also relevant to problems inherent within domestic economy that will be discussed below.

21. In fact, extended families are just as likely to be found today as in the past. See John Goode, *World Revolution and Family Patterns* (London: Free Press 1963), and Peter Laslett, *Household and Family in Past Time* (Cambridge: Cambridge University Press, 1972). My point is that this history of the family reflects the nineteenth-century view of the family. Numerous writers, including Ruskin, Carlyle, and Engels, evoke an idealized view of the extended family as do the works under discussion. A central document, one on which Engels drew, is Peter Gaskell's *Artisans and Machinery: The Moral and Physical Condition of the Manufacturing Population with Reference to Mechanical Substitutes for Human Labour* (London: John W. Parker, 1836); Gaskell's analysis of the problems of industrialization and urbanization focusses on their effects on the family. For an argument that the extended family increased in importance, rather than decreased, see Michael Anderson, *Family Structure in Nineteenth Century Lancashire* (Cambridge: Cambridge University Press, 1971).

22. *Bleak House,* edited by Norman Page (Harmondsworth: Penguin, 1971), p. 116.

23. Kirk Jeffrey, discussing the American family, makes this clear when he compares the family to nineteenth-century utopian ventures. The utopians often did attempt to reproduce what was felt to be an older, more communal social structure, which usually meant a rural setting as well as experimentation with social structures, and Jeffrey argues that the formation of the nucleated family was a similar venture accommodated to the needs of urban life.

24. This passage has become the *locus classicus* of discussions of the importance of the home to the Victorian middle class, but in most cases the analysis simply accepts the Victorian explanation of the division between home and world rather than trying to discover its structural significance. The following is a far from exhaustive list of those who cite the passage: Walter E. Houghton, *The Victorian Frame of Mind* (New Haven: Yale University Press, 1964), p. 343; Carol Bauer and Lawrence Ritt, *Free and Ennobled: Source Readings in the Development of Victorian Feminism* (Oxford: Pergamon, 1979), p. 16; Jenni Calder, *The Victorian Home* (London: Batsford, 1977), p. 10; Susan Casteras, *The Substance or the Shadow: Images of Victorian Womanhood* (New Haven: Yale Center for British Art, 1982), p. 14; Erna Olafson Hellerstein, Leslie Parker Hume, and Karen M. Offen, eds., *Victorian Women: A Documentary Account of Women's Lives in Nineteenth-Century England, France, and the United States* (Stanford: Stanford University Press, 1981), p.

278; Christopher Wood, *Victorian Panorama: Paintings of Victorian Life* (London: Faber and Faber, 1976), p. 59; Eli Zaretsky, *Capitalism, The Family, and Personal Life* (New York: Harper, 1976), p. 51.

25. Kate Millett partially untangles it in "The Debate Over Women: Ruskin vs. Mill," in *Suffer and Be Still: Women in the Victorian Age,*" edited by Martha Vicinus (Bloomington: Indiana University Press, 1972), pp. 121-139.

26. Fredric Jameson, *The Political Unconscious: Narrative as a Socially Symbolic Act* (Ithaca, N.Y.: Cornell University Press, 1981), pp. 217-218.

27. Alexander Welsh, *The City of Dickens* (Oxford: Clarendon Press, 1971), chapter 11.

28. Eli Zaretsky, p. 27 and passim; Rayna Rapp, "Household and Family," 175-178, in Ellen Ross Rapp and Renate Bridenthal, "Examining Family History," *Feminist Studies,* 5 (1979), 174-200; and Michele Barrett, *Women's Oppression Today: Problems in Marxist Feminist Analysis* (London: Verso, 1980), chapter 6, "Women's Oppression and 'the Family'."

29. Sarah Ellis, *The Wives of England* (London: Fisher, Son, & Co., 1839), pp. 239-240, and Eliza Warren, *A Young Wife's Perplexities* (1886), p. 35, cited in Calder, p. 111.

30. On the relationship between family and pastoral in *Middlemarch,* see Anthony G. Bradley, "Family as Pastoral: The Garths in *Middlemarch,*" *Ariel,* 6:4 (1975), 41-51.

31. For a very useful discussion of the work ethic in Dickens, see Welsh, pp. 75-84. The relationship between Evangelical religion and middle-class values is explored in Catherine Hall, "The Early Formation of Victorian Domestic Ideology," in *Fit Work for Women,* edited by Sandra Burman (London: Croom Helm, 1979), pp. 15-32.

32. Edgar Johnson, *Charles Dickens: His Tragedy and Triumph,* 2 vols. (New York: Simon and Shuster, 1952), II, 714-718, 593-594, 621.

33. To a certain degree this process of exclusion reverses Dickens' own practice. While David excludes his novels from his domestic autobiography, Dickens excludes his domestic life from his novels. At this point, one could follow another trajectory than that I have followed here, and examine how Dickens attempts to differentiate his representation of the family from that found in the domestic manuals and social histories. Placing himself outside of the novel's domestic realm by injecting it with humor, sentiment, and linguistic excess, just the converse of David's attempt to put

his art outside of his autobiography, Dickens attempts to distinguish the economy of his novel from the taut economies of the middle class. But this division between the novelistic and the domestic is tenuous at best, and in Eliza Action's cookery book, Dora would have found a recipe for "Ruth Pinch's Beef-Steak Pudding." The cookbook writers were quick to employ the means of the novelist, recognizing its appeal to the housewife: Soyer's book is in the form of an epistolary novel, Eliza Warren's domestic advice is written as an autobiographical narrative, and Isabella Beeton originally published her cookbook in twenty-four monthly parts. This sort of analysis has been carried out in other discussions of Dickens; see David A. Miller, "Discipline in Different Voices: Bureaucracy, Police, Family and *Bleak House,*" *Representations* (1983), 59-89, and Catherine Gallagher, "The Duplicity of Doubling in *A Tale of Two Cities,*" *Dickens Studies Annual,* 12, edited by Michael Timko, Fred Kaplan, and Edward Guiliano (New York: AMS Press, 1983), pp. 125-145.

Margaret Myers (essay date 1986)

SOURCE: Myers, Margaret. "The Lost Self: Gender in *David Copperfield.*" In *Gender Studies: New Directions in Feminist Criticism,* edited by Judith Spector, pp. 120-32. Bowling Green, Ohio: Bowling Green State University Popular Press, 1986.

[*In the following essay, Myers views* David Copperfield *as principally concerned with David's search for identity, conditioned by his reintegration of the feminine qualities embodied by Agnes Wickfield into his masculine persona.*]

Whether *David Copperfield* is read as a *bildungsroman,* a novel of individual growth to artistic and moral maturity, or as an Oedipal drama in which David quests for an idealized version of the lost mother, it remains quintessentially a novel about the search for self.[1] Indeed both the Freudian interpretation of the novel and the more conventional literary exegesis share ground insofar as the autobiographical narrative voice articulates—and therefore imposes—a coherence upon his own experience. While criticism has amply expanded upon the moral, artistic and sexual content of David's narrative, it has at best only obliquely recognized the sequence of gender role-playing that vitally informs his journey to self-discovery. For the adult David Copperfield must rediscover and re-integrate into a coherent sense of self those aspects of his male selfhood culturally designated as feminine. It is a task finally too radical in its es-

pousal of an achieved state of androgyny to be affirmed at novel's end, but until then *David Copperfield* clearly indicts the cultural extremes of masculinity and femininity. All that is best in David—his artistic and moral impulses—are identified as feminine, and these he loses in early adulthood when he adopts the culturally approved and strictly masculine persona. His rebirth in the Swiss Alps and his marriage to Agnes appear to reclaim the feminine aspects of that androgynous selfhood. Through David's development, his loss and recovery of selfhood, the key figures of Agnes Wickfield and Tommy Traddles act as harbingers of what should be and what may be. Moral barometers, both, they also offer the promise of reconciling the feminine with the masculine, the moral and the imaginative with the social, the private and the public.[2]

The novel itself, of course, structures the literal journey of self-discovery in David's symbolic rebirth during his Wordsworthian encounter with the grandeur of the Swiss Alps following Dora's death.[3] David's prolonged stay in Europe enables him to recover that which he had lost. The novel focuses that loss on Agnes as the appropriate wife for David, though many critics now argue that Agnes more significantly represents a selfhood which David also needs to discover and recover. J. Hillis Miller is one who sees Agnes as the creator of David's selfhood "without whom he would be nothing."[4] In the religious analogy which Miller uses, "David has that relationship to Agnes which a devout Christian has to God." Alexander Welsh goes on to refine Miller's thesis by noting that the definition of self "becomes crucial at death, after which he [the hero] will be nothing unless the heroine can save him."[5] Finally, Stanley Friedman in his subsequent discussion of the novel picks up Welsh's delineation of Agnes as the familiar of death and argues that she offers the necessary consolation to the older narrator as he confronts his own death, and that in such consolation the narrator is able to reconcile with a Providence over which he has no control.[6] All this criticism correctly follows Dickens' lead in designating Agnes the "heroine" of the novel.[7] She functions in the novel as the agent of male destiny rather than as the creator of her own, although Friedman concludes his discussion by quoting Milton, arguing that since, like Adam and Eve, "their state cannot be sever'd," both David and Agnes "serve together as the hero of David's life."[8]

This line of criticism invites further refinement. *David Copperfield* is structured around the ironic juxtaposition of simultaneous loss and achievement. At one crucial point in his life David acquires a conventionally masculine demeanor, but he does so at the unrecognized expense of a selfhood which at a later stage in his life is only recovered by his wife's death. That lost selfhood is feminine-identified insofar as the moral, the emotional and the artistic are culturally associated with the feminine, an association which the novel itself confirms. Finally the novel seeks to reconcile that feminine selfhood with a masculine identity, not simply in individuals and their private relationships, but also by implication in the larger social context. The last chapter overtly attempts to expound a social optimism based on such a reconciliation. The attempt proves futile. The story of conventional success, and even triumph, is permeated with a sense of irrevocable loss so that even at its end the novel holds true to the ironic pattern of its basic structure. While it attempts at a covert narrative level to deny the pattern by which achievement is inevitably alloyed with loss, a haunting sadness permeates the novel's end. In part that sadness derives from the recognition in the final chapter of the proximity and permanence of death, but death's closeness is a recognition that has informed the novel from its beginning (and David's caul): in *David Copperfield* birth always has death in attendance. There is, I think, a further source for the subdued atmosphere of the final chapter, and that can be found in the novel's inability to achieve an effective and convincing optimism for life while it is lived. Whatever the promise of an androgynous reconciliation, the masculine-identified world of *David Copperfield* cannot finally admit the feminine-identified into the prevailing social and economic structures. Psychological truth must give way finally to cultural convention.

Modern criticism has marvelled at the psychological insight of the novel, and there is no need here to recapitulate David's loss of Eden with the intrusion of the sexually potent adult male, Murdstone. David's consequent expulsion to Salem House moves him into a "homosocial" world, an exclusively male company which in common with all such societies still divides experience into masculine and feminine domains. The emotional, the moral, and the artistic are all feminine-identified, and it is here as schoolboys that both Tommy Traddles and David Copperfield are most overtly identified with the feminine. In this enclosed environment, James Steerforth enacts the masculine role and here, as in later life and in the larger social world, he comes to represent the worst aspects of indulged cultural manhood. Socially successful, revered by his male peers, he is sensual, amoral, and self-absorbed. The moral and the emotional Tommy Traddles suffers much in this exclusively masculine community, and in Salem House his moral sensibility and his emotional sensitivity are contemptuously identified with the feminine. After Steerforth's public mistreatment of Mr. Mell, an incident in which Mell is not only humiliated but is also dismissed from his only means of livelihood, David feels "self-reproach" and "contrition," though he does not reveal his feeling for fear of Steerforth's contempt. Traddles, unlike David, is afraid neither to weep in sor-

row for Mr. Mell nor to upbraid Steerforth for his cruel mistreatment of the impoverished teacher. Steerforth's response to Traddles is to call him "a girl," and "Miss Traddles," and all the other boys, on hearing that Steerforth plans to compensate Mr. Mell with money (the masculine substitute for feeling), are "extremely glad to see Traddles so put down" (Chapter VII).[9]

David's inability to act upon his best moral instincts, a weakness crucial to his subsequent life, does not deny that at Salem House, he too is feminine-identified. No sooner has he arrived at the school than the handsome Steerforth asks David if he has a sister:

> 'You haven't got a sister, have you?' said Steerforth, yawning.
>
> 'No,' I answered.
>
> 'That's a pity,' said Steerforth. 'If you had had one, I should imagine she would have been a pretty, timid, little, bright-eyed sort of a girl. I should have liked to know her. Good night, young Copperfield.'
>
> (Chapter VII)

Not for the only time in his life, David is identified with a mythic sister (although clearly Steerforth could just as well be describing David's surrogate sibling, Little Em'ly). Steerforth, from their first meeting, identifies a feminine in David which is central to the nature and development of their friendship. Moreover, this exchange takes place late at night in the bedroom David shares with several other boys, including Steerforth, and it follows the feast of cakes and wine which David's pocket-money has purchased under the magisterial supervision of Steerforth. The experience of secrecy and sensuality is very much in keeping with subsequent revelations of Steerforth's character, particularly in his treatment of Little Em'ly. Such secret sensuality is further associated with David's imagination and artistic abilities. While at Salem House, David is the "plaything" of his dormitory because of his night-time story-telling.

> Whatever I had within me that was romantic and dreamy, was encouraged by so much story-telling in the dark; and in that respect the pursuit may not have been very profitable to me.
>
> (Chapter VII)

The evaluative disassociation of the narrative voice from his "romantic and dreamy" youthful self seems curious given the nature of the adult's professional success as a writer—such earlier practice has indeed "proved profitable." It is a clue that the narrator is anxious about the feminine identification. Uncertain and ambivalent about both sensuality and artistic ability, the adult male artist distances himself from those "feminine" characteristics on which, ironically, his art and worldly success are founded. By the time David reaches cultural manhood, feminine art will have been transformed into masculine enterprise. The suspect will have been made culturally safe.

Meantime, David's boyhood continues to engage in gender role-playing. The enactment of male and female roles survives through the shared experience of Salem House to the renewal of David and Steerforth's friendship in London. The intervening years have been spent by David in a household where sexual role-playing does not conform to traditional precepts. Davey, the son of David and Dora, is transformed into Trotwood Copperfield, the adopted child of Mr. Dick and Betsey Trotwood. The emotional and artistic Mr. Dick, florid, full of childish delight, without a strong rational sensibility is in marked antithesis to the Victorian paterfamilias. Betsey Trotwood, on the other hand, is explicitly masculine-identified. When David first meets her in Dover, he describes her as "handsome," her dress is severe and neat with "linen at her throat not unlike a shirt-collar, and things at her wrists like little shirt-wristbands" (Chapter XIII). She wears a man's watch, with chain and seals, and when, much later, she visits Dora's aunts Lavinia and Clarissa, she is regarded as "an eccentric lady, and somewhat masculine with a strong understanding" (Chapter XL). In such an environment, David is not identified as exclusively masculine. Constantly encouraged to think and act as would his imaginary sister, Betsey Trotwood Copperfield, he is also confirmed in an identification with both natural parents, for he "would be as like his father as it's possible to be, if he was not like his mother, too" (Chapter XIII). Even his new name, Trotwood, defines gender identity.

Names play a telling role in David's life. Significantly it is not until they meet again as young men that Steerforth coins the nickname "Daisy" for David Copperfield. In an act of sensitive generosity Betsey Trotwood has given the eighteen-year-old David the freedom and the money to spend a month as he wishes while travelling to visit Yarmouth. Stopping in London for his first night, intimidated by waiters, abashed by the palpable fact that he has no need of the hot shaving water the maid leaves outside his door in the morning, David runs into Steerforth, now an Oxford undergraduate. The dynamics of their boyhood friendship continue into adulthood. Steerforth is masterful and knowledgeable while David is full of romantic enthusiasm, "as fresh as a daisy at sunrise" (Chapter XIX), ready to be tutored and eager to be liked by the older man. They visit Steerforth's mother and spend a week "in a most delightful manner" with Steerforth giving lessons in the manly arts of riding, boxing and fencing:

> The week passed rapidly, as may be supposed, to one entranced as I was; and yet it gave me so many occasions for knowing Steerforth better, and admiring him more in a thousand respects, that at its close I seemed to have been with him for a much longer time. A dashing way he had of treating me like a plaything, was more agreeable to me than any behavior he could have adopted.

> (Chapter XXI)

Steerforth, of course, then joins David in his visit to Yarmouth, thereby initiating the sequence of events which leads to the seduction of Little Em'ly, Steerforth's new "plaything," and all the betrayals of family and friends attendant upon their elopement.

Until that disillusionment, the friendship of David and Steerforth continues in the pattern of their childhood. Steerforth is the dominant, experienced, condescending superior in a relationship comfortable in its operating assumption of inequality. Their relationship has only the subtlest of moral content, and the nature of that content explicitly lies within the power of the superior Steerforth. Though founded on genuine love, the friendship of David and Steerforth hints at the corruption of innocence in its best moral impulses. Thus David represses his sympathy for Mr. Mell; thus Steerforth allows the inexperienced David to spend a drunken night on the town. As Agnes warns David, Steerforth is his "bad angel," a charge which at the time David vehemently denies. In so doing, David is covertly defending that aspect of self which is most akin to Steerforth: the social male self. Throughout their early relationship, David is morally superior to Steerforth only in the innocence of his instinct, never in an actual choice in terms of action or behavior.

The loss of Steerforth marks David's movement from androgynous boyhood to masculine adulthood. It is a loss which coincides with two other markers in this rite of passage. The first is his love for Dora. The second is David's initiation into cultural manhood when, with the news of his aunt's financial ruin, he shoulders the traditional male burden of economic responsibility for his family. For David, social and cultural maturity means the adoption of a rigorously masculine role, a role which relies for its definition on the clear separation of the feminine from the masculine. David becomes earnest, rational and hardworking. He masculinizes his own selfhood. The art of writing is turned into the enterprise of Parliamentary reporting so that he can make a living. Simultaneously, David looks for his domestic and personal happiness to a woman who matches the extremity of his own cultural role-playing. Conforming to stereotype, their differences come to represent the separation of the instinctive from the rational; neither is able, however, to make moral or emotional coherence out of the polarity. As such their relationship develops into an indictment of extreme sexual roles, an indictment confirmed by the parallels which exist between their marriage and the friendship of David with Steerforth. While Doady is never Dora's "bad angel," their relationship, in its content, the dynamic of its development and even, in some measure, the nature of its eventual outcome, echoes the earlier and older friendship. In giving priority to a social male self, David diminishes his emotional sensitivity and blunts his moral sensibility. In so doing he hurts Dora, he betrays the child of nature, the "young innocence" whom experience cannot teach.

The audience of *David Copperfield* is warned from the outset of the inherent moral ambivalence of David's masculine role-playing. The famous incident of the beggar in the street calling "Blind! Blind! Blind" refers to the matrix of experience in which it occurs, not solely to David's choice of Dora over Agnes. Part of that matrix is his espousal of the work ethic, which happens simultaneously, and from which the narrator deliberately and ironically distances himself. Chapter XXXVI, "Enthusiasm," follows immediately upon the beggar's call of "Blind! Blind! Blind!" and opens:

> What I had to do, was, to turn the painful discipline of my younger days to account, by going to work with a resolute and steady heart. What I had to do, was, to take my woodman's axe in my hand, and clear my own way through the forest of difficulty, by cutting down the trees until I came to Dora. And I went on at a mighty rate, as if it could be done by walking.

The single most important source of David's manifold "blindness" is his capacity for uncritical and exuberant enthusiasm. Agnes, who like the narrator is also a major source of moral comment in the novel, tempers David's youthfully passionate response to life, though she always does so with a gentle humor, as when, for example, she teases him by "threatening to keep a little register of [his] attachments with the dates, duration, and termination of each . . ." (Chapter XXV) when David confesses that he is half in love with Rosa Dartle. Unlike either his relationships with Agnes or Tommy Traddles, David's relationships with both Steerforth and Dora are characterized by an early passionate enthusiasm which blinds him to the moral implications of personality and behavior, both in himself and in those he loves. So it is with work.

Meanwhile, the loss of Steerforth intensifies David's passionate love for Dora, though, as with Walter Gay's devotion to Florence Dombey, his early love is centered on an ideal rather than an actuality:

> All this time, I had gone on loving Dora, harder than ever. Her *idea* [italics mine] was my refuge in disappointment and distress, and made some amends to me, even for the loss of my friend. The more I pitied myself, or pitied others, the more I sought for consolation in the image of Dora. The greater the accumulation of deceit and trouble in the world, the brighter and purer shone the star of Dora high above the world. I don't think I had any definite idea where Dora came from, or in what degree she was related to a higher order of beings; but I am quite sure I would have scouted the notion of her being simply human, like any other young lady, with indignation and contempt.

> (Chapter XXXIII)

It reads almost as purely as Ruskin and hence the parody. But the humor does not disguise the serious consequences of this culturally-condoned view of women. It is David's inability to comprehend the reality of Dora which causes his failure to mediate between her perceptions of life and his excessive enthusiasm, a failure compounded by his disastrous attempt at playing the teacher and mentor in Dora's life, which Steerforth has played in his.

David alone fails to understand Dora's essential nature, and, as becomes the pattern, their relationship is in fact mediated through other women: Julia Mills, Betsey Trotwood and Agnes Wickfield. David and Dora are thus trapped in the contradictions of their own culture. David has enthusiastically espoused the ideals of masculinity and femininity: he will work earnestly toward an inevitable worldly success while relying on a "Cottage of Content" for his domestic happiness. He has fallen in love with an ideal of decorative womanhood, a woman who is childish, without intellectual depth or strong understanding, but one who delights and pleases him, and who, by every implication, excites him physically. He is superior, she is inferior: he will teach her, she is his "plaything." It is one of the further ironies, of course, that David is attempting to amalgamate the divided maternal image of the two Claras. He wants Dora to acquire the domestic skills of Peggotty. The undoubted, if narratively unacknowledged, sensuality of David and Dora's relationship connects significantly with the secrecy of their engagement: it is a constellation of moral ambivalence which marks all the disastrous relationships in the novel, and one which is most clearly identified with Steerforth. In upbraiding David for this deceit towards Dora's aunts, Agnes serves to remind the audience of David's moral fallibility; it undercuts any claim David might make to moral superiority in his relationship with Dora.

The pleasures of courtship prove to be the dilemmas of marriage, and so David pursues the painful pedagogical course of attempting "to form Dora's mind." The profound unhappiness he causes her rests on David's conviction of the superiority of the rational, a conviction which operates in defiance of the "natural" realities of Dora's personality and capabilities. David, for all his sense of the superiority of the masculine-identified attribute, that of rationality, is the very last to comprehend the fixed nature of his marital relationship. Agnes,

Betsey Trotwood, even Dora herself, all understand and warn David about the nature of his choice in marriage. The "instinctively" feminine has a moral sensitivity denied to the intellectually based. Thus Betsey Trotwood who, like David, regains a feminine selfhood which she had denied in the bitterness of experience, refuses to repeat the pattern of the past. She declines to interfere in the marriage by advising Dora on practical matters, as David had requested, and instead accepts "Little Blossom" as she is without criticism. It is Dora herself who asks to be called "child-wife"; she too comprehends that she can never be what David wants her to be. He, however, does not take the warning seriously, and so he sets about making Dora "reasonable," with the only palpable results being his own loneliness and her unhappiness. Finally deciding it had been a wrongheaded scheme, David brings home gifts and a good mood to reconcile himself to his wife. Their conversation works around the key polarities of the rational and the instinctive:

> I sat down by my wife on the sofa, and put the earrings in her ears; and then I told her that I feared we had not been quite as good company lately, as we used to be, and that the fault was mine. Which I sincerely felt, and which indeed it was.
>
> 'The truth is, Dora, my life,' I said; 'I have been trying to be wise.'
>
> 'And to make me wise too,' said Dora, timidly. 'Haven't you, Doady?'
>
> I nodded assent to the pretty inquiry of the raised eyebrows, and kissed the parted lips.
>
> 'It's not a bit of use,' said Dora, shaking her head, until the ear-rings rang again. 'You know what a little thing I am, and what I wanted you to call me from the first. If you can't do so, I am afraid you'll never like me. Are you sure you don't think, sometimes, it would have been better to have—'
>
> 'Done what, my dear?' For she made no effort to proceed.
>
> 'Nothing!' said Dora.
>
> 'Nothing?' I repeated.
>
> She put her arms around my neck, and laughed, and called herself by her favorite name of a goose, and hid her face on my shoulder in such a profusion of curls that it was quite a task to clear them away and see it.
>
> 'Don't I think it would have been better to have done nothing than to have tried to form my little wife's mind?' said I, laughing at myself. 'Is that the question? Yes, indeed, I do.'
>
> 'Is that what you have been trying?' cried Dora. 'Oh what a shocking boy!'
>
> 'But I shall never try any more,' said I. 'For I love her dearly as she is.'
>
> 'Without a story—really?' inquired Dora, creeping closer to me.

> 'Why should I seek to change,' said I, 'what has been so precious to me for so long! You can never show better than as your own natural self, my sweet Dora; and we'll try no conceited experiments, but go back to our old way, and be happy.'
>
> 'And be happy!' returned Dora. 'Yes! All day! And you won't mind things going a tiny morsel wrong, sometimes?'
>
> 'No, no,' said I. 'We must do the best we can.'
>
> 'And you won't tell me, any more, that we make other people bad,' coaxed Dora; 'will you! Because you know it's so dreadfully cross!'
>
> 'No, no,' said I.
>
> 'It's better for me to be stupid than uncomfortable, isn't it?' said Dora.
>
> 'Better to be naturally Dora than anything else in the world.'
>
> 'In the world! Ah, Doady, it's a large place.'
>
> She shook her head, turned her delighted bright eyes up to mine, kissed me, broke into a merry laugh and sprang away to put on Jip's new collar.
>
> (Chapter LIII)

David, of course, is remarkably obtuse as to the hidden content of this conversation, which is founded on Dora's accurate perception that he regrets the marriage. The failure of David's "wisdom," of his male-identified rationality, to engage successfully with Dora's naturalness, represents the failure of the culturally-endorsed concepts of masculinity and femininity. There is appeasement, but there can be no reconciliation between such fixed extremes: David and Dora's marriage is a thoroughgoing indictment of the "Cottage of Content." It is only after the loss of such sexual extremes that a structure of possible reconciliation can be discovered when David regains those feminine aspects of selfhood which he has repressed or denied.

The deaths of Dora and Steerforth are narratively fortuitous. They relieve David of a life-long commitment to erroneous youthful choice, an instance of authorial generosity common in mid-Victorian novels. Their deaths, moreover, take on further significance if the characters do indeed represent the culturally-approved concepts of masculinity and femininity. Steerforth, readily admired, forever associated with money and easy social success, is without moral instinct, a lack he himself recognizes, and for which he blames his mother.[10] Dora, on the other hand, pretty and foolish, enjoys a moral innocence, a native inability for conscious malice, one which qualifies (if never actually compensates for) her complete lack of intellectual comprehension.[11] David, potentially androgynous, has loved them both and loses them both. Neither Daisy, the feminized male, nor Doady, the corrupted male, survives: it is Trotwood Copperfield who returns, renewed, from Europe. As Trotwood (the name which Agnes uses), David is able to make a living as an artist, he is able to weep openly (when he was married to Dora, David would weep only in secret), and perhaps most important of all, he is able to acknowledge his love for the "right" woman, Agnes. At the same time, David loses none of the quality of masculine enterprise; he retains his capacity for earnest hard work, an earnestness "thorough-going, ardent, and sincere" which David claims he owes all to Agnes (Chapter XLII).

Agnes is central to the significance of David's rediscovery of selfhood while in Switzerland, but the sequence by which David reaches Dover after his return to England is equally telling. Apart from Mr. Chillip, as much in attendance at this spiritual birth as he was at David's natural birth, the only people David visits in London en route to Agnes are Tommy Traddles and Sophy, "the dearest girl," whom Tommy has married. Tommy Traddles plays an extremely important role in *David Copperfield,* not least of which is his apparent representation of a social no less than personal reconciliation between the masculine and the feminine. In his selfhood, Tommy is posited as an ideal: emotional and intensely moral, Tommy is nonetheless capable of the hard work and intellectual endeavor necessary for eminence in the public domain. Thus he appears to reconcile internally the masculine with the feminine, the rational with the moral and the emotional, but even more significantly he appears to reconcile the private with the public. Married to the woman he loves, together they serve with maternal self-sacrifice the whole impoverished Crewler family. The image of Tommy Traddles in the dusty chambers of the Inns of Court surrounded by laughing women, all enjoying the best of communal and familial times, attempts a genuine optimism. Hidden away, at the very heart of the very driest male institution, an institution which deliberately excludes the emotional and the moral from the structure on which it rests, is a group of happy women chatting around a fire while a contented and busy man makes tea for everyone. The scene is as overtly optimistic as is Traddles' eventual success in law. The assumption, at novel's end, of his appointment to the Bench represents the most positive view of the law in Dickens' novels. With Traddles a judge, there would be an active moral agent at the highest levels of a major social institution. Moreover, that agent is identified as possessing the feminine qualities of sensibility and domesticity. The difficulty of the final chapter which embodies this social optimism, derives in part from its failure to make this optimism convincing. It is a failure which operates in conjunction with the portrayal of Agnes, a character who has always provoked critical unease.

It is a cliche of literary criticism that nothing is more difficult than to portray sympathetically and convincingly a positive idea of good. As with all cliches, it has a strong measure of truth to it. Certainly one of the difficulties surrounding Agnes Wickfield is that she is supposed to represent an ideal of womanhood, an ideal which has mercifully lost favor with the passing years. The ideal is of a woman who is domestically competent yet who has the "softened beauty of a stained-glass window"; a woman who embodies the best moral impulses, impulses which are instinctively structured on selflessness, yet one who simultaneously enjoys a calm and serious intelligence. Whatever the problems of this cultural ideal of womanhood, there are certain specific elements in the portrayal of Agnes which are essential to an understanding of the novel's final failure to carry through on its promise of espousing an unconventional sexual and social ideology.

Agnes Wickfield is the great lost character of *David Copperfield.* Although Dickens gives little real narrative substance to her extraordinary life, he was fascinated as an author with the nexus of family character and experience which constitute the main details of her biography. As with almost every other major Dickens character (and thus the exceptions become significant[12]), Agnes is motherless. Her mother, having married socially beneath her family and against its wishes, dies shortly after Agnes' birth. Throughout her childhood and early adulthood, Agnes has thereby provided the sole rationale for her alcoholic father's obsessive and criminally unethical behavior, much as Little Nell is her grandfather's own excuse for his compulsive gambling. The male burden of economically supporting women (and this seems especially so when the women are explicitly identified as "good angels") often takes a neurotic, and finally criminal cast in Dickens' novels. Simultaneously Agnes plays housekeeper to her widowed father, another key and recurrent relationship in Dickens' writings. Moreover, in love from childhood, Agnes must bear the additional burdens, not only of unrequited love, but of loving a man too blind to comprehend the nature of her feelings, and one who marries a woman thoroughly and entirely different from herself. In this sea of troubles other dangers lurk: she is desired by the morally odious and physically repulsive Uriah Heep, her father causes the bankruptcy of their dearest friends, and she must over a period of several years run a school to support herself and her father following the public revelation of his dubious work habits. Yet despite a life so ripe for artistic exploration and revelation, Agnes as an autonomous character remains hidden from the audience. We know nothing of her emotional or intellectual responses to these traumatic events; we never even discover what she feels about Uriah Heep and his courtship of her, or of her father's public disgrace. Agnes is presented entirely from David's point of view, a view which is always egocentric and often unperceptive.

In part the difficulty of revealing Agnes may derive from the nature of autobiographical technique. It is a technique which, as used by Dickens, inherently subordinates all other characters, limiting the audience's access to them to the agency of the first-person persona. David, unlike Nick Carroway, for example, is never off-stage: events and characters are all revealed through his presence, if not his consciousness. But the limitations of first-person narration cannot be blamed entirely for the unavailability of Agnes as an autonomous character. Dickens demonstrates, for example, an easy capability of using the possibilities of retrospective in the revelations of Steerforth: the superior knowledge of the narrator constantly qualifies the limited awareness and understanding of the character of David Copperfield at the various stages of the narrative. No such technique is ever used to generate a complexity of characterization for Agnes; not once does the narrator reflect or concede an enhanced understanding of Agnes as a character who has suffered great pain and humiliation: retrospective experience merely confirms the stereotype. Moreover, other characters are demonstrated to have experiences and feelings unknown to David Copperfield, and for the audience to be aware of the depth and significance of that unknown life, if ignorant of the details. Betsey Trotwood has enjoyed a complex and profound range of experience and emotions in her marriage to, separation from, and blackmail by a man she has loved passionately. It is as apparent to David as to the audience that her fear of fire is a symptom of this hidden life, that it reveals the presence, but not the nature, of deep feelings held under severe control. With the exception of her love for David, and then only at the very end when David himself is suffering the pangs of unrequited love, Agnes is never implicitly granted an autonomous moral or emotional life. Finally, it is a perverse comment on the significance which Agnes has in the novel that she must remain hidden from the audience, hidden, that is, except as David perceives her. If she were revealed as a character, Agnes Wickfield would threaten to displace David from the center of his own narrative, a displacement which would run counter to the egocentric nature of the novel's theme and structure.

Agnes, then, exists only as an idea in the mind of the narrator. What the idea of Dora is to the young David Copperfield, Agnes is to the older narrative persona: as the heroine of his life she exists only in relationship to him. Agnes, moreover, is not simply the heroine of the narrator's life; she is also, as Alexander Welsh has argued, the prefiguration of his death.[13] The last chapter of *David Copperfield* is haunted by a preoccupation with the inevitability of the narrator's own death, at whose dying and at whose wake Agnes will stand guard, harbinger and protector both. The fear of the feminine resides in part in the anxiety inspired by death and its human guardians. Even the feminine-identified Tommy Traddles doodles constantly the skeletal image of human morality. But the problem posed by the final chapter of *David Copperfield* resides not only (and perhaps

not even primarily) in the fear of the feminine identification with death; that fear is significantly compounded by the male anxiety of feminization, an anxiety which helps create a conventionality at the novel's end which defies its own sexual radicalism. The portrayal of the Copperfield household in the last chapter is socially and sexually safe: he and Agnes (a soundly conventional couple) are blessed with healthy children, those they love are enjoying a golden old age, and David's writing, his "feminine" art, is acknowledged only in terms of successful worldly enterprise. The narrator has retreated from the true heroism of David Copperfield, the individual recognition of the complexity of sexual identity and the necessity of incorporating the feminine into that which is masculine identified. The intensity of Romantic experience, the self lost and found again in defiance of social convention and definition, is embourgeoised: *David Copperfield* retreats from the radical into a safe domestic harbor, a Victorian middle-class home.

Notes

1. For an excellent reconciliation of the "intentionalist" and psychoanalytic readings of the novel, see Gordon D. Hirsch, *Victorian Newsletter,* 58 (Fall 1980), pp. 1-5.

2. Throughout this discussion of *David Copperfield*, I use the term "feminine" much as Marilyn French characterizes the "inlaw" (i.e. culturally approved) characteristics designated as feminine in "The Garden Principles," *Shakespeare's Division of Experience* (New York: Summit Books, 1980).

3. *The Prelude* was of course published in the same year as *David Copperfield*. John Lucas argues that Dickens may well have read the poem (which appeared in July 1850) before beginning work on the number which includes Dora's death: *The Melancholy Man: A Study of Dickens' Novels* (London: Methuen and Company, 1970), pp. 169-70.

4. J. Hillis Miller, *Charles Dickens: The World of His Novels* (Bloomington: Indiana University Press, 1969), p. 157.

5. Alexander Welsh, *The City of Dickens* (Oxford: Clarendon Press, 1971), p. 181.

6. Stanley Friedman, "Dickens' Mid-Victorian Theodicy," *Dickens Studies Annual,* 7 (1978), pp. 128-150.

7. John Butt and Kathleen Tillotson, *Dickens At Work* (London: Methuen and Company, 1957), pp. 128-30.

8. Friedman, p. 150.

9. As Bert G. Hornback has noted, Dickens took some care over the choice of these epithets; Dick-

ens changed the text in manuscript from "stupid" to "you girl," and the phrase "Miss Traddles" is an interlinear addition. *"The Hero of My Life": Essays on Dickens* (Athens: Ohio University Press, 1981), p. 82.

The text used is from *The Oxford Illustrated Dickens* (London: O. U. P., 1948). All subsequent references are by the chapter, and are included in parentheses in the text.

10. Blaming the mother for a moral failure in self is not simply an abdication of individual responsibility. It also represents an additional burden women bear in a culture which deems them the moral standard-bearers.

11. The incident of the page finally transported after repeated revelations of theft from the Copperfield household is one small demonstration of the central differences between a rationally-based and an instinctively-held morality. David attempts to explain the moral "contagion" of their domestic incompetence (that it leads their servants into theft and other nefarious activities); Dora emotionally understands the accusation (that *she* is being blamed and compared to a transported page), but is incapable of understanding the intellectual concept of responsibility by default (Chapter XLVII).

12. Arthur Clennam is the single most important exception to the general Dickens rule of motherless central characters.

13. Welsh, pp. 180-183.

Rosemary Mundhenk (essay date fall 1987)

SOURCE: Mundhenk, Rosemary. "*David Copperfield* and 'The Oppression of Remembrance.'" *Texas Studies in Literature and Language* 29, no. 3 (fall 1987): 323-41.

[*In the following essay, Mundhenk explores David's suppression, acceptance, and transcendence of painful memories in* David Copperfield.]

Early in his "Personal History," David Copperfield, fictional autobiographer, describes a childhood battle with his mother's new husband. In response to Murdstone's brutality, David bites his stepfather's hand, suffers a retaliatory beating, and is imprisoned in his lonely room. Recalling the incident and its aftermath, the mature Copperfield calls attention to both the child's immediate recollections and the narrator's retrospective memories:

> How well I recollect, when I became quiet, what an unnatural stillness seemed to reign through the whole house! How well I remember, when my smart and pas-

sion began to cool, how wicked I began to feel! . . . I shall never forget the waking, next morning; the being cheerful and fresh for the first moment, and then the being weighed down by the stale and dismal oppression of remembrance.[1]

Both the child's and the narrator's acts of memory are oppressive. Both levels of recollection suggest the haunting and potentially debilitating effect of memory. As a child and as an adult, David Copperfield is obsessed with his past, a past largely painful to experience and to remember. Throughout the "slow agony" (145) of Copperfield's youth "runs an undercurrent of loss and sadness" that, as Robin Gilmour has suggested, subverts the novel's success story and lesson of prudence.[2] *David Copperfield* is a particularly complex novel about remembering, for it dramatizes the paradoxical force of memory as both a source of creativity and morality and a burden, potentially oppressive and debilitating.

In looking backward, David Copperfield is, of course, very much the Victorian. Just as the central moral statement of his autobiography, the disciplining of an undisciplined heart, emphasizes the Victorian virtue of prudence, Copperfield's preoccupation with the past places him in the company of other nineteenth-century historicists. From the medievalism of Thomas Carlyle's *Past and Present* and Alfred, Lord Tennyson's *Idylls of the King* and the classicism of Matthew Arnold's *Empedocles on Etna,* to the personal journeys into the more recent past in *Jane Eyre, Pendennis,* John Stuart Mill's *Autobiography,* and **Great Expectations,** the Victorians use the past to define their time and themselves.[3] Most of Charles Dickens's novels are structured around an embedded return to the past in order to discover or clarify the meaning of the present: witness the rummaging through old documents and dust mounds and the discoveries of concealed parentage (of Oliver Twist, Smike, Estella, Esther, Arthur Clennam) and of identity (Monks, John Rokesmith, and Mr. George, to name but a few). In his later fiction in particular, Dickens emphasizes the difficulty of dealing constructively with the remembered past: in characters like Mr. Wickfield, Miss Havisham, Mr. Boythorn, Louisa Gradgrind, Lady Dedlock, Bradley Headstone, Mrs. Clennam, and Flora Finching, Dickens catalogs the debilitating effects of memory, its unhealthy suppression or indulgence and its capacity to arrest development and pervert natural feeling. Most particularly, in **David Copperfield,** Dickens focuses directly, through the central plot and protagonist, on the complexities and paradoxes of the act of remembering.

In its exploration of the process of memory, Copperfield's autobiography most obviously resembles William Wordsworth's poetic excursions into the past, especially his *Prelude,* coincidentally published the same year as Dickens's novel. Both autobiographical works focus on the incremental mingling of memory and perception, and both simultaneously lament the loss of heightened feeling and champion the morally edifying effect of memory. Yet for all its overt resemblances to Wordsworth's poetry, especially in chapter 58, where David experiences a Wordsworthian awakening, this "most Wordsworthian of Dickens's novels"[4] often seems closer to another personal exploration published in 1850, Tennyson's *In Memoriam,* which shares its intense struggle with grief. Try as he may, David Copperfield never attains Wordsworth's "philosophic mind," the qualified optimism that finds, "For such loss, . . . Abundant recompense."[5] Like the melancholic singer of *In Memoriam,* Copperfield's voice reveals an uneasy tension between recovery from personal grief and the oppressive effects of remembered loss. *David Copperfield*'s refusal to "oversimplify the relationship between past and present" is, in Alan Shelston's words, "disturbing and honest."[6] So too is its refusal to resolve the conflict between the constructive and destructive forces of memory.

By the time young David Copperfield reaches Miss Trotwood's cottage at Dover to begin a "new life" (184), he carries a burdensome mass of oppressive memories. His childhood security has been destroyed by the Murdstones; his mother has died; he has been separated from Peggotty and from his Salem House companions; he has suffered the humiliation of Murdstone and Grinby's; and he has known the hunger and the alienation of poverty. At Dover and Canterbury, he encounters two characters who provide alternative ways of dealing with the pain of memory: Mr. Wickfield and Miss Trotwood.

For Mr. Wickfield, memory has become destructive. Grief for his dead wife and guilt over her estrangement from her family after her marriage obsess him. Wickfield's present constantly reminds him of his past. His daughter Agnes's face bears the same "placid and sweet expression" (191) that characterizes her dead mother's portrait, prominently hanging on the wall. He tells David that he has "'always read something of her poor mother's story, in her character'" (721). In the evenings, after too much port, "sometimes his eyes rested on her, and he fell into a brooding state, and was silent" (192). "'If it is miserable to bear, when she is here,'" Wickfield confesses to David, "'what would it be, and she away? No, no, no. I can not try that'" (199). Self-aware, he can diagnose his problem: "'Weak indulgence has ruined me. Indulgence in remembrance, and indulgence in forgetfulness. My natural grief for my child's mother turned to disease; my natural love for my child turned to disease'" (493). Wickfield's indulgence in the forgetfulness vainly promised by wine is a conscious act of refusal to accept the painful reality of the past. Ironically, his indulgence in forgetfulness only increases

the pain of his grief and makes him easy prey for the scheming Uriah Heep. Wickfield's melancholic indulgence in remembrance perverts his natural relationship with Agnes—a "morbid father-love," Q. D. Leavis calls it.[7] His possessiveness is clear; inviting David to join the household, Wickfield concedes that theirs is "'a monotonous life; but I must have her near me. I must keep her near me'" (199). Refusing to accept the present, he attempts to form the present into a perverse version of the past. He substitutes his daughter for his lost wife. Agnes becomes his little housekeeper; she does not go to school because "'Papa couldn't spare me to go anywhere else'" (196). She is forced to become his emotional parent. Not only does he limit Agnes's life, but he narrows his own; in Agnes's words: "'I know what a multitude of things he has shut out for my sake, and how his anxious thoughts of me have shadowed his life, weakened his strength and energy, by turning them always on one idea'" (316).

Wickfield's predicament is clearly central to Dickens's development of the theme of memory in *David Copperfield.* Indeed, a sketch of Mr. Wickfield's character was one of Dickens's earliest seeds for the novel. In January 1849, Dickens wrote to John Forster: "What should you think of this for a notion of a character? 'Yes, that is very true: but now, *What's his motive?*' I fancy I could make something like it into a kind of amusing and more innocent Pecksniff."[8] Between this early notion and the introduction of Mr. Wickfield in the fifth monthly number, Dickens decided to make Wickfield a less amusing character and a more tortured human being. Dickens retains the insistence on single motives, but adds the implication that Wickfield's attempt to find the one secret motive in everyone else's actions derives from his reduction of his own life to one motive. That motive centers, of course, on Agnes, the constant reminder of his dead wife. His limitation of life's possibilities and mysteries to one motive—"his poor little inch-rule," according to Betsey Trotwood (716)—is destructive and unnatural. Not only does it increase his melancholy and cut short his daughter's childhood, but the effects of his severe, "inch-rule" judgments extend beyond his family circle of two. His misunderstanding of Dr. Strong's motives in sending Jack Maldon abroad and his misjudgment of Annie Strong's "motives" increase the tension, suffering, and guilt in their marriage. His misunderstanding of Uriah Heep—"'I was satisfied that I had bound him to me by motives of interest'" (493)—leads to Heep's mastery of Wickfield and to the financial woes of Betsey Trotwood and others who depend upon Wickfield's advice. Wickfield's perverse indulgence in memory weakens his hold on the reality of the present and nearly destroys his own life and the lives of others.

Betsey Trotwood's method of dealing with the pain of the past is strikingly different from, almost schematically opposite to, Wickfield's indulgence in memory.

Rather than attempt to make her memories ever present, as Wickfield does, she tries to suppress memory. Next to Mr. Wickfield, Miss Trotwood seems to have made the more healthful choice. Recoiling from a disastrous marriage to a man who treated her cruelly, she moves "a long way off" (3) and reassumes her maiden name. She attempts to raise David in accordance with the same lesson. She renames him "Trotwood Copperfield," and he begins a "new life, in a new name, and with everything new about" him (184). Later, she advises David, "It is in vain, Trot, to recall the past, unless it works some influence upon the present" (296). Miss Trotwood's decision, however, to forget the past unless it can constructively influence the present is neither as successful nor as healthy as her juxtaposition with Mr. Wickfield would seem to indicate. First, the grotesque quirks of her behavior, marvelously comic though they are, bear the mark of the past she tries to forget. Her gruffness and her avoidance of affection in chapter 1 reveal her attempt to avoid more emotional pain. Her plans for the infant girl she hopes David's mother will bear—"'There must be no mistakes in life with *this* Betsey Trotwood. There must be no trifling with *her* affections'" (6)—and her hopes to educate her servant Janet "in a renouncement of mankind" (166) show her desire to spare others the suffering she has experienced and remembered. Second, the reprobate husband whom she tries to forget periodically intrudes upon her present life, tracking her from Dover to London, begging for money, until his death. Third, as her care for her husband in his final days shows, she is unable to forget the memory of her early love for him, despite her efforts.

Clearly neither of these alternatives is ideal. Mr. Wickfield's indulgence in memory becomes a debilitating disease. Miss Trotwood's attempt to suppress the past hardens her, cuts her off from affection for a time, and ultimately fails. The examples of both Mr. Wickfield and Miss Trotwood, however, suggest the complexities and paradoxes of remembrance. The past cannot be changed. Yet it cannot be escaped; it continues to affect the present, if only by remaining in memory. Furthermore, although memory is the source of identity and the foundation of creativity and growth, it can also cause debilitation and stasis, as it does in Wickfield, when the memories are predominantly painful and haunting.

Dickens's investigation of the complexity and paradoxes of memory led him to populate the novel with characters who are troubled by memory. The scar on Rosa Dartle's face is a reminder of Steerforth's thoughtless cruelty; like Wickfield, Rosa Dartle indulges in remembrance, but, unlike Wickfield's, her humanity is consumed by anger and bitterness. Mrs. Gummidge dwells so much on the loss of her "'old 'un'" that she becomes a grotesque parody of grief for most of the novel. Ham has loved Emily too much to forget her, yet he is so deeply scarred by the memory of her elopement with Steerforth that his life is narrowed and determined by memory: "'I loved her—and I love the mem'ry of her—too deep—to be able to lead her to believe of my own self as I'm a happy man. I could only be happy—by forgetting of her'" (631). Mr. Dick, who sometimes pretends to have no memory, cannot forget his brother's unkindness and his sister's calamitous marriage—"'the recollection of it is oppressive to him even now,'" according to Betsey Trotwood (175). The futility of Mr. Dick's suppression of memory is demonstrated grotesquely in the spontaneous, unwilled appearances of Charles I's head in nearly everything Mr. Dick writes. Mr. Micawber optimistically submerges his past failures in the hope that something will be turning up, but is plagued by bill collectors; only emigration releases him. This catalog of characters for whom the past is nightmare suggests at the least the breadth and complexity of Dickens's treatment of memory in the novel. It suggests further that finding and sustaining a healthy way of dealing with painful memories—somewhere between Miss Trotwood's attempted amnesia and Mr. Wickfield's indulgence—are not easy tasks.

The history of David Copperfield himself dramatizes more fully the struggle to deal with the complexity of memory, to reconcile the irretrievability of the past with the remembrance of it, to avoid the oppression of remembered pain and loss while simultaneously drawing upon memory constructively and creatively. At Dover and Canterbury, young Trotwood Copperfield tries to separate himself from his painful memories and to begin a "new life." Like his aunt, he hides the past from public view; as he begins school at Doctor Strong's, he is worried that the other boys will discover his secret: "My mind ran upon what they would think, if they knew of my familiar acquaintance with King's Bench Prison?" (195). At Dr. Strong's school, Trotwood Copperfield seems to succeed in escaping his past. By the time he is head boy, "That little fellow seems to be no part of me; I remember him as something left behind upon the road of life . . . and almost think of him as someone else" (229). But the secure havens of Canterbury and Dover offer only temporary and partial respite. As Q. D. Leavis remarks, "Life has consisted of fresh starts, but each phase is penetrated by characters from his pasts or related to the others by parallels in incident."[9] Steerforth, Traddles, Micawber, the Murdstones, and Creakle reappear. Dr. Strong's school replaces Mr. Creakle's; Traddles replaces Copperfield at the Micawber's lodging; Uriah Heep's scheming parallels Murdstone's; and Dora resembles David's mother. Even if young Copperfield's memory were not "traunt," as Gilmour rightly calls it,[10] he would be drawn frequently into the past by circumstance. Betsey Trotwood's hope to exorcise memory thus proves as futile for her nephew as for herself.

The structure of the novel emphasizes the intrusion of the past or of memory on the present. Most obviously, as an autobiographer, the adult Copperfield narrates retrospectively, and, as he does so, he calls more attention to the effects of recollecting and narrating on the narrator than do such other nineteenth-century autobiographers as John Stuart Mill, Phillip Pirrup, and Jane Eyre. Moreover, the structure of *David Copperfield* is not only linear but circular as well. The plot moves forward temporally only by circling back geographically over the same terrain. David Copperfield progresses toward maturity through time only by returning geographically and emotionally to familiar territory—to Yarmouth, Blunderstone, and Canterbury. Although nearly every Dickens novel dramatizes the effects of the past on the present, none—including *Great Expectations*—contains as much revisiting of earlier settings as does *David Copperfield.* As some critics have noted. David Copperfield seems to mark each movement into the future with a return to a familiar scene of his past.[11] Each revisit measures the changes in the surroundings, the changes in David, or both. When the protagonist returns to the places of his earlier experiences, his current perceptions both evoke and become colored by his memories.

For example, David's returns to Yarmouth trigger a Wordsworthian commingling of memory and observation that results in a painful sense of loss. Returning after his mother's death, he is at first "rather disappointed" by the place, as a result of his recent loss (121). When he returns again at Mr. Barkis's death, Yarmouth itself speaks of loss. When he next returns with Mr. Peggotty, David has experienced the frustrations of marriage, Dora's illness, Em'ly's elopement with Steerforth and reunion with her uncle. Hence his perceptions of Yarmouth are complicated by memories of loss and a painful sense of change in himself and the town. With a "sorrowful wish to see the old place once more" (630), he revisits the deserted boathouse: "I thought of myself, lying here, when the first great change was being wrought at home. I thought of the blue-eyed child who had enchanted me. I thought of Steerforth" (632). Unlike Wordsworth, David here can find little strength in what is left behind. The physical changes in the setting complement and reinforce his personal sense of loss. David's growing association of Yarmouth with pain and loss—the pain made more poignant by the earlier cheerful memories of the place—culminates in his return after Dora's death to visit Ham. David finds all "the remembrances of the place naturally awakened" and experiences such a "jumble in my thoughts and recollections, that I lost a clear arrangement of time and distance" (676). The jumble of time increases as he witnesses Ham's death on the same sea that he associates with his idyllic memories of Yarmouth and discovers Steerforth's body lying, as David recollects it once did in sleep, on the same shore, where David played with Em'ly:

. . . he led me to the shore. And on that part of it where she and I had looked for shells, two children—on that part of it where some lighter fragments of the old boat, blown down last night, had been scattered by the wind—among the ruins of the home he had wronged—I saw him lying with his head upon his arm, as I had often seen him lie at school.

(681)

As the past and the present merge in his mind, the reality of the present is made more painful by the memories.

Similarly, the idyll of David's early childhood at Blunderstone is soon destroyed, and the memory of it marred. After his first visit to Yarmouth, the child returns home to find his mother married to Murdstone and the Rookery "so altered" (33). Later, coming home from Salem House for a holiday visit, he discovers that the happy memories evoked by Blunderstone only increase his feelings of loss: "every object I looked at, reminded me of the happy old home, which was like a dream I could never dream again!" (93). Even Canterbury, the scene of David's deliverance from poverty and abandonment, does not sustain his idealizing association of it with changelessness and security. Although he hopes with each revisit to find in the calm serenity of Canterbury a balm for his own increasingly complicated life, Canterbury itself becomes a painful reminder of "change in everything" (634-35).[12] Mr. Wickfield declines and Heep ascends. David's "old adversary the butcher" is "now a constable" (720). When the mature Copperfield, after his spiritual convalescence on the Continent, returns to find the Wickfield home, with the Heeps now expelled, "just as it used to be in the happy time," his joy is immediately overcome by a sorrowful memory: "The feeling with which I used to watch the tramps, as they came to town on those wet evenings . . . came freshly back to me; fraught, as then, with the smell of the damp earth . . . and the sensation of the very airs that blew upon me in my own toilsome journey" (718). Even if David Copperfield chose to suppress his memories, as his aunt once advised, he could not avoid the pain of memory, for the events and coincidences of his life, the reappearing characters, the recurring incidents, and the revisited settings continually remind him of his past.

Many of David's returns suggest a willingness, if not an inclination, to "indulge" in memory. Most obvious are his visits to Blunderstone long after his mother's death and his escape from the Murdstones, when no exigencies of plot require him to return. Visiting Yarmouth with Steerforth, David chooses to make several "solitary pilgrimages" to "the old familiar scenes" of his childhood:

. . . my occupation in my solitary pilgrimages was to recall every yard of the old road as I went along it, and to haunt the old spots, of which I never tired. I haunted them, as my memory had often done, and lingered among them as my younger thoughts had lingered when I was far away. The grave beneath the tree, where both my parents lay—on which I had looked out, when it was my father's only, with such curious feelings of compassion, and by which I had stood, so desolate, when it was opened to receive my pretty mother and her baby.

(272)

Like Tennyson, returning to gaze at the "dark house" where Arthur Hallam lived, David studies the Rookery from the outside. His deliberate evocation of painful memories is intensified by the changes he sees: the rooks' nests are gone; the trees, "lopped and topped out of their remembered shapes"; the garden, wild; and the house occupied by "a poor lunatic gentleman" (272).[13] Later, on the occasion of Mr. Barkis's death, David deliberately arrives at Blunderstone "early in the morning" in order to spend some time alone at his parents' graves. He describes his emotions on these visits as a "jumble of sadness and pleasure" (273). Orphaned and once outcast, he returns to his birthplace to reaffirm his sense of self and to mark his progress into the future: "My reflections at these times were always associated with the figure I was to make in life" (272). Yet his pleasure in evoking the memory of his mother and in meditating on the future—"as if I had come home to build my castles in the air at a living mother's side" (272)—is inextricably tied to the sad reality of the loss of his mother and the decay of his home. David has earlier displayed his need to return to, even indulge in, the past when, on his flight to Dover from London, he goes out of his way to spend a painful night outside the walls of Salem House (155).

The decision of the mature David Copperfield to write his own "Personal History . . . Which he never meant to be Published on any Account" is itself a conscious, deliberate return to the past.[14] If we accept both the fiction that the novel is Copperfield's autobiography and his statement that the "manuscript is intended for no eyes but mine" (517), then we must assume that he intends neither to instruct nor to entertain others but to summon memories for his own purposes. Copperfield is curiously vague about his reasons for doing so, whether to transcend, exorcise, come to terms with, order, or merely indulge his memories. Creative though his imaginative return is, he clearly risks that "indulgence in memory" that nearly destroys Mr. Wickfield. Copperfield himself is aware of the dangers, for as he begins to describe the tempest in which Ham and Steerforth die he writes that "from the beginning of my narrative, I have seen it growing larger and larger as I advanced, like a great tower in a plain, and throwing its forecast shadow even on the incidents of my childish days" (672). In the act of recreating his own past, the autobiographer consciously courts the dangers of indulgence in memory.

With surprising frequency, Copperfield interrupts his narrative to reveal the effect that his deliberate remembering has upon him as he recollects. With phrases like "How well I remember," "Never, while I live, shall I forget," and "How vividly I recollect," he draws attention away from the experience of his younger self and to the act of remembering. Such phrases serve not only to convey "the impression of truthfulness"[15] but also to emphasize the tenacious persistence of memories and their emotional effect on the mature narrator in the present. Dickens's Esther Summerson and Pip use similar exclamations in their narratives with much less frequency; in fact, the comparison of the three first-person narrators suggests the idiosyncrasy of *David Copperfield* in its emphasis on the act of retrospection. Moreover, the overwhelming majority of such interruptions in *David Copperfield* occur when the experience remembered is painful: the deprivation and loneliness of his childhood, the estrangement and the death of his mother, the unfortunate marriage to Dora and her death, the elopement of Steerforth and Em'ly, and the deaths of Steerforth and Ham.

As he describes his childhood, for instance, Copperfield interrupts his narration to reveal the oppressive persistence of those memories associated with deprivation and loneliness. The Murdstone invasion of his home is so painful and persistent a memory that, as he describes the solemn lessons and church visits, the present David experiences them as the past David did—and fears that the future David will as well: "Shall I never forget those lessons!" (45). His biting of Murdstone's hand "sets my teeth on edge to think of it" (50), and the subsequent hours of punishment with the accompanying "oppression of remembrance" are memories that the narrator will "never forget" (51). Most vivid in the narrator's mind is the London warehouse of Murdstone and Grinby: "I now approach a period in my life, which I can never lose remembrance of, while I remember anything; and the recollection of which has often, without my invocation, come before me like a ghost, and haunted happier times" (129). As he writes, the details of the warehouse appear "all before me, just as they were in the evil hour" (132). Recollecting his escape from London, the narrator remembers most vividly his loneliness: "Never shall I forget the lonely sensation of first lying down, without a roof above my head!" (155).

Although in life and in art David Copperfield tries to master the oppression of remembered pain by emotionally distancing himself from his memories, his frequent exclamations in the present indicate the nearness and intensity of the past. Emphasizing Copperfield's artful strategies for recalling and shaping his memories into a meaningful whole, Jean Ferguson Carr argues that his writing "can thus become a way to free him from the obsessive repetition of his past and move him beyond ethnocentric concerns."[16] Surely, by shaping the past into writing, David Copperfield attempts to control and master, perhaps even transcend, his past, but his attempt is not so successful as he wishes. As he evokes the past in order to control it, he finds that he lacks the mastery and distance he seeks. For example, as he begins his account of Em'ly's elopement, Copperfield confesses his fear of evoking the painful memory: "A dread falls on me here. A cloud is lowering on the distant town, towards which I retrace my solitary steps. I fear to approach it. I cannot bear to think of what did come, upon that memorable night; of what might come again, if I go on" (382).

The day of Steerforth's and Ham's deaths at sea is prominent in his memory, like "a great tower in a plain" (672). He acknowledges that he cannot control its painful intrusions in his mature life: "For years after it occurred, I dreamed of it often. I have started up so vividly impressed by it, that its fury has yet seemed raging in my quiet room, in the still night. I dream of it sometimes, though at lengthened and uncertain intervals, to this hour" (672). As he writes, "I do not recall it, but see it done: for it happens again before me" (672). According to J. Hillis Miller, Copperfield's tendency "to be, in certain states of excitement, thrown into tumultuous confusion by memory" is countered by an opposing tendency to distance himself from his memories and to hold "them at arm's length."[17] Yet, these two tendencies in Copperfield's narrative coexist in uneasy balance, in unresolved tension. Even as Copperfield tries to achieve emotional distance, some memories, especially those associated with pain and loss, touch the narrator with such force that he interrupts his narration to exclaim, "Never shall I forget."

Copperfield's most obvious attempts to distance himself, to control and transcend the oppressive pain of remembering, occur in his handling of the memories of Clara Copperfield, Dora, and Steerforth. He consciously tries to mold his complicated memories of these figures into idealized, timeless images.[18] He asserts, for instance, that, as a newly orphaned child, he learned from Peggotty to remember his mother "only as the young mother of my earliest impressions, who had been used to wind her bright curls round and round her finger, and to dance with me at twilight in the parlor" (115). By focusing on the timeless image of "the mother of my infancy" (115), he tries to erase the pain of Clara Copperfield's second marriage, his separation from her, and her early death. Harry Stone, calling attention to Copperfield's partial blindness, notes that the son "will not look at the reality of his dead mother's face, but he will bow in unconscious, lifelong homage to the false image of her."[19] Yet, Copperfield's idealization of Clara is neither as unconscious nor as unqualified as Stone suggests. Although Copperfield may be sustained and comforted by the "fanciful picture" of his mother (160), his selective transformation of a complex of memories into

one timeless image is not completely successful. The frequency and the nature of his present-tense exclamations about the poignancy of his memories of Clara subvert his claim to have supplanted the pain with a timeless image. Her death, not her dancing in the parlor, is "a high rock in the ocean" of memory (113): "How well I recollect the kind of day it was! I smell the fog. . . . I see the hoar frost" (105). The regret, the bitterness, and the guilt, associated with his loss of his mother to Mr. Murdstone, remain: "It touches me nearly now, although I tell it lightly, to recollect how eager I was to leave my happy home" (23). Thus, the fanciful image alleviates, but does not exorcise the pain of memory. Indeed, Copperfield's ability to describe vividly the painful events in his relationship with his mother, in chapters 2 through 8, shows that he remembers what he would forget.

Copperfield also attempts to create idealized, timeless images of Dora, as "the dear child as I knew her first" (658), and of Steerforth, "at his best." Despite his idealization of Dora, remembering brings pain, both because he has lost her and because he now realizes that theirs was a marriage of incompatible minds.[20] As he writes, the recollection of Dora's "pretty joy . . . brings tears to" the mature Copperfield's eyes (553). The sight of a ring of forget-me-nots, like the one for Dora, evokes memories that interrupt his mature peace: "Yesterday, when I saw such another, by chance, on the finger of my own daughter, there was a momentary stirring in my heart, like pain!" (417-18). Memory, unconsciously awakened, eludes Copperfield's conscious attempts to control it. Similarly, despite his claim to remember Steerforth only as a cherished friend— "No need, O Steerforth, to have said . . . , 'Think of me at my best!' I had done that ever" (681)—the fuller realization of Steerforth's lost promise and irresponsibility remains in Copperfield's memory. Although Steerforth's betrayal is never given the full examination that Dora's lesser faults are (in chapters 44 and 48), Copperfield cannot divorce the memory of Steerforth from Em'ly's misfortunes either in his narrative or in his mind.[21]

The images of Clara, Steerforth, and Dora that Copperfield chooses to remember, and in his narration to emphasize, resemble what Freud would later call "screen memories," memories that displace, reduce, or substitute for the original or "real" experience. According to Freud, because "strong forces from later life . . . work on the capacity of childhood experiences for being remembered," an individual's "so-called earliest childhood memories" are not "the genuine memory-trace but a later revision of it."[22] Recurring early memories can serve as distorting screens that filter out feelings of remorse, regret, and disappointment. David Copperfield's remembering of Clara as "the mother of my infancy" is thus a revision of historical fact, a psychological truth rather than a historical one.[23] Indeed, Copperfield's account of his reaction to the story of Clara's last days underlines this psychological revision of history:

> Thus ended Peggotty's narration. From the moment of my knowing of the death of my mother, the idea of her as she had been of late had vanished from me. I remembered her from that instant, only as the young mother of my earliest impressions. . . . What Peggotty had told me now, was so far from bringing me back to the later period, that it rooted the earlier image in my mind. It may be curious, but it is true. In her death she winged her way back to her calm untroubled youth, and cancelled all the rest.
>
> (114-15)[24]

While Freudians emphasize the unconscious, unwilled screening of memory, David Copperfield's screening seems often conscious and deliberate; at least he is aware of the process. He consciously chooses to remember Clara, Dora, and Steerforth at their best. And partly because he consciously chooses, the screening effect is incomplete and temporary. The memory of Clara's "calm untroubled youth" does not in fact cancel all the rest, as his full narrative of childhood illustrates. Nor do the consciously screened memories of Dora and Steerforth block David's knowledge of their shortcomings and his experience of pain.

David Copperfield's idealization of his mother, his wife, and his friend recapitulates Dickens's own manner of dealing with grief. Haunted by the loss of his sister-in-law Mary Hogarth, in particular, he consciously sought to defend himself from the melancholy of loss by remembering Mary at her best, at her happiest moments. She thus became in recollection Dickens's "better Angel":[25] "The first burst of anguish over, I have never thought of her with pain—never. . . . I have long since learnt to separate her from all this litter of dust and ashes, and to picture her to myself with every well remembered grace and beauty heightened by the light of Heaven."[26] Although Dickens wrote these words in March 1839, we know that afterward he experienced haunted dreams of Mary Hogarth, that he painfully relived his loss of her in writing of Little Nell's death, and that he always marked the anniversary of her death with sadness. He fulfilled his promise to Mary's mother to "take a melancholy pleasure in recalling the times when we were all so happy."[27] Thus, although Gilmour is correct in asserting that David Copperfield and his creator share "the capacity to partition off" their "deepest responses and experiences,"[28] the timeless images do not completely screen from consciousness the painful realities of loss and disappointment.

As a boy, David Copperfield shows the reader that not only is his memory good but also that, like Wickfield, he cannot experience the present without reference to the past. The young boy who awakens to feel "weighed down by the stale and dismal oppression of remembrance" and the mature narrator who proclaims "I shall never forget the waking" (51) are surely akin to the tormented Mr. Wickfield who indulges in memory. As if to emphasize the kinship, Hablot K. Browne's final illustration for the novel, "A Stranger Calls to See Me," shows a portrait of Dora prominently displayed between smaller pictures of the boat house and the Rookery above the mantlepiece in Copperfield's home, much as earlier the portrait of Mrs. Wickfield dominated the Wickfield household. In the foreground, David, Agnes, and three of their children greet Mr. Peggotty, visiting from Australia, but, as Michael Steig suggests, the "emblematic details" of the background "take precedence over the characters." Of the significance of Dora's portrait, Steig offers three possible explanations: first, that Dora blesses the marriage of David and Agnes; second, that her portrait and the other pictures represent "the past which David has outgrown"; finally, "in another sense David and Agnes are permanently haunted by his earlier loves."[29] Given the implication that David and Agnes have chosen to place Dora's picture so centrally in their home and the revelation that the Copperfields have named a daughter after Dora, Dickens is clearly emphasizing the parallels between Copperfield and Wickfield. Copperfield, like Wickfield, is a man who deliberately summons sorrowful memories of his past to his happier present.

What then, aside from sobriety, distinguishes David Copperfield's penchant for reviving painful memories from Wickfield's self-destructive "indulgence in memory"? In part, David's ability to construct a more productive life is an accident of psychology and temperament, just as Martha Endell is inexplicably more able than Em'ly to recover from the mistakes of her past and construct a healthy present in Australia. For both Wickfield and Copperfield, indulgence in memory is a form of mourning, but Wickfield's mourning has turned to melancholy. Freud's comparison of melancholia and mourning is instructive here.[30] Both are reactions to loss of a loved one or a cherished abstraction. Yet, while the mourner engages in a progressive "testing of reality," a struggle between the psychological need to hold on and the fact of absence, the melancholic's energies are directed not outwardly toward a testing of reality but monotonously and inwardly on the self, resulting in a kind of psychic paralysis. As a result, the melancholic, unlike the normal griever, experiences "an extraordinary diminution in his self-regard, an impoverishment of his ego on a grand scale."[31] In Dickens's novel, Wickfield becomes subsumed in his lack of self-respect, as demonstrated by his frequent self-abasement and his drinking, but David can mourn without suffering the paralytic loss of self-esteem. Furthermore, Copperfield's ability as novelist and autobiographer to transform his painful memories into art allows him a method of recovery that Wickfield lacks: writing both permits

David to use creatively the oppression of remembrance and serves as the basis of his self respect and identity.[32] Furthermore, although Copperfield's memories frequently intrude upon his present, he is able to regard the past as irrevocable and final. While Wickfield unnaturally attempts to stop time and to live psychologically in the past, Copperfield attempts to assimilate the past into the present. Despite the pain and potential oppression of remembrance, Copperfield frequently returns to his past, in life and in writing, neither to deny it nor to submit to it, but to incorporate it into his present. Thus, although the novel's final illustration suggests the similarity between Wickfield and Copperfield, it also implies a difference; for the haunting presence of David's dead wife's portrait is balanced by the living presence of Agnes and her children. When Wickfield indulges in memory and forgetfulness, he denies the totality of the past and the present. Copperfield, on the other hand, both as protagonist and narrator, attempts to accept all.

His attempt is not always successful. For instance, his way of dealing with the painful memories of his mother, Dora, and Steerforth by idealizing them, by thinking of them only at their best, denies the totality he seeks. The resulting tension in the narrative between his idealizing and the reality he remembers indicates the emotional trauma that still attends those memories. Furthermore, as he narrates, his attempt to distance himself from his younger self and to transform experience into art is frequently foiled by the intrusion of painful memories, the feelings he cannot forget. Indeed, the novel implies that the *pain* of memory should not be deadened, because it fosters moral growth. The edifying force of painful memories, for instance, prompts Aunt Betsey, the woman who tries to forget but cannot, to care for Mr. Dick and finally for her dying husband. Memory is a moral faculty not only because it keeps alive "the child's undisciplined purity of heart . . . the source of love and therefore of morality"[33] but also because remembered pain fosters moral sympathy. As Willis Konick argues, "Without the force of childhood memory," and I would emphasize painful memories, "one loses humanity and never feels a natural union to the souls of others."[34] Looking back on his lonely flight from London to Dover, Copperfield cherishes the edifying power of one painfully remembered event: "I remember how I thought of all the solitary places under the night sky where I had slept, and how I prayed that I never might be houseless any more, and never forget the houseless" (170).

A few months before beginning work on *David Copperfield,* Charles Dickens, who like his protagonist was haunted, sometimes oppressed, by his past, wrote to John Forster: "Of course my point is that bad and good are inextricably linked in remembrance, and that you could not choose the enjoyment of recollecting only the good. To have all the best of it you must remember the worst also."[35] Dickens was referring to his Christmas story, **"The Haunted Man"** (1848), in which Redlaw, haunted by painful remembrances, accepts his ghostly double's offer to expunge his memory of the sorrowful wrongs done him only to find that he has forfeited his identity and his capacity for sympathy and moral feeling.[36] Redlaw and all those he infects with the "blessing" of forgetfulness become cold and brutish, until their memories and their humanity are restored by the angelic influence of Milly William, who cherishes her own sorrowful memory. The story closes with the invocation, "Lord, keep my memory green."[37] The simple platitude about the inextricable linkage of good and evil in memory is handled simplistically in this moral fable, the least successful of Dickens's Christmas books. When Dickens turned the following year to *David Copperfield,* he moved beyond platitudes and drew upon his own unmastered memories to create a novel of memory, rich and haunting in its exploration of the mixed blessing of remembrance. Indeed, the complexity of Dickens's treatment of David's struggle between the two extremes represented by Betsey Trotwood and Mr. Wickfield shows how inadequate are the terms that critics often use to characterize David's psychological growth. We find ourselves saying that he "recreates," "selects," "masters," and "transcends" his memories, when in fact he partially does so and partially does not. We say that he "distorts," "suppresses," or "refuses to examine" his past, when in fact at times he does and at times he does not. Throughout the novel, David Copperfield struggles to balance the tendency to submit to the oppression of remembrance and the inclination to suppress or distort painful memories. Even as he closes his autobiography, the struggle continues: as he temporarily dismisses "the shadows" of his past, he must "subdue" his "desire to linger yet" (751).

Notes

1. Charles Dickens, *David Copperfield,* ed. Nina Burgis (Oxford: Clarendon, 1981), 50-51; subsequent references to this edition will be noted parenthetically.

2. Robin Gilmour, "Memory in *David Copperfield,*" *Dickensian* 71 (1975): 31. Gilmour investigates the rhythm of memory in the novel and the conflict between the reality David remembers and his attempt to discipline his heart. Other significant discussions of memory in *David Copperfield* include Phillip D. Atteberry, "The Fictions of David Copperfield," *Victorian Institute Journal* 14 (1986): 67-76; Murray Baumgarten, "Writing and *David Copperfield, Dickens Studies Annual* 14 (1985): 39-59; Jean Ferguson Carr, "David Copperfield's Written Memory," in *Approaches to Teaching Dickens' "David Copperfield,"* ed. Richard J. Dunn (New York: Modern Language Asso-

ciation, 1984), 88-94; Albert A. Dunn, "Time and Design in *David Copperfield*," *English Studies* 59 (1978): 225-36; K. J. Fielding, "Dickens and the Past: The Novelist of Memory," in *Experience in the Novel*, ed. Roy Harvey Pearce (New York: Columbia University Press, 1968), 107-31; Gordon D. Hirsch, "A Psychoanalytic Reading of *David Copperfield*," *Victorian Newsletter* 58 (1980): 1-5; Bert G. Hornbeck, "*The Hero of My Life*" (Athens: Ohio University Press, 1981); Willis Konick, "The Chords of Memory: Teaching *David Copperfield* in the Context of World Literature," in *Approaches to Teaching Dickens' "David Copperfield*," 61-70; William T. Lankford, "'The Deep of Time': Narrative Order in *David Copperfield*," *ELH* 46 (1979): 452-67; Robert E. Lougy, "Remembrances of Death Past and Future: A Reading of *David Copperfield*," *Dickens Studies Annual* 6 (1977): 72-101; Carol Hanbery MacKay, "Surrealization and the Redoubled Self: Fantasy in *David Copperfield* and *Pendennis*," *Dickens Studies Annual* 14 (1985): 241-65; Sylvia Manning, "David Copperfield and Scheherazada: The Necessity of Narrative," *Studies in the Novel* 14 (1982): 327-36; James E. Marlow, "Memory, Romance, and the Expressive Symbol in Dickens," *Nineteenth-Century Fiction* 30 (1975): 20-32; Alan Shelston, "Past and Present in *David Copperfield*," *Critical Quarterly* 27 (1985): 17-33; and Barry Westburg, *The Confessional Fictions of Charles Dickens* (DeKalb: Northern Illinois University Press, 1977), 3-71.

3. Carl Dawson (*Victorian Noon* [Baltimore: Johns Hopkins University Press, 1979]) traces the importance of historicism, autobiography, and memory in much midcentury literature.

4. Lougy, 97. For discussions of *David Copperfield*'s affinities with and debt to Wordsworth, see also Dawson, 123-43; Gilmour, 40; Hornbeck, 70-83; Marlow, 22-25; and Shelston, 17-22. Distinguishing between *David Copperfield* and other nineteenth-century treatments of the relationship between past and present, Shelston convincingly argues that whereas the subject becomes in Wordsworth and George Eliot a great public theme, emphasizing "the significance of it all" and providing "a sustaining faith for both present and future," *David Copperfield* remains a private reflection of the difficulty of relating the past to the present in a significant way (22).

5. William Wordsworth, "Lines composed a few miles above Tintern Abbey," ll. 87-88.

6. Shelston, 17.

7. F. R. Leavis and Q. D. Leavis, *Dickens the Novelist* (London: Chatto & Windus, 1970), 81.

8. *The Pilgrim Edition of the Letters of Charles Dickens*, vol. 5, ed. Graham Storey and K. J. Fielding (Oxford: Clarendon, 1981), 483.

9. Leavis, 99.

10. Gilmour, 36.

11. See Dunn, 233; Lankford, 460-61; and Westburg, 47-48.

12. Lankford discovers in the description of David's walk through Canterbury a conflict between viewing the past as an unchanging order and viewing the past as a destructive process, and argues that the conflict is temporarily reconciled in the passage by the image of "the deep of time" (457-59). Yet, like all Copperfield's attempts to overcome his oppression by memory, this one is only temporary.

13. I agree with Lougy's argument that the poor lunatic gentleman "threatens David because David sees in him a vision of his own possibilities—the Romantic artist's fear of sinking into despondency and madness—and David flees from him toward a vision of a serene and distinguished future that is not threatening" (80).

14. The novel's full title as it appears on the number wrappers is "The Personal History, Adventures, Experience, and Observation, of David Copperfield the Younger. Of Blunderstone Rookery. Which He never meant to be Published on any Account."

15. Sylvere Monod, *Dickens the Novelist* (Norman: University of Oklahoma Press, 1968), 308.

16. Carr, 94.

17. J. Hillis Miller, *Charles Dickens: The World of His Novels* (Bloomington: Indiana University Press, 1958), 154.

18. Gilmour argues: "David Copperfield shares with Dickens the capacity to partition off his deepest responses and experiences in an area of his being where they remain inaccessible to, or at least unaffected by, the larger processes of thought by which he attempts to account for the past. David's mother has an imaginative existence for him in a 'changeless past'" (35).

19. Harry Stone, *Dickens and The Invisible World* (Bloomington: Indiana University Press, 1979), 207.

20. Rebecca Rodolff, in her analysis of chapter 53 in "What David Copperfield Remembers of Dora's Death," *Dickensian* 77 (1981): 32-40, also argues that David does not stop mourning Dora.

21. William Marshall's "The Image of Steerforth and the Structure of *David Copperfield*," *Tennessee*

Studies in Literature 5 (1960): 57-65, remains the most useful study of Copperfield's remembering of Steerforth.

22. Sigmund Freud, "Childhood and Screen Memories," *The Standard Edition of the Complete Psychological Works of Sigmund Freud,* ed. and trans. James Strachey (London: Hogarth, 1957-65), 6:43-52. This essay elaborates on Freud's earlier "Screen Memories," *Works,* 3:303-22.

23. I rely on the more recent approaches to psychoanalysis by Paul Ricoeur, *Freud and Philosophy: An Essay in Interpretation* (New Haven: Yale University Press, 1970), and Donald Spence, *Narrative Truth and Historical Truth: Meaning and Interpretation in Psychoanalysis* (New York: Norton, 1982). Both Ricoeur and Spence seek to correct the Freudian notion of psychoanalysis as a kind of mental archaeology, a notion that assumes that, if one digs deeply enough, he may find historical truths or valid memory traces. Both argue that the reductive and creative process of recollection and the transforming power of language in verbalizing memories make the retrieval of the actual image or experience in the past impossible. In place of Freud's archaeological search, both advocate the creation of "narrative truth" (Spence's phrase), a coherent narration of the past that forms meaningful sequences and connections out of the chaos of isolated remembered events. In a sense, the tension between what David Copperfield proclaims he remembers and what the narration reveals he actually remembers anticipates this recent distinction between narrative and historical truth. In another sense, the tension and the contradictions in Copperfield's narration suggest that he has not achieved the coherence that Ricoeur and Spence speak of.

24. In "Childhood and Screen Memories," Freud distinguishes between three types of chronological relationships between "the screen memory and the content that is screened off by it": first, a retroactive or retrogressive displacement, in which the content of the screen memory belongs early in childhood while the mental experience replaced by the screen memory belongs chronologically later; second, a forward displacement, in which a later impression displaces an earlier one; and finally, contemporary or contiguous displacement (44). Copperfield's memory of his mother and most of his screen memories are characteristically retrogressive. Furthermore, David's appearance in this memory of Clara as the babe in her arms (115) is significant not only because his image replaces that of his half brother but also because his own image appears visually in his memory. According to Freud, "Whenever in memory the subject himself appears . . . as an object among other objects

this contrast between the acting and the recollecting ego may be taken as evidence that the original memory has been worked over" ("Screen memories," 321).

25. Dickens to H. W. Longfellow, 29 December 1842, *Pilgrim Edition of Letters,* vol. 3, ed. Madeline House, Graham Storey, and Kathleen Tillotson (Oxford: Clarendon, 1974), 409.

26. Dickens to William Bradbury, 3 March 1839, *Pilgrim Edition of Letters,* vol. 1, ed. Madeline House and Graham Storey (Oxford: Clarendon, 1965), 516.

27. *Letters,* 1:323.

28. Gilmour, 35.

29. Michael Steig, *Dickens and Phiz* (Bloomington: Indiana University Press, 1978), 129.

30. Freud, "Mourning and Melancholia," *Complete Psychological Works of Freud,* 14:239-60.

31. Ibid., 246.

32. Stanley Friedman ("Dickens' Mid-Victorian Theodicy," *Dickens Studies Annual* 7 [1978]: 128-50) calls David's composing "effective therapy" (146). John P. McGowan ("*David Copperfield:* The Trial of Realism," *Nineteenth-Century Fiction* 34 [1979]: 1-19) refers to David's writing as a "talking cure" (19). Murray Baumgarten discusses the potentially recuperative powers of writing "as a culturally binding action" (41). Finally, Sylvia Manning argues that "despite pitfalls and shortcomings of language," the power of language provides "the defense against memory that the dreamer lacks" (327).

33. Lankford, 454.

34. Konick, 65.

35. *Letters,* 5:443.

36. John Lucas (*The Melancholy Man* [London: Methuen, 1970], 167-78) and Westburg, 57-67, have explored the connection between *The Haunted Man* and *David Copperfield.* See also Alexander Welsh, *The City of Dickens* (Oxford: Clarendon, 1971), 101-05, on Dickens's treatment of the subject of the forgiveness of past wrongs, and Marlow, 23-27, on the softening influence of memory.

37. "The Haunted Man," in *Christmas Books,* New Oxford Illustrated Dickens (London: Oxford University Press, 1954), 398.

Edwin M. Eigner (essay date 1987)

SOURCE: Eigner, Edwin M. "Death and the Gentleman: *David Copperfield* as Elegiac Romance." *Dickens Studies Annual* 16 (1987): 39-60.

[*In the following essay, Eigner concentrates on the relationship in* David Copperfield *between Dickens's nar-*

rator and James Steerforth in order to elucidate the novel's qualities as elegiac romance and illustrate its themes associated with gentility and the fear of death.]

Mortality and gentility, two concepts central to an understanding of *David Copperfield,* have become the subjects of important, recent studies of the nineteenth century. Philip Mason's *The English Gentleman: The Rise and Fall of an Ideal* (1982) and Robin Gilmour's *The Idea of the Gentleman in the Victorian Novel* (1981) both pay considerable attention to the works of Dickens, and Garrett Stewart's *Death Sentences: Styles of Dying in Victorian Fiction* (1984) uses *David Copperfield* as one of its primary texts. The themes appear to have little in common with one another and to require, indeed, quite different sorts of critical approaches, but still another recent book, *Elegiac Romance* (1983) by Kenneth A. Bruffee, although it deals with neither Dickens nor his times, provides nevertheless a way of discussing the pervasive Victorian aspiration toward gentility and the obsessive nineteenth-century preoccupation with the fear of death as they relate to one another in *David Copperfield,* the central novel in Dickens' career.

Most simply described, an elegiac romance is a first-person retrospective narration recounting the death of a romantic figure who has captured the imagination of the less heroic narrator. A few examples are *Moby-Dick, Heart of Darkness, The Great Gatsby,* Thomas Mann's *Doctor Faustus,* Ford Madox Ford's *The Good Soldier,* Salinger's "Seymour: An Introduction," R. P. Warren's *All the King's Men* and Saul Bellow's *Humboldt's Gift,* but Bruffee's impressive list of eighteen well-known novels and twice as many shorter pieces offers convincing proof that we have to do here with an important fictional construct, full of significance to some of our best writers. By virtue of the *apparent* heros, these works descend, according to Bruffee, from medieval exemplary romances. However, the down-to-earth writing styles and the self-effacement typical of the narrators, who, although they always turn out at last to be the true heroes, characteristically begin with the sincerely avowed purpose only of coming to terms with their grief by discovering its meaning, connect these important novels and stories with the nondidactic, unpretentious elegiac mode.

As the examples indicate, this apparently self-contradictory form belongs mainly to our own century. Moreover, *David Copperfield* is far too long and complex a novel to be summed up in terms of such a discreet and so relatively simple a genre. There is a great deal more in Dickens' novel than can be explained by it, or indeed by any single critical approach. It remains, nevertheless, that when we focus on the narrator's relationship with James Steerforth, *David Copperfield* displays most of the characteristics of an elegiac romance and can be profitably read as such.

Indeed, the novel's opening sentence—"Whether I shall turn out to be the hero of my own life, or whether that station will be held by anyone else, these pages must show"—is a sentiment that might almost have been spoken by Marlow or Nick Carraway or John Dowell or Gene Forrester of *A Separate Peace* or any of the other elegiac romance narrators who struggle to recapture, through their writing, the sense of identity and personal worth they lost through their ambiguous relationship with the hero. It is late in the novel, for instance, before Jack Burden of *All the King's Men* is ready to concede that "This has been the story of Willie Stark, but it is my story, too. For I have a story" (435); and Salinger's Buddy Glass castigates himself in the last paragraph for his "perpetual lust to share top billing with" his dead brother.

The role of David Copperfield in the novel that bears his name is similarly confusing. As Lawrence Frank writes, "Steerforth threatens to usurp our interest" (67), and, more significant, he threatens also to usurp the interest of the narrator. At times David appears to be writing an autobiography, and the complexities of the character self-revealed, either consciously or unconsciously, have proved fascinating to such acute critics as Barry Westburg and Sylvère Monod. At other times, he seems to operate merely as a window, an insignificant observer, reporting the far more interesting doings of the Heeps, the Strongs, the Peggottys, Micawbers, and Steerforths, and to be so uninteresting in his own right as to have led such a great Dickens enthusiast as George Bernard Shaw to conclude that David "might be left out of his biography altogether but for his usefulness as a stage confidant, a Horatio or Charles his friend: what they call on the stage a feeder" (31).

In *Charles Dickens: The World of His Novels,* J. Hillis Miller puts these two David Copperfields together in a way that will be useful to our discussion. Miller writes that "David has, during his childhood of neglect and misuse, been acutely aware of himself as a gap in being. . . . The center of David's life . . . is the search for some relationship to another person which will support his life, fill up the emptiness within him, and give him a substantial identity" (156-157). This is the quest of all the twentieth-century elegiac romance narrators, who, again like David, discover at the death of the other person that by attempting to complete themselves in this questionable fashion they appear to have lost themselves entirely. They then proceed, like David, to recount the story of the tragic loss, to elegize the heroic dead man, to puzzle over the meaning of the gut experience they have survived, and in the process, hopefully to free themselves of the fallen hero's quest, perhaps indeed of all heroic questing, and, in the end, to find their own true identities, to become, indeed, the heroes of their own lives, or to reject, once and for all, the romantic notion of heroism (Bruffee, 49-50).

David Copperfield had sought in his friendship with the arch-gentleman, James Steerforth, just such an identity-giving relationship as Miller describes, the intellectual companionship he somewhat peevishly complains of having missed in his marriage to Dora and which Dickens himself felt he had never been able to find. Friendships and would-be friendships abound in the novel. Murdstone begins his acquaintance with David by saying, "Come! Let us be the best friends in the world!" (16), and while David is wisely on his guard from this quarter, he usually welcomes the friendships that are constantly offered him throughout the novel. He "soon became the best of friends" with Mr. Dick (185), and he responds so positively when Mr. Wickfield refers to him as "our little friend" (189) that he soon finds himself "feeling friendly towards everybody" (192), including even the sinister Uriah Heep, who much later in the novel insists on the friendship then established:

> "This is indeed an unexpected pleasure! [says Heep]. To have, as I may say, all friends round Saint Paul's, at once, is a treat unlooked for! Mr. Copperfield, I hope I see you well, and—if I may umbly express myself so—friendly towards them as is ever your friends, whether or not."
>
> (637)

David's substitute father, Mr. Micawber, refers to Uriah as "your friend Heep" (224) or "our friend Heep" (482). Poor Micawber, embattled though he is, perceives friends everywhere, even in the razor he sometimes thinks of using to cut his own throat (224). He regards David as "the friend of . . . [my] youth, the companion of earlier days!" (348); and Mrs. Micawber tells David "You have never been a lodger. You have always been a friend" (149). David thinks himself "blest . . . in having . . . such a friend as Peggotty" (273), and, of course, his relationship with Agnes Wickfield sails under the flag of a "pure friendship" (737) until the very conclusion of the novel.

But it is, of course, Steerforth whom we and the narrator think of as "the friend" in the novel ***David Copperfield***. Young David fastens onto this friendship as firmly and immediately as he does because, in the first place, Steerforth appears in his life at the moment when he is in most need of confirming his very nearly lost human identity. David's stepfather has beaten him like a dog, and David has responded, doglike, by biting his tormentor's hand. Now he walks around with a dog's sign tied to his back—"*Take care of him. He bites*" (67). In this state he is carried before Steerforth, "as before a magistrate," who enquires into the facts of the case and concludes "that it was 'a jolly shame;' for which," as David states, "I became bound to him ever afterwards" (72). Later on in the novel, when an older but still socially insecure David has been assigned a bed in "a little loft over a stable," Steerforth gives him a suitable, human identity once again. "Where," he demands of the innkeeper, "have you put my friend, Mr. Copperfield" (245). And David is immediately translated into a more genteel room "with an immense four-post bedstead in it, which was quite a little landed estate" (246).

Just what Steerforth sees in David besides an admiring plaything is perhaps somewhat more difficult to explain. Like most of the elegiac romance heroes Kenneth Bruffee describes, Steerforth does not reciprocate the affection entirely. At their reunion in London, for instance, David is overcome. "'I never, never, never was so glad! My dear Steerforth, I am so overjoyed to see you!'" Steerforth is more restrained: "'And I am rejoyced to see you, too!' he said, shaking my hands heartily. 'Why, Copperfield, old boy, don't be overpowered!' And yet he was glad too, I thought, to see how the delight I had in meeting him affected me" (245-246). After their final parting, David concedes that Steerforth's "remembrances of me . . . were light enough, perhaps, and easily dismissed" (388).

Like most romance heroes, Steerforth is too self-absorbed for satisfactory friendship, but, as his mother assures David, "he feels an unusual friendship for you" (253), and he is uncharacteristically solicitous of David's good opinion. "'If anything should ever separate us'," he says at their parting, "'you must think of me at my best. Come, let us make that bargain'" (373). George Bernard Shaw's belittling identification of David as a Horatio turns out to be inspired criticism. There is a great deal of Hamlet in James Steerforth, or at least he fancies so. Steerforth is broodingly suspicious of action, and he is cynically unable to direct his abundant energy to any goal except winning because he fails to see the value of any other goal. "'As to fitfullness'," he says, "'I have never learnt the art of binding myself to any of the wheels on which the Ixions of these days are turning round and round'" (274). He even feels troubled by "'a reproachful ghost'" (273), and he misses the presence of "'a judicious father'" (274). The Hamlet-like James Steerforth wears David Copperfield in his heart of hearts because he thinks David, whom he nicknames Daisy, is free of the romantic passions which govern *him*, and because, like Hamlet and such elegiac romance heroes as Lord Jim, Jay Gatsby, Willie Stark of R. P. Warren's *All the King's Men*, and the mad editor of Nabokov's *Pale Fire*, he needs desperately to be understood aright and to have his story told. "'I don't want to excuse myself;'" Lord Jim says, "'but I would like to explain—I would like somebody to understand—somebody—one person at least'" (69). And on his deathbed, Willie Stark of *All the King's Men* tells his flunky and future biographer, "'It might have been all different, Jack. . . . You got to believe that,' he said hoarsely. . . . 'You got to,' he said again. 'You got to believe that'" (400).

David Copperfield becomes a novelist, a storyteller, because that was the identity James Steerforth, who had an equal need of justification, gave him when they were children back at Salem House School. Previously, in the lonely days at the Rookery, David sat upon his bed in solitude and read, as he says, "as if for life" (48). Now in his new friend's bedroom, to which David "belong[s]" (80) and where he feels "cherished as a kind of plaything" (81), Steerforth proposes that they "make some regular Arabian Nights of it" (79). David, as official storyteller to Steerforth, likens himself to "the Sultana Scheherazade" (80), who, of course, *told* stories for her life.[1]

Later on, when David becomes what he calls "a little laboring hind" (132) and feels in danger once again of losing both his class and his human identity, he makes use of this resource Steerforth had taught him when he tells "some astonishing fictions" (143) to the Orfling who works for the Micawbers. And, at the end of the novel, he will tunnel out from his grief for Steerforth by writing a story. It is significant that when David mentions working on his "first piece of fiction" he finds himself coming by accident "past Mrs. Steerforth's house" (567). And, while it is perhaps too much to say that the one surviving work of our fictional novelist may be a life of James Steerforth, curiously titled ***David Copperfield,*** it *is* true that when Dickens shortened his complex novel into an evening-long public reading, he omitted almost everything in the novel which did not relate to Steerforth, and he ended the reading with Steerforth's death.[2]

Kenneth Bruffee, whose book on elegiac romance is subtitled *Cultural Change and Loss of the Hero in Modern Fiction,* sees his genre as the most recent phase of a long tradition. In the medieval quest romance, he writes, our attention is directed "exclusively to the task and character of the aristocratic seeker, the knight . . . [whose] story is always courageous and serious . . . seldom ironic." In the second phase, invented by Cervantes, "the whole story becomes ironic," because the knight must now share the stage with Sancho Panza, and "the reader is never allowed to feel quite sure whose values Cervantes means us to share: the knight's or the squire's. . . . For the first time in the quest romance tradition, the conventions and values of feudal life, courtly love, and [the] heroic knightly quest receive serious criticism in the light of everyday experience" (32). In the modern or elegiac romance phase, as Bruffee sees it, the irony disappears once again as the squire, after a tremendous struggle, rids himself of his obsession with his hero, and in so doing, utterly rejects the corrupt values of the society that the hero represents, including the concept of heroism itself.

It follows from this line of thinking that an individual elegiac romance will become significant when the values of the romantic hero that obsess the narrator and that he finally comes to reject are of deep cultural importance. Thus Jay Gatsby and Lord Jim can be said to embody the false dreams of the societies they represent. It is not enough, therefore, simply to explain the psychological reasons for David Copperfield's decision to lose himself, so to speak, in James Steerforth. We must ask ourselves what social values Steerforth represents, and how he may be regarded not only as David's personal hero, but as a significant hero of the Victorian age, perhaps as *the* significant hero. When we have done this, we may also be able to see why he is so important to David, and why David must ultimately outgrow him.

Ellen Moers writes in her study of *The Dandy* that with Steerforth "Dickens for the first time draws a character whose 'aristocratic' temperament, manners, and attitudes play a major part in the novel. Steerforth the wicked seducer [of Little Em'ly]," she writes, "is merely a repetition of immature melodrama [such as Dickens had frequently made use of in earlier novels], but Steerforth the schoolboy hero of David Copperfield is Dickens's first attempt to deal with a problem that would bedevil him in maturity" as he dealt with such ambiguous, gentlemanly characters as James Harthouse, Henry Gowan, and Eugene Wrayburn (229-230). It is not quite accurate to say that there had been no admirable or admired gentleman in Dickens before Steerforth, but it is true, nevertheless, that in ***David Copperfield,*** for the first time in Dickens, the idea of gentility, represented by such a problematical figure, becomes the obsessive goal of the principal point-of-view character.

David's background may account for his social ambitions. Early in the novel Little Em'ly distinguishes between herself and David by noting, "your father was a gentleman and your mother is a lady" (30). David does not contradict her, but the reader knows that his mother was a governess, not a lady, before her marriage and that, as David's Aunt Betsey has pointed out, she and her husband "were not equally matched" (7). Perhaps David, like Dickens himself, was sensitive on this score of a servant ancestry, for, in contrast to such earlier heroes as Nicholas Nickleby and Oliver Twist, he behaves like a boy, and later on like a man, who is shamefully uncertain of his own position in society. His difficulty with servants, who almost always refuse contemptuously to accept his authority, is one of the great comic strands of the novel. When David's stepfather, who has told him that he is "not to associate with servants" (103), condemns him to become a laborer, David is devastated mainly at the loss of his social position:

> No words can express the secret agony of my soul as I sunk into this companionship; compared these henceforth every-day associates with those of my happier childhood—not to say with Steerforth and Traddles and the rest of those boys; and felt my hopes for growing up to be a learned and distinguished man, crushed in my bosom.
>
> (133)

Later when he is rescued and again finds genteel companions at Dr. Strong's school, "My mind ran upon what they would think, if they knew of my familiar acquaintance with the King's Bench Prison" (195). And still later he becomes morbidly afraid that his enemy Uriah Heep will discover these secrets from Micawber, and publicly taunt him with them, as indeed Heep does, when he calls Micawber, "the very scum of the world—as you yourself were, Copperfield, you know it, before anyone had charity on you" (640).

David's extraordinary sensitivity on the score of Heep has been noted by several critics, and usually interpreted, mistakenly, I believe, as an unconscious revelation of class consciousness on Dickens' own part. Thus, A. H. Gomme writes:

> [Heep's] writhings are real enough, but it is impossible at times to avoid a feeling of special pleading against him, of Dickens with a knife in Uriah. . . . It is made a point against him that not only does he pretend to a humiliation he does not own, but that he has a coarse accent and drops his aitches. . . . That . . . snobbery in Dickens as well as in David . . . becomes vicious in the scene in which David is obsessed by Heep's physical repulsiveness.
>
> (176)

In *Great Expectations,* where Pip feels a similar repulsion to the lower-class Orlick and where Orlick responds with the same enmity, readers have no trouble distinguishing between the class attitudes of the character and those of the author. The confusion exists in *David Copperfield* partly because it is an elegiac romance, while *Great Expectations* is not, and because what Barry A. Marks has called the writing time of a story, the months or years during which we are to suppose the narrator is putting his experience on paper so that he can "seek and express an understanding of it,"[3] is consequently more important. Pip-the-narrator at least believes that he has already achieved his wisdom, his maturity, his sense of his own identity long before he begins writing his autobiography. Thus he is able compassionately to condemn his own childish snobbery and to make us understand that neither he nor Dickens shares it. David Copperfield-the-narrator is in the *process* of learning about himself as he writes his own (or is it James Steerforth's?) life story, and since he does not yet understand his own class consciousness, his obsession with gentility, the blindness appears also to be that of Dickens, the creator of David-the-narrator as well as David-the-character, neither of whom is yet free of the hero-worship of Steerforth and a thralldom to the false values of gentility he represents.

David-the-narrator's excessive hatred of Uriah Heep is also understandable in terms of the behavior of David-the-character, which, if given an unfavorable construction—the sort of critical construction a Heep internalized in David's own psyche might put upon it—is not very easily distinguishable from the actions of Heep himself. In *Dickens and the Invisible World,* Harry

Stone has written that Uriah personifies "David's most aggressive and covetous thoughts" (222). Certainly the two characters, both poor boys, are similarly determined to rise in the world. Keith Carabine believes that "Heep embodies and deflects those elements of David which . . . [he needs to] deny—namely his ambition and his sexuality" (161). And it must be admitted that as far as ambitious sexuality is concerned, neither David nor Heep is especially scrupulous in the business of secretly courting the daughter of his wealthy employer. Carabine sees Heep as "a rival and a double" of David's (161-162), and Harry Stone calls our attention to the Uriah-David rivalry over Bathsheba in the Bible, where, of course, King David, and not his subordinate Uriah, is the clear sexual aggressor. In light of this confusion and this combination of roles for Heep, we should note that David sees Uriah, as indeed Pip sees Orlick, in disgustingly phallic terms. The thought of his Agnes "outraged" by this "red-headed animal" makes David positively "giddy," so that Uriah "seemed to swell and grow before my eyes" (326).

Nevertheless, the aggressiveness and the aggressive sexuality of David or Heep are nothing when compared to these same qualities in Steerforth, a character David strives to exculpate as strongly as he works to incriminate Uriah. Steerforth, after all, succeeds in *his* seductions, and while he obviously disdains the tawdry business of rising in the world, he is clearly as determined as Heep is to win at any price:

> "Ride on! [he says] Rough-shod if need be, smooth-shod if that will do, but ride on! Ride over all obstacles, and win the race."
>
> "And win what race?" said I.
>
> "The race that one has started in," said he. "Ride on!"
>
> (364)

Dickens, who had already risen high enough by the time he was writing *David Copperfield* to enroll his eldest son at Eton, but who found himself still possessed by an excess of competitive energy, may have been as much or more disturbed by Steerforth's gratuitous aggression, when he saw it reflected in his own character, than he was by Uriah's self-help ambition.

Another servant who aspires to marry a woman David loves and against whom there is almost as much special pleading as there is against Heep is Steerforth's man, Lattimer. Why, after all, should David hold Littimer more guilty and in so much greater contempt than he does Steerforth in the business of Little Em'ly's seduction? And what is so outrageous, after all, in Littimer's desire to marry Em'ly when Steerforth has cast her off? Is he not, as he represents himself, "a very respectable person, who was fully prepared to overlook the past, and who was at least as good [socially] as anybody the young woman could have aspired to in a regular way" (511)? As George Orwell says in defense of Heep, "Even villains have sexual lives" (41). It appears that, just as David prefers to revile Heep instead of himself for the sexual fantasies both of them cherish regarding Agnes, he also prefers, in the matter of Em'ly's seduction, to hate the servant Littimer rather than the gentleman Steerforth.

And David is not the only one who indulges this preference. Littimer (I almost said poor Littimer) is everybody's scapegoat. Miss Mowcher, who also, after all, assisted in the seduction, prays, "May the Father of all Evil confound him [Steerforth] . . . and *ten times more* confound that wicked servant" (395). Rosa Dartle, whom Steerforth had previously seduced, holds Littimer in such deep contempt after the Little Em'ly business that she will not permit him to address her (395). Steerforth insults him (572), and even Little Em'ly, meek though she is, tries to murder him (571). Daniel Peggotty, who can keep his powerful emotions under control when speaking of Steerforth, the man who has abused his hospitality and ruined his niece, boils over with rage whenever he thinks of "that theer spotted snake . . . may God confound him!" who tried, from his own point of view, at least, to make an honest woman of her (619).

What all these characters have in common with one another and with David is an absolute fascination with James Steerforth and the gentility he represents. Miss Mowcher is an indefatigable name-dropper, and Rosa is a sycophantic dependent. Daniel Peggotty may seem a much more self-respecting character, but he is so charmed by Steerforth from the moment of their first meeting at David's school that we can feel pretty sure he was more of an ally than Littimer in the business of his niece's seduction, albeit, of course, an unwitting one. Not only did he talk Steerforth up on every occasion—

> "There's a friend!" said Mr. Peggotty, stretching out his pipe. "There's a friend, if you talk about friends! Why, Lord love my heart alive, if it ain't a treat to look at him!"
>
> (122)

—but it was he who first started Em'ly dreaming of becoming a lady when she was a small girl, wearing "a necklace of blue beads," which must have been a present from him.[4]

David's attraction to gentility is at least as strong as his need for friendship, and genteel people draw him out as easily as servants repel him. He finds his schoolmaster's daughter "in point of gentility not to be surpassed" (79), and Micawber impresses him "very much" at their first meeting with his "certain indescribable air of doing

something genteel" (134). Both David and his biological mother come close on a number of occasions to acknowledging Peggotty—"that good and faithful servant, whom of all the people on earth I love the best" (113)—as his true mother (11, 13-14, 17, 53), and at one point Peggotty asserts her claim to act as David's motherly protector—"who has such a good right?" she asks—and she assures David "that the coachfare to Yarmouth was always to be had for the asking" (212). But to accept Peggotty as his mother would mean an end to his dreams of gentility. Even Steerforth tells David that it is with Peggotty that he "naturally belong[s]" (265). And yet in his moments of deepest depression as "a little laboring hind" in London, he "never in any letter (though many passed between us) reveals the truth" to Peggotty (139), and when his situation becomes intolerable, David chooses to take his chances with Aunt Betsey, whom he has never seen and about whom he has heard nothing in the least bit encouraging, rather than come home to Peggotty, although he has to write a lie to Peggotty to get his Aunt's address and to borrow enough money to get to Dover in genteel fashion (151). As one critic writes, "David's walk to Dover is as irrepressible an assertion of individuality and the will to succeed as Heep's faith in his father's words, 'be 'umble, Uriah . . . and you'll get on'" (Carabine, 160). He also has a lot in common with Pip of *Great Expectations.* "I never could have derived anything like the pleasure from spending the money Mr. Dick had given me," David writes, "than I felt in sending a gold half-guinea to Peggotty, per post . . . to discharge the sum I had borrowed of her" (211). For David, as later for Pip, cutting the old, shameful though legitimate ties, is as important as weaving the new, highly questionable connections to the world of gentility.

With the help of his chosen mother, David, again like Pip, seems to have his fairy-tale wish of great expectations fulfilled. He gets a new name, becomes an heir, and is educated at a school for gentlemen. And when, like the hero of a fairy tale, he sets out into the great world to choose a genteel profession for himself, the first significant person he encounters, of course, is his old idol, the archetypal gentleman, whom he once chose over the skeleton-drawing Tommy Traddles and whom he soon acknowledges, in preference to Agnes Wickfield, as the guiding star of his existence (308). The profession David chooses, both at the suggestion of his lady Aunt, who wishes "to provide genteely" for him (299), and on the recommendation of his gentleman friend, could not be better suited to the goal he has set for himself. "A proctor is a gentlemanly sort of fellow," Steerforth tells David in a cancelled passage (293), and in a passage which was allowed to stand, Steerforth says, "On the whole, I would recommend you to take to Doctor's Commons kindly, David. They plume themselves on their gentility there" (293). So, in effect, it is Steerforth's advice that makes David a gentleman, just (and just as ambiguously) as it later makes Little Em'ly a lady.

Returning to the Em'ly plot and Daniel Peggotty's part in his niece's seduction, we can see just how Dickens connects his two themes of death and gentility, for it was Em'ly's concern to prevent her uncle's death that was the first cause of her dangerous ambition to become a lady. As she told the young David,

> "We should all be gentle folk together, then. Me, and uncle, and Ham, and Mrs. Gummidge. We wouldn't mind then, when there come stormy weather. Not for our own sakes, I mean. We would for the poor fishermen's, to be sure, and we'd help 'em with money when they come to any hurt. . . . I wake when it blows, and tremble to think of Uncle Dan and Ham, and believe I hear 'em crying out for help. That's why I should like so much to be a lady."
>
> (30-31)

This passage, one of the most poignant and meaningful in the novel, shows that for Dickens gentility was not only a question of social ambition or snobbish pride, but a life and death matter. In *Oliver Twist,* if you are not a gentleman, like Oliver, you are literally starved to death in the workhouse or hanged as a criminal. In *Bleak House* you are helplessly "moved on," carrying the plague that kills you. In *Great Expectations* the social alternatives are presented with a stunning simplicity: you can either be a hound (a gentleman) or a varmint; if you do not run with the hunters, you must inevitably and unsuccessfully run from them. In *David Copperfield,* according to Little Em'ly's experience, if you are not a lady, all the men around you will be "Drowndead." On the night of her elopement with Steerforth, David, who is attending the death of Barkis, has "leisure to think . . . of pretty little Emily's dread of death" (379).

Steerforth and the gentility he both stands for and appears to offer, for he is ready "to swear she was born to be a lady" (284), seems to provide an escape from death and the grief death causes. I believe that Steerforth stands for something similar in David's mind also, and that this is why David is initially fascinated by Steerforth and so unwilling to condemn him even after he has been found unworthy. Steerforth the gentleman is thus the false cultural hero of Victorian England, the romantic knight whom the narrator of one of the century's most significant elegiac romances must reject for himself and his age, so that he and his readers can find their true identities in the face of their otherwise overwhelming and paralyzing fear of death.

Saul Bellow's *Humboldt's Gift,* perhaps more than any of the other works on Kenneth Bruffee's list, demonstrates that elegiac romance, like pastoral elegy, pro-

vides an opportunity for a serious inquiry into the general question of death. The subject had always fascinated Dickens, but nowhere more powerfully than in *David Copperfield,* where the narrator is, after all, a "posthumous child" (2), and where his story includes the deaths of his mother, his infant brother, the previous tenant of his London rooms, his aunt's estranged husband, his beloved nurse's husband and her nephew, his own first child, who is stillborn, his first wife, her father and even her dog, and, finally, his own best friend and alternate identity. Moreover, David's childhood sweetheart is an orphan, motivated, as we have seen, with the dread of death; his first wife's mother is dead; and so is the mother of his second wife, who has been brought up in a mausoleum, haunted by a father, overcome with what he calls "disease[d]" and sordid "grief" (493-494). As Garrett Stewart has noted, *David Copperfield* is the only work "before *Malone Dies* that has invented a new word for death [drowndead, and] . . . the novel has, beyond this, far more than a word to add to the idea of death as a test of wording" (73).

If we are at first surprised at this quantity of deaths, it is perhaps because so few of them are actually rendered in the novel, so few of them directly witnessed by the narrator. I take this suppression to be in itself significant, for *David Copperfield* is a novel of suppressions, especially suppressions of death. Thus, Stewart suggests that Doctor Strong has been unable to get past the letter D in his unfinished dictionary because he cannot confront the word death. David apparently, or Dickens, cannot stand the sight of it, and so the writer who had sent Victorian England into profound mourning in his previous novel with the death of Paul Dombey and was to electrify them in his next book with the death of Jo the crossing-sweeper, shows David present at the dying moments only of the dog, Jip, and of the comic figure, Barkis. Moreover, both experiences are immediately overshadowed by so-called "Greater Loss[es]" (380), which David does not directly witness, the death of Dora and the elopement of Em'ly, who asks her family to "try to think as if I died when I was little and was buried somewhere" (386). When David remembers the last time he saw his mother alive, he writes, "I wish I had died. I wish I had died then with that feeling [of being loved?] in my heart!" (94). And soon his wish is symbolically fulfilled, although he has typically missed even his own death scene: When he describes his mother and his brother in their coffin, he thinks "The little creature in her arms was myself" (115).

David denies on the very first page of the novel that he was "privileged to see ghosts and spirits," but all the characters he subsequently introduces are referred to as "shadows" on the last page. Earlier he called them "phantoms" (541). The novel abounds with references to the ghosts in *Julius Caesar, Macbeth,* and especially *Hamlet.* Indeed, no other work of Dickens is so specter-ridden. The recollection of his unhappy youth, he writes, came upon David "without . . . invocation . . . like a ghost, and haunted happier times" (129), and after Steerforth's death David entered, what he calls "a long and gloomy night . . . haunted by the ghosts of many hopes, of many dear remembrances, many errors, many unavailing sorrows and regrets" (608).

As the presence as well as the denial of all this death in the novel would indicate, David Copperfield's reaction to death is both profound and ambiguous. "If ever a child were stricken with sincere grief," it was David at the news of his mother's death, yet he felt "distinguished" by it in the eyes of his schoolmates "and walked slowly" (107). When Mr. Spenlow dies David has "a lurking jealousy . . . of Death . . . [which might push him from his] ground in Dora's thoughts" (475). But, on the whole, he has a nightmare dread which dates back to his association with the best parlor and Peggotty's account of his father's funeral there. The story of "how Lazarus was raised up from the dead" so frightened him as a child that his mother and Peggotty were obliged to take him out of bed and show him the quiet churchyard out the bedroom window, "with the dead all lying in their graves at rest, below the solemn moon" (12). It is, of course, his own death David fears. When he returns from his first trip to Yarmouth and thinks that his mother is dead, he feels as though he "were going to tumble down" (36), and this is precisely his sensation later on when he hears of Mr. Spenlow's death—"I thought it was the office reeling, and not I" (474). Spenlow, whose posthumous son-in-law David will soon become, is another character paralyzed at the thought of death. He has been psychologically unable to make out a will. But the subject of death is as fascinating to David and the others as it is horrifying. The death-dreading Em'ly goes to work for an undertaker, and David ends his search for a genteel profession by binding himself apprentice to a probate attorney.

Barry Westburg argues that David's stepfather, Mr. Murdstone, is the personification of Thanatos himself. Westburg writes:

> When David is told, "You have got a Pa!" he says, [that] "Something . . . connected with the grave in the churchyard, and the raising of the dead, seemed to strike me like an unwholesome wind." [Later,] when two of his associates greet Murdstone they say, "We thought you were dead!" He is dark of dress, skin, and whiskers and professes a mortifying religiosity. . . . Murdstone is the resurrection of death itself, of life's primal antithesis.
>
> (46)

And as we have seen, it is Murdstone who initiates the friendship theme in the novel. "'Come! Let us be the best friends in the world!' said the gentleman, laughing. 'Shake hands!'" (16).

David offers Murdstone only his left hand, but to Steerforth, the second gentleman of the novel, he gives both hand and soul wholeheartedly, and with Steerforth he does become "the best friends in the world." It is a strange substitution, as profoundly ironic as Little Em'ly turning to this same gentleman-sailor as a protection against being "drowndead." The warnings come quickly in both cases. On the first evening, Steerforth entertains Em'ly with "a story of a dismal shipwreck" (269), and David, who is introduced to Steerforth "under a shed in the playground" (72), spends *his* first night sitting with Steerforth in the bedroom, thinking of ghosts. We have previously seen that Steerforth gives David a life-saving, artist's identity at school, but we should note that if David is Scheherazade in the relationship, Steerforth is the Sultan, who may choose to spare, but whose more usual course is to execute his brides after the wedding night.

Michael Slater has suggested that the invention of Steerforth, "handsome and captivating, entrancing company, yet ultimately shallow, selfish and cruelly frivolous . . . enables Dickens to create David's Maria [Beadnell] figure, Dora Spenlow, untouched by the unhappy memories of the way in which his real-life original had tormented and ultimately failed him" (62-63). Dora, who dominates the second half of the novel almost as powerfully as Steerforth had the first, and whose plot was the only one besides Steerforth's that Dickens kept for his public reading of *David Copperfield,* is, with her attractive vivacity and gentility, yet another ironically fragile safety-net against death. David's association of Dora with life and gentility becomes comically clear in his shocked horror when his landlady likens his love for the doomed "Little Blossom" to the passion of a dead lodger, David's predecessor, for a working-class girl. "I must beg you," David says, expressing far more than snobbery, "not to connect the young lady in my case with a barmaid, or anything else of that sort, if you please" (341).

But it is more frequently to Steerforth directly that David, like Em'ly, looks for salvation. David refers to Steerforth as his "protector" (307). Steerforth, David says, "was a person of great power in my eyes" (76), power which I submit David believes will save him from the dominance of Murdstone and the spell of death, as, indeed, at their reunion at the London inn it rescues David from his "small bedchamber," which David describes as "shut up like a family vault" (243). Em'ly seems actually to expect something like a rebirth through Steerforth, hoping for the day when "he *brings me back* a lady" (386, my emphasis). That this appearance is delusive goes perhaps without much saying— Steerforth is himself "drowndead"—but *In Memoriam,* and a host of important literary works glorifying the gentleman give evidence that it was the culture's delusion as well as David's and Em'ly's. Robin Gilmour believes that Pip's great expectations represent "some of the deepest hopes, fears, and fantasies of Dickens's class and generation" (118), and Arnold Kettle writes that the "day-dream nature . . . of Steerforth, the Byronic superman, aristocratic self-confidence and all, is revealed in the novel as no arbitrary personal 'weakness' in David's character, but as an important and complex social psychological problem of nineteenth-century England" (72-73). He seems, according to Lawrence Frank, "to have stepped out of David's dreams as the dazzling figure David wishes and fears to become" (92). "Steerforth was a myth," according to Garrett Stewart, "generated out of the . . . suspension of moral consciousness into which David was betrayed by his adolescent identification with his idol as the incarnated dream of invincible vitality and charm" (78); i.e., of life and gentility.

After Steerforth rescued David from the vault-like room above the stable at the Golden Cross Inn, David, who had just seen a performance of *Julius Caesar,*" fell asleep in a blissful condition, and dreamed of ancient Rome, Steerforth, and friendship, until the early morning coaches, rumbling out of the archway underneath, made me dream of thunder and the gods" (247). Steerforth is, of course, the principal god in question, but David's and Em'ly's hope that he will confer some of his immortality on them does not reckon with the fact that he regards them and all servants and the children of servants as belonging to a different species from himself. Their "feelings," he assures one of his schoolmates, "are not like yours" (86), and when a member of his own class asks him if the Peggottys and people of that sort are "really animals and clods, and beings of a different order," he allows "with indifference," that "there's a pretty wide separation between them and us" (251). When Steerforth dismisses Ham Peggotty as "a chuckle-headed fellow," David, who has been vaguely worried about Steerforth since the latter's gratuitous humiliation of their unoffending schoolmaster, Mr. Mell, finds it possible, or perhaps necessary, to convince himself that his friend and protector is only hiding his sympathies for the poor by making a joke (271). Obviously Em'ly is capable of the same kind of self-delusion, until Steerforth unmistakably shows how he regards her by trying to arrange a marriage for her with his own servant.

Both David and Em'ly have passed through a sort of fairy-tale experience, which can be called the motif of the bad wish granted and which Dickens employed to structure a number of his novels, most obviously **"The Haunted Man,"** *Little Dorrit,* and *Great Expectations.* In such works the beneficent fairy, who is sometimes only implied, makes the wish come true so that the hero can learn its falseness and try to save himself by unwishing it. David and Em'ly both wished for gentility through Steerforth, and they both seemed about to have

the desire fulfilled, but only so that, like Pip and the others, they might discover in time that the ambition was unworthy.

Em'ly began the necessary redemptive business of reversing the destructive wish when, after recovering from the fever which followed her flight from Steerforth and Littimer, she told the Italian children not to address her as "'pretty lady' [*bella donna*] as the general way in that country is, and . . . taught 'em to call her 'Fisherman's daughter' instead" (622). Then she became a servant at an inn in France. And finally, after her arrival in England, she walked from Dover to London, literally reversing David's earlier painful and heroic march to gentility.

David's way back is more difficult because he has invested still more of himself even than Em'ly has in Steerforth and what he represents. She has been Steerforth's mistress and has lost her good name; but David, like the narrator of the twentieth-century elegiac romances, has allowed himself to become Steerforth's double, and it is not too much to say that he has lost his soul. After the seduction of Little Em'ly, which occurs at the precise center of the novel, David declares his cherished friend dead. He claims that Steerforth "fascinated me no longer" and that "the ties that bound me to him were broken" (388). Steerforth disappears physically from the next seven numbers of the novel, but his name recurs regularly in each monthly installment. And like Tennyson to the dead Hallam's door, David keeps returning during these pages—"in an attraction I could not resist" (445)—to the garden under Steerforth's window. After the drowning, which takes place in the next to last number, David mourns for Steerforth as a potential hero "who might have won the love and admiration of thousands, as he had won mine long ago" (696).

Robin Gilmour writes that "there is no real awakening of David's undisciplined heart in relation to Steerforth" because "Dickens's imagination is not really engaged [in **David Copperfield**] as it will be later in **Great Expectations** in exploring the processes of moral and emotional self-discovery" ("Memory," 39). I have been arguing a greater similarity between the two novels in question. According to my reading, David and Pip are alike not only in regard to their social ambition and the fear of death which sparks it in both instances, but, to an even larger extent, in the burden of guilt they share. Pip is made to feel guilty about being an orphan, about being a boy, about being a laborer, and he makes himself guilty by wishing himself into becoming a snobbish, persecuting gentleman. In the last third of **Great Expectations,** Pip suffers various kinds of symbolic death, which have been seen as ritual attempts to expiate that guilt, to unwish the bad wish that had caused it. But in respect to guilt, David, I think, surpasses even Pip. As the projections on Littimer and Heep indicate, he feels guilty about his social background, about his ambition to rise above it, and about his sexual nature, which Dickens frequently saw as both motivation and means for social advancement. He even feels guilty about distrusting the perfidious Steerforth. More legitimately, perhaps, David appears to blame himself for his part in the seduction of Little Em'ly and for unconsciously wishing his unsatisfactory wife to death.[5] And the writing of *David Copperfield* can be seen as *David's* ritual attempt—the elegiac ritual, this time—to clear himself of this enormous load of guilt.

Elegy would seem to be a promising means of expiation in this case because the sins were all connected with the fascination for the dead Steerforth. It was David who introduced little Em'ly to her seducer and, according to John O. Jordan, gave her to Steerforth in an unconscious attempt to gain his idol's approval and thus rise in social class (69-70). Even the unsatisfactory wife recommended herself in the first place as a tangible representation of the Doctor's Commons gentility Steerforth had advised David to pursue. If David can come to terms with Steerforth through the act of writing *David Copperfield,* then he will perhaps have found the absolution he requires and will perhaps have unwished *his* evil wish.

And the ending of *David Copperfield,* which finds the hero comfortably married and the father of a growing family, might suggest that David's elegy has been more effective than the ritual expiations of Pip, who in the original version of *Great Expectations* remains a wanderer and a childless bachelor. Lawrence Frank believes that David has succeeded where Pip later fails, because at the end of *David Copperfield*—"at the successful end—one has come into possession of one's own story. At the end David's story stands in chronological and thematic coherence" (92), whereas Pip recoils "from his own imaginative achievement," glorifying Joe as he had previously falsified Miss Havisham (181). But I am not convinced that either hero really succeeds in overcoming his obsession with death, and Pip is, at least, a great deal clearer about the social significance of his guilt than David ever consciously becomes.

Nor, finally, am I certain that David Copperfield ever frees himself from his fascination for Steerforth, even after he has described the latter's death and supposedly ended the elegy. At the conclusion of the novel David has become a gentleman who keeps a respectful servant, and he has reached this station by exercising the identity of the storyteller which Steerforth has conferred on him as a schoolboy. *Steerforth's Gift,* Saul Bellow might have named the novel. There would be nothing wrong with this ending if the story that came before it had been in all respects an elegiac romance. But it seems to me that *if* David has attained the more significant "station" he wondered about in the first sen-

tence of the novel, if he has, in fact, become the hero of his own life, he has done so not by acknowledging his alternate identity and then letting it go, like the narrator in Conrad's "The Secret Sharer," not, as Frank maintains, by recognizing "the failings of Steerforth without rejecting what is redeeming in him," thus acknowledging "the ambiguity of his own moral condition in which good and bad intermingle" (72). Rather, he asserts his identity at the conclusion by rigorously suppressing even the name of his rival.

David Copperfield, like most of Dickens' novels, was originally published in eighteen equal, monthly parts and a bonus nineteenth installment of one and a half times the normal length. Steerforth's death is recounted in the eighteenth number. The final "double-number," seven chapters long, one-thirteenth of the entire novel, contains the most gratifyingly protracted set of curtain-calls in all of Dickens. Everyone is brought back for a final round of applause. Mr. Peggotty comes all the way from Australia so that we can learn not only about Em'ly, Martha, Mrs. Gummidge and the Micawbers, but even about Mr. Mell, whom we had long forgotten, and Mr. Creakle's son, who never appeared in the novel except to be briefly mentioned. Dickens even reminded himself in the Number Plan not to forget Aunt Betsey's donkeys. Most of the dead are recalled, including James Steerforth, whom David "mourns for" (696), but whom in this single case, he consistently avoids naming.

There are plenty of opportunities in the last seven chapters for David to write the name of Steerforth—he recollects the meeting at the Golden Cross Inn (702), he has an interview with Littimer, who mentions his master only through a reference to "the sins of my former companions" (730), and finally, in the last chapter, he encounters James's mother, whose name he also suppresses and who, in retaliation perhaps, has "forgotten this *gentleman's* [David's] name" (749, my emphasis). It has required considerable ingenuity on David's part to avoid writing the name of the character who has dominated so much of what has gone before. Perhaps Steerforth, the only major character in the novel without a counterpart in Dickens' biography and thus the only pure product of his imagination, is too powerful a force to be laid to rest, but an elegy which fails to commemorate does not legitimately permit a final shift of attention to an elegist, who free now for "fresh woods and pastures new," can become a true hero of his own life.

I mentioned earlier that death scenes are scarce in *David Copperfield*—another important suppression—and that the only death scene of a human being at which David is himself present is that of Barkis. The last words of the dying man, "Barkis is willin," are a reference to the private joke he shares with David, but, coming at this precise moment, they also express a willingness to face death, which the miserly Barkis had been previously re-luctant to do.[6] The most obvious and significant sup-pression in the novel occurs in an earlier speech of Barkis's:

> "It was as true," said Mr. Barkis, "as turnips is. It was as true," said Mr. Barkis, nodding his nightcap, which was his only means of emphasis, "as taxes is. And nothing's truer than them."

David has long since completed Barkis's suppressed thought, when he said "it is as certain as death" that greed and cunning will overreach itself (650), but he used this lesson not to redeem himself, but to cast into the teeth of his old scapegoat, Uriah Heep.

Garrett Stewart believes that David has "put his dead back together again" and has thus succeeded, where such suppressing characters as Mr. Dick and Doctor Strong failed, in completing "an articulate memorial or record" (80). I question whether he has even conceded that his dead are in fact dead. David-the-narrator tells us that he has been dreading "from the beginning of the narrative" (673) to recount the death of Steerforth, and when the doctor tells him of the approaching death of Dora, David-the-character "cannot master the thought of it" (656). This reluctance and inability is caused, per-haps, by the young David's failure, as Lawrence Frank would have it, to confront his mother's death. "Part of David," Frank writes, "has never left that room [at the Rookery], has remained within it, gazing longingly in dread and yearning at the graves in the churchyard" (66). If so, then it is unlikely that he ever does learn to make this confrontation, for his remembered image of Steerforth dead, like the image Peggotty leaves him of his dead mother, is of a child sleeping.

At least one critic shares my sense of disquiet at the ending of *David Copperfield.* Judith Wilt writes:

> the final pages seem to picture a "tranquility" achieved with "a better knowledge of myself" and Agnes. Yet the tranquility is a strange one. . . . David, in his last paragraph, imagines in the mirror of the future the hard-won "realities" melting from him "like shadows which I now dismiss." Further, this Prospero pictures Agnes, not joining him in a final Reality, but rather "pointing upward" where the restless heart rests at last. Perhaps.
>
> (305)

The ambiguity suggests that the fear of death remains potent enough with David Copperfield, and perhaps also with Dickens, to prevent proper dismissal of the concept of gentility and of the gentleman who, as both the author and the narrator of this most penetrating study of death and gentility must surely know by now, cannot afford them the least protection.

Notes

1. Sylvia Manning notes that "David's ability to tell stories is a saving social asset: his 'good memory'

and his 'simple, earnest manner of narrating' win him a special position of storyteller to Steerforth." She goes on to say that "Just as the Sultana Sche-herazade, whose image presides over the episode, told stories for her very life, her young successor David told them to save his sheltered niche—to save his boy's life—in the isolated world of Sa-lem House" (331-332).

2. Samuel Clemens, who attended one of these per-formances, wrote that Dickens' reading of the storm scene "in which Steerforth lost his life was so vivid and so full of energetic action that the house was carried off its feet, so to speak" (175).

3. Marks, whose article anticipates Bruffee's by sev-eral years, does not distinguish between kinds of retrospective narrators, or between authors who attempt to discover meaning through this tech-nique or discipline and those who use it merely as a device for "engaging the reader in order that he might be led to believe what he might otherwise have merely understood" (375). This last distinc-tion seems crucial to me, and I could wish Bruffee himself had confronted it more directly. Romance asserts. Elegy seeks rather to discover.

4. In Hugh Walpole's fine scenario for the 1930s film version, we actually see Mr. Peggotty, played by Lionel Barrymore, give the necklace to Em'ly and tell her it comes from France.

5. Perhaps the most persuasive of the critics who have argued this point is Carl Bandelin, "David Copperfield: A Third Interesting Penitent," but Christopher E. Mulvey and Harry Stone also make strong cases for David's guilt.

6. George Anastaplo, writing on *A Christmas Carol,* argues that avarice should be regarded as "a deter-mined attempt to fence oneself off from death" (127).

Works Cited

Anastaplo, George. *The Artist as Thinker: From Shake-speare to Joyce.* Chicago: Swallow Press, 1984.

Bandelin, Carl. "David Copperfield: A Third Interesting Penitent." *SEL* 16 (1976), 601-611.

Bruffee, Kenneth. *Elegiac Romance: Cultural Change and the Loss of the Hero in Modern Fiction.* Ithaca, N.Y.: Cornell University Press, 1983.

Carabine, Keith. "Reading *David Copperfield.*" In *Read-ing the Victorian Novel: Detail Into Form.* London: Vi-sion Press, 1980.

Clemens, Samuel. *The Autobiography of Mark Twain.* Ed. Charles Neider. New York: Harper, 1959.

Conrad, Joseph. *Lord Jim.* New York: Holt, Rinehart and Winston, 1965.

Dickens, Charles. *David Copperfield.* Ed. Nina Burgis. London: Oxford University Press, 1981.

Frank, Lawrence. *Charles Dickens and the Romantic Self.* Lincoln and London: University of Nebraska Press, 1984.

Gilmour, Robin. *The Idea of the Gentleman in the Victorian Novel.* London: Allen and Unwin, 1981.

———. "Memory in *David Copperfield.*" *Dickensian* 71 (1975), 38-42.

Gomme, A. H. *Dickens.* London: Evans, 1977.

Jordan, John O. "The Social Subtext of *David Copperfield.*" *Dickens Studies Annual* 14 (1985), 61-92.

Kettle, Arnold. "Thoughts on *David Copperfield.*" In *Review of English Studies* N. S. 2 (1961), 65-74.

Manning, Sylvia. "*David Copperfield* and Scheherazade: The Necessity of Narrative." *Studies in the Novel* 14 (1982), 327-336.

Marks, Barry A. "Retrospective Narrative in Nineteenth-Century American Literature." *College English* 30 (1970), 366-375.

Mason, Philip. *The English Gentleman: The Rise of an Ideal.* New York: William Morrow, 1982.

Miller, J. Hillis. *Charles Dickens: The World of His Novels.* Cambridge, Mass.: Harvard University Press, 1958.

Moers, Ellen. *The Dandy: Brummell to Beerbohm.* New York: Viking, 1959.

Monod, Sylvère. *Dickens the Novelist.* Norman: University of Oklahoma Press, 1968.

Mulvey, Christopher E. "*David Copperfield:* The Folk-Story Structure." *Dickens Studies Annual* 5 (1976), 74-94.

Orwell, George. "Charles Dickens." In *Dickens, Dali and Others.* New York and London: Harcourt Brace Jovanovich, 1973.

Salinger, J. D. *Raise High the Roofbeam Carpenter and Seymour: An Introduction.* New York: Bantam Books, 1981.

Shaw, George Bernard. "Epistle Dedicatory" to *Man and Superman.* Harmondsworth: Penguin, 1983.

Slater, Michael. *Dickens and Women.* London: J. M. Dent and Sons, 1983.

Stewart, Garrett. *Death Sentences: Styles of Dying in Victorian Fiction.* Cambridge, Mass.: Harvard University Press, 1984.

Stone, Harry. *Dickens and the Invisible World: Fairy Tales, Fantasy, and Novel-Making.* Bloomington: Indiana University Press, 1979.

Warren, Robert Penn. *All the King's Men.* New York: Bantam Books, 1981.

Westburg, Barry. *The Confessional Fictions of Charles Dickens.* DeKalb: Northern Illinois University Press, 1977.

Wilt, Judith. "Confusion and Consciousness in Dickens's Esther," *Nineteenth-Century Fiction* 32 (1977), 285-309.

David Kellogg (essay date 1991)

SOURCE: Kellogg, David. "'My Most Unwilling Hand': The Mixed Motivations of *David Copperfield.*" *Dickens Studies Annual* 20 (1991): 57-73.

[*In the following essay, Kellogg eschews autobiographical readings of* David Copperfield, *instead focusing on the social subtext of the novel and its thematic intersection of personal happiness and social utility.*]

This paper's subtitle reveals some of its basic oppositions. The word *motivations* implies a human subject, impelled by external forces toward some specific end; naturally we assume this subject to be, as the novel's larger title says, "David Copperfield the Younger, of Blunderstone Rookery"—a person tied to a time and place. Yet we know this to be false, for *David Copperfield* is a fiction "By Charles Dickens, With Illustrations by H. K. Browne." This paper touches on *David Copperfield* in both major roles: as unique psychic identity, and as endlessly reproducible words on a page, socialized and socializing text. Still, this name that is also title could lead to confusion. Add to the book's dual identity the widely shared conviction that *David Copperfield* is Dickens' "autobiographical" novel, packed with clues about its author and even in some sense derived from an abandoned autobiographical project, and it is easy to see how this text has become vulnerable to the kinds of suggestive but perhaps overly speculative psychological readings that have dominated *Copperfield* criticism in this century.

Recently, however, critical response to *David Copperfield* has decisively turned toward social concerns. This is as it should be. Edmund Wilson's well-known reading of the novel in terms of the young Dickens' ordeal at Warren's Blacking has been attacked on a number of fronts;[1] and though others, notably Stephen Marcus, have attempted ingenious psychoanalytic readings of the "autobiographical fragment" that records the warehouse experience and informs so many responses to

David Copperfield, recent trends in literary theory have allowed more sophisticated analyses of the novel, analyses which refuse to reduce it to an elaborate response to a single experience that "produced in Charles Dickens a trauma from which he suffered all his life" (Wilson 6). Indeed, we have come to understand *David Copperfield* not as a novel divorced from political concerns but rather as one with a deeply embedded social subtext.

One of the best of these new readings argues that "anxiety about social class infects David's narrative and produces significant displacements, distortions, and omissions in his self-presentation and in his accounts of other people" (Jordan 63). For this critic, David Copperfield as narrator submerges his own anxiety about social mobility, class anger, and aristocratic privilege into his representations of the people around him, thus legitimating his own social position. "[T]he search for social legitimacy . . . constitutes the course of [David's] career" also for Chris R. Vanden Bossche (87), who believes that the very profession of author is attractive to David partly because of its gentility; it can never be confused with the kind of alienated labor performed at Murdstone and Grinby's (103).

But the mention of Murdstone and Grinby's brings us back to childhood and models for self-development; and in fact political and psychoanalytic readings overlap considerably.[2] Differences in (social and "public" vs. psychological or private) emphases produce different assessments of the narrator: biographical critics such as Alexander Welsh maintain that "*David Copperfield* was written from the assured perspective of a relatively stable sense of identity . . ." (108), while political critics emphasize David's lingering insecurity about his own rise in social and monetary status (Jordan 66). Though some psychoanalytic readings will admit that David's "personal development is conspicuously mixed, partial, and incomplete" (Hirsh 92), most would agree with Lawrence Frank that David writes in order to heal his psychic wounds, and that this healing is (fairly) successfully realized (75).

If these forms of reading conflict and intersect, it may be because *David Copperfield* tracks the collisions of self and society. This paper will examine some of these collisions, specifically those involved in Copperfield's act(s) of writing. David Copperfield is wounded both psychologically and socially; he writes both for psychic healing and for social and financial advancement. However, the very existence of *David Copperfield* the unpublished autobiography may imply that these motivations for writing conflict, that writing fiction for a large consuming audience improves David's position in society but does not deal. David thus writes his autobiography in order to achieve the psychic healing that the novels could not give. However, novel-writing may have accomplished its goal of social and financial re-

spectability so well that David can no longer retrieve a position of innocence with respect to his public life; his entrenchment in the middle class may be so complete that David is blind to his own implication in that entrenchment. In this reading, *Copperfield* as autobiography attempts to reprivatize, by writing, a life which has become publicly implicated through that selfsame writing. Though David says of his book that "this manuscript is intended for no eyes but mine" (42.671), honesty does not necessarily follow.[3]

When David's aunt Betsy Trotwood adopts David, she asks Mr. Wickfield for advice on his education. David has just met Uriah Heep, on the representation of whom he "heaps" all his own pecuniary interests, and he is about to meet Agnes, his "better Angel" and the representative of all his purer motivations. In the gap between these encounters Mr. Wickfield inquires into Miss Trotwood's motives for educating David; and when she becomes indignant, Mr. Wickfield, "shaking his head and smiling incredulously," declares that "It must be a mixed motive" (15.277). His answer indicates that Miss Trotwood has not admitted mixed motives; yet her motives, while "on the surface," need not be pure: "to make the child happy and useful" (15.277). Happiness and utility hardly walk hand in hand, and indeed may conflict: *happy* implies a psychological state independent of others, while *useful* connotes an existence the worth of which depends on the value others assign. Happiness is essentially personal or private, utility social, public, and economic. *David Copperfield* explores and is caught up in their collision.[4]

1

> But under this difficulty, and under all the other difficulties of my journey, I seemed to be sustained and led on by my fanciful picture of my mother in her youth, before I came into the world.
>
> (Dickens 13.243-44)

The "difficulties of [David's] journey" should be neither downplayed nor inflated. That the book urges us to read it in terms of Dickens's life—that, as Welsh says, "alert readers . . . , without any special knowledge, could realize that certain games were being played" with the Dickens biography (115)—presents a number of dangers, encouraging diverse biographical readings and misreadings. This quality of oblique confession has some importance for this paper, and I will discuss it later. For now we must recognize that, though it is impossible to place ourselves in a position where we do not know that *David Copperfield* is Dickens' autobiographical novel, we must resist a Dickens-centered analysis if we are to understand the strained and contradictory motivations of the text.

David suffers a number of real and significant losses early in the story of his life, with the second half of the book enacting a drama of recovery from the losses experienced in the first. Gordon Hirsh believes that "the plot is actually *based* on recurring experiences of separation and loss" (85; emphasis added), though I would argue that the major losses of the second half, the deaths of Steerforth and of David's "child-wife" Dora, rather *close* wounds opened in the first half—the loss of Steerforth's friendship and the death of David's mother. This dual function of death as both wound and healing casts new light on what have become commonplaces of *Copperfield* criticism: Steerforth as David's alter ego, Dora as a recreation of David's mother, and David as fluctuating, insecure identity. In "The Beginning of a Long Journey," which effectively opens the second half of the novel, David refers to Steerforth as "a cherished friend, who was dead" (32.516); but when he finally sees the body, Steerforth is "lying with his head upon his arm, as [David] had often seen him lie at school" (55.866). Thus his death brings on for David not merely an attack of nostalgia but the imaginative recreation of an earlier, better time before Steerforth's moral and social fall.

This partial temporal reversal must be made complete, so David takes the responsibility for Steerforth's body: "I knew that the care of it, and the hard duty of preparing his mother to receive it, could only rest with me; and I was anxious to discharge the duty as faithfully as I could" (56.867). David is anxious faithfully to discharge his duty not merely because of his former closeness to Steerforth but also because of his earlier faithlessness regarding Little Em'ly. His implication in her fall has brought on the guilt and anxiety he feels at this point; in burying Steerforth, David performs a purgation or even an exorcism, a symbolic burial of his own guilt in effigy as Steerforth. Furthermore, that David in the midst of all this takes on "the hard duty of preparing [Steerforth's] mother" only underscores the connection in the text between the expurgation of guilt and the restoration of proper parent-child relationships. As we shall see, both this expurgation and this restoration are entangled in uneasy questions of personal identity.

Indeed, as has often been observed, David's own mother reenters the novel in another form soon after Steerforth's death. When he first loses Steerforth, David finds comfort in loving Dora: "Her idea was my refuge . . . and made some amends to me, even for the loss of my friend" (33.534). Her "idea" serves as refuge partly because Dora reminds David of his mother, and of a time of seeming innocence. Connections between David's mother and Dora are easily established. Both women are children in the home; neither has a sense of domestic economy; both defer to their husbands and to more dominating women. In these contexts, Betsy Trotwood calls David's mother "the Baby" (1.55) and Dora "Little Blossom" (44.705). David, blindsided by the double losses of Steerforth and Little Em'ly, creates in Dora a "fanciful picture" (13.244) of his mother, never fully seeing his wife at all. In marrying Dora, David re-

fuses to recognize the death of his mother, creating a substitute for her in his wife. Dora's death devastates David not because of his love for Dora but because he has recreated his mother *in* Dora. The loss of a parent is likely to destabilize anyone's identity; but for David, whose sense of self is repeatedly threatened from a number of quarters, the death of Dora comes as the last in a series of severe traumas.

We must recognize, in addition to other losses in the book, David's own repeated loss of identity. David holds, as has often been noted, multiple names and identities. Even before his birth, his aunt names him Betsy Trotwood, after herself (1.55), and when he runs to her later she refrains from calling him David, referring to him rather as "David's son" (13.254). Only after she adopts David does she call him by name—and then she renames him Trotwood (14.271) and persists in calling him "Trot" to the end of the book (62.938). Earlier, when his mother remarries, David receives a new name and is understandably uncomfortable with it. On his way to school he has a hard time getting a meal because of his confusion of identity:

> "What name?" inquired the lady.
>
> "Copperfield, ma'am," I said.
>
> "That won't do," returned the lady. "Nobody dinner is paid for here, in that name."
>
> "Is it Murdstone, ma'am?" I said.
>
> "If you're Master Murdstone," said the lady, why do you go and give another name, first?"
>
> (5.116)

Thus David's identity crisis is also a crisis of finance.

David must constantly adjust himself to the different names he receives and their varying social implications—David, Davy, Brooks of Sheffield, Mas'r Davy, Daisy, David Murdstone, Trotwood Copperfield, Master Copperfield, and my particular favorite, *Doady*—"which was a corruption of David" (41.667). Part of the drama of recovery, then, is a repeated fantasy of reestablishing his true name and identity in the face of recurring corruptions.

But true identity can be imagined apart from social class neither in *David Copperfield* nor in the Victorian society it represents. Despite increasing potential for social mobility, stratification remains powerful and pervasive. Personal worth in *David Copperfield* is bound up largely with personal *wealth* or station, with questions most often answered by reference to one's own (or one's father's) occupation. At school, however, David finds his identity (pre)determined largely by his earlier hostility to his stepfather, his own father having died before the son was born, making David "a posthumous child" (1.50). The traditional avenue of establishing identity through lineage is blocked off at the start. Nevertheless, David maintains throughout the novel a sense of personal nobility in spite of his own alienation from the usual paths to gentility.

When David runs away from Murdstone and Grinby's, he conjures the image of his mother as an aid. That he does so evidences how destabilized he is, since personal as well as public identity "naturally" (in David's mind and in British law) spring from the father. As we have seen, this line of descent is impossible for David. So he imaginatively fills the gap in an act which both prefigures his later imaginative writing and nullifies another script which had announced his severance from the father.

Earlier, when David goes off to school, he receives a placard to wear on his back: *"Take care of him. He bites"* (5.130). His stepfather Mr. Murdstone thus deprives him of a name and reduces him to a beast; and in spite of his own sense of having been wronged, David even begins to fear himself "as a kind of wild boy who did bite" (5.131), thus coming to inhabit the text that socially locates him. But most of all he fears what the other boys will think. Waiting for the others to return, David reads *their* names carved in a door, and he notices in particular that "there was one boy—a certain J. Steerforth—who cut his name very deep and very often . . ." (5.131). Such conviction frightens the truly selfless David, and later both this assurance of identity and Steerforth's social power become deeply attractive to David. David's realization that Steerforth's "great power," which "was, of course, the reason of [David's] mind running on him" (6.140), comes from his mother, who "was a widow, and rich, and would do almost anything . . . that he asked her" (7.154), may spur David's later resurrection of his own mother. In any case, Steerforth provides for David a close model of seemingly self-authorized identity and power.

Thus David experiences, in his schooling as elsewhere, both true decenterings of psychological identity and losses of social position and privilege. At Murdstone and Grinby's these losses come together. Surely the awfulness of the warehouse experience owes as much to David's own disoriented psyche, what with the recent death of his mother and his stepfather's utter neglect of him, as it does to the warehouse itself. At home he was lonely, at school decentered, but at Murdstone and Grinby's he is deprived even of the comforts of his books, without which he "should have been perfectly miserable" (10.215). We might think that a boy in David's position would jump at the chance for friends; David, however, dismisses his potential friends at Murdstone and Grinby's, Mick Walker and Mealy Potatoes, with a disparaging mention of their fathers' working-class occupations (11.209-10). It seems that the sons of, respec-

tively, a bargeman and "a waterman, who had the additional distinction of being a fireman" (11.210), are not good enough for David's society. They offend his "natural" gentility.

David compares "this companionship" with his "happier childhood—not to say with Steerforth and Traddles, and the rest of those boys." He "felt [his] hopes of growing up to be a learned and distinguished man, crushed in [his] bosom" (11.218) David himself locates this crush of hope in the shame in his "position," the loss of which leaves him "utterly without hope." David, however, if he is to keep a sense of self, must represent gentility to himself as well as to others throughout. He succeeds so well that the other workers call him "'the little gent', or 'the young Suffolker'" (11.218), in spite of the fact that "[he] worked, from morning until night, with common men and boys, a shabby child" (11.216). Among the few comforts David takes at Murdstone and Grinby's is that he held "some station" there (11.216). This maintenance of gentility in the midst of hardship culminates in the magnificent image of the shabby young David walking into a pub and asking for "your best—your *very best*—ale" to the amusement of the pub owner and his wife (11.216).

David, then, maintains his identity in the midst of the trauma of Murdstone and Grinby's by remembering *who he is*. And remembering who he is means representing an "original" place in genteel society which he imagines was his; this original space, created after the fact and by imaginative fiat, much of the novel will try to regain. Thus the first sentence of the novel, which couples David's potential heroism with his social station, as John O. Jordan has argued (64-65), also engages the act of writing:

> Whether I shall turn out to be the *hero* of my own life, or whether that *station* will be held by anybody else, *these pages* must show.
>
> (1.49; emphasis added)

Writing then turns out to be an act of personal recovery and an affirmation of privileged social standing. David Copperfield will take it a step further, actually using writing as the means to (re)gain what he conceives as his rightful place. But the economic motive for writing undercuts and subverts the psychological one, which is to (re)create from an irrecoverable past an absent identity already fixed and located "before [he] came into the world (13.243-44).

2

> I wallow in words.
>
> (Dickens 43.692)

Even in youth David has a touch of the artist about him; when he goes with Peggoty to visit Yarmouth for the first time, he remarks that:

a mound or two might have improved it; and also that if the land had been a little more separated from the sea, and the town and the tide had not been quite so much mixed up, like toast and water, it would have been nicer. But Peggoty said, with greater emphasis than usual, that we must take things as we found them, and that, for her part, she was proud to call herself a Yarmouth Bloater.

(3.77-78)

Peggoty's somber tone and sharpness rise mainly from her knowledge that David will soon change his identity when his mother marries Murdstone. We can also possibly detect elements both of class and of regional pride in her voice. In any case we find here David "improving" the scene through imagination, a pattern of both imaginative creation and a tendency toward self-deception that will occur throughout the book.

I have mentioned how David found reading a comfort after his mother's death. Even before that event, though, he takes refuge in his father's book collection, which consisted mainly of eighteenth-century novels. "They kept alive my fancy," David says, "and my hope of something beyond that place and time" (4.105). "[T]hat place and time," however, is not without reading at all, but rather filled with "solemn lessons," "the death-blow of [David's] peace, and a grievous daily drudgery and misery" (4.103). This marks David's first awareness in the novel of an important split between two divergent uses of signs. David reads to escape or transcend his social imprisonment, while Murdstone oversees his stepson's lessons in order to see that social place confirmed. We might dub these two (to the young David) opposing functions of signification as private and public, or possibly happy and useful, or perhaps best of all *alphabetic* and *numeric*. David associates the alphabet with his mother, with the pleasure of a "puzzling novelty," and with an "easy good-nature"—thus letters take on life and personality (4.103). He calls Murdstone's lessons, however, "very *numerous*" (4.103; emphasis added)—a modifier which might refer to content as well as form—and writes of their culmination in "an appalling sum" which is "invented" by Murdstone especially for David (4.103).

It should, then, come as no surprise to the reader to see David's control over alphabetic signs collapse under the numeric weight of Mr. Murdstone. Whereas with his mother David had learned well and happily, "the very sight of [the Murdstones] has such an influence over me, that I begin to feel the words . . . all sliding away, and going I don't know where" (4.103). In their place, significantly, rise involuntary reflections on number and finance:

> . . . I can't think about the lesson. I think of the number of yards of net in Miss Murdstone's cap, or of the price of Mr. Murdstone's dressing-gown, or any such

ridiculous problem that I have no business with, and don't want to have anything at all to do with.

(4.104)

But David has more business with such reflections than he yet knows, and these new problems hit closer to the ethical source than those his stepfather invents. It is easy to see how practical subjects—history, geography, and especially math—offend young David's imaginative sensibility. But it is far more important to note how the discourse of mathematics and numbers, especially financial calculation, serves throughout the novel as a form of *reading* opposing imaginative literature and alphabetical signification in general. The great force of this type of signification reduces David to financial metaphors even when he describes his own loss of language; his missed lessons become "a pile of arrears," the size of which is inversely proportional to David's intelligence: "The bigger it gets, the more stupid *I* get" (4.104). The Murdstones, practical as they are, threaten David's imagination and grasp over language as they destabilize his identity.

David's power over language continues to fail until he finds, he says, "the words of my lessons slipping off, not one by one, or line by line, but by the entire page" (4.107). When confined to his room for five days, he becomes desperate for any form of communication: "I listened to all the incidents of the house that made themselves audible to me" (4.109), he writes, and refers to "the strange sensation of never hearing myself speak" as a special torture (4.109-10). We must assume that, since David does not have access to his father's room, he has no books either, which is probably why the period "appears to have gone round and round for years instead of days" (4.110) in his mind.

All this is to say that David takes refuge in the imagination—a natural response for any child, one supposes, yet crucial to David's understanding of his own identity and gentility. In these early days, David occasionally creates imaginatively, but his youthful imagination is far more receptive than expressive. The older David Copperfield, the one who narrates, is aware of the social power of imaginative creation. In a suggestive metaphor, the narrator illustrates the limits of his youthful imagination, as well as its later force:

> I could observe, in little pieces, as it were; but as to making a net out of a number of these pieces, and catching anybody in it, that was, as yet, beyond me.

(2.70)

The vehicle of this metaphor images the power inherent in imagination, which might catch and restrain hostile persons or forces, in this instance specifically Murdstone. As both protection and power, shield and sword, metaphor has as many social as aesthetic implications.

In school David first learns the public power of his imagination. In Chapter 7 we find an interesting contest of observation between the young David and Mr. Creakle, in which first David is "humbly watching his eye" and then "eyeing him" (7.142). The center of perspective power shifts from Creakle to David, who "blink[s] at him like a young owl" (7.142) and then even "eyes" him through walls. Later, Copperfield gains admittance to Steerforth's inner circle through telling stories—the first instance of Copperfield gaining public rather than merely psychological power through his imagination (7.144). David's justification of his motive is worth noticing:

> I was moved by no interested or selfish motive, nor was I moved by fear of him. I admired and loved him, and his approval was return enough.
>
> (7.145)

Of course that approval itself carries perks, and Steerforth's public position clearly implicates David's own supposedly uninterested love and admiration.

The death of David's mother soon overwhelms and indeed suppresses the public functions of his imagination, and again David turns inward. Such turning is, of course, "social" through and through, as is any act of signification; however, we need to stress here that imaginative escape has its own reality for a Victorian society in which even the social space of the domestic is considered "private." Again David takes solace in books, both his father's books at home and Foxe's *Book of Martyrs* at the Barkis' (10.203). In fact, David has begun to see himself self-consciously as a victim, as martyr:

> I considered, after some hours were gone, if my tears were really hard to flow now, as they seemed to be, what, in connection with my loss, it would affect me most to think of when I drew near home—for I was going home to the funeral. I am sensible of having felt that a dignity attached to me among the rest of the boys, and that I was important in my affliction.
>
> (9.177)

Later, as he runs away from Murdstone and Grinby's, he "began to picture to myself, as a scrap of newspaper intelligence, my being found dead in a day or two, under some hedge" (13.236). *Under some hedge;* already David embellishes with the touch of the born novelist. Later he sits "looking at the moonlight on the water, as if I could hope to read my fortune in it, as in a bright book" (13.255); still later at his aunt's he will learn about Mr. Dick's Memorial, and will hear that some people "are paid to *be* memorialized" (14.261).

Clearly imagination and fortune are connected; small wonder, then, that the first of the present-tense imaginative retrospectives that puncture the book relives his rise in the school to head-boy, and the imaginative killing of his own youth: "I am the head-boy, now! I look down on the line of boys below me, with a condescending interest in such of them as bring to my mind the boy I was myself, when I first came there" (18.325). However, his newly found social superiority flies quickly; almost as soon as he leaves school and enters the world, he meets Steerforth again, who considers "Daisy" his property and who makes David painfully aware of his own youth (20.348). In an interesting exchange, David subconsciously offers the working-class Em'ly to Steerforth, while Steerforth's indifferent attitude toward Rosa encourages David to dream of her (Jordan 69). Steerforth, David learns, gave Rosa the scar upon her lip—David imaginatively recreates the scar on a painting of Rosa in his room:

> The painter hadn't made the scar, but *I* made it; and there it was, coming and going; now confined to the upper lip as I had seen it at dinner, and now showing the whole extent of the wound inflicted by the hammer, as I had seen it when she was passionate.
>
> (20.356)

"Passionate" must be taken in its sexual as well as its emotional sense; David remakes Rosa's wound, rewounds her in fact, and so participates in Steerforth's sexual domination of her (Jordan 69-70).

Later David visits Yarmouth with Steerforth and so ushers in Em'ly's fall. But while Steerforth orchestrates that, David haunts his parents' grave, and the themes of identity and ambition conflate:

> My reflections at these times were always associated with the figure I was to make in life, and the distinguished things I was to do. My echoing footsteps went to no other tune, but were as constant to that as if I had come home to build my castles at a living mother's side.
>
> (22.378)

We can read *figure* here in three senses: as social station, as writing itself (alphabetic signification or figuring), and as income (numeric signification). When David begins to write, these figurations of *figure* conflate.

The period of David's relation to Dora seems to cover roughly one period in his career, that of writing for financial gain. David tells of taking "with fear and trembling to authorship" in the same paragraph that he tells us that because of his authorship, "I am quite well off; when I tell the income on the fingers of my left hand, I pass the third finger and take in the fourth to the middle joint" (43.692-93). In this context of financial gain through writing, as well, he tells us that he is to be married to Dora. Significantly, his own hand measures his worth. Counting by knuckles was common in Victorian

England, but such a bodily measurement may also indicate that David is selling his self in his fiction. While he composes with his right hand, he ticks off the profits on his left; while the right hand spins out, the left takes in. We are perhaps reminded of the first chapter in the novel, of young David watching his own caul raffled off "at half-a-crown a head" (1.50). While at the time David was "uncomfortable and confused, at a part of myself being disposed of in that way" (1.50), he seems not at all uneasy at this later selling of the self in fictional bits and pieces.

Alexander Welsh has noted that David presents his new career so quickly that "as readers we are a little taken aback and have to remind ourselves that this is a novel about a novelist" (109). This reaction is part of the nature of the retrospective chapters, all of which telescope years into a few pages through the use of selected present-tense scenes. Additionally, they all cover times of social advancement for David; they allow David briefly to review his own social climb in the present tense, without the potential complications of reflection and judgement. Also, they present scenes quickly, in a kind of fluid succession. Even in other chapters, David talks about his success only in passing, always quickly and with some humility; but his references often reveal the way the novel is quite literally for David a socializing form: "my success had steadily increased with my steady application, and I was engaged at that time upon my first work of fiction" (46.733), he says, as though writing were a business like any other. Or again: "I have been very fortunate," he tells Mrs. Steerforth, "and find my name connected with some praise" (46.742). As in childhood, again the solidity and validity of the *name* become allied with social position and status.

But while David acquires a name, financial stability, and social/economic recognition as a gentleman, he remains psychologically battered and scarred. What might be called the Agnes-period of David's writing career begins while David is in Switzerland, recovering from his many wounds: the deaths of Steerforth, Dora, and Ham, the emigration of the Peggotys and the Micawbers. His "third work of fiction" seems written almost purely for the purposes of healing; David admits that the story rises "not remotely, out of . . . experience," and indeed "[i]t was not half written, when, in an interval of rest, I thought of returning home" (58.889). Immediately he speaks of his love for Agnes and his desire "to cancel the mistaken past" (58.890). Agnes has purified his motives for writing. Now, for instance, when he meets Chillip and Chillip wants to talk about his writing, David resists the narcissistic urge and "divert[s] [Chillip's] attention . . . to his own affairs" (59.907). Fiction has done for David what the sorrows of the Peggotys did for Mrs. Gummidge: it has released him from self-pity.

3

> "Has that Copperfield no tongue?" muttered Uriah. "I would do a good deal for you if you could tell me, without lying, that somebody had cut it out."
>
> (Dickens 52.827)

And yet we have these two strikingly different *David Copperfield*s: the autobiography, which the author "never meant to be Published on any Account," and the public fiction by one Charles Dickens, whose life bears remarkable resemblance to David Copperfield's and who seems to have encouraged the search for correspondences both in the text itself and outside it, in letters to Forster and in the Preface to the Charles Dickens edition of the work, calling it his "favorite child" (47). Thus we either talk about the novel from David's perspective, as fictional autobiography, or from Dickens' perspective (if we can find it), as autobiographical fiction. Interrogating the first perspective, John O. Jordan questions David's "reluctance to publish" and finds the answer in "a sense of social shame." "David's reluctance to publish his autobiography comes from his knowledge that to do so is to make his secret public" (66). "[H]is secret" is nothing less than his identity—to publish would be to admit that David has made his own name, an admission which conflicts with the apparent givenness of gentility itself. But perhaps a more relevant question than, Why didn't David publish his Autobiography?, is the question, Why did he write it in the first place?

First of all, because fiction conceals.

> I have made [the autobiography], thus far, with no purpose of suppressing any of my thoughts; for, as I have elsewhere said, this narrative is my written memory. I have desired to keep the most secret current of my mind apart, and to the last.
>
> (58.889)

The narrative voice here assumes that fiction is unable to accomplish this. Fiction always conceals, possibly because of its wide availability. In fact, one might say that fiction conceals because it is so revealed. In any case, though it will perhaps be inevitable that fiction take itself from the life—it might be impossible for Mr. Dick ever to keep the severed head of King Charles from rolling into his memorial—autobiography has the advantage of attempting to represent truth without regard to an audience other than the self. Fiction scatters the self; autobiography gathers.

On the other hand, if the social subtext of *David Copperfield* includes ambivalence over the motives for public writing, then perhaps the writing takes autobiographical form not only to gather the self but to keep it from participating in an economic system in which writing—and by implication self-healing and indeed self-creation—are commodities, bought and sold like any other for public consumption. Uriah Heep, David's shadowy double, to some extent embodies all of David's baser ambitions. He realizes David's love for Agnes even before David does, and he recognizes the parallel in their public situations almost immediately. In the explosion chapter we are made aware both of the parallels between the two and of David's position of power relative to Uriah. Uriah is aware of it, too, and speaks of his desire that David's tongue be cut out. But David hasn't spoken a word. He doesn't have to; Micawber and Traddles vocalize him. His power is manifest not in his speech but in his silence, in others' doing his dirty work. All through the chapter we are aware of Uriah Heep's body (as throughout the novel we are made aware of it by its twisting and writhing) and of David's power—his social voice made louder in its silence—through his mouthpieces, Traddles and Micawber. The entire chapter repudiates David's dark, money-grubbing side.

But David has gained a voice in society through his social rise, which itself results from his writing but does not equal it. In fact, David has gained his position, his voice, through an ambitious personality similar to Uriah's. The distance between Uriah Heep and David Copperfield might then be summed up, in a (perhaps too) neat division of labor, in the difference between body and voice. Copperfield's public, fictional voice, then, is not innocent, pure, or stable, but is implicated in the capitalist system by which it is established as a public commodity, being made by its relation to the audience even as it makes fictions out of life.

Early in *David Copperfield* we see the private, innocent Mr. Dick, flying kites made out of bits of his Memorial; late in the book we find a more peaceful but less conscious Mr. Dick.

> My aunt informed me how he incessantly occupied himself in copying everything he could lay his hands on, and kept King Charles the first at a respectful distance by that semblance of employment; how it was one of the main joys and rewards of her life that he was free and happy; and now (as a novel general conclusion) nobody but she could ever fully know what he was.

(60.909)

Is it too much to see a pun in "novel general conclusion," and to read in this passage a dispersal and loss of the auctorial self in the conclusion, generally speaking, of novels? Is it too much to see the novelist's selling of the self foreshadowed in the earlier disposal of the caul (1.50)?

If not, then *David Copperfield* the autobiographical *bildungsroman* attempts to bridge the gap between public and private worlds, between happiness and utility, be-

tween this new, public Mr. Dick, slavishly copying words, and the sadder (but more self-conscious) Mr. Dick of the earlier novel, flying lonely kites constructed of bits of his Memorial. In Mr. Dick's case we see happiness and utility combine, but the result, it seems, is a loss of consciousness. The disappointing end of *David Copperfield* as autobiography, as well, seems to admit a similar loss of awareness; the author who desires "to linger yet" on his life (64.950) at the end seems a far cry from the tortured and lonely autobiographer whose "most unwilling hand" (31.509) attempts, for a while at least, to expose the depths of the self. David's social rise through writing, then, subverts this quest; the autobiography of David Copperfield ends with the very burial or suppression of the conscious self that had been feared. On the other hand, the *novel David Copperfield* seems a highly self-aware literary hall of mirrors, with on the one side happiness and on the other side utility, confession and fiction in infinite regress. By keeping these elements in perpetual play, it tastes of both worlds.

Notes

1. Recently an entire book, Alexander Welsh's *From Copyright to Copperfield: The Identity of Dickens,* was written "as an assault on Warren's Blacking Warehouse . . . expressly denying that a trauma in childhood provides the best ground for biographical criticism" (vii). Welsh's book is a curious mix of social and biographical reading, arguing that Dickens' first visit to America was far more important for his development as a writer than anything in his childhood. But though society constantly impinges on Welsh's book, Welsh offers nothing like a political reading, remaining solidly biographical in emphasis.

2. John O. Jordan, for example, acknowledges his debt to Fredric Jameson's *The Political Unconscious* (Ithaca, N.Y.: Cornell UP, 1981) for its (political) view of textual repression (Jordan 90).

3. All references to *David Copperfield* are by chapter and page number and cite the edition edited by Trevor Blount (London: Penguin, 1966).

4. As usual with binary oppositions, these distinctions are less clear-cut than they seem and might well be challenged. We are hardly able, at this late date, to posit a "personal" identity which is not already "social" or public. I have no intention of recovering an uncontaminated privacy which never existed; but, however unsatisfactory and imprecise in the final analysis, public/private distinctions of many varieties weightly obtain in Victorian society and are thus worth keeping in *Copperfield,* if only as well-defined *strategies* to help us locate inevitable sites of struggle in the text.

Works Consulted

Dickens, Charles. *David Copperfield.* Ed. Trevor Blount. London: Penguin, 1966.

Frank, Lawrence. *Charles Dickens and the Romantic Self.* Lincoln: U of Nebraska P, 1984.

Hirsh, Gordon D. "A Psychoanalytic Reading of *David Copperfield.*" *Charles Dickens: New Perspectives.* Ed. Wendell Stacy Johnson. Englewood Cliffs, NJ: Prentice-Hall, 1982. 83-93.

Jordan, John O. "The Social Sub-Text of *David Copperfield.*" *Dickens Studies Annual* 14 (1985): 61-92.

Marcus, Stephen. "Who is Fagin?" *Dickens: From Pickwick to Dombey.* London: Chatto and Windus, 1965. 369-78.

Moretti, Franco. *The Way of the World: The* Bildungsroman *in European Culture.* London: Verso, 1987.

Musselwhite, David E. "Dickens: The Commodification of the Novelist." *Partings Welded Together: Politics and Desire in the Nineteenth-Century English Novel.* London: Methuen, 1987. 143-226.

Thompson, F. M. L. *The Rise of Respectable Society: A Social History of Victorian Britain, 1830-1900.* Cambridge: Harvard UP, 1988.

Tracy, Robert. "Stranger than Truth: Fictional Autobiography and Autobiographical Fiction." *Dickens Studies Annual* 15 (1986): 275-89.

Vanden Bossche, Chris R. "Cookery, not Rookery: Family and Class in *David Copperfield.*" *Dickens Studies Annual* 15 (1986): 87-109.

Welsh, Alexander. *From Copyright to Copperfield: The Identity of Dickens.* Cambridge: Cambridge UP, 1987.

Wilson, Edmund. *The Wound and the Bow.* New York: Oxford UP, 1959.

Irène Simon (essay date February 1992)

SOURCE: Simon, Irène. "*David Copperfield*: A Künstlerroman." *Review of English Studies* 43, no. 169 (February 1992): 40-56.

[*In the following essay, Simon approaches* David Copperfield *as a fictional representation of David's artistic development.*]

David Copperfield was, of all his books, Dickens's favourite child,[1] and readers have long felt that this is the novel in which he puts most of himself. As a *Bildungsroman* it traces the development of David from the innocence of childhood, through his confrontation with the world and his initiation into evil, to maturity and self-realization in a world very different from the Eden of childhood. Since David not only tells his own story but ends up as a novelist, he invites comparison with the author, so that *The Personal History and Experience of David Copperfield the Younger*—to quote the title Dickens used in the monthly numbers—may be expected to relate in some way the growth of a novelist's mind.[2] The relation between author and hero has often been pointed out, mainly to show the extent of the autobiographical material in the novel, notably by Sylvère Monod in his *Dickens the Novelist* (1968). Yet while critics have found this novel 'the clearest account we have anywhere of the secret springs of Dickens's imagination',[3] few seem to regard it as a *Künstlerroman*. The reason for this is not far to seek, for David tells us little about his own fiction or about his conception of art. Besides, the novel is as different as can be from the art novels we know best, such as *A Portrait of the Artist as a Young Man,* and the hero quite unlike the 'priest of the eternal imagination, transmuting the daily bread of experience into the radiant body of everlasting life' that Stephen Dedalus claims to be. It is therefore not surprising that, while one critic says that 'the David who writes *David Copperfield* seems to represent Dickens' ambition as a novelist, as an artist',[4] another remarks: 'David is presented to us as an author. But I cannot imagine *Edwin Drood,* or, indeed, *David Copperfield* among his works.'[5] Most readers would probably agree with Barbara Hardy that David is indeed 'one of the strangest portraits of an artist ever written'.[6] Yet it seems to me that the lack of *explicit* reference to David's artistic temperament and ideals is as significant of the Victorian novelist as Joyce's emphasis on Stephen's priest-like calling is of the *fin de siècle* novelist.

In writing this novel Dickens was no doubt seeking to come to terms with his own experience and, through conscious and unconscious projection of his own self, to discover a pattern in his own development and to define his identity. By the late 1840s he had established an intimate relationship with his readers that would guarantee their interest in his past, and the public could not fail to recognize in David's story some aspects of the author's life. In some respects *David Copperfield* is a success story and, if not quite a rags-to-riches novel, cannot but remind us, in spite of the differences, of the lives Samuel Smiles was to relate in *Self-Help* (1859). The confidence and security Dickens had achieved through success certainly enabled him to look back upon the traumatic experience of his childhood which was to remain a secret even to his closest friends: his working at the blacking factory and his father's imprisonment in the Marshalsea. Having entrusted his secret to Forster in the autobiographical fragment that was to be made public only after his death, Dickens was able to transmute this into the episode of David's life when the boy was 'a little labouring hind in the service of

Murdstone and Grinby' (Ch. 11, p. 208). Whereas to modern readers familiar with Forster's *Life of Dickens* this section of the novel emphasizes its autobiographical nature, Dickens had sufficiently covered his tracks for his public *not* to recognize the author in this episode any more than in the fatherless child driven away from his mother and home by the sinister Murdstones. In fact, David is at once like his creator and a persona, and the novel itself, as Dickens wrote to Forster, 'a very complicated interweaving of truth and fiction'.[7] If David is a fictional character, there was no need for Dickens to make him a novelist, *unless* his life was to be, partly at least, of interest through his development as a novelist. If, on the other hand, David's writing was merely a factual item intended to confirm the autobiographical nature of the novel, then we may still wonder what the image of a novelist that emerges from ***David Copperfield*** reveals about Dickens's conception of his craft.

We may begin with what Barbara Hardy found most baffling, 'David's chief professional characteristic as an artist', that is, hard work. We may find, as she does, that the Victorian admiration for industry is here placed in a strange collocation (p. 124); but I doubt whether we shall agree that this betrays Victorian limitations which the author does not see. True, there seems to be little difference between David's industry in mastering the strange symbols of shorthand and his hard work as a writer; but more important, it seems to me, is the insistence that, as a writer, he takes his work seriously, is entirely committed to it, a professional, not an amateur, especially as Dickens was often to satirize the latest forms of Dandyism. Obviously, David does not believe that art is a lucky hit, and his many references to hard work may be viewed as a restatement of the need for the artist to train himself for his task rather than rely on his natural gifts alone. The usual combination of genius with art has no doubt undergone a sea change and may therefore suggest Trollope's businesslike manner of setting to work; but the emphasis on David's seriousness as a writer certainly contributes to raise the prestige of the novel as a genre: this may have been all important in an age that was still reluctant to regard fiction as a serious species of literary composition.[8] We need only compare David's earnestness as a novelist with the offhand manner of the 'fashionable novelists' whom Hazlitt had attacked in his essay on 'The Dandy School' to grasp why this aspect of him figures so large in the novel.

What may put off the modern reader is the language in which this is expressed. From the following sentence, for instance, the reader is apt to remember only the success due to industry and to ignore the writer's absorption in the world he creates:

> . . . one evening, as I was returning *from a solitary walk, thinking of the book I was then writing*—for my

success had steadily increased with my steady application, and I was engaged at that time upon my first work of fiction—I came past Mrs Steerforth's house . . .

(Ch. 46, p. 733)

The parallelism between the steady application and the steadily increasing success too clearly echoes the gospel of *Self-Help* for a hasty reader to pay attention to the solitary walk. In the extended passage in which David dilates on the source of his success (Ch. 42) he had also stressed his habits of punctuality, order, and diligence when learning shorthand, so that the reader may be inclined to interpret the later passage quoted above as merely another glorification of hard work crowned by success. However, David had added in Ch. 42: 'many men have worked much harder, and not succeeded half so well' (p. 671); from this could be gathered that industry is not as such a sure guarantee of success. David is certainly not indifferent to the money his work brings him, since in the next chapter he tells us: 'Altogether I am well off; when I tell my income on the fingers of my left hand, I pass the third finger and take in the fourth to the middle joint' (Ch. 43, p. 693). Yet at the beginning of the same paragraph he says that he has 'taken with fear and trembling to authorship' (p. 692), not because he is afraid of financial failure since he has not burnt his boats yet, but because, as he explains:

> Having some foundation for believing by this time, that *nature and accident* had made me an author, I pursued my vocation with confidence. *Without such assurance* I should certainly have left it alone, and bestowed my energy on some other endeavour. I should have tried to find out what *nature and accident* really had made me, and to be that, and nothing else.

(Ch. 48, p. 758)

He may have started writing by accident, to eke out his income, when he first sent 'trifling pieces' to magazines (Ch. 43, p. 692), but he was prompted in that direction by his nature. Nor are we surprised when he turns to fiction since, when working at the warehouse, he often lounged about London Bridge and was there joined by 'the Orfling', i.e. the Micawbers' maid, who liked 'to be told some astonishing fictions respecting the wharves and the Tower; of which I can say no more than that *I hope I believed them myself*' (Ch. 11, p. 223). As David implies at the end of this quotation, these stories may have been of the same kind as W. H. Ainsworth's *Jack Sheppard* (1839), *The Tower of London* (1840), and *Old St Paul's* (1841), or rather as versions of these plagiarized and adapted to suit the taste of the new working-class public by Edward Lloyd, such as 'A *Legend of the Tower of London* by "W. H. Hainsforth"'.[9] At that time David also made stories for himself 'out of the streets, and out of men and women'; and, the narrator adds, 'some main points in the character I shall *unconsciously develop,* I suppose, in writing my life, *were gradually forming* all the while' (p. 224). About this habit of David's as a child, the narrator concludes:

> When my thoughts go back now, to that slow agony of my youth, I wonder how much of the *histories I invented for such people* hangs like a mist of fancy over well-remembered facts. When I tread the old ground, I do not wonder that I seem to see and pity, going on before me, *an innocent romantic boy, making his imaginative* [? imaginary, imagined] *world* out of such *strange experiences* and *sordid things*.
>
> (p. 225)

David does not regard himself as a Prometheus under Jove, nor invoke the artificer Dedalus as his father. What the narrator shows is that, as a boy, he was endowed with keen perceptions and imagination, that he had a gift for story-telling and could create an imaginary world out of the scenes he saw. All the same, he needed to develop his talents. This puts a different construction upon 'success', for what David needs above all is reassurance through confirmation of his ability to write, and he can only gauge this from his readers' response. At the same time he seems to be warning us not to expect him to let us into his secret, since he tells us that 'his fictions express themselves' (Ch. 48, p. 758). When he is engaged upon his first work of fiction he—or rather the narrator—will tell us what qualities go to the making of such a work. In order for us to see what, given his natural talents, David needed to learn before he could become a full-fledged novelist, we must turn to the narrative itself, since there we shall see what further qualities his older self as narrator has developed.

The presence in the story of a narrator who lets the film of his life linger before his eyes, reliving his past with the vividness of present experience and at the same time musing over it in order to extract significance from the events of his own life and from his experience of the world—this presence is intimated to us in the arresting second sentence of the opening paragraph: 'To begin my life with the beginning of my life, I record that I was born (as I have been informed and believe) on a Friday, at twelve o'clock at night.' This draws attention to the narrator's part in shaping his story—'my life' as novel as against the beginning of his actual life. The next sentence—'It was remarked that the clock began to strike, and I began to cry, simultaneously'—reminds us, though Dickens may not have intended it, of another narrator whose 'geniture' was interrupted by a reference to the clock and who was to battle with the problem of organizing the narrative of his *Life and Opinions*.[10] To those readers who make such an association, the contrast between the two writers emphasizes this narrator's careful selection and ordering of his materials.

When David ponders over his life at the warehouse, he recalls the secret agony of his soul at the time (Ch. 11, p. 210) and reflects that he might easily have become a little robber or a little vagabond. This intense misery had a lasting influence on him and made him pray at the time that he 'never might forget the houseless' (Ch. 13, p. 255). From this we may infer that one of David's characteristics as man and as writer is his fellow-feeling with those whose lives have been cramped by such soulless institutions as Murdstone and Grinby's. He has escaped this brutalizing world, but that period of his life is sealed off, though not forgotten (Ch. 14, p. 272). David can lift the curtain for a moment, though with a reluctant hand, on the harrowing experience which filled him with shame. On the contrary, his strange guardian at Aunt Betsey's, Mr Dick, is unable to recall his past, however hard he tries to work at his Memorial. At one point Aunt Betsey tells David that Mr Dick is 'memorializing the Lord Chancellor, or Lord Somebody or other' (Ch. 14, p. 261): this suggests that Mr Dick may be compared with David the narrator, who repeatedly calls his narrative 'his written memory' and is writing what may be called a remonstrance to the extent that he makes us aware of what is evil in the world around him. While Mr Dick's memory is blocked because his mind has given way under suffering, David did not submit for long to the dreadful life of the warehouse, but escaped through '[his] own act' (Ch. 12, p. 228) and can now integrate this experience into his life. Compared with David, Mr Dick figures the passive versus the active response to traumatic experience: his reaction is a regression into childhood, a temptation against which David is not always proof, but which as a narrator he resists successfully. As Aunt Betsey tells him: 'It's in vain, Trot, to recall the past, unless it works some influence upon the present' (Ch. 23, p. 407). This is further brought home to David when Mr Wickfield realizes how wrong he has been to indulge in fond memories (Ch. 39, p. 642).

Indulgence is the danger that threatens David when recalling his past, for the film of his life sometimes glides before his eyes as in a dream, and he must be warned against giving himself up to dreams. As a result, the need for discipline becomes a central theme, with the many changes that are rung upon it all through the novel, from the repressive firmness of the Murdstones to the self-imposed discipline of David, as well as from the irresponsibility of Mr Micawber to the early and long suppression of self at the foundation school where Uriah Heep was brought up 'to be umble' (Ch. 39, p. 639), which, as David finally understands, has made Uriah the more eager 'to recompense himself by using his power' (ibid.).

Although David the narrator muses with evident nostalgia on scenes from his early life, he is saved from indulgence by his gift for aesthetic distance, which marks him as an artist, that is, by his ability to re-create his younger self with his feelings and responses, and at the same time to judge him. In the chapters of Retrospect the narrator pauses or stands aside—deliberately, as he tells us—in order 'to see the phantoms of those days go by [him] accompanying the shadow of [himself], in dim procession' (Ch. 43, p. 691). The vividness of his recollections is an index to the truth of his narrative[11] and to the richness of his imagination, while the distance from his subject is achieved through control of his materials.

Most of his evocations from the past are indeed characterized by these two main qualities: vividness of feeling and of imagination on the one hand, and capacity to distance himself from his subject on the other. Aesthetic distance is largely a matter of control of tone and viewpoint, that is, a matter of discipline. By the time David starts writing his life, he has realized that the source of his youthful errors is his 'undisciplined heart' so that his 'written memory' has been shaped by this view of himself, a view which David the hero does not form until the last part of the novel, when Annie Strong confesses her error in yielding to 'the first impulse of an undisciplined heart' (Ch. 45, p. 730), and he realizes that his life with Dora has been an escape from reality into a mere dream-world.

This marks an important stage in the hero's growth to maturity; it may also be read as a metaphor for the narrator's stance towards his materials, achieved only after he had learnt to discipline his heart. What he must have learnt is the control he must exercise over his gifts if he is to develop as a novelist. With the possible exception of the treatment of the young man's relation with Agnes, the narrator's stance to his younger self is one of sympathy and detachment. In his evocations of the past we are often reminded of the presence of the older David, not only in the chapters of retrospect, but in the scenes he recalls or relives, through some stylistic device—mostly a shift from the past to the present tense—or through his comments. Some of these only serve to substantiate some facts, while others suggest interpretations that only the older David could have thought of.[12]

Sometimes the distance in time—hence the narrator's knowledge of events which at the moment he evokes were still in the womb of time—allows him to bring out or imply the significance of some gesture, words, or scene which will be confirmed later, but which the boy or young man could not have grasped at the time. Such is the prolepsis in Chapter 3, when the child David and Little Em'ly are walking along the sea: she tells him that she is afraid of the sea because it is cruel, yet she walks so close to the jetty's edge that the boy is afraid she may fall over (pp. 84, 86); she also tells him that she would like to be a lady because she and her family 'would all be gentlefolks together' (p. 85) and not mind the stormy weather for their own sakes. David the narrator remembers this scene so vividly, he says, that, 'if I were a draughtsman I could draw its form here, I dare

say, accurately, as it was that day, and little Em'ly *springing forward* to her destruction (as it appeared to me), with a look that I have never forgotten, directed far out to sea' (p. 86). This scene and the narrator's comment have often been quoted as evidence of Dickens's careful construction of his novel. Sylvère Monod, for instance, remarks that 'Every significant event in **Copperfield** is foreshadowed by a multiplicity of warnings and signs, which make it cast its shadow backward as well as forward', and among his examples he quotes the narrator's reflection on this scene:

> There has been a time since—I do not say it lasted long, but it has been—when I have asked myself the question, would it have been better for little Em'ly to have had the waters close above her head that morning in my sight; and when I have answered Yes, it would have been.
>
> This may be premature. I have set it down too soon, perhaps. But let it stand.
>
> (pp. 86-7)[13]

Monod's concern in this part of his study is Dickens's art as a novelist; my present purpose, on the other hand, is to answer the question: Did Dickens endow David with qualities that might account for his development into a novelist? From that point of view the important aspect of this scene is not the conscious comment by the narrator, but the *way he could draw it accurately*. While the boy David was frightened lest Little Em'ly should *fall* over, the narrator would draw her as *springing forward*. In his memory the little girl's wish to be a lady has thus blended with her sense of the sea's cruelty, hereby shedding on the innocent scene between the two children the tragic burden of the young girl's later infatuation with Steerforth, who will lure her away from her family. At the same time the picture the narrator could draw reveals his perception of why she was so easily attracted to Steerforth. This is not simply an anticipation or an association of ideas, but an instance of the esemplastic power which Coleridge attributed to the creative imagination. We hereby grasp that, besides the freshness and innocence common to children, as well as strong feelings, a keen perception of everything around him, and a vivid imagination—as has often been noted—David was also endowed with the kind of memory or imagination that is a requisite for the artist, and therefore that he might one day develop into a novelist since his *creative* power appears in the writing of his 'memory'.

In some other episodes we see that the hero and the narrator blend into one as the emotions recollected in tranquillity take on the vividness of present experience. In Chapter 5, for instance, David recalls listening to Mr Mell playing the flute to his mother and relives the experience to the point of falling asleep:

> I don't know what the tunes were—if there were such things in the performance at all, which I doubt—but the influence of the strain upon me was, first, to make

me think of all my sorrows until I could hardly keep my tears back; then to take away my appetite; and lastly, to make me so sleepy that I could not keep my eyes open. *They begin to close again, and I begin to nod, as the recollection rises fresh upon me.*

(p. 128)

David's response to the music and his reliving of the experience are altogether different from the creative act of the memory or imagination implied in the passage discussed before. It is closer to Wordsworth's conception of the poetic process originating in feelings and emotions which revive away from their source with the same intensity—as in 'I Wandered Lonely as a Cloud'—or are enriched by the meditation that followed and are thereby reproduced in the mind. The important point here is that both these passages of *David Copperfield* exemplify the creative power at work in the mind remembering the past. It is worth noting, too, that for Wordsworth as for David, the poet is not a different species of man, but has 'a more comprehensive soul', a finer sensitivity and deeper sympathy.

A more complex aspect of the narrator's stance is his capacity to be now in, now out of the child's or the young man's mind,[14] and at times to be *both* in and out of it. For instance, when, in Chapter 7, he recalls Mr Creakle's visit to the schoolroom on David's first schoolday at Salem House, he remembers the headmaster 'looking round upon [the pupils] like a giant in a story-book surveying his captives', while 'the boys were all struck speechless and motionless' (p. 140). He next remembers Mr Creakle coming to his own desk and warning him that if [David] were famous for his biting—a reminder of the placard that was hung on the child's back on his arrival—'he [Mr Creakle] was famous for biting too'. The boy's fear is conveyed powerfully, though implicitly, through his intent watching of the man's sadistic behaviour, first showing the boy the cane, then giving him 'a fleshy cut with it that made [him] writhe'. The narrator then 'steps out' of the past to remark: 'I am sure when I think of the fellow now, my blood rises against him with the disinterested indignation I should feel if I could have known all about him without having ever been in his power; but it rises hotly, because I know him to have been an incapable brute' (p. 141). Yet he also thinks that the children's attitude was 'mean and servile', without yet directly blaming them, implying rather that they were made so by such masters: 'Miserable little propitiators of a remorseless Idol, *how abject we were to him!* What a launch in life I think it now, on looking back, to be *so mean and servile* to a man of such parts and pretensions!' (p. 142). Shifting to the present tense, the narrator *is* next sitting at David's desk and wondering which of the schoolboys Mr Creakle will torture next, once more following the master's movements, watching his eye as it surveys the boys and 'morbidly attracted to it, in a dread desire to

know what he will do next' (p. 142). It is no wonder that the pupils should all 'droop over [their] books and tremble', nor that, when the master swoops down on his victim and 'cuts a joke before he beats him', David, like his schoolfellows, should laugh, while the narrator passes judgement on their behaviour and on his own as a child: '. . . and we laugh at it [the joke],—*miserable little dogs, we laugh, with our visages as white as ashes, and our hearts sinking in our boots*' (p. 142). The use of the present tense throughout this paragraph not only renders the fear and nervous tension among the pupils as well as the inevitable explosion of laughter as a release from it all, but suggests that the narrator's present comment may well have been the child's at the time also, as the 'white visages' suggest.

The same skill in the narrator's handling of the point of view is revealed in another scene at Salem House in the same chapter, the baiting of Mr Mell. When Steerforth insults their schoolmaster in the meanest manner and insolently stands his ground as master and pupil confront Mr Creakle, what David feels is 'what a noble fellow Steerforth is in appearance, and how homely and plain Mr. Mell looks opposed to him'; he even feels 'quite a glow' at what he terms Steerforth's 'gallant speech' (p. 151). Not until he realizes his own guilt in providing the youth with matter for insulting Mr Mell—having told him that the schoolmaster's mother lives in an almshouse—and Traddles points out that Steerforth has lost Mr Mell his situation, does David reproach himself and feel 'quite wretched' at having betrayed the only master that ever was kind to him (p. 152).

The scene certainly shows that as a boy David needed to discipline his impulses, though the narrator does not, on this occasion, express his view of him explicitly. The dramatic presentation of the whole episode indeed reveals to us the narrator's sure control of tone and point of view so that he manages to convey the boy's lack of loyalty to a man to whom he owes so much, without even trying to excuse it, yet also without letting us forget how strong is the attraction that such a glamorous rebel as Steerforth exerts on the weaker and defenceless David, a child compared with the young man of the world who from the first has impressed him so deeply. This episode foreshadows the part David will unwittingly play in the 'fall' of Little Em'ly by introducing Steerforth to the young girl and her family. It also shows how susceptible David is to glamour—in this case to the aristocratic arrogance of Steerforth—and how easily he will fall a prey to adventitious charms. Through this scene, and without any comment from the older David, we get a glimpse of the boy's uncertain loyalties; at the same time we grasp how much David must have developed before he was able to narrate this episode and yet forbear to charge the boy with this weakness. On the other hand, when the narrator evokes the boy's years at school at Canterbury, he notes with an ironical yet tender smile his successive 'passions' for various young girls or ladies; for instance his 'adoration' for Miss Shepherd, for whom he prays during the service, mentally inserting her name, putting 'her in among the Royal Family' (Ch. 18, p. 323); or later, his 'passion' for Miss Larkins, whom he *worships,* a passion which 'takes away [his] appetite' and makes him wear 'his newest silk neckerchief continually' (p. 326).

The ability of the narrator to sympathize with the boy or young man he used to be, yet also to look at him from outside, is best revealed in the evocation of David's friendship with Steerforth. From the time of their first meeting at Salem House we are granted a double vision of both. We are made to see not only the real qualities of Steerforth as well as his many defects—and also how far these were encouraged by his mother—but alongside David's genuine feelings for the older boy or young man, the less pleasant side of his infatuation, i.e. the satisfaction of his vanity at being made much of by the cock of the walk, as well as his hero-worship for the bigger boy who has taken him under his wing. What we also grasp from the scenes evoked is the discrepancy between the boy or young man David admires and the real Steerforth, whose gentlemanly sophistication David is too innocent to see through. Particularly striking in this respect is the scene in Chapter 22, when Miss Mowcher joins David and Steerforth at the inn in Yarmouth. David completely fails to see in what capacity she is associated with his friend, and her innuendoes escape him altogether. David is blind to the real nature of Steerforth and cannot understand why his friend is so often a prey to black moods, any more than he can grasp why, at the end of his visit to his friend in Chapter 29, Steerforth asks him to 'think of [him] at [his] best' (p. 497). David indeed cherishes Steerforth in his heart, and, before he leaves the house, sees him peacefully asleep, 'lying, easily, with his head upon his arm, as [he] had often seen him lie at school' (p. 498).

When David does discover his friend's unworthiness and his own guilt in the destruction of Mr Peggotty's home, he does not condemn Steerforth but thinks 'more about all that was brilliant in him, [and] soften[s] more towards all that was good in him' (Ch. 32, p. 516). These were his feelings at the time, though he knew 'that all was at an end between [them]' (p. 516); they are also the feelings of the older David, the narrator, who, looking back on this earlier day, comments: 'My sorrow may bear involuntary witness against you at the Judgment Throne; but my angry thoughts or reproaches never will, I know' (p. 517). At this point it is as though David the hero had caught up with David the narrator.

The last picture we are given of Steerforth, when his body is washed ashore and David is looking at him, is one that must have been formed in 'calm of mind, all passion spent'; one that, while combining the charm and the unworthiness of the young man, transcends all moral judgement and fixes him for ever in the silence of art: a picture of the young man in repose in the foreground, and in the background, the ruins of Mr Peggotty's home. The contrasting images of Steerforth are now reconciled in David's vision, as if he and the narrator were looking through one pair of eyes. David the hero is now able to see Steerforth *sub specie aeternitatis,* that is, with aesthetic distance. This scene alone confirms him as an accomplished artist: he is now able to *see* with the same sympathy and detachment as the narrator:

> But, [the fisherman] led me to the shore. And on that part of it where [Emily] and I had looked for shells, two children—on that part of it where some lighter fragments of the old boat, blown down last night, had been scattered by the wind—among the ruins of the home he had wronged—I saw him lying with his head upon his arm, as I had often seen him lie at school.
>
> (Ch. 55, p. 866)

From Chapter 55 on we may expect David to become a successful novelist.

The image of David's child-wife which in Chapter 53—another Retrospect—rises before his memory will be blotted out at the end of the chapter, when 'darkness comes before [his] eyes' (p. 834). But, through the evocation in the present tense of both the figure in his memory and of the three times that 'come freshest on [his] mind' (p. 834), the image of Dora seems to be at once fixed in the narrator's mind and evanescent in the hero's. Two kinds of memory seem to be at work here: 'the figure . . . quiet and still . . . in its innocent love and childish beauty', being, like that of Steerforth, formed 'in calm of mind, all passion spent', while the other revives his suffering at the impending death of Dora. This mixture of permanence and fluidity is characteristic of the narrator's search for pattern or identity through remembrance of things past,[15] as well as of the narrative procedure all through *David Copperfield*: the film of his past life interrupted by shorter or longer pauses as the narrator moves from the past—relating what he remembers or sees—to the present—reliving the past or thinking about it. In Chapter 18—A Retrospect—for instance, he evokes the 'silent *gliding* of [his] existence—the unseen, unfelt progress of [his] life—from childhood up to youth' and looks 'back upon the *flowing water*', trying to remember how that period of his life ran (p. 322). At times, however, David the hero, too, has a sense of permanence beyond the flux of time, as, for instance, when he returns to Canterbury and in the early morning saunters through the town, noting: 'The rooks were sailing about the cathedral towers; and the towers themselves, overlooking many a long unaltered mile of rich country and its pleasant streams, were cutting the bright morning air, *as if there were no such thing as change on earth*' (Ch. 52, p. 810). It is almost as if, at this late stage, David were developing the double vision that characterizes David the narrator, as if he were indeed growing into a novelist.

Dora's death stuns David, and a long and gloomy night gathers on him as he is left alone. From this listlessness and brooding sorrow he will be aroused, he says, by the example and advice of Agnes, and he will at last recognize that he has 'thrown away the treasure of her love' (Ch. 58, p. 890). From now on the narrator's stress on David's undisciplined heart (Ch. 58, pp. 885, 886), errant heart (p. 890), wayward boyhood (ibid.), etc. shows only too clearly the direction David's life will ultimately take. Whatever the lapses in the presentation of his relationship with Agnes—Agnes as the figure in the stained-glass window in the church, or as the figure pointing upward, is hard to take—one thing is clear: David is freed from his youthful fancies, he has become emotionally mature and can now see the truth about himself. He has left behind his infatuation for Steerforth and for Dora, but, and this is an important qualification, he remembers both with love, as he did his mother for all her frailties.

Those readers who find David's 'good angel' not entirely palatable will probably set greater emphasis in his final growth to maturity as a novelist on his three years' absence, particularly on his sojourn in the Swiss valley, where one evening, he says,

> some long-unwonted sense of beauty and tranquillity, some softening influence awakened by its peace, moved faintly in my breast. I remember pausing once, with a kind of sorrow that was not at all oppressive, not quite despairing. I remember almost hoping that some better change was possible within me.
>
> (Ch. 58, p. 887)

In Wordsworthian fashion David has found the true source of restoration: 'Nature, never sought in vain' and the human interest he had 'lately shrunk from' (p. 889). This is the less surprising if we remember the child David's natural pieties, best revealed perhaps on his visit to his old home, to the churchyard and to Peggotty when he returned to Yarmouth with Steerforth, whose presence there emphasizes by contrast David's sense of his links with the past and his natural affections. No wonder the last two numbers, Chapters 58 to 64, show that as a novelist, too, he has come into his own. He will now be able to transmute his experience into art, for the discipline he has taught his heart and the new insight he has gained without losing his sympathy for his younger self, go to the shaping of his story.

Writing a story born of his own experience clearly contributes to restore him fully, for after the favourable reception of his novel in London, he starts writing with renewed vigour and, before his third novel is finished, he feels able to return home. The little he tells us now about his work suggests more than the diligence and punctuality of his early efforts. Now, he says, 'I fell to work, in my old *ardent* way, on a new *fancy, which took strong possession* of me. As I advanced in the execution of my task, I *felt it more and more,* and *roused my utmost energies* to do it well' (Ch. 58, p. 889). The discipline has abated none of his energy, and he is now *possessed* by his fancy. This is a long way from the mere virtues of the businessman which his earlier comments might have suggested. Both as man and as writer he is now fully mature. Yet instead of dilating on his specific power as a novelist, he once more stresses his common humanity: he has made friends in the valley, and when he returns to it in the spring 'their cordial greetings [have] a homely sound to [him]' (p. 889). For all his newly acquired wisdom he has lost none of his sensitivity and human interest. The child who, after finding a home at his Aunt Betsey's, prayed 'that [he] never might be homeless any more, and never might forget the houseless' (Ch. 13, p. 255), may well have erred through the mistaken impulses of his heart; but by now he has learnt to face painful facts, as he learnt to bear life at Murdstone and Grinby's, and he is able to tell the truth *as he now sees it.*

The ability of the narrator to empathize, which we have noted all through the novel, is a guarantee that the discipline of the heart has not dried up his feelings, nor stifled his imaginative powers. The child lives on in the narrator, and his sensitive heart, beating with fear or with indignation, or moved to sympathy with all manner of men, is the source of the novel's life, as is the vivid imagination which was nourished in his childhood by the books he was reading. We remember that the heroes of these books were as real to him as the people around him, and that he related several of these stories to Steerforth at night when they were both schoolboys at Salem House. The narrator himself had remarked at that stage that 'Whatever [David] had within [him] that was romantic and dreamy, was encouraged by so much story-telling in the dark' (Ch. 7, p. 146). If imagination and feeling are a prime requisite of the artistic temper, the boy David *was* a potential artist. The parts of the novel that live on most vividly in every reader's memory are indeed those in which David is still a wayward boy and makes mistakes, and his romantic and dreamy nature is confirmed by his tendency as a boy and as a young man to escape into a dreamworld.

This is shown to be both an asset and a liability. As a response to the Murdstones' firmness, it is a child's natural reaction, and it also stirs his imagination;[16] as ignorance of evil, it is a retreat from life which might lead him astray. Together with other retreats from life in the novel—Mr Dick's regression into childhood and his flying a kite; Mr Peggotty's 'ark' perilously balanced on the edge of the troubled sea; Miss Betsey's retreat to Dover—David's life with Dora appears as a deliberate escape from reality: they are both unaware of evil and, unwittingly, lead their servants into temptation. Their life together is only make-believe, a retreat into the innocence of childhood, which is clinched by Dora's wish to be called his 'child-wife' (Ch. 44, p. 711).

Miss Betsey will be compelled to leave her house at Dover; Mr Peggotty's boat will be destroyed by the tempest: David's fairy-world cannot endure either. He does give way to the temptation to escape pain and evil when, after Dora's death, he sinks into listlessness. It is Nature, as we saw, that recalls him to life and to action. When he resumes his writing he also returns to life, just as Mr Dick is free from Charles I's head when he is copying documents. The temptation for David to prolong a state of innocence beyond his wayward childhood has ultimately been overcome. As Aunt Betsey told him, brooding over the past will not do, unless good is to come of it. The narrator's musing over his past might easily have become a retreat into a world of innocence, and his evident nostalgia is a measure of the danger he has escaped.

Writing a novel therefore appears as a way of accepting reality and of seeking order in a disorderly world. The narrator's story is to a certain extent a 'Memorial' or remonstrance, but it is first and foremost an ordering of experience guided by his insight into the nature of his own self and of the world. The link between the necessary discipline and the shaping power of the imagination working on emotions recollected in tranquillity is suggested in a passage that immediately follows on David's brooding over Annie Strong's words. He is returning from a solitary walk, thinking of the book he is then writing, and comes past Mrs Steerforth's house. He has passed that way pretty often, yet never done more than glance at the house, but this time:

> As it was, I thought of it as little as I might. But my mind could not go by it and leave it, as my body did; and it usually awakened a long train of meditations. Coming before me, on this particular evening that I mention, *mingled with the childish recollections and later fancies,* the ghosts of half-formed hopes, the *broken shadows of disappointments dimly seen and understood, the blending of experience and imagination, incidental to the occupation with which my thoughts had been busy,* it was more than commonly suggestive.

> (Ch. 46, p. 734)[17]

By now, it seems, David has grasped the truth of Wordsworth's *Inner Vision.*[18]

The reason why he still does not speak of his artistic powers more explicitly is, I believe, because he has no wish to single himself out as a man different from his fellow-men. This is conveyed, in Dickens's economy of

the novel, through the parallel with Tommy Traddles, whose virtues David recognizes only towards the end, but who from the first has proved to have a generous heart and has known how to bear his lot in a world that exploits and bruises him. We remember Traddles at Salem House, as 'the merriest and most miserable of all schoolboys, [who] was always drawing skeletons over his slate' (Ch. 7, p. 143). Traddles's name is the very antonym of 'Steerforth', and his part at Salem House is to be the anti-hero; yet he is also the only one to rebuke David for his lack of loyalty to Mr Mell, the master whom Steerforth has ruined.

In spite of the 'de-emphasis on David's work as a novelist',[19] *David Copperfield* is a *Künstlerroman,* but one in which the artist is not viewed as an outsider or as alienated from his society, even though he is aware of its shady sides. He does not choose for his motto *Non serviam;* on the contrary, he means ever to remember the houseless. He will bite the hands of the Murdstones of this world rather than submit to their soul-killing philosophy, but he will be welcomed with cordial greetings by as many friends in the Swiss valley as in Yarmouth, because he has kept the child's innocent eye and can see both the beauty and the horror of the world around him; because, too, he has been wounded too early ever to forget man's inhumanity to man or to deny the holiness of the heart's affections. It is clear that Dickens is a greater artist than David could ever be, for David does not appear to have the demonic power that his creator manifests in his greatest works. If Dickens saw himself as another David, he must have underestimated his own powers; yet the image of the artist he projects in this novel is no less characteristic of the mid-Victorian novelist than Stephen Dedalus is of the *fin de siècle* artist. David as a man fully integrated in his society, yet critical of it, as well as the rebel Stephen, define the relation of the artist to the society in which he lives, but at two different points in history. Implicit all through *David Copperfield* is a conception of the poet as a man speaking to men, communicating to them the emotions or feelings he has experienced. Explicit in *A Portrait* is the conception of the artist as exile, severing himself from home and country 'to forge in the smithy of [his] soul the uncreated conscience of [his] race', and to become the poet who, ultimately, in his great comic epic in prose, will pit the archetypal artist Shem against the archetypal philistine Shaun in a battle that involves all place and all time, as well as all—or at least many of—the languages of the world. C. D., like the fictional D. C., delighted a wide public, one that included such as 'the Orfling' as well as Forster and Jeffrey, and often moved them to laughter or to tears. The son of Dedalus, on the other hand, has exercised the ingenuity of a host of critics, no less than their lungs as their Homeric laughter has resounded from one shore of the Atlantic to the other.

Notes

1. Preface to the Charles Dickens edition, 1869, quoted in *David Copperfield,* ed. Trevor Blount, The Penguin English Library (Harmondsworth, 1969; 1973), 47. All quotations are from this edition, with chapter and page numbers in parentheses. All italics in quotations are mine, unless otherwise stated. (Place of publication is London unless otherwise specified.)

2. John Butt and Kathleen Tillotson, however, remark that 'After promising so much in the title of *Dombey and Son,* Dickens would seem to be returning to the non-committal type of *The Life and Adventures of Nicholas Nickleby*' (*Dickens at Work* (1957), 114). Sylvère Monod, on the other hand, believes that 'Dickens might also have called the book 'The Growth of a Novelist's Mind' (*Dickens the Novelist* (Norman, Okla., 1968), 317).

3. J. Hillis Miller, *Charles Dickens: The World of his Novels* (Cambridge, Mass. and London, 1958), 151.

4. Bert G. Hornback, 'Frustration and Resolution in *David Copperfield*', *Studies in English Literature* (Autumn 1968), 663.

5. A. E. Dyson, *The Inimitable Dickens* (1970), 153.

6. Barbara Hardy, *The Moral Art of Charles Dickens* (1970), 124.

7. Letter to Forster, 10 July 1849, in John Forster, *Life of Charles Dickens* (1872-4), ii. 48.

8. Herbert Spencer believed that no novels save those of George Eliot were sufficiently serious to be in the London Library.

9. See Louis James, *Fiction for the Working Class* (1963), 90.

10. The temptation to pursue the comparison—by linking Sterne's method of progress through digression with Dickens's pauses in the evocation of the past—must be resisted if only because, among the 18th-century books that David reads with relish, *Tristram Shandy* is conspicuously absent.

11. Monod rightly stresses that the episodes invented by Dickens are as vivid and sound as true as those derived from his own life (*Dickens the Novelist,* 308).

12. In Ch. 2 (p. 70), David is speaking of his 'uneasy jealousy' of Mr Murdstone, and says: 'No such thing came into my mind or near it' (at the time).

13. Monod, *Dickens the Novelist,* 304. He notes that 'the passage did not result from some irresistible impulse of the author's, soon to be deplored. For the whole passage, remorse and all, was inserted by Dickens while correcting the first set of proofs' (p. 305).

14. As Orwell already noted; see his *Critical Essays* (1946), 17.

15. I am using the phrase on purpose since it was the title of the first translation of *À la Recherche du temps perdu.* A comparison of Dickens's use of memory with Proust's is worth pursuing.

16. On the effect of reading on Dickens's imagination, see Angus Wilson, *The World of Charles Dickens* (1970), ch. 1.

17. See the quotation from the same chapter given on p. 42, above.

18. *David Copperfield* appeared in monthly numbers from May 1849 to November 1850. Wordsworth's *The Prelude, or Growth of a Poet's Mind* was published in 1850.

19. Hornback, 'Frustration and Resolution', 665.

Joseph Bottum (essay date March 1995)

SOURCE: Bottum, Joseph. "The Gentleman's True Name: *David Copperfield* and the Philosophy of Naming." *Nineteenth-Century Literature* 49, no. 4 (March 1995): 435-55.

[*In the following essay, Bottum studies the process of renaming in* David Copperfield *as it reveals a hidden language of deceit, power, and desire lurking among the novel's interpersonal relationships.*]

Never was there such a book as **David Copperfield** (1849-50) for the giving of names, and the changing of names, and the just plain getting wrong of names. David himself is called by dozens of names in the course of the novel, but in this he is not alone.[1] Every character in **David Copperfield** has multiple names. Richard Babley is called Mr. Dick to his face, and Mrs. Markleham is called the Old Soldier behind her back. Steerforth is misremembered as Rudderford, and Ham Peggotty is mispronounced as Am, "a morsel of English Grammar."[2] Betsey Trotwood calls the murderous Murdstone "Murderer" and the jelly-lipped Chillip "Jellips," but Betsey herself has arbitrarily resumed her maiden name. Barkis hides his wealth under the name Blackboy, while Micawber hides his poverty under Mortimer. Uriah Heep ends as model prisoner Twenty-Seven, Peggotty marries to become C. P. Barkis, the serving girl Clickett dubs herself the Orfling, and even the long-mislaid schoolmaster, Mr. Mell, makes a curtain call as Doctor Mell.

Names fascinate the characters in every Dickens novel: Bumble explains over gin the alphabetical system with which he "inwented" Oliver Twist; Nicholas Nickleby refuses to believe a Bobster could be his love; in **Hard Times** Mr. Gradgrind declares "Sissy is not a name" immediately upon hearing it. But the fascination in **David Copperfield** goes far beyond that in the other novels. Betsey Trotwood blusters into Blunderstone Rookery in the opening pages and promptly scorns the name of the house, disparages the name of the servant, and proposes for the unborn child the most unlikely name of the three. In his dramatic confrontation with Uriah Heep, Micawber not only scores off Uriah's name but introduces Mr. Dick as Dixon—and foolish Mr. Dick stops to consider his new name. The narrating David turns aside repeatedly to speak of names: at his most facetious he weighs the names in Doctors' Commons; at his most pathetic he comments on the name above a shop on the Dover road.

In part this heightened fascination is possible because names in **David Copperfield** are unlike names in the earlier novels. Perhaps Dickens learned something from naming **Nicholas Nickleby**'s Verisopht, whom he began satirically but subsequently had to make sympathetic. Or perhaps the difference is forced upon him by first-person narration, for **Great Expectations** also seems mostly to have names unlike those in the early novels (though Esther's narrations in **Bleak House** do not). But in **David Copperfield** the names are not a joke from which the characters are excluded. Dickens has let his characters in on their naming, and a richness and subtlety of names results. The broad humor of a pettifogger named Fogg and a nag named Knag, of Jingle and Humm and Snobb and Curdle, of an undertaker named Mould and another named Sowerberry, is too cruel to impose on characters who are conscious of their own names, and Dickens mostly leaves it behind. There are exceptions, of course: Dickens could never resist a jab at a schoolmaster, and the names of Creakle, Sharp, Mell, and Tungay are throwbacks to the humor of "Wackford Squeers" and "Doctor Blimber." But in general, **David Copperfield** avoids the in-joke of unconscious names.

The unconscious names soon reappear, however: **Bleak House,** Dickens's next novel, is a festival of cruel but funny names. This reappearance, when taken with the multiple names for the characters in **David Copperfield** and their fascination with names, suggests Dickens has a program in mind for the naming in **David Copperfield.** The tension between meaning and reference—the tension of *that* word for *this* thing—is no longer just in the author's struggle against his own writing but rather is translated into the story. The characters themselves feel the tension of naming and explore with the author what their names are for.

They find first much what we would expect them to find. The order of names—the hierarchy of terms by which the characters refer to and address one another—betrays the power and desire that stand behind the screens of politeness and grammatical necessity. As he grows David must overcome every attempt to name him: Murdstone's disinheriting "David," Micawber's premature "Copperfield," Steerforth's diminishing "Daisy," Dora's cloying "Doady." Even Betsey Trotwood proposes to rename him upon his arrival in Dover (though Mr. Dick, as the baptismal father who washes, robes, and names the boy, interprets her proposal as a given name rather than a patronym). And just as David finds sanctuary in Canterbury from the destruction Murdstone intended for him in London, so he finds sanctuary in "Trotwood" from the hurt Murdstone had done to "David." But he must at last overcome even his new-christened name to reclaim his usurped patrimony.

Dickens and his characters find more, however, than that a name expresses and enforces the desire of the namer. Certainly, names have a way in **David Copperfield** of coming true: David's mother blunders and brings the murdering Murd*stone* to Blunder*stone;* David's father called his house the Rookery "when there's not a rook near it" (p. 5), but with the Murdstones dressed in black the rooks have come; the lamb Agnes Wick*field* at last marries Copper*field,* after being struggled over just as Bathsheba was by David and Uriah. This is the threat of "Towzer" and "Master Murdstone," the names David dodges: a boy called Towzer will become a dog and a boy called Murdstone will become a stone of *merde,* just as a young man called Daisy must be seduced and a grown man called Doady ("a corruption of David" [p. 514]) must behave like a child. Extrinsic denomination—to borrow from Scholasticism a phrase for naming by relation—has a way of becoming intrinsic denomination, of becoming true of the person apart from any relation to the namer.

The possibility of names coming true, however, requires that there be such a thing as truth, just as an observation of the failure of extrinsic names requires that there be an alternative of intrinsic names against which to measure that failure. An analogy might make this clearer. **David Copperfield** (Dickens's only book with a writer as its hero) contains a serious attack on writing. The novel mocks the extravagance of Julia's diary and Micawber's letters as well as Dr. Strong's impossible dictionary, Mr. Dick's interrupted memorial, Dora's indecipherable housekeeping book, Traddles's unwritten letters to his uncle, and Spenlow's feigned will. But Dickens is not indulging some complicated self-critique: by mocking bad writing he looks to defend the possibility of good writing. Similarly, by indicting the abuse of names Dickens looks to demonstrate not only the power of false names but the possibility of true names as well.

No one has ever accused Dickens of being a philosopher. But *David Copperfield* offers an opportunity for thinking philosophically about naming. Dickens shows how a name imposed in the economy of power and desire pushes a person into an expression of that name. But he also shows how the essence to which a true name refers pushes back on that economy with the moral force of truth.

* * *

Victorian English prizes variation and provides an enormous set of vocatives and nominatives for reference and address. Characters in *David Copperfield* are addressed by title ("Doctor"), surname ("Traddles"), title and surname ("Mr. Murdstone"), Christian name ("Dora"), title and Christian name ("Master David"), title and both names ("Mr. Wilkins Micawber"), title and husband's name ("Mrs. David Copperfield"), and Christian name and both surnames ("Clara Peggotty Barkis"); by polite sign ("Ma'am"), ignorance marker ("What's-your-name"), and grammatical person ("You"). They have nicknames formed as diminutives ("Ury"), shortenings ("Tom"), and corruptions ("Doady"), and nonce-names taken directly from substance ("Man") or drawn metonymically from an accidental category: relation ("Aunt"), action ("Driver"), passion ("Dear"), possession ("Red Whisker"), location ("Londoner"), quality ("Young Innocence"), etc. Any of these may be subject to further metonymy ("Yarmouth Bloater"), metaphor ("Mealy Potatoes"), allusion ("Croesus"), or comic reversal ("Six-foot" for a three-foot child). We come to expect this variety, for it saves us from the weariness of repetition and matches our experience—an experience formed by rhetorical variation. And when we meet repetition, as when Uriah Heep calls David "Master Copperfield" twenty-three times in forty-two sentences (pp. 200-202), we know *something* (whether comic or serious) has occurred.

And yet, though the variation is wide, it is not unlimited. No finite language expresses completely the infinite distinctions among beings, but each language expresses most completely those distinctions in which its speakers are most interested—or at least were once interested, since English preserves distinctions long after their social necessity is gone. Victorian modes of reference and address express distinctions of (and thus reveal interest in) gender, age, education, marriage, family relation, military rank, priesthood, ownership of land, occupation, formality of occasion, mood of the speaker, and many other things. But, most of all, names in Victorian English express fine degrees of social status and personal affection—of rank and sentiment.

A world of linguistic convention is revealed the moment David first speaks aloud:

> "Peggotty," says I, suddenly, "were you ever married?"

> "Lord, Master Davy," replied Peggotty. "What's put marriage in your head!"

> (p. 14)

The fact that a language has titles for distinguishing married from unmarried women betrays an interest its speakers take in the distinction. And yet, while David's mother keeps "Mrs." in her widowhood, Betsey Trotwood resumes "Miss" despite her marriage. And titles are often omitted, as Peggotty's is. More, the contrast of "Miss" and "Mrs." is corrupted by the vocatives "Miss" and "Ma'am." "Don't *Missis* me, ma'am," screeches the enraged Fanny Squeers when called "child" by her newly married contemporary 'Tilda in *Nicholas Nickleby.* Victorian English imperfectly distinguishes married from unmarried women, and David's confusion about Peggotty's marriage is possible in the language.

No confusion is possible, however, about rank and sentiment. Peggotty is well loved, but just as Polly Toodle is called "Richards" in *Dombey and Son* merely for her employer's convenience, and Harriet Beadle called "Tattycoram" in *Little Dorrit,* so Peggotty's name reveals her rank in *David Copperfield*:

> "Do you mean to say, child," [asked Betsey,] "that any human being has gone into a Christian church, and got herself named Peggotty?"

> "It's her surname," said my mother, faintly. "Mr. Copperfield called her by it, because her Christian name was the same as mine."

> (p. 6)

An untitled surname implies at least equality. So David uses surnames with his schoolmates, and Micawber (taking the boy as an equal and thus someone for whom he need not be responsible) quickly comes to call him "Copperfield." David's use of "Peggotty," however, reveals both that he feels close to her and that his rank outweighs a child's conventional inferiority to an adult. And Peggotty's "Master Davy," a diminutive with a title, reveals the same relation from the other side: a close affection and a social gap.

Dickens does more, however, than echo the existing order of names. He shows the way in which, precisely because they mark degrees of rank and sentiment, names are available for the assertion of power and desire. In the closed world of the Rookery no one uses the Christian name that the mistress and servant share. But by concealing from the reader a name the narrator could have revealed, Dickens creates a mystery that makes the revelation more dramatic. We do not hear the name until Murdstone uses it to admonish his new wife for showing affection to her son, and this admonishment frames David's memory of their marriage: the novel reveals "Clara" in the first sentence the boy hears upon seeing his newly married mother, and "Clara" is the last word he hears as he leaves her forever. Murdstone's use of Clara's Christian name illustrates the new order in the Rookery as clearly as do his first words to Peggotty:

> "My friend," turning a darkening face on Peggotty, when he had watched my mother out, and dismissed her with a nod and a smile: "do you know your mistress's name? . . . I thought I heard you, as I came upstairs, address her by a name [*viz.,* Mrs. Copperfield] that is not hers. She has taken mine, you know. Will you remember that?"
>
> (p. 39)

Murdstone neither lies to David and Peggotty nor speaks in an unconventional way. Husbands in Victorian novels generally call their wives by Christian names; wives in Victorian novels generally take their husbands' surnames. But truth and convention are only accidentally in Murdstone's mouth. The man is a perverter of language because he uses grammatical necessity—the necessity to refer and address by *some* distinction—as a tool of desire. He uses naming not to name but to assert his power to name:

> "It's very hard," said my mother, "that in my own house—"
>
> "*My* own house?" repeated Mr. Murdstone. "Clara!"
>
> "*Our* own house, I mean," faltered my mother, evidently frightened—"I hope you know what I mean, Edward—it's very hard that in *your* own house I may not have a word to say."
>
> (p. 43)

Throughout *David Copperfield* Dickens uses naming to reveal rank and sentiment. David's schoolmasters employ his Christian name only in sympathy for his mother's death. "Little Gent" maintains a space around David at the warehouse, and he is called nothing personal except when he recounts some story to entertain the older men. In meeting David as an adult, Miss Murdstone refuses him "Mr." and is left with "David Copperfield," just as Mr. Wickfield (once Uriah Heep has grown great) refers to his former clerk by both Christian name and surname.

And throughout the novel Dickens uses the perversion of naming to expose power and desire. Murdstone is the type, but he is not alone. Creakle mocks Mell's poverty with "Mr. What's-your-name," only to become furious when the dismissed teacher does not reply with an employer's title: "Sir, to you!" Creakle screams (p. 86). Uriah Heep is clever, and his repeated "Master Copperfield,—I mean Mister Copperfield" is a wonderfully witty abuse of language. Miss Murdstone has flashes of this sort of abusive wit: "Generally speaking," she says, "I don't like boys. How d'ye do, boy?" (p. 41). And Miss Mowcher is also good at wicked

name play, as when she signals with the naming game of Forfeits that she understands her role in procuring Emily. Even the sponger and would-be seducer Jack Maldon, with his "I call him the old Doctor—it's all the same, you know" (p. 197), and the pandering Littimer, with his respectable lack of a Christian name and refusal of superlatives, pervert the order of names. All the villains in *David Copperfield* abuse language.

That all villains abuse language, however, does not necessarily mean that all who abuse language are villains. If the villainous characters use words to twist reality, there are nonetheless comic characters who take words themselves as real. The grim Murdstone stands at one side of *David Copperfield,* but standing at the other, like laughter holding both his sides, is Wilkins Micawber.

Perhaps all abusers of language *are* villains, however. Generous motives and innocuous consequences mark moral characters in Dickens's early novels. Everyone tells stories in the *Pickwick Papers,* but Jingle wants to help himself and Pickwick wants to help others; Job Trotter hurts people and Sam Weller does not. By this standard, Mr. Micawber is a villain. He is comic and congenial, larger than the life that jails him for his debts; he is Pickwick and Weller loosened a notch, and his manipulation of language can make a nondescript house a theater, a ruined dinner a feast, and debtors' prison a carnival. But he is also Jingle and Trotter tightened a notch, for he hurts people along the way. It is not really funny that the bootmaker wants to be paid and the milkman needs his money. Micawber may at last redeem himself, but only after helping to destroy Wickfield. Traddles, scrimping for marriage, has his furniture confiscated to pay Micawber's debts. Mr. Micawber does have some "moral (or rather immoral) resemblance" (p. 642) to Murdstone and Heep.

Of course, we join David in exempting Micawber from condemnation as a villain. And there is a moral difference, for Micawber is never systematically cruel—as Murdstone is in beating David to train Clara, as Heep is in robbing Betsey to ruin David. Micawber has the virtue of his vices and is as incapable of systematic harm as he is of systematic thrift. Indeed, he has an openness that Murdstone, Heep, and Creakle (with his "system" of silent prison discipline [p. 727]) could never know. Micawber is not selfish but only absorbed in the drama of himself, and when he meets a real villain in Heep he loses the dramatic power of words that is his charm for living.

Similarly, we join David in exempting Micawber from condemnation as a liar. An enormous amount of dishonesty occurs in *David Copperfield.* Heep is a forger, of course, and a systematic liar, but the fly-drivers in Dover lie to David, the inveiglers in Doctors' Commons lie to clients, and the servants that David and Dora hire lie to everyone. In sorting out Heep's chicanery, Traddles discovers not only that Wickfield has fraudulently remitted interest while aware of the loss of capital but that Betsey has lied about her destitution (just as she twice pushes David toward Agnes with "a pious fraud" [p. 740]). Traddles himself practices a naive subterfuge to redeem his flower stand, Steerforth misleads his mother, and Barkis shams poverty. The lie that Mr. Spenlow tells about his will may be excusable—"there is no subject on which men are so inconsistent," his clerk Tiffy declares, "and so little to be trusted" (p. 476)—but dishonesty is Spenlow's defining trait: he lies about his wealth, methodically misrepresents his partner Jorkins, and defends the Commons on the grounds that appearance is as good as truth.

Young David is a liar, too. "If you make a brag of your honesty to me," a tinker threatens on the road to Dover, "I'll knock your brains out" (p. 160), and David has no right to brag: he lies about his name on his birthday in London, tells the Orfling fantastic stories, and deceives Peggotty in a money-begging letter. "Never be false," Betsey advises him (p. 192), but nine pages later he lies about Betsey herself. David's anxiety of "imposture" at Dr. Strong's (p. 195) is finally the fear of being found out false—a fear that resurfaces after his drunken dissipation: "I could scarcely lay claim to the name. . . . However, I told [the ticket-porter] I was T. Copperfield, Esquire, and he believed it" (p. 311). Lies constantly tempt David: in the flurried thought of asking at Mr. Mills's door for Mr. Blackboy, in the dishonorable correspondence with Dora, even in his fiction writing. "Your being secret and clandestine, is not being like yourself," Agnes admonishes, "in the candor of your nature" (p. 485).

And yet Micawber's lies are somehow different. The interminable sentences and linguistic gestures, the synonymizing and circumlocution, are comic because Micawber creates not himself but language—because he sets words free. A lie typically strains language: it is just as constrained by truth as honesty is, and constrained further by the liar's desire for truth to be other than it is. Dickens shows with Micawber, however, a lying that frees rather than strains language. Micawber does not speak ungrammatically or nonsensically, but grammar and meaning are all the constraint his words admit: language in Micawber's mouth is released from the necessity to express its speaker's desire, to conform to truth, even to convince its hearers. Each phrase suggests not what next to say but a synonymous inflation of what he has said already. His circumlocution is not avoidance but inflation: a turning of words back on themselves.

Dickens's use of irony shows this same free play of words. There is some complicated verbal irony in *David Copperfield*, but Micawber's speech has the simple irony of comic hypocrisy: such truths from such a source. "Annual income twenty pounds, annual expenditure nineteen six, result happiness," the extravagant debtor famously informs David (p. 150). "Never do tomorrow what you can do today," he advises. "Procrastination is the thief of time. Collar him!" (p. 149). But Micawber *is* Procrastination, wearing an imposing collar and collared in the King's Bench prison. Even when he speaks the truth, the irony of his saying something true puts his words above their truth. Language finds in Micawber a nearly perfect medium through which to speak itself, for he wears language as he wears his quizzing-glass: "for ornament, I afterwards found, as he very seldom looked through it, and couldn't see anything when he did" (p. 134).

Dickens consistently exploits abused language for comedy. Even with Betsey's willful errors set aside, the novel is full of confusions about words. "A Baboo—or a Begum" is misremembered by Mrs. Copperfield as a "baboon," "crocodiles" misunderstood by Peggotty as vegetable "crorkindills," "sweethearts" misheard by David as "sweetmeats," "Doctor" misread by Mrs. Markleham as "Proctor," "jury" mispronounced by Mrs. Crupp as "judy," and "elements" misspoken by Micawber as "elephants." Mrs. Crupp mistakes her lodger's names as Copperfull, "firstly, no doubt, because it was not my name; and secondly, I am inclined to think, in some indistinct association with a washing-day" (p. 341).

And Dickens consistently shows the moral ambiguity of comic characters. Micawber is the type, but he is not alone. Mrs. Markleham is a comically ceaseless talker— "What a useful work a Dictionary is!" she declares; "what a necessary work! The meaning of words! Without Doctor Johnson . . . we might have been at this present moment calling an Italian-iron a bedstead" (p. 555)—but she nearly destroys the Strongs by forcing her notion of their marriage upon them. Julia Mills has "a wonderful flow of words" (p. 473), and the mixed metaphors, ambiguous initials, and bizarre queries make her diary entries as funny as Micawber's letters. But she takes a "dreadful luxury" in making the most of Dora's afflictions and settles at last for a rich, older husband. Emma Micawber is as prone to dramatic abuse of language as Wilkins is. The letters to David and Traddles match perfectly: both Micawbers have something to say, but nothing more is said by their wordy letters than that they have something to say. Abetting her husband in the delusion that something will turn up, sending a child into a pawnshop, weighing with hilarious prudence Mr. Micawber's chances of becoming a judge or the governor of Australia, Mrs. Micawber is just as comic and culpable as her husband. While the Micawbers are leaving London "a mist cleared from her eyes" (p. 150), allowing her to see how young the boy is. But it is only for a moment, and when they next see

David, Mrs. Micawber leads the room in a chorus of "Auld Lang Syne."

Comedy is no cure for what ails language. For all his bounce Micawber is not the father David needs and cannot prevent "the waste of promise" (p. 129) that Murdstone intends by sending the boy to the city. *David Copperfield* presents a London of falsity and abuse: spurious names on shop-fronts and warehouses, forgeries, meaningless signatures on bills and IOUs, a gentility so counterfeit that even lawyers and schoolmasters pretend to it—the whole commercial world as a systematic perversion of naming. "Nothing's genuine in the place, in my opinion, but the dirt," Betsey declares; "it would be no pleasure to a London tradesman to sell anything which was what he pretended" (p. 295). And to oppose that falsity and abuse Micawber has only more falsity and more abuse—delightful falsity and comic abuse, a joy in living that villains never know, but at last he has no remedy for the fatherless: leaving London, Micawber hands the "disbanded" Orfling back to the workhouse (p. 149) and the orphan David off to the carman Tipp. The comic characters may escape destruction, may act happily in their imaginary dramas, may even succeed on the distant stage of an opportune Australia, but they cannot prevent the abuse of names. Micawber has the rhetoric of heroic drama, which makes him comic, boisterous, and fun. But David must look elsewhere for the real order of naming, must trek to Dover to seek true names.

* * *

David as he grows is a victim of naming. At each new stage of life he receives a new name; and each name is a forecast, a symbol, and an example of the namer's treatment. But even while he is a victim of his namers he is actively gaining over naming the mastery that will release him from his namers. Names fascinate the boy. "Did you give your son the name of Ham," he asks Dan Peggotty, "because you lived in a sort of ark?" (p. 28). When Emily talks forebodingly of David's parents being gentlefolk while her "uncle Dan is a fisherman," blind David responds, "Dan is Mr. Peggotty, is he?" (p. 30). At Creakle's school, at Omer's shop, at the prison and the warehouse, reference and address always catch David's attention.

And names continue to fascinate him as he grows. Arriving at Betsey's he shows both his sensitivity to names and his imperfect understanding:

> "I suppose," said my aunt, . . . "you think Mr. Dick a short name? . . . You are not to suppose that he hasn't got a longer . . . Mr. Richard Babley—that's the gentleman's true name."
>
> I was going to suggest, with a modest sense of my youth and the familiarity I had been already guilty of, that I had better give him the full benefit of that name, when my aunt went on to say:

> "But don't call him by it, whatever you do. He can't bear his name."

(p. 172)

David assumes Annie is the Doctor's daughter and is surprised to hear her called "Mrs. Strong." At Betsey's house, at Wickfield's office, at Strong's school, David struggles to master the order of names.

He thinks, of course, that he has mastered that order before he actually has. Out on his own for the first time after his adoption, David answers a coachman with an assertion of rank by naming—"'Yes, William,' I said, condescendingly (I knew him)" (p. 242)—and is promptly bamboozled into sitting outside the coach. After graduation "Daisy" has fall after fall (from his drunken fall down the stairs to his fall in fortune) while seeking his place in the order of names. "We wasn't aware," a waiter apologizes to Steerforth, "as Mr. Copperfield was anyways particular" (p. 247)—meaning, of course, that they did not suppose David to be particular about his room, but suggesting that he is no one in particular. David is "dreadfully young," but first under Steerforth's tutelage and then under financial necessity he begins to assert himself. Dickens lets names show the young man's progress in the social order: David plays at calling Peggotty "Mrs. Barkis" only to call her Peggotty thereafter; he dreams of being allowed to call his employer's daughter "Dora"; he priggishly warns Traddles against lending Micawber his name. At the debauch with Steerforth, at Mrs. Waterbrook's "blood" dinner, at the party ruined by Littimer, at the encounters with the Murdstones, at Mrs. Crupp's "guerilla warfare" (p. 439), at the confrontation between Mr. Peggotty and Mrs. Steerforth, David learns the order of names—slowly but nonetheless firmly and with "earnestness" (p. 518).

At last, at twenty-one, David is a master of names, a namer of himself and others. Having "come legally to man's estate," David is the proper son of his "father-in-law" Murdstone. He has "tamed that savage stenographic mystery" and now, like Murdstone, sees through language: "I am quite an Infidel" about parliamentary speeches, he declares (p. 535). And like Murdstone, he takes a child-wife. Even without Betsey's nudgings the parallels between Clara and Dora are obvious: both are bewitching orphans and incompetent housekeepers, both have two-syllable names ending in -ra, both suffer a husband's desire to reform them, both lose an unnamed child. David's similarity to Murdstone is deepened when we remember that Murdstone is left unpunished at the novel's end. Not exactly excused by David's treatment of Dora, much less redeemed, Murdstone is nonetheless beyond David's power to sentence: the man is doubly guilty (as his second marriage proves), but the narrating

David cannot impose the penalty—for he had tried to make Julia, Traddles, and even Betsey his "instruments" (p. 182), his own Misses Murdstone, for reforming Dora.

Of course, David is not really Murdstone. He is as much Micawber, and though he wallows in politicians' words he also begins to spin his own. David and Dora keep house with even more comedy than the Micawbers (who never had the money to treat Emma as a doll or cookery as a game). Humor is Micawber's legacy: Clara did the same silly things Dora does, but Murdstone, "sitting stern and silent" (p. 21), lacked the grace to laugh. And yet, just as Micawber offered no cure to Murdstone for David as a child, so he offers no alternative for David as an adult. "I wish to God," Steerforth mourns, "I had had a judicious father these last twenty years" (p. 274). Every character of David's generation has lost at least one parent, and this general orphaning deprives them of good models for being adults. When the Micawberish life with Dora wears thin, David sees only the model of Murdstone to which he can turn.

G. K. Chesterton famously bemoaned the "wrong ending" of *David Copperfield*.[3] But had the novel ended without Dora's death and David's remarriage it would have marked the triumph of Murdstone—proving that words are empty, that names are screens for power and desire, that villains are at least epistemologically if not morally correct. David plays Murdstone badly, of course, because David is basically a good man. But his mastery of names has failed to make him happy, for he has not found the truth to match his morals.

* * *

Rival epistemologies argue about the transformation of percepts into concepts and concepts into words, and they argue about the way in which language reaches back to influence conception and conception reaches back to influence perception. But all epistemologies agree that there are no *pure* names, no linguistic gestures that somehow skip over concepts to point straight to things (for even "thing" is a concept). All speech—even naming—passes through its speaker and by passing through becomes vulnerable to desire. Convention may limit choices for a name (this is the screen of politeness) but it never eliminates choice: in a language as rich as Victorian English the name chosen for reference or address always reveals something of the namer.

We must speak, however, and when we speak we distinguish things with conceptual distinctions (this is the screen of grammatical necessity). The personal identity and self-knowledge David seeks may be delusions—the over-blessed ending of *David Copperfield* holds little promise of their reality—but seek them he does, and for there to be identity and knowledge there must be *truth:*

an intelligible and speakable correspondence of conceptual distinctions with distinctions in reality. David must find in names a unity of concept and thing beyond the power of the namer and the weakness of the named. Dickens must put in *David Copperfield* an alternative to Murdstone's grim success and Micawber's cheerful failure.

Hints of this alternative appear throughout the novel in odd asides about words and language. Just as the lettering on tombstones speaks to Pip in *Great Expectations,* so the names carved on school desks speak to David of the carvers, Clara's indecipherable numerals speak of her housekeeping, and the cabalistic shorthand signs speak of the words David will report with them. So, too, sounds speak to certain listeners: "Dora!" David thinks, "what a beautiful name!" (p. 333); "Sophy—pretty name, Copperfield, I always think?" Traddles returns (p. 421). Warping names to match their bearers, Betsey often hears names as significant.

And something *is* significant in names. Steerforth charms the Peggottys with his quick grasp of names. Micawber chants "Heep" as a "magic word" (p. 608). Just as Barkis announces his marriage by saying he should write "Clara Peggotty Barkis" on the cart-tilt, so David feels the "visionary connexion" (p. 536) of names on his marriage license. So, too, the first abuse of Doctors' Commons that David denounces is divorce by declaration of wrong name. But what this significance is, the young man has somehow missed before Dora's death, somehow fallen short of grasping in his first try at adulthood. David would imagine as a boy that he was a character from a book: Roderick Random or Tom Jones or Captain Somebody who never had his ears boxed with a Latin Grammar. And "the Captain was a Captain and a hero, in despite of all the grammars of all the languages in the world" (p. 48). But David as he grows loses this childish sense that names might name things as they are—that there is a real significance to names.

Both of David's Canterbury fathers try to give that sense back to him. Only Dr. Strong and Mr. Dick are called "philosophers" in *David Copperfield* (pp. 216, 426), and though the title is given ironically there is something philosophical about their sense of names. "I have sent [the Doctor's] name up, on a scrap of paper, to the kite, along the string, when it has been in the sky, among the larks," Mr. Dick declares; "the kite has been glad to receive it, sir, and the sky has been brighter with it" (p. 557). When young David called the sailor with "Skylark" on his chest "Mr. Skylark" he still had this philosophical sense, as he did when he first met the Doctor:

> the Doctor's cogitating manner was attributable to his being always engaged in looking out for Greek roots; which, in my innocence and ignorance, I supposed to

be a botanical furor on the Doctor's part, especially as he always looked at the ground when he walked about—until I understood that they were roots of words, with a view to a new Dictionary.

(p. 203)

David Copperfield is a novel of recollection; and all recollection is selective, organizing memory for a present purpose. "It's in vain," Betsey warns, "to recall the past, unless it works some influence upon the present" (p. 296). We must take seriously that the narrating David—seeking self-knowledge in recollection—takes an extraordinary interest in words. He remembers how the Murdstones robbed him of words and memory and wonders in the present tense where forgotten words go. Remembering the repeated phrases of Dora's aunts he remarks, "I had (and have all my life) observed that conventional phrases are a sort of fireworks" (p. 503). Remembering Micawber's thanks to Betsey "as between man and man" he comments, "I don't know that Mr. Micawber attached any meaning to this last phrase; I don't know that anybody ever does" (p. 660). Into Micawber's dramatic denunciation of Heep he intrudes with a 243-word present-tense complaint about the "piling up of words" (p. 645).

Certainly David pictures himself as born to use words to tell stories. He remembers taking refuge in his father's books and a desperate sort of reading—"reading as if for life" (p. 48). He read then not as a story-reader but as a storyteller, for he needed to create an "imaginative world" (p. 145) to escape the Murdstones. The power to make words come alive is something he had before the Murdstones came (with the epitaphs in church, the Lazarus story, the Crorkindills book). But looking back at that reading of his father's books (the only legacy Murdstone does not usurp) he sees the moment when he first understood he had this power, and he exploits it for the rest of his life.

There is a moment late in *David Copperfield,* however, when storytelling is no help. David's child is dead and his wife dying. Heep seems certain to marry Agnes, and Traddles unlikely to marry Sophy. Steerforth has thrown off Emily, while the Murdstones are beyond David's reach. Betsey is bankrupt and haunted by her nameless husband. Mr. Dick has rescued the Strongs, but only in a way that crystallizes David's worry about his own "undisciplined heart" (p. 564). Ironically, the moment comes just when David has succeeded as a writer. He can throw off reporting for fiction; he can support his wife; people recognize his name. But it is to no purpose. David has mastered names and earnestly made his way, but he is not happy.

It is at this moment, however, that David begins to see the alternative he missed in mastering names as screens for power and desire, for it is at this moment that Dora

rescues him. When David says he loves her Dora replies, in a telling circumlocution, "without a story—really?" (p. 594). As David settles into his new house his old fear of being found out false wells up again, and he feels like an imposter waiting for "the real master" (p. 537) to come home. But life with Dora is not a story, and David's mastery of words is no help for his imposture.

Dora had warned him, however, about true names: "I don't mean, you silly fellow, that you should use the name [Child-Wife]. . . . I only mean that you should think of me that way" (p. 550). David's project of reforming Dora must be given up because Dora is already formed; David's desires are vain because Dora is already complete. It is "better to be naturally Dora than anything else in the world," he at last decides (p. 594). Since he cannot adapt Dora to himself, he resolves to adapt himself to Dora.

And yet, through the failure of Wickfield's assumption of "some one master motive" in each person (p. 526), Dickens warns against oversimplification. "Things must shrink very much," Betsey declares, "before they can be measured off in *that* way" (p. 716). David's resolution still seeks, by an act of earnest will, to reshape things to match their concepts. This was the moral practice Betsey claimed to have: a reformation not of others but of the self, a self-shaping by self-naming. As Dora's illness deepens and "Little Blossom" fades despite Betsey's care, David begins to see that even earnestness is not enough. When Dora says that she was not fit to be a wife, he answers, "Oh, Dora, love, as fit as I to be a husband!" (p. 657). With Dora's death David at last gives up trying to form even himself. When he finds Steerforth and Ham "drowndead" (p. 28) together (making the connection of nautical and theological matters that Steerforth had mocked in Doctors' Commons and that had seemed so odd with the sailors in church at Dora's wedding), David at last reaches an adult grasp of names beyond the childish assumption of meaning and the adolescent assumption of emptiness. He sails for the continent and begins his autobiography.

* * *

The use Dickens makes of names in *David Copperfield* originates in dialogue, for speech requires that relations be shown by what people say, and the power and desire that lurk behind politeness and grammatical necessity are exactly what people do *not* say, are exactly what language hides. Of course, people sometimes say more than they intend. Heep comes closest to speaking aloud of power and desire, for he plays against the gentility that the other characters assume. With his "detestable cant of false humility" (p. 490) he has his own strategy to hide the quest for power, and his desire almost breaks through to words. The irony of consoling David for

Betsey's ruin nearly betrays Heep into saying that power is itself the aim of desire. While describing his upbringing Heep says what no one else would say: "I am very umble to the present moment, Master Copperfield, but I've got a little power!" (p. 491).

Few characters will speak this way within anyone's hearing, however, and first-person narration limits dialogue to what David hears. Early in the novel Dickens stretches David's hearing by a simulated eavesdropping, exploiting the gap between child and adult: Quinion (speaking in front of "Brooks of Sheffield") thinks only a boy hears, but an adult overhears in memory. Later in the novel Dickens can obtain this effect only by making David blind to signals of coming events. Rosa's excoriation of Emily—the novel's one explicit eavesdropping scene—is heavily rewritten in Dickens's manuscript, but the published form still leaves us uncomfortable with David's passivity. Dickens must in general accept the limitations of first-person narration. His primary means for indicating his characters' relations must be the terms by which they refer to and address one another—their places in the order of names.

Though his use of naming originates in dialogue, however, Dickens finds a deeper purpose. The order of names has caught his attention, and he does more than use it to express rank and sentiment. Dickens shows both the origin of abuse in extrinsic denomination and the power of names to mask that abuse. And he claims at the novel's end both the possibility of intrinsic denomination and the power of true names to speak the unity of concept and thing.

David Copperfield's growth into the writer of *David Copperfield*—the growth of speaker into narrator—requires that David grasp the failure of false names before he reaches to the fullness of true names. But he must find in that falsity and failure the possibility of truth and reform. Dickens always believed in truth: beneath the jokes and abuse of language there is for Dickens an order of reality that is finally moral and true. No Cheeryble angel descends at the end of *David Copperfield*; no reformed Scrooge or Chuzzlewit comes to fix the broken lives. But truth at last wells up in the novel, nonetheless. Agnes is, of course, David's true wife, just as Traddles is his true friend. But it is Dora and Steerforth who establish with their deaths the connections David could not make before. Only upon his return from grieving abroad can he see the truth in Agnes and in the life that Traddles has made with Sophy and her sisters. In the novel's concluding "Retrospect" Dickens reveals the goal of autobiography: David as an adult, grasping true names at last.

None of David's names at the end of *David Copperfield* are new. Though the novelty of Sophy's "Tom" (for Traddles) is accented repeatedly by quotation marks in

the final chapters, David reclaims only his old names: David, Trot, Trotwood, Master Dav'y, even Brooks of Sheffield. But his grasp of names has changed since these were given. True names are not destroyed by abuse but survive to signify the unity of concept and thing. When the re-met Chillip says he cannot remember David's name, David replies, "and yet you knew it, long before I knew it myself" (p. 711). Each of David's names points to a real distinction in the man, and each of his reclaimings reveals his grasp not just of the corresponding conceptual distinction but of the truth—the *correspondingness*—of that distinction. When David puts his name on Traddles's door but refuses to allow practice in the Commons "under cover of my name" (p. 724), we see his maturity. Only "Doady" and "Daisy" are left unreclaimed: "I have forgotten this gentleman's name," the grief-mad Mrs. Steerforth mourns (p. 749). David has not forgotten it. But he has at last, in Dickens's eyes, outgrown it.

Notes

1. See Sylvère Monod, *Dickens the Novelist* (Norman: Univ. of Oklahoma Press, 1968), pp. 301-3. Two other studies demand particular mention. In "The Naming and the Namers of the Hero: A Study in *David Copperfield*," *Southern Review: Literary and Interdisciplinary Essays,* 11 (1978), 267-82, Norman Talbot shows the interweaving of David's names and the novel's plot. In "David Copperfield's Names," *Dickensian,* 74 (1978), 81-87, Donald Hawes traces Dickens's creation of David's names. Though I am deeply indebted to both of these studies, neither takes up, as I wish to, the general linguistic effect of multiple names in *David Copperfield,* particularly for characters other than David.

2. Charles Dickens, *David Copperfield,* ed. Nina Burgis (Oxford: Clarendon Press, 1981), p. 22. Further quotations are from this edition and are included in the text.

3. See *Appreciations and Criticisms of the Works of Charles Dickens* (1911), in *Chesterton on Dickens,* vol. 15 of *The Collected Works of G. K. Chesterton,* ed. George J. Martin, et al. (San Francisco: Ignatius Press, 1989), p. 332.

Gareth Cordery (essay date 1998)

SOURCE: Cordery, Gareth. "Foucault, Dickens, and *David Copperfield*." *Victorian Literature and Culture* 26, no. 1 (1998): 71-85.

[*In the following essay, Cordery comments on* David Copperfield *not as a representation of David's learned acquisition of emotional self-discipline, but rather as a depiction of the processes of cultural conditioning and social disciplining (as conceptualized by Michel Foucault) centered on the novel's protagonist.*]

Margaret Atwood's narrator in *Bodily Harm,* reminiscing about her childhood, says: "I learned to listen for what wasn't being said, because it was usually more important than what was" (55). Making a similar point, in *The History of Sexuality* Foucault writes that "There is not one but many silences, and they are an integral part of the strategies that underlie and permeate discourses" (1: 27). If we read *David Copperfield* in this way—listening to the silences, as well as attending closely to what is being said—the narrative which emerges from the surface *bildungsroman* is very different from the traditional story of David who learns that "there can be no disparity in marriage like unsuitability of mind and purpose," and that his marriage to Dora was "the first mistaken impulse of an undisciplined heart" (ch. 45; 733). In this surface narrative David, suitably chastened, is released to marry the boring Agnes by the fortuitous death of the unfortunate Dora. Many critics have commented wisely on David's emotional and psychological development.[1] What I want to suggest is that, while the surface story traces the disciplining of David's emotions, there is another narrative which tells of a different kind of disciplining, one that subjects David to a variety of social norms, rules, and regulations.

In *The Novel and the Police,* D. A. Miller briefly traces the several stages of David's early disciplining (212-13), and goes on to show how in his profession as writer he is at once liberated and imprisoned. What is missing from this story is how the various forms of overt discipline to which David is subject in the first twelve chapters—family (at Blunderstone Rookery), education (at the Rookery and Salem House), and work (at Murdstone and Grinby's warehouse)—reappear, disguised as liberal humanitarianism, at Aunt Betsey's Dover Cottage, Dr. Strong's Canterbury school, and in David's various jobs, especially that of novelist. In other words, David's arrival at the comfortable, safe, middle-class haven of Dover Cottage and his subsequent experiences, far from being "another beginning" as the title to chapter 15 states, is a continuation of the more obviously coercive disciplining suffered at the hands of his earlier persecutors.[2] Thus David simply exchanges one form of social discipline that is openly repressive and corporeal for another that is covert and internal. Resisting the invitation to read the novel as David's "personal history" (part of the novel's full title), refusing to accept its bourgeois ideology, and listening carefully to its many silences, I read *David Copperfield* not as the disciplining of David's undisciplined heart but as his social disciplining and education. In this disciplining, which is due in no small part to the invisible influence of Agnes Wickfield, David imbibes the values and practices of mid-Victorian bourgeois liberalism, which enable him to achieve a position of respectability and power from which he speaks as narrator.

This particular narrative that I have outlined finds its wider cultural and historical parallel in the development, during the eighteenth and nineteenth centuries, of those disciplinary technologies which Michel Foucault has traced in *Discipline and Punish.* Foucault's subject is "the mechanisms of power that frame the everyday lives of individuals" (77) and that general investigation finds its specific historical grounding in the "birth of the prison" (Foucault's subtitle). During the eighteenth and nineteenth centuries, discipline shifted from punishment by a visible authority (the monarch or his representatives), a public spectacle which subjects the body to the tortures so graphically described by Foucault, to its location in various disciplinary institutions, arms of an anonymous state bureaucracy, such as new kinds of prisons, which isolate inmates rather than herding them together, lunatic asylums, homes for fallen women, orphanages, workhouses, and so on—the very institutions, in fact, that are settings for Dickens's novels. According to Foucault, punishment becomes hidden and not displayed, and its site is no longer the body but the mind and soul. It is this larger historical process that I see Dickens's novel replicating in the purportedly "personal history" of David Copperfield.

In this history, the overt disciplining of David Copperfield by the Murdstones at Blunderstone Rookery becomes the covert disciplining of David Copperfield by Aunt Betsey at Dover Cottage. While David's respective experiences in the two households appear to be totally different, and while Aunt Betsey's routing of the Murdstones on their visit to Dover Cottage to reclaim David suggests the victory of love and liberty over narrow-minded authoritarianism, a number of striking similarities link the two households and coalesce in the figures of Jane Murdstone and Betsey Trotwood.[3] The humanity of Dover Cottage should not disguise the efficiency and order that it shares with Blunderstone Rookery, and in many ways Aunt Betsey is like Jane Murdstone, herself a clone of brother Edward. Both women manage their households while employing servants, Peggoty and Janet, to perform the menial tasks. Both hate men, fear sex, but are man-like. Jane is "dark, like her brother, whom she greatly resembled in face and voice; and with very heavy eyebrows, nearly meeting over her large nose, as if, being disabled by the wrongs of her sex from wearing whiskers, she had carried them to that account" (ch. 4; 97). When David first sees his aunt she is "wearing a gardening pocket like a toll-man's apron, and carrying a great knife" (ch. 13; 246), and later he notices that "she wore at her side a gentleman's gold watch" (249). Much of the description of Betsey could easily be applied to Jane: "[m]y aunt was a tall, hard-featured lady . . . there was an inflexibility in her face, in her voice, in her gait and carriage . . . unbending and austere" (249), the last a trait specific to "the Murdstone religion" (ch. 4; 101). David is greeted in identical fashion by both women: "'I don't like boys'" says Jane (97), while Betsey "making a distant chop in the air with her knife" exclaims "'Go along! No boys here!'" (ch. 13; 247). Even if this is not, as Eigner suggests (12), a symbolic act of castration, there is little doubt that both ladies are inveterate enemies of the male sex. Jane suspects that "the servants had a man secreted somewhere in the premises" and "[u]nder the influence of this delusion, she dived into the coal-cellar at the most untimely hours, and scarcely ever opened the door of a dark cupboard without clapping it to again, in the belief that she had got him" (ch. 4; 98); similarly, Betsey hires female servants "expressly to educate [them] in a renouncement of mankind" (ch. 13; 250). Both fail in their attempts: Jane never gets her man, while Betsey's servants "generally completed their abjuration [of mankind] by marrying the baker" (250).

If Aunt Betsey is like Jane who is a clone of her brother, it should follow that Betsey is like Edward Murdstone. Betsey, an independent woman alone in a man's world, must act like a man: she dresses like one, owns her own property, controls her own money, acts as David's guardian, sends him to school and sets him up in lodgings. And in one crucial particular she is *very* like Edward Murdstone: her belief in firmness of character. Early in the novel David observes "nobody in his world was to be so firm as Mr Murdstone; nobody else in his world was to be firm at all, for everybody was to be bent to his firmness" (ch. 4; 99). It has often been remarked that in attempting to "form" Dora, David acts towards his young wife in the same way that Murdstone acted towards David's mother and towards David himself. But the important part that Betsey plays in the formation of David's character has largely been ignored.[4] The goal of disciplining David is the same for both Mr. Murdstone and for Aunt Betsey, even if their methods are different: while Murdstone overtly attempts to break David's will and force him to submit to an external authority (himself) by beating and then imprisoning him, Betsey's campaign is more subtle and persuasive because her lifestyle reveals the rewards (good food, clean sheets, and new clothes) of conforming to bourgeois values. David internalises that firmness which his step-father had tried to beat into him and which Betsey virtually talks into him: "'But what I want you to be, Trot,' resumed my aunt,—'I don't mean physically, but morally; you are very well physically—is, a firm fellow. A fine firm fellow, with a will of your own. With resolution,' said my aunt, shaking her cap at me, and clenching her hand" (ch. 19; 332). It is no great distance from Betsey's clenched hand to Murdstone's swishing cane. The resemblance between the two disciplinarians is particularly close when Betsey first takes David in. At Blunderstone Rookery David, having bitten Murdstone's hand, is imprisoned in his room for five days (he is allowed out for half an hour each day), with the door locked and Jane Murdstone his "jailer." On David's first night at Dover Cottage he is taken up to his room "like a prisoner" (ch. 13; 254), the door locked, and he is subsequently confined to the house "except for an hour after dark" (262), until the arrival of the Murdstones when he is put on trial, being fenced in "with a chair, as if it were a prison or a bar of justice" (264). After the defeat of the Murdstones David is measured for a new suit of clothes marked "Trotwood Copperfield" in "indelible marking-ink" (ch. 14; 271). This, in fact, does mark the decisive moment when David passes indelibly from one authority to another, no longer subject to the Murdstones' overt repression but to Betsey's covert moral and social discipline.

Nor is David Aunt Betsey's first disciplinary subject. Apart from the long line of young women (Janet is merely the latest) whom she has successfully instructed in household economy, Mr. Dick has already been covertly subjected to a regime of bourgeois domesticity, which is why Aunt Betsey can trust him to answer correctly her questions about what to do with David. His replies—that she should wash, clothe and put him to bed (David notes the "snow-white sheets" (ch. 13; 255) and white curtains)—embody those virtues (cleanliness, a respectable appearance, and purity) which are part of the bourgeois ethos. David and Dick are, in their different ways, children and, eventually, writers. Their background is virtually identical. Like David, Dick is a "distant connexion" (ch. 14; 260) of Betsey's and was similarly unwanted and "ill-used" (257) by an unfeeling male who imprisoned him in an insane asylum. Indeed, Mr. Dick's head reminds David of "one of Mr Creakle's boys' heads after a beating" (ch. 13; 250), David himself having been subject to Creakle's attentions (ch. 7; 141). In each case Betsey comes along and rescues the beleagured male; she "got" Mr. Dick from his brother (ch. 14; 260) just as she "gets" David from his step-father, an echo, perhaps, of Jane Murdstone's futile attempts to "get" her imaginary male intruder. The change in ownership is signalled by a change in name as well as by a suit of new clothes: Mr. Dick's original name was Richard Babley (257), while Betsey re-christens David "Trotwood." David first sees Mr. Dick in gentleman's clothes which David borrows, and he lives in a kind of sartorial limbo until, as we have seen, he can be measured for his own.

Once correctly attired, David can be correctly educated, and so becomes a pupil at Dr. Strong's which "was an excellent school; as different from Mr Creakle's as good is from evil" (ch. 16; 293). Although Dickens deliberately contrasts the two educational institutions, nonetheless they are connected. Collins (117-18) has shown that the identification of Dr. Strong's school with the historical King's Grammar at Canterbury is mistaken;

Dr. Strong's is a privately run institution, just like Creakle's. While there is nothing especially significant in their both being private houses converted to small schools, (this was common enough in educational institutions of the time), to David both schools appear prison-like. Salem House "was a square brick building with wings," enclosed "with a high brick wall," which is entered through a locked gate with a grating in it (ch. 5; 129); similarly, Dr. Strong's house is surrounded by "tall iron rails and gates" together with a red brick wall topped with stiff, heavy stone urns at regular intervals (ch. 16; 282).

This resemblance suggests that Canterbury is Salem House with a human face where discipline and control are covert, not overt. David passes via Aunt Betsey from one to the other: in Foulcauldian terms social control passes from a visible authoritarianism to a network of disciplinary technologies. At Salem House Creakle slashes away unmercifully at the boys (ch. 6; 138), leaving David "with a red ridge across [his] back" (ch.7; 142). However, this openly corporeal discipline is supplemented by Creakle's scrutinising eye, which "morbidly attract[s]" David: "Here I am in the playground, with my eye still fascinated by him, though I can't see him. The window at a little distance from which I know he is having his dinner, stands for him, and I eye that instead" (142). Creakle's visual control approaches but does not epitomize Foucault's ideal of the invisible gaze, for David, though he cannot actually see Creakle, is only too well aware of his presence. It is at Canterbury, where the disciplinary gaze is not absent so much as it is more discreet and diffused than at Salem House, that control is virtually invisible, because unperceived, and thus more complete:

> It [the school] was very gravely and decorously ordered, and on a sound system; with an appeal, in everything, to the honour and good faith of the boys, and an avowed intention to rely on their possession of those qualities unless they proved themselves unworthy of it, which worked wonders. We all felt that we had a part in the management of the place, and in sustaining its character and dignity. Hence, we soon became warmly attached to it—I am sure I did for one, and I never knew, in all my time, of any other boy being otherwise—and learnt with a good will, desiring to do it credit. We had noble games out of hours, and plenty of liberty; but even then, as I remember, we were well spoken of in the town, and rarely did any disgrace, by our appearance or manner, to the reputation of Doctor Strong and Doctor Strong's boys.

(ch. 16; 293-94)

Thus Canterbury, "decorously ordered, and on a sound system," successfully encourages in the boys the self-discipline and self-surveillance that, according to Foucault, leads to an "'integrated' system" of disciplinary power which functions as "a network of relations": "Discipline makes possible the operation of a relational

power that sustains itself by its own mechanism and which, for the spectacle of public events, substitutes the uninterrupted play of calculated gazes" (*Discipline* 176-77). Dr. Strong's school illustrates such an uninterrupted play of gazes. The ostensible reason for the success of Dr. Strong's is the traditional liberal-bourgeois appeal to the "honour and good faith of the boys," but this appeal disguises that network of discreet surveillance which ensures that the boys behave according to the norms the system perpetuates: in one of those revealing parentheses David says "I never knew, in all my time, of any other boy being otherwise [than attached to the school]," a discreet checking up on the behaviour of others, who no doubt return the compliment. Furthermore, the whole school is subject to an unobtrusive public scrutiny: "we were well spoken of in the town, and rarely did any disgrace, by our appearance and manner, to the reputation of Doctor Strong."

In addition to being, like Salem House, the site of a disciplinary gaze, Dr. Strong's school is not entirely free of the violence of Creakle's establishment, although significantly this violence is inflicted upon the lower class. David's resentment, which finds its release in the fights he has with the butcher, has two sources. The first is the physical victimisation suffered literally at the hands of Creakle and his partner in violence, the bull-necked Tungay (ch. 5; 129); his fight with the "bull-necked, young butcher" (ch. 18; 324) may be seen as David's revenge for his harsh treatment at Salem House. The second source of his resentment is David's sense of class superiority, his gentlemanliness, which the lower-class butcher, who is seconded in his fight with David "by two other butchers, a young publican, and a sweep" (324), so openly disparages. The butcher's challenge to David's new-found status as a young gentleman must be met with violence. Even Agnes condones it: "she thinks I couldn't have done otherwise than fight the butcher" (325). His glorious defeat of the butcher in his second bout of fisticuffs (329) signals David's triumph over his working-class experiences, and he can, from his superior position on the box seat of the London coach, contemplate throwing the butcher "five shillings to drink" (ch. 19; 340). David's gentlemanly superiority, learned from Aunt Betsey and Dr. Strong, is threatened from below, but its victory ironically is achieved by the very weapon to which the lower classes resort and which David so roundly condemns at Salem House, namely violence.

But the butcher, too, eventually learns the lessons of middle-class discipline. David, in one of his frequent trips to Canterbury, sees him "in business for himself" and suitably domesticated, "nursing a baby" (ch. 52; 811). He is now "a benignant member of society" (811) to the extent that he finally becomes a constable. The originally rebellious butcher has been completely absorbed into the fabric of bourgeois society, his potentially disruptive violence now controlled by and in the service of the class he formerly opposed. There is no more significant parenthesis (and significant *because* a parenthesis) than the one which reveals the marriage of capitalism and the police state: "I walked through the streets; and once more seeing my old adversary the butcher—now a constable, with his staff hanging up in the shop—went down to look at the place where I had fought him" (ch. 60; 913-14).

Until David is fully educated in the bourgeois self-discipline of Dr. Strong's school, Aunt Betsey ensures the continuation of her own surveillance. As David says, "While I was yet new at Doctor Strong's, she made several excursions over to Canterbury to see me, and always at unseasonable hours: with the view, I suppose, of taking me by surprise. But, finding me well employed, and bearing a good character, and hearing on all hands that I rose fast in the school, she soon discontinued these visits" (ch. 17; 306). Although she now finds the schoolboy David a fully fledged member of the Victorian bourgeoisie (he works hard, is morally upstanding, and is successful), she still keeps tabs on her nephew through his visits to Dover "every third or fourth week" (306), as well as through Mr. Dick's fortnightly visits to him at Canterbury. According to Foucault "from such trifles, no doubt, the man of modern humanism was born" (*Discipline* 141), just as David's humanism is nurtured by the mundane, apparently insignificant minutiae of his aunt's disciplining. Foucault also writes: "[d]iscipline is a political anatomy of detail . . . [t]here is a whole history to be written . . . of the utilitarian rationalization of detail in moral accountability and political control" (139). Betsey holds David morally accountable and subjects him to her political control.

After he graduates from Dr. Strong's, Aunt Betsey tests David's self-discipline by sending him on an expedition to London and Suffolk in order to "look about him." She maintains her surveillance under the guise of giving David his freedom: "I was at liberty to do what I would, for three weeks or a month; and no other conditions were imposed upon my freedom than the beforementioned thinking and looking about me, and a pledge to write three times a week and faithfully report myself" (ch. 19; 332-33). What kind of freedom is that, we may ask? And Agnes is ever present, hovering around David as his "good angel." We might prefer to apply to her Esther Summerson's phrase for Mrs. Pardiggle in *Bleak House*: "an inexorable moral Policeman" (ch. 8; 158). There is no escape for David from the moral and social imperatives which weave the network of disciplinary surveillance that entraps him.

This pattern of disciplinary surveillance is repeated in David's working life. As "a little labouring hind in the service of Murdstone and Grinby" (ch. 11; 208), he is subject to the vigilance of Quinion, who watches David "through a window above the desk" (209), and David knuckles down to the task of washing bottles so well that he becomes "at least as expeditious and as skilful as either of the other boys" (218). His first job after leaving Dr. Strong's school is as proctor in the firm of Spenlow and Jorkins, but this does not provide the necessary discipline required to make David a fully paid-up member of the bourgeoisie; Aunt Betsey once more steps in to supply the discipline by ceasing to supply the money. Betsey loses her fortune by unwisely investing it with Wickfield's firm, now run by the unscrupulous Heep, although she still has two thousand pounds, something she conceals from both David and the reader. Thus David is thrown back on himself, the self that has already been formed by the Murdstones, Salem House, the bottling warehouse, Aunt Betsey, and Dr. Strong: "what I had to do, was, to turn the painful discipline of my younger days to account, by going to work with a resolute and steady heart" (ch. 36; 582). It is, perhaps, the only time in the novel that David uses the word "discipline" to refer not to "the first mistaken impulse of an undisciplined heart" but to the totality of his past experiences. And so he becomes, in addition to a proctor, a parliamentary reporter, secretary to Dr. Strong, and, of course, famous writer. He remarks that Mr. Dick feared "no galley-slave or convict worked as I did" (589), and his seventeen-hour working day includes the immense discipline, determination and perseverance needed to master the "despotic characters" (ch. 38; 609) of the system of shorthand.[5] This "desperate firmness" (ch. 37; 600) as he calls it is, of course, in the service of Dora, but it also confirms his aunt's faith in him, so much so that he passes her "trial" of him with flying colors. Anticipating Magwitch's praise of Pip in *Great Expectations,* she says: "'you came out nobly—persevering, self-reliant, self-denying!'" (ch. 54; 847). In a word, disciplined.

Dora, however, fails her husband's test of her. That firmness which he has inherited from his stepfather and aunt David does not find in his wife. His attempt to "form her mind" (ch. 48; 762) as Murdstone had formed his mother's, is a failure, and discipline in the domestic sphere is as essential for Victorian bourgeois success as it is in the public. Beneath the comic extravagance of those chapters which describe the domestic chaos of the Copperfield's housekeeping, Dickens drives home his point: "system and management" (760) in the house are twin pillars of middle-class domestic ideology.

Dora's want of household system and management, symbolised by the cookery book which becomes Jip's "plaything" (Vanden Bossche 96), is supplied by Aunt Betsey and Peggoty as David strives to make his own way in the world. Ultimately they relinquish this role to Agnes who, from her very first appearance, carries by her side that perennial symbol of Dickensian household management, a basket of keys, and who "looked as staid and as discreet a housekeeper as the old house could have" (ch. 15; 280). In Foucault's book, the most effective disciplinary technologies are those which are invisible: Agnes may be David's invisible spiritual icon, the stained-glass window that is his guiding moral principle, but it is her domestic discretion that so powerfully attracts David. At one point David asks her what is the secret of her influence over him, to which she does not reply: "Her head was bent down, looking at the fire" (ch. 39; 631). She is crestfallen at David's blindness to her love for him, but the gesture also suggests that her secret is her secrecy, that unstated and invisible skill at managing the home, the center of which is the fire. Agnes is the angel in the house not just because of her spirituality but because, without a flutter of her wings, she brings about that calm orderliness which David's domestic life so desperately needs. Subsequent to her financial losses, Aunt Betsey arrives at David's London rooms where Agnes's "noiseless presence" at once tidies, orders, and arranges: "I knew who had done all this, by its seeming to have quietly done itself . . . and I [looked] on, thinking how little Peggotty seemed to do with a good deal of bustle, and how much Agnes did without any bustle at all" (ch. 35; 576). David's observations point up, if they do not explain, why, of these two housekeepers, one remains angelically pure and the other's forefinger is roughened by a pocket nutmeg grater.

How Agnes manages to keep her various households clean and tidy without actually *doing* any cleaning and tidying is never explained. Servants, of course, are the answer—except for David and Dora who are subject to the "Ordeal of Servants" as David calls it (ch. 44; 707). They are continually exploited by a series of supremely inefficient domestics ranging from the thieving page to the Paragon, whose "cousin in the Life-Guards" (702) deserts in favor of the newly-weds' coal-hole, only to be arrested "by a piquet of his companions in arms, who took him away handcuffed" (707). The law interrupts even domestic bliss, especially when it is chaotic. Clearly the efficient management of servants is a cornerstone of domestic harmony: even the Micawbers have the Orfling. But at the Wickfield household there *are* no servants—or at least none are mentioned.[6] Agnes is so efficient that she has managed *not* to dispense with them (they are, after all, indispensable): rather she has them disappear. They are even less than children: they are neither seen nor heard. For Foucault control is most complete when it is subtle, insidious, and invisible (because unlocatable); it is the idea of surveillance rather than surveillance itself that controls. Agnes is the supreme embodiment of surveillance in ***David Copperfield.*** The invisible network of servants which sustains the household economy of the Wickfields is "seen" again at the end of the novel where David and Agnes, after ten years of domestic bliss, are shown "sitting by the fire, in our house in London, one night in spring, and three of our children were playing in the room" (ch. 63; 939). And not a servant in sight. The "discreet housekeeper" we first meet in chapter 15 maintains her discretion to the end. For David she has always been identified with the idea of Home. On his return from Switzerland his sense that he will never marry Agnes is expressed in the following way: "Home, in its best sense, was for me no more," while his consolation is that he will "calmly hold the place in her home which she had calmly held in mine" (ch. 59; 902-03). We expect "heart" rather than "home"; at this point they are one and the same. When David and Agnes visit Aunt Betsey to break the news of their love for one another, she asks "'who's this you're bringing home?' 'Agnes,' said I" (ch. 62; 937). Aunt Betsey can now cease her surveillance of David safe in the knowledge that Agnes will continue her role. Thus the disciplining of David Copperfield has passed from the steely gaze of Jane Murdstone, to the more discreet watchfulness of Aunt Betsey, and finally to the more or less invisible "presence" of Agnes.

As David's wife, mother of his children, supervisor of the household, in short his Home, Agnes is the one who "controls" David, not in the sense of dominating him but in the Foucauldian sense of control and power as a function of relationships; power is not on the "outside" to be owned but is embedded in the "practices and relations that constitute it" (Seltzer 153). As Foucault says in *The History of Sexuality,* "power is tolerable only on condition that it mask a substantial part of itself. Its success is proportional to its ability to hide its own mechanisms . . . For it, secrecy is not in the nature of an abuse; it is indispensable to its operation" (1: 86). In that sense Agnes, the "presence" who haunts David and embodies the notion of Home which is only fleetingly glimpsed at the end of the novel, is the most powerful figure of all. She presides over the family which, according to Musselwhite, is "the principal means by which the 'idea of the state' comes to be internalized and subjectivized" (9).

I have traced the process from David's earliest incarceration in his bedroom by Murdstone through the various disciplinary mechanisms, both overt and covert, to which he is subjected, until he arrives at that most discreet and tactful institution of social control, the family. Several critics have argued persuasively that the family became in the nineteenth century an instrument of social discipline, a self-regulating institution whose differences from the prison were more apparent than real.[7] Only if families failed to regulate themselves did formal institutions such as orphanages, workhouses, homes for fallen women, and prisons impose external discipline. Thus the carceral and the familiar were two sides of the same coin and though the lines of demarcation were clear, "it was alarmingly easy to cross them"

(Miller 59). The Micawbers are a wonderful example of this, as there is no difference between the Micawbers in prison and out of it. While at home Mr. Micawber is a prisoner because, on occasions, he cannot leave it for fear of being arrested for debt, but while in prison he is at home: he supervises a dinner of mutton, his wife and children move in, they play skittles and cards, Micawber acquires his own room, and presides over an informal club within the prison walls (ch. 11; 221-25). In fact Micawber's life is far more ordered and disciplined at the King's Bench Prison than in his various lodgings. The family demands self-regulation, a lesson that David, of course, must learn from bitter experience, but he, unlike the reader, fails to see the relevance of the Micawbers to his own later marriage to Dora. If the family, like the Micawbers, does not regulate itself, regulation is imposed, whether it be through imprisonment or emigration to Australia, that colonial dust heap for criminals and social outcasts. If there is no essential difference between the prison and the family, then neither is there between the prison and Australia whose shores are a somewhat larger version of the walls of the prison in Borough High Street. Is it so surprising, then, that the improvident Micawber, formerly father of the King's Bench, should end up as magistrate of Port Middlebay? "Is it surprising," asks Foucault, "that prisons resemble factories, schools, barracks, hospitals, which all resemble prisons?" (*Discipline* 228).

Agnes is thus the culmination of that process which Foucault traces in *Discipline and Punish* and which is David's destiny. She represents "a new kind of power, not repressive or authoritarian, but concerned and caring" (Nead 208), a figure who, like Maggie Verver in James's *The Golden Bowl,* deploys a "vigilance of 'care'" which operates as a strategy of control (Seltzer 59). The home or the family is the site for such regulatory operations, such "disciplinary intimacy," and such a "gentle way in punishment."[8] Agnes exercises the "power of domestic surveillance" (19) which Nancy Armstrong identifies as crucial to changes in the political and social economy of the nineteenth century,[9] and that contributed to the rise of female authority both in the home and in the novel. Agnes's invisible work which magically orders the household and is the emblem, paradoxically, of her disciplinary intimacy, finds its parallel in the more or less invisible work of David as writer. Mary Poovey has brilliantly analysed how this invisibility actually masks the contradictions in class and gender inherent in the novel:

> If Agnes and the home implicitly collude in covering over the hypocrisy and alienation that pervade class society, then so does the literary man. In fact, the literary man derives the terms of his ideological work from the idealized vision of domestic labour epitomized in Agnes. Like a good housekeeper, the good writer works invisibly, quietly, without calling attention to his labor; both master dirt and misery by putting things in their

proper places; both create a sphere to which one can retreat—a literal or imaginative hearth where anxiety and competition subside, where one's motives do not appear as something other than what they are because self-interest and self-denial really are the same.

(122)

I would like to emphasise that Agnes is not, as most critics see her, simply David's spiritual guide with finger pointing ever upwards, or the supreme household manager, but, in Poovey's phrase, is "the idealized vision of domestic labor," the young writer's muse.[10] Dora can only sharpen David's pens and copy the odd page of manuscript, whereas Agnes is David's creative inspiration and helpmate. The more famous and successful an author David becomes, the closer he approaches union with Agnes; she symbolises that goal of artistic perfection he seeks. In finding and marrying her David discovers his own identity and purpose. That identity, in Micawber's phrase, is "David Copperfield . . . Eminent Author" (ch. 63; 945), and that purpose is to write. When, following Dora's death, he returns from Switzerland to England and to Agnes, the rest of David's working life is spent writing novels—at home. Hence the famous separate spheres of public and private here merge because David's work is true domestic labor—performed at home with Agnes. The penultimate paragraph of the novel, presumably written as Agnes is beside David, reads: "My lamp burns low, and I have written far into the night; but the dear presence, without which I were nothing, bears me company" (ch. 64; 950). As Alexander Welsh points out, the lamp "is literally the writing lamp that burns low, figuratively the lamp of life" (113); here the spiritual, the domestic and the professional come together.

While Poovey works out in terms of class and gender the implications of this merging of private and public spheres, I want to pursue the implications of David as writer, in terms similar to those which I used to explore his disciplinary training. To do this, I find it useful to invoke Bentham's notion of the panopticon, an architectural structure which consisted of a courtyard made up of separate cells on the perimeter watched over by an observer in a central tower. Its crucial feature was that prisoners could neither see one another nor know whether they were subject to observation from the central tower. Thus discipline was enforced by a power that was ultimately invisible: the observer could leave the central tower and the inmates would not know this, yet they would act as if they were under overt surveillance. For Foucault the panopticon became the model for the new disciplinary technologies, "a generalizable model of functioning; a way of defining power relations in terms of the everyday life of men . . . the diagram of a mechanism of power reduced to its ideal form . . . which can be implemented in hospitals, workshops, schools, prisons" (*Discipline* 205). And in the novel.[11]

David, having fully absorbed and internalized Agnes's discipline, now speaks from his comfortable middle class station as writer and observer. His panoptical position as central character and only narrator gives him total control and omniscience.[12] All characters are subject to David's disciplinary gaze: he controls, observes, and allocates roles in the prison that is his novel within which his characters (and himself) are trapped.

Dickens experienced considerable difficulty deciding on a title for his novel. Four of his trial titles begin "The Copperfield Survey of the World" (the novel was actually advertised in this way), before he settled on the existing title which reads in full "The Personal History, Adventures, Experience, & Observation of David Copperfield the Younger of Blunderstone Rookery (Which He never meant to be Published on any Account)".[13] As this title implies, David is the observer *par excellence;* as soon as he is physically able to observe, he does. "I Observe" is the title of chapter 2, and he also lays claim to being a "child of close observation" (61). In that chapter he remarks: "I could observe, in little pieces, as it were; but as to making a net of a number of these pieces, and catching anybody in it, that was, as yet, beyond me" (70). The "as yet" is important. By the end of the novel, David has disciplined himself sufficiently to be able to catch anything and everybody in the net of his observation. But, as in the panopticon, nobody is aware of David's observation. It is not the structure of *David Copperfield* which replicates the panopticon (Musselwhite 216), so much as it is the idea of surveillance and invisibility that informs both. The ultimate effect of the panopticon is that the central observer is himself the object of scrutiny; in this case David, as we have seen, is observed primarily by Aunt Betsey and Agnes, but also by the reader, a point to which I shall return. Rabinow, who writes that "[t]hose who occupy the central position in the panopticon are themselves thoroughly enmeshed in a localization and ordering of their own behavior," quotes Foucault: "Such is perhaps the most diabolical aspect of the idea and of all the applications it brought about" (19).

Thus the novel is David's panoptic prison: he is at once the prison guard, surveying his characters (including his younger self), who are unseen by him, in his all-seeing position as retrospective narrator and novelist, and he is also prisoner *of* his own novel, entrapped by his own construction, enmeshed in his own web of words, that network of observations which catches everybody, including himself, incarcerated within the walls (the covers) of his own book, without which he would and could not exist. Hence he can have no existence other than that of prisoner; the condition for his very being is entrapment at the moment he believes himself most liberated—as husband, father, and successful novelist. The title of the novel is thus multiple-edged. Where we might expect the plural "observations" we get the singular: the "observation" *by* David *of* others; also *of* David *by* Murdstone, Betsey, and the rest; the observation *of* the younger David *by* his elder self; and, in the final instance, the observation *of* this mature narrator *by* the reader.

The reader observes David but the reader is also observed by Dickens, and vice-versa. It is at the point where the Victorian reader of 1850 buys the final monthly number, or the first full volume of the novel, that I wish to conclude. As Terry Eagleton says, the reading and experience of a novel is part of the individual's cultural formation: "Literature is a vital instrument for the insertion of individuals into the perceptual and symbolic forms of the dominant ideological formation" (52). The Victorian novel was not merely an instrument for this process but, as we all know, one of the great institutions of the period, an institution as influential as any of the more obvious state apparatuses which exercised power and control over its people. If *David Copperfield* is socially disciplined by the discreet influence of his aunt and of Agnes, so too is the reader, by being inscribed as a member of a middle class which holds certain values and assumptions. The text positions the reader in such a way as to demand compliance with its ideological underpinnings. The reader of the 1990s can resist such demands; the reader of the 1850s was less able to do so. In this sense, the immense popularity of *David Copperfield* shows its readers willingly embracing its value system. Thus the reviewer in *Fraser's Magazine* of December 1850 states that Dickens is so popular "above all, because of his deep reverence for the household sanctities, his enthusiastic worship of the household gods" (qtd. in Poovey 109). The following comment on the novel by Forster might well stand as the establishment's pronouncement on the high noon of Victorian middle-class ideology: "By the course of the events we learn the value of self-denial and patience, quiet endurance of unavoidable ills, strenuous effort against ills remediable; and everything in the fortunes of the actors warns us, to strengthen our generous emotions and to guard the purities of home. It is easy thus to account for the supreme popularity of *Copperfield*" (2: 106-7). There is a reciprocation of intent and reception, an agreeable collusion of author and audience who share a comfortable *view* of the world. Unlike his other novels which so disturbed the complacency of his middle-class readers by their trenchant social criticism, Dickens's *David Copperfield* confirms, constructs, and simultaneously (yet unknowingly) challenges this complacency in the tensions, contradictions, omissions, and silences which are inevitably the hallmark of literature that seeks to mask them. *David Copperfield* is, in Feinberg's paraphrase of Fredric Jameson, "an imaginary construct which pretends to resolve cultural antinomies by casting such contradictions into intelligible narratives" (16).

The reception in 1850 of the novel *David Copperfield* was part of a process of cultural formation, a historical event as important in its own way as the Great Exhibition of the following year. Like no other novelist of his day, Dickens was a public figure, the publication of his novels significant cultural events at which his readers could celebrate and thus confirm the tastes and values that they shared with their author. That agreeable collusion of author and audience that I have just mentioned is most obvious in Dickens's response to his readers' complaints or compliments, the best example in *David Copperfield* being, of course, the change in Miss Mowcher's character subsequent to Dickens reading a letter from Mrs. Seymour Hill, who was greatly offended by his original portrait. But Dickens was never one to defer to anybody, and, while his audience influenced his novels locally, it was the Inimitable who surely exercised a greater degree of influence and control over his readers than they did over him. He obviously immensely enjoyed his relationship with his audience but nonetheless wielded the ultimate authority. In the public readings, those cultural phenomena of the late 1850s and 1860s, Dickens relished his hold on his listeners. He wrote "what a thing it is to have power," and that it was "a great sensation to have a large audience in one's hand" (*The Public Readings,* xviii, xxii). And, in turn, his audiences loved the readings so much that, like Oliver, they asked for more. Foucault's notion of power is a perfect explanation for what went on between Dickens and his audience at these public readings. Power is not hierarchical, a force that those on top use to oppress those at the bottom, but "it traverses and produces things, it induces pleasure, forms knowledge, produces discourse" (qtd. in Rabinow 61). In 1846, anticipating the power and control he later exercised as a public reader, Dickens wrote to Lord Morpeth: "I have hoped, for years, that I may become at last a Police Magistrate" (*Letters* 566-67). This reminds one of Zola's definition of the novelist: "We novelists," he wrote in 1893, "are the examining magistrates of men and their passions" (qtd. in Seltzer 85).

If Agnes is David's "inexorable moral policeman," then Dickens is that of his contemporary readers: his novel, written and read, "as a form and as an institution, reinscribes and supplements social mechanisms of policing and regulation" (Seltzer 19). Nowhere is disciplinary control felt more acutely or exercised more effectively than in the bosom of the family. It is at home that David writes *David Copperfield*; it was at home that Dickens wrote it;[14] and it was, for the most part, at home that it was read: both silently in the privacy of bedroom or boudoir, and, increasingly in the nineteenth century, aloud by the father standing at the family hearth. As Brodhead notes (90) the *practice* of reading novels aloud, like saying grace at meal times or reciting biblical passages before the assembled household, became another mechanism which established the family as a

unit of control. And this control was extended beyond the family, in an attempt to enlarge the very definition of family, through the well-known practice of reading Dickens's monthly numbers in pubs and on street corners or, as just mentioned, in Dickens's own, later, public readings which were the *paterfamilias*'s domestic readings writ large.[15] Such practices established a sense of community, of family, and they were accompanied by that intimacy with which Agnes seeks to discipline David. The disciplining of David Copperfield's personal history is thus also the story of the radical entanglement of Dickens, his readers, and the institutions of the novel and the family with the processes of cultural formation and social control.

Notes

1. The classic exposition is Needham's.

2. I am considerably indebted to Miller's ch. 6, but whereas he writes that "the discipline from which he [David] has escaped to become the 'subject of the Novel' reappears as his own self-discipline" (216), I emphasize the crucial roles played by Aunt Betsey and Agnes Wickfield and the continuity between his childhood, adolescent and adult experiences. Miller (214ff) convincingly shows how David's writing at once both conceals and reveals his self, but mentions Agnes only briefly (218). Building on Poovey's analysis of Agnes in relation to David as writer, I elaborate on her role as David's muse and invoke Foucault's version of Bentham's panopticon to discuss David's status as invisible, all-powerful, yet incarcerated novelist. I deliberately omit discussing David's visit to the model prison in chapter 62 because of Miller's brilliant analysis (217-19). On this point see also Musselwhite (215-16).

3. I am indebted in the following discussion to the Schroeders, who draw attention to the numerous parallels between Aunt Betsey and Jane Murdstone. But whereas they focus on Betsey's psychological progress as she rejects her double as "an unwholesomely manipulative and misanthropic part of her own nature" (269), I emphasise the cultural and historical dimensions of the relationship (especially as it pertains to David's so-called development), and also the connections between Aunt Betsey and Edward Murdstone rather than, as the Schroeders do, the links between the two women.

4. A notable exception is Eigner, to whom I am indebted for my discussion of Betsey's firmness.

5. Significantly Foucault specifies handwriting as one of those practises which ensures a "well-disciplined body" (152), a point illustrated by the photograph overleaf from page 169. David's hand-

book was *Brachygraphy, or an Easy and Compendious System of Shorthand* (1750), by Thomas Gurney, the first official shorthand writer at the Old Bailey. The link between discipline, handwriting, and the law is also exemplified by that most undisciplined of characters, Mr. Dick, a neat penman (ch. 36; 590) who, as copyist of Traddles's legal documents, learns "instructions," resoluteness, and an "orderly business-like manner" (591), a comic parallel to David's more serious endeavors. Later Sophy, as her husband's copying clerk, displays an "extraordinarily legal and formal . . . stiff hand" acquired "from a pattern" (ch. 61; 918-19). Dickens himself, of course, was famous for his accurate and rapid shorthand reporting of Parliament's proceedings.

6. A point also noted by Vanden Bossche who, however, explains this as merely "because she [Agnes] is herself a housekeeper" (99) without pursuing the implications of this invisible control.

7. For an excellent brief account see section B in Feinberg. See also Brodhead 70-74, Malone 16-17, Miller ch. 3, esp. 102-05, and Seltzer 122-24.

8. The first phrase is Brodhead's, whose discussion (70-74) is relevant here; the second phrase is the title of ch. 4 of Foucault's *Discipline and Punish*.

9. My interpretation supports the argument of *Desire and Domestic Fiction* and adds *David Copperfield* to the tradition of domestic fiction which Armstrong traces from Richardson to Woolf. *David Copperfield* is undoubtedly Dickens's most domestic novel; that it is narrated by a man need not disturb us, for as we have seen, not only does David cede, as all good middle class Victorian husbands did, control of the home to Agnes, but as we shall see, he writes his novel at home: in this sense, *David Copperfield* is true domestic fiction.

10. The point is also discussed by Welsh 112-15.

11. Foucault's reticence on the role played by literature, both as text and as institution, in the disciplinary process is noted by Miller who quotes Foucault himself: "On every occasion I made literature the object of a report, not of an analysis and not of a reduction to, or an integration into, the very field of analysis" (viii). However, Seltzer (170) argues that Foucault's attitude changed from viewing literature in opposition to politics to identifying it as just one among many discourses, functioning as part of a more general ideology of power. This latter position is clearly my own.

12. See also Musselwhite who, in his discussion of the Pentonville system in the problematic ch. 61 ("I am shown Two Interesting Penitents"), briefly notes that "[t]he book is like a panopticon with the magisterial 'I observe' at the centre surrounded by sets of relationships which exist in forlornly separate cells" and that "Dickens is, by this time, locked in his own class 'system'" (216). Unlike Musselwhite, however, I pursue the idea of David as observer (see n. 13) and controller.

13. Is it a coincidence that both Dickens and Foucault had trouble with the notion of observation/ surveillance in their titles? Alan Sheridan, in attempting to translate into English the original title *Suveiller et punir,* discusses the various options which Dickens himself must have canvassed before settling on "observation":

> The verb 'surveiller' has no adequate English equivalent. Our noun 'surveillance' has an altogether too restricted and technical use. Jeremy Bentham used the word 'inspect' which Foucault translates as 'surveiller'—but the range of connotations does not correspond. 'Supervise' is perhaps closest of all, but again the word has different associations. 'Observe' is rather too neutral, though Foucault is aware of the aggression involved in any one-sided observation. In the end Foucault himself suggested *Discipline and Punish,* which relates closely to the book's structure.

(Translator's Note)

14. Although Dickens wrote the novel at various places (London, Brighton, Broadstairs, Bonchurch), his family was present throughout. For a different interpretation see Vanden Bossche 105-06.

15. Miller, in discussing *Bleak House* and its serial format (82-83), writes interestingly of how reading that novel replicates the rhythms of public and private life, as readers move from one to the other and back again. Dickens's public readings are also central to this process.

Works Cited

Armstrong, Nancy. *Desire and Domestic Fiction: A Political History of the Novel.* New York: Oxford UP, 1987.

Atwood, Margaret. *Bodily Harm.* London: Virago Press, 1982.

Brodhead, Richard. "Sparing the Rod: Discipline and Fiction in Antebellum America." *Representations* 21 (1988): 67-96.

Collins, Philip. *Dickens and Education.* London: Macmillan, 1965.

Dickens, Charles. *Bleak House*. Ed. Norman Page. Harmondsworth: Penguin, 1971.

———. *David Copperfield*. Ed. Trevor Blount. Harmondsworth: Penguin, 1966.

———. *The Letters of Charles Dickens*. Pilgrim Edition. Ed. Kathleen Tillotson. Vol. 4. Oxford: Clarendon Press, 1977.

———. *The Public Readings*. Ed. Philip Collins. Oxford: Clarendon Press, 1975.

Eagleton, Terry. *Criticism and Ideology*. London: Verso, 1977.

Eigner, Edward M. "David Copperfield and the Benevolent Spirit." *Dickens Studies Annual* 14 (1985): 1-15.

Feinberg, Monica. "Family Plot: The Bleak House of Victorian Romance." *Victorian Newsletter* 76 (1989): 5-17.

Forster, John. *The Life of Charles Dickens*. Ed. A. J. Hoppe. 2 vols. London: Dent, 1969.

Foucault, Michel. *Discipline and Punish: The Birth of the Prison*. Trans. Alan Sheridan. New York: Vintage Books, 1979.

———. *The History of Sexuality*. 2 vols. New York: Random House, 1980.

Malone, Cynthia Northcutt. "The Fixed Eye and the Rolling Eye: Surveillance and Discipline in *Hard Times*." *Studies in the Novel* 21 (1989): 14-26.

Miller, D. A. *The Novel and the Police*. Berkeley: California UP, 1988.

Musselwhite, David. *Partings Welded Together: Politics and Desire in the Nineteenth Century Novel*. London: Methuen, 1987.

Nead, Lynda. *Myths of Sexuality: Representations of Women in Victorian Britain*. New York: Blackwell, 1988.

Needham, Gwendolen. "The Undisciplined Heart of David Copperfield." *Nineteenth Century Fiction* 9 (1954): 81-107.

Poovey, Mary. *Uneven Developments: The Ideological Work of Gender in Mid-Victorian England*. London: Virago Press, 1989.

Rabinow, Paul, ed. *The Foucault Reader*. Harmondsworth: Penguin, 1984.

Schroeder, Natalie, and Ronald A. Schroeder. "Betsey Trotwood and Jane Murdstone: Dickensian Doubles." *Studies in the Novel* 21 (1989): 268-78.

Seltzer, Mark. *Henry James and the Art of Power*. Ithaca: Cornell UP, 1984.

Vanden Bossche, Chris R. "Cookery Not Rookery: Family and Class in *David Copperfield*." *Dickens Studies Annual* 15 (1986): 87-109.

Welsh, Alexander. *From Copyright to Copperfield: The Identity of Dickens*. Cambridge: Harvard UP, 1987.

Steve Hake (essay date 1998)

SOURCE: Hake, Steve. "Becoming Poor to Make Many Rich: The Resolution of Class Conflict in Dickens." *Dickens Studies Annual* 26 (1998): 107-19.

[*In the following essay, Hake considers Dickens's resolution of* David Copperfield's *class conflicts in Christian terms—with the poor sacrificing for the rich.*]

Class conflict worried Dickens. He announced that the purpose of *Household Words* was no less than "'to bring the greater and lesser in degree, together . . . and mutually dispose them to a better acquaintance and a kinder understanding.' In a word, he was promising to root out social disharmony" (Marlow 145). Myron Magnet, in *Dickens and the Social Order,* argues that Dickens believed that the upper classes have a responsibility to educate and humanize the lower classes: "No ruling class has a right to withhold the means—material, social, spiritual—of raising life above the merely brutal and savage" (200).

However, if we look carefully at his novels, we can see that it is often the "brutish" lower classes who humanize those above them. Marxists also see "salvation" as coming from below—the lower classes overthrow the upper—but Dickens' views are not necessarily those of Karl Marx. Perhaps this explains why the socialist playwright and critic George Bernard Shaw sees a gap in Dickens at this point. Dan H. Laurence and Martin Quinn observe that, "although both Shaw and Dickens were extremely sensitive to social disorder. Shaw, the Socialist, had a cause while Dickens—and, by extension, Shakespeare—did not" (xxii).

Because Dickens' "cause" was not that of socialism, it went unrecognized by critics such as Shaw. English and American critics in general have been very slow to recognize the depth of Dickens' Christian faith, particularly as reflected in his major novels.[1] His resolution of class conflict is a striking instance of this.

In Dickens, class tensions are resolved by a Christian concept of salvation through a forgiving and self-sacrificing love. Christianity always works from the bottom up. God was not incarnated as an aristocrat, but rather as a son in a poor, working-class family. Christ, though He was rich, became poor that He might make many rich (cf. II Cor.8:9). We see this pattern reflected in the way working-class people in Dickens suffer for and save the rich and sophisticated, or those who aspire to be rich and sophisticated. Dickens thus reflects the Bible's emphasis that it is often the poor and socially despised who are the first to enter the kingdom of God (Matt. 21:31 and Luke 7:29) and the rich and sophisticated who are scarcely able to enter at all (Matt. 19:24, Mark 10:25 and Luke 18:25). In Dickens it is most often the poor who are portrayed as having solid Christian values (cf. the Peggottys, Ham, Joe Gargery, and Lizzie Hexam). The rich, however, are seen as vain, tormented and in need of salvation (cf. Steerforth, his mother, Estella, Miss Havisham and Eugene Wrayburn). Those who aspire to "raise" themselves to a higher class (cf. Emily and Pip) are often seen as losing in the attempt much more than they gain. I will examine this aspect of *David Copperfield,* yet also make comparisons to *Great Expectations* and *Our Mutual Friend.*

Not only can we see class conflict resolved by the suffering and death of the poor for the rich, but we can also see a definite development of this idea as it took deeper root in Dickens' mind and art. Emily aspires to be a lady even before she meets Steerforth. She is thus ripe for Steerforth's deceptive promises and plunges herself into misery. She is saved by her own repentance and by the suffering love of Mr. Peggotty and Ham. Neither Emily nor the Peggotties, however, are able to save Steerforth, though Ham dies in the attempt, perhaps because there is a tinge of Steerforth even in them. They also encouraged Emily, though inadvertently, in her desires to be a lady, and they were also deceived by Steerforth. In this they are in significant contrast to both Joe and Biddy in *Great Expectations,* who were consistently aware of what was happening to Pip. Pip aspires to be a gentleman only after meeting Estella and only in order to win Estella. He too is saved by the long-suffering, forgiving love of Joe Gargery, no less real than, though not so dramatic as, the wanderings of Mr. Peggotty and the death of Ham. As Pip's warped values come back into focus, he is able in turn, by the vivid example of his own suffering and forgiving love, to rescue first Miss Havisham and finally even Estella[2] from their own unbending aristocratic pride and bitterness. So the upwardly aspiring person in *David Copperfield,* Emily, is able only barely to save herself and not able to save her aristocratic lover. In *Great Expectations,* Pip is not so early set on upward aspirations and so is able to save both himself, Estella, and Estella's mother.[3] In Dickens' last completed novel, *Our Mutual Friend,* Lizzie Hexam does not aspire to be a lady at all and so in a sense needs no salvation herself, and she succeeds in redeeming her Steerforth-like lover, Eugene Wrayburn. That social station to which Lizzie did not aspire, she is yet granted as the novel concludes, in that Eugene makes her a lady. Yet what she gives to Wrayburn is infinitely greater than what he gives to her. Wrayburn lifts her up socially, but she lifts him up spiritually. He

makes a "lady" of her, but she makes a man of him. So we can see a clear progression in the art of Dickens in which the poor grow in confidence in their spiritual riches in Christ, and thus in their ability to withstand the temptations of the deceptive worldly riches of the upper classes.

Emily's "Fall" Into the Upper Class

In *David Copperfield* Mr. Peggotty and Ham suffer for and save the would-be lady, Emily. Emily aspires to be a lady long before she meets Steerforth. When she and David first meet as little children, she already has very definite ideas about the clothing she would give to her uncle if she were a lady. Although she expresses this desire in generous terms, David even as a child can see the inappropriateness of this method of expressing her gratitude to her uncle. Perhaps the fact that she was "spoiled by them all [e.g., all the Peggottys]" (141) accounts in part for this aspiration. They set her apart, and in this way perhaps contribute, however inadvertantly, to her later fall. Mr. Omer observes that she has "elegant taste in the dress-making business" (305), so much so that no duchess can touch her, and that all the village women are jealous of her beauty and resentful of her aspirations to be a lady.

David, Mr. Peggotty, and Ham also contribute, albeit unwittingly, to Emily's fall in that they are first captivated by Steerforth: Emily learns of him through these men already so close to her. As they praised him, she sat "listening with the deepest attention" (143). When she meets him, she, too, is captivated: "She soon became more assured when she found how gently and respectfully Steerforth spoke to her; how skilfully he avoided anything that would embarrass her" (316). David says that Steerforth brought them all, "by degrees, into a charmed circle" and Mrs. Gummidge says she felt "bewitched" (316).

Emily is thus removing herself gradually from the solid world view of the working-class Peggoties, and transforming her allegiance to the outwardly impressive but ultimately empty values of the upper-class Steerforth. Even she has already begun to do this before meeting him in her desire to become a "lady"; his appearance accelerates, gives specific focus to, and completes the process. Dickens continues to prepare us for Emily's outward flight and to chronicle her gradual inward fall in many subtle ways. After meeting Steerforth, Emily keeps away from Ham in his presence. Martha also appears as a "disturbing shadow" (325) of a fallen woman. Emily is associated with the devouring sea and shipwrecks. Mr. Peggotty cannot bear to see Emily and Martha side by side "for all the treasures that's wrecked in the sea" (337). Steerforth's boat was originally named the "Stormy Petrel," a harbinger of trouble, as the petrel was believed to be most active before a storm (suggesting Steerforth's feverish activity before the abduction). The name petrel itself is believed to be a diminutive form of Peter, alluding perhaps to his attempt to walk on the stormy waters and his sinking when he took his eyes off Christ and looked rather at the more impressive wind and waves (as Emily takes her eyes off Ham and is fascinated by the more impressive Steerforth). These associations are reinforced when Steerforth renames the boat "The Little Em'ly" (325). There is one final reminder of this imagery when Mr. Peggotty finds Emily in Martha's room, and David notices that there are ships on the walls.

Emily experiences one final struggle as she talks with Martha, taking a last look at the people and values she is rejecting. She thinks she is not as good or as thankful as she ought to be for the opportunity to marry a good man and lead a peaceful life. In a slight but symbolic action, Peggotty "recall[s] her [Emily's] stray ringlets," even as Emily "innocently kiss[es] her chosen husband on the cheek, and creep[s] close to his bluff form as if it were her best support" (340). Both the Peggottys and David put the best construction on things, as David thinks that Martha's effect on Emily only intensifies her purity and grace (341), and Mr. Peggotty thinks that Emily's trembling and clinging to him "even to the avoidance of her chosen husband" is a result of the fact that Barkis is dying (443). Even the repetition of the word "chosen" before husband heightens for the reader the struggle in Emily's mind.

When Emily abandons the Peggottys and Ham for Steerforth, the contrast between the two families, and the two world views they represent, becomes increasingly clear. She hopes initially that Steerforth will make her a lady, but this hope is gradually abandoned. Her low spirits and his restlessness reflect the rapid breakdown in their foundationless relationship—she is unable to respect him and he is unable to commit himself to her in love. David says to Mrs. Steerforth:

> . . . if you suppose the girl, so deeply wronged, has not been cruelly deluded, and would not rather die a hundred deaths than take a cup of water from your son's hand now, you cherish a terrible mistake.
>
> (673)

The cup of water image, taken from the gospels of (cf. Matt. 10:42 and Mark 9:41) suggests that the salvation Steerforth holds out to Emily, in his invitation to her to become his "lady" and join the upper class, is a bogus one of which she no longer wants any part.[4]

This is confirmed when Rosa confronts Emily. For all her shrewdness, Rosa completely misreads Emily's personality and motives when she calls her "bold, flaunting [and] practiced" (718) and thinks that Emily can use her money to console the Peggottys. Emily is re-entering, or perhaps entering for the first time, the Christian world of the Peggottys, a world about which Rosa knows nothing. Emily alludes to the Lord's prayer as she desperately pleads with Rosa, ". . . for Heaven's sake spare me, if you would be spared yourself" (719), but it is precisely this forgiving love that Rosa never receives and can never give. Emily says that Rosa knows, perhaps, Steerforth's power with a weak, vain girl. (The reader is vividly shown Steerforth's ability to soften even Rosa in his final time with her before running off with Emily—Rosa too is taken in and then recoils in disgust). Emily then goes on to say that Steerforth "used all his power to deceive me, and that I believed him, trusted him, and loved him!" (720).

Emily abandons the world of the Peggottys before she realizes the full value and inner beauty of that world, even as Pip abandons the world of Joe Gargery in *Great Expectations* without beginning to understand what it is he is walking away from until it is almost too late. Both Emily and Pip eventually see through the superficially impressive world of Steerforth and Estella and are brought back to their senses by the long-suffering and sacrificial love of the Peggottys and Joe Gargery. As the Old Testament tabernacle was ordinary-looking on the outside, but resplendent on the inside, so one of the deepest movements in both these novels is toward the eventual recognition of one's true self and true home in that which at first is despised as outwardly common and unimpressive.

EMILY'S REDEEMERS: MR. PEGGOTTY AND HAM

Mr. Peggotty resolves, as soon as he learns of Emily's flight, not simply to wait for his prodigal daughter as the father does in that gospel story (Mrs. Gummidge does that, with the candle burning), but to seek her over land and sea.[5] His one message for her (that he sends out in every way he can) is one not of condemnation, but of love and forgiveness, a message that Steerforth intercepts and prevents Emily from receiving.[6] Mr. Peggotty's willingness to sacrifice himself to save Emily is shown in many ways. He confronts Mrs. Steerforth with her son's responsibility and demands that if Emily is low Steerforth should "raise her up!" (468). He is even willing never to see Emily in this life, if that would embarrass her new family, "till all of us shall be alike in quality afore our God!" (468). He asserts that he suffers as much as Mrs. Steerforth does and he despises her attempt to offer him "compensation." In all these things he reminds us strongly of the contrast between inner and outer nobility seen when Joe Gargery stands before Miss Havisham.

As Emily lies near death in the home of the Italian peasant woman, her one desperate need is for some word of forgiveness, and she fears she will not receive it. Mr. Peggotty remarks that this woman who helped

Emily at such a time of need will have "treasure in heaven" (728), a reference to Matthew 6 and a further reminder of the eternal perspective that characterizes his own outlook as well as that of Ham. When Mr. Peggotty finally does find Emily, she faints and he covers her face with a handkerchief and carries her home. This covering serves as an emblem of atonement and forgiveness.[7] He also returns every shilling of money that he ever received from the Steerforths so that his motives are perfectly clear to all. Finally, he takes Martha with him as well as Emily to a new life in a new world. David says, ". . . if ever I have loved and honored any man, I loved and honored that man in my soul" (811). Steerforth's influence on David is profound, but that of Mr. Peggotty and Ham is even more so, and it is this good influence that enables him finally to see Steerforth in the right light (as I hope to show below). As the ship leaves, taking the emigrants away, David reflects: "Aye, Emily, beautiful and drooping, cling to him with the utmost trust of thy bruised heart; for he has clung to thee with all the might of his great love" (812).

Emily's eventual redemption is accomplished not only by the forgiving and self-sacrificing love of Mr. Peggotty, but also by that of Ham. Just as Mr. Peggotty contrasts strongly with Mrs. Steerforth as the inwardly noble parent figure, so Ham contrasts strongly with Steerforth as the inwardly noble lover. Ham is described as "iron-true" to Emily, enabling Mr. Peggotty to die in peace with Emily in Ham's care (314), as opposed to Steerforth, who causes Mr. Peggotty to suffer so much for his falseness to Emily. We are told that "nature had given [Ham] the soul of a gentleman" (443), though not the wealth and articulate speech of one.

Ham's redemption or reclamation of Emily is developed along the lines of the lost childhood motif. In her initial note, Emily tells Ham to think of her as someone who died as a child and "was buried somewhere" (452). In a later letter, she speaks of Ham as "so brave and so forgiving" (587). This courage and forgiveness enable her to rise from the dead, as it were, and recover the lost innocence of her childhood, as can be seen in her near death by fever after her flight from Steerforth, her crying out for forgiveness, and her final experiencing of the "weakness of the littlest child" (727). We are reminded of Jesus' words, ". . . unless you change and become like little children, you will never enter the kingdom of heaven" (Matthew 18:3).[8]

Shortly before his death, Ham is described as the "serenest of the party" (736). As he is being prepared for sacrifice, he is described as broken-hearted, yet full of courage, sweetness, and a willingness to work harder and better than others. He talks of Emily as a child, but not as a woman, as her entrance into womanhood coincides with her yielding to the false values of Steerforth. In his last letter to her, he attempts very delicately both to ask Emily's forgiveness for pressing his affections and putting her in a difficult position, and also to assure her that he is not too greatly hurt by her betrayal. He hopes finally to see Emily "without blame, where the wicked cease from troubling and the weary are at rest" (738). This reference to Job 3:17 is both apt for obvious reasons and interesting, as Job also refers to a pre-Steerforth-like innocence and joy of childhood when he asks, ". . . why was I not hidden in the ground like a stillborn child, like an infant who never saw the light of day?" (vs. 16).

Though the sea is portrayed in the novel most frequently as an angry devourer and devours Ham himself, a detail suggests a heaven beyond it for Ham, as he concludes his final message to Emily and "turns his face towards a strip of silvery light upon the sea" (738). David later says of Ham's last message to Emily that it consisted of a "deep fidelity and goodness not to be adorned" (785). This is thoroughly consistent with the novel's presentation of Ham's character and perhaps explains the decidedly unadorned way in which Ham's death is recorded. The event contains within itself its own eloquence which does not need rhetorical heightening. If this is true, then the understated description of Ham's death, which might be taken as implicitly favoring the upper classes, confirms rather the novel's view that it is the rugged, self-sacrificing nobility of the poor, inward, and unadorned, that redeems the upper classes. Emily says of this last message that its very goodness is like "sharp thorns" (785) that hurt, but also heal, like the crown of thorns worn by Christ at his trial. She says finally, "When I find what you are, and what uncle is, I think what God must be, and can cry to him. . . . In another world, if I am forgiven, I may wake a child and come to you" (785). Emily learns of God's love and mercy through Ham and Mr. Peggotty, and makes one final reference to her hope of eventually recovering fully through this love and mercy the innocence of her lost childhood.

Ham's death can be seen as a sacrificial, even substitutionary, death for Emily. The angry sea demands Emily, but Ham offers himself instead, so that the sea can take Emily rather to a new life far away. David says of Ham as Ham is getting ready to save the drowning sailor, that "the determination in his face, and his look out to sea—exactly the same look as I remembered in connexion with the morning after Emily's flight—awoke me to a knowledge of his danger" (793). While this look refers most specifically to Ham's attitude toward Steerforth (I discuss this in detail below), it can also be thought of as bringing to mind Ham's willingness to die for Emily when he learns of her flight:

> "My love, Mas'r Davy—the pride and hope of my heart—her that I'd have died for, and would die for now—she's gone!". . . .

The face he turned up to the troubled sky, the quiver-
ing of his clasped hands, the agony of his figure, remain associated with that lonely waste, in my remembrance, to this hour.

(451)

Ham finally has his opportunity to lay down his life for
Emily. Mr. Peggotty's last news of Emily at the novel's
end shows her to be as she was in childhood, only better (i.e., without foolish aspirations to become "a lady").
His carrying to her, at her request, some grass and earth
from Ham's grave, shows that Mr. Peggotty has not
lived for her, and Ham has not died for her, in vain.

STEERFORTH REDEEMED AS WRAYBURN

Having looked at how Emily is first lost then found, let
us look at how Steerforth is lost in *David Copperfield,*
but redeemed as Wrayburn in *Our Mutual Friend.* Perhaps the two things that most characterize Steerforth
are his many abilities and his waste of those abilities.
The very first time his name is mentioned in the novel,
David sees it cut deep and often in the table top (79),
suggesting Steerforth's inflated view of himself. Steerforth replaces Mr. Mell briefly as a teacher and teaches
"in an easy amateur way, and without any book (he
seemed to know everything by heart)" (101). Both his
abilities and his underuse of them are suggested by this
detail. At Yarmouth David praises Steerforth's abilities
as athlete, speaker, singer—it seems there is nothing he
cannot do. David thinks Steerforth could distinguish
himself at Oxford as a scholar, but he has no interest in
this, almost a contempt for it, and his manner is again
characterized by "carelessness and lightness" (291).
Steerforth proposes a toast: ". . . and the lilies of the
valley that toil not, neither do they spin, in compliment
to me—the more shame for me!" (295). His mother
says of their choice of Mr. Creakle's school that they
looked for one where Steerforth would be deferred to,
that he soon became king there and could have totally
broken out, but rather he "haughtily determined to be
worthy of his station" (296). This school gives Steerforth an opportunity to make a somewhat more constructive use of his abilities, at least for awhile. Mrs.
Steerforth further says of him that he "can always [when
he wants to] outstrip every competitor" (296). At
Yarmouth Steerforth also shows himself to be a good
sailor who loves rough toil just as a change of pace.

Eugene Wrayburn is also characterized as someone with
many abilities that are not being used. He drifts through
life until he meets Lizzie Hexam. She gives him at last
something to strive for and someone to live for. Her
goodness acts as a moral rebuke to him, gradually un-
dermining his cynicism. In his efforts to clear her father's name and help with Lizzie's education he begins
to experience the satisfaction of doing things for others.
Even his elaborate tormenting of Bradley Headstone,

while perverse in motivation, gives him an opportunity
to exert himself over a sustained period of time with a
sense of vigor so new to him that it surprises his friend
Mortimer Lightwood. His final death and rebirth are
dramatized in his being struck from behind by Headstone (hence his name, I suppose, both as blow to the
head and as gravestone), his near drowning in the river,
and his protracted battle with death before his eventual
recovery. The old, indolent Eugene dies forever and a
new, resolute one emerges, willing to sacrifice everything for his wife:

> I will fight it out to the last gasp, with her and for her,
> here, in the open field. When I hide her, or strike for
> her, faint-heartedly, in a hole or a corner, do you [Mor-
> timer Lightwood] whom I love next best upon earth,
> tell me what I shall most righteously deserve to be
> told—that she would have done well to turn me over
> with her foot that night when I lay bleeding to death,
> and spat in my dastard face.

> (*OMF* [*Our Mutual Friend*] 885, 886)

Lizzie is the one who rescues Eugene from drowning
and who inspires him to pull through the deep waters of
his fever and illness. She is able to do this for him because she, unlike Emily, does not cave in to his twisted
values, but rather raises him up to her healthy ones.
She, like Mr. Peggotty, Ham, and Joe Gargery, believes
in her loved one no matter what, and willingly risks her
own life to save him.

Wrayburn gets Lizzie only after a very long, difficult
and life-changing struggle, and only on Lizzie's own
terms. Steerforth gets Emily all too easily, and on his
own terms. His pursuit of her is a game, a momentary
excitement, "a mere wasteful careless course of winning what was worthless to him, and next minute
thrown away" (311). Lizzie's goodness rebukes and inspires Wrayburn. Steerforth sees goodness in David, but
this is not enough to stop him: "I believe you are in
earnest, and are good. I wish we all were!" (318).

In a final revealing scene before their separation, David
comes upon Steerforth looking at pictures in the fire,
anticipating a similar scene involving Lizzie Hexam in
the later novel. But Lizzie sees salvation for Eugene in
the fire, while Steerforth sees only ruin for himself and
Emily. Lizzie reveals what she sees to her friend Jenny
Wren, but Steerforth hides what he sees from David; he
spoils the fire and strikes out of it a "train of red-hot
sparks that went careering up the little chimney, and
roaring out into the air" (321), suggesting the train of
disastrous events about to take place.

Steerforth wishes that he had been better guided and
could guide himself better. He sees himself as the boy
in the nursery tale who "didn't care" and became food
for the lions (322). Wrayburn's father is no more "stead-
fast and judicious" (*DC* [*David Copperfield*] 322) than

Steerforth's and is also a primary cause of his drifting lifestyle. David marvels that Steerforth can master anything so easily, yet make such a fitful use of his powers. In a final irony, Steerforth exhorts David to "Ride on over all obstacles, and win the race!" (426), and David "wished, for the first time, that he [Steerforth] had some worthy race to run" (426). The contrast between Steerforth's pursuit of Emily and Wrayburn's of Lizzie could scarcely have been focussed more sharply. In Steerforth's final meeting with David, he wishes that David could give to him freshness and innocence—it is just these qualities that Lizzie gives to Wrayburn.

STEERFORTH'S WOULD-BE RESCUER: HAM

Having looked at Emily, her rescuers, and Steerforth, it remains only to look briefly at his would-be rescuer, Ham. The roles of worthy and unworthy lover reverse themselves. Ham, as the worthy lover who humbles himself, is of the lower class, while Steerforth the unworthy lover is of the upper class. Eugene as the worthy lover who humbles himself is of the upper class, while Headstone as the unworthy lover is of the lower class, aspiring in foolish pride to exalt himself. There is an interesting contrast too in Ham as the diligent and skillful boat builder (recall the Emily-as-boat imagery) and Steerforth as the boat buyer and stealer.

Ham's initial response to Steerforth's abduction of Emily is to condemn him as "a damned villain" (453). Mr. Peggotty's initial response is no less violent and vengeful: he is ready to sink Steerforth's boat and wishes he could sink him instead. David himself is ready to curse Steerforth. At this critical point Mrs. Gummidge intervenes and first asks Mr. Peggotty to forgive her for all the grief she's ever caused him. She then reminds him of how he had pity on her, on Ham, and on Emily, and how he has sheltered them all these years. Finally, she reminds him of the promise, "As you have done it unto one of the least of these, you have done it unto me" (454, cf. Matthew 25:31-40). This passage in Matthew is one of the most moving in all the Bible on the subject of mercy, and this finally moves Mr. Peggotty (and David) to tears and to mercy as they yield to "better feeling" (454). David remembers Steerforth at his best not necessarily because he is unwilling to denounce him because he is of the upper class (he is ready to curse him, and even now says that the fascination, the evil spell, is gone; 454), and not simply because Steerforth himself asked him to do so, but most of all because he is moved to mercy. He feels "as weak as a spirit-wounded child" (454), recalling again the childhood motif of humility where mercy triumphs over judgment.

Dickens introduces a deliberately misleading ambiguity in his description of Ham's response to Emily's disappearance that functions in a way analogous to his treatment of Mrs. Strong's innocence. Dickens casts doubt on Mrs. Strong, not to tease the reader, but to make the eventual disclosure of her faithfulness the more powerful. So David wonders whether revenge or mercy are upper most in the mind of Ham, to make the nobility of his final sacrifice the more pronounced. Ham, after Emily's flight, is described as living a good life, though cut very deeply, as always strong to face danger to help and save others, yet very gentle. Yet the morning after the flight David sees a look, not of anger, but of determination in Ham's face and thinks the determination is to kill Steerforth (456). Later David asks Mr. Peggotty about Ham's state of mind and what he might do if he met Steerforth. Mr. Peggotty replies that he can't plumb the deep waters of Ham's mind on that point and would rather not ask him, but that he thinks its best if they never meet (677). Mr. Omer, on the other hand, says "all [Ham's] life's a kindness" (735).

In the climactic tempest chapter David suggests that many disparate threads of his story are to be brought together by an event to which he is "bound by an infinite variety of ties" (784). Ham's conduct continues tender, manful, quiet, even serene, though he is most tried. As the storm builds, the wreck is spotted, and the sailors on it begin to perish, the expectation of the narrative is that Ham will risk his life again to save others as he has so often in the past. As Ham is preparing to do so, indications that the last survivor is Steerforth begin to appear. The look of determination on Ham's face reminds David of the look that he originally took to be a murderous one. He says that this woke him up to a knowledge of Ham's danger, and he implores the other men on the beach "not to do murder" (793) by allowing Ham to go after the man about to drown. The men on the beach no doubt understood his words to mean murder in the sense of allowing Ham to throw his life away in a hopeless situation, but the suggestion is still there that Ham might be motivated as much by justice as by mercy in his determination to go out after Steerforth. Yet if Ham merely wants to ensure Steerforth's death, all he need do is wait a few moments, as Steerforth's death is immanent. He could easily have simply stood on the beach with the others, thinking that Steerforth is at last being justly destroyed by the sea over which he carried Emily away. Yet his last words are words, not of revenge, but of blessing: "Mas'r Davy,' he said, cheerily grasping me by both hands, 'if my time is come, 'tis come. If 'tan't, I'll bide it. Lord bless you, and bless all! Mates, make me ready! I'm a-going off!'" (793). Ham's valiant attempt fails, and David says of him that "his generous heart was stilled for ever" (794).

Steerforth speaks of his greatest nightmare as his own self (322). Like Kurtz in *Heart of Darkness*, he looks inside himself and is horrified. He is to an almost satanic extent taken up with himself and his own desperate fancies, no matter how destructive. He bewails his upbringing and his inability to break free from this bondage to self. His mother, too, is like him in her unbending pride. As she learns of his death there is some indication that her stony heart might be beginning to break. As Rosa justly rebukes her pride, Mrs. Steerforth's mouth is rigid and her teeth are closed, "as if the jaw were locked and the face frozen up in pain" (799). She finally feels the hammer blow to the face that Rosa felt so many years before. Rosa says, "Now is your pride appeased, you madwoman? Now has he made atonement to you—with his life! Do you hear?—His life!" (799). Class conflict is resolved in Dickens in a distinctively Christian way. The poor suffer and die for the rich, often succeeding in rescuing them from their mad pride and bondage to self:

> God chose the foolish things of the world to shame the wise; God chose the weak things of the world to shame the strong. He chose the lowly things of this world and the despised things—and the things that are not—to nullify the things that are, so that no one may boast before him.

> I Cor. 1:27-29

Notes

1. As early as his preface to *Pickwick,* Dickens made it clear that while he was a severe critic of the *abuses* of religion, he maintained a deep respect for religion itself. While his own faith had many weaknesses, it was still very real, particularly as reflected in his novels. Such astute foreign readers as Leo Tolstoy and Fyodor Dostoevsky recognized this.

2. Even Estella, though suffering is stressed as her teacher, is helped in the end by Pip's example. While I merely assert Pip's influence over Miss Havisham and Estella here, I demonstrate it in my as yet unpublished doctoral dissertation "The Power of a Life: *Great Expectations* as a Christian Novel."

3. Grahame Smith, in *Dickens, Money, and Society,* stresses both the greed for money and the intense class consciousness in *G. E.* (171).

4. Some readers might find this suggestion somewhat fanciful. I make is because I think it has critical merit. However, my overall argument does not depend upon it.

5. The New Testament metaphor "fishers of men" (cf. Matt. 4:19 and Mark 1:17) is perhaps in the background here.

6. Cf. John 8:1-11 and the woman taken in adultery.

7. The ideas of covering and atonement are closely linked in the Bible. We are covered with the blood of Christ even as the mercy seat covered the ark of the covenant.

8. Taken from the *Holy Bible: New International Version* copyright 1978 by the New York International Bible Society, used by permission.

Works Cited

Dickens, Charles. *David Copperfield.* London: Oxford UP, 1960.

——. *Our Mutual Friend.* Harmondsworth, Middlesex: Penguin Books, 1985.

Magnet, Myron. *Dickens and the Social Order.* Philadelphia: U of Pennsylvania P, 1985.

Marlow, James E. "Social Harmony and Dickens' Revolutionary Cookery." *Dickens Studies Annual* Vol. 17. New York: AMS, 1988.

Shaw, Bernard. *Shaw on Dickens.* Ed. Dan H. Laurence and Martin Quinn. New York: Frederick Ungar, 1985.

Smith, Grahame. *Dickens, Money, and Society.* Berkeley: U of California P, 1968.

Terence Wright (essay date spring 1999)

SOURCE: Wright, Terence. "Caresses that Comfort, Blows that Bind: Sex, Sentiment and the Sense of Touch in *David Copperfield*." *English: The Journal of the English Association* 48, no. 190 (spring 1999): 1-16.

[*In the following essay, Wright discusses Dickens's refashioning of eighteenth-century sentimentalism in* David Copperfield *through an exploration of the "intermingling of eroticism and cruelty" in the novel's human relationships.*]

In the lonely, gloomy period of his life following his mother's remarriage, David Copperfield finds consolation in a small collection of books left by his father—a 'glorious host to keep me company' (55). The eighteenth-century writers' names he lists are in a robust, extrovert tradition—Smollett, Defoe, Fielding—but of the inturned, subtly comic, sentimental Sterne he makes no mention. This is surprising, knowing that Dickens was certainly well acquainted with his works from his youth, and frequently quotes him in his letters. It is the more surprising when one considers how concerned *David Copperfield* is with time and memory, the power of sentimental recall lodged in objects, self-investigation and sympathetic comedy, all major preoccupations of Sterne. Sterne's influence is surely pervasive throughout Dickens' novel, from Mrs. Copperfield's recollection of her dead husband's belief that 'a loving heart was better and stronger than wisdom' (131)—doubly reinforced by being spoken on *her* deathbed—to such particularities as Miss Betsey Trotwood's exclamation:

'Bless the Baby!' exclaimed Miss Betsey, unconsciously quoting the second sentiment of the pincushion in the drawer up-stairs, but applying it to my mother instead of me, 'I don't mean that. I mean your servant.'

(6)

This is a memory in the manner of at least two moments in *Tristram Shandy* where Tristram's irascible father directs irritable exclamations at the wrong object (and in one instance bites into a pincushion in his agitation!).

I have not raised the question of this literary debt for its own sake, but in order to introduce a matter which Dickens may have owed to Sterne emotionally and imaginatively, but which his temper and age transforms into something very much his own. A powerful sensitivity to touch informs all Sterne's fiction. We may remember the admonitory tap on the arm which Mrs. Shandy delivers to her spouse as they are walking arm-in-arm and which Walter, who is 'all sensibilities from head to foot', interprets aright (Book IX Chapter One, 571). Or here is Sterne in the guise of Parson Yorick, holding the hand of a young woman before the remise door in Calais:

I fear, in this interval, I must have made some slight efforts towards a closer compression of her hand, from a subtle sensation I felt in the palm of my own—not as if she was going to withdraw hers—but, as if she thought about it—

(42-3)

The super-subtle awareness of minute changes in feeling and intention are not characteristic of Dickens, especially when those feelings are slyly erotic (and this may be part of the reason why Sterne is not included in David's early reading). Nevertheless, the hands are eloquent of the whole person for Dickens, and of much else besides, as we may see from the moment when David, travel-worn, ragged, dusty and sunburnt, unrecognisable as the gentleman's son and near relation which he is, presents himself to his Great Aunt in her garden at Dover. Her reaction is comically hostile (a guise in which she often appears):

'Go away!' said Miss Betsey, shaking her head, and making a distant chop in the air with her knife. 'Go along! No boys here!'

(191)

Before he speaks a word to her, David, 'without a scrap of courage, but with a great deal of desperation' goes softly in, stands beside her where she is working unconscious of his approach, and touches her with his finger. If there is any point on which this novel turns, we are now at it. At this moment we are taken back to a period before the hero was even born, when Betsey makes her brief and terrifying descent on the Rookery.

Mrs. Copperfield admits, crying, that 'she was afraid she was but a childish widow, and would be but a childish mother if she lived' (5). But then:

In a short pause which ensued, she had a fancy that she felt Miss Betsey touch her hair, and that with no ungentle hand; but, looking at her, in her timid hope, she found that lady sitting with the skirt of her dress tucked up, her hands folded on one knee, and her feet upon the fender, frowning at the fire.

(5)

This gesture, confirmed by feeling rather than sight, is the one talisman David carries with him on his quest for recognition and a new life. It is the only chink in the armour of this formidable 'discontented fairy' to suggest that she could be this little prince's Fairy Godmother. He receives the precious secret from his mother, carries it in his bosom, and when the moment comes triumphantly returns it to the giver. And finally, as confirmation of his trust, David re-enacts his mother's experience as he lies exhausted on the couch at Dover, recognised and taken in, but still not sure of his ultimate fate:

It might have been a dream, originating in the fancy which had occupied my mind so long, but I awoke with the impression that my aunt had come and bent over me, and had put my hair away from my face, and laid my head more comfortably, and had then stood looking at me.

(196)

Like his mother he looks up to see no sign that this impression has actually been the case, his aunt being seated on the far side of the room looking out of the window.

A number of points are contained in this exchange of touches. First, as with Sterne, it suggests sensitivity, the Feeling Heart (and, by implication, as we shall see, the lack of these qualities in some other people). It is also, as I have suggested, part of a fairytale or mythic story. David holds a secret key which has been passed to him by one now dead—a key which, used at the right moment, will unlock the door of his kingdom, despite abuse, abandonment and privation. But there is a further dimension to the business. When he is robbed of his money and realises he must walk to Dover, he reflects that he is:

taking very little more out of the world, towards the retreat of my aunt, Miss Betsey, than I had brought into it, on the night when my arrival gave her so much umbrage.

(179)

David has been experiencing a process of paring-down, in terms of domestic attachments from the moment his mother remarries. He is forbidden the company of Peggotty, he is sent away to school, his mother dies, he is turned off to fend for himself in a strange city. Absconding, he is robbed, sells his clothes, and finally appears before his aunt, as he says, almost as innocent of possessions, as indeed of family and past acquaintances, as at the moment of his birth. It is on the one hand a preparation for rebirth, the chance to start his life again as the person he might have been and should be. But that talismanic touch reminds us that no rebirth is ever really possible (or perhaps desirable). Attenuated though they may be, David never loses those things that feed his hopes and keep his integrity intact. The strain placed upon this grasp of sanity, hope and truth is comically enacted when Peggotty communicates with the about-to-be banished David through the keyhole of his room. Nevertheless it is a hold maintained with persistence, strength and resourcefulness. As he is driving away in Barkis' cart, Peggotty bursts through a hedge and climbs up to him. She hugs him passionately (her special gesture, its abandon embodied in flying buttons!), gives him a purse and a bag of cakes 'but not one word did she say' (63). Words are not needed; gestures convey love and care, and are remembered.

Love and memory, with a third factor I shall come to later, are the great binding forces in this book. Despite concerning itself so much with loss—of father, mother, wife, step-brother, friend, childhood sweetheart—this is a book in which it might be said that nothing is lost, in that David's psychological resources enable him to use memory as a defence and self-preservation. At least it must be felt that 'Tho' much is taken, much abides.' In the last pages Peggotty is still present with her wax candle, yard measure and workbox. Traddles is still a friend, Mr. Peggotty revisits David and Agnes. Even the Murdstones are there to be reassessed and assimilated into the hero's mature personality. His mother is now long dead, but his last glimpse of her is a silent imprint, rescued for ever—even with the baby half-brother—from the Murdstones, and stored in the subconscious as a sustaining image:

> It was cold still weather; and not a hair of her head, nor a fold of her dress, was stirred, as she looked intently at me, holding up her child.

> So I lost her. So I saw her afterwards, in my sleep at school—a silent presence near my bed—looking at me with the same intent face—holding up her baby in her arms.

> (121)

Thus the spirit arms itself, confronting or evading the threats to its immaturity until the man can encompass the threats that would overwhelm the child.

With such poignancy of loss, threat to the self and concern with the power of dream we have reached the point, perhaps, where we move beyond Sterne to a Post-Romantic cast of mind, but let us return to the matter of touch and hands with which I began. Dickens never has that concentrated inner sensitivity to touch so characteristic of Sterne, but he uses hand gestures with intense suggestiveness as social signals for individual relationships. Think of the variety of greetings that are exchanged, each subtly suggesting an unspoken world of feeling. When Mr. Murdstone wants to be 'best friends in the world' with David he suggests they shake hands. But David is 'jealous that his hand should touch my mother's in touching me' and:

> My right hand was in my mother's left, so I gave him the other.

> 'Why, that's the wrong hand, Davy!' laughed the gentleman.

> My mother drew my right hand forward, but I was resolved, for my former reason, not to give it him, and I did not.

> (18-19)

There is no need to elaborate on the symbolic significance of this exchange, especially given Murdstone's sinister nature and the overtones of wrong of all kinds associated with the left hand. Mr. Peggotty's handshake is the epitome of solid honesty, like 'the power and force of character his sinewy hand expressed' (724)—a hand so powerful that on one occasion it split a table he had struck for emphasis (33). Dr. Strong's hand which, when offered, David 'didn't know what to do with' does 'nothing for itself' (226). Uriah Heep's damp, clammy handshake is one of his most notorious features. David's rubbing of his own hand to get rid of the touch of Uriah's suggests not only contamination, but an unpleasant self-association, reinforced when Uriah is older and more powerful:

> All this time he was squeezing my hand with his damp fishy fingers, while I made every effort I decently could to get it away. But I was quite unsuccessful. He drew it under the sleeve of his mulberry-coloured great coat, and I walked on, almost upon compulsion, arm in arm with him.

> (574)

Heep's insistent appropriation of David's hand betokens his threat as an appropriator of persons, since he is, of course, not only David's rival but a repulsive manifestation of a second self—ungenteel, self-educated and rapacious of place and person.

James Steerforth is a more welcome friend. When David, as a young man, makes his acquaintance again 'I grasped him by both hands, and could not let them go' (287) in one of the warmest welcomes David ever bestows on a fellow-being. His inability to relinquish Steerforth's hands is powerfully evocative of those themes of love and memory I have mentioned. Despite the latter's falsehood, David's first feelings for Steerforth can never alter; but to justify those affections he must hold him forever as he is at his best (as Steerforth requests his friend to remember him before he falls from grace in his elopement with Emily). His last sight of the false friend is 'with his head upon his arm, as I had often seen him lie at school' (795). For Steerforth is ambiguous in his relations with David—careless, as when 'shaking [David's] hand heartily, and throwing it gaily away' (424) yet revealing his greatest charm, together with his nearest approximation to self-reproach, in his relations with his younger friend. At their last meeting:

> He was unwilling to let me go; and stood, holding me out, with a hand on each of my shoulders, as he had done in my own room.
>
> (436)

The dependency is mutual, and the grasp on the shoulders (interestingly, a gesture repeated later by Agnes) indicates his trust in David, his need to 'take his picture' as David does of his mother, and the determination to look one man straight and honestly in the eye, if it is to be for the last time.

There are other lesser but nevertheless instructive instances of touching—the guiding hand such as the kindly Mr. Quinion places upon the boy David's shoulder, turning him about to walk with him when the little orphan goes to work in the blacking factory, or those of Mr. Mell and Dr. Strong. There is Mr. Peggotty's man-to-man gesture with the back of his hand on Ham's chest—identifying and personal, but lacking the aggression of a jabbing finger. When David returns to see his old nurse after many years' absence 'I noticed a quick movement of her hands towards each other', and she 'took a step backward, and put out her hands in an undecided frightened way, as if to keep me off' (307). Perhaps the most mysterious in its ambiguity is the touch bestowed on David by Miss Murdstone after they have met again at Mr. Spenlow's house. After initial recognition the lady proposes that they should agree not to remark on the past, meeting simply as 'distant acquaintances'. David gives his opinion that both he and his mother were ill-used by the Murdstones, but agrees to her proposal:

> Miss Murdstone shut her eyes again, and bent her head. Then, just touching the back of my hand with the tips of her cold, stiff fingers, she walked away.
>
> (393)

The two have only one more significant encounter, when Miss Murdstone is implicated as the betrayer of David's secret liaison with Dora, so their association can hardly be said to conclude on a happy note. And yet, when Jane does not know of the love affair to come, is it possible that in her touch, cold and distant though it is, despite the 'disdain' of the bent head and closed eyes there may be, in addition to a truce, an acknowledgement at least of the right of David to be a person in himself? Certainly neither she nor her brother are exceptions to the rule in this novel that nothing changes essentially—but perceptions change. Perhaps in that faint, cold touch we have a recognition that David can no longer, for good or ill, see her as an ogre—her adornments remain the same, but the touch is a voluntary gesture of communication; and on her part an understanding of this change. At the least it indicates that with maturity comes compromise.

Hitherto I have confined my observations to kindly touch: hands that are sensitive to greet and recognise with love, arms that reach out to guide and embrace. But there is a quite other use of the hands, and one which has not only as great a significance in *David Copperfield* but is also closely implicated in the gentler forms of communication, though its nature is so different. When Mr. Pickwick meets his old acquaintance Alfred Jingle, now destitute, in the Fleet prison, the former strolling actor and 'con. man' abjectly repents of his past misdeeds, and finally breaks down. Mr. Pickwick calls over the servant Job:

> "Come here, Sir," said Mr. Pickwick, trying to look stern, with four large tears running down his waistcoat. "Take that, Sir."
>
> Take what? In the ordinary acceptation of such language, it should have been a blow. As the world runs, it ought to have been a sound, hearty cuff;
>
> (537)

It is not, of course, a blow—it is money for their immediate relief. If there is any debt at all to Sterne in the more violent side of Dickens it must be here, in the novel most clearly written in the shadow of the eighteenth-century tradition. Jingle is the sentimental criminal, brought low and redeemed by the goodhearted erstwhile enemy who now finds a corresponding warmth of sentiment manifest itself in a benevolent tear. But if the deserved blow is here avoided, there can be no doubt that Dickens made up for this softheartedness in the rest of his career. His very next novel, *Oliver Twist,* contains his most notoriously violent scene, in which a defenceless young woman is beaten to death in a welter of blood. The fascination this terrible scene held for Dickens is well-known, but in fact he never repeated an act of physical violence with such deadly consequences in any of his other novels. Murders became 'cleaner'; nevertheless it did not stop the beatings. From Nicholas Nickleby, struck in the face by Squeers' 'instrument of torture' (222), and later himself laying open Sir Mulberry Hawk's face 'from the eye to the lip' (499), through the grotesque threats of Quilp to the frightful thrashing performed upon the 'cur' Fledgeby by Alfred

Lammle, the kind of personal physical abuse comprehended in the term 'laying hands on' was never far from the source of Dickens' imagination. Sometimes it is a part of melodrama, as when the rather stagily enraged Rosa Dartle makes motions of spurning Little Em'ly with her foot (720), and if we were to look for literary antecedents we would probably turn to Smollett. But though Dickens occasionally indulges in the casual slapstick violence of Smollett, he usually relegates it to the realm of the comic or parodic threat, as we shall see. There is perhaps a simple 'healthy' relish in seeing Nicholas Nickleby lay into Squeers with his own cane. The bully is getting his just deserts. But many of the recipients of violence, especially in *David Copperfield,* are innocents, and the motives and emotions involved in personal violence are far more complex than a comfortable theory of 'justice' would suggest.

David Copperfield features violence and strong demonstrations of affection in almost equal proportions. Some, but not all of it is accounted for by the fact that the point of view for the first third of the book is that of the most vulnerable member of society, a child. A part of this violence is comic, of the kind that I hinted at above as diverting the Smollett order of assault into threats and feints such as those practised by Betsey Trotwood:

> My poor dear mother, I suppose, had some momentary intention of committing an assault and battery upon my aunt, who could easily have settled her with one hand, even if my mother had been in far better training for such an encounter than she was that evening.
>
> (6)

As the 'discontented fairy' she 'pounce[s]' on Ham who is 'clutched' by her, and then 'shook him, rumpled his hair, made light of his linen, stopped *his* ears as if she confounded them with her own, and otherwise touzled and maltreated him' (11). She aims a blow with her bonnet at Mr. Chillip 'in the manner of a sling' (12) and winds up the most famous of her tirades with the threat to Jane Murdstone that:

> 'Let me see you ride a donkey over *my* green again, and as sure as you have a head upon your shoulders, I'll knock your bonnet off, and tread upon it!'
>
> (214)

Nevertheless there is a firm line to be drawn between this comedy and all the other brutality in the book. Not that humour is ruled out in the more realistic passages, but it is humour of a disturbing kind, which we are not invited to take part in. Mr. Creakle pinches David's ear 'with ferocious playfulness' (82). He tells the child that if David is famous for biting *he* is too, and 'at every question he gave me a fleshy cut that made me writhe' (89). He 'cuts a joke' before he beats a boy, and 'miserable little dogs, we laugh' (90). We do not need to be

psychoanalysts to perceive that Creakle is indulging a perverted pleasure. 'There never can have been a man who enjoyed his profession more than Mr. Creakle did. He had a delight in cutting at the boys, which was like the satisfaction of a craving appetite' (89-90). Creakle stands very well as a blueprint for much of what I am concerned with here—a general model for many of the features of particular relations.

David remarks that Creakle did not particularly single him out for ill treatment, but this is not the case with Mr. Murdstone. Creakle in fact has some incidental resemblances to Murdstone—in particular both pride themselves on their 'firmness' and dominate their women. But Murdstone's relationship with David is particular and intimate. The man will break the boy's spirit (a phrase used with ominous inappropriateness a propos himself by Mr. Chillip on the day David is born). He looks into David's eyes, and the boy feels 'my own attracted, no less steadily, to his':

> 'David,' he said, making his lips thin, by pressing them together, 'if I have an obstinate horse or dog to deal with, what do you think I do?'
>
> 'I beat him.'
>
> . . . . .
>
> 'I make him wince and smart. I say to myself, "I'll conquer that fellow;" and if it were to cost him all the blood he had I should do it.'
>
> (46)

But David's private resolution is that his spirit should remain intact. The concentration upon the battle of wills is emphasised by their being 'opposed . . . face to face', alone together. When they are in company the relationship may be interpreted, by Murdstone at least, in social terms—he as the just father urging firmness and restraint, David as the child needing these rules. But when they are alone, the relationship is reduced to animal instinct. David is reduced to 'a horse or a dog', and under the provocation of a blow he reacts as an animal:

> . . . in the same instant I caught the hand with which he held me in my mouth, between my teeth, and bit it through.
>
> (58)

The extreme unnaturalness of the act now 'sets my teeth on edge to think of it'. This violence is brutal in its origins and brutalises its victim, who then provokes the aggressor to further extremes of violence in which all control is lost: 'He beat me then as if he would have beaten me to death' (58).

But there are darker secrets in Murdstone's heart, revealed only inadvertently to a few who enter into intimate contact with him. Turning round as he rides before him, David sees a 'kind of shallow black eye . . .

which, when it is abstracted, seems, from some peculiarity of light, to be disfigured, for a moment at a time, by a cast' (22). This is, mythically speaking, the 'evil eye', the proper feature of an ogre. But if the eyes are the windows of the soul, this cast opens up that perverted part of the man's being which remains, he hopes, his private property, perhaps not acknowledged even by himself. It flashes out still when the grown David has a last sight of him:

> He smiled, and shot as evil a glance at me as could come from his dark eyes.
>
> (477)

The fact of the wickedness *is* the secret, but we may be more particular and point, as with Creakle, to sadism, the difference being that Creakle's sadism is general and, in a sense, extrovert, while Murdstone's is entwined with painful ambiguity in the feelings of love he has for David's mother. He binds up the cane and flourishes it in the presence of both the boy and the mother:

> 'Now, David,' he said—and I saw that cast again as he said it—'you must be far more careful to-day than usual.'
>
> (57)

David is sure that as he walks him 'slowly and gravely' up to his room Murdstone has 'a delight in that formal parade of executing justice' (57-8). The perception of this obscure and malign motivation is Betsey Trotwood's most telling blow at the wicked stepfather, referring to:

> the poor child you sometimes tormented her through afterwards, which is a disagreeable remembrance, and makes the sight of him odious now. Aye, aye! you needn't wince!' said my aunt. 'I know it's true without that.'
>
> (213-14)

The specific instance of physical pain is recalled in the word 'wince', and in Murdstone's reaction—'though the smile was on his face still, his colour had gone in a moment, and he seemed to breathe as if he had been running' (214)—we may recall David's heart beating 'fast and high' and the shortening of breath he feels as he confronts Murdstone.

If the hand is one of the first and most sensitive means of communication, it is doubly painful when this delicate part is injured. David bites Murdstone in the hand and guiltily sees the wounded limb 'bound up in a huge linen wrapper' (59). Mr. Creakle flattens boys' hands with a ruler, and Mr. Micawber makes use of the same weapon to break the hand of Uriah Heep. Perhaps the most intriguing instance of damage to the hand is that which is self-inflicted. Neither of the instances I am going to analyse is in *David Copperfield,* but they are

worth mentioning because they might be called a short-circuit of the abuser/abused relationship. First there is Edith Dombey, subjected to the mock-obeisance of Carker, who bends over her hand and 'touch[es] it with his lips'. She does not withdraw her hand, or 'strike his fair face':

> But when she was alone in her own room, she struck it on the marble chimney-shelf, so that, at one blow, it was bruised, and bled; and held it from her, near the shining fire, as if she could have thrust it in and burned it.
>
> (581)

The gesture is not of course simply expressive of her detestation of Carker, but is an act of self-torture—punishment for that part of her which stands for instrumentality, and which is guilty of those actions of hers which have placed her in such a situation. It is also a gesture of deepest frustration, and in this guise it is even more forcibly enacted in *Our Mutual Friend* by the schoolteacher Bradley Headstone when Lizzie Hexam tells him she cannot consider him as a lover:

> 'Then,' said he, suddenly changing his tone and turning to her, and bringing his clenched hand down upon the stone with a force that laid the knuckles raw and bleeding; 'then I hope that I may never kill him!'
>
> (456)

He holds out his 'smeared hand as if it held some weapon and had just struck a mortal blow', and indeed the act is premonitory insofar as he does try to kill his rival. But in the self-inflicted wound we find all the repressed pride and pain of his social and emotional situation linked to all the self-hatred for being the hybrid his aspirations have made him—professional, but not of the 'true' professions, educated but not cultured, respectable but stiff, able neither to return to his origins nor to feel easy with the class which remains above him. The fist, the hand as aggressor, strikes, but succeeds only in exposing the vulnerability of its flesh. The urge to damage is so intimately tied to the raw wound of damaged pride that one cannot have its being without the other.

Wounds denied action become scars. The marks of physical violence remain with us:

> I won't flinch. It will be no use your rubbing yourselves; you won't rub the marks out that I shall give you
>
> (90)

says Mr. Creakle. There is a self-tormentor in *David Copperfield* who bears a scar from a blow we never see delivered. But this scar is the ultimate defining feature of its recipient, that unwilling spinster and eager questioner Rosa Dartle. David speculates on her appearance before he knows the origin of that magnetic line which disfigures her face:

> She had black hair and eager black eyes, and was thin, and had a scar upon her lip. It was an old scar—I should rather call it, seam, for it was not discoloured, and had healed years ago—which had once cut through her mouth, downwards towards the chin, but was now barely visible across the table, except above and on her upper lip, the shape of which it had altered.
>
> (292)

The self-correction to 'seam' for 'scar' draws attention to a word evoking both a buried store or hoard and the seam where two edges join. The old wound was given her, Steerforth somewhat shamefacedly reveals, by his own hand when in childish rage he threw a hammer at her, by that act joining them whether he would or no. Not only is he implicated directly in a disfigurement which may have blighted her prospects for the married state David thinks she is so eager to attain, but she is thereby able to bind Steerforth to her in a bond of guilt which is the only emotional tie she is likely to enjoy with him. For of course she loves her injurer, while he, as far as we can see, is unaware of her passion. The scar is a repository of pain and love—'the most susceptible part of her face' (295). It lengthens and darkens when she is aroused, starting out 'like the old writing on the wall' (ibid). She strikes it herself when in a fury. Rosa sees herself as the only person truly united to Steerforth—mother, friend, mistress may come between them, but her scar is the unhealing badge of that closeness which can only find its consummation in James's death. Then at last she can declare herself. Steerforth specifically asks David to come and

> stand between Rosa Dartle and me, and keep us asunder.'
>
> 'Would you love each other too much, without me?'
>
> 'Yes; or hate,' laughed Steerforth; 'no matter which. Come! Say the next day!'
>
> (427)

The indissoluble mixture of love and hate she feels for him reemerges as she plays the harp. The right hand (symbol of her better self?), which has just been playing 'the most unearthly music', a moment later is used for a blow at the man who had persuaded her to play it. 'She has been an angel', says Steerforth, 'for a little while; and has run into the opposite extreme, since, by way of compensation' (435-6).

David too finds himself reluctantly bound to another person via an act of physical violence which, for once, he perpetrates himself. Uriah Heep resolves to foment dissension in Dr. Strong's household by drawing the Doctor's attention to the past affection between his wife and Jack Maldon. Not content with this, he implies that he and David were privy to the affair, and shared a point of view on the subject. Unable to bear the suggestion that 'we had been in discussion together', David is driven to violence:

> The whole of his lank cheek was invitingly before me, and I struck it with my open hand with that force that my fingers tingled as if I had burnt them.
>
> He caught the hand in his, and we stood in that connexion, looking at each other. We stood so a long time; long enough for me to see the white marks of my fingers die out of the deep red of his cheek, and leave it a deeper red.
>
> (620)

Uriah's catching David's hand in the very act of striking hints that the blow is reinforcing the bond between them, even as David declares that he is casting the villain off:

> 'I have taken leave of you,' said I, wresting my hand away. 'You dog, I'll know no more of you.'
>
> 'Won't you?' said he, constrained by the pain of his cheek to put his hand there.
>
> 'Perhaps you won't be able to help it.'
>
> (620)

David's attempt to bring his detestation into play as an act of violence, which will reinforce the desired feeling of apartness, backfires upon him. Heep uses the blow as a weapon himself, returning it not in kind, but as a profession of forgiveness:

> 'How can you make yourself so inferior to me, as to show such a bad spirit? But I forgive you.'
>
> 'You forgive me!' I repeated disdainfully.
>
> 'I do, and you can't help yourself,'
>
> (620)

He does not need to tell David 'you're in quite a wrong position . . . you can't make this a brave thing, and you can't help being forgiven.' for 'He knew me better than I knew myself' (ibid). And indeed the reader could have understood this bond from the reciprocal pain in David's own fingers. It is a blow that leaves no apparent scar, but within it dislodges a tooth, again binding aggressor and 'victim' in a shared secret.

This series of violent blows introduces a third element into the pairing of love and memory which I earlier suggested is at the heart of *David Copperfield*. Recalling the time of his engagement to Dora, David writes:

> What an idle time it was! What an unsubstantial, happy, foolish time it was! When I measured Dora's finger for a ring that was to be made of Forget-me-nots, and when the jeweller, to whom I took the measure, found me

out, and laughed over his order-book, and charged me anything he liked for the pretty little toy, with its blue stones—so associated in my remembrance with Dora's hand, that yesterday, when I saw such another, by chance, on the ring of my own daughter, there was a momentary stirring in my heart, like pain!

(489)

It is, apart from anything else, a wonderfully elegant and sinuous sentence, drawing together the elements of love and memory, but crowning them with that third element of 'pain'. If it said nothing else, it would reiterate powerfully the message that nothing is lost. A part of Dickens wishes to say that all this is 'foolish' and 'unsubstantial', the product of an 'undisciplined heart'; that in marrying Agnes he will 'cancel the mistaken past' as though it were a separate story, a false start to be wiped out. But the man who wrote this sentence is recognising that if in one sense it is foolish and unsubstantial, in another sense this love has been an experience so profound that it can never be outlived, any more than David's first feelings for Steerforth, or his mother, or Murdstone, or that talismanic touch he carries with him to unlock his aunt's heart in Dover. It is also, like his feeling for Steerforth, an experience in which joy is inextricably bound up with pain, one instance of a great many in the book. The association presents itself in comic guise with a little play on the word 'tender' when Peggotty breaks through the hedge to say goodbye to David on his way to school:

> She took me in both her arms, and squeezed me to her stays until the pressure on my nose was extremely painful, though I never thought of that till afterwards, when I found it very tender.

(63)

David cannot help glancing at Rosa Dartle's scar 'with a painful interest' (295). He observes the newly-betrothed couple, Ham and Emily, 'with an indescribably sensitive pleasure, that a very little would have changed to pain' (315). The remembrance of Dora's 'pretty joy' when he allows her to hold his pens 'brings tears into my eyes' (64). As Mr. Peggotty tells Emily's story he combines religious compassion, pain and gratitude:

> and see her humbled, as it might be in the dust our Saviour rote in with his blessed hand—I felt a wownd go to my 'art, in the midst of all its thankfulness.

(725)

The association of the painful and the moving in itself has nothing new about it of course. It is part of the stock-in-trade of eighteenth-century sentiment, and indeed of Victorian sentimental fiction too. But *David Copperfield* is a book of violent affections and antipathies, as my treatment of the eloquence of the hand has, I hope, suggested, and pleasure and pain are given a further, darker twist by the penetration Dickens brings into the obscurer corners of human nature and motivation.

Nor is the comic element divorced from these serious explorations. Dickens is an inveterate parodist of his own deepest concerns. Those poles of pain and joy I cited above have their comic counterpart, blown up until they overbalance into the ridiculous, in Mr. Micawber's manic plunges from elation to despair and back again. In him, the emotions, rather than being mingled, are laid out linearly, one after another, and, as often happens, the 'mechanisation' of a complex experience makes the business comic. It is allied also to the fact that Micawber enjoys, indeed revels in, his own despair, even to the extent of threatening self-violence by 'making motions at himself with the razor' from an upstairs window for the benefit of a pressing creditor in the street below (159).

Here, however, is a different kind of parody, and a different kind of humour:

> On my way through the hall I encountered her little dog, who was called Jip—short for Gipsy. I approached him tenderly, for I loved even him; but he showed his whole set of teeth, got under a chair expressly to snarl, and wouldn't hear of the least familiarity.
>
> . . . . .
>
> He was mortally jealous of me, and persisted in barking at me. She took him up in her arms—oh my goodness!—and caressed him, but he persisted in barking still. He wouldn't let me touch him, when I tried; and then she beat him. It increased my sufferings greatly to see the pats she gave him for punishment on the bridge of his blunt nose, while he winked his eyes and licked her hand, and still growled within himself like a little double-bass.

(395)

Where have we encountered this situation before? Surely in the first chapters, where David refuses to be seduced by Mr. Murdstone's blandishments, shows his teeth to good purpose and is savagely beaten for his aggressiveness. Not only does the scene with Dora suggest comically that David may be repeating the Murdstone/Clara relationship, it also reminds us darkly of the intimate connection between pain and sexual love, in that though lighthearted, there is a powerful erotic overtone for David in seeing this delicate, fascinating creature 'beating' her dog (the word is his—he need not have chosen it).

This intermingling of eroticism and cruelty is at the heart of relationships which have a real imaginative conception in *David Copperfield.* It is for this reason that Agnes (whose characteristic gesture shows the least humanly engaged hand in the book—pointing upwards, away from worldly concerns) can never arouse those sentiments in David that Dora and Steerforth evoke. For Rosa Dartle, as we have seen, her whole being is tied up with love and pain, *her* erotic impulses transformed into deliberately extreme images of sadistic desire:

The air of wicked grace: of triumph, in which, strange to say, there was yet something feminine and alluring: with which she reclined upon the seat between us, and looked at me, was worthy of a cruel princess in a legend.

(667)

'And tell that to *me*,' she added, 'with your shameful lips? Why don't they whip these creatures? If I could order it to be done, I would have this girl whipped to death.'

(721)

To the extent that she mingles desire, pain and memory Rosa is a more vibrant figure than Agnes can ever be.

I began this paper on the note of sensitivity, and all ultimately hinges on this. When David reminds Traddles of Salem House, the cheerful extrovert recalls:

But dear me, there was a good deal of fun going on. Do you remember the nights in the bedroom? When we used to have suppers? And when you used to tell the stories? Ha, ha, ha! And do you remember when I got caned for crying about Mr. Mell? Old Creakle! I should like to see him again, too!'

(403)

It is left to the sensitive introvert to feel for him:

'He was a brute to you, Traddles,' said I, indignantly; for his good humour made me feel as if I had seen him beaten but yesterday.

(ibid)

To which Traddles responds: 'But it's all over, a long while.' And so it is, but to the man of feeling nothing is ever over.

It might be said that there is nothing in the nineteenth century man of feeling, Dickens, which might not be found in the eighteenth century sentimentalist with whom we began, Laurence Sterne. Both deal in closely associated experiences of pleasure, pain and humour, drawn together in memory. In Dickens, nevertheless, we are dealing with the sensibility of another age and another genius. *Tristram Shandy* is a fundamentally comic view of life. Hands, as parts of the body trying to cope with life, are as likely to hinder as help the process (witness Dr. Slop's futile efforts with nails and teeth to open his bag of obstetrical implements) (180). Dickens' humour, in *David Copperfield* at least, is often a parodic means of focusing our attention upon problems of intense joy and pain. Memory is for Dickens a more dynamic and interactive business than it is in Sterne. Not least among the new dimensions Dickens brings to the sentimental vision he inherits from the eighteenth century is a thoroughgoing psychological treatment of the power and persistence of memory, not merely for local effect but as a principle which brings

half-conscious repetition and reenactments of the past as a defence mechanism, as a rebirth, or simply (as in the case of Dora) because the hero cannot help it.

Most significant of all perhaps is the role played by sex in the eighteenth and nineteenth century writers. Sexuality in Sterne (*pace* the oft-noted threats of impotence in *Tristram Shandy*) is most frequently comic—the subject of bawdry and sly innuendo. Dickensian gesture reveals a more threatening world than was apparent to Sterne—a world much closer to that of Sterne's nearer contemporary, Richardson, involving a recognition that sexuality is perhaps the most powerful driving force in our natures, and that this drive compounds pain with joy, fascination with repulsion and cruelty with desire in a manner only to be encompassed imaginatively by those who, like David (and Dickens) have a sensibility capable of responding to the darkest, most violent and cruel springs of human motivation.

Works Cited

All references to *David Copperfield* are to the 'Oxford Illustrated Dickens' (1948).

The quotations from *Nicholas Nickleby* are taken from the 'Penguin Classics' edition, edited by Michael Slater (Harmondsworth 1978).

The quotation from *Dombey and Son* is taken from the 'Everyman' Dickens edited by Valerie Purton (London, 1997)

The quotation from *Our Mutual Friend* is taken from the 'Penguin Classics' edition, edited by Stephen Gill (Harmondsworth 1971).

The quotation from *The Life and Opinions of Tristram Shandy* is taken from the 'Penguin English Library' edition edited by Christopher Ricks (Harmondsworth 1967).

The quotation from *A Sentimental Journey* is taken from the 'Penguin English Library' edition, edited by Graham Petrie (Harmondsworth 1967).

S. D. Powell (essay date 2002)

SOURCE: Powell, S. D. "The Subject of David Copperfield's Renaming and the Limits of Fiction." *Dickens Studies Annual* 31 (2002): 47-66.

[*In the following essay, Powell contends that* David Copperfield *should be viewed as a semi-autobiographical novel, and claims that Dickens extensively renames his protagonist throughout the novel as a sophisticated means of maintaining authorial distance.*]

"I have in my heart of hearts a favourite child. And his name is DAVID COPPERFIELD."

Preface to the Charles Dickens Edition of *David Copperfield* (1867)[1]

Notwithstanding the insistence of Dickens himself about the name of his "favourite child," the hero of *David Copperfield* is seldom shown using that name. Called everything from Brooks of Sheffield to Doady, from Mas'r Davy to Trotwood, young David oddly never comments on his lack of a fixed name—nor on the plethora of temporary names he is given throughout the text. "He takes his names as they come," as A. E. Dyson has neatly put it (119).[2] The adult David, narrating the formation of his identity, is not much more forthcoming about the instability of his name; Dickens has him record but not editorialize the renamings. This essay seeks to explain the young hero's silence and, inextricably linked to it, the older narrator's unremarked persistence in recording all of the provisional names. Both the record of renaming and the narrator's uncharacteristic decision to silence both his own and his youthful alter ego's responses to the renaming are worth understanding. For, although David Copperfield's initials mirror the author's, and his life details are similar, David passively rejects his own name, that link to his textual progenitor, reminding the reader again and again that he is doing so. What, I ask, does this unexplained rejection say about Dickens's understanding of his creative enterprise in this novel, typically seen as one of his most autobiographical?

The immediate but not uncomplicated narrative explanation of David's renamings is probably to be sought in his immaturity. Throughout the novel, Dickens hints at the incompleteness of David's development, signaled, for example, by his unabated reverence for Steerforth and his infatuation with Dora. David's unremarked willingness to take on the names of those around him bespeaks a reason for that incompleteness: his unfilled need for the kind of parental care bestowed by the namers. Through much or perhaps all of the book, he is unable to identify himself except in terms of those around him. By allowing and even encouraging his many companions to name him—and through his adult failure to consider the full implications of that renaming, David reinforces our impression that he is, even as an adult, still in search of a parent to care for him. He is, to use Dyson's terms, more clay than potter (119), though as an adult he is complicit in the efforts of his renamers to mold him.

It should also be noted that David's nicknames advance the characterization of those around him and thus, as Sylvère Monod has argued, contribute "both firmly and subtly to creating the unity of the novel" (303).[3] Some critics have worked their way mechanically through David's many names, delineating the significance and symbolic effect of each one.[4] Norman Talbot has analyzed the entire novel, finding three plots (concerning the search for spouse, Steerforth and Emily, and Aunt Betsey and Uriah) and suggesting that in each of these plots David is given a good name (David Copperfield, Mas'r Davy, and Trotwood, respectively) and an ill name (Doady, Daisy, and Master Copperfield). "The three ill names all try to imprison David in a childish or blissfully childlike state, rendering him impotent where he should be heroically constructive and mature," Talbot writes (268).

What must be added to this approach, however, is that David permits these intrusions on his development. In fact, initially, at least, he welcomes almost all of the alternatives. And, except for Uriah's name for him, Master Copperfield, he never overtly rejects any of them. In short, David repeatedly has a chance to assert his own identity by insisting on proper forms of address, but the older David almost never shows his younger self taking this crucial step toward adulthood. His reluctance to do so allows Dickens to reveal David's continuing uncertainty about the stability of his personhood.[5]

Beyond that, I argue that David's willingness to be renamed must also be related to Dickens's larger mimetic goals. Specifically, it must be considered in light of his decision, as he planned the novel, to rename the hero—initially to be called David or Thomas Mag—David Copperfield, a clear echo of his own name.[6] For in renaming Mr. Mag, Dickens reverses his own initials, but he then refuses the hero the uncomplicated use of those initials. This paradox reflects Dickens's ambivalence towards autobiography, a genre he seems eager to approach, yet from which he also holds himself firmly away. If we see David's naming and renaming in this light, the novel may be read, internally, as a complex meditation on David's quest for parental care and, externally, as Dickens's deliberate consideration of his own personal and authorial identity, his bifurcated role as the textual creator of his favorite child and the autobiographical recorder of his own life story.

Dickens's trial titles for the novel, along with Hablot K. Browne's famous design for the cover of the serialized parts of the novel, neatly hint at the complexity of the relationship between creator and created, both textual and biological.[7] Externally, the assignment of the name David Copperfield to his hero allows Dickens to imply a direct relationship to his own life; internally, calling his memoirs those of "David Copperfield the Younger of Blunderstone Rookery" gives the older David a chance to reclaim his patrimony. Browne's rendering of the title, then, which was surely inspired by the trial titles, emphasizes Dickens's desire for a child, a symbolic offspring or an idealized projection, a desire that is disrupted by the continual renaming, which serves to obscure the genetic link between himself and David.

Similarly, the title implies that David's life story is in part a reflection of his desire to associate himself with his dead father.[8] But just as Dickens is uncertain about his relationship to David, so, too, is David ambivalent about his father, whose name he bears only intermittently and whose station in life is lost to him. In short, David's internal ambivalence about his parentage echoes Dickens's own ambivalence about his relationship to David. And the fake insistence that the work was "never meant to be Published on any Account," a phrase that recurs in the trial titles and survives in Browne's engraving, only adds to the sense that this work is, and is not, autobiographical; and is, and is not, a public recounting of private deeds.

David's original naming is only the first of a number of more or less problematic christenings, each a sort of "re-parenting" of the growing boy and young man. Indeed, *David Copperfield* may be read, on one level, as the record of David's serial attempts to find suitable substitutes for his parents.[9] These substitutes, some chosen and some thrust upon him, almost all exercise the parental prerogative of naming their child. David allows these new names to be granted and used, for he wishes, at some level, to see himself as a product of his namers, their surrogate son, and, even as an adult, he feels the need for their formative influences on his life. By changing David's initials or at least by obscuring the association of biological parent with named offspring, moreover, each new name also complicates the equation of Dickens with his favorite child, distancing Dickens from David. That distance is a subject to which I return at the end of this essay.

Naming—specifically the failure of naming—is, in many ways, the major topic of the novel's first chapter, just as it figures so prominently in Browne's design. The name of the family home, Blunderstone Rookery, is one of the first things Betsey Trotwood remarks on. As Aunt Betsey later will with young David's name, she shows little patience for the father's naming: "David Copperfield from head to foot! Calls a house a rookery when there's not a rook near it, and takes the birds on trust, because he sees the nests" (I.5).[10] Peggotty's name is also a subject of Betsey's scorn (I.6).

In this context, which foregrounds naming, the narrator's expression of his acute awareness of his father's absence takes on a new meaning. With dual time references showing that the narrator shares young David's feelings, the narrator reveals the way in which his father's role in his naming is excluded from his perception. "There is something strange to me, *even now,* in the reflection that he never saw me," he writes, "and something stranger yet in the shadowy remembrance that I have of my first childish associations with his white grave-stone in the churchyard, and of the indefinable compassion *I used to feel* for it lying out alone

there in the dark night, when our little parlor was warm and bright with fire and candle, and the doors of our house were—almost cruelly, it seemed to me sometimes—bolted and locked against it" (I.2, my emphases). These recollections show that, even much later, David feels in some way complicit in that absence and responsible for its effects; his passive safety behind the bolted doors is transmuted into an active rejection of every kind of paternal influence. The result is that the father's posthumous "involvement" in his son's naming is correspondingly and paradoxically overlooked. Indeed, as if to emphasize and foreshadow the name's failure, the actual naming is placed to the side of Betsey's failed effort to name the goddaughter she is anticipating, a prominent portion of the chapter, and is relegated to the void of early infancy between chapter I, "I am born" and chapter II, "I observe." No more is made of his name, until he begins to be addressed by Peggotty as Master Davy (II.14).

But if the narrator foregrounds Betsey's attempt to name him (or his unborn sister), he also feels similarly complicit in that naming's failure, for, by being born a boy, he drives her (seemingly) permanently out of his life, "like a discontented fairy" (I.10). "From the moment of this girl's birth, child," she had told Clara Copperfield, "I intend to be her friend. I intend to be her godmother, and I beg you'll call her Betsey Trotwood Copperfield. . . . She must be well brought up, and well guarded from reposing any foolish confidences where they are not deserved. I must make that *my* care" (I.6). When Betsey's attempted naming fails, so too does her plan to begin early the control she hopes to exert over her niece's life. Chapter I, then, records the loss of two parental figures, implicitly relating each loss to the topic of David's naming and to the loss of influential figures who might have helped to form his identity.

Chapter I's double sorrow—the loss of father and of godmother—nevertheless leaves David with a good name and in loving hands. Yet, unhappy as he quickly becomes about his mother's remarriage, it is surely indicative of his wish to have a father that it is he who brings the matter up, however obliquely (and even though prompted by Murdstone's accompaniment home from church the previous Sunday). He asks, "if you marry a person, and the person dies, why then you may marry another person, mayn't you, Peggotty?" (II.14). The account of his mother's courtship is necessarily tinged with knowledge of what came later, but young David is not altogether opposed to it, perhaps because he desires a stronger influence on his identity than his delicate mother: for Clara, unlike Betsey, lacks the gumption or flair to make his name stick. And the name Clara gives reflects another person's identity, rather than her own. Given all of this, David is at least taken with the idea of accompanying Murdstone to Lowestoft (II.17), and his complexion made him think Murdstone, "in spite of my misgivings, a very handsome man" (II.18).

It is at this point that David receives his next name, Brooks of Sheffield, a name of which young David is not even aware. The narrator uses this naming to signal the reader that Murdstone's intentions are less than fatherly, for this name assures that Murdstone can keep David in the childish state of ignorance that Talbot describes, rather than assisting constructively in his development. It does not take much longer for young David to realize that this surrogate father will be no happy substitute for his dead one, as he may initially have hoped.

Only a little later, Murdstone, halfheartedly attempting to fill the role of father, bestows a new name on his new stepson. Although he greets David's return from Yarmouth with a controlled, but possibly friendly "Davy boy" (III.34), the next morning he begins imposing on him the grown-up version of his name (IV.36), rejecting the name his mother uses. Again, naming serves as a shorthand commentary on Murdstone. Already then David recognizes Murdstone's cruelty, but his awareness has become more acute since (note again the double time reference): "I had little doubt *then,* and I have less doubt *now,* that he would have knocked me down without the least compunction, if I had hesitated" (IV.36, my emphases). Just as "Brooks of Sheffield" imprisons David in ignorance, "David" catapults him into a premature (and violent) adulthood. Hawes points out, "Mr Murdstone wants to emphasize to David and his mother that David is a boy and not a baby, and that he is not to be treated any longer as a mother's darling" (85), but young David is not ready for such treatment. Murdstone picks the one name, horrible as it is when he uses it, that David will not, may not reject, the name that his dead father had borne and that is, undeniably, his actual name. Yet Murdstone is virtually the only person in the book to call him David (Monod 302), and the narrator uses this fact to emphasize the cruelty of the naming. Ironically, then, by not using a nickname, Murdstone reveals his final rejection of the paternal role in which David had originally imagined him. For the rest of the novel, each conferring of a new name will signal the possibility of a new parental figure.

David's two forays away from Blunderstone Rookery, to Yarmouth and then to school, bring with them new father figures, more agreeable to him. The first of these, the kindly Mr. Peggotty, however, turns out to be, to David's surprise, no father, for, as Mr. Peggotty tells him in their first conversation, he had never given Ham his name, "his father giv it him" (III.26). Here again, the narrator equates naming with fatherhood, an equation that is complicated by the parental care Mr. Peg-gotty does in fact provide to Ham. In any case, David relates well to Mr. Peggotty's oddly-assembled family, for he is drawn to it by the orphanhood (partial at first, but soon complete) he shares with Ham and Em'ly (see III.27). But their kinship is always incomplete. Em'ly points out the difference between them: "your father was a gentleman and your mother is a lady; and my father was a fisherman and my mother was a fisherman's daughter, and my uncle Dan is a fisherman" (III.27). David never does become another adopted son for Mr. Peggotty, and so throughout his stay at Yarmouth and in later years, he retains the name that Peggotty uses, Master Davy (or Mas'r Davy). Hawes believes that name "nicely combines [the family's] affection with a proper respect" (85), and Talbot characterizes it as "good." John O. Jordan is right, however, to point out the social condescension that is implicit in David's relations with the Peggottys and that ultimately leads to their tragedy (see 70-76).

In his quest for a family (and thanks to his upbringing and society), young David is oblivious to the implications of the reverential, if affectionate, title the family uses for him. He does not consider why they call him what they do. He is only too willing to let them mold him into an honored part of the family. But the name reveals that he never does assume a place in the family and remains, instead, an intruder, adored even after he betrays them by introducing them to their downfall. In fact, in the novel's world, his failure to incorporate himself fully into the Peggotty family is signaled precisely by their reluctance to give him a new name, to mark him as one of their own instead of as a cherished outsider, whose naming reveals not familial or parental but rather social duty. In that respect, they are like Murdstone, but more kindly and wisely refusing to parent David. The naming shows all of that, but the narrator, embarrassed, perhaps, by his betrayal of the family, or bitter that they did not or could not adopt him, will not make the connections explicit.

David's sojourn at Salem House, on the other hand, leads him to a very different sort of father figure—one who, at last, willingly takes on that role. Although his fascination with Steerforth may strike readers today as homoerotic, it is worth considering David's reverence in other lights, as well. Indeed, his attempts to emulate the suavely elegant Steerforth suggest as strongly the relationship between a younger and an older brother as between lovers. Steerforth's command and manliness, moreover, also cast him in the role of surrogate father. One of the first things David does upon their meeting is yield to him the governance of all his worldly possessions, all of his seven shillings (VI.67). Steerforth controls other aspects of David's life, as well, including his sleeping and waking (see VII.73-75), and protects him from other boys: "nobody dared to annoy one whom he honored with his countenance" (VII.73). Steerforth also commands David's unquestioning affection, a fact made clear time and again through the novel.

None of this necessarily means that Steerforth fills anything more than a fraternal role, but later Steerforth moves definitively into the paternal role when he names David. "Daisy" is not a juvenile nickname, at least in the way Steerforth uses it, although it might be considered to be so if its usage were strictly mocking, if David were being called a sissy. But Steerforth does not hit upon this name until he is a young adult, "an Oxford man," while David has finished his schooling (XIX.235), and the name is not directly mocking or, at least, not perceived by David to be so. Steerforth asks, "'Will you mind my calling you Daisy?' 'Not at all!' said I. 'That's a good fellow!'" (XX.237). David's love for Steerforth, of course, will permit no other answer, although he blushes when Rosa Dartle asks about the name: "Is it—eh?—because he thinks you young and innocent?" (XX.242). Steerforth trespasses so on David's affections, then, as to impose on him a name as irrevocable as the one a parent bestows. This is a name, however, unlike his own, which "must have a touch of contempt," for it symbolizes David's innocence, which Steerforth "admires and violates" (Dyson 122). In short, recording the naming allows the narrator, on the one hand, quietly to show the extent to which his personal identity is controlled, not as lover but as parent, for good and ill, by Steerforth. The narrator's failure to editorialize the naming, on the other hand, is tantamount to young David's blush, a tacit but unspoken acknowledgment of an uncomfortable truth.

Upon leaving Blunderstone for good, David begins his new life as a child-laborer, lodging with the Micawber family. The Micawbers, so clearly modeled on Dickens's own parents, nevertheless remain a respectful distance away from David with their forms of address. Mr. Micawber's "Copperfield" or Mrs. Micawber's "Master Copperfield," Hawes points out, would not have been unusual forms of address at the time (85), but they do show that David maintains a greater distance from the Micawbers than he does from the Peggottys. And the contrast in their naming of David echoes the unsuitability of the Micawbers as parents. David says of his time as their lodger, "From Monday morning until Saturday night, I had no advice, no counsel, no encouragement, no consolation, no assistance, no support, of any kind, from any one, that I can call to mind, as I hope to go to heaven!" (XI.129).[11] Despite their mutual affection, the relationship remains based on the household economics that are the subject of Mrs. Micawber's first discussion with David and that remain an issue throughout the novel: he is first their boarder, eventually their pawning expert, then their financial adviser and, at the end of the Heep affair, (along with Tommy Traddles) their financial rescuer. Indeed, it seems that David is often the member of the household most in charge and most to

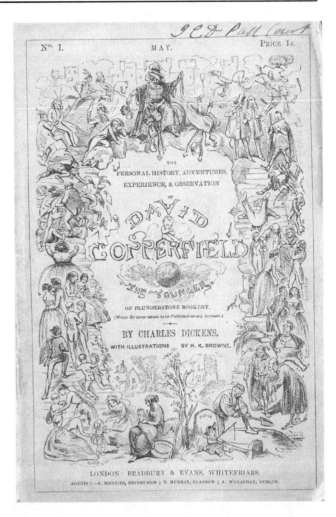

Title page for a nineteenth-century edition of David Copperfield, *by Charles Dickens.*

be respected. For this reason, perhaps, David's identity is stronger in this period than it has been before. He knows what he wants; he knows what he can do for others. The Micawbers' naming signals, and also reinforces, this stronger self-awareness.

We might imagine that David's maturation is complete. The Micawbers' use of his real name and their failure to take on parental roles at least points in that direction. More importantly, young David never sees the Micawbers as potential surrogate parents, and he assumes adult, and even parental, responsibilities in their household. At this point, then, the narrative search for parents appears to have ended.

But it is at most replaced by Dickens's autobiographical renegotiation of the betrayal of children by adults, for if young David does not see the Micawbers as potential parents, the narrator surely does. That larger concern transcends the absence of his parents through death, pointing up the not so humorous failure lying behind the Micawbers' humorous treatment of their youthful lodger. As do Dickens's own parents, the Micawbers fail their charge, rendering him toughened and seemingly mature but still in need of parental guidance. They are good to him, then, but not good enough, for they fail to treat him as a child. The narrator's emphasis on the Micawbers' name for David quietly reveals his sense of betrayal by them and his insistence that David is not yet ready to retain one and only one name, to achieve independent adulthood. Simultaneously, the Micawbers' failure to name David allows for Dickens's excoriation of the Victorians for their refusal to protect children.

When David is taken under the wing of his great-aunt, the theme of children's betrayal is tied even more directly to his search for parents who will name him. Betsey, again displaying her sensitivity to naming, tells him Mr. Dick's true name. "He can't bear his name," she says. "That's a peculiarity of his. Though I don't know that it's much of a peculiarity, either; he has been ill-used enough, by some that bear it, to have a mortal antipathy for it, Heaven knows" (XIV.164). Her recognition of the maltreatment of Mr. Dick at the hands of those who should have protected him and the consequences of it—his desire for a different name—lead Betsey to declare that David, too, must be renamed.[12] Having decided that she and Mr. Dick will care for him as surrogate parents, she works to erase the betrayals he has suffered, declaring, "I have been thinking, do you know, Mr. Dick, that I might call him Trotwood?" (XIV.175). She has, after all, reassumed the role she forfeited when David was born, as protector of her nephew's child, as that child's godmother. And so David observes, "Thus I began my new life, in a new name, and with everything new about me" (XIV.175). As Harry Stone puts it, "The fairy godmother who presided imperiously at his original birth presides with equal imperiousness at his rebirth" (193), though my reading of Betsey's motivations is more favorable than Stone's.

C. A. Bodelsen claims, "There is an air of bustle and goings to and fro about Trotwood, and also a touch of good-natured eccentricity, perhaps because one is reminded, via 'trot', of a little pony" (46). But "Trotwood," of course, is not an original coinage for Aunt Betsey. It is her own name and was to have been part of the name of his unborn sister. By accepting Trotwood as a name, then, David is defining himself, not only in terms of his aunt, but also in terms of his alter ego, the girl he was not.[13] His acceptance of the name means he has not just a new name, but a new family of sorts, a father and mother who name him, and a sister whose presence is murkily alluded to by the name (as it will be again by Steerforth's name, Daisy). Aunt Betsey has at last fulfilled her role as godmother, and she provides him a family in which he may safely grow up.

The name also suggests that she has bestowed on him a new identity, one less sturdy and predictable, more eccentric than "David" could ever be.[14]

It is from this new family that David ventures forth, coming into his own academically and personally. Nearly all of his new acquaintances in Kent call him Trotwood, significantly including Agnes, who retains this name for him right up to their mutual declaration of love (see LXII.706) and presumably after their marriage. But Dora does not, perhaps because she is unable to understand the eccentricity and quick wit in David, which "David" so nicely conceals but which "Trotwood" lays bare. Dora's usual name for him is "Doady," "which was a corruption of David" and may be an attempt to simplify David's personality even further (XLI.491). Monod calls this name "charming" (302), and Dyson declares it "as affectionate as 'Daisy' and far more innocent: a beautiful instance, in the tone surrounding it, of Dora's love, trust, tenderness and unfitness for life" (126). It is a mistake, however, to follow these critics in examining this name from the point of view of the namer, rather than the named. Dora certainly means no harm in calling David Doady, just as she never means any harm in anything she does or does not do. His willing acceptance of this name, however, and the narrator's refusal to criticize himself for it, should be an immediate tip-off that his attraction to Dora is wrongheaded, that the narrator recognizes, as we do, that "Doady" represents a step back from the mature freedom of "Trotwood" and the family that bestowed that name.

It would be too blunt to say that David is attracted to Dora only because she reminds him of his dead mother. Instead, once again, he is still in search of a surrogate parent, even despite his relationship with Betsey Trotwood. Thus, he is willing to be renamed—however inappropriately—by this new "mother," and, while Clara's affectionate "Davy" was acceptable for a young boy, Dora's new corruption of "David" strikes one as very wrong for a young man, just come of age. "Doady" allows David to imprison himself in a blissfully ignorant state, as Talbot points out, and thus in a wretchedly inappropriate and immature love and marriage.[15] These are subjects the narrator will leave the reader to figure out.

David is rescued from this marriage, however, as he is from so many other disasters, and he eventually enters a much more fulfilling and appropriate marriage with Agnes, who never finds it necessary to name David. She does not see herself as a shaper of his life and identity, and what shaping she does is unconscious. When he tells her, ". . . all my life long I shall look up to you, and be guided by you, as I have been through the darkness that is past," she shrugs off the praise: "She put her hand in mine, and told me she was proud of me, and of what I said; although I praised her very far beyond her worth" (LX.688). Agnes, in other words, does not aspire to shape David as a mother would, and her strength not to do so is symbolized by her not giving him a new name. Again, though, it is important not to focus too exclusively on the motives of the namer. What is more interesting is David's reaction to the lack of naming. It is Agnes's strength, not his, that makes him start to see her as more than a mother figure. And he becomes more of a husband than a son to her. Yet the incompleteness of that development is signaled by the two names with which he ends the novel, David and Trotwood, and the fact that Agnes uses the latter name.

As he matures, of course, David's many names cease to have a formative effect on him. The hurtfulness, even of Uriah's scornful "Master Copperfield," diminishes, and, as he gains assurance about his maturity, Miss Murdstone's "boy" (VIII.93), Mr. Murdstone's "Brooks of Sheffield," the waiter's "six-foot" (V.53), the factory boys' "little gent" (XI.131), and the "six-penn'orth of bad ha'pence" used by the young man who steals David's trunk (XII.143-44), all seem far less painful, and even a source of merriment for the narrator. That it takes him so long to reach the state of maturity in which sticks and stones hurt worse than names, however, is made clear by the effect that names given by those in his adopted families have on him, his willingness to accept new names from these families, and his later reluctance to explore the names more fully.

In a book full of orphans, David Copperfield is the one orphan who is in many ways not an orphan. He has many sets of parents, and many adults who take him into their protection and treat him as much like a son as they can. But even the older David searches for more fulfilling parental relationships, and his story may thus be read as the story of a quest for replacements for the family which he has lost but not forgotten at Blunderstone Rookery and for the identity which that family never could give him. That he ends the novel with two names just as he had begun it—as Betsey and David—suggests that this quest is not yet complete, that his identity remains only partially formed. His personal life as Trotwood Copperfield remains separated from his public life as David Copperfield. He must still identify himself in terms of another, though the narrator's acknowledgment of that fact is only glancing. As he writes at the end of his story, Agnes is "the dear presence, without which I were nothing" (LXIV.717). His need for Agnes "pointing upward," we can see, is yet the need of a child for a guiding mother.

Much earlier in the novel, Mr. Murdstone's actions have foreshadowed David's state of perpetual bifurcation. When his mother remarries, David is both a Copperfield and a Murdstone. Indeed, Murdstone even makes a fleeting attempt to change David's last name,

when his dinner on the way to school is paid for in the name Murdstone, not Copperfield (see V.52). The confusion that results is symbolic of the confusion he feels about his own identity and his parents'.

Yet this episode—and thus the novel's close—may be read in a different way, too. If Murdstone drops his attempts to rename David, "because Murdstone hates the thought of him far too much by now to persevere," as Dyson argues (121), then we have here a textual acknowledgment of the ways in which names and renaming can be used both to achieve intimacy and to create distance. Murdstone's renaming of David implies a paternal relationship that, from hatred, Murdstone almost immediately aborts by renaming him Copperfield again. Similarly, the narrator uses his many renamings as a way of signaling his newfound maturity and his distance from his younger self, a distance that is belied by his own continuing need for Agnes's parental care, not to mention Agnes's use of Trotwood rather than David to name her husband. Even as an adult, then, the narrator embraces his nickname as suitable for his interior life and rejects his birthname as appropriate only for the outside world. In doing so, he opens a space in his identification with the younger David Copperfield, rejecting, at a fundamental, personal level, his association with the life story he is in the process of writing. Dickens's feelings toward David are considerably kinder than Murdstone's, but they are as complex as David's about his younger self; his use of David's multiple names performs a function similar to the one sought by the narrator, the creation of distance. Dickens's emphasis on the consistent renaming of David invites us to see his feelings towards David as less warm than his own statements imply.

Indeed, the renaming suggests that Dickens wants his public life as a famous author to remain separate from the fictional and yet, clearly, also autobiographical projection of that life onto David. Both internally and externally, however, the novel remains deeply ambivalent about that split. The reasons for this complication, manifested in part by the narrator's failure to editorialize in the face of David's renaming, are to be found in Dickens's own life story. Specifically, I believe that Dickens is uncomfortable with the romanticization of his childhood that *David Copperfield* implies. Although both David and Dickens are betrayed by their parents' failings, the key difference cannot have escaped the author: the betrayal of young Charles was real, his degradation in the blacking factory was real, his parents' failure to educate him properly was real, his poverty and shame were real. They were, in fact, so real and so painful that he hardly wrote about them, and he kept many of the details even from his wife. In this semi-autobiographical novel, then, which editorializes almost every aspect of David's life, the fundamental fact of David's incomplete quest for parental figures and his concomitant inability to achieve fully adult relationships, even with Agnes, are effaced, hinted at only by his perpetual renaming.

And so it is with Dickens writing about himself: the author's reluctance to confide his most intense life details, which, like David's, stem from parental betrayal and affect marital relations, is a constant theme of the long autobiographical fragment about the blacking factory period woven into John Forster's *Life of Charles Dickens,* which was published shortly after Dickens's death. This fragment describes the time his father spent in debtor's prison, when Charles was a child laborer. As Dickens writes, "The deep remembrance of the sense I had of being utterly neglected and hopeless; of the shame I felt in my position; of the misery it was to my young heart to believe that, day by day, what I had learned, and thought, and delighted in, and raised my fancy and my emulation up by, was passing away from me, never to be brought back any more; cannot be written." (Forster 1:22). And, again, "From that hour until this at which I write, no word of that part of my childhood . . . has passed my lips to any human being . . . I have never, until I now impart it to this paper, in any burst of confidence with anyone, my own wife not excepted, raised the curtain I then dropped" (Forster 1:32-33). Although there is some indication that Dickens did in fact tell his wife about his experience as a child laborer,[16] even within marriage, Dickens, like his narrator, hesitated about confiding his true feelings about his parents. But the fact that he stresses this hesitation so fully suggests the depth of his desire to tell all.

Dickens also knew the inadequacy of autobiography to relay such details, to capture the horror he had experienced. As he writes in the concluding sentence of the autobiographical fragment (or so it appears in Forster), "[This writing] does not seem a tithe of what I might have written, or of what I meant to write." Moreover, Dickens abandoned autobiography after writing this fragment, choosing fiction instead. As Forster explains, it was "when the fancy of *David Copperfield* . . . began to take shape in his mind, that he abandoned his first intention of writing his own life" (1:20). In fiction, then, Dickens hoped finally to tell his story. But even fiction must not have seemed safe or sharp enough, and so he subverts the equation between his autobiography and his fiction that Forster and subsequent biographers have all taken for granted.[17] To take only one comparatively straightforward example, Charles's experiences as a boarder remind one of David's with the Micawbers, and both end the same way: with a return to a more conventional, though not unproblematic, childhood, David with Betsey, Charles with his parents. Yet the real and tragic failings of his real parents are displaced onto the Micawbers' fictional and risible failings as landlords.

In less fictive writings, Dickens's awareness of childhood's terrors is much more sharply delineated, though it is still veiled. In **"Gone Astray,"** an ostensibly autobiographical story about being inadvertently abandoned on an outing to St. Giles, for example, eight or nine-year-old Charles's anxieties about the need to support himself are so much in the forefront that he never stops to imagine that he might be able to rely further on his own parents. "To the best of my belief," Dickens writes, "the idea of asking my way home never came into my head . . . I have a serious conviction that in the wide scope of my arrangements for the future, I had no eyes for the nearest and most obvious course" (381-82). Instead, he planned to make his own way in the world, if necessary "to go into the army as a drummer" (382). The retrospective recollection of both his childhood panic and his melancholy sense that he would have to provide for himself was surely colored by his parents' more serious, later failure to provide for him. Indeed, the ferocity of the impressions may plausibly be thought to stem from that later period in his life. But, as the older David does in *David Copperfield,* the older Dickens resists making such connections overt or permanent.

Like his novel's narrator, he only intermittently hints at parental duties and parental betrayals. The true causes of his disappointment in his parents are conveyed only in private, autobiographical jottings and rare, confidential conversations with Forster and other close friends. His disappointment and the secrecy of it are especially evident in his comments on his removal from the blacking factory, following his father's release from debtor's prison. It is not till quite some time after that release that Dickens stops working and returns to school, a change that seems to have been a belated paternal expression of support for the boy. But Dickens knew well that his mother opposed the change, and he confides to his autobiography, "I do not write resentfully or angrily: for I know how all these things have worked together to make me what I am: but I never afterwards forgot, I never shall forget, I never can forget, that my mother was warm for my being sent back [to the factory]" (Forster 1:32).

Forster records a number of Dickens's other disappointments. When they had first moved to Camden Town (before his father's bankruptcy), for example, Charles had not been sent to school, as he had hoped to be, and, as he tells Forster, his father "appeared to have utterly lost at this time the idea of educating me at all, and to have utterly put from him the notion that I had any claim upon him, in that regard, whatever" (1:13). Having confided such betrayals to Forster, and having recollected the depth of his miseries, Dickens retreats to fiction and leaves it to his biographers to fill in the connections. But he complicates that task.

The work began with Forster's *Life,* and his assessment of the blend of fact and fiction in *David Copperfield* is still pertinent and forms an implicit basis of many critical and biographical treatments of Dickens, even today. Forster argues: "many as are the resemblances in Copperfield's adventures to portions of those of Dickens, and often as reflections occur to David which no one intimate with Dickens could fail to recognise as but the reproduction of his, it would be the greatest mistake to imagine anything like a complete identity of the fictitious novelist with the real one . . . or to suppose that the youth, who [in the factory] received his first harsh schooling in life, came out of it as little harmed or hardened as David did. The language of the fiction reflects only faintly the narrative of the actual fact . . . Here was but another proof how thoroughly Dickens understood his calling, and that to weave fact with fiction unskilfully would be only to make truth less true" (Forster 2:105).

But my study shows that Forster's emphasis is wrong. It is not that Dickens is spicing his fiction with carefully selected facts, as Forster would have it, but rather that he uses fiction to cancel or blunt fact: he *does* want to make truth either less true or at least more open to revision.

By writing a semi-autobiographical novel, Dickens might have hoped to renegotiate his parents' failures and his childhood deprivation, to understand them better, to come to terms with his own rise from childhood degradation (that is, at least, Forster's implicit argument). But the insistence on the renaming of David, which breaks the stated and implicit bond between him and "his favourite child," shows that the renegotiation is only partially complete. Dickens does not so much weave fact with fiction as he hides fact behind the veil of fiction, rendering fact both commercially viable and personally comfortable. And though he decides to lift that veil a bit in the title of the novel and in the hero's real name, the pains lingering from childhood are still too powerful to be easily repackaged as fiction. Like his narrator, in short, Dickens is drawn to tell his life story but works to break the bonds between his youth and his adult self.

Dickens acknowledged the problems with and limitations of his artifice, though only glancingly, in his preface to the 1850 edition: "I do not find it easy to get sufficiently far away from this Book, in the first sensations of having finished it, to refer to it with the composure which this formal heading [i.e., "Preface"] would seem to require."[18] The continuation might make us think that Dickens is going to confess to the autobiographical element: "My interest in it, is so recent and strong . . . that I am in danger of wearying the reader whom I love, with personal confidences, and private emotions." But this impulse is stopped quickly in the next sen-

tence, set aside, as if for emphasis, in its own paragraph: "Besides which, all that I could say of the Story, to any purpose, I have endeavoured to say in it." And, again, a few sentences later: "I have nothing else to tell . . ." These statements, in their alternation between confession and defense, between openness and secrecy, between truth and fiction, confirm that David Copperfield must—and, equally, must not—be seen as a reflection of Charles Dickens.

Notes

1. See *David Copperfield,* ed. Nina Burgis (Oxford: Clarendon, 1981) 752.

2. Dyson and most other commentators on the novel treat the broad range of naming practices as more unified in kind than they actually are. I will follow this practice here, though I am oversimplifying social conventions, for example, in calling "Mas'r Davy" a new name. Nevertheless, the general critical tendency to consider Mas'r Davy and Brooks of Sheffield as analogous is justified by the similarity of their artistic effects; both names, and all the others, are used by Dickens to reveal the nature of David's interaction with the rest of his world. It is more important to show the variation in these interactions, as revealed by different forms of appellation, than to categorize each of the names as nickname, diminutive, honorific, or the like.

3. Monod builds on a long history in Dickens criticism. In 1917, Elizabeth Hope Gordon was among the first to attempt to categorize Dickens's names, which she called "the last noteworthy appearance in fiction of names that pertinently distinguish the characters" (4). Gordon identifies four categories of names: those whose originals have been identified (6-9), "directly-descriptive names" (10-21), "vaguely suggestive names" (21-32), and those which are neutral (32-34). She concludes, "Names are with him not mere tags for puppets serving but to prevent confusion in the assemblage of characters. Rather they partake of the nature of the people to whom they belong" (34). The next year, however, E. de Laski, studying the surnames in *Pickwick Papers, Nicholas Nickleby,* and *Our Mutual Friend,* found that fully seventy-four percent of these names were "British or derived from British family names," while many others are English words or derived from English words. Fewer than a tenth of the names (only four percent in *OMF*) are "original" coinages. This, de Laski reasons, "raises a strong presumption that Dickens was not as original in his selection of surnames as is ordinarily supposed" (341). Lionel Stevenson assumes the source of Dickens's names is of minor importance: "whether he adopted an existing name or

coined a new one, the artistic effect is less in the source than in the application" (242).

Dickens's use of names remains a source of interest to more recent critics. Kelsie B. Harder points out that his names, in context, "obviously type a character or object, or they give tone and atmosphere to the situation. Individually, they reflect an Al Cappish sort of waggery, often vulgar and grotesque. But when they are placed in clusters they exemplify something more serious, an unconscious attitude that works out and repeats itself over and over" (42). C. A. Bodelsen is also interested in the role of the unconscious in naming in Dickens's novels. Bodelsen claims that "'symbolic' names are inventions of Dickens and form part of a general symbolic technique that permeates his work. What happens is that the sound, or spelling, of the name directs the reader's mind towards certain associations, which in their turn impart their own overtones to the name . . . Even the writer is no doubt often ignorant of how the effect is produced." Harry Stone writes of Dickens's naming: "That there was a right name he had no doubt. It was the name that conveyed the outward show and inward mystery of a character of a book, the name which revealed and yet concealed" (191).

4. See, for example, Dyson 119-26, one of the most complete treatments of the subject, or Hawes.

5. My argument here builds on Joseph Bottum's examination of the novel's naming and his claim that Dickens uses naming in order to examine the philosophical underpinnings of fiction. Bottum writes, "The order of names has caught his attention, and he does more than use it to express rank and sentiment. Dickens shows both the origin of abuse in extrinsic denomination and the power of names to mark that abuse. And he claims at the novel's end both the possibility of intrinsic denomination and the power of true names to speak the unity of concept and thing" (454).

6. For a complete record of Dickens's trial titles, see Burgis's edition of *David Copperfield,* 753-55. Two early titles have the hero's name as Charles Copperfield.

7. See Burgis's edition, frontispiece [ii].

8. John O. Jordan notes that "the title emphasizes that he [David] is well-born, that he has a father whose name he is proud to bear, and that he has an estate with a rather grand-sounding name" (67). Jordan supposes this reveals David's social ambivalence, but it also shows, more directly, that he wishes to associate himself with his dead father, to show clearly that it is his father who has conferred a name on him, however indirectly.

9. See Hochman and Wachs, especially 55-85, for a more complete consideration of this reading of the novel. Such a reading, admittedly, runs the risk of simplifying complex and multifaceted motivations. That risk seems justified here, given the trial titles and the centrality of problematic parenting in Dickens's own life story.

10. References to *David Copperfield* are to Burgis's edition, and are given parenthetically by chapter and page number.

11. Dickens's autobiographical recollection of his parents' abandonment during the blacking factory period is strikingly similar: "I certainly had no other assistance whatever . . . from Monday morning until Saturday night. No advice, no counsel, no encouragement, no consolation, no support, from any one that I can call to mind, so help me God" (Forster 1:27).

12. Herbert Barry has pointed out to me that, in this context, the echo of Dickens's surname in "Mr. Dick" provides further evidence of the author's interest in the relationship of the novel's names to his own life story.

13. Monod expands on the significance of this identification with Betsey Trotwood Copperfield, arguing that she "is something like the embodiment of the feminine side of David's personality" (323).

14. Hawes is especially thorough in his analysis of David's real first and last names. Pointing out that David was a fairly unusual name in Victorian England, Hawes suggests "the name 'David' was likely to convey impressions of fallibility as well as strength—impressions, that is, of a hero with certain flaws—to nineteenth-century readers with their ready and knowledgeable acquaintance with the Bible" (84). After describing the component parts of "Copperfield," Hawes writes, "The complete name . . . can . . . suggest not only the hero's essential but not extraordinary worthiness, durability, and malleability, but also the area and scope relating to the exercise and development of those personal qualities; there are, in addition, suggestions of familiar Englishness and perhaps . . . of characteristics that can loosely be called natural and Wordsworthian" (83).

15. The name is only one indication of this, of course. David's over-reliance on Dora manifests itself in the kind of complete and utter trust which a child has for a parent: "Her idea," he writes after Emily and Steerforth are lost to him, "was my refuge in disappointment and distress, and made some amends to me, even for the loss of my friend. The more I pitied myself, or pitied others, the more I sought for consolation in the image of Dora . . . I

don't think I had any definite idea where Dora came from, or in what degree she was related to a higher order of beings; but I am quite sure I should have scouted the notion of her being simply human, like any other young lady, with indignation and contempt" (XXXIII.387). The unsuitability of the marriage is recognized by Aunt Betsey, who calls Dora and David "a pair of babes in the wood," although she is, on the whole, much less scornful than she had been of Clara, whom she had, in similar fashion, dismissed as "a wax doll" (XLIV.522, I.3). Betsey comes to love Dora very much, as perhaps she would have come to love Clara.

16. In the 1892 edition of *David Copperfield*, Charles Dickens, Jr. reported that his father had shown the autobiographical fragment to Catherine. See Ackroyd's biography *Dickens*, 553 and 1118n. See also Michael Slater's essay "How Dickens 'Told' Catherine about His Past." Slater points out that in 1835, Dickens presented Catherine with a copy of the volume of *Lives of the English Poets* that contained Johnson's life of Richard Savage. By calling her attention to Savage's life, Dickens signaled a parallel between the poet's childhood miseries and his own. Slater's conclusion about the presentation to Catherine is similar to my own about his representation of David Copperfield: "Dickens wanted his Desdemona's pity for the perils he had passed but wanted also to conceal the sordid, inglorious nature of those perils" (3).

17. There are notable connections. For two twentieth-century understandings of these connections, see Edgar Johnson's *Charles Dickens: His Triumph and Tragedy* and Peter Ackroyd's *Dickens,* both of which return frequently and justifiably to *David Copperfield* and other novels to fill in details from Dickens's life.

18. See Burgis's edition, [lxxi].

Works Cited

Ackroyd, Peter. *Dickens*. London: Sinclair-Stevenson, 1990.

Bodelsen, C. A. "The Physiognomy of the Name." *Review of English Literature* 2.3 (July 1961): 39-48.

Bottum, Joseph. "The Gentleman's True Name: *David Copperfield* and the Philosophy of Naming." *Nineteenth-Century Literature* 49 (1995): 435-55.

Brook, G. L. *The Language of Dickens*. London: André Deutsch, 1970.

de Laski, E. "The Psychological Attitude of Charles Dickens toward Surnames." *American Journal of Psychology* 29 (1918): 337-46.

Dickens, Charles. *David Copperfield*. Ed. Nina Burgis. Oxford: Clarendon, 1981.

Dickens, Charles. "Gone Astray." *The Works of Charles Dickens*. Vol. 18. New York: Bigelow, Brown and Co., n.d. 380-92.

Dyson, A. E. *The Inimitable Dickens*. London: Macmillan, 1970.

Forster, John. *The Life of Charles Dickens*. Ed. A. J. Hoppé. 2 vols. London: Dent, 1966.

Gordon, Elizabeth Hope. "The Naming of Characters in the Works of Charles Dickens." *University of Nebraska Studies in Language, Literature, and Criticism* 1 (1917): 3-35.

Harder, Kelsie B. "Charles Dickens Names his Characters." *Names* 7 (1959): 35-42.

Hawes, Donald. "David Copperfield's Names." *The Dickensian* 74 (1978): 81-87.

Hochman, Baruch, and Ilja Wachs. *Dickens: The Orphan Condition*. Madison, NJ: Fairleigh Dickinson UP, 1999.

Johnson, Edgar. *Charles Dickens: His Tragedy and Triumph*. 2 vols. New York: Simon and Schuster, 1952.

Jordan, John O. "The Social Sub-text of *David Copperfield*." *Dickens Studies Annual* 14 (1985): 61-92.

Monod, Sylvère. *Dickens the Novelist*. Norman: U of Oklahoma P, 1968.

Slater, Michael. "How Dickens 'Told' Catherine about His Past." *The Dickensian* 75 (1979): 3-6.

Stevenson, Lionel. "Names in *Pickwick*." *The Dickensian* 32 (1936): 241-44.

Stone, Harry. "What's in a Name: Fantasy and Calculation in Dickens." *Dickens Studies Annual* 14 (1985): 191-204.

Talbot, Norman. "The Naming and the Names of the Hero: A Study in *David Copperfield*." *Southern Review* (Adelaide) 11 (1978): 267-82.

FURTHER READING

Criticism

Ablow, Rachel. "Labors of Love: The Sympathetic Subjects of *David Copperfield*." *Dickens Studies Annual* 31 (2002): 23-46.

　　Maintains that *David Copperfield* provides a model of sympathy based upon "the ethically valuable desire for another person's love and approval" rather than one designed to elicit a reader's identification with the novel's individual characters. The critic thus interprets *David Copperfield* in the context of its evocation of an idealized love object for David (Agnes), rather than its depiction of his emotional maturation.

Andrade, Mary Anne. "Pollution of an Honest Home." *Dickens Quarterly* 5, no. 2 (June 1988): 65-74.

Concentrates on *David Copperfield* as a celebration of family life, and particularly of the bonds between parent and child.

Berlatsky, Eric. "Dickens's Favorite Child: Malthusian Sexual Economy and the Anxiety over Reproduction in *David Copperfield.*" *Dickens Studies Annual* 31 (2002): 87-126.

Stresses the position of *David Copperfield* with regard to Victorian sexual discourse, as a work informed not only by the need to suppress and sublimate deviant or inappropriate sexuality, but also as one that encodes Malthusian fears of sexual reproduction as a source of overpopulation and consequent economic deprivation.

Berman, Ronald. "The Innocent Observer." *Children's Literature* 9 (1981): 40-50.

States that *David Copperfield* is the definitive Victorian novel of lost childhood innocence, and compares its use of a child narrator to reveal social inequities with that of Charlotte Brontë's *Jane Eyre*.

Buckton, Oliver S. "'The Reader Whom I Love': Homoerotic Secrets in *David Copperfield.*" *ELH* 64, no. 1 (spring 1997): 189-222.

Characterizes *David Copperfield* as rewriting the Victorian *Bildungsroman* in terms of its narrative construction of the past as secret, then continues by tracing hints of suppressed homosexual desire— principally focused on David's relationship to James Steerforth—in the novel.

Cain, Tom. "Tolstoy's Use of *David Copperfield.*" In *Tolstoi and Britain,* edited by W. Gareth Jones, pp. 67-78. Oxford: Berg Publishers Limited, 1995.

Details Tolstoy's application of *David Copperfield* as a model for certain characters, themes, and specific episodes in his novel *War and Peace*.

Carmichael, Virginia. "In Search of Beein': Nom/Non du Père in *David Copperfield.*" *ELH* 54, no. 3 (fall 1987): 653-67.

Reads *David Copperfield* as a novelistic search for "home" conditioned by the absence of Copperfield's father and expressed in terms of its hero's efforts to find both an appropriate vocation and sexual partner.

Chaston, Joel D. "Crusoe, Crocodiles, and Cookery Books: *David Copperfield* and the Affective Power of Reading Fiction." *University of Mississippi Studies in English* 9 (1991): 141-53.

Cites instances of individuals reading fiction in *David Copperfield* in order to underscore the benefits and potential dangers of reading for characters in the novel.

Clay, George R. "In Defense of Flat Characters." *Midwest Quarterly* 62, no. 3 (spring 2001): 271-80.

Claims that the wide cast of "flat," eccentric, secondary characters in *David Copperfield,* while having no direct bearing on the novel's main plot, nevertheless is central to the effectiveness of the work in engaging the reader's attention and interest.

Crick, Brian. "'Mr. Peggotty's Dream Comes True': Fathers and Husbands; Wives and Daughters." *University of Toronto Quarterly* 54, no. 1 (fall 1984): 38-55.

Focuses on the character of Mr. Peggotty in order to highlight Dickens's equivocal treatment of relations between older men and young women in *David Copperfield*.

Eiger, Edwin M. "The Lunatic at the Window: Magic Casements of *David Copperfield.*" *Dickens Quarterly* 2, no. 1 (May 1985): 18-21.

Highlights Dickens's extensive use of characters gazing or peering through windows in *David Copperfield,* but declines to make an overall interpretation of the motif's function in the novel.

Garnett, Robert R. "Why Not Sophy? Desire and Agnes in *David Copperfield.*" *Dickens Quarterly* 14, no. 4 (December 1997): 213-31.

Confronts the problem of Agnes's ostensibly unsympathetic characterization in *David Copperfield* by interpreting the novel as "a Dickensian allegory of spiritual ascent" in which Agnes offers precisely the symbolical and spiritual qualities that Copperfield lacks.

Hager, Kelly. "Estranging *David Copperfield*: Reading the Novel of Divorce." *ELH* 63, no. 4 (winter 1996): 989-1019.

Offers a radical reading of *David Copperfield* as a novel of adultery and divorce, rather than as one of marriage and romantic love.

Hochman, Baruch and Ilja Wachs. "Straw People, Hollow Men, and the Postmodernist Hall of Dissipating Mirrors: The Case of *David Copperfield.*" *Style* 24, no. 3 (fall 1990): 392-407.

Presents a deconstructionist interpretation of identity and character in *David Copperfield*.

Houston, Gail Turley. "Gender Construction and the *Künstlerroman: David Copperfield* and *Aurora Leigh.*" *Philological Quarterly* 72, no. 2 (spring 1993): 213-36.

Compares *David Copperfield* and Elizabeth Barrett Browning's *Aurora Leigh* as, respectively, male- and female-gendered versions of the Victorian *Künstlerroman.*

Jacobson, Wendy S. "Brothers and Sisters in *David Copperfield.*" *English Studies in Africa* 25, no. 1 (1982): 11-28.

Conducts an autobiographical appraisal of *David Copperfield* concentrated on Dickens's belief in the sanctity of the family and desire to fictionally recreate the idealized family life that he was himself denied.

Jordan, John O. "The Social Sub-text of *David Copperfield.*" *Dickens Studies Annual* 14 (1985): 61-92.

Illuminates repressed social themes concentrated on class tensions and class anxiety in *David Copperfield.*

Joseph, Gerhard. "Prejudice in Jane Austen, Emma Tennant, Charles Dickens—and Us." *Studies in English Literature, 1500-1900* 40, no. 4 (autumn 2000): 679-93.

Comparative analysis of literary prejudice illustrated by Jane Austen's *Pride and Prejudice* and in the differing estimations of Annie and Dr. Strong associated with David and Uriah Heep in *David Copperfield.*

Lankford, William T. "'The Deep of Time': Narrative Order in *David Copperfield.*" *ELH* 46, no. 3 (fall 1979): 452-67.

Considers the relationship between narrative and memory in *David Copperfield* as the principal thematic focus of the novel, exemplified in Copperfield's effort to reconcile the innocence of childhood perception with his mature understanding of events.

Lettis, Richard. "The Names of David Copperfield." *Dickens Studies Annual* 31 (2002): 67-86.

Explores the ways in which Dickens constructs David Copperfield's identity through the various names given to him over the course of the novel.

Lund, Michael. "Novels, Writers, and Readers in 1850." *Victorian Periodical Review* 17, nos. 1-2 (spring-summer 1984): 15-28.

Documents the redefinition of the novelist's position in Victorian society undertaken by Dickens in *David Copperfield* and William Thackeray in his *Pendennis.*

Magee, Mary Margaret. "Postscript: Theatricality and Dickens's End Strategies." In *Dramatic Dickens,* edited by Carol Hanbery MacKay, pp. 184-93. New York: St. Martin's Press, 1989.

Exposes Copperfield's role as theatrical impresario, the stage-managing source of plot, drama, and fictive closure in *David Copperfield.*

McGlamery, Gayla S. and Joseph J. Walsh. "Mr. (H)Omer and the Iliadic Heroes of *David Copperfield.*" *Classical and Modern Literature* 20, no. 2 (winter 2002): 1-20.

Chronicles mock-heroic and mock-epic allusion and spectacle in *David Copperfield.*

McGowan, John P. "*David Copperfield*: The Trial of Realism." *Nineteenth-Century Fiction* 34, no. 1 (June 1979): 1-19.

Argues that *David Copperfield* represents a turning point in Dickens's understanding of the tensions between literary realism and "fancy," in the sense of an artist's imaginative reconstruction of reality through fiction.

McSweeney, Kerry. "*David Copperfield* and the Music of Memory." *Dickens Studies Annual* 23 (1994): 93-119.

Regards *David Copperfield* as Dickens's most adept study of memory, viewing the novel as a search for identity and affirmation of temporal continuity rather than as the expression of a transcendental impulse.

Miller, D. A. "Secret Subjects, Open Secrets." *Dickens Studies Annual* 14 (1985): 17-38.

Probes Copperfield's autobiographical subjectivity and desire for liberation in *David Copperfield.*

Millhauser, Milton. "*David Copperfield*: Some Shifts of Plan." *Nineteenth-Century Fiction* 27, no. 3 (December 1972): 339-45.

Speculates about possible changes of character and plot Dickens may have made while composing *David Copperfield* for serial publication.

Muggleston, Lynda. "Fictions of Speech: Literature and the Literate Speaker in the Nineteenth-Century Novel." *Yearbook of English Studies* 23 (1995): 114-27.

Treats the equivocal and deceptive relationship between language use and social class depicted in *David Copperfield.*

Poussa, Patricia. "Dickens as Sociolinguist: Dialect in *David Copperfield.*" In *Writing in Nonstandard English,* edited by Irma Taavitsainen, Gunnel Melchers, and Paivi Pahta, pp. 27-44. Amsterdam: John Benjamins Publishing Co., 1999.

Affirms the authenticity of Dickens's recreation of dialect in *David Copperfield* through sociolinguistic analysis.

Preston, Shale. "True Romance? Dirty Davy and the Domestic Sublime: From Alps to the Abject in *David Copperfield.*" *Australasian Victorian Studies Journal* 3, no. 2 (May 1998): 59-69.

Claims that the true object of David Copperfield's love is his mother, Clara, and contends that in order to surmount this unattainable desire Copperfield must find a woman—like Agnes—who is his mother's moral antithesis.

Puttock, Kay. "'The Fault . . . Of Which I Confusedly Felt Guilty Yet Innocent': Charles Dickens's Evolving Championship of the Child." *Children's Literature Association Quarterly* 17, no. 3 (fall 1992): 19-22.

Appraises Dickens's sympathetic fictional portrayals of outcast, exploited, or oppressed children, with particular emphasis on *Great Expectations* and *David Copperfield.*

Rodolff, Rebecca. "What David Copperfield Remembers of Dora's Death." *Dickensian* 77, no. 1 (spring 1981): 32-40.

Studies Chapter 53 of *David Copperfield,* in which David recalls his wife Dora's illness and premature death, as a thematic microcosm of the novel.

Rogers, Philip. "A Tolstoyan Reading of *David Copperfield.*" *Comparative Literature* 42, no. 1 (winter 1990): 1-28.

Begins with a survey of Dickens-inspired characters in Tolstoy's fiction, followed by a reading of *David Copperfield* that applies the Russian author's analytic system of literary morality to the novel.

Ruth, Jennifer. "Mental Capital, Industrial Time, and the Professional in *David Copperfield.*" *Novel* 32, no. 3 (summer 1999): 303-30.

Marxist-materialist assessment of *David Copperfield* as it depicts the Victorian world of industrialized capitalism.

Saville, Julia E. "Eccentricity as Englishness in *David Copperfield.*" *Studies in English Literature, 1500-1900* 42, no. 4 (autumn 2002): 781-97.

Comments on Dickens's exploitation of eccentricity and memorably eccentric characters in *David Copperfield* to suggest a theme of reconciliation between individualism and communal responsibility.

Sell, Roger D. "Projection Characters in *David Copperfield.*" *Studia Neophilologica* 55, no. 1 (1983): 19-30.

Proposes that the secondary characters of *David Copperfield* can be understood as projections of submerged traits in Copperfield himself, allowing Dickens's narrator to explore the potentially negative qualities of his own persona once these characteristics have been displaced onto others.

Shelston, Alan. "Past and Present in *David Copperfield.*" *Critical Quarterly* 27, no. 3 (autumn 1985): 17-33.

Probes the quintessentially Victorian literary theme of the isolated individual struggling to understand present realities through the power of conscious reflection depicted in *David Copperfield.*

Welsh, Alexander. "I Am Transported Beyond the Ignorant Copperfieldian Present." *Modern Philology* 88, no. 3 (February 1991): 292-98.

Examines *The Letters of Charles Dickens* in order to suggest a tangible shift in the author's literary concerns between *David Copperfield* and *Bleak House.*

Additional coverage of Dickens's life and career is contained in the following sources published by Thomson Gale: *Authors and Artists for Young Adults,* Vol. 23; *Beacham's Guide to Literature for Young Adults,* Vols. 1, 2, 3, 13, 14; *British Writers,* Vol. 5; *British Writers: The Classics,* Vols. 1, 2; *Children's Literature Review,* Vol. 95; *Concise Dictionary of British Literary Biography, 1832-1890; Dictionary of Literary Biography,* Vols. 21, 55, 70, 159, 166; *DISCovering Authors; DISCovering Authors: British; DISCovering Authors: Canadian Edition; DISCovering Authors Modules: Most-studied Authors* and *Novelists; DISCovering Authors 3.0; Exploring Novels; Junior DISCovering Authors; Literary Movements for Students,* Vol. 1; *Literature and Its Times,* Vols. 1, 2; *Literature and Its Times Supplement,* Vol. 1; *Literature Resource Center; Major Authors and Illustrators for Children and Young Adults,* Eds. 1, 2; *Nineteenth-Century Literature Criticism,* Vols. 3, 8, 18, 26, 37, 50, 86, 105, 113; *Novels for Students,* Vols. 4, 5, 10, 14, 20; *Reference Guide to English Literature,* Ed. 2; *Reference Guide to Short Fiction,* Ed. 2; *St. James Guide to Crime and Mystery Writers,* Vol. 4; *St. James Guide to Horror, Ghost and Gothic Writers; Short Story Criticism,* Vols. 17, 49; *Something About the Author,* Vol. 15; *Supernatural Fiction Writers,* Vol. 1; *Twayne's English Authors; World Literature and Its Times,* Vol. 4; *World Literature Criticism; Writers for Children;* and *Writers for Young Adults.*

Victor Hugo
1802-1885

(Full name Victor Marie Hugo) French poet, playwright, novelist, essayist, and critic.

The following entry presents criticism on Hugo's works from 1990 to 2002. For further discussion of Hugo's complete career, see *NCLC,* Volume 3; for discussion of the novel *Les misérables,* see *NCLC,* Volume 10; for discussion of the novel *Notre-Dame de Paris* (*The Hunchback of Notre-Dame*), see *NCLC,* Volume 21.

INTRODUCTION

Hugo is considered one of the leaders of the Romantic movement in French literature as well as one of its most prolific and versatile authors. Although chiefly known outside France for the novels *Notre-Dame de Paris* (1831; *The Hunchback of Notre-Dame*) and *Les misérables* (1862), he is renowned in his own country primarily for his contributions as a Romantic poet. Hugo's verse has been favorably compared to the works of William Shakespeare, Dante, and Homer; and has influenced such diverse poets as Charles Baudelaire, Alfred Lord Tennyson, and Walt Whitman. Hugo's technical virtuosity, stylistic experimentation, range of emotion, and the variety and universality of his themes not only established him as a leader of the French Romantic school but also set the stage for the development of modern poetry.

BIOGRAPHICAL INFORMATION

Born into a military family, Hugo traveled extensively during his childhood until age twelve when his parents separated. He settled with his mother in Paris, where he attended school. At a young age, he attained literary recognition. In 1819, Hugo founded with his brothers a prominent literary journal, *Le conservateur littéraire,* and published his first volume of poetry, *Odes et poésies diverses* (1822). This volume, which celebrated the monarchy, earned him a pension from French king Louis XVII that enabled him to marry his childhood sweetheart Adéle Foucher. Hugo's home was the center of intellectual activity, and he counted among his devoted friends literary critic Charles Sainte-Beuve and writer Théophile Gautier. In 1841, Hugo was elected to the Académie française, and four years later he was made a peer. Hugo was also elected to the National As-

sembly in 1848 when Louis's regime collapsed and Napoléon Bonaparte established the Second Republic. Distressed by Napoléon's dictatorial ambitions, which were made evident when Napoléon seized power in a coup d'etat in 1851, Hugo fled to Belgium. He moved to the English Channel island of Jersey and, later, to the island of Guernsey; he lived in exile on the islands for eighteen years. There he conducted séances, wrote speeches and appeals concerning world politics, and published some of his greatest poetical works. Hugo returned to Paris as a national hero one day after the Third Republic was proclaimed in 1870. He continued to write prolifically even as he became increasingly detached from the outside world. When he died in 1885, Hugo was given a state funeral and was eventually buried in the Panthéon, although his body was transported in a poor man's hearse in accordance with his last wishes.

MAJOR WORKS

Hugo's early verse consists primarily of odes, ballads, and lyrics. His odes, which are collected in such volumes as *Odes* (1823) and *Nouvelles odes* (1825), were written in the neoclassical style and contain traditional poetic devices. In his ballads, Hugo used more experimental forms of versification and began to address such romantic themes as faith, love, and nature. He explained in the preface to *Odes et ballades* (1826) that the ballad form was a "capricieux" or whimsical genre that lent itself to the telling of superstitions, legends, popular traditions, and dreams. Hugo continued his experiments with versification in *Les orientales* (1829; *Eastern Lyrics*), which is set in North Africa and the Near East and which focuses on such subjects as the Greek war of independence, passionate love, and exotic cultures. Considered a protest against the materialism of western society, this volume was extremely popular and widely read in France.

His lyrical poetry of the 1830s primarily addressed such themes as nature, love, and death in a style that was both personal and uninhibited. Collections of this period include *Les feuilles d'automne* (1831), *Les chants du crépuscule* (1835; *Songs of Twilight*), *Le voix intérieures* (1837), and *Les rayons et les ombres* (1840). Edward K. Kaplan has noted that these four collections "are unified by the poet's discovery of faith through uncertainty and doubt. Not a Christian faith, but a modern faith which understood anxiety as an appropriate response to rapid social, political, and intellectual change."

During the 1840s, Hugo concentrated on his social and political activities and published little poetry. In the 1850s, however, when he lived in exile on the islands of Jersey and Guernsey, Hugo wrote *Les contemplations* (1856) and the three-volume collection *La légende des siècles* (1859-1883; *The Legend of the Centuries*). Both of these works have been hailed as poetic masterpieces and are considered among Hugo's best works. *Les contemplations,* which explores the metaphysical aspects of death and life as well as the mysteries of human consciousness, is divided into two parts. "Autrefois" celebrates innocence, youth, love, and creation, while "Aujourd'hui" revels Hugo's grief over the drowning death of his daughter Léopoldine in 1843 and addresses such issues as the incomprehensibility of the universe, religion, and good versus evil. *La légende des siècles* presents a panorama of human history from the Old Testament to the nineteenth century. Hugo wrote that he intended to work to trace "the development of the human race over the centuries, mankind rising out of the shadows on its way to the ideal, the paradisiacal transfiguration of earthly hell, the low, the perfect coming to the full bloom of freedom."

Hugo's later poetry comprises a diverse body of work. *Les chansons des rues et des bois* (1865) consists of light and fanciful pieces; *L'année terrible* (1872) centers on French history, particularly the establishment of the Third Republic in 1870; and *L'art d'être grandpère* (1877) contains poems that reflect Hugo's delight in his grandchildren Georges and Jeanne.

CRITICAL RECEPTION

At the time of Hugo's death, many of the works that were praised upon their publication were still highly regarded; *La légende des siècles* has been called the best work of the nineteenth century and has been favorably compared to John Milton's *Paradise Lost* by late twentieth-century critics. Scholars have examined Hugo's novels for their political and aesthetic value, finding symbolism that evokes the events of the social upheavals of his time. Although commentators have faulted the romantic excesses and pretentiousness sometimes evident in Hugo's writing, they have also acknowledged that his sentimentalism is often conveyed with grace, power, and technical virtuosity.

PRINCIPAL WORKS

Odes et poésies diverses (poetry) 1822
Han d'Islande [*Hans of Iceland*] (novel) 1823
Odes (poetry) 1823
Nouvelles odes (poetry) 1825
Bug-Jargal [*The Slave-King*] (novel) 1826
Odes et ballades (poetry) 1826
Cromwell (play) 1827
Amy Robsart (play) 1828
Le dernier jour d'un condamné [*The Last Day of a Condemned*] (novel) 1829
Les orientales [*Eastern Lyrics*] (poetry) 1829
Hernani (play) 1830
Les feuilles d'automne (poetry) 1831
Marion de Lorme [*The King's Edict*] (play) 1831
Notre-Dame de Paris [*The Hunchback of Notre-Dame*] (novel) 1831
Le roi s'amuse [*The King's Fool*] (play) 1832
Lucrèce Borgia [*Lucretia Borgia*] (play) 1833
Marie Tudor (play) 1833
Angelo, Tyran de Padoue (play) 1835
Les chants du crépuscule [*Songs of Twilight*] (poetry) 1835
Les voix intérieures (poetry) 1837
Ruy Blas (play) 1838
Les rayons et les ombres (poetry) 1840
Les burgraves (play) 1843
Les châtiments (poetry) 1853
Les contemplations (poetry) 1856
La légende des siècles. 2 vols. [*The Legend of the Centuries*] (poetry) 1859-83
Les misérables (novel) 1862

CRITICISM

Gilbert D. Chaitin (essay date fall 1990)

SOURCE: Chaitin, Gilbert D. "Victor Hugo and the Hieroglyphic Novel." *Nineteenth-Century French Studies* 19, no. 1 (fall 1990): 36-53.

[*In the following essay, Chaitin connects the symbolic use of stonework, alchemy, gypsies, and hieroglyphics in* Notre-Dame de Paris *and examines how the structure of the novel reflects the same principles that govern hieroglyphic writing.*]

In his monumental novel, **Notre-Dame de Paris,** Victor Hugo considers Notre-Dame de Paris, the edifice, to be a monument of medieval France. It is significant that the word "monument" did not acquire its modern meaning until the seventeenth century, at least in France. In the sixteenth century, according to Edmond Huguet's *Dictionnaire de la langue française du sieizième siècle,* a monument was a tomb, a sepulcher, or crypt. From the Latin *moneo,* to warn, the monument warned of death and pointed out the place of the cadaver; it was the physical mark, or trace, of the absent presence of the dead person. The warning, signifying, function of the monument was retained in the modern period, but its reference was now expanded to include any great

military, historic, or cultural event or accomplishment, and the physical mark became any structure made for, or capable of, evoking such an event. By Victor Hugo's time, a monument was any imposing structure or geographical formation (Chateaubriand writes of "natural monuments" such as Mount Etna in *René*) precisely because, for the Romantics, all such "monuments" had a meaning, signified a moment in the history of humanity or of a particular nation. "Il faut relire le passé sur ces pages de marbre" (**Notre-Dame de Paris** 187).

For the early French Romantics, the past had become a kind of architectural panorama, a landscape dotted with speaking stones whose messages added up to the history, and therefore the identity, the essence of the modern nation. This conception imposed on the Romantic writer a threefold task: 1) to find and preserve all such monuments; 2) to read, or decipher, their meanings, that is, to listen to the voices of the dead; 3) to reconstruct the world constituted by the synthesis of these meanings. Antipositivists before the fact (or the *lettre),* the Romantics were triply concerned, not with what was there, but with what was absent: 1) with monuments being destroyed, that is, signs being erased; 2) with meanings hidden behind those signs; 3) with the dead worlds of the past, that is, with the world of the dead. Their three R's were thus: reading, restoring, resuscitating. And these three R's form the ABC that gives so many productions of the Romantlc Era their coherence: the retrospective narration of the confessional novel, the preoccupation with ghosts, spectres and the supernatural in the Gothic novel, the will to resurrect the past in the new history of Michelet and in the historical novel of Hugo's model, Walter Scott; the new era of Egyptology ushered in by Napoleon and then Champollion; the movement to preserve France's heritage of Gothic architecture led by Hugo's mentor, Nodier, and by Hugo himself, especially in his outspoken text **"Sur la destruction des monuments en France."**

Although the goal of making absences present is clear in theory, in practice it is very much like reading between the lines, which may produce greater pleasure than reading the text, since there are no words to slow the reader's progress or inhibit the free exercise of one's creative powers; but that pleasure can easily turn to horror, if it threatens to become what Stendhal once called, in a different context, a hand to hand combat with nothingness, gazing into the bottomless abyss of hidden meanings. The novel proposes two competing methods of crypt-ography, of making absences present. The one is practiced by Claude Frollo, the priest whose profundity is a sign both of his intelligence and of his capacity for passion, suffering and evil, the Faust figure who studies alchemy, the occult science supposedly originated by the mysterious Hermes Trismegistus, an amalgamation of the Egyptian God Thoth and the Greek Hermes, forged in fact in the Hellenistic period from

Egyptian, gnostic and neo-Platonic conceptions. It is a method designed to unlock hermetically sealed mysteries, a method which searches for deep and hidden meanings and is called the hermeneutic method. Its main principle is expressed in a work supposedly written by Hermes Trismegistus, or rather inscribed by him into an emerald table which was found "in the hands of Hermes's mummy . . . situated, according to tradition, in the great pyramid of Gizeh: 'That which is above is like that which is below, to perpetrate the miracles of one thing'" (Seligmann 85). It is the principle of universal analogy, of mirror images, of "Correspondances" as Baudelaire was to put it two decades after Hugo's novel.

The other method is that of the frivolous, superficial, vain, self-centered, easily contented, poet, Pierre Gringoire, who often plays Sancho Panza to Claude Frollo's Quixote. As a man of letters, Gringoire is interested in linguistic rather than analogic processes of signification, and in the meanings that arise from combinations of alphabetic elements. The mystery he cares most about is the theatrical genre of the mystery play; the alchemy he practices is what Rimbaud would later call the alchemy of the word. Instead of witchcraft, witcraft.

Gringoire is a lover of word-play, figures of speech, and rebuses. His allegorical, pseudo-mystery play involves a golden dolphin who represents the *Dauphin,* the king's son and heir, and a young girl carrying a daisy, symbolic of *Marguerite* of Flanders, the dauphin's fiancée. Much later in the novel, when Gringoire and Phoebus—the *miles gloriosus,* the Apollo who alone is loved by the heroine of the novel, Esmeralda—are going out for a drink together, the poet suggests they go to the "Tavern of old science" because its sign is an excellent rebus: *La Vieille Science* is signified by an old lady—*la vieille*—who is sawing through a handle—*scie anse.*

Within the novel, the two opposing attitudes emerge most clearly in relation to the sun. As is explained in the chapter entitled Ananké—necessity, fatality, destiny—for Claude and his masters in alchemy, the secret meaning of the various writings inscribed into the wall of his cell in the cathedral tower is to be sought on the axis of similarity. Fire gives birth to the sun, the sun to the moon; fire is the principle, the law of nature, the soul of the great all—light, heat, passion, life, gold. The object of the alchemical quest is the philosopher's stone, which will confer upon its possessor the power of riches, light, health, life, the ability to transmute lead into gold. As the *Emerald Table* puts it: "And as all things have been derived from one . . . so all things are born from this thing, by adoption. The sun is its father, the moon is its mother. Wind has carried it in its belly, the earth is its nurse" (Seligmann 85).

Elsewhere in the novel, the sun is represented by our friend, Phoebus, whose name is that of a sun god. And it is his name which contributes to Esmeralda's downfall, since her goat (with whom Gringoire is consistently identified, for both do tricks for a living, and both have an all-too-platonic love relation to their mistress) manages to arrange an alphabet into the letters of Phoebus's name, a trick which the narrator, in free indirect discourse, calls, a "miracle" (249) and which her accusers claim to be an act of sorcery.

It is tempting to dismiss the silly Gringoire as a simple source of comic relief in an otherwise grim novel of sadism and destruction. But it is a curious fact that in a novel which Victor Brombert has called "The Living Stones of Notre-Dame" (49), a novel overflowing with stones: Notre-Dame is called a symphony of stone; Paris in the fifteenth century is a chronicle of stone; Claude Frollo, because of his hard-heartedness, is called a man of stone; the name of Quasimodo, the hunchback of Notre-Dame who was left as a baby in the parvis of the cathedral on the Sunday after Easter in 1467, derives in part from the first word of the liturgy of that day, drawn from Saint Peter's *First Epistle* in which it is said that the faithful will enter the structure of the edifice (of the Church) like living stones; Quasimodo lives his life in a world of stone plants and trees—the decorations and columns of Notre-Dame; because of his deformities, he lives a stone-like existence, cut off from most human contact, and is called a monster of stone, a gargoyle come to life; in this world where "le genre humain a deux livres, deux registres, deux testaments, la maçonnerie et l'imprimerie, la bible de pierre et la bible de papier" (87); in this petrified forest of living pillars, it is worth remembering that Quasimodo goes directly from stone to bone, a skeleton found embracing that of Esmeralda in the grave, that Esmeralda's mother has her head crushed against a paving stone, that Frollo, losing his grip on the lead gutter from which he was hanging for dear life, slips, falls and bounces like a tile against the paving stones of the street below, those same paving stones which, used in popular insurrections as in the assault of the cathedral, are said to symbolize the people of Paris; that in this crescendo of crashing rocks, there is only one stone that goes unturned—Pierre, Pierre Gringoire, the poet, the only main character (other than Phoebus) to survive at the end of the novel.

Notre-Dame de Paris, the cathedral, is a work of transition, according to the first chapter of Book Three of the novel; it is half Romanesque, half Gothic in style, half theocratic, half democratic in politics, half open, half closed in legibility. ***Notre-Dame de Paris,*** the novel, is also a hybrid, half architectural, half poetic, half visual, half linguistic, half theory, half action, half analogic, half alphabetic, half hermeneutic, half semiotic. By hybrid, I do *not* mean that one thing is simply grafted onto another, like a satyr that is half man, half horse. What I do mean is that every image is at the same time part of an intricate network of signifiers, that every signifier is at every moment giving rise to images; thus the *pierre* in Gringoire's name motivates his passing infatuation with architecture: he becomes an *"amateur de pierre"* as the narrator tells us, and he composes a commentary on a work entitled "De cupa petrarum." Thus the spider and the fly, tracked down and captured by the image-hunters right in the very middle of Hugo's textual web—Book VII, Chapter V, just after the chapter on Ananké—is the image which serves as an analogy for the web of fatality in which it is located (Grant 49-52). But, as critics since Charles Baudoin have repeatedly stressed, the relation of the spider to destiny is not only that of an image but is also that of a name, a series of letters, the Greek word for spider, Arachne, being almost an anagram for Ananké (Baudoin 169). Moreover, the alchemical inscriptions on the wall of Claude's cell look like a spider's web to his younger brother, Jehan. Claude himself sees a relationship between the words Ananké and Anagneia, the impurity of his own desire. Thus the architectural novel, *Notre-Dame de Paris,* is said to have been built upon the foundation of the half-erased word Ananké, a trace of Claude Frollo's passion inscribed on the wall of the cathedral tower and still legible, but barely, in the nineteenth century.

More generally, the entire novel is such a double network which allows plot, character, theme, history, melodrama, rhetoric and scene to appear as separate and distinct building blocks, and yet which uses a poetic process to weave all of them together into a complex tissue of signifying relations. I have already had occasion to mention the theme of alchemy and to stress Gringoire's fascination with rebuses. Now these two elements are linked in a curious way in one of the main sources Hugo used for historical documentation, Henri Sauval's *Histoire et recherche des antiquités de la ville de Paris* (1724). In Book XIV Sauval has a section entitled "Vision des Chercheurs de Pierre Philosophale, touchant plusieurs figures d'Eglise," which explains that those whom Sauval calls "our Hermetics" have strange "visions" concerning the statuary and other figures on the doors or in the court of Notre-Dame. By "visions" he means the fantastic stories that have been concocted through the years concerning the origin and meaning of these figures: our Hermetics think that they were built by alchemists such as Guillaume de Paris and Nicolas Flamel and that they are actually hieroglyphs, pictographs whose secret meanings add up to the formula for achieving the "Great Work" of alchemy, the secret of the Philosopher's *Stone.* Sauval concludes his chapter by asserting: "Enfin la folie des Hermetiques est si grande, qu'il n'y a sorte de rebus sculptés dans les Eglises qu'ils n'interpretent. . . ." (57).

As though to emphasize the lexical identification of hieroglyph and rebus the next chapter, called "Enseignes," begins with the words, "As for shop signs,

their absurdity comes from poor rebuses." There follow seven examples, the fourth one of which is "La vieille science, une vieille qui scie une anse" (57). The lesson would seem to be that the "silly," poetic way of reading these rebuses is clearly preferable to the mad search for profound but serious meanings. What is certain is that the synonymy of 'hieroglyph' and 'rebus' forms a concrete link between the poet as dreamer and quester and the poet as wordsmith and jester, a link, moreover, that ties architecture to reading, and both to alchemy, the cathedral, and ancient Egypt.

Even the crucial image of the spider and the fly, whose "intricate working out" constitutes the novel according to Richard Grant (53), cannot be adequately explained as a pattern of metaphors however complicated, cannot be contained in relations of resemblance however extended. More than an image, it is also part of a series of intertexts which establish non-analogic relations between the spider and fate. There is a well known, fifteenth-century ballad, usually attributed to the Burgundian poet and chronicler, Jean Molinet, which begins "Souffle, Trithon, en ta buse argentine," and whose most famous line is the eighth: "Ay combattu l'universel yraigne" (Dupire 851-52). Molinet being a Burgundian chronicler, it is no surprise that the allegorical meaning of this line is that the Duke of Burgundy has fought the King of France, Louis XI, the universal spider whose reign was coming to an end in the year in which the action of *Notre-Dame de Paris* was set, 1482.

It seems highly probable that Hugo knew this poem because he does mention Molinet in *Notre-Dame de Paris* and because the ballad was printed in Volume 10 of J. A. Buchon's collection of *Chroniques nationales françaises* (xvii-xviii) published in Paris in 1825 and easily available to Hugo who, we may suppose, would have taken a lively interest in the re-edition of the chronicles that form part of the written monuments of French history.

What makes the connection between fate, the spider, and Louis XI all the more probable is, first, that Claude connects the spider with fate when he prevents Louis XI's prosecutor, Jacques Charmolue, from killing the spider in order to save the fly, just as Claude will force the prosecutor to indict, prosecute, torture, convict, sentence and punish the heroine Esmeralda. In fact, this interplay between Claude and Charmolue is a partial reversal of the plot as outlined in Hugo's first scenario, composed in June or July, 1830 and dating back perhaps to Hugo's first idea of the novel in 1828. According to that initial plan, it was the King Louis XI, who was supposed to command that Esmeralda be hanged and to refuse clemency for her, because he, Louis, could not bear to see her live when he knew that he was about to die. In short, it was Louis who was to play the role of the fatal, universal, spider.

Indeed, that early version was to be set in 1483, not 1482, precisely because the former was the year of Louis XI's death; his death was the fatality hanging over Esmeralda and France. In the final version of the novel, Louis XI still orders his soldiers to hang Esmeralda, but he does so out of political rather than personal reasons. It is neither his own fear of death nor a desire for vengeance but the perceived need to remove a rival for power and for the allegiance of the people that motivates his fatal command. In short, the people of Paris and their leader have taken the place of the now defeated Burgundians as the major rival to monarchical dominance, and thus have become the new prey of the universal spider. The image of the spider derives from a text in which that metaphor is linked metonymically to a series of political terms; by inserting the image into the signifying chain of **Notre-Dame de Paris,** Hugo imported into the latter the entire series.

It was in November of 1828 that Hugo got the idea of writing this novel, and I would suggest that the event which precipitated this first crystallization was seeing the stage production of the version of *Faust* on which his friend and teacher, Nodier, collaborated (see Picat-Guinoiseau). As scholars have often pointed out, 1828 was the "Faust year" in the annals of French Romanticism, since, in addition to the Nodier adaptation, 1828 also saw the publication of Gérard de Nerval's translation of Part I of Goethe's *Faust,* and the exhibition of Delacroix's "Faust and Mephistopheles" in the Salon of that year.

Although it might seem far-fetched to claim a connection between Louis XI and Faust, to a Frenchman of Hugo's time such a link would appear quite natural. Of the two main sources of information on *Faust* he would turn to, Mme de Staël's *De l'Allemagne* and Nerval's "Préface" to his translation of Goethe's play, the latter recounts the theory, popularized in the Faust novel of a *Sturm und Drang* author named F. M. Klinger, that the legendary Faust was none other than the historical personage, Johann Fust. Now this Fust was born about 1400 and died in 1466 and was thus an older contemporary of Louis XI. He lived in Mainz, was the business partner of Gutenberg, and claimed to be the co-inventor of the printing press. Nerval relays the story that the Faust legends were supposedly fabricated by monks irritated at the invention of the printing-press which took away from them their jobs as manuscript copyists (9). In *De l'Allemagne,* Mme de Staël repeats the legend that Faust invented the printing press (3: 70).

Many years earlier, Victor Hugo had written a review of Walter Scott's *Quentin Durward,* a novel about the struggle for supremacy between Louis XI and Charles the Bold. In that review, as Jacques Seebacher has insisted, Hugo takes Walter Scott to task for giving an overly optimistic reading of the operation of history even while he is praising Scott as the great innovator of the contemporary novel, the model whom he, Hugo, promises to emulate and surpass (Introduction 1063). What the critics do not seem to emphasize is that *Quentin Durward* contains an important scene in which the *astrologer* and supposed master of *occult* knowledge, Galeotti Martinvalle, predicts for Louis XI's benefit the dire consequences of the invention of the printing-press: there will be a greater, uninterrupted flow of science which will change "the whole form of social life, establishing and overthrowing religions, erecting and destroying kingdoms," it will bear "fatal fruit" like the tree of knowledge in the garden of Eden (151, 156).

In the mouth of this astrologer, who elsewhere is compared to one of the ancient Magi, we find one half of the argument that was to become the theoretical cornerstone of **Notre-Dame de Paris,** the argument that Hugo presents in the famous Chapter II of Book Five, entitled "Ceci tuera cela," the printing-press will kill architecture and the more or less theocratic systems that support the supremacy of architecture. Thus the chapter which the majority of critics take to be an afterthought added to the novel in order to give it a false patina of thought, a kind of pretentious intellectual *cachet* grafted onto a simple, not to say simple-minded, melodrama, begins to find its place as a hybrid in the sense I have defined, a joint where Faust, Louis XI, occult science and printing intertwine and give rise to new developments in each other. Need I add that, in *Quentin Durward,* Louis XI first comes into the action disguised as a bourgeois named Maître *Pierre*!

The connection between the spider, fate, the king, the printing-press, alchemy and Faust is reinforced by two additional sets of facts. The first concerns the changes Hugo made in the scenario of his novel in 1830. According to Seebacher, they were three in number. First, he introduced the character Phoebus; second, he decided to make the pillory scene the occasion for recounting the story of the recluse, called La Sachette, who is the real mother of Esmeralda and the woman who brought Quasimodo to the cathedral after the gypsies put him in the place of the girl they stole; third, he made Jean, a character already in his plan, into the brother of Claude Frollo (1056-1057).

Now the interest of the first and third changes is that both involve Jean Molinet. The first four lines of his ballad about Louis XI, the universal spider, read:

> Souffle, Trithon, en ta buse argentine,
> Muse en musant en ta doulce musette,
> Donne louenge et gloire celestine
> Au dieu Phebus, a la barbe roussette.

There is, perhaps, nothing extraordinary about mentioning Phoebus and Louis XI in the same poem. But it seems more than coincidence that the original of Jean

Frollo was one Joannes de Molendino, i.e. Jean du Moulin or, Jean Molinet, also written Moulinet. In fact, the first time the character's name is mentioned in the first chapter of the final version of the novel, the speaker calls him "Joannes Frollo de Molendino" (16).

The second set of facts derives from another external text. Hugo's main source of information on magic, alchemy and the occult, the *Dictionnaire infernal* of one Collin de Plancy, contains an entry under the heading "Jean Faust," which states that Faust took up magic because he was depressed due to his poverty and lack of recognition, and to his old father's illness; that the monks gave him over to the devil to avenge themselves for his invention of the printing-press—the story we've already heard. But Collin adds one highly significant element to the legend: "On sait que quand les premiers livres imprimés parurent, on cria à la magie! on poursuivait Faust pour le brûler; et, *sans la protection de Louis XI* et de la *Sorbonne. l'imprimerie était étouffée en naissant*" (3: 15). Louis XI allegedly took printing under his protection just as Claude Frollo saves Quasimodo from burning at his second birth, in the Cathedral, by adopting him as his own child. By another strange twist of fate, the destinies of Faust, printing and Louis XI are once again intertwined.

These intertexts demonstrate an essential link between one of the main plots of the novel—Claude Frollo's Faustian quest for alchemical knowledge and power—and its theoretical framework, summarized in the phrase, "ceci tuera cela," printing will replace architecture as the principal monument of human history. The connection between plot and theory is all the more apparent in the text, since it is Claude himself who utters the phrase (173). Like Scott's astrologer Martinvalle, Hugo's alchemist predicts the downfall of the *ancien régime* in front of Louis XI (and his physician Coictier). It is the narrator, however, who finds another interpretation of Claude's thought: "La presse tuera l'église" (174).

Like the legends of Faust-Fust transmitted by Klinger and Collin, this interpretation connects Claude to the Enlightenment idea that the invention of the printing press presages the downfall of the Church (Condorcet 185-192). This hybrid Faust, who finds his certitude in alchemy (169), is both horrified and dazzled by the "luminous press of Gutenberg" (174). The representative of the old, dogmatic, theocracies which clothe their knowledge in hermetic secrecy, Claude also expresses the model of history envisaged by the Enlightenment, whose main arm in the battle for human freedom is the spread of knowledge through the use of the book.

The other main plot involves Claude's quest for Esmeralda, who, as woman, image and signifier, forms the hub around and through which the signifying relations of the novel radiate, the erotic, the alchemical, and the

historic. As a woman, she is the object of the passions of the typical Hugolian love quadrangle, three men for one woman, as is stated in **Hernani,** in this case Claude, Quasimodo, Gringoire. As image, she represents the maternal, the Notre-Dame of the gypsies as she is repeatedly called, a living replica of the cathedral who gives asylum to Gringoire just as the church does to Quasimodo. "Notre-Dame 'lieu d'asile' et . . . symbole maternel s'il en fut" (Baudoin, 169). As signifier, she is a name, a word whose meaning and function are to be discovered by a semiotic, a cryptographic, process.

Although her "real" name is Agnès, a word whose partial homophony with *agnus, agneau* gave rise to associations of innocence and sacrifice, throughout most of the novel she is known as La Esmeralda, which means emerald. She is thus, first and foremost, a stone, a gemstone, like that other object of the quest, the philosopher's stone. In the context of the action, she is called Esmeralda because she wears a talisman around her neck that contains green glass jewelry; the image determines the sign here. But not entirely. For La Esmeralda is her *gypsy* name, and as the English word indicates, as Hugo's French text emphasizes, a gypsy is a member of a nomadic group thought to have come from *Egypt.* The narrator as well as almost all the characters in **Notre-Dame de Paris** consistently refer to the gypsy queen as "the Egyptian." And gypsies, as we know, are fortune-tellers, purveyors of curses and the evil eye, generally uncanny people who have access to supernatural, perhaps diabolical, power and knowledge. Our heroine, moreover, is not just any gypsy, she is the emerald, and the *Emerald Table,* as we have noted, is the basic text of the supposed Egyptian master of alchemy, Hermes Trismegistus. We have also seen that Sauval reproaches "our Hermetics" with attempting to construe the figures in Notre-Dame as secret picture-writing, or hieroglyphics, inscribed by the famous alchemists of the past, most notably, Nicolas Flamel. And it is certainly no secret that hieroglyphics have always been associated with Egypt in the European mind, nor that for Hugo Egyptian hieroglyphs were the sign of theocracy.

But Hugo also knew and used a different theory of the origin of the gypsies, that of Collin de Plancy (vol. 1: 406-420). The latter thought the gypsies were none other than the disguised remnants of the European Jews who had been persecuted, killed or driven into hiding during the fourteenth century. Collin was not alone in embracing this theory. In *Quentin Durward,* the central role of the traitor is played by a gypsy named Hayraddin, whose presence in the novel gives rise to a series of comments about the gypsies: the peasants call them "Jews" (as well as "Mohamedans"), and Louis XI believes that they are descended from the Chaldeans, the originators of astrology and occult science (71, 138).

Now this 'Jewish theory' is highly significant for Hugo's novel and Esmeralda's role in it. It supplies another, more precise, connection between the gypsies and Esmeralda on the one side, and alchemy and hieroglyphics on the other. Both Collin de Plancy and a writer named Paul Lacroix, who published the first volume of his collection of short stories called *Soirées de Walter Scott* in 1829, under the pseudonym "Jacob, the Bibliophile," accept and explain a theory mentioned by our friend Sauval, according to which the greatest French alchemist, Nicolas Flamel, actually owed his vast fortune, and thus his reputation of having discovered the philosopher's stone, to the Jews.

Like the Egyptians, the Jews were considered to be the repository of ancient, secret, and more or less forbidden, knowledge; knowledge, moreover which they wrote down using an alphabet almost as strange as Egyptian hieroglyphs, and which, according to Hugo, at least, they inscribed into their architecture, especially King Solomon's temple (176). Indeed, according to several of the stories recounted in Collin's *Dictionary,* Solomon was held to be the originator of alchemical wisdom, which he had received from God and passed on to the Egyptians.

The Jewish theory also makes explicit a connection that critics have acknowledged for some time, that between *Notre-Dame de Paris* and a second novel by Walter Scott, *Ivanhoe*; more specifically, the similarity between Esmeralda the gypsy and Rebecca the Jewess. Like Esmeralda, Rebecca is tried for sorcery, like Esmeralda, she is accused falsely, and like Esmeralda her role is that of an outsider, member of an uncanny race, reviled and feared, yet (or therefore) the object of desire *par excellence.* But there are crucial differences between the young women. Whereas Esmeralda is accused of evil things—transmuting a metal coin into a dried leaf, owning a goat possessed by a spirit and thus able to spell, killing Phoebus by magic—the main evidence of Rebecca's occult powers are her sexual attraction for the Knight Templar, Brian de Bois-Guilbert, and her occult knowledge of medicine. There is, of course, a direct parallel between Rebecca's hold over Bois-Guilbert, and Esmeralda's over Claude Frollo. But the element of medicine, of healing, is what is most strikingly different and also most significant, for it points to the main purpose, goal, desire of alchemy, of Faust, of all the mystery religions and initiatic rites associated with Hermeticism, and indeed of Judaism and Christianity, too; namely, the power over and desire for *life.*

In *Ivanhoe,* Rebecca is able to nurse the wounded hero (Ivanhoe) back to life, because she was trained in medicine by Miriam, daughter of Rabbi Manasses of Byzantium (294); and Jewish physicians, associated by dress, customs, ancestry and acquaintance with the mysterious Orient, are supposed to be familiar with occult sciences, cabalistic art, the supernatural and magic (295). In Western tradition dating back to the *Asclepius* the Egyptian

Magi, or priests, were supposed to be able to invoke the gods so that they would come and inhabit their statues in the temples and begin to move and speak (*Corpus Hermeticum* 325-326). What better image of bringing stones to life could one find? And of course the philosopher's stone is supposed to confer immortality on its possessor, to protect him from disease, illness and old age. What is more, Collin de Plancy tells us that since time immemorial, "superstition" has attributed miraculous curative powers to the emerald, thus establishing a covert similarity between Rebecca and Esmeralda (2: 294).

The mystery religions with their phallic cults and orgiastic rites also promised a renewal of life. Hermes, the patron of alchemy is also the phallic god of the Greeks, no doubt due to his creative, life-giving, power, in both cases. And it is not by chance that Hugo begins the action of his novel precisely on January 6, Epiphany, the day of the visit of the Magi and the Festival of Fools, which Hugo explicitly likens to the Roman Saturnalia. It is at the latter festival that Quasimodo, the cyclops, is crowned Pope of Fools. Indeed, the deaf, one-eyed hunchback, whose name indicates both that he is like a newborn child (*Quasimodo geniti infantes*) and a half-formed creature (*un à peu près*), is the primary phallic figure in the novel. Brombert has described the sexual connotations of Quasimodo's bell-ringing in the cathedral (60). The women of the people call him "Chevaucheur de manche à balai!" (229). The narrator explains that he is the life-principle of the stone cathedral:

> La présence de cet être extraordinaire faisait circuler dans toute la cathédrale je ne sais quel souffle de vie. Il semblait qu'il s'échappât de lui . . . *une émanation mystérieuse qui animait toutes les pierres de Notre-Dame. . . .*
>
> (153-54, emphases added)

As though to emphasize the reference to the *Corpus Hermeticum* passage, Hugo ends the paragraph with the statement, "L'Egypte eût pris [Quasimodo] pour le dieu de ce temple" (154).

In short, in a cryptic way, Esmeralda and Quasimodo form the phallic couple that, like Rebecca, *is* life; and her secret, the secret of alchemy, the secret that Claude tried to decipher whether in the figures of the cathedral or while spying on her and her lover in a cheap, rented room, is the secret of life.

The second important difference between the two young heroines concerns their relations to fate. In *Ivanhoe,* Brian de Bois-Guilbert, the Templar who has fallen under Rebecca's irresistible spell, pleads his case to her by saying: "thou and I are but the blind instruments of some irresistible fatality, that hurries us along, like goodly vessels driving before the storm, which are dashed against each other, and so perish" (445). Rebecca rejects this plea as an excuse for de Bois-Guilbert's own "wild passions," and repeats her expectation that God will protect her from sin and corruption, but also from being convicted as a sorceress—and will "raise up a deliverer" for her at her trial (502). As you would expect in a novel by Walter Scott, God takes due notice of Rebecca's request and even goes her one better. Not only does He raise up Ivanhoe, but when the latter is clearly incapable of defending her innocence, still weak from the wounds he suffered earlier, God causes de Bois-Guilbert to die of "contending passions" before he can harm Rebecca's champion (506)!

In *Notre-Dame de Paris,* Esmeralda's deliverer and defender is the grotesque Quasimodo, who in fact defends her from her deliverers, the truants, and thus assures her death. Critics have long wondered at this ironic denouement. If Hugo had wanted to depict the inexorable force of historical destiny in Esmeralda's death, why did he not simply have Esmeralda fall prisoner in a battle in which the King's soldiers would win out over the truants, without Quasimodo's misguided intervention? If Hugo wanted to make of Esmeralda the hope for a better future, why didn't he have Quasimodo spirit her away secretly, or perhaps have the truants free her and hide her in their midst?

I suggest that the answer is that the denouement of *Notre-Dame de Paris* is a direct reply to Walter Scott, a re-writing that is a repetition and a reversal at the same time. In his review of *Quentin Durward,* Hugo wrote: "[Durward and Louis XI] réagissent l'un sur l'autre de manière à exprimer l'idée fondamentale. C'est en obéissant fidèlement au roi que le loyal Durward sert sans le savoir ses propres intérêts," while "les projets de Louis XI dont Durward devait être à la fois l'instrument et la victime tournent en même temps à la confusion du rusé vieillard et à l'avantage du simple jeune homme" (Seebacher 1063). Moreover, the instrument of this peculiar manner of operation is none other than the gypsy, Hayraddin, who is supposed to carry out Louis XI's orders to betray Quentin and his beloved, Isabel de Croy, precisely at the moment when they are to visit a shrine to the three Magi.

Quasimodo's ironic intervention is thus a repetition of the Durwardian *modus operandi* in that the former unwittingly and even against his will becomes the instrument that actualizes the outcome. (And like Hayraddin, Quasimodo is almost certainly a gypsy, since the gypsies put him into Esmeralda's cradle when they took her away). But that outcome is just the reverse of the denouements of *Quentin Durward* and *Ivanhoe*; it is not Providence but Ananké whose will is worked in the most mysterious ways. The very fatality of fate, its total inescapability, could only be demonstrated by the fact that its victory is brought about by and through all the good will and well-meaning actions of every character sympathetic to Esmeralda. The language that Scott puts into Rebecca's mouth—"raise up a deliverer"—brings out another way in which the Egyptian connection links the plot of each novel to its political theme. In *Ivanhoe,* Rebecca's reference is surely to the Jews' plight under the Pharaohs in Egypt and to their subsequent deliverance recounted in *Exodus.* It is not the Jews, however, but the Saxons who are the enslaved tribe in *Ivanhoe,* and the Normans who play the role of the Egyptian slave drivers. In *Notre-Dame de Paris,* the slaves are not so much the gypsies or the truants as they are the French people; the slave-drivers are the theocrats and the monarchs (read '*le trône et l'autel,*' as they said during the Restoration); and the Moses, the deliverer, is not some individual person, but the process of history working primarily through the spread of enlightenment and manifested in the shift from theocracy to democracy, from the hidden signs of the priests to the open alphabet used in the printing-press.

I referred earlier to the prediction of Scott's astrologer, Martinvalle, concerning the historical effects that the invention of printing would have, a prediction that Hugo took over as the basis for one half of his chapter, "Ceci tuera cela." The very title of the chapter indicates how different Hugo's view of the historical process is from Scott's; where Martinvalle talks of "changing" forms of social life, of "erecting and destroying" kingdoms, of "establishing and overthrowing" religions as though these were all separate, unrelated effects, as though one kingdom or religion were as good or bad as another, Hugo describes the process in terms of direct conflict between one side and another, where the victory of one entails the downfall of the other: theocracy cannot persist where democracy rules; printing must supplant architecture. The key word is *tuer,* kill. Fate, after all, is death.

For this reason the chapter itself, like the novel as a whole, is dialogic, recounting the historical struggle between two opposing principles. The similarity between the structure of this theoretical chapter and the structure of the novel indicates that this chapter is a kind of *mise-en-abyme,* a part of the novel that by its shape as well as by its contents, outlines the theory of the novel in which it is found, gives a set of instructions for its own reading (Zarifopol-Johnston 23-24). In a sense this chapter is itself a hieroglyph, a rebus like those supposedly found in the parvis of the cathedral. The directions for reading given in this chapter state that the novel is constructed according to the same principles that govern hieroglyphic writing.

It may seem strange to claim that this novel, which excoriates hieroglyphic writing as a tool by means of which the priestly castes of theocracies had succeeded in monopolizing knowledge and power, is actually structured like a hieroglyph. Yet if, as Suzanne Nash has argued persuasively, Hugo condemns sacerdotal, symbolic writing as monologic, monolithic, ungenerative, in a word, dead (125), he also praises the alchemists' use of hermetic writing: "Dès le treizième siècle Guillaume de Paris, Nicolas Flamel au quinzième, ont écrit de ces pages séditieuses. Saint-Jacques-de-la-Boucherie était toute une église d'opposition" (179).

Nash explains that the new freedom which Hugo saw in the Gothic period was able to express itself in architecture when form and message were "once and for all severed" (126). The priests retained control of the interior of the building, but the religious message was henceforth confined there; the four walls, as Hugo puts it, belonged to the artist (178), who could inscribe into the structure a more varied, supple, and human, tenor. In short, the Gothic cathedral consisted of a living structure encasing a dead (sacerdotal) interior; whereas in the theocratic edifice, "le verbe était enfermé dans l'édifice, mais son image était sur son enveloppe comme la figure humaine sur le cercueil d'une momie" (176). Instead of a living skin surrounding the dead skeleton, a dead husk around those same bones. Hugo expresses the dead unity of theocracy by an analogy which highlights the resemblance of outside to inside, a resemblance marked by the sign of analogy, the image (of the human face).

For Hugo, then, the image is suspect, not only because it is a dead representation of a once living being, but also because the signifier is tied to the signified in an allegedly rigid relation, that of similarity. One of his reproaches against hieroglyphics can thus be explained as a rejection of their imagistic quality: hieroglyphs are, after all, primarily pictographs, images of real objects such as the sun, the moon, and various animals and plants. But, as Lacan reminds us in his discussion of the dream as rebus in "Agency of the Letter in the Unconscious, Or Reason since Freud":

> the value of the image as signifier has nothing whatever to do with its signification [as representation] . . . [in] Egyptian hieroglyphics in which it would be sheer buffoonery to pretend that in a given text the frequency of a vulture, which is an *aleph,* or of a chick, which is a *vau* . . . prove that the text has anything at all to do with those ornithological specimens.
>
> (*Ecrits* 159)

Hieroglyphs, like rebuses, are a series of pictographs, in which the name of the thing functions as a letter or a signifying sound, the first letter of the name, a syllable like the 'scie' of 'la vieille science,' or a word like the *dauphin* or *marguerite* indicated by the image of the aquatic mammal or the flower. A pictograph thus operates according to a double process of signification, in which an image stands not for a thing or concept but for a signifier that is part of a system of signifiers, usually an actual language such as French, in which a *dauphin* is both a denizen of the sea and the heir to the throne.

The hieroglyphic structure of the novel allows it to foreshadow the freedom of the future without pretending to have attained it. Hugo insists that in the Gothic period it was necessary and possible to use hermetic writing to evade the censorship of the Church (179). In *Notre-Dame de Paris* as in the cathedral of the same name, form and message are not simply severed; the dead unity of similarity between signifier and signified is not merely disrupted. The image of the dead interior must both be killed and preserved so that it can become an element in the new signifying system. The image of the saw is needed to represent the *scie,* but then that representational value must be suppressed in order to insert the syllable 'scie' into the word 'science.' Just as printing kills architecture, so hieroglyphic writing must 'kill' the picture in order to function as writing. *Notre-Dame de Paris,* the piece of writing, had to use and replace Notre-Dame de Paris, the structure of stones. The novel could preserve the cathedral from destruction only by translating it into writing, just as literate enlightenment had to use and supplant the Church of Peter, of Pierre, of the stone.

If freedom is to prevail, on the personal or the political level, then this poetic system of double rewriting must be in operation. When it is not, the result is death, as the events of the novel attest. As object of the quest, as signifier of desire, the emerald brings *aphanisis,* disappearance and death to those who approach it too closely. Quasimodo, Claude, Jean, La Sachette, all live as long as Esmeralda is absent; all die when she is present, through her presence to them. Only the writer, Pierre, who sublimates his sexual desire for her, survives.

Quasimodo meets his death in the cellar of Montfaucon, frozen in the deadly embrace of Esmeralda's skeleton. Many readers see in this last, ghastly, scene, an occasion for optimism, the reunion of the two innocent outcasts signifying the possibility of hope for the future; strangely enough, I find myself in basic agreement with this view, although for different reasons. Reading, restoring and resuscitating were the three R's of early, conservative Romanticism in France, that of Walter Scott, Chateaubriand, Nodier and the young Hugo. The main thrust in the movement was to return to the past, to bring back the past in the present, or to fear the vengeance the past might wreak on the present. This infatuation with the image of the past, the attempt to enter into direct contact with it, entails the same loss of sublimations that afflicts Claude, the return of repressed desires which threaten the subject with dissolution. The hieroglyphic novel, on the other hand, is not a mere representation of history; it exercises the performative function of defining and enacting through its own writing a new relation to the past, a new historicization (Lacan, *Ecrits* 88). The intertextual, monumental, hieroglyphic functions whose operation I have described in *Notre-Dame de Paris,* the attitude of "Ceci tuera cela," puts the present into a very different relation with the past, the subject with the signifier of desire, the letter with the image, print with architecture, text with intertext. This relation can best be characterized as one of mourning (Lacan, "Desire . . . in Hamlet"). In it the attempt is no longer made, as in alchemy, literally to bring the dead, the stone-dead, (back) to life, that is, against all reason and experience, simply to deny the reality of death; rather the image, the model, the past, the dead, are marked and preserved in the monument, but they are preserved as dead. Like the pictograph and the intertext, their remnant, their corpse is then used in a process of rewriting; the killing, preservation and redeployment of the past are effected in the present in order to open the way for a new future.

"Quasimodo's marriage," as Hugo calls the last chapter of his monumental novel, the image of the skeletons of the phallic couple locked in a fatal embrace, is therefore a hieroglyph of the mourning process, a monument to the death of the fatal denial of death, and the first letter of the story of a new life.

Works Cited

Baudoin, Charles. *Psychanalyse de Victor Hugo.* Paris: A. Colin, 1972.

Brombert, Victor. *Victor Hugo and the Visionary Novel.* Cambridge: Harvard UP, 1984.

Buchon, Jean Alexandre. *Collection des chroniques nationales françaises.* Vol. 10. Paris: Verdiere, 1825. 47 vols. 1824-29.

Collin de Plancy, Jacques-Albin-Simon. *Dictionnaire infernal.* 2nd ed. 5 vols. Paris: P. Mongie aîné, 1825-1826.

Condorcet, Marquis de. *Esquisse d'un tableau historique des progrès de l'esprit humain.* Paris: Agasse, A n III (1795).

Dupire, Noël. *Les faictz et dictz de Jean Molinet.* Paris: Société des anciens textes français, 1936. 2 vols.

Festugière, A.-J., trans., and A. D. Nock, ed., *Corpus Hermeticum.* Vol. 2. Paris: Les Belles Lettres, 1945. 3 vols.

Grant, Richard. *The Perilous Quest: Image. Myth and Prophesy in the Narratives of Victor Hugo.* Durham: Duke UP, 1968.

Hugo, Victor. *Notre-Dame de Paris.* Paris: Gallimard, 1975.

Huguet, Edmond. *Dictionnaire de la langue française du seizième siècle.* 7 vols. Paris: Champion, 1925-1973.

Lacan, Jacques. *Ecrits: A Selection.* Trans. Alan Sheridan. New York: Norton, 1977.

———. "Desire and the Interpretation of Desire in *Hamlet.*" *Yale French Studies* 55/56 (1977): 11-52.

Lacroix, Paul. *Soirées de Walter Scott.* Vol. 1. Paris: Renduel, 1829. 2 vols. 1829-31.

Nash, Suzanne. "Writing a Building: Hugo's *Notre-Dame de Paris.*" *French Forum* 8 (1983): 122-133.

Nerval, Gérard de. "Préface de la première édition de *Faust.*" *Œuvres complémentaires de Gérard de Nerval.* Vol. 1:3-9. Ed. Jean Richer. Paris: Minard, 1959. 7 vols. 1959-81.

Picat-Guinoiseau, Ginette. *Une oeuvre méconnue de Charles Nodier. Faust imité de Goethe.* Paris: Didier, 1977.

Sauval, Henri. *Histoire et recherches des antiquités de la ville de Paris.* Paris: C. Moette, 1724. 3 vols.

Scott, Walter. *Ivanhoe.* New York: Penguin, 1984.

———. *Quentin Durward.* London: Black, 1932.

Seebacher, Jacques. Introduction. *Notre-Dame de Paris.* By Victor Hugo. Paris: Gallimard, 1975. 1045-1076.

Seligmann, Kurt. *Magic. Supernaturalism and Religion.* New York: Pantheon, 1971.

Staël, Madame de. *De l'Allemagne.* Vol. 3. Paris: Hachette, 1959. 5 vols. 1958-60.

Zarifopol-Johnston, Ilinca. "*Notre-Dame de Paris*: The Cathedral in the Book." *Nineteenth-Century French Studies.* 13 (1985): 22-35.

E. S. Burt (essay date December 1990)

SOURCE: Burt, E. S. "Hallucinatory History: Hugo's *Révolution.*" *Modern Language Notes* 105, no. 5 (December 1990): 965-91.

[*In the following essay, Burt uses the epic poem* Le Révolution *to illustrate the duplicitous nature of language in poetry; namely, the referential use of language and language as a reflection of the poem's historicity.*]

Readers of poetry and its criticism have long been accustomed to mixed reviews of its alleged autonomy. The lyric is generally the target here, although other poetic forms are also open to the charge of retreat from the public arena of history and politics. The loss of reference to empirical experience, deplored by some, has been felt by others to be a sacrifice made for gain: what poetry loses in concrete historical veracity, in attachment to a context, it makes up for by its achievement of the self-sufficiency and meaningful ideality of a fiction. What poems sacrifice in the way of a capacity to portray events or historical personages, they regain by depicting the human in all its generality.

Structuralist and post-structuralist critiques of the subject have modified this assessment somewhat. A theory of texts as self-reflexive structures has dispelled the illusion that poems represent a generalized, fictional self. One tends in recent times to praise poetry for its undoing of ideal fictions, rather than for its production of them.

It is no doubt natural that, in the wake of the undoing of the self as the meaning of the lyric, critics should cast around for something to put in its place and should ask whether they had not been too hasty in accepting the poem's autonomy. Even a poem understood to forego the representation of empirical experience can be considered in terms of a referent—for instance, as portraying a subject's wishful production of a self.[1] Poems do more than signify, they also refer. Words are not only interpretable figures, they are also signs that point. Some critics have therefore felt justified in asking whether, having passed through the bath of the theory of language as the locus of the poem's meaning, we cannot now place poems in a larger historical picture. In short, they have sought for poetry a place in the new historicism.

The return to questioning poetry as to its possible referent in experience has of course not meant the return to a literal referent provided by the author's biography or by a single historical event. Instead, the self-reflexive language of poetry having been identified as the source of meaning and its undoing in the poem, it becomes possible to suggest that the referent of modern poems could be precisely the historical event of a change in the way that poets think about language and poetry, the event of the establishment of a new and more modern understanding of literature and literariness. A Foucauldian epistemic shift moves a poet away from the naive wish to polish language so it can prove the perfect mirror of the self, toward a more sophisticated understanding, where language, recognized to be the stuff of poetry, stands revealed as always duplicitous, a structure always capable of saying more and less than the ideality of the self.

An historical thesis of this sort shows up in an admirable essay by Joel Fineman entitled "Shakespeare's 'Perjur'd Eye.'"[2] Fineman finds in the space of the slim volume of Shakespeare's *Sonnets* two conflicting poetic practices that suggest to him just such an epistemic shift. Fineman explains:

> . . . Shakespeare's sonnet sequence marks a decisive moment in the history of lyric, for when the dark lady sonnets forswear the ideally visionary poetics of the young man sonnets, when poetic language comes in this way to be characterized as something verbal, not visual, we see what happens to poetry when it gives over a perennial poetics of *ut pictura poesis* for . . . a poetics of *ut poesis poesis,* a transition that writes itself out in Shakespeare's sonnets as an unhappy progress from a poetry based on visual likeness . . . to a poetry based on verbal difference. . . .
>
> ("Eye" 71)

For Fineman, the visionary, idealizing poetics of the young man sonnets implies a metaphorical system based on vision in which sensuous form and idea have an adequate relation to one another, and poetic language is Cratylic, its signifiers and signifieds brought by the poet's craft into harmonious relation. In the dark lady sonnets, on the other hand, language is not the transparent language of pure visibility, but a verbal, performative language, full of artifices and duplicity, and one that, capable as it is of showing the idealism of the homogeneous vision-centered sonnets to be predicated on an illusion, has a life and force to be reckoned with. Language does not mirror without distorting; the ideal image is, upon closer examination, itself a distortion, since metaphor makes things look alike that are in fact very different. Shakespeare's sonnets thus serve Fineman as the index of a decisive move from a poetry that wants to reflect only the self and its self-sameness, to a poetry far shrewder about language as difference. That poetry, he claims, is the product of a subjectivity that has undergone alteration in its understanding of language and has recognized itself to be belated and historical. It takes only a little forcing to make the sonnet sequences—whose organizing principle is not necessarily that of a progressive narrative—into a *Bildungsroman* ordered around a moment of conversion that entails an increased awareness in poetic consciousness.

Thus, the highly-formalized construct that is the poem finds itself cleared of any charge of ahistoricity. Shakespeare's sonnets refer to the event of a change in consciousness within Shakespeare's history as a poet, an event that marks the appearance of a new subjectivity ("Eye" 71-2) and that corresponds to a shift from the Elizabethan lyric, with its tired Petrarchan themes, to a more modern and sophisticated literature of belatedness. Fineman is then able, in a polemical move, to suggest that recent language-centered theories are an epiphenomenon, a coming-into-theoretical consciousness of the crucial insight that Shakespeare had already figured in the dark lady sequence ("Eye" 78-79) as long ago as the Renaissance.

But to make the lady and her sexual difference stand for the difference of language is a decisive, stabilizing move on Fineman's part. On the one hand, it establishes the possibility of each poem or poem sequence operating autonomously as a system of meaning in which things as unlike as women and words can substitute for one another by way of a shared property, here, their difference. The dark lady is a figure within the sonnets for the language of the sonnets. On the other hand, it also establishes the possibility of reference for each poem or poem sequence, since a language known to be false can be a reliable vehicle for communication, at least about its own gainsaying ("Eye" 77). The figure of the lady consoles us for the revelation that language is a lie by telling us that we can trust it at one point, at the point that it identifies itself as lie: we can know, in a word, when we are dealing with liars and literary language, and when not. What Fineman calls a second degree of Cratylism makes the signifiers of lying language correspond to their signified, the lie of language.[3] Any language that tells us that it lies reveals the truth about language, and is literary. Any language that does not tell us about its lie, lies with respect to itself, but we can then know it is not poetry, and so does not mean to deceive us by what it says. Fineman's interpretation of the figure of the dark lady thus allows a distinction between a poetic space where an interrogation into the verbal nature of literary language goes on, and the public, historical space where language aims to represent the world as in a painting.[4]

But one can wonder whether poems (and poets) are as certain about the status of their language as Fineman wants them to be. The indeterminacy of texts touches on the impossibility of deciding whether a given use of language is a referential use or a self-referring one. One would expect poems to address this undecidability and the pressures exerted toward deciding it in their self-referential discussion of their language. To reanchor a poem too quickly in a context by a referential determination is to foreclose on the very place where poems could be speaking to the question of their historicity.

The question to be pursued in what follows, then, is the question of what poems have to say about the pressures in language toward reference and signification, as also what they have to say about their historicity. My example will be a poem by Victor Hugo that ostensibly refers to the historical event of the French Revolution, an event credited by the idealist tradition of Kant and Hegel with having opened modern history as the actualization of the idea of history itself.

The poem, entitled *La Révolution,* dates from 1857 and was originally to have been included in a group called the *Petites épopées,* the little epics.[5] Reworked and expanded in 1870, shortly before Hugo's return to France, it was destined to figure in a collection called *Les Quatre vents de l'esprit,* as the single example of the epic spirit. The title—translatable as *The Revolution* or as *Revolution*—suggests that the poem will be about the famous Revolution of 1789, or else about revolution in general.[6] But to all appearances, the poem takes neither

tack. Instead, it seems an hallucinatory history. It recounts the coming to life of the equestrian statues of three French kings, which it follows as they trot through Paris (in the first section, *Les Statues*); it apostrophizes the long-dead sculptor of the Pont-Neuf, and then sets down the thoughts of that downtrodden and speechifying bridge about the reigns of the kings (in the second section, *Les Cariatides*); it concludes with a brief dialogue concerning the meaning and authorship of the guillotine, a dialogue between the statues of the kings and the talking head of Louis XVI, which floats by (in the third section, *L'Arrivée*). An epilogue affirms that the outcome of all this delirium is progress toward peace, harmony and love. If the poem has a bearing on the real Revolution, or on the reality of revolution in general, it is as an hallucination relates to the real.[7]

A brief commentary on the term "hallucinatory" is in order. Hugo's hallucinations and his experiments with the occult in the *tables tournantes* during his exile are not at issue here. Riffaterre has already demonstrated that one does not have to have recourse to Hugo's biography or psychology to understand the hallucinatory effect of his poetry, which is produced by linguistic structures and figures. I will not be attempting the formal description of those structures either, Riffaterre having already done so in *Essais de stylistique structurale*; besides, the hallucinatory raises issues for consciousness that are not accounted for by the formalism of that early essay.[8] Nor will I be seeking to establish a causal connection between the events of the French Revolution and a psychology, be it that of an individual Revolutionary, or of the Parisian masses.[9] The poem does not support a crude causality of this sort. Finally, however tempting it would be to explore *La Révolution* as a history written within a psychoanalytic framework, there are reasons for preferring to start with a less subjective landscape. One reason for resisting psychoanalytic terms is that it is entirely uncertain whether the poem presents itself as the description of an hallucinatory vision or is rather the fiction of an hallucination, made up to elucidate something else, say the effect of figuring poetic language in terms of a subject and its experience of language.

The etymology of the word "hallucinate" supports the contention that a relation between consciousness and signs is at stake. "Hallucinate" is derived from the Latin *alucinari,* a term meaning "to wander in mind, to dream," but also, "to talk idly, to prate, to discourse freely." The etymology suggests that Hugo's hallucinatory poems might best be considered in the line passing from Montaigne's logorrhaeic *Essais* through the Cartesian digressive *Discours* and *Méditations,* to the discursive vagaries of Rousseau's *Rêveries du promeneur solitaire.* The locus of exile from which the later Hugo speaks is analogous to the dislocation of the I of the *Rêveries,* whom a catastrophic loss of intersubjective and subject-object relations forces back upon itself and its own resources. The Rousseauian *I* has nothing left to affirm itself over and against the void except its experience of memory and memory-signs. A similar intense epistemological uncertainty and a resultant forcing back of the self onto its experience of signs are characteristic of the hallucinatory poems of the second half of *Les Contemplations,* as well as of *La Révolution.*[10]

And it is indeed into a landscape from which human subjects and their objects of perception have disappeared that the poem introduces us, offering its horrific visions of mobile bronze, "visions où jamais un oeil humain ne plonge" (220) to "on ne sait quels spectateurs funèbres" (218). Against the landscape denuded of human subjects, in a night too dark to see anything but more darkness, move the statues with their human visages, endowed with sight, hearing, speech, and motion.

The walking statue is a redoubled prosopopeia. A statue is a work of art that gives a face to a dead or absent entity—the definition of prosopopeia—in a material very unlike that of the entity, be it granite or bronze in the case of sculpture, or, as Hugo says in the case of poetry, "le bronze dithyrambe et le marbre épopée" (230). To call such a work to life and motion is a prosopopeia to the second power, the prosopopeia of a prosopopeia. The poem is thus allegorizing its central figure, which is precisely the kind of figure by which Fineman decrees the lady's difference to stand for language's difference. Like a metaphor for metaphor, the walking statue meditates on itself as statue, as prosopopeia. But unlike a metaphor for metaphor, which tends toward the stasis of a revelation, giving a face to the giving of face has to concern itself with an open and undeterminable series of effects. It asks about the responsibility of and for the human face incurred by the work of art when it endows an inhuman material with human characteristics, about what Hugo calls the "Responsabilité de la figure humaine / Prise dans le granit ou le bronze fatal" (220). Prosopopeia faces the possibility of ungovernable referential effects engendered by the making of fictions about man. This possibility is carried to an extreme in the poem when the poet credits an obscure artist under Henri IV, the putative sculptor of the mascarons of the Pont-Neuf, with having unwittingly roughed out a sketch of Robespierre in one of his farcical masks: "Mais à ton insu même . . . tu mettais la lueur / Des révolutions dans le regard des faunes . . . Et ta fatale main, o grand tailleur de pierre / Dans Trivelin sinistre ébauchait Robespierre" (230). The prosopopeia to the second power, then, raises the specter of ungovernable repetition. For even should the poem manage to bring a closure to the effects of a first giving of human face to an inhuman material, it would nonetheless incur a second set of debts and responsibilities by the second prosopopeia, the very one that lets it assume a discourse of responsibility for the effects of the first.

And it is in their effects that the statues reveal their nature as redoubled prosopopeias. In the following passage these effects are divisible into two rough categories: the statues bring the immutable and the dead to life; they chill or petrify the mutable:

> Visions où jamais un oeil humain ne plonge!
> Et comme par la rampe invisible d'un songe,
> La statue à pas lents du socle descendit.
>
> Alors l'âpre ruelle au nom fauve et maudit,
> L'échoppe, la maison, l'hôtel, le bouge obscène,
> Les mille toits mirant leurs angles dans la Seine,
> Les obscurs carrefours où, le jour, en tous sens,
> Court l'hésitation confuse des passants,
> Les enseignes pendant aux crocs de fer des portes,
> Les palais crénelés comme des villes fortes,
> Le chaland aux anneaux des berges retenu,
> S'étonnèrent devant ce cimier inconnu
> Dont aucun ouragan n'eût remué la plume,
> Entendirent le sol tinter comme une enclume
> Et, tandis qu'au fronton des tours l'heure étouffait
> Sa voix, n'osant sonner au cadran stupéfait,
> Virent, dans l'épaisseur des ténèbres accrues,
> Droit, paisible et glacé, s'avancer dans les rues,
> Accompagné d'un bruit funèbre et souterrain,
> L'homme de bronze assis sur le cheval d'airain.
>
> L'eau triste frissonnait sous la rondeur de l'arche.
>
> (220)

Note that, upon the dramatic passage of the statue of Henri IV, a structure, the city of Paris, takes on human features: it sees, hears and is surprised. A little further on, a bone structure, a skeleton, turns in its grave and voices questions. Similarly, in the poem as a whole, each monument mobilized will ride up to the next and, by an apostrophe—"Viens voir si ton fils est à sa place encore"—will awaken it.[11] On the other side, however, the fugitive and figural is arrested in the passage. Time does not flee, but is, on the contrary, paralysed; the temperature of the Seine drops and it becomes chilly enough to shiver; further on, the dream loses its transforming and distinguishing capacities. A double movement is uncovered: the work of art endows with and deprives life, or what is the same thing here, feeling, movement, voice, distinctness.

What does this chilling and mobilizing mean with respect to a dynamic pressure toward reference and signification? Hugo is commenting upon the problem in this passage where, as exchanges take place between the spatial and temporal dimension of the text, the city, the text as structure or semiotic system, starts to take on intention and meaning, while time, the text as figural system, loses its mobility and gets fixed into a denominative system.

The arresting of time is indeed one of the most notable effects of the statue's passage. It would seem that a poem ostensibly about the historical event of the French Revolution, and one appearing, at that, as the example of the epic spirit, ought to be regulated by some overriding temporal scheme. Instead, among the various astonished spectators of the mobile statues an immobilized clock informs us of the suspension of objective time: "Et, tandis qu'au fronton des tours l'heure étouffait / Sa voix, n'osant sonner au cadran stupéfait. . . ."

The odditiy of the figure lies partly in the fact that the hour is not perceivable by the means that human beings have found to make their rational constructs of time felt, i.e., by the clock. Time cannot make itself heard or seen; its bell is silenced, its hands stunned into immobility. With the loss of time as we perceive it by the clock are also lost the constructs that go with it. The linear progression made perceptible by the sounded hour as it disrupts a continuum of silence is not operative.[12] Nor is the cyclical model for which the turning hands of the clockface is the visual analogy. The familiar rational structures—both of which are associated with the modern meaning of revolution—are suspended along with the familiar sensible manifestations that are their correlative.[13]

Hugo is well aware that we do not experience time directly, but as a language, by way of signs. The rest of the poem bears out the contention that the arrested clock signals an end to objective time. The poem does not narrate the events of the Revolution or suggest that the Revolution returns man to a more originary state of virtue and freedom, as Hugo's novel *Quatre vingt treize* will do. Only in the most oblique of ways—by an allegory developed in *Choses vues*[14] which says that a statue off its pedestal is like a dethroned king—can the moving statues be said to point to such empirical events of the Revolution as the destruction of the royal statues, the renaming of the Place Louis XV, or the beheading of Louis XVI. Hugo's stilled clock stops correlating the perception one has of the clock as signifier to an objective construct.

But, in another sense, the clock does not cease to keep time. It is still a sign and can refer to itself as an empty order or construction. The clock stilled is still a clock, just as a representation that represents nothing is nonetheless something, i.e., a representation or sign of nothing.

Is the objective time scheme then voided in order to open time and revolution to a subjective interpretation? The poem might be asserted to be self-referential in order to allow Hugo to focus on the Revolutionary crisis as a crisis of spirit in which the French nation found its identity, and watching Europe found confirmation that history was not a set of random events but reason actualizing itself.

By way of prosopopeia, the gift of voice, of feeling, and of the capacity for voluntary action associated with the inner time of the self is conferred upon the hour:

". . . l'heure étouffait / Sa voix, n'osant sonner au cadran stupéfait." But the gift of life is only equivocally a gift. The hour is endowed with human characteristics so that it may have more of which to be deprived. It gets the passion of fear to petrify passion's mobility, action to deprive itself of action. More tellingly, in a poem where the human is represented by the qualities specific to the poet, the hour is given voice only to mute it. Even its vestigial ears—for the root of *oser,* to dare, is *audere,* to hear—are taken away from it: *n'osant,* not daring / not hearing. The hour is made human so as to assert its striking resemblance—death-like stillness and stupefaction—to a suicide. The prosopopeia gives us to know the hour by an odd likeness to ourselves: it is like us when we have called into question our selfhood by an act of self-annihilation. The hour is the time ushered in when, in an act of Mallarmean self-doubt, the self ceases to exist as an operative category. Thus, the hour's stifled voice undoes the harmonious correlation between signifier and meaning. Time is not a signified expressed by ringing bells, as voiced language expresses human feeling; just as the stupefied clock interrupts the passage by way of meaning from the sign to an outside referent, so the stifled voice, the suicidal hour interrupts the process of signification itself, the passage from the outside of perception to the inside of meaning.

Bergsonian duration, introspective time, is not operative in the poem either. It is a poem about statues and masks, things devoid of inner life. The most human figure is that of the dead sculptor, Germaine Pilon. But even this representative artist is no self-conscious genius; he is said to have been a prophet who was not in on his own secret, a soul who did not have the revelation of his whole thought, a dreamer who did not know what symbol he had thrown across the Seine in the Pont-Neuf. *La Révolution* does not promise the great interpretative wealth of an introspective poem, centered on a self's return to itself, or on a radical transformation it brings about in its mental or moral order. The stifled voice of the hour speaks rather of a discrepancy between consciousness' understanding of poems as expressive totalities and the actual structure of the poetic text, which is non-homogeneous, non-totalizing and cannot necessarily be reduced to meaning.

The point is made in part by the undoing of prosopopeia as seductive human figure. Prosopopeia transfers face and voice to a dead or absent entity; here, the transfer also works in the reverse direction: the humanized hour is made a dead or absent entity. The figure speaks against the construction of the language of time along the model of the self.

But the hour is an houri, *l'heure est un leurre,* a lure, a trap, a Nervalian will o' the wisp, a gleam (or *lueur*). It is seductive in the first place because, in undoing itself as human figure, it becomes convincingly more and more like a human figure, endowed as it seems with a purposiveness in its act of self-stifling. It turns itself into a not-self by a fearsome, murderous gesture, and in so doing, hides itself as not-self by the apparent intentionality of its turn. The prosopopeia undoes the first figure only by reconstituting it.

The seductiveness involved in the reconstituting of the figure is, however, a blind that conceals a less graceful and more threatening spectacle. For we should remember that the hour and the clock are not coming to life in this passage, but are tending toward progressive petrification. The distinctive feature of the passage on time is: the seizing of the mobile, the figural, the human, in stone. The clock is stupefied, the hour is strangled; the fronton of towers turns to us a stony forehead (*fronton* derives from *front,* forehead). A rigor mortis seizes the temporal, after its reference to the objective word and its meaning for a self have both been evacuated in favor of a self-referential structure of uncertain or no meaning.

The syntagm *fronton des tours* accomplishes the rigidification by freezing in a single place the two functions evacuated. It is by way of the plural, *des tours,* which effaces the gendered article, that two different kinds of *tours,* both of which have been at work in the passage, are coupled: on the one hand, *tour* as tower, la Tour de la Bastille, la Tour de Nesle or La Tour de Babel; on the other hand, all the turns of *le tour,* from trope and turn of phrase, from sleight of hand or trick, from circuit or circular walk to rotation or revolution. As in Baudelaire's *Thyrsus,* where the hieratic emblem of a wand around which dances a snaky line of flowers allegorizes the indissociability of trope and sign, Hugo's twin *tours,* the referential and the tropological, are yoked together by a single—indeed a singular—*fronton.*

For a *fronton*—an architectural term designating a frontal or small pediment—like its near synonyms, pediment and façade, names by catachresis, that is, by abusive metaphor. A catachresis does not exchange terms between known entities but rather sets up an unequal exchange by means of which a known entity can give a term to an unknown entity so that the latter can get a name for one of its parts. The human body is often pillaged for these unequal exchanges, to name the teeth of a comb, the arm of a chair, the eye of a camera, or the face of a building. As catachresis *fronton* is both a name and a figure, and as such can successfully bridge the gap between signification and reference, trope and name, turn and tower.

However, the *fronton des tours* presses the passage—as passage allegorical of its language—away from the seductions of the self-undoing hour toward a rigid system of names, of conventional, referential language. As proper term for a part of a tower it makes the figurality

of the passage recede, giving to it the quality of a description of the literal scene of a tower on whose pediment is a stopped clock. One could, for example, read the passage as inspired by an event of the 1848 revolution described by Hugo in *Choses vues*: "Le cadran des Tuileries arrêté à 3 heures. (N'a pas été remonté depuis la révolution.) Marque l'heure de la chute de la monarchie."[15] As name, the catachresis presses the passage about the undecidability of language toward reference, and thence toward such referential towers as the *Bastille,* and such referential events as the French Revolution.

The figure is not far off, of course. We have been talking about language in this passage because time can come before us only by a process of signification, by the mediation of a language.[16] In a word, talking about time is to talk figuratively about a language, as to talk about the arresting of time arrested is to talk figuratively about bringing a stasis to a mobile, figural system. If the passage tends toward a sudden collapse into reference, that is precisely what it has been preparing all along in its discussion of rigidification. The figurative meaning of the catachresis is: meaning and reference are collapsed into reference when language stops meaning the self or referring to the world outside, and starts referring to itself as undecidably trope or sign. The stopped clock of *Choses vues* confirms the insight of *La Révolution* that there is a pressure in language toward the loss of a distinctness between names and tropes.

The loss of that distinction is here considered to be a pre-condition for the revolutionary turn. Of course Hugo is not claiming that the shots of the 1848 Revolution were fired by language. But he is suggesting that the collapse of the two disparate functions of language into a single referential function is necessary for revolution to be conceivable.[17] This is not a delirious notion on Hugo's part. We can certainly understand that, in order for the attack on the Bastille to touch off a revolution, the Bastille had not only to be the name of a literal tower and a symbol for the king's power, but also that, for the time it took to destroy it, it be treated as if those two functions were collapsed into its very stones. The Revolution is defined here as the collapse of the figure into a name.

This collapse has an equivalent on the other side of the equation, in a collapse taking place in the city. The city is a spatial structure standing for other structures, which is given the pathos of a human subject, and an object of knowledge—the moving city monument—that can well represent it. The poem sets up an opposition between space and time that suggests how we are to read this animation and attempt at self-understanding on the part of the city. While, *tandis que,* time is seized in stony structures and signification falls into reference, spatial constructs, the text as organized grammar, starts to move or get emotional, and language as structured set of conventional signs takes on meaning for a subject. The dramatic change takes place around the monumental statue.

Now the statue is of the city, insofar as it is a structure, but insofar as it advances, it is not entirely like the city. It has some of the features of the time system, and can be said, if not absolutely to be replacing time broken down on the other side of the equation, at least to have appropriated some of its properties. Its advance, its passage, is the signified that clock and bells ordinarily mean: time does not advance or pass, but the statue advances and passes. Furthermore, the ringing that should be the perceptual sign of time passing shows up here as a funereal and subterranean noise, the ringing of the ground itself that accompanies the statue's advance. The hour stifles its voice, but the earth rings. The clock hands cease to turn, and the turn of *tour* tends to disappear, but, as I will show in a minute, the towering statue can be said to turn. When we look to one of the representative structures of a text—the organization of its signifiers—for understanding, we do so by importing the discredited interpretive framework from the other side. In the structure that is the work of art the inside/outside polarity that reigns when we think of a perception corresponding to an understanding is not the primary function. But when the work of art as structure is taken to be representative, to be a figure, it is by way of the worn-out relation.

It is to the poem's signifiers, as to its very ground, that we need to look for the meaning. It is there that we hear time advancing, for example. For *heure* continues to sound its passing in odd ways and places: *épaisseur, rondeur, horreur, roideur, leur, grandeur, stupeur,* etc. Similarly, although time's turns are no longer visible on the dial, they can be sighted in a signifier, indeed in the signifier of vision itself, the peculiar *virent,* the past tense of the verb *voir,* to see, but which is also the present tense of *virer,* to veer, to round a corner. A strategic placement makes this *virent* turn to turn. It is distanced from its subject by the clause about time, and is thus close to the *tour* and the unturning hands; the object of vision, the man of bronze and the horse of brass, are quite capable of serving as the subject of *virent,* giving us a wheeling man and horse.[18]

The poem is commenting on itself as a structure that offers itself, by way of a new figuration, as a perception of sorts. Language is getting phenomenalized in the passage, its grammar and signs being treated as audible and visible. This phenomenalization is described as the descent of the dream into a mental maelström ("comme par la rampe invisible d'un songe / . . . dans l'égarement d'un orage mental . . . / Le rêve . . . / . . . s'épouvante . . . / Et frémit . . ." [220-1]) and what it raises is the issue of whether the text *advances* by way of such play with signifiers. For the system of signifiers, with the accidents of grammar and the sonorous plays it brings into view, does not merely serve as the correlative of meaning, as the voice expressing a thought. It seems actually to advance meaning. Thus, the *épaisseur des ténèbres* seems more than just a nonsensical tolling of "heure," a resounding of its signifier after its meaning has been emptied out. It seems to ring the changes of a new hour, an hour substantializable, spatializable, an hour made thick (*épaisse-heure*), an hour outside of the hour, *hors-heure,* a weighty hour, *une lourde heure,* an upright and kingly hour, *roi d'heure roide-heure,* a great hour, *une grande heure,* the impersonal hour itself, *l'heure elle-même, enfin!*

We are familiar with the engenderment of texts around their babbling, prating signifiers. This is one model for engendering texts at work in Rousseau's *Rêveries.* What is striking about the passage from **La Révolution,** however, is that, as it refers to its own phenomenalization of language, it moves away from the original comparison of the vision to dreaming and thus from the hope of achieving a Cratylic correspondence between signifier and signified. It suggests, as I will show in a minute, that the phenomenalization of language involves a kind of madness, for the dream collapses into hallucination. The prosopopeia endowing the city with intention reintroduces a dysfunctional model that first has us rubbing our eyes, wondering if we see or just think we see a turn in *virent,* and has us checking our ears, wondering if we hear the voice of the stifled *heure* or the sound of the wind, favored topos of Hugo, in *devant, s'avancer, s'avança,* etc. But the dream begins to turn toward hallucination as the poet starts to ask about the status of the event on which he is focussing and of the subject who sees it: ". . . qu'est-ce qui passait? . . . / Qui donc a vu lentement passer les statues?" (220) The point is less whether we see or don't see any one of these phenomena, and whether they actually have a meaning or not, than the fact that one apparently prefers to make sense of nonsense rather than to have no meaning at all. The pressure toward meaning is great enough that when all sense has been evacuated and we are left with just a "nom fauve et maudit," one prefers to hallucinate meaning and intention rather than that there be none.[19]

Laplanche and Pontalis, in an article on "Fantasy and the Origins of Sexuality," suggest that when signifiers get treated as objects of perception, we are in the domain of hallucination.[20] When an infant hallucinates a breast, it is not attempting to get milk, which it knows is not there. Its "vision" of the breast is not the means by which it tries to satisfy its physical hunger. For the child, in the dearth of milk and breast, thinks it sees "not the real object, but the lost object; not the milk, but the breast *as a signifier*" (15). The infant substitutes the signifier for the milk, a substitution that is possible because the signifier, like an object, has a phenomenal existence. Whatever satisfaction the child gets from the hallucination comes from the linguistic operation of substituting signifier for object, and then from sucking it for all it's worth, that is, for mental nourishment, for extra signifieds, to give nascent consciousness some sense of its own life and operation.

In "Hypogram and Inscription" de Man further elaborates the distinctive character of hallucination: "in hallucination, the difference between *I see* and *I think I see* has been one-sidedly resolved in the direction of apperception[.] Consciousness has become consciousness only of itself" ("Hypogram," 49). Toward the end, the passage from **La Révolution** talks about such a collapse in the dreamspace itself:

> . . . et le rêve lui-même,
> Qui distingue à minuit dans l'immensité blême
> Tout un monde terrible à travers l'oeil fermé,
> Le rêve, aux habitants de l'ombre accoutumé,
> S'épouvante de voir cette lugubre espèce
> De fantômes entrer dans sa nuée épaisse,
> Et frémit, car le pas de ces noirs arrivants,
> N'est ni le pas des morts ni le pas des vivants.
>
> (221)

The dream can see with a closed eye because it knows no difference between waking and sleeping. But it is accustomed to distinguishing between the dreamspace (*dans l'immensité blême*) and the dream world with which it furnishes that space (*tout un monde terrible*). When the lugubrious phantoms arrive, however, they render the space into which they enter (*dans une nuée épaisse,* into a thick cloud) indistinct from themselves as intruders (they enter *dans une nuée épaisse,* that is, *as* a thick cloud or swarm). The dream no longer knows how to distinguish its habitual space from the inhabitants that occupy that space. It cannot differentiate between what it "sees" with its closed eye, the cloud of phantoms, and itself as dreaming consciousness, the thick cloud of thought. Phantom thought grips itself in phantom perceptions.

The lines that explain the cause of the dream's terror yield an example of the way that reference and signification get conflated into a meaning undifferentiated from perception when language is phenomenalized. The explanation reads: "Car le pas de ces noirs arrivants / N'est ni le pas des morts ni le pas des vivants." It is hard to seize the distinctions the poet is trying to make, as the attempt to translate them shows. If we translate them with respect to the referential event of stepping as "For the step of these black arriving ones / Is neither the step of the dead nor the step of the living" we suggest that, for the poet, there are three distinct ways of walking, one for the living, one for the dead, and one for the statues. The living do indeed have a step, but what madman has seen the dead or a town's monuments walking? The step of the dead is a no-step, a *pas de pas,* that is, a *pas* in its other sense, of negation. To translate *pas* as step is to lose the distinction between the dead and the living, as well as what separates both dead and living from the statue.

Could we then translate them, by way of the *pas de pas,* as the difference between three kinds of negativities: "For the negativity of these black arriving ones / Is neither the negativity of the dead nor the negativity of the living"? But can the living be said to have a negativity? There are no negatives in nature; the living have to take a positive step, to posit a death to get an idea of negativity, which thus involves a move to the level of signification. And what about the black arriving ones? They are said to be arriving. Even if their arrival does not involve a referential step, it is at any rate not the no-step of the dead. The lines are trying to distinguish the referential event (the *pas* of the living), and the event for signification (the *pas de pas* of the dead), which exist in a specular opposition, from a third *pas,* the *pas* of the statues.

One could propose a third translation that would try to take this distinctness into account: "For the *pas* of these black arriving ones / Is neither the negativity of the dead nor the step of the living." What distinguishes the *pas* of the statues is that it has neither the meaning of negation nor does it point to a referential event, a step: it is a signifier, a sounded *pas,* distinct by virtue of its indifference to the difference between steps and negations. It functions as an empty piece of language, irrespective of all questions of reference and significance.

But the third translation is problematic in a different way. When we translate the lines in this way, we lose their triple *pas,* reducing it to a single *pas.* We localize in one place the rule of "es-*pa*-cement" giving rhythm to the poem throughout. Furthermore, the translation makes the problem into that of distinguishing between three separate species of signifieds (step, negation, the signifier itself), when in fact, the difference that language makes appears phenomenally here—to ear and eye—as a slide from one *pas* to another to another. In rhythm, an aspect of poetic language everywhere available, signifier and signified are not yet distinct sign features for consciousness. It is a reduction to make a rhythm either a signified, an object of knowledge, or a mere set of signifiers sounded to the inner ear of readers. Rhythm is at once perception and meaning, insofar as it is organized perception. It is also a reduction to discover rhythm at a single point when the suggestion is that any understanding of the *pas,* as step or negation, necessarily rests on the insistent recalling of the signifier.

The hallucinatory passage of the statues signals the movement of the poem away from specular oppositions of dead and living, reference and signification, to the level of a language treated as an object of the senses undifferentiated from its signified.

The effect Fineman notes in Shakespeare's dark lady sonnets, namely, the effect of a secondary Cratylism in which a language that does not say what it means ends by saying exactly what it means, i.e., "I lie," is under discussion in this kind of text. The *pas* of the statues declares itself to mean neither step nor negation but to be just a signifier, *pas*. In so doing it reintroduces the equivalency of sound and meaning previously undone when the hour was stifled, since the sound *pas* gives us access to the meaning of the poem as rhythm, as ordered signifiers. But Hugo does not find this secondary Cratylism to be just a problem of poetic language, nor does he see it as the proof of an advance in understanding, as does Fineman. He sees it as hallucinatory and he sees it as laying the groundwork for the real. Consciousness in its infancy, prior to any distinction between its inside as consciousness and the outside of perception, is only conscious of itself in apperception. As de Man graphically puts it: "In that sense [the sense of consciousness as conscious only of itself], any consciousness, including perception, is hallucinatory" (49). A consciousness that subsists by producing meaning out of empty signifiers, milkless breasts, is certainly not a "wiser" consciousness, either. The triple *pas* of the statue gives access to an organization at work in the poem and can be said to add the signified "language" to *pas*. But this is emphatically not a poem in which sound echoes or engenders meaning or theme (except in the mode of illusion). Rather sound gives us access to a consciousness that cannot advance past the stage of hallucinatory, apperceptive consciousness. Hallucinatory consciousness just glides from *pas* to *pas* to *pas,* in what can be called a *pas-sage,* a wise step, only to the extent that a canniness is evinced with respect to the poem's rhythmic, sonorous dimension. This consciousness lives in proximity to a kind of terror, the terror of the sign that seems to engender thoughts instead of representing them. But there is a certain consolation even in this obsessive consciousness. One may not move ahead by way of this kind of play, but at least there is an organization that provides evidence that there is a consciousness around. When the possibility arises that we may not escape out of language to an outside referent, at the very least, the poem suggests, we can get evidence of the reality of consciousness.

Are we then to consider that, for Hugo, the track through the poem is finally that of a consciousness that constitutes itself over and over as apperception each time it gets deconstituted as self and finds itself confronted with a meaningless set of names?

In such a view, the poem would get its title from its understanding of the Terror as the equivalent, for a collectivity, of the threat of a disintegration into sheer difference, a threat over and against which it would constitute itself as a one-sided consciousness of consciousness. The very term "Reign of Terror" is instructive here.

Fear is alienated from subject and object in the term "Reign of Terror." We do not say the Terror of Robespierre, for example. We do not think of it as the fear he invokes in others, or as his own fear. It is a structural Terror, it is the law as producing not the unity of the collectivity living under it, but sheer, uncollectable difference. The Terror, as defined by the *Petit Robert,* is exactly the reign in which laws are measures of exception. The rule of difference, of exception, can indeed be said to be a rule of law of sorts: the rule of producing rules out of exceptions, of which the rule of *pas* would be one example. Against the threat of a chaos, utter loss, no order, to find an overall sense of patterning, even of the unlikely sort that rhythms the poem as the pursuit of *pas,* or that makes rules of exception into the rule, is consoling. Is Hugo then proposing, in lieu of a poem on the French Revolution, or on the meaning of revolution, to track the subterranean, hallucinatory history of revolution, defined as the rule by which signifiers operate to produce meaningful effects for consciousness, independent of any literal reference or signification? Unlike Kant or Hegel, for whom the French Revolution turns out to be proof that the idea of history actualizes itself in events, which are thus demonstrably not random, for Hugo, the Revolution would provide evidence that consciousness can only grasp itself in the textualized event by superimposing upon it a phenomenal grid that is in point of fact lacking. The Revolution would be the turning point when, faced with the likelihood of an ungovernable chaos, consciousness would have preferred the mad assertion of mastery and of law to a recognition of the true state of affairs.[21]

But the hallucinatory is a permanent interpretative possibility, and indicates the underlying possibility of consciousness as non-historical, as a-progressive, as obsessive repetition.[22] In its first part, the poem does concern itself with the phenomenalization of the signifier, and with the Terror as the equivalent of such a concern, but that is not where its historicity is situated. One would also have to take into account the second and third parts of the poem, which follow to its conclusion the logic of the promenading statues, and more especially, the epilogue, originally a separate poem whose title indicated a different and opposed logic. The poem from which the epilogue was excerpted was to have been called "Le Verso de la page."[23] From its first words, "Soit. Mais . . .", it sets itself up as a postscript opposing the main thesis. The epilogue tells us that the Revolution is a stage, the lair of a divine monster into which Progress strays, but from which it then departs: "Le Progrès n'a pas peur d'entrer, lui qui s'envole, / Chez ce monstre divin, la Révolution. / . . . Puis il sort de la haute et grondante tanière . . ." (246). The poem insists that it *traverses* hallucinatory consciousness and that its historicity is not to be reduced to that dark moment of madness when reference and meaning are collapsed into one another, be it by the abusive naming of catachresis, or by a one-sided, hallucinatory consciousness recognizing itself in a prosopopeia.

The passage we have been reading contains a clue as to where Hugo situates the historicity of poetry. There is a dominant element in the passage, an element characterized by a repose beyond the reach of all the vertiginous activity of the figural system, and that, as unknown, excites its transports. This element makes the immobile clock towers and the advancing statues appear as inadequate translations of a source for all rest and energy. The element is the feather that no hurricane can move, found on an unknown cimier: "Ce cimier inconnu / Dont aucun ouragan n'eût remué la plume."[24]

It is perched atop a *cimier,* a helmet crest, from the word for summit, *cime*. A feather on a helmet crest can be said to dominate even the high forehead of the towers. This feather is not a feather of the sort that birds shed and that could be tossed about by a light wind. By virtue of its immobility, it is not even a feather of the sort that one might find atop the forehead of a man of bronze. Bronze men are moved by the wind of inspiration in this poem, just as the hurricane that was the Revolution had no trouble melting down Henri IV's statue. "Rien, pas même l'airain, pour jamais ne s'arrête" (219), Hugo tells us in the passage just preceding this one. Nothing, no *thing,* even something made of bronze, can be arrested forever. Insofar as it can be made into a thing, even a creature of language, a work of art, can be moved. What is this feather atop this unknown helmet crest, that stands for the nonthing, for language as non-phenomenalizable, and that cannot be budged even by a hurricane?

Why is the *cimier* characterized as "unknown," anyway? A *cimier,* the *Petit Robert* tells us, is not only a term for a part of a helmet; it is also a heraldic term, indicating the uppermost part of an escutcheon. The whole of the passage can then be read as an escutcheon, of which this is just the uppermost part, the part that indicates that it is an escutcheon. Certainly, unknown escutcheons can come one's way. Indeed, the whole art of blazonry can be said to be pretty well unknown in our day. Of it, Hugo says: "Le blazon est une langue. . . . Ce sont les hiéroglyphes de la féodalité."[25] The language of blazonry is not an oral language to which the phenomenalized signifier could be the key. It is a written language which has as a pre-condition for its understanding an act that is not an act of perception but rather of reading, and that involves a preliminary organizing of its marks as a meaningful language system. The act of reading is active; it confers orderliness onto potentially random marks. One has, at the very least, to recognize that it is writing, to know anything about it. The *cimier* that reveals that we are reading an escutcheon, a written passage, part of the archive, suggests that the question of reading and of writing is the unknown

around which the rest is elaborated; the feather atop this escutcheon signals the writerly pen.

The quiet eye of the hurricane is writing, material inscription. Around it systems of exchange get set up and undone. In the face of its materiality, consciousness feels threatened enough to grasp at the straw of language as phenomenalizable. But also with respect to writing's materiality, the hallucinatory and repetitive history of the first part can be considered just a bad passage inscribed in a longer poem, or a bad reading of what shows up as inscription on the page's other side.

The unruffled emblem doesn't move partly because inscriptions don't move or get moved by hands, or even by whatever consciousness confers perceptibility and meaning on them. It also doesn't move because the wind that blows from it blows in one direction, forward, *devant*. It blows all its signs toward the future-oriented history of the epilogue. I'd like to conclude with an example from that epilogue which gives an idea of why, for Hugo, the historicity of poems resides in inscription, and is future-oriented. Two lines tell us:

> A qui te cherche, ô Vrai, jamais tu n'échappas.
> Une étape après l'autre. Après un pas, un pas.

The short sentences restate the old cliché about the seeking of truth as the only way to grab hold of it. The ideology it defines, Progress with a capital p, seems equally a cliché. But the last sentence, which repeats the problematic found in the earlier passage on the stepping statues, does so with a difference worth noting. Unlike the earlier lines about the statue's step, which ordered apparently alternative translations but in fact made sense only in the light of the system of meaning provided by the sounded signifier, this line defining Progress is very generous to the translator. One can translate it in many different ways, according to various systems of meaning: after a step, another step; after a negation, another negation; after a negation, a step; after a step, a negation. All these translations of the line are possible. All affirm, albeit in very different ways— from the pre-dialectical to the dialectical to the negatively dialectical—that progress toward truth is the law of history. The poem—and indeed, the Hugolian corpus—can be understood in the light of each of these differing ideologies of progress. To those interpretations can be added a commentary on the obsessive *pas* that gives rhythm to the poem; after a *pas,* another *pas*. The definition of progress in this translation would be repetition, consciousness of consciousness as obsessive, as advancing madness. In short, progress would be the repetitive move whereby consciousness persists in seeing itself in structures voided of meaning for it. To that reading can be added another reading, however. A difference could be being made between the obsessive *pas* of rhythm from which one can escape by forgetting about it, and the *pas* which one has more trouble getting away from, namely, the *p-a-s* of the inscription: after the sound *pas,* still another kind of *p-a-s.* This new *pas* is a stilled *pas,* and one that allows the poem to proffer to whoever seeks it, not only all the erroneous readings of which it is susceptible, but also the inescapable truth of its materiality as what makes it possible to denounce those errors. On the other side of the page of the hallucinatory history of Terror, or rather, on the same side of the page, as its support, we find Hugo writing through the madness of the Revolution as Terror toward an opening. His understanding of revolution in linguistic terms is a double understanding. If, on the one hand, its worst moments came about as it tried to refigure an insight into language's inhuman difference in human terms, on the other, its best involved the discovery anew of inscription as the source of historicity. With that it became possible to glimpse an opening, within the text of **La Révolution,** toward a definition of revolution as text, as "poème inouï (231)," the unheard, the unheard of, the magnificent poem, the yea-saying, or rather, yea-writing (*oui*), future-oriented poem which broadcasts the wherewithal to undo its ideologies of progress as far as or farther still than the ideologies themselves.

The materiality of writing is threatening to consciousness because it denies its power to progress to a certainty of anything beyond it—to an outside referent, to the inside of consciousness, or even, as in Fineman, to a progress in consciousness' understanding of how language functions. But it also provides a resistance to consciousness that gives it a handle on, an opening to, an outside of consciousness. Given the delusions of which consciousness showed itself capable at the end of the Enlightenment, we must consider that a good thing. There is, I would maintain, in a final polemical outburst, a *yes* worth thinking about in this darkest and most-nihilistic seeming of deconstructive texts, **La Révolution.**

Notes

1. An example, by now classic, of the way that language's undecidability can operate at a greater level of complexity than that of a mere option between fiction or history can be found in Rousseau's dialogued preface to *Julie.* Paul de Man, in *Allegories of Reading: Figural Language in Rousseau, Nietzsche, Rilke, and Proust* (New Haven: Yale University Press, 1979) discusses the insistent assertion by one of the two interlocutors, "R," who says he really does not know whether he is the author of a tableau, a fiction of man, or the editor of documents portraying particular men and women. De Man shows a re-emergence—at the very moment when the question seems resolved in favor of the self-signifying tableau—of a referential moment: ". . . the more the text denies the actual existence of a referent, real or ideal, and the more fantastically fictional it becomes, the more it becomes the representation of its own pathos. . . . In the terminology of the text, the "tableau" has become a "portrait" after all, not the portrait of universal man but of the deconstructive passion of a subject" (198-199).

2. Appearing in *Representations* 7 (Summer 1984) 59-86; rpt. in *Shakespeare's Perjured Eye: The Invention of Poetic Subjectivity in the Sonnets* (Berkeley: University of California Press, 1986). All references to the work will henceforth appear in the text.

3. Fineman explains the effect aimed at:

    Language thus speaks *for* its own gainsaying. The result is a new kind of Cratylism, a second degree of Cratylism, that, like the Liar's Paradox Shakespeare often flirts with in his sonnets—"Those lines that I before have writ do lie" (115), "When my love swears that she is made of truth" (138)—is proof of its own paradoxicality. In this gainsaying way—a speech acquired on condition that it speak against itself—Shakespeare accomplishes a limit case of the correspondence of signifier to be signified."

    ("Eye" 77)

4. Until fairly recently, New Historicism neglected poetry and Fineman's work could seem idiosyncratic. In the past few years, however, as attention has been turned to English Romanticism and Wordsworth, tacks similar to Fineman's have been taken. Alan Liu, for example, in his *Wordsworth: The Sense of History* (Stanford: Stanford University Press, 1989), starts by suggesting the pastoral to be an anti-historical or pre-historical mode: "The purpose of the mirror of georgic nature is to hide history in order, finally to reflect the self" (19). The thesis about poetry's a-historicism is then refined by a turn: "the denials of history are also the deepest realizations of history" (32). This turn, Liu suggests, is the one by which the self-referential language of poetry ends by referring to the ideology of its age: "the very scheme of differences that allows certain ages to define a "literary text" separate from historical event (for example, as representation rather than action, aesthetic object rather than utilitarian artifact, medium of the cultured rather than of popular culture) is a reference to, or mimesis of, the scheme of differences that divides and organizes the historical context of that culture" (47). Liu's notion that each age has its ideology of literature follows Fineman's idea of a shift in Shakespearian subjec-

tivity taking place around a more sophisticated understanding of language's deceitfulness. Both share the further assumption that a literary text and an historical event are two distinct objects for study and that texts in no way tend to interfere with that distinction. Whereas Liu merely asserts the distinction, however, Fineman finds a basis for it in the Liar's paradox.

5. *La Révolution,* in *Oeuvres complètes,* vol. X, ed. Jean Massin (Paris: Club français du livre, 1969) 217-247. The passage with which I will be working can be found pp. 220-221. All page references will henceforth be found in the body of the text. See the "Présentation" by Jean Massin, pp. 199-216, for further details as to the poem's composition and publication.

Only published in 1881, the poem might very well serve as a reflection on the major revolutions of the nineteenth century (1830, 1848, 1870) in which Hugo was more or less closely implicated.

6. The definite article, *la,* is a first indicator of the poem's hesitation between signification and reference. The definite article may modify a noun that designates a unique and well-known thing. *The* revolution, for a Frenchman, is, of course, the French Revolution. *La* may, on the other hand, modify a generic noun about which something is predicated, in a usage roughly synonymous to the English suppression of the article, as in the phrase "*Revolution* consists in a radical break with past forms of government." In the first case, the article suggests a referential language use; in the second, it introduces a meaningful fiction.

7. The choice of Hugo to pursue the argument with Fineman is not purely arbitrary. We have the testimony of Hugo on Shakespeare's influence. He not only admired Shakespeare and referred to his works often, but indeed he mentions him in this poem as one in a series of unconscious geniuses with whom the poetic voice is identified. Furthermore, the play that scholars generally agree to have been Shakespeare's last, "The Tempest," shows at least one important parallel to this poem: the court is driven mad by a series of hallucinations, as the invisible is rendered visible by Ariel's agency. The dark lady's deceptions are a relatively mild form of a problem that surfaces in Hugo's poem as a paralyzing terror and in Shakespeare's play as insanity.

8. Michael Riffaterre, "La vision hallucinatoire chez Victor Hugo," in *Essais de stylistique structurale* (Paris: Flammarion, 1971) 222-241.

9. The tendency to psychologize the revolution, to make of it a kind of Racinian tragedy in which is represented a conflict of forces within a single personality, is very strong. François Furet, in his *Interpreting the French Revolution,* trans. Elborg Forster (Cambridge: Cambridge University Press, 1981) warns against the 200-year-old tendency of historians to perpetuate the notion of the Revolution as a mythic tale of new beginnings and thus of the formation of a self. Historians tend, he claims, to identify with the actors, to commemorate the founders, to execrate the deviants, as if compelled to re-enact the dramatic conflict they are writing about. In that they do a disservice to an analytical understanding of the event (which is not a tale of self-constitution), as well as to Leftist political thought. The latter has become imprisoned, Furet suggests, by thinking in terms of a promise of unity that has failed, in lieu of thinking new political alternatives (11). His argument against reading the Revolution in psychological terms has not been much heeded.

10. See, for example, "Pasteurs et troupeaux," a re-writing of one of the earliest poems figuring in *Les Contemplations,* "Le firmament est plein. . . ." Riffaterre explains that in Hugo's hallucinatory poems "la métaphore disparaît du style" (*Essais* 239), as the figure gets treated as a "réalité littérale" (*Essais* 239). The most frequently commented lines in "Pasteurs et troupeaux"—"Le pâtre promontoire au chapeau de nuées / S'accoude et rêve au bruit de tous les infinis" contain such a figure treated literally. "Pâtre promontoire" does not compare shepherd and rock, but rather sees the rock as if it really were the ocean's shepherd.

11. Riffaterre defines this giving of movement to the immutable as hallucinatory: "Non le mouvement de vie qu'un bon écrivain sait donner à ses créations, et sans lequel certains mythes de Hugo ne seraient que des allégories, des rébus racontant des histoires, mais un mouvement anormal, et qui transforme la réalité à laquelle nous sommes habituées. Non le mouvement de ce que nous savons être vivant, mais le mouvement de ce qui devrait être immuable. Voilà qui alarme l'imagination et suggère l'hallucination" (*Essais* 226).

12. In *Choses vues,* Hugo remarks à propos of the death of the son of Louis-Philippe, then king of France, that the law of history has recently gone against the law of patrilinear descent. This leads him to speculate not only about the failure of human attempts to foresee and regulate the succession of rulers, but also, more generally, about the failure of the teleological model and of linear progression to account for history's laws. The laws of history, he suggests, are not rational, human schemes, but are as necessary as the laws that

regulate "les faits matèriels." The passage is worth quoting at some length:

> . . . quand on médite l'histoire des cent cinquante dernières années, une remarque vient à l'esprit. Louis XIV a régné, son fils n'a pas régné; Louis XV a régné, son fils n'a pas régné; Louis XVI a régné, son fils n'a pas régné; Napoléon a régné, son fils n'a pas régné; Charles X a régné, son fils n'a pas régné; Louis-Philippe règne, son fils ne régnera pas. Fait extraordinaire! Six fois de suite la prévoyance humaine désigne dans tout un peuple un tête qui devrait régner, et c'est précisément celle-là qui ne règne pas. Six fois de suite la prévoyance humaine est en défaut. Le fait persiste avec une redoutable et mystérieuse obstination. Une révolution survient, un universel tremblement d'idées qui engloutit en quelques années un passé de dix siècles et toute la vie sociale d'une grande nation; cette commotion formidable renverse tout, excepté le fait que nous venons de signaler; elle le fait jaillir au contraire du milieu de tout ce qu'elle fait crouler; un grand empire s'établit, un Charlemagne apparaît, un monde nouveau surgit, le fait persiste; il semble être du monde nouveau comme il était du monde ancien. L'empire tombe, les vieilles races reviennent, le Charlemagne se dissout, l'exil prend le conquérant et rend les proscrits; les révolutions se reforment et éclatent, les dynasties changent trois fois, les événements passent sur les événements, les flots passent sur les flots,— toujours le fait surnage, tout entier, sans discontinuité, sans modification, sans rupture. Depuis que les monarchies existent, le droit dit: *Le fils aîné du roi règne toujours,* et voilà que, depuis cent quarante ans, le fait répond: *Le fils aîné du roi ne règne jamais*. Ne semble-t-il pas que c'est une loi qui se révèle, et qui se révèle, dans l'ordre inexplicable des faits humains, avec ce degré de persistance et de précision qui jusqu'à présent n'avait appartenu qu'aux faits matériels? N'est-il pas temps que la providence intervienne pour déranger elle-même cela, et ne serait-il pas effrayant que certaines lois de l'histoire se manifestassent aux hommes avec la même exactitude, la même rigidité, et pour ainsi dire la même dureté, que les grandes lois de la nature?
>
> —*Choses vues: 1830-1846,* t. 1, ed. Hubert Juin (Paris: Gallimard, 1972) 234-236

13. The two time schemes suspended are both associated with the interpretation of the French Revolution. Hannah Arendt, in her discussion of "The Meaning of Revolution" (in *On Revolution* [Middlesex: Penguin, 1984], 21-58) suggests that the modern concept of revolution involves linear time: it is "inextricably bound up with the notion that the course of history suddenly begins anew, that an entirely new story, a story never known or told before is about to unfold . . ." (28). "It is obvious," she states, "that only under the conditions of a rectilinear time concept are such phenomena as novelty, uniqueness of events, and the like conceivable at all" (27).

Arendt also reminds us of the persistence of an earlier meaning, carried over from the time when revolution was an astronomical term "designating the regular, lawfully revolving motion of the stars, which . . . was certainly characterized neither by newness nor by violence. On the contrary, the word clearly indicates a recurring, cyclical movement" (42). When the term is carried over into the political domain, it gives a distinctly restorative flavor to revolution, as revolutionaries "pleaded in all sincerity that they wanted to revolve back to old times when things had been as they ought to be" (44).

We can correlate Arendt's problematic to the one raised by Hugo's stupefied clock because in both cases it is the correspondence of an ideal, rational model to a perceptual experience by way of a mediating sign—clock, or narrative construct—that is at stake.

14. In 1841, describing the Invalides where Napoleon's casket is provisionally lying upon its return to France, Hugo comes upon three statues off their pedestals and develops their allegory:

> J'ai retrouvé là, dans l'ombre, trois autres statues de plomb, descendues de je ne sais où, que je me rappelle avoir vues, à cette même place, étant tout enfant, en 1815, lors des mutilations d'édifices, de dynasties et de nations qui se firent à cette époque. Ces trois statues, du plus mauvais style de l'Empire, froides comme ce qui est allégorique, mornes comme ce qui est médiocre, sont là debout le long du mur, dans l'herbe, parmi des tas de chapiteaux, avec je ne sais quel faux air de tragédies sifflées. L'une d'elles tient un lion attaché à une chaîne et représente la Force. Rien n'a l'air désorienté comme une statue posée à plat sur le sol, sans piédestal; on dirait un cheval sans cavalier ou un roi sans trône. Il n'y a que deux attitudes pour le soldat, la bataille ou la mort; il n'y en a que deux pour le roi, l'empire ou le tombeau; il n'y

en a que deux pour la statue, être debout dans le ciel ou couchée sur la terre.

Une statue à pied étonne l'esprit et importune l'oeil. On oublie qu'elle est de plâtre ou de bronze et que le bronze ne marche pas plus que le plâtre, et l'on est tenté de dire à ce pauvre personnage à face humaine, si gauche et si malheureux dans sa posture d'apparat: "—Eh bien! va donc! va! marche! continue ton chemin! démène-toi! La terre est sous tes pieds. Qui te retient? qui t'empêche?" Du moins le piédestal explique l'immobilité. Pour les statues comme pour les hommes, un piédestal, c'est un petit espace étroit et honorable, avec quatre précipices autour."

—*Choses vues: 1830-1846,* 213-214

15. *Choses vues: 1847-48,* ed. Hubert Juin (Paris: Gallimard, 1972) 311.

16. See Paul de Man's "Hypogram and Inscription," (in *The Resistance to Theory* [Minneapolis: University of Minnesota Press, 1986] 27-53. All page references to the work will henceforth appear in the body of the text). De Man explains that the relationship between carillon and time "is analogous to the relationship between signifier and signified that constitutes the sign. The ringing of the bells . . . is the material sign of an event (the passage of time) of which the phenomenality lacks certainty." (48). He further explains that "the phenomenality of experience cannot be established *a priori,* it can only occur by a process of signification" (48). I have drawn heavily on de Man's analysis of prosopopeia and hallucination in this essay.

17. See Alexis de Tocqueville, *L'Ancien régime et la révolution* (in *Oeuvres complètes,* t. II. ed. J.-P. Mayer [Paris: Gallimard, 1953]) 56, 80. Tocqueville attributes a revolutionary force to the transfer of the exaggerated language by which Parlement traditionally remonstrated with the king onto a new stage, in front of an audience unfamiliar with usage. The violence with which the Parlement addressed the king was a conventionalized figure, whose decoding was not problematic for Parlement and king. To those unfamiliar with the convention, however, the clichéd form of address appeared a literal, referential use of language. Tocqueville is then describing as a pre-condition for revolutionary violence, the conflation of language's two functions into its single referential function.

18. A play earlier in the passage prepares the play of *virent* by suggesting that the city's corners can be thought as eyes: *mirer,* in "Les mille toits mirant leurs angles dans la Seine," can mean either to reflect, to mirror, or to sight, to look at. The roofs reflect or look at their angles, that is, depending on the perspective, at their corners or their eyes. The placement of a signifier, the angles it makes with other strategically-located signifiers are, so to speak, the "eyes" of the text.

19. The engendering of a text by way of a play with the signifier takes place at various moments in the poem. In the discussion of the reigns of Henri IV, Louis XIII, Louis XIV and Louis XV, the most referential of signs, the proper name, is treated as if it were a signifier devoid of meaning or reference from which the other elements in the passage can be discovered. Of Henri, we are told "Il fit tout *en ri*ant / Il *ri*ait à la guerre, il *ri*ait *en*priant." His wind of inspiration is a "b*ri*se", and what puts his reign into question, "non loin de ces jeux et de ces *ri*s" are the "b*ru*its" and débris of skeletons, ". . . b*ri*sés / Nus. . . ." Similarly, Louis XIV shines, "*lui*t" at Versailles, but his crimes "*Lui* firent dans son *Lou*vre un colossal trophée / De ruine. . . ." There are a multitude of such "streets" running through the poem.

However, Hugo lets us know that this textual model is a game with serious consequences. Henri IV, the ruler of an aesthetic kingdom of laughter where the play of signifiers is the rule, is undone, broken, because he is blind to a dimension of language that makes it escape the phenomenalization on which such play is based.

20. "Fantasy and Origins of Sexuality," in *The International Journal of Psycho-analysis,* 49, 1 (1968) 1-18. All references to this work will henceforth appear in the text.

21. Laplanche and Pontalis suggest that by means of the phenomenalization of the sign the subject gets a glimpse of its own original fantasy, and thus of its origin. Further, by way of the sense of hearing, the subject inserts itself into "the history or legend of parents, grandparents and the ancestors: the family *sounds* or *sayings,* the spoken or secret discourse, going on prior to the subject's arrival, within which he must find his way. Insofar as it can serve retroactively to summon up the discourse, the noise—or any other discrete sensorial element that has meaning—can acquire this value" (11). For Laplanche and Pontalis, the noise of the signifier, which often appears in a fantasy and is in fact the starting point for its elaboration, is eminently historical. It gives the subject its origins as subject, and inserts it as well in a family history.

22. Hugo thought the revolutions of the nineteenth century, particularly the 1848 Revolution, largely in terms of a parody of a repetition at work in the

French Revolution. At most the hallucinatory can explain the parody of the Revolution by the nineteenth century, parody which, for Hugo, does not constitute a genuine historical move. He returns over and over again in his writings on the 1848 Revolution to lament its plagiaristic bent: "O parodistes de 93! . . . Quoi la Terreur parodie! Quoi la guillotine plagiaire! . . . 93 a eu ses hommes, il y a de cela cinquante-cinq ans, et maintenant il aurait ses singes." (*Choses vues: 1847-8,* 315). What is parodic about 1848 is not the fact that it repeats 1793. Rather it is the fact that it provides the repetition available in the Terror and the guillotine in 1793, with a friendlier face: a prosopopeia conflates mechanical repetition and man, bringing repetition into view in the humanoid, monkey-like features of today's revolutionaries. Both man and knowledge of repetition stand the losers by the conflation.

23. The text can be found as it has been reconstructed by Pierre Albouy in Victor Hugo, *Oeuvres complètes,* vol. X, ed. Jean Massin (Paris: Club français du livre, 1969) 261-287.

24. A reader of Baudelaire's *Tableaux parisiens* cannot help but notice the affinity between this passage and "A une passante" with its "jambe de statue," its hurricane's eye, etc.

25. Victor Hugo, *Notre-Dame de Paris,* in *Oeuvres complètes,* vol. IV, ed. Jean Massin (Paris: Club français du livre, 1967) 100.

Kathryn M. Grossman (essay date fall-winter 1991-92)

SOURCE: Grossman, Kathryn M. "Narrative Space and Androgyny in *Les Misérables.*" *Nineteenth-Century French Studies* 20, nos. 1 & 2 (fall-winter 1991-92): 97-106.

[*In the following essay, Grossman proposes that in* Les Misérables, *the character of Jean Valjean, by incorporating the male and female characteristics of his two antagonists, rises above traditional gender dichotomy.*]

In one of the few passages in *Les Misérables* that directly links politics and poetics, Hugo claims that "un peuple civilisateur doit rester un peuple mâle. . . . Qui s'effémine s'abâtardit. Il ne faut être ni dilettante, ni virtuose; mais il faut être artiste. En matière de civilisation, il ne faut pas raffiner, mais il faut sublimer. A cette condition on donne au genre humain le patron de l'idéal" (864).[1] This provocative statement would seem to fix the author's notion of the sublime, both moral and artistic, under the sign of "maleness." The "pattern"

of the ideal is also a paternal "patron." However, as my analysis will demonstrate, the novel elaborates a far richer relationship between gender and romantic narrative.

In a dualistic interpretation of Hugo's text, the exemplary Jean Valjean would embody a purely "masculine" ideal, while more self-centered characters like Thénardier would represent the kind of effeminate bastardization—the antithesis of vigorous art—to which our passage refers. But the ex-convict is clearly associated with such "feminine" qualities as compassion and maternity, and in many ways the authoritarian Javert seems the most typically "male" personage in the book. In resolving these contradictions, I will show that Jean Valjean transcends the conventional dichotomy of gender by incorporating the feminine and masculine principles of his two antagonists into a hybrid system of his own. I adopt Bachelard's notions of gender-related space in *La Poétique de l'espace* (1957) to explore the various moral worlds depicted in ***Les Misérables*** and to consider their aesthetic and historical implications.

From the very outset, the unscrupulous Thénardier appears to occupy shifting territory: "Ce gredin de l'ordre composite était, selon les probabilités, quelque flamand de Lille en Flandre, français à Paris, belge à Bruxelles, commodément à cheval sur deux frontières" (306). Without a political or moral base, he is a crossbreed who exploits circumstances to his own ends, a *mélange des genres* both passionate and calculating, "féroce" and "adroit" (581), "chat" and "mathématicien" (330).[2] Mme Thénardier is equally heterogeneous. A "minaudière hommasse" (154), this "ogresse" (305) feeds on silly romantic fiction as her husband delights in concocting devious plots. Together, they represent "ruse et rage mariés ensemble" (307), their monstrous appetite knowing no bounds.

As in Dante's *Inferno,* these miscreants distort Bachelard's warm, curving, "feminized" universe into a tortuous, discontinuous world.[3] Because Thénardier lacks any integrity: "Le flux et le reflux, le méandre, l'aventure, était l'élément de son existence; conscience déchirée entraîne vie décousue" (306). The "meandering" of malefaction implies not so much aimless wandering as the winding path through Hell. Twisted mentalities thrive in nonlinear space. Thus, one bandit, "accoutumé à aller de travers," fails to catch Jean Valjean in the Montfermeil woods when he opts for the more "respectable" approach of the "ligne droite" (920). Likewise, the wreckage in front of the Thénardiers' inn, "tout enchevêtré de courbes et d'angles farouches, s'arrondissait comme un porche de caverne" (152)— doubtless "la grande caverne du mal" (533) inhabited by all those who undermine society. And the inside of the couple's Parisian garret belies the symmetry of the building's exterior: "Cela avait des saillies, des angles, des trous noirs, des dessous de toits, des baies et des promontoires. De là d'affreux coins insondables . . ." (548). Thénardier's semblance of respectability similarly houses a "crooked" inner space. That this "homme petit, maigre, blême, anguleux, osseux, chétif" (305) appears less manly than his bearded spouse seems appropriate in light of his identification with a feminine architectonics.

The master of truncated relationships, Thénardier dreams of living abroad in a three-story pueblo where doors are replaced by hatches and stairs by ladders: "le soir on ferme les trappes, on retire les échelles" (983) to escape from cannibals.[4] Formed in his own image, this habitation of endless loopholes makes a virtue of destroying all connections and articulations, in other words, all genuine communication, for the sake of self-preservation. This is the extreme of disjointed, paratactic space, where meaning vanishes altogether. A version of Hell, it also resembles the Gorbeau tenement, that quintessential place of gaps and erasures where the first two floors are separated by a "plancher qui n'avait ni trappes ni escalier" (343).

In this realm of fictionality, criminal chaos partakes of figurative, if not literal, garbage. Like the early Paris sewers, lawlessness is: "Tortueux, . . . coupé de fondrières, cahoté par des coudes bizarres, montant et descendant sans logique, fétide, sauvage, farouche, . . . épouvantable . . ." (881).[5] From an aesthetic standpoint, then, evil is closely related to verbal sewage. Along with argot inhabiting its "cloaque" (697) or the flatterers in Dante's Hell (*Inf.* XVIII), bad writing wallows in its own filth. Mme Thénardier's relish of "des romans bêtes" (157) thus corresponds to her spouse's inelegant *cuirs* and horrendous spelling, his maudlin sentimentality and hollow compassion, his pathetic attempts at painting and drama, and his fraudulent letter-writing. His emphasis on "la mode, . . . qui change presque à chaque vent" (540) is a symptom of *aesthetic*—not just moral—debasement. Under his "jolie petite barbiche romantique" (561), Thenardier has no ethical or artistic sensibility whatsoever, just an instinctive sense of how to prosper at the expense of others. Fulfilling the author's warning that human progress depends upon the proper use of one's talents—"Qui s'effémine s'abâtardit. Il ne faut être ni dilettante, ni virtuose . . ."—Thénardier appears as a dark cultural force conspiring to thwart historical perfection. His *mélange des genres* undermines and subverts human intercourse instead of enriching it. To understand Hugo's corollary vision of authentic art, we now turn our attention first to his conventional characters, then to his outlaw hero.

Like Thénardier, Fantine's lover Tholomyès is an insatiable predator. Appetite and the law are indissolubly linked when he exclaims, "Complétons notre cours de droit par la folie et la nourriture. Indigestion et digeste. Que Justinien soit le mâle et que Ripaille soit la femelle!" (147). Reducing love to the same level as food, Tholomyès balances merry-making ("Ripaille") with control ("Justinien"), passion with order, Thénardier with Javert. But his dichotomy of a "male" Apollonian principle and a "female" Dionysian principle projects his own licentiousness onto the other. On one hand he claims, "La femme est perfide et tortueuse. Elle déteste le serpent, par jalousie de métier" (145). The image of tortuosity allies woman with the forces of evil, though it is Tholomyès himself who is perfidious. When he and his friends desert their sweethearts with the accusation, "l'abîme, c'est vous" (150), they pretend to escape engulfment in order to conceal their own heedless consumption. Rejecting the female principle, they return to utter conventionality: "Nous rentrons dans la société, dans le devoir et dans l'ordre. . . . Il importe à la patrie que nous soyons, comme tout le monde, préfets, pères de famille, gardes champêtres et conseillers d'Etat" (150). Their embrace of paternalism signals a moral decline not wholly unrelated to Thénardier's.

The world to which they flee, however, is Javert's, one that is stiff, straight, rectilinear—that is, "masculine"—both inside and out. Though free of internal contradictions, the lack of imagination here corresponds to geometric configurations as infernal in their own way as the tortuous space of villainy. That Javert is regular right down to his invisible atomic structure is suggested by his status in the text as "ce crystal" (911). The "meanders" of society's Thénardiers are systematically cancelled out by his directness: "Il avait introduit la ligne droite dans ce qu'il y a de plus tortueux au monde . . ." (169)—including his own criminal heritage. It is therefore fitting that he should meet his end when he cannot choose between "deux routes également droites" (911):

> Ce qui se passait dans Javert, c'était le Fampoux d'une conscience rectiligne, la mise hors de voie d'une âme, l'écrasement d'une probité irrésistiblement lancée en ligne droite et se brisant à Dieu. Certes, cela était étrange, . . . que l'incommutable, le direct, le correct, le géométrique, le passif, le parfait, puisse fléchir!
>
> (915)

Unable to bend before the three-dimensional justice that suddenly looms large in Jean Valjean, Javert breaks. The irresistible force is crushed by an immovable object: divine love. Linear "geometry" is defeated by a completely different form of harmony.

Hugo also connects conventionality with the static space of symmetry. For example, Javert's orderly, obedient nature—a doubling of military and hieratic mentalities—is figured in the neighborhood around the Gorbeau tenement. In this avenue, the factories look like barracks or monasteries because of their "longues lignes froides et la tristesse lugubre des angles droits" (339). The effect is distinctly dystopian: "Pas un accident de terrain, pas un caprice d'architecture, pas un pli. C'était un ensemble glacial, régulier, hideux. Rien ne serre le coeur comme la symétrie. C'est que la symétrie, c'est l'ennui, et l'ennui est le fond même du deuil" (339). More insufferable than the hell of villainy is the spiritual death caused by monotony.[6] The transfiguring power of the "pli" or gap is as absent here as in Javert, that "caractère complet, ne faisant faire de pli ni à son devoir, ni à son uniforme" (245). Without contrast or contradiction, place and character remain hopelessly dull.

The limits of uniformity resurface in Hugo's discussion of the modern sewer:

> Aujourd'hui, l'égout est propre, froid, droit, correct. Il réalise presque l'idéal de ce qu'on entend en Angleterre par le mot «respectable». Il est convenable et grisâtre; tiré au cordeau. . . . Là, tout doit être subordonné au chemin le plus court. . . . Les rapports mêmes de la police dont il est quelquefois l'objet ne lui manquent plus de respect.
>
> (881)

Mirroring the city above, the sewer repeats other patterns as well. The references to neatness, to correctness, to the police, to the efficiency of the direct approach recall the traits of Javert in particular and of conventionality in general.

But dullness is not innocence. Evil lurks in excessive regularity, like Thénardier hiding out in the sewer. A ramp that once led to the Seine has been removed for the sake of symmetry. Horses die of thirst, "mais l'oeil est flatté" (891). Too much orderliness is as bad as none at all. The very geometry of the 1848 Temple barricade reflects the diabolic forces of illegitimate revolt. With the sewer, it is "droit, correct, froid, perpendiculaire, nivelé à l'équerre, tiré au cordeau, ligné au fil de plomb. . . . C'était ajusté, emboîté, imbriqué, rectiligne, symétrique, et funèbre. Il y avait là de la science et des ténèbres" (824). Obsessive, mechanical uniformity is not the opposite but the counterpart of lawless chaos. A certain mindlessness informs both the beast and the machine. Orthodox "masculinity" can never touch the sublime.

Affiliated with the hypotactic structures of orderly, well-disciplined reasoning, linearity is thus, in the novel, the space of prose. Thinking metonymically, in logical sequences, supplies a strong sense of "reality"—an authoritarian belief system that the text consistently deflates. If Javert considers that "la vérité est la vérité" (194), his unimaginative tautology merely echoes the symmetries that he inhabits. To a great extent, his preference for what is "défini, coordonné, enchaîné, précis, exact, circonscrit, limité, fermé" (915) expresses the classical aesthetic. Geometry, symmetry, categories, and compartments—all correspond to Hugo's notion of harmonious but uninspired art.[7] Despite his appreciation for theatrical effect, Javert is remarkably prosaic. He simply fails to aim high enough: his ideal is to be not "sublime," but "irréprochable" (914). Only when "l'absolu fictif" of perfection that he has always embraced is suddenly eclipsed by "le véritable absolu" (915) of perfectibility does he notice this flaw. The transformational process of history opposes not only the unprincipled flexibility of lawlessness but also its contrary, "l'incommutable, le direct, le correct, le géométrique, le passif, le parfait." The unyielding world of tidy, literal interpretations is as limited as the ungrounded, figurative illusions of villainy.

By way of contrast, Jean Valjean incorporates both anarchy and regularity into a more complex, hybrid order that corresponds to his multiple gender roles in the novel. Thus, as a parent figure, he embraces motherhood and fatherhood alike. His paternal might is evident when, after returning from Arras, he detaches Javert's tenacious hand "comme il eût ouvert la main d'un enfant" (248). In the same scene, his maternal concern also manifests itself when he attends to Fantine "comme une mère eût fait pour son enfant" (248). More important, he mothers children. Nine months after Fantine's death, Valjean "sentit se remuer ses entrailles" and experiences "des épreintes comme une mère" (342) when he rescues Cosette from the Thénardiers. His true vocation is not as *maire* of Montreuil-sur-*mer* but as *mère* to Cosette. The adolescent girl imagines that "l'âme de sa mère avait passé dans ce bonhomme. . . . [C]'est peut-être ma mère, cet homme-là!" (639). Their union lasts for nine years, a "gestation" after which the ex-convict symbolically gives birth to Marius, carrying him through the sewers as, in old paintings of the flood, "une mère . . . fait ainsi de son enfant" (897). Hugo's virile hero possesses a woman's creative power.[8]

Demonstrating heart as well as muscle in all his benevolent actions, where "feminine" compassion impels "masculine" power, Jean Valjean may at first appear oxymoronic. A *"mendiant qui fait l'aumône"* (344), a "malfaiteur bienfaisant" (912), a "galérien qui obéit à sa conscience" (960), he seems inherently defined as a contradiction in terms. But the morality of this "Caïn tendre" (966) is structured not by logical contraries, but by the interplay of tenor and vehicle in the metaphorical process itself. The outlaw resembles that countryside "un peu bâtarde . . . et composée de deux natures"—that "amphibie" (434), the outskirts of Paris—so attractive to poets. In this environmental "mélange du sauvage et du bourgeois" (434), of Thénardier and Javert, Hugo suggests a way of reading his hero as well. By living in mongrel territories—the Gorbeau tenement set in a suburban no man's land, or the "constructions hybrides" (384) of the convent, or his two-faced residence on the rue Plumet and the rue de Babylone—Valjean indicates his continuing rejection of *either/or* propositions.

For conscience is an all-inclusive infinite within an infinite, an "abîme concentrique à un autre abîme" (394). The crossroads of moral quandaries are embedded in larger, curling patterns. Saving both oneself and others is a recursive function. As in Dante, the journey of the saintly spirit follows a spiraling, indirect path upward. Myriel deflects a cathedral's stolen treasure into the hands of the poor. Gavroche lifts Valjean's purse from Montparnasse and throws it over a wall to feed Mabeuf. And the ex-convict's errant course after his conversion, in which "il revenait à chaque instant sur ses pas" (124), evolves from turning in this vicious circle—wherein he robs Petit-Gervais—to mastering the twists and turns of his conscience, the streets of Paris, and the labyrinthine sewer. Unlike Thénardier's haphazard "meander," his "itinéraire obscur et ondulant" (335) follows a moral direction.

In this way, Jean Valjean figures a specifically *romantic* architectonics by combining the linear space of law, Javert, "masculinity," and prose with the twisting, tortuous space of lawlessness, Thénardier, "femininity," and bad fiction. His two shadow selves conjoin in a stunning new alliance.[9] Tangled chaos and boring symmetry are integrated into a higher, "androgynous," *poetic* order characterized by circles, cycles, and spirals. Like Bachelard's notion of poetic reverie, which diverts us from "la lecture linéaire,"[10] the good is not straightforward at all: "Les prédestinations ne sont pas toutes droites; elles ne se développent pas en avenue rectiligne devant le prédestiné; elles ont des impasses, des coecums, des tournants obscurs, des carrefours inquiétants offrant plusieurs voies" (951). Illustrating the usefulness of nonlinear, recursive motion, Valjean's artful "détours" (366) to elude the police lead him to the convent; his hidden escape route from the house on the rue Plumet is "sinueux," full of "détours" and "angles" (631); and he falls in the sewers "d'un cercle de l'enfer dans l'autre" (886). All these "spirales visionnaires comme dans Dante" (202) enable him to rise when he most appears to descend, just as the revolutionaries on the verge of defeat retreat heavenward up the "escalier de bois en spirale perçant le plafond" (766) in the Corinthe tavern.[11] The novel's protagonists reject the closed worlds represented by Thénardier's pueblo, the Gorbeau tenement, and Javert's self-contained crystal for more open-ended, communicating structures.

Thus, we see that in Hugo's work spiritual and historical progress is neither unilinear nor continuous, the unfolding of some absolute in the here and now. Winding, cyclical, poetic space depicts the path of conscience and history alike. "Masculine" becoming is not incompatible with Bachelard's spiraling, "feminine" form of being.[12] Indeed, true civilization can be achieved only

through recycling everything, including society's waste. God recuperates the Bastille elephant and turns this abandoned monument into a home for orphans, just as the junk-laden barricades momentarily protect France's utopian dreams. What humanity rejects—whether outlaws or *misérables* or revolution or refuse or *le mot de Cambronne*—God and poets may yet find a use for. This redemption of the worthless is perhaps the deepest nonlinear subversion of all. The spiral of history will repeat itself many times over, metaphorically transforming and recycling itself in ever more useful forms. Fantine's illegitimate daughter is triumphantly reintegrated into society as a baroness. Thénardier remains unrepentant, but his children achieve moral stature. In this way, the text presents a dialectic rather than a dualistic vision not just of gender and history but of the romantic novel itself. For Hugo, great literature is a dynamic process, not a static product, a conception perhaps justified by his continued worldwide acclaim long after the official demise of the romantic movement.

In the labyrinthine sewer of *Les Misérables* manure transmuted thus becomes food for all, literally as well as figuratively. In one form it nourishes bodies. Properly channeled and treated, waste can engender everything from "la prairie en fleur" to "du pain sur votre table" to "la vie" (873) itself. It can be *other.* This metaphorical transfiguration of death and decay into life-giving forces once again integrates apparent opposites at a higher level. In another, literary form, sewage can nourish minds. The offal of society constitutes a major *topos* of Hugo's book. Garbage is a metaphor for Jean Valjean, that "cloaque" who gives birth to Cosette just as "le fumier" (967) helps to create the rose. Moreover, to dredge up argot, "cet idiome abject qui ruisselle de fange" (697), to wrest the language of *les misérables* from its "cloaque," requires an author as courageous as his hero, who emerges from the sewers "tout ruisselant de fange" (898). Jean Valjean's redemptive nature points to Hugo himself as he attempts to recover language, from silence to grandiloquence, from the sublime to the grotesque, from unspeakable transcendence to "obscenities" and argot. Recuperating the French language, with all its masculines and feminines, is analogous to saving souls. In the androgynous space of his novel, the besmirched and exiled poet sublimates the raw materials of literature into a new "*patronne* de l'idéal."

Notes

1. All references to Hugo are to *Les Misérables,* vol. 11 (1969) of the *Œuvres complètes,* ed. Jean Massin, 18 vols. (Paris: Le Club Français du Livre, 1967-70).

2. As I have shown elsewhere, the malevolence of Biassou, Habibrah, and other "mulâtres" in *Bug-Jargal* (1826) is directly related to their status as a failed union of opposites. *In Notre-Dame de Paris* (1831), on the other hand, Hugo's cathedral repre-

sents the epitome of successful heterogeneity. Cf. Kathryn M. Grossman, *The Early Novels of Victor Hugo: Towards a Poetics of Harmony* (Genève: Droz, 1986) 71-89 and 165-70.

3. Bachelard analyzes at length the *poetic* rationale for considering that "l'angle est masculin et la courbe féminine" (*La Poétique de l'espace* [Paris: Presses Universitaires de France, 1957] 138). In the underworld, the warmth normally attributed to the latter reaches infernal proportions and is eventually transformed into its contrary, extreme cold.

4. It is therefore no accident that the swindler uses an abbreviated pseudonym—"Thénard"—when he confronts Marius with this scheme. We might also recall that the destiny of truncation is, for the author of *Le Dernier Jour d'un condamné* (1829), the emasculating force of the guillotine.

5. In his book on argot, Hugo depicts certain political eruptions as anarchy from below: "Nous ne sommes plus aux temps où . . . apparaissaient à la surface de la civilisation on ne sait quels soulèvements de galeries de taupes, où le sol se crevassait, où le dessus des cavernes s'ouvrait . . ." (708). Later, he decribes a collapse inside the Paris sewer in similar terms: "le désordre . . . se traduisait en haut dans la rue par une espèce d'écart en dents de scie entre les pavés; cette déchirure se développait en ligne serpentante dans toute la longueur de la voûte lézardée . . ." (896). These passages contribute to the network of connections between chaos, caverns, sewers, and sinuous space.

6. Bachelard would add that the only truly human space is that shaped from within by imagination, rather than imposed from without by geometric order (see esp. *La Poétique de l'espace* 100-01).

7. In *Victor Hugo philosophe* (Paris: Presses Universitaires de France, 1985) 49, Jean Maurel finds that Hugo systematically transgresses and dislocates this "logique positiviste d'un rationalisme substantialiste, propriétaire et calculateur." Cf. Bachelard's "philosophe intellectualiste" who, in using words "comme les petits outils d'une pensée lucide," attempts to crystallize them into "des solides parfaits" (*La Poétique de l'espace* 138). As I determine in *The Early Novels* 198-99, the association in Hugo between geometry and dogmatism dates back to *Notre-Dame de Paris*. Cf. also my article on "Hugo's Romantic Sublime: Beyond Chaos and Convention in *Les Misérables*," *Philological Quaterly* 60 (Fall 1981): 477-79 and 482-83 for a more detailed analysis of Javert's "neoclassicism."

8. We might note that the patriarchal Gillenormand ends by imitating Valjean when he becomes a nurturing "grand-mère" (922) to Marius. Ironically,

he must disrupt his own obsession with virility, becoming at once more feminine and more child-like, to discover the realm of humane concerns.

9. Thénardier, of course, represents the old Adam in Jean Valjean, the monster that he continues to dominate throughout his life. Javert, on the other hand, represents the ex-convict's strictly law-abiding ethos. See my discussion of the moral interrelationship of these three characters in "Hugo's Romantic Sublime" 474-76. For Jean-Pierre Richard, "Petite lecture de Javert," *Revue des Sciences humaines* 156 (October-December 1974): 597-611, Javert is Jean Valjean's "envers noir et légal, . . . tout comme Thénardier figure . . . sa tentation noire et illégale . . ." (598). Jacques Dubois, in "L'Affreux Javert: *the champ you love to hate*," *Hugo dans les marges,* ed. Lucien Dällenbach and Laurent Jenny (Genève: Zoe, 1985) 9-34, elaborates further on the fraternal pairing of outlaw and policeman, in which "Javert serait l'envers de Valjean comme l'ombre est celui de la lumière" (13).

10. Bachelard, *La Poétique de l'espace* 151. See also 154, where the critic insists that "[l]a rêverie n'est pas géométrique."

11. Cf. Richard B. Grant, *The Perilous Quest: Image, Myth, and Prophecy in the Narratives of Victor Hugo* (Durham: Duke U Press, 1968) 159-65 and 170-72, who amply demonstrates the mythical dimensions of the hero's Dantesque ascension.

12. Bachelard, *La Poétique de l'espace* 193. In *Victor Hugo and the Visionary Novel* (Cambridge: Harvard U Press, 1984), Victor Brombert shows that Hugo opposes a "cyclical reading" of history to the notion of "linear development" (128) in a complex binary system that leads out of history altogether (cf. also 133 and 135-39). The spiral image is developed as early as "La Pente de la rêverie" (*Feuilles d'automne,* 1831). Its central role in *Les Misérables* tempers to some extent the optimism of "Plein ciel" (*La Légende des siècles,* 1859), where progress appears far more linear. In a forthcoming book-length study of the novel, I discuss further Hugo's attempt to reconcile the notions of historical evolution and utopian timelessness.

Kathryn M. Grossman (essay date 1991)

SOURCE: Grossman, Kathryn M. "Homelessness, Wastelands, and Barricades: Transforming Dystopian Spaces in *Les Misérables*." In *Utopian Studies IV,* edited by Lise Leibacher-Ouvrard and Nicholas D. Smith, pp. 30-4. Lanham, Md.: University Press of America, 1991.

[*In the following essay, Grossman states that in* Les Misérables *Hugo unites utopian values with aesthetic concerns by describing the dystopian plight of the orphaned and homeless.*]

The plight of the orphaned and homeless is a major theme of Victor Hugo's *Les Misérables* (1862), one that unites utopian values with aesthetic concerns. Many of the novel's characters—the ex-convict Jean Valjean, the martyred Fantine, Cosette and her future spouse Marius, Gavroche and his abandoned siblings, and the young revolutionary Feuilly—have lost their parents either through death or neglect. As a result, they can forge their existence only by embracing a variety of parental or fraternal models. Valjean incorporates the bishop Monseigneur Myriel as the voice of conscience, then follows Fantine's maternal example by adopting and raising Cosette. Marius learns to love the father he never knew and, through him, revolutionary France. Gavroche treats strangers as brothers—which they indeed turn out to be. And the insurgents claim kinship on the 1832 barricades with their brave ancestors of 1789.

But less fortunate characters suffer from a loss of identity that entails even age and gender. Without models, whether ethical or artistic, they merge into an amorphous conglomerate. Destitution provides a hideous version of nothingness, an extreme of mongrelization:

> Fathers, mothers, sons, daughters, brothers, men and women alike merge into a composite, like a mineral alloy, in the murky promiscuity of sexes, relationships, ages, infamy and innocence . . . How pale they are, those unfortunates, how cold they are! They might be the inhabitants of a planet far more distant from the sun than our own.
>
> (I. 639)[1]

In this enactment of what Thomas Weiskel calls the metaphorical sublime, we find "a massive underdetermination [of meaning] that melts all oppositions or distinctions into a perceptional stream."[2] Lumped together in indefinable promiscuity, the wretched are no longer differentiated nor differentiating. They have reached the point where all meaning—including the distinction between good and evil—disappears.

The disintegration of identity thus entails that of moral and perceptual differentiation. Fantine's physical degradation is marked by a profound "resignation" (I. 180) that signals the end of any caring, and hence of any discrimination. Because apathy is the lot of the poor in general, the villainous Thénardiers' lack of feeling for their own children is not wholly voluntary: "There is a level of poverty at which we are afflicted with a kind of indifference which causes all things to seem unreal: those closest to us become no more than shadows . . ." (II. 117). Faceless larvae, the image of death itself, replace one's beloved offspring. Hugo's social outcasts do not constitute a vibrant eclectic mixture, but an in-

distinguishable amalgam of identities. Chaos is their source and chaos their destiny. Such terms as "mineral alloy," "pale," and "cold" in Hugo's description of their promiscuity suggest that these grotesques of poverty have lost not only their identity, their power of discernment, and their humanity but life itself. The flatness of their world is that of the grave. A close reading of the novel reveals that, far from being an incidental image, horizontal space is consistently associated with all forms of spiritual death. In the remainder of this paper, I first consider more fully the book's horizontal dimension, then investigate its contrary—the vertical spaces that figure spiritual, political, and artistic resurrection.

As we might expect, the loss of selfhood and the subsequent hybridization of humanity corresponds in *Les Misérables* to an array of wastelands. In other words, the dislocation of the family, repeated in the dislocation of self, is figured by the barren, dystopian landscapes that characterize Weiskel's metaphorical sublime. These include the outskirts of Digne, whose inhabitants refuse to house Jean Valjean; the countryside in the ex-convict's dream before he denounces himself to save another; and three aspects of the Paris suburbs—the neighborhood around the Gorbeau tenement, the Lark's Field, and the revolutionary Saint-Antoine district. Fantine's "cropped head" (I. 178) resembles the terrain around Digne, where the "hillock covered with the stubble of the recent harvest . . . looked like a shaven head" (I. 79), which in turn recalls Valjean's "shorn but stubbly [head]" (I. 71) after his release from prison. The same imagery appears in the fugitive's dream before he denounces himself at the court in Arras as both a "vast, barren landscape" and a man with a "bare skull" (I. 222). And it reemerges in the tedious no man's land between Paris and the area surrounding the tenement where he, Cosette, Marius, and the Thénardiers all live at one time or another.

In the horizontal space of these mongrel regions, all meaning tends to collapse. The errant personages who wander there have little sense of their identity or moral direction. In a way, then, we can read literally the many references in the novel to Hell and damnation. "Hunger and thirst are the point of departure and to be Satan is the final goal" for those who occupy what Hugo calls the "great cavern of evil" (I. 621). Jean Valjean alludes to this infernal existence when he predicts how the young Montparnasse will trick himself into an endless prison sentence; the criminal is destined to repeat his sins forever, like those who inhabit Dante's Inferno. A powerful portrait of this eternity of incarceration appears when Cosette and Valjean witness the passing of the chain gang in the Lark's Field. In this "march of the condemned on the way to torment"(II. 89), the desire to become Satan has been realized. Here, "wild spirits nakedly exposed" (II. 88) have lost their earthly disguises and assumed their final form. This "chaos" (II. 88) merges every manner of human and animal face in a communal *danse macabre*. In their living death, the galley slaves have lost, with Hugo's other *misérables,* any individual distinction.

Rather, there has been an erasure of any diversity among them: "They had been chained together haphazard, probably in alphabetical order, and loaded haphazard onto the carts" (II. 88). Linked by the logic of ersatz order, the convicts form a single beast that consumes their personal identities. They are forever trapped in the undifferentiated metaphorical sublime, forfeiting selfhood to the communal soul of each chain.[3] And the text leaves no doubt that this soul is not just condemned but also damned: "Dante might have seen in them the seven circles of Hell on the move" (II. 89). The convicts have already entered the afterlife to which they are destined, one where the shared body of the Eucharist finds in "the imagery of cannibalism . . . its demonic parody."[4] This collective dissolution is perpetuated in and by all penal communities, where society minimally cares for its outcasts and where vicious alliances are constituted in the absence of any true sense of the human family.

After the Thénardiers lose their home in Montfermeil— the inn where Cosette spends a wretched childhood boarded as a slave—they follow Valjean and Cosette by taking up residence in the Gorbeau tenement. Situated on the fringe of Paris, this "home" carries two street numbers and thus a confused identity of its own: "Where exactly was one? No. 50 on the outside, 52 inside" (I. 386). In such places, one can quickly lose one's physical and moral bearings. Hugo links this confusion with the static space of symmetry in his description of the street where the building is located. In this avenue, the "featureless edifices in long, cold lines, with the monotony of right angles," form a distinctly dystopian ensemble:

> No accident of terrain, not an architectural flourish, not a bend or curve: a glacial setting, rectilinear and hideous. Nothing chills the heart like symmetry, for symmetry is ennui and ennui is at the heart of grief. Despair is a yawn. It is possible to conceive of something even more terrible than a hell of suffering, and that is a hell of boredom.

> (I. 388)

More insufferable than the abyss inhabited by *les misérables* is the death of the soul caused by monotony. However regimented life may be in prison or in the galleys, it does not approach the torment of the metaphorical sublime propagated by collective bad taste. The Paris suburbs of 1823 bear a striking resemblance to Haussmann's neoclassically reconstructed city under the Second Empire.

In this hideout, Thénardier generates a wide range of aliases as his family comes apart at the seams, replaced by criminal collegiality. In their squalor, they need not

die—or even go to prison—to enter the demonic realm. Thus, in certain lights, Marius finds that their garret resembles "a gateway to the inferno" (I. 671). The fire heating instruments of torture there masks a sinister chill. The Thénardiers' coldheartedness signals more than just material and moral destitution: it is the mark of death itself. Cosette's "bleak world" (I. 347) at their inn is an icy grave, just as those who feed sexually on Fantine's need are as deeply frozen as she: "To touch her is to feel a chill" (I. 180). As in the center of Dante's Inferno, the damned consume each other, completely "wedged in ice" (*Hell* XXXII. 34)[5] Hugo's alienated *misérables* could well be on Pluto, the frigid planet of Dis. Good will alone cannot revive these souls "groping in darkness and sundered from the living world" (I. 639). They have become fixed, like Dante's dead, in their own abjection, crying out against the rest of creation with "a vast malediction, a gnashing of teeth, . . . a rage against all human kind, and a mockery of Heaven" (I. 489). Hell is, in the end, a self-perpetuating prison.

Jean Valjean and Cosette, on the other hand, escape from the harmful environs of prison, the Thénardiers' inn, and the Gorbeau tenement to a different kind of boarding house—the Petit-Picpus convent. As the convent gardener, Valjean greatly improves the yield of its "mixed strain" (I. 487) fruit trees through pruning and grafting. He also applies these horticultural talents to himself: a fertile crossbreed of good and evil, of principle and chaos, he produces the best fruit by grafting Cosette onto his existence. He resembles that "bastard countryside, ugly as a rule but fascinating for its twofold nature"—that "amphibious world" (I. 498), the outskirts of Paris—that attracts urchins and poets alike. In this environmental "mingling of wilderness and order" (I. 498), of the outlaw Thénardier and the policeman Javert, Hugo suggests a way of reading his hero as well. By inhabiting mongrel territories—the Gorbeau tenement, or the "hybrid bloc of houses" (I. 445) comprising the convent, or his two-faced residence on the rue Plumet and the rue de Babylone—Valjean indicates his continuing rejection of *either/or* propositions.

This inclusiveness is reflected on the novel's macrocosmic level. Thus, the familial relations developed in monastic institutions are founded on brotherly principles that expand to embrace the whole of humanity. In losing oneself through devotional sacrifice, one finds and recuperates the *other.* Countering the horizontal plane of homelessness and anonymity, the verticality of prayer permits a re-articulation of self and place in the convent. Those who pray share many features with the saintly Myriel, whom they follow in the novel, and with the young revolutionaries, whom they foreshadow:

> They have dissolved the family of the flesh and constructed within their community the family of the spirit. They have no relations other than this assembly of

men. They assist the poor and care for the sick. They
elect those to whom they owe obedience. They call
each other "brother."

(I. 707)

Their fraternal, egalitarian spirit extends first to each
other, then to the rest of society. Their silent voices are
raised to heaven, not in the galley slaves' "rage against
all human kind" but in "blessedness and love" (I. 489).

Articulated by kneeling, this communication can take
place either directly or through an intermediary. In the
convent, Valjean channels his prayer through a nun expiating the sins of others: "When he thought of these
things his whole being was abased before the mystery
of the Sublime" (I. 491). As his pride tumbles into an
inner abyss, his reflection reaches sublime heights, just
as Cosette's anguished cry to God in the Montfermeil
woods is answered by an agent of divine intercession,
Valjean himself. The ex-convict also intervenes at the
barricades to model "the vast, virtuous evolution of
mankind" that the revolutionaries "would have prayed
on [their] knees" (I. 559) to see arrive. Like utopian action, prayer is oriented toward the "Ideal" (I. 711),
namely God. According to Hugo, there is "no more
sublime work" than that of those who pray, and "perhaps none more useful" (I. 712). This utility matches
God's own useful creativity—and the practical labors
of both utopianism and romantic literature.

In this perspective, religious communities approach the
political ideal. Because "[o]nly liberty is needed to
transform the monastery into a republic" (I. 708), such
communities are located between the dystopia of prison
and the republican utopia. Ironically, when Marius asks
his friends what could be a greater destiny for France
than to be Napoléon's nation, they reply "To be free"
(I. 580). To achieve its aspirations, France must become
a republic. It is perhaps not accidental that one of their
barricades, "an irregular quadrilateral, sealed on all
sides" (II. 237), has the same basic shape as the "large
irregular quadrilateral" (I. 444) of the Petit-Picpus convent.

But monastic institutions are an anachronism and the
Petit-Picpus convent is almost a ruin: according to the
author, it no longer exists in 1862, when his novel is
published. With French romanticism, this fictive construct has long been outmoded. Still, through its confra-
ternal spirit, the convent is related to two other ruins in
the work, the Bastille elephant—a monument celebrating Napoleon's glory—and the barricades, both of
which also serve as temporary shelters from a hostile
world. The barricades of 1832 and 1848 protect the
revolutionaries fighting for the rights of all French citizens, while the monolithic elephant generously houses
orphans like Gavroche and his little brothers. Their
tenuous security amid the invading rats prefigures that

of the barricade resisting governmental assault. In har-
boring lost children, the elephant also resembles the
wall around the convent, which proves so hospitable to
Valjean and Cosette. At the same time, the Saint-
Antoine barricade, erected upright at the outskirts of
Paris in 1848, echoes the elephant as a supreme construct of rubbish. This horrendous amalgam adheres
equally to the sublime and the grotesque: "It was a pile
of garbage, and it was Sinai" (II. 294). The abandoned
elephant, too, "has a contradictory quality of garbage
waiting to be swept away and majesty waiting to be beheaded" (II. 127). As in Valjean's dual character, such
oxymoronic terms may not be mutually exclusive or
unworthy of recuperation. Similarly, the poor, the illiterate, and even imprisoned villainy can, in Hugo's system, be redeemed by social reform. The nation must
adopt its people as one family; it must become their
temporal home.

The Republic is therefore a kind of monastery, but one
suffused by liberty. In the vertical, apocalyptic imagery
of Weiskel's metonymical sublime, where "meaning is
overwhelmed by an overdetermination which in its extreme threatens a state of absolute metaphor,"[6] the novel
depicts the revolutionaries' struggle for a *different* future from atop the barricades. According to their vision,
all refuse—sewage, barren land, *les misérables* themselves—will be recovered and transformed into something of value. To stem this wastefulness demand seeing waste—like Cambronne's famous expletive at the
battle of Waterloo or the "garbage" suggested by the
Bastille elephant or the barricades—in new ways: "If
our gold is so much waste, then, on the other hand, our
waste is so much gold" (II. 365). Utopia hides in the
depth of human detritus; sewage has many pastoral, if
not Edenic, forms:

> It is the flowering meadow, green grass, marjoram and
> thyme and sage, the lowing of contented cattle in the
> evening, the scented hay and the golden wheat, the
> bread on your table and the warm blood in your veins—
> health and joy and life. Such is the purpose of that
> mystery of creation which is transformation on earth
> and transfiguration in Heaven. Return all that to the
> great crucible and you will reap abundance.

(II. 365)

The poet's vision is the practical reality of tomorrow.
Specifically, he proposes to replace the sewer, "which is
mere impoverishment" with "drainage, with its double
function of restoring what it takes away" (II. 366).
When the metaphorical exchange of drainage systems
supersedes the one-way, metonymical flow of sewers,
the problem of poverty will be resolved. Pragmatic wisdom born of reflective imagination will impel history
toward a just, prosperous, and peaceful future for everyone.

Manure transmuted thus becomes food for all, both literally and figuratively. In one form it nourishes bodies.

Properly channeled and treated, sewage can become *other.* This metaphorical transfiguration by which death and decay become life-giving forces denies any absolute distinction between being and nothingness. Once again, apparent opposites are integrated at a higher level. In another, literary form, sewage can nourish minds. The offal of society constitutes the primary subject of Hugo's book. Properly nurtured, these voiceless masses will become articulate; they will differentiate themselves from nothingness; they will rebuild the glory not of French military might but of French civilization. Related to the notion of conscience as mounting a vertical axis, this thunderous voice of the multitude resembles that of the ubiquitous author himself. Speaking through the work that bears their name, *les misérables* clamor for attention. If they leave fewer traces than their rulers, they communicate through such "symbols of the popular will" (II. 127) as barricades and the Bastille elephant.

In the meanwhile, the absent voice raised on their behalf is that of Hugo himself. Exiled from France during the Second Empire, the author is in a sense as homeless as those whose cause he espouses. He lives, not so much in the no man's land of Guernsey on the outskirts of France, but in the monumental constructs of his literary and polemic works. For writing recuperates the nothingness of words and fashions them into new associative families. Like the Saint-Antoine district, his novel should be considered a "powder-mill of suffering and political thought" (II. 37), ready to spark off renewed political commitment. From these paper barricades Hugo joins the struggle for the universal Republic, both modeled by and located in the confraternity of reading great literature.

Notes

1. All references are to Victor-Marie Hugo, *Les Misérables,* trans. Norman Denny, 2 vols. (Harmondsworth: Penguin, 1980).

2. In *The Romantic Sublime: Studies in the Structure and Psychology of Transcendence* (Baltimore: John Hopkins UP, 1976), 26.

3. Hugo uses much the same imagery to depict the chaining of the prisoners in his early novel, *The Last Day of a Condemned Man* (1829). Valjean's identification with this scene from his past repeats the condemned man's own empathy and horror. Cf. Kathryn M. Grossman, *The Early Novels of Victor Hugo: Towards a Poetics of Harmony* (Genève: Droz, 1986), 147-49.

4. Northrop Frye, *Anatomy of Criticism: Four Essays* (Princeton: Princeton UP, 1957), 148.

5. Dante Alighieri, *Hell,* trans. Dorothy L. Sayers (Harmondsworth: Penguin, 1973), 272.

6. Weiskel, 26.

John E. Coombs (essay date fall 1993)

SOURCE: Coombs, John E. "State, Self and History in Victor Hugo's *L'Année Terrible.*" *Studies in Romanticism* 32, no. 3 (fall 1993): 367-78.

[*In the following essay, Coombs suggests that* L'année terrible *should be considered a great epic, achieving status similar to Milton's* Paradise Lost.]

> ". . . coupable aussi moi d'innocence . . ." ("A ceux qu'on foule aux pieds.")

Hugo's last major poem sequence, and perhaps the last major poetic statement of European romanticism, was written in 1870-72, throughout the historical events with which it is concerned: the Franco-Prussian war, the Commune and their aftermath. Its articulation upon those events is thus very different from that of Wordsworth's *The Prelude,* with its attempt at a monolithic tranquillity of retrospection upon the Revolution, or indeed—to cite a less evidently conservative/conservatory instance—Heine's *Deutschland, Ein Wintermärchen,* generated out of the depressing yet constant condition of political exile.

Rather, the conditions of writing of *L'Année Terrible*—from the last months of Republican exile in Jersey through residence in the Paris of siege and civil war, to brief renewed exile in, and expulsion from, Belgium after the Commune—resemble the vicissitudes of that other great epic of mixed political hope and despair, *Paradise Lost.* And indeed, in its invective power, its coruscations and intercalations of mythology, its problematic convictions of righteousness, *L'Année Terrible* deserves the epithet "Miltonic," with its further connotations of classical virtue and the imperatives of resistance to political degeneracy, as specified in Hugo's **"Prologue"**:

> La république anglaise expire, se dissout,
> Tombe, et laisse Milton derrière elle debout;
> La foule a disparu, mais le penseur demeure
>
> [The English republic fades, dissolves,
> Falls, leaves Milton standing there;
> The crowd has disappeared, the thinker remains][1]

Particularly, the negotiations in Hugo's work, of poetic/textual truth and political/historical fact, are oblique. The text contains relatively little explicit reference to the "major" historical events with which it is closely involved; historical references, obscure to the modern reader, are often made in passing with the result that recourse to the footnotes of a scholarly edition has the effect of engendering, for the reader, a certain sense of fragmentariness, of structured chaos both within the writing and in its further communication. In general, the relation of text and context in *L'Année Terrible* comes to seem very like that perceived in those configurations of ground and figure with which we are all familiar, those complementary silhouettes where each constitutes the other by its momentary absence and where the branches of a tree may, in the blinking of an eye, be transformed into a donkey's head, and vice versa. Such a paradoxical relationship—arguably the condition of all textuality, particularly evident here—is signally achieved in the three poems of invective against the hapless and subsequently (deservedly) obscure general Trochu (Janvier v, "Sommation"; Janvier XII; Juin XVII). In the first, a "Sommation" of extreme agitated tension, directed at the unnamed but identifiable military butt, deployment of proto-expressionist chiaroscuro effects enacts the contrast between action and inaction, popular will and military timidity:

> L'heure est sombre; il s'agit de sauver l'empyrée
> Qu'une nuée immonde et triste vient ternir,
> De dégager le bleu lointain de l'avenir,
> Et de faire une guerre implacable à l'abîme.

> [The hour is dark; now to save the firmament
> Threatened by a ghastly deadening cloud,
> To free the future's distant blue,
> and fight to the end against the abyss.]

The tendency of the poem is to cast its ostensible historical subject, Trochu, into a gulf of nothingness (it is notable to what extent familiar Hugolian imagery—"gouffre," "abîme," "ombre"—gains a new preponderance throughout the text); the corresponding imaging of inchoate viscosity has more in common with Rimbaud (and later Sartre and Malraux) than with the relatively stable identities of earlier romantic utterance:

> Quand tous les êtres bas, visqueux, abjects, jaloux,
> L'affreux lynx, le chacal boiteux, l'hyène obscène,
> L'aspic lâche, ont pu, grâce à la brume malsaine,
> Sortir rôder, glisser, ramper, boire du sang . . .

> [When all those creatures, vile, viscous, abject, jealous
> Hideous lynx, lame jackal, obscene hyena,
> Creeping asp, have, through the foetid mist
> Come to slide, slither, crawl, suck blood . . .]

Similarly, in the second poem against Trochu-Tartuffe—"ce pauvre homme" (Janvier XII)—the motor forces of history, "Audace, Humanité, Volonté, Liberté," are juxtaposed/deadlocked against the personality of their conjunctural bearer, "dont le suprême instinct serait d'être immobile" ["whose primordial instinct would seem to be remaining still"]; the resultant articulation is of madness, nothingness:

> . . . notre démence,
> Devant le noir nadir et le zénith vermeil,
> Ajoute un chien d'aveugle aux chevaux du soleil.

> [. . . our madness
> Before the black nadir and the crimson zenith,

> Sends a blind man's dog towards the horses of the sun.]

Intriguingly, Trochu's last poetic (dis)appearance (in Juin XVII) involves his reduction to a suggestive epistemological trace, to the status—in a brilliantly apposite pun—of the past participle of the invented verb *tropchoir* (to fall too far); a reflexive evocation of the collapse, not only of the ruling state order and its dominant notions of subjectivity, but of its very possibilities for signification itself.

The eclipse of the established, individualist, notion of the subject and of his/her language is central to the work as a whole; *L'Année Terrible* may be seen, indeed, as a notation of the disintegration of the romantic ideology of subjectivity and its quasi-mythological certainties under the pressure of events, notably the transition from foreign to civil war and the accompanying destabilization of perceptions of self and world as political discourses.

Thus the Prologue, "Les 7 500 000 oui (Publié en Mai 1870)"—ostensibly an attack on Napoléon III's last, successful, plebiscite—articulates at a high level of concentration the contradictions of liberal romantic Republicanism; it may be seen, in major ways, to assert the continuation from exile of the Second Republic which had been Hugo's project ever since the *Coup d'état*. In it we find much classic Republican élitism, manifest in the familiarly Olympian self-imaging of the poet:

> La foule passe, crie, appelle, pleure, fuit;
> Versons sur ses douleurs la pitié fraternelle.

> [The crowd goes by, shouts, calls out, weeps, flees;
> Let us assuage its pain with fraternal pity.]

Romantic poetic subjectivity is, then, initially manifest in a distanced sympathy for the coherent entity represented by the "peuple," as against the inchoate anarchy of the (lumpenproletarian) "foule." The uncertainty of the distinction was to be made explicit by Marx in his text on the Commune, *The Civil War In France,* where capacity for both "the highest and the lowest deeds" is ascribed to the lumpenproletariat; it is, moreover, reminiscent of perennial tensions in the romantic social thinking of 1848, of Michelet, Renan, George Sand. To the suggested plenitude of "le peuple"—"Ce vieux dormeur d'airain"—however, is counterposed "la foule," as later in Yeats, seen as fluctuating and contradictory, as ". . . la sombre faiblesse et . . . la force sombre." More socially specific, yet suffused with a certain conservatism, is the critique of modern individualist rootlessness as the product of capitalist property-relations:

> Ah! le premier venu, bourgeois ou paysan
> L'un égoïste et l'autre aveugle, parlons-en!

[Oh! anyone at all, bourgeois or peasant
Whether selfish or blind, let us speak of them!]

Yet running counter to this ideological set we perceive in the text a latent critique of it; a critique which, in its self-betraying language, may be seen, for instance, to demonstrate through its deployment of an obscure imagery which approaches oxymoron, the insubstantiality of Olympian "truth" as a commodity to be distributed rather than a process collectively elaborated:

La vérité, voilà le grand encens austère
Qu'on doit à cette masse où palpite un mystère.

[See now the truth, great austere incense
Owed to the masses throbbing with mystery.]

The distanced formulations of post-enlightenment optimism can still be made with notable banality:

On interrompt Jean Huss; soit; Luther continue
La lumière est toujours par quelque bras tenue . . .
Des justes sortiront de la foule asservie
Iront droit au sépulcre et quitteront la vie.

[Maybe Jan Huss is stopped; but Luther carries on
The light is always passed on from hand to hand . . .
Just men will come out from the oppressed masses
To go to the tomb, give up their life.]

Yet their notional effect is subsequently undercut by a dynamic and graphic realization of the workings of ideology itself:

L'ombre?
. . . On dirait que la vie éternelle recule
La neige fait, niveau hideux du crépuscule,
On ne sait quel sinistre abaissement des monts;
Nous nous sentons mourir si nous nous endormons;
. . . on ne distingue plus son chemin. Tout est piège.

[The dark?
. . . It is as if life eternal slips away
The snow, dread surface of the dusk,
Bears ominously down upon the hills;
We feel that sleeping we are already dead
. . . We can no longer find our way. All's trap.]

The perceived drive towards nothingness—"[la] mort à la vertu donne un baiser farouche" ["death gives a wild kiss to virtue"]—outruns the text's manifest assertion of reformist palliatives, just as fluid contortions of language and imagery outrun banal assertion:

Qui donc s'est figuré
. . . Que j'entrasse au cachot s'il entre au cabanon!

[Who had ever thought
. . . that I should go to the dungeon as he to the madhouse!]

Thus does the verse attain the contradictory position which its ostensible discourse ascribes to "le premier venu," the average individual representative of the nineteenth-century status quo: "Il est sa propre insulte et sa propre ironie" ["He is his own insult, his own irony"]. Such fluctuations and contradictions extend across the corpus of *L'Année Terrible* as a whole, their critical and problematic nature becoming increasingly evident. Thus in the sequence "Août" we have, repeatedly, the arresting sense of the writing of a new conjuncture, the impact of *total* war as the consequence of Napoleon III's modern manipulation of mass politics as disorientation and dream:

Jamais les siècles le passé,
L'histoire n'avaient vu ce spectacle insensé,
Ce vertige, ce rêve, un homme qui lui-même,
. . . Prend la peine d'ouvrir sa fosse . . .

[Never had centuries past,
Had history seen this senseless spectacle
This dizzying dream, a man himself,
. . . Working to open up his tomb . . .]

The perennial structured confusions of the late Napoleonic project are of course innovatory; their dimensions are more systematically explored both in Hugo's *Histoire d'un Crime* and in Marx's *Eighteenth Brumaire of Louis Bonaparte*; their significance for developments of right-wing totalitarianism in the twentieth century is now apparent. Yet at this point the discourse presented in opposition is still one of liberal balance; Hugo's elegiac suggestion of a decline from the status of the Napoleon for whom "le côté de clarté cachait le côté d'ombre" ["the side of light hid the side of darkness"] seems a notable escape from contemporary engagement into past myth.

In the same way we perceive in Octobre III—a poem notably shackled, so to speak, by residual bourgeois ideology—a retreat, a considerable reduction of dynamic range; first the Miltonic imaging of the chaos of battle, in which the rapid intermingling of concepts and levels ensures that chaos becomes not merely the topic but the condition of the poem:

Le gouffre est comme un mur énorme de fumée
Où fourmille on ne sait quelle farouche armée;
. . . Et les bruits infernaux et les bruits souterrains
Se mêlent, et, hurlant au fond de la géhenne,
Les tonnerres ont l'air de bêtes à la chaîne.
. . . Et ce chaos s'acharne à tuer cette sphère.
Lui frappe avec la flamme, elle avec la lumière.

[The gulf is like a massive wall of smoke
In which some wild army rages;
. . . And sounds infernal, subterranean
Are mingled, and, shrieking in hellish depths,
Thunder has the sound of beasts enchained.
. . . Such chaos seeks to kill the very sphere.
Which, struck by its flame, strikes back with light.]

But then follows the imposition of uncertain stability, implicit—if momentary—confirmation of a pathetically serene liberal ideology:

Tout à coup un rayon sort par une trouée
Une crinière en feu, par les vents secouée,
Apparaît . . . le voilà!

[A sudden shaft of light shines through a crack
A fiery mane, swept by the winds,
Comes forth . . . see!]

In the opposite direction, however, we observe in the series "Novembre" and "Décembre" the eventual eclipse of a series of articulations of conventional bourgeois moralism. In "Du haut de la muraille de Paris" (Novembre I), notably, is to be found a reversionary poetic tendency more characteristic of Vigny than Hugo. Here, evocation of the twilight is anything but conventionally harmonious,

La nuit se fermait ainsi qu'une prison
. . . Le couchant n'était plus qu'une lame sanglante

[Night closed in like a prison
. . . The setting sun just a dripping blade]

yet the last stanza obliterates the immediacy of the effects which precede it by a dogmatic specification of explicit significance: "Cela faisait penser à quelque grand duel . . ." ["It called to mind some great duel . . ."].

The procedure—of dogmatic pedagogics rather than of poetic logic—has its correlatives in the inadequate, explicit politics of much of the series, with their simple manicheism ("Paris diffamé à Berlin"), banal moralism ("A tous ces princes") and—perhaps the nadir of the tendency—the vindictive banality of "En voyant flotter sur la Seine des cadavres prussiens":

'Allons chez la prostituée
. . . Paris, cette ville publique,
. . . Nous ouvrira ses bras . . .'
Et la Seine son lit.

['Let us go whoring
. . . Paris, strumpet city,
. . . Will open her arms to us . . .'
And the Seine her bed.]

But against such an image of Paris must be set the emergent notation of the city as collective subjectivity. Already apparent in "Lettre à une femme" (Janvier II), in which poetic Olympian individuality is occluded— "On est un peuple, on est un monde, on est une âme" ["Being a people, being a world, being a soul"]—the tendency is later more fully manifest, not just as a mode of being, but in a sense of shared practice:

Ce tumulte enseignant la science aux savants
Ce grand lever d'aurore au milieu des vivants.

(Janvier 1871, IV)

[This tumult teaching science to the scholar
This great dawning in the middle of the living.]

Such a perception of the transformation of "normal" human and social relations may be seen to provide the narrative context for the negative primordial charge of three centrally important poems, "Sommation," "Une bombe aux Feuillantines," and "Le Pigeon" (Janvier 1871, V, VI, VII). Here we have a coruscation of expressionist effects *avant la lettre*—of light and dark, of emptiness, focus and flux, of presence and absence, infinite space and minute detail ("Le pigeon")—which collectively constitutes a clear notation of political and cultural crisis to which received notions of writing are clearly no longer adequate.

The nature of the crisis—and of the work's figuration of it—is already apparent in the positive centrality of "Loi de formation du progrès" (Février V). The significance of the poem may be seen, in a sense, as the transition it effects from the world of 1848 to the world of the Commune, from the abstract post-enlightenment suggestion, reminiscent of Pope and Voltaire, of

quelque but final, dont notre humble prunelle
N'aperçoit même pas la lueur éternelle,

[Some final end, whose everlasting light
Cannot be glimpsed by our humble gaze,]

to the implicit and forceful denunciation of such abstractions as projections of order, authority and social privilege:

Qui se promènera dans les éternités
Comme dans les jardins de Versailles Lenôtre?

[Who shall stroll through eternity
As did Lenôtre in the gardens of Versailles?]

From the distanced assertion of Olympian judgment

On voit la loi de paix, de vie et bonté
Pardessus l'infini dans les prodiges luire

[The law of peace, of life, of goodness
Is seen to shine beyond infinity in its marvels]

to the evocation of the self as discontinuous, problematic:

La loi!
Qui la connaît? Quelqu'un parmi nous, hors de soi,
Comme en soi . . .
A-t-il percé ce gouffre?

[The law!
Who knows it? Who amongst us, beside himself,
As in himself . . .
Has penetrated this chasm?]

From affirmation of the isolate self to that of positive human relations through and with others, the poem significantly moves from its earlier bland assertion that slavery is at least an advance on cannibalism to a final denunciation of imperialism very different in tone:

> Le plus grand siècle peut avoir son heure immonde;
> Parfois sur tous les points du globe un fléau gronde.
>
> [The greatest age of all may have its darkest hour;
> And all across the globe rumbles the scourge's sound.]

From these central movements on, reversion to liberal individualist discourse in *L'Année Terrible* is increasingly disrupted, offset, outweighed by radical shifts in understanding in which "literature" and "politics" are often merged. Thus, characteristically, the bloody repression of the Commune is denounced as "Alceste . . . aujourd'hui fusillé par Philinte" ["Alceste today . . . shot down by Philinte"], a Rousseau-esque reading of Molière which breaks drastically with bourgeois notions of good sense and rationality. Thus does the poem **"Les fusillés"** (Juin XII) proclaim its indivisible radicalism; further, it incorporates a shift to a point in political understanding (of the "otherness" of opposing classes and their forms of reason) unrivalled in contemporary writing (or indeed in the early sequences of the work itself).

A stupendous realization of empathy with the Communard insurgents is throughout apparent:

> Il semble
> qu ils ont hâte de fuir un monde âpre, incomplet.
>
> [It seems
> They long to leave a world so harsh, so incomplete.]

(Politicization of romantic notions of totality)

> . . . ils ne tiennent pas à la vie; elle est faite
> De façon qu'il leur est égal de s'en aller.
>
> [They do not care for life; it is such
> That they do not mind leaving it behind.]

(Discretion and laconic respect);

> Ils sont étrangers à tout ce qui se passe.
>
> [They are apart from everything that happens.]

(Recognition of alienation both as a social variable and as an ontological category);

> Etre avec nous, cela les étouffait.
> Ils partent.
>
> [Being with us stifled them.
> They leave.]

(Recognition of the writer's social distance; an elegy rather than an affirmation).

Moments such as these are indeed extraordinary. They culminate in the transformation of the Hugolian trope of "l'abîme" into the realization that this abyss is indeed the hell of oppressive social relations. And the transforming recognition is complemented by that of the narrating subject as, necessarily, the bearer of privilege. The import of such a transformation—how far, so to speak, the poem has come—may be demonstrated by a comparison of two poems, **"Choix entre deux nations"** (Septembre I) and **"A qui la faute?"** (Juin VIII), which use virtually identical effects of narrative retardation to achieve their effect.

In the first, a contrived and rather effete climax is achieved by the brief exclamation—"O ma mère!"—which constitutes the entirety of the poem's second part ("A la France"), the first part consisting of a lengthy enumeration of the qualities of German culture ("A L'Allemagne"). The touching simplicity of conventional patriotism is quite evidently the sought-after effect, and no doubt achieved within its limits which are, after all, merely those of ritual confirmation. In the later poem, the narrator's interrogation of a Communard who has just set fire to a library carries an altogether different impact. Here, the contrast between the interrogator's prolonged, sonorous, idealist abstractions

> "As-tu donc oublié que ton libérateur,
> C'est le livre?"
>
> ["Can you have forgotten that the book,
> Is your liberator?"]

and the worker's one line reply—"Je ne sais pas lire" ["I cannot read"]—points to the material superficiality of pretentions to exclusive cultural power in a situation where two divergent class-discourses, two languages, can have little contact. Clearly, between the two poems the discourse of nation has been supplanted by the discourse of class; a manner of discursive disruption emerges which, in its laconic questioning of the axiomatic validity of established notions of language and culture themselves, looks forward notably to the poetry of Brecht.

In **"Flux et reflux"** (Juillet II), the awareness of discontinuity and structural diversity which we have already noted is warranted, amplified, by a consciousness of the significance of *will* as a necessary shaping principle, if human experience is not to be enclosed in a mechanistic fatalism:

> Ces flux et ces reflux,
> Ces recommencements, ces combats, sont voulus.
>
> [These ebbs and flows,
> These new beginnings, struggles, all are willed.]

Stress on the will as a determinant natural factor, paradoxical though it may seem, places Hugo's poem here in a line of rational materialist thinking that leads from Marx to Gramsci and Althusser. In the same text, notably, the awareness of possible universal degeneracy—

> Le pauvre a le haillon, le riche a le lambeau,
> Rien d'entier pour personne; et sur tous l'ombre infâme.
>
> [To the poor his rags, to the rich his tatters,
> Nothing whole for anyone; and over all the dread shadow.]

—has evident affinities with Marx's warning of the possible "common ruin of all classes," the very antithesis of the mechanistic optimism so perennially ascribed to revolutionary thinking.

The alternative to such a distortion is suggested, finally, in Hugo's articulation of a revolutionary, collective optimism far removed from the text's initially distanced representation of the "peuple," in **"Le Procès à la Révolution"** where material conflict rather than abstract harmony is frankly asserted as the motor of history:

> Le monde ténébreux râle; que d'agonies!
> Il fait jour, c'est affreux! . . .
> Le rayon sans pitié prend l'ombre et la dévore . . .
>
> [The world of shadows slowly rattles out its last!
> And now the dreadful birth of day! . . .
> Its heartless light seizes and devours the gloom . . .]

Darkness at noon? At any event, the collusive stance of individualist romanticism has been supplanted by a discourse revolutionary in both procedure and effect.

Note

1. Victor Hugo, *Oeuvres poétiques* III, ed. P. Albouy (Paris: Bibliothèque de la Pléiade, 1974). All quotations from Hugo are from this edition; all translations are my own.

Angelo Metzidakis (essay date December 1993)

SOURCE: Metzidakis, Angelo. "On Rereading French History in Hugo's *Les Misérables*." *The French Review* 67, no. 2 (December 1993): 187-95.

[*In the following essay, Metzidakis considers Hugo's treatment of two historical dates in* Les Misérables *and traces Hugo's attempts to influence his readers to take political action against the regime of Napoleon III.*]

In *Les Misérables,* Hugo presents a very selective reading of nineteenth-century French history in order to convince the bourgeoisie of the Second Empire of the virtues of republicanism. Hugo's historical commentary underscores the unwitting role that the bourgeois class

had played in the development of republicanism in France as a means to persuade his readers that conscious opposition to the government of Napoleon III would serve their own interests as well as those of France as a whole. Hugo's reading of French history contains an implicit critique of the Second Empire during the early 1860s. By praising various aspects of political life during the Restoration and the July Monarchy in his novel, Hugo makes oblique references to specific changes in contemporary political life which he deplores. In this way, he educates his readers with respect to their political opportunities in the hope that they will renounce their tacit collusion with the regime of Napoleon III by taking action through the political process.

The bulk of Hugo's commentary centers on two dates: 1814, the year of Napoleon's first abdication and of the first Bourbon Restoration and, 1830, the year of the July Revolution and of the rise to power of Louis Philippe. Both of these dates represent stages of political transition during which the powers of the throne were diminished in favor of the bourgeoisie which, in each case, prolonged the monarchy for the sake of national stability.[1]

In a discussion on the result of the July Revolution, Hugo draws a parallel between the events of 1814 and 1830 in order to underscore the bourgeois role in them:

> Qui arrête les révolutions à mi-côte? La bourgeoisie. Pourquoi? Parce que la bourgeoisie est l'intérêt arrivé à la satisfaction. Hier c'était l'appétit, aujourd'hui c'est la plénitude, demain ce sera la satiété. Le même phénomène de 1814 après Napoléon se reproduisit en 1830 après Charles X. On a voulu, à tort, faire de la bourgeoisie une classe. La bourgeoisie est tout simplement la portion contentée du peuple. Le bourgeois, c'est l'homme qui a maintenant le temps de s'asseoir. Une chaise n'est pas une caste. Mais, pour vouloir s'asseoir trop tôt, on peut arrêter la marche même du genre humain. Cela a été souvent la faute de la bourgeoisie. On n'est pas une classe parce qu'on fait une faute. L'égoïsme n'est pas une des divisions de l'ordre social.
>
> (11: 600)[2]

Hugo describes 1814 and 1830 as "halts," moments during which the bourgeoisie consolidated its gains and forces in view of further progress at some more auspicious moment in the future. At the time, republicanism was seen as a threat against which a weakened throne was a safeguard. It seemed that the monarchy would preserve liberal policies that would assure national stability.

Hugo's commentary on 1814 and 1830 has negative implications for the political situation in which the original readers of *Les Misérables* found themselves. Although the aspirations of the bourgeoisie in the early

1860s had not changed, the government of Napoleon III was no longer the guarantor of liberalism and stability. As the Second Empire had already begun its gradual decline, government opposition grew on many fronts. For example, the industrialists were alienated by Napoleon III's free trade agreements with Britain (Plessis 196-97), and the Catholics were furious with his military involvement in Italian affairs which touched off the "Roman Question" (193-96). Faced with such growing opposition, Napoleon III changed his despotic policies for more liberal ones in order to gain support (Plesis 200-01). Unfortunately, his politically motivated liberalism only gave more ground to the Opposition[3] and fostered political activity among the French.

Having intimated that support of Napoleon III is no longer in the interest of the bourgeoisie, Hugo shifts the focus of his historical criticism to the early years of the Second Empire. Two of Hugo's remarks, one concerning the Bourbons, the other Louis Philippe, are of particular interest in this context since they amount to indirect accusations of Napoleon III's rule during the authoritarian phase of the Second Empire which had entered into its so-called "liberal" phase[4] only a few years prior to the publication of *Les Misérables*. Given this time frame, the reader cannot possibly ignore Hugo's intent.

In his first critical remark, Hugo favorably stresses the relative liberties that prevailed during the Restoration until the signing of the July Ordinances:

> [C]'est sous Louis XVIII et Charles X que vint le tour de parole de l'intelligence. Le vent cessa, le flambeau se ralluma. On vit frissonner sur les cimes sereines la pure lumière des esprits. Spectacle magnifique, utile et charmant. On vit travailler pendant quinze ans, en pleine paix, en pleine place publique, ces grands principes, si vieux pour le penseur, si nouveaux pour l'homme d'état: l'égalité devant la loi, la liberté de la conscience, la liberté de la parole, la liberté de la presse, l'accessibilité de toutes les aptitudes à toutes les fonctions. Cela alla ainsi jusqu'en 1830.
>
> (11: 597)

The "flambeau de l'intelligence" that shone on France from on high is Hugo's main concern here. He is referring to the "sacred" tribune[5] of the Chamber of Deputies in which long parliamentary debates were fought between the Liberals and the Ultraroyalists during public sessions throughout the Restoration.[6] Napoleon III suppressed such free debate during which the will of the people, as expressed by the Liberals, was heard and not without effect. Clearly, by extolling selected aspects of past political life, Hugo is emphasizing the fact that the first nine years of the Second Empire was a period of dictatorial rule during which the legislature was gagged and powerless.[7]

Furthermore, the history of the tribune from the French Revolution until its destruction by Louis Napoleon's coup d'état is detailed in the fifth book of *Napoléon le Petit* entitled "Parlementarisme" (8: 484-92). One typically Hugolian sentence from the ninth chapter of this book, "La Tribune détruite," suffices to revive Hugo's incisive criticism of Napoleon III which is shrouded under the veil of historical commentary in *Les Misérables*:

> Donc 'le parlementarisme', c'est-à-dire la garantie des citoyens, la liberté de discussion, la liberté de la presse, la liberté individuelle, le contrôle de l'impôt, la clarté dans les recettes et dans les dépenses, . . . la liberté de conscience, la liberté des cultes, le point d'appui de la propriété, le recours contre les confiscations et les spoliations, la sécurité de chacun, le contrepoids à l'arbitraire, la dignité de la nation, . . . tout cela n'est plus.
>
> (8: 490-91)

It should be remembered, however, that the bourgeois reader of *Les Misérables* needed no such reminders since many of the practices of the despotic regime were still in recent memory: wide press censorship, unconstrained government spending, official lists of approved candidates for elections, and the arbitrary arrest and deportation of many persons suspected of antigovernment activity after Orsini's attack on Napoleon III.[8]

A second indirect accusation of Napoleon III is found in Hugo's appreciation of Louis Philippe's apparent good faith in his ascendance to the throne:

> Louis-Philippe était entré dans l'autorité royale sans violence, sans action directe de sa part, par le fait d'un virement révolutionnaire, . . . dans lequel lui, duc d'Orléans, n'avait aucune initiative personnelle. Il était né prince et se croyait élu roi. Il ne s'était point donné à lui-même ce mandat; il ne l'avait point pris; on le lui avait offert et il l'avait accepté; convaincu, à tort certes, mais convaincu que l'offre était selon le droit et que l'acceptation était selon le devoir.
>
> (11: 605)

Hugo's characterization of Louis Philippe dramatically underscores the extent of Louis Napoleon's bad faith[9] while preparing the rise of the Second Empire: once elected President of the Second Republic, on the strength of his Napoleonic ancestry,[10] he intended to remain in power, no matter what the cost. He began by manipulating the "Parti de l'Ordre" in order to crush the democratic movement of the Republicans. After failing in his attempt to revise the Constitution so as to permit his reelection,[11] his last recourse was the coup d'état.[12] After having exploited this chaotic situation by evoking the threat of the "spectre rouge,"[13] Louis Napoleon polled the Frenchmen on an exacting plebiscite: "Le peuple français veut le maintien de l'autorité de Louis-Napoléon Bonaparte et lui délègue les pouvoirs nécessaires pour faire une constitution."[14] That is how Louis Napoleon legitimized his cause, procured his new mandate, and became Napoleon III on the first anniversary of the coup d'état which conveniently coincided with the date of the great battle of Austerlitz.[15]

Hugo's limited presentation of the Restoration and of the July Monarchy makes the bourgeois readers aware of their unwitting participation in France's political transformations. Their political strength grew under the rule of the "legitimate" Bourbons and continued to do so under the "illegitimate" (Howarth 155-60) duc d'Orléans, "le roi citoyen," the bourgeois king. One very real aspect of their power was the national guard which was organized in March 1831 (Daumard 306-12). It was a bourgeois army, a type of police force, whose function was to protect Louis Philippe's regime from its adversaries. When its support of the July Monarchy ended in 1848, the regime collapsed. What followed was the troubled Second Republic during which the interests of the French people were split into two antagonistic groups: the bourgeois, along with the peasants, versus the workers, the truly afflicted class. The former group was horrified by the latter, while the latter hated the former. This marks the beginning of the counterproductive or, to use more lenient language, the "irresponsible" role of the bourgeois in French society. From this point on, Hugo's moral instruction of the bourgeois, his plea for the spirit of revolution and Christianity (8: 526-27) in the service of the ideal—and therefore of the people—is applicable.

In *Les Misérables,* Hugo's interest in the Second Republic is limited to a discussion of the socialist insurrection of June 1848. The complexity of this situation, which required bourgeois participation, is clear in the following passage: "Juin 1848 fut . . . un fait à part, et presque impossible à classer dans la philosophie de l'histoire. . . . [C]ette émeute extraordinaire où l'on sentit la sainte anxiété du travail réclamant ses droits. Il fallut la combattre, et c'était le devoir, car elle attaquait la République. Mais, au fond, que fut juin 1848? Une révolte du peuple contre lui-même" (11: 822).[16] Although the "duty" of the bourgeois was to save the Republic from mounting socialist protest and disorder, these stringent measures could have been avoided had the government had the will to initiate legislation that could have eased the poverty-stricken condition of the workers.[17] The need for such legislation was chronic because the French economic crisis, which had begun during the July Monarchy, worsened during the Second Republic, especially after the February Revolution. Socialist agitation had brought commerce to a virtual standstill.

In order to discredit the Socialists—and, in particular, Louis Blanc, theoretician of *L'Organisation du travail*—the provisional government intentionally founded a warped version of the "Ateliers nationaux" (Agulhon 44-45).[18] When these workshops proved to be obvious failures, the government closed them, ordering indigent workers either to join the army, or to leave for work in the provinces. The barricades of the June Revolt, "l'acropole des va-nu-pieds," arose from this tragic situation. The bourgeois and the peasants were ready for order, even if it meant Louis Napoleon's order: the suppression of the Republic and of its ideals. They would be content if material order were restored, but would they remain content if moral order were not also restored in the long run? The question of moral grandeur, inspired by the contemplation of the ideal, is crucial to Hugo's argument against the premises of the Second Empire. Hugo does not situate this grandeur with the bourgeois position, but rather with the socialist one.[19] The Socialists were directly concerned with the social issues that the politically oriented bourgeoisie wanted to ignore.[20] By analyzing the abortive revolt of 1832 and the temporarily successful one of 1848, Hugo presents his reader with the ideal side of the socialist position. He disengages its lofty goals from its violent acts by characterizing the insurrectionists as "essayeurs de l'avenir" (11: 862) whose aim was to build a truly equitable republic in which global growth would be uninhibited by artificial means.

Hugo's advocacy of the ideals of the revolution of 1848 constitutes a call for political action that seems to have been heard by his readers of the Second Empire. The legislative elections of 1863, approximately one year after the publication of *Les Misérables,* established a sizeable anti-Empire group within the government thanks to the growing idea of an "union libérale" (Plessis 208). This wide-ranging shift in public opinion, gradual though it was, raised the moral consciousness of the bourgeois who, during the regime of silence, had rather apathetically concerned themselves with material considerations.

The reason for Hugo's interest in the bourgeois reader, especially in the young generation that had matured during the Empire, is quite simple. This group, having been given a certain education and culture, was the most receptive to what he called the peaceful "philosophie de la révolution" (11: 483) which is, in short, ideal republicanism. Up until Napoleon III's rise to power, republican ideals were associated with the violent anarchy and militant socialism surrounding 1832 and 1848. During the period that preceded the Second Empire, the workers who revolted, "les barbares de la civilisation," received "la souterraine éducation de l'émeute" which was, judging from Enjolras' speech to the insurgents of 1832,[21] a course in the force of the ideal without any concern for its implementation through peaceful means. The bourgeois, among others, was to receive later a similar form of education beginning with the brief, but violent repression that followed the coup d'état. The education of the bourgeois in the value of the ideal was to be much slower and, so to speak, more reasoned than had been the case for the insurgents of the Republic.

The role of *Les Misérables* in the "subterranean" education of the bourgeois can be seen in Hugo's evaluation of the political and social climate of France in the early 1830s. To a great extent, this historical description is applicable to the 1860s, with the difference that the bourgeois is called upon to act "appropriately" against the Empire:

> Entre l'attaque du passé et l'attaque de l'avenir, l'établissement de juillet se débattait. . . . Une harmonie voulue à contre-sens est souvent plus onéreuse qu'une guerre. De ce lourd conflit, toujours muselé, mais toujours grondant, naquit la paix armée, ce ruineux expédient de la civilisation suspecte à elle-même. . . . Cependant, à l'intérieur, paupérisme, prolétariat, salaire, éducation, pénalité, prostitution, sort de la femme, richesse, misère, production, consommation, répartition, échange, monnaie, crédit, droit du capital, droit du travail, toutes les questions se multipliaient au-dessus de la société; surplomb terrible. En dehors des partis proprement dits, un autre mouvement se manifestait.

(11: 606)

Clearly, "la paix armée" is an indictment of Napoleon III's "peaceful" Empire which began warring early on; for example, the Crimean War in 1854, the war in Italy in 1859, and the beginning of the ruinous Mexican Involvement in 1861-1862. Furthermore, the economic factors concerning monies, credits, capital investment, and the like, all point to Napoleon III's financial ventures which, although having done much for the nation's economy and prestige, did much less for the workers.[22] This produced a cleavage between the bourgeois and the workers, the "misérables" of the Second Empire, that is referred to indirectly in the previous passage by the relative terms: "paupérisme, . . . salaire, éducation, pénalité, prostitution, sort de la femme, richesse, misère." In the 1860s, all of these factors taken together produced a new movement in France, a movement that was to form a coalition that would cut across party lines, namely the Opposition.[23] If Hugo addressed the bourgeois element of this growing opposition, he did so in the hope that its members would channel their efforts and influence towards the building of the Republic that they had once scorned, the same Republic that the majority of the Opposition was still against.

Hugo's selective rereading of French history in *Les Misérables* presents a multifaceted analysis of the republican ideal that goes far in the education of its bourgeois reader. While it is true that the social question posed by the "misérables" has a moral dimension that transcends the time frame of the novel,[24] Hugo's political intent—his credo—is very specific and posits the political inevitability of the Republic. In short, Hugo maintains that if bourgeois readers become politically active, they will thereby reconcile their power with their moral obligations, and thus join the revolutionary movement of which they are part with the truly Christian fervor (in Hugo's sense) that blind "égoïsme" had previously dampened. Conversely, if they do not act,

they will be an "obstacle" (8: 478-79) to be done away with when the Republic is at hand. This is Hugo's message to his readers of the Second Empire, and this is precisely the wider, political point of view to which he alludes at the end of his preface to *Les Misérables*: ". . . en d'autres termes, et à un point de vue plus étendu encore, tant qu'il y aura sur la terre ignorance et misère, des livres de la nature de celui-ci pourront ne pas être inutiles" (11: 49).

Notes

1. In order to put Hugo's views in perspective, see Daumard's analysis of the political role of the Parisian bourgeoisie (295-318).

2. Throughout this article, references to volume and page citations are to the chronological edition of Hugo's works: *Œuvres complètes*. Ed. Jean Massin. 18 vols. Paris: Le Club français du livre, 1967-1970.

3. In August 1859, people who had been banished or deported for political reasons were permitted to return to France; in November 1860, the Senate and the Legislature were permitted discussion of government policies, and—a detail of prime importance—a complete transcript of these discussions could be published in the newspapers (Bury 87). The revival of the "tribune" increased public interest and political activity among the French.

4. For a discussion of the interpretation of the "liberal" phase of the Second Empire, see Thompson (225-28).

5. For a brief explanation of why Hugo glorified the tribune of the Chamber of Deputies in several of his works of the exile period, see footnote 52 in the Massin edition of *Paris* (13: 598).

6. In *La Restauration,* Bertier de Sauvigny, after demonstrating why the Chamber of Deputies was much more efficacious in politics than the Chamber of Peers, concludes: "La Chambre des députés était donc sans conteste le centre et le pivot de la vie politique. Là seulement les grandes tendances entre lesquelles se partageait la nation—ou, du moins, son élite cultivée—se trouvaient clairement représentées par des hommes et des partis; là seulement elles pouvaient s'exprimer librement à la face du pays" (290).

7. Plessis décrit la situation du "corps législatif" in the following terms: "Aux élus du suffrage universel n'est réservée qu'une place secondaire et subordonnée. Même les mots choisis pour les désigner sont révélateurs d'un souci de les rabaisser: ils forment, non plus 'une assemblée nationale' de 'représentants' de la volonté du pays, mais un 'corps' de 'députés' envoyés, en assez

petit nombre (270 environ), pour aider le chef de l'Etat. Les journaux ne peuvent plus rendre compte du détail de leurs séances, ce qui diminue leur audience dans le pays. Leur président et leurs vice-présidents sont nommés parmi eux par l'empereur, et il n'est prévu pour les sessions ordinaires qu'une durée de trois mois. Ils n'ont pas la possibilité de renverser le gouvernement ou d'exercer un droit de regard sur son action" (32).

8. For a summary of the brief, but brutal repression that followed Orsini's attack on Napoleon III on January 14, 1858, see Plessis (192-93).

9. Although Hugo is greatly responsible for the vilification of Napoleon III, judgments on this rather enigmatic figure have varied. For a survey of twentieth-century appraisals of Napoleon III, see Spitzer. For an analysis of Hugo's reaction against Louis Napoleon, see Seebacher.

10. Thompson notes that Hugo supported Louis Napoleon's candidacy to the presidency by appealing to the Napoleonic legend: "'It is not a Prince who returns to the country', wrote Victor Hugo in 'L'Evénement' (Louis' most eloquent supporter now, as afterwards his most eloquent enemy), 'it is an Idea. The people have been waiting for Napoleon ever since 1815. The man whom the people have just elected to represent them is not the victim of a scrimmage at Boulogne; he is the victor of Jéna. . . . His candidature dates from Austerlitz!'" (95).

11. He did not succeed in this venture because the "Parti de l'Ordre" intended to restore the old monarchy, a project that naturally excluded Louis Napoleon. For a survey of the conflicts between Louis Napoleon and the "Parti de l'Ordre," see Agulhon (140-63).

12. The coup-d'état entailed the following: Louis Bonaparte broke his presidential oath to uphold the Constitution of 1848, and he authorized massive repressive measures: shootings, arrests, and the later deportations through the institution of the infamous "commissions mixtes." For a detailed account of the coup d'état and of the repressive measures that followed it, see Guillemin (355-418).

13. At various times, Louis Napoleon used the threat of another Red Revolution in order to gather popular support—a fact which is particularly evident in his two proclamations, "Appel au Peuple" and "A l'Armée," published the morning of the coup d'état (Thompson 118-19). Over time, however, the political effectiveness of this threat waned (Cf. *Napoléon le Petit* (8: 438) and *Les Misérables* (11: 708)).

14. In *Napoléon le Petit,* Hugo parodies this plebiscite: "Le peuple français entend-il se remettre pieds et poings liés à la discrétion de M. Louis Bonaparte?" (8: 432).

15. December 2 is, in fact, a quadruple anniversary: in 1804, Napoleon I was crowned; in 1805, Napoleon I was victorious at Austerlitz; in 1851, Louis Napoleon carried out the coup d'état; and in 1852, Louis Napoleon became Napoleon III when the Second Empire was proclaimed. Thus, Louis Napoleon placed his career under the sign of Napoleon I.

16. See Delabroy for a thought-provoking examination of the status of 1848 in *Les Misérables.*

17. For a detailed analysis of the growing conflict between the government and the socialists, see Agulhon (27-72).

18. It should be pointed out that Hugo's opinion on the intentions of the provisional government is quite biased, a point which can be inferred from Wright's analysis (136).

19. I agree with Kahn on the point that Hugo had never been a socialist (685). Hugo's use of the word "socialism" and its derivatives is politically motivated. See Prélot and Lescuyer for an informative analysis of the different occurrences and meanings of the word "socialism" in France during the nineteenth century (599-603).

20. Various interpretations of the conflict between the socialists and the bourgeoisie are possible. For a presentation of the Marxist point of view, see Wright (133-38).

21. Enjolras's speech appears in "Quel horizon on voit du haut de la barricade" (11: 833-35). See Gusdorf for a study that shows the importance of Enjolras's speech in the context of the philosophy of *Les Misérables.* For another point of view on Enjolras's speech, see Leuilliot (104). See Sayre and Löwy for a well-documented study on the historical, social, and literary contexts concerning the insurrection portrayed in *Les Misérables.*

22. One example of the way in which the Second Empire placed workers at a disadvantage is found in the "Haussmannization" of Paris (Plessis 165-66).

23. For a list of the results of the legislative elections during the Second Empire, see Plessis (209). Based on the vote, the growth of the Opposition nearly tripled between 1857 and 1863.

24. Strictly speaking, *Les Misérables* covers the period extending from the beginnings of the Bourbon Restoration to the year after the June Insurrection of 1832 during the July Monarchy. In

"Quelques pages d'histoire," Hugo provides the reader with a survey of this period whose political climax, as far as the narrative of *Les Misérables* is concerned, is reached during the republican insurrection in Paris on the occasion of General Lamarque's funeral. See Gohin for a detailed discussion of the chronology of *Les Misérables*.

Works Cited

Agulhon, Maurice. *1848 ou l'apprentissage de la République: 1848-1852*. Paris: Seuil, 1979. Vol. 8 of *Nouvelle histoire de la France contemporaine*. 18 vols. 1979.

Bertier de Sauvigny, G. de. *Au soir de la monarchie: la Restauration*. 3rd ed. ("revue et augmentée"). Paris: Flammarion, 1974.

Bury, J. P. T. *Napoleon III and the Second Empire*. London: English UP, 1964.

Daumard, Adeline. *Les Bourgeois de Paris au XIXe siècle*. Paris: Flammarion, 1970.

Delabroy, Jean. "1848 et *Les Misérables* de Victor Hugo." *Lendemains* 28 (1982): 59-66.

Gohin, Yves. "Une histoire qui date." *Lire* Les Misérables. Eds. Anne Ubersfeld and Guy Rosa. Paris: José Corti, 1985. 29-57.

Guillemin, Henri. *Le coup du 2 décembre*. Paris: Gallimard, 1951.

Gusdorf, Georges. "'Quel horizon on voit du haut de la barricade'." *Hommage à Victor Hugo*. Strasbourg: Bulletin de la Faculté des Lettres de Strasbourg, 1962. 175-196.

Howarth, T. E. B. *Citizen-King: The Life of Louis-Philippe, King of the French*. London: Eyre and Spottiswoode, 1962.

Hugo, Victor. *Œuvres complètes*. Ed. Jean Massin. 18 vols. Paris: Le Club français du livre, 1967-1970.

Kahn, Jean-François. *L'Extraordinaire métamorphose: ou cinq ans de la vie de Victor Hugo (1847-1851)*. Paris: Seuil, 1984.

Leuilliot, Bernard. "*Quatrevingt-Treize* dans *Les Misérables*." *Romantisme* 60 (1988): 99-107.

Plessis, Alain. *De la fête impériale au mur des fédérés*. Paris: Seuil, 1979. Vol. 9 of *Nouvelle histoire de la France contemporaine*. 18 vols. 1979.

Prélot, Marcel and Georges Lescuyer. *Histoire des idées politiques*. 7th ed. Paris: Dalloz, 1980.

Sayre, Robert and Michael Löwy. *L'Insurrection des Misérables: romantisme et révolution en Juin 1832*. Archives des Lettres Modernes 253. Paris: Lettres Modernes, 1992.

Seebacher, Jacques. "La prise à partie de Louis-Napoléon." *Romantisme* 60 (1988): 77-82.

Spitzer, Alan. "The Good Napoleon III." *French Historical Studies* 2. 3 (1962): 308-29.

Thompson, J. M. *Louis Napoleon and the Second Empire*. 1955. New York: W. W. Norton, 1967.

Wright, Gordon. *France in Modern Times*. 3rd ed. New York: W. W. Norton, 1981.

Angelo Metzidakis (essay date fall-winter 1994-95)

SOURCE: Metzidakis, Angelo. "Victor Hugo and the Idea of a United States of Europe." *Nineteenth-Century French Studies* 23, nos. 1 & 2 (fall-winter 1994-95): 72-84.

[*In the following essay, Metzidakis traces Hugo's fervent support for the idea of the United States of Europe.*]

The idea of the United States of Europe was popularized in the aftermath of the crisis of 1848.[1] Its formation drew upon the idea of a federation of European states, whose origin predates the nineteenth century and was expounded by such thinkers as William Penn, the Abbé de Saint-Pierre and Kant. By 1848, the idea of such a federation was gaining momentum and would be discussed in the various peace congresses that would continue to meet throughout the latter half of the nineteenth century (Pegg 4-5).

Victor Hugo was one of the most influential proponents of the idea of the United States of Europe. He became the champion of the republican cause in France as a member of the Legislative Assembly during the late 1840's. As chair of the Paris Peace Conference, on August 21, 1849, Hugo exposed his vision of the seminal idea of the United States of Europe before an international audience. Although he was not the first to coin the term, Hugo played a decisive role in its dissemination both in France and beyond. The appeal of Hugo's vision is evident in the following excerpt from his speech:

> Un jour viendra où la guerre paraîtra aussi absurde et sera aussi impossible entre Paris et Londres, entre Pétersbourg et Berlin, entre Vienne et Turin, qu'elle serait impossible et qu'elle paraîtrait absurde aujourd'hui entre Rouen et Amiens. . . . Un jour viendra où vous . . . , nations du continent, sans perdre vos qualités distinctes et votre glorieuse individualité, vous vous fondrez dans une unité supérieure, et vous constituerez la fraternité européenne. . . . Un jour viendra où il n'y aura plus d'autres champs de bataille que les marchés s'ouvrant au commerce et les esprits s'ouvrant aux idées. Un jour viendra où les boulets et les bombes se-

ront remplacés par les votes, par le suffrage universel
des peuples, par le vénérable arbitrage d'un grand sénat
souverain. . . .

(7: 219)[2]

Hugo then announces, for the first time in his *oeuvre,*
the creation of the United States of Europe whose commercial and cultural ties with the United States of
America would influence the entire world (7: 220).

Within the context of Hugo's work, the origin of the
idea of the United States of Europe can be traced back
to a diplomatic incident in 1827. During a reception at
the Austrian embassy on January 24, 1827, four mar-
shals of the Empire were announced by their names and
not by their ducal titles. This action was construed as
an insult to the glory of France's imperial past. French
public opinion, especially in liberal circles, became indignant.

Two weeks later, Hugo responded to the Austrian affront by writing the ode entitled *A la colonne de la
place Vendôme.* Hugo's ode is more than just a patriotic cry in response to Austria's diplomatic pettiness; it
is an expression of his frustration with the Bourbon
monarchy. In Hugo's view, Bourbon policies should
reconcile the grandeur of France's imperial past with
the present aspirations of the French for a relatively
more liberal future, a future in which the Vienna Settlements of 1814-1815 would no longer be a prime consideration in French political decision-making.

In this ode, Hugo glorifies Napoleon and equates his
legacy with that of France's other "giant," Charlemagne.
By doing so, Hugo evokes the dream of French empire,
a preliminary form of the idea that would later become
the United States of Europe in his work. From 1827 to
1849, the growth of the idea of a unified Europe under
French guidance, if not control, would parallel the development of Hugo's liberalism.

Although Hugo pays hommage to the Bourbon monarchy in *A la colonne de la place Vendôme,* his liberalism is evidenced by his allusions to the various movements of independence of that time:

> Quoi! le globe est ému de volcans électriques;
> Derrière l'océan grondent les Amériques;
> Stamboul rugit; Hellé remonte aux jours anciens;
> Lisbonne se débat aux mains de l'Angleterre . . .
> Seul, le vieux peuple franc s'indigne que la terre
> Tremble à d'autres pas que les siens!

(2: 788)

For example, the mention of the wars of independence
in Latin America against the legitimate monarchies of
Spain and Portugal shows that Hugo has turned away
from the ultra-royalist position of his youth. Some two

years later, Hugo's allusion to the Latin American wars
of independence would take on a much deeper significance with the publication of *Fragment d'histoire.*

Fragment d'histoire was originally written in 1827 and
was to be a part of the preface to *Cromwell.* However,
before being published separately in 1829, Hugo added
to his text passages referring indirectly to the struggle
for independence in the Americas.[3] For example, at the
end of *Fragment d'histoire,* Hugo foresees that a main
characteristic of European civilization will be surpassed
by a new, American principle:

> Nous voulons parler ici du principe d'émancipation, de
> progrès et de liberté, qui semble devoir être désormais
> la loi de l'humanité. . . . Aussi, si ce principe est ap-
> pelé, comme nous le croyons avec joie, à refaire la so-
> ciété des hommes, l'Amérique en sera le centre. . . .
> Aux trois théocraties successives d'Asie, d'Afrique et
> d'Europe succédera la famille universelle. Le principe
> d'autorité fera place au principe de liberté . . .

(5: 154-155)

When Hugo speaks of America in the preceding passage, he is referring only in part to the United States of
America. In the mid-1820's at the Pan-American congress in Panama, Simon Bolivar had proposed the creation of a "holy alliance of nations" (Juin 547) incorporating all American states in order to oppose the
despotic policies of the European monarchies in the
New World. Although Bolivar's proposal would fail, his
idea provided Hugo with the hope that a similar system
could rejuvenate France and allow France to assume a
leading role in the reorganization of Europe.

Between 1830 and 1840, Hugo had not yet elaborated
his ideas on the exact role that France would play in the
new Europe of the future. With Bolivar's death at the
end of December 1830, Hugo's hopes for a United
States of the Americas, and what would later become
the idea of the United States of Europe, were dashed
(Juin 622). What remained in his mind was the grandeur of the Napoleonic Empire whose memory was
maintained throughout this period and beyond by the
continued development of the Napoleonic myth of
which he was one of the main propagators.

In 1840, an international crisis would force Hugo to
formulate clearly his political ideas. Europe seemed to
be on the verge of war, and France was in isolation, its
national pride seemed to be on the line as it had been in
1827.

Here is a summary of the events that led to the crisis of
1840. In June 1839, Mehemet Ali, pacha of Egypt, defeated the Turkish sultan whose forces were attempting
to retake Syria. The French had been aiding Mehemet
Ali, and French public opinion rallied to the side of
Egypt. In June 1840, Palmerston arranged an agreement

with Austria, Prussia and Russia that would limit the influence of Mehemet Ali by depriving him of most of his gains. By July 1840, French public opinion was in an uproar because France seemed to be confronted by the same coalition that had humiliated her after Napoleon's defeat![4] This action appeared to renew the Vienna Settlements of 1814-1815. Concurrently, there was a swelling of anti-German sentiment in France. In the end, the Pasha rejected Palmerston's ultimatum counting on French support. When the British forces moved to help the Turks drive Mehemet Ali from Syria, the French did nothing. The crisis of 1840 ended when France accepted the settlement arranged by England and the other powers.

Although the Egyptian Crisis had been settled, Franco-German relations remained problematic on account of a quarrel concerning the status of the west bank of the Rhine river, which the French wanted to claim as belonging to France. The uproar that Nicolas Becker's poem, the *Rheinlied,* had caused when it was published on September 18, 1840, provoked an even greater reaction on June 1, 1841, when it was republished by the *Revue de Paris,* along with Lamartine's conciliatory response *La Marseillaise de la Paix.* Two weeks later, other, harsher responses to Becker's poem would be published, notably, the *Rhin allemand* by Musset and *Le Rhin* by Quinet.

Although Hugo's well-known response to the Rhine controversy would be published in the conclusion to *Le Rhin* in 1842, his concerns about France and its role in Europe are sketched out in his induction speech to the Académie Française on June 3, 1841. His speech restates and develops further his ideas from *A la colonne de la place Vendôme.* While in 1827 his ode opposed the pettiness of the Austrian insult with the grandeur of the Napoleonic Empire, his speech at the Académie Française is, in effect, a subdued call for action, for Hugo seems to offer his political services to the government of Louis Philippe.

One of the main themes of his speech is that Napoleon was Charlemagne's successor and that he had established the basis for a new Europe through, among other things, the creation of the Rhenish Confederation (Descotes 27): "Il avait construit son état au centre de l'Europe comme une citadelle, lui donnant pour bastions et pour ouvrages avancés dix monarchies qu'il avait fait entrer à la fois dans son empire et dans sa famille" (6: 146). Hugo goes on to maintain that, even though the Napoleonic Empire has been undone, France's territorial integrity, its "God-given form," can never be altered permanently, in spite of the actions of "coalitions, reactions and congresses." Hugo thereby intimates that a new Europe can only be viable if the west bank of the Rhine river is returned to France. At this point, however, he offers no concrete proposal, but

he hopes for the appearance of a new Malesherbes who would counsel the king in order to diffuse the growing tensions in Franco-German relations in the aftermath of the Egyptian Crisis of 1840. The government quickly put an end to Hugo's timid candidacy by having Salvandy say, in its official response before the Académie Française, that Malesherbes was not one of Hugo's ancestors.

The heart of Hugo's solution to the Franco-German crisis would be formulated in a poem entitled *Hymne pour l'inauguration de la colonne de Napoléon à Boulogne,* dated July 30, 1841:

> Dieu veut la grande France et la grande Allemagne.
> Il fit Napoléon comme il fit Charlemagne,
> Pour donner à l'Europe un centre souverain.
> Que Stamboul meure, alors vers l'orient tournée,
> Teutonia, de gloire et de paix couronnée,
> Reprendra le Danube et nous rendra le Rhin!
>
> (6: 976)

In this poem, Hugo yearns for a new European empire whose center would be based on the confederation of two states, France and Prussia. Hugo's correspondence shows that he knew that his poem was too bellicose and that it was too adventurous for France's foreign affairs (6: 1212-1213). He also must have known that such an idea would have been rejected by the government, given Louis Philippe's repeated efforts for the establishment of closer ties with the British.

In spite of governmental policies favoring the development of Franco-British entente, Hugo pursued his idea of a European confederation that would ally France with Prussia by publishing *Le Rhin, lettres à un ami* in January 1842. In its conclusion, which was written during the previous July, Hugo exposes in detail his argument: "L'alliance de la France et de l'Allemagne, c'est la constitution de l'Europe. L'Allemagne adossée à la France arrête la Russie; la France amicalement adossée à l'Allemagne arrête l'Angleterre" (6: 535). When Hugo says "Allemagne," he means Prussia. He favored a united Germany under Prussian rule to the detriment of Austria, which he associated with blows to France's national pride, namely, the Vienna Settlements and the Austrian insult at its Paris embassy in 1827. The same can be said about the reference to England and Russia, for they are also enemies as far as Hugo's Bonapartist sentiments are concerned.

In his conclusion to *Le Rhin,* Hugo describes a united Europe whose unity and strength would be produced by the peaceful coexistence of the French and German empires. He views Europe in terms of a balance of power, as an entity to be constructed in terms of a military metaphor:

> Il faut, pour que l'univers soit en équilibre, qu'il y ait
> en Europe, comme la double clef de voûte du conti-
> nent, deux grands états du Rhin, tous deux fécondés et

étroitement unis par ce fleuve régénérateur; l'un sep-
tentrional et oriental, l'Allemagne, s'appuyant à la Bal-
tique, à l'Adriatique et à la mer Noire, avec la Suède,
le Danemark, la Grèce et les principautés du Danube
pour arc-boutants; l'autre méridional et occidental, la
France, s'appuyant à la Méditerranée et à l'Océan, avec
l'Italie et l'Espagne pour contre-forts.

(6: 519-520)

Although Hugo claims to support his reasoning by
drawing on the plans of Charlemagne, Louis XIV and
Napoleon, the influence of the Napoleonic legend is unmistakable in his thought in the early 1840's. Hugo
would become greatly disillusioned, some thirty years
later, by the siege of Paris during the Franco-Prussian
war.[5]

Hugo's ideas on Germany that were exposed in *Le Rhin*
would be illustrated in *Les Burgraves* in 1843. There
is, however, a change of scope that Hugo is careful to
underscore in his preface to this play. Hugo now envi-
sions Europe as an independent entity that is no longer
considered in terms of a Franco-Germanic confederation. According to the preface, "le poète qui raconte la
lutte des burgraves fait aujourd'hui pour l'Europe une
oeuvre . . . nationale" (6: 574). By saying so, Hugo
maintains that the theme of German unity in *Les Burgraves* is symbolic of the international unity that will
one day be characteristic of a united Europe in which
France would be the first among nations. Furthermore,
Hugo's fervent wish is to extend France's cultural he-
gemony to all of the world: "avoir pour patrie le monde
et pour nation l'humanité" (6: 575).

The preface to *Les Burgraves* provides the transition
between the united Europe under Franco-Prussian domination that was portrayed in *Le Rhin* and the United
States of Europe that Hugo would proclaim in his 1849
speech as chair of the Paris Peace Conference. Hugo
seems to confirm this evolution in his thought by alluding to the initial state of his idea of the United States of
Europe in *Le Rhin* during his 1849 speech: "Un jour
viendra où la guerre paraîtra . . . absurde entre Paris et
Londres, entre Pétersbourg et Berlin . . ." (7: 219). The
allusion to the ideas in *Le Rhin* is clear: Paris and Berlin, i.e., France and a Prussian dominated Germany,
would form the core of a united Europe, and London
and Petersburg, i.e., England and Russia, would be held
in check by France and Germany, respectively. It is important to note, however, that Hugo, in his 1849 speech,
has transcended the opposition or, better, the balance of
powers on the Continent that had been characteristic of
his earlier thought. Furthermore, the wish for global
peace that had been expressed at the end of the preface
to *Les Burgraves* has been fully developed in his 1849
speech; the united Europe of 1843 has been transformed
into the United States of Europe, with the hope of becoming, one day, a global body.

In his speech at the Paris Peace Conference, Hugo presents a utopian vision of the future in which Europe
and the world will develop and prosper in peace. He asserts in evangelical fashion that the concept of universal
peace is a logical extension of the revolutionary ideal of
fraternity: fraternity among citizens is extended to all of
the human race. He maintains that such an expansion
can be achieved through the progressive implementation of universal suffrage, first within the framework of
a European federation and, eventually, within that of a
world federation. Universal suffrage would be the expression of the common good and, through the mediation of a supranational senate, all disputes could be
solved, thus eliminating the possibility of war. The
elimination of the threat of war would then necessitate
the disbanding of national armies and would free fund-
ing for all kinds of programs and development that
would promote interdependence and the continued expansion of republican ideology. Hugo claims that this
would eventually result in unification for the common
good and would entail the founding of the United States
of Europe.

Hugo's heralding of "European fraternity" in the form
of the United States of Europe has been criticized for
not giving much thought to how such a supranational
political entity could be realized in practical terms.
While political scientists have berated Hugo for not
having pondered what form the United States of Europe
might take, historians have taken him to task for the
content of his thought. Denis de Rougemont wrote that
Hugo "effected the 'transfiguration' of the ideals of
1848 into a sublime Europeanism and universalism,
thus consummating—but in the realm of the imagination only—the nationalist dialectics of political romanticism" (264). From the historian's point of view, Hugo
is only a visionary with utopian ideas. The poetic content of Hugo's thought would therefore provide sufficient grounds for its rejection.

As cogent as Hugo's prophecy may be for the world today, the importance of this speech is not to be found in
Hugo's ability to elucidate the future through a form of
"poetic projection" (Kahn 621), but rather in the development of his political thought. Generally speaking,
Hugo's use of the United States of Europe is politically
motivated and is related to the growth of his republican
beliefs.[6] Hugo had taken up the cause of the ideals of
revolution of 1848 at a time when former liberals had
become disillusioned and had rejected them. For example, during his political speeches in the Legislative
Assembly, Hugo was increasingly ridiculed by the Right
when he spoke on such issues as the elimination of abject poverty ("misère") from French society (7: 207-
216),[7] the political implications for the Second Republic
of sending French soldiers to Italy in support of Pope
Pius IX who had been expulsed from Rome by republican revolutionaries (7: 239-254), the bill on the free-

dom of education that would, on the contrary, assure a preponderant role for the Church in the public schools (7: 254-267), and the political motives behind the bill that would restrict universal suffrage (7: 280-298). By addressing these issues in a polemical fashion, Hugo intended to bring out into the open the antirepublican agenda of the Right.[8]

Hugo was frustrated with the growing conservatism of the Legislative Assembly, especially after the elections of May 1849 (Bruhat 1284). His appointment as chair of the Paris Peace Conference in August of the same year provided him with a ready-made forum in which he could present a précis of his liberal beliefs to a receptive audience. Later, after the fall of the Second Republic, the ideas associated with this speech would assume their full importance in Hugo's *oeuvre*. By that time, he had become a militant republican. The idealistic themes attendant to the idea of the United States of Europe became radically politicized. Throughout the exile period, Hugo would use them to attack the supporters of the Second Empire.[9]

Although the term "United States of Europe" virtually disappears in prose texts that address the general reading public during the exile period,[10] the themes associated with this term have been transposed and developed further in these texts. The untempered republican vision of a super republic on the European continent presented in Hugo's Paris Peace Conference speech in 1849 has been toned down in the form of a European federation that would apparently preserve the national identity and predominance of the French in what Hugo calls "l'Europe des peuples" (8: 532). The label may have changed, but the ideological content of this idea has remained basically the same since the 1849 speech.

The wavering between the choice of a super republic and a federation of European states is most evident in *Napoléon le Petit* (1852), in which Hugo excoriates Louis Napoleon Bonaparte for betraying his constitutional oath and for causing the destruction of the Second Republic. The United States of Europe appears in the original manuscript of *Napoléon le Petit* in the following passage:

> [S]ouhaitons cette dernière guerre que j'ai appelée quelque part *la guerre des patries contre les royaumes,* et d'où sortiront les Etats-Unis d'Europe, d'où sortira le parlement continental, la fédération des nations, la fusion des races, la civilisation suprême, la Paix! Ne l'oublions pas, on ne clora la révolution universelle que par la république universelle.
>
> (8: 539)

This passage, which was not published in *Napoléon le Petit,* appears in a much longer text that deals with universal peace in much the same terms as the peace speech in 1849; it even includes many of the same analogies.

In the published version of *Napoléon le Petit,* however, the excised text mentioned above is recouped in a way that demonstrates the importance of Hugo's Paris Peace Conference speech in 1849. The United States of Europe is now referred to as "l'union de l'Europe et de la fédération démocratique du continent" (8: 516). Hugo maintains, as he had in 1849, that its eventual realization was in the divine scheme of things, adding that the Second Empire was only a temporary obstacle on the way to the creation of the predestined European federation. Significantly, Hugo reasserts the themes associated with the United States of Europe in the conclusion to *Napoléon le Petit,* where he reevaluates the significance of the revolution of 1848 while appealing to the moral grandeur of the French nation and to its role in the reorganization of Europe in view of the messianic character of the French Revolution. In the concluding section of *Napoléon le Petit,* entitled "Deuil et foi," Hugo mourns the demise of the misunderstood Second Republic, and he professes his faith in the future Republic and the advent of universal peace. In the latter part of this text, the idealistic themes of the political credo that Hugo had formulated in relatively benign terms in 1849 have been radically politicized to suit the militant aims of his anti-imperial republicanism.

In 1862, almost ten years after the publication of *Napoléon le Petit,* another avatar of the United States of Europe would appear in *Les Misérables,* in a chapter entitled "Quel horizon on voit du haut de la barricade" (11: 833-835).[11] Hugo had originally thought of omitting this chapter because of the growing length of *Les Misérables,* but he decided to keep it, citing the crucial importance of the barricade scene in his novel.[12] Although Hugo's barricade is located on Chanvrerie Street during the insurrection of 1832, it evokes with precision the decor and events surrounding the very real Saint-Merry barricade. Furthermore, based on the speech by Enjolras, the head of the revolutionaries in the novel, the barricade scene is emblematic of those of other revolutionary moments in French history, including those of the revolution of 1848, to the extent that Enjolras' speech seems "to sum up the profession of faith of the French revolutionaries of the nineteenth century" (Gusdorf 177-178). More importantly, this scene contains a statement of Hugo's own profession of faith transposed from his 1849 Paris Peace Conference speech.

Before the barricade is attacked in *Les Misérables,* Enjolras proclaims the following:

> Nous allons à l'union des peuples; nous allons à l'unité de l'homme. Plus de fictions; plus de parasites. . . . La civilisation tiendra ses assises au sommet de l'Europe, et plus tard au centre des continents, dans un grand parlement de l'intelligence. . . . La France porte cet avenir sublime dans ses flancs. C'est là la gestation du dix-neuvième siècle.
>
> (11: 834)

In his pronouncement, Enjolras speaks of the idea of European federation and fraternity while at the same time reemploying most of the themes and analogies that Hugo had used in his Paris Peace Conference speech in 1849, and again in *Napoléon le Petit,* but without the mordant style encountered in his polemical writing of the early 1850s.

Why did Hugo attach so much importance to Enjolras' speech in the barricade scene? The answer to this question must take into account the changing political climate in France at the time that Hugo decided to revise and complete the manuscript of *Les Misérables.* In the years following the legislative elections of 1857, the political base of the Second Empire began to erode (Plessis 191-201). The fragility of Napoleon III's personal rule was brought to light, especially after Orsini's attempted assassination of the Emperor on January 14, 1858. In response to this attack, the government instituted repressive measures, which included a wave of arrests that led to the deportation of many republicans. The imperial regime was not able to root out the small, but growing opposition movement that several of Napoleon III's so-called liberal, personal initiatives would only foster in the years to come. In view of this new political climate in France, Hugo began the revision and completion of *Les Misérables* at the start of the 1860s in an attempt to bring all those who were growing disenchanted with the Second Empire into the republican camp.

Given the changing political climate in France in the early 1860s, the significance that Hugo attached to Enjolras' speech is clear: if he hoped to attract those who were becoming ever more disaffected with the conservative policies of the Second Empire, what better platform could he devise other than the one that he had used himself in his Paris Peace Conference speech in 1849? To the extent that Hugo was seeking the support of a liberal, if not republican, audience for his anti-Empire position, the ideas that he had put forth when he himself was about to break away from the conservative Right and become a republican were exemplary. Hugo's sense of timing was quite opportune, for the growing unpopularity of the regime would be witnessed by the elections of 1863, just one year after the enormously successful publication of his novel.

With the exception of Enjolras' speech, Hugo does not devote much space in *Les Misérables* to his ideas on European federation. This is quite understandable because his primary political goal was to reestablish republicanism in France in order to do away with Napoleon III. The themes of European federation are present nevertheless because they are part and parcel of the aspirations of the revolution of 1848, whose idealistic principles became leitmotifs in *Les Misérables.*

The importance of Hugo's Paris Peace Conference speech in 1849 stretches far beyond his literary production, his political career and even his lifetime. Hugo had popularized the idea of a United States of Europe which would reappear, now and then, in the context of discussions on European integration.[13] With the passage of time, Hugo's vision of the United States of Europe seems closer to being realized. A new Europe has emerged within the past forty years: in 1957, the Treaty of Rome established the original European Economic Community; in 1965, the Brussels Treaty approved the 1967 formation of the present Commission of European Communities, the EC; and in 1986, the Single European Act set 1992 as a target date for a "Europe without frontiers."

Will the Hugolian utopia ever come to term and thereby inaugurate the reign of universal peace? The author of *Les Misérables* responds indirectly to this question in a passage on the nature and power of revolutionary beliefs: "Rien n'est tel que le dogme pour enfanter le rêve. Rien n'est tel que le rêve pour engendrer l'avenir" (11: 481).

Notes

1. In the introduction to this article, I have drawn upon Pierre Renouvin's work on the emergence of the idea of the United States of Europe and on European federation. His work was drawn to my attention indirectly while I was reading Morin's highly synthetic and thought-provoking study on the evolution of the concept of Europe. I noticed that Morin, in a single paragraph (63), referred to Victor Hugo, the idea of the United States of Europe, the liberation of national groups, republican democracy and European federation; he does this while citing Duroselle, Rougemont and Voyenne as sources, all three of whom, I later realized, refer back to Renouvin's seminal work (Duroselle 217; Rougemont 270; Voyenne 243). Although Renouvin's observations were initially formulated during the late 1940s, they have become part of the established canon and, for the most part, have withstood the test of time.

2. Throughout this article, references to volume and page citations are to the chronological edition of Hugo's works: *Œuvres complètes* (Le Club français du livre), ed. Jean Massin.

3. Such reference to the Americas in 1829 develops the significance that can be attributed to the Americas in the 1827 ode *A la colonne de la place Vendôme.* In fact, Hugo does so retrospectively by republishing *Fragment d'histoire* in 1834 as part of *Littérature et Philosophie mêlées* and attributing the 1829 version of this text to the year 1827. And at an even later date, Hugo would underscore

the perceived relationship between his ode and his historical fragment by claiming that 1827 had been the year when he became a liberal (9: 1020).

4. See Gaudon for an insightful analysis of the French public's reaction to the 1840 London treaty (6: 175-177). His commentary on the relationship between the Orient and the grandeur of France's imperial past in the popular imagination is particularly revealing. It helps to explain, in part, why Hugo proposed Ali Pasha as Napoleon's replacement at the end of the preface to *Les Orientales* (January 1829).

5. See Messières for a detailed discussion of Hugo's disillusionment with Germany (427-428). For further commentary, see Savey-Casard (430-432).

6. It is true, as one of the anonymous readers remarked, that some of the motivation in the 1840s is personal ambition.

7. In *L'Homme qui rit* (1869), the chapter entitled "Les Tempêtes d'hommes pire que les tempêtes d'océans" contains a fictionalized account of Hugo's reception by the Right (14: 346-355). This chapter contains several allusions to his speech on *la Misère* (July 9, 1849).

8. Kahn's book is devoted to the study of Hugo's "extraordinary metamorphosis" in terms of his political evolution from 1847 to 1851. His vivid presentation of the parliamentary debates within the ideological context of this period is very useful.

9. Hugo used the term "United States of Europe," after 1849, on the following, major occasions: 1) on July 17, 1851, when he opposed the proposal for the revision of the constitution that would have permitted Louis Napoleon Bonaparte, the future Napoleon III, to renew his mandate as president of the Second Republic; 2) on August 1, 1852, in Antwerp, before a group of fellow French republicans in exile, upon embarking for London in order to avoid the possible consequences of the publication of *Napoléon le Petit,* his diatribe against Louis Napoleon Bonaparte; 3) on November 29, 1853, in Jersey, to commemorate the twenty-third anniversary of the Polish revolution; 4) on February 24, 1854, to commemorate the revolution of 1848; 5) on February 24, 1855, to commemorate again the revolution of 1848; 6) on September 4, 1869, at the International Peace Conference in Lausanne; 7) on September 9, 1870, in a text published both in French and German, to the Prussians forces that would besiege Paris after the French military defeat at Sedan; 8) on September 20, 1872, in a letter to the members of the International Peace Conference in Lugano; 9) on July 18, 1874, in a letter to Saint-Martin; 10) on September 4, 1874, in a

letter to the members of the Peace Conference in Geneva; 11) on April 16, 1876, in a speech during a fundraiser for sending a workers' delegation to Philadelphia; 12) on August 29, 1876, in a speech dealing with the Serbian crisis before the National Assembly; 13) on March 25, 1877, in a speech during a fund-raiser for the workers of Lyon; 14) on May 18, 1879, in a speech commemorating the abolition of slavery in 1848; and 15) on August 31, 1881, in his last will and testament, in which he bequeathed the totality of his manuscripts and drawings to the future National Library of the United States of Europe. Other occurrences of the United States of Europe are found in the chronological edition of Hugo's works, for example, in 7: 659-660, in 9: 1021, in 10: 736, and in 14: 873, 1306 and 1307. They are, however, of minor significance.

10. I agree with another one of the anonymous readers who pointed out the reason why Hugo makes little mention of the United States of Europe in the literary texts of the exile period. The idea of the United States of Europe is linked to Hugo's notion of imperialism as a missionary force. When imperialism became a colonizing force under Napoleon III, Hugo stopped using this term.

11. I basically agree with Gusdorf, who has written a comprehensive analysis of this chapter of *Les Misérables.*

12. See Leuilliot's book, Victor Hugo publie *Les Misérables,* for the text of the letter in which Hugo explains why the barricade scene must be retained (328). See Leuilliot's article, "Les barricades mystérieuses," for an interesting analysis of Hugo's portrayal of his experiences in 1848.

13. Here are but a few examples: 1) After an international congress in Geneva in 1867, a group of delegates established the International League for Peace and Freedom whose journal *Les Etats-Unis d'Europe* would be published in Bern fairly regularly until 1922, and in Paris from 1922 until 1938 (Pegg 5, 166); 2) In July 1921, a German economist named Johannes Bell spoke in the Reichstag and referred to the United States of Europe and to the idea of the "solidarity of the peoples of Europe" in the context of one of Hugo's speeches (Pegg 20); 3) In 1930, Hugo's Paris Peace Conference speech was read in its entirety at the Second Pan-European Congress (Pegg 144); 4) In the early 1940's, the French resistance proclaimed its support of a United States of Europe (Schmitt 15); and 5) In September 1946, Sir Winston Churchill in a speech at Zurich University recommended the building of "a kind of United States of Europe." With respect to the 1867 Geneva conference, Pegg states the following: "At the larger and more im-

posing international conference in Geneva in 1867, the delegates, inspired by such well-known personalities as Guiseppe Garibaldi, John Stuart Mill, Edgar Quinet, Charles Lemonnier, *as well as Victor Hugo,* debated the idea [of the United States of Europe]. . . ." (5; my emphasis). Hugo did not attend the conference. See Hugo's correspondence in 13: 875, 877 and 878-9.

Works Cited

Bruhat, Jean. "Situation historique: 1844-1851." *Œuvres complètes.* By Victor Hugo. Ed. Jean Massin. Vol. 7. Paris: Le Club français du livre, 1967-1970. 1259-1298. 18 vols.

Descotes, Maurice. *La Légende de Napoléon et les écrivains français du XIXe siècle.* Bibliothèque de littérature et d'histoire 9. Paris: Lettres modernes-Minard, 1967.

Duroselle, Jean-Baptiste. *L'idée d'Europe dans l'histoire.* Paris: Denoël, 1965.

Gaudon, Jean. "Présentation du *Rhin.*" *Œuvres complètes.* By Victor Hugo. Ed. Jean Massin. Vol. 6. Paris: Le Club français du livre, 1967-1970. 173-191. 18 vols.

Gusdorf, Georges. "'Quel horizon on voit du haut de la barricade'." *Hommage à Victor Hugo.* Strasbourg: Bulletin de la Faculté des Lettres de Strasbourg, 1962. 175-196.

Hugo, Victor. *Œuvres complètes.* Ed. Jean Massin. 18 vols. Paris: Le Club français du livre, 1967-1970.

Juin, Hubert. *Victor Hugo: 1802-1843.* Vol. 1. Paris: Flammarion, 1980-86. 3 vols.

Kahn, Jean-François. *L'extraordinaire métamorphose: ou cinq ans de la vie de Victor Hugo: 1847-1851.* Paris: Seuil, 1984.

Leuilliot, Bernard. *Victor Hugo publie* Les Misérables. Paris: Klincksieck, 1970.

————. "Les barricades mystérieuses." *Europe* (Mar. 1985): 127-136.

Messières, René de. "Victor Hugo et les États-Unis d'Europe." *French Review* 25 (1952): 413-429.

Morin, Edgar. *Penser l'Europe.* Paris: Gallimard, 1987.

Pegg, Carl H. *Evolution of the European Idea, 1914-1932.* Chapel Hill: U of North Carolina P, 1983.

Plessis, Alain. *De la fête impériale au mur des fédérés.* Vol. 9 of *Nouvelle histoire de la France contemporaine.* Paris: Seuil, 1979. 18 vols.

Renouvin, P. "L'idée des Etats-Unis d'Europe pendant la crise de 1848." *Actes du Congrès historique du Centenaire de la Révolution de 1848.* Paris: PU de France, 1949. 31-45.

————. *L'idée de la fédération européenne dans la pensée politique du XIXe siècle.* Oxford: Clarendon Press, 1949.

Rougemont, Denis de. *The Idea of Europe.* Trans. Norbert Guterman. 1966. Cleveland: Meridian-World Publishing, 1968.

Savey-Casard, Paul. "Le Pacifisme de Victor Hugo." *Revue de littérature comparée* 35 (1961): 421-432.

Schmitt, Hans A. *The Path to European Union: From the Marshall Plan to the Common Market.* Baton Rouge: Louisiana State UP, 1962.

Voyenne, Bernard. *Histoire de l'idée européenne.* Paris: Payot, 1964.

Mary Anne O'Neil (essay date 1994)

SOURCE: O'Neil, Mary Anne. "Classical Terror/Gothic Terror: Victor Hugo's *Quatrevingt-treize.*" *Poetica* 39-40 (1994): 259-73.

[*In the following essay, O'Neil avers that* Quatrevingt-treize *is not just a fictionalized account of the political events of 1793 (the Reign of Terror), but a study of the terrors that have hindered mankind's progress throughout history: "fanaticism, intransigence, war and capital punishment."*]

It is hardly an exaggeration to claim that Victor Hugo maintained a life-long obsession with the Middle Ages. In her exhaustive study of the subject, *The Medievalism of Victor Hugo,* Patricia Ward has traced Hugo's interest in medieval architecture, history, and literature that manifests itself in his early novel *Notre-Dame de Paris,* as well as in his poetry from 1826 through *La Légende des Siècles* and his drama from *La Préface de Cromwell* of 1827 to *Les Burgraves* of the 1840s. While Ward believes that Hugo's admiration for the Middle Ages waned considerably after the 1860s (100-108), his final novel, *Quatrevingt-treize* of 1873, quite obviously returns to medieval literary motifs, which may provide a clue to this work's highly ambiguous treatment of historical material.

Quatrevingt-treize does take place, as the title suggests, in the summer of 1793 and concentrates on two crucial events of the Terror, the Committee of Public Safety's rise to power and the Vendean civil war. In addition, Parts I and II, which comprise about half of the novel, rely on extensive historical documentation[1] to evoke the political events of this period and to recreate, in a detailed, realistic manner, the ambiances of Paris and Brittany, as well as the appearance, speech and psychology of the revolutionaries and the reactionaries. However, the third part of the novel curiously seems to veer away from history. The long descriptions of battle scenes between the Whites or Royalist insurrectionists, and the Blues, the Republican soldiers, are highly melodramatic. The plot focuses upon the rescue of three Breton peasant children held hostage by the Royalists in a burning castle rather than on the civil war. Moreover, the characters Hugo specifically patterns after real historical types act in ways that strike the reader as historically uncharacteristic. Lantenac, the aristocratic leader of the Breton insurrectionists, whom Hugo describes as the only man capable of thwarting the Revolution, sacrifices the royalist cause by saving the children and delivering himself into his enemy's hands. His nephew Gauvain, a noble-turned-fervent-republican and brilliant military strategist, undoes his defense of the fatherland by freeing Lantenac and thus perpetuating the political conflict. Cimourdain, expriest and rigid ideologue, the representative of the Committee of Public Safety, places the Terror's laws in an ironic light by committing suicide after ordering the execution of his protégé Gauvain for treason. The final symbol that Hugo offers of 1793 is of the guillotine, hardly a positive souvenir of the Terror's contribution to progress. If we recall how Hugo defended the Revolution throughout his mature writings as well as how painstakingly he researched his subject before putting pen to paper, we may well wonder why *Quatrevingt-treize,* his only published prose work devoted uniquely to this pivotal moment in world history, takes such an unusual turn.[2]

The almost mystical transformation of Gauvain in the novel's final pages suggests a rapprochement between this work and Hugo's masterpieces of the 1850s and 1860s, *La Légende des siècles* and *Les Misérables,* which interpret history as a progression from darkness to light and matter to spirit through the awakening of the human conscience, self-sacrifice, and the victory of divine love over earthly justice. In addition, as in both the early *Préface de Cromwell* and the much later *William Shakespeare* (1864), Hugo seems obsessed in *Quatrevingt-treize* with understanding the literature that expresses, but also shapes, this simultaneously intellectual and moral evolution. Hugo makes special references to the Greco-Roman world in his description of the Convention in Part II of *Quatrevingt-treize* and then switches his attention to Arthurian legends and Romance literature in the initial chapters of Part III, *En Vendée.* Through these allusions, which associate the Revolutionaries with classical antiquity and the Royalists with the Middle Ages, Hugo examines two conflicting worldviews that contribute to the formation of the protagonists of 1793 and that propose radically different ways of understanding the individual's duty to society as well as the individual's potential for participating in society's redemption. These allusions also enable Hugo to analyze the myriad forms of evil that accompany political change. *Quatrevingt-treize* thus becomes not just a fictional recreation of 1793, the Terror, but rather an intertext for the study of fanaticism, intransigence, war and capital punishment, the terrors that have thwarted human progress throughout history.

In *Quatrevingt-treize,* the streets of Paris resemble the Forum of Ancient Rome. "On y vivait en public" (*Q. T.,* I, 116), exposed to revolutionary propaganda in the form of posters, sculpture and theatre. The city's parks are immense training grounds for this modern republic's army. Hugo evokes the fad of classical first names through a pun: "Ce pitou raillait la mode des noms grecs et latins; sa chanson favorite était sur un savetier qu'il appelait Cujus, et dont il appelait la femme Cujusdam" (*Q. T.,* I, 117). French versions of Latin terms such as "civisme," "unité," "égalité," "fraternité," visible in governmental decrees and on statues, furnish the intellectual foundations of the age.

Hugo insists upon this imitation of classical antiquity even more clearly in his description of the Convention Hall. He portrays the hastily erected home of this constitutional assembly as a neoclassical structure of strict geometrical lines: "des bancs symmétriques, une tribune carrée, des pilastres parallèles . . . de longues étraves rectilignes, des alvéoles rectangulaires" (*Q. T.,* I, 165), reminiscent of Roman architecture and city planning. Hugo tells us that the great Roman architect Vitruvius reigned unchallenged in the Paris of 1793 (*Q. T.,* I, 168). Decorating the building are "une grande grisaille peinte par David" (*Q. T.,* I, 164-165), "un vélarium romain, des draperies grecques" (*Q. T.,* I, 165), statues of the Spartan and Athenian lawgivers Lycurgus and Solon, plaster *fasces,* bundles of rods with an ax that symbolized the power of the Roman lectors, "la hache en dehors" (*Q. T.,* I, 169).

Hugo's insistence upon a Greco-Roman ambiance is historically accurate. The intellectual leaders of the French Revolution did look to the classical world for role models. R. R. Palmer, the great historian of the Terror, tells us that "they remembered their ancient history, or moral episodes they took to be history, and they saw more idealized republics, the polished citizens of Athens, the stern patriots of Sparta, the incorruptible heroes of early Rome" (19). Moreover, they translated this admiration for the governments of Greece and Rome into concrete symbols that became part of popular Parisian culture: "they wore phrygian caps, built triumphal arches, and erected statues . . . to all the classical virtues, crowned their heroes with laurel wreaths" (Cobban, I, 174). Hugo's neoclassical Paris is not picturesque, however; it is ironic and disquieting. Instead of evoking the eternal, this décor appears unstable. No more than a temporary framework between the permanent pavilions of the Tuileries palace, its columns and arches made from barrel staves, crates and putty, the Convention Hall could neither survive the Revolution nor even contain the tempestuous debates between the

Mountain and the Gironde held within its walls (*Q. T.,* I, 165). Rather than reason or nature, this edifice suggests repression: "Tout cet ensemble était violent, sauvage, régulier. Le correct dans le farouche" (*Q. T,* I, 170). It is, in fact, a perversion of the neoclassical style. We sense that its designers have emptied eighteenth-century art of all of its fantasy and indulgence: "C'était quelquechose comme Boucher guillotiné par David" (*Q. T.,* I, 171).

The Convention Hall serves as a fitting backdrop for the presentation of the Revolutionaries, the most significant of whom is Cimourdain. Hugo characterizes him as "par dessus tout un opiniâtre" (*Q. T.,* I, 123); "il avait en lui l'absolu" (*Q. T.,* I, 123). Brombert remarks that Cimourdain incarnates the ideological intransigence that led to the Terror's atrocities (213-214), while Moore compares Cimourdain to Javert of *Les Misérables,* another man "blind to everything but the law" (391). Although Cimourdain is an ex-priest, his philosophy derives nothing from the Bible. He is a republican along classical lines: "De quelle république? De la république de Platon peut-être, et peut-être aussi de la république de Dracon" (*Q. T.,* I, 124). If Cimourdain considers the Revolution the apogee of wisdom, "Il voulait que cette Minerve, couronnée des étoiles de l'avenir, fût aussi Pallas, et eût pour bouclier le masque aux serpents" (*Q. T.,* I, 125). His desire for justice results in a limited vision rather than objectivity: "Il avait les yeux bandés comme la Thémis d'Homère" (*Q. T.,* I, 127). Ultimately, Hugo associates Cimourdain with the classical underworld. The only "coin non trempé dans le Styx" (*Q. T.,* I, 130) in the personality of this delegate from the Committee of Public Safety is his affection for his former pupil Gauvain.

The pagan underworld becomes the dominant classical reference in the subsequent chapters on Robespierre, Danton, and Marat, entitled "Le Cabaret de la Rue du Paon." In this, perhaps the most baffling episode of the novel, the reader senses that Hugo's admiration for these heroes constantly gives way to a fascination with their vindictiveness. As Suzanne Guerlac has remarked, although Hugo tries to infuse these pages with an aura of sublimity, "the sublime of the Terror" is so contaminated by violence that it approaches "the Terror of the grotesque" (870). At first, the three revolutionaries recall the triumvirate of Octavian, Antony, and Lepidus as they plot a dictatorship that will save the Republic from external war and internal factionalism. Hugo soon switches his attention, however, to their insults and threats to each other, their espionage and struggle for dominance. He fittingly connects them to Minos, Aeacus, and Rhadamanthys, mythological judges of the dead. They condemn moderation and debate alternative battle plans as might "les trois têtes de Cerbère" (*Q. T.,* I, 145). Hugo refers to them as both titans and hydras (*Q. T.,* I, 152), but in his insistence upon their craving for wars, their anger and their days passed in the dark-

ness of taverns, he seems to draw on Virgil's description of the Fury Alecto, who excites the Latins against Aeneas's troops:

> Dweller in Hell's dark shadows, sorrow-bringer,
> Lover of gloom and war and plot and hatred.

(VII, 342-43)

Let us note, finally, that allusions to classical literary genres initiate and conclude the description of Paris under the Terror. "Rien de plus tragique," Hugo claims, than 1793, "l'Europe attaquant la France, et la France attaquant Paris. Drame qui a la stature de l'épopée" (*Q. T.,* I, 125). The significant moments of the Terror must be understood as "tragédies nouées par les géants et dénouées par les nains" (*Q. T.,* I, 178). In his earliest theoretical pronouncements on the development of genres in *La Préface de Cromwell* of 1828, Hugo posited that the epic poem and its variant tragedy arose during an historical period with definite parallels to revolutionary France, namely the period of Greek civilization when a national conscience surfaced. These genres reflect the great events of such an age: "les chocs d'empires," "la guerre" (*P. C.,* 49). They require of their audience a devotion to national interest: "la famille a une patrie; tout l'y attache" (*P. C.,* 50). Their protagonists, like Hugo's Cimourdain, Robespierre, Danton, Marat, are superhuman, godlike. At the same time, there is an ironic undertone in this comparison of the Terror to the epic poem and tragedy since these are, for Hugo, fairly primitive genres that correspond to the adolescence of humanity. Again, if we refer to *The Preface of Cromwell* we find it clearly stated that neither the classical epics nor tragedies are capable of expressing the complex emotions of modern life. They are inferior to both medieval literature and the Romantic drama because they celebrate the material world and glorify humanity at God's expense (*P. C.,* 52).[3] Hugo also implies that these genres are a dead end: "Ainsi que la société qu'elle représente, cette poésie s'use en pivotant sur elle-même" (*P. C.,* 52). Stuck on the same subjects—war and revenge, the same conflicts between intractable personalities and often the same predictable endings, the epic genres do not evolve and seem strangely unfit to translate the dynamic character of 1793, a turning point in history.

If we regroup these three types of classical allusions in Part II of *Quatrevingt-treize*—the Greco-Roman décor, the comparisons of the revolutionaries to Greek mythological figures, the references to genres deemed inadequate—we suspect that Hugo is defining a type of evil that threatened the First French Republic from its incipience. This Classical Terror is a psychic rigidity, an excessive reliance upon reason, a bloodthirstiness that runs counter to the Hugolian notion of the true movement of history, which is a spiritual progress, a liberation of the imagination, an ascension from earth to the stars that alone can bring about political progress. Unconsciously, in patterning themselves upon the Ancients, the leaders of the Terror perpetuate tyranny. They become the lords of the guillotine and the inadvertent predecessors of both *Napoléon le grand* and *Napoléon le petit*. The fear of the Greco-Roman world Hugo expresses in *Quatrevingt-treize* is altogether in keeping with his earlier thought. Pierre Albouy, in his *Création mythologique chez Victor Hugo,* characterizes Hugo's dissatisfaction with Greek mythology, voiced throughout his life, as a dislike for a mythical system that is too anthropomorphic, that takes away the mystery of religion and that ultimately concentrates too heavily on the conflicts between the deity and mortals (62-97). Such a mythology constrains humanity excessively, like the Convention Hall, which Hugo compares in *Quatrevingt-treize* to "un gigantesque tiroir de commode" (*Q. T.,* I, 167). Small wonder that in his summation of the positive contribution the Terrorists made to civilization, our author judges these men pawns of a higher power:

> La Revolution est une action de l'Inconnu . . . Elle semble l'oeuvre en commun des grands événements et des grands individus mêlés, mais elle est en réalité la résultante des événements . . . Desmoulins, Danton, Marat, Grégoire et Robespierre ne sont que des greffiers. Le rédacteur énorme et sinistre de ces grandes pages a un nom, Dieu, et un masque, Destin.
>
> (*Q. T.,* I, 188)

The novel's setting changes radically as we move from Paris to the Vendée. Here, Gothic elements predominate. The Breton forests are a maze of secret passages for the rebellious peasants and traps for the revolutionary soldiers. Hugo initially compares these woods to open tombs: "Rien de plus sourd, de plus muet et de plus sauvage que ces inextricables enchevêtrements d'épines et de branchages, ces vastes broussailles étaient des gîtes d'immobilité et de silence; pas de solitude d'apparence plus morte et plus sépucrale" (*Q. T.,* II, 6). A labyrinth of caves extends the length of the forest floor to lodge the peasants in time of danger. Inspired by recollections of Dante's hell,[4] Hugo imagines this subterranean world as a funnel dotted by pockets: "Des puits ronds et étroits, verticaux, puis horizontaux, s'élargissant sous terre en entonnoir, et aboutissant à des chambres ténébreuses" (*Q. T.,* II, 6). The inhabitants of these holes are not unlike Dante's sinners in that they have degenerated from the human into animalistic creatures of darkness. They sneak about like moles (*Q. T.,* II, 8) or emerge snake-like from the underbrush (*Q. T.,* II, 21). Hugo transforms this anonymous mass of peasants into a symbol of the remnants of feudalism that challenged the Revolution's push for progress. Cowed by centuries of repression, their fear of tyrants has turned into the "méprise habituelle aux esclaves" (*Q. T.,* II, 7) of innovation. If the Parisian revolutionaries are guilty of an overreliance on reason, this troglodytic people is still ruled by superstition and religious fanaticism: "On leur faisait accroire ce qu'on voulait;

les prêtes leur montraient d'autres prêtres dont ils avaient rougi le cou avec une ficelle serrée et leur disaient: 'Ce sont des guillotinés ressuscités'" (*Q. T.,* II, 14). Unkempt, ignorant, hungry for violence, these troops are the modern successors of the *vilains* of medieval romance.

La Tourgue or *la Tour Gauvain,* where the confrontation between the two armies takes place, is a fitting site for the rebels' defeat. A romanesque fortress complete with torture chamber, "oubliette," iron door and secret staircases, it resembles, above all, the wall of the centuries in "La Vision d'où est sorti ce livre," the opening poem of *La Légende des siècles,* that evokes the state of brute matter from which the Spirit must be liberated. La Tourgue rises from the plain as "la muraille colossale, quinze pieds d'épaisseur à la base et douze au sommet, ça et là des crevasses et des trous . . . par où l'on entrevoyait des escaliers dans l'intérieur ténébreux du mur" (*Q. T.,* II, 73). Inhabited by a variety of nocturnal animals—owls, goatsuckers, bats—it soon becomes the home of the hideous White lieutenant, l'Imanus, whose name signifies ogre and who indeed attempts to devour the three children he has imprisoned in the castle. However strongly Hugo felt attracted by the medieval world throughout his life, he seems here to present the reader with its most distasteful elements. Patricia Ward judges *Quatrevingt-treize* "an important example of the negative medievalism of his final year," when Hugo "no longer turns to the Middle Ages to represent the injustices of his own time. . . . Rather, he looks for vestiges of the past which carry over into the present—vestiges of obscurantism, dogmatism, and authoritarianism—and these he labels medieval" (103). Taken together, the rebel army and the tower suggest a second type of terror—a Gothic Terror—that threatens the forward motion of civilization with fear and prejudice.

Hugo's evocation of the Vendée is not, however, without ambivalence. La Tourgue's foundation is in stone and shadow, but it moves to the heavens and light, again in imitation of Dante's cosmology: "Le passant voyait sous ses pieds des ronces, des pierres, des reptiles, et sur sa tête une rondeur noire qui était le haut de la tour et qui semblait la bouche d'un puits énorme, les étoiles" (*Q. T.,* II, 73). It thus becomes a possible locus of redemption. For all of his condemnation of the insurrectionists' fanaticism and backwardness, Hugo does recognize the Vendean rebellion as a truly popular movement (*Q. T.,* II, 19). He admires, moreover, this people's profoundly spiritual nature which results from their daily immersion in the mysteries of nature, their Celtic roots and Christianity:

> "Croyant à la sainte Vierge et à la Dame blanche, dévot[s] à l'autel et aussi à la haute pierre mystérieuse debout au milieu de la lande . . . pensif[s], immobile[s] souvent des heures entières sur la grande grève déserte, sombre[s] écouteur[s] de la mer."
>
> (*Q. T.,* II, 5)

Grotesque and sublime, creatures of violent passion but also of religious aspirations, they eminently fit the description of the Romantic character Hugo proffers in *La Préface de Cromwell* (*P. C.,* 65) because they incarnate the human duality of flesh and soul, and the desire of the soul to be freed from the bondage of flesh whose social equivalent is governmental repression.

It is fair to say that the dominant theme of *Quatrevingt-treize*'s second half is liberation, which Hugo develops partially through subtle allusions to medieval literature. The peasants in battle recall the peers of France commanded by Roland at Roncevaux. Militant defenders of the Church against the modern infidel, "s'ils rencontraient sur le champ de combat une croix ou une chapelle, tous tombaient à genoux et disait leur prière sous la mitraille; le rosaire fini ce qui restait se relevaient et se ruaient sur l'ennemi" (*Q. T.,* II, 14). Cannons baptized with the names of the Virgin and saints are their technologically advanced *Durandal* (*Q. T.,* II, 17).

We find even more frequent allusions to Arthurian romance interwoven throughout the story of La Tourgue's siege. Interestingly, Hugo establishes these connections not with the conservative troops but with his final protagonist and ultimate hero, the revolutionary leader Gauvain. Many critics have noted Hugo's pointed references to the forest of Brocéliande as well as his naming his hero after one of King Arthur's best known knights;[5] however, the pattern of romance runs much deeper than names and furnishes, in good measure, the structure of the novel's ending. Hugo seems to have in mind the Grail legends. Gauvain, like his medieval predecessor, is a great warrior, able to fight without becoming fatigued, never vanquished in battle: "Toujours rué éperdument dans les mêlées, il n'avait jamais été blessé" (*Q. T.,* II, 34).[6] He accepts the commission from his superiors to defeat his demonic uncle Lantenac, who is, quite literally, the lord of this land, and who has thrown down the gauntlet to Paris. Gauvain must cross an enchanted forest, peopled by an invisible army. He discovers, there, a wasteland, "cette misérable Brétagne éperdue" (*Q. T.,* II, 7), rendered barren by centuries of repression enacted by each successive political régime, "le despotisme sous toutes ses espèces, la conquête, la féodalité, le fanatisme, le fisc" (*Q. T.,* II, 7), which begs to be liberated from this evil spell. The situation of the land is mirrored in that of the three Breton children, innocents captive in the castle. In his quest to free Brittany, Gauvain must undergo a series of trials by the sword with monstrous figures: at Dol, where his miniscule battalion takes on the rebel masses; against the unrepentant Imanus in the tower and, finally, against the guillotine. The castle becomes the locus of Gauvain's spiritual transformation, as is so often the case in courtly novels, a transformation which gives him the ability to complete his mission. This transformation is effectu-ated, moreover, not by the knight's own prowess, but through his contact with the ancient lord of the castle, a Fisher King, here represented by Lantenac, who holds the secret to both individual and social redemption.[7]

During the siege of La Tourgue, classical allusions again come to the fore, although it is perhaps more accurate to state that the Greco-Roman world and that of the *chanson de geste* come together to create a timeless vision of Civil War. The two armies' calls to battle, enumeration of their warriors, engagement in hand-to-hand combat, and the suggestion offered by Cimourdain that the dispute be settled by a confrontation between himself and Lantenac (*Q. T.,* II, 153) are episodes reminiscent of *The Iliad, The Aeneid,* and *The Song of Roland.* Far from approving this convergence of history, Hugo regrets how easily each new age reverts to the worst moments of the past: "Les guerres entre parents sont toute l'histoire du moyen âge; les Etéocles et les Polynices sont gothiques aussi bien que grecs, et Hamlet fait dans Elseneur ce qu'Oreste a fait dans Argos" (*Q. T.,* II, 93).[8] Such an outmoded literary paradigm cannot truly advance the Revolution.

In Book VI, "C'est après la victoire qu'a lieu le combat," the classical and medieval worldviews again diverge and clash, with Gauvain's soul as battleground. After the arrest of Lantenac, who has voluntarily relinquished his freedom to save the infants from the conflagration, Cimourdain states that he will ignore this act of bravery, conform to the Convention's decrees, and guillotine Lantenac after a summary trial. This steadfastness in duty, this insistence upon subordinating individual merit to civic interest, this impassive reasoning, also take on the character of an act of revenge which in turn promises to perpetuate the cycle of terror that threaten to transform France into a modern Troy or Argos.

Although Lantenac does not speak to Gauvain at this point, his example proves more eloquent and provides greater guidance than Cimourdain's terse judgment. In the chapter "Gauvain pensif," the young officer conceives of Lantenac's unexpected reversal from childkiller to child-savior as an allegorical reenactment of the soul's struggle for redemption: "Le combat du bien contre le mal" (*Q. T.,* II, 208). This victory instigates a metamorphosis: "Un héros sortait du monstre; plus qu'un héros, un homme. . . . Ce n'était plus un tueur que Gauvain avait devant lui, mais un sauveur" (*Q. T.,* II, 212). Hugo presents Lantenac's transformation, moreover, as a victory of new life over old age, "le berceau" winning over "la vieillesse farouche" (*Q. T.,* II, 208-209), fertility over barrenness. Lantenac appears as the Fisher King who has healed his own flesh and, thus, liberated his kingdom from the curse that laid it waste. Since he accomplishes this feat through an act of self-sacrifice, by which he rediscovers "la haute loi divine de pardon, d'abnégation, de rédemption" (*Q. T.,* II, 211), he has, in a metaphorical sense, retrieved the Holy Grail of medieval quest literature. A true knight, who has become the champion of the stranger, the orphan, the poor (*Q. T.,* II, 210), Lantenac offers, ironically, a better example of a leader contributing to the triumph of the People than the revolutionary Cimourdain.

Gauvain's subsequent spiritual awakening also closely follows the pattern established by twelfth and thirteenth-century Grail romances. In his study of the Grail legends, Roger Sherman Loomis explains that the knight Gawain is forced to spend the night in the Grail Castle, where he witnesses a series of supernatural events while in a dreamlike state. He fails to liberate the castle because he does not ask the questions that would explain the Grail's mystery. This experience allows him, however, to understand his inadequacies, and he sets out for further adventures with the hope of gaining the prowess necessary to complete his mission (Loomis, 67-73). In *Quatrevingt-treize,* Gauvain is also revealed as an inadequate warrior. He has conquered the castle, but his enemy has escaped him and he has been unable to rescue the children. Although he spent his youth in La Tourgue, he does not know the mystery of the castle, the secret passageway that allows Lantenac to reenter the burning library where the babes are trapped. After Lantenac's capture Gauvain spends a night in a dreamlike state of meditation, a "rêverie . . . insondable" (*Q. T.,* II, 206), in which he has recurrent visions of Lantenac's heroism. Hugo refers to this, as we have already noted, as a supernatural event: "Gauvain venait de voir un miracle:

> La victoire de l'humanité sur l'homme.
> L'humanité avait vaincu l'inhumain.

(*Q. T.,* II, 208)

Gauvain is initially tempted to avoid questioning himself about the significance of Lantenac's rescue. Cimourdain's injunction "cela ne te regarde pas" (*Q. T.,* II, 207) implies that Gauvain's duties as a military leader do not extend to problems of justice. He nevertheless overcomes this temptation, undertaking a painful examination of conscience on both his own behalf and that of the French Revolution. He comes to reject not only Cimourdain's conception of justice but even his former tutor's reliance upon reason. As he weighs Lantenac's good and evil deeds, Gauvain finds it equally logical to condemn or to pardon his noble uncle. He must turn inward, Hugo tells us, to fathom this mystery:

> Le raisonnement disait une chose; le sentiment en disait une autre; les deux conseils étaient contraires. Le raisonnement n'est que la raison, le sentiment est souvent la conscience; l'un vient de l'homme, l'autre de plus haut.

(*Q. T.,* II, 218)

This willingness to question himself finally allows him to succeed where his medieval predecessor failed. He too discovers the spiritual mystery ignored by the law, that one act of self-sacrifice requires another. The liberation of humanity and the foundation of a truly moral republic can only come about through clemency. While Gauvain does die at the novel's conclusion, his death is an apotheosis. Like the legendary Gawain, whose strength derived from that of the sun,[9] Hugo's Gauvain appears most heroic as he faces the guillotine at the first rays of dawn.

The heroic roles played by Lantenac and Gauvain in the conclusion may mislead the reader into thinking that Hugo somehow advocates a return to the pre-Revolutionary political order. This is certainly not the case. Hugo takes pains to condemn the insurgents' "feudalism." La Tourgue incarnates Humanity's physical enslavement to matter in the form of the soil and social bondage to the nobility that the Revolution mercifully terminated. His harsh judgment of Breton history extends to attributing responsibility for the Revolution's excesses to the feudal order. As the guillotine approaches the tower, it provokingly accuses: "Je suis ta fille" (*Q. T.,* II, 255). At the same time, Hugo pointedly expresses his admiration for medieval literary models over those classical paradigms chosen by the Terror's adherents because the medieval models better translate the complexities of the human soul while they inspire higher spiritual ambitions.[10] Like the plaster columns of the Convention hall, the classical tradition proves itself at once too rigid and flimsy to carry the moral weight of the Revolution. During Gauvain's court-martial, le capitaine Guéchamps condemns his young commander since in "L'an 414 de Rome, Manlius fit mourir son fils pour le crime d'avoir vaincu son ordre" (*Q. T.,* II, 237). Sargent Radoub, perhaps the novel's best representative of the People, immediately decries the inadequacy of such reasoning, which restricts the definition of goodness to legal conformity. Radoub, like Gauvain, looks to the Middle Ages when he proclaims: "Mon commandant . . . je vous donnerais la croix de Saint-Louis, s'il y avait encore des croix, s'il y avait encore des saints, et s'il y avait encore des louis" (*Q. T.,* II, 238). Finally, Lantenac, in his prison interview with Gauvain, warns that Breton legends offer a conception of the superior leader that the Revolutionaries will sorely miss in their new society: "Vous ne voulez plus avoir de nobles, eh bien, vous n'en aurez plus. Faites-en votre deuil. Vous n'aurez plus de paladins, vous n'aurez plus de héros . . . vous êtes un peuple fini; . . ." (*Q. T.,* II, 228-229). Hugo proves Lantenac's judgement correct, for, in the conversation between Cimourdain and Gauvain on the eve of Gauvain's execution, it is Cimourdain, the Revolutionary, who ironically envisages the future as a new age of repression: "le service militaire obligatoire, le nivellement, aucune déviation, et audessus de tous et de tout, cette ligne droite, la loi" (*Q. T.,* II, 245), whereas Gauvain, now the Committee of Public Safety's enemy, dreams of "la république de l'idéal" (*Q. T.,* II, 245), where evil and war will disappear.

This opposition between Greco-Roman and medieval models helps clarify Hugo's attitude toward the past. Brombert, again, has best pointed out ***Quatrevingt-treize***'s ambiguous representation of the past, especially evident in the description of La Tourgue which our author makes into a simultaneous repository of feudal fanaticism, through its dungeons and torture chambers, yet also of civilization, through its library (215-218). In addition, Gauvain envisages his liberation of his Uncle Lantenac, in part, as a duty he owes to his personal past, his family (*Q. T.,* II, 213). This fictional ambivalence accurately reflects the very real ambivalence Hugo felt throughout his life for the French Revolution. According to Jean Boudout, it was only during the final decades of his career, after the publication of ***Les Misérables,*** that Hugo found himself capable of writing impartially about the Revolution, in ways that highlighted its positive accomplishments yet condemned its excesses (xvi). ***Quatrevingt-treize*** contains just such a balanced judgment of the year of the Terror. Hugo lauds the Committee of Public Safety's efforts to establish a republic but does not shy away from the ironies involved in their struggle. Because the Revolutionaries, incarnated in Cimourdain, turned to an outmoded past, one that stresses impersonality, discipline and revenge, they unwittingly perpetuated the fanaticism they sought to destroy. It is impossible to miss this vicious cycle into which the nineteenth century had trapped itself. It is revealed by both Lantenac and Radoub in the novel's final pages. The great-uncle explains that nothing has really changed, since war, repression, imprisonment and capital punishment still rule France: "Ceci est une ancienne chambre de ma maison; jadis les seigneurs y mettaient les manants; maintenant les manants y mettent les seigneurs. Ces niaiseries-là se nomment une révolution" (*Q. T.,* 224). Radoub echoes the same sentiment when he declares that Cimourdain's refusal to reward good deeds empties the Revolution of its moral content: "Il n'y a plus de raison pour qu'on s'arrête . . . Sapristi! nous nous abrutissons à la fin" (*Q. T.,* II, 238-237). In a gesture of reconciliation with his Breton roots and poetic ancestors reenacted fictionally through Gauvain's reunion with his great uncle, Hugo highlights the rich spiritual legacy furnished by medieval literature to his own age. Gauvain, much more easily than Cimourdain, can envisage the future because he has retrieved the spiritual legacy of the past. The ethics of generosity (Boudout, xxxii), the belief in the possibility of transformation through forgiveness might have allowed the men of 1793, Hugo suggests in his novel's dénouement, to fuse family and nation into a unified force, the People.

Notes

1. The best studies of Hugo's historical documentation for *Quatrevingt-treize* are Olin H. Moore's "The Sources of Victor Hugo's *Quatrevingt-treize*" and "Further Sources of Victor Hugo's *Quatrevingt-treize.*"

2. Victor Brombert traces Hugo's fascination with 1793 in his chapter on *Quatrevingt-treize* in *Victor Hugo and the Visionary Novel.* This problematic use of history has been the central concern of critical studies of *Quatrevingt-treize.* For some scholars, Hugo was simply too limited by ideological prejudices to treat the Terror properly. Thus, Richard Grant, in *The Perilous Quest,* judges *Quatrevingt-treize* disappointing because Hugo indulges too obviously his penchant for prophecy. Lukács has best expressed this view in *The Historical Novel,* where he praises Hugo for his portrayal of "tragic conflicts, which are real ones, sprung of the soil of the Revolution" but finds the novel nevertheless marred by the author's bourgeois idealism, which distorts "the real, human and historical collisions of the protagonists into "ingenious conflicts of duty based on . . . abstract humanism" rather than on economic struggle (257). Hugo's defenders, however, point out that *Quatrevingt-treize* is concerned not only with the French Revolution but with a larger interpretation of history that accounts for the novel's unexpected ending. For Sandy Petrey, Jeffrey Mehlman, and Winfred Engler *Quatrevingt-treize* was strongly influenced by Hugo's experience of the Commune and his sympathy for the Communards. As Mehlman succinctly explains, "Hugo judges 1793 in the light of 1848 in the wake of 1871" (46). Victor Brombert, in his final chapter of *Victor Hugo and the Visionary Novel,* feels that this novel attempts to place history "in a transcendental context" (222), by presenting the reader with an interpretation of the Terror as part of the divine scheme for cosmic redemption. Taking a different tack, Guy Rosa suggests that Hugo purposefully created a split between recorded historical accounts of 1793 and his narrative to underscore the notion that individuals are not determined by history: "La fiction atteste que chacun reste responsable de ses actes et qu'ils sont passibles d'un jugement moral auquel la nécessité historique n'apportera aucune circonstance atténuante" (341-342). Similarly, Raser suggests that it is the resistance of historical facts to "purely formal analysis that indicates history's presence" in *Quatrevingt-treize*" (60). Petrey offers an analogous judgement: Hugo forces his protagonist Gauvain to "struggle against men who represent the world historically in order to preserve the pastoral simplicity of the 'langue humaine' in which amnesty is a universal and eter-

nal value" (91). Finally, Suzanne Guerlac and Timothy Raser point out that Hugo's obsessions in the novel are more aesthetic than historical. For Guerlac, especially, *Quatrevingt-treize* reveals the admirable coherence between Hugo's "literary and critical essayistic writings" (875), specifically the early *Préface de Cromwell* and the late *William Shakespeare.*

3. Hugo expresses much the same idea in his 1826 preface to *Odes et ballades,* where he claims that classical literature is simply a regularity invented by humans whereas Romantic literature aims at a freedom of the imagination that allows the divine order of the cosmos to reveal itself (*O. P.,* I, 279-283).

4. For a detailed study of the influence of Dante on Hugo's writing, see Patricia A. Ward, *The Medievalism of Victor Hugo.*

5. Winfried Engler notes the mythological foundations Hugo's Breton landscape: "La route qui conduit au château présuppose une riche tradition typologique sans que cette relation intertextuelle explique le fond du récit" (45). For Donald Aynesworth, "The Breton forest is an area in which reality has been eroded by fiction, and nature itself ravaged by the excesses of the imagination . . . the forest is haunted by the supernatural. It is a locus of the transformation of fact into fantasy, a place at once legendary and historical . . ." (207-208). Brombert speaks of Gauvain as a character "who bears the name of the purest of medieval knights" (222), while Claudie Bernard reminds us that "the Lantenac-Gauvain relationship, that of great-uncle to nephew, has resonances of the relationships between Charlemagne-Roland, Arthur-Mordred, Marc-Tristan" (339).

6. We find such a Gauvain in Chrétien de Troyes' *Yvain.* Gawain is also a mighty warrior in *Sir Gawain and the Green Knight.* For a comprehensive study of Gawain and the Grail romances, see Roger Sherman Loomis, *The Grail. From Celtic Myth to Christian Symbol,* 65-76, 147-156.

7. In his insightful "Anonymity, Identity, and Narrative Sovereignty in *Quatrevingt-treize,*" Donald Aynesworth takes pains to underline the critical role of Lantenac as regenerator of Brittany and of Gauvain: "He reestablishes himself in his paternal domain and there, appropriately in a subterranean setting, reclaims his patrimony in a finished critical narrative of French history, feudal and revolutionary" (210).

8. Brombert notes that, in *Quatrevingt-treize,* as in *William Shakespeare,* Hugo refers to the epic tradition as bloodthirsty (217-218).

9. In *The Arthurian Handbook,* Lacy and Ashe note that a peculiar quality of Gawain's, "that his strength increases till noon and then declines, hints that he had a background in solar myth" (340).

10. For Brombert, Gauvain can look to the future because he has retrieved the lyricism of past culture. Brombert believes, however, that this return to the past is actually a revival of the Homeric epic (222-223).

Works Cited

Albouy, Pierre. *La Création mythologique chez Victory Hugo.* Paris: Corti, 1963.

Aynesworth, Donald. *Anonymity, Identity, and Narrative Sovereignty in "Quatrevingt-treize."* Kentucky Romance Quarterly 29: 2 (1982): 201-213.

Boudout, Jean. Introd. *Quatrevingt-treize.* By Victor Hugo. Paris: Garnier Frères. 1963.

Brombert, Victor. *Victor Hugo and the Visionary Novel.* Cambridge: Harvard University Press, 1984.

Cobban, Alfred. *A Brief History of Modern France,* vol. 1. Baltimore: Penguin Books, 1963.

Engler, Winfried. "Une Poétique du regard ou la mise en perspective de la Révolution: *Quatrevingt-treize.*" *Texts réunis et presentés par Mireille Calle-Gruber et Arnold Rothe.* Paris: Nizet, 1988.

Grant, Richard. *The Perilous Quest.* Durham: Duke University Press, 1968.

Guerlac, Suzanne. "Exorbitant Geometry in Hugo's *Quatrevingt-treize.*" *MLN* 96: 4 (May 1981): 856-876.

Hugo, Victor. *La Légende des siécles. La Fin de Satan. Dieu.* Paris: Gallimard, 1950.

———. *Oeuvres poétiques.* Paris: Gallimard, 1964.

———. *La Préface de Cromwell* and *Hernani.* Ed. John R. Effinger, Jr. Chicago: Scott, Foresman and Company, 1960.

———. *Quatrevingt-treize.* 2 vols. Paris: J. Hetzel, 1874.

———. *William Shakespeare.* Trans. by Melville B. Anderson, Freeport, NY: Books for Libraries Press, 1970.

Lacy, Norris J. and Ashe, Geoffrey. *The Arthurian Handbook.* New York: Garland Publishing, 1988.

Loomis, Roger Sherman. *The Grail. From Celtic Myth to Christian Symbol.* Princeton: Princeton University Press, 1991.

Lukács, Georg. *The Historical Novel.* Trans. by Hannah and Stanley Mitchell. Lincoln: The University of Nebraska Press, 1962

Mehlman, Jeffrey. *Revolution and Repetition: Marx/ Hugo/Balzac.* Berkeley: The University of California Press, 1977.

Moore, Olin. "Further Sources of Victor Hugo's *Quatrevingt-treize*." *PMLA* 41 (1926): 452-61.

———. "The Sources of Victor Hugo's *Quatrevingt-treize*." *PMLA* 39 (1924): 368-405.

Palmer, R. R. *Twelve Who Ruled.* Princeton: Princeton University Press, 1941.

Petrey, Sandy. *History in the Text: Quatrevingt-treize and the French Revolution.* Amsterdam: John Benjamins, 1980.

Raser, Timothy. "Revolution and Aesthetics in Hugo's *Quatrevingt-treize*." *Esprit Créateur* 29. 2 (Summer 1982): 50-61.

Rosa, Guy. "*Quatrevingt-treize* ou la critique du roman historique." *Revue d'Histoire littéraire de la France*, 75. 2-3 (March June 1975): 329-343.

Virgil. *The Aeneid.* Trans. by Robert Fitzgerald. New York: Random House, 1983.

Ward, Patricia A. *The Medievalism of Victor Hugo.* University Park: The Pennsylvania State University Press, 1975.

Karen Masters-Wicks (essay date 1994)

SOURCE: Masters-Wicks, Karen. Introduction to *Victor Hugo's* Les Misérables *and the Novels of the Grotesque*, pp. 1-10. New York: Peter Lang, 1994.

[*In the following essay, Masters-Wicks provides an introduction to her book-length study of Hugo's works and considers how his "concept of the grotesque and the sublime esthetic" is woven into his texts to portray a certain meaning to the reader.*]

> The author makes his readers, just as he makes his characters.[1]

In the ***Préface de Cromwell*** of 1827 and later in ***William Shakespeare*** (1864), Victor Hugo defines the modern novel in terms of a union between the "grotesque" and the "sublime" as being part of "le génie moderne" [***Préf. de Cromwell***, 70[2]]. The genre of the novel is characterized as "cette merveilleuse nouveauté littéraire qui est en même temps puissance sociale . . . l'épique, le lyrique et le dramatique amalgamés" [***WS***, I,4,1,306[3]], or to use Mikhail Bakhtin's term, a "genre-in-the-making."[4] The novel thus defined is a suitably monstrous form wherein the hyperbolic language of the grotesque, of extremes, and antithetical constructions can be played out for mass consumption. For Hugo each of the genres combines to form the novel. As a free and flexible form, the novel is "the only developing genre and therefore it reflects more deeply, more essentially, more sensitively and rapidly, reality itself in the process of its unfolding."[5] The emphasis in the ***Préface de Cromwell*** on the "liberty" of the poetic voice demonstrates its importance in Hugo's concept of literature. For Hugo, both the epic and the lyric are "high" forms, whereas the drama signifies an intrusion of the grotesque into the sublime,[6] a retrieval of what had been left "à côté," repressed or suppressed in the epic (***Préface de Cromwell***). As we shall see in one of Hugo's last novels, ***L'Homme qui rit,*** the lyric, epic, and dramatic registers of discourse combine to form a three-dimensional, polyglot, and open-ended narrative environment where the exaggerated "figure" of the grotesque hero Gwynplaine becomes the metaphor for inadequacy and failure of presentation of the poetic voice.

The major focus of this study is on the Hugolian novel and how Hugo's concept of the grotesque and the sublime esthetic is interwoven within the texts in such a way as to clue his reader to a certain reading, metaphorically demonstrated in the ever-pervasive image of the spider slowly weaving a tight web around her subject. A detailed study of each of the novels will expose the different problems of "reading the grotesque." The methodology of our "reading" is thus closely linked to the evolution of narrative structures in the novels.

The incorporation of both the grotesque and the sublime esthetic in Hugo's theory of the novel reverses a traditional identification of the sublime in opposition with the grotesque in art and literature. The problematic, or slippery nature of the term "sublime" in French romanticism (for example in the prose poems, poetry, and essays on art of Baudelaire and the poetry of Lautréamont) has been treated by others.[7] However, for purposes of our study, a cursory look at the classical concept of the sublime esthetic is important to fully appreciate Victor Hugo's premise that the grotesque esthetic is essential to modern "drama."

From the neoclassical use of the word "sublime" by writers such as Longinus and Boileau as a critical, esthetic term dealing with the concept of poetic purity, beauty, and taste to Kant's eighteenth-century theoretical placement of the sublime in the realm of moral law and reason, the history of the sublime esthetic is grounded in cultural coding and valorization. However, as Suzanne Guerlac points out, the definitions of the sublime are difficult to formulate, with the Longinian sublime not always in agreement with the Kantian sublime or with Boileau's use of the term. "Significant ruptures or displacements in the conceptions of the sublime as we move from one text to another . . ."[8] occur. For Hugo "le beau [est] serviteur du vrai" [***WS***, II,6,1,399]: "être utile, ce n'est qu'être utile; être beau, ce n'est qu'être beau; être utile et beau, c'est être sublime." [*WS,* II,6,2,403]. The "real" has more validity than "the beautiful" per se. The Hugolian sublime thus becomes a kind of "déformation grandiose" [*WS,* I,4,9,323]. The "subversion" of the sublime in Hugo's discussion of drama is, therefore, a part of the historical evolution of the term.

On the one hand, in Hugo's 1827 *Préface de Cromwell* exists the concept of excess, of the nondemonstrability and the inaccessibility of the sublime, and an attack against the classical restrictions of the theatre (an overcodified sublime). On the other hand is the inclusion of that which has been excluded (the grotesque) within classical esthetics. The play, *Cromwell,* attempts to surpass classical restrictions and presents a new romantic "drame" that is more true to reality ("le réel"), although this theatrical production is in fact unplayable on stage, lending itself much better to the genre of the novel. Hugo thus heralds the dialogic nature of literature in the *Préface* and demonstrates an attraction toward everything that is not yet completed (or perfect in classical esthetics), and he specifically places the sublime within the rubric of the grotesque:

> Le sublime sur le sublime produit malaisément un contraste, et l'on a besoin de se reposer de tout, même du beau. Il semble, au contraire, que le grotesque soit un temps d'arrêt, un terme de comparaison, un point de départ d'où on s'élève vers le beau, avec une perception plus fraîche et plus excitée.
>
> [*PC,* 72]

The fact that Hugo champions in his later treatise *William Shakespeare* (1864) only those "sublime" writers who combine the grotesque and sublime in their works further reiterates a rejection of the classical codification of beauty and suggests the dialogic, malleable nature of the terms in his rhetoric. He refers to "génies" such as Shakespeare and Molière and to their works of genius as "monstres du sublime" [*WS,* II,3,6,377], a dramatic oxymoron which incorporates both sides of "le réel." As we shall see, this concept of "sublime" monsters will surface in Hugo's novels, for example, in the hybrid "figure" of *93,* which represents the horror of La Terreur within the sublimity of the revolution, and in the disfigurement of the enigmatic "l'homme qui rit." As Hugo points out in his "Notices" to *L'Homme qui rit,* "son grotesque vous constate sublime . . . Rien ne vous affirme à vous-même comme cette présence gaie du malheur" [*HQR, Notices,* 1085]. Both the sublime and the grotesque thus become part of Hugolian deformations. Hugo takes as his starting point the breakdown of all esthetic codes and creates a new framework for fiction.

In this study, we will elaborate the problematic of Hugo's use of the terms grotesque and sublime as a heuristic device for the reading of his narratives. Our methodology has drawn upon the work of Gérard Genette and Mikhail Bakhtin in narrative discourse; on the work of Peter Brooks, Ross Chambers, Seymour Chatman, Gerald Prince, and other narratologists; upon the research of Inge Crosman Wimmers, Umberto Eco, Stanley Fish, Wolfgang Iser, Susan Suleiman, Jane Tompkins, and other theorists of "Reader-Response"; and, to a lesser degree, on the work of descriptive theorists such as Philippe Hamon. This list does not pretend to be exhaustive, but rather to provide a sampling of reader-oriented critics whose efforts to redefine the aims and methods of literary study through a focus on the reader has been useful in our effort to present a fresh approach to an analysis of Hugolian narrative. The dialectic nature of Hugo's novels lends itself well to such an approach. As Jane P. Tompkins has noted in her study of reader-response criticism, it is "not a conceptually unified critical position, but a term that has come to be associated with the work of critics who use the words *reader, the reading process,* and *response* to make out an area for investigation."[9] We will be borrowing numerous terms from reader-response critics in our study and will be starting from the theoretical premise that Hugolian narrative invites participation on the part of the reader and, for the most part, guides the reader in the interpretation of the tale through a reading of the grotesque. As Wolfgang Iser notes,

> In this way, every literary text invites some form of participation on the part of the reader . . . In view of our preceding discussion, we might say that here the author himself removes the gaps; for with his comments, he tries to create a specific conception of his narrative . . . The author himself tells the reader how his tale is to be understood.[10]

As we will demonstrate, within the novels a preoccupation with their correct reading is evidenced by specific elements in the fabric of the narrative structure which are intended to be elicited by the "inscribed" or "encoded reader"[11] to create specific "frames of reference"[12] to guide our reading of the grotesque and to establish a rapport between the reader and the grotesque hero.[13] The dialogic nature of Hugolian narrative will be discussed, strictly applying the Bakhtinian notion of "dialogic" reading, to demonstrate the significance of the constant juxtaposition of opposites and the simultaneous presence of opposing realities in the novels.

As we shall see, the problematic of "reading the grotesque" in Hugolian narrative is that the paradigm of reading shifts from text to text. The reader's function is thus structured and manipulated by the texts. An evolution in the author's concept of the grotesque esthetic can be seen from his "oeuvres de jeunesse" to his later fiction. The novels before the 1827 *Préface de Cromwell* (*Han d'Islande* and *Bug-Jargal*) present simplistic dualities and straight-forward, clearly defined comic grotesque (evil) and sublime (good) characterizations.

The novels after the *Préface* (*Le Dernier jour d'un condamné* and *Notre-Dame de Paris*) examine perturbations in the meaning of the grotesque and the sublime, and the later narratives which were written around the time of the writing of the 1864 treatise *William Shakespeare* (*Les Misérables, Les Travailleurs de la mer, L'Homme qui rit,* and *Quatrevingt-treize*) offer more ambiguous characterizations of the grotesque esthetic.

From the early novels, the psycho-projections of implied narrators (Léopold in *Bug-Jargal* and the Condemned Man in *Le Dernier jour d'un condamné*) and the inter-subjectivization of the third-person narrator in *Han d'Islande* and *Bug-Jargal* and of the first-person narrator in *Le Dernier Jour* ask the reader to participate in the narrative through identity with the protagonists and/or sympathy for them. Polysemy and semantic instability are highlighted in the metaphor of "argot" in *Le Dernier Jour, Notre-Dame de Paris,* and particularly in *Les Misérables.* Hugo uses theatricality to depict a crisis of language within the novels, symbolized in the cannon scene in *Quatrevingt-treize* and Gwynplaine's dramatic, yet displaced speech in the House of Lords in *L'Homme qui rit.* Spectatorship dominates the narratives of *Han d'Islande, Bug-Jargal, Notre-Dame de Paris,* and *L'Homme qui rit,* in which the author examines the erotic and often pornographic invasion of the spectacle (particularly in *Notre-Dame de Paris*). This invasion is linked to the sacred and the obscene (the sublime and the grotesque) and contaminates the reader's field of vision through the shift between the domain of seeing, hearing, and reading due to the predominant presence of slang, for example, in *Le Dernier Jour* and in *Les Misérables.* As we shall see, in the later novels, particularly in *Les Travailleurs de la mer,* in *L'Homme qui rit,* and in *Quatrevingt-treize,* the reader is confronted with the problematization of reading, that is, with the deconstruction of reading. The author is obsessed with the potential unreadability or illegibility of his own words (for example, the "page blanche" of the first pages of *Les Travailleurs de la mer*), where the breakdown and inflation of meaning permeate the texts.

The "dialogic" reading which Hugo presupposes in his theoretical manifesto of 1827, the *Préface de Cromwell,* begins with his elevation of the term "grotesque" in the *Préface* to the level of an esthetic concept: "Ainsi voilà un principe étranger à l'Antiquité, un nouveau type introduit dans la poésie . . . voilà une forme nouvelle qui se développe dans l'art. Ce type, c'est le grotesque. Cette forme, c'est la comédie." [*PC,* 69]. As A. R. W. James has demonstrated in his lexographic study, "Crotesques, Grotesque," Hugo uses the word "grotesque" as a hallmark of romanticism, uniting the varied connotations of the word, to make "du *laid* un type d'imitation, du *grotesque* un élément de l'art" [*PC,* 69].

The word 'grotesque' acquired sudden prominence in French, when Victor HUGO published the preface to *Cromwell* in 1827. Its origins go back to sixteenth century Italy whence the adjective or substantive—usually in the plural—came to France, with connotations of abundance and relief-work. The extension of the sense to 'caricature', usually held to date from the seventeenth century, belongs in fact to the sixteenth, though the reasons for it are not sufficiently elucidated. A further change is the use of the substantive in the singular to denote a *genre* and despite some earlier examples this is where HUGO's major contribution lies. He left his mark, not merely by using the word as a banner, but by the linguistic inventiveness of the context, where variety and multiplicity are everywhere present and all the connotations the word had previously had are united.[14]

The theory that Hugo establishes in the *Préface* (1827) and reemphasizes later in *William Shakespeare* (1864) makes the grotesque esthetic the cornerstone of the differentiation between modern romantic and classical literature, where he suggests that the relationship of the sublime and the grotesque is the primary code of romantic drama: ". . . Que ferait le drame romantique? . . . le drame, c'est le grotesque avec le sublime . . ." [*PC,* 105].

Prior to the *Préface,* Hugo's visionary mind had been stimulated by the paintings of Callot, Salvator Rosa's *Tentation* and *Mêlée,* and works of other painters which reflected his concept of the grotesque.[15] Hugo thus overtly assimilates the pictorial tradition which inspired romantic painters into his own theory of the grotesque. As we shall see, the primary descriptive technique of Hugolian novels hinges on visual metaphors, where the theatricalization of the grotesque predominates. This theatrical code is extended on the level of content (preoccupation with horror, deformation, monstrosity, the macabre, masking and unmasking, the notion of hybridity, and the blending and blurring of opposites) and on the level of form (the abundant use of antitheses, oxymorons, and hyperboles, the juxtaposition of disparate elements, extravagant enumerations and lists, and the elements of polysemy and dialogism, to name but a few).

Hugo's concept of the grotesque in art is important to his overall use of the term in literature. As an art form, the grotesque is not limited to literary discourse in romantic narrative; it is always presented in the realm of cultural coding, where dominant codes of beauty, logic, and vraisemblance are put into question. It most often functions as a counter-code in opposition to the established norm, creating its own esthetic, forcing the reader or spectator to look at art and literature in a new way. In contrast with the "renaissance grotesque" (to use Bakhtin's terminology[16]), with its regenerative and carnivalistic aspects, the "romantic grotesque" became an expression of a subjective, isolated, and individualistic world outlook. We see this concept in the Gothic or "roman noir" and in the *Sturm und Drang* novels, which greatly influenced the French romantic novelists of the 1820's and 1830's. The hybrid quality of the grotesque, this constant mixing of dissimilar elements, appealed to writers like Baudelaire, Flaubert, Gautier, and Hugo, whose interest in hybridization and the overlapping of genres fits within this framework. The many aspects of this esthetic can be found in various forms within nineteenth century French literature, be it parody, satire, black humor, or caricature. The obvious interest of Baudelaire in "L'Essence du rire" (1855), of Gautier in *Les Grotesques* (1844), of Hugo in the **Préface de Cromwell** (1827), and others with codifying a new esthetic, a "drame" based on a mixture of genres and tones, where comedy and tragedy are present in the same text and where the grotesque and the sublime overlap and invert meanings, reflects the importance of the grotesque as a major topos in the esthetics of romanticism. As we shall see, Hugo, in particular, guides the reader into a fictional universe through narrative and descriptive techniques and built-in reading models that underscore a reading of the grotesque, not only from a visual frame of reference, but most importantly as it relates to the problematic of language and its readability.

Notes

1. Henry James.

2. *Cromwell,* Éd. Garnier-Flammarion, 1968, Paris.

3. *William Shakespeare, Oeuvres complètes, Critique,* Éd. Robert Laffont, S.A., Paris, 1985.

4. Bakhtin, Mikhail, *The Dialogic Imagination,* University of Texas Press Slavic Series, No. 1, Austin, 1981, p. 11.

5. Bakhtin, *The Dialogic Imagination,* p. 7.

6. For example, note the title of the preface to *Le Dernier jour d'un condamné,* "Une Comédie à propos d'une tragédie."

7. Note in particular Guerlac, Suzanne, *'Monsters of the Sublime'—Hugo, Baudelaire, Lautréamont and the Esthetics of the Sublime,* Ph.D. Thesis, The Johns Hopkins University, Baltimore, 1984; and Weiskel, Thomas, *The Romantic Sublime: Studies in the Structure and Psychology of Transcendence,* The Johns Hopkins University Press, Baltimore, 1976.

8. Guerlac, p. 11.

9. Tompkins, Jane P., "An Introduction to Reader-Response Criticism," *Reader-Response Criticism: From Formalism to Post-Structuralism,* The Johns Hopkins University Press, Baltimore, Maryland, 1980, p. ix.

10. Iser, Wolfgang, *Prospecting: From Reader Response to Literary Anthropology,* The Johns Hopkins University Press, Baltimore, 1989, pp. 10, 12.

11. Suleiman, Susan R.; Crosman, Inge (ed.), *The Reader in the Text: Essays on Audience and Interpretation,* Princeton Univ. Press, Princeton, 1980.

12. Wimmers, Inge G., *Poetics of Reading. Approaches to the Novel,* Princeton Univ. Press, Princeton, 1988, p. 121. We will be referring to "frames of reference," "conflicting frames of reference," "interlocking frames of reference," and "systems of reference" throughout our study. These are terms used in Wimmers' descriptions of the act of reading and the relationship of the reader to the text.

13. The lack of reciprocity, or the fear of non-reciprocity of the view between the spectator and the spectacle is pervasive in Hugolian narrative. See particularly Chapter IV of this study on *Notre-Dame de Paris.*

14. James, A. R. W., "Crotesques, Grotesque," *Cahiers de Lexicologie,* No. 51, 1987, *Revue Internationale de Lexicologie et Lexicographie,* publ. Bernard Quemada, pp. 159-176; p. 159.

15. Thompson, C. W., *Victor Hugo and the Graphic Arts (1820-1833),* Librairie Droz, Genève-Paris, 1970, p. 54.

16. Bakhtin, Mikhail, *Rabelais and His World,* Indiana University Press, Bloomington, 1984.

Galya Gerstman (essay date spring-summer 1996)

SOURCE: Gerstman, Galya. "Fictional Fathers and Fathers by Fiction: The Surrogate Father as Novelist in the Work of Victor Hugo." *Nineteenth-Century French Studies* 24, nos. 3 & 4 (spring-summer 1996): 370-80.

[*In the following essay, Gerstman states that Hugo's novels provide a focal point for examining the destabilization of the paternal figure during the eighteenth and nineteenth centuries. Gerstman shows how this theme and Hugo's treatment of paternity and parricide in his works offer insight into his personal psychology.*]

"Cette guerre," writes Victor Hugo in **Quatrevingt-Treize,** "mon père l'a faite, et j'en puis parler."[1] It is through his father that Hugo obtains the authority—in the sense either of permission or of capacity, due to the ambiguity of the verb "pouvoir"—to depict the revolt in Vendée. Paternal participation thus empowers or *authorizes* Hugo to author his novel. The war in question, however, is described in the same work as an "essai inconscient de parricide" (*QT* 926). In effect, the titular year 1793 indicates an exemplary form of parricide: the beheading of the king of France. Though the revolutionary Gauvain, the novel's hero, refuses to burn the Lantenac library because, among other reasons, "il semblait à Gauvain que brûler les archives, c'était attaquer ses pères" (*QT* 966), he is nonetheless in the very process of attacking one of his "fathers" in the person of his great-uncle, the marquis de Lantenac: "Ce sang qu'il allait répandre, . . . est-ce que ce n'était pas son sang, à lui Gauvain?" (*QT* 1037)

The patriarchal authority initially invoked is thus subsequently subverted. Indeed, the destabilization of the paternal figure is a predominant motif in the nineteenth-century, and not solely French, novel. This no doubt reflects the violent uprooting of authority engendered by both the American and French Revolutions of the late eighteenth century, as well as by the Industrial Revolution that weakened, if not eliminated, the father's role in the imparting and instruction of a trade or livelihood. The novels of Victor Hugo, spanning most of the century from 1823 to 1873, provide an exemplary focal point for the examination of this paternal vacuum. These works, which almost invariably include an episode of popular revolt, echoing the Revolution, are significant more than merely because they offer a great number of examples in which paternity suffers a threat of one form or another. It is foremost the insistent presence of a surrogate fatherhood which constitutes their relevance and importance in connection with paternal authority. The phenomenon of threatened paternity lends itself to largely historical and psychoanalytical interpretations, which will make up the first part of this study. Yet it is the adoptive father, through whom Hugo attempts to refill a paternal void, who will provide the focus for the second part of this essay. Possessing historico-political significance, the surrogate father may also and more provocatively be read as a general figure for the artist, and specifically, the novelist.

The most obvious theme with which to begin an examination of problematized paternity in Hugo's novels would seem to be parricide. In fact, however, the novels display a virtual absence of biological fathers through no criminal wrongdoing. Fatherhood is often simply glossed over. Nevertheless, this does not prevent the institution from being frequently linked to criminality and perversion. Biassou labels "dénaturés" the white fathers of slave mixed-bloods in *Bug-Jargal*: "ils ne vous ont jamais traités en pères" (*BJ* 332), thus legitimizing their parricides. In the same vein, fathers in Hugo's novels are on occasion guilty of abandoning their offspring, and even guilty of infanticide. By these acts, moreover, they lose the status of father, for they have removed the very element that constitutes their paternity. The death of children, however, occurs at times through no fault of the parent, perhaps evoking the death of one of Hugo's own children, Léopoldine. This theme is in effect highly visible in Hugo's work, reinforcing Jacques Seebacher's claim that his daughter's drowning in 1843 became "le centre de gravité de la vie de Hugo."[2] Yet the prevalence of offspring mortality is not solely a reflection of the author's own life, as examples of this thematic already occur in works published before 1843. By far, finally, the most prevalent threat to the paternity of Hugolian heroes is chastity, which precludes the very possibility of siring. The reader of *Les Travailleurs de la mer,* for instance, learns that Gilliatt "était probablement vierge" (*TM* 104). Only the early novel *Han d'Islande* reveals in its closing sentence the hero's reproductive success, which contrasts with the violent deaths of Han's and the Count d'Ahlefeld's[3] sons. Apart from this early work, all the heroes of Hugo's novels fail either to obtain or to maintain the status of father.[4]

We must thus begin by seeking the significance of what appears to be a failed fatherhood. As noted, the historical relevance of this literary phenomenon would seem to point to the reverberations in the nineteenth century of the overthrow and murder of the king of France during the French Revolution. Sade's pamphlet, "Français, encore un effort si vous voulez être républicains," implied that fatherlessness was par for the Revolutionary course, as all citizens "ne doivent avoir d'autre mère que la patrie,"[5] that is, the fatherland. Yet even before the Revolution, as Lynn Hunt demonstrates, French novels throughout the eighteenth century were "inherently antipatriarchal," depicting a threatened, and then effaced, father (28). Furthermore, the weakening of paternity viewed in pre-revolutionary painting and literature more than merely predicted the fate of the king. According to Hunt, the art of the era actually aided in producing the regicide, for the disparaging depictions of paternity "fatally undermined the absolutist foundations of the monarchical regime" (34).

A Freudian interpretation of parricide, however, reverses the significance attributed above. For Freud, the murder of the paternal figure entails the elimination of the father, but not of fatherhood entirely. As the goal is actually to take the place of the father, the act of parricide is directed toward not the destruction of paternity, but rather the reaffirmation of it. The revolutionary regicide therefore does not abolish an authoritative rule, but merely permits the replacement of one ruler by another; the king is superseded by the people. Exploring another angle of paternity, Freud observes that the name of the dead is regarded by primitive societies as endowed with a portion of the deceased's personality (13: 112). To take the father's name[6] would in this manner be another means of taking his place, joining the basis of genealogy, that is, history, or more precisely historiography, with this same drive to usurp the father. We have seen that it is due to his father—a dead father—that Hugo is able to recount history, for **Quatrevingt-Treize** is an historical novel.

The absent father is also explained by another Freudian notion, that of the "family romance," in which the child imagines replacing his mother and father with what he considers to be more ideal parents. Though the French Revolution appears to be an enactment of a family romance, Hunt argues that on the contrary, the French sought to replace their monarchical "family" with "one in which the parents were effaced and the children, especially the brothers, acted autonomously" (xiv). This configuration, however, fares just as badly as the original, for the conflict between revolutionary "brothers" likewise produced fodder for the guillotine. In view of this reading, the prevalent theme of warring brothers in Hugo's work might indicate more than a reflection of the early competition with his brother Eugene.[7] It may also suggest a failure to resolve, by substituting fraternal equality, the absence of paternal authority. This would appear to be illustrated in **Quatrevingt-Treize,** which describes the Reign of Terror following the king's execution, and also the civil war in Vendée.

This Freudian family romance is pursued in a different direction by Marthe Robert. In order to have a mysterious or altogether mythical origin, and hence to fulfill one of the requisites for heroism, claims Robert, the hero of a novel must be either a foundling or a bastard. In other words, he must in some way eliminate his natural father. The effacement of the father thus becomes, according to Robert, the necessary condition for the composition of a novel. Hugo's introductory acknowledgment can be read this time to reveal recognition of a debt towards his absent father in connection with the writing of **Quatrevingt-Treize** not simply as history but as novel.

Contrary, however, to the above proposition that artistic promise emerges from the *effacement* of the father, Hugo seems to view a parallel to such invention in paternity itself. For Hugo, sexual reproduction is a form of artistic creation[8]: "l'autorité étant incluse dans l'auteur, il n'y a point d'autre autorité que la paternité" (*QT* 1037). Already in his second preface (April 1823) to **Han d'Islande,** Hugo compares himself and his novel to a father and child. In bestowing artistic significance upon paternity, the implicit stake involved in the act of parricide is transformed into a power that is creative in more than merely a sexual sense. Similarly, the analogy between a natural and a crafted production would appear to increase any failure of paternity from a uniquely biological register to an aesthetically creative lack. Is the failure of paternity consequently equivalent to a failure of art? If so, how can this reading of creative failure be reconciled with the very existence of Hugo's aesthetic achievement, that is, the book itself?

It is at this point that the concept of art must be examined more closely, for it implies not only creation, but also artifice. Though the Hugolian hero does not manage to claim the status of father due, in the largest number of instances, to his chastity, there remains open to him yet one more avenue towards paternity, that of adoption.[9] It is still a matter of taking the place of the father, with the difference here that the hero usurps the place not of his own father but rather of another's. In order, ultimately, for the adoptive father to truly succeed in his endeavor, he must eclipse the natural father and forge his own paternity. The term "forge" is appropriate because it means to form, even to invent, but also to counterfeit. The successful adoptive father is he whose simulation of the genuine article is "seamless," whose adoptive distance disappears while the artificial aspect of his claim to paternity is forgotten. Adoption is in fact a creation, but a creation of an illusion, at the same time as it is the illusion of a creation.[10]

This may perhaps explain an additional source of Hugo's preoccupation with the figure of Christ, who becomes more than exclusively the representative of love, pity and sacrifice—one more means of taking the place of another—but recalls as well a substitution of fathers between God and Joseph.[11] What is of added interest here is that Christ's origin entails no biological reproduction. A physical paternity is replaced by a divine, non-sexual siring. Indeed, God's creative power is not by nature sexual but very often verbal, as Hugo emphasizes: ". . . Dieu . . . dit à l'ombre: / Je suis. Ce mot créa les étoiles sans nombre" (**La Fin de Satan,** Poésie IV, 28). As described by Saint John, God is a "creative writer" in a very literal sense, for his creativity is wrought through words.

The adoptive father, then, inserts himself in the place of another's authority and assumes this power that is at heart artistic—in a generally creative sense, as expressed by Hugo—in order to construct a paternity that is artistic, this time in the sense of a creation by means of artifice. Biological fatherhood allows its simulated replacement to occupy the foreground in Hugo's novels, reflecting the artistic rather than natural productions that are the novels themselves. In effect, this surrogate paternity symbolizes a literary endeavor, as the illusion of fatherhood is created not through language alone but primarily through narrative. The adoptive father fabricates a different history with which to replace the real one. He is a storyteller, a composer of fiction. In the final analysis, he is the novelist.

The adoptive father is in fact a prevalent figure in Hugo's novels. Undoubtedly the most celebrated is Jean Valjean, self-appointed father to Cosette. Having been abandoned by her natural father at a very early age, Cosette does not remember him, nor does she recall her mother Fantine, who on her deathbed entrusted her daughter to Valjean. The memory of her mother is so weak in Cosette's mind that she professes twice to be unsure of even having had one (*LM* 314, 705). "Cette mère," we are told, "elle ne savait pas même son nom. Toutes les fois qu'il lui arrivait de le demander à Jean Valjean, Jean Valjean se taisait. . . . Était-ce prudence? Était-ce respect? était-ce crainte de livrer ce nom aux hasards d'une autre mémoire que la sienne?" (*LM* 705) Cosette's ignorance regarding her mother is consequently not merely a result of a faulty memory, but also caused by the silence of Jean Valjean.

The reason for this silence, the reader learns, is to protect Fantine, by covering up her impure past. In effect, the sexual nature of her genesis is particularly relevant to Cosette, in that her mother had been a prostitute. Yet it is also pertinent to the tie binding Fantine to Cosette's father, which is reduced to a purely sexual bond, as the two never entered into a legal attachment by marrying. Valjean's silence may thus be interpreted as an effort to erase the negatively-charged biological aspect of Cosette's birth.

At this point, however, an allusion is raised concerning another source of Valjean's reticence:

> Tant que Cosette avait été petite, Jean Valjean lui avait volontiers parlé de sa mère; quand elle fut jeune fille, cela lui fut impossible. Il lui sembla qu'il n'osait plus. Était-ce à cause de Cosette? était-ce à cause de Fantine? il éprouvait une sorte d'horreur religieuse à faire entrer cette ombre dans la pensée de Cosette, et à mettre la morte en tiers dans leur destinée.
>
> (*LM* 705)

The "horreur religieuse" experienced by Valjean would indeed appear to corroborate the assumption that his taciturnity stems from a purifying intention, but what is additionally revealed is a far less disinterested aim. The hero does not speak of Fantine because he does not want to share Cosette with her mother, who would insert herself as a "tiers" into their duo. The assertion that Valjean had spoken to her of her mother, willingly even, as the text stresses ("Jean Valjean lui avait volontiers parlé de sa mère"), is rendered rather dubious by the fact that Cosette does not even know Fantine's name. Thus among the questions regarding the hero's motivations, "Était-ce à cause de Cosette? était-ce à cause de Fantine?" the one significantly lacking is "Était-ce à cause de Jean Valjean lui-même?"

In effect, the erasure of Fantine's name from Cosette's mind procures its desired impact: "C'est peut-être ma mère, cet homme-là!" reflects Cosette (*LM* 705). She also refers to him as "père." Victor Brombert observes that "[t]he accession to paternity [of Valjean] . . . takes place exactly nine months after the death of Fantine" (103). In revolutionary France, argues Carol Pateman, an ideal arose of "men's creation of new political life"

in which women were "defeated and declared procreatively and politically irrelevant" (36).[12] In fact, an engraving of the era shows Deputy Target literally giving birth to the constitution of 1791.[13] Valjean's fathering of Cosette on his own may indeed reflect historical and political concerns, yet on an artistic level, he is above all the "creator" of Cosette:

> Jean Valjean avait travaillé à Cosette. Il avait un peu fait cette âme. C'était incontestable.
>
> (*LM* 1108)

> Il [Dieu] avait construit cette charmante Cosette, et il y avait employé Jean Valjean. Il lui avait plu de se choisir cet étrange collaborateur.
>
> (*LM* 1109)

These two citations suggest the efforts of the artisan, for whom the creative act entails "travail," "faire," "construction" and "emploi." The second reference, however, on the one hand withholds a portion of the hero's creative authority by making him share it with God, yet on the other hand augments this authority by ascribing precisely a divine aspect to this col*labor*ative production. One may recall once more the origin of Christ, it too was removed of its carnal nature and replaced instead with a celestial character. Valjean appears likewise to compose a false paternity in which Cosette's origin is purged of its sexual component and imbued with religious overtones.

This collaboration, moreover, manages to reinforce intertextually a properly "authorial" authority in its resemblance to another cooperation with God for the purpose of producing an equally "heavenly" creature. The angel Liberty in *La Fin de Satan* is the daughter of both God and Satan, for she is born when the divine gaze rests upon a feather fallen from the archangel's wing just before his fall. Satan hence becomes God's partner in this creative enterprise by dint of a *plume*—denoting "feather" and also "pen".

The significance of this detail concerning the adoptive father as novelist is reaffirmed towards the end of *Les Misérables,* when Jean Valjean fabricates a story of a crushed thumb that "l'avait empêché de rien signer" (*LM* 1074). What is of import is not particularly the lie itself but the reason for the lie: to avoid the act of signing. The hero refuses to sign, and thus to legitimize, documents that would establish a familial bond between himself and his adopted daughter. By withholding his signature, Jean Valjean, the cooperator with God in *Les Misérables,* expresses his renunciation of paternal rights over Cosette (described, incidentally, as an "angel").[14] A rejection of paternity thus involves a rejection of writing. His fatherhood and his writing are consequently linked. For both Jean Valjean and Satan, whose nonsexual procreations coincide with a shared fatherhood, paternity is allied with the pen.[15]

It is more abstractly through discourse that Cimourdain, the former priest of **Quatrevingt-Treize,** obtains his "plagiarized" paternity. Incapable of becoming a biological father, it is in an intellectual manner that Cimourdain, one-time religious "father," manages to take the place of his orphaned pupil Gauvain's natural father: "O mon maître," exclaims the young hero to his tutor, "je vous remercie. C'est vous qui m'avez créé" (*QT* 1056). A close link indeed is revealed between father and preceptor, in that their functions are both compared to a creative act:

> [Cimourdain] l'aimait de toutes les tendresses à la fois, comme père, comme frère, comme ami, comme créateur. C'était son fils; le fils, non de sa chair, mais de son esprit. Il n'était pas le père, et ce n'était pas son œuvre; mais il était le maître, et c'était son chef-d'œuvre. De ce petit seigneur, il avait fait un homme.
>
> (*QT* 868)

The role assigned to Cimourdain, furthermore, possesses a stronger artistic or creative value than the role of the father; the latter produces merely a "work," whereas the former produces a "masterpiece." In artistic terms, he is more esteemed than a father, and Cimourdain surpasses even traditional artistic ideals:

> Modeler une statue et lui donner la vie, c'est beau; modeler une intelligence et lui donner la vérité, c'est plus beau encore. Cimourdain était le Pygmalion d'une âme.
>
> (*QT* 869)

Adoptive paternity is consequently valorized at the expense of a biological one, while a creation forged by speech is preferable to one wrought by touch. Cimourdain, as an instructor, becomes "creator" and "sculptor" of Gauvain's mind by means of language; once again, what is evoked is a creation linguistically achieved. It is no coincidence, then, that the myth chosen to relate this relationship between spiritual father and son is that of Pygmalion and Galatea, in which the initial "conception" of the creation occurs not through sex but through art.

Cimourdain eventually usurps the place of biological father: "Quelquefois le précepteur est plus père que le père" (*QT* 868). The authority procured by this new father appears moreover limitless, for Cimourdain does not consider his work finished: "Une jeune destinée se levait, magnifique, et, ce qui ajoutait à sa joie profonde, il avait plein pouvoir sur cette destinée" (*QT* 943). Cimourdain's ambition extends to Gauvain's "destiny," his future, to not merely what he has become but also what he will become. In fact, the hero's tutor wishes to "faire un général" (*QT* 943) and with this aim, chooses Gauvain:

> Il y avait en Cimourdain deux hommes, un homme tendre, et un homme sombre; tous deux étaient contents;

car, l'inexorable étant son idéal, en même temps qu'il voyait Gauvain superbe, il le voyait terrible.

> (*QT*, 944)

Cimourdain desires Gauvain to be both magnificent and fearsome, splendid and dreadful, just as his own personality is split between tenderness and severity. His desire to produce a mirror of this torn self reveals that the preceptor dreams of fashioning Gauvain according to his own image; he seeks essentially to recreate himself. Cimourdain's paternity thus evokes divine creation, yet also human procreation. The preceptor's vision reveals the intention to spawn another version of himself, to discover an avenue other than sexual in order to reproduce.

One final example of artificial authority may be viewed in **Les Travailleurs de la mer,** in which Mess Lethierry is surrogate father to his niece Déruchette, daughter of his deceased brother. In addition to her uncle, Lethierry is also the young woman's godfather, once again a spiritual father. This status of godfather endows the old sailor with a further function: "C'était lui qui lui avait trouvé cette patronne: sainte Durande, et ce prénom: Déruchette" (*TM* 89). Lethierry is thus the "author" of Déruchette by having created her linguistic identity. The adoption is finally complete, as his ward "n'appelait jamais son oncle autrement que 'mon père'" (*TM* 90).

It is not long, however, before the artificial nature of this paternity manifests itself, in the guise of the steam engine constructed by Lethierry and bearing the name of "Durande": "Durande et Déruchette," we are told, "c'est le même nom" (*TM* 88). In effect, the Durande appears to occupy in Lethierry's eyes a position similar to that of Déruchette, for the beloved ship is also referred to as his "daughter". This point in common unites them all the more in that this filiation is in both cases the result of a *fabrication*. Lethierry is "father" of the Durande (*TM* 89) because he has constructed it, and father to Déruchette because he has adopted her; he has arrived at a paternity not natural but manufactured.

It is in this respect that the ship's figurehead proves especially meaningful. "La poupée de la Durande," the reader learns, "était particulièrement chère à mess Lethierry. Il l'avait commandée au charpentier ressemblante à Déruchette" (*TM* 94). As he himself has not produced a Déruchette of flesh and blood, Lethierry produces one in wood; the link with artisanry emphasizes quite strikingly his artificial parenting. The creation of the second Déruchette, moreover, is as indirect as the first, for this creation passes likewise through a third party, the carpenter. Lethierry consequently attains even this fashioned fatherhood by procurement and substitution. Once again, he is not the original author.

The wooden effigy, however, signals more than the simple relation between art and adoption. Both the art and the hollow paternity are devalorized by the fact that the figure on the prow resembles Déruchette "à coups de hache" (*TM* 94); the artistic effort is botched. This description is revealing, because it introduces the notion of failure involved in the thematic of adoptive paternity. In effect, on the narrative level, the figurehead is a fore-shadowing of failure: the sculpted image symbolizing Lethierry's idolatrous affection for his niece proves later to be one of the parts of the Durande that Gilliatt does not manage to rescue, prefiguring in this manner the loss of Déruchette both by Gilliatt and by Lethierry.

Yet Lethierry's loss is foreshadowed elsewhere as well in *Les Travailleurs de la mer,* and precisely in connection with the loss of parenthood, when we are apprised of the religious beliefs of the new rector, Ebenezer Caudray:

> Il faisait le rêve de la primitive église . . . où Frumen-tanus, évêque d'Hiérapolis, enlevait une fille pour en faire sa femme en disant aux parents: . . . vous n'êtes plus son père et vous n'êtes plus sa mère. . . .
>
> (*TM* 106)

Unsurprisingly, Déruchette leaves Lethierry to run off with Ebenezer. There is, in the end, no doubt that this abandonment is more than a mere withdrawal of her presence: "C'était la première fois de sa vie que Déruchette disait en parlant de mess Lethierry, *mon oncle.* Jusque là elle avait toujours dit *mon père*" (*TM* 329). "Un oncle," Ebenezer summarizes, "n'est pas un père" (*TM* 330). Lethierry loses Déruchette in a pro-vocative manner: by means of a letter written by him-self to the parish minister, authorizing her marriage to her unnamed suitor, whom he intends to be Gilliatt. By his writing, Lethierry manifests his paternal authority, yet loses it when this writing is subverted: the suitor is mistaken to designate Ebenezer. When he loses control of his writing, when his words lose their intended mean-ing, Lethierry loses his daughter.

In a similar manner, Cimourdain's aspirations to make of Gauvain an "ange exterminateur" are short-lived, for the pupil is discovered to be a "clément" (*QT* 944), that is, splendid, but not fearsome. Cimourdain does not succeed in the artificial reproduction of himself, and the result is the very dissolution of his paternity. It is pre-cisely the reason for the young revolutionary's "fail-ure," in the eyes of the ex-priest—a failure due to the youth's conception of a merciful rather than immovable justice—that prompts Gauvain to condemn himself to death in order to spare the life of Lantenac. In losing his "son" Gauvain, Cimourdain is deprived of the one who had constituted him as a father. In addition, the ab-sence of this paternal *raison d'être* causes the former priest to forfeit his *raison d'être* entirely: at the moment that the hero is guillotined, Cimourdain shoots himself. The loss of fatherhood results in a loss of his very life.

Such is, we know, the fate of Jean Valjean as well, whose paternity gradually slips away by undergoing the same sort of disappearance as that to which the memory of Fantine was subjected. The obliteration of the hero moreover surpasses in pathos that of Fantine, for Co-sette begins to forget him before he is even dead. The following are but a few examples among many that stress this elimination:

> Elle avait Marius. Le jeune homme arrivait, le bonho-mme s'effaçait; la vie est ainsi.
>
> (*LM* 1063)

> Le fauteuil occupé [par Marius], M. Fauchelevent [Jean Valjean] fut effacé; et rien ne manqua.
>
> (*LM* 1083)

> Il [Marius] s'était borné à éloigner peu à peu Jean Val-jean de sa maison et à l'effacer le plus possible dans l'esprit de Cosette.
>
> (*LM* 1125)

This disappearance is caused not only by the preoccu-pying happiness of Cosette, nor only by Marius's machinations, but additionally by the efforts of Jean Valjean himself. The hero distances himself from his beloved daughter both physically and linguistically: re-moving himself little by little from her presence, he asks that she no longer refer to him as "père" but in-stead as "monsieur." His sacrifice becomes a true mar-tyrdom, as Jean Valjean's death appears to be a direct result of Cosette's absence. It was earlier noted that this paternal abdication coincides with a withholding of his signature—a lack of writing. In a parallel manner, the termination of fatherly status is described each time above as an "effacement," yet another lack of writing.

The erasure of Jean Valjean from the mind of Cosette and from life in general continues well beyond his death. His final testament is a letter left for Cosette in which nothing is spoken of him but which details in-stead a summary of his financial wealth ("'tu vas voir les chiffres'" *LM* 1129). Just as he forgoes writing of himself here, he requests that the inscribing of his name be omitted from his tombstone. The hero of *Les Mis-érables* thus appears to die without leaving a written trace of himself.

"[O]n n'a pas le droit de s'éterniser" (*LM* 1144), con-cludes Jean Valjean upon his abandonment by Cosette. By "s'éterniser" we understand him to mean immortal-ity. Valjean, however, does not desire immortality. On the contrary, he allows himself to die after having in-curred the loss of Cosette: "Il mourut quand il n'eut plus son ange" (*LM* 1151). The privilege of immortality that Valjean seeks would appear instead to be that of paternity, as a reproduction of oneself. The hero has no right to this type of perpetuity either, yet not because he is replaced by another, Marius. In marrying off a daugh-ter, it has been observed, the father loses his legal but not his paternal rights; he will always remain a father. Instead, Valjean has no right to this eternity because he has never possessed any paternity but a borrowed and fundamentally artificial one. And just as this eternity proves beyond his grasp, so too another type of eternity escapes him, that offered by writing. By refusing himself as well the right to write, Jean Valjean is not an author in this sense either.

One must finally wonder at the frequent problematizing of the role of father and stepfather in Hugo's novels. The surrogate father may provide a response to parricide by filling the vacant seat of authority, yet his jurisdiction is a very different one. Rather than possessing a natural paternal right, his authority stems from his acceptance by the object of his caretaking. Adoptive paternity may thus echo the political movement from monarchy to democracy, from an imposed rule to an elected one. Marius rejects his grandfather's fatherly command at precisely the moment in **Les Misérables** when he rejects royalism. When reunited at the end, there has been a "coup," a reversal: the grandfather Gillenormand has become the "petit-fils de son petit-fils," a transformation referred to as an "abdication" (**LM** 1053). The surrogate father thus appears also to reflect the change in the locus of political power, from the governor to the governed. Déruchette and Ebenezer are those responsible for Lethierry's stepping down as father; Jean Valjean himself resigns this title when he feels he can no longer serve the interests of Cosette and Marius; and Cimourdain sacrifices his own paternal position—he does not save Gauvain—for the greater good of the people. Jean Valjean's rejection of the "droit de s'éterniser" may consequently be read from this political perspective as a rejection of absolute rule, and an acknowledgment of earned rights rather than inherited privileges determined by blood.

Such paternal surrender, however, is nevertheless bewildering in the context of the association between art and paternity explicitly established by the author. All the more perplexing, then, is the case of adoption, which links fatherhood with fiction, and which likens the act of fathering to an act of writing. If the surrogate father does indeed share some common ground with the novelist, why do his efforts ultimately not triumph? The father is like God, we have seen Hugo affirm, yet the adoptive father is not a true father and not a true God, just as the author is not God. His words are merely signs and symbols but never real, never made flesh. "L'art," concludes Hugo in **La Préface de Cromwell,** "ne peut donner la chose même" (25). The adoptive father thus manages to create perhaps less in the image of God, but in the final analysis, more in the image of the novelist himself. Unlike God, he can only create fictions.

Notes

1. Victor Hugo, *Œuvres complètes,* Roman 3, Bouquins edition (920). Further references to Hugo's works will be from this same edition and will henceforth appear in parentheses in the body of the text, with the acronym corresponding to the novel in question.

2. "Poétique et politique de la paternité chez Victor Hugo" in Hugo, *Œuvres complètes,* édition Massin (12: xxii).

3. The text also implies that Lieutenant d'Ahlefeld is not the son of the Count but of his subordinate Musdoemon, thus problematizing further the issue of paternity.

4. The narrator of *Le Dernier jour* does have a child, but this daughter has so profoundly forgotten her father that she calls him "monsieur," a reference that provokes in the narrator the following comment: "Quoi! déjà plus père!" (*DJC* 477).

5. Quoted in Lynn Hunt 139.

6. As opposed to the Lacanian "nom du père,", it is Freud's example that is more appropriate here, due to the necessity that the name be that of the *dead* father.

7. See Charles Baudoin, *Psychanalyse de Victor Hugo,* particularly the first chapter, "Caïn: le motif des frères ennemis," 23-40.

8. See, for example, the proximity between erotic and artistic creation in Hugo's *Les Contemplations* as examined by Suzanne Nash, *Les Contemplations of Victor Hugo: An Allegory of the Creative Process,* in particular chapter 4: Aurore, 79-107.

9. For Kathryn M. Grossman, the rejection of the old, paternalistic order in Hugo's early novels indicates a sort of "literary oedipal complex," a "desire for originality" (*The Early Novels of Victor Hugo* 50). She disagrees, however, with the fearsome view of fathers in Harold Bloom's vision of literary heritage (*The Anxiety of Influence: A Theory of Poetry*). Rather than displace patrimony, in Hugo's eyes "[t]he nineteenth century must . . . embrace and include its neoclassical heritage within its modern concerns if its values are to endure" (51). Fatherhood must be preserved, yet not unaltered. It is my contention that this accommodation of paternity is embodied by the adoptive father.

10. D. A. Miller proposes disillusionment as a model for the workings of nineteenth-century society and, more provocatively, the novel itself. Disillusionment, as a metaphor for narration, espouses "a

logic of displacement" and "exchange," yet the novel's "insights need to seduce us, and insofar as we are seduced, in entranced 'possession' of truth, the novel has succeeded in escaping our critical scrutiny" (178-179). The novels Miller examines as the basis for his analysis are those in which appear Vautrin, the archetypal artificial father. Though Miller does not delve into this paternity per se, the adoptive father embodies, as I have stated, the logic of displacement and thus, following from Miller's argument, the model of narrative, the success of which also depends upon an escape from critical scrutiny.

11. Christ's origin has already been interpreted as an example of the parricidal aspect of the Oedipal complex by both Freud and Robert. Freud signals the divine origin of Christ in order to insist, in *Moses and Monotheism,* on the sacrifice of the son of God as a psychological expiation of the guilt of a parricide transformed into a deicide. According to the primitive law of the talion, only the sacrifice of a divine being may atone for a crime committed against another divine being, into which the guilty imagination has transformed the dead father. Robert's analysis, on the other hand, comes closer to that of the present study, in that she centers her analysis on the aspect of a false origin. For Robert, Joseph's paternal authority is denied to make way for an origin evidently far more magnificent, thus removing both the banal nature as well as the physical presence of an (other) authority. The hero is thereby constituted as a proper hero by an extraordinary origin and by his freedom from a tangible figure of authority.

My interpretation and that of Robert resemble one another in that both observe a link between parricide and the writing of a novel. The point at which the two diverge is to be found in the distinction of perspective: Robert approaches the Oedipal scene from the point of view of the child-hero, whereas it is viewed in this essay through the optics of a different "killer" of the father, he who dispatches the father of another in order to become the new adoptive father.

12. It is interesting in this context to note that the loathing and disgust inspired by women in the public sphere prompted the exclusion of "public" women from political creation, just as Fantine, a different sort of "public" woman, is being erased from the scene of procreation.

13. See Hunt 100.

14. One might object that this refusal to sign documents preparing the marriage evokes not a resignation of rights over Cosette but rather a refusal of this resignation. This would be so if there were not other indications of the hero's intentions, such

as his request that Cosette refrain from naming him "father" and address him instead as "sir." Moreover, a marriage contract is understood to deprive a father of his legal rights, but not of the paternal status that is at stake here. The father of the bride may no longer be legal guardian over his daughter, but he will always remain her father.

15. Vautrin, alias Carlos Herrera, tells his protégé Lucien in *Splendeurs et misères des courtisanes,* "Je suis l'auteur, tu seras le drame . . ."

Works Cited

Baudoin, Charles. *Psychanalyse de Victor Hugo.* 1943; Paris: Armand Colin, 1972.

Bloom, Harold. *The Anxiety of Influence: A Theory of Poetry.* New York: Oxford UP, 1973.

Brombert, Victor. *Victor Hugo and the Visionary Novel.* Cambridge, Mass.: Harvard UP, 1984.

Freud, Sigmund. *Totem and Taboo.* Trans. James Strachey. *The Origins of Religion.* The Pelican Freud Library, Vol. 13. Penguin, 1985.

————. *Moses and Monotheism.*

Grossman, Kathryn M. *The Early Novels of Victor Hugo: Towards a Poetics of Harmony.* Geneva: Droz, 1986.

Hugo, Victor. *Œuvres complètes.* Sous la direction de Jacques Seebacher, assisté de Guy Rosa. Roman 3. Editions Bouquins. Paris: Robert Laffont, 1985. 16 vols.

Hunt, Lynn. *The Family Romance of the French Revolution.* Berkeley: U California P, 1992.

Miller, D. A. "Balzac's Illusions Lost and Found." *Yale French Studies* 67 (1984): 164-181.

Nash, Suzanne. *Les Contemplations of Victor Hugo: An Allegory of the Creative Process.* Princeton: Princeton UP, 1976.

Pateman, Carol. *The Sexual Contract.* Stanford: Stanford UP, 1988.

Robert, Marthe. *Roman des origines et origines du roman.* Paris: Gallimard, 1972.

Seebacher, Jacques. "Poétique et politique de la paternité chez Victor Hugo." *Œuvres complètes de Victor Hugo.* Ed. Jean Massin. Vol 12. Paris: Le Club français du livre, 1967-70. 18 vols.

Galya Gerstman (essay date 1996)

SOURCE: Gerstman, Galya. "The Mastery of Language and the Language of Mastery in Victor Hugo's *L'Homme qui rit.*" In *Repression and Expression: Literary and Social Coding in Nineteenth-Century France,* edited by Carrol F. Coates, pp. 81-7. New York: Peter Lang, 1996.

[*In the following essay, Gerstman discusses the correlation between language and power and how the verbal inadequacy and silence in* L'homme qui rit *reflects the powerlessness of the masses.*]

"Le bonheur de l'Olympe est au prix du silence du Co- cyte," muses the philosopher Ursus in Victor Hugo's *L'Homme qui rit.* "Donc, peuple, tais-toi."[1] Though the references are to the mythically divine and damned, the context is a social one, as the word "peuple" indicates. The author of *Les Misérables* is well-known for having raised social issues in both his literary and political life, yet his works also reveal an understanding of the dy- namics between power and language. In effect, in order to properly employ language, according to Pierre Bour- dieu, one must possess not only a technical but also a social competence, "celle du locuteur légitime, autorisé à parler et à parler avec autorité."[2] Whereas a purely formal linguistic competence may enable one to under- stand a sentence, explains Bourdieu, it is not enough to require that one listen to it. "Les locuteurs dépourvus de la compétence légitime se trouvent exclus en fait des univers sociaux où elle est exigée, ou condamnés au si- lence."[3]

This notion of silence as linguistic disempowerment is one which occupies a preponderant place in the work of Victor Hugo. Language, in the Hugolian universe, is not simply a reflection of power but also contributes to and even appears to constitute it. Conversely, a lack of political and social influence is shown to accompany verbal incapacity. And, as the opening quotation illus- trates, the linguistic inability of some is also portrayed as a foundation upon which is based the very social for- tune of others.

Such linguistic inability translates, in *L'Homme qui rit,* Hugo's penultimate novel, not as a faulty or inadequate speech, but rather as a non-existent one. "Le peuple," muses the young hero Gwynplaine, "est un silence. Je parlerai pour les muets" (757). The theme of silence, in fact, occupies a crucial position in this work, published in 1869, and centering on the inequality between classes in seventeenth-century England. According to the hero, whose face has by royal order been disfigured to re- semble a laughing man, and whose fortune leads him from commoner to nobleman to revolutionary, the pow- erlessness of the masses is expressed in terms of verbal incapacity:

> Je parlerai pour tous les taciturnes désespérés. Je tra- duirai les bégaiements. Je traduirai les grondements, les hurlements, les murmures. . . . Le bruit des hommes est inarticulé . . . ils crient. Mais on ne les comprend pas, crier ainsi équivaut à se taire, et se taire est leur désarmement.
>
> (757-8)

The downtrodden populace, he reflects, does not have access to speech at all but rather to inarticulate, and thus ineffectual, sounds. Speech is perceived as a weapon, and the lower classes, deprived of such, are "disarmed" into silence.

Muteness, however, is not specific to the lower classes but is characteristic of social disempowerment in gen- eral, by the fact that arbiters of justice themselves are relegated in the House of Lords to the status of mere observers. "Les juges," explains the narrator, ". . . ne sont à la chambre haute que de simples assistants ne pouvant parler qu'interrogés . . ." (732). The insinua- tion that the judges' authority is less than that of the lords is apparent in that they may only speak when questioned, that is, when permitted. As Ursus empha- sizes to his adopted son Gwynplaine, "Bavarder est défendu. Es-tu un lord, imbécile?" (662).

Indeed, the lords represent the upper echelon of both socio-political as well as linguistic potency. "Le lord," continues Ursus, "ne prête jamais serment, ni au roi, ni en justice. Sa parole suffit. Il dit: *sur mon honneur*" (757). The lord is not required to swear, for it is not necessary that his word be reinforced by any higher au- thority to any higher authority, implying that there is no authority above the lord. Judges are certainly less pow- erful, and even God is rendered if not inferior, at least equal by dint of being addressed as "mylord" (359). In an unpublished passage, the duchess Josiane's word is so commanding that by simply keeping her love letter to the hero on her night table instead of sending it, she is told it will have the effect she desires and will bring him to her (1096). When Gwynplaine and Josiane fi- nally come face to face, he is reduced to silence both by her incessant chatter preventing him from getting a word in, and more explicitly by her placing a hand over his mouth, as Jean Gaudon remarks.[4] Even in love, lin- guistic capacity parallels social rank.

"Moi," states Gwynplaine, "je ne suis rien qu'une voix. Le genre humain est une bouche, et j'en suis le cri" (739). He will become the voice to fill the soundless orifice of humanity, and what enables him to do so is the revelation that he is not one of the masses but is ac- tually a member of the fortunate élite. Indeed, this up- heaval provides him with more than social status alone: "Et puis, disait-il, je serai éloquent" (659). Linguistic mastery is thus a privilege which he has been "granted": "la parole lui était donnée, à lui formidable échantillon social, . . . [par une] langue de feu tombant d'en haut" (757). His social insignificance has become a thing of the past, for he has since been given "la parole" from above. The reference, of course, is to a heavenly tongue, as Gwynplaine purports to enact divine justice. Yet the fact that this verbal power comes from above is signifi- cant as well in that it is, in fact, on a higher social level that linguistic ascendancy resides. For the lower ech- elon, in constrast, silence appears to be the only pos- sible option.

Such silence, however, is more than single-faceted. It is described as a symbol and as a result of the social, po- litical and economic insufficiencies of the proletariat, and is at the same time employed as a means of protection. In other words, through elite oppression, the brutalized peasant is rendered incapable of speech, is officially forbidden to raise his voice, and himself adopts silence as a protective shield: "Se taire sur quelqu'un, il semble que c'est l'éloigner" (595). The comprachicos, a roving band of artisans responsible for Gwynplaine's disfigurement, cautiously keep silent as they board their ill-fated ship, in order to escape capture and punishment. Thus Gwynplaine's seditious rumination on economic inequality, translated as "un propos mal sonnant" (579), prompts Ursus to caution his pupil accordingly: "Il y a une règle . . . pour les petits, ne rien dire. Le pauvre n'a qu'un ami, le silence" (579). Hence it is that an otherwise unfortunate occurrence, the effacement of an inscription on Ursus's carriage, is "par la bonté de la Providence . . . heureusement illisible," as the philosophy it expressed "n'eût pas été du goût des . . . portes-perruques de la loi" (357). A few misplaced words risk becoming a legal offense.

Providence, however, does not always come to the rescue of the aging dramatist: "Lui qui recommandait tant le silence aux autres, il avait là une rude leçon" (582), for Ursus does not follow his own advice: "Il avait l'effronterie de se servir des mots qui rendaient sa pensée. Il n'avait pas plus de goût que Voltaire" (587). This audacity is more than a matter of taste, for the ambulant playwright consequently finds himself before a tribunal: "Vous parlez en public? [. . .] De quel droit?" As a showman, Ursus is permitted to speak, but as a philosopher, the judges warn, "vous devez vous taire" (583). Speech is only acceptable when emitted as frivolous and insignificant entertainment, but forbidden when it risks becoming meaningful and influential knowledge.

The judges thereupon continue their examination of Ursus, whom they accuse of linguistic indiscretions judged to be, like Gwynplaine's, "mal sonnantes" (583). Ursus's defense will reside largely in the denial of his various blasphemous and treacherous remarks: "Je n'ai pas dit cela" (583). Earlier, Ursus was similarly threatened with punishment for having spoken rashly to the Archbishop of Canterbury. His escape from punishment appeared to have been linguistically enacted by composing a sermon to charm the irate minister. Yet rather than being saved by his speech, it is the loss of his speech which saves him: the archbishop appropriates his sermon and publishes it as his own. In both instances, Ursus evades retribution—of a linguistic offense—by agreeing to "not say." For Ursus, this is furthermore an acceptance of the loss of his status as author. Before the tribunal, his defense was "I did not say that"; before the archbishop, his defense becomes essentially "I did not write that." It is no coincidence, then, that Ursus is also a ventriloquist: as an artist, he is capable of imitating the voices of others, but his insufficient political status renders his own voice dangerous to himself. On the pretext, moreover, of inculcating to

Gwynplaine prudent conduct, Ursus almost always repeats the repressive discourse of the powers that be.

This discourse, however, is repressive more than solely through the act of silencing all others. Gwynplaine's sudden prestigious accession from showman to lord has shut out his formerly cherished life, all as a result of a linguistic act. The message in a bottle, revealing the orphan Gwynplaine's true identity to be that of Lord Fermain Clancharlie, seems to have established his fate. It is subsequently discovered, however, that the other side of the parchment upon which this message appears contains a determining force even more authoritative than the first. While one side of the document displays the comprachicos' revelation of Gwynplaine's hidden heritage, the other exhibits the royal decree by which the comprachicos were ordered to disfigure and hence disguise the young hero. The fact that one of the original titles of this novel was to be "Par ordre du roi" attests to the importance of this discovery. The royal order thus claims foremost authority first in the sense of a recognized legal power above which there is no other, and second in the sense of author (*auctor*itas), for the comprachicos are revealed to be only the scribes rather than the "dictating" force. The king's political power passes through his pen.

Aside from being merely criminal, moreover, the royal order erects yet another obstacle to popular communication, in a very general sense. What is learned by means of the monarch's edict ordering Gwynplaine's face to be disfigured, is that not only has the royalty of England cut out the tongues of its subjects, it has additionally cut out their faces. The populace has, in essence, been doubly mutilated. In this manner, Gwynplaine's miscarried speech in the House of Lords reflects his own physical distortion as well as that of his countrymen: "Sa parole avait paru plus difforme que sa figure" (759). The double mutilation of the lower castes is therefore a double silencing, for they have been denied the ability of both verbal and facial expression. As a result, the silence of the popular classes becomes a blank sheet upon which the ruling body may impose its own meaning. Gwynplaine is forced to mask his true emotions with an indelible smile forever signaling approval or acquiescence. Effacing the populace's expression, the aristocracy substitutes its own self-representation: Gwynplaine's "masque de joie fait par la torture . . . signifi[ait] *jussu regis* [by order of the king]" (758).

The effect of such royal muscle is far-reaching. Due to Gwynplaine's disfigurement, Ursus's play, effected through mime—and thus itself likewise mute—fails to impress upon its spectators the spiritual apotheosis which Ursus intended to depict. This failure is due to the irrepressible eruption of hilarity upon the sight of Gwynplaine's face, an effect which Jean-Pierre Reynaud refers to as a "gag".[5] The play is a "gag" in the sense of comedy, evidently, yet also in the sense of silencing. The laughter evoked in the populace is not the subversive, Rabelaisian mirth which threatens to unseat tyranny, but is instead the laughter of oblivion: "faire rire, c'est faire oublier" (558). The laughter of the populace in this novel is nothing more than a narcotic, a sedative, useful in controlling the masses, and Gwynplaine is a dispenser of this drug, a "distributeur d'oubli" (558), rather than the bearer of light which he has imagined himself. As a philosopher, we recall, Ursus is forbidden to speak, yet as a showman, the interdiction is lifted. The entertainer, therefore, *l'homme qui fait rire,* serves the upper classes well, in that he lulls the populace, numbing them of their pain. They are once more silenced, by means of such "gags."

Thus the lyrics in Ursus's play "Chaos vaincu"—"Prie! pleure! Du verbe naît la raison. Le chant crée la lumière" (552)—are ultimately false in this work. Or rather, as Anne Ubersfeld explains, these lyrics express a "mythe populaire" which does not manage to transform itself into a "parole de vérité."[6] Neither reason nor light is produced by the stutterings of the oppressed classes. Indeed, as Reynaud evokes, laughter impedes communication between Ursus and the populace, and also between Gwynplaine and the lords.[7] The laughter of the lords, however, is characteristic yet again of the nobility in that it is a laughter which imposes silence on others. In fact, Gwynplaine is mocked by the lords not solely as a result of his grimace, but primarily by dint of his revolutionary speech. Gaudon likewise recognizes Gwynplaine's language as the butt of the joke. The source of merriment is in the hero's "extravagant" discourse, characteristic of the romantic poet, which constrasts with the suitable parliamentary rhetoric, according to Gaudon. It is "la poésie qui fait rire."[8] Thus Gwynplaine's speech is the target of noble mirth by virtue of a technical incompetence, of the inappropriate nature of the words themselves. Yet such a sanction of speech is also a product of a social incompetence. Because of the insufficient social status which he claims to represent—"Mylords, je vous le dis, le peuple, c'est moi" (745)—and which he purports to force the lords to recognize—"Vous m'entendrez" (739), Gwynplaine's diatribe is deformed and he is "gagged."

But the "power" of language, finally, is not limited to its socio-political influence. For language is both a means and an end, that is, both political and esthetic. For Bourdieu, literature is yet another pillar upon which linguistic inequality rests, one reason for which is that great writers must employ an original linguistic style "distinct" from a clichéd, or "common" language,[9] despite professed attempts to place a "bonnet rouge sur le vieux dictionnaire," as Hugo boasts in "Réponse à un acte d'accusation." Yet whether the author is viewed as a linguistic tyrant or as Hugo's poet-victim, the socio-political vantage point reveals only part of the picture.

The mention of Daniel Defoe in this novel is in this respect significant. "[O]n a tourné au pilori," Ursus asserts, "un scélérat appelé Daniel de Foë, lequel avait eu l'audace d'imprimer les noms des membres des communes qui avaient parlé la veille au parlement" (580). The fact that he is depicted as a political subversive intimates the link between literature and politics to which Hugo was so committed. Yet what is particularly provocative is that though the author of *Robinson Crusoe* is shown here to be subjugated, the reader is well aware that this will not be the last one hears of Defoe. Though politically he has been beaten, esthetically he has triumphed. Napoléon III did indeed, though temporarily, thwart Hugo politically. Just as Ursus is forced into exile, Hugo's novel was published during his own exile. This parallelism places in doubt whether "Chaos vaincu" is in fact vanquished. ***L'Homme qui rit,*** it would appear, despite or perhaps because of its portrayal of socio-linguistic oppression, is ultimately an affirmation of a different sort of verbal power. In the final analysis, no force is so powerful as to still the voice of the artist.

Notes

1. Victor Hugo, *L'Homme qui rit,* in *Oeuvres complètes. Romans,* T. III (Paris: Robert Laffont "Bouquins," 1985), 563. All following references to this text will appear in parentheses in the body of the essay.

2. Pierre Bourdieu, *Ce que parler veut dire. L'économie des échanges linguistiques* (Paris: Fayard, 1982), 20.

3. Bourdieu, 42.

4. Jean Gaudon, "*L'Homme qui rit* ou la parole impossible," *L'Information Littéraire* 1984; 36: 199-200.

5. Jean-Pierre Reynaud, "Le rire monstre," in *"L'Homme qui rit" ou la parole-monstre de Victor Hugo. Colloque de la Société des Etudes Romantiques* (Paris: SEDES, 1985), 172.

6. Anne Ubersfeld, *Paroles de Hugo* (Paris: Editions Sociales, 1985), 76.

7. Reynaud, 172.

8. Gaudon, 204.

9. Bourdieu, 50.

Texts Cited

Albouy, Pierre (1963) *La Création mythologique chez Victor Hugo.* Paris, Corti.

Baudoin, Charles (1943/1972). *Psychanalyse de Victor Hugo.* Genève/Paris, Mont-Blanc/Armand Colin.

Bénichou, Paul (1988). *Les Mages romantiques*. Paris, Gallimard.

Bourdieu, Pierre (1982). *Ce que parler veut dire. L'économie des échanges linguistiques*. Paris, Fayard.

Brombert, Victor (1984). *Victor Hugo and the Visionary Novel*. Harvard University Press.

Gaudon, Jean (1984). "*L'Homme qui rit* ou la parole impossible." *L'Information littéraire* 36: 197-204.

«L'Homme qui rit» ou la parole-monstre de Victor Hugo (1985). Colloque de la Société des Etudes Romantiques. Paris, SEDES.

Hugo, Victor (1985-86). *L'Homme qui rit* in *Oeuvres complètes, Romans*. Vol. III. (Coll. «Bouquins».) Paris, Robert Laffont.

Kessler, Joan C. (1984). "Art, Criminality and the *Avorton*: The Sinister Vision of Hugo's *L'Homme qui rit*." *Romanic Review* 1975: 312-34.

Pacaly, Josette (1986). "Une lecture psychanalytique de *L'Homme qui rit*." *Littérature* May; 62: 25-47.

Reynaud, Jean-Pierre. "Le rire monstre." In *La parole-monstre de Victor Hugo* [supra], pp. 169-180.

Robert, Guy (1976). *"Chaos vaincu": quelques remarques sur l'oeuvre de Victor Hugo*. Paris, Les Belles-Lettres.

Seebacher, Jacques and Anne Ubersfeld, dirs. *Hugo le fabuleux. Colloque de Cérisy*. Paris, Seghers.

Ubersfeld, Anne (1985). *Paroles de Hugo*. Paris. Éditions Sociales.

Patricia Mines (essay date autumn 1997)

SOURCE: Mines, Patricia. "The Role of the Marquis de Sade in the Late Novels of Victor Hugo." *Nottingham French Studies* 36, no. 2 (autumn 1997): 10-23.

[*In the following essay, Mines surveys the influence of the Marquis de Sade on Hugo's three late novels:* Les travailleurs de la mer, L'homme qui rit, *and* Quatrevingt-treize.]

For some years, scholars have tended to interpret Hugo's works in terms of the philosophy of *immanence,* asserting the author's belief in the omnipresence of a benevolent God and in the absolute certainty of progress.[1] The predominance of this critical approach has therefore caused the negative aspects of *Les Travailleurs de la mer, L'Homme qui rit* and *Quatrevingt-treize* to be almost entirely overlooked.[2] The references Hugo made to the marquis de Sade in his late novels remain especially neglected. The prevalence of *imma-*nence might cause readers to think that there could be no possible connection between Hugo and this infamous figure, but critics have shown that the majority of writers of Hugo's generation were familiar with his work because it had many similarities with the European *romans terrifiants* or *romans noirs* which fired their imaginations so intensely.

It is well known that in their youth the Romantics had all shown a fascination for English *romans noirs,* such as *The Monk* and *The Castle of Otranto*:

> ceux qui formeront plus tard l'école romantique sont en train de nourrir leurs jeunes imaginations des romans de Lewis et d'Anne Radcliffe. Stendhal recommande à sa soeur Pauline la lecture des *Mystères d'Udolphe* et de *l'Italien* [. . .] Gautier dévorait dans sa jeunesse tous ces ouvrages, nous dit-il dans la préface des *Jeunes France*: 'j'ai épuisé tous les cabinets du quartier. Que d'amants malheureux, que de femmes persécutées m'ont passé devant les yeux! . . .' George Sand raconte aussi les délicieux frissons que lui donna, dans sa jeunesse, la lecture de ces histoires palpitantes: 'nous nous persuadions entendre des soupirs, des gémissements partir de dessous les pavés ou s'exhaler par les fissures des portes et des murs'.[3]

The Romantics seem to have been obsessed with narratives involving the forces of evil and the unjust suffering they seek to inflict. Their work began to reflect the novels they were reading. *Han d'Islande,* Hugo's second novel which was published in 1823, is a 'sombre récit, dominé par le personnage hideux et monstrueux du brigand d'Islande, qui boit dans les crânes de ces victimes' and this work illustrates 'crimes horribles'.[4] But what is the relation between the works of Sade and the novels which were so esteemed by the Romantics? R. Virolle has indicated that in 1797, the same year in which *The Monk, The Italian, The Mysteries of Udolpho* and *The Castle of Otranto* appeared in Paris, 'Sade offre aux amateurs de cruauté sa *Nouvelle Justine*'.[5] Sade's novel possesses many of the characteristics of the English *romans noirs* which terrified and at the same time inspired the young writers. The heroine Justine is a 'femme persécutée' who endures torments and sheds tears, but whose sobs and cries remain unheard because of the thick walls of the impenetrable Gothic prisons in which she is held against her will. In *La Nouvelle Justine,* Sade also depicts human beings who are not monstrous in their physical appearance but who nevertheless prove to be utterly depraved. Thus, Sade's work had much to offer the *amateurs* of the English *romans noirs.* The Romantics' interest in Sade can also to some extent be explained by the reasons behind their passion for *The Monk*: 'aux environs de 1830, Lewis jouit d'une très grande popularité et fait appel à un romantisme devenu moins chrétien, moins moral, et qui se plaît à étaler des tableaux de prêtres corrompus et de nonnes débauchées'.[6] In her recent work on Sade, Chantal Thomas asserts that his infamy alone automatically guaranteed that some of his work at least would continue to be read in the 19th century: 'l'enfer des bibliothèques, le secret des collections privées, la curiosité de certains psychiatres et de quelques écrivains peuvent seuls témoigner d'une survivance précaire, souterraine, déformée, amputée, de l'œuvre du marquis'.[7] Indeed, Chantal Thomas insists that Sade was an important preoccupation of many major authors throughout the 19th century.[8] Even if the Romantics were initially attracted to Sade's work in the 1820s because of his notoriety, upon inspection they would have found that many features of his writing intensified their interest in him.

Of all the Romantics, however, it seems that the works of Sade had the most profound and enduring of impressions on Hugo and Lamartine. Jean Gaudon has indicated that Lamartine's heroines resemble Sade's Justine and he has suggested that 'la quasi-totalité des œuvres non-autobiographiques de Lamartine pourraient être réunies sous un titre commun déjà utilisé par le marquis de Sade: Les infortunes de la vertu'.[9] In *Antoniella,* a novel which was published in 1867, Gaudon remarks that 'la cruauté s'exerce sans contrôle avec quelque chose de quasi-frénétique'.[10] Lamartine was therefore still preoccupied with Sade in his sixties and seventies and this article will demonstrate that in his later years, Hugo also published novels which compare with those of Sade. In his article on Lamartine, Gaudon does not mention that Hugo was reading the works of Sade in the 1860s, a point that I will discuss later. It is remarkable to note that whilst Lamartine's heroines are reminiscent of Justine, the female characters in Hugo's late novels mirror Sade's Juliette in their derivation of sexual pleasure from their assaults upon males in their presence.[11]

Hugo mentions Sade by name in *Les Travailleurs de la mer* and in *Quatrevingt-treize,* which were published in 1866 and 1874 respectively. *L'Homme qui rit,* published in 1869, is a novel in which children are sold, kidnapped and mutilated for the entertainment of adults, and this work has several parallels with the evocation of merciless humanity provided by Sade. This article will endeavour to show that Sade was highly significant in each of Hugo's three late novels. These works suggest that Hugo was inspired by Sade and, furthermore, that he agreed with much of the Marquis's thinking.

It is perhaps only to be expected that Sade would be found in *Quatrevingt-treize,* Hugo's illustration of 1793. It could be argued that for the sake of verisimilitude, Hugo had no choice but to include Sade in his depiction of France under the Terror: 'le marquis de Sade présidait la section des Piques, place Vendôme' (15: 344-345). The Club Français du Livre edition of *Quatrevingt-treize* states that Hugo made a 'grosse erreur' in regard to the period in which Sade held this office.[12] However, Hugo could have been concentrating on atmospheric repleteness, rather than historical precision. By elevating Sade to a more prominent position than he actually held at this point in 1793, Hugo emphasises the debauchery of Paris at that time:

> Après le 9 thermidor, Paris fut gai, d'une gaieté égarée. Une joie malsaine déborda [. . .] en même temps que l'impudeur, l'improbité reparut; il y eut en haut les fournisseurs et en bas 'la petite pègre'; un fourmillement de filous emplit Paris, et chacun doit veiller sur son 'luc', c'est-à-dire son portefeuille: un des passe-temps était d'aller voir, place du Palais-de-Justice, les voleuses au tabouret; on était obligé de leur lier les jupes.
>
> (15: 344)

In *Quatrevingt-treize,* the Paris of the Terror is in a state of absolute frenzy, as exemplified by Sade. The Parisian backcloth of *Quatrevingt-treize* is made more complete by the presence of Sade, but Hugo did not necessarily have to include references to his philosophy in this text. Nevertheless, his ideas can also be detected in *Quatrevingt-treize.* As in Sade's own novels, satisfaction is shown to be obtained from killing helpless people. It is interesting to note that like Sade, Hugo attributes ruthlessness not only to the male characters in his fiction. In *Quatrevingt-treize,* there are women who are reminiscent of Sade's anti-heroine Juliette and her fellow murderess Clairwil, since they delight in inflicting grievous injury: 'Ce temps épique était cruel. On était des furieux. Madame de Lescure faisait exprès marcher son cheval sur les républicains gisant hors de combat; *morts,* dit-elle; blessés peut-être' (15: 394).

Most of the male characters in *Quatrevingt-treize* are fighting in the civil war, but rather than being sickened by human destruction, the majority show that pleasure is to be found in slaughtering innocent civilians: 'ceux qui ont tout massacré sont partis. Ils étaient contents' (15: 336). Masochism is also to be witnessed in *Quatrevingt-treize.* Whilst murder is shown to be pleasing, death can be a peculiar source of delectation to those who are closest to it. During the siege of la Tourgue, the character l'Imânus is torn in two by an enemy sword, but he shows us that masochistic relish can be derived even from fatal war wounds: 'la blessure était effroyable. Le ventre était fendu de part en part. L'Imânus ne tomba pas. Il grinça des dents, et dit:- C'est bon!' (15: 463) Whilst Sade was necessary to the historical fabric of *Quatrevingt-treize,* his thinking intensifies the violence of the period which Hugo seeks to accentuate. Hugo was less concerned with giving a precise record of a past era than with testifying to the human passion for cruelty. Hugo conveys the Terror not as a singular episode in history, but as only one of many bloody epochs, such as the Fall of the Roman Empire and the Commune: 'les fusillés tombaient dans la fosse parfois vivants; on les enterrait tout de même. Nous avons revu ces mœurs' (15: 393). According to Hugo, all these events have occurred because there is an innate lack of compassion within man and *Quatrevingt-treize* seems to lend its support to Sade's view of human activity:[13] 'le mal étant plus piquant, plus attravant que le bien' (8: 304).

It could be argued that in his final novel Hugo is merely bearing witness to the violent deeds which fear drives men to commit in times of war and social unrest. However, there is no political upheaval in *L'Homme qui rit* and yet this work is perhaps Hugo's most powerful evocation of sadism. As in *L'Histoire de Juliette,* children are kidnapped and mutilated for pleasure and for financial gain, but this practice is not confined to France in Hugo's text. In *L'Homme qui rit,* children fall victim to the *comprachicos,* who wander across Europe preying upon infants: 'sous ce nom, *comprachicos,* fraternisaient des Anglais, des Français, des Castillans, des Allemands, des Italiens [. . .] Dans cette fraternité de bandits, des levantins représentaient l'Orient, des ponantais représentaient l'Occident' (14: 49). These criminals have originated from diverse regions and their offence is not only committed in Europe:

> Les *comprachicos,* pendant l'opération, assoupissaient le petit patient au moyen d'une poudre stupéfiante qui passait pour magique et qui supprimait la douleur. Cette poudre a été de tout temps connue en Chine, et y est encore employée à l'heure qu'il est. [. . .] En Chine, de tout temps, on a vu la recherche d'art et d'industrie que voici: c'est le moulage de l'homme vivant. On prend un enfant de deux ou trois ans . . .
>
> (14: 48)

People who are capable of disfiguring children are therefore to be found all over the world and Hugo indicates that their atrocity continues still. In *L'Homme qui rit,* sadism is not limited to one time or one place and the blackness of this novel is largely created by the universal, timeless nature of this evil.

As in *Quatrevingt-treize,* the focus is on the human body and the tortures inflicted upon it, but *L'Homme qui rit* is particularly Sadean because of the enormity of the deeds related. It is children who are most often the victims of torture and their sufferings are nauseating: 'quelquefois ils laissaient la colonne dorsale droite, mais ils refaisaient la face [. . .] Les produits destinés aux bateleurs avaient les articulations disloquées d'une façon savante. On les eût dit désossés' (14: 48). Children are branded in *L'Homme qui rit*: 'Jacob Astley [. . .] eut dans sa famille un enfant vendu, sur le front duquel le commissaire vendeur avait imprimé au fer chaud une fleur de lys' (14: 49). In *L'Histoire de Juliette,* children do not usually suffer long because their lives are extinguished after brutal treatment, but the sadists in *L'Homme qui rit* condemn their infant victims to a life of unceasing pain: 'cela faisait des êtres dont la loi d'existence était monstrueusement simple: permis-

sion de souffrir, ordre d'amuser' (14: 46). For those who delight in the anguish of others, the *comprachicos* are in possession of a skill that is greater than that of the executioner: 'défigurer vaut mieux que tuer' (14: 48). In the *comprachicos,* therefore, it can be seen that Hugo created characters more 'sadiques' than those of the 'roi du sadisme'.

Since most of those who experience evil do so because they are made of frail flesh and since the physical tortures usually enrich those who perpetrate them, the emphasis is very much on evil materialism. In *Les Contemplations,* Hugo had written 'le mal, c'est la matière',[14]—and his re-reading of Sade in 1865 would appear to have confirmed his belief in this concept: 'j'ai sous les yeux le livre du marquis de Sade. C'est le dernier mot logique du matérialisme'.[15] This statement was made in the same year in which *Les Travailleurs de la mer* was being written.[16] Thus it is indisputable that during the period in which Hugo was writing his last three novels, the works of Sade were among his preoccupations. The words 'logique' and 'matérialisme' are to be noted, since they would seem to indicate that Hugo accepted Sade's view of existence as an entirely rational one and *L'Homme qui rit* appears to demonstrate this pessimistic outlook.

The parallels between Sade's novels and *L'Homme qui rit* can be perceived in the characters of Barkilphedro and Hardquanonne. Barkilphedro is unique among the evil males invented by Hugo: *L'Homme qui rit* is the only novel in which the villain is utterly triumphant at the conclusion. (The eponymous character in *Torquemada* is also victorious at the end of this drama, which was published in 1869, the same year as *L'Homme qui rit.* The success of these two villains thus points to one of Hugo's preoccupations at the end of the 1860s.) Barkilphedro's character testifies to 'the pleasure of comparison', a theory discussed by Pierre Klossowski in *Sade my Neighbour.*[17] According to this concept, an individual can only experience happiness if he is witnessing the anguish of another person and Barkilphedro intends to revel in the tortures he will inflict: 'nuire, c'est jouir' (14: 361). Sade's anti-heroes would no doubt have thoroughly approved of Barkilphedro's plan for the duchess Josiane, to whom he owed his professional success. Josiane is the Justine of Barkilphedro's sadistic fantasy: 'faire subir à Josiane ce qu'on appellerait aujourd'hui une vivisection, l'avoir, toute convulsive, sur sa table d'anatomie, la disséquer, vivante, à loisir dans une chirurgie quelconque, la déchiqueter en amateur pendant qu'elle hurlerait, ce rêve charmait Barkilphedro'(14: 166-167). Hugo's villain aspires to be a Sadean debauchee. He practises a 'religion of evil'[18] since he is determined to adhere to the maxim 'fais ce qui nuit, advienne que pourra' (14: 167), even if this principle results in his own physical harm. His masochistic tendencies are revealed because he insists that he would be oblivious to any injury he sustained if he succeeded in forcing his victim to experience agonising pain: 'être un peu pris dans la torture de Josiane lui eût été égal. Le bourreau, manieur de fer rouge, a sa part de la brûlure, et n'y prend pas garde. Parce que l'autre souffre davantage, on ne sent rien. Voir le supplicié se tordre vous ôte votre douleur' (14: 167).

The truth of this last statement can be witnessed in the execution of Hardquanonne, at which Barkilphedro officiates. Hardquanonne is the real *auteur de l'homme qui rit,* and although he is being crushed to death, he bursts out laughing in an expression of rebellion and sadistic delight, when he sees Gwynplaine, his *supplicié* standing before him. His laughter would seem to suggest that Hardquanonne was finding a perverse pleasure in the ironies of his own execution. The death penalty is a source of delectation to Hardquanonne, because its severity indicates that he has been judged responsible for absolute evil, knowledge which flatters the pride of Sadean villains and merely makes them appreciate their atrocities even more. As Klossowski has elucidated, to a criminal psyche such as that of Hardquanonne, 'the greater the punishment deserved, the more valuable the offence is in its eyes'.[19] Hugo is certainly making the inference, however, that this villain is not being chastised severely enough and that his attitude is a threat to justice itself. In *L'Histoire de Juliette,* Sade showed his concern with punishment as well as with crime, insisting that men have never invented sufficiently harsh sentences for criminals and that those who commit atrocities should receive grave penalties: 'la paresse et l'imbécillité des législateurs leur firent imaginer la loi du talion. Il était bien plus simple de dire: *faisons-lui ce qu'il a fait,* que de proportionner spirituellement et équitablement la peine à l'offense' (8: 162). Hardquanonne's fate would seem to lend weight to this argument.

Critics invariably comment upon the spirituality of *L'Homme qui rit,* but the ideological emphasis on the value of the non-corporeal is more than tempered by the sheer weight of matter, by the universal revelling in flesh and by the merciless treatment meted out to Gwynplaine, who is forced to endure interminable humiliation because of his visage. Like any novel written by Sade, *L'Homme qui rit* testifies to an unjust world in which the benevolent suffer ceaselessly.

Whilst Hugo appears to further Sade's discussion of crime and punishment with his depiction of the wicked and the inadequate means devised for dealing with them, the cosmos of *L'Homme qui rit* also compares with that in Sade's work. Like the barbaric judge Saint-Fond in *L'Histoire de Juliette,* the sea intends no swift or merciful end for its victim, the *Matutina*: 'l'océan s'amuse. Toutes les nuances de la férocité fauve sont dans cette vaste et sournoise mer [. . .] La mer a le

temps. Les agonisants s'en aperçoivent' (14: 100). The sea is personified in all of the late novels and together with the other elements it is constantly portrayed as a sadist. It is apt that Hugo portrays the sea as an omnipotent, terrifying killer, since Roland Barthes has revealed that this cosmic force was deeply feared by Sade.[20]

In Livre Deuxième of *Quatrevingt-treize,* Hugo combines the determination to kill with sexual desire in his interpretation of the sea. When a cannon becomes unleashed in the body of the royalist ship, *la corvette Claymore,* the sea intensifies its deadly momentum: 'le flot, aveugle, dirigeait le combat' (15: 304). The *Claymore* is wilfully and irreparably damaged by the waters of the English Channel and they surround the stricken vessel, in order, seemingly, to gain sexual gratification from the devastation they have caused, 'de grosses vagues venaient baiser les plaies béantes de la corvette, baisers redoutables' (15: 306). Hugo's interjection 'redoutables' signals that these are not soothing kisses, but the indication that the sea is eager to consume its prey. These murderous depths resemble Sadean villains who embrace those they kill after they have tortured them and who are aroused by the weals and the cuts they inflict. This representation of the sea demonstrates that Hugo was anxious to show that men could be treated no more kindly by the elements than by their fellows. The title of the Première Partie of *Quatrevingt-treize* is 'En mer', so that all those embroiled in the civil war in the Channel and in the Vendée can be seen to be immersed in a ruthless universe.

In *Les Travailleurs de la mer,* vessels are violated and destroyed by the wrath of the waters upon which they sail. The wrecking of the *Durande* is described as a rape and a murder: 'la Durande offrait toutes les traces d'une voie de fait épouvantable. C'était le viol effrayant de l'orage. La tempête se comporte comme une bande de pirates. Rien ne ressemble à un attentat comme un naufrage. La nuée, le tonnerre, la pluie, les souffles, les flots, les rochers, ce tas de complices est horrible' (12: 672). The collaboration between these evildoers recalls the fearful intimacy of the murderous clerics in *La Nouvelle Justine ou les malheurs de la vertu* (7: 63-81). In this passage, as in many others, Hugo relates that nature is employing its energies not to reproduce and to nurture, but to enjoy the obliteration of the beneficent creation that already exists. This emphasis upon the ruthlessness of nature echoes the ideas Sade expressed in *L'Histoire de Juliette ou les prospérités du vice*: 'nous ne concevons pas qu'un homme de plus ou de moins dans le monde, que tous les hommes ensemble, que cent millions de terres comme la nôtre, ne sont que des atomes subtils et déliés, indifférents à la nature' (9: 174). It is not only surprising to see that a parallel can be drawn between the thinking of these two writers, but also that the present tense is used by both of them in their observations regarding nature. Hugo, like Sade before him, was not speaking metaphorically, but actually defining the condition of the universe. Furthermore, the present tense indicates the writers' belief that this malevolent state is constant. Hugo depicts the natural world perceived by Sade, in which the strong defeat the weak, but he also describes the elements in a manner recalling Sade's portrayal of human beings. The entire universe in the late novels seems to be indulging in an endless orgy of destruction.

The late novels do appear to demonstrate that Hugo had a considerable interest in Sade and further research needs to be done to explain the reasons for it. *Les Travailleurs de la mer,* which Hugo was writing while he was reading Sade in the 1860s, and which has the sadistic ocean for one of its central characters, is perhaps the work which can be seen to most sharply reflect *L'Histoire de Juliette* and *La Nouvelle Justine.* The very title of the chapter in which Sade is first mentioned, 'Un intérieur d'abîme, éclairé', is suggestive of Chapitre XII of *La Nouvelle Justine,* in which Roland informs his new slave Justine about his lethal use for the 'abîme' at the side of his workhouse. In 'Un intérieur d'abîme, éclairé', Hugo reveals the truly heinous nature of the highly respected seafarer Clubin and this chapter is the climax to 'Sieur Clubin', the Première Partie of *Les Travailleurs de la mer.* Sade is referred to in connection with the hypocrisy of Clubin: 'Escobar confine au marquis de Sade. Preuve: Léotade. L'hypocrite, étant le méchant complet, a en lui les deux pôles de la perversité. Il est de l'un côté prêtre, et de l'autre courtisane' (12: 650).[21] It is at first surprising that Hugo should allude to the marquis merely in connection with hypocrisy, although it must be admitted that Clubin is an exceptionally treacherous hypocrite, like those belonging to the criminal fraternity in the works of Sade. The fact that the Première Partie of *Les Travailleurs de la mer* takes its title from the name of the Sadean villain could indicate the importance of Sade in this novel. Hugo makes an analogy between his villain Clubin and le frère Léotade, who in 1850 was found guilty of the rape and murder of a fourteen year old girl, a crime which his fellow brothers in the monastery helped to conceal.[22] And Hugo seems to rhyme 'Sade' with 'Léotade' in order to cast doubt on the progress made since the Revolution, and seems to infer that Sadean evil was very much alive in the society of the mid-nineteenth century. Léotade can convincingly be compared to Sade's priests. In *La Nouvelle Justine,* the Benedictine monks dom Severino, Jérôme and the ironically named Clément rape, torture and kill trusting young girls (6: 255-414, 7: 9-82).

The marquis interested Hugo because he called into question the fallibility of human cognition, a failing which is a prevalent theme in the late novels. The apparently impeccable citizen Clubin, 'aucune réputation de religion et d'intégrité ne dépassait la sienne' (12: 605), repays the trust of his employer by destroying his revolutionary ship and depriving him of a vast fortune. Both Sade and Hugo suggest that believing in the goodness of others can be extremely perilous. On the contrary, Sade insists in *L'Histoire de Juliette* that people who seek dominance and success must practise duplicity: 'mettez l'hypocrisie en pratique: elle est nécessaire dans le monde' (9: 40) and to some extent Hugo would seem to agree with this view. Although Clubin does not ultimately profit from his crime, his fellow traitor Rantaine achieves considerable personal gain, and the hypocrisy of Barkilphedro in *L'Homme qui rit* enables him to attain an immensely powerful position.[23]

The allusion to Sade would seem a rather grandiloquent treatment of Clubin's deception, unless we recognise that Hugo is relating the nature and psychology of hypocrisy to the ideas of Sade upon this subject. In 1837, almost thirty years before he created the villain Clubin, Hugo was already considering the behaviour of the individual who feigns goodness: 'l'hypocrite imite le juste. C'est une loi éternelle: ce qui cherche à vous nuire cherche aussi à vous ressembler'.[24] Hugo was therefore clearly absorbed by Sade's association between evil and concealment. Indeed, in his delineation of Clubin, Hugo employs the same imagery that Sade had used in his discussion of hypocrisy in his *L'Histoire de Juliette.* In maintaining a guise of impeccable probity, Clubin has conducted himself in strict accordance with Juliette's code: 'si vous devez retirer quelque bénéfice de votre crime, cachez soigneusement cet intérêt' (9: 39). Clubin has always worn what Juliette recommends, 'le masque nécessaire à tromper les autres' (9: 40) and like Sade's traitors, he shows that intense joy is to be found in casting it off: 'être démasqué est un échec, mais se démasquer est une victoire' (12: 650).

Additionally, on the Douvres, the 'abîme' of Clubin's soul is a representation of boundless evil, into which Juliette's pupil is told to immerse herself: 'plongez-vous entièrement dans l'abîme' (9: 40). It would seem that an association between Sade and 'l'abîme' had embedded itself in Hugo's consciousness, since Jacques Seebacher has informed us that in his works the abyss is the ultimate representation of nihilism: 'l'abîme est tous les abîmes, de l'histoire, de la société, de la pensée, de l'amour et de Dieu'.[25] The similarity between Clubin's career and the passages in *L'Histoire de Juliette* is particularly striking because they are voiced by a whore, a person with whom Clubin strangely admits he has deep affinity: 'il enviait la fille publique [. . .] il se sentait plus fille publique qu'elle, et avait le dégoût de passer pour vierge' (12: 650). In the past, even though he has alluded to Sade in his assessment of Hugo,[26] Jacques Seebacher has still warned against a closer study of the two authors, but the bonds between the hypocrite of *Les Travailleurs de la mer* and *L'Histoire de Juliette* are quite strong.[27]

In the world of *immanence,* everything is visible, since light is synonymous with good. But in the novels of Sade, Hugo found its inversion, a world of murky opaqueness where the hypocrite is able to thrive entirely unseen. Sade's evil is always clandestine, taking place behind the high walls and thick closed doors of monasteries or convents and the most evil designs in the late novels are also plotted in secret. Sade indicates that evil operates out of sight and Hugo reinforces his point of view by creating his own hidden places of dread. The slum dwelling *la Jacressarde* is a focal point of evil in *Les Travailleurs de la mer,* and it is to be found on the margins of Saint-Malo society, out of public scrutiny in 'une ruelle' (12: 621). *La Jacressarde* bears more than a passing resemblance to Roland's secluded counterfeiting workhouse in Sade's *La Nouvelle Justine* (7: 296). It is simple to notice that the last syllable of *la Jacressarde* echoes the marquis's name.[28] Like the majority of Roland's counterfeiting slaves, most of the inhabitants of *la Jacressarde* find themselves in a woeful place which will ultimately claim their lives: 'la cour était traversée par une poutre horizontale sur poteaux, figure d'un gibet pas trop dépaysée là' (12: 623). Furthermore, *la Jacressarde* is important to the Sadean hypocrite, because it is from there that Clubin is able to purchase a gun (12: 626). By profiting from weapons of destruction, the female owner of *la Jacressarde* displays the same indifference towards human life as Roland.

Evil in *Les Travailleurs de la mer* and in Sade's novels is imperceptible and unfathomable since it is associated with concealment, but in particular it is concerned with hidden voids. Hugo defines a hypocrite as 'une caverne' (12: 649), a reduction of the 'abîme' of Clubin's unmasking. *La pieuvre,* nature's 'hypocrite' (12: 741), is also a void, 'il n'y a rien dedans' (12: 741). Hugo and Sade seemed to believe that a void suggests a complete absence of any goodness whilst simultaneously implying an inexhaustible capacity for unimaginable malevolence.

Evil emptiness is frequently conveyed by the plummeting space inside a well in Hugo's late novels. As a conspirator with a void for his innermost being, Clubin compounds his malevolence in *la Jacressarde,* which is defined as the gaping hole of a large well: '*la Jacressarde* était plutôt une cour qu'une maison, et plutôt un puits qu'une cour' (12: 622). By now, readers will not be surprised to learn that Roland's counterfeiting workhouse also has a deep hole in its midst: '"vois-tu ce puits", continua-t-il [Roland] [. . .] en montrant à Justine une grande et profonde grotte, située au fond de la cour, où quatre femmes, nues et enchaînées, faisaient mouvoir une roue' (7: 296).

La Jacressarde's resemblance to the slave factory in *La Nouvelle Justine* indicates that the more widely experienced reader is evidently meant to catch the Sadean reference. The well that is contained by *La Jacressarde* is as deep and as perilous as that in Roland's slave camp: 'le puits, sans parapet et sans couvercle, toujours béant, avait trente pieds de profondeur' (12: 623). It is true that the well recurs as a negative image in Hugo's work, in *Les Contemplations,*[29] and most notably, perhaps, in 'Waterloo' in *Les Misérables* (11: 258), where the loss of life is emphasised by a well which is overflowing with bodies. Indeed, Hugo's earliest recollection was of a well and in pondering the reasons for the association between this memory and pessimism in the writer's consciousness, Yves Gohin seems to imply that in his childhood Hugo had firmly associated the well with a forlorn awareness of an unalterable absence: 'son destin commença dans une île, la première femme dont il répéta les mots était une étrangère. "Il semble toujours qu'il a perdu quelque chose"'.[30]

In *La Nouvelle Justine* and *Les Travailleurs de la mer,* the well indicates that human compassion is missing. Although the well had always been a source of sad reflection for Hugo, he found the fullest expression of its grievousness in Sade's *La Nouvelle Justine.* The world of *immanence* is one in which the spirit of God is ubiquitous and replete, but its frightening antithesis is suggested by the limitless void of the well at the heart of Roland's prison and of *la Jacressarde.*

Sade and Hugo use the well not only to suggest the ungodliness of men, but also to demonstrate it. In Sade's fiction and in Hugo's late novels, the well is either itself a killer, or it is made to kill. Both writers employ the well to demonstrate that men expend the lives of their fellows with the same unconcern as nature shows to the people it destroys. In *La Nouvelle Justine,* Roland expresses his contempt for the life of his prisoners by ironically juxtaposing a life-giving 'puits' with his own peculiar method of execution: '"quand tu seras morte à la peine, on te jettera dans le trou que tu vois à côté de ce puits, avec deux cents autres coquines de ton espèce qui t'y attendent, et l'on te remplacera par une nouvelle"' (7: 296). *La Jacressarde* is an amalgamation of Roland's well and of his lethal pitfall and it allows its victims no dignity in death: 'les immondices y suintaient, tous les ruissellements de la cour y filtraient' (12: 623). In a reversal of the classic myth, rather than being a fount of life, this well is indifferent to those it poisons and to those it kills: 'qui avait soif, y buvait. Qui avait ennui, s'y noyait' (12: 623). The unfortunate of *la Jacressarde* are committed to 'la tombe qui lave' like the *comprachicos* in *L'Homme qui rit* (14: 104), but unlike them they are without sin: the iniquitous remain alive and unthwarted. They thus bear witness to a Sadean universe, in which the innocent are mistreated and destroyed while the wicked thrive unchecked.

The charge could be made that Roland's slaves are put to death by a ruthless individual, whereas the inhabitants of *la Jacressarde* take their own lives, but they do so because of the indifference which is shown to them by their fellow men and which is represented by the chasm of the well. Roland will be able to kill relentlessly 'et l'on te remplacera par une nouvelle' and the absence of compassion in the Saint-Malo of **Les Travailleurs de la mer** is such that it causes children to commit suicide in the well of *la Jacressarde*: 'en 1819, on en retira un enfant de quatorze ans' (12: 623).

During his travels in 1837, Hugo wrote a passage in which he makes the old association between a well and the truth: 'j'ai à ma gauche un vieux puits et l'océan à ma droite, si bien que je pourrais voir surgir subitement la beauté à ma droite et à ma gauche la vérité'.[31]

The wells in *La Nouvelle Justine* and *la Jacressarde* testify to the bitter truth concerning the defencelessness of the innocent in human society. The malevolent are indomitable and they are obliged to make little effort to vilify and obliterate the good. Besides its relationship with emptiness, the well would have interested Sade and Hugo because it can be seen to signify a point of intersection between nature and human civilisation, since wells can exist naturally or can be man-made. The writers suggest that men are not making progress, because they demonstrate the intense predilection for destruction that can be witnessed in the cosmos. The immeasurable depth of the wells is an expression of immensity, but the greatness which it suggests is a boundless preference for ruthlessness rather than for beneficial improvement. Civilisation is being transformed into a mass grave.

That no assessment has been made of Hugo's interest in Sade is surprising, given that in the late novels and in **Les Travailleurs de la mer** in particular, Hugo does refer to him explicitly, appears to recreate his ideas and portrays characters who are almost indistinguishable from any of the maleficent in Sade's fiction. As Klossowski has pointed out, Sade believed that 'only motion is real: creatures are but its changing phases'[32] and whilst Hugo seems to have accepted this pessimistic vision of the world, it was nevertheless a view he acknowledged with some bitterness and regret. For Sade, perpetrating evil was essential in order to prove the existence of the freedom of the individual,[33] and, moreover, as Bressac affirms in *La Nouvelle Justine*, human misdeeds are necessary to nature: 'il faut que l'équilibre se conserve; il ne peut l'être que par des crimes; les crimes servent donc la nature: s'ils la servent, si elle les exige, si elle les désire, peuvent-ils l'offenser? et qui peut être offensé, si elle ne l'est pas?' (3: 88). Hugo is the 'offensé' whom Bressac seeks. To Sade, 'crime is a tribute paid to life'[34] but to Hugo crime only vilifies human existence. Whilst violence is synonymous with lib-

erty and energy in the Sadean consciousness, to Hugo it is the execrable residue of the barbarous past: 'Hugo seems almost to espouse a Voltairean view of history as a succession of horrible acts [. . .] History is hell. And Hugo's dream is the abolition of all gehennas'.[35]

The idea of improvement is as important to Hugo as malevolent desire is to Sade and Sade's thought 'is contrary to every idea of progress'.[36] Hugo believed that human beings should not simply imitate the devastation of the cosmos and the past. He desired that they should unceasingly devote themselves to the cause of progress, but this idea is no more than a wish, because Hugo is forced to admit that rather than fashion lasting works for the benefit of mankind, men dedicate themselves to obliterating anything positive which already exists: 'la mer édifie et démolit; et l'homme aide la mer, non à bâtir, mais à détruire'. (12: 537). What is more, Hugo's late novels seem to imply that mankind must struggle for advancement without divine assistance. Sade's Justine is left in no doubt about the absence of a benevolent God, 'voilà le plus misérable des êtres . . . le plus lourd imposteur qui eût encore paru, le voilà Dieu' (3: 82) and the hostility of such an empty universe is the final impression of **L'Homme qui rit**: 'God's responsibility for evil is more than hinted at in Gwynplaine's bitter and blasphemous hypothesis that if Dea were to die, this would prove that God is a 'traitor' and man a dupe (XIV, 382). Dea dies within the hour'.[37] Although he continues to yearn for progress in the 1860s and 1870s, Hugo seems to have become convinced, like Sade, that God is an illusion and that the only certainty is the existence of evil: 'un certain mauvais fond humain est presque irréductible' (14: 396).

In the latte, years of his exile, Hugo clearly did reject Rousseau's perception of the universe in favour of the harsh reality propounded by Sade. It is in **L'Homme qui rit** that Hugo again insists upon the association between human evil and unfathomable depths, 'notre côté ténébres est insondable' (14: 167), a statement which is evidently more akin to Sade than to any teaching of Rousseau or to the philosophy of *immanence*. Critics should accept that if we are to hold a proper debate about Hugo's philosophy, his concern with the radical pessimism and materialism of Sade must be addressed.[38] It is time to dispel the radiant myth of *immanence* and to confront the Sadean shadows in which Hugo immersed himself in his late novels.

Notes

1. See, for instance, Yves Gohin's introduction to the most recent edition of Hugo's late novels, published together in one volume, *Œuvres complètes de Victor Hugo* (Paris: Robert Laffont, 1985), Romans III, pp. i-v.

2. Victor Brombert, C. W. Thompson and Jean-Pierre Reynaud have all drawn our attention to the darker clements in Hugo's late novels, however.

3. Alice Killen, *Le Roman terrifiant ou roman noir de Walpole à Anne Radcliffe* (Paris: Librairie Ancienne Edouard Champion, 1923), pp. 123-4.

4. Ibid., p. 181.

5. 'Vie et Survie du Roman Noir', *Manuel d'Histoire Littéraire de la France,* Co-ordination assurée par P. Barbéris et C. Duchet (Paris: Editions Sociales, 1972), tome IV, 1789-1848, p. 38. See also Claude Duchet, 'L'image de Sade à l'époque romantique', in *Le Marquis de Sade* (Paris: Armand Colin, 1968), pp. 219-40.

6. Killen, *Le Roman terrifiant ou roman noir de Walpole à Anne Radcliffe,* p. 142.

7. Chantal Thomas, *Sade* (Paris: Editions du Seuil, 1994) pp. 236-7.

8. Thomas indicates to us that 'régulièrement dans les soirées ou les diners, dont ils [les frères Goncourt] notent les conversations, il est question de "M. de Sade". Comme Flaubert, le XIXe siècle est hanté et presque entièrement muet sur cette hantise ou ne l'exprimant qu'indirectement.' (*Sade,* p. 236) Besides Flaubert and the Goncourt brothers, Thomas includes Balzac, Baudelaire, Huysmans, Michelet, Jules Jann and Barbey d'Aurevilly in the group of writers who were fascinated by Sade (Ibid., pp. 236-7).

9. Jean Gaudon, 'Les infortunes de la vertu', *Lamartine: le livre du centenaire,* Etudes recueillies et présentées par Paul Viallaneix (France: Flammarion, 1971), 31-43, p. 31.

10. Ibid., p. 31.

11. Consider, for instance, the lubricious duchess losiane in *L'Homme qui rit,* who attacks and miures the virginal hero with whom she yearns to copulate: 'et elle le mordit d'un baiser' (14: 317). All quotations of works by Hugo and page references are from the *Œuvres completes,* ed Jean Massin, 18 vols (Paris: Club Français du Livre, 1967-1969) and will be indicated in the text.

12. 15: 345, footnote 15.

13. Page references are from the Pauvert edition of the *Œuvres completes du marquis de Sade,* 15 vols (Paris: Société Nouvelle des Editions Pauvert, 1987) and will be indicated in the text.

14. *Les Contemplations,* VI, 26 (9: 373).

15. Barrère, *Victor Huge à l'Œuvre* (France: Klincksieck, 1965), p. 172. Barrère points out that this extract is to be found in *En Voyage.* Edition Imprimerie Nationale, tome 2, p. 595.

16. *Les Travailleurs de la mer* was published in March, 1866.

17. Pierre Klossowski, *Sade my Neighbour.* translated by Alphonso Lingis (Illinois: Northwestern University Press, 1991), p. 78 First published as *Sade mon prochain* (Paris: Editions du Seul, 1947).

18. Ibid., p. 76.

19. Ibid., p. 75.

20. Roland Barthes, *Sade, Fourier, Loyola,* translated by Richard Miller, (London Jonathan Cape, 1977): 'Sade had a phobia: the sea' (p. 179). First published in French (Paris: Editions du Seuil, 1971).

21. None of the editions of the *Œuvres completes de Victor Hugo* makes any comment about this reference to Sade.

22. See 7: 927.

23. Rantaine writes to Lethierry from the *Tamaulipas* (12: 760), a ship which enables miscreants to travel to exotic lands and oppress their innocent inhabitants (12: 607-8). In Hugo's earlier novels, Han, Frollo and Javert all lose their lives, but Barkilphedro is still on the ascendant at the end of *L'Homme qui rit.*

24. *France et Belgique,* '1837', *Voyages, Œuvres Completes de Victor Hugo* (Paris: Robert Laffont, 1987), p. 627.

25. *Roman* 24798, folio 198-180/217, 1854-55, in 'Portefeuille Romanesque, Du Roman Serk aux Travailleurs de la Mer', 10: 1149.

26. See Jacques Seebacher's article, 'Poétique et politique de la paternité', in *Romantisme et politique,* 1815-51, Colloque de l'ENS de St. Cloud, avril 1965, (France: A. Colin, 1969), pp. 110-28.

27. The plot relating the crimes committed by Rantaine and Clubin seems to have emanated from the advice given by Juliette (9: 38-40).

28. The name 'la Jacressarde' does, of course, also suggest 'la Jacquerie', the uprising of the *paysans* in the 14th century. However, in the context of Hugo's slum dwelling, this connotation is quite ironic, since there is no 'association' or 'révolte' among its tenants 'ces être se connaíssaientils entre cux? Non' (12: 623). Hugo informs us that the *jacques* of la *Jacressarde* seldom have the courage even to speak 'parlait qui osait [. . .] On tâchait de s'oublier dans le sommeil [. . .] On prenait de la mort ce qu'on pouvait' (12: 623).

29. *A ma fille* (9: 66).

30. Gohin provides us with this fact in *Victor Hugo, Que sais-fe?*, (Paris: P.U.E., 1987), p. 8.

31. *Le Bourg d'Ault / ou le Crotoy (Voyage), fragment numéro 2, France et Belgique, '1837', Voyages, Œuvres Complètes de Victor Hugo* (Paris: Robert Laflont, 1987), p. 654.

32. Klossowski, *Sade my Neighbour,* p. 90.

33. 'The Sadean mind reproduces in its reflection the perpetual motion of a Nature who creates but arouses obstacles for herself with those very creations and, for a moment, finds her freedom only in destroying her own works' (Ibid., p. 98).

34. Ibid., p. 138.

35. Victor Brombert, *Victor Hugo and the Visionary Novel* (Massachusetts: Harvard University Press, 1984), p. 229.

36. Klossowski, Sade my Neighbour, p. 100.

37. Brombert, *Victor Hugo and the Visionary Novel,* p. 202.

38. In *Victor Hugo and the Visionary Novel,* Victor Brombert insists on the 'inadequacy' of a 'naive reading of Hugo' (p. 242).

Charles Nunley (essay date 1997)

SOURCE: Nunley, Charles. "(En)gendering Terror: Women and Violence in *Quatrevingt-treize*." In *The Play of Terror in Nineteenth-Century France,* edited by John T. Booker and Allan H. Pasco, pp. 35-44. Newark, N.J.: University of Delaware Press, 1997.

[*In the following essay, Nunley discusses the character of Michelle Fléchard in* Quatrevingt-treize *and states that Hugo accurately reflects women's revolutionary roles in the novel, offering a vision in which feminine values could be essential to the revolutionary process.*]

Just a few months before he began work on **Quatrevingt-treize,** Hugo wrote a poem in praise of Louise Michel, recently captured, tried, and sentenced to six years of exile in New Caledonia for having been one of the leaders of the Paris Commune of 1871. In his poem—tellingly entitled **"Stronger than a Man"**—Hugo speaks highly of Louise Michel's contribution to the short-lived Commune, praising her for her abnegation, what he calls her "working-class woman's pride,"[1] and her heroic defense of the barricades (Hugo 1986, 199). Prior to becoming an anarchist, Louise Michel was not only a school teacher and poet, but also an avid reader of Hugo. It is thus hardly surprising that she should be hailed as an important woman revolutionary by Hugo, who had on several occasions expressed sympathy and support for women in their struggle for equality.

So why, one might ask, is the main female character of **Quatrevingt-treize**—unlike the novel's verbally assertive male protagonists—an inarticulate mother who depends solely upon her intuitions to see her and her children through some of the darkest days of *la Terreur*? Did Hugo mean to suggest that women like Louise Michel did not exist during the French Revolution, or that those like Charlotte Corday had transgressed sexual boundaries, making them unsuitable for the kind of maternal heroism he had in mind?[2] In a word, what could Louise Michel and Michelle Fléchard possibly have in common other than their homonymous names?[3] While Fléchard's role as woman-revolutionary in **Quatrevingt-treize** clearly differs from Louise Michel's intellectually motivated engagement with her fellow Communards of 1871, I will argue in the following that, despite her limitations, Fléchard is not belittled in Hugo's text.[4] In examining her place in the novel, it is possible to glimpse a vision of the French Revolution according to which feminine values would be recognized as an essential component of the revolutionary process.

In a particularly insightful passage of her recent study of the role of women in the public sphere during the French Revolution, Joan Landes observes that, in his *Serment des Horaces,* "David removes his dutiful Roman matrons to the sidelines of political life; still, they are there" (Landes 158). By situating women in the margin of his painting, David underscores their limited role as spectators to events in which they appear unable to partake. According to Landes, the marginalization of women in David's painting—as passive spectators of patriarchy—is emblematic of the fear of female subjectivity one often finds on the part of male leadership during the French Revolution (Landes 158). On the contrary, critical allusion in **Quatrevingt-treize** to Marat's well-known suspicion of women's clubs (156)[5] would suggest a reluctance on Hugo's part to foreclose on possible forms of feminine involvement in the revolutionary process. It remains to be seen, however, what the exact nature of women's contribution to revolution and specifically to *la Terreur* in Hugo's novel actually is. For while the boudoir politics of the Old Regime have been carefully filtered out of Hugo's epic tale, women and mothers or women as mothers—in the novel, the two are synonymous—continue to exercise a modicum of influence within the public sphere. Like the Roman matrons of David's painting, women in **Quatrevingt-treize** have perhaps been moved by Hugo to the sidelines of political life; still, they are there.

Throughout **Quatrevingt-treize,** Michelle Fléchard's presence reveals important aspects of Hugo's understanding of written language as a strictly masculine form of Terror. Like the traces left on the walls of La Tourgue's feudal *oubliette* by the instruments of torture previously used to tear victims limb from limb, the traces of the Republican clerk's pen that writes out

Gauvain's death sentence toward the end of the novel (464) underscore Hugo's equivocal view of written words as modern, abstract agents of Terror that are as cutting as the guillotine's blade and—I would argue—gendered in ways that preclude Fléchard's use of them.[6] While able to bring men to act through the woeful cry of her own private grief, Fléchard herself is unable to participate verbally in the revolutionary process that Hugo's historical novel portrays, trapped as it were for safe keeping within the author's gendered view of language, deprived of the instruments that might allow her to play a more reasoning role in Hugo's épopée of social change.

In the opening scene of the novel, Michelle Fléchard is found by the *batallion du Bonnet Rouge* on its way through the dark Saudraie forest in search of Vendée insurrectionists. Instead of the enemy, however, the soldiers find Michelle Fléchard and her three children housed within what Hugo calls "a kind of *chamber* of foliage, half open like an *alcove*" (9, emphasis added). There they see the mother nursing one child, with two others asleep at her side. From the beginning, Fléchard is portrayed as a consummate mother, one, to be sure, who has been forced to flee her home, but one that continues, nonetheless, even in the deepest thicket, to occupy what Victor Brombert has called an "unexpectedly feminine setting" (Brombert 210), a domestic space where Fléchard continues to perform her maternal duties.[7]

Throughout the scene, Fléchard is unable to comprehend sergeant Radoub as he aggressively attempts to determine her political opinions, while the battalion's *vivandière* plays the role of interpreter, translating the sergeant's formal discourse into terms the mother might comprehend. Indeed, if Fléchard speaks to the *vivandière*, it is because both fulfill similar functions: while Fléchard nurses her young, the *vivandière* "nurses" wounded soldiers. As she explains, "I give everybody and anybody a sip, yes . . . Whites the same as Blues, though I am a Blue myself, and a good Blue too; but I serve them all alike" (16). Like the maternal statue of Nature, depicted as a female sphinx with huge breasts spouting the water of regeneration built in Paris in celebration of the Festival of Unity in August 1793 (Hunt 154), both the *vivandière* and Michelle Fléchard are cast as maternal agents of revolution through the biological act of nursing.[8] Although Fléchard is unable to comprehend what the soldiers want to know—is she royalist or republican?—she intuitively trusts them. The scene ends happily with the adoption of Fléchard and her children into the ranks of the battalion. The soldiers' initial suspicions give way to an overwhelming sense of paternal compassion as the sergeant cries out: "I conclude that the regiment is going to become a father" (20). Once a widow with three orphans at her side, Michelle Fléchard has miraculously become—in

the closing line of the first chapter—*citoyenne,* a new member of that large family known as *la République.*

It would be possible to analyze the first chapter of Hugo's novel in terms of the ambivalence that surrounds Fléchard's initiation into the battalion's ranks and more generally into *la République,* an ambivalence specifically reinforced by the coercive way in which her new title of *citoyenne* is imposed upon her by the sergeant. Having replaced Fléchard's father and dead husband, sergeant Radoub's paternal control guarantees that the mother remain subordinate by granting her titular status as *citoyenne.* In her study, *The Family Romance of the French Revolution,* Lynn Hunt convincingly argues that "the shift toward the good father [in the late eighteenth century] fatally undermined absolutist royal authority" while safeguarding patriarchy as such (Hunt 25). In the opening scene of **Quatrevingt-treize,** the sympathetic image of a tear rolling down the sergeant's cheek as he looks into the eyes of Fléchard's daughter indeed confirms Radoub's dual vocation as leader and "good father" to the battalion. At a time when the king of France was about to lose his head—an event that bothered Hugo throughout his life—Radoub's benevolent paternal presence seals Fléchard's fate as mother, relegating her to the realm of domesticity and effectively silencing her in his very respect for her maternal function.

Shortly after Fléchard's assimilation into the battalion, the group is captured by Vendée insurrectionists under the leadership of the *ci-devant* marquis de Lantenac, who orders that the children be taken hostage and the mother shot along with the soldiers. After miraculously surviving execution, Fléchard sets out on the quest to find her children, who, she discovers, are held prisoner at La Tourgue, a feudal tower belonging to Lantenac. Here again, Hugo underscores the degree to which Michelle Fléchard enters *la République* as mother and not as a reasoning *citoyenne*: upon hearing the words "La Tourgue," the name begins to take on the mysterious air of an incantation: "Had there been any one near, he might have heard her ceaselessly murmur, half aloud, 'La Tourgue.' Except the names of her children, this word was all she knew" (350). With such a limited command of the French language, it is hardly surprising that Fléchard should have a difficult time finding her way not only through the unfamiliar woodlands she has been forced to inhabit but also through the thicket of a new, Republican lexicon. A few pages later, upon hearing the word "guillotine," her response is again intuitive: "This rude peasant, Michelle Fléchard, did not know what that was, but instinct warned her. She shivered *without being able to tell why*" (353, emphasis added). Once again, the lexical blinders Hugo has placed on the indigent mother keep her from becoming sidetracked on the quest to find her children, for anything other than Fléchard's intuitive comprehension of *la Terreur*'s verbal trappings—the most emblematic of which is no doubt the word "guillotine" itself—would only lead her astray, distancing her even further from the domestic sphere to which she desperately seeks to return.

Fléchard's propensity to pop up every now and then in public settings without risk of opprobrium is directly related to her ability to remain silent and thus stay out of trouble. However, at least one scene in *Quatrevingt-treize* suggests that motherhood and citizenship are not always compatible. On her way to La Tourgue, Michelle Fléchard stumbles onto a village square in search of food, only to find a crowd standing before a public crier wearing a tricolored scarf over his peasant dress and holding a placard. To be sure, reference to the crier's revolutionary and pre-revolutionary dress aptly underscores the pointedly transitional stage of *la Terreur,* when new identities had not yet effaced older ones, but it also distinguishes the male peasant's eagerness and ease of assimilation from that of Michelle Fléchard, who carries no visible sign of her sympathy for the Republic, no phyrigian cap—no *bonnet rouge*. In ways reminiscent of her initial encounter with the *bataillon du Bonnet Rouge,* Fléchard is unable to comprehend the crier's message, and only hears him when he mentions La Tourgue, where Lantenac and his royalist sympathizers are holding Fléchard's children hostage. As in the first scene of the novel, in which the *vivandière* is the only member of the battalion able to communicate directly with the mother, another woman on the village square urges Fléchard to keep silent: "Listen, traveller. In times of revolution you mustn't say things that cannot be understood; you may get yourself taken up in that way" (361). By virtue of the fact that Fléchard is a stranger to the village and that she says things "that cannot be understood," she is viewed with mistrust, as a potential threat. As some of the suspicious male peasants observe: "She looks like a bandit" (357); and "She might easily be a spy" (359). Fléchard need only keep silent in order to maintain the modicum of respect necessary for her survival. Like the Roman matrons of David's painting, she must remain a passive spectator of the crier's address if she is to keep out of trouble. Ironically, however, it is precisely Fléchard's inability to keep still during the public crier's speech that testifies to her sincerity—her authentic expression of motherhood—while instilling the village people's mistrust of her as a potential spy. Here, as in the earlier scenes of the novel I have analyzed so far, Hugo imparts a keen awareness of the problematic, indeed dangerous place women held in the public sphere during the French Revolution.[9] As the concluding words to this chapter of *Quatrevingt-treize* make absolutely clear, there is no place on the village square for babbling mothers: "She plunged into the forest" (362).

Fléchard's most significant contribution to plot in *Quatrevingt-treize* no doubt occurs upon arriving at La Tourgue. When she realizes that the forms she sees through the library window are in fact her own children about to be swept up in the growing conflagration, the narrator tells us "She uttered a terrible cry" (413). Fléchard's cry—what Hugo calls "inarticulate, heart-rending; sobs rather than words" (415)—momentarily enables her to speak and be heard without being perceived suspiciously as a spy or a mad-woman as was the case on the village square, but as a mother whose exclusive concern is the welfare of her children. For this to occur, Fléchard has had to surrender articulate speech. While her words on the village square had included "They shot me;" "I am doing no harm. I am looking for my children;" "I must go to La Tourgue! Show me the way to La Tourgue" (359-60), here she is limited to "that cry of indescribable agony [that] is only given to mothers" (413). It is the force of what Hugo would like us to perceive as Fléchard's unequivocally maternal cry that sways the royalist Lantenac to return to La Tourgue after a narrow escape in order to free the children from the locked library to which he alone holds the key.

Indeed, had Lantenac not heard the mother's voice, Fléchard's role in *Quatrevingt-treize* would have remained isolated from the larger picture of Hugo's epic narrative as it depicts the Republican army's impending victory over the Vendée insurrectionists. Instead, Hugo uses Fléchard's cry to bolster his familial understanding of the French Revolution—"To abolish feudality is to found families" (438)—since her cry serves more than anything else to reunite the royalist Lantenac with his Republican nephew, Gauvain. In the final analysis, figures of patriarchy in *Quatrevingt-treize* are restored *because* Lantenac chooses to heed Fléchard's plea for mercy. Thanks to his ability to hear the mother's voice, the father figure is resurrected, if only temporarily, as progenitor of the newly engendered Republican family.[10]

Once Michelle Fléchard's scream is heard by the royalist Lantenac, she and her children all but disappear from the novel, swept up by the sea of Republicans who receive Fléchard's children from the hands of Lantenac as the library at la Tourgue goes up in flames. While it is not clear what Fléchard's personal fate as mother and *citoyenne* will be in post-revolutionary France, it is fair to assume that her early retreat from the novel—some fifty pages still remain—puts an end to her short-lived, intuitive engagement with Revolution. Indeed, Fléchard's absence at the end of the novel from Gauvain's public execution would appear to suggest the desire on Hugo's part to prevent Fléchard from witnessing Terror as an event that symbolically "beheads" the strictly familial nature of her role in the novel. Unlike the well-documented popularity of public executions among women in Paris during the French Revolution, Hugo's restricts his audience to four thousand *men,* who obediently look on as Gauvain is beheaded and Cimourdain shoots himself through the heart. In contrast to the chaotic, whimsical dynamics of non-gendered crowds evoked elsewhere in the novel, the movements of the male spectators in the closing scene of *Quatrevingt-treize* are rigidly regimented along lines that are in accordance with Cimourdain's heartlessly mathematical view of France's future: "They surrounded the guillotine on three sides in such a manner as to form about it the shape of a letter E; the battery placed in the center of the largest line made the notch of the E. The red machine was enclosed by these three battle fronts; a sort of wall of soldiers spread out on two sides of the edge of the plateau; the fourth side, left open, was the ravine, which seemed to frown at La Tourgue. These arrangements made a long square, in the center of which stood the scaffold" (487). Hugo's allusion to the shape of the *written* letter E in the above passage is not inconsequential. Not only is it the first letter of such words as "Echafaud" and "Egalité," it also testifies to the exclusively masculine nature—"l'E" evoking the definite article "le"—of those scenes in Hugo's novel where writing occurs in the absence of women and in the proximity of death: "Cimourdain was *writing—writing* these lines: 'Citizen Members of the Committee of Public Safety, Lantenac is taken. He will be executed tomorrow.' He dated and signed the dispatch" (459, emphasis added). Or, later, when Guéchamp votes in favor of Gauvain's execution: "'Gauvain is guilty. I vote—*death.*' 'Write, registrar,' said Cimourdain. The clerk *wrote,* 'Captain Guéchamp: *death*'" (464, emphasis added). In the end, writing as a silent and silencing agent of Terror unfolds in a strictly masculine space.[11]

Indeed, as *Quatrevingt-treize* draws to a close, all traces of feminine involvement are effaced, beheaded, as it were, like Gauvain himself, whose white neck—about to be severed—"reminded one of a woman" (490). Like his earlier description of the architectural coldness of the Convention—"these hard rectilinear angles, cold and sharp as steel; it was something like Boucher guillotined by David" (188)—the epitome of what Hugo perceives as Cimourdain's quintessential terrorist aesthetic precludes any feminine presence. There is simply no room for women in *Quatrevingt-treize* as the blade begins to fall.[12]

In Hugo's portrayal of *la Terreur,* women's roles are defined exclusively in terms of intuition, emotion, and biological function. One might say that Fléchard's sublime inability to comprehend revolution keeps her from indulging in intrigue and thus neglecting her duties as mother. Unlike Marie-Antoinette, whom Hunt calls the most celebrated "bad mother" (Hunt 99) of late eighteenth-century France, Michelle Fléchard is incapable of any kind of deception, verbal or otherwise. Moreover, it is her illiteracy that gives Hugo's archetypical mother the means to rise above the written word as an even greater emblem of truth. Although Hugo is careful to suggest in his novel that—to borrow a phrase from Lantenac—"[The Revolution] came from the scribblers and the rhymesters" (452), authorship as a means of precipitating the revolutionary process lies strictly in the hands of men.

Following the Commune and just prior to his 1872 retreat to Guernesey where he would write *Quatrevingt-treize,* Hugo sent a letter to the editor of *L'avenir des femmes,* a Paris newspaper voicing the opinions of the "Association pour le Droit de la Femme," of which Louise Michel was one of the founders. In his letter, Hugo expresses the following sympathetic position: "In our legislation as it is, woman does not own, she has no existence in courts of justice, she does not vote, she does not count, she does not exist. There are male citizens, there are no female citizens."—"Il n'y a pas de *citoyennes.*" He concludes: "This is an extraordinary situation; it must cease" (Moses 194). One wonders whether Hugo might have thought back to this statement as Michelle Fléchard, *citoyenne,* began to emerge in his writing. While he imparts an ironic awareness of this predicament when he speaks of Fléchard's servile station in life—"She was indeed a slave. The slave of her lost children" (365)—Hugo does so without suggesting that Fléchard's slavery is perhaps more the result of her illiteracy than the result of her being a mother. But that would have entailed writing another novel, one whose author might have been Fléchard herself. And who knows what stories she might have told.

Notes

1. Unattributed translations are my own.

2. Charlotte Corday is briefly mentioned at one point in Hugo's novel: "Outside the door was stationed Marat's 'watch-dog'—a certain Laurent Basse, porter of number 18, Rue de Cordeliers, who, some fifteen days after this 28th of June, on the 13th of July, was to deal a blow with a chair on the head of a woman named Charlotte Corday, at this moment vaguely dreaming in Caen" (1963, 147). The fact, however, that Corday's assassination of Marat is only obliquely evoked and in a way that underscores the violence of Marat's "guard dog" and not that of Corday herself would suggest that Hugo saw no place for violent women in his novel.

3. In addition to echoing "Louise Michel," the name of Hugo's ficticious mother also contains resonances that suggest strong masculine characteristics including, but not limited to those of the sword-bearing archangel, Saint Michael, bolstered

by the "virile" and indeed distinctly phallic patronym "Fléchard." Although such "manly" attributes clearly suggest that Hugo's peasant-heroine will have an important role in the novel, it remains to be seen to what degree the mother actually plays the part of peasant-revolutionary as the tale unfolds.

4. On the contrary, the only women who are belittled in Hugo's novel are those in Paris who, following Robespierre's execution, took pleasure in parodying revolution, seeing in the end of Robespierre's reign of Terror an opportunity for decadence and self-indulgence: "The artist Boze painted his daughters, innocent and charming heads of sixteen, 'en guillotinées;' that is to say, with bare necks and red shifts. . . . To grave citizenesses making lint succeeded sultanas, savages, nymphs; to the naked feet of the soldiers covered with blood, dust, and mud, succeeded the naked feet of women decorated with diamonds" (131). Hugo is quick, however, to counter such decadence with a reminder that his story has nothing to do with these latter days of the Revolution: "But in '93, where we are, the streets of Paris still wore the grandiose and savage aspect of beginnings" (132). We will see that Fléchard's archetypical status as mother remains spatially and temporally distant from the contagion of parody characteristic of Parisian street life after the fall of Robespierre as Hugo depicts it in his novel.

5. In Hugo's novel, Marat expresses his mistrust of women as follows: "Robespierre, Danton, the danger is in this heap of cafés, in this mass of gaming-houses, this crowd of clubs—Clubs of the Blacks, the Federals, the Women . . ." (Hugo 156).

6. To be sure, Hugo's choice of an illiterate peasant woman from the Vendée region was not the only one available to him. As Catherine Marand-Fouquet argues, there were peasant women from the Vendée who were able to read and write. We can assume therefore that Hugo's choice of an *illiterate* mother is intentional. It is also significant, I believe, to note that Fléchard's male peasant counterpart in the novel, Halmalo—while also unable to write—has the ability to remember Lantenac's long message in a chapter entitled "The peasant's memory is as good as the captain's science" (74-86). While perhaps no better equipped than Michelle Fléchard to grasp the weighty implications of words, Halmalo's ease in assimilating Lantenac's discourse and accurately communicating it to others is unique in the novel and, I would argue, gender-specific.

7. In his engaging discussion of *Quatrevingt-treize,* Brombert's depiction of the batallion's ambush as "a trap of tenderness" (Brombert 210) aptly characterizes Fléchard's predicament throughout the

novel, caught within a new form of patriarchy from which there appears to be no escape.

8. As Madelyn Gutwirth observes, "Women's biology . . . comes to the fore, defining their 'nature' and obscuring in them all else that might allow them to be perceived as civic beings" (1992, 161).

9. As Dorinda Outram observes, "the woman who refused to be respected but excluded [during the French Revolution] was faced with a series of difficult choices, in the actual act of speaking in public as much as in the choice of words to speak. If she was not respected, there was no way of being heard; if heard, the way was open for all sorts of attacks on a consequent loss of virtue—just the sort of attacks that were in fact made on the female activists of the political clubs and especially on the women's political club, the Société des républicaines révolutionnaires" (126). While Michelle Fléchard belongs to no club or organization, the dynamics Outram speaks of here closely resemble those operative in the scene that unfolds on the village square in *Quatrevingt-treize* (120-35).

10. For an interesting discussion of Lantenac's role as founder in Hugo's novel, see Aynesworth.

11. Needless to say, Hugo's own writing of *Quatrevingt-treize,* while safeguarding certain stereotypes that are gender-distinct, does little to uphold the qualities of Cimourdain's unfailingly terrorist rhetoric. On the contrary, it would be possible to argue that Hugo's discourse constitutes an attempt to legitimize Gauvain's egalitarian view of post-revolutionary France by assuming intentionally a-geometrical, protean, indeed, androgynous characteristics that are opposed to the angular, uncompromising regularity of Cimourdain's exclusively "male" agenda, according to which, as Cimourdain himself concedes, "Man is master. I admit only one royalty, that of the fireside. Man in his house is king" (475).

12. It is appropriate that Cimourdain's final gesture as *nourrice* (143) or wet-nurse to Gauvain should simultaneously entail the execution of his "offspring" and his own suicide. In confirmation of the gendered view of Terror played out in *Quatrevingt-treize,* Cimourdain is unable to engender anything other than his own destruction and that of his "son."

Timothy Raser (essay date May 1998)

SOURCE: Raser, Timothy. "Victor Hugo's Politics and Æsthetics of Race in *Bug-Jargal.*" *The Romanic Review* 89, no. 3 (May 1998): 307-19.

[*In the following essay, Raser analyzes Hugo's treatment of race in* Bug-Jargal.]

In March of 1818, Victor Hugo published the first installment of a short story in his *Conservateur Littéraire*; this story was taken up again and greatly amplified seven years later, republished anonymously as the novel *Bug-Jargal.* Five years later, on the occasion of yet another edition, this one signed, Hugo explained that the first version had been written to win a bet, but that the later novel was being republished in order to inform readers what the author's early interests had been, "comme ces voyageurs qui se retournent au milieu de leur chemin et cherchent à découvrir encore dans les plis brumeux de l'horizon le lieu d'où ils sont partis" (I, 278). Hugo thus, at thirty years of age, presented the novel as a curiosity, interesting, if not in itself, at least for the light it might shed on its now-famous author. Further, he implied that the views of potential interest were those of the novel, not those of the story: it is the circumstances of the story's composition, not its content, that he explains.[1]

And yet the novel, set during the slave revolt in Santo Domingo of August, 1791[2], sits uneasily with late 20th-century racial sensibilities: it recounts the progress whereby a young white colonialist comes to recognize a black leader of the rebellion, Bug-Jargal. What is at stake in this recognition is Bug-Jargal's identity (as the son of an African king), his courage, his strength, and, most importantly, his moral worth. But all is measured by the hero's own standard: it is not a question of whether Bug-Jargal is strong, good, or brave, but whether he is as strong, as good, or as brave as his white adversaries. The hero's sidekick, Thadée, even comes to say of Bug-Jargal: ". . . c'était le premier brave de la terre, après vous . . . mon capitaine" (I, 904). Despite these tips of the hat in the direction of racial equality, the phrase "pour un nègre", as in "comme sa figure était belle pour un nègre" (I, 884), returns frequently enough to make modern readers prefer to take *Bug-Jargal* as Hugo himself suggested in 1832, as a curiosity rather than as an exposition of his views on race.

Nevertheless, one must give Hugo credit: other public stands on issues of race should suffice to indicate commitment to a cause of racial equality. In 1859, for example, he wrote a letter on the trial of John Brown protesting the institution of slavery: "Il y a des esclaves dans les états du Sud, ce qui indigne, comme le plus monstrueux des contre-sens, les états du Nord" (X, 513). And after Brown's hanging, writing to the editor of the Haitian journal *Le Progrès,* he wrote:

> Puis qu'il n'y a qu'un père, nous sommes tous frères
> . . . Poursuivez votre œuvre, vous et vos dignes conci-
> toyens. Haïti est maintenant une lumière. Il est beau
> que parmi les flambeaux du progrès, éclairant la route
> des hommes, on en voie un tenu par la main d'un nègre.
>
> (X, 526)

Of course, these are relatively safe positions to occupy: a self-exiled Frenchman, and a world-famous one at that, Hugo could easily afford to criticize slavery, and he did so. But why was he so ashamed of *Bug-Jargal* that he presented it as a curiosity rather than as a work of which to be proud? The modifications that Hugo made to the story in the course of its 1825-6 revision, the revision that made it into a novel, did indeed, as Georges Piroué and Kathryn Grossman have argued, transform it from a novel into a Hugolian novel. At the same time, however, those changes represent a retreat from the political engagement of the first *Bug-Jargal,* and make of it a more coherent work, even if it is the curiosity that Hugo presented in 1832. In a word, *Bug-Jargal* represents the two poles of a fundamental choice made by Hugo in the late twenties, between politics and æsthetics. This choice defined his later æsthetics, and rendered some of his later political positions ambiguous.

Let me summarize the story from 1818, and indicate what additions Hugo made to it when he published it as a novel; it runs thus:

The hero, Delmar, is asked to explain how he came to own the dog Rask, so beloved of him and his men that one of the latter, Thadée, risks his life to save him. First owned by Pierrot, a slave on Santo Domingo, where Delmar grew up, Rask's story is thus also Pierrot's.

Pierrot, admired by all the slaves for his self-sacrifice and his majesty, is condemned to death by the hero's uncle for having raised his hand against him to protect a fellow-slave. He is at once befriended by Delmar; he escapes, and shortly after his escape from prison, there is a slave rebellion which the white colonialists unite to put down. In battle, Delmar is captured by one of the black leaders, Biassou, while the whites capture a black leader, the mysterious Bug-Jargal. Biassou frees Delmar on his word as a Frenchman that he will return for his execution; during this period of liberty, Delmar finds Pierrot, who, it turns out, is none other than Bug-Jargal, the rival leader of the black slaves. He in turn has been freed by his French captors, leaving ten hostages in his place, in order to enable him to save Delmar; Bug-Jargal explains that even if the French colonialists have lost much in this rebellion, their loss is nothing compared to that of the slaves: he, for example, is the son of an African king, was sold into slavery, his wife was killed, and his children also died. Bug-Jargal orders the execution party to spare Delmar, but the treacherous Biassou nonetheless waves the black flag that signifies that Delmar has been put to death. Thus when Bug-Jargal returns to his French captors to take the place of the hostages, he is summarily executed, by Thadée, before Delmar can return.

Almost all of the modifications Hugo made to the story as he turned it into the novel are additions; it is more than twice as long as the first version. The smaller changes include a name-change for the hero, from Delmar to D'Auverney, and changes in the names of the secondary characters. But it is the insertion of two new characters, and one group of characters that changes the story most: the hero acquires a love-interest, Marie, who serves as a point of opposition between D'Auverney and Bug-Jargal, rivals for her affections. At the same time, another slave leader is added, Habi-brah, who serves before the revolt as the tyrannical supervisor of his brothers, and afterwards, as the *obi,* or witch-doctor of the ex-slaves. And the colonialists as a group are fleshed out by the addition of several individuals, who first discuss gruesome means of putting down the revolt, and then, having been captured, display a cowardice matched only by their earlier brutality, begging for a mercy that is then denied to them. Finally, the novel has an epilog that closes the fate of its protagonist.

Hugo qualifies these additions as efforts to complete its "local color" and to verify its "historical truth": ". . . rectifier ce que le récit du capitaine d'Auverney présentait d'incomplet sous le rapport de la couleur locale, et d'incertain relativement à vérité historique" (I, 277). Hugo thus adds to the story in order to increase its verisimilitude, or, as Michael Riffaterre says, its fictional truth. What is important to note here is that while the additions have an æsthetic aim—to increase narrative coherence—they also have a political effect, and the acknowledged effort to increase verisimilitude is doubled by an unacknowledged reduction of its political import.

Verisimilitude, Riffaterre argues, is an effect produced solely by textual mechanisms: a reader needs possess no knowledge of a text's ostensible referent to appreciate its mimesis. This effect is produced by overdetermination, that is, the use of multiple textual mechanisms at a single point of the narrative, and thus, longer texts, with more mechanisms, produce greater verisimilitude: "In other words, verisimilitude increases (rather than decreases, as Genette would have it) as motivation goes from implicitness to explicitness and occupies more and more textual space" (Riffaterre, 7). Such an effect is evident in *Bug-Jargal,* and, indeed, in Hugo's preface to the novel: making it longer makes it more true. But what is understood here is verisimilitude, not reference: the novel is not more accurate, but more convincing, because of the additions. Correlatively, if the novel is pointing more insistently at its text through its multiple devices, it cannot be pointing away from itself, or, put more succinctly, its referentiality (or whatever hope of referentiality it had) decreases as its verisimilitude increases.

When we look at the individual additions, it is important to understand that, by definition, they do not affect the plot: the hero still struggles with a black prince whose valor he finally recognizes, Bug-Jargal still dies while aiding the young man who originally despised

him; the hero still regrets his belated recognition of Bug-Jargal's worth. In terms of this overarching plot, the effect of an addition can only be zero: the outcome remains the same. Thus while the men now struggle over Marie, they still fight, die, or live to regret their struggle; while the *obi* now occupies a place in the plot, he serves to indicate how worthy Bug-Jargal is, and must disappear before the end. The contribution of these additions is in narrative coherence or depth of characterization rather than in their effect on outcomes.

For Georges Piroué, it is the addition of Marie that is most significant, for the inclusion of a love rivalry to oppose D'Auverney and Bug-Jargal both separates and binds the two men: from a simple story of military values, Bug-Jargal becomes far more complex through the addition of Marie:

> . . . un élément qu'on pourrait tenir pour secondaire et conventionnel, pour un ornement ajouté en vue de plaire et d'émouvoir, modifie tout de fond en comble. Une femme est entrée dans l'arène . . . La femme dans ***Bug-Jargal*** ouvre un monde de ténèbres dont l'exploration pour Hugo n'aura désormais plus de fin.
>
> (iv-v)

Indeed, Bug-Jargal must overcome his resentment of D'Auverney and surrender to his rival the woman he loves; D'Auverney must acknowledge the bravery, etc., of a man he can only call his rival. And certainly, the presence of Marie changes the static opposition of the two male characters and makes it dialectic, as it were, anticipating the antithetical constructions of ***Ruy Blas*** or ***Les Misérables.***[3] For Grossman, though, the changes go further: if Marie is a typical, virginal Hugolian heroine, she is herself opposed to the new character of Habi-brah, who is a typical Hugolian villain, related to Han, to Claude Frollo, and to Hardquanonne.[4] A pairing of angel and devil results, like those of Claude and Esmeralda, Marie and Salluste, Josiane and Gwynplaine.[5] As Grossman has convincingly shown, this construction exemplifies the pairing of grotesque and sublime that was first advocated in the "Préface" of ***Cromwell*** (59). Since, however, Bug-Jargal's love is unrequited, since there is never any question that Marie reciprocate his love, since, in a word, Bug-Jargal loves from a safe distance, through song rather than through dialog, one should qualify this love more as an æsthetic attribute of his character than as a real plot possibility. Indeed, other than declaring his love, Bug-Jargal does nothing with it or for it: it has no future. One could say that he is destined to fail in love, just as Hernani is destined to die, Ruy Blas destined to fail, Jean Valjean destined to be persecuted. Such a concept of destiny is antithetical to the presupposition of a future and the freedom of choice implicit in political engagement.

At the earliest mention of Marie, the narrator's desire is paired with political considerations from which he is distracted by his desire:

. . . mon oncle avait fixé cette époque pour mon union avec Marie. Vous comprenez aisément que la pensée d'un bonheur si prochain absorbait toutes mes facultés, et combien doit être vague le souvenir qui me reste des débats politiques dont à cette époque la colonie était déjà agitée depuis deux ans.

(I, 288)

Or again: "Les yeux fixés sur mon bonheur, qui s'approchait, je n'apercevais pas le nuage effrayant qui déjà couvrait presque tous les points de notre horizon politique, et qui devait, en éclatant, déraciner toutes les existences" (I, 289). In other words, Marie is conceived from the very beginning of the narrative as a distraction from the central political conflict. It can hardly be surprising, given this status, that Marie is kidnapped on her wedding-night before the marriage can be consummated, for her purpose is to sharpen the conflict of the storie's heroes. If so, the stories concerning Marie— how she is rescued from a crocodile by Bug-Jargal, how he pines for her, but nonetheless relinquishes her to D'Auverney, how he saves her from the *obi*—merely constitute a subtext whose function is to increase verisimilitude, and accordingly, the character of D'Auverney appears more plausible. But by the same token, the plight of the slave, or slavery itself, becomes less important.

While Marie's presence makes the story more engaging, the same cannot be said of the addition of Habibrah, the supervisor/witch-doctor, whose primary purpose seems to be to exercise cruelty and strike terror on blacks and whites alike. It is this use of stereotype in the second version that attracts Christopher Miller's attention: "The story juxtaposes a stereotype of the 'good Negro,' le nègre généreux et révolté, named Bug-Jargal, to that of the 'bad Negro,' the 'Bizarre' *obi*" (109). Certainly Habibrah goes beyond the requirements of his office, meting out more severe punishments than D'Auverney's cruel uncle ever demanded. And as *obi*, he carries out a sacrilegious black mass parodying the catholic mass; at his death, literally struggling to take D'Auverney into the abyss with him, and that, after having been spared by the hero, he incarnates treachery and blind vengeance, willing to die if he can thereby cause the death of his enemy. As a negative version of white values, he simply reinforces stereotypes of Africa and Africans.[6]

But beyond the issue of stereotype another question comes to the surface in Miller's reading: that of opposition. A good and a bad black are opposed, and this antithesis is part of a more general tendency in western writing, from Herodotus onwards, to deny representation to Africa, for such self-cancelling formulations leave Africa a blank: "Consciousness is 'utterly' denied to these specific groups [the Garamantes and Atalantes reported by Pliny]; for them a complete nullity is reserved, and they represent a complete refutation of the notion of civilization as based on consciousness and inter-subjectivity. . . . Africanist discourse in the West is one in which the head, the voice—the logos if you will—is missing" (27). There can hardly be any denying the political effect of this use of stereotype, but I would also argue that it springs precisely from Hugo's desire for verisimilitude: by opposing good and bad, Hugo makes his portrait of the good slave more verisimilar (even if definitely not more accurate).

The mechanisms of this stereotyping show how textual coherence and political engagment are opposed: the *obi* is defined entirely in opposition to Bug-Jargal, and his relations to Bug-Jargal constitute another sub-text: he is as deformed physically as Bug-Jargal is exemplary of classical beauty; while Bug-Jargal is noble and serious, the *obi* Habibrah is a grotesque caricature; while Bug-Jargal never accepts his status as slave, Habribrah revels in his; and while the hero is attracted by Bug-Jargal's royal demeanor, he immediately despises Habibrah: "Je n'aimais pas cet esclave" (I, 288) It is hardly surprising then that Bug-Jargal is a model of constancy, consistent in his actions and faithful, unto death, in his word; Habribrah is treachery personnified, as vindictive towards his former masters as he was servile while in their service. Each action and characteristic is a counterpoint to some feature of Bug-Jargal, to the point that every word of description of the *obi* must be read as a negative image of Bug-Jargal, and by opposing Bug-Jargal, the *obi* presupposes him, making him appear more true.[7] As he does so, however, the *obi* makes the character of Bug-Jargal more heroic, and, by the same token, less exemplary of the slaves he represents. In detail, this reading still holds true: Habibrah's deformities include "jambes grêles et fluettes" even if he is "gros, court, ventru;" his head is "énorme . . . hérissée d'une laine rousse et crépue;" his ears are "si larges que ses camarades avaient coutume de dire qu'Habibrah s'en servait pour essuyer ses yeux quand il pleurait" (I, 287). All of these traits are presented as deviations from the norms of beauty and elicit rejection; to ensure this rejection, Hugo guides the reader's reaction with this summary: "Je n'aimais pas cet esclave." But the point here is that all of our reaction is directed against "cet esclave" rather than against slavery: the political dimension decreases as textual coherence increases.

The group of colonialists is another matter, and its presence significantly modifies the story: first, it must be noted that its members are revolutionary stereotypes. There are, for example, an economist, a *négrophile* and a *philanthrope* among them. Their presence draws **Bug-Jargal** into relation with contemporary events in France, and makes of its slave revolt a commentary on the Revolution. Representing an insurrection of slaves, **Bug-Jargal** offers a reversed image of the French revolution:

slaves revolting against their masters, but those masters are "enlightened;" a king dying, but that king is king of slaves; mass decapitation, but of the insurgents, not of the masters. Irony pervades this representation of revolt: in order to intimidate the rebellious slaves, one colonialist, and the *philanthrope* at that, generously offers to behead five hundred of his slaves and to display their severed heads before the fort. At this point, it should be noted that the novel ends with D'Auverney's condemnation to death by the Convention for having recounted the anti-revolutionary story we have just read; by contrast, the story has no such ending, and indeed, is supposed to have been recounted fully fifteen years after the events it relates, that is, in 1806 or 1807. Returning to the colonialists, I point out that while punctuating their speeches with revolutionary rhetoric—the adjective "ci-devant" comes back frequently, even to modify the word "noirs"—no revolutionary ideal informs their speech. As slave-owners, they hardly believe in *liberté* or *égalité,* and they certainly deny *fraternité* to the slaves, who frequently use the word *frère.*

As a comment on the revolution, the royally-subsidized Victor Hugo, who eight months previously had attended the coronation Charles X and had written a poem celebrating the event, could not have said anything plainer: the revolution was an exercise in hypocrisy. Its leaders did not believe in equality or brotherhood; the use of terror was at odds with humanitarian ideals; its control of speech denied it the right to claim liberty as one of its aims. Finally, the coda appended to the story also attacks the revolution: D'Auverney is killed in the attack which follows the telling of Bug-Jargal's story, and the news of his death arrives at the same time as a decree from the Convention that he is to be put to death for having told it. The government he defends decides to take his life, and not only that, but at the very moment he gives his life for that government, and does so for having told a story. Here, the modification is decisive. In the story, the adventure of Bug-Jargal was recounted in the past tense, but since the narrator is left alive at the end, it was possible to ask: "What happened after Bug-Jargal died?" In the novel, a "Note" tells us that D'Auverney has died defending the Republic that has just condemned him for his subversive story: there is no future for D'Auverney, and, indeed, there is no future for the story: its very terms are condemned. It would be a capital crime even to repeat it, for its language is what offends.[8] The narrative itself is thus a crime. No possibility of relating it, no possibility of learning more about its protagonists, its future is doubly blocked, and such blockage is antithetical to the postulation of a future required by ethical and political pronouncements. Further, since this "Note" takes as its pre-text the story of Bug-Jargal, commenting on the circumstances and consequences of its narration, it serves as a "subtext," heightening the verisimilitude of the original text (Riffaterre, 28). By adding this subtext, Hugo has, evidently, increased the effect of his narrative, but has done so at the expense of its political message.

In any event, the irony of the Convention's decision can only leave one speechless. There is no recognition, no gratitude, no understanding, not even tragedy here: an inhuman, inflexible power simply refuses to acknowledge its adversaries: Bug-Jargal, D'Auverney, or others. Here Hugo uses a structure that will be reemployed in *Le Dernier Jour d'un condamné, Hernani, L'Homme qui rit,* and other works, and that he will sometimes call destiny.

To summarize, a story of racial inequality and oppression in the first version becomes, in the second, a more personal and more heroic story, where a struggle of egos displaces the struggle of equals. As it becomes more heroic, its political message becomes confused, for the struggle for equality implied by the opposition of D'Auverney and Bug-Jargal is neutralized by comments on how unjust egalitarian government is. The story also becomes more abstract and extreme: from a study in black and white, the story becomes a study in good and evil too. At that point, *Bug-Jargal* becomes more verisimilar, that is, more racist: in order to produce heroes and villains, it must resort to stereotypes of the kind exemplified by Habibrah; in order to produce antitheses, it must abandon the ideological thrust of the first version; in order to imply destiny it must forsake the future.

What I'd like to point out here is just how big these changes are, and just how Hugolian they are too. If the first version was a story of honor, valor, and belated recognition of those qualities, the second is quite different. If one accepts conventions that reduce soldiers to embodiments of strength and weakness, courage and cowardice, honor and treachery, it must follow that there is a very egalitarian thrust to the admittedly schematic first version of *Bug-Jargal.* If the whites are brave, their black enemies are just as brave; if the blacks are cruel, their cruelty is more than matched by that of the whites; if whites suffer in the rebellion, that suffering is not to be compared with that of their black slaves. And it is thus not by accident that the story is punctuated, as Piroué has noted, by Bug-Jargal's recurrent vocatives: *frère.* By contrast, the second version loses this thrust and acquires a different dimension: one stops, amazed. Amazed by Bug-Jargal's generosity, by the *obi*'s treachery, by Biassou's cruelty, by the colonialists' cowardice. We're not encouraged to act, or even to speak on behalf of the oppressed slaves; we are dumbfounded, speechless before this compound of betrayals, and even if we could name it, with which treason would we start? In a word, the second version is a particular species of the verisimilar: it is sublime. The pairing of extremes of virtue and evil in the opposition of Marie and Habibrah, the postulation of a blind, relentless, overpowering, and inhuman force called the revolution, the terror practiced by whites and blacks alike are characteristics of that æsthetic. Indeed, the very notion of terror, whether that practiced by the *Comité de Salut Public* or that practiced in *Bug-Jargal,* is sublime. Kant indicated that in some cases, fear was an attribute of an æsthetic reaction: even a fearful object, if contemplated from a safe distance, can inspire awe and be sublime.

> Bold, overhanging, and, as it were, threatening rocks, thunderclouds piled up the vault of heaven, borne along with flashes and peals, volcanoes in all their violence of destruction . . . make our power of resistance of trifling moment in comparison with their might. But, provided our own position is secure, their aspect is all the more attractive for its fearfulness; and we readily call these objects sublime.
>
> (110)

At another point, Kant calls war "sublime," and clearly, the bravery of the blacks, the cowardice of the whites, the cruelty shared by both races, are fearful, but sublime when contemplated from a safe distance. If an ideological message requires of us some course of action, before the sublime, we simply stop in awe and amazement, unwilling to relinquish the safe position we occupy. In other words, the first version of *Bug-Jargal* was, at some level, an exhortation to action, while the second leaves us in an attitude of passivity. I'd call the second attitude contemplation.[9]

Here I point out, confirming Piroué's and Grossman's theses, that the second version of *Bug-Jargal* is a first step towards a definitive Hugolian æsthetic: here we find the contrasts, the antitheses, the paradoxes that Baudelaire so disliked[10], but that do characterize his dramatic and novelistic forms; here also we find the attitude that will characterize his lyrical poetry, and that is absent from his political poetry: ideological theses are incompatible with contemplation, just as Hugo had to finish *Les Châtiments* in order to write *Les Contemplations.* Here we find too the amplification that is a defining characteristic of Hugo's writing, and one function of which is to increase the coherence, and thus, the verisimilitude, of the narrative.

One could even say that this attitude of "contemplation" informs and deforms all of Hugo's considerations of race: if the first version of *Bug-Jargal* was a cry against racial injustice, Hugo's subsequent writings on race made race a marker of an æsthetic, not a political, orientation. There are in fact very few texts about race in the rest of Hugo's works, as if this question were no longer appropriate material for his new æsthetics: an allusion to race in *Ruy Blas,* the letters on the trial and execution of John Brown that have already been mentioned, an address to women exiled from Cuba in 1870.

The passages from *Ruy Blas* are perhaps exemplary of Hugo's definitive attitude: in the fourth act of the play, Don César returns to Seville, only to land in Don Sal-

luste's hideaway, where, entirely by accident, he must play the role of the man who is playing the role of César. By a series of extraordinary coincidences, he first undoes Salluste's wicked machinations, and then, just as accidentally, allows Salluste to reconstruct them. The situation at the end of the fourth act is identical to that at its beginning, and one could consider César's actions an exercise in futility. In the midst of this comic interlude, two black pages wait on César: I quote the second of two passages[11] *in extenso*:

> *(Il agite la sonnette. Entre un des noirs.)*
> Tu sais écrire?
> *(Le noir fait un signe de tête affirmatif. Étonnement de don César.)*
> *(A part.)*
> Un signe!
> *(Haut.)*
> Es-tu muet, mon drôle?
> *(Le noir fait un nouveau signe d'affirmation. Nouvelle stupéfaction de don César.)*
> *(A part.)*
> Fort bien! continuez! des muets à présent!
> *(Au muet, en lui montrant la lettre, que la vieille tient appliquée sur la table.)*
> —Écrivez-moi là: Venez.
> *(Le muet écrit. Don César fait signe à la duegne de reprendre la lettre, et au muet de sortir. Le muet sort.)*
> *(A part.)*
> Il est obéissant!
>
> (VIII, 113)

The scene is comic, but the circumstances are quite serious: César's blind actions affect the life and happiness of the play's protagonists; more generally, set in the decadence of seventeenth-century Spain, the play unfolds against a backdrop of the colonial exploitation of the New World, which has corrupted the Spanish nobility; Salluste, for example, has sold César as a slave; Ruy Blas, the hero, represents the oppressed classes who see none of the wealth that the conquest of the New World has brought to the aristocracy. And while the blacks are not Salluste's slaves as such, they might as well be: mute, obedient, the pure executors or orders coming from elsewhere, they are nothing but the instruments of another's will. Indeed, their comic function is to provide incongruous obedience to their new, illegitimate master. In sum, while there is an ample context for an ethical discussion of the politics of race, Hugo envisages only the comic effects race might contribute to a discussion of the unauthorized exercise of power: the political has become æsthetic.

The passages from Ruy Blas are however parts of a work of fiction, and might thus be ambiguous indicators of Hugo's attitudes on race; let's look at something that is less equivocal. In 1859, on the occasion of John Brown's failed raid on Harper's Ferry, Hugo wrote twice about the problem of slavery in the United States.

First came an open letter to the United States of America, published in several European newspapers, and then a letter to the editor of the Haitien *Le Progrès*. In the open letter, he protests both the institution of slavery and the miscarriage of justice that John Brown's trial: exemplified the first with relation to the notion of freedom that America is supposed to incarnate, and the second by depicting the appalling circumstances of Brown's trial, which are of course opposed to the noble intentions the failure of which made the trial take place. Along the way however, the rhetoric of Hugo's letter gains the upper hand: blacks are opposed to whites, slaves to free men, North to South, light to darkness. The passage ends: "Oui, que l'Amérique le sache et y songe, il y a quelque chose de plus effrayant que Caïn tuant Abel, c'est Washington tuant Spartacus" (XI, 514). As the antitheses are multiplied, the probability of Brown's death becomes more and more certain: the comparisons with Abel and Spartacus promise as much. It is as if, even as he argues that Brown should be spared, Hugo was constructing an argument that would glorify him in death; it is as if even as he pleads for Brown's life, he is starting to build his tomb. I can think of no better illustration of destiny. In his subsequent letter to Heurtelou, editor of *Le Progrès,* when he argues that race is of no consequence, he comes out with this startling statement: "Il n'y a sur la terre ni blancs ni noirs, il y a des esprits; vous en êtes un. Devant Dieu, toutes les âmes sont blanches" (X, 525). The æsthetic value of whiteness is so compelling that, in addition to assuming that "white" is a complimentary adjective, for its sake Hugo sacrifices the political argument that the difference between white and black is of no consequence.

In 1870, while France was preoccupied with the question of the succession to the Spanish throne, a revolt in Cuba was harshly repressed by Spain. Three hundred Cuban women who had fled to New York asked Hugo for his support, and he responded with a letter and a declaration of the rights of Cubans. In the letter, he condemned the Spanish repression of the insurrection, qualifying it as the suppression of liberty and of self-determination, as racism, as colonialism:

> Aucune nation n'a le droit de poser son ongle sur l'autre, pas plus l'Espagne sur Cuba que l'Angleterre sur Gibraltar. Un peuple ne possède pas plus un autre peuple qu'un homme ne possède un autre homme. Le crime est plus odieux encore sur une nation que sur un individu: voilà tout. Agrandir le format de l'esclavage, c'est en accroître l'indignité. Un peuple tyran d'un autre peuple, une race soutirant la vie à une autre race, c'est la succion monstrueuse de la pieuvre, et cette superposition épouvantable est un des faits terribles du dix-neuvième siècle.

(X, 639-40)

The clarity of this declaration is admirable, as is Hugo's uncompromising political stand. As the declaration develops, however, Hugo multiplies the analogies and an-

titheses typical of his æsthetics, producing such statements as "Eh bien, si la France avait encore Haïti, de même que je dis à l'Espagne: Rendez Cuba! je dirais à la France: Rends Haïti!" (X, 640). To obtain the parallelism Hugo invokes an unreal condition, immediately associating his statements regarding Cuba with hypothetical statements regarding Haiti, and distancing himself from the cause of the Cuban women as he does so. And thus in his declaration of the rights of Cuba he comes to an apparent compromise regarding Spain's colonial conquests: "Il (the Spanish people) a colonisé; mais comme le Nil déborde; en fécondant" (X, 642). What was an incitement to action has become an invitation to appreciation.

I think that two conclusions may be made on the basis of this analysis, one having to do with Hugo's evolution as a thinker, and the other having to do with his æsthetics. It is tempting, given Hugo's fascination with progress, that slow but steady evolution of things towards the Good, to think that the same principle is true of Hugo's life. This is not the case. If anything, the second version of **Bug-Jargal** shows a young man who has abandoned his position in favor of the revolution for the sake of a new æsthetic.

Secondly, for Hugo, ideology and æsthetics are opposed, and not simply in the conventional sense that politics don't make good subjects of novels, the famous *coup de pistolet* that Stendhal scorned. Rather, the æsthetic attitude he seeks requires an entirely passive view of opposed forces, where their symmetry and balance can be appreciated without for a moment requiring or even implying the choice of one side or the other, for to do so would be to leave the position of safety that allows contemplation. One doesn't simply avoid politics in good books, it must be neutralized, neutralized by carefully balancing opposed positions, and even if that neutralization can only imply a different politics and a different ideology, that of contemplation. For the function of contemplation is to produce fictional truth and so doing, to neutralize politics.

Notes

1. Indeed, Hugo writes that the second *Bug-Jargal* eclipses not only the first, but also the intervening *Han d'Islande*: "Ce livre a donc été écrit deux ans avant *Han d'Islande*. Et quoique, sept ans plus tard, en 1825, l'auteur l'ait remanié et récrit en grande partie, il n'en est pas moins, et par le fond, et par beaucoup de détails, le premier ouvrage de l'auteur" (I, 275). What has changed, of course, with the second version of *Bug-Jargal,* is that Hugo has started to sign his works, and it is especially significant that he starts to sign works the ideology of which diverges markedly from that of the first *Bug-Jargal*: it is as if he can only sign Hugo when the too-explicit message of the first version has been made to disappear.

2. The blacks of Santo Domingo revolted in August, 1791 when the white colonialists refused to apply the decrees of equality promulgated by the National Assembly. In 1800, Toussaint-Louverture, leader of the insurrection, proclaimed Haiti's independence, only to be captured by Napoleon's armies two years later, and to die in prison in France in 1804.

3. In *Ruy Blas,* for example, Ruy Blas and Don Guritan vie for the queen's affections, but the queen elevates Ruy Blas to a high position, from which his acceptance of Don Guritan's challenge to a duel appears all the stranger; further, Ruy Blas' *alter ego,* Don César, actually goes about killing Don Guritan. Each character here takes on a different value as it is contrasted with another one.

4. From *Han d'Islande, Notre-Dame de Paris,* and *L'Homme qui rit,* respectively.

5. From *Notre-Dame de Paris, Ruy Blas,* and *L'Homme qui rit,* respectively.

6. These, Miller argues in *Blank Darkness,* can be summarized in such self-canceling formulations as "virtueless slaves", and have been in use since Herodotus and Aristotle (26).

7. Riffaterre explains the relation between subtext and verisimilitude thus: ". . . the subtext always constitutes a second reading of what the text surrounding it is about, a poetic or humorous metalanguage of the narrative. The subtext thus actualizes the relationship of referentiality. Whether it metonymically develops a specific aspect of the story in which it is embedded or whether it substitutes a metaphor for it, the subtext is like an illustration or an example isolating and emphasizing a moment of the story. The main story is therefore presupposed to be true" (28).

8. D'Auverney used several "expressions réprouvées par tous les bons sans-culottes pour caractériser divers événements mémorables," used "monsieur," instead of "citoyen" in his story, and merely by relating the story, conspired to overthrow the Republic (X, 396).

9. For the definitive study of the æsthetic dimension of *contemplation,* see Jean Gaudon, *Le Temps de la contemplation,* Paris: Flammarion, 1971. Here of course it is the withdrawal from politics implicit in contemplation that's under discussion. It is worth noticing that Flaubert also shared this æsthetic: Gérard Genette points out in his "Silences de Flaubert" (*Figures,* Paris: Seuil, 1966, 223-43) that Flaubert used the term "amour de la contemplation" to justify extended descriptions: here the withdrawal from politics is doubled with a withdrawal from narrative.

10. "M. Victor Hugo laisse voir dans tous ses tableaux, lyriques et dramatiques, un système d'alignement et de contrastes uniformes. L'excentricité elle-même prend chez lui des formes symétriques. Il possède à fond et emploie froidement tous les tons de la rime, toutes les ressources de l'antithèse, toutes les tricheries de l'apposition" (II, 431). I point out that in the same *Salon,* Baudelaire praised "political" criticism, albeit without mentioning Hugo: ". . . la critique doit être partiale, passionnée, politique . . ." (II, 418). While Hugo is only mentioned much later in the article, it is clear that Baudelaire's rejection of him is due at least in part to what Baudelaire perceives as his apolitical stance.

11. The other passage is structurally identical. After witnessing one of the black pages dutifully execute the orders of a lackey, César exclaims: "Je suis chez Belzébuth, ma parole d'honneur!" (VIII, 108).

Works Cited

Baudelaire, Charles. *Œuvres complètes.* Paris: Laffont, 1980.

Hugo, Victor. *Œuvres complètes.* 16 vols. Jacques Seebacher, ed. Paris: Laffont, 1985-.

Gaudon, Jean. *Le Temps de la contemplation.* Paris: Flammarion, 1969.

Genette, Gérard. "Silences de Flaubert." In *Figures.* Paris: Editions du Seuil, 1966, 223-43.

Grossman, Kathryn. *The Early Novels of Victor Hugo: Towards a Poetics of Harmony.* Geneva: Droz, 1986.

Kant, Immanuel. *The Critique of Judgement.* James Creed Meredith, trans. New York: Oxford University Press, 1951.

Miller, Christopher, *Blank Darkness. Africanist Discourse in French.* Chicago: The University of Chicago Press, 1985.

Piroué, Georges. "Les Deux Bug-Jargal." In Victor Hugo, *Œuvres complètes,* ed. Jean Massin, Paris: Club du Meilleur Livre, 1970.

Riffaterre, Michael. *Fictional Truth.* Baltimore: Johns Hopkins University Press, 1990.

Albert W. Halsall (essay date 1998)

SOURCE: Halsall, Albert W. "The Romantic Drama after Victor Hugo." In *Victor Hugo and the Romantic Drama,* pp. 207-12. Toronto: University of Toronto Press, 1998.

[*In the following essay, Halsall maintains that Hugo's influence helped move Romantic drama in France away from the neo-classical model and toward an alternative aesthetic norm.*]

As we have already seen, Fernand Baldensperger, writing in 1929, declared that Hugo's Romantic manifesto, the Preface to **Cromwell,** changed 'forever' the history of the theatre in France by 'liberating' it once and for all from the neo-classical rules governing the genres forming literary theatre.[1] Clearly, Hugo's rhetorical presentation of the theory of dramatic genres proved convincing and its influence has lasted into our own day. But Hugo's Romantic dramas themselves, as we have also seen, did not always find a public, at the State-funded theatres or elsewhere, 'grateful' for this liberation. Because they were ahead of their time, in both symbolic complexity and advanced staging techniques, Hugo's dramas needed time to find acceptance by the French theatre-going public. By 1867, however, we already find Gautier reporting that, on the revival of **Hernani** at the Comédie-Française, the new public fully realized Hugo's confident optimism by taking in their stride innovations which in 1830 had caused a scandal:

> When you attend a performance of **Hernani** nowadays, [Gautier wrote], as you follow the actors on an old copy that [in 1830] you marked in the margin with your finger nail in order to record those audiences' interruptions, outcries, and whistles . . . , you [now] feel a surprise not easy to express and one that the present-day public, whom our valiant efforts succeeded in ridding of such nonsense, will never be able to fully understand. How can one imagine that a line such as: 'What time is it?—Midnight soon,' could have provoked such stormy scenes, and that we would have had to fight for three days for its first half? [In 1830] it was declared trivial, familiar, improper. A King asks the time like any bourgeois, and he receives the answer 'Midnight,' as if he were some bumpkin. That's well done. It would have been 'polite' if he had used some fine periphrasis like: 'The hour / Will soon attain its final resting place.' As well as wanting to exclude precise, concrete terms from verse, [previous audiences] tolerated just as impatiently any epithet, metaphor, or simile, in fact any poetic expression at all—in a word, lyricism itself.[2]

In fact, the history of the Romantic drama after Hugo begins with the growing acceptance that his plays provided the alternative aesthetic norm to the neo-classical model that had until 1830 governed the production and reception of dramatic works in France.

But opposition to the Romantic drama and to Romanticism itself did not die out as more and more dramas of mixed generic makeup appeared and as, after Ponsard, neo-classical imitations entirely dried up. Opposition to, or espousal of, Hugo's theatre often reflected the political affiliations of his critics, friendly and unfriendly. In France, where aesthetic questions soon become openly politicized, the history of the reception of Hugo's dramas since his death displays the ever-present dialectic between right-wing and left-wing French critics. From the 1920s on, the most striking example of the political oppositions underlying the criticism of his dramas found

expression when the extreme Right, represented by Maurras and the *Action Française,* came into conflict with the Surrealists whose sympathies were Marxist. In 1923 Eugène Marsan, writing in *Paris-Journal* on the first production of Hugo's **Les Deux Trouvailles de Gallus,** revealed that ideological bias lay at the base of his criticisms both of Hugo and of Romanticism:

> In the matter of Victor Hugo, I must be suspect on several counts. In fact, I belong to the critical school, founded by Charles Maurras, which has not ceased over the last 20 years in its attacks against Romanticism in general, and against the enormous errors of Victor Hugo in particular.
>
> As is well known, our attacks have not been in vain. Not long ago, the epithet 'Romantic' was currently understood as a term of praise, synonymous with poetic, lyrical, even generous and magnanimous. Today all that has changed; the same epithet has gradually taken on a pejorative sense so marked and clear that anyone called Romantic nowadays no longer feels flattered. That is our work. Our analyses, our definitions have won the day. Who nowadays remains unconvinced of the psychological inanity of *Romanticism*? . . . Romanticism = lies, puerility, bombast.
>
> (*PF,* 275)

Obviously, no rhetoric, by any writer of a liberal or left-wing persuasion could hope to convince such a dramatic critic for, as Aristotle reminds us, in order to persuade, an orator must appeal to the generally accepted beliefs of his public.[3]

Thirty years later, Louis Aragon, eminent Surrealist poet, Resistance hero and uncontested Communist leader of intellectual France at that time, writing after a 1952 performance of **Hernani** at the Comédie-Française, during which the well-heeled audience had misbehaved, also chose to couch his condemnation in socio-political rather than in literary or aesthetic terms: 'A public that calls itself *le Tout-Paris* (Everybody who is Anybody in Paris) and that remains unknown to Parisians, and which, being composed of a few cretins and their ladies, dares to call itself 'Society,' had the indecency to celebrate France's greatest poet with its sniggering' (*PF,* 278). And the same year, Paul Éluard, another Resistance hero and also a principal Surrealist poet, speaking at a meeting celebrating International Communism in Moscow, declared:

> I read, understood, and loved Victor Hugo at 13 . . . Hugo was for me at 13, the illumination of poetry and I might say of the world . . . La Fontaine taught me to read, as it were, but Hugo taught me to speak . . .
>
> What will best preserve Hugo's works from time's assaults is the vulgarity with which the 'enlightened' have reproached him. Is Victor Hugo vulgar? Yes, if to be vulgar is to reveal his emotion without doubting that of others. Yes, if it is to assert boldly the exclusive importance of Good (over Evil). Yes, if it means not fear-

ing any single word, be it the rarest or most banal . . .
How also could one excuse the bad taste he showed in
celebrating the poor, better and more highly than anyone else, in words sparkling with truth and generosity.

(*PF,* 336)

It is only to be expected that Aragon and Éluard would,
as Marxist poets, respond so severely against the intellectual snobbery of a self-declared Right-wing élite and,
equally, that they would favour the passion for social
justice that forms, as we have seen, one of the principal
rhetorical appeals made in Hugo's works, notably his
Romantic dramas.

Such ideological squabbling in the world comprising
literary Paris did nothing, however, to reduce the place
Hugo's Romantic dramas carved out for themselves in
the canon of performed works in France. His dramas
have occupied the stage at the Comédie-Française much
more frequently than the works of any other Romantic
dramatist. In her 1979 history of France's premier theatre, Sylvie Chevalley provided statistics which, for instance, establish that out of thirty-three authors whose
works have been featured at the Comédie-Française 'at
least 1000 times between 25 August 1680 and 31 December 1978,' Victor Hugo stood in twelfth place, with
2,685 performances. Further, out of seventy 'plays featured at least 500 times' between the same dates, ***Hernani*** and ***Ruy Blas*** were in twenty-ninth and thirtieth
place with 979 and 957 performances, respectively.
Their only 'Romantic' rival was Rostand's affectionate
caricature of a Romantic hero, *Cyrano de Bergerac,* in
thirty-fifth place, with 854 performances. Finally, Chevalley shows that out of forty-nine 'plays featured at
least 100 times in the 25 years between 1 January 1954
and 31 December 1978,' ***Ruy Blas*** with 150 performances took twenty-eighth place. Only in this more recent period do plays—other than Rostand's—that show
the influence of the Romantic drama begin to appear:
Cyrano is notable in second place with 438 performances, but there are others. Montherlant's three
historical dramas, set in Portugal, Spain, and France in
the seventeenth century (*Port-Royal, La Reine morte,*
and *Le Cardinal d'Espagne*) take twelfth, twenty-sixth,
and fortieth places, with 325, 155, and 119 performances respectively in the 25 years. Also in the list is
Anouilh's historical confrontation between Henry II and
his Archbishop of Canterbury, *Becket ou l'Honneur de
Dieu* (forty-fourth place, 110 performances) and, for the
first time, we find the only Romantic drama comparable
to Hugo's in scope and dramatic effect, Musset's *Lorenzaccio* (in forty-seventh place with 102 performances).[4]
Strikingly absent from the list are the Romantic dramas
of Alexandre Dumas and Alfred de Vigny.

But this empirical, statistical proof of Hugo's success
as a dramatist is contradicted by the relative failure of
his plays in the Anglo-Saxon world. In fact, outside the
francophone world, *Lorenzaccio* may well be better
known than any of Hugo's dramas, given their infre-
quent performance. (It is fair to say that, as the twentieth century draws to an end, the musical version of
Hugo's great novel, ***Les Misérables,*** represents almost
the only 'dramatic' work by Victor Hugo occupying
stages outside France.)[5] Nowadays in England and North
America, Hugo's plays find themselves in something
like the void to which Shakespeare's plays were banished in France in the seventeenth and early eighteenth
centuries. Lacking adequate translations, and without
exciting productions, they have failed to attract the attention of Anglo-Saxon theatrical directors or audiences. Until 1996 the only French Romantic drama to
have played successfully since the 1960s in London, at
Stratford, Ontario, and on Broadway was Musset's
Lorenzaccio, partly, perhaps, because of the tradition—
since Sarah Bernhardt created the role in 1896—that its
eponymous (and androgynous) hero has usually been
played by a woman. Richard Eyre's 1996 production at
London's Royal National Theatre of Hugo's ***Le Roi
s'amuse,*** as adapted by Tony Harrison, has set a powerful precedent for future directors.

Hugo's Romantic dramas would seem obvious candidates for any of the four principal kinds of production
that Ralph Berry sees as characterizing modern productions of Shakespeare.[6] Whether played in the sets and
costumes appropriate to their historical period, or in
modern dress, or in what Berry calls the 'Period
Analogue' style, that is, with 'elegant and appealing'
costumes and sets and serving some overriding
'concept,' aesthetic, political or historical in nature, or
finally in some 'eclectic' or metaphorical version,
Hugo's dramas have been adapted to fit such categories
much less frequently, even in France, than have those
of Shakespeare throughout the world. While one can
think easily and quickly of many examples of Shakespeare's plays fitting into all four of Berry's categories,
even Ubersfeld, the great specialist on Hugo's Romantic dramas both in their written form and in performance, admits that for about a hundred years, from
1850 to 1950, the only kind of performances Hugo's
dramas received were strictly of what she calls the
'commemorative' kind, content merely to repeat the
style of previous successful productions.

Only with Jean Vilar in the 1950s did Hugo's dramas
begin to receive in France the kind of dramatic treatment likely to attract modern audiences. With stars like
Gérard Philippe and Maria Casarès, ***Ruy Blas*** and ***Marie
Tudor*** achieved, on the vast sets provided by the Courtyard of the Palais des Papes in Avignon or at the Palais
de Chaillot in Paris, the kind of popular success in
France that Shakespeare's plays have found the world
over. Later, modern productions came from French directors like Hubert Gignoux (***Mille Francs***), Antoine
Vitez (***Les Burgraves,*** 1977; ***Hernani,*** 1985), and Jean-

Louis Barrault (*Angelo,* 1984). Most recently, the Comédie-Française presented within the single 1994-5 season both **Lucrèce Borgia,** in a powerful *mise en scène* by Jean-Luc Boutté which leant towards the 'Period Analogue' approach and **Mille Francs de récompense,** finally admitted to the canonical repertoire. In all cases, modern theories and practice of theatrical production have revealed new dimensions in Hugo's Romantic dramas.

Finally, Hugo's dramas have successfully made the transition to other media: radio, film and television have extended the possibilities for displaying the spectacular effects that Hugo wrote into his dramas. On TV, for instance, the striking visual effects and sequences in **Marie Tudor, Torquemada, Les Burgraves,** have all, by their ability to enhance the performance of Hugo's dramas, tempted directors working for the small screen (*PF,* 377-80). And for decades, all of Hugo's dramas have been fairly regularly presented on French radio, with some of them being issued on disk or cassette (ibid., 369-71). But it is in the cinema that Hugo's dramas have found their most frequent modern medium. In its first hundred years, the French cinema, as well as producing versions of Hugo's novels—**Notre-Dame de Paris** and **Les Misérables** being the most popular—has produced (sometimes several) versions, faithful or otherwise, of **Lucrèce Borgia, Le Roi s'amuse, Ruy Blas, Hernani, Marion de Lorme, Marie Tudor,** and even **Cromwell** (*PF,* 372-6). We may confidently expect that in the twenty-first century such transfers will extend to other media—both videodisc and CD-ROM readily suggest themselves. It is to be hoped that the increasing accesibility that such media transfers make possible will introduce Hugo's Romantic dramas to a wider international audience.

Notes

1. Fernand Baldensperger, 'Les Années 1827-28 en France et au dehors,' *Revue des Cours et Conférences,* 30 June 1929, 529.

2. Quoted in V. Hugo, *Théâtre complet* (Pléiade edition), 1, 1766.

3. Aristotle, *On Rhetoric: A Theory of Civic Discourse,* Book 1, Chapter 2, 1356b, 33-4; trans. George A. Kennedy (New York: Oxford University Press 1991), 41.

4. Chevalley, *La Comédie-Française, hier et aujourd'hui,* 83-6.

5. Richard Eyre's 1996 production at London's Royal National Theatre of *Le Roi s'amuse* in Tony Harrison's translation/adaptation, entitled *The Prince's Play* is a notable exception.

6. Berry, ed., *On Directing Shakespeare,* 14-23.

Works Consulted

Hugo, Victor, *Oeuvres complètes.* Ed. Jean Massin. 18 vols. Paris: Le Club Français du Livre 1967-70.

———, *Cromwell.* Ed. Anne Ubersfeld. Paris: Garnier-Flammarion 1968.

———, *Les Deux Trouvailles de Gallus.* Ed. John J. Jane. New York: University Press of America 1983.

———, *Mangeront-ils?* Ed. René Journet and Guy Robert. Paris: Flammarion 1970.

———, *Preface de Cromwell.* Ed. Pierre Grosclaude. Paris: Larousse 1949.

———, *Ruy Blas.* Ed. Anne Ubersfeld. 2 vols. Paris: Les Belles Lettres 1971-2.

———, *Théâtre complet.* 2 vols. Paris: Gallimard. 'Bibliothèque de la Pléiade' 1963.

———, *Théâtre.* 2 vols. Paris: Robert Laffont 1985.

———, *Torquemada.* Ed. John J. Jane. New York: University Press of America 1989.

V. Hugo/Tony Harrison. *Le Roi s'amuse/The Prince's Play.* London: Faber & Faber 1996.

Laster, Arnaud. *Pleins Feux sur Victor Hugo.* Paris: Comédie-Française 1981.

Chevalley, Sylvie. *La Comédie-Française hier et aujourd'hui.* Paris: Didier 1979.

Gautier, Théophile. *Histoire de l'art dramatique en France depuis vingt-cinq ans.* 6 vols. Paris: Hetzel 1858-9.

Aristotle, *On Rhetoric: A Theory of Civic Discourse.* Trans. George A. Kennedy. New York: Oxford University Press 1991.

Baldensperger, Fernand. 'Les Années 1827-28 en France et au dehors,' *Revue des Cours et Conférences* (30 June 1929), 528-42.

List of Abbreviations

CI	D. C. Muecke, *The Compass of Irony* (1969)
DR	Anne Ubersfeld, *Le Drame romantique* (1993)
DRGC	Descotes, *Le Drame romantique et ses grands créateurs* (1955)
FS	M. Carlson, *The French Stage in the Nineteenth Century* (1971)
HADF	T. Gautier, *Histoire de l'art dramatique en France* 6 vols. (1858-9)
HR	M. Carlson, '*Hernani*'s Revolt from the Tradition French Stage Composition' (1972)
MSF	M.-A. Allévy. *La Mise en scène en France* (1938)
PF	A. Laster, *Pleins Feux sur Victor Hugo* (1981)

PVH   H. Lyonnet, *Les 'Premières' de Victor Hugo* (1930)

RB   Anne Ubersfeld, *Le Roi et le bouffon* (1974)

RBL   Anne Ubersfeld, *Ruy Blas,* critical edition, 2 vols. (1971-2)

RH   Anne Ubersfeld, *Le Roman d''Hermani'* (1985)

RS   Stendhal, *Racine et Shakespeare* (1965)

SG   W. D. Howarth, *Sublime and Grotesque* (1975)

TF   J. de Jomaron (ed.), *Le Théâtre en France* (1992)

VHR   *Victor Hugo raconté par Adèle Hugo* (1985)

VHT   J. Gaudon, *Victor Hugo et le théâtre* (1985)

VHTL   V. Hugo, *Théâtre* (Laffont edition), 2 vols. (1985)

Constance Sherak (essay date 1999)

SOURCE: Sherak, Constance. "Investing in the Past: Victor Hugo's 'La Bande Noire.'" *Romance Languages Annual* 10, no. 1 (1999): 157-63.

[*In the following essay, Sherak declares that Hugo's portrayal of* la bande noire—*a group of thieves who demolished old monuments to sell the stone—in his poem "La Bande noire" suggests an inextricable link between violence and preservation.*]

"Je créai le mot pour tuer la chose."[1] Abbé Grégoire's famous denunciation of the destruction of France's national treasures introduced one of the rare neologisms into post-revolutionary France. Grégoire, the Constitutional Bishop of Blois and one of the deputies of the Constitutional Assembly, coined the word "vandalisme" in his *Rapport sur les destructions opérées par le vandalisme et sur les moyens de le réprimer* of 1794 to protest the confiscation and demolition of France's national monuments: "On ne peut inspirer aux citoyens trop d'horreur pour ce vandalisme qui ne connaît que la destruction."[2] Writing one of his many reports to the Convention on the fate of art in post-revolutionary France, he cautioned against the removal, destruction and sale of painting, statuary, monuments, and libraries:

> L'Assemblée nationale, considérant qu'en livrant à la destruction les monuments propres à rappeler les souvenirs du despotisme, il importe de préserver et de conserver honorablement les chefs-d'oeuvre des arts, si dignes d'occuper les loisirs et d'embellir le territoire d'un peuple libre, décrète qu'il y a urgence.
>
> (Grégoire, *Rapport sur les destuctions*)

Grégoire condemned revolutionaries who went about destroying monuments, churches, abbeys and châteaux, and selling their stone for profit. Indeed, he criticized those who went so far as to justify this new economy of violence in the name of revolutionary messianism. Grégoire's newly-minted word lent currency to the important debates surrounding the future and the past of France's cultural heritage and were pointed indictments of the governmental bodies that regulated the purchase and sale of national property.

Grégoire saw this kind of destruction as legitimate grounds for inciting cultural warfare and decided to retaliate with words. He wrote numerous tracts condemning the effacement of public monuments and libraries, declaring that such violence constituted barbarous acts of national treason. "Les barbares et les esclaves," Grégoire proclaimed, "détestent les sciences et détruisent les monuments des arts; les hommes libres les aiment et les conservent" (Grégoire, *Rapport sur les destructions*). He perceived these new aggressors, in their revolutionary zeal, to be as and destructive as the Vandals who first invaded France in the Third Century. Thus by coining the word "vandalisme," he had recontextualized a word that had come to lose its historical specificity. Vandalism became a figure for counter-revolutionary verbal assaults used to inveigh against terrorist acts of violence and cultural ruin. Fighting fire with verbal fire seemed to be the best possible means of winning the war on this form of terrorism. These tactics gave way to a public dialogue that was to last through the century, as the concern for the protection of France's national heritage grew and became increasingly politicized.

How did this economy of cultural banditry mirror attitudes towards history following the French Revolution, and later during, the Restoration? The conflicting principles of violence and preservation introduced a set of duplicitous cultural practices into Restoration France that ultimately influenced the conceptualization and disciplinarization of such fields as art history, historiography, philology, and philosophy and played a crucial role in laying the epistemological foundations of institutions such as the museum, the archive, and national conservation commissions. Michelet's celebrated declaration that "[L]e Moyen Age nous a laissé de lui un si poignant souvenir que toutes les joies, toutes les grandeurs des âges modernes ne suffiront pas à nous consoler" (7:193), confirmed the possibility of redemption offered by the relics of the past. Linked to religion and to the feudal past, France's Medieval heritage came to symbolize cultural and political redemption in the aftermath of revolutionary destruction. Classicism no longer expressed the spirit of the age, and Christian and chivalric mythology replaced the archetypes of ancient Greece and Rome in the attempt to recreate a collective national past. The wave of Bonapartism that swept France sought a Christian ideal incarnate in chivalric codes. Historiographers exploited the secular associations of the Middle Ages. The Baron de Barante, in his *Histoire des ducs de Bourgogne,* imitated medieval chroniclers "dans le détail vivant des faits et des moeurs, de façon à offrir au lecteur le récit le plus concret et coloré possible, sans intervention critique ou philosophique du narrateur" (21:124).

The debates surrounding the preservation of France's *biens nationaux,* or public property, manifested themselves in a variety of political and literary forms in Republican and Restoration France. A rigorous process "desymbolization," what Frank Bowman describes as "the historical modulation of the relation between language and the symbol,"[3] was of fundamental concern for many Romantic thinkers who wished to reinvest pre-Revolutionary iconography with new meaning relevant to their day. Jules Michelet in his *Origines du droit français cherchées dans les symboles et formules du droit universel* from 1837, argued that law in France was verbal in its formulations and thus subject to historical influence, just as a symbol grows, changes, and gradually changes its signification. His excursions into jurisprudence helped prove that interpretation was a manifestation of historical progress.

Throughout the nineteenth century, the ambivalent attitudes towards architecture and the ruins mirrored equally ambivalent attitudes toward history and progress. The radical displacement of history in the first part of the nineteenth century stemmed from a fundamental ambivalence towards the past: whether to seek reinscription of the past or to dispense with the burden of history. The young Republic saw itself as a clean slate on which could be written new formulas for conceptualizing the past. The interest in a single national heritage reflected this attempt to unify France through its historical markers. At the same time, these new formulas constituted a predicament for those who, clinging tenaciously to the past, also understood that the past was no longer viable for present conditions. The incompatibilities of statehood and monarchy became the central issue around which most political, historical, and literary debates turned. Such ideological conflicts characterized the century in its preoccupation with innovation, progress, and originality on the one hand, and the interest in tradition and history, on the other. The conflicting ideologies surrounding was filtered through a variety of symbolic practices that began to take hold for the explicit purposes of creating a new citizenry.

One of the most important practitioners in archictecture was Eugène Emmanuel Viollet-le-Duc whose politics of restoration revolutionized architecture from the nineteenth century forward. An architectural theorist, Viollet-le-Duc was one of those rare architects who gave his name to a style rather than to a historical site or period. Unlike his detractors whose idealized versions of history and whose fascination with the Middle Ages led to a revival of interest in the Gothic style, Viollet-le-Duc advanced a theory of architecture which rejected the Gothic as frivolous decorum that under-

mined the French spirit of rationality and consequently invalidated the spirit of progress. For Viollet-le-Duc, restoration did not mean to maintain or repair a building but to lend the restored edifice itself originality: ". . . restaurer un édifice, ce n'est pas seulement 'l'entretenir, le réparer, le refaire,' c'est en fait 'le rétablir dans un état complet qui peut n'avoir jamais existé à un moment donné" (16). Viollet-le-Duc and his disciples also maintained that each stone served as an index of different architectural styles. Mérimée and Hugo, on the other hand, regarded Viollet-le-Duc's basic premise as a kind of violent architecture that betrayed historical accuracy, and the expression "faire du Viollet-le-Duc" signified the abusive restitution of an edifice. Hugo, in particular, considered Viollet-le-Duc's project to be vulgar and capricious, a sacrilegious affront to the past. For Hugo, the vandalism of France's national monuments during the French Revolution mirrored the destruction of French national identity and the collapse of the social order.

These debates are best characterized by the opposing impulses of restoration and renovation. The idea that monuments could be preserved in their original condition meant that they could faithfully restore the past to the present and thereby offer a sense of living history. Alternatively, if the notion of abolishing the institutions of the ancien régime constituted progress during post-revolutionary France, the fundamental renovation of monuments would best reflect this preoccupation with originality, past and present. To renovate a structure meant that it would not necessarily resemble its original state but would be embellished by a new architectural idea, as in the term "faire du Viollet-le-Duc," which signified for the 1850s and 1860s the abusive restitution of an edifice. Hugo, in particular, considered Viollet-le-Duc's project to be vulgar and capricious, a sacrilegious affront to the past. In contrast, to preserve a monument was to express the sensibilities of the past in the most faithful reconstruction possible. Partisans of faithful restoration such as Victor Hugo, Prosper Mérimée and Charles Nodier clashed with supporters of architectural innovation in this conflict over the image of historic France.

Similarly, the expressions of post-revolutionary national identity that reflected this architectural quarrel were expressed in Romantic poetry by two divergent modes: the elegiac mode and the iconoclastic mode. As I will later demonstrate in my reading of the Hugo ode, with the elegiac mode, reverence for the past was refigured as nostalgia. The iconoclastic mode suggested here points to the original meaning of iconoclasm as a rhetoric of violence aimed at shattering cherished beliefs and traditions. In the cultural and literary debates of the early nineteenth century, the institutions and language of the ancien régime were intended for destruction in order to generate this new identity. Republican vandals sought to profit from the spoils of revolution and engage in destructive acts of vandalism. These two modes also played themselves out in the contentious space of the museum. Bound up with the museological impulse was the anxiety over architectural renovation and restoration. To the extent that a society defines itself just as much by the ways in which it destroys as by its production and construction, architecture appears to contain, though it does not reconcile, such contradictions. Many of these seemingly duplicitous practices relate to the collection, cataloguing, and exhibiting of art.

The French Revolution would affect the fate of enormous numbers of works of art as they became available to the public, and it was becoming increasingly evident that too many churches, abbeys, and cathedrals were being destroyed for anyone to watch passively as France's cultural heritage was unraveling. The mounting interest in conservation was precipitated by the widespread agreement in France that the art and architecture of the Republic were in a lamentable state and that systematic classification of its national treasures had to be registered. Considered public property freed from the kings, the Church and the emigrating aristocracy, many works of art and monuments were requisitioned for public use. In compliance with a decree of the Convention, works confiscated over the whole of France were sent to a few key repositories; newly secularized convents, now vast and empty spaces, were often utilized for this purpose. In Paris, the principal storehouses for national relics were the *Couvent of the Petits-Augustins* (now the *Ecole des Beaux Arts*), the *Capucins,* the *Grands Jésuites,* the *Cordeliers* and the *Hôtel de Nesles.* A great many works in some way marked with feudal, religious or royal devices forbidden by law, were set aside to be destroyed and were broken, melted down or burned.

Museum-going also resulted in a deeper allegiance by the people to the new Republic. The myth of Napoleon and the people was sustained by the codification of symbolic and cultural practices introduced into republican society. Citizens paid homage to the revolutionary state by visiting the *Musée Napoléon,* or what we now call the Louvre. Politicians and writers projected their vast theories of history onto the monuments of France's past. Most notably, Jules Michelet's commentary on Alexandre Lenoir's chronological arrangement of medieval statuary displayed in Lenoir's *Musée des Petits-Augustins* (now the *Ecole des Beaux Arts*), still remains one of the most valuable testimonies of the sense of the past that each fragment conveyed to the nineteenth-century beholder; it is said that, not unlike Gibbon, Michelet discovered his calling as an historiographer in Lenoir's museum while contemplating the ruins in the Elysée garden of the Petits-Augustins:

> Que d'âmes ont pris dans ce musée l'étincelle historique, intérêt des grands souvenirs, le vague désir de remonter des âges! [. . .] A la puissante voix de la Révolution, tout un monde de morts historiques était venu se rendre dans cette vallée de Josaphat. [. . .] Pour la première fois, l'ordre regnait parmi eux, le seul vrai, celui des âges. La France se voyait enfin elle-même dans son développement de siècle en siècle, d'hommes en hommes. De tombeau en tombeau, elle pouvait faire son examen de conscience.[4]

Romantic historiography of the 1830s and 1840s was born of this obsession with the past and with the desire to "remonter des âges," especially the recent past of the French Revolution. Inspired by statuary and by the archival impulse, Jules Michelet instilled the sense of optimism, innovation, and progress in historical thinking of the period. Conservationists borrowed from these ideas of history to establish the notion of cultural heritage through the preservation and restoration of French national monuments.

The mounting interest in conservation and the preservation of antiquities was precipitated by the widespread agreement in France that national art and architecture were in a deplorable state. This interest was actively promoted by learned societies and conservation movements. Ludovic Vitet was appointed to the post of Inspector General of French Historical Monuments in 1830. Vitet's role as inspector involved the safeguarding and classification of national monuments in this "guerre aux démolisseurs," a term Hugo used to title his essay of the same name (1832) to vilify the architect and to lament the neglect of France's national monuments. Prosper Mérimée inherited the position from Vitet in 1834 and became a vital force in the rehabilitation of Gothic art. From 1835 to 1848, Hugo was a member the *Commission des Arts et Monuments* and was assigned the task of classifying antiquities and medieval statuary and assessing their condition. The publication between 1820 and 1840 of Charles Nodier's and Baron Taylor's *Voyages pittoresques et romantiques dans l'ancienne France* also contributed to the widespread appeal of the conservation movements. Hugo's descriptions of the picturesque in his early verse and especially in his ode, **"La Bande noire"** parallel at various points the lithographs of the *Voyages.*

Just twenty years after the French Revolution, Victor Hugo had joined forces with Charles Nodier and Baron Taylor in the crusade against the notorious *Bande noire,* those brigands, thieves, and landowners who demolished old monuments to sell their stone. Such bandits were reacting against the symbols of a feudal past which they understood to be an oppressive political and cultural system. Even prior to the French Revolution, the expression "Bande noire" was used to designate a certain form of peasant violence, more destructive than deadly. During the Restoration, the *Bande noire* came to be associated with the threat of destruction to nature and to public, or nationally-owned, and private property. Those who decried this group of brigands operated through monetary or ideological motivation to invest in a system that protected family or national heritage. This type of investment assured the preservation of the past and protection against the violent erasure of history. It slowly evolved into the association with the first years after the Revolution and with the period up through the July Monarchy during which a considerable amount of land as well as innumerable national monuments and ruins were sold. Most notably, the legal and commercial versions of vandalism incited a host of debates over property rights, the conservation of France's architectural treasures, and, ultimately, French national identity. Whether a mere detail of history or an indelible cultural blemish, the fact that these brigands left their mark on France reminds us that central to the narratives of national identity and social construction are the stories of how a society destroys. In 1987, an international colloquium held in Clermont-Ferrand brought together historians, political scientists, sociologists, and literary critics under the banner of "Révolution française et vandalisme révolutionnaire." In the introduction to the published proceedings of this conference, the conveners queried "[D]ans quelle mesure le thème controversé du 'vandalisme révolutionnaire' appartient-il à la légende noire de la Révolution française ou à son histoire?" (Bernard-Griffiths, Chemin, and Ehrard, *Révolution francaise* ix). They were interested in exploring the ideology of destruction and acts of cultural repression in the wake of the Revolution, this "légende noire." The destruction of symbols, destruction for destruction's sake, utilitarian destruction, destruction in the name of progress versus preservation in the name of nationalism, the juridical and etymological definitions of vandalism. These were the issues that came to the fore during the conference and were the subject of the four-hundred and fifty-six-page volume of the proceedings.

The *Bande noire*'s inscription into literature has extended its meaning to suggest a broader notion of cultural repression through violence, namely violence to property, nationhood, and national memory. For instance, in his *Les Paysans,* Honoré de Balzac treats peasant revolt as a form of banditry associated with *La Bande noire*. Gustave Flaubert's odd couple, Bouvard and Pécuchet, in their archaeological pursuits, "arrivèrent à ne plus tolérer la moindre marque de décadence. Tout était de la décadence et ils déploraient le vandalisme, tonnaient contre le badigeon" (Flaubert, *Bouvard et Pécuchet* 166). It might be said that poets and novelists such as Hugo used language to avenge the iconoclasts of French national identity. Hugo invests his verse with rhetorical figures borrowed from medieval warfare to reinforce his please and to shield his Restoration armies from the onslaught of the *Bande noire* bandits.

In exploring the political, historical, and rhetorical uses of *Bande noire,* I would like to examine the different ways in which the term's inscription into literature extended its meaning to a broader notion of cultural repression through violence, namely violence to property, nationhood, and national memory. I am also interested in the etymological richness of the verb "to invest" because it resonates both with feudal iconography. What I have found is a rich arsenal of meaning, both military and economic, that helps me read Hugo's poem with attention to the rhetoric of medieval warfare and to link such warfare to the debates surrounding the uses of the past in Restoration France. The nexus of meanings that "invest" conveys articulates some of the complicated dualities inherent in the early conservation movements mentioned above and sheds light on Hugo's position as conservator and poet. The term "invest" is of multiple origins, and it is worth exploring the evolution of its meaning as it has come to light over past centuries. The verb "to invest" can be traced back to the Latin *investire,* meaning to clothe, cover, or adorn. A related meaning has to do with the symbolic power of investing as a means of signifying power and dignity. Thus the idea of enveloping something or someone of value in a garment is at the root of the term's origin. The French *envestir* can be traced back to 1241 with the definition: "to acquire a fiefdom." Here the verb prefigures its later military reference to surrounding or besieging. In the sixteenth century, with *investir* and a shift in spelling, the meaning was modified to include personal benefits ("to acquire wealth"). In the seventeenth century, the notion of "assuming the power of dignity" introduced the concept of attribution or endowment. The idea of investment as endowment reminds us of its contemporary economic resonance; yet the idea of putting down money doesn't gain currency, as it were, until much later on.

The early use of *envestir* as a reference to military strategy invites us to read the poetry of the ruins in terms of a violent struggle waged in the cultural battlefields of France. As in battle, when troops invest a citadel, they are hemming in with hostile forces so as to cut off approach or escape. They are surrounding and occupying a territory, "clothing" it through invasion. The hostile forces were the group of people who sought to confiscate France's monuments in exchange for a currency that could buy progress and a warranty for the future. Here, for the purposes of reading Hugo, I am moving towards a reading of the ruins as texts, rather, onto which were projected politics of preservation. Thus, when troops invest a citadel, they are hemming it in with hostile forces so as to cut off approach or escape. They are surrounding and occupying a territory, "clothing" it through invasion. The hostile forces in this case are the group of people who wished to confiscate France's monuments in exchange for a currency that would buy progress and a warranty for the future.

Machicolations, fortresses, and crenellations are scattered throughout the marble wilderness of Hugo's early verse. In these poems, fragmented religious architecture reflects the erosion and repression of Christian doctrine since 1789. These architectural fragments are virtually the protagonists of the author's early *Odes* (1822-1828) written during the Restoration. Both sacred and secular monuments comprise the over-arching emblem of social cohesion in his writings and concretize a conception of history, individual and collective, as well as a metaphorical staging of daily life. Hugo's articulation of Royalist Romanticism in his ode **"La Bande noire,"** illustrates the inextricable link between violence and preservation, the ruins constituting the very agency and subject of cultural repression. His preoccupation with the conservation of monuments corresponded to his early campaigns against a kind of dangerous cultural amnesia born of the profound fear that post-revolutionary France would forget its own past. **"La Bande noire"** integrates aesthetic considerations with political invective. In this poem, the chivalry allegorizes the crusade against the iconoclastic practices of thieves who sought to profit from the spoils of 1789 by stealing and selling architectural fragments. The medieval landscapes conjured by Hugo the Royalist in this poem reminds us of his belief in the redemptive powers of the restored monarchy. In an accompanying note to the 1824 publication of his ode **"La Bande noire,"** in *La muse française,* Hugo justifies the poem's ostensibly unimaginative title by reminding us of the Bande noire's importance in revolutionary history: "On reprochera peut-être au titre de cette ode sa trivialité; mais la Bande noire est une des institutions laissées par la révolution; et en parlant des choses de cette révolution, la trivialité est souvent un défaut inévitable."[5]

The poet's treatment of the *Bande noire,* in his ode of the same name, incorporates the features of cultural banditry with the opposing rhetorical impulses of preservation and progress. Hugo's troping of the ruins in his ode extends the meaning of *Bande noire* to a more generic idea of violence, namely violence to the memory of a unified French identity before the cataclysm of revolution did its damage. This ode is a rallying cry for the defenders of history to don their armor, to clothe, adorn or invest themselves and attack the enemy in the theater of battle, both actual and rhetorical. The ruins signify the reward for and guarantor of victory in this crusade against the destruction to the past. The ramparts and machicolations invest, in the sense of "surround," the fragmented past, granting the ruins immunity from the likes of the *Bande noire.* And Hugo, from the watchtower of poetry, invests his words with a call to arms against the vandals of history, these prosaic destroyers of France's glory. Joan DeJean has written on literary fortresses as texts dedicated to the constraint and repression of disorder (*Literary Fortifications*). Hugo's *Odes* can be perceived as texts dedicated to the liberation of the spirit and to the preservation of order: "Mes odes, c'est l'instant de déployer vos ailes / Cherche d'un même éssor les voûtes immortelles / Le moment est propice . . . Allons" (*Oeuvres poétiques* 1:340).

From the opening of **"La Bande noire,"** Hugo reanimates the past by invoking France's military strongholds. Fortresses, cathedrals, and abbeys are central foundation upon which the poet constructs his plea for historical preservation. He accomplishes this by apostrophizing component architectural features of the fortress: "O murs! ô crénaux! ô tourelles! / Remparts! fossés aux ponts mouvants! / Lourds faisceaux de colonnes frêles" (1-3). Other monuments are invoked here. They include the hallowed houses of worship ("Modestes couvents / Cloîtres poudreux" (4-5) and military fortresses: "tours où combattaient nos aïeux" (10). The oxymoron of the "lourds faisceaux" and the "colonnes frêles" emphasizes the fading stability of ecclesiastical and military strongholds brought on by the ravages of 1789. We know that as the poet laments the destabilization and the looting of such cultural strongholds his public acts are to build a rock-solid program of conservation and restoration. Through a poetic investment of monuments he can restore old symbols for use in the present.

In this ode, the architecture frames a Royalist fervor for past military, ecclesiastical, and political glory. Note Hugo's address to the ruins as guardians of a glorious chivalric past:

> Parvis où notre orgueil s'enflamme!
> Maisons de Dieu! manoirs des rois!
> Temples que gardait l'oriflamme,
> Palais que protégeait la croix!
> Réduits d'amour! arcs de victoires!
> Vous qui témoignez de nos gloires,
> Vous qui proclamez nos grandeurs!
> Chapelles, donjons, monastères!
> Murs voilés de toute de mystères!
> Murs brillants de tout de splendeurs!
>
> (11-20)

The four walls meet here to protect and offer up the great institutions of the feudal past to the new generation of Royalists seeking to undo the damage of revolution. Hugo's verse-text becomes the *tectum,* the roof protecting and buttressing France's medieval past while sheltering the symbols of the restored monarchy. For Hugo, poetry shields and defends against the Bande noire "rubble-rousers." He juxtaposes the decay of the monuments with the relative youth of the newly-restored monarchy:

> O débris! ruines de France,
> Que notre amour en vain défend,
> Séjours de joie ou de souffrance,
> Vieux monuments d'un peuple enfant!
>
> (21-24)

Despite their dilapidated condition, these monuments symbolically reconstruct the mythology surrounding the heroes of the Middle Ages. These heroes "people" the rubble; indeed, they loom larger than life:

> Ces débris, chers à la patrie
> Lui parlent de chevalerie;
> La gloire habite leurs néants;
> Les héros peuplent ces décombres;
> Si ce ne sont plus que des ombres,
> Ce sont des ombres de géants!
>
> (95-100)

Hugo calls upon his compatriots not only to venerate and inventory the ruins but also to defend and protect the Bourbon kings; he invests the rubble with his words:

> O Français! respectons ces restes!
> Le ciel bénit les fils pieux
> Qui gardent, dans les jours funestes,
> L'héritage de leurs aïeux.
> Comptons chaque pierre tombée;
>
> (101-105)

The poem becomes the very fortress of language constructed primarily to crusade against the *Bande noire* and against all forms of religious and cultural desecration; and his fellow soldier or adventurer muse ("muse adventurière") is the errant knight of conservation. He is the messenger of (the) R/restoration whose mission it is to preserve the past of pre-revolutionary France. This knight, like Hugo the poet, is urged to don his medieval armor ("Ceignit la cuirasse guerrière / Et l'écharpe des paladins") (43-44), to invest himself "d'un fer rongé de rouille" (45) and set off "vers des régions nouvelles / Pour hâter son coursier, sans ailes," (49). On his poetic mission, this soldier of fortune rides out to defeat the vandals of time and to raise the dead monarchs. Hugo seeks to buy back France's original glory lost in the violence of 1789 and to destroy all threats to the past. The economic resonances of investing did not come into use until this century with the notion that through the placing of money in a sector of the economy one is saving up monetarily for the future.

Let us also not forget the psychoanalytic uses of investing. One could argue that as an analogue to the economic reference, one can also invest affectively or libidinally by conferring a charge of psychic energy or attaching a psychic value to an object or person. Freud's use of the word *besetzen,* as libidinal attachment, parallels Hugo's affection for his country and the role that the monuments play in his (Hugo's) universalizing histories. He figures the anachronism of (the) R/restoration itself by investing in the return of the Bourbon king through an evocation of France's royal lineage:

> Honneur à ces vaillants que notre orgueil renomme!
> Gloire à ces braves! Sparte et Rome

> Jamais n'ont vu d'exploits plus beaux!
> Gloire! ils ont triomphé de ces funèbres pierres
>
> (125-128)

France, now stripped of its history, would remain a naked and belittled body, a sacred and maternal body above all. Hugo calls upon the people clothe this body in its former renown untainted by recent events:

> Quand de ses souvenirs la France dépouillée,
> Hélas! aura perdu sa vieille majesté,
> Lui disputant encore quelque pourpre souillée,
> Ils riront de sa nudité!
> Nous, ne profanons point de cette mère sacrée,
> Consolons sa gloire éplorée.
> Chantons ses astres éclipsés.
> Car notre jeune muse, affrontant l'anarchie,
> Ne veut pas secouer sa bannière blanchie
> De la poudre des temps passés.
>
> (171-180)

Here, the poet is reassuring the people of France that in the future and by subscribing to the terms of the restored monarchy, they will be the rightful inheritors of the past. Just as Grégoire had to declare a new era of *vandalisme* thirty years earlier in order to destroy its evil, Hugo's rhetorical weapon is poetic language.

Gesturing forward to another poem, I refer below to a poem, Gérard de Nerval's "Notre-Dame de Paris." The poem fuses the elegiac with the iconoclastic, finding beauty in the slow degradation of this archetypal monument. The prophecy of a cathedral ruined by the time, taste, and fashion so much through revolution as time conflates a familiar topos of Hugo's theory of universal history, themes of salvation and human progress. Nerval wrote his poem in 1832, a year after the publication of Hugo's novel of the same name, to remind us of the Cathedral's precarious reputation as locus of history and fiction. It is a fragile monument subject to the ravages of time and evolving revolutions. Just as a predatory wolf destroys its prey, time will strip away the layers of history that have filled Notre-Dame Cathedral recounted by Victor Hugo. For Nerval, the Cathedral locates an important semiotic reversal, a complex teasing out of the conundrum of literature where, in the future, he can imagine people pointing to Notre-Dame and claiming that it is Victor Hugo who brought it out of the shadows of destruction:

> Notre-Dame est bien vieille; on la verra peut-être
> Enterrer cependant Paris qu'elle a vu naître.
> Mais, dans quelque mille ans, le temps fera broncher
> Comme un loup fait un boeuf, cette carcasse lourde,
> Tordra ses nerfs de fer, et puis d'une dent sourde . . .
> Bien des hommes de tous les pays de la terre
> Viendront pour contempler cette ruine austère,
> Rêveurs, et relisant le livre de Victor . . .
> Alors ils croiront voir la vieille basilique,
> Toute ainsi qu'elle était puissante et magnifique,
> Se lever devant eux comme l'ombre d'un mort!
>
> (476)

Notes

1. Quoted from Abbé Grégoire's *décret du 16 septembre 1792*, *Rapport sur les destructions opérées par le vandalisme et sur les moyens de le réprimer* (14 Fructidor, An II de la République). Cited in Deluche, Bernard and Jean-Michel Leniard. *La culture des sans-culottes he premier dossier du patrimoine, 1789-1998*. Paris: Les Editions du Paris, 1989.

2. L'Abbé Grégoire, *Rapport sur les inscriptions des monuments publics* (22 Nivôse, An II de la République).

3. Frank Bowman has analyzed this process of de-symbolization with respect to the relation of nineteenth-century French theology and law to religion and philosophy of the period. See his *French Romanticism: Intertextual and Interdisciplinary Readings*.

4. Quoted in André Chastel, "La Notion de patrimoine." *Les Lieux de mémoire II: La Nation*, ed. Pierre Nora 418.

5. Victor Hugo, Preface to "La Bande noire," *Oeuvres poétiques* 1: 1239. Unless stated otherwise, all quotations from "La Bande Noire" will be from Volume 1 of this edition.

Works Cited

Baron de Barante, Guillaume. *Histoire des ducs de Bourgogne de la maison de Valois*. 2ⁿᵈ ed. 2 vols. Cited in Patricia A. Ward, *The Medievalism of Victor Hugo*. University Park: The Pennsylvania State UP, 1975.

Bernard-Griffiths, Simone, Marie-Claude Chemin, and Jean Ehrard, eds. *Révolution française et "vandalisme révolutionnaire."* Proceedings of Colloque international de Clermont-Ferrand, December 15-17, 1988. Paris: Universitas, 1992.

Bowman, Frank. *French Romanticism: Intertextual and Interdisciplinary Readings*. Baltimore: The Johns Hopkins UP, 1990.

Chastel, André. "La notion de patrimoine." *Les lieux de mémoire: La nation*. Ed. Pierre Nora. Vol. 2. Paris; Gallimard, 1986.

DeJean, Joan. *Literary Fortifications: Rousseau, Laclos, Sade*. Princeton: Princeton UP, 1984.

Flaubert, Gustave. *Bouvard et Pécuchet*. Paris: Gallimard, 1979.

Grégoire, L'Abbé. *Rapport sur les inscriptions des monuments publics* (22 Nivôse, An II de la République). Cited in Bernard Deloche and Jean-Michel Leniaud, *La culture des sans-culottes: Le premier dossier du patrimoine, 1789-1798*. Paris: Les Editions de Paris, 1989.

———. *Rapport sur les destructions opérées par le vandalisme et sur les moyens de le réprimer*. (14 Fructidor, An II de la République). Cited in Bernard Deloche and Jean-Michel Leniaud, *La culture des sans-culottes: Le dossier du patrimoine, 1789-1798*. Paris: Les Editions de Paris, 1989.

Hugo, Victor. *Oeuvres poétiques*. 3 vols. Paris: Gallimard, 1967.

Michelet, Jules. *Histoire du dix-neuvième siècle. Oeuvres complètes*. Paris: Flammarion, 1982.

Nerval, Gérard. *Oeuvres complétes*. Paris: Gallimard, 1974.

Viollet-le-Duc, Eugène Emmanuel. *Dictionnaire raisonné de l'architecture française du XIᵉ au XVIᵉ siécles*. 10 vols. Paris: Bance et Morel, 1854-1868.

Mary Anne O'Neil (essay date summer 1999)

SOURCE: O'Neil, Mary Anne. "Pascalian Reflections in *Les Misérables*." *Philological Quarterly* 78, no. 3 (summer 1999): 335-48.

[*In the following essay, O'Neil attempts to document the full extent to which the philosophy of Blaise Pascal informs* Les Misérables.]

Hugo only refers to Pascal by name in the opening chapters of *Les Misérables,* in the course of his description of Monseigneur Myriel, the Bishop of Digne.[1] Here, Hugo ambivalently calls the seventeenth-century Jansenist both a genius and a madman, a thinker devoted entirely to contemplation of the absolute but so dazed by "la vision terrible de la montagne infine" that his mind slipped into insanity.[2] Many other paragraphs of *Les Misérables,* in which Hugo speaks of the distant heavens and the importance of prayer, suggest, however, that he felt an affinity and even an admiration for the author of the *Pensées*. Even the title of his novel, especially the original title, *Les Misères,* points the reader in the direction of Pascal's thoughts.

The resemblance between Hugo and Pascal is not a new idea to critical studies of *Les Misérables,* although most scholars see these resemblances as coincidences resulting from common religious preoccupations.[3] Henri Peyre best explains these overlaps in "After 1850: God," where he notes Hugo's increasing obsession with God in the works composed during exile and the fact that "Hugo had personal experience of God, experience that he considered as irrecusable as the sign that Pascal, the Jansenist, believed that he had received from Jesus Christ."[4] In *Victor Hugo and the Visionary Novel*, Victor Brombert suggests a further reason for these similarities: "*Les Misérables,* in Hugo's mind, grew to be an increasingly religious book. All of human destiny, as the narrator explains, is summed up in the dilemma: "loss or salvation"[5]—the same dilemma that inspired the *Pensées.* Still other critics have proposed a deliberate connection between the two writers. Kathryn Grossman, in *Figuring Transcendence in Les Misérables,* cites a number of concepts, most specifically "the affinities between creatures and creation (or Creator), that is, between the infinitesimal and the boundless"[6] that originated in the *Pensées.* Bernard Leuilliot establishes that Hugo reread the *Pensées* in Brussels in 1852 and found it "un vrai livre d'exil."[7] Finally, Jacques Neefs points out imagistic and stylistic similarities between the two works. In *Les Misérables,* Hugo weaves thousands of reflections on the human condition into the plot; he has a habit, like Pascal, of dramatizing philosophical debates through contrasts of light and dark, ascents and falls, vertigo.[8] While all of these comments draw our attention to the curious way in which Hugo's novel so often echoes Pascal's obsessions, they fail to compare the texts of *Les Misérables* and the *Pensées* in a coherent fashion.

The author's frequent allusions to such key Pascalian concepts as "les deux infinis" and "Dieu sensible au coeur" suggest that the *Pensées* serves as a more prominent intertext in *Les Misérables* than critics have previously recognized. Moreover, a close examination of Hugo's conception of the deity, the relationship between the human and the divine, and redemption reveals that he understands these issues in the same way, and often in the same terms, as his Jansenist predecessor. A comparison between *Les Misérables* and Pascal's work allows us to approach the novel's protagonist, Jean Valjean, as a character who embodies the efficacy of faith and moral commitment advocated in the *Pensées* and to interpret the story of this hero's progress from crime to sanctity as a nineteenth-century version of Pascal's wager.

Les Misérables, like the *Pensées,* attempts to persuade its readers to wager in favor of God's existence and the soul's immortality. The 1861 revisions of the 1848 manuscript clearly orient the novel in the direction of theological argumentation. Albouy and Brombert have commented upon the most significant additions: the Bishop of Digne appears in the novel before Jean Valjean and engages in discussions with both believers and non-believers in which the defenders of God carry off victory; the curious digression after the introduction of the Petit Picpus convent entitled "Parenthèse" pleads for the necessity of religious faith; the long exposition of the Battle of Waterloo insists upon the deity's supervision of history.[9] We may add to this list of revisions, "Les Mines et les mineurs," the chapter opening "Patron Minette," where Hugo affirms that all philosophers who have bettered the human condition have kept their eyes on the heavens (1:856). An urgency to prove the value of religion suffuses the novel. As Albouy states the case: "Il s'agissait moins, en effet, de raconter ou de décrire, que de prouver. *Les Misérables* sont, aux yeux de Hugo, une gigantique preuve de Dieu et de l'âme."[10]

As they argue in favor of religion, both writers criticize similar categories of secular thinkers. In the *Pensées,* Pascal takes aim at the seventeenth-century libertines, who place their faith in science, and the skeptics, or Pyrrhonians, whom he associates with Montaigne and who deny the mind's ability to arrive at any precise notion of truth, goodness, or an afterlife.[11] Writing over two hundred years later, Hugo obviously fears the influence of both contemporary philosophers and political thinkers who either eliminate the notion of a supreme being from metaphysics or whose enthusiasm for science results in unadulterated materialism. Albouy and Leuilliot have suggested that Hugo's opponents probably include several atheistic schools that had developed in France at the beginning of the Second Empire such as the positivists and the Feuerbachian materialists.[12] Brombert further points out that the author's "private quarrel with his fellow 'socialists' at a time when French socialism, abandoning earlier utopian leanings, tended to link revolutionary values with impiety" certainly motivated the composition in 1860 of the "Philosophical Preface" Hugo intended as an introduction to his novel.[13] While this preface does not appear in twentieth-century editions of *Les Misérables,* modern readers can find Hugo's polemic against profane thinkers in the digression of *Les Misérables* most concerned with religion, "Parenthèse." Here, Hugo rejects all forms of atheism as intellectual blindness: "Il y a, nous le savons, une philosophie qui nie l'infini. Il y a aussi une philosophie, classée pathologiquement, qui nie le soleil; cette philosophie s'appelle cécité" (1:619). He goes so far as to prefer to atheism the fanaticism of cloistered nuns, since this fanaticism is motivated by true religious conviction.

Neither Pascal nor Hugo is an abstract philosopher. Both fall into the French moralist tradition which regards thought as a basis for action. Both counter atheism within this practical framework. Pascal especially fears those who deny the immortality of the soul—a tenet that determines our entire conduct: "Toutes nos actions et nos pensées doivent prendre des routes si différentes, selon qu'il y aura des biens éternels à espérer ou non, qu'il est impossible de faire une démarche avec sens et jugement, qu'en réglant la vue de ce point, qui doit être notre dernier objet" (24). Hugo expresses much the same sentiment in his explanation of the value of religion in *Les Misérables.* In "Parenthèse," he condemns atheism for eliminating the possibility of an afterlife while interpreting progress exclusively in scientific or economic terms. Such a materialistic philosophy cannot offer individual citizens the necessary incentives to sacrifice present pleasures for the future happiness of mankind. Only the desire to know the absolute can motivate the unselfishness required to realize social progress. As for Pascal, for Hugo this absolute is God:

> Le progrès est le but; l'idéal est le type.
> Qu'est-ce que l'idéal? C'est Dieu.
>
> (1:621)

In the early pages of *Les Misérables,* the dying "ancient constitutionnel" foreshadows the above-mentioned discussion of religion when he states: "Le bien ne peut pas avoir de serviteur impie. C'est un mauvais conducteur du genre humain que celui qui est athée" (1:59). Hugo creates several atheistic characters whose actions prove harmful to society. The first, the hedonistic senator of the chapter "Philosophie après boire," denounces charity as foolishness based on the erroneous concept of an afterlife. Monseigneur Myriel explains that such an attitude, especially in a public servant, makes it all too easy to ignore the poor and oppressed. For the bishop, progress requires that "la croyance au bon Dieu soit la philosophie du peuple" (1:43). In later chapters, Hugo includes among "Les Amis de l'ABC" Grantaire, a youthful cynic indisposed to sacrifice his pleasure for the unprovable existence of God. Although a quasi-comic character—Grantaire passes out drunk at the start of the insurrection and revives only to die from a gunshot—Hugo includes him to underscore the uselessness of atheists in political revolutions. A more important character, Javert, has no notion of a transcendent ideal informing human justice. At the moment of crisis preceding the policeman's suicide, the reader learns that "depuis qu'il [Javert] avait l'âge d'homme et de fonctionnaire, il mettait dans la police toute sa religion. . . . Il n'avait guère songé jusqu'à ce jour à cet autre supérieur, Dieu" (2:583). This *de facto* atheism plays a role in the perpetuation of prostitution, child neglect and the suppression of the lower classes. M. Gillenormand, Marius's grandfather, also "croyait fort peu en Dieu" (1:721). His selfishness and *libertinage* cause him, first, to separate Marius from the Baron Pontmercy and, later, to impede Marius's marriage. Finally, Thénardier, the novel's true villain, is a materialist (1:457). All of these characters point out Hugo's conviction that atheism provides a shaky foundation for the amelioration of society and must be countered by strong arguments in favor of the soul's immortality.

How much does the divinity Hugo promotes in *Les Misérables* have in common with the "Dieu d'Abraham, Dieu d'Isaac, Dieu de Jacob" acknowledged by Pascal in his "Mémorial" (4)? Hugo presents himself as separate from the Judeo-Christian tradition in "Parenthèse" where he claims to stand "pour la religion contre les religions" (1:623).[14] Nevertheless both the *Pensées* and *Les Misérables* present the reader with a first cause who has ordered the cosmos into a series of parallel infinities, stretching from the infinitely large to the infi-

nitely small, all interdependent and reflecting the infinity of their creator. Pascal's celebrated text of "La Disproportion de l'homme" evokes the astonishment of an observer who confronts, from an intermediate position, first the heavens stretching limitlessly above and then the endless complexity of the animalcule (87-89). At certain points in his novel, Hugo copies Pascal's imagery. The description of the Bishop of Digne's garden, for example, shows the saintly cleric dividing his time between "Un petit jardin pour se promener, et l'immensité pour rêver" (1:73). The child Cosette, during her night errand in the Montfermeil forest, is compared to a bit of matter lost in a universe: "D'un côté toute l'ombre; de l'autre un atome" (1:467). The introduction to "L'idylle Rue Plumet" affirms the unity of the natural world in almost the same terms used by Pascal to describe the interdependence of the microcosm and macrocosm. For Pascal, "L'un dépend de l'autre et l'un conduit à l'autre. Ces extrémités se touchent et se résument en Dieu, et en Dieu seulement" (89-90). For Hugo

> Où finit le télescope, le microscope commence. Lequel des deux a la vue la plus grande? . . . Les éléments et les principes se mêlent, se combinent, s'épousent, se multiplient les uns par les autres, au point de faire aboutir le monde matériel et le monde moral à la même clarté . . . ramenant tout à l'âme atome, épanouissant tout en Dieu. . . .
>
> (2:81)

The digression on "Les Mines et les mineurs" suggests that God has even ordered intellectual history in imitation of the cosmos. Concentric circles of thinkers, "qu'une divine chaîne invisible lie entre eux à leur insu" (1:856) work for the moral progress of humanity.

However clear the notion of infinity may be to our authors, neither believes that the mind can directly apprehend the creator. In Pascal's view, original sin has cast a veil between the mortal soul and the immortal object of the soul's desires: ". . . les hommes sont dans les ténèbres et dans l'éloignement de Dieu, . . . il s'est caché à leur connaissance . . . c'est même le nom qu'il se donne dans les Ecritures, *Deus absconditus*"(123). For Hugo, the situation is both different and analogous. While he does not accept the permanent consequences of the Fall, he demonstrates in his novel that the distance between divine perfection and human imperfection is so great that it can never be fully surmounted in this life.[15] For the Bishop of Digne, whose secure faith spares him the need for metaphysical speculation, this hidden God gives cause for wonder: "sans chercher à comprendre l'incompréhensible, il le regardait. Il n'étudiait pas Dieu. Il s'en éblouissait" (1:73). However, the *Deus absconditus* is a source of anguish to the novel's hero who desperately seeks moral guidance. Hugo's portrayal of his protagonist's spiritual misery most closely resembles Pascal's description of "La Misère de l'homme sans Dieu" in the Petit-Gervais chapter, where the former prisoner wanders beyond Digne, trapped between the immensity of the night sky and the endless, empty plain. The Bishop's charity shines as a light in this dark night of the soul, but only to impress upon Valjean his precarious spiritual situation between salvation and damnation, "ange" and "monstre" (1:139). Pascal invokes much the same dilemma in his thoughts on "La Disproportion de l'homme." His contemplator feels dizzy and lost, "se considérant soutenu dans la masse que la nature lui a donnée entre ces deux abîmes de l'infini et du néant," realizing that his gaze is limited to "[quelque] apparence du milieu des choses" (88). Throughout the moral struggles in the Champmathieu affair, the insurrection and the Paris gutters, Jean Valjean must resign himself to acting upon faith rather than revelation. Even in the novel's conclusion, during the sleepless night preceding the confession of his true identity to Marius, the protagonist only perceives God as "Le On qui est dans les ténèbres" (2:655).

Like his Jansenist predecessor, Hugo accords more importance to the emotions than to reason as a means of attaining faith. Neither writer disparages thought; indeed, for both, the ability to think is at once the most fundamental and highest attribute of the human mind. Pascal's "toute notre dignité consiste donc en la pensée" (163) finds an echo in Hugo's "Penser, voilà le triomphe vrai de l'âme (1:620). By thought, each includes a variety of introspective activities that lead to a proper assessment of our human condition. For Pascal, thought is the opposite of the "divertissement" that numbs our awareness of our mortality. True thought begins with an appraisal of the self, then moves to meditation on God: "Or l'ordre de la pensée est de commencer par soi, et par son auteur et sa fin" (116). Hugo similarly signals thought as a function, like prayer, that directs the conscience toward eternity: "Certaines facultés de l'homme sont dirigées vers l'Inconnu: la pensée, la rêverie, la prière" (1:618). Yet both authors remain skeptical about the application of mathematical or scientific reasoning to religious questions. Pascal admits that the human mind can gain some understanding of the deity through the mathematical concepts of unity and infinity, but such analogies do not lead far: "S'il y a un Dieu, il est infiniment incompréhensible, puisque n'ayant ni parties ni bornes, il n'a nul rapport à nous" (135). Hugo, for his part, points out the limits of science,[16] which he calls "un cordial," or stimulant to the mind contemplating ethical problems, whereas faith serves as the "élixir," or medicine capable of curing the mind beset by metaphysical or moral dilemmas (1:620).

In his thoughts on "Les Moyens de croire," Pascal signals the advantage of the heart over reason as an avenue to faith: "C'est le coeur qui sent Dieu et non la raison. Voilà ce que c'est que la foi: Dieu sensible au coeur et non à la raison" (147). The seat of both intuition and the emotions, the heart's superiority lies in its ability to grasp first principles, for example the fact that the soul exists and yearns for God, without demonstration. The heart cuts through the myriad complications and doubts plaguing reason and responds quickly and accurately. Because "Le sentiment . . . agit en un instant, et toujours est prêt à agir" (143), Pascal advises his readers to put their faith in their feelings—the best guide, except for direct revelation, in religious matters.

In *Les Misérables* Jean Valjean proves the wisdom of Pascal's advice, for, at every crucial step of his development, his heart serves as the compass to right behavior. In the Petit Gervais episode, his realization of his spiritual misery occurs simultaneously with the stirring of emotion in his numbed heart:

> Je suis un misérable! Alors son coeur creva et il se mit à pleurer. C'était la première fois qu'il pleurait depuis dix-neuf ans.
>
> (1:138)

The description of the sleepless night of the Champmathieu affair underscores the inadequacy of reason in the resolution of moral dilemmas. After endless deliberations, Valjean remains incapable of determining the better of two equally desperate actions: to hide his name and thus condemn an innocent man to the galleys or to reveal his past and deprive Montfermeil of its leading citizen. Only after a nightmare causes him to relive the fear and loneliness he experienced as an outcast can he envision the path to justice (1:289-93). His final struggle between his own desires to remain close to Cosette and his conviction that he must confess his identity to Marius is facilitated by emotional release: "Ce fut un bonheur pour Jean Valjean d'avoir pu pleurer. Cela l'éclaira peut-être" (2:653). Like Pascal, Hugo teaches the reader through his hero's trials that the heart has its reasons that are unknown to reason (146), especially in those cloudy areas that oppose personal interest to the more general interest of society.

When Jean Valjean performs extraordinarily good deeds, such as his rescue of Cosette from the Thénardiers or, later, from Javert and Marius, he does so intuitively as if responding to an inner voice whose call becomes ever more distinct in the course of the novel. Hugo names this inner voice the conscience and describes it as the human faculty most capable of establishing contact with the hidden God. In a pointed reference to Pascal, the final chapter of "Parenthèse" reinterprets "les deux infinis" as God and the soul:

> En même temps qu'il y a un infini hors de nous, n'y a-t-il pas un infini en nous? . . . Ce second infini est-il intelligent aussi? Pense-t-il? Aime-t-il? Veut-il? Si les deux infinis sont intelligents, chacun d'eux a un

principe voulant, et il y a un moi dans l'infini d'en haut comme il y a un moi dans l'infini d'en bas. Ce moi d'en bas, c'est l'âme; ce moi d'en haut, c'est Dieu.

(1:618)

Hugo may have rewritten Pascal's thoughts in reaction to the intermediate position in the cosmic order the Jansenist assigns to humanity.[17] In Hugo's revision, God and the soul emerge asfundamentally similar beings, both immortal, endowed with understanding, volition and the ability to love. This definition of "les deux infinis" provides the basis for *Les Misérables'* version of the doctrine of progress which proclaims individuals, such as the novel's hero, capable of overcoming evil both in themselves and in society if they are willing to respond to the divinity within.

This is not to say that Hugo presents an idealized view of humanity through his hero. As Albouy has noted, "[La] notion de l'homme grotesque et sublime, touchant à l'ange et tenant à la bête" is an integral element of Hugo's conception of human nature as early as *The Preface of Cromwell* of 1827,[18] and one which explains the imagery of extremes used to describe mankind in general and Jean Valjean in particular. The author assures the reader that nowhere can the mind encounter "plus d'éblouissements ni plus de ténèbres que dans l'homme" (1:270). Jean Valjean is composed of "La Boue mais l'âme." Albouy suggests that Hugo's conception of *homo duplex* shares a certain resemblance with Pascal's thought on our grandeur and misery: "L'homme n'est ni ange ni bête, et le malheur veut que celui qui veut faire l'ange fait la bête" (164).[19] At the climax of the Petit Gervais episode, the protagonist's moral awakening involves a realization of this dual nature:

Une voix lui disait-elle à l'oreille . . . que si désormais il n'était pas le meilleur des hommes il en serait le pire, qu'il fallait pour ainsi dire que maintenant il montât plus haut que l'évêque ou retombât plus bas que le galérien, que s'il voulait devenir bon il fallait qu'il devînt ange; que s'il voulait rester méchant il fallait qu'il devînt monstre?

(1:139)

Once again, however, Hugo rewrites Pascal's text to his own purpose.[20] For Pascal, any extreme pursuit of virtue makes vice all the more attractive. Thus, "qui veut faire l'homme fait la bête"(164). Hugo considers this intermediate moral position the most pernicious, since, for him, good and evil coexist in equally strong measures, pulling the soul at once between hatred, ignorance and selfishness on the one hand and enlightenment and charity on the other. Jean Valjean's struggles impress upon the reader the ease with which even the most conscientious individual can slip backwards into egotism. In *Les Misérables,* indeed, "qui ne veut pas faire l'ange fait la

bête." Jean Valjean's transformation from a brutish criminal without a moral conscience into an honest father and citizen requires vigilance and commitment.

A belief in God's existence, an awareness of the limits of human knowledge, as well as the necessity of choosing religion over atheism, are matters that inspire *Les Misérables* as much as the *Pensées*. In the most crucial stage of his argument, Pascal reminds his interlocutor that our inability to answer the question of the soul's immortality does not excuse us from taking a stance for or against eternity:

Il se joue un jeu, à l'extrémité de cette distance infinie, où il arrivera croix ou pile. Que gagerez-vous? Par raison, vous ne pouvez faire ni l'un ni l'autre; par raison, vous ne pouvez défendre nul des deux . . . Oui, mais il faut parier . . . vous êtes embarqué. Lequel prendrez-vous donc?

(135-216)

In *Les Misérables,* Jean Valjean finds himself embarked when the Bishop of Digne's forgiveness of the theft of silver offers him an initial opportunity for redemption. The bishop's words: "Jean Valjean, mon frère, vous n'appartenez plus au mal, mais au bien. C'est votre âme que je vous achète; je la retire aux pensées noires et à l'esprit de perdition; et je la donne à Dieu" (1:133) present the former criminal with two clear options: heads, to lift his soul into sainthood; tails, to fall into bestiality. The wager that the hero accepts at the conclusion of the Petit Gervais incident is only the first of a series of choices which consume his entire existence. Hugo insists upon the anguish suffered by his protagonist, who most often contemplates his alternatives alone in a darkness that suggests imagistically his doubts. Choice becomes more difficult rather than easier. During "Une Tempête sous un crâne," Jean Valjean realizes that all of his efforts to live as an honest bourgeois did nothing to prepare him for the sacrifice required to save Champmathieu: "tout ce qu'il avait fait jusqu'à ce jour n'était autre chose qu'un trou qu'il creusait pour y enfouir son nom" (1:274). In "La Nuit Blanche" the author asserts that, even after a lifetime of moral decisions, his hero finds this last step as arduous as the first: ". . . cette fois encore, comme cela lui était déjà arrivé dans d'autres péripéties douleureuses, deux routes s'ouvraient devant lui; l'une tentante, l'autre effrayante. Laquelle prendre" (2:651)? Conceived as a Pascalian character, Jean Valjean is deprived of certainty but required to choose and, moreover, to choose correctly.

Recognizing that belief may not come easily to his interlocutor who has accepted the necessity of the wager, Pascal recommends prayer, the imitation of saintly people and the suppression of the passions as the most efficient spiritual exercises preparing the way to faith. Hugo speaks of these same three avenues to faith in

Les Misérables. Both writers insist on the primacy of prayer,[21] which, for Pascal, acknowledges our dependence upon the deity (138). Hugo, for his part, advocates prayer as a means of overcoming the separation between the human and the divine: "Mettre par la pensée, l'infini d'en bas en contact avec l'infini d'en haut, cela s'appelle prier" (1:619). He broadens his definition of prayer to include meditation and reverie: "Quant au mode de prier, tous sont bons, pourvu qu'ils soient sincères" (1:619). When Hugo presents Jean Valjean absorbed in consideration of some moral dilemma, he wishes the reader to understand that his hero is praying. Valjean often appears, as well, in traditional postures of supplication. At the conclusion of the Petit Gervais episode, for example, a passerby notices "un homme dans l'attitude de la prière, à genoux sur le pavé dans l'ombre, devant la porte de monseigneur Bienvenu" (1:195). Following Pascal's advice: ". . . apprenez de ceux qui ont été liés comme vous, et qui parient maintenant tout leur bien" (1:137), Hugo's hero remains attentive, until the moment of death, to the Bishop of Digne's example and imitates his mentor's charity and forgiveness.

Valjean also comes to imitate more and more vigorously in the course of the novel the bishop's renunciation of worldly pleasures. Hugo demands extreme asceticism of the novel's hero, who must give up not only his desires for vengeance but also his paternal feelings, wealth and comfort. Like Pascal (138), Hugo seems to feel that passions are great obstacles to faith and that even the simplest satisfactions lead us too easily astray into egotism, the modern manifestation of Pascal's deceptive "amour-propre." Hugo signals this danger at several crucial points, most notably during the Champmathieu affair, when Jean Valjean recognizes that his seemingly worthwhile existence as Monsieur Madeleine has tainted "tant d'années de repentir et d'abnégation" (1:272) and in "L'Idylle Rue Plumet," where the discovery of Cosette's romance with Marius turns the hero's love into a revolt described as "l'immense réveil de l'égoïsme" (2:390). The emphasis on sacrifice explains, further, the constant comparisons of Jean Valjean to Christ, which, as Brombert notes, abound in the later chapters of *Les Misérables.*[22] The death scene enacts dramatically Pascal's conviction that renunciation of the world opens the door to faith (137), for, as Jean Valjean leaves the world, a celestial light floods his eyes and an angel welcomes his soul into paradise.

It is the notion of faith, a faith drawn from the depths of the heart, unfathomable by logic, yet capable of transforming our moral life, that most closely links Hugo to Pascal. *Les Misérables* demonstrates the author's own faith in human perfectibility and the values of the French Revolution, and it does so at a point of consummate difficulty in his life, when his exile not only separated him from his compatriots but when the repressive atmosphere of the Second Empire would have made his message of social progress and liberty appear naïve. Hugo was certainly aware that his audience, prepared by a quarter century of secular thought to dismiss religion, might prove skeptical toward his defense of God and the immortality of the soul. In some personal comments at the end of the "Parenthèse," Hugo seems to reassure his readers that his faith in the deity is not only sincere, but indeed the primary reason for the composition of his novel. Contrasting the nuns of the Petit Picpus Convent, who live even on earth in the divine presence, with French men and women of the late-nineteenth century, "cette heure où tant d'hommes ont le front bas et l'âme plus haute" (1:629), Hugo places himself squarely in the nuns' camp with the declaration "Quant à nous . . . [nous] vivons comme elles par la foi" (1:624). Indeed, like Pascal's *Pensées*, *Les Misérables* is a protest against a world over-confident yet unhappy in its materialism. A bold and courageous wager, Hugo's novel invites us to look beyond the present to a more just future and, ultimately, to eternity.

Notes

1. I wish to thank Whitman College for the Abshire grant I received in 1996 that enabled me to do the research for this paper. I am especially indebted to Dana Miller, a senior French major, who helped me not only in the compilation of a bibliography but also in taking notes and organizing my ideas on Pascal and Hugo. I would also like to recognize another former student, Karen Boscher, whose seminar paper, "La Source de la douleur dans *Les Misérables*," written in 1993, first suggested the possibility of a comparison between Pascal and Hugo.

2. Victor Hugo, *Les Misérables,* ed. Marius-François Guyard, 2 vols. (Paris: Classique Garnier, 1963), 1:5. Subsequent references will be included in the text.

3. See Pierre Albouy, *Mythographies* (Paris: José Corti, 1976), 163; Paul Bénichou, "Victor Hugo et le Dieu caché," *Hugo le fabuleux: Colloque de Cérisy,* ed. Anne Ubersfeld (Paris: Seghers, 1985), 146-64; Frank Bowman, "Le Système de Dieu," *Hugo le fabuleux: Colloque de Cérisy,* 165-77; Kathryn Grossman, *Figuring Transcendence in Les Misérables* (Southern Illinois U. Press, 1994), 313; Bernard Leuilliot, "Philosophie(s): Commencement d'un livre," *Lire Les Misérables,* ed. Anne Ubersfeld and Guy Rosa (Paris: José Corti, 1985), 59-75; Jacques Neefs, "L'Espace démocratique du roman," *Lire Les Misérables,* 77-95; Henri Peyre, "After 1852: God," *Modern Critical Views: Victor Hugo,* ed. Harold Bloom, (New Haven: Chelsea House Publishers, 1988), 61-82.

4. Peyre, 167.

5. Victor Brombert, *Victor Hugo and the Visionary Novel* (Harvard U. Press, 1984), 117.

6. Grossman, 313, n50.

7. Leuilliot, 64, n8.

8. Neefs, 78-79.

9. See Albouy, 135-37; Brombert, 119-21, and Peyre, 166-67, for a discussion of the revisions of *Les Misères*.

10. Albouy, 137.

11. Blaise Pascal, *Pensées* (Paris: Garnier, 1964), 170-71; 86. Subsequent references will be included in the text.

12. Albouy, 122-23; Leuilliot, 60-61.

13. Brombert, 118-19.

14. For a fuller treatment of Hugo's conception of God, see Albouy, 98-137; Bénichou, Bowman, and Peyre.

15. As Bénichou notes, for Hugo, God "n'est caché que par un mystère de grandeur et non d'interdiction" (154).

16. For an extensive treatment of Hugo's ideas on this subject see Albouy's "Raison et science chez Victor Hugo," *Mythographies* (98-118).

17. Neefs has pointed out that Pascal's notion of the two infinities stresses the distance that separates the mind from the object of its contemplation as well as the mind's inability to know, whereas Hugo's text provides a means for the infinitely large and the infinitely small to come together (80, n2).

18. In the chapter of *Mythographies* entitled "Des Hommes, des bêtes et des anges," Albouy suggests that, unlike Pascal's notion of man as an "être moyen, ni tout à fait bon ni tout à fait mauvais," Hugo conceives of a man as simultaneously grotesque and sublime, "Touchant à l'ange et tenant de la bête" (155).

19. Albouy, 155.

20. Hugo's rewriting of Pascal's thought on "l'ange et la bête" may be another instance of his criticism of classicism in *Les Misérables* which Grossman studies (107, 110-16).

21. Leuilliot sees Hugo's conception of prayer as an answer to Pascal's thought: "Incompréhensible que Dieu soit, incompréhensible qu'il ne soit pas" (64).

22. Brombert, 123. Albouy notes that some early twentieth-century critics have considered Hugo a Christian writer (100). For a contrary view see Peyre, 162.

Ariane Smart (essay date August 2000)

SOURCE: Smart, Ariane. "The Darkness and Claustrophobia of the City: Victor Hugo and the Myth of Paris." *Modern & Contemporary France* 8, no. 3 (August 2000): 315-24.

[*In the following essay, Smart highlights Hugo's depiction of the city of Paris as a dark and gloomy prison.*]

According to Roger Caillois,[1] a new literary representation of Paris appeared in the 1840s which had such a powerful effect on the imaginary that its truth was never challenged. During this period, Paris became a central figure: as soon as Paris was mentioned, lyricism, adventure, heroism, and mystery were evoked. A dark and mysterious Paris was presented as the 'real' Paris, the Paris that normal people in their everyday routines might not see, but which was 'real' precisely because it went beyond its surface appearance:

> Comment [. . .] ne se développerait-il pas en chaque lecteur la conviction intime [. . .] que le Paris qu'il connaît n'est pas le seul, n'est pas même le véritable, n'est qu'un décor brillamment éclairé, mais trop *normal,* [. . .] et qui dissimule un autre Paris, le Paris réel [. . .] d'autant plus puissant qu'il est secret, et qui vient à tout endroit et à tout moment se mêler dangereusement à l'autre?[2]

It is within this complex interaction between a 'fantastic' and 'realistic' representation of Paris that the essence and the power of this modern and urban myth lay. The urban imaginary expressed in the literature of the 19th century is therefore not a matter of pure imagination, but is rather a consequence of concrete, political/historical realities which were being collectively interpreted during the same historical period.[3] The literary interest in describing Paris as a dark and claustrophobic place highlighted, in other words, the fears and obsessions of a new, urban, civilisation.

Like the Greek masks of comedy and tragedy, the myth of Paris contains two opposing faces. On the one hand, the bright, positive side glorifies the capital of progress, of modernity; the city of lights, magnificence, and power. As the city of 1789, Paris is also the *capitale du genre humain,* the capital of the world. On the other hand, the dark, negative side represents Paris as dirty, unhealthy, gloomy, and dangerous. Both sides were repeatedly explored by Hugo. Although he is probably better known as the 'prophet' of Paris, I have chosen to focus on an equally important aspect of Hugolian representations of the capital: its darkness.

The importance of Hugo in the mythmaking of the capital is fundamental; first, because Paris was 'la grande affaire de sa vie'[4] and his passion for the capital is to be found in much of his work. Second, because his sense of the epic together with his use of symbolism and his 'metaphysics' make him a major contributor to what Claude Millet called 'le dispositif légendaire' of 19th-century France.[5] Finally, it can be argued that Hugo was characteristic of a period in French history which produced a rather optimistic discourse while, at the same time, being submerged by a very dark imaginary (and particularly a dark *urban* imaginary).

Nineteenth-century France lived in the shadow of the guillotine (to put it in a Hugolian way), and had to cope with the ambivalent legacy left by the French Revolution. Uncomfortable with the past, uncertain about the present, France rushed frantically into the future, a process which, far from healing its deep anxiety, increased it dramatically. The faith in science and progress barely hid the bourgeoisie's social phobia of darkness, both material (how the city looked) and moral (what kinds of perversion it generated). Hugo's work, it may be argued, is a particularly pertinent illustration of this anxiety: anguished, oppressive, suffocating, claustrophobic and fearful, the Hugolian imaginary highlights the fears of his time as much as it encapsulates the dark side of a phantasmagoria where 'l'humanité [. . .] fait figure de damné'.[6]

Hugo will be considered mainly as a symbolist and poet, even when he writes novels. In his use of metaphors—which are never gratuitous, but are carefully chosen[7]—Hugo leaves symbolic clues which the reader must decode. Recurrent metaphors, which are to be found both in his poems and novels, play a central role in the texts' construction of meaning, rather than acting as mere poetic illustrations.[8] 'Closer to romance and myth than the realist tradition, projecting linguistic and metaphoric structures that achieve what has been called the *roman-poème,* [. . .] he translates private obsessions into collective symbols'.[9] In other words, not only is Hugo representative of the imaginary of his time (in his expression of its obsessions), he also appears as a main contributor to the myth of Paris, first because his use of symbolism makes him a natural 'mythmaker', and, second, because of his devotion to Paris.

As we have seen, parallel with the official, optimistic, and perhaps naive glorification of Paris (as the symbol of a bright future) there existed a dominant, pessimistic representation of Paris, in which darkness illustrated the moral concern felt by 19th-century France towards this ever-growing urban monster. According to the physiology of the time, darkness is not only the city's prevalent tone; it also reveals its moral depravation. Hugo, through his combination of the fantastic and the realistic, the sublime and the horrific, is part of a tradition which, since Balzac, has delighted in representing Paris as a dark, and, consequently, as an evil place. The perception of the city as evil was not created by the 19th century. There was already a Rousseauesque tradition

of suspicion towards the city in general, as opposed to an idealistic vision of the country. For Paris, this tradition was reinforced by the trauma caused by the Terror: the people of Paris leading the whole country into a bloodbath was a nightmarish memory in France. According to Jean Tulard, the September Massacres in particular remained engraved on the collective memory: '[D]ésormais, Paris inspire peur et dégoût. Les massacres de Septembre pèseront lourd sur l'avenir de Paris, un Paris que l'on souhaite à nouveau enchaîner.'[10] From Napoleon onwards, the capital was kept under tight surveillance. As a revolutionary city, it was still able to overthrow regimes, but its power over the rest of France was to decrease throughout the 19th century. Nevertheless, the image of a bloodthirsty capital remained: 'le sang effacé des pierres de la capitale s'est incrusté dans les mémoires'.[11] Paris still represented a threat.

Moreover, the trauma of the Revolution was intensified by the socio-historical context of the time: Paris had to contend with massive immigration from the country, and dramatic changes in society.[12] The tradition of a country in which people died where they were born was undermined for thousands of *provinciaux* who rushed to the capital to find a job or seek their fortune. To them, the city appeared a dangerous place: isolated, the new migrant became the easy prey of a world about which he was ignorant, a new world that obeyed different rules, rules that he was unable to master. Nineteenth-century French literature is frequently peopled by such young, naïve *provinciaux,* who are destabilised by a frantic rhythm of life to which they are unaccustomed; they are both fascinated and frightened by the unfamiliar city. Everything was new, everything happened at breakneck speed: 'la vie y est d'une effrayante rapidité', notes Balzac's newcomer Lucien Rubempré.[13] Opposed to the provinces, Paris represented a world of complexity, fluidity, and mobility, and gave an impression of chaos, resembling a modern Capernaum, a new Inferno. Separated from any roots or points of reference, tempted by petty con-men and whores, the new migrant was forced to learn quickly the rules of the urban game, and, in so doing, definitively cut himself off from his past, traditions and social group: 'le provincial installé à Paris, avide de reconnaissance, doit pour sa part se désolidariser du milieu dont il émane'.[14]

As for the poorest among the newcomers, they found themselves in what remained a medieval town, ill-prepared to face the ever-growing number of migrants—at least before *haussmannisation* (and, to a large extent, afterwards). Many of the jobs offered by the capital were seasonal, and, once jobless, the poor stayed in Paris, becoming concentrated in the many blocks of poverty where epidemics spread; the unhealthy and overcrowded places described by Hugo as the 'bas-fonds'. There, a different world emerged which developed its own rules and its own language ('l'argot').

The underworld quickly transformed poverty into criminality, the only way to survive in this kind of urban environment.

Paris as the capital of crime became a recurring image in 19th-century French literature: the anonymity of the big city protects and hides the criminals whilst it hampers police efficiency. A literature influenced by the success of the *roman noir* encapsulated this dreadful vision, combining all the dangers of Paris into a very potent recipe: crime, mystery and power. This tendency reached its climax with the phenomenal success of Eugène Sue's *Les Mystères de Paris* (1842-1843), which participated in elaborating the literary image of the city of crime and mystery. Paris, at once capital of crime and revolutionary city, became a reference point as a place of conspiracy, where mysterious people dressed in black gathered at night, for some obscure purpose, in a city they had learned to tame perfectly. This recalls the opening passages of Balzac's *L'Histoire des treize.* Hugo's representation of Paris also shares deep similarities with that of Balzac.

For Balzac, the ugliness of Paris reveals its moral deprivation; its darkness reveals its evil. Paris and its inhabitants share the same gloomy and infernal physiology: 'Peu de mots suffiront pour justifier physiologiquement la teinte presque infernale des figures parisiennes, car ce n'est pas seulement par plaisanterie que Paris a été nommé un enfer.'[15] Balzac's Paris can be particularly dark, but his representation also contains elements of the fantastic:[16] describing the tiny streets by night, Balzac creates suggestive images of dust, dampness and mud. Paris is depicted as a grey, dirty and miserable place with narrow and tortuous streets leading to dark courts and *impasses*. The walls are grey, dark, and yellowish; Paris bears the stigma of misery and is on the verge of decay; the city is crumbling away, metaphorically exuding its misfortune: 'illustre vallée de plâtras incessamment prêts de tomber, et de ruisseaux noirs de boue'.[17] Balzac conjures up a sordid reality, but his vision transforms the abject into something grandiose and powerful: 'Alors apparaît un Paris obscur en surface, redoutable en profondeur [. . .]. Tel est le Paris de Balzac, *réellement et fantastiquement* noire, violente et ténébreuse gravure'.[18] This 'gravure' is, to a large extent, a Hugolian one. Balzac's numerous allusions to Dante, to the *égouts sociaux,* his fascination for the figure of the convict, his interest in the *Paris souterrain,* and the combination of the grotesque and the grandiose, bring the two authors together. But whereas Balzac sees Paris as the scene of human passions (particularly in terms of money), Hugo sees it in a much more metaphysical way, as the *capitale du genre humain*. Not only does Paris represent the promise of a better future, it also serves as the allegory of the contemporary, urban human condition, characterised by its carceral oppression. There are strong similarities between the gloomy, though powerful, representation of the city that dominates Hugo's literary imaginary, and that of a cell: a sense of oppression, sweating walls, the predominance of grey, black and yellow. Darkness is common to both, and Hugo emphasises the analogies between the two oppressive places.

The image of the prison and metaphors and allusions related to imprisonment are omnipresent in Hugo's work. There are countless references, throughout Hugo's work, to caves, cages, tombs, cells, dungeons, chains, keys, locks and bars. One example will serve to illustrate the many allusions, references and metaphors that Hugo uses to connote a prevailing tone of suffocation. In a scene in *Les Misérables,* Hugo's narrator describes the arrival of Valjean, the protagonist, in Paris.[19] Valjean is a convict on the run. He is in charge of Cosette, a young girl whose mother has just died and whom he is trying to protect. On his arrival in Paris, he finds refuge in the 'masure Gorbeau', a sinister place—'plus morne qu'un cimetière' (1/462)—near the 'mur d'enceinte', the guillotine and the Salpêtrière: incarceration, the death penalty and madness enhance the 'innombrables traditions patibulaires du lieu' (1/466). The dark place is a promise of the trap yet to come: 'On croyait pressentir des pièges dans cette obscurité, toutes les formes confuses de l'ombre paraissaient suspectes' (1/466). Soon after, Inspector Javert, believing he has recognised the convict, starts the hunt again—and a hunt is precisely what it is, for the prey (1/510) is chased by a pack of dogs ('les limiers de meutes')[20] led by a 'chien fils d'une louve' (1/198), who was himself born in a prison. Valjean tries to find his way into the labyrinth of the streets.[21] He finally finds himself trapped in a dead-end: the 'cul-de-sac Genrot': 'Là, barrage'; 'Jean Valjean se sentait pris comme dans un filet qui se resserrait lentement' (1/486). He manages to escape by climbing over a wall, and lands in a convent.[22] In order to find refuge in this convent, 'Le Petit-Picpus', he first has to leave it without being noticed. He achieves this by hiding inside a coffin, and is then buried alive in the *cimetière Vaugirard,* the cemetery where religious victims of the September Massacres were buried, and a cemetery that was later used to bury the *guillotinés.*[23] Unfortunately, there is a new warden who undermines Fauchelevent's attempts to deliver his friend. Ultimately, Valjean will be saved, but the fact that he faints emphasises how close he was to dying in his coffin.

Such an example is even more convincing if we place *Les Misérables* in the context of Hugo's work during the late 1850s and early 1860s, that is, as a continuation of his earlier poetic work, *Dieu* and *La Fin de Satan.* The third and final part of the latter was left unfinished under the suggestive title of 'La Prison'. Instead of finishing it, Hugo resumed work on a 12-year-old manuscript entitled *Les Misères,* the story of a convict. I suggest that *Les Misérables* not only shares the same obsession for metaphysical confinement, but also operates according to the same symbolic pattern.[24] In *Notre-Dame de Paris,* Hugo had already drawn on an elaborate series of variations on the themes of oppression and incarceration, themes symbolised by the recurrent imagery of spiders. The spider (*arachne* in Greek) serves as a symbol of Fate (*ananke* in Greek) throughout the novel. This symbolism culminates in the famous scene where Maître Jacques attempts to save a fly from being eaten by a spider. He is stopped by Frollo, shouting in anguish 'laissez-faire la fatalité!',[25] before comparing himself both to the spider and to the fly. The 'prison-spider' relationship developed by Hugo intensifies the oppressive claustrophobia of the city, and stresses the power of Fate over an individual isolated by the city.

Moreover, the spider's web is reminiscent of the urban web: the labyrinth. The labyrinth defines the city: 'le Paris moral est un labyrinthe où il est besoin d'un fil d'Ariane', notes Balzac.[26] The labyrinth is the ultimate test. It symbolises the need either to master the set of rules imposed by the city, or to be swallowed by its monster. It is a demanding test, particularly for the new arrivals, *les provinciaux.* In this sense, it can be seen as a modern variation on archaic initiation. Surviving in the city requires an urban epistemology[27] to master 'les zigzags de la stratégie' (1/479-82), to borrow Hugo's terms. In *Le Père Goriot,* Balzac distinguished between the neophytes and those who mastered the urban code: Vautrin tries to save Rastignac from becoming Paris's next victim, which is likely to happen if he refuses to see 'la vie telle qu'elle est'.[28] Hugo's main characters often do not possess this code; they are described as being trapped in a destiny against which they are blind and defenceless.

In order to increase the effect of oppression, not only does the labyrinth serve to define the city, it is also to be found *within* the narrative structure. The plot of *Notre-Dame de Paris* develops a number of individual dramas, all linked in some way to the architecture of the cathedral (the prison) and to the labyrinth of the city.[29] According to Bachelard, the labyrinth corresponds to 'l'imagination du mouvement *difficile,* du mouvement *angoissant*'.[30] Although the complexity of this symbol cannot be analysed in detail here, its use in 19th-century literature stresses a specific urban perception of space: '[D]égoût, angoisse, secrète solitude, labyrinthe *immense* où l'on n'aperçoit dans les ténèbres que des lieux de *perdition,* comme si le chaos n'était qu'un *vaste* désert fait de bruit, de fumée et de boue.'[31] The image of the 'void', with which Hugo is fascinated, echoes the figure of the labyrinth. They both reflect the same fantastic imaginary of urban space. Whether the trap is horizontal or vertical, it symbolises both oppression and vastness. Thus, claustrophobia and vertigo are not contradictory; rather, they are complementary. For as much as Hugo develops an oppressive urban atmosphere, he also surrenders to the 'hantise de la chute vertigineuse'.[32] *Les Misérables* revolves around images of falling and descent:[33] Fantine's fall from the status of a *grisette* to the worst destitution; the Thénardiers's decline from the poverty of an inn to the misery of their *galetas*; the descent into the underworld (in the two suggestive chapters entitled 'Les mines et les mineurs' and 'Le Bas-fond'); and also Valjean's descent into the sewers: 'Abîme, gouffre, trou et chute suggèrent sans doute l'espace, mais ne sont pas étrangers au sentiment de clôture [. . .]. Satan après tout, est prisonnier de l'infini.'[34] Satan is, in fact, a major figure in Hugo's work. Mention of Satan, just like the image of darkness, always refers to 'materiality', to *la matière*: 'la dualité de l'ombre et de la lumière [. . .] est la dualité cartésienne de la matière et de l'esprit'.[35] Hugo seems obsessed with his century's lack of spirituality and with the dramatic development of urban civilisation, or, in other words, with the apparent triumph of 'materiality'. For Hugo, the darkness of the city and its claustrophobia come from its inherent 'materiality', as the then fashionable assimilation of Paris as a 'new Babylon' illustrates.

Ancient Babylon was understood to be the antithesis of Jerusalem and of Paradise. Although a magnificent city, it was ultimately destroyed because it was only based on temporal values. The symbolism of Babylon is one of a *splendeur viciée* that dooms itself by distracting humankind from its spiritual duties. Babylon symbolises the transitory triumph of a material world that will eventually destroy humankind. What is striking in the process of the 19th-century condemnation of 'materiality' is the discourse and the imaginary it produces. Criticising the materiality of urban civilisation, Hugo, amongst others, describes it as very much *alive*: as a monster. 'Paris-matière' is not made of cold stones, it is a monster of flesh and blood in the purest Biblical tradition. A vast set of demonic and hideous figures serve to emphasise Paris's ability to swallow those who disobey or ignore its mysterious rules: 'ce gouffre énorme qui ingurgite tout'.[36] The image of the monster reflects Hugo's vertigo in a very suggestive scene that refers, once again, to the image of the spider. In *Notre-Dame de Paris,* Louis XI, 'l'Universelle Aragne', descends into the depths of the Bastille, visiting his brand new and costly cage (whilst superbly ignoring his victim who has spent the past 14 years agonising in a tiny cell).[37] The figures of the 'gouffre', the labyrinth and the spider mingle into one single image of a monster swallowing its prey, or of *Ananke* devouring its victims. Those who do not master the urban code, in other words, are devoured and digested.

Thus the constant references to an ugly, hideous, and dangerous Paris transfigure the whole city into something organic. Hugo refers to the sewers of Paris as 'l'intestin du Léviathan' (3/284-303).[38] The image of the 'ventre' is also to be found in Zola (*Le Ventre de Paris*) and in Balzac: '[E]spèce de ventre parisien, où se digèrent les intérêts de la ville et où ils se condensent sous la forme dite *affaires,* se remue et s'agite, par un âcre et fielleux mouvement intestinal, la foule [. . .].'[39] Although it is a symbol of materiality, the urban monster remains a classical monster: gigantic, voracious, pitiless, bloodthirsty, powerful and, above all, alive: 'énorme organisme en mouvement, beau parce que vivant, animé, dans son devenir par une vie souterraine pleine d'ombres et profonde'. The urban monster is characterised by its 'vie morte et terrible'.[40] The apparent paradox of a living death stresses the specificity of materiality as being alive, but not *humanly* alive. The kind of 'death-in-life' evoked in these urban tombs is reminiscent of that in Baudelaire's 'Une Charogne':

> Les mouches bourdonnaient sur ce ventre putride,
> D'où sortaient de noirs bataillons
> De larves, qui coulaient comme un épais liquide
> Le long de ces vivants haillons.[41]

It is within its very decay, in the wriggling of the worms, that an illusion of life is created, although it is anarchic, hideous and non-human.

What increases the power of the metaphor of the monster to an even greater extent is its blurred and undefined image: the people, the buildings and the city are confused in one single hideous figure. The buildings, for example, such as 'la masure Gorbeau', in *Les Misérables,* are described as particularly dark and threatening places: 'le jour, c'était laid; le soir, c'était lugubre; la nuit c'était sinistre' (1/467). The *galetas* where the Thénardiers live is even worse; a hideous slum, with dark corners which might hide some terrible creatures: 'De là d'affreux coins insondables où il semblait que devaient se blottir des araignées grosses comme le poing, des cloportes larges comme le pied, et peut-être même on ne sait quels êtres humains monstreux' (2/274). As for the people, the gang of con-men and criminals, *la bande à Patron-Minette,* is described as 'un mystérieux voleur à quatre têtes [. . .] le polype monstrueux du mal habitant la crypte de la société' (2/253) (a vision recalling the then fashionable image of the *hydre de l'anarchie*). People, then, are also reshaped into a monster.

Furthermore, the city seems to turn those who can survive in it into small replicas of the urban monster: the people of the 'bas-fonds', like the people of the 'Cour des miracles', are repeatedly compared to every possible infernal creature one might think of, whether animal (spiders, bats) or supernatural (demons, devils, ghouls, vampires, ghosts and spectres). Moreover, the comparison goes beyond mere physical resemblance. In *Les Misérables,* for instance, the character of Eponine is repeatedly compared to a spectre and a ghoul, and thus appears as a sign of death and malediction, both to herself and to Marius.

The population of Hugo's dark Paris bears the stigma of its 'living death'. But, more importantly for Hugo, it also bears the stigma of ignorance, of spiritual darkness: the monster, hiding in the dark, is opposed to God and to Light. The rhetoric which opposes Evil to God, Light to Darkness, and which sees Evil *within* the urban space, stresses that only the city contains places where light no longer penetrates ('où la lumière s'éteint'; 2/249). This may be related to the Hugolian notion of fall and descent, and, once again, echoes *La Fin de Satan*:

> Depuis quatre mille ans il tombait dans l'abîme [. . .]
> Les ténèbres sans bruit croissaient dans le néant. [. . .]
>   Et déjà le soleil n'était plus qu'une étoile. [. . .]
> L'étoile maintenant n'était plus qu'une étincelle [. . .]
>   Et l'archange comprit, pareil au mât qui sombre,
>   Qu'il était le noyé du déluge de l'ombre;
>   Il reploya son aile aux ongles de granit
>   Et se tordit les bras.—Et l'astre s'éteignit.[42]

The vision of Paris by Hugo is related, inevitably, to his metaphysics and to his religious concerns. The dark side of his imaginary, which, I would argue, is prevalent in his literary and poetic representation of Paris, depicts the capital as oppressive, suffocating, claustrophobic, dark, ugly, and, most of all, as evil. Although typically Hugolian, this representation is in tune with the dominant urban imaginary and discourses of the period: the belief that Paris resembled a monster.

Although it may appear Manichean, such a representation is also highly ambivalent, and is thus characteristic of the myth of Paris. Paradoxically the darkness of the city reveals some positive aspects. There is a certain beauty in the ugliness in the writing of both Balzac and Zola—authors who, amongst others, enhanced the darkness of the city and who were vehemently criticised for what was perceived as scandalous vulgarity. Moreover, the personification of the city as monster can have positive connotations. When attacked by an army of pickaxes ('une armée de pioches') in Zola's *La Curée,* for example, Paris, victimised, dying and defenceless, regains its humanity through martyrdom. Finally, for Hugo, salvation comes from below, from the 'bas-fonds' which is, then, somehow necessary. Paradoxically, though, the 'bas-fonds' remains, for those who live in it, a locked tomb, the ultimate cell. As the examples of Valjean, Fantine, Eponine and Gavroche illustrate, the people who live in darkness can only find redemption through martyrdom and, ultimately, through death.

Hugo has depicted Paris as an oppressive, claustrophobic place that symbolises the power of 'materiality' over humanity. His use of symbolism, his obsession with the image of the prison, his attitude towards materiality and his concern with Evil, make him a brother to Baudelaire, who, incidentally, dedicated three of his major Parisian poems to him ('Le Cygne', 'Les Sept Vieillards', and 'Les Petites Vieilles'). I would argue that there are deep similarities between the two poets, and a common anguished imaginary that merits more attention than it currently receives.[43]

However, one major difference remains: despite Hugo's attraction to darkness, chaos and the void, he never surrenders to it. Ultimately, he chooses light and order. Baudelaire, on the other hand, encapsulates everything with which Hugo is fascinated, but allows himself to be taken in by it, and makes the opposite choice, that of evil. Nevertheless, because of their common imaginary, which, in my view, is more prevalent than their well-known oppositions, Baudelaire and Hugo represent a culmination in the elaboration of the 'dark side' of Paris: as a place of Evil, an urban prison of modern society, and a modern cell of the human condition.

Notes

1. Caillois, R., *Le Mythe et l'homme* (Gallimard-Folio, 1992), pp. 152-75.

2. *Ibid.*, p. 160.

3. I shall use the problematic notion of the 'imaginary' which is, in a sense, close to the idea of 'collective representation'. It embodies the political context, recent history and collective memory of a particular historical period. The study of France's collective imaginary contributes to an understanding of certain discourses and concerns (such as the politics of hygiene) in postrevolutionary France.

4. Hugo stated: 'J'ai eu deux affaires dans ma vie: Paris et l'océan.' Quoted by J. Massin in his presentation of Paris in HUGO, V., *Œuvres complètes* (Club Français du livre, 1967-1970), vol. 13, p. 563.

5. Millet, C., *Le Légendaire au XIXe siècle: Poésie, mythe et vérité* (PUF, 1997).

6. Benjamin, W., *Paris, capitale du XIXe siècle: le livre des passages* (Éditions du Cerf, 1997), p. 47.

7. Albouy, P., *La Création mythologique chez Victor Hugo* (Corti, 1963), p. 147.

8. Villiers, C., *L'Univers métaphysique de Victor Hugo* (Vrin, 1970), pp. 85-93, and Seebacher J., *Victor Hugo ou le calcul des profondeurs* (PUF, 1993), p. 219.

9. Brombert, V., *Victor Hugo and the Visionary Novel* (Harvard University Press, 1984), p. 7.

10. Tulard, J., *Le Consulat et l'Empire: nouvelle histoire de Paris* (Hachette, 1983), p. 218.

11. Corbin, A., *Le Temps, le désir, l'horreur* (Flammarion, 1991), p. 218.

12. Marchand, B., *Paris, histoire d'une ville: XIXe-XXe siècle* (Seuil, 1993), pp. 9-21.

13. Balzac, H., *Illusions perdues* (Librairie générale française, 1962), p. 185.

14. Corbin, A., 'Paris-province', in P. Nora (ed.), *Les Lieux de mémoire* (Gallimard-Quarto, 1997), vol. 2, pp. 2852-3.

15. Balzac, H., *La Fille aux yeux d'or* (Gallimard-Folio, 1976), p. 246. On the infernal image of Paris, see Citron, P., *La Poésie de Paris dans la littérature française de Rousseau à Baudelaire* (Minuit, 1961), pp. 101-8.

16. Poncin-Bar, G., 'Aspects fantastiques de Paris dans les romans réalistes de Balzac', *L'Année balzacienne* (1974), pp. 227-44.

17. Balzac, H., *Le Père Goriot,* quoted in Poncin-Bar, 'Aspects fantastiques', p. 235. The 'teint hâve, jaune et tanné' of the Parisians echoes the yellowish and 'plâtreux' appearance of Paris—constants of the Balzacian description of 'Paris lépreux'.

18. *Ibid.*, p. 240; my emphasis.

19. Hugo, V., *Les Misérables* (3 vols, Garnier-Flammarion, 1967), vol. 1, pp. 479-510; vol. 2, pp. 52-91. Further references will appear in parentheses in the text with volume and page number.

20. The title of the *Livre cinquième* is suggestive in this regard: 'A Chasse noire, meute muette'.

21. For a close description of the chase in the streets of Paris, see Tersen, E., 'Le Paris des *Misérables*', *Europe,* 394-5 (1962), pp. 98-103.

22. Hugo, in one of his many digressions, stresses the carceral nature of a convent. Like the prison, the convent, for Hugo, is an aberration that underlines the spiritual darkness, ignorance and weakness of contemporary society. *See* Brombert, *Victor Hugo,* p. 129.

23. Tersen, 'Le Paris des *Misérables*', pp. 102-3.

24. A short example illustrates this crucial aspect of Hugo's work. Eponine, the sister of Gavroche and daughter of the Thénardiers, may be reinterpreted from the perspective initiated in *La Fin de Satan* with Lilith-Isis, with whom she shares some symbolic similarities (such as allusions to *Anankeldestinée* and darkness, and comparisons with a ghoul and a spectre). Such a rereading may thus help us to understand the powerful influence of this secondary character, both in the life of Marius and in the plot of the novel.

25. Hugo, V., *Notre-Dame de Paris* (Le Livre de poche, 1972), p. 360.

26. *Le Père Goriot* quoted in Poncon-Bar, 'Aspects fantastiques', p. 240.

27. Hannosh, M., 'La femme, la ville, le réalisme: fondements épistémologiques dans le Paris de Balzac', *Romanic Review* 82 (1991), pp. 127-45.

28. Balzac, *Le Père Goriot* (Gallimard-Folio, 1971), p. 153.

29. Brombert, *Victor Hugo,* p. 49. The same goes for *Les Misérables*—although in a different way— where the barricade operates as the central focus of all the individual dramas.

30. Bachelard, G., *La Terre et les rêveries du repos* (Corti, 1948), p. 185.

31. Macchia, G., *Paris en ruines* (Flammarion, 1988), p. 172; my emphasis.

32. Brombert, V., *La Prison romantique* (Corti, 1975), p. 105.

33. In *Les Misérables,* 'La chute' is the title of the *Livre deuxième* and 'La Descente' is the title of the *Livre cinquième*.

34. Brombert, *La Prison,* p. 105.

35. Villiers, *L'Univers,* p. 226. *See* also CELLIER, L., *L'Epopée humanitaire et les grands mythes romantiques* (SEDES, 1971), p. 298.

36. Balzac, *La Fille,* p. 372.

37. Hugo, *Notre-Dome de Paris,* pp. 564-8.

38. The title of Part II of the *Livre cinquième* of *Les Misérables,* 'Leviathan' is traditionally the monster of primal chaos. Although temporarily dormant, Leviathan remains a threat and may awake at any time.

39. Balzac, *La Fille,* p. 256.

40. Macchia, G., *Le Mythe de Paris* (Einaudi, 1965), p. 411.

41. Baudelaire, C., *Les Fleurs du mal* (Flammarion, 1964), p. 58.

42. Hugo, *La Fin de Satan,* in *Œuvres complètes,* vol. 11, pp. 1621-6.

43. If we subscribe to this view, it would be possible to reread Hugo as a modernist, in accordance with Benjamin's well-known reading of Baudelaire.

William Graham Clubb (essay date winter-fall 2000)

SOURCE: Clubb, William Graham. "Quasimodo, Quasi-Man: A Man of the Woods in Victor Hugo's *Notre-Dame de Paris*." *Italian Quarterly* 37, nos. 143-146 (winter-fall 2000): 267-79.

[In the following essay, Clubb studies Hugo's treatment of the motif of monstrosity in the character of Quasimodo in Notre-Dame de Paris.*]*

No one reads Hugo nowadays, they say. The point is arguable, but even after all necessary qualifications are conceded, there remains a sense in which the statement is true. For if Hugo's lyric poetry and novels nourish our being, to borrow Thibaudet's metaphor,[1] if they have influenced our development and so become a part of our mental functioning, it is generally true also that having read him once in youth, we do not return to feed on him throughout life, as the adult French reader does on Racine and Molière, the English on Shakespeare, the Italian on Dante, and so forth. Exception could be made for Hugo's theater and the adaptations of his work for the stage: the musical *Les Misérables* continues its long run, while *Hernani, Ruy Blas, Angelo* remain present to us whether we will or no by way of grand opera, the genre in which his drama found its natural home.

Granted then, we have all read *Notre-Dame de Paris,* but probably not after the age of eighteen, except perhaps as one of those professional duties that lend a half-life to shelves full of dead literature. If we have some fresher memory it is probably owed to one of the many film versions still available in archives and on television. But as translation from novel to film is notoriously more treacherous even than translation from one language to another, the authentic substance of Hugo's novel remains for the most part in dimmed memory. A brief review, therefore, of Hugo's first novel worth serious attention may serve to recall the specific character, psychology, and actions of Quasimodo, who, if not the protagonist, is certainly the pivotal character of the novel. He saves Esmeralda, the beautiful gypsy dancer from death by hanging, only to throw her all the more surely into the executioner's hands. Of the four men who love her, Quasimodo alone willingly joins her in death. This privilege was transferred by Hugo himself to another character when, six years after publication, it was necessary to extract an opera libretto from Notre-Dame, but the structure as it appeared in 1831 and in the augmented definitive edition of 1832 is superior to all subsequent versions, and Quasimodo, with his cathedral, is the only element of the novel to survive the shipwreck of the rest. Filmmakers who entitle their versions *The Hunchback of Notre-Dame* are not wholly in error.

A review of the novel's organization is also a necessary preparation for the question this essay poses: whence comes this troubling, paradoxical personage, this "monster," this "presqu'homme"? It is properly a two-fold question: what are the literary antecedents of Quasimodo as a character; and, more significantly, how, though not much more mature as a novelist than when in 1821 he feverishly (if with tongue in cheek, as he later suggests) sketched the quasi-monstrous but ridiculously exaggerated portrait of Han d'Islande for his eponymous first novel in 1823, was Hugo able by 1830 so to enrich, deepen, and transform the topos of the physically and mentally anomalous outcast, that Quasimodo seems more convincing and significant than all his antecedents or counterparts in literature? (With rare exceptions: Shakespeare's Caliban rivals Quasimodo in power and significance, but not in verisimilitude.) Furthermore, how was he able, without the usual recourse to sickly sentiment, so to develop the character from first to last that Quasimodo becomes not so much quasi-man as man, purely and simply?

Notre-Dame is, as we know, a historical romance structured in the manner of Walter Scott but with diction and *dianoia* in the style of Chateaubriand: it is partly an attempt at detailed and faithful reconstruction of a past era. The year is 1482, the place Paris in the final months of the reign of Louis XI. From the opening tableau of the capital on double holiday for the Feast of the Epiphany, coincident with the popular anti-Feast of Fools—*la Fête des Rois* and *la Fête des Fous*—which is a brilliant diptych of the pomps of royal rule: processions, church rites, and dramatic performances commissioned for the event, in dramatic contrast with the orgiastic (Hugo's word) celebrations of the day of popular misrule. From this diptych to the final atrocious scenes of judicial torture and public execution, the author, in emulation of his precursor and master, performs the by then conventional multiple roles of tour guide, art historian, museum curator, philologist, and philosopher. One chapter (Livre III, ch. ii) is a panorama of Paris at the end of the fifteenth century, "Paris à vol d'oiseau."[2] Another (III, i) is an analysis and somewhat heated defense of the Gothic style in architecture. Still another (V, ii) is an essay on the consequences to architecture in general that Hugo foresees in the spread of movable-type printing. Throughout the novel the speech of minor figures (but not that of major characters) is relentlessly studded with archaisms, dialectisms, Latinisms, not to reproduce—Hugo has not this pretension—but to evoke the everyday speech of 1482. This vast, turbulent and motley historical matrix was intended to lend authenticity to a story of epic grandeur, and with customary energy Hugo immersed himself in documents for the task, remaining sufficiently faithful to his sources, secondary though they were (Sauval, Du Breul, for example)[3] to have won fulsome praise for his reconstruction. For the admiring Michelet it was like a chapter of his own future *Histoire de France* come to life.[4] After *Notre-Dame* had run the first critical gauntlet, however, Hugo with prudence and *sprezzatura* abandoned all specific historical, aesthetic and philosophical pretensions. The setting, he said, was only

> une peinture de Paris au quinzième siècle et du quinzième siècle à propos de Paris. . . . Le livre n'a aucune prétention historique, si ce n'est de peindre . . . uniquement par aperçus et par échappées, l'état des moeurs, des croyances, des lois, des arts, de la civilisation enfin au quinzième siècle. S'il a un mérite, c'est d'être oeuvre d'imagination, de caprice et de fantaisie.[5]

It must be remembered, however, that when Hugo sketched the shape of the novel in 1828 he still took seriously his youthful philosophy of history, his theories of architecture and art, and his antiquarian lore. Léon Cellier reminds us of Hugo's earliest ambitions for a kind of historical novel yet to be created: one that would be poetic as well as picturesque, ideal as well as real, great as well as true, an epic, in short, as well as a drama.[6] But it has long been a critical truism that *Notre-Dame* is not all of these things: poetic it is, as well as picturesque, and dramatic too but neither sufficiently true nor epic, in Hugo's sense of the word. Nor is it either real or ideal, as we understand the words today. The fault, it is held, lies in the absurd melodrama at the center of the novel. Major figures of history appear but briefly, and the plot consists for the most part of rather lurid anagnoreses and peripeties in the lives of a handful of people of historically little or no note whom the author can manipulate with entire freedom. It was just this aspect that drew from an exasperated Goethe the frequently quoted: "pauvres marionettes en bois que l'auteur remue à son gré.[7] In 1831, however, Goethe was eighty-two years old, ill and near death, well beyond the reach of whatever enchantment this novel can work on young minds.

In the course of the festivities of January 6, then, all the central characters are introduced, the first of them in a tableau representing the unsuccessful efforts of an acting-troupe to perform for visiting dignitaries a morality play, *Le bon jugement de Madame la Vierge,* composed by the starveling poet Pierre Gringoire. The latter is based on the historical Pierre Gringore,[8] whose best-known work, *Le Jeu de Prince des Sots,* probably inspired Hugo to resurrect him as a character and to present a succeeding tableau of riotous violence in which the bell-ringer of Notre-Dame is elected New Year's King of Fools.

With Hugo's introduction of Quasimodo we encounter the motif of monstrosity which is the topic of this essay:

> Nous n'essaierons pas de donner au lecteur une idée de ce nez tétraèdre, de cette bouche en fer à cheval, de ce petit oeil gauche obstrué d'un sourcil roux en broussailles tandis que l'oeil droit disparaissait entièrement sous une énorme verrue, de ces dents désordonnées, ébréchées ça et là, comme les créneaux d'une forteresse, de cette lèvre calleuse sur laquelle une de ces dents empiétait comme la défense d'un éléphant, de ce menton fourchu, et surtout de la physionomie répandue sur tout cela, de ce mélange de malice, d'étonnement et de tristesse.

(I, v)

Hugo exaggerates less the grotesquerie than the horror of his portrait with details unnecessary to the significance of the whole, for reasons to be elucidated below.

Leaving aside the huge wart, the elephantine tusk, the forked chin, let us keep in mind the pyramidal nose, the horse-shoe mouth, the red bushy eyebrows and, above all, the expression compounded of malice, stupor, and sadness. Hugo develops the head into a full-length portrait: large head; red hair; humped back "dont le contre coup se faisait sentir par devant" (that is, as a caved-in chest); knock-kneed, but bowlegged also, so that the *système,* as Hugo calls it, looks like a pair of crossed sickles joined at the handle; big feet; and to complete the picture

> . . . avec toute cette difformité, je ne sais quelle allure redoutable de viguer, d'agilité et de courage; étrange exception à la règle éternelle qui veut que la force, comme la beauté, résulte de l'harmonie.

Reactions of the spectators, as Quasimodo is enthroned as king of fools, are to our purpose also: "Gare les femmes grosses! . . . Ou qui ont envie de l'être!" . . . "Oh! le vilain singe! C'est le diable!" To which they add, because of his enormous strength as well as because of the concealed eye, the epithet "Polyphème." Hugo will subsequently resort to the generic *cyclope* more often than to the word *bossu,* reminding us that the essential traits of Quasimodo's being are anomaly and deficiency rather than mere deformity. Finally, misery's crown of misery: Quasimodo's greatest joy, ringing his massive bells, has made him deaf.

It might seem that the unbelievable disorderliness, the bedlamite violence of the first chapters are intended merely to perform functions similar to those of the more mechanical horrors of Gothic novels: to frighten, to terrify the readers, his *lectrices,* as Hugo insists on feminizing them. Nor is he above such simple strategies; even in 1830 he cannot resist pinning tag-ends of mystery or horror to his works, like ornaments on a Christmas tree. Such is the silly and incongruous Greek inscription "ANAKH," signifying fate or necessity, that he claimed in the foreword to have found carved on the inner wall of a tower of Notre-Dame cathedral in letters plastered over or scratched out by 1829. Such tricks provide a *frisson* to naive readers but distress the judicious.

The portrait of Quasimodo is altogether different. Almost every detail of his presentation is carefully chosen, necessary, and double in meaning and function. Though elsewhere Hugo frequently adopted Chateaubriand's famous *rythme tenaire,* in *Notre-Dame* the essential strictures are more often binary or quaternary. Just as January 6 is a double feast day and the novel opens with a double tableau, so all meanings and functions are double. Moreover, while Hugo is deliberately episodic and disorderly on the literal level, he achieves perfect coherence and harmony on the allegorical: all the semantic doublings correspond not only with each

other but with a vision of reality shared more or less by most early Romantics, subject to the pervasive influence of German Romanticism from the beginning of the century. Since 1848, when that system of thought lost much of its penetrative power, an essential key to the allegories of the era has been lost; the early Hugo seems less to us than he is because we try to unlock him with another key, one that almost works, but not quite. If we demand from him the style of thought of, say, Flaubert or Baudelaire, even Zola, or of one of the great English Victorians, he disappoints and seems empty and bombastic. But whether the explicit messages Hugo claimed to have for us in *Notre-Dame* are there or not, implicitly the thought of his own era guides his hand. That he could have formulated it as idea may be doubted—Malraux did not err in remarking that no reality becomes an idea until it has died—but its moulding force is visible in Hugo's development of his plot.

The feast-day of January 6 brings about the meeting of all five principal characters: Esmeralda the gypsy dancer and her four lovers. The characters are, in fact, six, for a dramatic role is assigned also to the white goat Djali, an inseparable companion trained to take part in Esmeralda's performances: Djali triggers the charge of witchcraft and is condemned to the gallows with her—for in 1482 a witch's "familiar" (usually a cat) fully shared in her ordeals. From the outset the virginal Esmeralda is innocence itself: her dances blameless, her tricks harmless: all is grace, lightness, incorporeal beauty—and completely unaccountable as well, for we learn that she is the fatherless daughter of an aging whore and was kidnapped in infancy and raised by gypsies. For our time it seems unlikely that this genetic inheritance and upbringing could have brought forth such a model of purity of mind, heart and body, but the concept of bright flowers, even butterflies, springing from a dung-hill was dear to Romantics generally and to Hugo in particular. Theirs was the pre-Pasteur era, when the theory of spontaneous generation was still a scientific option. Hugo had presented Ruy Blas as just such another inexplicable bloom, but in *Notre-Dame* he gave the motif almost Baudelairian resonance.

The paragon Esmeralda acquires three of her lovers on the Feast of the Epiphany and her fourth, Quasimodo, the next day. Three of them represent principal professions of French medieval and Renaissance society: the archdeacon Claude Frollo, born into the petty nobility, belongs to the Church; the captain Phoebus de Châteaupers "de fort noble naissance" to the Army; and the poet Pierre Gringoire, of indeterminate origin, is by education a member of the *bourgeoisie,* probably a lawyer. In stark contrast to these conventional social and literary types Esmeralda's fourth lover, Quasimodo, like Esmeralda herself, has no status. The hunchback is an outcast, a foundling left on the steps of Notre-Dame on the feast day of Quasimodo.[9] Hearing the mob dub the infant "spawn of the devil" and advise burning the poor misshapen wretch, Frollo—"mauvais prétre," diabolist, and seeker after the philosopher's stone—adopted and baptized him

> Quasimodo, soit qu'il voulut marquer par là le jour où il l'avait trouvé, soit qu'il voulut caractériser par ce nom à quel point la pauvre petite créature était incomplète et à peine ébauchée. En effet, Quasimodo, borgne, bossu, cagneux, n'était guère qu'un *à peu près.*
>
> (IV, ii)

Hugo had informed the reader that the cathedral Notre-Dame de Paris, Quasimodo's future and only home, belonged achitecturally to a special category:

> Cette église centrale et génératrice est parmi les vieilles églises de Paris une sorte de chimère; elle a la tête de l'une, les membres de celle-là, la croupe de l'autre; quelque chose de toutes.
>
> (III, i)

Literally a sort of monster. Unlike structures of the pure type, these chimaeras show how primitive architecture may be. The greatest architectural monuments are not the product of an individual genius; they are

> . . . oeuvres sociales: plutôt l'enfantement des peuples en travail que le jet des hommes de génie; le dépôt que laisse une nation; les entassements que font les siècles; le résidu des évaporations successives de la société humaine; en un mot, des espèces de formations. Chaque flot du temps superpose son alluvion . . .

This passage is doubly significant. In history and in art there occur conjunctions so miraculously right and appropriate that they seem destined, inevitable. Each of the pair seems to be made for the other, to call for the other. But the sense of destiny or inevitability is almost always an illusion. In reality, if Versailles suits the Sun King, it is because he commissioned and almost daily supervised its construction and decoration. If Notre-Dame suits Quasimodo, Quasimodo Notre-Dame, it is because Hugo deploys all the seductions of his art to persuade us that they were made by nature, society and the slow workings of the centuries to become as he shows them to be, to convince us that some Fate has made them so, one for the other. This too is an illusion. Hugo himself—or the taste of his era—has designed and built this Notre-Dame that he compares to a mountain, the work of centuries; on the other hand it is a work interrupted sometimes for centuries: "pendent opera interrupta." And before the slow geologic processes can begin again, the art of architecture evolves, and a new growth is engrafted on the old. Of course, an essential plan remains, that of the primitive Christian structure: it is only on the additions and on the surface that time works freely, recomposing and adding its "prodigieuse variété": "Le tronc de l'arbre est immuable, la végétation est capricieuse."

The deliberate, expressionistic distortions of truth and evidence, the inexact geological and botanical analogies, suggest of themselves his precise purpose: to create an appropriately monstrous milieu to set his man-monster in, confirmed by the terms in which he characterizes both: disparate parts badly joined; interrupted growth; capriciously variegated florescence of the skin or exterior. Notre-Dame is a quasi-Gothic structure, an *ébauche* of the type, as Quasimodo is "almost a man," a rough draft of the human species. Hugo proposes this similarity to his reader as a natural phenomenon, by no means accidental: Quasimodo grew from infancy to manhood "dans le sens de la cathédrale," precisely because he grew in the cathedral.

Hugo's assumptions and propositions are revealed in steps scanned below in six statements made in IV, iii. It is here that he develops the character of Quasimodo most completely and systematically in one long, extended and extremely detailed Homeric simile, materialized in clusters of metaphors and images. At first the terms of the simile seem simple enough and familiar, accustomed as we are to Romantic comparisons drawn from the natural world. According to one definition of the age, the practice is a hallmark of the Romantic style. But the tenor of the passage, the meanings contained, are allusive, complex, floating. The core simile is based on the analogy drawn between the development of individual human beings from infancy to adulthood and the evolution of animal species, both processes then considered to be governed by a point-by-point, cause-and-effect correspondence of organisms with their environments, in short, by the so-called law of biological harmony.

1. *Notre-Dame avait été successivement pour lui . . . l'oeuf, le nid, la maison, la patrie l'univers.* We are to understand that, as he grew, Quasimodo had come to know and occupy successively larger and larger portions of the cathedral until he knew it all and occupied it all. And that the moment of knowing all of it marked the end of his growth and of his experience. From an expanding space his world is transformed into a prison cell.

2. *. . . il y avait une sorte d'harmonie mystérieuse et préexistante entre cette créature et cet édifice. Lorsque tout petit encore, il se traînait tortueusement et par soubresauts sous les ténébres de ses voûtes, il semblait avec sa face humaine et sa membrure bestiale le reptile naturel de cette dalle humide. . . .* Quasimodo's is not a teleological pattern of growth. It does not entail the incarnation of a pre-established and immutable archetypal structure, such as the ideal human form as worked out by, say, Leonardo, harmoniously well-proportioned in terms of itself. On the contrary, like all biological forms, he grows according to a law of harmonic development: there is a basic pattern of the species that remains, of course, but changing environmental circumstances determine absolutely the proportions of the parts and the arrangement and mode of connection of the parts with one another. The account given by Jean Baptiste Lamarck[10], the earliest of the French evolutionists, aside from Buffon, of the evolution of the giraffe, for example, illustrates this new concept of harmony: the basic equine structure is altered step by step—the

forelegs and neck become longer to reach the food that would otherwise be out of reach; and because they lengthen, in harmony the body and the hind legs become shorter. In Lamarck's biological organism as in Lavoisier's chemical equations, it is assumed that in the whole system there is but so much substance: nothing can be gained, and nothing, proportionately, can be lost. It is possible only to redistribute substance within the system. This is a biological adaption of the first law of thermodynamics, the physical and chemical demonstrations of which had just been made during Hugo's childhood, and his mind had been just as much formed thereby, whether he understood those laws or not, as was his Quasimodo's body by the cathedral.

3. . . . *il en avait pris la forme, comme le colimaçon prend la forme de sa coquille . . . Il y avait entre la vieille église et lui une sympathie instinctive si profonde, tant d'affinités magnétiques . . . matérielles, qu'il y adherait . . . comme la tortue à son écaille.* The cathedral was Quasimodo's shell, his armor. Here again is an allusion to a concept newly formulated in Hugo's time. There is no essential, material difference between the substances and laws of physical phenomena and biological phenomena: the animal feeds on, absorbs, and thus becomes cosubstantial with his milieu; hence the affinities, the magnetisms of which Hugo speaks.

4. . . . *non seulement son corps semblait s'être façonné selon la cathédral, mais encore son esprit. . . . Dans quel état était cette âme, quel pli avait-elle contracté. quelle forme avait-elle prise, c'est ce qu'il serait difficile de déterminer. . . . C'est à grande peine et à grande patience que Claude Frollo était parvenu à lui apprendre à parler.* Here the analogy is lifted onto another and more interesting level. As the cathedral is to the body, so the body is to the mind or soul. The same law, the same necessity, governs the ontogeny of the intellect.

5. *Il est certain que l'esprit s'atrophie dans un corps manqué . . . Son cerveau était un milieu particulier: les idées qui le traversaient en sortaient toutes tordues. . . . Le premier effet de cette fatale organisation, c'était de troubler le regard qu'il -jetait sur les choses. Le monde extérieur lui semblait beaucoup plus loin qu'à nous.* A deformed anomalous body demands a soul to match.

6. *Le second effet de son malheur, c'était de le rendre méchant. Il était méchant en effet parce qu'il était sauvage: il était sauvage parce qu'il était laid. Il y avait une logique dans sa nature comme dans la nôtre. . . . Sa force, si extraordinairement développée, était une cause de plus de méchanceté. "Malus puer robustus," dit Hobbes.* The second, as Hugo calls it, but more accurately, the ultimate consequence of Quasimodo's physical misfortune is expressed in his social and moral character: he is savage, he is wicked, he is strong.

This last feature is a curious one. The author himself made the point earlier, and himself limned the paradox: how could a creature of ill-made, disproportionate, badly joined and organized parts be both unusually agile and unusually strong, when, still according to the author, by the law of harmony strength should be joined to beauty and health? Obviously Hugo has not permitted himself this inconsistency, or error, simply to enable Quasimodo to perform the feats of strength required of him by the plot. The explanation must be sought within an informing system of thought.

For the organization of this chapter he is indebted not to a particular genre like the Gothic novel nor to the literary commonplaces of monstrosity he had used in *Han d'Islande.* What Quasimodo has in common either with the monsters of mythology or with the hunchbacks of antecedent fiction or anecdotal history is negligible. For constructing *Notre-Dame* Hugo found the "almost" or, more accurately, the "sub" human type in his contemporary actuality. Since 1789 the monstrous and the bestial in human kind and behavior had been a daily staple of both universal experience and report. Hugo remembered, even if we forget until reminded by Michel Foucault, that Louis XVI was prosecuted and guillotined by the Revolutionary courts not so much for personally committed crimes (he had committed none that a normally constituted court would not have forgiven) but because it was the view of that tribunal that kings are to society what monsters are to nature. At the moment of Louis' condemnation his judges doubtless had no very clear idea of what produced either kings or monsters in the first place. But by 1830 a Hugo, a Balzac, or a Vigny not only had precise ideas on the relation of individuals to milieu, and on that of different animal species to one other, but also on the ontogeny of the one and the phylogeny of the other, that is, on embryological development and physical growth in individuals and on the evolutionary development of species. They were confident of understanding the relation between the two processes and the sorts of things that can happen if something goes wrong or interferes with normal evolution or normal growth, for in their time had appeared the first successful scientific account of the genesis of physical anomalies or monsters. The widely-discussed new science of teratology created by Geoffroy Saint-Hilaire,[11] after Cuvier the best known of the French comparative zoologists, discredited once and for all the prejudices and superstitions that had hovered over the subject and had rendered the existence of unfortunates such as Quasimodo even more precarious, and an infinitely greater misery than it need have been, from the beginning of man to Hugo's century. Nevertheless many, perhaps most, of his contemporaries still held to the hoary prejudices: monsters are creatures cursed; they are created by the devil; or they are begotten by the devil on the bodies of human beings; or they are begotten by humans and animals copulating together. One idea disseminated in the eighteenth century by Christian apologists determined to halt the advance of rational mechanistic views was that God created monsters in order to demonstrate what nature would be without Him. Geoffroy Saint-Hilaire's teratology not only removed the Divine or diabolic curse from anatomical monsters but also, by implication, brought them back to the realm of nature and the fold of humanity. Hugo may well have been the first major poet to apply the lesson in art.

The key to the ideas shared by Romantic writers is the system of thought called *Naturphilosophie* in Germany, where it originated from multiple sources, and soon known in France as *la philosophie de la nature*. To paraphrase the well-known formulation of Schelling: Nature is universal and unifold, comprehending all existences and essences, all substances and phenomena, even those often held to be metaphysical or supernatural; and, in the course of time, human science will show that all things are created, evolve, and exist subject to one single allembracing and immutable law.[12] Now as far as that goes, *Naturphilosophie* is not unlike the kind of naturalism that took its place after 1848. But there are profound differences between the latter and the Romantics' application of Schelling's great law to organic nature. Their nature is animistic, teleological and platonic, if not frankly pantheistic: it is the "sensate garment of the living God" in which the spirit struggles ever upward to greater freedom and higher forms of conscious being. It is a disguised dualism. Later Naturalism, on the other hand, is monistic and dispenses with all teleologies and, indeed, with the very idea of spirit, at least for scientific purposes, replacing it with that of physio-chemical energies. But in the zoological sciences properly speaking, nature philosophers, from Goethe through Lamarck and Geoffroy Saint-Hilaire to Darwin, explain the evolution of animal species, including man, as a concrete manifestation of universal upward striving. It is in just these terms that Hugo means us to understand, for example, the dances of Esmeralda the gypsy. Through her physical beauty, grace, and rhythm she symbolizes the struggle toward perfection, the Life Force that nature philosophers saw everywhere, but especially in insect metamorphosis, from caterpillar to cocoon to butterfly. One recognizes here also the central concept of Bergson's *Evolution créatrice*,[13] and long after the Romantic period it continued to form the conscious or unconscious philosophical underpinnings of writers from Maeterlinck in Belgium to George Bernard Shaw and Aldous Huxley in England and to Thomas Mann in Germany, among others.

The scientific branch of Nature Philosophy, however, had reached its end by 1848, its ideas about evolution no longer tenable. According to the zoologists of this stamp, animal species evolved by altering the shape, size and proportion of parts, and the integuments of a hypothetical early, primitive forerunner of all the species, and by adding complication and refinement to the original structure. Both the structural idea and the number, arrangement and connection of parts remain essentially unchanged through all the ages of evolution and are to be found in every known species today, even if only as vestiges in some cases. This idea of the single plan, erroneous though it was, stimulated investigations in comparative anatomy that proved extremely useful. A corollary of the belief was the so-called recapitulation theory: ontogeny repeats phylogeny:[14] that is, the individual in his growth from seed to maturity repeats all the phases of the evolution of the species to which

he belongs. Each of us has been egg, worm, fish, salamander, reptile, dog, and ape; until at last, just previous to birth, we add a part of the character of man. But it is not until we are three or four years of age that we acquire human language and become, as it were, entirely human. And it is from this notion that Geoffroy Saint-Hilaire logically develops his teratology. Dividing monsters into three types, to wit, those from hybrid births, those from excessive or deficient growth, and those from anomaly or deformity of parts, he argues that all have been produced by damage to the seed or embryo or by long environmental interference with the normal patterns of growth. Ordinarily, the damage is the result of accident or of an inadequate or dangerous environment. He himself demonstrated his thesis by so manipulating chicken embryos in the egg that chicks were produced with two heads, or with one leg or three, or with both legs on the same side of the body, and so forth. If the cells that are to develop into limbs and organs are jumbled in the very early embryo, the adult will have jumbled and therefore necessarily defective parts. In these cases, furthermore, there will occur an arrest ("un arrêt"), a stoppage of growth, not only to particular parts but to the organism as a whole.

Logically, then, since growth means the addition or imposition of the specific traits of a higher form on those of a lower—traits in themselves not fully developed in the transitory phases of the ontology of higher species but nevertheless recognizably there (as in mammalian embryos in which primitive gills visibly develop at a very early stage but are then partly reabsorbed during subsequent development)—the defective embryo will never grow into the complete man. It will have been halted at an early "evolutionary" stage, be it fish, reptile or ape. And this, we must conclude, guided by the multiple signposts Hugo has provided, is exactly Quasimodo's case. What were the causes? Perhaps mechanical, a mother's fall from a carriage or a blow to the abdomen. Perhaps alcoholism or a disease of the mother, or even more commonly, inadequate or poisoned nourishment. Hugo's era believed also in unnatural causes, traumas to the mother's psyche during pregnancy. Whatever the precise causes, the parts of Quasimodo's organism grew jumbled, slowly and incompletely, and therefore he became a creature not quite man, neither in body nor in mind. Hugo's description of his monster's childhood coincides in too many details with Geoffroy Saint-Hilaire's account of the origins of organic anomaly for the coincidence to be fortuitous.

Still we may ask: precisely in what way does Quasimodo resemble another species lower than the human? That Hugo frequently compares him to other species means little: animal metaphors are a staple of both satiric and melodramatic literature in all ages. Moreover, might not Hugo have gleaned his zoological lore from any number of eighteenth-century writers on the topic, the *encyclopédistes,* for example, or the eccentric Scottish essayist Lord Monboddo, celebrated for his belief that there was once a race of men with tails and that the orang-outang does in fact belong to the human species, but is a man without language? In the response to the last question lies that to the first.

In 1830 the attention of all Europe, philosophical and literary as well as scientific, was focussed on a debate, held in public at the French *Académie des sciences,* between the two best-known comparative zoologists of the era, Cuvier[15] and Geoffroy Saint-Hilaire. These two, who had worked in collaboration more or less harmoniously for almost two decades, had recently fallen out on the question of the evolution of species. Before the voyage of the Beagle, or, rather, before Darwin's account of its results in *Origin of Species,* lacking any convincing theory of the mechanics of inheritance and therefore any theory of how transformations occur, it was still just possible for two eminent scientists who had studied all the evidence then available to disagree. Cuvier, the more precise and careful of the two, had found much to criticize, both in Lamarck's account of the causes and mechanism of evolution and in Geoffroy Saint-Hilaire's idea of the single plan or type from which all species are descended. To him both theories smacked not of science but of vain metaphysical speculation and of the German kind that he particularly disliked, being not without a touch of chauvinism. The debate was prolonged, violent, and inconclusive. But in the years that followed, the arguments and issues were reported and analyzed by everyone who had a public voice. Indeed, at the outset Goethe was invited to Paris to hear and judge the debate, for he himself had made and successfully defended his own anatomical discoveries, and was even then debating with Newtonian physicists the nature of light (here, unfortunately, with little reason on his side and with less success). Goethe refused to judge, but he wrote an account of the personalities and issues of the debate for German readers, and this, his last work, was published in Brussels in 1832 under the title "Naturalistes français, ou la Méditation de Goethe sur la marche et le caractére des sciences à Paris." It appeared in an issue of *Paris, ou le livre des cent-et-un* [sic]—a curious collection of essays, stories, anecdotes on subjects of general interest, appropriate to highbrow magazines and reviews,[16] which fairly demonstrates what the literate Frenchman was reading, thinking, and arguing in those years, bringing together pieces by many writers, among them Lamartine, Geoffroy Saint-Hilaire, Sainte-Beuve, Charles Nodier—and Hugo himself. *Le Livre des cent-et-un* attests the high degree of interest raised by the question of evolution, and ample evidence exists also of the authority wielded in this and in other realms of zoological science by Geoffroy Saint-Hilaire. It is impossible that Hugo was not as

au courant of these issues as any well-read Frenchman must have been in the very years he was composing *Notre-Dame de Paris.*

Finally, then, if Quasimodo's deformity was caused by embryonic damage, and therefore by developmental arrest, at what stage of evolutionary recapitulation did Hugo stop his growth? A suggestion is offered by August Barthélemy and Joseph Méry's poem "Le Jardin des plantes, poème en alexandrins," published in the same *Livre des cent-et-un*:

> On y voit à l'heure oú l'on donne à manger
> aux fauves, des tigres, des lions, des léopards
> . . . des taureaux réservés dépècent les chairs vives,
>
> . . . . .
>
> Plus loin l'orang-outan au geste scandaleux
>
> . . . . .
>
> Tous les types grossiers de la nature humaine
> De ces hôtes pervers là finit la domaine;
> Dans un Tartare noir Cuvier les enchaîne;
> Là, règne un bruit pareil au souffle de l'Etna,
> Un concert de pieds lourds et d'affreuses risées.
>
> (67-72)

Before publishing *Notre-Dame* in 1831 the only species of great ape Hugo could have seen with his own eyes was, precisely, the orang-outang.[17] The gorilla was known and written of, but it would not be captured and held in European zoos until much later. The orang-outang in particular had seized on popular imagination for several reasons: it had been immediately recognized as an astonishingly close relative of man partly because, to general surprise, it was observed to prefer a monogamous family life, partly because it seemed to have its own quasi-verbal language and therefore an almost human intelligence, and partly because it was called the Man of the Woods by the human inhabitants of its land of origin. According to reviews of Hugo's time, the myths of Borneo tell of orang-outangs capturing beautiful village maidens for brides and carrying them off to their forest bowers of bliss. It was natural and logical that Hugo, wanting to account for Quasimodo on well-approved and, at that time well-understood comparative zoological principles, should make him resemble the orang-outang: in his red hair, his triangular nose, his horseshoe mouth, his large head, his humpbacked silhouette (a feature that develops only in the adult male of the species), his bowlegs; and in that expression compounded of malice, stupor, and sadness; above all, in his extraordinary agility and strength. For on the principle that man's development of intelligence inevitably entailed a loss of physical powers, even a defective ape is much stronger than the most perfect man. So Quasimodo, "devenu en quelque façon singe" . . . "ne rêvait pas d'autres espaliers que les vitraux toujours en fleurs, d'autre ombrage que celui de ces feuillages de pierre qui s'épanouissent chargés d'oiseaux . . ." (IV, iii), climbs, leaps and clambers everywhere in and on his cathedral like a giant simian in a stone forest. Thus he is enabled twice to seize and carry off Esmeralda to his forest home, once to serve the lusts of his foster-father and once again to preserve her from Louis XI's executioners. This same fearful strength wreaks havoc on the cathedral's besieging mobs. He is accidentally frustrated in the first endeavor and only temporarily successful in the second, because he is almost inarticulate, cut off as much as the orangoutang from the rest of humanity, and so he ultimately loses Esmeralda to the hangman.

Quasimodo is almost a complete and coherent portrait and the protagonist of an almost perfect action. But Hugo faltered briefly at a crucial point. When Quasimodo holds Esmeralda in sanctuary in the cathedral, he temporarily turns into a quasi-courtly lover, on the pattern of Boccaccio's memorable, touching but unverisimilar Cimone, who is transformed by a glimpse of feminine beauty from shaggy savage into perfect cavalier.[18] "Awakened" by love, Hugo's monster suddenly acquires a gentleness, delicacy, eloquence, and self-abnegation that would do credit to a denizen of Scudéry's *pays de Tendre*[19] or some such dreamworld of literary preciosity and sensibility. Even this improbable metamorphosis might have been acceptable if it had been handled more subtly, for the quasi-man topos comprehends upward striving and therefore the possibility of some success, an awakening to some higher state of being. But the results of it should coincide with the painstakingly naturalistic design of the character. Instead, Hugo, whose rich literary culture naturally included the works of Scudéry,[20] commits the fatal error of lending Quasimodo for this moment, and this moment only, the language and vocabulary of the *pays de Tendre* in such speeches as:

> Quand je me compare à vous, j'ai bien pitié de moi, pauvre malheureux monstre que je suis! Je dois vous faire l'effet d'une bête, dites. Vous, vous êtes un rayon de soleil, une goutte de rosée, un chant d'oiseau! Moi, je suis quelque chose d'affreux, ni homme, ni animal, un je ne sais quoi plus dur, plus foulé aux pieds et plus difforme qu'un caillou!
>
> (IX, iii)

and in verse:

> La beauté est parfaite,
> La beauté peut tout,
> La beauté est la seule chose qui n'existe pas à demi.
> Le courbeau ne vole que le jour,
> Le hibou ne vole que la nuit,
> Le cygne vole la nuit et le jour.
>
> (IX, v)

Hugo gives these words to the inarticulate monster of whom he had written in IV, iii, "La parole humaine pour lui, c'était toujours une raillerie ou une maledic-

tion." The strain placed on the readers's willing suspension of disbelief is past bearing. If for this reason alone, the moving and powerful ***Notre-Dame de Paris*** remains in our estimation only a quasi-great novel.

Notes

[This is the text of an unpublished lecture that my late husband gave first at Berkeley and later at the University of Padua. I have added footnotes to the original English version in order to offer it to our friend Vittore Branca.—Louise George Clubb, University of California, Berkeley]

1. Albert Thibaudet, *Histoire de la Littérature française, de 1789 à nos jours.* Paris, 1931.

2. All references are to the Pléiade edition of *Notre-Dame de Paris,* eds. Jacques Seebacher et Yves Gohin. Paris, 1975.

3. Henri Sauval, *Histoire et Recherche des Antiquités de la Ville de Paris.* Paris, 1724; Jacques Du Breul, *Le Théâtre des Antiquités de Paris.* Paris, 1612.

4. Jules Michelet, *Histoire de France au Moyen Age.* Paris, 1833.

5. Mme. Victor Hugo, *Victor Hugo raconté par un témoin de sa vie.* Bruxelles, 1863.

6. Léon Cellier, *L'Epopée romantique.* Paris, 1954.

7. Johann Peter Eckermann, *Gespräche mit Goethe.* 1835.

8. The real Gringore would have been only eight years old in 1482.

9. The Introit for Low Sunday, octave of Easter, begins with St. Peter's Epistle: "Quasi modo geniti infantes, alleluia . . ."

10. Jean Baptiste Pierre Antoine de Monet de Lamarck, *Philosophie zoologique.* Weinheim, 1809.

11. Etienne Geoffroy Saint-Hilaire, *Philosophie anatomique, II. Discours d'introduction à l'ouvrage, Monstruosités humaines.* . . . Paris, 1822.

12. Friedrich Wilhelm Schelling's *Entwurf der Naturphilosophie and Einleitung zu seinem Entwurf der Naturphilosophie.* Both first printed at Jena, 1799.

13. Henri Bergson, *L'Evolution créatrice.* Paris, 1907.

14. For the history of this and related scientific ideas, see Stephen Jay Gould, *Ontogeny and Phylogeny.* Cambridge, Mass., 1977.

15. Georges Léopold Chrétien Cuvier, *Règne animal distribué d'aprés son organisation* had appeared in its augmented second edition, Paris, 1829-1830.

16. *Paris, ou le livre des cent-et-un,* 5. Bruxelles, 1832.

17. Petrus Camper's description appeared first in Dutch as *Natuurkundige verhandelingen van Petrus Camper over den orang outang.* . . . Amsterdam, 1782. The degree of popular interest in the orang-outang may be measured by the printing in Venice, c. 1790, of a comedy entitled *L'Orangoutang over L'Uomo del bosco incivilito. Commedia pantomima in cinque atti,* claiming to be "imitata dagli Inglesi; e tradotta da un manoscritto francese" and paid for "A spese degli uomini e degli orang-outanghi." It is said that when Hugo's friend Pierre Bruneseau charted the Paris sewer system he found the skeleton of an orang-outang known to have escaped from the zoo in 1800. Possibly Hugo received from Bruneseau not only the material for his description of the sewers in *Les Misérables* but also the germ of his creation of Quasimodo.

18. *Decameron* (V, 1).

19. Madeleine de Scudéry, *Clélie, histoire romaine.* Paris, 1654.

20. He even refers to *Le grand Cyrus* in *Notre-Dame* X, v.

Eric Ormsby (essay date October 2002)

SOURCE: Ormsby, Eric. "Victor Hugo: The Ghost in the Pantheon." *The New Criterion* 21, no. 2 (October 2002): 23-8.

[In the following essay, Ormsby surveys Hugo's literary and cultural legacy.]

Victor Hugo was born two hundred years ago this year and his countrymen have been trying ever since to contain him. They resorted first to the tried-and-true: ostracism and outrage at his brazen Romanticism followed by acclaim and fervid acceptance. When this failed to muzzle him, they elected him to a position in the Assemblée; the transcripts of his speeches there are punctuated with such exclamations as "great sensation among the audience" and "tumults of applause." They then accorded him a seat beneath the monumental cupola of the Immortals at the Académie Française.

Hugo, avid if not insatiable, gulped down outrage and prestige equally with the alacrity of a tomcat swallowing minnows. As his fame grew, he continued to overspill all bounds: manuscripts in every genre (as well as drawings and paintings) flowed so copiously from his fluent pen that his publishers fell into permanent backlog; decades after his death new works of his were still being published. Mounting acclaim failed to hobble him. Then, in 1851, his enemies contrived to force him into exile, ostensibly for criticizing Louis Napoleon—Napoleon III after 1852. But hadn't Hugo always been a bit too exuberantly Promethean, if not downright Shakespearean, to be genuinely French? Installed for eighteen years in comfortable exile on the Channel Island of Guernsey, he not only flourished but achieved his most resounding successes. Undeflectable, standing every morning before a writing lectern that faced the waters of the English Channel while he sipped coffee left over from the previous evening, Hugo composed thousands of lines of verse, most of it wonderful; he wrote novels, all still in print, still read and loved by millions the world over; he wrote plays, manifestos, epics, diatribes. His scattered jottings and observations of a long lifetime—he lived to be eighty-three—fill more than a thousand pages of fine print (collected under the title **Choses vues**). Returned from exile in 1870, Hugo found himself a national hero, admired by even such truculent younger contemporaries as Flaubert. Desperate, the French had only one recourse left: in 1876 he was made a senator. Even this failed to lull the Titan into complacency. When Hugo died, in 1885, he was given an immense state funeral followed by "Pantheonization"—who but the French could have devised the verb *panthéoniser?*—a terminal accolade that usually suffices to muffle even the most obstreporous for all eternity. The Hugolian colossus should have lain still; few spirits, marmorealized in *la Gloire,* ever re-arise, and an oblivious and grateful nation can go about its mundane affairs without disruption.

No such luck. Victor Hugo refuses to lie still. Like some restless, perpetually chattering Dracula he pops up at every turn, draining the anemic veins of his compatriots who prefer less rumbustious fare, say, the desiccated Beckett or the (God help us!) bloodless Paul Auster. To give but a few examples: on a visit to my local Gallimard bookstore in Montreal, I notice that in celebration of the great man's 200th birthday, one can now obtain Hugo's complete works in a sprawling set of fifteen overstuffed volumes, totalling 17,500 pages. I am told that the set is selling well. (Needless to say, it isn't really complete.) Again, on the French website "La Poésie Française," more poems by Hugo are available than by any other French poet: 357 Hugo texts appear compared to 156 for Baudelaire, 167 for Verlaine, or a measly 127 for La Fontaine, the latter, along with Paul Claudel, his only serious rivals as the greatest of French poets. (There are a number of other websites on Hugo in this bicentennial year, one of the most attractive and interesting being that of the Maison Hugo in the Place des Vosges.)

In a very real sense, of course, Victor Hugo has surpassed even himself, becoming as much a mythic figure as Quasimodo or Jean Valjean; thus, "Victor Hugo" has come to resemble the "Borges" which the "real" Jorge Luis Borges learned to fear and suspect. Hugo's egomania, his unquenchable amatory gusto, his political battles and debacles, have become as important to the legend as his writing. This phantom Hugo threatened to overwhelm Hugo the man even during his lifetime, prompting Jean Cocteau's quip that "Victor Hugo was a madman who thought he was Victor Hugo." But to English readers, sadly enough, Hugo is known almost exclusively as the author of *Notre-Dame de Paris* (*The Hunchback of Notre-Dame*) and *Les Misérables,* the former in its film versions and the latter in its highly successful musical comedy guise. Even his several other superb novels are closed books to English speakers. In a recent tribute to Hugo in a local newspaper I learned that we should all read him because in addition to his many celebrated gifts, he had a wonderful sense of humor: hadn't he written *The Man Who Laughs*? The critic clearly hadn't read the novel which is about a child who is deliberately mutilated by having a smile carved into his mouth for life to amuse a king; the book illustrates Hugo's love of the grotesque but it isn't rich in laughs. Hugo's great dramas and his even greater poetry remain utterly unknown; music lovers may appreciate the songs based on his verse (Hugo himself refused to allow his poetry to be set to music during his lifetime), especially in the sublime renditions of Dame Felicity Lott, but few Americans have any acquaintance with the poetry, in the original or in translation.

For various reasons, Hugo's poetry has not so far succeeded in English translation; the verse has suffered the fate of a few other marvelous nineteenth-century poets—one thinks of Goethe or Leopardi—whose lyrics simply do not travel well. This has a lot to do with the intrinsic differences between French and English poetry. In his indispensable survey *An Essay on French Verse,* Jacques Barzun pointed out that one reason for this is that French is a language of pure vowels whereas English is not. What we do to our poor long-suffering vowels, from stretching them on the rack of the Southern drawl to snapping them out of the eastern air like lizards catching flies, would appall a French speaker for whom the vowels, particularly in poetry, have a sculpted and crystalline integrity. We can appreciate the force of the French vowels in such a line as Hugo's "L'ombre était nuptiale, auguste et solennelle" ("The dark was nuptial, and august, and solemn," in Brooks Haxton's new translation[1] and in another new version: "The shade was a deep, nuptial, solemn thing."[2]). But we are less likely to swoon at the effect than a native speaker; in fact, we are liable to be wary of such effects as overly sonorous, excessively magniloquent. Our wariness is well founded: Hugo's poetry almost always strikes a high and sublime note. Though his intonations and accents permeate the work of such successors as Baudelaire and Rimbaud, Hugo does not rely on spleen and bitter sarcasm to the same degree as those poets, even if

he outdoes them both in sheer vituperation. Hugo is lofty, and this falls with a hollow clangor on our ironic ears. Furthermore, Hugo almost always composed both dramas and poetic sequences in strict forms; he is a supreme technician of rhyme. Should a translator attempt to duplicate his rhymes in English, or rely on blank verse, to convey the sweeping effect of the original?

Now Hugo's two-hundredth birthday has inspired several new translations of his poetry, and the results are by and large quite gratifying. The most impressive, and probably the best, is the huge selection lovingly prepared by E. H. and A. M. Blackmore. This pair of translators has had the audacity to translate much of the verse in strict rhyme and meter, and the results are often surprisingly fine. Arranged chronologically and illustrated throughout by Hugo's own drawings and paintings, their selection for the first time gives the English reader the full range of Hugo's accomplishment as a poet. Even better, they have prefaced each of Hugo's collections, from *Odes et ballades* of 1822 to *Océan,* published posthumously in 1942, with intelligent and informative prefaces which set each work within a biographical and historical context. Their notes to the poems are succinct but apposite. The Blackmores' devoted and lavish attention to the nuances and subtleties of Hugo's verse should prompt a re-evaluation of this poet, one of the greatest writers of the nineteenth century and, in fact, a European genius of the stature of Goethe and Pushkin.

Of course, in the end only one question matters: do the translations convince, if not as credible poems in their own right—an almost impossible criterion—but as convincing representations of Hugo's originals?

One of Hugo's greatest poems is **"Booz endormi"** from his vast epic cycle *La Légende des siècles.* The poem is based on Ruth 3:1-8, in which Ruth the Moabite woman spends the night sleeping at the feet of Boaz, the aged and wealthy Israelite. It is a poem not only about the consequences of this unexpected union, out of which the line from David to Jesus will be established, but about a young woman's preference for an old man (Hugo was fifty-seven when he wrote the poem). Hugo's poem has a quiet majesty which steadily builds as the poem progresses; this is in part because he avails himself of simple declarative lines that have a solemn Biblical plainspokenness about them:

> *Booz s'était couché de fatigue accablé;*
> *Il avait tout le jour travaillé dans son aire;*
> *Puis avait fait son lit à sa place ordinaire;*
> *Booz dormait auprès des boisseaux pleins de blé.*

Here is the Blackmores' version of this opening stanza:

> There Boaz lay, overcome and worn out.
> All day he'd labored at his threshing floor;

Now, bedded in his usual place once more,
He slept, with grain bagged everywhere about.

Brooks Haxton, in his much slimmer selection, translates the same lines:

Boaz, overcome with weariness, by torchlight
made his pallet on the threshing floor
where all day he had worked, and now he slept
among the bushels of threshed wheat.

Haxton's version reads well though it is quite far from the original French. Hugo says nothing about "torchlight" nor does he mention a "pallet." Moreover, Haxton has altered the motion of the lines by linking them together and employing enjambment. The Blackmores, by contrast, succeed at reproducing the rhyme scheme; they even manage to suggest the alexandrine line with its almost obligatory caesura. In the French, there is a pause in the first line before the phrase *de fatigue accablé* and the Blackmores convey this with their strategically positioned comma after *lay*. True, like Haxton, they pad a bit ("overcome and worn out"), but theirs is a reasonably measured and finished translation. If it lacks the true Hugolian grandeur, who will blame them when they have otherwise come so close?

The problems with Haxton's version appear as the poem moves on. He tends to extrapolate, and he changes the original in ways that I for one would not condone. Another effect of which Hugo is a master is to cap a stanza with an aphoristic line. In the fifth stanza, for instance, he writes:

Booz était bon maître et fidèle parent;
Il était généreux, quoiqu'il fût économe;
Les femmes regardaient Booz plus qu'un jeune homme,
Car le jeune homme est beau, mais le vieillard est
    grand.

One can easily imagine the grizzled older Hugo, no chilly Parnassian, whispering this final maxim into the ears of some young soubrette. Haxton, however, expands the line and abandons its axiomatic flavor:

. . . for youth is handsome,
but to him in his old age came greatness.

The Blackmores get it right: "Young men have beauty, but old men have might." This is properly pithy, and captures the tone of the French (and "might" excellently suggests the force of *grand*). Like La Fontaine (whose maxim this could be), Hugo often clinches high-flown sublimity with a tart punch-line. Again, in the final stanza of the first section, Haxton introduces Ruth before Hugo does; he writes: "And though fire burned in young men's eyes, / to Ruth the eyes of Boaz shone clear light." What Hugo actually wrote is this, again in the Blackmores' version: "In the eyes of the young men there is fire, / But in the eyes of the old, illumination."

The simple stratagem of translating "light" (lumière) as "illumination" (as opposed to Haxton's "clear light") makes Hugo's intention gently but forcefully transparent.

Towards the end of the poem Hugo wrote: *Tout reposait dans Ur et dans Jérimadeth.* As the Blackmores have it: "all slumbered in Jerimadeth and Ur." Now every French schoolkid knows that there is no such place as "Jerimadeth." Hugo invented the name for the sake of a rhyme and because he liked the sound of the word. This sovereign playfulness amid such solemnity of diction is a masterstroke, but Haxton fluffs it when he writes: "All slept, all, from Ur to Bethlethem." Perhaps he disapproves of Hugo's hijinx, perhaps he wishes to make more explicit the lineage culminating in Christ; whatever the reason, he takes too great a liberty here for my taste. The ending of "Boaz Asleep" is one of Hugo's finest achievements. Here, in the Blackmores' version, the plain, stately, end-stopped lines, cadenced yet declarative, flower open into a grand but simple vision:

All slumbered in Jerimadeth and Ur;
The stars enameled the deep, somber sky;
Westward a slender crescent shone close by
Those flowers of night, and Ruth, without a stir,
Wondered—with parting eyelids half-revealed
Beneath her veils—what stray god, as he cropped
The timeless summer, had so idly dropped
That golden sickle in the starry field.

Even here, Haxton cannot resist meddling. Instead of the simple phrase *ouvrant l'oeil à moitié sous ses voiles* ("half opening her eye beneath her veils"), he gives poor Ruth a sudden ophthalmic disorder: "eyes half opened, / under the twingeing of their lids." And the *faucille d'or* is not a "golden scythe," as Haxton translates it, but a golden sickle. The rich grains and crops of the opening—Boaz is a farmer, after all—here assume a transcendent form, with the moon acting as a sickle in the "field of stars."

Both Haxton and the Blackmores also tackle one of Hugo's finest late poems, the elegy for his old friend Théophile Gautier, who died in 1872. This grand poem had already been rendered partially by Robert Lowell in his *Imitations,* and it is hard to see how anyone could surpass his version. Lowell imitates the rhyming couplets of the original (which neither Haxton nor the Blackmores attempt) and captures the inmost feeling of the poem:

We die. That is the law. None holds it back,
all leans; and this great age with all its light
glides to the shadow, where we flee—pale, black!
The oaks felled for the pyre of Hercules,
what a harsh roar they make in the red night!
Death's horses throw their heads, neigh, roll their
    eyes—
they are joyful, for the shining day now dies

. . . the ancient sea that made us young is dry,
youth has no fountain, age has no more Styx,
and Time moves forward with his heavy blade,
thoughtful, and step by step, to the last ear.
My turn comes round; night fills my troubled eye,
which prophesies the future from the past,
weeps over cribs, and smiles at this new grave.

Without being literal, Lowell remains surprisingly accurate both to the sense and the feeling of the original. The same cannot be said of either Haxton or the Blackmores. The last five lines of the poem, rendered literally, read:

The harsh reaper with his wide blade moves forth,
thoughtful, step by step, towards the remaining wheat;
it's my turn; and night fills my troubled eye
which guessing—alas!—the future of doves,
weeps over cradles and smiles at tombs.

Haxton seems to me here to capture the cadence of Hugo's lines rather well, though he mangles the doves:

Lost in thought, the mower with his long blade
moves on step by step into the standing wheat.
My turn has come. My good eye, muddled now
by mightfall, straining to make out the shapes
of doves, weeps over cradles and smiles at tombs.

The magical phrase *l'avenir des colombes* (which Lowell shrewdly omits) puzzles at first. The Blackmores render this by: "and gloom is filling my / Troubled sight, as I guess what future the doves must face." Can this be what Hugo meant? That doves, like everything else that lives, must die? But the line is ambiguous and can mean not simply "guessing the future of the doves," but "divining the future from the doves." It is, in other words, a supreme flash of hope: at the very moment when darkness fills his eye, the poet augurs the luminous stir of a future life. And it is for this reason that, like some ancient saint, he cries over cradles and smiles at graves: death is discerned as a beginning.

It was, of course, for this very Christian-like attitude, sundered as it was from official Christianity or any formal church, that earned Hugo the undying obloquy of such ferocious Catholics as Paul Claudel who could announce, in one of his *Five Grand Odes,* that Hugo's soul was "with the dead dogs." Claudel mistrusted Hugo's passion for social justice, in part because of Hugo's pronounced anti-clericalism. But there was much more, I think, to Hugo's thirst for justice than mere sloganeering. From an early age he expressed a profound empathy with the outcast, the despised, the rejected. That empathy takes on melodramatic forms in the novels but in the verse, it can pierce the reader with sudden poignancy. Hugo was drawn not solely to galley slaves, prisoners, thieves and vagabonds, but to their analogues in the natural world. One of his deepest poems, from *The Contemplations,* his magnificent collec-

tion of 1856—one year, be it noted, before the publication of Baudelaire's *Fleurs du mal*—begins: "I love the spider and I love the nettle / Because they are hated." One of Hugo's most astute early commentators, the great Austrian poet and dramatist Hugo von Hofmannsthal, suggested that this plastic ability of identification developed early in Victor Hugo's childhood when he haunted the public gardens of Paris. "In the very soil of those gardens," von Hofmannsthal wrote, "Hugo's marvelous intimacy with trees and flowers, with birds' nest and stars, took root and those thousands of lines of verse, with their magisterial abundance and compression, those thousands of metaphors, . . . were also rooted there." And yet, this is perhaps too easy; for Hugo's plasticity extended beyond the small and insignificant and despised to other, more daunting exemplars. In *Les Misérables,* Hugo's affinity with the implacable policeman Javert is just as striking and just as deep as his sympathy for Jean Valjean. The public Victor Hugo was not a hollow shell within which the private, and authentic, Victor Hugo crouched; rather, the outer man and the inner man existed in a kind of agonized hypostasis. As von Hofmannsthal again put it, with regard to Hugo's drama *Hernani,* what is involved is "a world of inner antitheses hurled forth into a world of outer antitheses." Hugo teemed with antitheses, and it is perhaps this quality that constitutes the indissoluble riddle of his personality: the public man speaks in the most intimate of whispers; the private man thunders anathemas; and yet, somehow, the voice is one and unmistakable.

The ability to assimilate virtually anything—from a lowly spider to a vengeful magistrate to God Himself (a posthumous collection was entitled simply *Dieu*)—is amazing enough; even more astounding, however, is the countervailing ability to exteriorize and to cast such a profusion of identities into objective form. Hugo possessed both abilities in inexhaustible abundance and it was this perhaps which prompted an admiring Baudelaire to write of him (in his "Reflections on Some of My Contemporaries") in a strangely negative vein that only accentuates his reverence:

He who is not capable of painting everything—palaces and hovels, emotions both tender and cruel, the circumscribed affections of a family and universal love, the grace of the green world and the marvels of architecture; all that is sweetest and all that is most horrifying, both the inner significance and the outer beauty of every religion, the moral and the physical physiognomy of each nation, in short, everything, from the visible to the invisible, from heaven to hell—that man is no true poet in the widest sense of the word and in the heart of God.

Victor Hugo was such a poet for Baudelaire (whose verse the aging Hugo admired), as for every French poet who has followed after him, even those—especially those—who (like Paul Claudel) have most despised and repudiated him. Everyone probably knows the anecdote in which André Gide is asked who the greatest French poet is and replies, "Victor Hugo, hélas!" But, as the Blackmores recount in their excellent notes, Théophile Gautier put it both more justly and more admirably when he remarked, after Hugo returned from exile in 1870, "talking poetry with Hugo is like talking theology with the Lord God." Both of these new translations, despite wide variation and the occasional infelicity, give us back something of Hugo's distinctive accents and in so doing set a vivid ghost free from its pantheon.

Notes

1. *Victor Hugo: Selected Poems,* translated by Brooks Haxton, Penguin, 141 pages, $12.00 (paperback).

2. *Selected Poems of Victor Hugo: A Bilingual Edition,* translated by E. H. and A. M. Blackmore. University of Chicago Press, 661 pages, $35.00.

Jeffrey Spires (essay date winter 2002)

SOURCE: Spires, Jeffrey. "Victor Hugo's *Notre-Dame de Paris*: The Politics and Poetics of Transition." *Dalhousie French Studies* 61 (winter 2002): 39-48.

[*In the following essay, Spires analyzes other critical assessments of Hugo's treatment of political and social issues in* Notre-Dame de Paris *and concludes that the novel "needs to be viewed as a work of æsthetic, personal, social, and political transition."*]

As we have been approaching the 200th anniversary of the year of Victor Hugo's birth, we have been witnessing a renewal of interest in this author who did so much to define both letters and intellectual history in nineteenth-century France. Victor Brombert, in his study of Hugo's novels, provides us with a thought-provoking explanation for Hugo's capacity to be accepted even today as one who could ultimately be the conscience of his age and give voice to an entire cultural identity: "Hugo converts politics into myth, much as he translates private obsessions into collective symbols" (7). In this essay, I would like to examine Brombert's assertion more closely, and analyze precisely how Hugo effects this conversion from the political to the mythic. Specifically, temporal ambiguity at the beginning of the novel creates a sense of "eternal return," suggesting that the turmoil of 1830 is merely part and parcel of a long heritage of political upheavals. Perhaps more importantly, this essay concludes with a re-evaluation of the nature of the politics being mythologized. It has been generally agreed upon that by the time Hugo wrote his first major novel, *Notre-Dame de Paris* (1831), he

had both crystallized a world-view based on the importance of myth, and abandoned the socially-conservative royalist politics championed by his mother,[1] adopting instead a liberal-democratic, even populist, stance. Indeed, the narrative of *Notre-Dame de Paris* opens on the day of the feast of fools: a popular, rebellious festival *par excellence.* Yet a close examination of this feast as a socio-historical phenomenon, and of the use Hugo makes of it in his novel, shows a political position, and a mythologization of it, more uncertain and thus more ambiguous than generally thought, and demonstrates that above all *Notre-Dame de Paris* needs to be viewed as a work of æsthetic, personal, social, and political transition.

Cycles of Festive Temporality

In his study of carnival in literature, *Rabelais and His World,* Mikhail Bakhtin identifies the primary organizing principle of the carnivalesque: "Its hero and author is time itself, which uncrowns, covers with ridicule, kills the old world (the old authority and truth), and at the same time gives birth to the new" (207). As both hero and author, time is the nucleus of the carnival and its driving force. Questions of the nature of time and man's comprehension of it and relationship to it are at the heart of every festivity: "The feast is always essentially related to time, either to the recurrence of an event in the natural (cosmic) cycle, or to biological or historical timeliness" (Bakhtin 9). In the summer and autumn of 1830, the ideas, so essential to the Feast of Fools, of revolutionary uncrownings, of killing off the old world and creating a new one, of social crisis and rupture, and of biological and historical cycles, were a major preoccupation in all of France.[2] Hugo was of course no exception to this, and one of the most characteristic features of the opening of *Notre-Dame de Paris* is a strongly-felt juxtaposition of cyclical and linear time.

The very first sentence of the *fête des fous* episode, and thus of the novel itself, introduces the reader into a ludic universe where cyclical return and linear progression co-exist in a state of tension:

> Il y a aujourd'hui trois cent quarante-huit ans six mois et dix-neuf jours que les Parisiens s'éveillèrent au bruit de toutes les cloches sonnant à grande volée dans la triple enciente de la Cité, de l'Université et de la Ville.[3]

In this sentence, Hugo's use of time-markers initially establishes an opposition between the present and the past. The term "aujourd'hui" is expressive of a present-day narration, but it is followed by the distancing technique of an exact count of how many years, months, and days have passed since the events of the story took place. There is thus an initial separation between the story time and the time of narration, and also the reader's present.

Notre-Dame de Paris is an essentially linear narrative, with a clearly-defined temporal progression from the beginning of the story to its dénouement. A very strong non-linear element to the novel, however, takes the form of the extended use of this eternal and subjective present that Hugo uses in the first sentence. The present tense can be found throughout the novel, but it is perhaps most strongly felt during the *fête des fous* in the way it is employed to destabilize the reader's point of reference and to include the reader in the events being related through calling upon his or her own imaginative faculties to complete the descriptions. The present tense in the carnival scene is used primarily to situate the narrative voice temporally. The narrator places himself repeatedly at the moment of the composition of the novel, and includes himself in the same community as its initial reading public. In describing the general chaos of the *grand'salle,* the narrator's initial gesture is to remind his reader of the distance separating the time of narration and the time of reading from the action:

> S'il pouvait être donné à nous, hommes de 1830, de nous mêler en pensée à ces Parisiens du quinzième siècle et d'entrer avec eux, tiraillés, coudoyés, culbutés, dans cette immense salle du Palais, si étroite le 6 janvier 1482, le spectacle ne serait ni sans intérêt ni sans charme, et nous n'aurions autour de nous que des choses si vieilles qu'elles nous sembleraient toutes neuves.
>
> (27)

The opposition between 1830 and 1482 is reinforced by the implied negativity of the statement, "S'il pouvait être donné à nous . . . ," that serves to emphasize the impossibility of transcending temporal boundaries, and the opposition between "vieilles" and "neuves." In fact, the entire spectacle possesses the charm and attraction of something foreign or exotic. In this case, the distance thus established is both temporal and cultural in nature.

The narrator, however, does not limit himself to his perspective in the Paris of 1830. It quickly becomes apparent that he is also part of the world of Paris in 1482 and is capable of adopting the point of view of his characters, as when he recounts what Gringoire sees and feels first in the *grand'salle,* then later during Gringoire's wanderings through the streets of Paris, and finally in the *Cour des Miracles.* The narrator also conveys the emotions felt by "tout le populaire de Paris" (26) as it fills the Palais de Justice. The narrator takes the reader on a tour of the *grand'salle* and then provides a meticulous description of its interior as it could be seen "à l'époque où *nous la voyons*" (27, my emphasis):

> Et d'abord, bourdonnement dans les oreilles, éblouissement dans les yeux. Audessus de nos têtes une double voûte en ogive, lambrissée en sculptures de bois, peinte d'azur, fleurdelysée en or; sous nos pieds, un pavé alternatif de marbre blanc et noir [. . .].
>
> (27)

What we are seeing and feeling is the situation as it existed in 1482. The narrative perspective has shifted and the present tense has shifted with it. This dislocation of point of view leaves the narrator the possibility of being either simultaneously or alternatingly a part of the nineteenth or fifteenth century. Hugo thus gives the reader two different and in many respects contradictory points of reference, a sort of temporal oxymoron, and in doing so makes a powerful statement. He signals that the universe of this novel will be a creation springing from the constant tension between a present-day narration, a plot situated in the past, and a perspective that will be based not on a stable point of reference in time but rather on the constant shifting between these two poles of past and present, narrative and story. If we couple this fact with Hugo's recurring use of the timeless "nous" to refer to the Parisian population, what can already be observed here is a subtle erosion of the distance separating 1482 from 1830. In fact, if we return to the first sentence of the novel, it is interesting to note that the point of reference from which the reader is to count the 348 years, six months, and nineteen days is not a precise date but rather the universal and essentially timeless word "aujourd'hui." Hugo originally had a precise date pencilled-in on his manuscript, July 25, 1830 (Hugo 1966:25, note 1). While this date is of great use to his biographers and those interested in the genesis of the text, I feel that what is most noteworthy is its exclusion from the final version of the novel and the resulting ambiguity of the first sentence. The moment of reading, "aujourd'hui," is an eternal and subjective present, and the exact count of time separating "aujourd'hui" from 1482 becomes more meaningless with each passing year.

It is certain that Hugo uses the present tense, the "historical present," in this description as a technique for reporting events that are vivid and exciting, or for enhancing the dramatic effect of a story by making addressees feel as if they were present at the time of the experience, and witnessing events as they occurred. The peculiar play of temporality that is characteristic of this festival is not limited, however, to the effacement of distinctions between past and present. To a consciousness of temporality that is linear or timeless, is joined a conception of history that is circular in nature. The first sentence of the novel represents a problematization of classifications of past and present, and the issue is complicated further in the second sentence by naming the precise year 1482: the gesture is that of a return to an absolute, mythic origin and its reactualization in the present.

The years 1482-1483, punctuated by the death of King Louis XI, marked a period of transition in France. The Middle Ages were drawing to a close, and this period is thus considered by many to have been the origin of the modern era. Hugo's use of this era as the setting for

Notre-Dame de Paris has a dual significance. On the one hand it is a time in France that has historical importance, but on the other hand the details of the daily social and political life of the era remained fairly obscure to the general public of the 1830's. Thus the choice of this period seems natural for an author writing a historical novel[4]: the subject is both well-known enough to spark the reading public's interest, but not so well-known as to be a commonplace. Indeed, Sir Walter Scott's *Quentin Durward* also dealt with this time in French history, and it is obvious that the subject presented Hugo with an opportunity to follow in Scott's footsteps while at the same time distancing himself from the model. But this choice of 1482-1483 has a deeper, more festive significance:

> La fête se présente en effet comme une actualisation des premiers temps de l'univers, de l'*Urzeit,* de l'ère originelle éminemment créatrice qui a vu toutes les choses, tous les êtres, toutes les institutions se fixer dans leur forme traditionnelle et définitive.

> (Caillois 136)

Mircea Eliade supports Caillois' assertion, writing that "through the paradox of rite [. . .] the time of any ritual coincides with the mythical time of the 'beginning'" (20).

The year 1482 in the novel thus functions as an origin, the point in time when all the foundations of modern-day France were established. Caillois goes on to state that the *Urzeit* was the time in which "divine" ancestors lived and established the social and cultural norms and practices of civilization. The *Urzeit* also represents the origin of the self and self-consciousness, and the origin of the Other and of consciousness of the Other; this extends to the society as a whole, in the recognition of itself as a community. Thus the reader of *Notre-Dame de Paris* is presented with a mythologized setting: medieval France on the threshold of the modern era, a state of relative chaos immediately preceding the order and return to classical reason of the Renaissance. The force behind this gesture of a return to the source is the festival itself. It is as repetition that the festival succeeds in recreating the original creation: "Through repetition of the cosmogonic act, concrete time, in which the construction takes place, is projected into mythical time, *in illo tempore* when the foundation of the world occurred" (Eliade 20). The effect of a festival or ritual constituting the making present of a past time or event is so powerful on those involved, that "on ne fait [. . .] aucune distinction nette entre le fondement mythique et le cérémonial actuel" (Caillois 144). The *fête des fous* is the ritual re-enactment of a revolution: a King or Pope is deposed and his replacement is elected from among the general population. Just as the *fête des fous* harkens back to an Ur-event, the novel *Notre-Dame de Paris* takes on an increasingly festive character as it ritually

reactualizes 1482 and makes it present in 1830. The novel's carnival becomes an Ur-event around which is built a mythology and a collective memory and identity. Hugo's preoccupations with and predilections for Greek, Norse, and Christian mythology lead him to create a medieval mythology[5] and to project a myth-based consciousness on the emerging cosmology of France in 1830.

What the traditionalizing element of festival and a myth-based consciousness have in common is the concept of cyclicity; in a conception of the world based on myth, all things belong to the great cosmic cycle of creation, destruction, and re-creation. Obviously, one of the major themes of *Notre-Dame de Paris,* Hugo's history of art, literature, and architecture, is based on the concept of a linear progression of time: the romanesque architecture of the cathedral gives way to the gothic, the architectural work of art will be replaced by the printed word, theocratic art will be replaced by popular art. Yet there is one theme in the novel that is firmly grounded in a cyclical apprehension of history: if the cosmic cycle is based on creation, destruction, and re-creation, the socio-political cycle consists of monarchy, revolution, and restoration. For Hugo the combination of politics and myth was natural and an integral part of his world-view. Indeed, as Victor Brombert has argued, one of the underlying subjects of the novel is the mythologization of revolution, starting with the Revolution of 1789: "The French Revolution, which is not the overt subject of *Notre-Dame de Paris,* is nonetheless its mythical time: it lies both behind and ahead" (55).

In *Notre-Dame de Paris* revolution is used as a framing device: the book opens with a symbolic revolution in the *fête des fous,* and the action reaches its dramatic climax in the popular assault on the cathedral. As a frame, or socio-political setting, revolution becomes the dominant theme of the novel. Thus Hugo's gesture of a return to the source acquires a deeper meaning: the novel is a ritual or festive re-enactment of the *Urzeit,* at the center of which we find popular revolt in its various forms. Hugo is proposing a cycle of revolution in which 1830 is a re-enactment of 1789, which is itself a ritual reenactment of the "original" revolt of 1482. In typical Hugolian fashion, the gesture is paradoxical: he invents a new tradition. As Eric Hobsbawm relates:

> "Traditions" which appear or claim to be old are often quite recent in origin and sometimes invented. "Invented tradition" is taken to mean a set of practices, normally governed by overtly or tacitly accepted rules and of a ritual or symbolic nature, which seek to inculcate certain values and norms of behavior by repetition, which automatically implies continuity with the past.

> (1)

Revolution and myth consequently come together as Hugo invents an entire French tradition of popular revolt.

The recurring revolution is a concept that can be found both in Hugo's political writings and in ***Notre-Dame de Paris.*** In his *Journal [. . .] d'un révolutionnaire de 1830* he writes about steps in the revolutionary process that are repeated: "Ainsi les révolutions ont de certaines phases qui reviennent invariablement. La révolution de 1789 en était alors où en est la révolution de 1830 aujourd'hui, à la période des insurrections" (1967:V:116). The revolution itself as a cyclic phenomenon is hinted at in a note that Hugo added to the fifth edition of ***Notre-Dame de Paris***:

> Les Tuileries ne sont plus simplement un chef-d'œuvre de l'art du seizième siècle, c'est une page de l'histoire du dix-neuvième siècle. Ce palais n'est plus au roi, mais au peuple. Laissons-le tel qu'il est. *Notre révolution* l'a marqué deux fois au front. Sur l'une de ses deux façades, il a les boulets du 10 août sur l'autre, les boulets du 29 juillet. Il est saint.
>
> (109; my emphasis)

The dates referred to in the text, August 10 and July 29, belong respectively to the Revolution of 1789 and that of 1830. It is interesting that Hugo should refer to these two historical events, separated by forty-one years of history, in the singular, as "notre révolution." The implication here is of continuity, of an unfinished project: revolution as a grotesque image[6]. At the same time there is a strong hint of repetition, of the same event happening over and over again. The novelistic 1482 thus suggests that 1789 and 1830 are all part of a great cycle, and are no different in nature from the *fête des fous*: a recurring ritual of social renewal and rebirth[7].

The suggestive power of this revolutionary return is remarkable. By positing recurring revolutions, Hugo is actually inserting revolution in a long-standing tradition of calendrical rituals such as the *fête des fous*. He is also inventing what Anne Ubersfeld has paradoxically called a "tradition of rupture" (461): it is the institutionalization of revolution. The revolutions of 1789 and 1830 were seen as crises, social upheavals that called into question not only the institutions and long-standing practices of life in France, but the very foundations of French history itself. As Lukàcs writes in his work on the historical novel in Europe (23), the last years of the eighteenth century and the first decades of the nineteenth saw an enormous concentration of political upheavals and social changes in Europe, so much so that "history" came for the first time to be seen as a man-made product rather than a "natural occurrence." Hugo's "social mythmaking" in his novel "naturalizes" revolution, and imposes some order into those chaotic decades. It is this proposal of revolution as part of the natural cycle and not as a traumatic break, that can be seen as a gesture that both reconciles and reassures. In the French society of the time as well as in Hugo's own personal life, 1830 marked a phase of transition and

worry. In an age of crisis, doubt, transition, and the *remise en question* of all certainties, there is a natural grasping for that which is permanent. Hugo posits cyclical history and thereby stabilizes his and society's cosmos; a long-standing tradition of popular unrest, uprising and revolution normalizes and attenuates the radicalism of 1789 and 1830 in France. Thus Hugo's claims for progress in a linear narrative are confronted with a deeply conservative nostalgia for circularity: history becomes predictable, present and future events are demystified.

THE CONSERVATIVE CARNIVAL

Despite the conservatism of his views on socio-political temporality, there is little doubt that in ***Notre-Dame de Paris*** Hugo demonstrates some decidedly democratic leanings. Practically every fundamental element of Hugo's novel has a close connection to "common classes": the use of all the festive/grotesque imagery is taken from popular origins and thus on the surface signifies Hugo's deep affinities with the *peuple*. As Anne Ubersfeld has observed, Hugo's first formulation of his theory of the grotesque in the ***Préface de Cromwell*** reveals the influence of his growing social consciousness:

> À chaque page de la *Préface,* le grotesque est indiqué comme *peuple,* en opposition aux privilégiés: superstition populaire, art populaire, personnages populaires, le grotesque peut être tenu dans ce texte comme une image de la force populaire aliénée.
>
> (463)

This is a reading of Hugo's populism in his early works that many critics share. Richard Grant, for example, affirms: "Hugo as early as 1830 has cast the common people in the role of the new sun" (67-68). Married to this populism is Hugo's apparently wholehearted belief in the salutary effects of revolution in all its forms[8]. It is true that both the ***Préface de Cromwell*** and ***Notre-Dame de Paris*** display a carnivalesque conception of the world, and no doubt in this conception the will of the popular collective can overcome, reverse, or topple the established hierarchy of social and political institutions, ideas, privileges and values that act as barriers to freedom and equality.

It would be a misrepresentation, however, to characterize Hugo's identification with the *peuple* and with forces of popular revolt and revolution as total and unqualified. Indeed, a distinction must be made between Hugo's treatment of the masses and his conception of a more ideal population touched by spiritual and intellectual enlightenment. If we turn to Quasimodo, we are reminded that even though he comes from the people, is elected Pope of Fools by it, and physically resembles it as a harmony of contradictory and conflicting elements, he nonetheless despises and fears the people and is despised and feared by it. In the climactic scene of the popular assault on the cathedral, of course, Quasimodo becomes the active enemy of the mass of *truands*. The highly ambivalent status of the relationship of Quasimodo to the *peuple* is much more in line with Hugo's own sometimes contradictory statements about mass movements and the ambivalence that lies at the heart of references to the popular classes in **Notre-Dame de Paris.** The novel does open with a popular festival scene, which can be interpreted as a gesture toward the participants in the recent July Revolution; it is, all in all, a positive depiction of a mass celebration. Yet there are unmistakable signs in the scene of a sense of unease with the collective, of Hugo's fear of the uncontrolled passions and violence among the crowds who have not yet fully become an enlightened *peuple*.

In fact, it is in the very use of the *fête des fous* that Hugo's ambivalence about change and stability finds its richest expression. The symbolism of this festival is that of a ritual crowning and uncrowning, but other symbolic elements of the carnival as well as its historical practices combine to suggest that the celebration is equally one of traditional institutions and the *status quo*. In his writings on carnival, Mikhail Bakhtin sees the feast as a wholly popular practice that ridicules, and even temporarily abolishes, the dominant official ideology. Although he decries the monological nature of official culture, his insistence on seeing only the subversive side of the carnival borders on a monologic oversimplification of the phenomenon. The fundamental nature of carnivalized literary works is that of a contradictory duality: all carnivalesque literature contains tradition, the discourse of the dominant ideology or *status quo*, as well as rupture, the carnivalesque subversion of the dominant ideology. The same is true of the carnival itself, and Anne Ubersfeld identifies the fundamental flaw in Bakhtin's analysis of the carnival when she writes: "À beaucoup de points de vue, il n'est pas sûr que le Carnaval de Bakhtine, incontestablement populaire, soit toujours aussi « progressiste » qu'il le dit" (501, note 195). For Bakhtin there are "popular" and "official" festivals, but he seems to admit no mixture of the two. The official feast simply serves to "sanction" and "reinforce" the existing order of life, and was thus the consecration of the "predominant truth" (Bakhtin 9). What is so interesting about these characterizations is that for Bakhtin they all applied equally to "popular" carnival throughout the ages.

Hugo's *fête des fous*, however, like most feasts of this kind in history, retains certain characteristics of an "official" celebration. The mystery play, the reception of the Flemish delegation, and the election of the Pope of Fools all take place not in the public square, but rather in the Hall of Justice: the heart of the State apparatus for judging and condemning, it is in this building that the secular authorities exercise their power of oppression and control. That the carnival should take place there at all can perhaps be seen as a subversion, as an instance of the people taking control of the legal institution and the administration of justice. Yet to hold the festival in an enclosed space symbolic of official power and imprisonment, rather than in the open square that belongs to all the people and symbolizes limitless freedom, is to inscribe the carnival carefully within the dominant power structure. The Hall represents restraint and constraint, and makes the State a major participant in the festivities.

This participation is extended to the financing of the carnival activities: the May tree, the *feu de joie,* and Gringoire's mystery play are all sponsored and financed by the Church in the *Cité,* and by the *Prévôté* in the *Ville.* The very condition making this feast day possible is thus the indulgence and active participation of the city and church officials. What we observe here is a process of assimilation, whereby chaotic, revolutionary and potentially explosive forces are brought under control and regulated in such a way as to become either part of the daily reality or an instrument of the perpetuation of the *status quo*[9]. The ritual of status reversal that constitutes the carnival is a temporary status reversal, not a permanent revolution. The *fête des fous* is not only a symbol of revolt but also a medium through which Hugo can make a commentary on popular uprisings, and through its use he implicitly questions the efficacy of revolutions, and perhaps especially the revolution of 1830, in bringing about real and lasting change.

That there might be some ambivalence on Hugo's part about the power of revolution as a force for positive change is born out in his statement, made in *Journal [. . .] d'un révolutionnaire de 1830,* about the goals of and the means for achieving this change:

> Une révolution, quand elle passe de l'état de théorie à l'état d'action, débouche d'ordinaire par l'émeute. L'émeute est la première des diverses formes violentes qu'il est dans la loi d'une révolution de prendre. L'émeute, c'est l'engorgement des intérêts nouveaux, des idées nouvelles, des besoins nouveaux, à toutes les portes trop étroites du vieil édifice politique. Tous veulent entrer à la fois dans toutes les jouissances sociales. Aussi est-il rare qu'une révolution ne commence pas par enfoncer les portes. Il est de l'essence de l'émeute révolutionnaire, qu'il ne faut pas confondre avec les autres sortes d'émeute, d'avoir presque toujours tort dans la forme et raison dans le fond.

> (1967:V:116-17)

The core element of Hugo's hesitation about popular revolt lies in the notion of the riot, of the destructive potential of any popular movement. Indeed, throughout the *fête des fous* episode and the rest of the novel, the threat of popular violence, or its actualization, lies close to the surface.

The *fête des fous* itself, in its pagan form as *Saturnalia,* was predicated on violence as the slave who was elected carnival king was ritually executed by the crowd at the end of his reign (Orloff 27). We find an echo of this in *Notre-Dame de Paris* when Quasimodo is tortured in the public square. Hugo takes great care to chronicle the cruelty of the crowd as Quasimodo asks for relief from his suffering:

> Cette exclamation de détresse, loin d'émouvoir les compassions, fut un surcroît d'amusement au bon populaire parisien qui entourait l'échelle, et qui, il faut le dire, pris en masse et comme multitude, n'était alors guère moins cruel et moins abruti que cette horrible tribu des truands chez laquelle nous avons déjà mené le lecteur, et qui était tout simplement la couche la plus inférieure du peuple.

(171)

The violent character of the festival is retained throughout the centuries, with outbreaks of destructive or murderous behavior by the mob being all too common: "[P]our la paix et le bon ordre, ces divertissements populaires, ces grands rassemblements de foules provoquent souvent des situations ambiguës ou dangereuses" (Heers 23).[10] It is from the "couche inférieure" of the brigands of the *Cour des Miracles* that the greatest threat of violence springs. There is no positive characterization of either the place or its inhabitants in the narrator's description:

> [. . .] hideuse verrue à la face de Paris; égout d'où s'échappait chaque matin, et où revenait croupir chaque nuit ce ruisseau de vices, de mendicité, et de vagabondage toujours débordé dans les rues des capitales; ruche monstrueuse où rentraient le soir avec leur butin tous les frelons de l'ordre social.

(75)

Indeed, the use of the playful gaiety of the *grand'salle* and the *Cour des Miracles* as frames for the *fête des fous* episode, and of the Feast episode itself and the assault on the cathedral as frames for the novel, traces the progression the festival can make from a joyful symbolic revolution and popular celebration to a sinister, cruel and destructive uprising.

Hugo's choice of the *fête des fous* to open his novel is thus indicative, I believe, of the spirit of transition that will dominate the novel[11]. In the realm of æsthetics, Victor Brombert has written: "Hugo appears at the origin of the modern 'polycentric' novel—as the creator of a liberating but always problematic countercode" (7). The *fête des fous,* with its polysemous grafted imagery, its mixture of popular and official sources, its diverse and conflicting temporalities and points of reference, its communal and participatorial aspect, and its cross-cultural dialogism, becomes a vehicle for the expression of a "modern" polycentrism in the novel and even for the renewal of novelistic discourse. Hugo's use of this festival is also an indication of the ambivalence many people of 1830 felt towards the processes of revolutionary change and especially their agents. *Notre-Dame de Paris* is a novel of political passage, marking the change from a conservative royalist Hugo to a liberal and progressive Hugo, and on a social scale from a repressive monarchy to a more progressive one. In December of 1830, Hugo is still far from giving his total endorsement to the masses in their quest for more rights and greater power: "Ne demandez pas des droits pour le peuple tant que le peuple demandera des têtes" (1967:V:115). Although he became more and more socially progressive and a champion of popular democracy as the years passed, as part of the French intellectual elite Hugo would never entirely lose his distrust of the masses and of their potential for cruelty and destruction. That in *Notre-Dame de Paris,* at the age of 28, he should give expression to this ambivalence and nuance his generally favorable position towards the revolution, should come as no surprise.

Notes

1. This conservatism of course extended to his literary undertakings. From 1819 to 1821 he was an editor of and a frequent contributor to *Le conservateur littéraire,* a review founded by Abel Hugo whose main goal seemed to be to decry any form of literary experimentation or novelty (Robb 75).

2. Hugo started working on his novel on July 25, just before the onset of the Revolution. This social unrest and the birth of his daughter Adèle on July 28 kept him from writing more than a few pages, and it was only on September 1 that he was able to return to his writing on a full-time basis (Sacy 25, note 1).

3. Hugo 1967:IV:25. Subsequent reference's to *Notre-Dame de Paris* will be to this edition (pages only), unless noted otherwise.

4. Hugo's original contract with the editor Gosselin called for him to write a historical novel "à la Walter Scott" (Seebacher 1052). The remainder of this paragraph in the novel, however, is little more than a list of all the events of historical importance that did *not* take place on that day and thus will not be the subject of the story to be told. That Hugo should distance himself in this way is not surprising, for in 1823 he was already writing: "[I]ci j'aime mieux croire au roman qu'à l'histoire, parce que je préfère la vérité morale à la vérité historique" (1967:V:133), and in his *Préface de Cromwell,* he states: "Il [le drame] laisse à l'historien l'exacte série des faits généraux, l'ordre des dates, les grandes masses à remuer, les batailles, les conquêtes, les démembrements d'empires, tout l'extérieur de l'histoire. Il en prend l'intérieur" (1967:III:57). Thus *Notre-Dame de Paris* opens by simultaneously invoking and distancing itself from the model of the historical

novel: the gesture here is one of irony, of admitting to noting that which is not noteworthy, of remembering that which is not inherently memorable. By simultaneously appropriating the historical novel and distancing his work from it, Hugo *subverts* the genre as well as notions of historical progression and historicism itself. As Brombert has observed, all of Hugo's novels are "deeply historical" but they also all challenge the basic tenets of the historical novel (9), and even raise the problematic of the mixture of historical fact and novelistic fiction (52).

5. Following a Gothic tradition established by Chateaubriand's *Génie du Christianisme.*

6. As Hugo advances in his *Préface de Cromwell,* the grotesque image is an inherently hybrid construct. By dint of being formed through the *bricolage* of parts of different totalities, the grotesque image (as well as the hybrid festival and the mixed genre) itself gives rise to a dislocation of traditional meaning and a destruction of the unity that characterizes what Bakhtin terms monologic cultural forms. They also "depict or imply an essential *incompleteness*" (Bakhtin 26) or open-endedness. Hugo himself champions this notion of the incomplete, open-ended work in the "new æsthetic" he is proposing in the *Préface de Cromwell*: "[C]'est le moyen d'être harmonieux que d'être incomplet" (1967:III:50). It is characteristic of Hugo that his poetics should be based on the paradoxical notion of incompleteness engendering a more harmonious, total completeness.

7. Mehlman argues: "One senses in this somewhat improbable parallel between the events of 1482 and 1789 that liberal teleology of history which would see in the year of the bourgeois revolution a culmination of all that preceded it" (134). Hugo's ambiguous use of temporality, as we have seen, argues against Mehlman's notion that Hugo is proposing 1830 as the end of the revolutionary era and the realization of its ideals. As we shall see, Hugo's ambivalence about the means, the ends, and the actors of France's revolutions also supports the more nuanced view that 1830 is merely the continuation, rather than the culmination, of 1789 and its aftermath.

8. In her study of Hugo's chapter on the advent of the printing press and the other forces changing art ("Ceci tuera cela"), Kessler states that Hugo's "sympathies will appear manifestly on the side of this revolutionary process in artistic and cultural development" (183). Likewise, for Grossman the Hugo of *Notre-Dame de Paris* is optimistic about the future of French society: "As the faithful link bewteen past, present, and future, Victor Hugo remains true to the ethico-æsthetic universe of his earliest prose works. Only, in 1830, French politics have at last caught up with French literature. Romanticism has, since the start, proclaimed the necessity of a genuinely new society. In the July Monarchy it obtains, so Hugo appears to hope, the realization of that vision of harmony" (196).

9. Hugo will comment on this appropriation of carnival by the forces of order more explicitly in *Les Misérables.* At a time when all of France, but especially Paris, has willingly surrendered its political will and is letting itself be amused, distracted and ultimately pacified by Napoleon III's "fête impériale," Hugo writes about revolutionary laughter become "suspect": "Le rire de tous est complice de la dégradation universelle. De certaines fêtes malsaines désagrègent le peuple et le font populace. Et aux populaces comme aux tyrans il faut des bouffons. Le roi a Roquelaure, le peuple a Paillasse. Paris est la grande ville folle toutes les fois qu'il n'est pas la grande cité sublime. Le carnaval y fait partie de la politique. Paris, avouons-le, se laisse volontiers donner la comédie par l'infamie. Il ne demande à ses maîtres,—quand il a des maîtres,—qu'une chose: fardez-moi la boue" (1967:XI:942).

10. Le Roy Ladurie has devoted *Le carnaval de Romans* to the study of how carnival joy and laughter suddenly turned murderously violent in the small town of Romans in 1580.

11. Zarifopol-Johnston's assertion (47-48) that in its form *Notre-Dame de Paris* is above all a hybrid construction, is incontestable. Her further claim, however, that hybridity is also the major theme of the novel fails, I think, to account for the importance of the idea of æsthetic, personal, social and political transition that I have argued in this essay. To my mind, hybridity serves in the novel to underline liminality, passage, transition, and not, as she suggests, as an end unto itself.

Works Cited

Bakhtin, Mikhail M. *Rabelais and His World.* Bloomington: University of Indiana Press, 1984.

Bloom, Harold, ed. *Victor Hugo.* Modern Critical Views. New York: Chelsea House Publishers, 1988.

Brombert, Victor. *Victor Hugo and the Visionary Novel.* Cambridge: Harvard University Press, 1984.

Caillois, Roger. *L'homme et le sacré.* Paris: Gallimard, 1950.

Eliade, Mircea. *The Myth of the Eternal Return.* Trans. Willard R. Trask. New York: Pantheon Books, 1954.

Grant, Richard. *The Perilous Quest: Image, Myth, and Prophesy in the Narratives of Victor Hugo.* Durham: Duke University Press, 1968.

Grossman, Kathryn M. The Early Novels of Victor Hugo: Towards a Poetics of Harmony. Geneva: Droz, 1986.

Heers, Jacques. *Fêtes des fous et carnavals.* Paris: Fayard,1983.

Hobsbawm, E. J., and Terence Ranger, eds. *The Invention of Tradition.* Cambridge: Cambridge University Press, 1983.

Hugo, Victor. 1966. *Notre-Dame de Paris.* Ed. Samuel de Sacy. Paris: Éditions de poche.

———. 1967. *Œuvres complètes.* Édition chronologique. Ed. Jean Massin. 17 vols. Paris: Club français du livre.

Kessler, Joan C. "Babel and Bastille: Architecture as Metaphor in Hugo's *Notre-Dame de Paris.*" *French Forum* 11. 2 (May 1986):183-97.

Le Roy Ladurie, Emmanuel. *Le carnaval de Romans: de la Chandeleur au Mercredi des cendres 1579-1580.* Paris: Gallimard, 1979.

Lukàcs, Georg. *The Historical Novel.* Trans. Hannah and Stanley Mitchell. London: Merlin Press, 1962.

Mehlman, Jeffrey. "Revolution and Repetition in *Notre-Dame de Paris.*" *Victor Hugo.* Ed. Harold Bloom. Modern Critical Views. New York: Chelsea House Publishers, 1988. 129-45.

Orloff, Alexander. *Carnival: Myth and Cult.* Worgl, Austria: Perlinger Verlag 1981.

Robb, Graham. *Victor Hugo.* New York: W. W. Norton, 1997.

Sacy, Samuel de. See Hugo 1966.

Seebacher, Jacques. Introduction. *Notre-Dame de Paris.* Bibliothèque de la Pléiade. Paris: Gallimard, 1975. 1045-76.

Ubersfeld, Anne. *Le roi et le bouffon: étude sur le théâtre de Victor Hugo de 1830 à 1839.* Paris: Corti, 1974.

Zarifopol-Johnston, Ilinca. *To Kill A Text: The Dialogic Fiction of Hugo, Dickens, and Zola.* Newark: University of Delaware Press, 1995.

FURTHER READING

Criticism

Affron, Charles. "The Time of the Lyric: *Hernani.*" In *A Stage for Poets: Studies in the Theatre of Hugo & Musset,* pp. 21-61. Princeton, N.J.: Princeton University Press, 1971.

Detailed analysis of *Hernani,* Hugo's 1830 Romantic drama, discussing the author's treatment of political and aesthetic concerns.

Andrews, Larry R. "Hugo's Gilliatt and Leskov's Golovan: Two Folk-Epic Heroes." *Comparative Literature* 46, no. 1 (winter 1994): 65-83.

Juxtaposes the "folk-epic heroes" Gilliatt, Hugo's protagonist of *Les travailleurs de la mer,* and Golovan, protagonist of Nikolaj Leskov's *Nesmertel'nyj Golovan.*

Cardinal, Roger. "Victor Hugo, Somnambulist of the Sea." In *Artistic Relations: Literature and the Visual Arts in Nineteenth-Century France,* edited by Peter Collier and Robert Lethbridge, pp. 209-21. New Haven, Conn.: Yale University Press, 1994.

Compares the imagery found in Hugo's nautical-themed drawing, *Le Bateau-vision* (c. 1865-66), to Hugo's writings from the same period, highlighting the author's "oceanic fixation."

Grant, Richard B. *The Perilous Quest: Image, Myth, and Prophecy in the Narratives of Victor Hugo.* Durham, N.C.: Duke University Press, 1968, 253 p.

Discusses common symbols and structures in Hugo's works.

Grossman, Kathryn M. "Louis-Napoléon and the Second Empire: Political Occultations in *Les Misérables.*" In *Correspondances: Studies in Literature, History, and the Arts in Nineteenth-Century France,* edited by Keith Busby, pp. 103-11. Amsterdam: Rodopi, 1992.

Traces the relationship between the story and historical facts in *Les Misérables,* with particular attention paid to the reign of Louis-Napoléon.

———. *Figuring Transcendence in* Les Misérables: *Hugo's Romantic Sublime.* Carbondale: Southern Illinois University Press, 1994, 358 p.

Comprehensive study of *Les Misérables* that examines the novel within Hugo's oeuvre, using theories on metaphor and the Romantic sublime to demonstrate how Hugo merges politics, aesthetics, and ethics.

———. "From Classic to Pop Icon: Popularizing Hugo." *The French Review* 74, no. 3 (February 2001): 482-95.

Discusses the animated, Walt Disney depiction of Hugo's *Notre-Dame de Paris,* and other modern adaptations of Hugo's works, addressing "[w]hat happens to Hugo—and to those who teach his works—when his characters have become pop icons" by "looking first at the process by which both [Hugo] and his works have become so thoroughly popularized, then at the particular attraction of his fiction for other forms of media, and finally at three kinds of relationships between literary classics and their transformations."

Guerlac, Suzanne. "Phantom Rights: Conversations across the Abyss (Hugo, Blanchot) Post-Mortem: The State of Death as a Modern Construct." *diacritics* 30, no. 3 (fall 2000): 73-89.

Investigates how the relationship between writing and death in Hugo's *Le dernier jour d'un condamné* is treated in Maurice Blanchot's critical writings.

Hamilton, James F. "Terrorizing the 'Feminine' in Hugo, Dickens, and France." *Symposium* 48, no. 3 (fall 1994): 204-15.

Studies works by Hugo, Charles Dickens, and Anatole France to demonstrate how the feminine principle was oppressed during the Reign of Terror.

Nash, Suzanne. "In the Wake of Victor Hugo: The Poetry and Politics of Indebtedness." In *Literary Generations: A Festschrift in Honor of Edward D. Sullivan by His Friends, Colleagues, and Former Students,* edited by Alain Toumayan, pp. 125-40. Lexington, Ky.: French Forum Publishers, 1992.

Asserts that "[b]y looking at shifts in the reception of Hugo's poetry since the 1860s . . . one can better understand certain key issues underlying the creative activity which has accompanied serious cultural redefinitions in our century."

Pendell, William D. *Victor Hugo's Acted Dramas and the Contemporary Press.* Baltimore, Md.: The Johns Hopkins Press, 1947, 135 p.

Full-length, scholarly assessment of the attitude of nineteenth-century critics toward Hugo's works in particular, and Romantic theater in general.

Petit, Susan. "Michel Tournier and Victor Hugo: A Case of Literary Parricide." *The French Review* 68, no. 2 (December 1994): 251-60.

Examines the literary and biographical significance of the themes of parricide and fatherhood found in Michel Tournier's *Angus,* a children's story that comprises a revision of Hugo's poem "L'Aigle du casque."

Phillips, James M. *Representational Strategies in* Les Misérables *and Selected Drawings by Victor Hugo: An Intermedial Comparison.* New York: Peter Lang, 1999, 155 p.

Considers how Hugo's drawings and novels informed and influenced one another, and demonstrates Hugo's strategy of blending language and image to transcend traditional boundaries of both literature and visual art.

Saint-Amand, Pierre. "Hot Terror: *Quatrevingt-treize.*" *SubStance: A Review of Theory and Literary Criticism,* no. 86 (1998): 61-72.

Uses the physics concept of thermodynamics as a metaphor to analyze the Reign of Terror in Hugo's *Quatrevingt-treize* (Ninety-three).

Schick, Constance Gosselin. "Death Comes to the Cathedral: Romantic Allegorizations of the Symbol." *French Forum* 22, no. 2 (May 1997): 149-64.

Discusses the use of the cathedral as a symbol in Hugo's *Notre-Dame de Paris* and in Théophile Gautier's *La Comédie de la Mort.*

Zarifopol-Johnston, Ilinca. "Bakhtin's Dialogue with Hugo." In *To Kill a Text: The Dialogic Fiction of Hugo, Dickens, and Zola,* pp. 33-46. Newark, N.J.: University of Delaware Press and Associated University Presses, 1995.

Presents Mikhail Bakhtin's theory of dialogism in the novel and argues that some of Hugo's writings in *Preface to Cromwell* and *Notre-Dame de Paris* support Bakhtin's theory.

Additional coverage of Hugo's life and career is contained in the following sources published by Thomson Gale: *Authors and Artists for Young Adults,* Vol. 28; *Dictionary of Literary Biography,* Vols. 119, 192, 217; *DISCovering Authors*; *DISCovering Authors: British*; *DISCovering Authors: Canadian Edition*; *DISCovering Authors Modules: Dramatists, Most-studied Authors, Novelists,* and *Poets*; *DISCovering Authors 3.0*; *Epics for Students,* Vol. 2; *European Writers,* Vol. 6; *Exploring Novels*; *Guide to French Literature,* 1789 to the Present; *Literature and Its Times,* Vols. 1, 2; *Literature Resource Center*; *Nineteenth-Century Literature Criticism,* Vols. 3, 10, 21; *Novels for Students,* Vols. 5, 20; *Poetry Criticism,* Vol. 17; *Reference Guide to World Literature,* Eds. 2, 3; *Something About the Author,* Vol. 47; *Twayne's World Authors*; and *World Literature Criticism.*

John Neal
1793-1876

(Has also written under the pseudonym Jehu O'Cataract) American novelist, poet, short story writer, autobiographer, essayist, historian, playwright, speech writer, and translator.

INTRODUCTION

Neal is remembered today for his ardent support of American literary nationalism, for his associations with Edgar Allan Poe, and for his fiction and essays that often anticipated the themes and styles used by his more famous contemporaries, including Nathaniel Hawthorne and James Fenimore Cooper. As a literary critic, Neal was among the first to identify as innovative and masterful the narratives of such authors as Poe, Nathaniel Hawthorne, Henry Wadsworth Longfellow, and Washington Irving.

BIOGRAPHICAL INFORMATION

Neal was born on August 25, 1793 in Falmouth, in what was then the District of Maine, to Quaker parents. Neal's father, John, a teacher, died in September of 1793. Following her husband's death, Rachel Neal taught school as a means of providing financially for Neal and his twin sister. Neal's own formal education ended when he was twelve, and he was expelled from the Society of Quakers for fighting in 1820 after many years of expressed dissatisfaction with his community's pacifist philosophy. Neal worked as a store clerk beginning in 1805, and later became a partner in a wholesale dry-goods business. Following the War of 1812 and the bankrupting of his business, Neal studied law and was admitted to the bar of the State of Maryland. In 1816, along with his close friend and former business partner John Pierpont and seven other Baltimore-area literary men, Neal founded the Delphian Club, whose members published works by contemporary authors and held extensive literary discussions. Each of the Delphians used a pseudonym; Neal was known as Jehu O'Cataract. As a Delphian, as the editor of numerous periodicals, including *The Portico, Federal Republican and Baltimore Telegraph, Brother Jonathan* and *The Yankee,* and as a contributor of essays on literary, political, and philosophical subjects, Neal was heavily involved and influential in New England intellectual discourse. In 1823 Neal traveled to England. There he contributed many

reviews of works by American writers to *Blackwood's Magazine* and served as Jeremy Bentham's secretary. Neal returned to the United States in 1827, married Eleanor Hall in 1828, and settled in Portland, Maine. Neal was an active participant in the American women's suffrage movement; he belonged to several formal women's rights organizations, published many articles on women's rights, and delivered speeches in support of women's rights and suffrage at numerous conferences and events. In addition to his support for women's rights, Neal was also a social activist associated with a number of other causes. He was an abolitionist, argued against the custom of dueling, advocated an end to capital punishment and, as a proponent of physical exercise, was credited with popularizing athletic gymnasiums in the United States. In 1851 Neal joined the Congregational Church, and during the remainder of his life he actively expressed his religious and spiritual beliefs. Neal died on June 20, 1876 and was buried in Portland. He was survived by his wife and their daughters, Mary and Margaret Eleanor, and their son, John

Pierpont. He was predeceased by another daughter, Eleanor, who died before the age of one, and a son, James, who died in 1856.

MAJOR WORKS

Neal claimed to have written his first novel, *Keep Cool* (1817), in part to disparage dueling. During the next several years, Neal wrote five more novels. *Seventy-Six* (1823) and *Brother Jonathan* (1825)—historic novels set during the American Revolution—were informed by Neal's co-authorship with Tobias Watkins of *A History of the American Revolution* (1819), which was attributed to Paul Allen when it was published. *Logan, a Family History* (1822), set prior to the American Revolution, is a Gothic novel containing numerous depictions of violence and features an Englishman—Logan—turned Mingo chief as its protagonist. The novel treats the issue of conflict between Native Americans and Europeans over rightful ownership of American land; Logan himself is torn between love for his two sons, one of whom is raised in Mingo culture and the other in English society. *Seventy-Six* is characterized by colloquial language, including profanity, and involves narrator Jonathan Oadley's relation of his own, his brother's, and his father's experiences while serving in George Washington's army, as well as his own and his brother's romances with two sisters. *Brother Jonathan,* in which Neal incorporates the same colloquial language he employed in *Seventy-Six,* portrays a year in the life of Walter Harwood, a conscript in Washington's army. *Randolph* (1823) is a novel presented in epistolary form, and involves Sarah Ramsey's journey to discover the hidden nature of Edward Molton. The novel's plot is interspersed with commentary on numerous real-life writers, artists, and periodicals of the early nineteenth century. *Errata; or, the Works of Will. Adams* (1823) centers on protagonist Will Adams, who becomes insane after murdering his close friend in a jealous rage; Neal also includes in this novel various biographical details from his childhood as a Quaker and his experiences in commerce as a young adult. *Rachel Dyer* (1828) is a fictionalized account of the Salem witchcraft trials in which Neal highlights the consequences of the prejudice and social injustice involved in this infamous historical event. The main characters in the novel, preacher George Burroughs, and sisters Rachel and Elizabeth Dyer, decry the accusations of witchcraft made against their neighbors and are ultimately accused of witchcraft themselves. Burroughs is executed, and Rachel, who forgives her accusers and prays for them, dies before her execution can take place. Following the deaths of Burroughs and Rachel, the residents of Salem become aware of their error and Elizabeth's life is spared. In his "Unpublished Preface" to *Rachel Dyer,* Neal expounds on his literary inspirations and predecessors, and discusses his conception of a uniquely American literary tradition. Neal published the religious tract *One Word More* in 1854. The death of his son James in 1856, which deepened Neal's religious faith, informed the novel *True Womanhood* (1859), in which the religious revivals held in New York during the 1850s are portrayed. During the 1860s, Neal agreed to write *The White-Faced Pacer* (1863), *The Moose-Hunter* (1864), and *Little Moccasin* (1866), a series of popular "dime novels," to earn money. The last of Neal's works published during his lifetime were his autobiography *Wandering Recollections of a Somewhat Busy Life* (1869), *Great Mysteries and Little Plagues* (1870), a collection of essays written for and about children, and *Portland Illustrated* (1874), a history of the city of Portland, Maine.

CRITICAL RECEPTION

Critical commentary on Neal's works has always been mixed, with some critics dismissing his works outright as amateurish and rambling and others lauding him as an innovative and thoughtful chronicler of the unique aspects of American life. Many commentators have focused on the representation of Neal's political and philosophical views in both his essays and works of fiction, particularly of his defense of the rights of women. Alexander Cowie has judged Neal's works as meriting scholarly consideration principally for their influence on other writers and as examples of American literary nationalism. Hans-Joachim Lang, a leading Neal scholar, has asserted that Neal's literary talents are somewhat lacking, but has maintained that Neal deserves recognition for his role as a proponent of American letters and as a prescient admirer of such authors as Poe, Hawthorne, and Irving. William J. Scheick has illustrated that in *Rachel Dyer* Neal demonstrates how the establishment of a distinctly American social order and "American art" results from the process of conflict between Old World and New World notions of individual autonomy and authority. Fritz Fleischmann has closely studied Neal's feminist writings as well as his social activism, and has argued that Neal has been incorrectly and unfairly excluded from his rightful place in the history of American literature.

PRINCIPAL WORKS

Keep Cool, A Novel. 2 vols. (novel) 1817
Battle of Niagara, A Poem, without Notes; and Goldau, or the Maniac Harper (poetry) 1818; enlarged edition, 1819
*A History of the American Revolution; Comprehending All the Principle Events Both in the Field and in the Cabinet [with Tobias Watkins] (history) 1819

Otho: A Tragedy, in Five Acts (play) 1819
Logan, a Family History. 2 vols. (novel) 1822
Errata; or, the Works of Will. Adams. 2 vols. (novel) 1823
Randolph, A Novel. 2 vols. (novel) 1823
Seventy-Six. 2 vols. (novel) 1823
Brother Jonathan; or, the New Englanders. 3 vols. (novel) 1825
Rachel Dyer; A North American Story (novel) 1828
Authorship, a Tale (novel) 1830
Principles of Legislation: From the MS. of Jeremy Bentham . . . Translated from the Second Corrected and Enlarged Edition with Notes and a Biographical Notice of Jeremy Bentham and of M. Dumont [translator] (essays) 1830
The Down-Easters. 2 vols. (novel) 1833
One Word More: Intended for the Reasoning and Thoughtful among Unbelievers (religious tract) 1854
True Womanhood: A Tale (novel) 1859
The White-Faced Pacer: or, Before and After the Battle (novel) 1863
The Moose-Hunter; or, Life in the Maine Woods (novel) 1864
Little Moccasin; or, Along the Madawaska. A Story of Life and Love in the Lumber Region (novel) 1866
Wandering Recollections of a Somewhat Busy Life (autobiography) 1869
Great Mysteries and Little Plagues (essays) 1870
Portland Illustrated (history) 1874
Observations on American Art: Selections from the Writings of John Neal (1793-1876) (essays) 1943
The Genius of John Neal: Selections from His Writings (essays, short stories, speeches, and novel extracts) 1978

*This work was originally attributed to Paul Allen.

CRITICISM

John Neal (essay date 1828)

SOURCE: Neal, John. "Preface and Unpublished Preface." In *Rachel Dyer: A North American Story,* pp. iii-xx. Portland, Maine: Shirley and Hyde, 1828.

[*In the following essays, which prefaced his novel,* Rachel Dyer, *Neal regards his literary inspirations and predecessors, and discusses his conception of a uniquely American literary tradition.*]

PREFACE

I have long entertained a suspicion, all that has been said by the novel-writers and dramatists and poets of our age to the contrary notwithstanding, that personal beauty and intellectual beauty, or personal beauty and moral beauty, are not inseparably connected with, nor apportioned to each other. In **Errata,** a work of which *as* a work, I am heartily ashamed now, I labored long and earnestly to prove this. I made *my* dwarf a creature of great moral beauty and strength.

Godwin, the powerful energetic and philosophizing Godwin, saw a shadow of this truth; but he saw nothing more—the substance escaped him. He taught, and he has been followed by others, among whom are Brown, Scott and Byron, (I observe the chronological order) that a towering intellect may inhabit a miserable body; that heroes are not of necessity six feet high, nor of a godlike shape, and that we may be deceived, if we venture to judge of the inward by the outward man. But they stopped here. They did not perceive, or perceiving, would not acknowledge the whole truth; for if we consider a moment, we find that all their *great* men are scoundrels. Without one exception I believe, their heroes are hypocrites or misanthropes, banditti or worse; while their good men are altogether subordinate and pitiable destitute of energy and wholly without character.

Now believing as I do, in spite of such overwhelming authority, that a man may have a club-foot, or a humpback, or even red hair and yet be a good man—peradventure a great man; that a dwarf with a distorted shape may be a giant in goodness of heart and greatness of temper; and that moral beauty *may* exist where it appears not to have been suspected by the chief critics of our age, and of past ages—namely, in a deformed body (like that of Æsop,) I have written this book.

Let me add however that although such was my principal, it was not my only object. I would call the attention of our novel-writers and our novel-readers to what is undoubtedly native and peculiar, in the early history of our Fathers; I would urge them to believe that though there is much to lament in that history, there is nothing to conceal; that if they went astray, as they most assuredly did in their judgments, they went astray conscientiously, with what they understood to be the law of God in their right hands. The "*Salem Tragedie*" is in proof—that is the ground-work of my story; and I pray the reader to have patience with the author, if he should find this tale rather more serious in parts, and rather more argumentative in parts, than stories, novels and romances generally are.

I do not pretend to say that the book I now offer to my countrymen, is altogether such a book as I would write now, if I had more leisure, nor altogether such a book as I hope to write before I die; but as I cannot afford to throw it entirely away, and as I believe it to be much better, because more evidently prepared for a healthy good purpose, than any other I have written, I have concluded to publish it—hoping it may be regarded by the wise and virtuous of our country as some sort of atonement for the folly and extravagance of my earlier writing.

The skeleton of this tale was originally prepared for Blackwood, as the first of a series of North-American Stories: He accepted it, paid for it, printed it, and sent me the proofs. A misunderstanding however occurred between us, about other matters, and I withdrew the story and repaid him for it. It was never published therefore; but was put aside by me, as the frame-work for a novel—which novel is now before the reader.

JOHN NEAL

Portland, October 1, 1828

P. S. After some consideration, I have concluded to publish a preface, originally intended for the North American Stories alluded to above. It was never published, nor has it ever been read by any body but myself. Among those who are interested for the encouragement of our native literature, there may be some who will not be sorry to see what my ideas *were* on the subject of novel-writing, as well as what they *are*. Changes have been foretold in my views—and I owe it to our people to acknowledge, that in a good degree, the prediction has been accomplished. I do not feel now as I did, when I wrote **Seventy-Six, Randolph,** and the rest of the works published in America; nor even as I did, when I wrote those that were published over sea. The mere novel-reader had better skip the following pages and go directly to the story. The introductory chapter in all human probability will be too much for him.

J. N.

UNPUBLISHED PREFACE

To the North-American Stories, Alluded to in Page V

The author of this work is now under the necessity of bidding the novel-readers of the day, on both sides of the water, farewell, and in all probability, forever. By them it may be considered a trivial affair—a time for pleasantry, or peradventure for a formal expression of what are called good wishes. But by him, who does not feel like other men—or does not understand their language, when they talk in this way, it will ever be regarded as a very serious thing. He would neither conceal nor deny the truth—he would not so affront the feeling within him—and he says therefore without affectation or ceremony, that it goes to his heart even to bid the novel-readers of the age, the few that have read his novels, it were better to say—farewell.

These volumes are the last of a series which even from his youth up, he had been accustomed to meditate upon as a worthy and affectionate offering to his family and to those who have made many a long winter day in a

dreary climate, very cheerful and pleasant to him—the daughters of a dear friend—of one who, if his eye should ever fall upon this page, will understand immediately more than a chapter could tell, of the deep wayward strange motives that have influenced the author to say thus much and no more, while recurring for the last time to the bright vision of his youth. And the little that he does say now, is not said for the world;—for what care they about the humble and innocent creatures, whose gentleness and sincerity about their own fireside, were for a long time all that kept a man, who was weary and sick of the great world, from leaving it in despair? No, it is not said for them; but for any one of that large family who may happen to be alive now, and in the way of remembering "the stranger that was within their gates"—when to the world he may be as if he never had been. Let them not be amazed when they discover the truth; nor afraid nor ashamed to see that the man whom they knew only as the stranger from a far country, was also an author.

In other days, angels were entertained in the shape of travellers and way-faring men; but ye—had ye known every stranger that knocked at your door to be an angel, or a messenger of the Most High, could not have treated him more like an immortal creature than ye did that unknown man, who now bears witness to your simplicity and great goodness of heart. With you it was enough that a fellow-creature was unhappy—you strove to make him happy; and having done this, you sent him away, ignorant alike of his people, his country and his name.

* * *

This work is the last of the sort I believe—the very last I shall ever write. Reader—stop!—lay down the book for a moment and answer me. Do you feel no emotion at the sight of that word? You are surprised at the question. Why should you feel any, you ask. Why should you?—let us reason together for a moment. Can it be that you are able to hear of the final consummation of a hope which had been the chief stay of a fellow-creature for many—many years?—Can it be that you feel no sort of emotion at hearing him say, Lo! I have finished the work—it is the last—no sensation of inquietude? Perhaps you now begin to see differently; perhaps you would now try to exculpate yourself. You are willing to admit now that the affair is one of a graver aspect than you first imagined. You are half ready to deny now that you ever considered it otherwise. But mark me—out of your own mouth you are condemned. Twice have I said already—three times have I said already, that this was the last work of the sort I should ever write, and you have read the declaration as you would, the passing motto of a title-page. You neither cared for it, nor thought of it; and had I not alarmed you by my abruptness, compelled you to stop and think, and awed you by steadfastly rebuking your inhumanity, you would not have known by to-morrow whether I had spoken of it as my last work or not. Consider what I say—is it not the truth?—can you deny it? And yet you—*you* are one of the multitude who dare to sit in judgment upon the doings of your fellow men. It is on what you and such as you say, that authors are to depend for that which is of more value to them than the breath of life—character. How dare you!—You read without reflection, and you hear without understanding. Yet upon the judgment of such as you—so made up, it is that the patient and the profound, the thoughtful and the gifted, are to rely for immortality.

To return to what I was about saying—the work now before you, reader, is the last of a series, meditated as I have already told you, from my youth. It was but a dream at first—a dream of my boyhood, indefinite, vague and shadowy; but as I grew up, it grew stronger and braver and more substantial. For years it did not deserve the name of a plan—it was merely a breathing after I hardly knew what, a hope that I should live to do something in a literary way worthy of my people—accompanied however with an inappeasable yearning for the time and opportunity to arrive. But so it was, that, notwithstanding all my anxiety and resolution, I could not bring myself to make the attempt—even the attempt—until it appeared no longer possible for me to do what for years I had been very anxious to do. The engagement was of too sacred a nature to be trifled with—perhaps the more sacred in my view for being made only with myself, and without a witness; for engagements having no other authority than our moral sense of duty to ourselves, would never be performed, after they grew irksome or heavy, unless we were scrupulous in proportion to the facility with which we might escape if we would.

This indeterminate, haunting desire to do what I had so engaged to do, at last however began to give way before the serious and necessary business of life, and the continually augmenting pressure of duties too solemn to be slighted for any—I had almost said for any earthly consideration. Yea more, to confess the whole truth, I had begun to regard the enterprise itself—so prone are we to self-deception, so ready at finding excuses where we have a duty to perform—as hardly worthy of much power, and as altogether beneath an exalted ambition. But here I was greatly mistaken; for I have an idea now, that a great novel—such a novel as might be made—if all the powers that could be employed upon it were found in one man, would be the greatest production of human genius. It is a law and a history of itself—to every people—and throughout all time—in literature and morals—in character and passion—yea—in what may be called the fire-side biography of nations. It would be, if rightly managed, a picture of the present for futurity—a picture of human nature, not only here but every where—a portrait of man—a history of the

human heart—a book therefore, written not only in a universal, but in what may be considered as an everlasting language—the language of immortal, indistructable spirits. Such are the parables of Him who spoke that language best.

Again however, the subject was revived. Sleeping and waking, by night and by day, it was before me; and at last I began to perceive that if the attempt were ever to be made, it must be made by one desperate, convulsive, instantaneous effort. I determined to deliberate no longer—or rather to stand no longer, shivering like a coward, upon the brink of adventure, under pretence of deliberation; and therefore, having first carefully stopped my ears and shut my eyes, I threw myself headlong over the precipice. Behold the result! If I have not brought up the pearls, I can say at least that I have been to the bottom—and I might have added—of the human heart sometimes—but for the perverse and foolish insincerity of the world, which if I had so finished the sentence, would have set their faces forever against my book; although that same world, had I been wise enough—no, not wise enough but cunning enough, to hold my peace, might have been ready to acknowledge that I had been sometimes, even where I say—to the very bottom of the human heart.

I plunged. But when I did, it was rather to relieve my own soul from the intolerable weight of her own reproach, than with any hope of living to complete the design, except at a sacrifice next in degree to that of self-immolation. Would you know what more than any other thing—more than all other things determined me at last? I was an American. I had heard the insolent question of a Scotch Reviewer, repeated on every side of me by native Americans—"*Who reads an American Book?*" I could not bear this—I could neither eat nor sleep till my mind was made up. I reasoned with myself—I strove hard—but the spirit within me would not be rebuked. Shall I go forth said I, in the solitude of my own thought, and make war alone against the foe—for alone it must he made, or there will be no hope of success. There must be but one head, one heart in the plan—the secret must not even be guessed at by another—it must be single and simple, one that like the wedge in mechanics, or in the ancient military art, must have but one point, and that point must be of adamant. Being so it may be turned aside: A thousand more like itself, may be blunted or shivered; but if at last, any one of the whole should make any impression whatever upon the foe, or effect any entrance whatever into the sanctity and strength of his tremendous phalanx, then, from that moment, the day is our own. Our literature will begin to wake up, and our pride of country will wake up with it. Those who follow will have nothing to do but *keep* what the forlorn hope, who goes to irretrievable martyrdom if he fail, has *gained*.

Moreover—who was there to stand by the native American that should go out, haply with a sling and a stone, against a tower of strength and the everlasting entrenchments of prejudice? Could he hope to find so much as one of his countrymen, to go with him or even to bear his shield? Would the Reviewers of America befriend him? No—they have not courage enough to fight their own battles manfully.[1] No—they would rather flatter than strike. They negociate altogether too much—where blows are wanted, they give words. And the best of our literary champions, would they? No; they would only bewail his temerity, if he were the hold headlong creature he should be to accomplish the work; and pity his folly and presumption, if he were any thing else.

After all however, why should they be reproached for this? They have gained their little reputation hardly. "It were too much to spend that little"—so grudgingly acquiesced in by their beloved countrymen—"rashly." No wonder they fight shy. It is their duty—considering what they have at stake—their little all. There is Washington Irving now; he has obtained the reputation of being—what?—why at the best, of being only the American Addison, in the view of Englishmen. And is this a title to care much for? Would such a name, though Addison stood far higher in the opinion of the English themselves, than he now does, or ever again will, be enough to satisfy the ambition of a lofty-minded, original thinker? Would such a man falter and reef his plumage midway up the altitude of his blinding and brave ascent, to be called the American Addison, or even what in my view were ten thousand times better, the American Goldsmith.[2] No—up to the very key stone of the broad blue firmament! he would say, or back to the vile earth again: ay, lower than the earth first! Understand me however. I do not say this lightly nor disparagingly. I love and admire Washington Irving. I wish him all the reputation he covets, and of the very kind he covets. Our paths never did, never will cross each other. And so with Mr. Cooper; and a multitude more, of whom we may rightfully be proud. They have gained just enough popular favor to make them afraid of hazarding one jot or tittle of it, by stepping aside into a new path. No one of these could avail me in my design. They would have everything to lose, and nothing to gain by embarking in it. While I—what had I to lose—nay what *have* I to lose? I am not now, I never have been, I never shall be an author by trade. The opinion of the public is not the breath of life to me; for if the truth must be told, I have to this hour very little respect for it—so long as it is indeed the opinion of the public—of the mere multitude, the careless, unthinking judgment of the mob, unregulated by he wise and thoughtful.

To succeed as I hoped, I must put everything at hazard. It would not do for me to imitate anybody. Nor would it do for my country. Who would care for the *American* Addison where he could have the English by asking for it? Who would languish, a twelvemonth after they appeared, for Mr. Cooper's imitations of Sir Walter Scott, or Charles Brockden Brown's imitations of Godwin? Those, and those only, who after having seen the transfiguration of Raphael, (or that of Talma,) or Dominichino's St. Jerome, would walk away to a village painting room, or a provincial theatre, to pick their teeth and play the critic over an imitation of the one or a copy of the other. At the best, all such things are but *imitations*. And what are imitations? Sheer mimicry—more or less exalted to be sure; but still mimicry—wherever the *copies* of life are copied and not life itself: a sort of high-handed, noon-day plagiarism—nothing more. People are never amazed, nor carried away, nor uplifted by imitations. They are pleased with the ingenuity of the artist—they are delighted with the closeness of the imitation—but that is all. The better the work is done, the worse they think of the workman. He who can paint a great picture, cannot copy—David Teniers to the contrary notwithstanding; for David never painted a great picture in his life, though he has painted small ones, not more than three feet square, which would sell for twenty-five thousand dollars to day.

Yes—to succeed, I must imitate nobody—I must *resemble* nobody; for with your critic, resemblance in the unknown to the known, is never anything but adroit imitation. To succeed therefore, I must be unlike all that have gone before me. That were no easy matter; nor would be it so difficult as men are apt to believe. Nor is it necessary that I should do *better* than all who have gone before me. I should be more likely to prosper, in the long run, by worse original productions—with a poor story told in poor language, (if it were original in spirit and character) than by a much better story told in much better language, if after the transports of the public were over, they should be able to trace a resemblance between it and Walter Scott, or Oliver Goldsmith, or Mr. Addison.

So far so good. There was, beyond a doubt, a fair chance in the great commonwealth of literature, even though I should not achieve a miracle, nor prove myself both wiser and better than all the authors who had gone before me. And moreover, might it not be possible—*possible* I say—for the mob are a jealous guardian of sepulchres and ashes, and high-sounding names, particularly where a name will save them the trouble of judging for themselves, or do their arguments for them in the shape of a perpetual demonstration, whatever may be the nature of the controversy in which they are involved—might it not be possible then, I say, that, as the whole body of mankind have been growing wiser and wiser, and better and better, since the day when these great writers flourished, who are now ruling "our spirits from their urns," that authors may have improved with them?—that they alone of the whole human race, by some possibility, may not have remained altogether stationary age after age—while the least enquiring and the most indolent of human beings—the very multitude—have been steadily advancing both in knowledge and power? And if so, might it not be *possible* for some improvements to be made, some discoveries, even yet in style and composition, by lanching forth into space. True, we might not be certain of finding a new world, like Columbus, nor a new heaven, like Tyho Brahe; but we should probably encounter some phenomena in the great unvisited moral sky and ocean; we should at least find out, after a while—which would of itself be the next greatest consolation for our trouble and anxiety, after that of discovering a new world or a new system,—that there remained no new world nor system to be discovered; that they who should adventure after us, would have so much the less to do for all that we had done; that they must follow in our steps; that if our health and strength had been wasted in a prodigious dream, it would have the good effect of preventing any future waste of health and strength on the part of others in any similar enterprize.

Islands and planets may still be found, we should say, and they that find them, are welcome to them; but continents and systems cannot be beyond where we have been; and if there be any within it, why—they are neither continents nor systems.

But then, after all, there was one plain question to be asked, which no honest man would like to evade, however much a mere dreamer might wish to do so. It was this. After all my fine theory—what are my chances of success? And if successful, what have I to gain? I chose to answer the last question first. Gain!—of a truth, it were no easy matter to say. Nothing *here,* nothing *now*—certainly nothing in America, till my bones have been canonized; for my countrymen are a thrifty, calculating people—they give nothing for the reputation of a man, till they are sure of selling it for more than they give. Were they visited by saints and prophets instead of gifted men, they would never believe that they were either saints or prophets, till they had been starved to death—or lived by a miracle—by no visible means; or until their cast-off clothes, bones, hair and teeth, or the furniture of the houses wherein they were starved, or the trees under which they had been chilled to death, carved into snuff-boxes or walking-sticks, would sell for as much as that sympathy had cost them, or as much as it would come to, to build a monument over—I do not say over their unsheltered remains, for by that time there would be but little or no remains of them to be found, unmingled with the sky and water, earth and air about them, save perhaps in here and there a museum or college where they might always be bought up, however, immortality and all—for something more than compound interest added to the original cost—but to build a monument or a shed over the unappropriated

stock, with certain privileges to the manufacturer of the walking-sticks and snuff-boxes aforesaid, so long as any of the material remained; taking care to provide with all due solemnity, perhaps by an act of the legislature, for securing the monopoly to the sovereign state itself.

Thus much perhaps I might hope for from my own people. But what from the British? They were magnanimous, or at least they would bear to be told so; and telling them so in a simple, off-hand, ingenuous way, with a great appearance of sincerity, and as if one had been carried away by a sudden impulse, to speak a forbidden truth, or surprised into a prohibited expression of feeling by some spectacle of generosity, in spite of his constitutional reserve and timidity and caution, would be likely to *pay well.* But I would do no such thing. I would flatter nobody—no people—no nation. I would lie to nobody—neither to my own countrymen, nor to the British—unless I were better paid for it, than any of my countrymen were ever yet paid either at home or abroad.

No—I choose to see for myself, by putting the proof touch like a hot iron to their foreheads, whether the British are indeed a magnanimous people. But then, if I do all this, what are my chances of reward, even with the British themselves? That was a fearful question to be sure. The British are a nation of writers. Their novel-writers are as a cloud. True—true—but they still want something which they have not. They want a real American writer—one with courage enough to write in his native tongue. *That* they have not, even at this day. *That* they never had. Our best writers are English writers, not American writers. They are English in every thing they do, and in every thing they say, as authors—in the structure and moral of their stories, in their dialogue, speech and pronunciation, yea in the very characters they draw. Not so much as one true Yankee is to be found in any of our native books: hardly so much as one true Yankee phrase. Not so much as one true Indian, though you hardly take up a story on either side of the water now, without finding a red-man stowed away in it; and what sort of a red-man? Why one that uniformly talks the best English the author is capable of—more than half the time perhaps out-Ossianing Ossian.

I have the modesty to believe that in some things I am unlike all the other writers of my country—both living and dead; although there are not a few, I dare say who would be glad to hear of my bearing a great resemblance to the latter. For my own part I do not pretend to write English—that is, I do not pretend to write what the English themselves call English—I do not, and I hope to God—I say this reverently, although one of their Reviewers may be again puzzled to determine "whether I am swearing or praying" when I say so—

that I never shall write what is now worshipped under the name of *classical* English. It is no natural language—it never was—it never will be spoken alive on this earth: and therefore, ought never to be written. We have dead languages enough now; but the deadest language I ever met with or heard of, was that in use among the writers of Queen Anne's day.

At last I came to the conclusion—that the chances were at least a thousand to one against me. A thousand to one said I, to myself, that I perish outright in my headlong enterprise. But then, if I do not perish—if I triumph, what a triumph it will be! If I succeed, I shall be rewarded well—if the British *are* what they are believed to be—in fair proportion to the toil and peril I have encountered. At any rate, whether I fail or not, I shall be, and am willing to be, one of the first hundred to carry the war into the very camp, yea among the very household gods of the enemy. And if I die, I will die with my right arm consuming in the blaze of their altars—like Mutius Scævola.

But enough on this head. The plan took shape, and you have the commencement now before you, reader. I have had several objects in view at the same time, all subordinate however to that which I first mentioned, in the prosecution of my wayward enterprise. One was to show to my countrymen that there are abundant and hidden sources of fertility in their own beautiful brave earth, waiting only to be broken up; and barren places to all outward appearance, in the northern, as well as the southern Americas—yet teeming below with bright sail—where the plough-share that is driven through them with a strong arm, will come out laden with rich mineral and followed by running water: places where—if you but lay your ear to the scented ground, you may hear the perpetual gush of innumerable fountains pouring their subterranean melody night and day among the minerals and rocks, the iron and the gold: places where the way-faring man, the pilgrim or the wanderer through what he may deem the very deserts of literature, the barren-places of knowledge, will find the very roots of the withered and blasted shrubbery, which like the traveller in Peru, he may have accidentally uptorn in his weary and discouraging ascent, and the very bowels of the earth into which he has torn his way, heavy with a brightness that may be coined, like the soil about the favorite hiding places of the sunny-haired Apollo.

Another, was to teach my countrymen, that these very Englishmen, to whom as the barbarians of ancient story did by their gods when they would conciliate them, we are accustomed to offer up our own offspring, with our own hands, whenever we see the sky darkening over the water—the sky inhabited of them; ay, that these very Englishmen, to whom we are so in the habit of immolating all that is beautiful and grand among us—

the first born of our youth—our creatures of immortality—our men of genius, while in the fever and flush of their vanity, innocence and passion—ere they have had time to put out their first plumage to the sky and the wind, all above and about them—that they, these very Englishmen, would not love us the less, nor revere us the less, if we loved and revered ourselves, and the issue of our blood and breath, and vitality and power, a little more. No—the men of England *are* men. They love manhood. They may smile at our national vanity, but their smile would be one of compassionate benevolence and encouragement, if we were wise enough to keep our young at home, till their first molting season were well over—and then, offer to pair them, even though there would be a little presumption in it, high up in the skies, and the strong wind—with their bravest and best: not, as we do now, upon the altars of the earth—upon the tables of our money-changers—half fledged and untrained—with their legs tied, and wings clipped; or, peradventure, with necks turned, and heads all skewered under their tails—a heap of carrion and garbage that the braver birds, even among their enemies, would disdain to stoop at. Such would be their behavior, if we dealt as we ought with our own; there would be no pity nor disdain with them. They would cheer us to the conflict—pour their red wine down our throats if we were beaten; and if their birds were beaten, they would bear it with temper—knowing that their reputation could well afford an occasional trumph, to the young of their favorite brood. The men of England are waiting to do us justice: but there is a certain formality to be gone through with, before they will do it. We must claim it. And why should we not? I do not mean that we should claim it upon our knees as the condemned of their courts of justice are compelled to claim that *mercy,* which the very law itself, has predetermined to grant to him—but will not, unless that idle and unworthy formality has been submitted to; no—I mean no such thing. We do not want mercy: and I would have my countrymen, when they are arraigned before any mere *English* tribunal—not acting under the *law of nations* in the world of literature, to go at once, with a calm front and untroubled eye, and plead to their jurisdiction, with a loud clear voice, and with their right hand upon the great book of English law, and set them at defiance. This, they have the right, and the power to do; and why should they not, when some of the inferior courts, of mere *English* criticism, have the audacity at every little interval, to call upon a sovereign people, to plead before them—without counsel—and be tried for some infringement of some paltry municipal provision of their statute book—some provincialism of language—or some heresy in politics—or some plagiarism of manner or style; and abide the penalty of forgery—or of ecclesiastical censure—or the reward of petit-larceny; re-transportation—or re-banishment to America.

It is high time now, that we should begin to do each other justice. Let us profit by their good qualities; and let them, by ours. And in time, we shall assuredly come to feel like brothers of the same parentage—an elder and a younger—different in temper—but alike in family resemblance—and alike proud of our great ancestry, the English giants of olden time. We shall revere *our* brother; and he will love his. But when shall this be?—not, I am sorely afraid—till we have called home all our children, from the four corners of the earth; from the east and from the west; from the north and from the south—and held a congress of the dead—of their fathers, and of our fathers—and published to the world, and to posterity—appealing again to Jehovah for the rectitude of our intentions—another DECLARATION OF INDEPENDENCE, in the great REPUBLIC OF LETTERS. And, yet this may soon be. The time is even now at hand. Our representatives are assembling: the dead Greek, and the Roman; the ancient English, and the fathers of literature, from all the buried nations of all the earth, and holding counsel together, and choosing their delegates. And the generation is already born, that shall yet hear the heavens ringing with acclamations to their decree—that another state has been added to the everlasting confederacy of literature!

And now the author repeats to the people of America, one and all, farewell; assuring them that there is very little probability of his ever appearing before them again as a novel-writer. His object has been, if not wholly, at least in a great degree accomplished. He has demonstrated that a bold and direct appeal to the manhood of any people will never be made in vain. Others may have been already, or may hereafter be incited to a more intrepid movement; and to a more confident reliance upon themselves and their resources, by what he has now accomplished—where it is most difficult to accomplish any thing—among his own countrymen: and most devoutly does he pray, that if they should, they may be more fortunate, and far more generously rewarded, than he has ever been; and if they should not, he advises them to go where he has been already—and trust to another people for that, which his own have not the heart to give him, however well he may deserve it. Abroad—if he do not get a chaplet of fire and greenness—he will, at least, get a cup of cold water,—and it may be, a tear or two of compassion, if nothing of encouragement—whatever he may do. At home—he may wear himself out—like one ashamed of what he is doing, in secrecy and darkness—exhaust his own heart of all its power and vitality, by pouring himself into the hearts of others—with a certainty that he will be called a madman, a beggar and a fool, for his pains—unless he persevere, in spite of a broken heart, and a broken constitution, till he shall have made his own countrymen ashamed of themselves, and afraid of him.

It is a sad thing to say good bye, even for an author. If you mean what you say—it is a prayer as well as a blessing, an audible breathing of the heart. And if you do not—it is a wicked profanation. So far, reader, you have been the familiar companion of the author; and you may be one of those, who have journied with him before, for many a weary day, through much of his wandering and meditation:—that is, you may be one of those who, having been admitted before, to touch his heart with a naked hand—have felt in one pulsation—in one single hour's fellowship with it, all that he had felt and thought for many a weary year. You have been *with* him to a more holy place than the fire-side; *to* him, more like the invisible creatures—for he hath never seen your face, and peradventure never may, though you have been looking into his very soul—that hover about the chamber of prayer—the solitude of the poet—or the haunted place under the shadow of great trees, where the wearied man throws himself down, to muse upon the face of his Creator, which he sees in the sky over him, or beneath the vast blue water before him. Is it wonderful therefore that there should be a little seriousness about his brow—although ye *are* invisible to him—when he is about to say farewell to you—farewell forever—without having once heard the tone of your voice—nor one of the many tears, that you may have dropped over him, when you thought yourself altogether alone:—

Nor can he look back, without some emotion, upon the labour that he has undergone, even within that flowery wilderness, where he hath been journeying with you, or lying and ruminating all alone, for so long a time; and out of which, he is now about to emerge—forever—with a strong tread, to the broad blue sky and the solid earth; nor without lamenting that he cannot go barefooted—and half-naked among men;—and that the colour and perfume—the dim enchantment, and the sweet, breathing, solemn loneliness of the wild-wood path, that he is about to abandon, for the broad dusty highway of the world, are so unpropitious to the substantial reputation of a man: nor, without grieving that the blossom-leaves, and the golden flower-dust, which now cover him, from head to foot, *must* be speedily brushed away;—and that the scent of the wilderness may not go with him—wherever he may go—wandering through the habitation of princes—the courts of the living God—or, the dwelling places of ambition—yea, even into the grave.

* * *

I have but one other request to make. Let these words be engraven hereafter on my tomb-stone: "WHO READS AN AMERICAN BOOK?"

Notes

1. Or had not before this was written. Look to the *North-American Review* before 1825, for proof.

2. I speak here of Goldsmith's prose, not of his poetry. Heaven forbid!

William B. Cairns (essay date 1922)

SOURCE: Cairns, William B. "Fiction." In *British Criticisms of American Writings, 1815-1833*, pp. 208-14. Madison: University of Wisconsin Press, 1922.

[*In the following excerpt, Cairns chronicles critical responses to Neal's works written during the 1820s and early 1830s.*]

Three novels by John Neal—*Logan, Seventy-Six,* and *Brother Jonathan*—were read and criticised in England between 1820 and 1830; and in the closing years of the period under consideration some slight notice was given to *Rachael Dyer,* and *Authorship, a Tale.*

The *Magazine of Foreign Literature*[1] places the author of *Logan* in the group of American writers who fail because they are too proud to form themselves on English models:

> It would be difficult, indeed, to guess what end he purposed to accomplish by his singular work. It could not be to amuse his readers, because it is unintelligible; if he wished to frighten them he has failed of his end, for he only makes them laugh. . . . We laugh not with him, but at him. His style is the most singular that can be imagined—it is like the raving of a bedlamite. There are words in it, but no sense. . . .
>
> The incidents are such as fill a sick man's dream. . . . We have taken some pains to inquire who the author may be, but without success;—it is, perhaps, as well that we are in ignorance of his name; the knowledge must be painful, as we have no doubt that the poor gentleman is at this time suffering the wholesome restraint of a straw cell and a strait waistcoat. If he is not, there is no justice in America.

The review concludes: "Absurdity is sometimes more amusing than wit; the author's folly has been a source of much mirth to us, and we trust it may contribute to that of our readers."

Very different in tone is a notice in the *Literary Chronicle and Weekly Review*[2] which considers *Logan* as a Minerva Press novel, and says nothing of the name or the nationality of the author.

> *Logan* is a novel purporting to be written by a descendant of the celebrated Mingo chief, who relates his own history in a manner which is no bad imitation of the abrupt but startling eloquence of the much-abused Aborigines of America. The story, too, possesses considerable interest, and the work will be no discredit to the shelves of a modern circulating library, improved as they have now become.

The same journal[3] gives an early notice of the Baltimore edition of *Seventy-Six,* in which it raises the question whether the author may not be ranked with Irving, Brown, and Cooper, and continues: "There is, indeed, an occasional abruptness in the style but the effect on the whole is not unpleasing; and *Seventy-Six* may be considered as a work which will meet with many admirers; and which no lover of fiction should omit to read." The *Monthly Magazine or British Register*[4] is disturbed by the peculiarities of the novel.

> It is rude and boisterous; every chapter being covered with blood, or heaving with the throes of lacerated flesh. The style, too, is affectedly precipitous; and its metaphors as incongruous as those of the poets of the Lakes. In addition to the regularly formed oaths, which are very numerous, the name of God is invoked in every page; and in such a manner as to make it difficult to discover whether the author meant to pray or to swear.

The *Magazine of Foreign Literature*[5] refers to its earlier judgment that the author of *Logan* is insane:

> He is not yet in a straight waistcoat. He has written and published another novel; and a London bookseller, with that desperate sort of courage which is nearly allied to madness, has republished it here. As it is in every respect a curiosity, and by no means destitute of interest, it may answer the purpose of the latter very well. . . .
>
> The style [is] a delightful jumble of bad English, worse German, superfine Irish, and elegant American. . . .
>
> If the author would only condescend to write intelligibly, and agreeably to the rules which govern other persons, he would yet, we think, notwithstanding his eccentricities, become eminent as a novelist. . . .
>
> There are a great many things to make us laugh in these volumes; the author's coarseness is often ridiculous, and always disagreeable. The conversation which he puts into the mouths of ladies and gentlemen is of that description which, in England, is only used by costermongers and hackney-coachmen, and their fair partners. The incidents are impossible, the style inflated, and the grammar deplorably vicious: and yet, with all this, there is so much talent, so much of surprisingly amusing madness, that we cannot blame it as we ought.

The *Monthly Review Enlarged*[6] is well-disposed, but not enthusiastic:

> [*Seventy-Six*] relates to the unfortunate contest between this country and the American colonies which raged in the year *seventeen hundred and seventy-six*. We know not that any good purpose can be answered by recalling the events of that lamentable warfare, vividly and painfully as they are here depicted to the eye, by one who certainly must have been an actor in them;

and whose sentiments are so violently anti-Anglican, and anti-monarchial, that they by no means soften the effect produced by his delineations.

Still the interest excited by this tale, and the command over our feelings which the writer exerts, are very far from trifling and ordinary. His energies are somewhat rough, indeed, but they are powerful; like much of his vast continent, not cultivated but fertile, not polished but naturally impressive; his battle pieces plunge us into the midst of them; [sic] and his hero is "every inch" a hero. . . .

The language of this narrative is often inelegant and peculiar.

Brother Jonathan seems to have called forth more comment than either of its predecessors. The *Literary Chronicle and Weekly Review,*[7] which had spoken with some favor of *Logan* and *Seventy-Six* became enthusiastic.

The work displays a vigour and pathos which are only to be found in novels of the first rank. In Brother Jonathan, there are scenes which the 'Great Unknown' might be proud to acknowledge; and the whole construction and management of the story is such as no person but an author possessing powers of the first order could have executed.

The attitude of the reviewer toward American institutions is shown in his praise of the people of New England for their devotion to freedom. He concludes: "We are sure our readers will agree with us, that there are few novels—few indeed, which display so much talent or possess such a fearful interest as *Brother Jonathan.*"

The *Lady's Magazine*[8] as usual gives many extracts and says nothing unfavorable, though its praise is not very significant:

We do not expect the high features of romance in tales connected with so new an establishment as the republic of the United States: yet pleasing and striking stories may be drawn by a man of talent from the varied incidents of American life and society; and the present author has contrived, by skilful management, to keep up a continuity of interest, instead of diffusing languor over the feelings of his readers.

Colburn's New Monthly Magazine[9] recognizes the identity of the author, saying, "These volumes are, it is said, the production of an American gentleman, who has contributed a series of articles on the literature of his country to the pages of one of our well-known periodical publications." It pronounces *Brother Jonathan* better than *Logan* and *Seventy-Six,* though still too extravagant: Of the characters it says: "His heroes and heroines, though worthy citizens of the United States, possess passions, and beauty, and language more powerful, more transcendent and more lofty than ever fell to the share of creatures not born in the land of romance. . . . Upon the whole, we regard *Brother Jonathan* as a work

of a very mixed character, though displaying throughout the marks of great intellectual power." The *Ladies Monthly Museum*[10] says that the "striking delineations of New England manners are interesting as well as amusing, notwithstanding their coarseness." The *Monthly Review Enlarged*[11] decides that "this novel, though published in Edinburgh, is, we have reason to believe, written by an American." It assumes that the object of such writers is "to communicate to strangers, by living pictures, a knowledge of the manners, habits, characters, and transactions of their countrymen of this present and former time." It finds that "in this work there are some traces of genius; . . . however, his work as a representation of life, is a failure." The plot is confused, the characters are contradictory and absurd; the descriptions and some of the dialogues have merit; "but the general character of the style is that of exaggeration." The *Dumfries Monthly Magazine*[12] also praises the descriptions, finds fault with the structure of the plot and the unreality of the incidents, and assumes that Neal portrays actual American life: "*Brother Jonathan* is the first publication of the kind that introduces us to anything like an accurate and Waverley-novel-kind of acquaintance with the inhabitants of the great continent—aborigines as well as colonists."

The *British Critic*[13] in the first of a series of two articles on American novels, says that Neal "has evidently formed his style on that of Brown in his wildest vagaries."

The characters described in Brown are downright men and women, whom, with all their weaknesses and eccentricities, we are almost sure we know or have known. Neal's dramatis personae are for the most part stalking moody spectres with glaring eyeballs and inflated nostrils, towering above the common height, and exhibiting the play of their muscles and veins through their clothes in the most trivial action; atrocious two-legged nightmares such as might have been engendered in the brains of Edgar Huntley, if he had washed down his raw panther collop with new Yankee rum, and slept in the reeking skin.

His able article on American writers, in *Blackwood's Magazine,* as well as much in his novels, shows him to be well worth the trouble of breaking in; and since, to judge from the conclusion of *Logan,* he is so jealous of English criticism, we will content ourselves with a matter-of-fact abstract of the said novel, the first of his works, and thus let him review himself.

Later the critic speaks of Neal as a Quaker broken loose.

In the second article of the series[14] he again has much to say of Neal. The most serious fault which he finds is that the reader cannot follow the story, or make out the relations of the characters to each other. He devotes most attention to *Seventy-Six,* in which he thinks the accounts of the treatment of American prisoners must be untrue, and remarks that Neal is inconsistent with his own professions in reviving offensive matters from the war. He raises the question whether the novelist in some passages is not "bantering himself and his own style of expression." He finds Jonathan Peters "an obvious plagiarism of Carwin." Of Neal's eccentricities and improbabilities he says:

> It is provokingly unaccountable that an author of the strong sense and acuteness evinced by Mr. Neal's articles in Blackwood, should thus persevere in outraging truth and nature; that with the power of conceiving and vividly executing characters of the stamp of the elder Oadley and his son Archibald, he should wilfully devote three huge close-printed volumes to the adventures of profligates, misanthropes, maniacs, liars, and louts, for such are the serious personages of **Brother Jonathan.** We are really at a loss to divine any thing like a moral or a leading idea in the book. . . .
>
> In the more familiar and every-day parts of the book, where nothing superfine or miraculous is attempted, the author is himself again. We are not only introduced to the wrestling matches and quilting frolics of the country, and divertingly jumbled in a stage waggon, passengers, pigs, gunpowder, hardware and all, but, which is better and more difficult, fairly seated round a New England fireside, a genial scene, we conceive, of that rough old-fashioned kindliness which marks our common origin. . . .

The *Edinburgh Literary Journal,*[15] in printing a poem, **"The Birth of a Poet,"** by John Neale [sic] pays this compliment:

> We doubt whether sufficient justice has hitherto been done in this country to the talents of the author of **Brother Jonathan.** His book is full of vigour and originality, making you feel at every page that you have to do with one who thinks freely, boldly, and efficaciously. It contains descriptions of scenery, and illustrations of the natural passions of the human heart and soul, worthy of that prodigious continent, whose hills are mountains, and whose mountains are immeasurable,—whose streams are rivers, and whose rivers are seas,—whose woods are forests, and whose forests are eternal. The verses we have now the pleasure of presenting to our readers, do credit even to the novelist.

The *Englishman's Magazine,* a short-lived periodical of little importance, gives to its review of Neal's **Authorship, a Tale** and **Rachael Dyer**[16] the title *England and the United States.* It bestows unstinted praise on Neal, who "exults in the name of Yankee, and Yankees should be proud of him." This article is bombastic enough to have been written by Neal himself. The *Westminster Review*[17] in its review of Miss Mitford's *Stories of American Life,* says, "There is no mistaking the hand of John Neal, whilom during his sojourn in England a collaborator of half our periodicals, and the author of some half hundred of unreadable romances." Some fairly severe criticism of Neal follows. The *Monthly Review*[18] describes **Authorship, a Tale** as "a common love story of our own Isle of Wight," and finds it of little moment.

There can be little question that part of Neal's vogue as a novelist after 1824 was due to his articles on American literature in *Blackwood's,* and to his comments on himself. In the opening article of the series[19] he names himself, with Brown and Paulding as one of the only three American writers who would not pass just as readily for English. He also praises himself in his discussion on Brown; and in the appropriate place in the alphabetical list he devotes eight pages to himself, in contrast to about a half page given to Cooper. Much of this discussion is given in quotation marks as the author's own judgment of himself, and it mingles some condemnation of faults with the praise. In a later article in *Blackwood's*[20] he asks the question, "Where shall we go for a North American story? Is there such a thing on earth?"; and answers in a footnote: "Yes, **Brother Jonathan** is a real North American story; and [Catharine Maria Sedgwick's] *Redwood,* we have reason to believe, is another, and a very good one." Englishmen were only too ready to accept his assertion that the roughness, oddity, and turgidity of his writings were distinctive American characteristics, and that his grotesque characters were truly representative of American life. He was one of the earliest of several Americans who were heartily welcomed because they conformed to the Englishman's uncomplimentary notions of what an American writer should be.

Notes

1. I (April, 1823) 102.

2. V (April 26, 1823) 282.

3. V (June 28, 1823) 409.

4. LV (July 1823) 545.

5. I (July 1823) 308.

6. CII (Oct. 1823) 212.

7. VII (July 16, 1825) 449.

8. VI (July 1825) 421.

9. XV (Aug. 1825) 362.

10. XIII (Aug. 1825) 102.

11. CVII (1825) 484.

12. I (Aug. 1825) 172.

13. II (April 1826) 53.

14. II (July 1826) 406.

15. I (May 9, 1829) 386.

16. I (April 1831) 65.

17. XIV (April 1831) 395.

18. n. and i. ser. (July 1831) p. 438.

19. *Blackwood's,* XVI (1824) 304.

20. XVIII (Sept. 1825) 317.

Alexander Cowie (essay date 1948)

SOURCE: Cowie, Alexander. "Contemporaries and Immediate Followers of Cooper, I." In *The Rise of the American Novel.* 1948. Reprint, pp. 165-227. New York: American Book Company, 1951.

[*In the following excerpt from an essay originally published in 1948, Cowie traces Neal's life and asserts that Neal's works merit scholarly consideration principally for their influence on more accomplished writers and as examples of American literary nationalism.*]

JOHN NEAL (1793-1875)

Among the contemporaries of [James Fenimore] Cooper none was more original than John Neal (1793-1875), a Maine Yankee of Scotch or English or Irish descent.[1] He was possessed of a limitless exuberance which explained both his success and his failure as a writer. His enormous ambition, his warm imagination, his generous sympathies, his passionate convictions, his genially quarrelsome nature, and his boundless egotism tempered by keen humor marked him as a man who must write vividly if at all. Unable or unwilling to discipline himself, however, he substituted a sort of wild improvisation for hard work. The violence and velocity of his early novels commanded instant attention but soon wearied the public. Story and style alike were splintered by the hurricane of his inspiration; and the reader, stunned by his experience, scarcely knew what had happened. With more art Neal might have rivalled Cooper as a writer of romance or Poe as an exponent of the tale of terror. In his rarer moods of quiet reflection he might have produced charming regional stories of New England. As it was, he never fully developed any one of his brilliant abilities. Accordingly Neal is now remembered chiefly as the eccentric and slightly choleric author of a few freakish novels and as a friend of Poe. Most of his books are out of print and they are largely inaccessible. Nevertheless no writer can be wholly ignored whose romances could intoxicate Hawthorne's "boyish brain."[2] In any case Neal deserves attention as an early experimenter with native materials in fiction and as a colorful critic of literature during the difficult days when American writers were just beginning to *be* American.

Neal was born in Portland, Maine. Destined to be a fighter all his life, he was brought up a Quaker. Capable of the most prodigious literary productivity, he spent twelve years in mercantile life. He was the commercial partner for a time of the poet John Pierpont, but they were forced into bankruptcy not long after the War of 1812. Neal profited, however, by his association with Pierpont, whose *Airs of Palestine,* published in 1816, presently made him one of the best-known poets in America. In Baltimore, Pierpont was one of the founders of a literary club, the "Delphians," and out of that club grew a magazine, the *Portico,* which was destined to be the theatre of Neal's first literary appearance. One day when Pierpont declined to write a review of Byron's works, Neal, who happened to be present at the time, intrepidly offered himself as a substitute. The offer was regarded as a joke by everyone but Neal. Then followed four frenzied days, during which "Jehu O'Cataract" (such was Neal's nickname and pen-name) read all of Byron's published works and produced a fifty-five page review, which was greeted enthusiastically upon its serial appearance in the *Portico.*[3] Thus Neal's career as a writer was characteristically launched. At the same time he was studying law, but although he was admitted to the Maryland bar in 1819, he practiced only intermittently: letters would be his prime vocation for the next decade or so at least.

Contributing to the *Portico* brought fame but not funds. Accordingly Neal dashed off a novel, peddled it unsuccessfully, rewrote it, changed its title, and finally "entrapped" a publisher, who paid him two hundred dollars for it. This, Neal's first novel, was published in 1817 under the title ***Keep Cool: A Novel.*** It is a story of a man who suffers remorse after killing his opponent in a duel. On the title page Neal facetiously referred to the book as "Written in Hot Weather, by Somebody." Apparently cold weather soon overtook the novel, and its author remained a nobody except to a small circle of friends who kept insisting that Neal was a genius. Neal himself later admitted that ***Keep Cool*** contained much of which "even a young writer might well be ashamed; much indeed that was boyish, if not absolutely childish."[4] During the interval between ***Keep Cool*** and his next novel, Neal was busy with a number of projects including writing poetry[5] and considerable literary hackwork, besides his law studies. In 1822 he reappeared as a novelist with ***Logan,*** which, though crude in many respects, was successful enough to encourage the author to write stories furiously for a number of years to come.

Logan, A Family History (1822) arose out of Neal's desire to see justice done to the Indian. The humanitarian interest in it—which, besides the plight of the Indian, touches on slavery,[6] imprisonment for debt, and capital punishment—is in fact considerable, but it is overshadowed by the amazing narrative of Logan and his family. Neal's Logan, an Englishman, is a partly real and partly legendary character—a sort of superman—married to an Indian queen. His gigantic stature and his implacably cruel temperament make him an ideal warrior-leader among the Indians. When part of his wife's family is murdered by white people he vows vengeance, but is prevented from consummating it when the Indians discover that *he* is a white man and attempt to kill him. On what he supposes to be his death bed he entreats Harold, his son, who has been brought up as an Indian, to take up the red man's burden. This ultimately involves Harold's going to England and addressing Parliament on behalf of the Indians. Returned to America, he is shot down by his father on the spot where his father was believed to have died. Actually Logan had lived on, a raving maniac, killing everyone who crossed his path. Harold's brother now completes the catastrophe by shooting Logan before he recognizes him as his own father. He himself soon after dies a madman. In the meantime many complications have been brought about by Harold's synchronous love for the wife of a governor who has befriended him and for Loena, an Indian princess, the last direct descendant of the historic old Indian chief Logan. Harold had taken Elvira (the governor's wife) by violence, but later suffered remorse, which was rendered the more acute by his discovery that his brother had once loved her too. His final devotion, however, had been to Loena—who upon Harold's death herself fell dead upon his body. It should be added in a story in which four out of the five principal characters apparently die and are reanimated, that these last-cited deaths are permanent.

Logan is not a nice story. Superstition, supernatural suggestions, brutality, sensuality, colossal hatred, delirium, rape, insanity, murder are the stuff out of which Neal weaves a Gothic tapestry never quite paralleled by Charles Brockden Brown or Poe. Characters live constantly on the peak of extreme emotions generally of the more horrible sort. On one occasion the heroine is fain to restore her failing strength by drinking the blood of a pigeon shot by Harold:

> He fired, and a pigeon came fluttering, from midheaven, almost to his feet. Loena started at the sound of the shot, and in the first terrour of the moment, shrieked to find herself alone. The next, her head was supported upon his knee, the bosom of the bird was laid open, and applied, bleeding, to her lips. She shut her eyes, in her loathing, but still, with an unconquerable eagerness, that showed how nearly famished she was, she pressed her mouth to it, and, if her newly opened eyes told true, she drew new life with the red moisture from its heart. Harold leant over her with looks of unutterable fondness.[7]

A fight is not complete without the most harrowing and sometimes incredible details:

> Their blades met. Harold was the more wary, the more lightning-like, but the stranger was bolder, and stronger. Both were resolute as death. Several wounds were given, and received. Harold's sword broke to the hilt. He threw himself upon the stranger and bore him to the earth, wrenched his sword from him, and twice, in his blindness and wrath attempted, in vain, to pass it

through and through his heart, as they grappled together. But twice the Englishman caught the sharp blade in his hands, and twice Harold drew it, by main force, through his clenched fingers, slowly severing sinew, and tendon, and flesh, and grating on the bones, as it passed. Harold gasped—the Englishman held him by the throat—the blood gushed from his ears and nostrils—once more!—he has succeeded! The blood has started through the pores of the brave fellow below him! His arteries are burst—He is dead—dead!—nailed to the earth, and Harold is sitting by him, blinded, and sick.

> A half hour has passed. The horse stamps, impatiently, by the corse. Why stands Harold thus, gazing upon the red ruin before him, with such a deadly hatred?[8]

The reader is at first shocked by the ghastly detail of the book, but he soon becomes calloused to further attack on his sensibilities, the more so because of the fact that in his hot pursuit of blood and bombast Neal allows the larger action of the story to become almost hopelessly confused.

Sometimes, however, Neal's penchant for horror carried him into psychological realms where his methods are a trifle less objectionable. His analysis of Harold's mental distress is distinctly suggestive of Poe in this respect:

> Alas, for Harold! A continual and confused ringing was about him, all night long. Worn, and trembling, and sick at heart, time appeared to stand still, as he turned, again and again, and adjusted his limbs to the rugged cordage, upon which he lay, until he was utterly exhausted.

> . . . . .

> And then his conscience would awake, and put on her bloody robes, and sit over him with a terrible countenance—and he would feel himself pinioned, naked, hand and foot—helpless, alone—with just enough of light to see the far off and dim movement of innumerable feet, incessantly approaching in the darkness, as of some cumbrous, and interminable monster—and to feel ten thousand detestable and obscene creatures crawling slowly over his very lips and eyes, which he had no power to shut—slimy, loathsome reptiles, slipping lazily over his naked fingers; while his very flesh crawled and quivered, and rotted, in the poison that they left in their trail. Anon, this would be changed. The light would break out upon him—he would be sleeping in a delicious green solitude—the earth flowering all about him, with fountains flowing 'in odour and gold'—and violets—'but the trail of the serpent was over them all.' He would lie, *so* happy, so purely, so perfectly happy—he would feel an approaching face—his hair would be stirred by a gentle breathing—he would awake, and behold two miniature pictures of himself—a pair of the loveliest blue eyes over him, dissolving in lustre—with an image of himself in each—damp, luminous—transparent—like the swimming azure of heaven—or violets exhaling colour, and substance, and perfume, all in the red sunshine!

> . . . . .

> Then, a strange obscurity would arise, like the vapour of charnel houses, offensive and sickening—and some

other violent transition would succeed, alternately—from heaven to hell, from hell to heaven, would he vibrate, like a pendulum.

> 'It was, as if the dead could feel
> The icy worm around them steal;
> And shudder, as the reptiles creep,
> And revel in their rotting sleep;
> Without the power to scare away
> The cold consumers of their clay;'

And then, as if the very dead were suddenly thrilling with life, and borne away—to the tranquillest climes:

> Where—'light breezes *but* ruffle the flowers sometimes.'[9]

A gruesome scene certainly, and yet a scene betokening uncommon literary powers. Poe was guilty of similar extravagant indulgences in *The Narrative of A. Gordon Pym* and elsewhere, but on other occasions Poe exercised that artistic restraint which was almost completely foreign to Neal. *Logan* maintains its dizzying pace throughout. The public read it with astonishment. Some persons took it seriously as an almost epic work; others "took it as they took opium, or exhilarating gas."[10]

Having once well begun to write novels Neal continued with the feverish intensity which characterized his activity throughout life. No less than three novels appeared bearing the date 1823. *Seventy-Six* was avowedly suggested by, though not imitative of, Cooper's *Spy*.[11] Its psychological content is greater than that of Cooper's Revolutionary stories, and it gives space to discussions of love and passion that Cooper, if he read the book, must have regarded as unwholesome. Mainly, however, *Seventy-Six* was a patriotic tale of adventure. Not Neal's most original work, it was possibly, as Neal thought, his best story.[12]

Randolph (1823) is a story (in letter form) so full of inflammable comment on current events and on celebrities of all sorts—writers, painters, orators, statesmen—that it was "received like a lighted-thunderbolt, dropped into a powder magazine."[13] Neal was not a malicious man by nature, but he was sometimes dreadfully plainspoken in his adverse comments. At all times he was supremely confident in his judgments. The story of *Randolph* as such is slight and chaotic: its burden is to dispel the clouds around a mysterious, fascinating young "villain" and finally show him forth as a hero. A contemporary reviewer remarked that "the various incidents have about as much coherence as the thoughts of a maniac."[14] At the same time the reviewer discerned signs of real power in Neal—power which, in the reviewer's opinion, was destined never to be controlled:

> We think Mr. Neal a man of unquestionable and inexhaustible resources. We know him personally, and have wondered at his energy and power of achievement. We always believed him possessed of a moral and intellectual nature, which, with due culture and discipline, might have borne most rare and valuable fruits. But it is too late . . . and . . . we cannot resist the conviction, that either from some inherent defect in his disposition or faculties, or from the irresistible dominion of confirmed habit, he never will be other than what he is—a man whose talents are various and powerful, but perverted and worse than useless.[15]

But Neal was soon to be visited with more material protest against his arbitrary judgments of men. The book had appeared anonymously, and indeed the author gravely included his own literary portrait (with his name deliberately misspelled "Neale") among the celebrities. But the authorship was soon guessed. One of the sparks from *Randolph* inflamed Edward C. Pinkney, the poet, to the point of challenging Neal to a duel on account of his disparaging comments on Pinkney's father, who died just after the book was written. Here was an irony indeed: that a man who had written a book (*Keep Cool*) in denunciation of duelling should himself be called to the "field of honor." Neal conceived that he could best show his originality by ignoring the challenge (even though he was stigmatized as "craven" for his restraint and, it was whispered, "soundly thrashed" as well), and he utilized the whole affair in his next novel, *Errata, or the Works of Will Adams* (1823), "purporting to be the confessions of a coward."[16]

Despite the mixed reception of his books, Neal had received enough commendation, including favorable foreign comment,[17] to lead him to believe that he could swing a literary career abroad. Accordingly, having made arrangements for the accommodation of his legal clients, he sailed for England, arriving there January 8, 1824. The *Quarterly*'s impudent inquiry as to "who reads an American book" had aroused his ire as it did Paulding's, and he proposed to

> see what might be done, with a fair field, and no favor, by an American writer. Irving had succeeded; and, though I was wholly unlike Irving, why shouldn't I? Cooper was well received; and I had a notion, that, without crossing his path, or poaching upon his manor, I might do something, so American, as to secure the attention of an Englishman.[18]

He was confident of his own high powers, and he knew that he could "write faster than any man that ever yet lived."[19] Personally he was well received, and he lived for a time with Jeremy Bentham in the capacity of secretary. His literary work consisted chiefly of articles written for *Blackwood's Magazine*.[20] In his first article he pretended to be an English traveler writing his impression of America—even referring again to "Neal" as if to another writer—for he "had good reason to believe, that communications from an American, if he did not abuse America, would go into the Balaam-basket."[21] After an initial success he became a regular contributor to *Blackwood's* and received very satisfactory sums for his work, though nothing comparable to what Irving could ask. His aim in his periodical writing was to present a series of brief, vivid sketches of American writers from an impartial point of view. The sketches, done entirely from memory, were often faulty in factual detail, occasionally unfair in judgments, but generally rich in acute critical perceptions.

Neal came to London with high hopes of becoming a permanent addition to the literary coterie there. He expected to pour forth novels which would make his name forever illustrious. But despite the fact that *Logan* and *Seventy-Six* had been promptly pirated in England, he found London publishers strangely indifferent to his actual presence and his proffer of new manuscripts. Indeed it was only after he had completely rewritten it a second time that he finally secured a publisher (Blackwood of Edinburgh) for his next novel *Brother Jonathan: or, The New Englanders* (1824).

Brother Jonathan, the longest of Neal's novels, is about as much of a hodge-podge as anything he wrote: reviewers complained that they couldn't even follow the story. It differs from the other novels in containing (besides rant and rubbish) a considerable amount of local realism pertaining to New England.[22] The action of the story is set in Ginger Town, Connecticut, beginning about a year before the Battle of Lexington. Here a stranger arrives—one Jonathan Peters, a mysterious, sorrowful person about whose past nothing can be learned. He can talk down the preacher, the lawyer, and the military, and he is a vaguely awe-inspiring man—not unlike a character out of Hawthorne. Perhaps he is the spirit of the times: "It was [says Neal] a time of rebellion. A whole people had become rebels. It was a time of warfare and sedition.—The face of Jonathan Peters corresponded finely with it . . ."[23] Presently Peters is swept up in the welter of the Revolutionary War: he is suspected as a spy, his house is burned. But he has a personal problem as well as a political one, for he enters into a controversy with one Abraham Harwood, a minister, over the latter's too harsh treatment of his son. A reader oriented in the American novel of this period naturally suspects that Harwood's "son" is in reality the son of Peters—and this proves to be the case. But many, far too many, other matters arise to complicate the story of *Brother Jonathan*; and in the end, the reader, wearied by an anarchy of incident, takes what comfort he may in the incidental New England lore distributed throughout the book. The book is drenched with superstition, prophecy, and legend. It contains pages of Yankee dialect, carefully marked by Neal to indicate proper stresses in pronunciation. It tells of a New England husking, a "raising," a quilting "frolick."[24] Quaker dialect, dress, and customs receive authoritative and none too complimentary treatment by Neal.[25] To see unity in the vast conglomeration of *Brother Jonathan* is impossible. Perhaps Neal thought he was expressing all of

New England in its various aspects—political, personal, domestic, household—at the time of a crisis. A few reviewers were favorable toward the book, but almost all of them were puzzled by it. One critic compared Neal with Charles Brockden Brown, to the disparagement of the former:

> The characters described in Brown are downright men and women, whom, with all their weaknesses and eccentricities, we are almost sure we know or have known. Neal's dramatis personae are for the most part stalking moody spectres with glaring eye-balls and inflated nostrils, towering above the common height, and exhibiting the play of their muscles and veins through their clothes in the most trivial action; atrocious two-legged nightmares such as might have been engendered in the brains of Edgar Huntley, if he had washed down his raw panther collop with new Yankee rum, and slept in the reeking skin.[26]

The same critic suggested that Jonathan Peters was plagiarized from Brown's Carwin, and added his regret that Neal should have

> devote[d] three huge closely-printed volumes to the adventures of profligates, misanthropes, maniacs, liars, and louts, for such are the serious personages of *Brother Jonathan.* We are really at a loss to divine any thing like a moral or a leading idea in the book . . .[27]

In 1827, after about three and a half years spent abroad, Neal returned to America. He was received none too warmly by his compatriots at Portland, Maine. Occasionally he was assailed in language as unrestrained as his own.[28] His works were not being reissued in this country. New writers were competing for public favor, and Neal's flare as a novelist would seem to have burned out. Yet he was as cocky as ever, and he was far from finished with literature. Many more stories were yet to come from his pen, and he was to be connected with a number of journalistic ventures. The first of these latter after his return from Europe was the establishment of *The Yankee,* a weekly newspaper, as editor of which Neal gave Poe "the very first words of encouragement" he remembered having received in print.[29] As for fiction, he wrote *Rachel Dyer* (1828), *Authorship* (1830), *The Down-easters* (1833), *True Womanhood* (1859), besides a number of dime novels produced in the 1860's. Of the novels, perhaps the most fruitful for modern readers is *Rachel Dyer* (1828), not only because it constitutes an early treatment of an important American theme but because it reveals a new aspect of Neal as a writer.

Rachel Dyer is in several respects Neal's best novel. He seems to have turned to the subject of witchcraft not as a professional writer in quest of "copy" but as a genuine student of early American history. Nor was he interested merely in the external history of the Salem tragedies, with their gruesome data of torture and death;

rather, he sought to incorporate these data in a story which should lead finally to a philosophical understanding of the whole phenomenon. He does not indicate his sympathy with the victims of witchcraft by the simple expedient of railing at the judges. He tries, as his preface shows, to be objective:

> I would call the attention of our novel-writers and our novel-readers to what is undoubtedly native and peculiar, in the early history of our Fathers; I would urge them to believe that though there is much to lament in that history, there is nothing to conceal; that if they went astray, as they most assuredly did in the judgments, they went astray conscientiously, with what they understood to be the law of God in their right hands.[30]

An introductory first chapter bespeaks the reader's imaginative sympathy even with those of our ancestors who were deluded. After all, they had their warrant in Scripture, their precedent in the statutes of the mother-country. Most of all, the belief in witchcraft was a natural one in man:

> We may smile now to hear witchcraft spoken seriously of; but we forget perhaps that a belief in it is like a belief in the after appearance of the dead among the blue waters, the green graves, the still starry atmosphere and the great shadowy woods of our earth; or like the beautiful deep instinct of our nature for worship,—older than the skies, it may be, universal as thought, and sure as the steadfast hope of immortality.[31]

The tale itself, of course, does not attempt to exculpate the leaders of the Salem persecutions.[32] Rather it is focussed upon the victims of the delusion and on their heroic, pitiful efforts to oppose it. Action begins with the partly mischievous, partly nervous behavior of the children whose complaints led to the rapid spread of hysteria, and it ends with brief allusion to the recantation of Sewall. Dynamic courtroom scenes bring out the full horror of the situation. Persons actually involved in the Salem tragedies appear in active roles: Samuel Parris (called Matthew Paris in the novel), Samuel Sewall, Increase and Cotton Mather, the Indian Tituba, Sarah Good, George Burroughs, and others.[33] The hero of the story is George Burroughs, the minister, who carries on courageously against impossible odds, including distorted evidence. The heroine is Rachel Dyer, a Quaker woman "without youth or beauty,"[34] who is drawn into the vortex of suspicion and hatred by reason of her association with the minister Burroughs. Toward the end of the book a moving scene occurs in a dungeon cell when Burroughs beseeches Rachel to save herself by confessing: her confession, he believes, will delay her execution until the accusers are themselves accused. But Rachel disdains to "save herself by a lie." When she in turn asks him if he means to confess, he pleads that as "a preacher of the word of truth" he would be unable to force his conscience. Elizabeth, a sister of Rachel, who also refuses to confess, is saved by an ill-

ness which delays legal action. But Burroughs is executed, and Rachel's execution is appointed for the following day. As it turns out, Rachel is spared the gallows, for when the executioners come for her, she is found in her last "sleep," her arm thrown over the Bible she has been reading. The novel ends as quietly as it had begun. No unnecessary exploitation of physical or mental distress has been resorted to, for Neal was so deeply moved by the cruel errors he was recording, that he was fain to let the most agonizing events speak for themselves. A kind of sombre repose characterizes the style of *Rachel Dyer*. Constrained, perhaps, by his great theme, Neal for once abandoned his literary monkey-shines and wrote in simple sincerity of real people whose tragedy was the heavier for having resulted from the religious convictions of their oppressors.

Even *Rachel Dyer*, arresting as it is, has now passed into oblivion for all but historians and special students.[35] Neal left no single work of fiction which deserves to be revived for its sheer merit. In most of his stories he was the victim of his own lust for words. In his torrential flow of uninhibited language he surprisingly foreshadows Thomas Wolfe, but he is even less controlled than Wolfe. Whatever idea or image came to the surface of his subconscious mind was hastily tumbled on to his page, wholly unedited by his judgment. Inevitably he reaped the harvest of haste: poor proportion, loose ends, slip-shod diction, and general incoherence. As if to make up for these defects, he tried to hold the reader by the passionate intensity of his expression. But the reader finally fled from such disorder and violence.

What, then, can be the excuse for regarding Neal as of any consequence in the history of American literature? The answer can only be that, however badly he used them, he possessed extraordinary literary powers. Flashes of something very like genius gleamed from his most gaudy pages. Critics who were aghast at Neal's excesses could not forbear to praise his brilliance. Poe regarded him highly.[36] Hawthorne fed—selectively, one may be sure—at the mountainous repast Neal offered. Moreover in a day when the average literary ambition of Americans yearned toward an Irving-like success in the Anglo-American essay, Neal sturdily mined his native land for materials. Crude ore he undoubtedly turned up for the most part, but along with it came more valuable materials which the curious amateur of Americana may yet discover in John Neal of Portland, Maine.

For it never could be forgotten that Neal was staunchly loyal, first to his section[37] and then to his nation. From a practical point of view perhaps this has been his greatest service: that he energized American literature at a time when such a service was badly needed. Sometimes he wrote scornfully of his fellow-American writers as sycophantic; sometimes he singled out individual writers for attack. But always his aim was to stimulate more and better narrative production. His gibes were tonic in effect. Thus in the second preface to **Rachel Dyer** he wrote:

> The British are a nation of writers. Their novel-writers are as a cloud. True—true—but they still want something which they have not. They want a real American writer—one with courage enough to write in his native tongue. *That* they have not, even at this day. *That* they never had. Our best writers are English writers, not American writers. They are English in every thing they do, and in every thing they say, as authors—in the structure and moral of their stories, in their dialogue, speech and pronunciation, yea in the very characters they draw. Not so much as one true Yankee is to be found in any of our native books: hardly so much as one true Yankee phrase. Not so much as one true Indian, though you hardly take up a story on either side of the water now, without finding a red-man stowed away in it; and what sort of a red-man? Why one that uniformly talks the best English the author is capable of—more than half the time perhaps out-Ossianing Ossian.
>
> I have the modesty to believe that in some things I am unlike all the other writers of my country—both living and dead; although there are not a few, I dare say who would be glad to hear of my bearing a great resemblance to the latter. For my own part I do not pretend to write English—that is, I do not pretend to write what the English themselves call English—I do not, and I hope to God—I say this reverently, although one of their Reviewers may be again puzzled to determine "whether I am swearing or praying" when I say so—that I never shall write what is now worshipped under the name of *classical* English. It is no natural language—it never was—it never will be spoken alive on this earth: and therefore, ought never to be written. We have dead languages enough now; but the deadest language I ever met with or heard of, was that in use among the writers of Queen Anne's day.[38]

It was not easy to produce a good indigenous literature; Neal recognized as much in 1822 when (in **Randolph**) he cited the usual obstacles to such an end. Yet it is to be observed that Neal answered his own objections and that at bottom he is optimistic:

> But in our country, there is every thing to discourage a novelist—nothing to incite him. The very name . . . of a novel writer would be a perpetual reproach to a man of genius . . . We have no old castles—no banditti—no shadow of a thousand years to penetrate—but what of that. We have men and women—creatures that God himself hath fashioned and filled with character. And what more do we want? . . . You laugh at my enthusiasm. I am sure of it. But why need we go back to the past for our heroes?—There is no such necessity; and he who shall first dare to grapple with the *present,* will triumph, in this country. Remember, my prediction.
>
> Another very serious reason why, whatever were the merit of our writers, we could not enter into competition with the men of Europe is, that we cannot afford to write for nothing; and yet, if we would write for nothing; and *give* the copy right of a novel, for in-

stance, to a publisher, it would still be a perilous adventure to him. Shall I tell you the reason? Our booksellers here can publish your costliest poems, and novels, and dramas, without any expense for the copyright. You give Byron or Moore five thousand guineas for a poem; and, in forty days, there will be an American edition published here, for the copy right of which, our publishers have not given a cent. Names will sell anything. We all know that . . .

> But will this last forever? No. The time is rapidly approaching, when, it will be enough to sell a work, if it be called American. We are getting to feel a national pride; and men are already beginning to put in their title pages, "*by an American*"—and "*an American Tale*"—words, that, a few years ago, would have been as politick, as "by a Choctaw" or "*or a Narragansett tale.*"[39]

It was in this spirit that John Neal wrote. He could be pugnacious, whimsical, blood curdling, or idealistic in his own writing. He could attack his contemporaries smartly. But finally he was an eager apostle of American literature. He lived so long that he was lost to view the nation over. In 1846 Hawthorne wrote that Neal must be dead: "else he never could keep himself so quiet."[40] No, Neal was not dead, he had merely contracted his circle of activity. Within that circle (finally no larger than Portland, Maine) he lived on until 1875.

Notes

1. Neal never was sure what strain predominated, but he inclined to regard himself as Scotch.

2. "P's Correspondence," *Mosses from an Old Manse* (Boston, 1864), II, 159.

3. John Neal, *Wandering Recollections of a Somewhat Busy Life: An Autobiography,* Boston, 1869, pp. 193-95.

4. *Ibid.,* p. 221.

5. His first book of verse, *The Battle of Niagara,* appeared in 1818.

6. Neal, however, "opposed the extreme abolitionist views of William Lloyd Garrison" just as he also disapproved "the extreme prohibitionism of his distant cousin Neal Dow." Irving T. Richards, "The Life and Works of John Neal," *Summaries of Harvard Theses 1933,* Cambridge, 1934, p. 297.

7. *Logan,* Philadelphia, 1822, I, 242.

8. *Ibid.,* I, 216.

9. *Ibid.,* I, 291-94.

10. *Wandering Recollections,* p. 224.

11. "I had got charged to the muzzle with the doings of our Revolutionary fathers, while writing my portion of 'Allen's History,' and wanted only the hint, or touch, that Cooper gave in passing, to go

off like a Leyden jar, and empty myself at once of all the hoarded enthusiasm I had been bottling up, for three or four years." *Wandering Recollections,* p. 224.

12. *Seventy-Six* seems to have had its extremely loyal devotees. Of one lady reader, it was said—in phrasing slightly ambiguous—that she "died with 'Seventy-Six' in her hand." *Ibid.,* p. 228.

13. *Ibid.,* p. 229.

14. *The United States Literary Gazette* (April 1, 1824) I, 6.

15. *Ibid.*

16. *Wandering Recollections,* p. 238.

17. See Cairns, *British Criticisms of American Writings 1815-1833,* pp. 208-10.

18. *Wandering Recollections,* p. 239.

19. *The New York Mirror* (September 28, 1833), XI, 101, quoted in *American Writers, A Series of Papers Contributed to Blackwood's Magazine (1824-1825) by John Neal,* ed. by F. L. Pattee, Durham (N. C.), 1937, Introduction, p. 15.

20. The articles Neal wrote for *Blackwood's* have been collected and reprinted by F. L. Pattee. See note above. Neal seems to have written for a number of other periodicals as well (see Pattee's Introduction, p. 19, n. 18), but he addressed himself chiefly to *Blackwood's* as "the cleverest, the sauciest, and the most unprincipled of all our calumniators." *Wandering Recollections,* p. 245.

21. *Wandering Recollections,* p. 246.

22. Indeed the entire subject of Neal as a New England writer still awaits detailed treatment. In his *Flowering of New England* Van Wyck Brooks refers to Neal's novels as valueless. Actually there is in them a great deal of native material which would have been germane to Mr. Brooks' study.

23. *Brother Jonathan,* Edinburgh, 1824, I, 17.

24. *Ibid.,* I, 52, 53 ff.

25. *Ibid.,* II, 166-70.

26. *British Critic* (April, 1826) II, 53, quoted in Cairns, p. 212.

27. *Ibid.,* II, 406. Quoted in Cairns, p. 213.

28. In 1829 he was accorded these plain terms of contempt: "Your ravings are the dreams of a sick monkey—and your ideas hang as awkwardly together as so many bits of old rope spliced by a land lubber. Look at your novels. Why, you can't, to save your ears, sell them for four-pence the bushel. After having been a 'poor Devil Author' so long as to be starved first out of America into G. Britain, and back again into America, it hardly looks well in you to put on airs, and swagger as is your wont. Be modest, John, be modest—you never *did* support yourself by your pen, and you never *will* . . ." Quoted in *The Ariel, A Semimonthly Literary and Miscellaneous Gazette* (July, 1829) III, 44.

29. A. H. Quinn, *Edgar Allan Poe, a Critical Biography,* New York, 1941, p. 154. The favorable notice appeared in *The Yankee* in September, 1829.

30. *Rachel Dyer: A North American Story,* Portland, 1828, Preface, p. iv.

31. *Ibid.,* p. 22.

32. Although for the most part calm in his treatment of the Massachusetts elders, Neal allows himself to draw a rather satiric portrait of Governor Phipps, who is represented as unduly covetous of power and rank. Indeed Neal enlarges his satire at one point to include all New England—a place, he says, "where birth is now, and ever will be a matter of inquiry and solicitude, of shame perhaps to the few and of pride to the few, but of inquiry with all, in spite of our ostentatious republicanism." *Rachel Dyer,* p. 45.

33. In an appendix Neal supplies certain "Historical Facts" which he used or altered for purposes of his story.

34. *Rachel Dyer,* p. 148. Rachel's lack of physical charm makes it the harder for her to secure a fair trial, for (she says) although there might be "some hope on earth for a beautiful witch. . . . with golden hair. . . . with large blue eyes. . . . and a sweet mouth," there can be no real hope for "a freckled witch. . . . with red hair and a hump on her back." *Ibid.,* p. 262.

35. Oddly enough, *Rachel Dyer* turns up in the conversation of two characters in a novel published in 1861—G. W. Curtis's *Trumps.*

36. Poe, who recognized Neal's limitations, was nevertheless "inclined to rank John Neal first, or at all events second, among our men of indisputable *genius.*" *Marginalia.* As late as 1843 Poe was hoping to secure the aid of Neal for his projected *Penn Magazine.* Quinn, *Edgar Allan Poe,* p. 366.

37. For his satirical comments on New York, see *Brother Jonathan,* II, 336 ff.

38. *Rachel Dyer,* Portland, 1828, Unpublished Preface to the North-American Stories, p. xv.

39. *American Writers,* ed. by Pattee, pp. 236-37.

40. *Mosses,* II, 159.

John J. Seydow (essay date 1973)

SOURCE: Seydow, John J. "The Sound of Passing Music: John Neal's Battle for American Literary Independence." *Costerus* 7 (1973): 153-82.

[*In the following essay, Seydow assesses Neal's oeuvre to provide context for the author's assertion of American literary nationalism in his "Unpublished Preface" to* Rachel Dyer.]

The year 1828 is a pivotal one in American civilization, a year in which the previously submerged battle for literary independence from England surfaced in the form of a capable militia of skilled, pen-wielding apologists.

In that year Andrew Jackson was elected President of the United States; and, almost overnight, the "people" of America symbolically attained the opportunity and equality granted them by the Constitution some forty years before. In that year, a "revolution" of another kind was announced by the publication of Noah Webster's "American" Dictionary, the preface to which proclaimed, in a militantly nationalistic tone, that the United States was now equal to England in population, and that in "arts and sciences, our citizens are very little behind the most enlightened people on earth; in some respects, they have no superiors."[1] With the appearance in 1828 of *Notions of the Americans*—"an attempt to answer what he believed to be gross misrepresentations by a full and calm presentation of the facts in the clear light of the democratic faith"—[2]James Fenimore Cooper, in the guise of a British traveler, is seen propagating a view of the American people diametric to the widespread British calumnies of them, incidentally observing that "it is rather a striking feature in the character of the lower orders of the Americans, that they rarely lose their native attachments. They have a great and fixed contempt for all monarchies."[3] Also in 1828, in what purported to be merely another "travel book," James Kirke Paulding castigated the English writer-traveler who exploited America by deriding the gaucheries of her people in order to sate a British audience eager for sardonic accounts of American callowness.[4]

But the most significant national literary outburst in America, likewise occurring in 1828, appeared in the preface to a novel by John Neal (1793-1876), **Rachel Dyer.** With the warning that his preface is only for "those who are interested for the encouragement of our national literature," Neal tells his readers what determined him to write the novel: "I was an American. I had heard the insolent question of a Scotch Reviewer, repeated on every side of me by native Americans— 'Who reads an American book?' I could not bear this—I could neither eat nor sleep till my mind was made up."[5] Although Paulding had earlier that same year used this question as an excuse for spawning more anglophobic

vituperation,[6] and despite the fact that Neal himself had recalcitrantly reiterated the "Scotch Reviewer's" taunt some four years previous,[7] **Rachel Dyer** emerged as the first real rebuttal of Sydney Smith's "verdict" of American literature.[8]

For, of course, it was the Reverend Sydney Smith who, in 1820, in the *Edinburgh Review,* rhetorically queried a largely partisan audience, "In the four quarters of the globe, who reads an American book?" It is difficult to believe that Smith's indictment about the primitive state of American letters remained unchallenged for so long, and perhaps only coincidental that the answer to that challenge should finally appear coeval with several American artists' articulated search for national identity. Whatever the reason, the actual intrusion of so many significant cultural documents upon the American scene in such a relatively brief time span argues the importance of the year 1828 for all Americans.

II

Among students of American literature, Sydney Smith is not unknown. But those same students may still ask, and perhaps rightly so, "Who is John Neal?" A recent critic justifies his mention of Neal by pointing out that he was an "apostle of American literature." Earlier critics praised Neal for writing the best criticism in America until the late nineteenth century, for being an early defender of American writers, for being the "archcritic" of his times, and for being the first "ambassador to the British, of American literature." One of Neal's contemporaries noted that he was the first American to "gain a living by literature," while another declared that Neal was "first, or at all events second, among our men of indisputable *genius.*"[9]

Edgar Allan Poe was the latter critic who ranked Neal so high among his contemporary Americans, and he had at least one very good reason for doing so. Neal's 1829 review amounted to, in Poe's words, "The very first words of Encouragement I ever remember to have heard";[10] and Neal gave the young poet "the first jog in my [Poe's] literary career."[11] In gratitude for being the first critic to publish a review of his poetry, a review which probably secured him a publisher for *Al Aaraaf, Tamerlane, and Minor Poems,*[12] Poe dedicated "Tamerlane" to John Neal.

Neal was also acknowledged by others of America's literati. He was a lifelong friend of Longfellow and, by his own admission, was the first critic to encourage Whittier as a poet.[13] He was a charter member of the Delphian Club in Baltimore, whose membership boasted such names as H. H. Brackenridge, John Howard Payne, Francis Scott Key, William Wirt, and Rembrandt Peale, and whose avowed purpose was mutual stimulation "to contribute to the progress of American letters."[14] He was also the first American writer to appear in the British quarterlies,[15] where he demonstrated his knowledgeableness of his native American literature in a series of anonymous articles written for *Blackwood's* in 1824 and 1825, an achievement which Howard Mumford Jones praises as the first attempt at American literary history.[16] Finally, in his novel *Randolph,* in his reviews in the *Portico* and *Yankee,* and in the prefaces to and contents of his many novels, John Neals exhibits a lifelong dedication to American literature and its practitioners.

III

John Neal's literary talents were manifold, but to discover them, and their contribution to America's battle for literary independence, it is essential to study the large body of material which he published prior to *Rachel Dyer* and the critical year of 1828. For if Neal was not America's most prolific writer of the first half of the nineteenth century, he was certainly its most rapid.

Between June, 1816 and November, 1823 he had written "fifteen or twenty volumes, large duodecimos," and newspaper and magazine articles "equal to at least six or eight volumes more." Neal also states that from October, 1821 to March, 1822 he "wrote and published no less than eight large duodecimos, which in England would have been equal to thirteen volumes; and this while pursuing my law studies, and writing for the *Telegraph* and the *Portico.*"[17]

Neal's first novel, published anonymously, was *Keep Cool* (1817), a partly comic, partly didactic tract against duelling. It has been damned by one critic as "immature," while another, referring to Neal's facetious subtitle, "Written in Hot Weather, by Somebody," concludes, "Apparently cold weather soon overtook the novel, and its author remained a nobody except to a small circle of friends who kept insisting that Neal was a genius."[18]

Neal's attitude toward the novel varied. In 1825, he wrote: "Much to the credit of my country, *Keep Cool* is forgotten: or, where it is known at all, is looked upon as a disgrace to her literature—perhaps to myself. I am glad of it." However, in his autobiography Neal insists that the characters and situations of the novel are "worthy of great praise," that the story is "dramatic, and earnest and plausible," and that the language is "far beyond the trash of the hour." He brags of the $200 he received for the novel, adding, "It seems a pitiful sum now for an American novel; but then, it was something handsome, since he [the publisher] could have the best English novels, in print, for nothing; and Charles Brockden Brown . . . got even less for *Ormond, Wieland,* and *Edgar Huntley.*" But perhaps the most telling effect which the novel produced is seen in an anecdote which Neal good-naturedly relates. He tells of dining at the house of a friend, and after dinner being taken into his host's library and handed the first volume of *Keep Cool,* "a tattered, dirty-looking book, the dog-eared leaves hardly kept in place by the cover, so much had it been used." After Neal "had sufficiently admired it," his host handed him the second volume, "which appeared quite new and fresh." Neal's only comment is that he hoped his friend enjoyed the joke as thoroughly as he.[19]

Although *Keep Cool* suffers as a novel—it is vague, partially incoherent, with poorly subordinated and disconnected subplots, and obtrusive puns—it is important in the canon of Neal's work because it introduces many of the themes which he later develops, and issues and ideas which he later propagandizes in his championing of American literary pride. It is also an American novel which, in those times of unprotected copyright, a publisher was willing to pay for.

Neal wittily prefaces the novel with his own review of it, in the first part of which he remarks, in the persona of an American reviewer:

> There seems to be a curse resting upon American scholarship and taste; and that taste, to *us* appears to be nothing less, than an egregious emulation;—a preposterous and idle ambition of doing something for the literary reputation of *our* country. True patriotism would inform *us* that the only way to do honour to *our* country, is to be silent.[20]

Then, reemerging in his own voice, Neal makes explicit his denunciation of that kind of American reviewer: "Reviewers suppose themselves to be, in the republick of letters, what our legislators are, in our national assemblies; the collective wisdom of our country;—the representatives of judgment and intellect;—the concentrated majesty of opinion. The body of the people are their slaves" (I, xv-xvi).

For years Neal continued this vendetta against the American reviews for their deprecation of native material, and their obeisance to British writers and British tastes. Thus, in one novel the chief character pillories Robert Walsh and the *North American Review* for omitting native American works in favor of "the refuse haberdashery of Great Britain," continuing, with nationalistic fervor:

> Are our reviews to be made up on that [British] side of the atlantic, and republished under the title of Walsh's Museum?—Or, as in the North American, are they to be confined to the works of another people; and now and then, as it will sometimes happen, of a *native* writer, after they have been amazed at meeting with his name in some European journal. . . . I am an American—I glory in the name. Were I an Englishman, I should glory in the name of an Englishman. But then, as now, I should lift up my voice, in unqualified denunciation of such conduct in my countrymen.[21]

In like manner, while writing in 1825 in the guise of an Englishman for *Blackwood's,* Neal declared that the American journals had done the literary people of the United States "little or no good," and that *Blackwood's,* severe as it had been in pointing out the faults of American writers, had "positively done more for their *encouragement,* fifty times over, than all their own journals together; and all of ours—except our own."[22] As late as 1828, in his preface to *Rachel Dyer,* Neal is still berating the *North American* and other native reviews for their lack of patriotism in failing to befriend American writers and their work (p. x). Therefore, in **Keep Cool,** when one young lady asks another if the poem they just heard recited by an American gentleman was a good one, and receives the response that "I am not sufficiently familiar with the English poets to judge" (I, 126), one realizes that Neal is making one more satirical comment on the heinous effect produced by that "concentrated majesty of opinion."

In his next published work, the **Battle of Niagara** (1818), a poem based on the War of 1812, Neal declared that he was again more concerned with propagating "American scenery and American character" than in versifying "the minutiae of battles."[23] E. T. Channing favorably reviewed the work in the *North American Review,* but felt that Neal had failed to achieve his announced goal, declaring that he, Channing, was "much better satisfied with the subject than the treatment."[24] Neal was actually attempting in the poem to set an American scene in American scenery, with the hope of an American character—heroic in stature and epic in proportion—arising out of the conflict. Channing admired what Neal was trying to do—the War of 1812 being the ideal "subject" from which the "national" American could emerge—but he felt that the work ultimately suffered from vagueness.

Despite its shortcomings, the poem does serve as a vehicle for advancing several of Neal's "causes." In speculating on the possibility of a favorable reception of the poem, Neal feels that, if it has merit, his countrymen will acknowledge it, "if not at this time, they will at some future hour when it shall have become the fashion for Americans to respect themselves" (p. iii). This optimism for the future respectability of American letters reiterates the patriotic confidence which Neal first displayed in the preface to **Keep Cool**; and just as the source of confidence in that novel lay in "our cataracts—our rivers—our mountains,"[25] so the American landscape is at the heart of this nationalistic paean in the preface to **"Niagara"**:

> My country,! my home! sunny land of my fathers!
>   Where empires unknown in bright solitude lie;
> Where Nature, august in serenity gathers
>   The wonders of mountain, and ocean, and sky:
> Where the blue dome of heaven scarce bounds her dominion;

> Where man is as free as the creatures of air;
> As thine Eagle—of fleet, uncontroulable pinion;
>   The gallant gray Bird of the Winds! that is there.

(p. ix)

Neal's repeated panegyrics to America, the "fatherland," and to its "Eagle" and its "Nature," are consistent with his mission to bring that "future hour" of self-respect a bit closer to his particular present.

One other way of honing self-respect, a way in which to instill in his fellow citizens that nationalistic pride and self-confidence which he constantly advocated, and which he realized was necessary if American literature were ever to be accepted and encouraged by the American public, was for Neal to destroy the spurious respect which the average American had for all things British, a respect which he felt subsequently led to the worst kind of unquestioned subservience. Thus Neal chose the war of 1812 as his battleground, and the American vanquishing of the British as the means whereby he could spur national feeling while attacking the myth of British superiority. For the poem is

> Of men, who have fought with the high Briton too,
> As he sat on his throne in his empire of blue,
> Till the scarlet-crossed banner that majesty bent
>   Had faded and fled from its home in the sky;
> Till its terrours went off, as its splendours were rent,
>   Like meteors that over the firmament fly,
> And threw, as they passed o'er the free-rolling tide,
> A deep ruddy tint—'twas the last blush of pride.

(p. xii)

Neal next turned his hand to drama, publishing **Otho: A Tragedy** in 1819. The play is unbelievably mediocre, especially considering the fact that Neal constantly deprecated Shakespeare, and in one of his works had a Neal-like character declare that he could write a play "that criticks would swallow for Shakespeare's."[26] Perhaps his character felt that way, but in **Otho** Neal offers conclusive evidence to the contrary concerning his own dramatic abilities.

Neal's next novel, **Logan,** published anonymously in 1822, and called by one admirer "one of the most extraordinary productions of the present age,"[27] states in its preface that it is "an American story" written by an American.[28] In its confused symbolism and its Biblical parallels, the novel most resembles the later published **Rachel Dyer,** although the most obvious critical failure of the work lies in its uneven mixture of lyricism and melodrama.

Logan does once again, however, illustrate Neal's preoccupation with the advancement of a national literature. Late in the novel an educated Englishman expresses the belief that the Greek and Roman poets were the greatest, and would always be the greatest, poets who ever lived. He then hypothesizes that if England, as the contemporary equivalent of Rome and Greece, were at the center of the cultural world, in all the arts "the old British model would be preferred, because *all* had preferred it, while its own modern imitations, would be considered the *next* best" (II, 186-188). Oscar, sidekick to Harold, the protagonist in the novel, promptly repudiates that analogy, with its colonial overtones, and is proudly lauded by the hero, who injects a topical simile into his otherwise straightforward encomium: "How he [Oscar] derides, and scorns, all the ridiculous ceremonies of life! They are tricks, he says, that patrician fools invent, like escutcheons, to distinguish their party. And when these are counterfeited by the plebians, or imitated, they manufacture others, like the Free Masons" (II, 191).

Neal here reinforces his "national" crusade in two new ways. Imitation of any kind is execrated. In later works Neal actually insists on American writers producing "bad originals" rather than good imitations.[29] In subsequent novels he constantly denounces the pomp and ceremony associated with the aristocracy, and condemns the affectation of the British "patrician fools" for titles.

Harold then becomes the spokesman for the American Indians against British exploitation, defending their cause before a British tribunal: "Gracious heaven! how blind and deaf they [the British legislators] are!—here they have parcelled out an empire, and given kingdoms to the petty, depredating pedlars of the country—loosened a set of hell hounds, hungry and fleet, among the naked population of a continent, to lay waste, and spoil" (II, 273). The obviousness of this parable becomes evident at the conclusion of the novel, when the dying narrator proclaims:

> I have now done. I am dying. I am an American. . . . Englishmen! Let me utter some plain truths before I depart. There are multitudes among you, who rank my countrymen with the men of Botany Bay, the refuse of your most degenerate and profligate children—multitudes that have never heard of our revolution, and know nothing of our history, but regard us yet, as *rebels*.
>
> (II, 338)

Harold's plea for the rights of the Indians thus becomes an allegorical cry for American independence.

But Neal is not yet finished. His "dying" American catalogues the still-existing British offenses against his country: a ministry which "blasphemes the destinies of my country," reviewers "drunk with arrogance and hatred toward us," and a "vagabond horde" of travellers who misrepresent the American people abroad (II, 339). Then he attempts to puff American pride while deflating British aloofness in this nationalistic reminiscence of the Revolutionary War:

> Forty years have passed away. Great God! what a revolution! My beloved country standing up, with her forehead in the sky, her bright hair streaming from ocean to ocean—helmeted and cuirassed—starred and glittering with 'intolerable light'!—and lo! her tyrant in the dust!—where is his manhood now?—where the presence, before which Europe trembled and was afraid?
>
> (II, 340)

The initial focus is on America, on his "beloved country." But then the other participant in the "revolution" appears, the "tyrant" who is "in the dust," and the focus turns toward him, questioning his "manhood" and gloating over his downfall. Finally, with undisguised patriotism, the narrator traces this incredible American progress, and his closing metaphor does Sydney Smith's "four quarters of the globe" one better:

> *I am an American.* I remember when I first set my foot upon your shores. *Then* was the name a reproach. Our Eagle too, was only a butt, for derision and ribaldry. How is it now? I have lived to see that name ringing from kingdom to kingdom—to see that Bird breaking onward, through cloud and storm, even to the four corners of the sky.
>
> (II, 338-339)

This ardent nationalism carries over into the previously cited *Randolph* (1823), a highly digressive epistolary novel whose plot alternates between a quest after the real identity of the hero and a series of dialogues on British and American literature. To an Englishman's sarcastic request for Neal's hero to tell him about America's "great men, if you have any," Edward Molton (the Randolph of the title) polemicizes about such American writers as Irving, Dana, Paulding, Everett, Percival, and "Neale." Then, referring to America's obeisance to British writers, he introduces a topic common to Neal's works:

> But will this last forever? No. The time is rapidly approaching when it will be enough to sell a work, if it be called American. We are getting to feel a national pride, and men are already beginning to put in their title pages, "by an American"—and "an American Tale"—words, that, a few years ago, would have been as politick, as "by a Choctaw" or "or a Narragansett tale."
>
> (II, 209)

As early as *Keep Cool* had Neal declared in his dedication that the author was an American; and as early as the *Battle of Niagara* he had expressed optimism for the future of American writers:

> And many a bard of my country who slumbers—
> Neglected—forgotten—oppressed—or unknown—
> May arise in his strength, in the grandeur of numbers,
> Sublime on the height of a star-lighted throne—
>   And chant to the skies! and assert his high claim
>   With those who are forth for the chaplet of Fame.
>
> (p. xiii)

Logan he called an "American story," and he would later call *Rachel Dyer* "A North American Story." And although he was acutely aware of several discouraging obstacles in the path of an American author—the lack of copyright and the onus associated with the name "writer" in America—[30] he could hardly have foreseen that these national inscriptions and anti-British outbursts would later help him in selling the book to Americans desirous of patronizing the artistic efforts of their countrymen.[31]

But the most interesting item in Molton-Randolph's ramblings concerns two issues which Hawthorne debates in his prefaces a generation later.[32] The first centers around a discussion of whether men should write "Novels or Romances." Novels neither "allure" nor "amaze"; they are "fine, *natural* models"; they are "useful, and uniformly attractive," but are "destitute of phrensy." Romances, on the other hand, are grounded not in naturalism, but in exaggeration: "I say *exaggeration*—because if there be no exaggeration, there will be none of that trance-like agitation and excitement" (II, 183-184). Neal's distinction between the Novel and the Romance thus bears a striking resemblance to Hawthorne's often quoted preface to *The House of the Seven Gables* (1851).

The second comment by Molton is an articulate response to a familiar complaint of American writers. In his preface to *The Marble Faun* (1860), Hawthorne expressed his feelings concerning the lack of a useable past:

> Italy, as the site of his [the author's] Romance, was chiefly valuable to him as affording a sort of poetic or fairy precinct, where actualities would not be so terribly insisted upon as they are, and must needs be, in America. No author, without a trial, can conceive of the difficulty of writing a romance about a country where there is no shadow, no antiquity, no mystery, no picturesque and gloomy wrong, nor anything but a commonplace prosperity in broad and simple daylight, as is happily the case with my dear native land. It will be very long, I trust, before romance-writers may find congenial and easily handled themes, either in the annals of our stalwart republic, or in any characteristic and probable events of our individual lives. Romance and poetry, ivy, lichens, and wall flowers, need ruin to make them grow.

Some forty years earlier Washington Irving, in introducing Ichabod Crane, ironically commented: "In this by-place of nature, there abode, in a remote period of American history, that is to say, some thirty years since, a worthy wight of the name of Ichabod Crane." And, in our germinal year of 1828, Cooper complained that in American there were "no annals for the historian; no follies (beyond the most vulgar and commonplace) for the satirist; no manners for the dramatist; no obscure fictions for the writer of romance; no gross and hardy offenses against decorum for the moralist; nor any of the rich artificial auxiliaries of poetry."[33]

But Irving, Cooper, and Hawthorne were not novel in their attacks. In the closing decades of the eighteenth century, American writers were debating the same question, and David Humphreys answered those artists who sought inspiration in the sublimities of the Old World by insisting on the advantages offered by the American landscape, unsullied as it was by "mystic obelisk, or storied wall," and by "ruin'd statues" and "crumbling arch."[34] But this "topographical fallacy" was not the answer, and so in *Randolph* Neal proposed his own solution:

> We have no old castles—no banditti—no shadow of a thousand years to penetrate—but what of that. We have men, and women—creatures that God himself hath fashioned and filled with character. And what more do we want? . . . why need we go back to the past for our heroes?—There is no such necessity; and he who shall first dare to grapple with the *present*, will triumph, in this country.

> (II, 208)

In predictable fashion, then, Neal turns his back on the past, and instructs the American artist to exploit the *"present"* in his work. Although occasionally using the American past as the setting for a novel, Neal thus interprets the historical past in light of the present, and his theme always reflects upon the issues and feelings of the audience of his day.

Neal's next novel, the already mentioned *Errata; or, the Works of Will. Adams* (1823), is a discursive account of duelling and divorce, and is perhaps best described by this prefatory speculation in the first chapter: "Quere, if *Digression* would not have been a good title for this novel?" Aside from several direct appeals to the "reader," the only noteworthy occurrence concerns this prediction by the poet Hammond:

> We are beginning to have respect for ourselves; and to be, *for that reason,* respected abroad; and, it is my firm belief, that the time is fast coming when it will be a better name for a literary work, to call it *American,* than *English,* or *Scotch.* The fashion of reading what our countrymen write, is gaining ground, every day.

> (II, 109)

This kind of optimism for American letters is interesting, not only because it is an essential fiber in the fabric of Neal's aesthetic, but because it represents a vision of future respectability for American literature. The aesthetic primacy of Neal's nationalistic campaign therefore helps to explain the presence of several seemingly non-organic comments in the novels, which themselves seem at times to be patterned after the principle which Neal abhorred in his contemporaries: "The essay does'nt [sic] fit the tale; let us make the tale fit the essay" (I, 92).

Seventy-Six, also published in 1823, is one of Neal's historical novels. As would be expected, the story treats of the Revolution (although having a subplot completely independent of the title and far out of proportion with the main plot), and Neal uses this as the frame on which to erect his recurring nationalistic platforms. From the "Our Country!—Right or Wrong" motto on the title page, to the naming of the hero Jonathan, to the patriotic adages prefacing several chapters,[35] *Seventy-Six* is the most obviously nationalistic of Neal's works.

The War of 1812 had spurred new feelings of nationalism and independence in the American people, but to many the "victory" which the United States achieved was a Pyrrhic one, and the ambiguous treaty which ended the war reinforced that opinion. But the War of Independence was viewed by nearly all nineteenth century Americans as a decisive conquest of a great nation by an outmanned, poorly trained, and generally uncultivated group of dedicated men; or, as the narrator of *Seventy-Six* expresses it: "We wrestled, children as we were, for eight years, with armed giants: and wrenched—*wrenched!* with our own hand, the spoil from the spoiler—overcame them all, at last, after eight years of mortal trial, and uninterrupted battle, even in their stronghold."[36]

Comments like that are plentiful in the novel. At the beginning of the work, by referring to his listeners' stake in the War, the narrator necessarily involves the reading audience in his story:[37] "I would have *your* thought go in pilgrimage over the same ground, remembering that the old men who travelled it, in the revolution, doing battle at every step, for *your* inheritance, were an army journeying, deliberately, to martyrdom" (I, 4; my italics). The author's keen awareness of his audience is evident in the frequent breaks in the narrative, with the narrator directing his listeners (and thus Neal's readers) how to feel: "My children! I must pause. I would have you realize the tremendous peril in which your father and uncle—all his family and friends—nay! all the hopes of America, were placed at this hour" (I, 254). This artificial method of heightening excitement through an irresistible appeal practically assures Neal of his desired response from an involved audience. Following several spectacular scenes in which the militia retakes New Jersey for the Americans, the narrator further comments: "There, my dear children, I have been willing to forget the battle and the subject for a while, and amuse you, for I know your taste and that of our people, with a few rockets, and—let me return—" (I, 350-351). This is a clear indication of the aesthetic that is functioning in the work, for the narrator, like Neal, is aware of what his audience wants.

Having guaranteed audience empathy for his story, Neal has his characters reaffirm the theme of nationalism. Sometimes their comments rely on anglophobia as the device for illustrating that theme, as when the neutral Mr. Arnauld cries out after seeing a wounded American soldier: "Henceforward I am an American—heart, blood, and pulse; there is the royal protection! (tearing a paper in pieces, and throwing it into the fire, indignantly as he spoke)—there let it be! No peace with the tyrants—no quarter" (I, 84). And sometimes, as in this comment by Jonathan Oadley to Mr. Arnauld, the theme arises from an attack on aristocracy, with overtones of xenophobia:

> There is a dangerous, discontented spirit among us; we seem to be . . . anxious to down with our natural-born men of America; our old fashioned republicans, and put any body, no matter whom, if he has been educated abroad, in their places. I use no disguise. Lee [a general] is a favourite with our patricians here, because he is a haughty, over-bearing aristocrat; has been trained in Europe, among their princes and nobility. . . .
>
> (I, 147)

One other way of either creating or expressing this national feeling was through the use of symbols. Conventional symbols like the eagle and the name Jonathan have been seen. When one character cries out, "O, Lord God of Israel! the prayer of an afflicted people. Lo!" (I, 100), Neal resurrects another symbol which the American people applied to themselves as early as the seventeenth century. For, as one character put it, the Americans (like the Israelites) had become slaves under British rule, but were "men who wanted [needed] only to be slaves, to be the best troops upon the earth" (I, 256).

Neal also created new symbols, based on classical analogues, to illustrate the character of his countrymen. Thus Washington's crossing of the Delaware River beat "all hollow" Xenophon's retreat (I, 264); the British exploitation of the American people only made them stronger, for they fell, "only to rise, like Antaeus, with renewed power" (III, 208); and the Romans and Greeks endured nothing compared to those Americans who wintered at Valley Forge: "Greeks and Romans! blisters on the American tongue, that shall dare to name them in comparison with our poor fellows" (II, 287)! The American people therefore appear as the real Spartans, strengthened by adversity, and saved by Yankee hardiness.

Neal's next novel, *Brother Jonathan: or, the New Englanders,* was published in Edinburgh in 1825 by William Blackwood, for whom Neal had been writing anonymous articles on American literature. Neal had gone to England, he said, because he was angered by Sydney Smith's question, and was going to write something "so American, as to secure the attention of Englishmen."[38] Because his *Logan* and *Seventy-Six* had been well received there, he felt he had good reason for expecting further success in Great Britain.

Brother Jonathan seems to be a book written particularly for foreign consumption. A whole chapter, for example, is devoted to detailing the American customs of that day of "husking," "raising," and "quilting." The setting is the Revolution, and the cast is a farina of Indians, bandits, murderers, bear-fighters, Tories, and Quakers. Probably because Neal is critical of the American "bucktails" (who are stereotypes of the "skinners" in Cooper's *The Spy*), and because he is wholly unsympathetic toward the unscrupulous merchants of New York and New England, Arthur Hobson Quinn implies that Neal's British audience is responsible for his uncomplimentary treatment of his countrymen.[39]

It is true that the novel sometimes places the United States and its people in an unattractive light, as in the description of an American as "one of that singular people, who know a little, and but a little, of everything."[40] But for every detraction, Neal offers several favorable views of the country; as, for example, this nostalgic and rhapsodic description of autumn in North America:

> It was autumn. Fires were lighted for about an hour, every day; in the morning and evening. The nights were cold, frosty and clear; the days were warm, delightful, and hazy;—like those of the Indian summer— that beautiful season of the south, in the United States. The woods were all in bloom. The magnificent foliage of the northern wilderness—gorgeous and heavy, with a profusion of colour; changing with every cloud; fluctuating with every wind—hung down, as it were, from the illuminated skies, over all the waters, and over all the mountains—colouring the very atmosphere;—shadowing the land, with a broad, lucid shadow; richer by far, than a carpet of crushed moss, or trodden flowers;—and covering the inaccessible rocks, with what appeared like the unsubstantial herbage of poetry. The mornings were wonderful; and so, were the evenings.
>
> The autumnal beauty of a North American forest cannot be exaggerated. It is like nothing else on earth.
>
> (II, 28-29)

Likewise, there is this further eulogy by Neal of another facet of the American landscape:

> People may talk of their fine Italian skies; of their hot bright East Indian skies; of the deep midnight blue of the South American skies. We have seen them all . . . and we say, that, in reality, they are dim, heavy—unclouded, uninteresting—compared with your North American skies, a little before, and after sunset.
>
> (II, 30)

As in *Keep Cool* and the *Battle of Niagara*, nationalistic pride in something so seemingly unimportant as nature serves Neal in advancing the cause of America.

The novel also contains some rather explicit anti-British comments. When one loyalist defends the King in an American town meeting, Neal uses his discourse to reflect what Cooper had called the American "fixed contempt for all monarchies": "George, King of Great Brit-

ain—whose groan was that" (I, 169)? When the enraged Tory then threatens the townpeople with hanging as traitors, they arise and slowly file from the hall. As in several of his other novels, Neal also depicts the American hatred of titles when Jonathan Peters, the most ambiguous character in *Brother Jonathan,* retorts after being called "'Squire," "No titles for me, that imply subordination. . . . I am an American; a native born Yankee. We have begun a war upon titles. It will end . . . mark me; it will end yet in bloodshed" (I, 62-63). Then Peters, after a three page harangue on the subject, sums up his feelings:

> Who are our nobility? . . . *men,* called out of the coarse earth, like Adam, by the will of Jehovah! what have we to do with ensigns and armorial bearings—the blazonry of an old people, any more than he had; he, the untitled Adam. We are a new people; we have no fathers, no progenitors.
>
> (I, 70-71)

This Adamic simile, new for Neal, captures the spirit of America in the 1820's. The American man becomes the "Original Man,"[41] becomes Adam before the Fall, without limitation in his preternatural state and infinitely perfectible; and the American landscape, beautiful and unsullied, becomes the Garden of Eden. The image is thus redolent with optimism, and suggests much of what is later embodied in the popular concept of "Manifest Destiny."

Neal also makes use of other symbols in *Brother Jonathan* to delineate the national character. The American people are said to suppose themselves "the chosen Israel of God" (II,116), an image which repeats the optimism of the Adamic one, and which is reminiscent of the Puritan concept of America as the New Zion. Bald Eagle, an Indian who appears at convenient times in the novel to render assistance to a frustrated hero or distressed heroine, becomes a worthy symbol of the American people. Shot twice at close range and roasted over a "slow fire," he is freed by his trusty dog, but lies on the hot ashes to formulate his plan of revenge, ultimately surviving long enough to slash the throats, take the scalps, and cleave the skulls of his six assailants. The "Jonathan" symbol functions in this novel to suggest the disguised relationship between Jonathan Peters and Walter Harwood when Walter is referred to as "a 'jinooine' Brother Jonathan" (II, 46). And Walter is immediately raised to the stature of a hero by the juxtaposing of his name with that of a renowned national hero, thus precluding the author's need to detail the desired heroic characteristics in the drawing of Walter's character: "Your country is in danger.—You are wanted! *you,* Nathan Hale—and *you,* Walter Harwood" (II, 117)!

At the turn of this century one American critic declared that *Brother Jonathan* "enjoyed the distinction of being the longest work in early American fiction, if not in all American fiction." Although the novel suffers by being excessively lengthy, it is unmistakably a concrete example of the "American" novel which Neal asked for in an 1825 issue of *Blackwood's:*

> It is American books that are wanted of America; not English books. . . . Give us a bad original, they would say, to every American writer, if they [the British people] had any hope of him; keep your good copy: No great man was ever able to copy. Come forth naked, *we* should say, to every real North American—savage or not; . . . do not come forth, in a court equipage, with fine lace over your broad knuckles, and your strong rough hair powdered.

Neal's emphasis on the need for a "bad original" to the exclusion of a "good imitation," anticipating by several years Melville's identical plea, effected a definite tactical victory in the battle of American literary independence. When considered within the context of the period in which Neal wrote, **Brother Jonathan**—as decidedly "bad" as it is "original"—is significant. Being, as Neal wrote in *Blackwood's,* "a real North American story," and being first published in the British Isles before being reprinted in the United States, **Brother Jonathan** points to a new market for the truly "American" writer—a writer interested in working with American materials and American themes—who might otherwise be discouraged by the lack of adequate copyright protection at home.[42]

Neal's next novel was also original, but it is distinguished from the rest of his work by being readable today. **Rachel Dyer,** the only one of Neal's many novels worthy to be reissued in the twentieth century,[43] does suffer from its author's usual confused symbolism and digressive plotting; but its achievement lies in the suspenseful reworking of an historical account in order to comment sensitively upon a universal condition. Admitting that one of his objectives for writing **Rachel Dyer** "was to show my countrymen that there are abundant and hidden sources of fertility in their own beautiful brave earth, waiting only to be broken up" (p. xvi), Neal anticipates Hawthorne in choosing the Salem witch trials as the setting in which to dramatize the lack of love among men.

But Neal had another motive for writing **Rachel Dyer,** and this concerned the aforementioned "verdict" of Sydney Smith. This initial intent, when combined with Neal's call for "another *Declaration of Independence,* in the great *Republic of Letters"* (p. xviii), helps explain some otherwise unrelated comments and events in the novel. For example, Neal's hero, George Burroughs, in defending a woman accused of being a witch, lashes out at the American judges who use British law as the basis for the trial procedure, and who refer to themselves as representatives of the "crown":

> Against the crown Sir! what on earth has the crown to do here?—what have we to do with such absurdity? . . . God help such crowns, I say! What an idea

of kingship it gives! What a fearful commentary on the guardianship, of monarchs! How much it says in a word or two of their fatherly care! He who is *for* the subject, even though a life be at stake, is therefore *against* the king!

(pp. 93-94)

Burroughs, characterized as an "American" by the narrator's insistence upon the hero's Indian blood and frontiersman qualities, gains further sympathy from Neal's American audience by his attack on the British monarchy, and the logic of his last sentence above provides no alternative for the would-be American of that time.

One other allusion in the novel is also explained in terms of Neal's desire to exploit the anti-British feelings of the American audience. After a group of fellow frontiersmen repulse an Indian attack on the fort in which they and their families are temporarily encamped, Burroughs cautions them not to relax their defenses but to anticipate a second attack. However, believing the Indians to have been routed completely, the men leave the fort, and climb to the summit of an adjacent hill in order to ascertain the whereabouts of any remaining savages. Previous to leaving, one of the camp's leaders urges on those of his comrades who feared disregarding Burroughs' advice: "Hourra then—*hourra for the king"* (p. 160; my italics). He then leads the men from the fort, and, upon reaching the top of the hill, they are all massacred by scores of Indians lying in ambush. Burroughs, the "American," had warned those "Tories," and the combined unheeding of his admonition and the salute to the King makes their death both predictable and justified to Neal's readers.

In his preface Neal had expressed the hope that, when Sydney Smith is answered, "Our literature will begin to wake up, and our pride of country will wake up with it" (p. 10). Until the appearance of **Rachel Dyer,** he had actually been trying to awaken a nationalistic pride in Americans for their country, which would then allow for the reception of an indigenous American literature, bad originals and all. Therefore, **Rachel Dyer** is a fitting culmination to Neal's campaign; for it is a novel which not only answers Sydney Smith, but one in which the American people could be *truly* proud, confirming Alexander Cowie's opinion that Neal's greatest benefit was that "he energized American literature at a time when such a service was badly needed."[44]

Authorship, published anonymously by Neal in 1830, has as its subtitle, "By a New Englander Over-Sea." Possibly capitalizing on the popularity of British travel books, Neal seems to have written one for the sheer enjoyment of his fellow Americans, for the "novel" possesses the popular ingredients of romance, mystery, adventure, and intrigue, as well as detailed sketches of London society with its drinking and gambling habits.

Although *Authorship* is not as anti-British as one would expect, especially since British works in that genre always put Americans in the worst possible light, the book is certainly nationalistic. For example, in looking out from Westminster Abbey, the narrator nostalgically exclaims:

> It would be altogether vain for me to try to describe what I saw from the top of the rock; for my thoughts were away, far, far away, and my heart was heavy, and I felt some how or other as if I myself were away among the solitudes of North-America, by the riverside or the water-fall, in the darkness and beauty of another world.[45]

Here is seen another of Neal's encomiums of the American landscape; and, "topographical fallacy" or not, this sentimental appeal was probably quite effective. The first person narrator is homesick, and whiles away his time by absent-mindedly playing "Yankee Doodle" on the chimes. Therefore, when he is respectfully greeted by a distinguished member of British society, the narrator can hardly restrain his delight: "I have seen a good deal of your country, said the man I speak of, with a bow which it was impossible for me not to return with a feeling of pride, for with that bow, he said more in praise of America than most others would have said in a long speech" (p. 157).

Another interesting technique which Neal uses in *Authorship* is the "American" simile. In *Brother Jonathan,* Neal had referred to the days being "like those of Indian summer," but the setting was North America in autumn, and the simile thus at best a cliche. *Authorship,* however, is set in England, and so comparisons like the following seem more original: "There was a deep dead silence—dead as that of a New-England meeting-house in the middle of a warm summer-afternoon" (p. 239). The American identity of the author is also evidenced in the simile used by the narrator to describe his pursuit of a mysterious woman: "I have pursued her as the North-American savage would pursue his prey" (p. 261). The novel ends, conveniently, with the woman returning to her birthplace, to "America—the United States of North America" (p. 267).

The Down-Easters, Neal's last "serious" novel, is a "wild tale" in which the author experiments with colloquial American speech. Long an advocate of what he called "natural" writing, Neal decries the "written" language—"made up to order from Dr. Blair, Allison on Taste, or the British classics hashed over"—[46] which he found in contemporary literature. Like Noah Webster and, later, Thoreau and Whitman, Neal was also an Americanist with respect to dialect and vocabulary,[47] and he asks his readers, in the preface to *The Down-Easters,* "What price would be too much to pay now, by any hearty lover of his country, or of his country's literature, for a dialogue of their day, faithfully reported from their lips" (I, iii)?

It is ultimately this kind of repeated nationalism which provides the most noteworthy element in the novel. In his preface, Neal writes:

> To judge by our novel-writers, playmakers and poets, with here and there a partial exception, rather by *accident* than otherwise, we have cottages and skylarks in our country; pheasants and nightingales, first families, youth of a 'gentle blood,' and virtuous *peasantry*; moss-grown churches, curfews and ivy-mantled towers . . . any thing and every thing in short which goes to the groundwork of a third-rate English or Scotch novel, and nothing—absolutely nothing—whereby a stranger would be able to distinguish an *American* story from any other.

> (I, v-vi)

This declaration places Neal in the mainstream of the campaign in the 1830's in America against the skylark and the nightingale, a campaign which was aimed at ridding American literature of any vestiges of British influence.[48] Thus, William Cullen Bryant counselled his brother, who had written a poem about a skylark, that it was "an English bird," and that he should draw his images from his surroundings. Longfellow, in advising American poets to describe only "natural" scenery, precluded the skylark and nightingale as being improper images, because for Americans "they only warble in books." And Thoreau lamented the habit of American authors to sing of "skylarks and nightingales, perched on hedges, to the neglect of the homely robin-red-breast, and the straggling rail fence of their native land."

Perhaps there were those "poets" who, as William Tudor remarked, "believed if the nightingale were out of the way, their own croaking would be music." But, although much of what he wrote was little better than "croaking," Neal's lifelong commitment to the "Independence" of American letters places his motives beyond Tudor's legitimate suspicions.

IV

After the *Down-Easters,* Neal published only a few religious tracts, several speeches, and two dime novels,[49] with the greatest portion of his second forty years being divided between the practice of law and the editorship of various journals and newspapers.

However, when American literature had needed a spokesman, he was there. He had been, as Griswold said, "an American author par excellence,"[50] and if the decade following the War of 1812 was filled "with an air of hopefulness" for American letters,[51] Neal was probably the one person most responsible for both creating and sustaining that optimism. By modern standards his methods are crude—arousing feelings of self-pride and militant nationalism in the American people—but they were duly necessary in order to convince his countrymen of the need to support a native literature independent of Great Britain. Thus, by the pivotal year of 1828, John Neal had sufficiently paved the way for the reception of a native novel of which America could be proud—not only because it was a "North American story" written by a North American—but because it was a *good* North American story written by, as Poe said, a man of "indisputable *genius.*"

As the man who asked to have "Who reads an American book?" engraved on his tombstone, John Neal finally made "all England, for a time, and perhaps Sydney Smith, aware of at least one American writer, one that for three years filled their magazines and molded their thinking of American literature." But, as one modern critic observes, "The question has been answered, the Reverend Sydney Smith silenced, and John Neal vindicated. Yet Smith may have his revenge after all: the question now is 'Who reads John Neal?'"[52]

John Neal, however, did fall victim to his own admonition to other American writers:

> Nothing is more short-lived than violent popularity. It is the tempestuous brightness of a moment—a single moment only—*the sound of passing music*—the brief blossoming of summer flowers.

> Let them [American writers] remember, that there is one law of nature, which governs alike through all creation. . . . It is this—That which is a given time in coming to maturity, shall abide a like time without beginning to decay.

And this description, when applied to Neal's works and the rapidity of their composition, explains James Russell Lowell's dismissal of him:

> Neal wants balance; he throws his mind always too far,
> And whisks out flocks of comets, but never a star;
>
>   . . . . .
>
> He has used his own sinews himself to distress,
> And had done vastly more had he done vastly less;
> In letters, *too soon is as bad as too late,*
> Could he only have waited he might have been great,
> But he plumped into Helicon up to the waist,
> And muddied the stream ere he took his first taste.[53]

One of Neal's expressed intentions in writing, though, was to be "popular," in the sense that his aesthetic was oriented towards the people,[54] and his novels expressed their feelings, hopes, and desires. The wide discrepancy between Neal's "popularity" (and thus his corresponding reputation) today and in his own time can only be explained in terms of that aesthetic: that to direct one's comments towards a particular people in a particular time is an unavoidable way of excluding future audiences. As an exploiter of the ideology of his time—which has been summed up in the term "democratic na-

tionalism," and which embodied the "popular" hatred for England, aristocracy, and imitation—and as an exponent of a theory of literature, a theory which can only be understood within the cultural and historical context of the United States of the 1820's and 1830's, John Neal merits a better fate than the present critical opinion that, "If history has obscured his works, it can only be said that, as usual, it has acted with justice."[55]

In order to evaluate properly Neal's contribution to American letters, the critic must first immerse himself in history, in the history of Neal's particular era, a history which damns to obscurity neither Neal nor his works; and he must likewise immerse himself in the aesthetic of that age, an aesthetic which enabled Neal to substitute a workable present for an unusable past. Perhaps Neal did write too much, too soon, as Lowell contended, but that was because he, like Jonathan Peters in **Brother Jonathan,** "corresponded finely" with his times (I, 17). However one finally judges him, it is this closing description of John Neal which justifies what one critic apoligized for doing, "to disinter the long dead":[56]

> He [Neal] was not only a Yankee of the New England limit, he was an American of the most ardent and pulsating force. He preached 'Americanism' in every other breath; and just as he could rap his fellow-men for their discipline, he could also boost for their encouragement. He urged that American ideals be adopted, that American art and standards of art be cultivated, that American books and American subjects be written, and that American pride be taken in all that belonged to this country.[57]

Notes

1. Noah Webster, "Preface" to *An American Dictionary of the English Language,* 2 vols. (New York, 1828), I, [3].

2. Robert E. Spiller, "Introduction to *Notions of the Americans,* Fac. ed., 2 vols. (New York, 1963), I,v.

3. [James Fenimore Cooper,] *Notions of the Americans Picked Up by a Travelling Bachelor,* 2 vols. (Philadelphia, 1828), II, 78-79.

4. [James Kirke Paulding,] *The New Mirror For Travellers; and Guide to the Springs* (New York, 1828), p. 79: "Of all the countries in the world, Old England, our kind, gentle, considerate old mamma, sends forth the largest portion of this species of literary 'riders,' who sweep up the materials for a book by the road side."

5. There are two prefaces to the novel. The first citation, concerning Neal's warning, is from the first preface, p.v. The second citation is from the second preface, p. x, or from what Neal entitled his "Unpublished Preface." All subsequent references

are to that second preface. John Neal, *Rachel Dyer* (Portland, Maine, 1828).

6. "'Who reads an American book?' No Englishman certainly, except with a view of borrowing its contents without giving the author credit for them." Paulding, p. 83.

7. [John Neal,] "A Summary View of America," *Blackwood's Edinburgh Magazine,* XVI (1824), 644-645.

8. Although Robert E. Spiller ("The Verdict of Sydney Smith," *American Literature,* I [1929,] 43) states that the American people and the American press were furious over Smith's indictment, and although Neal himself declared that "there has been the devil to pay, in America" over Smith's question, I agree with Professor Duane Schneider's contention (in unpubl. diss., "Sydney Smith's Reputation in America to 1900" [Colorado, 1965,] p. [1]) that there is little evidence "that there had been 'the devil to pay' between 1820 and 1824 as a result of Smith's query, and if the question needled the Americans, they surely were slow to show it (in print, at any rate)." Even considering Neal's comment in *Blackwood's,* and Paulding's in "The New Mirror," I would contend further that the first *real* response to Smith's question does not appear until *Rachel Dyer* in 1828, for that marks the first attempt to rebut Smith with an authentic, original American book.

9. Alexander Cowie, *The Rise of the American Novel* (New York, 1951), p. 177; Fred Lewis Pattee, ed., *American Writers, A Series of Papers Contributed to "Blackwood's Magazine" (1824-1825), by John Neal* (Durham, 1937), p. 10; Dane Yorke, "Yankee Neal," *American Mercury,* XIX (March, 1930), 368; Mary E. Phillips, *Edgar Allan Poe the Man,* 2 vols. (Chicago, 1926), I, 344; Windsor Daggett, *A Down-East Yankee From the District of Maine* (Portland, 1920), p. 9; Rufus Wilmot Griswold, *The Prose Writers of America,* 2nd ed., rev. (Philadelphia, 1847), p. 313; Edgar Allan Poe, "Marginalia," *The Complete Works of Edgar Allan Poe,* ed. James A. Harrison, 17 vols. (New York, 1902), XVI, 152.

10. Cited in Hervey Allen, *Israfel: The Life and Times of Edgar Allan Poe,* 2 vols. (New York, 1927), I, 257.

11. The letter from which this quotation is abstracted is quoted in full in John Neal, *Wandering Recollections of a Somewhat Busy Life: An Autobiography* (Boston, 1869), p. 256.

12. This is the opinion of Hervey Allen, *Israfel,* I, 258.

13. *Wandering Recollections,* p. 337.

14. John Earle Uhler, "The Delphian Club," *Maryland Historical Magazine,* XX, No. 4 (1925), 307.

15. Yorke, p. 365, and Daggett, p. 11. Neal himself makes this claim in *Wandering Recollections,* p. 251.

16. Howard Mumford Jones, *The Theory of American Literature* (Ithaca, 1948), pp. 7, 58.

17. *Wandering Recollections,* pp. 219, 173. These claims may seem apocryphal since Neal took almost three and a half years to complete his autobiography of 431 pages. However, most critics have taken Neal's words at face value, and Pattee facetiously comments that they are "hard to believe—until one reads the novels" (p. 5).

18. Arthur Hobson Quinn, "The Establishment of National Literature," *The Literature of the American People,* ed. Arthur Hobson Quinn (New York, 1951), p. 221; Cowie, p. 166.

19. *American Writers,* p. 161; *Wandering Recollections,* pp. 198, 259.

20. [John Neal,] *Keep Cool, A Novel,* 2 vols. (Baltimore, 1817), I, x.

21. [John Neal,] *Randolph, A Novel,* 2 vols. (Eastern District of Pennsylvania, 1823), I, 110.

22. *American Writers,* p. 187.

23. Jehu O'Cataract [Neal's pseudonym], *Battle of Niagara, A Poem, Without Notes; and Goldau, or The Maniac Harper* (Baltimore, 1818), p. iii.

24. [E. T. Channing,] "Neal's *Battle of Niagara,*" *North American Review,* VIII, No. 22 (1818), 144.

25. Referring initially to foreign reviewers, to whom Americans are "indebted for the degrading sentiments that are entertained of the genius of our countrymen," Neal concludes his preface with this nationalistic hope for his homeland: "The time will arrive, when these slanders, and these aspersions will be forgotten; when our posterity will wonder that we could have ever doubted the everlasting charter of greatness that is written upon our barriers:—our cataracts—our rivers—and our mountains" (*Keep Cool,* I, xvi).

26. [John Neal,] *Errata; or, the Works of Will. Adams,* 2 vols. (New York, 1823), II, 70.

27. Neal includes in his autobiography a letter from Dr. Watkins, the president of the Delphian Club, which extravagantly praises *Logan (Wandering Recollections,* p. 224).

28. [John Neal,] *Logan, A Family History,* 2 vols. (Philadelphia, 1822), I, 3.

29. For example, in an article in *The Yankee; and Boston Literary Gazette* (December, 1829) on

"The Encouragement of Native Literature," Neal writes: "Native writers in a time of peace are what native troops are in a time of war. *They must be had, whatever be the cost.* Mercenaries may be had *cheaper* than a native militia; natives that are not altogether so good soldiers nor so *cheap* at the time, though better citizens and better defenders" (p. 325).

30. In *Randolph,* Edward Molton laments the fact that in America "the very name of a novel writer would be a perpetual reproach to a man of genius" (II, 207); and he complains of the lack of copyright legislation in America. In the article on encouraging native writers mentioned above, Neal complains that in England "popular writers are paid on the average, from fifty to one hundred times as much for what they do, as they would receive in this country for the very same work" (p. 325), and he proposes "a small tariff on British literature, in the shape of a modification of the law of copyright" (p. 327).

31. This is the opinion of Lillie Deming Loshe, *The Early American Novel* (New York, 1907), p. 83.

32. Julian Hawthorne (*Nathaniel Hawthorne and His Wife: A Biography,* 2 vols. [Boston, 1885,] I, 145) reproduces a letter from Jonathan Cilley, dated November 17, 1836, which points to a possible influence of Neal on Hawthorne: "What sort of book have you written, Hath? I hope it is nothing like the damned ranting stuff of John Neal, which you, while at Brunswick, relished so highly."

33. Nathaniel Hawthorne, "Preface" to *The Marble Faun* (Boston, 1860), p. 15; Washington Irving, "The Legend of Sleepy Hollow," *The Works of Washington Irving* (New York, [1878]), p. 369, and quoted by Terence Martin, "Rip, Ichabod, and the American Imagination," *American Literature,* XXXI (1959), 142; *Notions of the Americans,* II, 108.

34. Quoted in Benjamin T. Spencer, *The Quest For Nationality* (Syracuse, 1957), p. 13.

35. For example, the motto introducing chapter two is: "Thy spirit, Independence! let me share! / Lord of the Lion-heart and eagle eye! / Thy steps I follow, with my bosom bare, / Nor heed the storm that howls along the sky"; that of chapter ten: "—Thou, land of the free! / Thou hope of the nations; what trance is in *thee*! / Thou parent of heroes!—the bravest and best, / That ere smote the plumage from Tyranny's crest"; and that of chapter seventeen: "I've loved to hear the warhorn's cry; / And panted at the drum's deep roll; / And held my breath, when, flaming high, / I've seen our starry banners flow, / As challenging the haughty sky, / They stirred the battle in my soul."

36. [John Neal,] *Seventy-Six,* 3 vols. (London, 1823), I, 4-5. The novel was first published in Baltimore, in two volumes, in the same year.

37. Or, as Neal said of the novel in *Blackwood's,* "The reader becomes an eyewitness in spite of himself" (*American Writers,* p. 169).

38. *Wandering Recollections,* p. 239.

39. Arthur Hobson Quinn, *American Fiction: An Historical and Critical Survey* (New York, 1936), p. 49.

40. [John Neal,] *Brother Jonathan: or, the New Englanders,* 3 vols. (London, 1825), I, 12-13.

41. In *Man: A Discourse Before the United Brothers' Society of Brown University, September 4, 1838* (Providence, 1838, p. 19), Neal described what he called the "Original Man," a person with all the Adamic attributes: "Without being an orator, a poet, a lawgiver, a statesman, or a mathematician, the Original Man, having all the faculties of a Man in their highest perfection, must have been capable of being all these; of being indeed whatever any other Man has been since, or may hereafter be."

42. Loshe, p. 93; *American Writers,* pp. 200-202; Melville felt that "it is better to fail in originality, than to succeed in imitation," and believed that America, in establishing an independent literature, should "first praise mediocrity even, in her children, before she praises . . . the best excellence in the children of any other land" (Spencer, pp. 96, 80); *American Writers,* p. 205n.

43. John Neal, *Rachel Dyer,* fac. ed. (Gainesville, 1964). The edition contains an "Introduction" by John D. Seelye.

44. *The Rise of the American Novel,* p. 175.

45. [John Neal,] *Authorship, A Tale; By a New Englander Over-Sea* (Boston, 1830), p. 31.

46. John Neal, *The Down-Easters, & c. & c. & c.,* 2 vols. (New York, 1833), I, iv.

47. Cf. Harold C. Martin, "The Colloquial Tradition in the Novel: John Neal," *New England Quarterly,* XXXII (1959), 455-475.

48. The campaign against the skylark and nightingale by American nationalistic writers was brought to my attention by Benjamin T. Spencer's *The Quest for Nationality (op. cit.,* pp. 86-87), a book to which I am highly indebted, and from which I have taken the quotations from Bryant, Longfellow, Thoreau, and William Tudor which follow.

49. For a complete bibliography of Neal's works, see Irving T. Richards, "John Neal: A Bibliographie," *Jahrbuch für Amerikastudien,* VII (1962), 296-319.

50. Griswold, p. 315.

51. R. W. B. Lewis, *The American Adam: Innocence, Tragedy, and Tradition in the Nineteenth Century* (Chicago, 1955), p. 13.

52. *Rachel Dyer,* p. 20; Pattee, p. 24; Harold C. Martin, p. 455.

53. *American Writers,* p. 31 (my italics); [James Russell Lowell,] *A Fable For Critics* (New York, 1848), pp. 46-47 (my italics).

54. Benjamin Lease ("Yankee Poetics: John Neal's Theory of Poetry and Fiction," *American Literature,* XXIV [1953,] 505-519) believes that "Neal's theory of literature is basically psychological; that is, in all of his practical and theoretical criticism he is primarily concerned with the varied emotional responses effected in readers by varied literary stimuli" (p. 506). Again, with respect to what I would call Neal's audience-oriented aesthetic, Lease says, "It is evident that Neal's scattered critical writings emerge as a unified theory of literature—a theory derived from his basic concern with the ways in which a literary work may arouse the faculties of the reader" (p. 519).

55. Harold C. Martin, p. 456.

56. Pattee, p. 21.

57. Daggett, pp. 7-8.

Benjamin Lease (essay date December 1974)

SOURCE: Lease, Benjamin. "John Neal and Edgar Allan Poe." *Poe Studies* 7, no. 2 (December 1974): 38-41.

[*In the following essay, Lease examines the relationship between Neal and Edgar Allan Poe to illuminate "the role each of these writers played in the American literary revolution."*]

Among the earliest and most dramatic responses to Sydney Smith's taunt—"who reads an American book?"—was that of the rambunctious New Englander John Neal (1793-1876), who invaded England and *Blackwood's Edinburgh Magazine* to further the cause of American literature and his own literary career. Neal's British campaign was climaxed by the appearance in *Blackwood's* of a series of articles, **"American Writers"** (1824-25), in which he complained that "with two exceptions, or at most three, there is no American writer who would not pass just as readily for an English writer. . . ."[1] (Neal was, predictably, one of those two or three.) I have told the story of this campaign elsewhere[2] and offer here a passage which, though it might well have been included, does not appear in that discussion:

There is not a more disgusting spectacle under the sun than our subserviency to British criticism. It is disgusting, first, because it is truckling, servile, pusillanimous—secondly, because of its gross irrationality. We *know* the British to bear us little but ill-will; we know that in the few instances in which our writers have been treated with common decency in England, these writers have either openly paid homage to English institutions, or have had lurking at the bottom of their hearts a secret principle at war with Democracy:—we *know* all this, and yet, day after day, submit our necks to the degrading yoek of the crudest opinion that emanates from the fatherland. Now if we *must* have nationality, let it be a nationality that will throw off this yoke.

The writer concludes: "In Letters as in Government we require a Declaration of Independence" and "A better thing still would be a Declaration of War—and that war should be carried forthwith 'into Africa.'"

The author of the preceding passage and concluding warlike sentiment was not John Neal but Edgar Allan Poe—in an 1845 *Marginalia* comment omitted from the Harrison edition of Poe's works.[3] Such ardent nationalistic sentiment is rarely associated with Poe; on the contrary he is usually identified with those who attacked uncritical praise of American literary productions in language like this:

. . . one is pretty sure to hear the most ridiculous and exaggerated misrepresentations, one way or the other, for or against *American* authorship. . . . But if we would not over-cuddle the young American writers; kill them with kindness; turn their heads with our trumpeting, or produce a fatal revulsion in the popular mind, let us never make a prodigious fuss about any American book, which, if it were English, would produce little or no sensation.

This passage is not Poe's but John Neal's—an excerpt from his *Blackwood's* series on American writers.[4] Poe was to express similar sentiments in his review of Drake and Halleck (1836) and in "Exordium" (1842); and it has been suggested that he joined the ranks of the literary nationalists and "Young America" in 1845-46 as a temporary expediency designed to promote his always precarious literary fortunes: "Who [asks Claude Richard] could reproach any half-starving young critic with a dying wife for forcing and somewhat colouring in brighter hues some of his opinions? Who would doubt Poe might yield to such temptation."[5] Poe's intensified attack on American subservience to British opinion has also been attributed to his disappointment over his rejection by *Blackwood's* and its editorial consultant, John Wilson ("Christopher North"). Michael Allen quotes from an 1845 review in which Poe, ridiculing Wilson at every point, muses wonderingly: "And this is the criticism—the British criticism—the Blackwood criticism—to which we have so long implicitly bowed down!"[6] Allen provides a detailed account of Poe's important involvement with *Blackwood's Edinburgh*

Magazine but says nothing about Neal's involvement with *Blackwood's* or Poe's involvement with Neal. The explanations of Claude Richard, Michael Allen, and others leave something to be explained about Poe's nationalism. I propose to review the Neal-Poe relationship for the light it sheds on the role each of these writers played in the American literary revolution.

Poe's first critical recognition—a recognition he never forgot—took place in the columns of *The Yankee and Boston Literary Gazette* for September 1829. Editor Neal notified correspondent "E. A. P. of Baltimore" that, despite his shortcomings, he "might make a beautiful and perhaps magnificent poem. There is a good deal here to justify such a hope." An excerpt from "Heaven" (later titled "Fairyland") followed this comment. In the December number, Neal suggested that, "with all their faults, if the remainder of *Al Aaraaf* and *Tamerlane* are as good as the body of the extracts here given . . . , he will deserve to stand high—very high—in the estimation of the shining brotherhood." Neal also quoted at length from an extraordinary letter in which the fledgling poet calls Neal's praise "the very first words of encouragement I ever remember to have heard," turns to his mentor as "a man that loves the same beauty which I adore," and identifies himself, plaintively, as one who has "no father—nor mother."[7] Two years later, reviewing *Poems* (1831), Neal called Poe "A fellow of fine genius" capable of "Pure poetry in one page—pure absurdity in another." "To Helen" is reprinted as an example of pure poetry, the production of one who "has the *gift,* and betrays the *presence . . .* that cannot be mistaken." Perhaps even more important, Neal concludes with the (for him) familiar complaint that he is "sick of poetry" and "would not have meddled with this volume" if not for the genius and promise of its young author.[8] Poe had returned to Baltimore from New York early in 1831 and it is almost certain that Neal's notice of his book in a prominent New York newspaper would come to his attention. Neal's tales were appearing in *The Token* and other literary annuals, and the struggling young poet might have found, in Neal's critique and example, encouragement for his own decision—made just about this time—to give up poetry for storytelling.[9]

Poe never forgot the critic who gave him "the first jog in my literary career" (as he put it in an 1840 letter to Neal). It was much more than a sense of personal gratitude, however, that led Poe to praise his mentor on numerous occasions and—as late as 1849—to rank John Neal "first, or at all events, second, among our men of indisputable *genius.*"[10]

But how did this budding Southern poet and Yankee editor come together in the first place? Young Poe first wrote to Neal from Baltimore where Neal's was still a name very much to be reckoned with. Shortly after the War of 1812, the Yankee from the District of Maine had settled in Baltimore for a career in law and literature. Neal's stormy literary career as critic, poet, and novelist came to a climax in late 1823 after a scandal over a love affair—a scandal aggravated by the fact that he incorporated details of the affair into two of his novels. He precipitously left Baltimore for a three-year visit to England where he scored a great success with William Blackwood and *Blackwood's Magazine* until the financial failure of a Neal novel published by Blackwood—*Brother Jonathan* (1825)—cooled off this intense association between the Yankee and the Scotsman. Neal became involved in other ventures and eventually returned to America in 1827. He had failed in his plan to match the success of Irving and Cooper; but Neal could claim for his British campaign a victory of a different kind:

> When it is remembered, that, up to this period, May, 1824, no American writer had ever found his way into any of these periodicals, and that American affairs were dealt with in short, insolent paragraphs, full of . . . downright misrepresentation, as if they were dealing with Fejee Islanders, or Timbuctoos, it must be admitted . . . that my plan was both well-conceived, and well-carried out.[11]

From its beginnings in 1817, *Blackwood's Magazine* had been an extremely influential force in America. Neal's phenomenal success as an American contributor can be partly attributed to his sympathy with its critical tenets. Poe's involvement with *Blackwood's,* early and late, is well known.[12] It is less well known that some of the numbers Poe studied while he was developing his critical theory featured articles on American writers by John Neal.[13]

Neal's psychological theory of literature has many similarities to Poe's. Both Neal and Poe were responsive to A. W. Schlegel's doctrine of "unity" or "totality" of effect—to what William Charvat has called *"Blackwood's* doctrine of the short poem, adopted from Schlegel."[14] More recently, G. R. Thompson has demonstrated the importance to Poe of Friedrich Schlegel's conception of irony: "the perception or creation of a succession of contrasts between the ideal and the real, the serious and the comic, the sinister and the absurd, through which the 'transcendental ego' can ambivalently mock its own convictions and productions from the height of the 'ideal.'"[15] Thompson suggests that Poe became familiar with A. W. Schlegel's views through John Black's translation of his *Lectures on Dramatic Art and Literature;* in addition, discussions of Schlegelian doctrine were pervasive in *Blackwood's* and its fiction characteristically embodied such views.

Neal's exposition of this doctrine was readily available to Poe in the *Blackwood's* series on American writers; in the lengthy Preface to *The Battle of Niagara* (2nd ed., 1819); and, most notably, in the series in *The Yankee* on **"The Drama."** Poe was familiar with *Niagara*; and in the same numbers of *The Yankee* in which he received his first encouragement and expressed his gratitude (September and December 1829) are two installments of Neal's five-part series on the drama. Young Poe almost certainly took note—in the number calling attention to "E. A. P. of Baltimore"—of Neal's explorations of "certain movements of the human heart" that must take place before a man is capable of committing murder. He probably read, too (in the October number), an explanation of the way the "heart" of the reader is aroused by an artistic manipulation of his relationship to the characters in a story.[16] Poe was, moreover, well acquainted with Neal's novels and tales—fiction charged with romantic irony. (See *Works*, XIII, 154; XVI, 46, 131, 152.)

John Neal struggled heroically (at times wildly and erratically) to combine this ironic vision—this intense serio-comic emphasis on self and the uncertitude of self—with his persistent quest for authentic nationality in literature. During the same decade in which Cooper said of a nursing foal that it "exacted the maternal contribution," Neal's adventurous experiments contributed significantly to our colloquial tradition. In the Preface to **The Down-Easters** (1833), he warned his readers that the rapid changes taking place in our country would soon leave us with hardly a vestige "of our strongest and sharpest peculiarities."[17] His sense of himself as an instrument for preserving a precious and vanishing heritage occasionally collided with the unity of effect he valued but rarely achieved. An anonymous critique of Neal's manuscript novel **Brother Jonathan** complained that "The style has the same eternal effect of italics—& breaks—& affectation; but in many passages & descriptions, I have met with *nothing* more beautifully strong and original." This critique, forwarded by William Blackwood to Neal, was to have its counterpart—some two decades later—in this observation by Poe:

> [Neal] always begins well—vigorously—startlingly— proceeds by fits—much at random—now prosing, now gossiping, now running away with his subject, now exciting vivid interest; but his conclusions are sure to be hurried and indistinct; so that the reader, perceiving a falling-off where he expects a climax, is pained, and, closing the book with dissatisfaction, is in no mood to give the author credit for the vivid sensations which have been aroused *during the progress* of perusal. Of all literary foibles the most fatal, perhaps, is that of defective climax. Nevertheless, I should be inclined to rank John Neal first, or at all events second, among our men of indisputable *genius*. Is it, or is it not a fact, that the air of a Democracy agrees better with mere Talent than with Genius?
>
> ("Marginalia" [1849], *Works*, XVI, 152)

Poe's recognition of greatness and genius despite glaring deficiencies in what he elsewhere calls the "con-struction" of Neal's works is reinforced by an 1848 pronouncement envisioning him as a force to be reckoned with in our emerging national literature:

> The Byronic poets were *all* dash. John Neal, in his earlier novels, exaggerated its use into the grossest abuse—although his error arose from the philosophical and self-dependent spirit which has always distinguished him, and which will even yet lead him, if I am not greatly mistaken in the man, to do something for the literature of the country which the country "will not willingly," and cannot possibly, "let die."
>
> ("Marginalia" [1848], *Works*, XVI, 131; Poe refers to the novels **Errata** and **Seventy-Six** in *Works*, XVI, 46)

That this high praise and deep concern for Neal's contribution to "the literature of the country" do not manifest a transient nationalist phase is evidenced by Poe's 1843 review of Cooper's *Wyandotte* (*Works*, XI, 205-220). Cooper is placed among those writers who, distrustful of their powers, choose an unfailingly popular subject—for example, life in the wilderness—and are widely read "with pleasure but without admiration." Poe contrasts those writers to others, "not so popular, nor so widely diffused," whose productions arouse "a distinctive and highly pleasurable interest, springing from our perception of the skill employed, or the genius evinced in the composition." Brown, Simms, Neal, and Hawthorne are grouped among the less popular writers of skill or genius; Cooper is "at the head of the more popular division. . . ." (Compare Neal's evaluation of Poe, in his 1850 tribute, as one "who would never be a popular Magazine-writer, although, as a man of genius, every man of genius he touched, would thrill with acknowledgment.")[18]

"It would not do for me to imitate anybody," proclaimed John Neal in 1828;[19] "All true men must rejoice to perceive the decline of the miserable rant and cant against originality," wrote Poe in 1845 (*Works*, XVI, 67-68). Both writers felt it important for them, as Americans, to break new ground. Originality for both Neal and Poe encompassed a sense of terror (and an ironic ambivalence about terror) both of Germany and of the soul— the American soul. William Carlos Williams identified the blend as peculiarly American and singled out Poe as *the* representative American writer—more representative than Fenimore Cooper. According to Williams, Poe shied away from the easy, attractive subjects (for example, Indians and forests) to originate a style that sprang from "the local conditions, not of trees and mountains, but of the 'soul.' . . ."[20] In his obituary tribute to Poe (a response to Griswold's slanderous attack), Neal anticipated Williams' view: Poe, he suggested, "saw farther, and looked more steadily, and more inquisitively into the elements of darkness—into the shadowy, the shifting and mysterious—than did most of the shining brotherhood about him."[21]

Despite their close ties, there were significant differences between John Neal and Edgar Allan Poe. Both writers clamored for individuality and originality but Poe, claims Benjamin T. Spencer, "Had little concern for that larger kind of originality which would involve the national as well as the individual mind, and which Emerson and Whitman sought to foster."[22] Neal's emphases on live talk and authentic character reflected an organicism that foreshadowed Emerson, Whitman, and Mark Twain. As a result, Neal's high praise of Poe—in his 1850 tribute—was accompanied by a recognition of what he considered shortcomings; while insisting on Poe's vast superiority over the polished, shallow Horne Tooke, he nonetheless sees a resemblance: "I hold that [Poe] was a creature of wonderful power; concentrated, keen, finished and brilliant: rather Ho[rn]e Tooke-ish in his literary slope; but with ten times the genius, quite as much learning, and forty times the imagination of Tooke. . . ."[23] John Neal was, in fact, a key transitional figure in the American literary revolution—one who shaped a rough and ready poetics that pulled him simultaneously in several different directions: toward Schlegelian unity of effect and Byronic sweep, toward authentic colloquialism and rhapsodic eloquence, toward the farcical and the tragic.

We have moved a considerable distance from Parrington's dismissal of "The problem of Poe" as "quite outside the main current of American thought" and from Matthiessen's decision to exclude Poe from his *American Renaissance* because his work seemed "relatively factitious when compared with the moral depth of Hawthorne or Melville."[24] The importance of John Neal has also begun to emerge. Poe stood almost alone in his praise of Neal's tales until 1962 when Hans-Joachim Lang, a German authority on nineteenth-century American literature, discovered and reprinted in Germany two powerful stories, **"David Whicher"** and **"Otter-Bag"**—along with a selection of Neal's critical writings.[25] These and other tragicomic stories of frontier travail are cruder than Poe's studies in self-destructiveness and madness, but at times they convey a greater poignance and horror than the younger man's more polished productions; they deserve wider critical attention.

In **"David Whicher"**—the best of Neal's stories and one that illustrates well his fictional method—an inoffensive, non-violent man of God is captured by four Indians. While playing for time by demonstrating his extraordinary skill as a woodsman, Whicher suddenly notices what seem to be the scalps of his two children—still bleeding—buckled on the chest of one of the warriors. He must have revenge; but he must be certain of the truth before violating his lifelong commitment to non-violent faith in God's providence. By a clever ruse, he pins the hands of the Indians in a tree prepared for this purpose and discovers that the scalps are indeed his children's. Unable to use his axe on the murderers, Whicher leaves them to God's providence and the wolves. On the anniversary of his terrible be-

reavement, the woodsman returns to the tree—and poignance suddenly dissolves into outrageous anticlimax as the auditor-narrator boggles at a tall-tale account of four skeletons "still striving to tear the tree asunder." Neal's ironic mode involves the telling of this harrowing tale by a ludicrous little man with green spectacles, and at the conclusion the narrator takes his leave from this mysterious storyteller, knowing "in my heart he intended to hoax me." The hoaxing conclusion of **"David Whicher"** echoes what Baudelaire has described as the agonized laughter of Melmoth, whose "double and self-contradictory nature" stirs him to a mocking laughter that "freezes and torments the bowels of mercy and love."[26] In Poe's ironic mode "a tragic response to the perversities of fortune and to the treacheries of one's own mind is contrasted by a near-comic perception of the absurdity of man's condition in the universe."[27] This statement has equal force for Neal. The bitter joke played by God upon the meek and mild and God-loving David Whicher has its counterpart in the "deceptive hoaxical" narrative framework—a joke played successively on the narrator-persona and the reader.

In turning to Indians, forests, and historical subjects, Neal transformed what he considered Cooper's excessively bland vision of the American landscape into his own wild, darkly ironic, and peculiarly American Gothicism. Neal's ironic vision is significantly reflected in Hawthorne; shortly before the publication of *Twice-Told Tales,* Jonathan Cilley wrote his old Bowdoin College classmate: "What sort of book have you written, Hath? I hope and pray it is nothing like the damned ranting stuff of John Neal, which you, while at Brunswick, relished so highly."[28] Hawthorne, in 1845, referred to "that wild fellow, John Neal, who almost turned my youthful brain with his romances. . . ."[29] A commentator on romantic irony in Hawthorne's tales, Alfred H. Marks, has observed that "Hawthorne knew the works and, at times, seems to have imitated the techniques of several of these writers [contemporaries immersed in the tradition of romantic irony]—techniques visible in John Neal, for instance. . . ."[30]

Neal's acknowledged influence on Hawthorne and his relationship with Poe are interrelated phenomena that clarify our understanding of Neal's—and Poe's—contribution to the American literary revolution. Poe's expressions of nationalistic sentiment, his involvement with *Blackwood's,* his ironic mode—all these facets of Poe's genius are better understood against the background of his protracted and important relationship with John Neal.

Notes

A different version of this paper was presented at the Midwest Modern Language Association meeting, November 2, 1973.

1. *American Writers: A Series of Papers Contributed to* Blackwood's Magazine *(1824-1825) by John Neal,* ed. F. L. Pattee (Durham, N.C.: Duke Univ. Press, 1937), p. 29.

2. *That Wild Fellow John Neal and the American Literary Revolution* (Chicago and London: Univ. of Chicago Press, 1973), esp. pp. 38-65. For quotations and references to Neal's life and writings in this essay, refer to the index of this book.

3. *Broadway Journal,* 2 (Oct. 4, 1845), 199-200. For evidence of Poe's authorship of this item, see E. H. O'Neill, "The Poe-Griswold-Harrison Texts of the 'Marginalia,'" *American Literature,* 15 (1943-44), 246-248.

4. *American Writers,* pp. 29-30.

5. "Poe and 'Young America,'" *Studies in Bibliography,* 21 (1968), 29. For other views of Poe's relationship to "Young America," see John Stafford, *The Literary Criticism of "Young America"* (Berkeley and Los Angeles: Univ. of California Press, 1952), esp. pp. 22, 33, 47-48, 75; Perry Miller, *The Raven and the Whale* (New York: Harcourt, Brace, 1956), esp. pp. 126-127, 133-134, 145-146, 199; Robert D. Jacobs, *Poe: Journalist & Critic* (Baton Rouge: Louisiana State Univ. Press, 1969), pp. 275, 286, 381 n.

6. *Poe and the British Magazine Tradition* (New York: Oxford Univ. Press, 1969), pp. 154-156; Allen quotes from Poe's review in the *Broadway Journal,* 1 (January 4, 1845), 7.

7. *The Yankee and Boston Literary Gazette,* n.s. 1 (September and December 1829), 168, 295-298.

8. "Poems by Edgar A. Poe," *Morning Courier and New-York Enquirer,* July 8, 1831.

9. For Poe's debut as a writer of tales, see Arthur Hobson Quinn, *Edgar Allan Poe: A Critical Biography* (New York and London: D. Appleton-Century, 1941), pp. 191-192.

10. Poe to Neal, June 4 [1840], *The Letters of Edgar Allan Poe,* ed. John Ward Ostrom (New York: Gordian Press, 1966), I, 137; "Marginalia" [1849], *The Complete Works of Edgar Allan Poe,* ed. James A. Harrison (New York: Thomas Y. Crowell, 1902), XVI, 152. Hereafter referred to as *Works.*

11. *Wandering Recollections of a Somewhat Busy Life* (Boston: Roberts Brothers, 1869), pp. 251-252.

12. The most comprehensive treatment of Poe's indebtedness to *Blackwood's* is in Margaret Alterton, *The Origins of Poe's Critical Theory* (Iowa City: Univ. of Iowa Press, 1925), pp. 7-45; see also Allen, *Poe and the British Magazine Tradition,* pp. 29-39.

13. Among Neal's contributions to *Blackwood's* available and probably familiar to Poe were: "American Writers," Nos. 1-3, 16 (1824), 304-311, 415-428, 560-571; Nos. 4-5, 17 (1825), 46-69, 186-207; "Late American Books . . . ," 18 (1825), 316-334.

14. *The Origins of American Critical Thought, 1810-1835* (New York: A. S. Barnes, 1961), p. 57. For a valuable discussion of Poe's psychological concept of effect, see Walter Blair, "Poe's Conception of Incident and Tone in the Tale," *Modern Philology,* 46 (1941), 228-240.

15. *Poe's Fiction: Romantic Irony in the Gothic Tales* (Madison: Univ. of Wisconsin Press, 1973), p. 27; the reference to A. W. Schlegel in the following sentence is based on Thompson, pp. 30-34.

16. Poe refers to Neal's *The Battle of Niagara* in "The Literati," *Works,* XV, 46. Neal's notices of Poe in *The Yankee,* n.s. 1 (1829) are on pp. 168 and 295-298; his articles on "The Drama" are on pp. 57-68, 134-145, 195-209, 249-258, 303-317.

17. For another example of this pervasive concern, see Neal's *Seventy-Six* (London: Whittaker, 1823), I, 1-11.

18. "Edgar A. Poe," *Portland Advertiser Weekly,* April 30, 1850.

19. "Unpublished Preface" [originally submitted to *Blackwood's*], in *Rachel Dyer: A North American Story* (Portland: Shirley and Hyde, 1828), p. xi.

20. *In the American Grain* (New York: Albert & Charles Boni, 1925), p. 227.

21. "Edgar A. Poe," *Portland Advertiser Weekly,* April 30, 1850.

22. *The Quest for Nationality: An American Literary Campaign* (Syracuse, N.Y.: Syracuse Univ. Press, 1957), p. 196.

23. "Edgar A. Poe," *Portland Advertiser Weekly,* April 30, 1850.

24. V. L. Parrington, *The Romantic Revolution in America, 1800-1860* (New York: Harcourt, Brace, 1927), p. 58; F. O. Matthiessen, *American Renaissance* (New York: Oxford Univ. Press, 1941), p. xii, n. 3.

25. Lang, ed., "Critical Essays and Stories by John Neal," *Jahrbuch für Amerikastudien,* 7 (1962), 204-319; the story discussed in the following paragraph, "David Whicher" (1832), is reprinted in Lang, pp. 278-288.

26. *The Essence of Laughter,* ed. Peter Quennell (New York: Meridian Books, 1956), pp. 116-117; the reference is to Charles Maturin's *Melmoth the Wanderer.*

27. Thompson, p. 166; the quoted adjectives in the following sentence are from Thompson's discussion of *Pym,* p. 183.

28. Cilley to Hawthorne, November 17, 1836; quoted in Julian Hawthorne, *Nathaniel Hawthorne and His Wife* (Boston: Houghton Mifflin, 1885), I, 145.

29. "P.'s Correspondence" [1845], *Mosses from an Old Manse* (Boston: Houghton Mifflin, 1882), p. 426; Hawthorne is being ironically jocular on the whole, but seems quite straightforward in his comments on Neal and Halleck.

30. "German Romantic Irony in Hawthorne's Tales," *Symposium,* 6 (1953), 274-275.

William J. Scheick (essay date autumn 1976)

SOURCE: Scheick, William J. "Power, Authority, and Revolutionary Impulse in John Neal's *Rachel Dyer.*" *Studies in American Fiction* 4, no. 2 (autumn 1976): 143-56.

[*In the following essay, Scheick argues that in* Rachel Dyer *Neal demonstrates how the establishment of a distinctly American social order and "American art" results from the process of conflict between Old World and New World notions of individual autonomy and authority.*]

Although John Neal (1793-1875) has not been entirely disregarded by literary critics and is in fact the subject of a recent book-length study, he still remains a relatively obscure figure in discussions of nineteenth-century American fiction. In part this neglect derives from the unavailability of his novels today, but principally it emanates from a critical consensus of the sort reflected in Alexander Cowie's conclusion that though "flashes of something very like genius gleamed from his most gaudy pages," Neal "reaped the harvest of haste: poor proportion, loose ends, slip-shod diction, and general incoherence."[1] Similarly, Harold Martin observes Neal's "mind is second rate and his energy, no matter the good purposes to which it was put, was never sufficiently concentrated to have more than local and temporary effect";[2] and Fred Lewis Pattee laments "could the cataract have been early directed, the headlong powers trained and subdued, [Neal] might have been America's literary master" during his time.[3]

Within the context of this overall assessment of Neal's literary career, *Rachel Dyer* (1828) has surfaced as the novel in which he most successfully restrained his defi-

ciencies. Cowie considers it Neal's best work, an opinion shared by John Seelye and intimated by Benjamin Lease, who speaks of it as "a significant development in Neal's career as a novelist."[4] To a certain extent Neal anticipated this latter-day response to *Rachel Dyer,* for in his introductory remarks to the novel he balances his complaint of insufficient leisure to create quite the book he had in mind with the claim that it nonetheless is "much better, because more evidently prepared for a healthy good purpose, than any other I have written" and should "be regarded by the wise and virtuous of our country as some sort of atonement for the folly and extravagance of my earlier writing."[5] These comments, perhaps accentuated by the author's "farewell, and in all probability, forever," to his readers, suggest that *Rachel Dyer* was, in Neal's opinion, his most accomplished work. Moreover, the likelihood that Nathaniel Hawthorne, who was strongly attracted to Neal's works, may have discovered several features in *Rachel Dyer* seminal to *The Scarlet Letter*[6] alerts the critic to take Neal's novel seriously. A careful reading of *Rachel Dyer* will, in fact, elevate an appreciation and estimation of Neal's management of theme and symbolic detail, for the belletristic achievement of the novel is far more accomplished than previous critical attention has indicated.

Neal's introductory assertion of greater mastery in this novel is underscored by his intentional distortion of factual details.[7] Neal knew many of the historical particulars concerning the Salem witch trials of 1692, apparently chiefly as presented in the 1823 edition of Robert Calef's *More Wonders of the Invisible World,* but he deliberately departed from them. His twelve-page addendum, entitled "Historical Facts," suggests the degree of artistic liberty he took in shaping factual matters to suit the contours of the aesthetic design of his book. Besides embellishing particulars pertaining to the historically incomplete background and portrait of George Burroughs, Neal made numerous alterations ranging from the significant creation of the Quaker Dyer sisters (in actuality Mary Dyer gave birth to no daughters, and no Quakers were placed on trail during the Salem disturbance),[8] to the symbolically significant and plot-facilitating omission of the wives of the real Burroughs and Reverend Parris (which change makes them widowers), to the unimportant modification of the historical Reverend Parris' name. In the addendum Neal remarks that "the true name of Mr. Paris was Samuel, instead of Matthew, and he spelt it [his patronymic] with two r's" (p. 265). Neal then abandons this matter as abruptly as he had introduced it, never intimating why he had made these innocuous changes or why he felt they ought to be brought to attention. The statement finally is an oblique assertion of artistic freedom in fictively treating historical events and an index to Neal's desire that his book be read as a work of art rather than as a factual study. Neal illuminated his attitude toward authorial fidelity to historical matters three years before the publication of *Rachel Dyer,* the very year in which he had written the original shorter version of the story. Reviewing Harriet Vaughn Cheney's *A Peep at the Pilgrims in 1636* (1825) in *Blackwood's Magazine,* Neal complained that the book was "surcharged with historical truth, which nobody cares for; crowded with sober stuff, the insupportable accuracy of which were enough to damp the poetical ardour of a whole nation."[9] Obviating the problem in *Rachel Dyer,* Neal permits his New England setting of 1692 to serve merely as a semi-imaginary stage for the dramatization of fundamental truths about America, "inner" truths more essentially revealing than would be a surfeit of "external" historical details.

The thematic center of *Rachel Dyer* lies, in fact, less with the limitations of the legal system (as most of Neal's critics have concluded) than with a cardinal tension underlying these deficiencies, with the conflict between the artificial power of established authority (expressed in the static laws of an Old World civilization emphasizing conformity to external prohibitive social norms) and the more elemental power of the independent self (expressed in the antinomian impulse of a New World experience emphasizing a self-reliant harkening to internal permissive asocial values). Neal dramatizes this antagonism by means of characterization and symbolic detail, implying that this tension results in a revolutionary impulse identifying the true American, providing the basis for a newly developing American society, and distinguishing genuine American art.

Of the images which Neal manages consistently in his depiction of the conflict between authority and the self, the most prominent derive from the archetypal contest between light and dark. These images do not, as Benjamin Lease concludes, merely establish emotional atmosphere;[10] they define, in a rudimentary manner, the two coordinates of the thematic center of the novel. Imagery pertaining to light identifies the force of social authority, whereas that pertaining to darkness relates to the puissance of the self. Light illuminates external reality, and throughout *Rachel Dyer* Neal impugns Salem society, particularly as reflected in its legal system, for focusing exclusively on circumstantial and superficial evidence. British law, "the law of the mother-country and therefore the law of colonies," embodies the power of an authority based on externals; with irony Neal refers to it as "a pillar of light for the sages of hereafter" and speaks of its administrators as people "*decorated with the badges of authority*" (pp. 23, 64, 93; italics added). Appropriately, at George Burroughs' trial the magistrates call for the lighting of torches in order to counter the sudden encroachment of darkness (p. 233)—the darkness of the mysterious, frightening, asocial energies of the self evident in Burroughs.

Burroughs, however, does not function as Neal's antithesis to Salem society. Opposed to the "illuminating" force of civilization is the Indian, "the *dark* Savage" inhabiting the "*shadow* of the great western wilderness" (pp. 21, 249; my emphasis). The "wild men" dwelling in the "great shadowy woods" (pp. 22, 152) evince the anarchistic instinct of the self at war (literally in Neal's novel) with the repressive voice of social authority arising from Salem's clearing in the wilderness. For Neal, human life is most valued "among the barbarians and the savages" because they represent the self's internal dark impulse which is essential to life but which the Old World civilization seeks to annihilate, the same shadowy force suggested by Neal's inclusion of the seemingly offhanded observations that witches never perform their mischief in the light of day and that Abigail Paris became increasingly darker in complexion the more she experienced the effects of witchcraft (pp. 104, 136, 196).

Both white (civilization) and dark (wilderness), Burroughs is a half-breed (p. 150) symbolizing Neal's notion of the true American. Burroughs' affinity for civilization is most apparent in those periods of his life when he "traversed the whole of Europe" and when he served as a Joshua to the residents of Casco Bay, a village under siege by Indians (pp. 153-54). More often, for reasons evident in the plot of *Rachel Dyer,* Neal stresses the darker features of his swarthy protagonist, who not only grew up in the midst of savage warfare but can with ease assume the identity of an Indian (pp. 149-50, 168). Neal readily reinforces this feature of Burroughs by carefully managing several conventional Gothic devices, such as introducing him in the novel as "a stranger . . . in the shadow of the huge trees that overhung the doorway like a summer cloud," having him ride a "great black stallion," allowing him to defy "the Power of Darkness" before which others tremble, and making him arrive at Paris' home in "pitch dark" (pp. 68, 88, 144, 174).

Accenting his ironic use of light imagery with regard to authority and contributing to his depiction of Burroughs as a representative of both civilization and the wilderness, Neal attributes to his protagonist an inner fire which, because of its mysterious nature, the Salem citizens interpret as darkness but which is the real foundation of society. Seemingly conventional references to Burroughs' "bright fierce look," to the "fire flash[ing] from his eyes," and to his tendency to probe a problem "as with fire" (pp. 68. 72, 174) emphasize his possession of an interior illumination. This feature prevails in accounts of his apparition; and "to the terror of the people" even his black stallion stares with eyes "like two balls of fire" and makes "fire fly" as he runs along a rocky path (pp. 85, 138, 144). Burroughs' possession of this inner illumination suggests that the "light" of social authority is related to the power of the self, a point intimated in Burroughs' assertion to the court, "my feet are upon the foundations of your strength" (p. 241). Compared to Burroughs' inner fire inflaming the wild power of the self, the flickering torchlight of authority proves artificial and weak. Those living in the wan illumination of authority, reflecting the once familiar and now abandoned "fire-sides in Europe" (p. 22), respond to hints of the genuine source of this light "with unspeakable terror," interpret them as expressions of a demoniac "dark" power, and so reduce Burroughs to the status of "an outcast and fugitive, pursued by the law" (pp. 82, 178).

However, as a half-breed combining the instinct of the red man and the ethics of the white man, Burroughs never polarizes his identity. Exemplifying Neal's conception of a true American, Burroughs does not choose one side over the other. In his younger years he had wrestled with the decision over whether he should pursue "further into the cities of Europe, or go back into the wilderness of America" (p. 104); but an older Burroughs fully embraces his double heritage in spite of the fact that at times he is ashamed of his relationship to civilization and that Neal uses him generally as a foil for social authority: "As a white man, I will not war with white men. As the adopted of the red men . . . with the blood of a red man boiling in my heart, as the captive and nursling of the brave Iroquois, I will not be the foe of a red man" (p. 171; author's ellipsis). Because the Indians fear his whiteness and the colonists fear his savage inner power—Burroughs is "a creature of tremendous power" in body, mind, and words (pp. 222, 225, 237) disproportionate to his external anatomical appearance[11]—he has learned to accept his twilight existence between the warring forces symbolized by the wilderness and civilization.

Elizabeth and Rachel Dyer likewise lead a twilight existence, literally "living on the outskirts of the wood" (p. 203) between the Indians and the colonists (perhaps adumbrating Hester's similar symbolic residence in *The Scarlet Letter*). Rachel, rather than Elizabeth, represents the feminine equivalent to Burroughs. When Neal reports that she stood "in the dark part of the [meeting] house" where "the shadow of a mighty tree fell so as to darken all the faces about her" (pp. 129, 147), he introduces her in a manner very similar to the initial appearance of Burroughs. Like Burroughs, moreover, Rachel not only lives between the wilderness and civilization but can readily interact with both white and red races (p. 200). Likewise, the Dyers "belong to neither side in the war" between the Indians and the Salem residents (p. 205); and Rachel's red hair, freed from the confines of her cap (a parallel symbolic detail occurs in *The Scarlet Letter*) and "shining . . . with a frightful fixed gleam" (p. 226), corresponds to Burroughs' terrifying fiery looks. A pariah, Rachel is said to lead a charmed life rather like that of Burroughs, who is thought insane (pp. 88, 206).

By introducing the detail that Rachel is a Quaker (p. 147),[12] Neal not only forges another link between his two protagonists but also broadens their symbolic function. As a Quaker, Rachel is an outcast in Salem (a community of Congregationalists) and, without totally repudiating civilization, she relies on an inspiring Inner Light, on the "inward prompting" of the shadowy power of the self so feared by the Salem witch-hunters. Rachel's Quaker faith in the Inner Light corresponds to Burroughs' trust in the antinomian impulse of the independent self, in spite of the fact that nominally he is a Congregationalist minister. At one point Burroughs concludes that he is "a messenger of the Most High"; he believes "the dead of the night," when one's thoughts turn inward, is the time when God, "the Searcher of Hearts," speaks most effectively (p. 173). When he asserts that his feet stand upon the foundation of the magistrates' strength, Burroughs declares that what the judges do by the power of their authority—"which is, to deal with the creatures of God, as God himself professes to deal with them" (p. 102)—he can similarly perform by the more elemental power of a divinely inspired interior light which is in fact the very source of external legal authority. Like a Quaker, Burroughs believes that he speaks "by authority of *one* who hath endowed me with great power" (p. 223).

Neal prepares the reader for this emphasis on Rachel and George's mutual trust in the interior power of the self by referring early in the novel to Elizabeth Hutchinson (he means Ann, of course). As Michael Colacurcio has observed about a similar allusion in *The Scarlet Letter,* "virtually all commentators have recognized that in New England, in dialectic with the Puritan Way, Ann Hutchinson and the Quakers go together; that the latter represent, chiefly a more organized and self-consciously sectarian espousal of the values of individualistic (or 'spiritual') freedom which is the essence of Ann Hutchinson's doctrine."[13] Emphasizing that Hutchinson was "one of the most extraordinary women of the age," that she was a close friend of Rachel's mother, and that she spoke with "awful power" about a "new faith" as if she had "authority from above" (pp. 36-41),[14] Neal intends the reader to detect this connection between antinomianism and Quakerism. The Salem residents believe that their trouble with the Indians signifies the actualization of Hutchinson's fearful prophecy, and they are correct: the Indians represent the dark power of the antinomian self which has once again returned to confront (warfare) and to haunt (witchcraft performed only at night) the force of authority denying its relation to the more fundamental power of man's interior and thereby making fugitives of such people as the Dyers and Burroughs.

Neal also dramatizes this conflict between the antinomian self and social authority in his portrait of the Reverend Paris. Initially a leader of his community, Paris becomes increasingly alienated during the trials. Now a widower dwelling "away and apart from all he knew,

on the very outskirts of the solitude" (p. 51), he encounters the inner wilderness of the self. For Neal, as
later for Hawthorne, marriage symbolizes one's tie to
the social community,[15] and it is noteworthy not only
that George and Rachel are unmarried and cannot wed
each other but also that Paris "had never been afraid of
witches till after the death of his wife," who significantly was "as beautiful as the day" (pp. 50, 186; in
fact the wife of the real Parris did not die until 1696).
While married, Paris dwelt in the illumination of society's clearing in the wilderness and enjoyed a community identity similar to that of Governor Phips, "who
lived in the very whirl of society, surrounded by the
cheerful faces of those that he most loved on earth"
(pp. 48-49). With the death of his wife this light vanished for Paris, and he "withdrew from the world and
shut himself up in a dreary solitude"; under these circumstances he encountered "the desolation of a widowed heart" (pp. 49, 50), that same shadowy wilderness
of the self known to George and Rachel.

Paris, however, experiences turbulent dreams and visions because, unlike George and Rachel, he symbolizes the inability of the Salem community, those Old
World emigrants who fearfully left behind their reassuring English fireside society, to cope with the inner
power of self symbolized and stimulated into expression by the "shadow of the great western wilderness."
Unable to reconcile the "dark savage" power of the self
and Old World social authority, Paris goes insane (p.
233); his insanity ironically undercuts Salem's sense of
Burroughs' dementia as well as symbolizes and explains the madness evident in Salem's crazed persecu-
tion of anyone who seems to evince the witchery or
dark powers of the self.[16] Confronted by the New World
environment, which encourages the expression of the
self, the Old World society, unable to suppress or to accommodate the New World forces, goes insane and
steadily destroys itself.

In ***Rachel Dyer*** Neal celebrates the promise of a fresh
society, one indigenous to the New World reconciling
self and community, a society of half-breeds, as it were.[17]
Sharing a faith in the self and experiencing similar circumstances, George and Rachel forshadow a new alternative society. At this early phase of American development, however, they suffer from loneliness. Although
they do not repudiate society, they are isolated from it
and are forced to experience, internally and externally,
"the desolate shores of a new world," the "shores of the
solitude" (pp. 21, 33). Like Burroughs and like Hawthorne's Hester (who is forced into the solitude of forest freedom as if she were a "wild Indian"),[18] Rachel is
"always alone" during her life at the edge of the forest
(p. 200). But when Neal's two protagonists join forces,
they represent the emergence of a new society, one in
which Burroughs feels supported by the Dyer sisters
and in which they, each in her own way, fall in love
with him (p. 226). At the conclusion of the novel Rachel

kisses George, an act suggestive of their own sense of
family or social cohesion. They can never marry—
Neal's symbol for the actualization of social identity—
because the new community they symbolize has not yet
arisen.

In order for this alternative society to emerge, sacrifices
must be made to the Old World civilization. Whereas
the Indians do not accept Burroughs' offer of himself as
"a sacrifice for [his] white countrymen," the residents
of Salem "would have the blood of a brother" (p. 170).
An act redressing his earlier failure to lead the Casco
Bay congregation to "their salvation," to prevent the
"sacrifice" (Neal's word) of Sarah Good, and to protect
his two deceased wives, who "had died, he believed in
his own soul, a sacrifice to the bitter though mute per-
secution they had to endure for marrying with one who
was not altogether a white man," Burroughs' death
saves two hundred lives (pp. 34, 96, 152, 154). Solitude
(estrangement) and sacrifice (death) are the initial requisites for an emerging New World society.

This new community will not annihilate but will accommodate the self. It will displace the life-destroying,
wilderness-leveling fears of an Old World society antagonistic to the vital impulse of the self; it will, in
Neal's opinion, supplant a Calvinistic life-negating belief in a transcendent God emphasizing external legalisms with a secular life-engendering trust in a social authority derived from the self's emphasis on internal
virtue. As Neal's prototype of the citizens of this new
community, Burroughs readily departs from Congregationalist dogma, most significantly when he advises
Rachel to prevaricate and confess her guilt so that she
may live to "do much good on earth" (p. 257). No conscientious New England Puritan minister of 1692 would
give this advice, least of all for the reason Burroughs
cites; for the Puritan, truth before God mattered above
all else regardless of its consequences in the material
world. Burroughs, however, responds to an inner authority and, consequently, he advocates a variety of
"situation ethics."[19] Explaining to Rachel: "What I have
said to you, I have been constrained to say, for it is a
part of my faith Rachel, that as we believe, so are we
judged: and that therefore, had you believed it to be
right for you to confess and live, it would have been
right, before the Lord" (p. 257). No orthodox Puritan
could have espoused such a notion, one clearly stressing the primacy of the self's authority. Burroughs, like
Hawthorne's Hester, affirms action based on the inner
self's sense of social ethics rather than on mere conformity to external authority and the fear of God.

Burroughs' concern over public welfare indicates Neal's
idea that the free expression of the self in America will
not result in anarchy but will somehow give rise to a
new society which proves less structured and more liberated than the Old World civilization yet which imparts broader social purpose to the energies of the self.

Although *Rachel Dyer* ostensibly dramatizes the conflict in seventeenth-century America between the self and social authority, the central focus of the novel highlights its two protagonists as prototypical Americans transforming the antinomian impulse stimulated by the New World experience into a burgeoning social order deriving from and somehow accommodating the self. Without the metamorphosis provided by the American experience, the mysterious "dark" self would tend toward anarchistic savagery and manifest the deformity the Old World associates with it. Neal acknowledges the external deformities which the eruptions of the self are prone to produce—hence Burroughs' altered swarthy appearance and small stature as well as Rachel's unattractive freckled face and "distorted shape" resulting from her humped back (p. 226); but he also warns against assessing value and beauty by superficial evidence or externals illuminated by a light merely revealing surfaces: "we may be deceived, if we venture to judge of the inward by the outward man" (p. iii). Rachel and George evince an inward force resulting in certain unattractive and anarchistic deformities in the external concerns of the Old World society but nonetheless proving potentially beautiful and valuable with regard to the internal virtue of an emerging New World community. As Neal explained in 1825, "we require of the American people, great power, stout, original power; productions, whatever else they may be, indigenous to the country; preferring those which are decidedly vicious, to those which are of a neutral character"; "give us that which is able to be mischievous, if unrighteously, or unworthily administered" because "whatever is incapable of doing mischief, is incapable of doing good."[20] In *Rachel Dyer* Neal depicts the shadowy power of the self as an apparent deformity (dark and savage) which in actuality provides the basis (an inner light) for the evolution of New World social ethics organic to the self.

For Neal, the most dramatic expression of this power occurred during the War of Independence, though the revolutionary impulse or inward prompting was experienced by true Americans before that time. Rachel and George represent types embodying the alienated, sacrificial revolutionary spirit which was manifested during the War of Independence. They would have found the society of post-Revolutionary America a more congenial environment than seventeenth-century Salem; they would have enjoyed a new society purchased by the sacrificial deaths of people like themselves. Quoting a remark about Burroughs, Neal stresses that "what he [George] was put to death for in 1692, he may be renowned for (if it please the Lord) in 1792" (p. 149). By means of a careful management of Burroughs' role in Sarah Good's trial, Neal places his protagonist's defense of the alleged witch in the context of a rebellion foreshadowing the American revolt against the authority of the British king. At one point during the trial Bur-

roughs complains, "I can perceive now why it is, if a man appear to testify in *favor* of human life that he is regarded as a witness *against* the crown"; and he continues, "God help such crowns, I say! What an idea of kingship it gives!" In reply the voice of Old World authority warns, "Beware of that Sir.—You are on the very threshold of treason," and threatens him with death if he speaks further in this manner (pp. 93-94). Neal reinforces this adumbration of the spirit and of the rhetoric of the Revolutionary War period when he has Burroughs observe, "where human life is thought much of, there liberty is" (p. 104). In post-Revolutionary America even "the very rabble of our earth deride" the fears and behavior of the Salem residents.

By alluding to the War of Independence Neal hoped to accomplish more fully one of the primary goals he set forth in his preface to the novel: to reflect artistically what is indigenous and unique in American people. "Our literature will begin to wake up, and our pride of country will wake up with it" (p. x), Neal explains, implying that the revolutionary impulse evident in the spirit of the War of Independence and of such sacrificial prototypes as Rachel and George will also increasingly permeate a developing American literature. The War of Independence serves Neal as a lodestar symbol of the spirit of the genuine American. Writing in his autobiography about another of his novels, *Seventy-Six* (1823), Neal recalls, "I had got charged to the muzzle with the doings of our Revolutionary fathers, while writing my portion of 'Allen's History,' and wanted only the heat, or touch, that Cooper gave in passing [in *The Spy*], to go off like a Leyden jar, and empty myself at once of all the hoarded enthusiasm I had been bottling up."[21] *Rachel Dyer* is a more disciplined expression of Neal's enthusiasm; and in their assertion of self against Old World authority, George and Rachel evince the revolutionary impulse which Neal believed indigenous to America, the impulse most dramatically manifested during the War of Independence and increasingly evident in American society and literature.

Although Neal considered the Revolutionary War as the *sine qua non* of symbols appropriate for portraying the American spirit, he did not maintain that a novelist should limit himself to that specific period of American history. In 1825, he had in fact disapproved of the many American authors who restricted themselves to this event; but he conceded that however dull this preoccupation with the period had become, it "augurs well for a new growth of literature" and indicates "the day of thorough emancipation is near," when American literature will clearly demonstrate that it too arises out of the indigenous Revolutionary War impulse:

> Who that wishes well to the great republic of literature,—who that knows what miracles may be wrought, with a spirit entirely free,—when a whole nation goes

forth to a generous warfare; every heart swelling with courage, heaving with joy, beating with hope; all on fire, with a new taste of immortality, ripe for adventure in every possible shape . . . will not pray for that hour to arrive?[22]

The American novelist, in Neal's opinion, does not need to set his book in the War-of-Independence period in order to depict the revolutionary impulse of the American people. Settings, historical events, local color characters, and colloquial speech (significantly, a "free" language uninhibited by Old World conventions)[23] drawn from the full range of American experience will reveal this autochthonous New World force existing before and continuing to thrive since 1776.

In the completed novel as well as in the earlier, shorter version of **Rachel Dyer,** Neal intended to employ "the language of immortal, indistructable [sic] spirits" in order to create "a portrait of man—a history of the human heart" (p. ix). By delving into the "dark" force of the self in its reaction to confining social authority, Neal explored not only the underlying power infusing an emerging American civilization and literature but also the antinomian inward promptings shared by all humans: "If I have not brought up the pearls, I can say at least that I have been to the bottom" (p. ix). Reiterating his purpose several pages later, Neal resorts to imagery suggesting his concern with the interior terrain of the self, with the inner impulse or "subterranean melody" of the American psyche: "One of my objects was to show to my countrymen that there are abudant and hidden sources of fertility in their own beautiful earth . . . barren places to all outward appearance . . . yet teeming with bright sail" (p. xvi).

For Neal, American literature reflects, particularly since the War of Independence, an evolving New World society derived from, accommodating, and containing without stifling the inward prompting of self stimulated into expression by contact with the free, life-loving "dark savage" dwelling in the shadowy wilderness (an externalization of the self's interior reality). Because this developing society recognizes the primacy of and remains responsive to the self's revolutionary impulse, its authority does not confront but directs the self's power. This more advanced human community is suggested at the conclusion of the novel when Rachel kisses George, her spiritual brother who might have been her lover in a more congenial environment. This kiss seals their mutual citizenry in the emerging New World society comprised of literal and figurative half-breeds who were initially reduced to alienated solitude and sacrificially slain by the Old World authority in order to give birth to a new community; indeed Elizabeth Dyer, who is spared, "will have sympathy" (p. 260). **Rachel Dyer** celebrates a vision of America's fresh future society in a prose style which, in Neal's opinion, is emancipated from Old World literary authority. Not rigid like the external artificial legalisms of Old World established authority or chaotic like the internal elemental power of the self's antinomian impulse, the prose in this novel was designed by Neal to convey, as it were, a halfbreed style mirroring George Burroughs' harmonious integration of revolutionary impulse (the self's power) and social ethics (community's accommodating authority), an ideal integration informing Neal's vision of a looming new American society and of its burgeoning indigenous literature.

Notes

1. *The Rise of the American Novel* (New York: American Book Co., 1951), p. 175.

2. "The Colloquial Tradition in the Novel: John Neal," *NEQ* [*New England Quarterly*], 32 (1959), 459.

3. In the introduction to his edition of Neal's *American Writers: A Series of Papers Contributed to "Blackwood's Magazine" (1824-1825)* (Durham: Duke Univ. Press, 1937), p. 21.

4. Cowie, p. 173; Seelye, in his introduction to a facsimile reproduction of the work (Gainesville, Florida: Scholars' Facsimiles and Reprints, 1964), p. viii; Lease, *That Wild Fellow John Neal and the American Literary Revolution* (Chicago: Univ. of Chicago Press, 1972,), p. 144. Oral Sumner Coad concludes, "Neal happily has no rival in the school of frenzied fiction" ("The Gothic Element in American Literature before 1835," *JEGP* [*Journal of English and Germanic Philology*], 24 [1925], 87).

5. *Rachel Dyer: A North American Story* (Portland: Shirley and Hyde, 1828), p. iv. Subsequent page references to quotations from this edition will be included parenthetically in the text of the article.

6. Lease refers to Hawthorne's addiction to Neal's romances (pp. 39, 94-95, 194).

7. Lease notes in passing that Neal took liberties with the facts but does not speculate about implications (p. 144).

8. James Savage, *A Genealogical Dictionary of the First Settlers in New England* (1860-1862) (Baltimore: Genealogical Pub. Co., 1965), II, 89; Marion L. Starkey, *The Devil in Massachusetts: A Modern Inquiry into the Salem Witch Trials* (New York: Knopf, 1949), p. 133.

9. *American Writers,* p. 197.

10. Lease, p. 143.

11. The word *power* is not only prevalent in *Rachel Dyer* but abounds throughout Neal's writings. It is

power that Neal admires in Cooper's *The Refugee* and that he perceives as his own strongest attribute (*American Writers,* pp. 220-21; 244-46).

12. Neal was raised as a Quaker but broke with the faith. His personal feelings apparently did not interfere with his use of Quakerism to symbolize certain features of his notion of the proper American.

13. "Footsteps of Ann Hutchinson: The Context of *The Scarlet Letter*," *ELH,* 39 (1972), 473. Neal's suggestion that Ann Hutchinson is a type for Rachel may have been seminal to Hawthorne's interest in her as a type for Hester. The observations of Nina Baym's "Passion and Authority in *The Scarlet Letter*" *NEQ,* 43 (1970), 209-30, read in the light of my discussion, implies still other similarities between *Rachel Dyer* and *The Scarlet Letter.*

14. In fact, the real Mary Dyer, who had no daughters, was a close friend of Ann Hutchinson and was executed in 1660 for her Quaker heresy. Neal's references to Ann Hutchinson, central to his view of Rachel, advance his favorable position on women's rights. For his views on this subject, see Neal, *Wandering Recollections of a Somewhat Busy Life* (Boston: Roberts Brothers, 1869), pp. 50-51, 88-103, 412-20; and Boyd Guest, "John Neal and 'Women's Rights and Women's Wrongs,'" *NEQ,* 18 (1945), 508-15.

15. Neal married in the year in which *Rachel Dyer* was published. He has remarked in his autobiography that he had a horror of "the dreariness, the loneliness, the desolation, the utter hopelessness of a bachelor's life," indicating the value of marriage as a symbol for him at the time (*Wandering Recollections,* p. 356).

16. In fact the real Parris never went insane and served Sudbury, Massachusetts as a teacher and petty merchant until the end of his life. For an excellent study of Parris' role in the Salem upheaval, see Paul Boyer and Stephen Nissenbaum, *Salem Possessed: The Social Origins of Witchcraft* (Cambridge: Harvard Univ. Press, 1974).

17. For a discussion of another literary use of the image of the half-breed by a contemporary of Neal, see my "Frontier Robin Hood: Wilderness, Civilization, and the Half-Breed in Irving's *A Tour on The Prairies*," *Southwestern American Literature,* forthcoming.

18. Nathaniel Hawthorne, *The Scarlet Letter* (Columbus: Ohio State Univ. Press, 1962), p. 199.

19. Joseph Fletcher uses this phrase to describe an approach to morality which is not limited by rigid notions based on natural law (Roman Catholicism) or on scriptural law (Protestantism) and which prevents the other extreme of pure antinomianism by admitting the single absolute of love as the criterion for a moral decision (*Situation Ethics: The New Morality,* Philadelphia: Westminister Press, 1966).

20. *American Writers,* p. 201.

21. *Wandering Recollections,* p. 224.

22. *American Writers,* pp. 193-94.

23. On Neal's use of the colloquial, see Harold G. Martin, "The Colloquial Tradition in the Novel" and his "The Development of Style in 19th Century American Fiction," in *Style in Prose Fiction,* ed. H. C. Martin (New York: Columbia University Press, 1959), pp. 114-41.

Donald A. Sears (essay date 1978)

SOURCE: Sears, Donald A. "Experiments in American Fiction." In *John Neal,* pp. 34-52. Boston: Twayne Publishers, 1978.

[*In the following essay, Sears discusses the six novels—* Keep Cool, Logan, Randolph, Errata, Seventy-Six, *and* Brother Jonathan—*written by Neal during the early 1820s.*]

In an eight year period John Neal published six novels,[1] each in many ways unpolished and hectic but each an experiment in treating American themes and scenes in an American way. That they were written with what Neal called "marvellous rapidity" and what critics damned as "fatal facility" is attested by the author himself; indeed he wishes to astound with his boast:

> *Keep Cool* was "written in hot weather" in 1816.
>
> *Logan* . . . I wrote in six or eight weeks, ending Nov. 17, 1821;
>
> *Randolph,* I began Nov. 26, 1821, and finished in thirty-six days;
>
> *Errata* . . . was begun Jan. 8, 1822, and finished in thirty-nine days;
>
> *Seventy-Six,* begun Feb. 16, 1822, and finished March 19, 1822—four days off—in twenty-seven days.[2]

All this feverish writing was while Neal was pursuing his law studies, and writing for the press. Only *Brother Jonathan* (1825), which he took in manuscript to England and there rewrote for *Blackwood's,* escapes his boast of speed. Actually the first as well as the last of this series of early novels was fully revised, yet these two are no better for it than the others. In fact, *Seventy-Six* is without doubt the best, despite its having been struck off in a month.

Neal's pride in speedy composition was intended as a boast. He was more than a little a showman, trained in his apprentice years to the sharp come-on of salesmanship. As he sets out to sell his writing, he is advertising himself as a rash and fiery genius. Perhaps he oversold his image, although there is scant evidence that he could have done better with more leisure. A touch of genius he had, but to the end it remained undisciplined and unchanneled.

I KEEP COOL

At twenty-three, Neal was struggling to support himself while reading for the law, and although stimulated by the publication of his poems and articles in *The Portico,* he had received no money for these contributions. As he put it, "I now began to cast about for something better to do—something, at least, that would pay better; and, after considering the matter for ten minutes or so, determined to try my hand at a novel" (*WR,* 196). Even then Neal was so constituted as to throw himself wholeheartedly into nearly hopeless causes. To make a living by writing was such a cause, for by this summer of 1816 fewer than seventy novels by Americans had been published and fewer still had been a financial success. There were the examples of Charles Brockden Brown's series of hurried novels, of Brackenridge's *Modern Chivalry,* and of Royall Tyler's *The Algerine Captive:* otherwise the field of fiction in America lay in the genteel hands of the women who wrote sentimental novels of seduction. To expect to increase his income by writing a novel was as unrealistic as it was typical of Neal.

But a novel it was to be; he proceeded to write in a fine frenzy, stating "I shall write as others drink, for exhilaration"[3]. The resulting outpouring was novel indeed, with its mock-serious title "Judge Not from First Appearances." The manuscript was entrusted to his friend Pierpont, by now in Massachusetts studying for the ministry, who sought without success among the Boston publishers for someone to buy the book (*WR,* 196-97). In rejecting it, they found the women too earthy, too susceptible to male overtures,[4] while lacking the higher flights of love: "There is not quite *love* enough in it to suit the ladies," was the judgment of Mrs. Read, wife of one of the publishers with whom Pierpont shared the manuscript. Neal accepted the criticism—tamely for him—and set about rewriting the work with a new title of *Keep Cool.* Another friend, Dr. Watkins, interested the Baltimore publisher Joseph Cushing in taking the toned-down version. Neal jumped at the offer of two hundred dollars "like a cock at a gooseberry" (*WR,* 197), but whether Neal had tamed his wild genius and outspoken Yankee realism sufficiently for the lady readers is, however, questionable.

In an age used to Richardsonian heroines of sentiment, Neal's women are too pert. Harriet teases the hero: "I can put you in good humor any time, by a little *flattery,* no matter how gross" (*KC,* I, 41). Treading on still more dangerous ground, she can fall in a faint in the hero's arms, only to revive enough to saucily admonish him to "keep cool" (*KC,* I, 40). Fainting, after all, confides the author, is "the last and highest of their witcheries, and the next after hysterics and tears." Such puncturing of the facade of female decorum could not be offset by Neal's dedication: "To his Country Women the Author, who is an American, respectfully dedicates this work." Neal does, however, defend American womanhood from the coquettry of Laura by having her born abroad albeit by American parents. She has become "Italianate." Her behavior is revealed as play-acting when, to be entertaining, she mimics her friends to perfection. The scene foreshadows by almost thirty years the similar unmasking of Major Bulstrode in Cooper's *Satanstoe.* The open honesty of Americans can see through the sophisticated role-playing of the European.

In spite of this patriotic bias, the book still had for novel readers of the day too many characters who relish their sins, and to them the author gave the best lines: the rakish Charles Percy likes all women, for "his mother and his sister were women, and he could have hugged to his heart all that resembled them. . . ." Further "Charles had the heart of a man; when he saw perfection—and every thing young and lovely seemed to him to be perfection—he worshipped it . . ." (*KC,* I, 25). Unfortunately, Charles also likes to tell of his adventures with women, a trait he shares with later Neal characters. He has in Laura a female counterpart who is allowed her defense of fickleness and flirtation: "Who can answer for the constancy of woman? Besides . . . it is not I who change, but the *object*" (*KC,* I, 172).

Neal was enjoying himself in this novel, enjoying being a bit outrageous, projecting his own O'Cataract character into the story, and writing with an eye on the ladies of the Baltimore circle who had first led him into literature. As a bachelor—by choice or the exegencies of bankruptcy—he was at the time of writing his first novel teasing his married friend Pierpont and boasting of the superior ability of an unmarried man to start, as they were doing, a new career: he wrote, "You are at that age when such misfortunes are most terrible—the sapling may be prostrated with little damage to the oak itself—but when the oak falls, a thousand dependences fall with it."[5] There is as much self-justification as gratuitous moralizing in such remarks to his friend; and there is certainly a young man's self-justification as well as crypto-confession in his treatment of the romantic tendencies of his fictional characters.

So also there is self-advertisement when he reprints his *Portico* poems **"To Genius"** and **"To Fancy"** as illustrations of a discussion of poetry (*KC,* I, 124-31), or when he argues that every author publishes because he has a high opinion of himself—and hence should not play at false modesty (*KC,* I, 114-15). Yet in the preface his boasts are tempered with coyness as he admits that for all its faults, the book is the best that the author can make it. In fact, the reader is constantly warned from title to introductory words at chapter openings, to "Keep Cool."

The result of this self-conscious playfulness is an ambiguity of tone. As much as anything, the shifting of tone from arch attempts at wit through mock seriousness to concern for social issues confuses the reader, who indeed must keep cool if he is not to lose all patience. As a first novel, *Keep Cool* is too rich a pudding; individual plums can be savored only when abstracted from the seething mass. The strangely modern ring of Earnest's insult to his landlord—"Keep cool, daddy" (*KC,* I, 61)—is followed by a republican attack on the use of titles, even those of military rank (*KC,* I, 62-63). An accurate description of the varied crowd on a Hudson River boat[6] turns into frontier-type horseplay as the group convinces a luxuriously bewhiskered man to shave himself clean because whiskers have been found to induce facial cancer. By the time the reader is swept into the second volume, his head spins with new characters, such as the Byronic poet Echo,[7] and with social issues ranging from arguments against capital punishment to defenses of the noble Indian. Yet the narrative dramatizes an opposite view, as bloodthirsty Indians drawn from captivity narratives provide a "glorious" chase for the rescuers.

Keep Cool is a young man's novel, filled with too many diverse elements and episodes through which a racing prose tumbles the weary reader. It is embellished with coy humor such as its titular refrain and false chapter epigraphs,[8] and is often marred by brashness: "I have no respect for Aristotle; his criticism is fast following his philosophy" (*KC,* II, 126).

Faulty as it may be, the book has energy, and deserves more than the passing reference afforded it in standard studies of early American fiction. The preface helps to set it in historical perspective. Alluding to foreign attacks on American writing, Neal proclaims

> The time will arrive, when the production of American science and genius, will bear some proportion to the scale of their inspiration. The time will arrive, when these slanders, and these aspersions will be forgotten; when our posterity will wonder that we could have ever doubted the everlasting charter of greatness that is written upon our barriers:—our cataracts—our rivers—and our mountains.
>
> (*KC,* I, xvi)

A great landscape will evoke a concomitantly great literature, boasts Neal in a fervor of literary nationalism built upon association psychology. And if *Keep Cool*

fails of greatness, as it does, it is eminently American in its individuality that achieves eccentricity, in its brashness, in its flashes of earthiness puncturing pretension, and in its moral earnestness regarding social reform.

It was this last that Neal later claimed as his major purpose. In retrospect, after he had been made notorious for his antiduelling stance following the publication of *Randolph,* Neal increasingly felt that he had written his first novel in order to strike a blow as a social reformer: "In writing this story, I had two objects in view: one was to discourage duelling; and another was—I forget what" (*WR,* 197). But even here the playfulness of the last clause undercuts the seriousness of the first statement. If indeed *Keep Cool* had been planned as an antiduelling novel, he waited overly long to introduce the topic—195 pages. It is true that Neal had debated the duelling question before the Delphian Club and had published his thoughts in *The Portico.* As a young Quaker boy he had doubtless been impressed by the public outcry when Burr had killed Hamilton in 1804; there is little doubt of Neal's sincere abhorrence of the *code duello* as an aristocratic holdover inappropriate to the democratic scene. He held flatly that "duelling is the worst of murders" (*KC,* I, 209) and stressed the class element whereby "in America, a *gentleman* may cut another's throat, or blow out his brains with complete impunity. Here, the vulgar only are hanged for murder" (*KC,* I, 231).

But one senses less of the social reformer than the novelist in the work itself. The few early American novels that served Neal as models generally had a strong didactic strain, often as defense against those who held the genre immoral. Here as elsewhere Neal seems to be using the didactic mainly to illustrate the towering intellect of his titanic heroes. Cast in the mold of Manfred, his supermen must project intellectual power. Further, Neal is developing a Godwinian plot. Like Godwin's Caleb Williams, a good man who is goaded into a justified murder but is destroyed by the guilt that haunts him, Neal's Sydney is a Byronic English officer who is provoked into a duel with the lady's man Charles Percy. With his antagonist fatally wounded, Sydney flees civilization to do penance among the Indians by whom, it is revealed, he had formerly been adopted. Neal seems to have intended an exploration of the effects of guilt and expiation. But he loses himself as well as his hero in the murky woods, bringing him back to an un-Godwinian happy ending: Sydney and Laura kneel penitently before the portrait of Percy, marry, and produce cherubic twins.

Keep Cool is finally a confused and confusing book, but one that pioneers in the use of American material, including the Indian. In its attempts to deal with sin and expiation it intrigued the undergraduate Hawthorne.

And, in what was then a predominantly feminine field (Cooper's *Pioneers* was six years in the future), Neal's novel is healthily masculine even in its faults. As a recent critic states, "Whatever objections may be raised against *Keep Cool* . . . the book can hardly be called monotonous."[9] The final judgment is Neal's: "The idea . . . was original enough . . . [but] there was much in it . . . that was boyish . . ." (*WR,* 221).

II *LOGAN*

Despite the cool reviews of his first novel, Neal was launched into prose. Like Pierpont he had vowed to give over poetry after the publication of his first volume, actually promising to write only in prose. The shift from his rhetorical poetry to poetic rhetoric was not a great one for him, and he supported his literary practice by his developing theory of poetry that was expanded to embrace a new prose-poetry. Some of his clearest statements were to appear in *Randolph,* but even before writing *Logan* he held that the literature of the future was to be heart literature in which "man must be the hero—and his heart the world which is convulsed in his career: the passions of man are the most terrible ministers—more terrible—infinitely more so, than the familiars of Milton's angel."[10] *Logan* presents in passionate prose such a hero.

Whereas his first novel had been rewritten out of deference to the lady reader, *Logan* was Neal unrestrained. He breaks violently from the genteel tradition that apologized for fiction as the product of an author's leisure hours, designed to improve the leisure hours of others by its good moral principles and exposure of vice.[11] Neal now proclaimed the novel as the very highest of literary forms. Just as he had broadened his concept of poetry to include all emotive language, he expanded the novel to include the best of all fiction, whether drama or verse, "where imaginary creatures, invested with all the attributes of humanity, agitated by the passions of our nature, are put to the task of entertaining or terrifying us."[12] Further, the novel, because it is read by people who never read anything else, is capable of greater influence than any other art form; it therefore calls to the man of greatest talent to provide the best possible novels. Men should enter a field that is too important to leave to "women and children," for "To write a good novel, a man should be a poet, a dramatist, a tragick and comick writer, a philosopher, a preacher, and an orator. . . ." (*S,* II, 228). In short, the novelist should be a John Neal, who setting flying pen to paper, poured his own passionate nature into *Logan,* his concept of a new novel for a new country.

At the time Neal had been managing to eke out a living from his writing. The two hundred dollars he received for *Keep Cool* had been followed by one hundred dollars worth of books for his volume of poetry and one hundred dollars for his drama *Otho.* Still desperate to support himself while he read the law, he engaged in the sheer drudgery—"sixteen hours a day, every day, including sabbaths . . . for four full months"—in indexing the first twelve volumes of *Niles' Weekly Register.* For this he received two hundred dollars plus the unexpected gift of a bound set of the *Register,* worth another one hundred dollars.[13] When a fellow Delphian, Paul Allen, was unable to fulfill a commitment for which subscriptions had already been sold, Tobias Watkins and John Neal teamed up to write Allen's *History of the American Revolution* (1819) on a payment per page basis. Neal hoped to do better with the more congenial work of his second novel.[14]

The resulting two volumes that burst upon the public in 1822 were, reflected Neal, a "wild, passionate, extravagant affair with some . . . of the most eloquent and fervid writing I was ever guilty of, either in prose or poetry" (*WR,* 223). Watkins, who received his copy in Washington, D.C., at once recognized O'Cataract's rhetoric in "every sentence, every line—nay, every thought, idea, phrase, expression." Somewhat ambiguously he concluded that *Logan* "is one of the most extraordinary productions of the present age . . . no other man on earth could have written such a book."[15] While no one knew just what to make of it, the book was a sensation, with readers taking it "as they took . . . exhilarating gas . . ." (*WR,* 224). Down to the present, critics have continued to have trouble dealing with this tale of American gothicism; Alexander Cowie states flatly, "*Logan* is not a nice story. Superstition, supernatural suggestions, brutality, sensuality, colossal hatred, delirium, rape, insanity, murder are the stuff out of which Neal weaves a Gothic tapestry never quite paralleled by Charles Brockden Brown or Poe."[16] Cowie forgot incest in his list of horrors.

Whereas Neal's first novel had ended among the Indians, *Logan* at the outset proclaims itself to be a truly American story by a native American, purportedly the last of the Mingos. Chapter 1 is in the form of a letter from the fictional narrator, written from exile in London at midnight on December 31, 1820. A second chapter leaves the epistolary device with its first person point of view to give a narrative review of the Virginia Indian Logan, a legendary chieftain who started as a friend of the whites but turned to vengeance after the massacre of his Indian wife and family. In actuality he is an Englishman gone renegade, begetting sons in wrath to carry on his vengeance before disappearing—à la King Arthur—leaving behind his mighty bow that none can draw. But unknown to Logan, his son Harold has survived the massacre and has been adopted by the governor. It is this son who is the central Byronic titan of the story. A word picture—*ut pictora poesis*—sketches his mother as an Indian queen in panther skin, sandaled feet, and carrying a bow; this dusky Diana is, however, no virgin huntress, for she is surrounded by naked children, a fruitful Eve of the forest.

With the background material behind him. Neal races into the story improper with Chapter 3. The gigantic Logan suddenly appears before the governor, who faints. The garrison is in a panic, but superhero Harold returns, assumes command, and restores order as Logan escapes with the Indian treaties. Harold goes on the warpath as an Indian killer, vying with Logan for the lovely Indian girl Loena. This father-son rivalry seems ended when Logan is reported to have wed Loena and started a new family. Meanwhile the governor's young wife, the Lady Elvira—a lively combination of pride and contrariness—harbors a secret passion for Logan whom she saw before her rescue by the governor from a massacre. Unconsciously in love with Harold as a surrogate for Logan, she ambiguously accepts his visit to her bedchamber.[17] The jealous governor banishes Harold to the forest where his parentage is revealed by an apparently mortally wounded Logan. Inheriting the feud to kill all whites, Harold also inherits Loena. As leader of the Indians, he runs amok in pillage and carnage, learning the uses of pain both as a protection of self and as a means of defining pleasure.

He becomes, however, a truly noble savage during his honeymoon idyll with Loena: "The moonlight shone upon their faces—they embraced, and slept, like two children, innocent and lonely, and helpless; without one impure thought, one throb of sensuality to disturb their beloved dreaming—'*Their priest was solitude.*'"[18] In their forest Eden they rise to wed one another by starlight, and then "They knelt together: her warm cheek rested upon his, her dark tresses hung waving over her bosom. . . . Heart throbbed against heart; mouth breathed upon mouth; and their intertwining arms, in the pure innocence of their embrace, trembled at the same moment, with the same sensation" (*L*, I, 239). The scene, with its echoes of *Paradise Lost,* is one of the first to present the American Adam as wilderness lover, and it ends with the further Edenic touch of the beasts passing by and leaving the couple unmolested as they drift into innocent sleep. Less innocent perhaps was Neal's titillation of his readers with the physical warmth of a passage that reveals something of his own heated imagination. His dream woman is like his Bill Frazier's "woman as she is by nature, the Woman of the Woods, the exalted creature that issues uncorrupted, untouched from the hand of her Almighty Father! Eves of the great wilderness! Angels of solitude!"[19]

Harold's forest idyll ends as he travels to Quebec where the governor sends him to Europe to be trained as a proper leader of his people. Loena is left behind to be trained by the governor's wife. As he embarks, the first volume is rapidly coming to a close with Harold heroically rescuing a child who falls overboard at sea and repulsing a French boarding party. He and a lovely girl faint together, he of wounds, she of passion, as the reader is teased on to the sequel volume.

The plot, which for all its fervor in Volume 1 had been that of a border romance, now runs out of control. The widowed Elvira shows up on shipboard with her child Leopold, who proves to be Harold's contribution to their not so ambiguous night. Oscar, a second romantic genius, is also aboard and turns out to be Harold's brother as Loena is his sister. To the incest motif is added further murky sexuality when it is known that Oscar once wooed and won Elvira. The meaning of Neal's subtitle "A Family History" is fast becoming family fiasco. After discoursing eloquently on slavery, including the legal slavery of those under twenty-one, the apprentice and the indentured, Oscar leaps into the sea, a suicide expiating the murder of a woman he once slew at sea. The ocean crossing is further enlivened with gory scenes of two dead captains,[20] the hanging of pirates from the yardarm, and the passing of a slave ship; dead slaves wash by the ship, described with chilling details of fish-eaten bodies.

Harold is brought safely to England, where he discovers that he is of royal blood. For all Neal's American democratic sympathy he does not escape the romantic stereotyping of his hero—noble blood will tell even on the frontier. Through Harold's innocent eye, Neal effects some reputable satire of society; Harold is surprised at the expense lavished on public monuments when the funds could have been used to build a hospital. He visits the seat of rural charm, his ancestral home. He discovers the correspondence of Oscar and Elvira, and much of the volume reverts to epistolary style in recounting their love affair. Even more than Harold, Oscar has demonstrated the unleashed pride, will and ambition of a titan: "from head to foot, a creature of desperate energies, irregular appetite, and sublime incoherency . . ." (*L*, II, 124).

Suddenly Oscar returns from drowning, is reunited with Elvira, the woman he thought he had killed. Harold delivers an impassioned speech to parliament in defense of the nobility of the Indians, and they all depart for America. As they make a family pilgrimage to the spot of Logan's death, Fate appears as the maddened father of so many of the characters: Logan, not dead but totally mad. He shoots down Harold; Loena falls dead across his body. Oscar fights and kills Logan who dies "like some wild beast strangling in his own blood." Having killed his own father and having learned from Elvira of her shameful affairs, Oscar goes mad and dies. With most of the cast dead, this time without hope of surprise resurrection, Neal ends on a patriotic note, asking the English to "acknowledge us, as we are, the strongest (though boastful and arrogant) progeny of yourselves . . . when your nation was a collossus . . ." (*L*, II, 34).

The importance of *Logan* was in its demonstration of the uses of native material within the tradition of the gothic novel as developed by Charles Brockden Brown; in its foreshadowing of elements of the border romance, particularly the more bloody variety such as Robert Montgomery Bird's *Nick of the Woods* (1837); in its tracing of the effects of the sin of the father upon later members of the family—a theme that Hawthorne was to develop so brilliantly; in its elements of diseased psychology that Poe was soon to exploit. As both Cowie and Lease have amply shown, there are passages in Neal where dream—or rather nightmare—imagery is brilliantly used to reveal the troubled soul of a character. Harold's near madness after learning of his incestuous relations transforms the ship's ropes upon which he tries to sleep into serpents of conscience:

> Alas, for Harold! A continual and confused ringing was about him, all night long. Worn, and trembling, and sick at heart, time appeared to stand still, as he turned, again and again, and adjusted his limbs to the rugged cordage, upon which he lay, until he was utterly exhausted. . . . And then his conscience would awake, and put on her bloody robes, and sit over him with a terrible countenance—and he would feel himself pinioned, naked, hand and foot—helpless, alone—with just enough of light to see the far off and dim movement of innumerable feet, incessantly approaching in the darkness, as of some cumbrous, and interminable monster—and to feel ten thousand detestable and obscene creatures crawling slowly over his very lips and eyes, which he had no power to shut—slimy, loathsome reptiles, slipping lazily over his naked fingers; while his very flesh crawled and quivered, and rotted, in the poison that they left in their trail. Anon, this would be changed. The light would break out upon him—he would be sleeping in a delicious green solitude—the earth flowering all about him, with fountains flowing "in odour and gold"—and violets—"but the trail of the serpent was over them all."

> (*L,* I, 291)

As an experimental novel, the influence of the book was great upon the rising generation of American writers, although it was not reprinted in America. To British readers it appealed on different grounds as the work of an erratic but near genius of the New World. Besides the 1822 edition, *Logan* was republished in London in 1840 and again in 1845. Today it is difficult to be fair to the book, for it is excessive in almost every way. Perhaps the best evaluation is that of Neal himself, writing from the perspective of England and seeing his novel in the context of the then scant range of American fiction. In his survey of American writers, he concludes,

> *Logan* is full of power—eloquence—poetry—instinct, with a more than mortal extravagance: Yet so crowded—so incoherent—. . . so outrageously overdone, that no-body *can* read it through. Parts are without a parallel for passionate beauty;—power of language: deep tenderness, poetry—yet every page . . . is rank with corruption—the terrible corruption of genius.—It should be taken, as people take opium. A grain may exhilarate—more may stupify—much will be death.[21]

His next novel will be more controlled; he had passed through a personal crisis by projecting his own unresolved pride and ambition into his titans—Logan, Harold, and Oscar.

III *Seventy-Six*

When he came to write *Seventy-Six* Neal found through the framework of history a greater control over his torrential prose, producing what he continued to feel was his best novel. Shortly after publication, pretending to be a British critic reviewing American literature, he treats his own work, and gives a fair summary of the achievement: "I pronounce this to be one of the best romances of the age. With a little care—some pruning: a few alterations, it might be made an admirable book of. So far as it goes, it is quite a faithful history of the old American War—told with astonishing vivacity. The reader becomes an eyewitness in spite of himself."[22] The seeming boast of the first sentence is a proper judgment, for *Seventy-Six* appeared in 1823, the same year as Cooper's *The Pioneers* and *The Pilot*. When he was writing it, virtually the only competition for Neal's new novel was Cooper's *The Spy* (1821) with which Neal's compares well in its evocation of actuality.

Neal had been in the preceding years filling himself to overflowing with reading for his share of Allen's *History of the American Revolution* (1819-1822). Now stimulated by Cooper's example, he drew on this historical background,[23] adding the zest of a style more personal and exciting than Cooper's. By narrating the story through the words of an old soldier, Jonathan Oadley, Neal gains the eyewitness viewpoint of a storyteller's story. Oadley ostensibly relates the events in the life of his brother, but they are events in which he also plays a part. From the moment of Oadley's opening words, "Yes, my children, I will no longer delay it," a colloquial tone of immediacy is set. Neal is deliberately experimenting with a new and American style of writing. Before him he had few models (and few after him until Twain) who tried to bring the prose of serious fiction closer to the speech of contemporary America. Earlier experiments had been restricted to stage Yankees like Jonathan of *The Contrast* or humorous newspaper pieces of frontier humor. Neal wanted to narrow the gap between spoken American English and the prevalent stilted style of romance. Even Natty Bumppo speaks in an elevated language for elevated thoughts, and as for the prose of *The Spy,* Neal found Cooper's style "without peculiarity—brilliancy, or force."[24] Neal's aim was to "talk on paper" (*S,* I, 17).

Oadley therefore begins to talk on paper, recording for his children an account of the family's participation in the Revolution. But first he warns them—and the reader—that the style will be unique:

> My style may often offend you. I do not doubt that it will. I hope that it will. It will be remembered the better. It will be the style of a soldier, plain and direct, where facts are to be narrated; of a man, roused and inflamed, when the nature of man is outraged—of a father—a husband—a lover and a child, as the tale is of one, or of the other.
>
>   (*S,* I, 17)

The very passage itself illustrates the directness of the soldier in the short sentences and repetition, but also the longer and looser sentence structure of passion— usually easily spotted on Neal's pages by the free use of dashes.[25]

Soon the language will reveal itself in another way as the language of soldiers; profanity and oaths occur with an outspokenness appropriate to the occasion, but nonethless surprising for the century. Especially from the fire-eating Clinton come frequent "damn its" and an occasional "what the devil." With complete vividness Clinton recounts the skirmish in which he was wounded:

> "It was *there,*" said he, "*there,* exactly where that horse is passing now, that they first fired upon me. I set off at speed up that hill, but, finding nine of the party there, I determined to dash over that elevation in front—I attempted it, but, shot after shot, was fired after me, until I preferred making one desperate attempt, sword in hand, to being shot down, like a fat goose, upon a broken gallop. I wheeled, made a dead set, at the son-of-a-bitch in my rear, unhorsed him, and actually broke through the line."
>
>   (*S,* I, 184-85)

Not until a century later was the same freedom allowed a writer; even the Twain of *Roughing It* reports a profane miner's oath as a "son of a skunk." Neal's frankness, of course, did not slip unrebuked past the critics, who faulted him for attributing oaths to the speech of honorable soldiers.[26]

In the dialogues, obviously, Neal is most able to achieve the effects of "talking on paper." He is bothered by the conventional labelling of speeches, and struggles to gain some variety through direct address (*S,* I, 131), then midway in the novel, he tries another device: the narrator speaks for him: "To save the constant repetition of *said he,* and *said she*—I shall give the names first, of each speaker, as in a dialogue [That is, as in a play]" (*S,* I, 198). He tries this for a time, but soon slips back to more traditional means of identifying speakers. This, however, was only the first of Neal's attempts to make his dialogue more closely approximate

the look as well as the sound of actual talk. In later novels he continued experimentation and actually found a more adequate solution.

This pursuit of a more colloquial style also had a salutary effect on Neal's narrative and descriptive passages. The images of meteors and cataracts that overweight his early poetry and prose—especially in *Logan*—are replaced from closer to earth. As a result Neal's writing at this period contains some of his most telling comparisons. For instance, he describes how the soldiers only become aware of their discomfiture after the heat of battle cools: ". . . and then it was—*then*—when it was necessary to move about the quieter operations of strife, that we began to feel the intense coldness of the night—the keen air cutting into our new wounds, like rough broken glass" (*S,* II, 160). The cutting of the winter air is realized with a vividness that can only make the feelings of the troops come alive on the readers' senses. Neal draws on natural observation to find a simile for the pent-up fury—and evil—of Copely: ". . . he opened his mouth, and his heart ran out, like a current dammed up,—and ready, at his bidding, to waste and thunder, like the spring tide, and swollen rivers of our country, loaded with ice, and foam, and blackened with wreck and ruin" (*S,* II, 79). When the same demonic Copely turns his enmity toward the narrator, the effect is more than chilling: ". . . my heart, upon my word, felt, as if it had been drifting about in a cold rain, for a week, drenched and soaked through—chilled" (*S,* II, 76). There is, of course, a certain heightened straining after special effect in such passages. But the style is capable of quiet understatement as well. A family interlude ends with the men departing once again for the battlefield. "Rodman and Copely then embraced their wives . . . and . . . set off, at full speed, from the house. It was a bitter cold morning for the season" (*S,* II, 222). The restraint of the final sentence, which is also the last sentence of the paragraph and chapter, is more powerful than all of Neal's earlier pyrotechnics in *Logan.*

Furthermore, the plot is the most straightforward that Neal has so far developed. While dramatizing the darkest days of the Revolution through the battles of New Jersey and on to Valley Forge, he also traces the adventures of the Oadley family—two brothers, a cousin, father, and friends. As the story opens the family has not yet been touched by the war and they debate whether the young men should enter service. When the Hessians burn their home and rape their mother, there is a rush to enlist. The young men mature and marry during their years of service. Archibald, the Byronic brother of the narrator and hero of the novel, has to kill two men in duels, but is afterward haunted by the blood he has spilled. Historical personages including Washington, Lafayette, Pulaski, and Burr appear briefly. The events of war are intertwined with the romances of the young men. The central couple, Archibald and Lucia, are ill-fated as each is tainted by sins of passion; the novel ends with their marriage at which Archibald falls dead. The scene and line end the novel in Neal's best (or worst) melodramatic manner. Archibald murmurs "Lucia, my *wife*" and then

> He stood suddenly erect upon his feet; the light flashed over his face. It was the face of a dead man. He fell upon the floor: a loud shriek followed. Where were we?—*Where!* We ran to him—we raised him up. It was too late! Almighty God! *it was too late!* HIS WIFE WAS A WIDOW!

> (*S,* II, 260)

It is not for such overwrought effects that the novel still appeals, but rather for the actualization of battle scenes from the viewpoint of ordinary soldiers, for honestly presented love affairs of real young men and women, for some touches of social comedy, and for the use of psychological material of visions and dreams.

One of the most effective battle scenes presents the retreat across the icy river at Trenton. When one of the great war chargers falls into the river and is carried downstream and under the ice, Jonathan recalls that ". . . either of us would have risked his own life, I have no doubt, for the safety of the animal—when we heard his last loud, convulsive sobbing, and saw the amazing strength of his blows, as he broke through the ice at every leap" (*S,* I, 165). Here as elsewhere, Neal is particularly good in dealing with horses; one of the best sections of his poem **"The Battle of Niagara"** had presented the night movements of the cavalry, and the passages in *Seventy-Six* dealing with cavalry remain stirring today.

Well presented is the enmity and rivalry between the Northern and Southern troops fighting under Washington. While Neal's native sympathy goes to the New Englanders as the "most substantial men for the service" (*S,* II, 39), he is fair in his praise for the more chivalric valor of the Virginians.

Interspersed with the historical scenes of battle is a secondary plot of romance. At a time when the daughters of Pamela dominated fiction, Neal's women, in contrast, are varied, warm, and even earthy. His lovers act as real young men and women involved in real affairs of the heart in which sexual attraction is felt on both sides. Archibald's love for Lucia falters when the seducer Copely comes between them for a time, but even in the role of seducer he is far from the stock villain of the sentimental novel. He is a brave officer, a close relative to Washington, who is admired for his good qualities by Archibald who is deeply affected by the developing triangle. The reader feels the impending tragedy of a situation that can only end in a challenge and duel. Archibald wins but suffers remorse that undermines both health and mind.

Concurrently Archibald's brother, the narrator Jonathan, is in love with Lucia's haughty sister Clara, but cannot resist the vivacity of flirtatious blonde Ellen. On leave in Philadelphia he finds himself alone with Ellen; the scene develops warmly, stopping just short of physical seduction, although it is a good question who seduces whom. Only Jonathan's sense of honor controls the situation. After the first passionate kiss upon the mouth, Jonathan remembers Clara and breaks off the love scene with the suggestion that they cool off with a walk through the snowy streets of the city. He admonishes Ellen that her flirtatious ways would with anyone else have been her undoing; he had only been teaching her a needed lesson! In this pious conclusion, Neal is himself involved. As a young bachelor, he had been caught out and "misunderstood" in a similar situation with the sister-in-law of his friend Pierpont.

With Ellen, Neal is presenting the realities of passion among the young and their complications. Jonathan still has to face Clara who has heard an exaggerated report of his behavior with Ellen. After she is convinced of his innocence, the scene develops into a love exchange which Neal breaks off, this time less effectively, by a Shandean device: At the crucial moment, the page is filled with asterisks and a note from the publisher to the effect that a whole page has been lost. The story takes up again as the lovers are parting (*S,* II, 111).

The love plots take place in the private homes of New Jersey and Philadelphia, allowing both for good insights into the effects of the Revolution upon domestic life and for scenes of social comedy. There are, for example, playful hits against the social awkwardness of some Quaker men: ". . . haw! haw! haw!—laughed the brace of Quakers, sprawling their legs about, and, leaning back in their chairs, with their hands in their breeches" (*S,* II, 241). At the opposite extreme are the overly ladylike airs of Lucia's and Clara's mother. Married to the Frenchman M. Arnauld, she likes to embellish her conversation with mangled French and Italian, an innocent ridiculousness which Neal satirizes (for example, *S,* I, 199-200). Neal's love of punning, however, gets out of hand when the discussion turns to the dog of Venice, the dolphin of France, and the clam of Tartary (*S,* I, 242). He is on surer ground with Yankee humor. A Down-East frontiersman named Hanson is serving in the army and brings news of Archibald. Ill at ease in the drawing room, Hanson shifts about in his chair, crosses his legs, tugs at the collar of his coat, and then reports in good Yankee dialect. The entire passage, of several pages, possesses a linguistic interest. Hanson gradually loses his shyness as he recounts the battle in which Archibald was wounded, and his terse, broken speech rises to Yankee rhetoric as he concludes: "Captain Rodman too, did famously; but the major!—well—Guns! how he rattled away at 'em!—hey—no quarter—none!—It soon became a race—whoop! Morgan's riflemen peppered 'em, fore and aft, well—the horse tumbled together, in heaps. . . . So, you see, they got a sound drubbin'" (*S,* II, 203). As elsewhere, Neal uses the dash freely to indicate the pauses and rhythms of actual speech. The passage also reveals the New England use of "famously" in the sense of "well." The archaic plural "horse" is true to the dialect as is the use of words like "drubbin'" and "peppered."

Some of the same broken rhythms of speech are found in remarkable passages of dream psychology used by Neal to reveal the inner passions of his characters. In a state that would be recognized today as battle fatigue, Jonathan's sleep is troubled with war images:

> I was asleep. At dead of midnight, I heard a trumpet, as I thought, sounding to battle. I rose, pained and dizzy,— unwilling to go out—and desirous to skulk, if I could, into the holes of the rocks. Then I thought that it began to rain fire upon me; and the earth shook, and battalions of men, armed all over in shining mail, spattered with blood, came, parading, column after column, from the earth—nation after nation—each of loftier, and yet loftier stature still,—warlike—and terrible, like the buried Apostles of liberty: and then, all at once, there was a tremendous explosion, and I felt myself sinking in a swamp—the loose earth quivering like jelly, at every tread, and cold serpents and bloated toads all slipping about me, so thickly, that, set my naked foot, wherever I would, something that had life in it—some fat icy reptile would stir under the pressure—and then I was entangled in the thorny creeping tendrils of many a plant that encumbered my path; dead bodies lay in my way; I was pinioned hand and foot, and serpents fed upon my blood, and vultures flapped over me. And then, out of the east, there blazed, all at once, a light, like a million of rockets, that blinded me. And then, I felt a hand—the hand of a murderer about my throat— God!
>
> (*S,* II, 54-5)

Similar use of psychological material reveals the approaching breakup of Archibald and the reactions of Jonathan to battle itself. Unlike his brother, Jonathan was not eager to enlist and confesses his fear of battle. As he reports his first battle, however, he reveals the excitement and "terrible delight" that catches him up until he fights with "a sort of religious fervour, exceeding wrath and indignation." He is knocked from his horse, senseless; when he comes to, the battlefield is dark and strewn with corpses. He staggers toward an enemy soldier, but the heat of battle is gone and he feels no hatred but sympathy for a fellow human being. Not until the scenes of *The Red Badge of Courage* were the varying emotions of war to be so well realized— and, interestingly, both Neal and Crane were of the generation after the war which each vivifies. An act of creative imagination brings both battle and soldier's reaction to life, as Robert Bain has correctly stated regarding this battle scene: "Neal explores in some depth, the consciousness of his narrator. The fear, the chaos, the exhilaration, the righteousness, the madness, the emptiness, the amazement, and finally the exhaustion are realized fictionally in the world outside Oadley *and* in his consciousness. . . ."[27] This realization is largely effected by repetition of highly sensuous imagery and contrasts of light and dark, noise and quiet, hatred and sympathy.

To dramatize thus the inner and outer battles has taken greater space than Neal had planned for. The reader is therefore not surprised by Oadley's sudden cry "I shall never be able to carry you through the whole war, as I intended to do, when I began" (*S,* II, 242). In the few remaining pages of the novel, the events are summarized by the use of letters that culminate in the final dramatized scene of Archibald's marriage and death. Nor is that last scene the only touch of gothicism in the story. Archibald has visions, a mysterious rapping three times is heard just before the death of the father, violent storms in the elements accompany storms of the passions in a deliberate reaching after an effect of the sublime. In fact, the sublimity of American nature is explicitly discussed by Archibald:

> Let a man go with me . . . out into the wilderness . . . sit with me as we sat together this afternoon, before the hurricane broke down upon us; and feel the soft air whispering about his heart; or hear the thunder breaking at his feet; and see the great trees bending and parting, in the wind and blackness of God's power—I care not who he is, or what he is—where born—or how educated—I defy him not to fall down, with his forehead in the dust, and acknowledge the presence of God.
>
> (*S,* II, 234)

It was not this reverential effect of the sublime, however, that infused Neal's next novels. In these he returned to the more extravagant style of ***Logan*** in order to explore human passion.

Notes

1. Neal's fiction is discussed by Herbert Ross Brown, *The Sentimental Novel in America 1789-1860* (Durham, North Carolina, 1940, reprinted New York, 1959) for attitudes toward women and the religious novel; by Alexander Cowie, *The Rise of the American Novel* (New York, 1948), pp. 165-77; by David Brion Davis, *Homicide in American Fiction, 1789-1860* (Ithaca, N.Y., 1957) for his Titanic heroes; by Ernest E. Leisy, *The American Historical Novel* (Norman, Oklahoma, 1950) in a brief treatment of *Rachel Dyer;* and by Lillie Deming Loshe, *The Early American Novel 1789-1830* (New York, 1907, reprinted 1958), especially pp. 92-94; and most recently by Henri Petter, *The Early American Novel* (Columbus, Ohio, 1971) and Lease, *That Wild Fellow,* chapters 7-10, 12-13.

2. *Wandering Recollections* [(Boston, 1869)], p. 173[; hereafter cited in text as *WR*].

3. Neal, *Keep Cool* (Baltimore, 1817), preface; hereafter cited in text as *KC*.

4. Lease, *That Wild Fellow*, p. 25.

5. Neal to Pierpont, April 17, 1816 (Pierpont Morgan Library, New York); quoted by Lease, p. 24.

6. *Keep Cool*, I, 74-76. Neal developed a similar setting in *The Down-Easters*, making it the scene of a comedy of national manners and an expose of sharpers. Melville developed such a setting further in *The Confidence Man* (1857).

7. His name may be intended to satirize *The Echo*, publication of the Connecticut wits.

8. Neal confesses the falseness of the epigraphs: ". . . inasmuch as it had become a settled fashion to head the chapters of a story with quotations, like those of Sir Walter Scott. . . . I sat down and wrote several pages of dislocated and fantastic verses, which I handed to the printer, with general directions to divide the chapters, according to his own good pleasure, and to prefix the mottoes, without any regard to their applicability . . . no wonder people could never quite satisfy themselves that I was not making fun of the reader" (*WR*, 197).

9. Henri Petter, *The Early American Novel* (Columbus, Ohio, 1971), p. 177.

10. Delphian Club records, quoted by Lease, *That Wild Fellow*, p. 74.

11. See, for example, the prefaces of *Julia* and *Dorval* by Sally Wood, a fellow native of Neal's home state of Maine.

12. Neal, *Seventy-Six* (Baltimore, 1823), II, 228; hereafter cited in text as *S*.

13. The index was published in Baltimore in 1818. Neal recounts the misery of his hack work at length in *Wandering Recollections* (pp. 210-14). He treated himself to a trip back to Portland with the proceeds.

14. Cary and Lea of Philadelphia brought out the American two-volume edition of *Logan, a Family History* (1822). A four-volume edition appeared in London the following year. As *Logan, the Mingo Chief. A Family History* it was republished in London in 1840 and again in 1845.

15. Letter to Neal, December 18, 1822; reprinted in *Wandering Recollections*, pp. 233.

16. Cowie, p. 167.

17. This scene is the first of several psychologically revealing scenes of a man's midnight visit to a girl's room. Here the "rape" is not only completed but half accepted by the victim (but see discussion in the following chapter).

18. Neal, *Logan* (Philadelphia, 1822), I, 238; hereafter cited in text as *L*.

19. Neal, *The Down-Easters* (New York, 1833), II, 160; hereafter cited in text as *D*. The story of "Bill Frazier—The Fur Trader" appears at the end of that novel (II, 112-72).

20. Compare the Portland burial of Captain William Borrows of the *Enterprise* and Captain Samuel Blythe of the *Boxer*. Both young men were killed in the naval engagement between their brigs on September 5, 1813. The American and British were given full and equal military honors and were buried side by side in Eastern Cemetery on September 8. (See William Willis, *The History of Portland* [Portland, 1865], pp. 759-60.) The occasion also impressed the very young Longfellow who includes the episode in one stanza of "My Lost Youth."

21. *Blackwood's Magazine* 17 (February, 1825); reprinted in *American Writers*, ed. F. L. Pattee (Durham, North Carolina, 1937); pp. 168-69.

22. *American Writers*, p. 169. For his similar opinion, written in old age, see *WR*, 224.

23. As Neal put it, "I had got charged to the muzzle with the doings of our Revolutionary fathers, while writing my portion of 'Allen's History,' and wanted only the hint, or touch, that Cooper gave in passing, to go off like a Leyden jar . . ." (*WR*, 224). Neal's preceding novel *Logan* had dealt with events on the eve of the Revolution; he now treated the central patriotic period itself, proclaiming on the title page "Our Country!—Right or Wrong."

24. *American Writers*, p. 70. For Neal's use of dialect and development of a colloquial style see Harold C. Martin, "The Colloquial Tradition in the Novel: John Neal," *New England Quarterly* 32 (1959), 455-75; Robert J. Menner, "Two Early Comments on American Dialects," *American Speech* 13 (1938), 8-12; Richard Bridgman, *The Colloquial Style in America* (New York, 1966); and Robert A. Bain, Introduction to *Seventy-Six*, facsimile edition (Bainbridge, N.Y., 1971), pp. xx, xxvi-xxviii.

25. Neal's punctuation was a feature, common to his age, of expressing emotion by free use of dashes and the like. On emotive punctuation, traceable to Sterne, see Ian Watt, *The Rise of the Novel* (London, 1960), pp. 196-97.

26. See Lease, *That Wild Fellow*, p. 95.

27. Bain, Introduction to *Seventy-Six*, p. xxxiii.

Selected Bibliography

PRIMARY SOURCES

1. BOOKS

Keep Cool, a Novel. Written in Hot Weather, by Somebody, M.D.C. & c. & c. & c. 2 vols. Baltimore: Joseph Cushing, 1817.

Battle of Niagara, a Poem, without Notes; and Goldau, or the Maniac Harper. By John O'Cataract. Baltimore: N. G. Maxwell, 1818. 2d. enl. 1819. International, 1978.

Otho: A Tragedy, in Five Acts. Boston: West, Richardson and Lord, 1819. Facsimile, Ann Arbor, Michigan: University Microfilms International, 1977.

Logan, a Family History. 2 vols. Philadelphia: H. C. Carey & I. Lea, 1822. London Editions, 1823, 1840, and 1845.

Seventy-Six. 2 vols. Baltimore: Joseph Robinson, 1823. London editions 1823 and 1840. Facsimile of Baltimore ed., with introduction by Robert A. Bain, Bainbridge, N. Y.: York Mail-Print Co., 1971.

Randolph, A Novel. 2 vols. [Philadelphia], 1823.

Errata; or, the Works of Will. Adams. 2 vols. New York: Published for the Proprietors, 1823.

Brother Jonathan: or, the New Englanders. 3 vols. Edinburgh: William Blackwood, 1825.

Rachel Dyer: a North American Story. Portland: Shirley and Hyde, 1828. Facsimile, with introduction by John D. Seelye. Gainesville, Fla.: Scholars' Facsimiles and Reprints, 1964.

Authorship, a Tale. By a New Englander Over-Sea. Boston: Gray and Bowen. 1830. Facsimile, Ann Arbor, Michigan: University Microfilms International, 1978.

The Down-Easters, & c. & c. & c. 2 vols. New York: Harper & Brothers, 1833.

True Womanhood: A Tale. Boston: Ticknor and Fields. 1859.

Wandering Recollections of a Somewhat Busy Life. Boston: Roberts Brothers. 1869.

SECONDARY SOURCES

1. BIBLIOGRAPHIES

Richards, Irving T. "John Neal: A Bibliography." *Jahrbuch für Amerikastudien* 7 (1962), 296-319.

2. BIOGRAPHIES

Lease, Benjamin. *That Wild Fellow John Neal and the Literary Revolution.* Chicago: University of Chicago Press, 1972. Sheds new light on Neal's years in England while stressing his role in literary nationalism.

Richards, Irving T. "The Life and Works of John Neal." 4 vols. Ph.D. dissertation, Harvard University, 1932. Fullest account but relatively inaccessible.

Yorke, Dane. "Yankee Neal." *The American Mercury* 19 (January-April, 1930), 361-68. Very readable and sympathetic portrayal.

3. STUDIES

Cowie, Alexander. *The Rise of the American Novel.* New York: American Book Company, 1948. Contains a full critical discussion of the major novels.

Guest, Boyd. "John Neal and 'Women's Rights and Women's Wrongs.'" *New England Quarterly* 18 (December, 1945), 508-15. Presents Neal's activity in the women's rights movement.

King, Peter J. "John Neal as Benthamite." *New England Quarterly* 39 (1966), 47-65. Examines Neal's role as a popularizer of Benthamism in America.

Lang, Hans-Joachim. "The Authorship of 'David Whicher.'" *Jahrbuch für Amerikastudien* 7 (1962), 288-93. First assignment of this story from *The Token* to Neal.

———. "Critical essays and stories by John Neal." *Jahrbuch für Amerikastudien* 7 (1962), 204-88. Reassessment of Neal's contribution to the genre of the short story, and examples of his work.

Lease, Benjamin. "Yankee Poetics: John Neal's Theory of Poetry and Fiction." *American Literature* 24 (January, 1953), 505-19. First study of Neal's literary theory and practice as it relates to Schlegel.

———. "The Authorship of 'David Whicher': The Case for John Neal." *Jahrbuch für Amerikastudien* 12 (1967), 124-36. Discussion of the publication of Neal's story and his dealings with Goodrich.

Martin, Harold C. "The Colloquial Tradition in the Novel: John Neal." *New England Quarterly* 32 (December, 1959), 455-75. Credits Neal with pioneer development of American colloquial style.

Menner, Robert J. "Two Early Comments on American Dialects." *American Speech* 13 (February, 1938), 8-12. Earliest study of Neal's use of dialect in his fiction.

Richards, Irving T. "John Neal's Gleaning in Irvingiana." *American Literature* 8 (May, 1936), 170-79. Presentation of Neal's meeting with Irving, and living in Irving's former rooms in London.

Rubin, Joseph J. "John Neal's Poetics as an Influence on Whitman and Poe." *New England Quarterly* 14 (June, 1941), 359-62. Study of those elements of Neal's literary theory that were developed more fully by the later poets.

Yoshe, Lillie Deming. *The Early American Novel.* New York: Columbia University Press, 1907. Pioneer study of the novel of Neal and his contemporaries.

Donald A. Sears (essay date 1978)

SOURCE: Sears, Donald A. "Critic, Patron, Hack." In *John Neal,* pp. 111-21. Boston: Twayne Publishers, 1978.

[In the following excerpt, Sears illustrates how Neal influenced American literature through his literary efforts and patronage of fledgling authors during his tenure as editor of The Yankee.]

Like Poe, Neal was at heart a magazinist, throwing his considerable energy and talent into the editing of various periodicals over a span of forty years. His first experience had come in Baltimore where he prepared the June, 1818, issue of *The Portico.*[1] The founding editor, Dr. Tobias Watkins, who had recently been appointed assistant surgeon-general of the United States, left the preparation of what turned out to be the final issue to Neal, its major contributor during the preceeding two years. The hoppers were nearly empty and the young substitute editor filled the pages with his own reviews, including a perceptive study of "Childe Harold's Pilgrimage, Canto IV." But his uncongenial excursion into philosophy—**"Man not a Free Agent"**—ran twenty-seven pages, and, said Neal, "knocked it in the head."[2] *The Portico's* days were, however, already numbered with the breaking up of the original group of the Delphian Club; the demise of its journal cannot be laid to Neal's editorship. Otherwise he would not, a few months later, have been asked by Paul Allen, another of the Delphians, to fill in for him as editor of the *Federal Republican and Baltimore Telegraph.* Neal had also contributed to this journal as early as 1817. Now during February through July, 1819, he saw its issues through the press. These two experiences with editing in Baltimore were a foretaste of his launching his own ambitious *Yankee*[3] in January, 1828. It marked his reentry into the American literary scene after his years abroad and was his platform for reestablishing his reputation.

I A YANKEE CIRCLE

During the two years of its existence *The Yankee* as edited by John Neal was a stimulating vehicle for new ideas, a voice for Neal's considerable critical talents, and an outlet for previously undiscovered writers. The forthrightness of the editor was reflected in every issue. It was this openness and honesty that impressed a contemporary who wrote of the weekly,

> Articles, which for their boldness and audacity could find place in no other columns, were as acceptable to our unflinching editor, as the mother's milk that gave him his incipient vigor. If they were erroneous, he retracted like a true man, in the next issue. Were they true, as soon prevent the soul of John Brown from marching on, as move him to a retraction.[4]

With characteristic lack of modesty, Neal himself knew the value and uniqueness of what he was doing. In the sixth issue he advised subscribers to get covers and pre-serve the paper, for "Our *Yankees* are worth it. . . ."[5] As editor he labored with love for five hundred dollars a year payable in books,[6] but his true reward was in earning back his place of acceptance in his hometown. Early issues, therefore, contain a good deal of self-vindication in long articles on England that demonstrate how little he had sold out his native land. Yet he refrained from a position of unexamined anti-British sentiment, for issues in March, 1828, contain praise of Shelley, followed the next month by defenses of Leigh Hunt and Byron. Neal also hoped to introduce to America the thought of Jeremy Bentham.

His interest in Benthamism had, of course, been reinforced by his residence in the philosopher's household, and he now dedicated his weekly to spreading Bentham's ideas, at least as he understood them. But he had quarreled in England with most of the younger utilitarians, and too often his columns contain splenetic attacks on John Bowring and John Stuart Mill. Even his portraits of Bentham reveal a crotchety and eccentric old man rather than a seminal thinker. His most positive contribution to the introduction of utilitarian principles into America turns out to be in the practical field of prison reform. Drawing on the *Panopticon* of Bentham, Neal ran a six-part series on **"Penitentiary Systems"** during 1829. Yet, in spite of the motto blazoned on *The Yankee*—"The greatest happiness of the greatest number"—Neal's service to popularizing utilitarianism was, at last, mixed in effect. He may actually have done the philosophy harm by his own intemperate espousal; one reviewer concluded,

> Bentham's views we believe, are not appreciated in this country owing to two causes—the fact that they were originally published in the French language, and the more unfortunate fact, that that versatile and unbearably egotistical genius, John Neal, undertook, from the very best motives, to introduce them to the American public.[7]

For all that Neal's Benthamism created intellectual excitement and ferment in the pages of *The Yankee,* the more lasting impact of the paper was upon the rising generation of writers, many of whom found in Neal their first sympathetic editor. Actively seeking native writers who would fulfil his dream of a truly native literature, his friendly and insightful responses were crucial to a number of struggling young hopefuls. Whittier, among them, would write to Neal in 1828: "I have just written something for your consideration. . . . If you don't like it, say so privately; and *I will quit poetry, and everything also of a literary nature,* for I am sick at heart of the business. . . ."[8] Neal responded by rushing the poem into print within the month, and later on wrote to Whittier with the good advice not to worry so much about hostile reviews.[9] In November, 1828, he was one of the few to see merit in Hawthorne's first novel *Fanshawe*; he reviewed it in encouraging terms while noting the signs of haste and inexperience. Neal was also perceptive in his reviews of Longfellow and N. P. Willis: of the poet he wrote "As for Mr. Longfellow, he has a fine genius and a pure and safe taste, and all that he wants, we believe, is a little more energy, and a little more stoutness" (January 23, 1828). He also had good words for the Boston poet J. G. Percival and Portland's own Grenville Mellen, but his early discovery of Poe was probably his most signal critical achievement.

The years of *The Yankee* were those of crisis in the life of Edgar Allan Poe: his recent break with John Allan had resulted in his enlistment in the army. A partial reconciliation, effected by Mrs. Allan in her deathbed, led Allan to help Poe gain an appointment to West Point. But by 1829 he was living on a small allowance in Baltimore with his brother and Mrs. Maria Clemm, while hoping that the new edition of his poems would be better received than had been the Boston edition of 1827. Personal crisis and professional discouragement in his hoped-for writing career had brought him to a point of low morale, when from Maine and the pen of John Neal came the first essential understanding of his poetic talent:

> If E. A. P. of Baltimore—whose lines about *Heaven* [later titled "Fairyland"], though he professes to regard them as altogether superior to anything in the whole range of American poetry. . . . , are, though, nonsense, rather exquisite nonsense—would but do himself justice, [he] might make a beautiful and perhaps a magnificent poem. There is a good deal here to justify such a hope.

So wrote Neal in the September issue of the paper. Certainly not unqualified praise, but just, and to the struggling Poe, sufficient to raise his battered hopes.

Poe responded with a long letter[10] detailing his orphaned childhood and his publication plans. He seized on Neal's words regarding the possibilities of his writing a beautiful and perhaps magnificent poem, calling them "the very first words of encouragement I ever remember to have heard." He was considering dedicating his new volume of poetry to Neal, who felt that such a dedication would be of little help to the young poet. The compromise was that "Tamerlane" was indeed dedicated to John Neal in Poe's *Al Aaraaf, Tamerlane, and Minor Poems* (1829). From the prepublication galleys Neal printed selections in the last issue of *The Yankee* (December, 1829), praising the poems, which he found to be a quality that entitle the poet to "deserve to stand high—very high—in the estimation of the shining brotherhood."[11]

Poe was soon to turn to the writing of tales, where he was influenced by Neal, particularly by the latter's theory of effect.[12] As late as 1840, Poe would recall to Neal the early encouragement he had received in *The Yankee*: ". . . you gave me the first jog in my literary career. . . ."[13]

Meanwhile, the stir created in Portland by the return of John Neal as its most famous, or infamous, author was not without its effect upon the younger writers of the area. Neal had long been friends with Grenville Mellen, who was to break with the family tradition of law (his father rose to be chief justice of Maine) and publish poetry and tales in the gift books and journals. Mellen's brother Frederic, a talented artist, was one of a group who had become acquainted with Neal's work while they were still undergraduates at Bowdoin College. These included Nathaniel Hawthorne and Henry W. Longfellow. At the nearby Waterville College, now Colby, Seba Smith and James Brooks were inspired by Neal to follow literary journalism. Brooks is typical of those in the young college groups:

> I was a college-boy when I first became acquainted with Mr. Neal as a writer; and late at night I used to read his ***Errata,*** not the best nor the worst of his novels, with an intense and thrilling interest, and feel strange thoughts as I was wrought upon by his wild but ungovernable imagination. He was the hero of our circle.[14]

Neal was selected to give the address to the alumni of Colby College in 1830, and in 1836 received an honorary masters degree from Bowdoin.

To this nucleus of writers, Neal drew also a number of women. Mrs. Sally Wood, novelist of the older generation, was a resident in Portland where her last volume, a collection of tales, appeared in 1827 and was reviewed favorably by Neal. The young Elizabeth Oakes, who was to marry Seba Smith, was strongly influenced by Neal, as was Ann Stephens, who in her Portland years edited *The Portland Magazine* (1836-1837) and *The Portland Sketch Book* (1836).

After 1836 many of the group scattered to Boston and New York, but Neal's first decade in Portland was filled with the stimulus of a congenial literary group. Thereafter he kept in touch by voluminous correspondence and travel, not only with the lesser known members of the circle, but with Longfellow, Whittier, Poe, N. P. Willis, and Lowell. He was also active in fostering music and painting, writing reviews, acting as patron, everywhere demanding American support for American arts. *The Yankee* was, as it were, a catalyst to the cultural strivings of the region, as struggling painters as well as writers found a patron in its editor.

Notes

1. See Frank Luther Mott, *A History of American Magazines* (Cambridge, Massachusetts, 1957), I, 293-96.

2. *Blackwood's Edinburgh Magazine* 17 (February, 1825), 190.

3. Launched at Portland, *The Yankee* merged on August 20, 1828, into *The Yankee and Boston Liter-*

ary Gazette. It remained a weekly through June, 1829, issuing a new series of monthly copies from July through December, 1829, when it expired.

4. Charles Holden, in Joseph Griffin, *History of the Press in Maine* (Brunswick, 1872), p. 56. Holden (1804-1875) was an early printer and later state senator who contributed articles on the press of Portland to Griffin.

5. *Yankee* 1 (February 6, 1828), 48, so printed in error for p. 42.

6. Neal, *Portland Illustrated* (Portland, 1874), p. 54.

7. Boston *Morning Post,* May 16, 1840, quoted by Peter King, "John Neal as a Benthamite," *New England Quarterly* 39 (1966), 65.

8. Dated "10th Mo., 1828" and reprinted in [Richards, Irving T. "The Life and Works of John Neal." 4 vols. Ph.D. dissertation, Harvard University, 1932], I, 610-11.

9. Manuscript letter of September 4, 1829, at the Essex Institute, Boston; quoted by John A. Pollard, "John Neal; Doctor of American Literature," *Bulletin of the Friends Historical Association* 32 (1943), 10-11,

10. The letter was sent from Baltimore in late 1829; it appears in *The Letters of Edgar Allan Poe,* ed. John Ward Ostrom (Cambridge, Massachusetts, 1948), I, 32-33.

11. The extracts and praise appear on pp. 295-98.

12. For probable influence of Neal's theory of effect, see Lease, pp. 130-32; Walter Blair, "Poe's Conception of Incident and Tone in the Tale," *Modern Philology* 41 (1944), 228-40; and J. J. Rubin, "John Neal's Poetics as an Influence on Whitman and Poe," *New England Quarterly* 14 (1941), 359-62.

13. Letter to Neal dated Philadelphia, June 4, 1840, in Ostrom, I, 138.

14. "Letters from the East—John Neal," *The New-York Mirror* 2 (1833), 69.

Works Cited

Lease, Benjamin. *That Wild Fellow John Neal and the Literary Revolution.* Chicago: University of Chicago Press, 1972. Sheds new light on Neal's years in England while stressing his role in literary nationalism.

Fritz Fleischmann (essay date 1983)

SOURCE: Fleischmann, Fritz. "The Last Phase: Feminist Journalism and Organizational Efforts." In *A Right View of the Subject: Feminism in the Works of Charles Brockden Brown and John Neal,* pp. 209-27. Erlangen, Germany: Palm & Enke, 1983.

[*In the following excerpt, Fleischmann examines Neal's treatment of women and feminism in his writings, and discusses the author's participation in the American women's suffrage movement.*]

From 1844 to 1864, Neal wrote about women almost exclusively in works of fiction. That he had not entirely withdrawn from practical agitation is shown by the occasional appearance of his name in records of the suffrage movement, and in feminist publications.

In 1852, Elizabeth Oakes Smith read a long letter from Neal to the delegates at the third national woman's rights convention at Syracuse[1]. The letter, addressed to Smith and dated July 18, 1852, is an extended summary of Neal's views on the status of American women, with numerous echoes from his writings in the **Brother Jonathan.** The writer is now a veteran in this struggle: "I have been laboring over twenty years in their behalf, and to this hour, the bitterest things that are ever said, or thought of me, are by the women whom I have been trying to raise up from the condition of bond-slaves, contented with their task-masters and their fetters, to a state of entire equality and companionship with man" (p. 25). Neal advises the convention to attend to one point, "at all hazards. With it, you will have accomplished everything—without it, nothing.—You must oblige men to pay women better wages" (p. 26). Women's suffrage is the only way to achieve this goal.

The letter ends on a religious note, an indication of the great change in Neal's religious life[2]. Neal writes that Jesus was the only teacher "who appeared to have understood the true character of woman. . . . He, of all the men that have labored for the elevation of mankind, acknowledged by solemn adjudication, the equality of woman" (p. 28).

At the afternoon session of September 10, the convention constituted a Central Committee, to which Neal was appointed as the representative for Maine (p. 93).

According to Windsor Daggett, "Neal contributed to the *Una* in 1853"[3], but this claim is not substantiated by fact. In 1854, Neal corresponded with the feminist journal edited by Paulina Wright Davis in Providence, Rhode Island. *The Una* printed the complimentary letter he had sent with his subscription[4]. "You are doing your work *womanfully,*" Neal had written, "which I take it is rather better for a woman, than *manfully.*"

In 1864, Neal published one of the most interesting essays of his career in a newly founded Maine magazine, *The Northern Monthly.* Its title, **"Masquerading,"** describes not only the topic (men and women dressing alike) but also the author's treatment[5]. An incisive piece of feminist social criticism, it camouflages itself as a conservative critique of current fashion: "What are we coming to? . . . what shall we say of . . . men dressing like women, and wearing perfumes and jewelry, and embroidered shirt-bosoms . . . ? Or of women wearing hats and feathers, boots and spurs, and cropped hair, and carrying canes, and walking the streets with a swagger . . . ?" (p. 1). It states that "the two sexes have seriously begun to interchange appearances, if not characters," and asks, "Shall the two sexes assimilate or approximate? or fly off still further from a common type in their attire? What are the true indications of progress and refinement?" (ibid.). The question of what constitutes barbarism and civilization in this ratter becomes the subject of a historical discussion of some length (pp. 1-4), during which the author inveighs against "unsex[ing] ourselves" (p. 3), denying that it is "any more creditable for a woman to be manly, than it would be for a man to be womanly" (p. 4). But Neal's familiar distinction of sexual characters has now become a mere assertion, as the cat is let out of its semantic bag: "A man may be gentle, or a woman dignified and brave, without changing character" (p. 4):

> To be of a womanly sensitiveness; to be affectionate and believing, as most women are, self-denying and self-sacrificing, as almost all women are by nature, would be a glory added to the highest type of manhood,—serious, earnest and uncorrupt; for, so much alike are we, nothwithstanding the distinctions of sex, that not only does it seem to be substantially true, as understood by the ancients, that man is but women [sic] turned inside out; but that while the highest type of manhood has a something of woman's tenderness and compassionate gentleness in it—for, "Jesus wept"—the highest type of womanhood has a something of man's hearty self-reliance, unflinching steadfastness, and solemn purpose, unchangeable as death.
>
> [p. 4]

Neal now comes down on the side of approximation, even "in all that relates to costume or decorations," as he hopes this will "bring about a salutary change, as all changes in fashion are brought about, by little and little" (p. 4). Women's clothes, he insists, have served to subjugate their wearers:

> petticoats were the contrivance of man, and not of woman. They are part of *his* machinery for enhancing the attractions of woman, and for keeping her satisfied with herself, and out of harm's way; and for making a prisoner of her with her own consent, regardless not only of expense, but of her health, comfort, and usefulness . . . just as crippling the feet in China, and roasting women alive in Hindostan . . . have come to be regarded as privileges and distinctions, by the sufferers themselves.
>
> [pp. 4-5]

This was the beginning of the last phase of Neal's feminist journalism. Hopes for women ran high after the Civil War. Obviously stimulated by the autobiographical project that was to become *Wandering Recollections* (begun in 1866 and published in 1869), Neal published two articles on women's rights in the *American Phrenological Journal* in 1867, and a series of minor

contributions to *The Revolution* in 1869-70. The long reminiscences of his earlier efforts in *Wandering Recollections* (especially the long final section on women's rights [pp. 409-20]) also belong to this last effort to aid the cause. What is more, Neal once again participated in the organized struggle for reform.

In May 1869, at the anniversary meeting of the American Equal Rights Association in New York, the committee on organization reported Neal as one of the vice-presidents for the states[6]. Six months earlier, he had attended the New England convention of the American Equal Rights Association in Boston on November 18-19, 1868, at which the New England Woman Suffrage Association was formed, with Julia Ward Howe as its first president. In the *History of Woman Suffrage,* Neal is named first in a long list of "distinguished men and women of the New England States" at the convention, "old-time advocates, together with newer converts to the doctrine, who then became identified with the cause of equal rights irrespective of sex"[7]. He was elected to the executive board of the new association as one of sixteen vice-presidents[8].

When Elizabeth Cady Stanton and Susan B. Anthony, soon after the New York convention of 1869, organized the National Woman Suffrage Association in support of a woman suffrage amendment to the Constitution[9], the New England association took steps to initiate the rival American Woman Suffrage Association[10], formalizing a schism that was to last for over twenty years. After a committee of correspondents (made up of members of the New England group) had prepared the ground, a call was issued for the first convention of the American Woman Suffrage Association to be held at Cleveland, Ohio on November 24-25, 1869. "John Neal, Maine" headed the list of signers to the call[11]. The American Association subscribed to the goals of the old abolitionist coalition, accepted the priority of black suffrage over woman suffrage, and was politically loyal to the Republican program for Reconstruction. The National Association represented a much wider spectrum of feminism, emphasized the urgency of women's enfranchisement along with that of black males, and consequently opposed the Fifteenth Amendment[12].

Although he must be considered a co-founder of the American, Neal continued to write for the National's paper, *The Revolution,* until its demise in 1870, whereas he never contributed to *The Woman's Journal,* the organ of the American Association. He regretted the split as a weakening of the movement, but his sympathies lay with the National and its goals of political and social emancipation for women. In William Lloyd Garrison, who was now a supporter of the American, he spotted an ancient foe[13], who was once again trying to weaken the cause of women. In a letter to *The Revolution* dated November 27, 1869, Neal took exception to

Garrison's criticism of the National[14]. (A letter from Garrison to this effect had been read at the American's founding convention in Cleveland.) Neal accused him of being "[not] satisfied with sowing division among those who, if they are to succeed, *must* pull together," of thinking "that to him and his" alone "we are indebted for the emancipation of our slaves," and of "running a tilt . . . against the only well-established organization of a national character for Woman's Suffrage." In his next contribution, dated December 6, 1869, Neal openly attacked the position (held by the American Association) that women must stand in line behind the freedmen to wait for their political emancipation. He criticized a New York *Times* editorial for suggesting that women might be just as disappointed by suffrage as the former slaves were:

> What! Because the poor ignorant blacks, wholly unprepared for the trumpet-blast that set them free, expected too much, and were disappointed, when they found out that Suffrage did not give them a homestead, nor a cotton-plantation, nor even a suit of clothes, nor pay off their debts, nor send them headlong into Congress, *therefore,* the women of this mighty people, are to forego their strivings for equality before the law, least they should be disappointed as the negroes were![15]

In rejecting the *Times* writer's animadversions against the National, Neal states "that a large proportion of those who were found in the Cleveland Convention were, and still are, actual members of the other organization" (p. 387). He then explains his own absence and the reason for his signature under the call for the Cleveland convention: "My own name headed the call, by special and urgent invitation, though I refused to go, after I understood the object, and how we were to be fooled" (ibid.). Such urgent solicitation did indeed take place. "Because they prized their connections with leading Republicans and abolitionists, the organizers of the American Association were particularly anxious to distinguish themselves from the hostility to male political influence that had been expressed in the National Association. They deliberately sought male supporters"[16].

In the same letter to *The Revolution,* Neal mentions a number of reformers not of "the Cleveland stripe" who were "[on] the platform with me at Providence" (p. 387). Neal's presence at a woman suffrage convention in Rhode Island (probably in December 1868[17]) indicates his support for local and regional efforts as well as the national movement. The New England Association which he helped found organized suffrage associations in all New England states except Connecticut between 1868 and 1873[18]. The "brilliant John Neal" is mentioned in the Rhode Island chapter in the third volume of *The History of Woman Suffrage* as among the speakers at the annual conventions[19].

Neal also became active in his own state. He called the first meeting in Portland on the subject of woman suffrage. In a letter to *The Revolution* published on May 5,

1870, he describes his efforts and the meeting itself. *The History of Woman Suffrage* prints the letter[20], praising the writer as having been "foremost in all good work in Maine" (p. 352). Neal gives a summary of each speaker's views, accompanied by his own, colorful commentary. He commends his home state for enlightened legislation as well as adjudication with regard to the property rights of married women, which are "far ahead of the age, and not only acknowledged, but enforced" (p. 353). One speaker, who took the anti-suffrage position and argued that women did not ask for suffrage (a suggestion which had already incensed Neal in his debate with Mrs. Farnham), is told that women have sent petitions and complaints by the thousands to their legislators—Neal once again feels justified by the course of history. His letter informs *The Revolution* that the meeting is "adjourned for a week. Probably no organization will be attempted, lest it might serve to check free discussion" (p. 354).

A month earlier, *The Woman's Journal* had printed a "Letter from Maine" by Eva M. Wilder, bemoaning the lack of suffrage agitation there, although "the first petition for Woman Suffrage has been presented to the Maine Legislature"[21]. Now, the readers of the *Journal* learned from a Mr. W. W. McCann about the Portland meeting; in a letter that gives most of its space to Neal's appearance:

> Hon. John Neal, who issued the call for the meeting, was the first to speak. He reviewed the history of this movement, both in this country and in England. He gave some entertaining reminiscences of his acquaintance with John Stuart Mill forty years ago. Mr. Mill was not then in favor of universal suffrage; he advocated the enfranchisement of the male sex only. Mr. Neal claimed the right for women also. He was happy to learn that since then Mr. Mill has thrown all the weight of his influence and his masterly intellect in favor of universal suffrage. He then entered into an elaborate discussion of some of the objections brought against woman suffrage, and, much to the surprise of many present, showed that the rights which women demand are just and reasonable, and ought to be granted.
>
> [*HWS,* III, p. 354]

Like so many women of his generation, Neal had adopted the role of historian without relinquishing that of participant in making history.

The sequel to this event is reported in Neal's last contribution to the *Revolution* on May 12, 1870[22]. He had called a meeting to discuss

> the following propositions—*against all comers:*
>
> 1. That the right of Suffrage is a natural right, incident to, and inherent in, every *rational* being.
>
> 2. That Woman Suffrage is provided for in the clearest and most positive terms by the Constitution itself.
>
> [p. 291]

Neal claims that the right of suffrage is not "a political or civil right, growing out of the constitution of society" (p. 292), but a natural right which neither can, nor needs to be acquired. To prove his second proposition, he examines the language of the Declaration of Independence ("We the people") and of the Fourteenth Amendment ("all *persons* born or naturalized in the United States, and subject to their jurisdiction, are *citizens* of the United States and of the State" [p. 292]).

As late as 1873, Neal was involved in organizing a suffrage movement in his state. His name (closely followed by that of his wife Eleanor) is the first on a long list of signers to a call for the first statewide woman suffrage convention. It is not known whether Neal had a hand in writing this appeal to the people of Maine, or whether he was simply content to sign it. Content he must have been, since the document surveys the grounds on which he had always believed the cause for women's equal rights should be based. It addresses those

> who believe in the extension of the elective franchise to women as a beneficent power for the promotion of the virtues and the correction of the evils of society, and all who believe in the principles of equal justice, equal liberty and equal opportunity, upon which republican institutions are founded, and have faith in the triumph of intelligence and reason over custom and prejudice.[23]

This meeting took place in Augusta on January 29, 1873 and was attended by over a thousand persons[24]. A State Woman Suffrage Association was founded, with Neal as one of the vice-presidents (p. 360). The resolutions passed at the convention included an appeal to the legislature for funds "for the establishment of an Industrial School for girls" (ibid.). Neal's role at the convention appears to have been a passive one. Lucy Stone, who reported at length on the Augusta meeting, did not mention his name[25].

Neal's journalistic efforts during the last active period of his life included his already-mentioned contributions to the *American Phrenological Journal* in 1867 and *The Revolution* in 1868-70.

"Woman's Rights—and Woman's Wrongs" in the *American Phrenological Journal*[26], a long essay published in two installments, is a major summary of Neal's feminist views in his old age. Unlike **Wandering Recollections,** which emphasizes the continuity of his beliefs, this article shows recent transformations as well as long-held and virtually unchanged convictions.

The two most prominent changes in outlook and rhetoric are responses to a national as well as a personal crisis—the Civil War, and Neal's discovery of religion. The first had led him to a new sense of urgency, the second to an even more principled position on the question of civil equality between the sexes. Neal realized that he had been wrong to oppose abolition[27]. Now, he writes that "denying a right, or abridging, or withholding a right . . . may be a wrong of such magnitude as to endanger the whole constitution of society. Have we not found it so already with one form of human bondage?" (p. 75). He is confident that the "spirit of the age will not brook delay" in the abolition of female bondage either (ibid.). Neal's embrace of Christianity now leads him to reduce the question "to its simplest elements": "Have women souls?—are they accountable beings?" (p. 75). He takes particular care to refute ministerial objections to woman suffrage, referring both to the Bible and church history. When God created human beings, "Was there but one soul for both, and that the soul of man?" Neal's frame of reference, his similes and analogies, have become predominantly theological, superseding (yet absorbing) his former, almost exclusively legal, categories. A husband's "virtual" representation of his wife is thus no longer merely a constitutional abomination but a threat to "her *individuality*"—

> that glorious prerogative which God himself appears to reverence in his creatures . . . that property which lies at the very foundation of the system, whereby he administers the affairs of the universe [,] that unshifting, unchangeable center to which all that we know of man's history and hope converges [,]—that wonderful microcosm we call *self*[.]
>
> [p. 75]

The argument that men as a group should rule over women as a group (advanced by those who cite the Bible to maintain that a wife should obey her husband) is "rather too much of a piece with that which seeks to justify another kind of human bondage, even slavery, by the curse pronounced upon Ham" (p. 78).

As in most of his earlier articles on the subject, Neal refutes popular objections to woman's rights (such as women's alleged inferiority, their alleged satisfaction with their present lot, etc.) with accustomed vigor. Here, again, recent American history furnishes a new illustration: "By far the largest portion of the slaves held in this country—the colored slaves, I mean now—never asked to be delivered from their bondage" (p. 77). Such deliverance is a civic and Christian duty: "it is not only expected, but required of us, to enlighten the ignorant, to help the helpless, and right the wrongs of all who are deceived or oppressed" (p. 77).

Familiar legal language appears when the text denounces taxation without representation. But this, too, shows a sense of heightened urgency, inspired by the nation's dear-bought recent survival: "A great principle is involved—the very germ of our nationality—the great seal of our charter of independence" (p. 76).

The second installment of the essay contains a long discussion of natural rights and refers to the recent enfranchisement of black males in the District of Columbia[28].

Neal affirms that the right to self-government is a natural right ("inherent and essential to man's nature[;] something, without which man is no longer man, nor woman, woman" [p. 106]). Suffrage, as a natural right, is not something that a majority may or may not grant to a minority, but an inherent right of each group, if government is to be derived from the consent of all governed.

> If there be any such thing as a natural right—any right even "to life, liberty, and the pursuit of happiness," independent of human concession, then the right of self-government is clear and conclusive; for what is the right of self-government, but the right of suffrage? all other rights being merged in that, all, however modified, and however changeable, being dependent upon that.
>
> [p. 106]

The writer finds it "shameful" and "astonishing" that a society should talk about natural rights "as man, the lawgiver, may choose to allow . . . no rights, in a word, which man is bound to respect" (ibid.). This, to him, constitutes slavery.

After pointing to women's performance in the Civil War, Neal returns to his main point—that the American system of government must live up to its premises. Women must be permitted to run for elective office because the voters alone may decide who should represent them:

> In a word, if the masses are capable of self-government, if they have wisdom enough to choose their rulers, and their lawgivers, why abridge the liberty of choice? . . . If they are unfitted to judge, so are you. Otherwise your pretensions are a ridiculous farce, and self-government—representative government—a sheer hallucination.
>
> [p. 107]

Familiar tones from Neal. But they are qualified by the historical context of early Reconstruction and the tension between black suffrage and woman suffrage advocates. Neal's discussion of natural rights makes explicit reference to this context. His opening statement warns reformers that "now is the time of danger. We may be going too fast and too far, if, in our hurry to reform an abuse, we do not weigh every word we utter, and calculate in advance, every step we take" (p. 106). The consequence may be another battle "likely to divide the whole nation" (ibid.).

Since this warning is preceded by a quotation from a newspaper report on a universal suffrage memorial to Congress ("*praying for the removal of all restriction of color or sex, in regard to suffrage*" [p. 106]), it is not clear whether universal suffrage, i.e., the simultaneous enfranchisement of blacks and women, is the "danger" or the proposed remedy. But Neal's position, were it

not already known, emerges clearly at the end of his essay, where he demands "*universal and impartial suffrage*" and concludes that the signs of the times are both "portentous" and "propitious" (p. 108). This position links him with the group of feminists around Elizabeth Cady Stanton and Susan B. Anthony who insisted that "the woman's hour" had arrived with that of the black man, and who felt bitterly disappointed by the refusal of their abolitionist allies and the Republican party to support this goal. In 1867, the Republican party worked openly against a woman suffrage referendum in Kansas[29], with the result that some of the leading feminists began to appeal to Democratic constituencies, going so far as to play on their fear of black suffrace. The enfranchisement of white women would help to offset the impact of the black vote[30]. Neal, a Unionist who had long distrusted abolitionists' motives and had no wish to see the defeated South humiliated, found it hard to go along with the Republican goal of using black suffrage to cement its national power and to create Republican bastions in the South. A contemporary historian of this period observes that "[southern] blacks were a pronorthern force in the heart of the Confederacy and this linked their enfranchisement to the preservation of the Union's victory and the protection of the Republican party's power"[31]. Neal mentions in his article that

> the Kentucky House of Representatives are listening to an address from Mrs. Blackwell, of New York city, asking the Legislatures of the Southern States to allow not only blacks, but black women and white women to vote; "for then," she says—and who shall gainsay her?—"then, the four millions of *Southern white women will counterbalance the four millions of negro men and women,* and the political supremacy of the white race *will* remain unchanged." Even so! The premises are clear—the result inevitable.
>
> [p. 108]

Lucy Stone ("Mrs. Blackwell"—Neal either did not know or ignored the fact that Stone had not changed her name upon marriage) and her husband, Henry Blackwell, supported the Kansas campaign of 1867 but sided with the American Association and the Republican party in 1869. Henry Blackwell had proposed woman suffrage to Southern legislatures as a counterbalance to black suffrage in January 1867[32]. Neal, hardly a white supremacist, supports that argument in this essay. His reasons for doing so are not entirely clear, although his old Southern sympathies show up in the following admonition:

> But are the eyes of the South opened far enough to see the consequences? Can they cipher? Have they courage enough, and will they bid promptly enough, to forestall the North? If so, then will they have their destinies in their own keeping, and become, of a truth, a regenerated people—a people "redeemed, regenerated, and disenthralled"—and forever.
>
> [p. 108]

In 1869-70, about a dozen communications from Neal appeared in *The Revolution*. Only a few are longer than one page, and most are responses to recent publications or events. His first piece was apparently not even submitted by him, but reprinted from a letter he had written to the Portland *Press*[33]. The excerpt in *The Revolution* consists mostly of Neal's role-reversal argument (if men had to live like women, they would understand the injustice of the present gender-role system), followed by an attack on the double standard of morals, and on unfair pay for women. Suffrage, of course, is suggested as a remedy, since it will bring about "such consideration as you will find ten thousand times more desirable than all the hypocritical deference and flattering courtesy which the men . . . pretend to feel for you."

"The Subjection of Women"[34] welcomes John Stuart Mill's recently published treatise as an "admirable essay" and paraphrases twelve "of the many strong positions taken by Mr. Mill"—essentially identical with Neal's own views. His summary emphasizes women's desire for emancipation, equal opportunity to earn a decent income and participation in government. Women's "nature" and "special function" are mentioned to show that the present restrictions are unnecessary. Suffrage "cannot make nor unmake them. It cannot give them another nature." This "nature" is highly individualized and varies by class and culture, making men's presumption to judge for all women collectively appear preposterous. The last point on Neal's list answers his own argument from his 1824 **"Men and Women"** essay in *Blackwood's,* where he had linked talent, gender, and temperament:

> Lastly—But women are of a more nervous temperament—meaning of a finer temperament—than men. Be it so. "And let me then ask," [John Stuart Mill] says, "are men of nervous temperament found to be unfit for the duties and pursuits usually followed by men? If not, why should woman [sic] of the same temperament be unfit for them?"
>
> Answer me that, my masters.

"A Contented Woman"[35] takes one Mrs. "C. P. B." to task for having slandered the suffragists in a letter to the *Rhode Island Bulletin*. Neal ridicules her rather mercilessly for claiming to be "one of the *contented* women of Rhode Island. One of the short-sighted, sleepy women, rather, who, not understanding their true condition, wholly mistake their duty" (p. 276). After a blow-by-blow refutation of each point he finds offensive, Neal suggests that "Mrs. C. P. B. had better review the case, and then, perhaps, I may not be obliged to deal with her as I would with a man, for his blundering audacity" (p. 277).

The "contented woman" is also referred to in a review of Epes Sargent's *The Woman who Dared*[36]: a "capital book," "a conclusive answer to most of the pettifogging objections that are urged against woman being allowed to have dominion over herself" (p. 296). Most of the review deals with the book's treatment of marriage, deploring social conditions which force women to marry for support. It also condemns the passive role women are expected to play in courtship, and encourages the author's suggestion that women should take the initiative: "why not? As these matters are now managed, though not openly and above board, do not most women take the *initiative in wooing?* Would any man with a thimble-full of self-respect, or common sense, offer himself to a woman without some encouragement?" (p. 296).—The reviewer also praises the "fine poetry" of the book but finds "all such objects subordinate to the grand idea of woman's emancipation" (p. 296).

"The Woman's Parliament"[37] contains some reactions to the proceedings of a recent woman suffrage meeting published in the New York *World*. One of the speakers there had described the force of public opinion as *"a mightier lever than the ballot,"* prompting this correction: "Granted—if public opinion be enforced by the ballot: otherwise not" (p. 322). Neal disagrees with another speaker on the historical origins of woman's subordination (he opposes the idea of a lost paradise of sexual equality) and with her description of an ideal marriage as one in which "[he] *never acts without her approval* any more than she would without his sanction" (p. 323). To Neal, this is pious fiction: "he would be a ninny if this were true; and she another, if she followed his example. Each must be independent of the other, within a particular sphere. Each must reverence the other's equality and rights, if they mean to be happy" (ibid.). This insistence on unabashed masculinity and femininity is familiar; independent personhood is to be realized, not suppressed by women's emancipation in and out of marriage. What is interesting in the 1869 text is the sovereignty with which Neal manipulates the semantics of separate "spheres" to suit the ends of his argument. He transforms the concept from a limiting to a liberating one. The speaker he criticizes had characterized a happy marriage as one in which "[all] *is common between them*" (p. 323)—a vision which Neal finds both unrealistic and confining for both parties. The "separate sphere" assumes a new meaning, the promise of independence.

Horace Greeley, who had been notorious for his wavering and idiosyncratic support for woman suffrage in the late 1860s[38], is next in line to receive Neal's strictures[39]. He, too, is criticized for his assumption that the sexes started out equal, and that women's oppression is the result of historical development ("When did the woman lose all her rights?" [p. 339]). Neal is most incensed by Greeley's opposition to women's activities outside the home, and by all his talk about the home as women's "kingdom" whose purity stands in contrast to the "promiscuous" mingling of men and women in public places. After citing numerous instances of socially accepted associations between women and men, the writer concludes, "Where men and women associate freely, and on equal terms, there both are free—the man strengthens the woman; the woman refines, purifies and *humanizes* the man" (p. 340). From this, he also makes a case for children's coeducation. Such "promiscuous intercourse," he lectures Greeley, is demanded by "the more enlightened, who desire not the emancipation of women only, but of men . . ." (p. 340). For the classroom (one of Greeley's examples), Neal refers to his own and his daughter's experience in teaching Sunday School—each, he says, prefers pupils of the opposite sex. There is no danger in such "promiscuity," he assures Greeley—and devotes the entire second half of the article to a burlesque ridicule of Greeley's fear of mixed assemblies, to which he attributes the editor's equivocating stance on woman suffrage.

> And this—*this*!—is the bugbear that frights Mr. Greeley from his propriety . . . ! a fear that such women as Mrs. Elizabeth Cady Stanton, Miss Susan B. Anthony, Mrs. Burleigh, Mrs. Howe, Mrs. Lucy Stone, Rev. Olympia Brown, and fifty others I might name, will be *closetted in committees* with our statesmen and lawgivers! To say nothing of the men, whatever they may be or not be, what must he think of the *women*?
>
> [p. 340]

Right after this article, Neal critizes an example of clerical opposition to woman suffrage[40]. He emphasizes the link he sees between suffrage and wages, and he ridicules the clergyman's reflections on the law and social order—both of which, he reminds him, are male products. Arguments like these show a "most amusing self-complacency," but "such nonsense ought never to pass unrebuked" (p. 341).

The next two contributions, letters attacking William Lloyd Garrison and the New York *Times,* have already been mentioned[41]. In January, Neal came to the defense of Harriet Beecher Stowe, who was under attack for "The True Story of Lady Byron's Life" (1869) and had just published her *Lady Byron Vindicated*[42]. His article asserts that Mrs. Stowe's summary is "not only a triumphant vindication of Lady Byron . . . but a complete justification of Mrs. 'Beecher Stowe' herself" (p. 36). After reviewing and approving the evidence, Neal recalls "that in a review of Manfred, in 1816-17, which appeared in the Portico . . . I was led to charge Byron with 'endeavoring to blind us to the guilt of incest'" (p. 37). Revering him as a poet, he viewed the man "as a sort of melo-dramatic personage turned adrift upon the world" (p. 37).

After this, Neal contributed only once more to *The Revolution.* His report on **"Progress in Maine"** has already been mentioned[43]. For Neal, the Civil War confirmed the strength of women under the worst condi-

tions, even on the battlefield. Now, he goes so far as to assert women's equality as citizens in all respects, even military service. While denying a reporter's allegation that he wished to see women going to war, he emphasizes their suitability as well as their willingness, "to take the burdens with the privileges of man" (p. 292). A quarter of a century earlier, Mrs. Farnham had accused him of holding precisely this view—now, he asserts it with full confidence. At the end of his life, his radicalism unabated, Neal felt justified by history.

Notes

1. *The Proceedings of the Woman's Rights Convention, held at Syracuse, September 8th, 9th & 10th, 1852* (Syracuse, J. E. Masters, 1852), pp. 24-28.

2. See Lease, *Wild Fellow,* pp. 196-199.

3. *Down-East Yankee,* p. 40.

4. *The Una* 2, p. 302. The journal also reprinted a piece of art criticism from the *Home Journal,* where it had appeared with a short note by Neal (2, p. 240). Richards also identified a short poem, "Patience" (*Una* 3, p. 13) as Neal's ("Life and Works," p. 1149). Even such meager contributions must have been appreciated, however, as we read in *HWS* [*The History of Women Suffrage*] that *The Una* "could boast for its correspondents some of the ablest men and women in the nation," after which Neal is mentioned in a list of prominent names (I, p. 246).

5. John Neal, "Masquerading," *The Northern Monthly* 1, no. 1 (March 1864), pp. 1-5.

6. *HWS,* II, p. 380.

7. *HWS,* III, pp. 266-67. Maine always appeared first on such lists, as the states were listed in a sequence from East to West.

8. I take this information from Samuel E. Sewall, *The Legal Condition of Women in Massachusetts.* Woman's Suffrage Tracts. No. 5 (Boston: The New-England Woman's Suffrage Association, 1869). Its appendix lists Neal among the officers of the organization. The account of the 1868 Boston convention in *HWS* III, just quoted, is by Harriet Hanson Robinson (who wrote the Massachusetts chapter in this volume) and lifted verbatim from her earlier book, *Massachusetts in the Woman Suffrage Movement: A General, Political, Legal and Legislative History from 1774, to 1881* (Boston: Roberts Brothers, 1881; 2nd printing 1883), pp. 47-48. There, she does not mention officers' names; in the *HWS,* Neal does not appear among the vice-presidents. In his place, his cousin and enemy Neal Dow is listed as "Neil Dow, Me." (p. 267). (This substitution is not implausible,

since Dow was also involved in the suffrage movement in Maine.)

The matter cannot be resolved to complete satisfaction. Lois Bannister Merk notes that the "records of the New England Woman Suffrage Association have apparently been lost, though Mrs. Robinson had them in 1881 when she wrote her account of the founding of the organization" (Lois Bannister Merk, "Massachusetts and the Woman Suffrage Movement," Ph. D. diss., Radcliffe College, 1958, 2 vols. [Cambridge, Mass.: General Microfilm Co., 1961], vol. 2, chapter 1, note 4). It is unclear whether the records were already lost in 1886, when *HWS* III was published. For a list of the officers of the association in 1870, Merk refers to the appendix of Woman Suffrage Tract No. 1, Henry Ward Beecher's *Woman's Influence on Politics* (Boston: The New-England Woman's Suffrage Association, 1870). There, John Neal is named as a vice-president (p. 20).

9. Cf. Flexner, pp. 154-56.

10. Robinson, pp. 54-55.

11. *HWS,* III, p. 757.

12. The best account of the origins and background of the two associations is to be found in Ellen Carol Du Bois, *Feminism and Suffrage: The Emergence of an Independent Woman's Movement in America 1848-1869* (Ithaca and London: Cornell University Press, 1978). See esp. chapters 2 ("The Fourteenth Amendment and the American Equal Rights Association") and 6 ("The Fifteenth Amendment and the Emergence of Independent Suffragism").

13. Lease, *Wild Fellow,* p. 126 n. 6 states that a reconciliation took place in 1865, but Neal apparently never quite trusted Garrison.

14. "What is the Meaning of This?", *The Revolution* 4, no. 23 (Dec. 9, 1869), p. 364.

15. "The New York 'Times,'" *The Revolution* 4, no. 25 (Dec. 23, 1869), p. 387.

16. Du Bois, p. 196.

17. See *HWS,* III, p. 340.

18. Du Bois, p. 180 (with reference to Merk, I, p. 200).

19. *HWS,* III, p. 340 n.

20. *HWS,* III, pp. 352-54. All page numbers in the text refer to this publication. The original letter appeared in *The Revolution* 5, no. 18 (May 5, 1870), pp. 277-78.

21. Eva M. Wilder, "Letter from Maine," *The Woman's Journal* 1, no. 14 (April 9, 1870), p. 107.

22. "Progress in Maine," *The Revolution* 5, no. 19 (May 12, 1870), pp. 291-92.

23. *HWS,* III, p. 358.

24. Ibid., p. 359. Further references in the text.

25. Lucy Stone, "Maine and Woman Suffrage," *The Woman's Journal* 4, no. 6 (Feb. 8, 1873), p. 44.

26. "Woman's Rights and Woman's Wrongs," *American Phrenological Journal* 45 (Jan.—June 1867), pp. 75-77, 106-8.

27. Lease, *Wild Fellow,* p. 126 n. 6.

28. Cf. Du Bois, p. 67.

29. See Du Bois, chapter 3 (pp. 79-104).

30. Ibid., pp. 92-101. On the racist tendencies among the *Revolution* feminists, see pp. 108, 174-79.

31. Ibid., p. 57.

32. Ibid., p. 100.

33. "Woman Suffrage," *The Revolution* 3, no. 1 (Jan. 7, 1869), p. 11.

34. "The Subjection of Women," *The Revolution* 4, no. 15 (Oct. 14, 1869), p. 226.

35. "A Contented Woman," *The Revolution* 4, no. 18 (Nov. 4, 1869), pp. 276-77.

36. "The Woman Who Dared," *Revolution* 4, no. 19 (Nov. 11, 1869, p. 296.

37. "The Woman's Parliament," *Revolution* 4, no. 21 (Nov. 25, 1869), pp. 322-23.

38. On Greeley's role in the 1867 Kansas campaign, see Du Bois, pp. 83, 87-91.

39. "Horace Greeley and his 'Notion of Woman's Rights,'" *Revolution* 4, no. 22 (Dec. 2, 1869), pp. 339-40.

40. "More Masculine Reasoning—from the Pulpit," *Revolution* 4, no. 22 (Dec. 2, 1869), pp. 340-41.

41. *Revolution* 4, no. 23 (Dec. 9, 1869), p. 364; and no. 25 (Dec. 23, 1869), pp. 387-88.

42. "Lady Byron," *Revolution* 5, no. 3 (Jan. 20, 1870), pp. 36-37. *The Woman's Journal* devoted two articles to the issue. See Mary H. Livermore, "Mrs. Stowe's Vindication," and Julia Ward Howe, "Lady Byron Vindicated," *Woman's Journal* 1, no. 3 (Jan. 22, 1870), pp. 17, 20.

43. See note [22] above.

Works Cited

BROWN, CHARLES BROCKDEN

Wieland, or The Transformation. An American Tale.— Memoirs of Carwin the Biloquist. Vol. 1 in *The Novels and Related Works of Charles Brockden Brown.* Bicentennial Edition. Edited by Sydney J. Krause and S. W. Reid. Kent, Ohio: Kent State University Press, 1977.

Ormond, or The Secret Witness. Vol. 2 in *The Novels and Related Works of Charles Brockden Brown.* Bicentennial Edition. Edited by Sydney J. Krause and S. W. Reid. Kent, Ohio: Kent State University Press, 1982.

Arthur Mervyn, or Memoirs of the Year 1793. Vol. 3 in *The Novels and Related Works of Charles Brockden Brown.* Bicentennial Edition. Edited by Sydney J. Krause and S. W. Reid. Kent, Ohio: Kent State University Press, 1980.

Edgar Huntly, or Memoirs of a Sleep-Walker. Edited by David Lee Clark. New York: Macmillan, 1928.

NEAL, JOHN

Keep Cool: A Novel. Written in Hot Weather, by Somebody, M. D. C. & c. & c. 2 vols. Baltimore: Joseph Cushing, 1817.

Logan, A Family History. 2 vols. Philadelphia: Carey & Lea, 1822.

Seventy-Six. By the Author of Logan. 2 vols. Baltimore: Joseph Robinson, 1823. Facsimile Reproduction with an Introduction by Robert A. Bain. Bainbridge, N. Y.: York Mail-Print, 1971.

Randolph, A Novel. . . . By the author of Logan—and Seventy-six. 2 vols. Published for Whom It May Concern. [Philadelphia,] 1823.

Errata; or, The Works of Will Adams. A Tale by the Author of Logan, Seventy-six, and Randolph. 2 vols. New York, 1823.

Brother Jonathan: or, The New Englanders. 3 vols. Edinburgh and London: William Blackwood and T. Cadell, 1825.

Rachel Dyer: A North American Story. By John Neal. Portland: Shirley and Hyde, 1828. Facsimile Reproduction with an Introduction by John D. Seelye. Gainesville, Fla.: Scholars' Facsimiles and Reprints, 1964.

Bentham, Jeremy. *Principles of Legislation: From the MS, of Jeremy Bentham. . . . Translated from the Second Corrected and Enlarged Edition with Notes and a Biographical Notice of Jeremy Bentham and of M. Dumont.* By John Neal. Boston: Wells and Lilly, 1830.

The Down-Easters, & c. & c. & c. By John Neal. New York: Harper and Brothers, 1833.

True Womanhood: A Tale. By John Neal. Boston: Ticknor and Fields, 1859.

Wandering Recollections of a Somewhat Busy Life. An Autobiography. . . . By John Neal. Boston: Roberts Brothers, 1870.

COLLECTIONS OF NEAL'S WORK

Dickson, Harold E., ed. *Observations on American Art: Selections from the Writings of John Neal.* Pennsylvania State College Studies No. 12. State College, Pa.: Pennsylvania State University Press, 1943.

Lang, Hans-Joachim, ed. "Critical Essays and Stories by John Neal." *Jahrbuch für Amerikastudien* 7 (1962): 204-88.

Lease, Benjamin, and Lang, Hans-Joachim, eds. *The Genius of John Neal: Selections from his Writings.* Studien und Texte zur Amerikanistik, vol. 1. Frankfurt on the Main: Peter Lang, 1978.

Pattee, Fred Lewis, ed. *American Writers. A Series of Papers Contributed to Blackwood's Magazine (1824-25), by John Neal.* Durham, N. C.: Duke University Press, 1937.

MANUSCRIPT SOURCES

Brunswick, Maine. Hawthorne-Longfellow Library, Bowdoin College. Letters from Charles Brockden Brown to Joseph Bringhurst.

Austin, Texas. Humanities Research Center, The University of Texas at Austin. Letter from Charles Brockden Brown to John Davidson.

Brown, Cheryl L., and Olson, Karen, eds. *Feminist Criticism: Essays on Theory, Poetry and Prose.* Metuchen, N. J.: Scarecrow Press, 1978.

Brown, Herbert Ross. *The Sentimental Novel in America: 1789-1860.* Repr. ed. New York: Octagon, 1975.

Buhle, Mari Jo; Gordon, Ann G.; and Ryan, Mary P. "Women in American History: An Historical Contribution." *Radical America* 5 (1971): 3-66.

Carroll, Berenice A., ed. *Liberating Women's History: Theoretical and Critical Essays.* Urbana: University of Illinois Press, 1976.

Chevigny, Bell Gale. *The Woman and the Myth: Margaret Fuller's Life and Writings.* Old Westbury, N. Y.: Feminist Press, 1976.

Chico, Beverly Berghaus. "Two American Firsts: Sarah Peale, Portrait Painter, and John Neal, Critic." *Maryland Historical Magazine* 71 (1976): 349-59.

Christadler, Martin. *Der amerikanische Essay 1720-1820.* Heidelberg: Carl Winter, 1968.

Cicardo, Barbara Joan. "The Mystery of the American Eve: Alienation of the Feminine as a Tragic Theme in American Letters." Ph. D. diss., St. Louis University, 1971.

Conrad, Susan P. *Perish the Thought: Intellectual Women in Romantic America 1830-1860.* London: Oxford University Press, 1976.

Cornillon, Susan Koppelman, ed. *Images of Women in Fiction: Feminist Perspectives.* Bowling Green, Ohio: Bowling Gree University Press, 1972.

Cott, Nancy F. *The Bonds of Womanhood: "Woman's Sphere" in New England 1780-1835.* New Haven and London: Yale University Press, 1977.

———. "Passionlessness: An Interpretation of Victorian Sexual Ideology, 1790-1850." *Signs* 4 (Winter 1978): 219-36.

Cott, Nancy, and Pleck, Elizabeth, eds. *A Heritage of Her Own: Toward a New Social History of American Women.* New York: Simon and Schuster, 1979.

Cross, Barahara. *The Educated Woman in America: Selected Writings of Catharine Beecher, Margaret Fuller, and M. Carey Thomas.* Classics in Education 25. New York: Columbia University Press, 1965.

———. "Catharine Esther Beecher." In *Notable American Women 1607-1950: A Biographical Dictionary,* edited by Edward T. James, Janet Wilson James, and Paul Boyer, vol. 1, pp. 121-24. Cambridge, Mass.: Harvard University Press, 1971.

Daggett, Windsor. *A Down-East Yankee from the District of Maine.* Portland: A. J. Huston, 1920.

Davis, Paulina Wright, comp. *A History of the National Woman's Rights Movement, for Twenty Years, from 1850 to 1870.* New York: Journeymen Printers' Cooperative Association, 1871. Repr. Kraus Reprint Co., 1971.

De Beauvoir, Simone. "[Excerpts from] *The Second Sex.*" In *The Feminist Papers,* edited by Alice S. Rossi, pp. 674-705. New York: Bantam, 1973.

Deegan, Dorothy Yost. *The Stereotype of the Single Woman in American Novels.* New York: Columbia University Press, 1951.

Diamond, Arlyn, and Edwards, Lee R., eds. *The Authority of Experience: Essays in Feminist Criticism.* Amherst: University of Massachusetts Press, 1972.

Donovan, Josephine, ed. *Feminist Literary Criticism: Explorations in Theory.* Lexington, Ky.: University Press of Kentucky, 1975.

Douglas, Ann. *The Feminization of American Culture.* New York: Avon, 1978.

Du Bois, Ellen Carol. *Feminism and Suffrage: The Emergence of an Independent Woman's Movement in America 1848-1869.* Ithaca and London: Cornell University Press, 1978.

D., W. [Dunlap, William?] "Attachments to Persons of the Same Sex." *Literary Magazine and American Register* 1 (Jan. 1804): 247-48.

Earnest, Ernest. *The American Eve in Fact and Fiction, 1775-1914.* Urbana: University of Illinois Press, 1974.

Ehrenreich, Barbara, and English, Deirdre. *Complaints and Disorders: The Sexual Politics of Sickness.* Old Westbury, N. Y.: Feminist Press, 1973.

———. *For Her Own Good: 130 Years of the Experts' Advice to Women.* Garden City, N. Y.: Anchor Press, 1978.

[F.] "Female Education." *The Yankee and Boston Literary Gazette* 2, no. 22 (May 28, 1829): 175; no. 24 (June 11): 189-90; no. 25 (June 18): 197-98.

Farnham, Eliza W. [Mrs. T. J.] "Rights of Women. Reply to Mr. Neal's Lecture." *Brother Jonathan* 5, no. 8 (June 24, 1843): 236-38; no. 9 (July 2, 1843): 266-68.

———. "The Rights of Women. Mrs. Farnham's Reply to John Neal, Esq." *Brother Jonathan* 5, no. 13 (July 29, 1843): 363-67.

Fetterley, Judith. *The Resisting Reader: A Feminist Approach to American Fiction.* Bloomington: Indiana University Press, 1978.

Field, Vera B. *Constantia: A Study of the Life and Works of Judith Sargent Murray 1751-1820.* University of Maine Studies. Orono, Me.: University of Maine Press, 1931.

Fishwick, Marshall W. "*The Portico* and Literary Nationalism after the War of 1812." *William and Mary Quarterly* 3rd series, 8 (1951): 238-45.

Flexner, Eleanor. *Century of Struggle: The Woman's Rights Movement in the United States.* Rev. ed. Cambridge, Mass.: Harvard University Press, 1975.

Freud, Sigmund. *The Interpretation of Dreams.* Translated by James Strachey. New York: Avon/Discus, 1965.

———. *Introductory Lectures on Psychoanalysis.* Translated by James Strachey. New York: Norton/Liveright, 1977.

Gilbert, Sandra M. "Life Studies, or, Speech After Long Silence: Feminist Critics Today." *College English* 40 (April 1979): 849-63.

Godwin, William. *Memoirs of the Author of "A Vindication of the Rights of Woman."* 1798. Facsimile Repr. Farnborough, England: Gregg International Publishers, 1970.

Grove, Gerald Robert. "John Neal: American Romantic." Ph. D. diss., University of Utah, 1974.

[H., W.] Letter to John Neal. *The Yankee and Boston Literary Gazette* 2, no. 12 (March 19, 1829): 94-95.

Hawthorne, Nathaniel. *The Blithedale Romance.* Vol. 3 in *The Centenary Edition of the Works of Nathaniel Hawthorne.* Columbus: Ohio State University Press, 1964.

Howe, Julia Ward. "Lady Byron Vindicated." *The Woman's Journal* 1, no. 3 (Jan. 22, 1870): 20.

Hymowitz, Carol, and Weissman, Michaele. *A History of Women in America.* New York: Bantam, 1978.

[J. . . .] "Capacities of Women." *The Yankee and Boston Literary Gazette* 2, no. 18 (April 30, 1829): 144.

James, Janet Wilson. "Judith Sargent Murray." In *Notable American Women 1607-1950: A Biographical Dictionary,* edited by Edward T. James, Janet Wilson James, and Paul Boyer, vol. 2, pp. 603-605. Cambridge, Mass.: Harvard University Press, 1971.

Janes, R. M. "On the Reception of Mary Wollstonecraft's *A Vindication of the Rights of Woman.*" *Journal of the History of Ideas* 39 (1978): 293-302.

Kelley, Mary, ed. *Woman's Being, Woman's Place: Female Identity and Vocation in American History.* Boston: G. K. Hall, 1979.

Kerber, Linda K. *Women of the Republic: Intellect and Ideology in Revolutionary America.* Chapel Hill: University of North Carolina Press, 1980.

King, Peter J. "John Neal as a Benthamite." *New England Quarterly* 39 (1966): 47-65.

Kolodny, Annette. "Some Notes on Defining a 'Feminist Literary Criticism.'" *Critical Inquiry* 2 (Autumn 1975): 75-92.

———. "Critical Response: The Feminist as Literary Critic." *Critical Inquiry* 2 (Summer 1976): 821-32.

Krouse, Agate Nesoule. "Toward a Definition of Literary Feminism." In *Feminist Criticism: Essays on Theory, Poetry and Prose,* edited by Cheryl L. Brown and Karen Olson, pp. 279-90. Metuchen, N. J.: Scarecrow Press, 1978.

Lang, Hans-Joachim. "Drei Wurzeln der Wahrheit im historischen Roman: John Neals *Rachel Dyer.*" In *Geschichte und Gesellschaft in der amerikanischen Literatur,* edited by Karl Schubert und Ursula Müller-Richter, pp. 9-32. Heidelberg: Quelle & Meyer, 1975.

Lease, Benjamin. "Yankee Poetics: John Neal's Theory of Poetry and Fiction." *American Literature* 24 (1953): 505-19.

———. "John Neal's Quarrel with the *Westminster Review.*" *American Literature* 26 (1954): 86-88.

———. *That Wild Fellow: John Neal and the American Literary Revolution.* Chicago and London: Chicago University Press, 1972.

Lemons, J. Stanley. *The Woman Citizen: Social Feminism in the 1920's.* Urbana: University of Illinois Press, 1973.

Leonard, Eugenie A. *The Dear-Bought Heritage.* Philadelphia: University of Pennsylvania Press, 1965.

Lerner, Gerda, ed. *The Female Experience: An American Documentary.* Indianapolis: Bobbs-Merrill, 1977.

———, ed. *The Majority Finds Its Past.* New York: Oxford University Press, 1979.

Lewis, W. David. "Eliza Wood Burhans Farnham." In *Notable American Women 1607-1950: A Biographical Dictionary,* edited by Edward T. James, Janet Wilson James, and Paul Boyer, vol. 1, pp. 598-600. Cambridge, Mass.: Harvard University Press, 1971.

Livermore, Mary H. "Mrs. Stowe's Vindication." *The Woman's Journal* 1, no. 3 (Jan. 22, 1870): 17.

Loshe, Lillie Deming. *The Early American Novel 1789-1830.* Repr. ed. New York: Fredrick Ungar, 1958.

Martin, Harold C. "The Development of Style in 19th-Century American Fiction." In *Style in Prose Fiction,* English Institute Essays, 1958, edited by Harold C. Martin, pp. 114-41. New York: Columbia University Press, 1959.

———. "The Colloquial Tradition in the Novel: John Neal." *New England Quarterly* 32 (1959): 455-75.

Martin, Wendy. "Profile: Frances Wright, 1795-1852." *Women's Studies* 2 (1974): 273-78.

McAlexander, Patricia Jewell. "The Cultural Dialogue on the Nature and Role of Women in Late Eighteenth-Century America." *Early American Literature* 9 (1975): 252-66.

Melder, Keith. "The Beginnings of the Woman's Rights Movement in the United States, 1800-1840." Ph. D. diss., Yale University, 1964.

———. "Ladies Bountiful: Organized Women's Benevolence in Early Nineteenth Century America." *New York History* 18 (1967): 231-54.

Merk, Lois Bannister. "Massachusetts and the Woman Suffrage Movement." 2 vols. Ph. D. diss., Radcliffe College, 1958. Cambridge, Mass.: General Microfilm Co., 1961.

[Mill, John Stuart.] "Edinburgh Review." *The Westminster Review* 1 (1824): 505-41.

Moers, Ellen. *Literary Women: The Great Writers.* New York: Doubleday, 1976.

Murray, Judith Sargent [Constantia]. *The Gleaner: A Miscellaneous Production.* 3 vols. Boston: I. Thomas and E. T. Andrews, 1798.

O'Neill, William. "Feminism as a Radical Ideology." In *Dissent: Explorations in the History of American Radicalism,* edited by Alfred F. Young, pp. 273-300. DeKalb: Northern Illinois University Press, 1968.

———. *The Woman Movement: Feminism in the United States and England.* London: Allen and Unwin, 1969.

———. *Everyone Was Brave: The Rise and Fall of Feminism in America.* Chicago: Quadrangle, 1969.

Parker, Gail, ed. *The Oven Birds: American Women on Womanhood, 1820-1920.* New York: Doubleday, 1972.

Parker, Patricia. *Charles Brockden Brown: A Reference Guide.* Boston: G. K. Hall, 1980.

Petter, Henri. *The Early American Novel.* Athens, Ohio: Ohio University Press, 1971.

Quinn, Arthur Hobson. *American Fiction: An Historical and Critical Survey.* New York: Appleton-Century, 1936.

Reed, James. *From Private Vice to Public Virtue: The Birth Control Movement and American Society Since 1830.* New York: Basic Books, 1978.

Richards, Irving T. "The Life and Works of John Neal." 4 vols. Ph. D. diss., Harvard University, 1932.

———. "Mary Gove Nichols and John Neal." *New England Quarterly* 7 (1934): 335-55.

———. "John Neal: a Bibliography." *Jahrbuch für Amerikastudien* 7 (1962): 296-319.

Riegel, Robert. "Women's Clothes and Women's Rights." *American Quarterly* 15 (1963): 390-41.

Riley, Glenda Gates. "The Subtle Subversion: Changes in the Traditionalist Image of the American Woman." *The Historian* 32 (1970): 210-27.

Roberts, Helene E. "The Exquisite Slave: The Role of Clothes in the Making of Victorian Woman." *Signs* 2 (1977): 558-66.

Robinson, Harriet Hanson. *Massachusetts in the Woman Suffrage Movement: A General, Political, Legal, and Legislative History from 1774, to 1881.* Boston: Roberts Brothers, 1881; 2nd printing 1883.

Rosenberg, Carroll Smith. "The Hysterical Woman: Sex Roles and Role Conflict in 19th-Century America." *Social Research* 39 (Winter 1972): 652-78.

———. "Puberty to Menopause: The Cycle of Femininity in Nineteenth-Century America." *Feminist Studies* 1 (1973): 58-72.

Rosenberg, Carroll Smith, and Rosenberg, Charles. "The Female Animal: Medical and Biological Views of Woman and Her Roles in Nineteenth-Century America." *Journal of American History* 80 (Sept. 1973): 332-56.

Rossi, Alice, ed. *The Feminist Papers: From Adams to de Beauvoir.* New York: Bantam Books, 1973.

Rousseau, Jean-Jaques. *La Nouvelle Héloïse: Julie, or the New Heloise. Letters of Two Lovers, Inhabitants of a Small Town at the Foot of the Alps.* Translated by Judith H. McDowell. University Park: Pennsylvania State University Press, 1968.

Rubin, Joseph Jay. "John Neal's Poetics as an Influence on Whitman and Poe." *New England Quarterly* 14 (1941): 359-62.

Ryan, Mary P. *Womanhood in America: From Colonial Times to the Present.* New York: New Viewpoints, 1975.

[S., R.] "Departure of Woman." *The Yankee and Boston Literary Gazette* 2, no. 21 (May 21, 1829): 162-63.

Scheick, William J "Power, Authority, and Revolutionary Impulse in John Neal's *Rachel Dyer.*" *Studies in American Fiction* 4 (1976): 143-55.

Sears, Donald A. *John Neal.* Twayne's United States Authors Series 307. Boston: G. K. Hall, 1978.

———. "Maine Fiction before 1840: A Microcosm." *Colby Library Quarterly* 14 (1978): 109-24.

Sewall, Samuel E. *The Legal Condition of Women in Massachusetts.* Woman's Suffrage Tracts. No. 5. Boston: The New-England Woman's Suffrage Association, 1869.

Seydow, John J. "The Sound of Passing Music: John Neal's Battle for American Literary Independence." *Costerus* 7 (1973): 153-82.

Showalter, Elaine. *A Literature of Their Own: British Women Novelists from Brontë to Lessing.* Princeton, N. J.: Princeton University Press, 1977.

———. "Feminist Criticism in the Wilderness." *Critical Inquiry* 8 (Winter 1981): 179-205.

Sklar, Kathryn Kish. *Catharine Beecher: A Study in Domesticity.* New Haven: Yale University Press, 1973.

Smith, Bonnie. "Judith Sargent Murray: The Making of an American Feminist." *Essays and Studies by Students of Simmons College* 34, no. 2 (May 1982): 14-19.

Smith, Elihu Hubbard. *The Diary of Elihu Hubbard Smith.* Edited by James E. Cronin. Philadelphia: American Philosophical Society, 1973.

Smith, Elizabeth Oakes. *Selections from the Autobiography of Elizabeth Oakes Smith.* Edited by Mary Alice Wyman. Lewiston, Me.: Lewiston Journal Co., 1924.

Smith, Henry Nash. "The Scribbling Women and the Cosmic Success Story." *Critical Inquiry* 1 (Sept. 1974): 47-70.

Smith-Rosenberg, Carroll. "The Female World of Love and Ritual: Relations between Women in Nineteenth-Century America." *Signs* 1 (1975): 1-29.

Sochen, June. Herstory: *A Woman's View of American History.* New York: Alfred, 1974.

Spengemann, William C. *The Adventurous Muse: The Poetics of American Fiction, 1789-1900.* New Haven and London: Yale University Press, 1977.

Stage, Sarah. *Female Complaints: Lydia Pinkham and the Business of Women's Medicine.* New York: Norton, 1979.

Stanford, Ann. "Images of Women in Early American Literature." *In What Manner of Woman: Essays on English and American Life and Literature,* edited by Marlene Springer, pp. 184-210. New York: New York University Press, 1977.

Stanton, Elizabeth Cady; Anthony, Susan B.; and Gage, Matilda Joslyn, eds. *The History of Woman Suffrage.* Vols. 1-3. Rochester, N. Y.: Susan B. Anthony, 1881-86.

Stearns, Bertha Monica. "Early Philadelphia Magazines for Ladies." *Pennsylvania Magazine of History and Biography* 64 (1940): 479-91.

Stone, Lucy. "Maine and Woman Suffrage." *The Woman's Journal* 4, no. 6 (Feb. 8, 1873): 44.

Taylor, William R. *Cavalier and Yankee: The Old South and American National Character.* New York: Doubleday Anchor, 1963.

Taylor, William R., and Rasch, Christopher. "Two 'Kindred Spirits': Sorority and Family in New England, 1839-1846." *New England Quarterly* 36 (1963): 23-41.

Thièbaux, Marcelle. "Mary Wollstonecraft in Federalist America 1791-1802." In *The Evidence of the Imagination: Studies of Interactions Between Life and Art in English Romantic Literature,* edited by Donald H. Reiman et al., pp. 195-245. New York: New York University Press, 1978.

Tolles, Frederick B. "Mary Dyer." In *Notable American Women 1607-1950: A Biographical Dictionary,* edited by Edward T. James, Janet Wilson James, and Paul Boyer, pp. 536-37. Cambridge, Mass.: Harvard University Press, 1971.

Uhler, John Earle. "The Delphian Club." *Maryland Historical Magazine* 20 (1925): 305-46.

Verbrugge, Martha H. "Women and Medicine in Nineteenth-Century America." *Signs* 1 (Summer 1976): 957-72.

Violette, Augusta Genevieve. *Economic Feminism in American Literature Prior to 1848.* Orono: University of Maine Studies, 1925.

Wardle, Ralph. *Mary Wollstonecraft: A Critical Biography.* Lawrence: Kansas University Press, 1951.

Welter, Barbara. "The Cult of True Womanhood: 1820-1860." *American Quarterly* 18 (1966): 151-74.

———. "The Feminization of American Religion." In *Dimity Convictions: The American Woman in the Nineteenth Century,* by Barbara Welter, pp. 83-102. Athens: Ohio University Press, 1976.

Wertheimer, Barbara Mayer. *We Were There: The Story of Working Women in America.* New York: Pantheon, 1977.

Wilder, Eva M. "Letter from Maine." *The Woman's Journal* 1, no. 14 (April 9, 1870): 107.

Williford, Miriam. "Bentham on the Rights of Women." *Journal of the History of Ideas* 36 (1975): 167-76.

Wollstonecraft, Mary. *A Vindication of the Rights of Woman.* 2nd ed., 1792. Facsimile Reproduction. Farnborough, England: Gregg International Publishers, 1970.

Wood, Ann Douglas. "The 'Scribbling Women' and Fanny Fern: Why Women Wrote." *American Quarterly* 23 (1971): 3-24.

———. "'The Fashionable Diseases': Women's Complaints and Their Treatment in Nineteenth-Century America." *Journal of Interdisciplinary History* 4 (1973): 25-52.

Fritz Fleischmann (essay date 1985)

SOURCE: Fleischmann, Fritz. "'A Likeness, Once Acknowledged': John Neal and the 'Idiosyncracies' of Literary History." In *Myth and Enlightenment in American Literature: In Honor of Hans-Joachim Lang,* edited by Dieter Meindl and Friedrich W. Horlacher, in collaboration with Martin Christadler, pp. 161-76. Erlangen, Germany: Universitätsbund Erlangen-Nürnberg, 1985.

[*In the following essay, Fleischmann uses some of Neal's works to illustrate the process through which works are entered into or excluded from a literary canon, and argues that some of Neal's works may have been erroneously and unfairly excluded because of the criteria by which they have been evaluated.*]

I

For literary historians of the United States, the 1980s promise to be a period of reconstruction. Two decades of vigorous challenges to established canons and ways of reading have produced a new wealth of texts that ask to be taken seriously, a vast amount of new historical knowledge, and an enormous increase in critical activity and sophistication. That our "current critical judgement" no longer beats at the "feeble pulse" diagnosed by Hans-Joachim Lang in 1962[1] but at a more invigorating throb is evident, not least, in the brave new attempts to outline a coherent story of "American" literature: *Reconstructing American Literature,* Paul Lauter's collection of "alternative" syllabi and course descriptions, has become an enormously popular reference work for literary Americanists,[2] and two renowned university presses (Columbia and Cambridge) have embarked upon a rewriting of American literary history. Much current critical debate is devoted to questions of canon formation.[3]

It is clear, however, that the enormous task of examining familiar critical categories has only begun and that a "heroic rereading" (Annette Kolodny)[4] is needed before we can see the literary past with new eyes. Such a rereading, as Kolodny puts it, "must proceed from the commitment to take seriously those works with which we are least familiar, and especially so when they challenge current notions of art and artifice" [107]. As a result, "the once-familiar will have been *de*familiarized" [ibid.], no longer eliciting the semi-automatic responses that constitute so large a part of critical "judgement." Defamiliarization, according to this view, also liberates "the historical and the evaluative impulses" [105] from their entrenched opposition, by rehistoricizing them. Drawing on the work of Jane Tompkins, Kolodny suggests that we try to understand "how a text works out 'problems inherent in the culture at the moment of composition' or how a text is reconstituted by some later cultural elite so as to work out the problems of another period—and thus how it achieves power at any given time." This, she argues,

> simultaneously enables both synchronic and diachronic analyses. On the one hand, this approach offers innovative procedures for analyzing the literary strategies of a single period or decade; on the other hand, it offers new ways of constructing lines of literary influence. Most importantly, in other words, this approach allows us to reassess our literary heritage *by means and in terms of* reembedding texts and authors into encompassing, complicated, and dense historical processes.
>
> [106]

This means, inevitably, a renewed interest in cultural contexts: "literary history becomes in part social history, in part economic history, in part the history of taste" *and* "in part, the history of the vocation of criticism itself" [107].

II

John Neal (1793-1876) is a decidedly non-canonical writer whose works have tended to fall through the grid of a critical perception schooled in the familiar "great works" and the critical theories designed to accommodate them. He shares this fate, needless to say, with writers from various marginalized groups that have recently begun to attract critical attention. Like theirs, Neal's reputation has suffered from notions of value based on a canon of familiar patterns and interconnections that have imposed on students of noncanonical writings "the nonsensical burden of trying to recuperate these materials on the grounds that they are 'just as good as canonical texts,' or, as Jane Tompkins phrases it, 'good in the same way canonical texts are.'"[5] Neal's chances for re-cognition, I wish to argue, are improved by a defamiliarizing approach that promises to take the hitherto excluded on its own terms rather than those of the canon.

Once assigned, a writer's place in literary history is difficult to adjust. Over two decades ago, Hans-Joachim Lang described how this "law" has affected Neal's repu-

tation. In the eyes of most critics, Lang wrote, "Neal seemed to resemble the drawing master and portrait painter of his novel **Randolph,**" who specialized in profiles that exaggerated some physical idiosyncrasy of the subject, making sure that others recognized the external resemblance. Neal's painter knew "that no blundering of mine, could ever destroy a likeness, once acknowledged: and, therefore, I went on, working as fearlessly with my India ink, as if I were blacking a pair of boots; and the *expression* was, generally worthy of the work."[6] Lang professed uncertainty as to "[w]hether this is a caricature of Neal's art or of the art of Neal's critics" but concluded, sadly, that "the indestructibility of 'a likeness, once acknowledged' is a law of literary history which works against any attempt to resurrect [Neal] as a writer." His case in point: F. L. Pattee had failed to recognize the stature of Neal's story **"Otter-Bag"** because of "the nefarious influence of the short-story theory" [ibid.].

But how can we liberate ourselves from such "nefarious" habits of reading? Even champions of Neal's literary fame find themselves comparing their man to some canonical figure or other to validate his work. Thus, Lang asserts "that **'Otter-Bag'** is as good as Kipling"; Benjamin Lease states that "the best stories of John Neal suffer only by comparison with the best productions of Irving, Hawthorne, and Poe"; both scholars claim in their 1978 introduction to *The Genius of John Neal* that his best work "invite[s] comparison with the best of Poe, Hawthorne, and Melville."[7] Lease characterizes **"Idiosyncrasies,"** a long tale published in 1843, as "Neal's 'Imp of the Perverse,' published two years before Poe's."[8]

However supportive of Neal's claim these comparisons may be, they argue the unarguable—that he is "good in the same way" as some of his contemporaries. It may be more helpful to contemplate the fact that he has been *neglected* in the same way as certain contemporaries, to some of whom (e.g., Herman Melville) critical tribute has since been paid, but many of whom (notably a number of women writers) are still in the process of being rediscovered.

I mention Melville's work because it is a case in point. If we apply to it Kolodny's explanation of how texts achieve power, the shoe seems to fit perfectly: Melville's best-known writings work out "'problems inherent in the culture'" of his time, and they attract(ed) the interest of a later period by addressing some problems of that period (even if, as Winfried Fluck has suggested, the problems of the later age may be largely those of the critical profession).[9] But Melville's case also shows that this approach may raise other canonical questions. To what extent do cultural configurations become the artist's personal "problem"? If, for instance, we agree with Ann Douglas that "America was the problem

[Melville] had to comprehend,"[10] how does that affect the rank of individual works within the Melville canon?

If we are to review texts in the framework of "encompassing, complicated, and dense historical processes" [106], we must have some general knowledge of these processes *before* we approach individual texts, and we expect to deepen our knowledge as a result of reading those texts. By merely looking at the reading process as a necessarily continuous, never-ending affair, however, we may well end up condemning this "hermeneutic circle," as many critics have, as a vicious circle of futility. The only way out is to understand what drives this mechanism—what causes critics to discover ever new "meanings" in texts that have already been subjected to apparently exhaustive treatment.

This question is intimately related to that of a text's canonicity. Canons are ideological constructs; they have certain functions and serve certain ends. The "mutability and diversity" of aesthetic value, as Barbara Herrnstein-Smith has pointed out, constitute its "most fundamental character": "All value is radically contingent, being neither an inherent property of objects nor an arbitrary projection of subjects but, rather, the product of the dynamics of an economic system."[11] This dynamics affects, among other things, the value of an aesthetic object to an individual subject whose "personal economy" is made up of "needs, interests, and resources—biological, psychological, material, and experiental" [11-12]; these are always changing and are, in turn, influenced by the entities used to satisfy them.

Within such a framework of personal and group economies, aesthetic entities are classified according to their functions. Not only is their value contingent upon a large variety of factors, but so is the "value" of critical judgments: the "value" of an evaluation depends on "how well it performs various desired/able functions for the various people who may at any time be concretely involved with it" [22].

Two recent case studies have demonstrated how personal and group interests affect literary status. For the period from 1960 to 1975, Richard Ohmann has described how U. S. novels were selected for publication and promoted to critical attention by a close network of people within "the Professional-Managerial class." Ohmann's analysis reveals "that the emergence of these novels has become a process saturated with class values and interests, a process inseparable from the broader struggle for position and power in our society, from the institutions that mediate that struggle, as well as from legitimation of and challenges to the social order."[12]

Jane Tompkins, in examining the making of Hawthorne's status as a classic American author, suggests "that a literary reputation could never be anything but a

political matter," and "that the literary works that now make up the canon do so because the groups that have an investment in them are culturally the most influential."[13] This is not to say that "classic" texts are not "good" in the sense that they "[reward] the scrutiny of successive generations of readers" [640], but only to suggest that their being read at all has more to do with the historical conditions of their publication and reception than with their allegedly timeless stability as aesthetic objects:

> The recognition that literary texts, like everything else, are humanly created, historically produced objects, whose value has been created and recreated by men and women out of their particular needs, suggests a need to study the interests, institutional practices, and social arrangements that sustain the canon of classic works. It also opens a way for the retrieval of the values and interests embodied in other, noncanonical texts, which the literary establishment responsible for the canon in its present form has—for a variety of reasons—suppressed.
>
> [641-42]

The last two decades of scholarship in women's studies have produced a powerful rearrangement of "values and interests" within the academy. Not incidentally, and as if to support Tompkins's thesis, the re-historicizing of value judgments follows an historical change in the judging institution.[14]

III

"Idiosyncrasies," a tale about the madness of patriarchy, is one of Neal's most mature and complex stories: "As for sheer horror, Poe's more artfully contrived stories are child's play as compared to the moral obliquities of Lee, the authoritarian, lovingly-murderous father and husband."[15] Neal's story exposes the need for complete control over women and children as a form of male hubris that cripples good intentions and destroys the objects of men's love. Most disturbingly, the story puts its male readers on the spot by questioning whether the destructive behavior it depicts grows out of one man's "idiosyncrasies"—or whether that man's psychic constellation, so far from being idiosyncratic, comes with the territory of manhood. How mad, in other words, is Lee, the narrator? How that question is answered depends, as we shall see, on the strength of the reader's own defenses.

Neal's story was published in **Brother Jonathan,** a New York magazine of which he was then the editor. The first part, subtitled "An Introductory Chapter," appeared on May 6, 1843, the second and major portion, divided into three chapters, on July 8.[16]

The tale is narrated in a hospital for the insane by an inmate, Lee, who is locked up there at the behest of his daughter. He is provoked into talking by an unnamed interviewer who has come to see him. This visitor's story provides the frame in which Lee's narrative is embedded; this narrative itself, however, contains a story within a story. Lee's "idiosyncrasy" for which he is locked up is his mad jealousy of his daughter, who is the exact image of his dead wife. His child "has fallen in love . . . without consulting her father, and now she wants to be married" [94]. This jealousy is traced back to the psychodynamics of Lee's marriage [70]. His recounting of the time he met his wife, their subsequent marriage, and her death encircles the core of his tale— the story of a disastrous mountain expedition, which brings out Lee's most self-destructive impulses.

At the outset of chapter II, the narrator begins the explanation of his jealousy by distinguishing the love of children from that between adults:

> Talk about the love of men and women! I tell you, sir, that between the mature and fully-grown of equal age, there is no such thing as love—high-hearted, strong, and pure, unconquerable love. Men and women have other and very different feelings towards each other, and wholly mistake the diviner impulses, and the deeper and warmer sensibilities, that belong to the pure of heart, the faithful by nature, and the *wholly inexperienced.*
>
> [70]

When he met his future wife, Lee was "a full grown, serious-looking man" [ibid.] with definite views of what women were and ought to be like; he espoused feminist positions identical with Neal's:

> I had loved the society of women, believing it to be a safeguard against every sort of debasing and soiling temptation. That I found them weak, changeable, frivolous—and everything but faithless, and heartless, and treacherous, I acknowledge. But, with all their faults, I always found them better than men, better-hearted, more trustworthy, and altogether more self-sacrificing—more unselfish. And so, I began to look about me, and tried for a long while to understand *why* it was, that women were so changeable, and weak, and frivolous; and having found it in the *Institutions of Society,* as we men call them, *we,* the founders, framers, and supporters of those very institutions, which imprison the soul of woman, and set a seal upon her faculties— and seven seals upon the fountain of her thoughts; forbidding her to reason for herself, to enquire for herself, to judge for herself—nay even to believe for herself; and allowing her no share whatever in the glorious birthright we claim, of governing ourselves: Having found the cause, I say, in these institutions, the handywork of Man, and believing in my heart . . . that where the evil was, there the remedy must be sought for, I went to work, with a determination to help the first woman I should meet with, having the courage and steadfastness of purpose, needed for such a struggle, up—up—and *into* the place she had been created for— that of entire companionship with Man.
>
> [71]

When he offers this kind of help to "a young and lovely woman," however, he only succeeds in putting her to sleep. Prompted by vanity and self-delusion, he lectures her "upon her duties to herself," while pretending that "I saw nothing, and felt nothing, as my look wondered over her divine countenance and richly-moulded person—but a magnificent flower: a spirituality in blossom . . ." [71]. This is the kind of self-absorbed male sentimentalism Neal had ridiculed as early as 1817 in his first novel, **Keep Cool**: when James Earnest says about his love for Laura, "'her *mind* is the reason—it was that I first loved,'" he is rudely interrupted by the narrator: "Nonsense, Earnest; no man ever fell in love with a pretty girl's mind *first.*"[17] In our story, Lee finds his audience "fast asleep on the sofa." A little girl who had witnessed the whole scene first giggled at, then felt sorry for him; as he was about to leave, he explains, "I felt her little warm hand stealing into mine; and when I looked down upon her, I started, for tears were in her eyes and her sweet mouth trembled, as if I had been rough with her" [72]. Scorned by the woman, Lee found the sympathy he craved in this child: "That child understood me; and after a few more years, we were married, and she became the mother of a child, so like herself, when I first saw her" [72]—except that he "never *saw* her" until her gesture of sympathy, which restored his wounded pride. Because of his daughter's likeness to the child her mother once was, Lee "never could bear the thought of her loving anybody on earth but me" [73]. His marriage was marked by inequality of age, temper, and power. Lee always refers to his wife in childlike terms ("poor little Jenny" [86]) and reveals that "she seldom spoke to me above her breath, when we were alone" [73]. He boasts that he "could depend upon her" [73], but his jealousy makes him doubt her love even now: "She thought she loved me—poor girl— she persisted in that belief all her life long, though I labored mightily to undeceive her, and she died at last to prove that I was mistaken" [73-74].

Two children were born: Willy, a self-willed and independent boy whom his father "used to try . . . as with fire and water, almost every day of his life" [74], and Biddy, a sweet, angelic little creature, the apple of her parents' eye.

The story proper begins when the children are twelve and ten years old. The family is travelling in the winter, stopping at an inn near a snow-covered mountain. In a scene that reveals much about the jealous insecurity which makes him play the tyrant over his wife and children [75-76], Lee discovers that Willy would like to go up on the mountain the next morning to watch the sunrise. At first opposed to the idea ("I hope you didn't encourage the simpleton"), the father begins to support it when he hears that his wife fears for the boy's safety: "I hope you didn't discourage the boy" [76-77]. Lee switches sides (here and in several later instances) because, as a husband "who knew his rights, and know-ing, must maintain them" [77], he cannot bear the fact that his wife thinks for herself. But he allows her and Biddy to join the expedition because he wants to test their courage [78].

When asked if he has made "all the proper inquiries about the best path" [79], he is "nettled at this. The question itself implied a doubt, and a reproach." After all, he is "well acquainted with this neighbourhood—my father used to live within a hundred miles of it. I have Greenleaf's Map and the Gazetteer." He cuts off further discussion: "Her mouth was finally stopped, hey? Didn't I make her know her place!" [79]

Still, the next morning he brings a length of bedcord along, "half ashamed" [81] of himself for taking even the slightest preparation. All goes well, however, and three and a half hours later the family is descending the mountain again, the children and their dog Pompey scampering in the snow after Biddy's fur cap. Suddenly they find themselves on a large overhanging snowdrift—their mother "pale and speechless with terror," her hus-band "vexed" by her behavior. So provoked is he by her anxieties that he stifles his own impulses to call the children back. As the drift begins to move, Biddy man-ages to return to her mother; Willy is told to lie down in the snow while his father fumbles for the rope he brought. His wife implores him to save the boy, and this "interference," Lee recalls,

> vexed me more than anything she ever did in her life.
>
> Nonsense! I said—and put the line back into my pocket. And then, to punish her for such untimely interference, I called out to Willy to send Pompey for the cap, and make him fetch it.
>
> Yes, father.
>
> But the dog wouldn't stir an inch. He would neither go for the cap, nor leave his young master.
>
> What ails the dog? said I.
>
> He's frightened, father.
>
> Well, and what if he is?—and are you frightened, my boy?
>
> Yes, father.
>
> Well, then, fetch me that cap!
>
> [83]

Willy goes forward, and his mother faints; Lee represses his own urge to call the boy back; his wife awakens from her swoon and screams "—and then—oh, Lord God of the childless, be merciful to me!—I heard him say, *father! father!*—and he was gone!" [84]

Here begins the father's hair-raising rescue attempt [84-92] which, by itself, should have established Neal's place in the annals of American literature. Lee ties his

rope around some bushes and prepares to descend after his boy—a foolishly heroic act from which he is dis-suaded by his wife, not without great resistance: "A plague on the counsels of a woman! If she had let me alone, I should have thought of all these things myself" [87]. Finally, he agrees to her proposal that she, being of lighter weight, should descend into the gulf after Willy [ibid.]. Biddy, who weighs even less, then asks to take her mother's place, and goes down into the dark. She finds her brother, but he is lost a second time when an avalanche tears him away. Biddy's rope is stuck, and Lee himself goes down to find the children [90]. An-other avalanche thunders by; he follows it and discov-ers his boy, half-dead "with cold and terror": "when I lifted him up, and began to rub him and speak to him, he knew me, and . . . laid his cheek to mine, and be-gan to sob with a violence that frightened me—he was only twelve, you must know" [91].

The children are rescued, but Willy dies within a year—"perhaps of fright, and perhaps of something else" but, Lee explains, "I never could bring myself to forgive his mother": "But for that confounded scream, just as he had his hand upon the cap, the boy would have got back safely enough, and all would have been well" [92].

The listener arises to go, but Lee holds him back with the statement that he put his "wife to death for that very scream" [92]. Years later, he explains, he and his wife were walking near Wentworth Falls, talking about their children, the husband saying:

> I do in my heart believe, that if I had commanded ei-ther of those children to leap into the whirlpool yonder, I should have been obeyed instantly.
>
> And if you were—what then? said she.
>
> Why then, said I, somewhat nettled, I acknowledge, at the strange propriety of the question; and the difficulty I found in answering it: Why then said I, with a biting emphasis, and looking into her large clear eyes, as if I could see into the very depths of her heart—I wish to Heaven I could find any other living creature capable of such obedience.
>
> You would!—said my wife.
>
> Yes—I *would*.
>
> And it would really make you happier?
>
> It would indeed, I replied.
>
> We were walking together, a few feet from the bank. She stopped and kissed me—and whispering, *Be hap-pier then!* Sprang into the whirlpool.
>
> [93]

Although Lee jumped after her, his wife drowned, and he was accused of pushing her in. His disclaimer neatly summarizes his impossible expectations of a wife—a woman who can think for herself but who nevertheless strictly obeys her husband: "what business had she to drown herself without my leave! what a fool to do so at the bidding of a husband! and such a husband!" [93]

IV

"Idiosyncrasies" illustrates the symbiotic relationship between text and context; to miss the context is to misunderstand the functioning of the text. With Poe's "Imp" in mind, critics have tended to read this story as a study of the perverse that uses Nealian autobiographical props, an illustration of "the nearly self-destructive element of the perverse in a strong-willed man not unlike the author."[18] By itself, neither analogy—with Poe, or with aspects of Neal's own life and character—takes us far enough. Poe's imp is "a mobile without motive, a motive not *motivirt* [sic]";[19] Neal's *is* motivated since it asks: whose imp is it? The autobiographical details also impinge on that question (*whose* "idiosyncrasies" is the story about?) and should therefore be handled with caution.

The question itself is addressed in the very first sentence of the story: "And what the plague are Idiosyncrasies?" [67]. It takes the reader to Neal's own aesthetic premises:[20] "Why not tell us in good wholesome English what your meaning is?" Criticizing "the language of books" and "parade of learning" as unsuited to engage an audience, the visitor exhorts Lee: "No, no, my friend; if you are to tell your story to any good purpose, it should be in that household speech, whereof we hear so much and read so little" [67].

The man who preaches such Nealian doctrine then ascribes to Lee a career and a role that appear to reflect Neal's sense of his own role in history at this time— that of the misunderstood prophet whose greatness goes unrecognized by those he seeks to benefit: "I see you wondered at—reverenced—reviled, and as I believe, shamefully misunderstood, not to say misrepresented" [ibid.]. By attributing some of his own biographical and literary hallmarks to both sides of the dialogue, Neal avoids being identified with either side. This is a dramatic technique he had used already in his early novels, most strikingly in his *succès de scandale*, **Errata; or, The Works of Will. Adams** (1823).[21] It allows him to create characters that explore various aspects of his own experience; but none of them can plausibly be identified with the author.

We can only get further if we are fully aware of Neal's history as a campaigner for women's rights and his involvement in feminist advocacy at the time of publication. In the history of the American woman movement, the decade from 1838 to 1848 is marked by three milestone documents: in 1838, by Sarah Grimké's *Letters on the Equality of the Sexes and the Condition of*

Women; in 1843, by Margaret Fuller's long essay, "The Great Lawsuit. Man versus Men. Woman versus Women" (revised and published as *Woman in the Nineteenth Century* in 1845); in 1848, by the "Declaration of Sentiments" of the Seneca Falls Convention. Also in 1838, however, John Neal was invited by Margaret Fuller to address her students at the Greene Street School in Providence, Rhode Island, "on the destiny and vocation of Woman"; in 1841, the feminist activist Mary Gove Nichols addressed him as "the man who gave the first impetus to the cause of women in this country";[22] and in 1843, he gave his most controversial and widely reported performance as a public speaker on women's rights.

On January 24, 1843, John Neal spoke about the **"Rights of Women"** at the Broadway Tabernacle, New York's largest hall with a seating capacity of 2500, returning a week later to expand upon his views. On February 8, he made a third appearance there to participate in a debate with editors Park Benjamin of the *New World* and William Leete Stone of the *Commercial Advertiser.* Each time, the press reaction was vitriolic.[23] The debate was resumed in the pages of *Brother Jonathan,* whose chief editor Neal was to become in May. An editorial notice on April 29 defended his opinions, and *Brother Jonathan* published his Tabernacle address on June 17. A critical response by Eliza Wood Farnham appeared on June 24 and July 2. More replies followed on both sides, and the controversy continued into September.[24] A note in the second volume of *The History of Woman Suffrage* (1881) testifies that the affair "roused considerable discussion": "Mr. Neal's lecture . . . was extensively copied, and as it reviewed some of the laws relating to woman and her property, it had a wide, silent influence, preparing the way for action. It was a scathing satire, and men felt the rebuke."[25]

Further articles by Neal on the subject of women's rights appeared in *Brother Jonathan* on September 23, October 21 and 28, December 2 and 16. In his last contribution of the year, Neal placed himself in the mainstream of the reform movement: "die when we may, we shall not have lived in vain! There is a spirit at work throughout this land, which *must* lead to the complete emancipation of our mothers and sisters and wives and daughters, before many years have gone by."[26] For Neal, who had first publicly advocated woman suffrage in 1823 and continued to do so into his old age, this was indeed his life's work.[27]

When **"Idiosyncrasies"** appeared in 1843, its publication in *Brother Jonathan* overlapped, as the following timetable shows, with the Neal/Farnham debate in the same magazine (and, incidentally, with Fuller's "Great Lawsuit," which was published in the July issue of *The Dial*):

Clearly, any reading of **"Idiosyncrasies"** must pay attention to this immediate and literal context. Its presence in the story is unmistakable.

V

What, then, are we to make of the fact that Neal puts his feminist philosophy into the mouth of a domestic tyrant confined in a madhouse? Our answer depends on our interpretation of Lee's madness. If we believe his visitor, who claims to have barely escaped with his life [95], Lee is "crazed" and therefore a completely unrealiable narrator. The jury that tried him for killing his wife also found him insane [94]. Lee himself disputes that interpretation, arguing that it is easy to counterfeit madness before a jury—using his own case as an indictment of the insanity defense [69]. He tells his visitor, "I am no more of a madman than you are" [68] and explains: "however mad a man may be north-north-west, as our friend Hamlet the Dane has ist, he may still know a hawk from a handsaw . . . when the wind is easterly" [ibid.]. And he claims, "I am not now—I never have been beside myself" [69].

That, precisely, is his problem—that he cannot escape from himself. When his wife died, he says, she "left me to quarrel with mankind for having allowed such a creature to belong to me. . . . I did not deserve such a Woman—*I, altogether a Man; and therefore it is, that I deserved her not*" [74; emphasis mine]. As a consequence, he distrusts all men as he distrusts himself. How can his daughter want to get married "to a man"? He asks his visitor, "Did you ever see a man in your life you would be fool enough to marry, if you were a woman? *I* never did! They are all alike, selfish and heartless and exacting" [94]. What Lee calls his "idiosyncrasies" is the fact that he has wanted to be a liberator but has acted as an oppressor. As Benjamin Lease recently wrote, "Neal had a profound understanding of the divided self—of the ways the power and integrity of men are inevitably undermined by their exploitation of women; in a man's world, both men and women are victims."[28] The title of Margaret Fuller's famous essay of July 1843, "The Great Lawsuit. Man versus Men. Woman versus Women," makes precisely the same point—that the existing gender arrangements and the attitudes they have created force men and women to be-

have against their own best interests. Like Fuller's essay, Neal's story can be read as a manifesto for human rights which challenges established notions of masculinity and femininity. **"Idiosyncrasies,"** more focussed than some of Neal's other work, goes beyond a purely intellectual appreciation of women's oppression to probe the mechanisms ("idiosyncrasies," indeed!) which force men to behave in destructive ways. It is left to the reader to decide whose "idiosyncrasies" these are. But now we should pay attention to Poe's comment on the "Imp": "No one who trustingly consults and thoroughly questions his own soul, will be disposed to deny the entire radicalness of the propensity in question."[29]

In rereading Neal's story for possible inclusion in a (not "the") canon of American literature, it is not enough to argue that embedding it in the context of feminist debate makes it an important text. When Irving T. Richards, in 1962, doubted Neal's authorship of **"David Whicher,"** he argued that "[t]he story is written with a compression, restraint, and general narrative skill that Neal rarely attained, and almost never maintained."[30] Neal maintained it in **"Idiosyncrasies,"** at least: so far from being a "rambling tale,"[31] it is carefully constructed and uses its materials with economy and purpose. We can only appreciate that purpose, however, if we read it in its own proper context. I invite the reader to judge for herself.

Notes

1. "Critical Essays and Stories by John Neal," ed. Hans-Joachim Lang, *Jahrbuch für Amerikastudien,* 7 (1962), 207.

2. *Reconstructing American Literature: Courses, Syllabi, Issues,* ed. Paul Lauter (Old Westbury, NY: Feminist Press, 1983).

3. See, among others, Nina Baym, "Melodramas of Beset Manhood: How Theories of American Fiction Exclude Women Authors," *American Quarterly,* 33 (Summer 1981), 123-39; Deborah S. Rosenfelt, "The Politics of Bibliography: Women's Studies and the Literary Canon," and Elizabeth A. Meese, "Archival Materials: The Problem of Literary Reputation," in *Women in Print I: Opportunities for Women's Studies Research in Language and Literature,* ed. Joan E. Hartman and Ellen Messer-Davidow (NY: MLA, 1982), pp. 11-35 and 37-46; Paul Lauter, "Race and Gender in the Shaping of the American Literary Canon: A Case Study from the Twenties," *Feminist Studies,* 9 (Fall 1983), 435-63; *Critical Inquiry,* 10, No. 1 (September 1983), special issue: *Canons,* ed. Robert von Hallberg; Adrienne Munich, "Feminist Criticism and the Literary Canon," forthcoming in *Feminist Criticism,* ed. Coppelia Kahn and Gayle Greene (NY: Methuen, 1985). See also Jane Tomp-

kins's forthcoming book, *Sensational Designs: The Cultural Work of American Fiction, 1790-1860* (NY: Oxford University Press, 1985).

4. Annette Kolodny, "The Integrity of Memory: Creating a New Literary History of the United States," *American Literature,* 57 (May 1985), 104. I am grateful to Professor Kolodny for sending me a galley copy of her essay and for permission to quote from it. (All subsequent references will be in the text.)

5. Kolodny, p. 107. The reference here is to Jane Tompkins, "But Is It Any Good?': The Institutionalization of Literary Value," in *The Grip Report: Second Draft,* Vol. 2 (March 1984), p. 26.

6. Lang, "Critical Essays and Stories," p. 206.

7. Lang, "Essays and Stories," p. 207; Lease, *That Wild Fellow: John Neal and the American Literary Revolution* (Chicago and London: University of Chicago Press, 1972), p. 159; *The Genius of John Neal: Selections from His Writings,* ed. with an Introduction by Benjamin Lease and Hans-Joachim Lang (Frankfurt: Peter Lang, 1978); "Introduction," p. xix.

8. *Wild Fellow,* p. 174; cf. *Genius,* p. xx.

9. See Winfried Fluck, "Das ästhetische Vorverständnis der *American Studies,*" *Jahrbuch für Amerikastudien,* 18 (1973), 127 and passim.

10. Ann Douglas, *The Feminization of American Culture* (NY: Avon, 1978), p. 353.

11. Barbara Herrnstein-Smith, "Contingencies of Value," *Critical Inquiry,* 10, No. 1 (September 1983), 11. (Subsequent references will be in the text.)

12. Richard Ohmann, "The Shaping of a Canon: U.S. Fiction, 1960-1975," *Critical Inquiry,* 10, No. 1 (September 1983), 209, 200.

13. Jane Tompkins, "Masterpiece Theater: The Politics of Hawthorne's Literary Reputation," *American Quarterly,* 36, No. 5 (Winter 1984), 618. (Subsequent page references will be in the text.)

14. See Carolyn G. Heilbrun, "The Profession and Society, 1958-83," and Paul Lauter, "Society and the Profession, 1958-83," *PMLA,* 99, No. 3 (Centennial Issue, May 1984), 408-413 and 414-426.

15. *Genius of John Neal,* p. 281.

16. *Brother Jonathan,* 5, No. 1 (May 6, 1843), 25; 5, No. 10 (July 8, 1843), 274-80. Citations in my text follow the version reprinted in *The Genius of John Neal,* pp. 67-95. The actual story title is merely "Idiosyncrasies."

17. *Keep Cool: A Novel.* Written in Hot Weather, by Somebody, M.D.C. & c. & c. (Baltimore: Joseph Cushing, 1817), I, 156.

18. Donald A. Sears, *John Neal,* Twayne's United States Authors Series, 307 (Boston: G. K. Hall, 1978), pp. 95-96. Cf. Lease, *Wild Fellow,* pp. 174-78; *Genius,* p. xx.

19. "The Imp of the Perverse," in *Collected Works of Edgar Allan Poe,* ed. Thomas Ollive Mabbott (Cambridge, Mass.: Belknap Press of Harvard University Press, 1978), III, 1220-21.

20. See Benjamin Lease, "Yankee Poetics: John Neal's Theory of Poetry and Fiction," *American Literature,* 24 (1953), 505-19; cf. chapter 6 in *This Wild Fellow* (pp. 69-80).

21. For a discussion of Neal's technique, see Fritz Fleischmann, *A Right View of the Subject: Feminism in the Works of Charles Brockden Brown and John Neal,* Erlanger Studien, 47 (Erlangen: Palm & Enke, 1983), pp. 261-63.—*Errata,* too, is a story of jealous tyranny and paternal failure. Will Adams, convinced that nobody can love him for himself, must constantly subject his wife and son's affection to cruel tests. See, for instance, I, 109-10.

22. Bell Gale Chevigny, *The Woman and the Myth: Margaret Fuller's Life and Writings* (Old Westbury, NY: Feminist Press, 1976), p. 234; letter from Mary Gove Nichols to John Neal, April 4, 1841, quoted in Irving T. Richards, "Mary Gove Nichols and John Neal," *New England Quarterly,* 7 (1934), 346.

23. See Irving T. Richards, "The Life and Works of John Neal" (Ph.D. diss., Harvard University, 1932), pp. 1035-41; Sears, *John Neal,* p. 101. For a view from the audience, see *Selections from the Autobiography of Elizabeth Oakes Smith,* ed. Mary Alice Wyman (Lewiston, Me.: Lewiston Journal Co., 1924), p. 69.

24. For a detailed discussion, see Fleischman, *Right View,* pp. 187-204.

25. *The History of Woman Suffrage,* ed. Elizabeth Cady Stanton, Susan B. Anthony and Matilda Joslyn Gage, II (Rochester, NY: Susan B. Anthony, 1881), pp. 435-36, n.

26. "Rights of Women—Acknowledged!" *Brother Jonathan,* 6, No. 16 (Dec. 16, 1843), 438.

27. For an overview of his feminist reform activities, see Fleischman, *Right View,* pp. 155-227.

28. Review of Fleischmann, *A Right View, New England Quarterly,* 57 (1984), 597.

29. "The Imp of the Perverse," p. 1221.

30. "A Note on the Authorship of 'David Whicher,'" *Jahrbuch für Amerikastudien,* 7 (1962), 293.

31. Lease, *Wild Fellow,* p. 174.

FURTHER READING

Bibliography

Richards, Irving T. "John Neal: A Bibliography." *Jahrbuch für Amerikastudien* 7 (1962): 296-319.
>   Considered the definitive bibliography of Neal's works; also includes secondary sources.

Biographies

Lease, Benjamin. *That Wild Fellow John Neal and the American Literary Revolution.* Chicago, Ill.: The University of Chicago Press, 1972, 229 p.
>   Detailed biography that examines Neal's various contributions to American literature.

———, and Hans-Joachim Lang. Introduction to *The Genius of John Neal: Selections from His Writings,* edited by Benjamin Lease and Hans-Joachim Lang, n.p. Frankfurt, Germany: Peter Lang, 1978.
>   Provides an overview of Neal's life and work as an introduction to a collection of Neal's stories, essays, and speeches.

Criticism

Guest, Boyd. "John Neal and 'Women's Rights and Women's Wrongs.'" *The New England Quarterly* 18, no. 4 (December 1945): 508-15.
>   Surveys Neal's activism in the women's rights movement and his treatment of the subject in his works.

King, Peter J. "John Neal as a Benthamite." *The New England Quarterly* 34, no. 1 (March 1966): 47-65.
>   Details Neal's analyses of the theories and essays of Jeremy Bentham.

Lease, Benjamin. "Yankee Poetics: John Neal's Theory of Poetry and Fiction." *American Literature* 24, no. 4 (January 1953): 505-19.
>   Discusses Neal's essays in which he examines and espouses literary theory.

———. "The Authorship of 'David Whicher': The Case for John Neal." *Jahrbuch für Amerikastudien* 12 (1967): 124-36.
>   Traces the clues to the authorship of the short story "David Whicher," which he ultimately attributes to Neal.

Martin, Harold C. "The Colloquial Tradition in the Novel: John Neal." *The New England Quarterly* 32, no. 4 (December 1959): 455-75.
>   Asserts Neal's importance as an influential and innovative American writer.

Pattee, Fred Lewis. Introduction to *American Writers: A Series of Papers Contributed to Blackwood's Magazine (1824-1825) by John Neal,* edited by Fred Lewis Pattee, pp. 3-26. Durham, N.C.: Duke University Press, 1937.
>   Offers a biographical introduction to a collection of Neal's essays written for *Blackwood's Magazine.*

Richards, Irving T. "John Neal's Gleanings in Irvingiana." *American Literature* 8, no. 2 (May 1936): 170-79.
>   Discusses Neal's relationship with Washington Irving.

Rubin, Joseph Jay. "John Neal's Poetics as an Influence on Whitman and Poe." *The New England Quarterly* 14, no. 2 (June 1941): 359-62.
>   Briefly recounts the reactions of Walt Whitman and Edgar Allan Poe to Neal's theories of poetry.

Seelye, John D. Introduction to *Rachel Dyer,* pp. v-xii. Gainesville, Fla.: Scholars' Facsimiles & Reprints, 1964.
>   Examines Neal's life and work leading up to the writing of *Rachel Dyer.*

Additional coverage of Neal's life and career is contained in the following sources published by Thomson Gale: *Dictionary of Literary Biography,* **Vols. 1, 59, 243;** *Feminist Writers;* *Literature Resource Center;* **and** *Reference Guide to American Literature,* **Ed. 4.**

How to Use This Index

The main references

> **Calvino, Italo**
> 1923-1985 .... CLC **5, 8, 11, 22, 33, 39,**
> **73; SSC 3, 48**

list all author entries in the following Gale Literary Criticism series:

AAL = *Asian American Literature*
BG = *The Beat Generation: A Gale Critical Companion*
BLC = *Black Literature Criticism*
BLCS = *Black Literature Criticism Supplement*
CLC = *Contemporary Literary Criticism*
CLR = *Children's Literature Review*
CMLC = *Classical and Medieval Literature Criticism*
DC = *Drama Criticism*
HLC = *Hispanic Literature Criticism*
HLCS = *Hispanic Literature Criticism Supplement*
HR = *Harlem Renaissance: A Gale Critical Companion*
LC = *Literature Criticism from 1400 to 1800*
NCLC = *Nineteenth-Century Literature Criticism*
NNAL = *Native North American Literature*
PC = *Poetry Criticism*
SSC = *Short Story Criticism*
TCLC = *Twentieth-Century Literary Criticism*
WLC = *World Literature Criticism, 1500 to the Present*
WLCS = *World Literature Criticism Supplement*

The cross-references

> See also CA 85-88, 116; CANR 23, 61;
> DAM NOV; DLB 196; EW 13; MTCW 1, 2;
> RGSF 2; RGWL 2; SFW 4; SSFS 12

list all author entries in the following Gale biographical and literary sources:

AAYA = *Authors & Artists for Young Adults*
AFAW = *African American Writers*
AFW = *African Writers*
AITN = *Authors in the News*
AMW = *American Writers*
AMWR = *American Writers Retrospective Supplement*
AMWS = *American Writers Supplement*
ANW = *American Nature Writers*
AW = *Ancient Writers*
BEST = *Bestsellers*
BPFB = *Beacham's Encyclopedia of Popular Fiction: Biography and Resources*
BRW = *British Writers*
BRWS = *British Writers Supplement*
BW = *Black Writers*
BYA = *Beacham's Guide to Literature for Young Adults*
CA = *Contemporary Authors*
CAAS = *Contemporary Authors Autobiography Series*
CABS = *Contemporary Authors Bibliographical Series*
CAD = *Contemporary American Dramatists*
CANR = *Contemporary Authors New Revision Series*
CAP = *Contemporary Authors Permanent Series*
CBD = *Contemporary British Dramatists*
CCA = *Contemporary Canadian Authors*
CD = *Contemporary Dramatists*
CDALB = *Concise Dictionary of American Literary Biography*
CDALBS = *Concise Dictionary of American Literary Biography Supplement*
CDBLB = *Concise Dictionary of British Literary Biography*

CMW = *St. James Guide to Crime & Mystery Writers*

CN = *Contemporary Novelists*

CP = *Contemporary Poets*

CPW = *Contemporary Popular Writers*

CSW = *Contemporary Southern Writers*

CWD = *Contemporary Women Dramatists*

CWP = *Contemporary Women Poets*

CWRI = *St. James Guide to Children's Writers*

CWW = *Contemporary World Writers*

DA = *DISCovering Authors*

DA3 = *DISCovering Authors 3.0*

DAB = *DISCovering Authors: British Edition*

DAC = *DISCovering Authors: Canadian Edition*

DAM = *DISCovering Authors: Modules*

    DRAM: *Dramatists Module;* **MST:** *Most-studied Authors Module;*

    MULT: *Multicultural Authors Module;* **NOV:** *Novelists Module;*

    POET: *Poets Module;* **POP:** *Popular Fiction and Genre Authors Module*

DFS = *Drama for Students*

DLB = *Dictionary of Literary Biography*

DLBD = *Dictionary of Literary Biography Documentary Series*

DLBY = *Dictionary of Literary Biography Yearbook*

DNFS = *Literature of Developing Nations for Students*

EFS = *Epics for Students*

EXPN = *Exploring Novels*

EXPP = *Exploring Poetry*

EXPS = *Exploring Short Stories*

EW = *European Writers*

FANT = *St. James Guide to Fantasy Writers*

FW = *Feminist Writers*

GFL = *Guide to French Literature,* Beginnings to 1789, 1798 to the Present

GLL = *Gay and Lesbian Literature*

HGG = *St. James Guide to Horror, Ghost & Gothic Writers*

HW = *Hispanic Writers*

IDFW = *International Dictionary of Films and Filmmakers: Writers and Production Artists*

IDTP = *International Dictionary of Theatre: Playwrights*

LAIT = *Literature and Its Times*

LAW = *Latin American Writers*

JRDA = *Junior DISCovering Authors*

MAICYA = *Major Authors and Illustrators for Children and Young Adults*

MAICYAS = *Major Authors and Illustrators for Children and Young Adults Supplement*

MAWW = *Modern American Women Writers*

MJW = *Modern Japanese Writers*

MTCW = *Major 20th-Century Writers*

NCFS = *Nonfiction Classics for Students*

NFS = *Novels for Students*

PAB = *Poets: American and British*

PFS = *Poetry for Students*

RGAL = *Reference Guide to American Literature*

RGEL = *Reference Guide to English Literature*

RGSF = *Reference Guide to Short Fiction*

RGWL = *Reference Guide to World Literature*

RHW = *Twentieth-Century Romance and Historical Writers*

SAAS = *Something about the Author Autobiography Series*

SATA = *Something about the Author*

SFW = *St. James Guide to Science Fiction Writers*

SSFS = *Short Stories for Students*

TCWW = *Twentieth-Century Western Writers*

WLIT = *World Literature and Its Times*

WP = *World Poets*

YABC = *Yesterday's Authors of Books for Children*

YAW = *St. James Guide to Young Adult Writers*

Literary Criticism Series
Cumulative Author Index

al-Hariri, al-Qasim ibn 'Ali Abu Muhammad al-Basri 1054-1122 .... **CMLC 63**
See also RGWL 3

Ali, Ahmed 1908-1998 .... **CLC 69**
See also CA 25-28R; CANR 15, 34; EWL 3

Ali, Tariq 1943- .... **CLC 173**
See also CA 25-28R; CANR 10, 99

Alighieri, Dante
See Dante

Allan, John B.
See Westlake, Donald E(dwin)

Allan, Sidney
See Hartmann, Sadakichi

Allan, Sydney
See Hartmann, Sadakichi

Allard, Janet .... **CLC 59**

Allen, Edward 1948- .... **CLC 59**

Allen, Fred 1894-1956 .... **TCLC 87**

Allen, Paula Gunn 1939- .... **CLC 84, 202; NNAL**
See also AMWS 4; CA 112; 143; CANR 63, 130; CWP; DA3; DAM MULT; DLB 175; FW; MTCW 1; RGAL 4

Allen, Roland
See Ayckbourn, Alan

Allen, Sarah A.
See Hopkins, Pauline Elizabeth

Allen, Sidney H.
See Hartmann, Sadakichi

Allen, Woody 1935- .... **CLC 16, 52, 195**
See also AAYA 10, 51; CA 33-36R; CANR 27, 38, 63, 128; DAM POP; DLB 44; MTCW 1

Allende, Isabel 1942- ... **CLC 39, 57, 97, 170; HLC 1; SSC 65; WLCS**
See also AAYA 18; CA 125; 130; CANR 51, 74, 129; CDWLB 3; CLR 99; CWW 2; DA3; DAM MULT, NOV; DLB 145; DNFS 1; EWL 3; FW; HW 1, 2; INT CA-130; LAIT 5; LAWS 1; LMFS 2; MTCW 1, 2; NCFS 1; NFS 6, 18; RGSF 2; RGWL 3; SSFS 11, 16; WLIT 1

Alleyn, Ellen
See Rossetti, Christina (Georgina)

Alleyne, Carla D. .... **CLC 65**

Allingham, Margery (Louise) 1904-1966 .... **CLC 19**
See also CA 5-8R; 25-28R; CANR 4, 58; CMW 4; DLB 77; MSW; MTCW 1, 2

Allingham, William 1824-1889 ...... **NCLC 25**
See also DLB 35; RGEL 2

Allison, Dorothy E. 1949- .... **CLC 78, 153**
See also AAYA 53; CA 140; CANR 66, 107; CSW; DA3; FW; MTCW 1; NFS 11; RGAL 4

Alloula, Malek .... **CLC 65**

Allston, Washington 1779-1843 .... **NCLC 2**
See also DLB 1, 235

Almedingen, E. M. .... **CLC 12**
See Almedingen, Martha Edith von
See also SATA 3

Almedingen, Martha Edith von 1898-1971
See Almedingen, E. M.
See also CA 1-4R; CANR 1

Almodovar, Pedro 1949(?)- .... **CLC 114; HLCS 1**
See also CA 133; CANR 72; HW 2

Almqvist, Carl Jonas Love 1793-1866 .... **NCLC 42**

al-Mutanabbi, Ahmad ibn al-Husayn Abu al-Tayyib al-Jufi al-Kindi 915-965 .... **CMLC 66**
See also RGWL 3

Alonso, Damaso 1898-1990 .... **CLC 14**
See also CA 110; 131; 130; CANR 72; DLB 108; EWL 3; HW 1, 2

Alov
See Gogol, Nikolai (Vasilyevich)

al'Sadaawi, Nawal
See El Saadawi, Nawal
See also FW

Al Siddik
See Rolfe, Frederick (William Serafino Austin Lewis Mary)
See also GLL 1; RGEL 2

Alta 1942- .... **CLC 19**
See also CA 57-60

Alter, Robert B(ernard) 1935- .... **CLC 34**
See also CA 49-52; CANR 1, 47, 100

Alther, Lisa 1944- .... **CLC 7, 41**
See also BPFB 1; CA 65-68; CAAS 30; CANR 12, 30, 51; CN 7; CSW; GLL 2; MTCW 1

Althusser, L.
See Althusser, Louis

Althusser, Louis 1918-1990 .... **CLC 106**
See also CA 131; 132; CANR 102; DLB 242

Altman, Robert 1925- .... **CLC 16, 116**
See also CA 73-76; CANR 43

Alurista .... **HLCS 1**
See Urista (Heredia), Alberto (Baltazar)
See also DLB 82; LLW 1

Alvarez, A(lfred) 1929- .... **CLC 5, 13**
See also CA 1-4R; CANR 3, 33, 63, 101, 134; CN 7; CP 7; DLB 14, 40

Alvarez, Alejandro Rodriguez 1903-1965
See Casona, Alejandro
See also CA 131; 93-96; HW 1

Alvarez, Julia 1950- .... **CLC 93; HLCS 1**
See also AAYA 25; AMWS 7; CA 147; CANR 69, 101, 133; DA3; DLB 282; LATS 1:2; LLW 1; MTCW 1; NFS 5, 9; SATA 129; WLIT 1

Alvaro, Corrado 1896-1956 .... **TCLC 60**
See also CA 163; DLB 264; EWL 3

Amado, Jorge 1912-2001 ... **CLC 13, 40, 106; HLC 1**
See also CA 77-80; 201; CANR 35, 74; CWW 2; DAM MULT, NOV; DLB 113, 307; EWL 3; HW 2; LAW; LAWS 1; MTCW 1, 2; RGWL 2, 3; TWA; WLIT 1

Ambler, Eric 1909-1998 .... **CLC 4, 6, 9**
See also BRWS 4; CA 9-12R; 171; CANR 7, 38, 74; CMW 4; CN 7; DLB 77; MSW; MTCW 1, 2; TEA

Ambrose, Stephen E(dward) 1936-2002 .... **CLC 145**
See also AAYA 44; CA 1-4R; 209; CANR 3, 43, 57, 83, 105; NCFS 2; SATA 40, 138

Amichai, Yehuda 1924-2000 .. **CLC 9, 22, 57, 116; PC 38**
See also CA 85-88; 189; CANR 46, 60, 99, 132; CWW 2; EWL 3; MTCW 1

Amichai, Yehudah
See Amichai, Yehuda

Amiel, Henri Frederic 1821-1881 .... **NCLC 4**
See also DLB 217

Amis, Kingsley (William) 1922-1995 ...... **CLC 1, 2, 3, 5, 8, 13, 40, 44, 129**
See also AITN 2; BPFB 1; BRWS 2; CA 9-12R; 150; CANR 8, 28, 54; CDBLB 1945-1960; CN 7; CP 7; DA; DA3; DAB; DAC; DAM MST, NOV; DLB 15, 27, 100, 139; DLBY 1996; EWL 3; HGG; INT CANR-8; MTCW 1, 2; RGEL 2; RGSF 2; SFW 4

Amis, Martin (Louis) 1949- .... **CLC 4, 9, 38, 62, 101**
See also BEST 90:3; BRWS 4; CA 65-68; CANR 8, 27, 54, 73, 95, 132; CN 7; DA3; DLB 14, 194; EWL 3; INT CANR-27; MTCW 1

Ammianus Marcellinus c. 330-c. 395 .... **CMLC 60**
See also AW 2; DLB 211

Ammons, A(rchie) R(andolph) 1926-2001 ...... **CLC 2, 3, 5, 8, 9, 25, 57, 108; PC 16**
See also AITN 1; AMWS 7; CA 9-12R; 193; CANR 6, 36, 51, 73, 107; CP 7; CSW; DAM POET; DLB 5, 165; EWL 3; MTCW 1, 2; PFS 19; RGAL 4

Amo, Tauraatua i
See Adams, Henry (Brooks)

Amory, Thomas 1691(?)-1788 .... **LC 48**
See also DLB 39

Anand, Mulk Raj 1905-2004 ...... **CLC 23, 93**
See also CA 65-68; CANR 32, 64; CN 7; DAM NOV; EWL 3; MTCW 1, 2; RGSF 2

Anatol
See Schnitzler, Arthur

Anaximander c. 611B.C.-c. 546B.C. .... **CMLC 22**

Anaya, Rudolfo A(lfonso) 1937- ...... **CLC 23, 148; HLC 1**
See also AAYA 20; BYA 13; CA 45-48; CAAS 4; CANR 1, 32, 51, 124; CN 7; DAM MULT, NOV; DLB 82, 206, 278; HW 1; LAIT 4; LLW 1; MTCW 1, 2; NFS 12; RGAL 4; RGSF 2; WLIT 1

Andersen, Hans Christian 1805-1875 .... **NCLC 7, 79; SSC 6, 56; WLC**
See also AAYA 57; CLR 6; DA; DA3; DAB; DAC; DAM MST, POP; EW 6; MAICYA 1, 2; RGSF 2; RGWL 2, 3; SATA 100; TWA; WCH; YABC 1

Anderson, C. Farley
See Mencken, H(enry) L(ouis); Nathan, George Jean

Anderson, Jessica (Margaret) Queale 1916- .... **CLC 37**
See also CA 9-12R; CANR 4, 62; CN 7

Anderson, Jon (Victor) 1940- .... **CLC 9**
See also CA 25-28R; CANR 20; DAM POET

Anderson, Lindsay (Gordon) 1923-1994 .... **CLC 20**
See also CA 125; 128; 146; CANR 77

Anderson, Maxwell 1888-1959 .... **TCLC 2, 144**
See also CA 105; 152; DAM DRAM; DFS 16, 20; DLB 7, 228; MTCW 2; RGAL 4

Anderson, Poul (William) 1926-2001 .... **CLC 15**
See also AAYA 5, 34; BPFB 1; BYA 6, 8, 9; CA 1-4R; 181; 199; CAAE 181; CAAS 2; CANR 2, 15, 34, 64, 110; CLR 58; DLB 8; FANT; INT CANR-15; MTCW 1, 2; SATA 90; SATA-Brief 39; SATA-Essay 106; SCFW 2; SFW 4; SUFW 1, 2

Anderson, Robert (Woodruff) 1917- .... **CLC 23**
See also AITN 1; CA 21-24R; CANR 32; DAM DRAM; DLB 7; LAIT 5

Anderson, Roberta Joan
See Mitchell, Joni

Anderson, Sherwood 1876-1941 .. **SSC 1, 46; TCLC 1, 10, 24, 123; WLC**
See also AAYA 30; AMW; AMWC 2; BPFB 1; CA 104; 121; CANR 61; CDALB 1917-1929; DA; DA3; DAB; DAC; DAM MST, NOV; DLB 4, 9, 86; DLBD 1; EWL 3; EXPS; GLL 2; MTCW 1, 2; NFS 4; RGAL 4; RGSF 2; SSFS 4, 10, 11; TUS

Andier, Pierre
See Desnos, Robert

Andouard
See Giraudoux, Jean(-Hippolyte)

Armah, Ayi Kwei 1939- . **BLC 1; CLC 5, 33, 136**
See also AFW; BRWS 10; BW 1; CA 61-64; CANR 21, 64; CDWLB 3; CN 7; DAM MULT, POET; DLB 117; EWL 3; MTCW 1; WLIT 2

Armatrading, Joan 1950- .... **CLC 17**
See also CA 114; 186

Armitage, Frank
See Carpenter, John (Howard)

Armstrong, Jeannette (C.) 1948- .... **NNAL**
See also CA 149; CCA 1; CN 7; DAC; SATA 102

Arnette, Robert
See Silverberg, Robert

Arnim, Achim von (Ludwig Joachim von Arnim) 1781-1831 .. **NCLC 5, 159; SSC 29**
See also DLB 90

Arnim, Bettina von 1785-1859 ...... **NCLC 38, 123**
See also DLB 90; RGWL 2, 3

Arnold, Matthew 1822-1888 ..... **NCLC 6, 29, 89, 126; PC 5; WLC**
See also BRW 5; CDBLB 1832-1890; DA; DAB; DAC; DAM MST, POET; DLB 32, 57; EXPP; PAB; PFS 2; TEA; WP

Arnold, Thomas 1795-1842 .... **NCLC 18**
See also DLB 55

Arnow, Harriette (Louisa) Simpson 1908-1986 .... **CLC 2, 7, 18**
See also BPFB 1; CA 9-12R; 118; CANR 14; DLB 6; FW; MTCW 1, 2; RHW; SATA 42; SATA-Obit 47

Arouet, Francois-Marie
See Voltaire

Arp, Hans
See Arp, Jean

Arp, Jean 1887-1966 .... **CLC 5; TCLC 115**
See also CA 81-84; 25-28R; CANR 42, 77; EW 10

Arrabal
See Arrabal, Fernando

Arrabal, Fernando 1932- ... **CLC 2, 9, 18, 58**
See Arrabal (Teran), Fernando
See also CA 9-12R; CANR 15; EWL 3; LMFS 2

Arrabal (Teran), Fernando 1932-
See Arrabal, Fernando
See also CWW 2

Arreola, Juan Jose 1918-2001 .... **CLC 147; HLC 1; SSC 38**
See also CA 113; 131; 200; CANR 81; CWW 2; DAM MULT; DLB 113; DNFS 2; EWL 3; HW 1, 2; LAW; RGSF 2

Arrian c. 89(?)-c. 155(?) .... **CMLC 43**
See also DLB 176

Arrick, Fran .... **CLC 30**
See Gaberman, Judie Angell
See also BYA 6

Arrley, Richmond
See Delany, Samuel R(ay), Jr.

Artaud, Antonin (Marie Joseph) 1896-1948 .... **DC 14; TCLC 3, 36**
See also CA 104; 149; DA3; DAM DRAM; DLB 258; EW 11; EWL 3; GFL 1789 to the Present; MTCW 1; RGWL 2, 3

Arthur, Ruth M(abel) 1905-1979 ..... **CLC 12**
See also CA 9-12R; 85-88; CANR 4; CWRI 5; SATA 7, 26

Artsybashev, Mikhail (Petrovich) 1878-1927 .... **TCLC 31**
See also CA 170; DLB 295

Arundel, Honor (Morfydd) 1919-1973 .... **CLC 17**
See also CA 21-22; 41-44R; CAP 2; CLR 35; CWRI 5; SATA 4; SATA-Obit 24

Arzner, Dorothy 1900-1979 .... **CLC 98**

Asch, Sholem 1880-1957 .... **TCLC 3**
See also CA 105; EWL 3; GLL 2

Ascham, Roger 1516(?)-1568 .... **LC 101**
See also DLB 236

Ash, Shalom
See Asch, Sholem

Ashbery, John (Lawrence) 1927- .. **CLC 2, 3, 4, 6, 9, 13, 15, 25, 41, 77, 125; PC 26**
See Berry, Jonas
See also AMWS 3; CA 5-8R; CANR 9, 37, 66, 102, 132; CP 7; DA3; DAM POET; DLB 5, 165; DLBY 1981; EWL 3; INT CANR-9; MTCW 1, 2; PAB; PFS 11; RGAL 4; WP

Ashdown, Clifford
See Freeman, R(ichard) Austin

Ashe, Gordon
See Creasey, John

Ashton-Warner, Sylvia (Constance) 1908-1984 .... **CLC 19**
See also CA 69-72; 112; CANR 29; MTCW 1, 2

Asimov, Isaac 1920-1992 ..... **CLC 1, 3, 9, 19, 26, 76, 92**
See also AAYA 13; BEST 90:2; BPFB 1; BYA 4, 6, 7, 9; CA 1-4R; 137; CANR 2, 19, 36, 60, 125; CLR 12, 79; CMW 4; CPW; DA3; DAM POP; DLB 8; DLBY 1992; INT CANR-19; JRDA; LAIT 5; LMFS 2; MAICYA 1, 2; MTCW 1, 2; RGAL 4; SATA 1, 26, 74; SCFW 2; SFW 4; SSFS 17; TUS; YAW

Askew, Anne 1521(?)-1546 .... **LC 81**
See also DLB 136

Assis, Joaquim Maria Machado de
See Machado de Assis, Joaquim Maria

Astell, Mary 1666-1731 .... **LC 68**
See also DLB 252; FW

Astley, Thea (Beatrice May) 1925-2004 .... **CLC 41**
See also CA 65-68; 229; CANR 11, 43, 78; CN 7; DLB 289; EWL 3

Astley, William 1855-1911
See Warung, Price

Aston, James
See White, T(erence) H(anbury)

Asturias, Miguel Angel 1899-1974 .... **CLC 3, 8, 13; HLC 1**
See also CA 25-28; 49-52; CANR 32; CAP 2; CDWLB 3; DA3; DAM MULT, NOV; DLB 113, 290; EWL 3; HW 1; LAW; LMFS 2; MTCW 1, 2; RGWL 2, 3; WLIT 1

Atares, Carlos Saura
See Saura (Atares), Carlos

Athanasius c. 295-c. 373 .... **CMLC 48**

Atheling, William
See Pound, Ezra (Weston Loomis)

Atheling, William, Jr.
See Blish, James (Benjamin)

Atherton, Gertrude (Franklin Horn) 1857-1948 .... **TCLC 2**
See also CA 104; 155; DLB 9, 78, 186; HGG; RGAL 4; SUFW 1; TCWW 2

Atherton, Lucius
See Masters, Edgar Lee

Atkins, Jack
See Harris, Mark

Atkinson, Kate 1951- .... **CLC 99**
See also CA 166; CANR 101; DLB 267

Attaway, William (Alexander) 1911-1986 .... **BLC 1; CLC 92**
See also BW 2, 3; CA 143; CANR 82; DAM MULT; DLB 76

Atticus
See Fleming, Ian (Lancaster); Wilson, (Thomas) Woodrow

Atwood, Margaret (Eleanor) 1939- ... **CLC 2, 3, 4, 8, 13, 15, 25, 44, 84, 135; PC 8; SSC 2, 46; WLC**
See also AAYA 12, 47; AMWS 13; BEST 89:2; BPFB 1; CA 49-52; CANR 3, 24, 33, 59, 95, 133; CN 7; CP 7; CPW; CWP; DA; DA3; DAB; DAC; DAM MST, NOV, POET; DLB 53, 251; EWL 3; EXPN; FW; INT CANR-24; LAIT 5; MTCW 1, 2; NFS 4, 12, 13, 14, 19; PFS 7; RGSF 2; SATA 50; SSFS 3, 13; TWA; WWE 1; YAW

Aubigny, Pierre d'
See Mencken, H(enry) L(ouis)

Aubin, Penelope 1685-1731(?) .... **LC 9**
See also DLB 39

Auchincloss, Louis (Stanton) 1917- .. **CLC 4, 6, 9, 18, 45; SSC 22**
See also AMWS 4; CA 1-4R; CANR 6, 29, 55, 87, 130; CN 7; DAM NOV; DLB 2, 244; DLBY 1980; EWL 3; INT CANR-29; MTCW 1; RGAL 4

Auden, W(ystan) H(ugh) 1907-1973 . **CLC 1, 2, 3, 4, 6, 9, 11, 14, 43, 123; PC 1; WLC**
See also AAYA 18; AMWS 2; BRW 7; BRWR 1; CA 9-12R; 45-48; CANR 5, 61, 105; CDBLB 1914-1945; DA; DA3; DAB; DAC; DAM DRAM, MST, POET; DLB 10, 20; EWL 3; EXPP; MTCW 1, 2; PAB; PFS 1, 3, 4, 10; TUS; WP

Audiberti, Jacques 1899-1965 .... **CLC 38**
See also CA 25-28R; DAM DRAM; EWL 3

Audubon, John James 1785-1851 . **NCLC 47**
See also ANW; DLB 248

Auel, Jean M(arie) 1936- .... **CLC 31, 107**
See also AAYA 7, 51; BEST 90:4; BPFB 1; CA 103; CANR 21, 64, 115; CPW; DA3; DAM POP; INT CANR-21; NFS 11; RHW; SATA 91

Auerbach, Erich 1892-1957 .... **TCLC 43**
See also CA 118; 155; EWL 3

Augier, Emile 1820-1889 .... **NCLC 31**
See also DLB 192; GFL 1789 to the Present

August, John
See De Voto, Bernard (Augustine)

Augustine, St. 354-430 .... **CMLC 6; WLCS**
See also DA; DA3; DAB; DAC; DAM MST; DLB 115; EW 1; RGWL 2, 3

Aunt Belinda
See Braddon, Mary Elizabeth

Aunt Weedy
See Alcott, Louisa May

Aurelius
See Bourne, Randolph S(illiman)

Aurelius, Marcus 121-180 .... **CMLC 45**
See Marcus Aurelius
See also RGWL 2, 3

Aurobindo, Sri
See Ghose, Aurabinda

Aurobindo Ghose
See Ghose, Aurabinda

Austen, Jane 1775-1817 ...... **NCLC 1, 13, 19, 33, 51, 81, 95, 119, 150; WLC**
See also AAYA 19; BRW 4; BRWC 1; BRWR 2; BYA 3; CDBLB 1789-1832; DA; DA3; DAB; DAC; DAM MST, NOV; DLB 116; EXPN; LAIT 2; LATS 1:1; LMFS 1; NFS 1, 14, 18, 20; TEA; WLIT 3; WYAS 1

Auster, Paul 1947- .... **CLC 47, 131**
See also AMWS 12; CA 69-72; CANR 23, 52, 75, 129; CMW 4; CN 7; DA3; DLB 227; MTCW 1; SUFW 2

Austin, Frank
See Faust, Frederick (Schiller)
See also TCWW 2

Baraka, Amiri 1934- .... **BLC 1; CLC 1, 2, 3, 5, 10, 14, 33, 115; DC 6; PC 4; WLCS**
See Jones, LeRoi
See also AFAW 1, 2; AMWS 2; BW 2, 3; CA 21-24R; CABS 3; CAD; CANR 27, 38, 61, 133; CD 5; CDALB 1941-1968; CP 7; CPW; DA; DA3; DAC; DAM MST, MULT, POET, POP; DFS 3, 11, 16; DLB 5, 7, 16, 38; DLBD 8; EWL 3; MTCW 1, 2; PFS 9; RGAL 4; TUS; WP

Baratynsky, Evgenii Abramovich
1800-1844 .... **NCLC 103**
See also DLB 205

Barbauld, Anna Laetitia
1743-1825 .... **NCLC 50**
See also DLB 107, 109, 142, 158; RGEL 2

Barbellion, W. N. P. .... **TCLC 24**
See Cummings, Bruce F(rederick)

Barber, Benjamin R. 1939- .... **CLC 141**
See also CA 29-32R; CANR 12, 32, 64, 119

Barbera, Jack (Vincent) 1945- .... **CLC 44**
See also CA 110; CANR 45

Barbey d'Aurevilly, Jules-Amedee
1808-1889 .... **NCLC 1; SSC 17**
See also DLB 119; GFL 1789 to the Present

Barbour, John c. 1316-1395 .... **CMLC 33**
See also DLB 146

Barbusse, Henri 1873-1935 .... **TCLC 5**
See also CA 105; 154; DLB 65; EWL 3; RGWL 2, 3

Barclay, Alexander c. 1475-1552 .... **LC 109**
See also DLB 132

Barclay, Bill
See Moorcock, Michael (John)

Barclay, William Ewert
See Moorcock, Michael (John)

Barea, Arturo 1897-1957 .... **TCLC 14**
See also CA 111; 201

Barfoot, Joan 1946- .... **CLC 18**
See also CA 105

Barham, Richard Harris
1788-1845 .... **NCLC 77**
See also DLB 159

Baring, Maurice 1874-1945 .... **TCLC 8**
See also CA 105; 168; DLB 34; HGG

Baring-Gould, Sabine 1834-1924 ... **TCLC 88**
See also DLB 156, 190

Barker, Clive 1952- .... **CLC 52, 205; SSC 53**
See also AAYA 10, 54; BEST 90:3; BPFB 1; CA 121; 129; CANR 71, 111, 133; CPW; DA3; DAM POP; DLB 261; HGG; INT CA-129; MTCW 1, 2; SUFW 2

Barker, George Granville
1913-1991 .... **CLC 8, 48**
See also CA 9-12R; 135; CANR 7, 38; DAM POET; DLB 20; EWL 3; MTCW 1

Barker, Harley Granville
See Granville-Barker, Harley
See also DLB 10

Barker, Howard 1946- .... **CLC 37**
See also CA 102; CBD; CD 5; DLB 13, 233

Barker, Jane 1652-1732 .... **LC 42, 82**
See also DLB 39, 131

Barker, Pat(ricia) 1943- ...... **CLC 32, 94, 146**
See also BRWS 4; CA 117; 122; CANR 50, 101; CN 7; DLB 271; INT CA-122

Barlach, Ernst (Heinrich)
1870-1938 .... **TCLC 84**
See also CA 178; DLB 56, 118; EWL 3

Barlow, Joel 1754-1812 .... **NCLC 23**
See also AMWS 2; DLB 37; RGAL 4

Barnard, Mary (Ethel) 1909- .... **CLC 48**
See also CA 21-22; CAP 2

Barnes, Djuna 1892-1982 .... **CLC 3, 4, 8, 11, 29, 127; SSC 3**
See Steptoe, Lydia
See also AMWS 3; CA 9-12R; 107; CAD; CANR 16, 55; CWD; DLB 4, 9, 45; EWL 3; GLL 1; MTCW 1, 2; RGAL 4; TUS

Barnes, Jim 1933- .... **NNAL**
See also CA 108; 175; CAAE 175; CAAS 28; DLB 175

Barnes, Julian (Patrick) 1946- . **CLC 42, 141**
See also BRWS 4; CA 102; CANR 19, 54, 115; CN 7; DAB; DLB 194; DLBY 1993; EWL 3; MTCW 1

Barnes, Peter 1931-2004 .... **CLC 5, 56**
See also CA 65-68; CAAS 12; CANR 33, 34, 64, 113; CBD; CD 5; DFS 6; DLB 13, 233; MTCW 1

Barnes, William 1801-1886 .... **NCLC 75**
See also DLB 32

Baroja (y Nessi), Pio 1872-1956 .... **HLC 1; TCLC 8**
See also CA 104; EW 9

Baron, David
See Pinter, Harold

Baron Corvo
See Rolfe, Frederick (William Serafino Austin Lewis Mary)

Barondess, Sue K(aufman)
1926-1977 .... **CLC 8**
See Kaufman, Sue
See also CA 1-4R; 69-72; CANR 1

Baron de Teive
See Pessoa, Fernando (Antonio Nogueira)

Baroness Von S.
See Zangwill, Israel

Barres, (Auguste-)Maurice
1862-1923 .... **TCLC 47**
See also CA 164; DLB 123; GFL 1789 to the Present

Barreto, Afonso Henrique de Lima
See Lima Barreto, Afonso Henrique de

Barrett, Andrea 1954- .... **CLC 150**
See also CA 156; CANR 92

Barrett, Michele .... **CLC 65**

Barrett, (Roger) Syd 1946- .... **CLC 35**

Barrett, William (Christopher)
1913-1992 .... **CLC 27**
See also CA 13-16R; 139; CANR 11, 67; INT CANR-11

Barrett Browning, Elizabeth
1806-1861 ... **NCLC 1, 16, 61, 66; PC 6, 62; WLC**
See also BRW 4; CDBLB 1832-1890; DA; DA3; DAB; DAC; DAM MST, POET; DLB 32, 199; EXPP; PAB; PFS 2, 16; TEA; WLIT 4; WP

Barrie, J(ames) M(atthew)
1860-1937 .... **TCLC 2, 164**
See also BRWS 3; BYA 4, 5; CA 104; 136; CANR 77; CDBLB 1890-1914; CLR 16; CWRI 5; DA3; DAB; DAM DRAM; DFS 7; DLB 10, 141, 156; EWL 3; FANT; MAICYA 1, 2; MTCW 1; SATA 100; SUFW; WCH; WLIT 4; YABC 1

Barrington, Michael
See Moorcock, Michael (John)

Barrol, Grady
See Bograd, Larry

Barry, Mike
See Malzberg, Barry N(athaniel)

Barry, Philip 1896-1949 .... **TCLC 11**
See also CA 109; 199; DFS 9; DLB 7, 228; RGAL 4

Bart, Andre Schwarz
See Schwarz-Bart, Andre

Barth, John (Simmons) 1930- ... **CLC 1, 2, 3, 5, 7, 9, 10, 14, 27, 51, 89; SSC 10**
See also AITN 1, 2; AMW; BPFB 1; CA 1-4R; CABS 1; CANR 5, 23, 49, 64, 113; CN 7; DAM NOV; DLB 2, 227; EWL 3; FANT; MTCW 1; RGAL 4; RGSF 2; RHW; SSFS 6; TUS

Barthelme, Donald 1931-1989 ... **CLC 1, 2, 3, 5, 6, 8, 13, 23, 46, 59, 115; SSC 2, 55**
See also AMWS 4; BPFB 1; CA 21-24R; 129; CANR 20, 58; DA3; DAM NOV; DLB 2, 234; DLBY 1980, 1989; EWL 3; FANT; LMFS 2; MTCW 1, 2; RGAL 4; RGSF 2; SATA 7; SATA-Obit 62; SSFS 17

Barthelme, Frederick 1943- ...... **CLC 36, 117**
See also AMWS 11; CA 114; 122; CANR 77; CN 7; CSW; DLB 244; DLBY 1985; EWL 3; INT CA-122

Barthes, Roland (Gerard)
1915-1980 .... **CLC 24, 83; TCLC 135**
See also CA 130; 97-100; CANR 66; DLB 296; EW 13; EWL 3; GFL 1789 to the Present; MTCW 1, 2; TWA

Bartram, William 1739-1823 .... **NCLC 145**
See also ANW; DLB 37

Barzun, Jacques (Martin) 1907- ..... **CLC 51, 145**
See also CA 61-64; CANR 22, 95

Bashevis, Isaac
See Singer, Isaac Bashevis

Bashkirtseff, Marie 1859-1884 .... **NCLC 27**

Basho, Matsuo
See Matsuo Basho
See also PFS 18; RGWL 2, 3; WP

Basil of Caesaria c. 330-379 .... **CMLC 35**

Basket, Raney
See Edgerton, Clyde (Carlyle)

Bass, Kingsley B., Jr.
See Bullins, Ed

Bass, Rick 1958- .... **CLC 79, 143; SSC 60**
See also ANW; CA 126; CANR 53, 93; CSW; DLB 212, 275

Bassani, Giorgio 1916-2000 .... **CLC 9**
See also CA 65-68; 190; CANR 33; CWW 2; DLB 128, 177, 299; EWL 3; MTCW 1; RGWL 2, 3

Bastian, Ann .... **CLC 70**

Bastos, Augusto (Antonio) Roa
See Roa Bastos, Augusto (Antonio)

Bataille, Georges 1897-1962 .... **CLC 29; TCLC 155**
See also CA 101; 89-92; EWL 3

Bates, H(erbert) E(rnest)
1905-1974 .... **CLC 46; SSC 10**
See also CA 93-96; 45-48; CANR 34; DA3; DAB; DAM POP; DLB 162, 191; EWL 3; EXPS; MTCW 1, 2; RGSF 2; SSFS 7

Bauchart
See Camus, Albert

Baudelaire, Charles 1821-1867 . **NCLC 6, 29, 55, 155; PC 1; SSC 18; WLC**
See also DA; DA3; DAB; DAC; DAM MST, POET; DLB 217; EW 7; GFL 1789 to the Present; LMFS 2; PFS 21; RGWL 2, 3; TWA

Baudouin, Marcel
See Peguy, Charles (Pierre)

Baudouin, Pierre
See Peguy, Charles (Pierre)

Baudrillard, Jean 1929- .... **CLC 60**
See also DLB 296

Baum, L(yman) Frank 1856-1919 .. **TCLC 7, 132**
See also AAYA 46; BYA 16; CA 108; 133; CLR 15; CWRI 5; DLB 22; FANT; JRDA; MAICYA 1, 2; MTCW 1, 2; NFS 13; RGAL 4; SATA 18, 100; WCH

Benary-Isbert, Margot 1889-1979 .... **CLC 12**
See also CA 5-8R; 89-92; CANR 4, 72;
CLR 12; MAICYA 1, 2; SATA 2; SATA-
Obit 21

Benavente (y Martinez), Jacinto
1866-1954 .... **DC 26; HLCS 1; TCLC 3**
See also CA 106; 131; CANR 81; DAM
DRAM, MULT; EWL 3; GLL 2; HW 1,
2; MTCW 1, 2

Benchley, Peter (Bradford) 1940- .. **CLC 4, 8**
See also AAYA 14; AITN 2; BPFB 1; CA
17-20R; CANR 12, 35, 66, 115; CPW;
DAM NOV, POP; HGG; MTCW 1, 2;
SATA 3, 89

Benchley, Robert (Charles)
1889-1945 .... **TCLC 1, 55**
See also CA 105; 153; DLB 11; RGAL 4

Benda, Julien 1867-1956 .... **TCLC 60**
See also CA 120; 154; GFL 1789 to the
Present

Benedict, Ruth (Fulton)
1887-1948 .... **TCLC 60**
See also CA 158; DLB 246

Benedikt, Michael 1935- .... **CLC 4, 14**
See also CA 13-16R; CANR 7; CP 7; DLB
5

Benet, Juan 1927-1993 .... **CLC 28**
See also CA 143; EWL 3

Benet, Stephen Vincent 1898-1943 ..... **PC 64;**
SSC 10; TCLC 7
See also AMWS 11; CA 104; 152; DA3;
DAM POET; DLB 4, 48, 102, 249, 284;
DLBY 1997; EWL 3; HGG; MTCW 1;
RGAL 4; RGSF 2; SUFW; WP; YABC 1

Benet, William Rose 1886-1950 ..... **TCLC 28**
See also CA 118; 152; DAM POET; DLB
45; RGAL 4

Benford, Gregory (Albert) 1941- ..... **CLC 52**
See also BPFB 1; CA 69-72, 175; CAAE
175; CAAS 27; CANR 12, 24, 49, 95,
134; CSW; DLBY 1982; SCFW 2; SFW
4

Bengtsson, Frans (Gunnar)
1894-1954 .... **TCLC 48**
See also CA 170; EWL 3

Benjamin, David
See Slavitt, David R(ytman)

Benjamin, Lois
See Gould, Lois

Benjamin, Walter 1892-1940 .... **TCLC 39**
See also CA 164; DLB 242; EW 11; EWL
3

Ben Jelloun, Tahar 1944-
See Jelloun, Tahar ben
See also CA 135; CWW 2; EWL 3; RGWL
3; WLIT 2

Benn, Gottfried 1886-1956 .. **PC 35; TCLC 3**
See also CA 106; 153; DLB 56; EWL 3;
RGWL 2, 3

Bennett, Alan 1934- .... **CLC 45, 77**
See also BRWS 8; CA 103; CANR 35, 55,
106; CBD; CD 5; DAB; DAM MST;
MTCW 1, 2

Bennett, (Enoch) Arnold
1867-1931 .... **TCLC 5, 20**
See also BRW 6; CA 106; 155; CDBLB
1890-1914; DLB 10, 34, 98, 135; EWL 3;
MTCW 2

Bennett, Elizabeth
See Mitchell, Margaret (Munnerlyn)

Bennett, George Harold 1930-
See Bennett, Hal
See also BW 1; CA 97-100; CANR 87

Bennett, Gwendolyn B. 1902-1981 .... **HR 2**
See also BW 1; CA 125; DLB 51; WP

Bennett, Hal .... **CLC 5**
See Bennett, George Harold
See also DLB 33

Bennett, Jay 1912- .... **CLC 35**
See also AAYA 10; CA 69-72; CANR 11,
42, 79; JRDA; SAAS 4; SATA 41, 87;
SATA-Brief 27; WYA; YAW

Bennett, Louise (Simone) 1919- ...... **BLC 1;**
CLC 28
See also BW 2, 3; CA 151; CDWLB 3; CP
7; DAM MULT; DLB 117; EWL 3

Benson, A. C. 1862-1925 .... **TCLC 123**
See also DLB 98

Benson, E(dward) F(rederic)
1867-1940 .... **TCLC 27**
See also CA 114; 157; DLB 135, 153;
HGG; SUFW 1

Benson, Jackson J. 1930- .... **CLC 34**
See also CA 25-28R; DLB 111

Benson, Sally 1900-1972 .... **CLC 17**
See also CA 19-20; 37-40R; CAP 1; SATA
1, 35; SATA-Obit 27

Benson, Stella 1892-1933 .... **TCLC 17**
See also CA 117; 154, 155; DLB 36, 162;
FANT; TEA

Bentham, Jeremy 1748-1832 .... **NCLC 38**
See also DLB 107, 158, 252

Bentley, E(dmund) C(lerihew)
1875-1956 .... **TCLC 12**
See also CA 108; DLB 70; MSW

Bentley, Eric (Russell) 1916- .... **CLC 24**
See also CA 5-8R; CAD; CANR 6, 67;
CBD; CD 5; INT CANR-6

ben Uzair, Salem
See Horne, Richard Henry Hengist

Beranger, Pierre Jean de
1780-1857 .... **NCLC 34**

Berdyaev, Nicolas
See Berdyaev, Nikolai (Aleksandrovich)

Berdyaev, Nikolai (Aleksandrovich)
1874-1948 .... **TCLC 67**
See also CA 120; 157

Berdyayev, Nikolai (Aleksandrovich)
See Berdyaev, Nikolai (Aleksandrovich)

Berendt, John (Lawrence) 1939- ...... **CLC 86**
See also CA 146; CANR 75, 93; DA3;
MTCW 1

Beresford, J(ohn) D(avys)
1873-1947 .... **TCLC 81**
See also CA 112; 155; DLB 162, 178, 197;
SFW 4; SUFW 1

Bergelson, David (Rafailovich)
1884-1952 .... **TCLC 81**
See Bergelson, Dovid
See also CA 220

Bergelson, Dovid
See Bergelson, David (Rafailovich)
See also EWL 3

Berger, Colonel
See Malraux, (Georges-)Andre

Berger, John (Peter) 1926- .... **CLC 2, 19**
See also BRWS 4; CA 81-84; CANR 51,
78, 117; CN 7; DLB 14, 207

Berger, Melvin H. 1927- .... **CLC 12**
See also CA 5-8R; CANR 4; CLR 32;
SAAS 2; SATA 5, 88; SATA-Essay 124

Berger, Thomas (Louis) 1924- .. **CLC 3, 5, 8,**
11, 18, 38
See also BPFB 1; CA 1-4R; CANR 5, 28,
51, 128; CN 7; DAM NOV; DLB 2;
DLBY 1980; EWL 3; FANT; INT CANR-
28; MTCW 1, 2; RHW; TCWW 2

Bergman, (Ernst) Ingmar 1918- ...... **CLC 16,**
72, 219
See also CA 81-84; CANR 33, 70; CWW
2; DLB 257; MTCW 2

Bergson, Henri(-Louis) 1859-1941 . **TCLC 32**
See also CA 164; EW 8; EWL 3; GFL 1789
to the Present

Bergstein, Eleanor 1938- .... **CLC 4**
See also CA 53-56; CANR 5

Berkeley, George 1685-1753 .... **LC 65**
See also DLB 31, 101, 252

Berkoff, Steven 1937- .... **CLC 56**
See also CA 104; CANR 72; CBD; CD 5

Berlin, Isaiah 1909-1997 .... **TCLC 105**
See also CA 85-88; 162

Bermant, Chaim (Icyk) 1929-1998 ... **CLC 40**
See also CA 57-60; CANR 6, 31, 57, 105;
CN 7

Bern, Victoria
See Fisher, M(ary) F(rances) K(ennedy)

Bernanos, (Paul Louis) Georges
1888-1948 .... **TCLC 3**
See also CA 104; 130; CANR 94; DLB 72;
EWL 3; GFL 1789 to the Present; RGWL
2, 3

Bernard, April 1956- .... **CLC 59**
See also CA 131

Bernard of Clairvaux 1090-1153 .. **CMLC 71**
See also DLB 208

Berne, Victoria
See Fisher, M(ary) F(rances) K(ennedy)

Bernhard, Thomas 1931-1989 ..... **CLC 3, 32,**
61; DC 14; TCLC 165
See also CA 85-88; 127; CANR 32, 57; CD-
WLB 2; DLB 85, 124; EWL 3; MTCW 1;
RGWL 2, 3

Bernhardt, Sarah (Henriette Rosine)
1844-1923 .... **TCLC 75**
See also CA 157

Bernstein, Charles 1950- .... **CLC 142,**
See also CA 129; CAAS 24; CANR 90; CP
7; DLB 169

Bernstein, Ingrid
See Kirsch, Sarah

Beroul fl. c. 1150- .... **CMLC 75**

Berriault, Gina 1926-1999 .... **CLC 54, 109;**
SSC 30
See also CA 116; 129; 185; CANR 66; DLB
130; SSFS 7,11

Berrigan, Daniel 1921- .... **CLC 4**
See also CA 33-36R, 187; CAAE 187;
CAAS 1; CANR 11, 43, 78; CP 7; DLB 5

Berrigan, Edmund Joseph Michael, Jr.
1934-1983
See Berrigan, Ted
See also CA 61-64; 110; CANR 14, 102

Berrigan, Ted .... **CLC 37**
See Berrigan, Edmund Joseph Michael, Jr.
See also DLB 5, 169; WP

Berry, Charles Edward Anderson 1931-
See Berry, Chuck
See also CA 115

Berry, Chuck .... **CLC 17**
See Berry, Charles Edward Anderson

Berry, Jonas
See Ashbery, John (Lawrence)
See also GLL 1

Berry, Wendell (Erdman) 1934- ... **CLC 4, 6,**
8, 27, 46; PC 28
See also AITN 1; AMWS 10; ANW; CA
73-76; CANR 50, 73, 101, 132; CP 7;
CSW; DAM POET; DLB 5, 6, 234, 275;
MTCW 1

Berryman, John 1914-1972 ... **CLC 1, 2, 3, 4,**
6, 8, 10, 13, 25, 62; PC 64
See also AMW; CA 13-16; 33-36R; CABS
2; CANR 35; CAP 1; CDALB 1941-1968;
DAM POET; DLB 48; EWL 3; MTCW 1,
2; PAB; RGAL 4; WP

Bertolucci, Bernardo 1940- ...... **CLC 16, 157**
See also CA 106; CANR 125

Berton, Pierre (Francis Demarigny)
1920-2004 .... **CLC 104**
See also CA 1-4R; CANR 2, 56; CPW;
DLB 68; SATA 99

Bertrand, Aloysius 1807-1841 .... **NCLC 31**
See Bertrand, Louis oAloysiusc

Bertrand, Louis oAloysiusc
See Bertrand, Aloysius
See also DLB 217

Bertran de Born c. 1140-1215 .... **CMLC 5**

Besant, Annie (Wood) 1847-1933 ..... **TCLC 9**
See also CA 105; 185

Bessie, Alvah 1904-1985 .... **CLC 23**
See also CA 5-8R; 116; CANR 2, 80; DLB 26

Bestuzhev, Aleksandr Aleksandrovich
1797-1837 .... **NCLC 131**
See also DLB 198

Bethlen, T. D.
See Silverberg, Robert

Beti, Mongo .... **BLC 1; CLC 27**
See Biyidi, Alexandre
See also AFW; CANR 79; DAM MULT; EWL 3; WLIT 2

Betjeman, John 1906-1984 ...... **CLC 2, 6, 10, 34, 43**
See also BRW 7; CA 9-12R; 112; CANR 33, 56; CDBLB 1945-1960; DA3; DAB; DAM MST, POET; DLB 20; DLBY 1984; EWL 3; MTCW 1, 2

Bettelheim, Bruno 1903-1990 .... **CLC 79; TCLC 143**
See also CA 81-84; 131; CANR 23, 61; DA3; MTCW 1, 2

Betti, Ugo 1892-1953 .... **TCLC 5**
See also CA 104; 155; EWL 3; RGWL 2, 3

Betts, Doris (Waugh) 1932- ..... **CLC 3, 6, 28; SSC 45**
See also CA 13-16R; CANR 9, 66, 77; CN 7; CSW; DLB 218; DLBY 1982; INT CANR-9; RGAL 4

Bevan, Alistair
See Roberts, Keith (John Kingston)

Bey, Pilaff
See Douglas, (George) Norman

Bialik, Chaim Nachman
1873-1934 .... **TCLC 25**
See also CA 170; EWL 3

Bickerstaff, Isaac
See Swift, Jonathan

Bidart, Frank 1939- .... **CLC 33**
See also CA 140; CANR 106; CP 7

Bienek, Horst 1930- .... **CLC 7, 11**
See also CA 73-76; DLB 75

Bierce, Ambrose (Gwinett)
1842-1914(?) ..... **SSC 9, 72; TCLC 1, 7, 44; WLC**
See also AAYA 55; AMW; BYA 11; CA 104; 139; CANR 78; CDALB 1865-1917; DA; DA3; DAC; DAM MST; DLB 11, 12, 23, 71, 74, 186; EWL 3; EXPS; HGG; LAIT 2; RGAL 4; RGSF 2; SSFS 9; SUFW 1

Biggers, Earl Derr 1884-1933 .... **TCLC 65**
See also CA 108; 153; DLB 306

Billiken, Bud
See Motley, Willard (Francis)

Billings, Josh
See Shaw, Henry Wheeler

Billington, (Lady) Rachel (Mary)
1942- .... **CLC 43**
See also AITN 2; CA 33-36R; CANR 44; CN 7

Binchy, Maeve 1940- .... **CLC 153**
See also BEST 90:1; BPFB 1; CA 127; 134; CANR 50, 96, 134; CN 7; CPW; DA3; DAM POP; INT CA-134; MTCW 1; RHW

Binyon, T(imothy) J(ohn) 1936- .... **CLC 34**
See also CA 111; CANR 28

Bion 335B.C.-245B.C. .... **CMLC 39**

Bioy Casares, Adolfo 1914-1999 ... **CLC 4, 8, 13, 88; HLC 1; SSC 17**
See Casares, Adolfo Bioy; Miranda, Javier; Sacastru, Martin
See also CA 29-32R; 177; CANR 19, 43, 66; CWW 2; DAM MULT; DLB 113; EWL 3; HW 1, 2; LAW; MTCW 1, 2

Birch, Allison .... **CLC 65**

Bird, Cordwainer
See Ellison, Harlan (Jay)

Bird, Robert Montgomery
1806-1854 .... **NCLC 1**
See also DLB 202; RGAL 4

Birkerts, Sven 1951- .... **CLC 116**
See also CA 128; 133, 176; CAAE 176; CAAS 29; INT CA-133

Birney, (Alfred) Earle 1904-1995 .. **CLC 1, 4, 6, 11; PC 52**
See also CA 1-4R; CANR 5, 20; CP 7; DAC; DAM MST, POET; DLB 88; MTCW 1; PFS 8; RGEL 2

Biruni, al 973-1048(?) .... **CMLC 28**

Bishop, Elizabeth 1911-1979 ..... **CLC 1, 4, 9, 13, 15, 32; PC 3, 34; TCLC 121**
See also AMWR 2; AMWS 1; CA 5-8R; 89-92; CABS 2; CANR 26, 61, 108; CDALB 1968-1988; DA; DA3; DAC; DAM MST, POET; DLB 5, 169; EWL 3; GLL 2; MAWW; MTCW 1, 2; PAB; PFS 6, 12; RGAL 4; SATA-Obit 24; TUS; WP

Bishop, John 1935- .... **CLC 10**
See also CA 105

Bishop, John Peale 1892-1944 ..... **TCLC 103**
See also CA 107; 155; DLB 4, 9, 45; RGAL 4

Bissett, Bill 1939- .... **CLC 18; PC 14**
See also CA 69-72; CAAS 19; CANR 15; CCA 1; CP 7; DLB 53; MTCW 1

Bissoondath, Neil (Devindra)
1955- .... **CLC 120**
See also CA 136; CANR 123; CN 7; DAC

Bitov, Andrei (Georgievich) 1937- ... **CLC 57**
See also CA 142; DLB 302

Biyidi, Alexandre 1932-
See Beti, Mongo
See also BW 1, 3; CA 114; 124; CANR 81; DA3; MTCW 1, 2

Bjarme, Brynjolf
See Ibsen, Henrik (Johan)

Bjoernson, Bjoernstjerne (Martinius)
1832-1910 .... **TCLC 7, 37**
See also CA 104

Black, Robert
See Holdstock, Robert P.

Blackburn, Paul 1926-1971 .... **CLC 9, 43**
See also BG 2; CA 81-84; 33-36R; CANR 34; DLB 16; DLBY 1981

Black Elk 1863-1950 .... **NNAL; TCLC 33**
See also CA 144; DAM MULT; MTCW 1; WP

Black Hawk 1767-1838 .... **NNAL**

Black Hobart
See Sanders, (James) Ed(ward)

Blacklin, Malcolm
See Chambers, Aidan

Blackmore, R(ichard) D(oddridge)
1825-1900 .... **TCLC 27**
See also CA 120; DLB 18; RGEL 2

Blackmur, R(ichard) P(almer)
1904-1965 .... **CLC 2, 24**
See also AMWS 2; CA 11-12; 25-28R; CANR 71; CAP 1; DLB 63; EWL 3

Black Tarantula
See Acker, Kathy

Blackwood, Algernon (Henry)
1869-1951 .... **TCLC 5**
See also CA 105; 150; DLB 153, 156, 178; HGG; SUFW 1

Blackwood, Caroline 1931-1996 .... **CLC 6, 9, 100**
See also BRWS 9; CA 85-88; 151; CANR 32, 61, 65; CN 7; DLB 14, 207; HGG; MTCW 1

Blade, Alexander
See Hamilton, Edmond; Silverberg, Robert

Blaga, Lucian 1895-1961 .... **CLC 75**
See also CA 157; DLB 220; EWL 3

Blair, Eric (Arthur) 1903-1950 .... **TCLC 123**
See Orwell, George
See also CA 104; 132; DA; DA3; DAB; DAC; DAM MST, NOV; MTCW 1, 2; SATA 29

Blair, Hugh 1718-1800 .... **NCLC 75**

Blais, Marie-Claire 1939- .... **CLC 2, 4, 6, 13, 22**
See also CA 21-24R; CAAS 4; CANR 38, 75, 93; CWW 2; DAC; DAM MST; DLB 53; EWL 3; FW; MTCW 1, 2; TWA

Blaise, Clark 1940- .... **CLC 29**
See also AITN 2; CA 53-56; CAAS 3; CANR 5, 66, 106; CN 7; DLB 53; RGSF 2

Blake, Fairley
See De Voto, Bernard (Augustine)

Blake, Nicholas
See Day Lewis, C(ecil)
See also DLB 77; MSW

Blake, Sterling
See Benford, Gregory (Albert)

Blake, William 1757-1827 . **NCLC 13, 37, 57, 127; PC 12, 63; WLC**
See also AAYA 47; BRW 3; BRWR 1; CDBLB 1789-1832; CLR 52; DA; DA3; DAB; DAC; DAM MST, POET; DLB 93, 163; EXPP; LATS 1:1; LMFS 1; MAICYA 1, 2; PAB; PFS 2, 12; SATA 30; TEA; WCH; WLIT 3; WP

Blanchot, Maurice 1907-2003 .... **CLC 135**
See also CA 117; 144; 213; DLB 72, 296; EWL 3

Blasco Ibanez, Vicente 1867-1928 . **TCLC 12**
See also BPFB 1; CA 110; 131; CANR 81; DA3; DAM NOV; EW 8; EWL 3; HW 1, 2; MTCW 1

Blatty, William Peter 1928- .... **CLC 2**
See also CA 5-8R; CANR 9, 124; DAM POP; HGG

Bleeck, Oliver
See Thomas, Ross (Elmore)

Blessing, Lee 1949- .... **CLC 54**
See also CAD; CD 5

Blight, Rose
See Greer, Germaine

Blish, James (Benjamin) 1921-1975 . **CLC 14**
See also BPFB 1; CA 1-4R; 57-60; CANR 3; DLB 8; MTCW 1; SATA 66; SCFW 2; SFW 4

Bliss, Frederick
See Card, Orson Scott

Bliss, Reginald
See Wells, H(erbert) G(eorge)

Blixen, Karen (Christentze Dinesen)
1885-1962
See Dinesen, Isak
See also CA 25-28; CANR 22, 50; CAP 2; DA3; DLB 214; LMFS 1; MTCW 1, 2; SATA 44; SSFS 20

Bloch, Robert (Albert) 1917-1994 .... **CLC 33**
See also AAYA 29; CA 5-8R, 179; 146; CAAE 179; CAAS 20; CANR 5, 78; DA3; DLB 44; HGG; INT CANR-5; MTCW 1; SATA 12; SATA-Obit 82; SFW 4; SUFW 1, 2

Blok, Alexander (Alexandrovich)
1880-1921 .... **PC 21; TCLC 5**
See also CA 104; 183; DLB 295; EW 9; EWL 3; LMFS 2; RGWL 2, 3

Brown, Sterling Allen 1901-1989 ...... **BLC 1;**
CLC 1, 23, 59; HR 2; PC 55
See also AFAW 1, 2; BW 1, 3; CA 85-88;
127; CANR 26; DA3; DAM MULT;
POET; DLB 48, 51, 63; MTCW 1, 2;
RGAL 4; WP

Brown, Will
See Ainsworth, William Harrison

Brown, William Hill 1765-1793 .... **LC 93**
See also DLB 37

Brown, William Wells 1815-1884 ...... **BLC 1;**
DC 1; NCLC 2, 89
See also DAM MULT; DLB 3, 50, 183,
248; RGAL 4

Browne, (Clyde) Jackson 1948(?)- ... **CLC 21**
See also CA 120

Browne, Thomas 1605-1682 .... **LC 111**
See also BW 2; DLB 151

Browning, Robert 1812-1889 . **NCLC 19, 79;**
PC 2, 61; WLCS
See also BRW 4; BRWC 2; BRWR 2; CD-
BLB 1832-1890; CLR 97; DA; DA3;
DAB; DAC; DAM MST, POET; DLB 32,
163; EXPP; LATS 1:1; PAB; PFS 1, 15;
RGEL 2; TEA; WLIT 4; WP; YABC 1

Browning, Tod 1882-1962 .... **CLC 16**
See also CA 141; 117

Brownmiller, Susan 1935- .... **CLC 159**
See also CA 103; CANR 35, 75; DAM
NOV; FW; MTCW 1, 2

Brownson, Orestes Augustus
1803-1876 .... **NCLC 50**
See also DLB 1, 59, 73, 243

Bruccoli, Matthew J(oseph) 1931- ... **CLC 34**
See also CA 9-12R; CANR 7, 87; DLB 103

Bruce, Lenny .... **CLC 21**
See Schneider, Leonard Alfred

Bruchac, Joseph III 1942- .... **NNAL**
See also AAYA 19; CA 33-36R; CANR 13,
47, 75, 94; CLR 46; CWRI 5; DAM
MULT; JRDA; MAICYA 2; MAICYAS 1;
MTCW 1; SATA 42, 89, 131

Bruin, John
See Brutus, Dennis

Brulard, Henri
See Stendhal

Brulls, Christian
See Simenon, Georges (Jacques Christian)

Brunetto Latini c. 1220-1294 .... **CMLC 73**

Brunner, John (Kilian Houston)
1934-1995 .... **CLC 8, 10**
See also CA 1-4R; 149; CAAS 8; CANR 2,
37; CPW; DAM POP; DLB 261; MTCW
1, 2; SCFW 2; SFW 4

Bruno, Giordano 1548-1600 .... **LC 27**
See also RGWL 2, 3

Brutus, Dennis 1924- ... **BLC 1; CLC 43; PC**
24
See also AFW; BW 2, 3; CA 49-52; CAAS
14; CANR 2, 27, 42, 81; CDWLB 3; CP
7; DAM MULT, POET; DLB 117, 225;
EWL 3

Bryan, C(ourtlandt) D(ixon) B(arnes)
1936- .... **CLC 29**
See also CA 73-76; CANR 13, 68; DLB
185; INT CANR-13

Bryan, Michael
See Moore, Brian
See also CCA 1

Bryan, William Jennings
1860-1925 .... **TCLC 99**
See also DLB 303

Bryant, William Cullen 1794-1878 . **NCLC 6,**
46; PC 20
See also AMWS 1; CDALB 1640-1865;
DA; DAB; DAC; DAM MST, POET;
DLB 3, 43, 59, 189, 250; EXPP; PAB;
RGAL 4; TUS

Bryusov, Valery Yakovlevich
1873-1924 .... **TCLC 10**
See also CA 107; 155; EWL 3; SFW 4

Buchan, John 1875-1940 .... **TCLC 41**
See also CA 108; 145; CMW 4; DAB;
DAM POP; DLB 34, 70, 156; HGG;
MSW; MTCW 1; RGEL 2; RHW; YABC
2

Buchanan, George 1506-1582 .... **LC 4**
See also DLB 132

Buchanan, Robert 1841-1901 .... **TCLC 107**
See also CA 179; DLB 18, 35

Buchheim, Lothar-Guenther 1918- .... **CLC 6**
See also CA 85-88

Buchner, (Karl) Georg
1813-1837 .... **NCLC 26, 146**
See also CDWLB 2; DLB 133; EW 6;
RGSF 2; RGWL 2, 3; TWA

Buchwald, Art(hur) 1925- .... **CLC 33**
See also AITN 1; CA 5-8R; CANR 21, 67,
107; MTCW 1, 2; SATA 10

Buck, Pearl S(ydenstricker)
1892-1973 .... **CLC 7, 11, 18, 127**
See also AAYA 42; AITN 1; AMWS 2;
BPFB 1; CA 1-4R; 41-44R; CANR 1, 34;
CDALBS; DA; DA3; DAB; DAC; DAM
MST, NOV; DLB 9, 102; EWL 3; LAIT
3; MTCW 1, 2; RGAL 4; RHW; SATA 1,
25; TUS

Buckler, Ernest 1908-1984 .... **CLC 13**
See also CA 11-12; 114; CAP 1; CCA 1;
DAC; DAM MST; DLB 68; SATA 47

Buckley, Christopher (Taylor)
1952- .... **CLC 165**
See also CA 139; CANR 119

Buckley, Vincent (Thomas)
1925-1988 .... **CLC 57**
See also CA 101; DLB 289

Buckley, William F(rank), Jr. 1925- . **CLC 7,**
18, 37
See also AITN 1; BPFB 1; CA 1-4R; CANR
1, 24, 53, 93, 133; CMW 4; CPW; DA3;
DAM POP; DLB 137; DLBY 1980; INT
CANR-24; MTCW 1, 2; TUS

Buechner, (Carl) Frederick 1926- . **CLC 2, 4,**
6, 9
See also AMWS 12; BPFB 1; CA 13-16R;
CANR 11, 39, 64, 114; CN 7; DAM NOV;
DLBY 1980; INT CANR-11; MTCW 1, 2

Buell, John (Edward) 1927- .... **CLC 10**
See also CA 1-4R; CANR 71; DLB 53

Buero Vallejo, Antonio 1916-2000 ... **CLC 15,**
46, 139; DC 18
See also CA 106; 189; CANR 24, 49, 75;
CWW 2; DFS 11; EWL 3; HW 1; MTCW
1, 2

Bufalino, Gesualdo 1920-1996 .... **CLC 74**
See also CA 209; CWW 2; DLB 196

Bugayev, Boris Nikolayevich
1880-1934 .... **PC 11; TCLC 7**
See Bely, Andrey; Belyi, Andrei
See also CA 104; 165; MTCW 1

Bukowski, Charles 1920-1994 ... **CLC 2, 5, 9,**
41, 82, 108; PC 18; SSC 45
See also CA 17-20R; 144; CANR 40, 62,
105; CPW; DA3; DAM NOV, POET;
DLB 5, 130, 169; EWL 3; MTCW 1, 2

Bulgakov, Mikhail (Afanas'evich)
1891-1940 ..... **SSC 18; TCLC 2, 16, 159**
See also BPFB 1; CA 105; 152; DAM
DRAM, NOV; DLB 272; EWL 3; NFS 8;
RGSF 2; RGWL 2, 3; SFW 4; TWA

Bulgya, Alexander Alexandrovich
1901-1956 .... **TCLC 53**
See Fadeev, Aleksandr Aleksandrovich;
Fadeev, Alexandr Alexandrovich; Fadeyev,
Alexander
See also CA 117; 181

Bullins, Ed 1935- ... **BLC 1; CLC 1, 5, 7; DC**
6
See also BW 2, 3; CA 49-52; CAAS 16;
CAD; CANR 24, 46, 73, 134; CD 5;
DAM DRAM, MULT; DLB 7, 38, 249;
EWL 3; MTCW 1, 2; RGAL 4

Bulosan, Carlos 1911-1956 .... **AAL**
See also CA 216; RGAL 4

Bulwer-Lytton, Edward (George Earle
Lytton) 1803-1873 .... **NCLC 1, 45**
See also DLB 21; RGEL 2; SFW 4; SUFW
1; TEA

Bunin, Ivan Alexeyevich 1870-1953 ... **SSC 5;**
TCLC 6
See also CA 104; EWL 3; RGSF 2; RGWL
2, 3; TWA

Bunting, Basil 1900-1985 ...... **CLC 10, 39, 47**
See also BRWS 7; CA 53-56; 115; CANR
7; DAM POET; DLB 20; EWL 3; RGEL
2

Bunuel, Luis 1900-1983 ... **CLC 16, 80; HLC**
1
See also CA 101; 110; CANR 32, 77; DAM
MULT; HW 1

Bunyan, John 1628-1688 ..... **LC 4, 69; WLC**
See also BRW 2; BYA 5; CDBLB 1660-
1789; DA; DAB; DAC; DAM MST; DLB
39; RGEL 2; TEA; WCH; WLIT 3

Buravsky, Alexandr .... **CLC 59**

Burckhardt, Jacob (Christoph)
1818-1897 .... **NCLC 49**
See also EW 6

Burford, Eleanor
See Hibbert, Eleanor Alice Burford

Burgess, Anthony . **CLC 1, 2, 4, 5, 8, 10, 13,**
15, 22, 40, 62, 81, 94
See Wilson, John (Anthony) Burgess
See also AAYA 25; AITN 1; BRWS 1; CD-
BLB 1960 to Present; DAB; DLB 14, 194,
261; DLBY 1998; EWL 3; MTCW 1;
RGEL 2; RHW; SFW 4; YAW

Burke, Edmund 1729(?)-1797 .... **LC 7, 36;**
WLC
See also BRW 3; DA; DA3; DAB; DAC;
DAM MST; DLB 104, 252; RGEL 2;
TEA

Burke, Kenneth (Duva) 1897-1993 ... **CLC 2,**
24
See also AMW; CA 5-8R; 143; CANR 39,
74; DLB 45, 63; EWL 3; MTCW 1, 2;
RGAL 4

Burke, Leda
See Garnett, David

Burke, Ralph
See Silverberg, Robert

Burke, Thomas 1886-1945 .... **TCLC 63**
See also CA 113; 155; CMW 4; DLB 197

Burney, Fanny 1752-1840 .... **NCLC 12, 54,**
107
See also BRWS 3; DLB 39; NFS 16; RGEL
2; TEA

Burney, Frances
See Burney, Fanny

Burns, Robert 1759-1796 ... **LC 3, 29, 40; PC**
6; WLC
See also AAYA 51; BRW 3; CDBLB 1789-
1832; DA; DA3; DAB; DAC; DAM MST,
POET; DLB 109; EXPP; PAB; RGEL 2;
TEA; WP

Burns, Tex
See L'Amour, Louis (Dearborn)
See also TCWW 2

Burnshaw, Stanley 1906- .... **CLC 3, 13, 44**
See also CA 9-12R; CP 7; DLB 48; DLBY
1997

Burr, Anne 1937- .... **CLC 6**
See also CA 25-28R

Burroughs, Edgar Rice 1875-1950 . **TCLC 2, 32**
See also AAYA 11; BPFB 1; BYA 4, 9; CA 104; 132; CANR 131; DA3; DAM NOV; DLB 8; FANT; MTCW 1, 2; RGAL 4; SATA 41; SCFW 2; SFW 4; TUS; YAW

Burroughs, William S(eward)
1914-1997 .. **CLC 1, 2, 5, 15, 22, 42, 75, 109; TCLC 121; WLC**
See Lee, William; Lee, Willy
See also AAYA 60; AITN 2; AMWS 3; BG 2; BPFB 1; CA 9-12R; 160; CANR 20, 52, 104; CN 7; CPW; DA; DA3; DAB; DAC; DAM MST, NOV, POP; DLB 2, 8, 16, 152, 237; DLBY 1981, 1997; EWL 3; HGG; LMFS 2; MTCW 1, 2; RGAL 4; SFW 4

Burton, Sir Richard F(rancis)
1821-1890 .... **NCLC 42**
See also DLB 55, 166, 184

Burton, Robert 1577-1640 .... **LC 74**
See also DLB 151; RGEL 2

Buruma, Ian 1951- .... **CLC 163**
See also CA 128; CANR 65

Busch, Frederick 1941- ... **CLC 7, 10, 18, 47, 166**
See also CA 33-36R; CAAS 1; CANR 45, 73, 92; CN 7; DLB 6, 218

Bush, Barney (Furman) 1946- .... **NNAL**
See also CA 145

Bush, Ronald 1946- .... **CLC 34**
See also CA 136

Bustos, F(rancisco)
See Borges, Jorge Luis

Bustos Domecq, H(onorio)
See Bioy Casares, Adolfo; Borges, Jorge Luis

Butler, Octavia E(stelle) 1947- .. **BLCS; CLC 38, 121**
See also AAYA 18, 48; AFAW 2; AMWS 13; BPFB 1; BW 2, 3; CA 73-76; CANR 12, 24, 38, 73; CLR 65; CPW; DA3; DAM MULT, POP; DLB 33; LATS 1:2; MTCW 1, 2; NFS 8; SATA 84; SCFW 2; SFW 4; SSFS 6; YAW

Butler, Robert Olen, (Jr.) 1945- ...... **CLC 81, 162**
See also AMWS 12; BPFB 1; CA 112; CANR 66; CSW; DAM POP; DLB 173; INT CA-112; MTCW 1; SSFS 11

Butler, Samuel 1612-1680 .... **LC 16, 43**
See also DLB 101, 126; RGEL 2

Butler, Samuel 1835-1902 .... **TCLC 1, 33; WLC**
See also BRWS 2; CA 143; CDBLB 1890-1914; DA; DA3; DAB; DAC; DAM MST, NOV; DLB 18, 57, 174; RGEL 2; SFW 4; TEA

Butler, Walter C.
See Faust, Frederick (Schiller)

Butor, Michel (Marie Francois)
1926- .... **CLC 1, 3, 8, 11, 15, 161**
See also CA 9-12R; CANR 33, 66; CWW 2; DLB 83; EW 13; EWL 3; GFL 1789 to the Present; MTCW 1, 2

Butts, Mary 1890(?)-1937 .... **TCLC 77**
See also CA 148; DLB 240

Buxton, Ralph
See Silverstein, Alvin; Silverstein, Virginia B(arbara Opshelor)

Buzo, Alex
See Buzo, Alexander (John)
See also DLB 289

Buzo, Alexander (John) 1944- .... **CLC 61**
See also CA 97-100; CANR 17, 39, 69; CD 5

Buzzati, Dino 1906-1972 .... **CLC 36**
See also CA 160; 33-36R; DLB 177; RGWL 2, 3; SFW 4

Byars, Betsy (Cromer) 1928- .... **CLC 35**
See also AAYA 19; BYA 3; CA 33-36R, 183; CAAE 183; CANR 18, 36, 57, 102; CLR 1, 16, 72; DLB 52; INT CANR-18; JRDA; MAICYA 1, 2; MAICYAS 1; MTCW 1; SAAS 1; SATA 4, 46, 80; SATA-Essay 108; WYA; YAW

Byatt, A(ntonia) S(usan Drabble)
1936- .... **CLC 19, 65, 136**
See also BPFB 1; BRWC 2; BRWS 4; CA 13-16R; CANR 13, 33, 50, 75, 96, 133; DA3; DAM NOV, POP; DLB 14, 194; EWL 3; MTCW 1, 2; RGSF 2; RHW; TEA

Byrd, Willam II 1674-1744 .... **LC 112**
See also DLB 24, 140; RGAL 4

Byrne, David 1952- .... **CLC 26**
See also CA 127

Byrne, John Keyes 1926-
See Leonard, Hugh
See also CA 102; CANR 78; INT CA-102

Byron, George Gordon (Noel)
1788-1824 ..... **DC 24; NCLC 2, 12, 109, 149; PC 16; WLC**
See also BRW 4; BRWC 2; CDBLB 1789-1832; DA; DA3; DAB; DAC; DAM MST, POET; DLB 96, 110; EXPP; LMFS 1; PAB; PFS 1, 14; RGEL 2; TEA; WLIT 3; WP

Byron, Robert 1905-1941 .... **TCLC 67**
See also CA 160; DLB 195

C. 3. 3.
See Wilde, Oscar (Fingal O'Flahertie Wills)

Caballero, Fernan 1796-1877 .... **NCLC 10**

Cabell, Branch
See Cabell, James Branch

Cabell, James Branch 1879-1958 .... **TCLC 6**
See also CA 105; 152; DLB 9, 78; FANT; MTCW 1; RGAL 4; SUFW 1

Cabeza de Vaca, Alvar Nunez
1490-1557(?) .... **LC 61**

Cable, George Washington
1844-1925 .... **SSC 4; TCLC 4**
See also CA 104; 155; DLB 12, 74; DLBD 13; RGAL 4; TUS

Cabral de Melo Neto, Joao
1920-1999 .... **CLC 76**
See Melo Neto, Joao Cabral de
See also CA 151; DAM MULT; DLB 307; LAW; LAWS 1

Cabrera Infante, G(uillermo) 1929- . **CLC 5, 25, 45, 120; HLC 1; SSC 39**
See also CA 85-88; CANR 29, 65, 110; CD-WLB 3; CWW 2; DA3; DAM MULT; DLB 113; EWL 3; HW 1, 2; LAW; LAWS 1; MTCW 1, 2; RGSF 2; WLIT 1

Cade, Toni
See Bambara, Toni Cade

Cadmus and Harmonia
See Buchan, John

Caedmon fl. 658-680 .... **CMLC 7**
See also DLB 146

Caeiro, Alberto
See Pessoa, Fernando (Antonio Nogueira)

Caesar, Julius .... **CMLC 47**
See Julius Caesar
See also AW 1; RGWL 2, 3

Cage, John (Milton, Jr.)
1912-1992 .... **CLC 41; PC 58**
See also CA 13-16R; 169; CANR 9, 78; DLB 193; INT CANR-9

Cahan, Abraham 1860-1951 .... **TCLC 71**
See also CA 108; 154; DLB 9, 25, 28; RGAL 4

Cain, G.
See Cabrera Infante, G(uillermo)

Cain, Guillermo
See Cabrera Infante, G(uillermo)

Cain, James M(allahan) 1892-1977 .. **CLC 3, 11, 28**
See also AITN 1; BPFB 1; CA 17-20R; 73-76; CANR 8, 34, 61; CMW 4; DLB 226; EWL 3; MSW; MTCW 1; RGAL 4

Caine, Hall 1853-1931 .... **TCLC 97**
See also RHW

Caine, Mark
See Raphael, Frederic (Michael)

Calasso, Roberto 1941- .... **CLC 81**
See also CA 143; CANR 89

Calderon de la Barca, Pedro
1600-1681 .... **DC 3; HLCS 1; LC 23**
See also EW 2; RGWL 2, 3; TWA

Caldwell, Erskine (Preston)
1903-1987 .... **CLC 1, 8, 14, 50, 60; SSC 19; TCLC 117**
See also AITN 1; AMW; BPFB 1; CA 1-4R; 121; CAAS 1; CANR 2, 33; DA3; DAM NOV; DLB 9, 86; EWL 3; MTCW 1, 2; RGAL 4; RGSF 2; TUS

Caldwell, (Janet Miriam) Taylor (Holland)
1900-1985 .... **CLC 2, 28, 39**
See also BPFB 1; CA 5-8R; 116; CANR 5; DA3; DAM NOV, POP; DLBD 17; RHW

Calhoun, John Caldwell
1782-1850 .... **NCLC 15**
See also DLB 3, 248

Calisher, Hortense 1911- ..... **CLC 2, 4, 8, 38, 134; SSC 15**
See also CA 1-4R; CANR 1, 22, 117; CN 7; DA3; DAM NOV; DLB 2, 218; INT CANR-22; MTCW 1, 2; RGAL 4; RGSF 2

Callaghan, Morley Edward
1903-1990 ..... **CLC 3, 14, 41, 65; TCLC 145**
See also CA 9-12R; 132; CANR 33, 73; DAC; DAM MST; DLB 68; EWL 3; MTCW 1, 2; RGEL 2; RGSF 2; SSFS 19

Callimachus c. 305B.C.-c.
240B.C. .... **CMLC 18**
See also AW 1; DLB 176; RGAL 2, 3

Calvin, Jean
See Calvin, John
See also GFL Beginnings to 1789

Calvin, John 1509-1564 .... **LC 37**
See Calvin, Jean

Calvino, Italo 1923-1985 .... **CLC 5, 8, 11, 22, 33, 39, 73; SSC 3, 48**
See also AAYA 58; CA 85-88; 116; CANR 23, 61, 132; DAM NOV; DLB 196; EW 13; EWL 3; MTCW 1, 2; RGSF 2; RGWL 2, 3; SFW 4; SSFS 12

Camara Laye
See Laye, Camara
See also EWL 3

Camden, William 1551-1623 .... **LC 77**
See also DLB 172

Cameron, Carey 1952- .... **CLC 59**
See also CA 135

Cameron, Peter 1959- .... **CLC 44**
See also AMWS 12; CA 125; CANR 50, 117; DLB 234; GLL 2

Camoens, Luis Vaz de 1524(?)-1580
See Camoes, Luis de
See also EW 2

Camoes, Luis de 1524(?)-1580 . **HLCS 1; LC 62; PC 31**
See Camoens, Luis Vaz de
See also DLB 287; RGWL 2, 3

Campana, Dino 1885-1932 .... **TCLC 20**
See also CA 117; DLB 114; EWL 3

Campanella, Tommaso 1568-1639 .... **LC 32**
See also RGWL 2, 3

Campbell, John W(ood, Jr.)
1910-1971 .... **CLC 32**
See also CA 21-22; 29-32R; CANR 34; CAP 2; DLB 8; MTCW 1; SCFW; SFW 4

Casares, Adolfo Bioy
See Bioy Casares, Adolfo
See also RGSF 2

Casas, Bartolome de las 1474-1566
See Las Casas, Bartolome de
See also WLIT 1

Casely-Hayford, J(oseph) E(phraim)
1866-1903 .... **BLC 1; TCLC 24**
See also BW 2; CA 123; 152; DAM MULT

Casey, John (Dudley) 1939- .... **CLC 59**
See also BEST 90:2; CA 69-72; CANR 23, 100

Casey, Michael 1947- .... **CLC 2**
See also CA 65-68; CANR 109; DLB 5

Casey, Patrick
See Thurman, Wallace (Henry)

Casey, Warren (Peter) 1935-1988 .... **CLC 12**
See also CA 101; 127; INT CA-101

Casona, Alejandro .... **CLC 49**
See Alvarez, Alejandro Rodriguez
See also EWL 3

Cassavetes, John 1929-1989 .... **CLC 20**
See also CA 85-88; 127; CANR 82

Cassian, Nina 1924- .... **PC 17**
See also CWP; CWW 2

Cassill, R(onald) V(erlin)
1919-2002 .... **CLC 4, 23**
See also CA 9-12R; 208; CAAS 1; CANR 7, 45; CN 7; DLB 6, 218; DLBY 2002

Cassiodorus, Flavius Magnus c. 490(?)-c. 583(?) .... **CMLC 43**

Cassirer, Ernst 1874-1945 .... **TCLC 61**
See also CA 157

Cassity, (Allen) Turner 1929- .... **CLC 6, 42**
See also CA 17-20R; 223; CAAE 223; CAAS 8; CANR 11; CSW; DLB 105

Castaneda, Carlos (Cesar Aranha)
1931(?)-1998 .... **CLC 12, 119**
See also CA 25-28R; CANR 32, 66, 105; DNFS 1; HW 1; MTCW 1

Castedo, Elena 1937- .... **CLC 65**
See also CA 132

Castedo-Ellerman, Elena
See Castedo, Elena

Castellanos, Rosario 1925-1974 .... **CLC 66; HLC 1; SSC 39, 68**
See also CA 131; 53-56; CANR 58; CD-WLB 3; DAM MULT; DLB 113, 290; EWL 3; FW; HW 1; LAW; MTCW 1; RGSF 2; RGWL 2, 3

Castelvetro, Lodovico 1505-1571 .... **LC 12**

Castiglione, Baldassare 1478-1529 ...... **LC 12**
See Castiglione, Baldesar
See also LMFS 1; RGWL 2, 3

Castiglione, Baldesar
See Castiglione, Baldassare
See also EW 2

Castillo, Ana (Hernandez Del)
1953- .... **CLC 151**
See also AAYA 42; CA 131; CANR 51, 86, 128; CWP; DLB 122, 227; DNFS 2; FW; HW 1; LLW 1; PFS 21

Castle, Robert
See Hamilton, Edmond

Castro (Ruz), Fidel 1926(?)- .... **HLC 1**
See also CA 110; 129; CANR 81; DAM MULT; HW 2

Castro, Guillen de 1569-1631 .... **LC 19**

Castro, Rosalia de 1837-1885 ... **NCLC 3, 78; PC 41**
See also DAM MULT

Cather, Willa (Sibert) 1873-1947 . **SSC 2, 50; TCLC 1, 11, 31, 99, 132, 152; WLC**
See also AAYA 24; AMW; AMWC 1; AMWR 1; BPFB 1; CA 104; 128; CDALB 1865-1917; CLR 98; DA; DA3; DAB; DAC; DAM MST, NOV; DLB 9, 54, 78, 256; DLBD 1; EWL 3; EXPN; EXPS;

LAIT 3; LATS 1:1; MAWW; MTCW 1, 2; NFS 2, 19; RGAL 4; RGSF 2; RHW; SATA 30; SSFS 2, 7, 16; TCWW 2; TUS

Catherine II
See Catherine the Great
See also DLB 150

Catherine the Great 1729-1796 .... **LC 69**
See Catherine II

Cato, Marcus Porcius
234B.C.-149B.C. .... **CMLC 21**
See Cato the Elder

Cato, Marcus Porcius, the Elder
See Cato, Marcus Porcius

Cato the Elder
See Cato, Marcus Porcius
See also DLB 211

Catton, (Charles) Bruce 1899-1978 . **CLC 35**
See also AITN 1; CA 5-8R; 81-84; CANR 7, 74; DLB 17; SATA 2; SATA-Obit 24

Catullus c. 84B.C.-54B.C. .... **CMLC 18**
See also AW 2; CDWLB 1; DLB 211; RGWL 2, 3

Cauldwell, Frank
See King, Francis (Henry)

Caunitz, William J. 1933-1996 .... **CLC 34**
See also BEST 89:3; CA 125; 130; 152; CANR 73; INT CA-130

Causley, Charles (Stanley)
1917-2003 .... **CLC 7**
See also CA 9-12R; 223; CANR 5, 35, 94; CLR 30; CWRI 5; DLB 27; MTCW 1; SATA 3, 66; SATA-Obit 149

Caute, (John) David 1936- .... **CLC 29**
See also CA 1-4R; CAAS 4; CANR 1, 33, 64, 120; CBD; CD 5; CN 7; DAM NOV; DLB 14, 231

Cavafy, C(onstantine) P(eter) .... **PC 36; TCLC 2, 7**
See Kavafis, Konstantinos Petrou
See also CA 148; DA3; DAM POET; EW 8; EWL 3; MTCW 1; PFS 19; RGWL 2, 3; WP

Cavalcanti, Guido c. 1250-c. 1300 .... **CMLC 54**
See also RGWL 2, 3

Cavallo, Evelyn
See Spark, Muriel (Sarah)

Cavanna, Betty .... **CLC 12**
See Harrison, Elizabeth (Allen) Cavanna
See also JRDA; MAICYA 1; SAAS 4; SATA 1, 30

Cavendish, Margaret Lucas
1623-1673 .... **LC 30**
See also DLB 131, 252, 281; RGEL 2

Caxton, William 1421(?)-1491(?) .... **LC 17**
See also DLB 170

Cayer, D. M.
See Duffy, Maureen

Cayrol, Jean 1911- .... **CLC 11**
See also CA 89-92; DLB 83; EWL 3

Cela (y Trulock), Camilo Jose
See Cela, Camilo Jose
See also CWW 2

Cela, Camilo Jose 1916-2002 .... **CLC 4, 13, 59, 122; HLC 1; SSC 71**
See Cela (y Trulock), Camilo Jose
See also BEST 90:2; CA 21-24R; 206; CAAS 10; CANR 21, 32, 76; DAM MULT; DLBY 1989; EW 13; EWL 3; HW 1; MTCW 1, 2; RGSF 2; RGWL 2, 3

Celan, Paul .... **CLC 10, 19, 53, 82; PC 10**
See Antschel, Paul
See also CDWLB 2; DLB 69; EWL 3; RGWL 2, 3

Celine, Louis-Ferdinand .. **CLC 1, 3, 4, 7, 9, 15, 47, 124**
See Destouches, Louis-Ferdinand
See also DLB 72; EW 11; EWL 3; GFL 1789 to the Present; RGWL 2, 3

Cellini, Benvenuto 1500-1571 .... **LC 7**

Cendrars, Blaise .... **CLC 18, 106**
See Sauser-Hall, Frederic
See also DLB 258; EWL 3; GFL 1789 to the Present; RGWL 2, 3; WP

Centlivre, Susanna 1669(?)-1723 .... **DC 25; LC 65**
See also DLB 84; RGEL 2

Cernuda (y Bidon), Luis
1902-1963 .... **CLC 54; PC 62**
See also CA 131; 89-92; DAM POET; DLB 134; EWL 3; GLL 1; HW 1; RGWL 2, 3

Cervantes, Lorna Dee 1954- ..... **HLCS 1; PC 35**
See also CA 131; CANR 80; CWP; DLB 82; EXPP; HW 1; LLW 1

Cervantes (Saavedra), Miguel de
1547-1616 .... **HLCS 1; LC 6, 23, 93; SSC 12; WLC**
See also AAYA 56; BYA 1, 14; DA; DAB; DAC; DAM MST, NOV; EW 2; LAIT 1; LATS 1:1; LMFS 1; NFS 8; RGSF 2; RGWL 2, 3; TWA

Cesaire, Aime (Fernand) 1913- .... **BLC 1; CLC 19, 32, 112; DC 22; PC 25**
See also BW 2, 3; CA 65-68; CANR 24, 43, 81; CWW 2; DA3; DAM MULT, POET; EWL 3; GFL 1789 to the Present; MTCW 1, 2; WP

Chabon, Michael 1963- ... **CLC 55, 149; SSC 59**
See also AAYA 45; AMWS 11; CA 139; CANR 57, 96, 127; DLB 278; SATA 145

Chabrol, Claude 1930- .... **CLC 16**
See also CA 110

Chairil Anwar
See Anwar, Chairil
See also EWL 3

Challans, Mary 1905-1983
See Renault, Mary
See also CA 81-84; 111; CANR 74; DA3; MTCW 2; SATA 23; SATA-Obit 36; TEA

Challis, George
See Faust, Frederick (Schiller)
See also TCWW 2

Chambers, Aidan 1934- .... **CLC 35**
See also AAYA 27; CA 25-28R; CANR 12, 31, 58, 116; JRDA; MAICYA 1, 2; SAAS 12; SATA 1, 69, 108; WYA; YAW

Chambers, James 1948-
See Cliff, Jimmy
See also CA 124

Chambers, Jessie
See Lawrence, D(avid) H(erbert Richards)
See also GLL 1

Chambers, Robert W(illiam)
1865-1933 .... **TCLC 41**
See also CA 165; DLB 202; HGG; SATA 107; SUFW 1

Chambers, (David) Whittaker
1901-1961 .... **TCLC 129**
See also CA 89-92; DLB 303

Chamisso, Adelbert von
1781-1838 .... **NCLC 82**
See also DLB 90; RGWL 2, 3; SUFW 1

Chance, James T.
See Carpenter, John (Howard)

Chance, John T.
See Carpenter, John (Howard)

Chandler, Raymond (Thornton)
1888-1959 .... **SSC 23; TCLC 1, 7**
See also AAYA 25; AMWC 2; AMWS 4; BPFB 1; CA 104; 129; CANR 60, 107; CDALB 1929-1941; CMW 4; DA3; DLB 226, 253; DLBD 6; EWL 3; MSW; MTCW 1, 2; NFS 17; RGAL 4; TUS

Chang, Diana 1934- .... **AAL**
See also CA 228; CWP; EXPP

Chomsky, (Avram) Noam 1928- ..... **CLC 132**
    See also CA 17-20R; CANR 28, 62, 110,
    132; DA3; DLB 246; MTCW 1, 2
Chona, Maria 1845(?)-1936 .... **NNAL**
    See also CA 144
Chopin, Kate .... **SSC 8, 68; TCLC 127;**
    WLCS
    See Chopin, Katherine
    See also AAYA 33; AMWR 2; AMWS 1;
    BYA 11, 15; CDALB 1865-1917; DA;
    DAB; DLB 12, 78; EXPN; EXPS; FW;
    LAIT 3; MAWW; NFS 3; RGAL 4; RGSF
    2; SSFS 17; TUS
Chopin, Katherine 1851-1904
    See Chopin, Kate
    See also CA 104; 122; DA3; DAC; DAM
    MST, NOV
Chretien de Troyes c. 12th cent. - . **CMLC 10**
    See also DLB 208; EW 1; RGWL 2, 3;
    TWA
Christie
    See Ichikawa, Kon
Christie, Agatha (Mary Clarissa)
    1890-1976 .. **CLC 1, 6, 8, 12, 39, 48, 110**
    See also AAYA 9; AITN 1, 2; BPFB 1;
    BRWS 2; CA 17-20R; 61-64; CANR 10,
    37, 108; CBD; CDBLB 1914-1945; CMW
    4; CPW; CWD; DA3; DAB; DAC; DAM
    NOV; DFS 2; DLB 13, 77, 245; MSW;
    MTCW 1, 2; NFS 8; RGEL 2; RHW;
    SATA 36; TEA; YAW
Christie, Philippa .... **CLC 21**
    See Pearce, Philippa
    See also BYA 5; CANR 109; CLR 9; DLB
    161; MAICYA 1; SATA 1, 67, 129
Christine de Pizan 1365(?)-1431(?) .... **LC 9**
    See also DLB 208; RGWL 2, 3
Chuang Tzu c. 369B.C.-c.
    286B.C. .... **CMLC 57**
Chubb, Elmer
    See Masters, Edgar Lee
Chulkov, Mikhail Dmitrievich
    1743-1792 .... **LC 2**
    See also DLB 150
Churchill, Caryl 1938- .... **CLC 31, 55, 157;**
    DC 5
    See Churchill, Chick
    See also BRWS 4; CA 102; CANR 22, 46,
    108; CBD; CWD; DFS 12, 16; DLB 13;
    EWL 3; FW; MTCW 1; RGEL 2
Churchill, Charles 1731-1764 .... **LC 3**
    See also DLB 109; RGEL 2
Churchill, Chick
    See Churchill, Caryl
    See also CD 5
Churchill, Sir Winston (Leonard Spencer)
    1874-1965 .... **TCLC 113**
    See also BRW 6; CA 97-100; CDBLB
    1890-1914; DA3; DLB 100; DLBD 16;
    LAIT 4; MTCW 1, 2
Chute, Carolyn 1947- .... **CLC 39**
    See also CA 123; CANR 135
Ciardi, John (Anthony) 1916-1986 . **CLC 10,**
    40, 44, 129
    See also CA 5-8R; 118; CAAS 2; CANR 5,
    33; CLR 19; CWRI 5; DAM POET; DLB
    5; DLBY 1986; INT CANR-5; MAICYA
    1, 2; MTCW 1, 2; RGAL 4; SAAS 26;
    SATA 1, 65; SATA-Obit 46
Cibber, Colley 1671-1757 .... **LC 66**
    See also DLB 84; RGEL 2
Cicero, Marcus Tullius
    106B.C.-43B.C. .... **CMLC 3**
    See also AW 1; CDWLB 1; DLB 211;
    RGWL 2, 3
Cimino, Michael 1943- .... **CLC 16**
    See also CA 105

Cioran, E(mil) M. 1911-1995 .... **CLC 64**
    See also CA 25-28R; 149; CANR 91; DLB
    220; EWL 3
Cisneros, Sandra 1954- .... **CLC 69, 118, 193;**
    HLC 1; PC 52; SSC 32, 72
    See also AAYA 9, 53; AMWS 7; CA 131;
    CANR 64, 118; CWP; DA3; DAM MULT;
    DLB 122, 152; EWL 3; EXPN; FW; HW
    1, 2; LAIT 5; LATS 1:2; LLW 1; MAI-
    CYA 2; MTCW 2; NFS 2; PFS 19; RGAL
    4; RGSF 2; SSFS 3, 13; WLIT 1; YAW
Cixous, Helene 1937- .... **CLC 92**
    See also CA 126; CANR 55, 123; CWW 2;
    DLB 83, 242; EWL 3; FW; GLL 2;
    MTCW 1, 2; TWA
Clair, Rene .... **CLC 20**
    See Chomette, Rene Lucien
Clampitt, Amy 1920-1994 .... **CLC 32; PC 19**
    See also AMWS 9; CA 110; 146; CANR
    29, 79; DLB 105
Clancy, Thomas L., Jr. 1947-
    See Clancy, Tom
    See also CA 125; 131; CANR 62, 105;
    DA3; INT CA-131; MTCW 1, 2
Clancy, Tom .... **CLC 45, 112**
    See Clancy, Thomas L., Jr.
    See also AAYA 9, 51; BEST 89:1, 90:1;
    BPFB 1; BYA 10, 11; CANR 132; CMW
    4; CPW; DAM NOV, POP; DLB 227
Clare, John 1793-1864 .. **NCLC 9, 86; PC 23**
    See also DAB; DAM POET; DLB 55, 96;
    RGEL 2
Clarin
    See Alas (y Urena), Leopoldo (Enrique
    Garcia)
Clark, Al C.
    See Goines, Donald
Clark, (Robert) Brian 1932- .... **CLC 29**
    See also CA 41-44R; CANR 67; CBD; CD
    5
Clark, Curt
    See Westlake, Donald E(dwin)
Clark, Eleanor 1913-1996 .... **CLC 5, 19**
    See also CA 9-12R; 151; CANR 41; CN 7;
    DLB 6
Clark, J. P.
    See Clark Bekederemo, J(ohnson) P(epper)
    See also CDWLB 3; DLB 117
Clark, John Pepper
    See Clark Bekederemo, J(ohnson) P(epper)
    See also AFW; CD 5; CP 7; RGEL 2
Clark, Kenneth (Mackenzie)
    1903-1983 .... **TCLC 147**
    See also CA 93-96; 109; CANR 36; MTCW
    1, 2
Clark, M. R.
    See Clark, Mavis Thorpe
Clark, Mavis Thorpe 1909-1999 ...... **CLC 12**
    See also CA 57-60; CANR 8, 37, 107; CLR
    30; CWRI 5; MAICYA 1, 2; SAAS 5;
    SATA 8, 74
Clark, Walter Van Tilburg
    1909-1971 .... **CLC 28**
    See also CA 9-12R; 33-36R; CANR 63,
    113; DLB 9, 206; LAIT 2; RGAL 4;
    SATA 8
Clark Bekederemo, J(ohnson) P(epper)
    1935- .... **BLC 1; CLC 38; DC 5**
    See Clark, J. P.; Clark, John Pepper
    See also BW 1; CA 65-68; CANR 16, 72;
    DAM DRAM, MULT; DFS 13; EWL 3;
    MTCW 1
Clarke, Arthur C(harles) 1917- .... **CLC 1, 4,**
    13, 18, 35, 136; SSC 3
    See also AAYA 4, 33; BPFB 1; BYA 13;
    CA 1-4R; CANR 2, 28, 55, 74, 130; CN
    7; CPW; DA3; DAM POP; DLB 261;
    JRDA; LAIT 5; MAICYA 1, 2; MTCW 1,
    2; SATA 13, 70, 115; SCFW; SFW 4;
    SSFS 4, 18; YAW

Clarke, Austin 1896-1974 .... **CLC 6, 9**
    See also CA 29-32; 49-52; CAP 2; DAM
    POET; DLB 10, 20; EWL 3; RGEL 2
Clarke, Austin C(hesterfield) 1934- .. **BLC 1;**
    CLC 8, 53; SSC 45
    See also BW 1; CA 25-28R; CAAS 16;
    CANR 14, 32, 68; CN 7; DAC; DAM
    MULT; DLB 53, 125; DNFS 2; RGSF 2
Clarke, Gillian 1937- .... **CLC 61**
    See also CA 106; CP 7; CWP; DLB 40
Clarke, Marcus (Andrew Hislop)
    1846-1881 .... **NCLC 19**
    See also DLB 230; RGEL 2; RGSF 2
Clarke, Shirley 1925-1997 .... **CLC 16**
    See also CA 189
Clash, The
    See Headon, (Nicky) Topper; Jones, Mick;
    Simonon, Paul; Strummer, Joe
Claudel, Paul (Louis Charles Marie)
    1868-1955 .... **TCLC 2, 10**
    See also CA 104; 165; DLB 192, 258; EW
    8; EWL 3; GFL 1789 to the Present;
    RGWL 2, 3; TWA
Claudian 370(?)-404(?) .... **CMLC 46**
    See also RGWL 2, 3
Claudius, Matthias 1740-1815 .... **NCLC 75**
    See also DLB 97
Clavell, James (duMaresq)
    1925-1994 .... **CLC 6, 25, 87**
    See also BPFB 1; CA 25-28R; 146; CANR
    26, 48; CPW; DA3; DAM NOV, POP;
    MTCW 1, 2; NFS 10; RHW
Clayman, Gregory .... **CLC 65**
Cleaver, (Leroy) Eldridge
    1935-1998 .... **BLC 1; CLC 30, 119**
    See also BW 1, 3; CA 21-24R; 167; CANR
    16, 75; DA3; DAM MULT; MTCW 2;
    YAW
Cleese, John (Marwood) 1939- .... **CLC 21**
    See Monty Python
    See also CA 112; 116; CANR 35; MTCW 1
Cleishbotham, Jebediah
    See Scott, Sir Walter
Cleland, John 1710-1789 .... **LC 2, 48**
    See also DLB 39; RGEL 2
Clemens, Samuel Langhorne 1835-1910
    See Twain, Mark
    See also CA 104; 135; CDALB 1865-1917;
    DA; DA3; DAB; DAC; DAM MST, NOV;
    DLB 12, 23, 64, 74, 186, 189; JRDA;
    LMFS 1; MAICYA 1, 2; NCFS 4; NFS
    20; SATA 100; SSFS 16; YABC 2
Clement of Alexandria
    150(?)-215(?) .... **CMLC 41**
Cleophil
    See Congreve, William
Clerihew, E.
    See Bentley, E(dmund) C(lerihew)
Clerk, N. W.
    See Lewis, C(live) S(taples)
Cleveland, John 1613-1658 .... **LC 106**
    See also DLB 126; RGEL 2
Cliff, Jimmy .... **CLC 21**
    See Chambers, James
    See also CA 193
Cliff, Michelle 1946- .... **BLCS; CLC 120**
    See also BW 2; CA 116; CANR 39, 72; CD-
    WLB 3; DLB 157; FW; GLL 2
Clifford, Lady Anne 1590-1676 .... **LC 76**
    See also DLB 151
Clifton, (Thelma) Lucille 1936- .... **BLC 1;**
    CLC 19, 66, 162; PC 17
    See also AFAW 2; BW 2, 3; CA 49-52;
    CANR 2, 24, 42, 76, 97; CLR 5; CP 7;
    CSW; CWP; CWRI 5; DA3; DAM MULT,
    POET; DLB 5, 41; EXPP; MAICYA 1, 2;
    MTCW 1, 2; PFS 1, 14; SATA 20, 69,
    128; WP

Clinton, Dirk
　　See Silverberg, Robert
Clough, Arthur Hugh 1819-1861 ... **NCLC 27**
　　See also BRW 5; DLB 32; RGEL 2
Clutha, Janet Paterson Frame 1924-2004
　　See Frame, Janet
　　See also CA 1-4R; 224; CANR 2, 36, 76,
　　135; MTCW 1, 2; SATA 119
Clyne, Terence
　　See Blatty, William Peter
Cobalt, Martin
　　See Mayne, William (James Carter)
Cobb, Irvin S(hrewsbury)
　　1876-1944 .... **TCLC 77**
　　See also CA 175; DLB 11, 25, 86
Cobbett, William 1763-1835 .... **NCLC 49**
　　See also DLB 43, 107, 158; RGEL 2
Coburn, D(onald) L(ee) 1938- .... **CLC 10**
　　See also CA 89-92
Cocteau, Jean (Maurice Eugene Clement)
　　1889-1963 ...... **CLC 1, 8, 15, 16, 43; DC
　　17; TCLC 119; WLC**
　　See also CA 25-28; CANR 40; CAP 2; DA;
　　DA3; DAB; DAC; DAM DRAM, MST,
　　NOV; DLB 65, 258; EW 10; EWL 3; GFL
　　1789 to the Present; MTCW 1, 2; RGWL
　　2, 3; TWA
Codrescu, Andrei 1946- .... **CLC 46, 121**
　　See also CA 33-36R; CAAS 19; CANR 13,
　　34, 53, 76, 125; DA3; DAM POET; •
　　MTCW 2
Coe, Max
　　See Bourne, Randolph S(illiman)
Coe, Tucker
　　See Westlake, Donald E(dwin)
Coen, Ethan 1958- .... **CLC 108**
　　See also AAYA 54; CA 126; CANR 85
Coen, Joel 1955- .... **CLC 108**
　　See also AAYA 54; CA 126; CANR 119
The Coen Brothers
　　See Coen, Ethan; Coen, Joel
Coetzee, J(ohn) M(axwell) 1940- ..... **CLC 23,
　　33, 66, 117, 161, 162**
　　See also AAYA 37; AFW; BRWS 6; CA 77-
　　80; CANR 41, 54, 74, 114, 133; CN 7;
　　DA3; DAM NOV; DLB 225; EWL 3;
　　LMFS 2; MTCW 1, 2; WLIT 2; WWE 1
Coffey, Brian
　　See Koontz, Dean R(ay)
Coffin, Robert P(eter) Tristram
　　1892-1955 .... **TCLC 95**
　　See also CA 123; 169; DLB 45
Cohan, George M(ichael)
　　1878-1942 .... **TCLC 60**
　　See also CA 157; DLB 249; RGAL 4
Cohen, Arthur A(llen) 1928-1986 ...... **CLC 7,
　　31**
　　See also CA 1-4R; 120; CANR 1, 17, 42;
　　DLB 28
Cohen, Leonard (Norman) 1934- ...... **CLC 3,
　　38**
　　See also CA 21-24R; CANR 14, 69; CN 7;
　　CP 7; DAC; DAM MST; DLB 53; EWL
　　3; MTCW 1
Cohen, Matt(hew) 1942-1999 .... **CLC 19**
　　See also CA 61-64; 187; CAAS 18; CANR
　　40; CN 7; DAC; DLB 53
Cohen-Solal, Annie 19(?)- .... **CLC 50**
Colegate, Isabel 1931- .... **CLC 36**
　　See also CA 17-20R; CANR 8, 22, 74; CN
　　7; DLB 14, 231; INT CANR-22; MTCW
　　1
Coleman, Emmett
　　See Reed, Ishmael
Coleridge, Hartley 1796-1849 .... **NCLC 90**
　　See also DLB 96
Coleridge, M. E.
　　See Coleridge, Mary E(lizabeth)

Coleridge, Mary E(lizabeth)
　　1861-1907 .... **TCLC 73**
　　See also CA 116; 166; DLB 19, 98
Coleridge, Samuel Taylor
　　1772-1834 ...... **NCLC 9, 54, 99, 111; PC
　　11, 39, 67; WLC**
　　See also BRW 4; BRWR 2; BYA 4; CD-
　　BLB 1789-1832; DA; DA3; DAB; DAC;
　　DAM MST, POET; DLB 93, 107; EXPP;
　　LATS 1:1; LMFS 1; PAB; PFS 4, 5;
　　RGEL 2; TEA; WLIT 3; WP
Coleridge, Sara 1802-1852 .... **NCLC 31**
　　See also DLB 199
Coles, Don 1928- .... **CLC 46**
　　See also CA 115; CANR 38; CP 7
Coles, Robert (Martin) 1929- .... **CLC 108**
　　See also CA 45-48; CANR 3, 32, 66, 70,
　　135; INT CANR-32; SATA 23
Colette, (Sidonie-Gabrielle)
　　1873-1954 .... **SSC 10; TCLC 1, 5, 16**
　　See Willy, Colette
　　See also CA 104; 131; DA3; DAM NOV;
　　DLB 65; EW 9; EWL 3; GFL 1789 to the
　　Present; MTCW 1, 2; RGWL 2, 3; TWA
Collett, (Jacobine) Camilla (Wergeland)
　　1813-1895 .... **NCLC 22**
Collier, Christopher 1930- .... **CLC 30**
　　See also AAYA 13; BYA 2; CA 33-36R;
　　CANR 13, 33, 102; JRDA; MAICYA 1,
　　2; SATA 16, 70; WYA; YAW 1
Collier, James Lincoln 1928- .... **CLC 30**
　　See also AAYA 13; BYA 2; CA 9-12R;
　　CANR 4, 33, 60, 102; CLR 3; DAM POP;
　　JRDA; MAICYA 1, 2; SAAS 21; SATA 8,
　　70; WYA; YAW 1
Collier, Jeremy 1650-1726 .... **LC 6**
Collier, John 1901-1980 . **SSC 19; TCLC 127**
　　See also CA 65-68; 97-100; CANR 10;
　　DLB 77, 255; FANT; SUFW 1
Collier, Mary 1690-1762 .... **LC 86**
　　See also DLB 95
Collingwood, R(obin) G(eorge)
　　1889(?)-1943 .... **TCLC 67**
　　See also CA 117; 155; DLB 262
Collins, Hunt
　　See Hunter, Evan
Collins, Linda 1931- .... **CLC 44**
　　See also CA 125
Collins, Tom
　　See Furphy, Joseph
　　See also RGEL 2
Collins, (William) Wilkie
　　1824-1889 .... **NCLC 1, 18, 93**
　　See also BRWS 6; CDBLB 1832-1890;
　　CMW 4; DLB 18, 70, 159; MSW; RGEL
　　2; RGSF 2; SUFW 1; WLIT 4
Collins, William 1721-1759 .... **LC 4, 40**
　　See also BRW 3; DAM POET; DLB 109;
　　RGEL 2
Collodi, Carlo .... **NCLC 54**
　　See Lorenzini, Carlo
　　See also CLR 5; WCH
Colman, George
　　See Glassco, John
Colman, George, the Elder
　　1732-1794 .... **LC 98**
　　See also RGEL 2
Colonna, Vittoria 1492-1547 .... **LC 71**
　　See also RGWL 2, 3
Colt, Winchester Remington
　　See Hubbard, L(afayette) Ron(ald)
Colter, Cyrus J. 1910-2002 .... **CLC 58**
　　See also BW 1; CA 65-68; 205; CANR 10,
　　66; CN 7; DLB 33
Colton, James
　　See Hansen, Joseph
　　See also GLL 1

Colum, Padraic 1881-1972 .... **CLC 28**
　　See also BYA 4; CA 73-76; 33-36R; CANR
　　35; CLR 36; CWRI 5; DLB 19; MAICYA
　　1, 2; MTCW 1; RGEL 2; SATA 15; WCH
Colvin, James
　　See Moorcock, Michael (John)
Colwin, Laurie (E.) 1944-1992 .... **CLC 5, 13,
　　23, 84**
　　See also CA 89-92; 139; CANR 20, 46;
　　DLB 218; DLBY 1980; MTCW 1
Comfort, Alex(ander) 1920-2000 .... **CLC 7**
　　See also CA 1-4R; 190; CANR 1, 45; CP 7;
　　DAM POP; MTCW 1
Comfort, Montgomery
　　See Campbell, (John) Ramsey
Compton-Burnett, I(vy)
　　1892(?)-1969 .... **CLC 1, 3, 10, 15, 34**
　　See also BRW 7; CA 1-4R; 25-28R; CANR
　　4; DAM NOV; DLB 36; EWL 3; MTCW
　　1; RGEL 2
Comstock, Anthony 1844-1915 ...... **TCLC 13**
　　See also CA 110; 169
Comte, Auguste 1798-1857 .... **NCLC 54**
Conan Doyle, Arthur
　　See Doyle, Sir Arthur Conan
　　See also BPFB 1; BYA 4, 5, 11
Conde (Abellan), Carmen
　　1901-1996 .... **HLCS 1**
　　See also CA 177; CWW 2; DLB 108; EWL
　　3; HW 2
Conde, Maryse 1937- ..... **BLCS; CLC 52, 92**
　　See also BW 2, 3; CA 110, 190; CAAE 190;
　　CANR 30, 53, 76; CWW 2; DAM MULT;
　　EWL 3; MTCW 1
Condillac, Etienne Bonnot de
　　1714-1780 .... **LC 26**
Condon, Richard (Thomas)
　　1915-1996 .... **CLC 4, 6, 8, 10, 45, 100**
　　See also BEST 90:3; BPFB 1; CA 1-4R;
　　151; CAAS 1; CANR 2, 23; CMW 4; CN
　　7; DAM NOV; INT CANR-23; MTCW 1,
　　2
Condorcet 1743-1794 .... **LC 104**
　　See also GFL Beginnings to 1789
Confucius 551B.C.-479B.C. .... **CMLC 19, 65;
　　WLCS**
　　See also DA; DA3; DAB; DAC; DAM
　　MST
Congreve, William 1670-1729 ... **DC 2; LC 5,
　　21; WLC**
　　See also BRW 2; CDBLB 1660-1789; DA;
　　DAB; DAC; DAM DRAM, MST, POET;
　　DFS 15; DLB 39, 84; RGEL 2; WLIT 3
Conley, Robert J(ackson) 1940- .... **NNAL**
　　See also CA 41-44R; CANR 15, 34, 45, 96;
　　DAM MULT
Connell, Evan S(helby), Jr. 1924- . **CLC 4, 6,
　　45**
　　See also AAYA 7; AMWS 14; CA 1-4R;
　　CAAS 2; CANR 2, 39, 76, 97; CN 7;
　　DAM NOV; DLB 2; DLBY 1981; MTCW
　　1, 2
Connelly, Marc(us Cook) 1890-1980 . **CLC 7**
　　See also CA 85-88; 102; CANR 30; DFS
　　12; DLB 7; DLBY 1980; RGAL 4; SATA-
　　Obit 25
Connor, Ralph .... **TCLC 31**
　　See Gordon, Charles William
　　See also DLB 92; TCWW 2
Conrad, Joseph 1857-1924 ..... **SSC 9, 67, 69,
　　71; TCLC 1, 6, 13, 25, 43, 57; WLC**
　　See also AAYA 26; BPFB 1; BRW 6;
　　BRWC 1; BRWR 2; BYA 2; CA 104; 131;
　　CANR 60; CDBLB 1890-1914; DA; DA3;
　　DAB; DAC; DAM MST, NOV; DLB 10,
　　34, 98, 156; EWL 3; EXPN; EXPS; LAIT
　　2; LATS 1:1; LMFS 1; MTCW 1, 2; NFS
　　2, 16; RGEL 2; RGSF 2; SATA 27; SSFS
　　1, 12; TEA; WLIT 4

Curtis, Price
See Ellison, Harlan (Jay)
Cusanus, Nicolaus 1401-1464 .... **LC 80**
See Nicholas of Cusa
Cutrate, Joe
See Spiegelman, Art
Cynewulf c. 770- .... **CMLC 23**
See also DLB 146; RGEL 2
Cyrano de Bergerac, Savinien de
1619-1655 .... **LC 65**
See also DLB 268; GFL Beginnings to
1789; RGWL 2, 3
Cyril of Alexandria c. 375-c. 430 . **CMLC 59**
Czaczkes, Shmuel Yosef Halevi
See Agnon, S(hmuel) Y(osef Halevi)
Dabrowska, Maria (Szumska)
1889-1965 .... **CLC 15**
See also CA 106; CDWLB 4; DLB 215;
EWL 3
Dabydeen, David 1955- .... **CLC 34**
See also BW 1; CA 125; CANR 56, 92; CN
7; CP 7
Dacey, Philip 1939- .... **CLC 51**
See also CA 37-40R; CAAS 17; CANR 14,
32, 64; CP 7; DLB 105
Dacre, Charlotte c. 1772-1825? ... **NCLC 151**
Dafydd ap Gwilym c. 1320-c. 1380 ..... **PC 56**
Dagerman, Stig (Halvard)
1923-1954 .... **TCLC 17**
See also CA 117; 155; DLB 259; EWL 3
D'Aguiar, Fred 1960- .... **CLC 145**
See also CA 148; CANR 83, 101; CP 7;
DLB 157; EWL 3
Dahl, Roald 1916-1990 .... **CLC 1, 6, 18, 79**
See also AAYA 15; BPFB 1; BRWS 4; BYA
5; CA 1-4R; 133; CANR 6, 32, 37, 62;
CLR 1, 7, 41; CPW; DA3; DAB; DAC;
DAM MST, NOV, POP; DLB 139, 255;
HGG; JRDA; MAICYA 1, 2; MTCW 1,
2; RGSF 2; SATA 1, 26, 73; SATA-Obit
65; SSFS 4; TEA; YAW
Dahlberg, Edward 1900-1977 .. **CLC 1, 7, 14**
See also CA 9-12R; 69-72; CANR 31, 62;
DLB 48; MTCW 1; RGAL 4
Daitch, Susan 1954- .... **CLC 103**
See also CA 161
Dale, Colin .... **TCLC 18**
See Lawrence, T(homas) E(dward)
Dale, George E.
See Asimov, Isaac
Dalton, Roque 1935-1975(?) ..... **HLCS 1; PC
36**
See also CA 176; DLB 283; HW 2
Daly, Elizabeth 1878-1967 .... **CLC 52**
See also CA 23-24; 25-28R; CANR 60;
CAP 2; CMW 4
Daly, Mary 1928- .... **CLC 173**
See also CA 25-28R; CANR 30, 62; FW;
GLL 1; MTCW 1
Daly, Maureen 1921- .... **CLC 17**
See also AAYA 5, 58; BYA 6; CANR 37,
83, 108; CLR 96; JRDA; MAICYA 1, 2;
SAAS 1; SATA 2, 129; WYA; YAW
Damas, Leon-Gontran 1912-1978 .... **CLC 84**
See also BW 1; CA 125; 73-76; EWL 3
Dana, Richard Henry Sr.
1787-1879 .... **NCLC 53**
Daniel, Samuel 1562(?)-1619 .... **LC 24**
See also DLB 62; RGEL 2
Daniels, Brett
See Adler, Renata
Dannay, Frederic 1905-1982 .... **CLC 11**
See Queen, Ellery
See also CA 1-4R; 107; CANR 1, 39; CMW
4; DAM POP; DLB 137; MTCW 1
D'Annunzio, Gabriele 1863-1938 ... **TCLC 6,
40**
See also CA 104; 155; EW 8; EWL 3;
RGWL 2, 3; TWA

Danois, N. le
See Gourmont, Remy(-Marie-Charles) de
Dante 1265-1321 .... **CMLC 3, 18, 39, 70; PC
21; WLCS**
See also DA; DA3; DAB; DAC; DAM
MST, POET; EFS 1; EW 1; LAIT 1;
RGWL 2, 3; TWA; WP
d'Antibes, Germain
See Simenon, Georges (Jacques Christian)
Danticat, Edwidge 1969- .... **CLC 94, 139**
See also AAYA 29; CA 152, 192; CAAE
192; CANR 73, 129; DNFS 1; EXPS;
LATS 1:2; MTCW 1; SSFS 1; YAW
Danvers, Dennis 1947- .... **CLC 70**
Danziger, Paula 1944-2004 .... **CLC 21**
See also AAYA 4, 36; BYA 6, 7, 14; CA
112; 115; 229; CANR 37, 132; CLR 20;
JRDA; MAICYA 1, 2; SATA 36, 63, 102,
149; SATA-Brief 30; WYA; YAW
Da Ponte, Lorenzo 1749-1838 .... **NCLC 50**
Dario, Ruben 1867-1916 .... **HLC 1; PC 15;
TCLC 4**
See also CA 131; CANR 81; DAM MULT;
DLB 290; EWL 3; HW 1, 2; LAW;
MTCW 1, 2; RGWL 2, 3
Darley, George 1795-1846 .... **NCLC 2**
See also DLB 96; RGEL 2
Darrow, Clarence (Seward)
1857-1938 .... **TCLC 81**
See also CA 164; DLB 303
Darwin, Charles 1809-1882 .... **NCLC 57**
See also BRWS 7; DLB 57, 166; LATS 1:1;
RGEL 2; TEA; WLIT 4
Darwin, Erasmus 1731-1802 .... **NCLC 106**
See also DLB 93; RGEL 2
Daryush, Elizabeth 1887-1977 ...... **CLC 6, 19**
See also CA 49-52; CANR 3, 81; DLB 20
Das, Kamala 1934- .... **CLC 191; PC 43**
See also CA 101; CANR 27, 59; CP 7;
CWP; FW
Dasgupta, Surendranath
1887-1952 .... **TCLC 81**
See also CA 157
**Dashwood, Edmee Elizabeth Monica de la
Pasture** 1890-1943
See Delafield, E. M.
See also CA 119; 154
da Silva, Antonio Jose
1705-1739 .... **NCLC 114**
Daudet, (Louis Marie) Alphonse
1840-1897 .... **NCLC 1**
See also DLB 123; GFL 1789 to the Present;
RGSF 2
d'Aulnoy, Marie-Catherine c.
1650-1705 .... **LC 100**
Daumal, Rene 1908-1944 .... **TCLC 14**
See also CA 114; EWL 3
Davenant, William 1606-1668 .... **LC 13**
See also DLB 58, 126; RGEL 2
Davenport, Guy (Mattison, Jr.)
1927-2005 .... **CLC 6, 14, 38; SSC 16**
See also CA 33-36R; CANR 23, 73; CN 7;
CSW; DLB 130
David, Robert
See Nezval, Vitezslav
Davidson, Avram (James) 1923-1993
See Queen, Ellery
See also CA 101; 171; CANR 26; DLB 8;
FANT; SFW 4; SUFW 1, 2
Davidson, Donald (Grady)
1893-1968 .... **CLC 2, 13, 19**
See also CA 5-8R; 25-28R; CANR 4, 84;
DLB 45
Davidson, Hugh
See Hamilton, Edmond
Davidson, John 1857-1909 .... **TCLC 24**
See also CA 118; 217; DLB 19; RGEL 2

Davidson, Sara 1943- .... **CLC 9**
See also CA 81-84; CANR 44, 68; DLB
185
Davie, Donald (Alfred) 1922-1995 .... **CLC 5,
8, 10, 31; PC 29**
See also BRWS 6; CA 1-4R; 149; CAAS 3;
CANR 1, 44; CP 7; DLB 27; MTCW 1;
RGEL 2
Davie, Elspeth 1919-1995 .... **SSC 52**
See also CA 120; 126; 150; DLB 139
Davies, Ray(mond Douglas) 1944- ... **CLC 21**
See also CA 116; 146; CANR 92
Davies, Rhys 1901-1978 .... **CLC 23**
See also CA 9-12R; 81-84; CANR 4; DLB
139, 191
Davies, (William) Robertson
1913-1995 .... **CLC 2, 7, 13, 25, 42, 75,
91; WLC**
See Marchbanks, Samuel
See also BEST 89:2; BPFB 1; CA 33-36R;
150; CANR 17, 42, 103; CN 7; CPW;
DA; DA3; DAB; DAC; DAM MST, NOV,
POP; DLB 68; EWL 3; HGG; INT CANR-
17; MTCW 1, 2; RGEL 2; TWA
Davies, Sir John 1569-1626 .... **LC 85**
See also DLB 172
Davies, Walter C.
See Kornbluth, C(yril) M.
Davies, William Henry 1871-1940 ... **TCLC 5**
See also CA 104; 179; DLB 19, 174; EWL
3; RGEL 2
Da Vinci, Leonardo 1452-1519 ..... **LC 12, 57,
60**
See also AAYA 40
Davis, Angela (Yvonne) 1944- .... **CLC 77**
See also BW 2, 3; CA 57-60; CANR 10,
81; CSW; DA3; DAM MULT; FW
Davis, B. Lynch
See Bioy Casares, Adolfo; Borges, Jorge
Luis
Davis, Frank Marshall 1905-1987 ...... **BLC 1**
See also BW 2, 3; CA 125; 123; CANR 42,
80; DAM MULT; DLB 51
Davis, Gordon
See Hunt, E(verette) Howard, (Jr.)
Davis, H(arold) L(enoir) 1896-1960 . **CLC 49**
See also ANW; CA 178; 89-92; DLB 9,
206; SATA 114
Davis, Natalie Z(emon) 1928- .... **CLC 204**
See also CA 53-56; CANR 58, 100
Davis, Rebecca (Blaine) Harding
1831-1910 .... **SSC 38; TCLC 6**
See also CA 104; 179; DLB 74, 239; FW;
NFS 14; RGAL 4; TUS
Davis, Richard Harding
1864-1916 .... **TCLC 24**
See also CA 114; 179; DLB 12, 23, 78, 79,
189; DLBD 13; RGAL 4
Davison, Frank Dalby 1893-1970 ..... **CLC 15**
See also CA 217; 116; DLB 260
Davison, Lawrence H.
See Lawrence, D(avid) H(erbert Richards)
Davison, Peter (Hubert) 1928- .... **CLC 28**
See also CA 9-12R; CAAS 4; CANR 3, 43,
84; CP 7; DLB 5
Davys, Mary 1674-1732 .... **LC 1, 46**
See also DLB 39
Dawson, (Guy) Fielding (Lewis)
1930-2002 .... **CLC 6**
See also CA 85-88; 202; CANR 108; DLB
130; DLBY 2002
Dawson, Peter
See Faust, Frederick (Schiller)
See also TCWW 2, 2
Day, Clarence (Shepard, Jr.)
1874-1935 .... **TCLC 25**
See also CA 108; 199; DLB 11
Day, John 1574(?)-1640(?) .... **LC 70**
See also DLB 62, 170; RGEL 2

Doblin, Alfred .... **TCLC 13**
See Doeblin, Alfred
See also CDWLB 2; EWL 3; RGWL 2, 3

Dobroliubov, Nikolai Aleksandrovich
See Dobrolyubov, Nikolai Alexandrovich
See also DLB 277

Dobrolyubov, Nikolai Alexandrovich
1836-1861 .... **NCLC 5**
See Dobroliubov, Nikolai Aleksandrovich

Dobson, Austin 1840-1921 .... **TCLC 79**
See also DLB 35, 144

Dobyns, Stephen 1941- .... **CLC 37**
See also AMWS 13; CA 45-48; CANR 2,
18, 99; CMW 4; CP 7

Doctorow, E(dgar) L(aurence)
1931- .... **CLC 6, 11, 15, 18, 37, 44, 65,
113**
See also AAYA 22; AITN 2; AMWS 4;
BEST 89:3; BPFB 1; CA 45-48; CANR
2, 33, 51, 76, 97, 133; CDALB 1968-
1988; CN 7; CPW; DA3; DAM NOV,
POP; DLB 2, 28, 173; DLBY 1980; EWL
3; LAIT 3; MTCW 1, 2; NFS 6; RGAL 4;
RHW; TUS

Dodgson, Charles L(utwidge) 1832-1898
See Carroll, Lewis
See also CLR 2; DA; DA3; DAB; DAC;
DAM MST, NOV, POET; MAICYA 1, 2;
SATA 100; YABC 2

Dodsley, Robert 1703-1764 .... **LC 97**
See also DLB 95; RGEL 2

Dodson, Owen (Vincent) 1914-1983 .. **BLC 1;
CLC 79**
See also BW 1; CA 65-68; 110; CANR 24;
DAM MULT; DLB 76

Doeblin, Alfred 1878-1957 .... **TCLC 13**
See Doblin, Alfred
See also CA 110; 141; DLB 66

Doerr, Harriet 1910-2002 .... **CLC 34**
See also CA 117; 122; 213; CANR 47; INT
CA-122; LATS 1:2

Domecq, H(onorio Bustos)
See Bioy Casares, Adolfo

Domecq, H(onorio) Bustos
See Bioy Casares, Adolfo; Borges, Jorge
Luis

Domini, Rey
See Lorde, Audre (Geraldine)
See also GLL 1

Dominique
See Proust, (Valentin-Louis-George-Eugene)
Marcel

Don, A
See Stephen, Sir Leslie

Donaldson, Stephen R(eeder)
1947- .... **CLC 46, 138**
See also AAYA 36; BPFB 1; CA 89-92;
CANR 13, 55, 99; CPW; DAM POP;
FANT; INT CANR-13; SATA 121; SFW
4; SUFW 1, 2

Donleavy, J(ames) P(atrick) 1926- .... **CLC 1,
4, 6, 10, 45**
See also AITN 2; BPFB 1; CA 9-12R;
CANR 24, 49, 62, 80, 124; CBD; CD 5;
CN 7; DLB 6, 173; INT CANR-24;
MTCW 1, 2; RGAL 4

Donnadieu, Marguerite
See Duras, Marguerite

Donne, John 1572-1631 ... **LC 10, 24, 91; PC
1, 43; WLC**
See also BRW 1; BRWC 1; BRWR 2; CD-
BLB Before 1660; DA; DAB; DAC;
DAM MST, POET; DLB 121, 151; EXPP;
PAB; PFS 2, 11; RGEL 3; TEA; WLIT 3;
WP

Donnell, David 1939(?)- .... **CLC 34**
See also CA 197

Donoghue, Denis 1928- .... **CLC 209**
See also CA 17-20R; CANR 16, 102

Donoghue, P. S.
See Hunt, E(verette) Howard, (Jr.)

Donoso (Yanez), Jose 1924-1996 ... **CLC 4, 8,
11, 32, 99; HLC 1; SSC 34; TCLC 133**
See also CA 81-84; 155; CANR 32, 73; CD-
WLB 3; CWW 2; DAM MULT; DLB 113;
EWL 3; HW 1, 2; LAW; LAWS 1; MTCW
1, 2; RGSF 2; WLIT 1

Donovan, John 1928-1992 .... **CLC 35**
See also AAYA 20; CA 97-100; 137; CLR
3; MAICYA 1, 2; SATA 72; SATA-Brief
29; YAW

Don Roberto
See Cunninghame Graham, Robert
(Gallnigad) Bontine

Doolittle, Hilda 1886-1961 . **CLC 3, 8, 14, 31,
34, 73; PC 5; WLC**
See H. D.
See also AMWS 1; CA 97-100; CANR 35,
131; DA; DAC; DAM MST, POET; DLB
4, 45; EWL 3; FW; GLL 1; LMFS 2;
MAWW; MTCW 1, 2; PFS 6; RGAL 4

Doppo, Kunikida .... **TCLC 99**
See Kunikida Doppo

Dorfman, Ariel 1942- .... **CLC 48, 77, 189;
HLC 1**
See also CA 124; 130; CANR 67, 70, 135;
CWW 2; DAM MULT; DFS 4; EWL 3;
HW 1, 2; INT CA-130; WLIT 1

Dorn, Edward (Merton)
1929-1999 .... **CLC 10, 18**
See also CA 93-96; 187; CANR 42, 79; CP
7; DLB 5; INT CA-93-96; WP

Dor-Ner, Zvi .... **CLC 70**

Dorris, Michael (Anthony)
1945-1997 .... **CLC 109; NNAL**
See also AAYA 20; BEST 90:1; BYA 12;
CA 102; 157; CANR 19, 46, 75; CLR 58;
DA3; DAM MULT, NOV; DLB 175;
LAIT 5; MTCW 2; NFS 3; RGAL 4;
SATA 75; SATA-Obit 94; TCWW 2; YAW

Dorris, Michael A.
See Dorris, Michael (Anthony)

Dorsan, Luc
See Simenon, Georges (Jacques Christian)

Dorsange, Jean
See Simenon, Georges (Jacques Christian)

Dorset
See Sackville, Thomas

Dos Passos, John (Roderigo)
1896-1970 ... **CLC 1, 4, 8, 11, 15, 25, 34,
82; WLC**
See also AMW; BPFB 1; CA 1-4R; 29-32R;
CANR 3; CDALB 1929-1941; DA; DA3;
DAB; DAC; DAM MST, NOV; DLB 4,
9, 274; DLBD 1, 15; DLBY 1996; EWL
3; MTCW 1, 2; NFS 14; RGAL 4; TUS

Dossage, Jean
See Simenon, Georges (Jacques Christian)

Dostoevsky, Fedor Mikhailovich
1821-1881 .. **NCLC 2, 7, 21, 33, 43, 119;
SSC 2, 33, 44; WLC**
See Dostoevsky, Fyodor
See also AAYA 40; DA; DA3; DAB; DAC;
DAM MST, NOV; EW 7; EXPN; NFS 3,
8; RGSF 2; RGWL 2, 3; SSFS 8; TWA

Dostoevsky, Fyodor
See Dostoevsky, Fedor Mikhailovich
See also DLB 238; LATS 1:1; LMFS 1, 2

Doty, M. R.
See Doty, Mark (Alan)

Doty, Mark
See Doty, Mark (Alan)

Doty, Mark (Alan) 1953(?)- .... **CLC 176; PC
53**
See also AMWS 11; CA 161, 183; CAAE
183; CANR 110

Doty, Mark A.
See Doty, Mark (Alan)

Doughty, Charles M(ontagu)
1843-1926 .... **TCLC 27**
See also CA 115; 178; DLB 19, 57, 174

Douglas, Ellen .... **CLC 73**
See Haxton, Josephine Ayres; Williamson,
Ellen Douglas
See also CN 7; CSW; DLB 292

Douglas, Gavin 1475(?)-1522 .... **LC 20**
See also DLB 132; RGEL 2

Douglas, George
See Brown, George Douglas
See also RGEL 2

Douglas, Keith (Castellain)
1920-1944 .... **TCLC 40**
See also BRW 7; CA 160; DLB 27; EWL
3; PAB; RGEL 2

Douglas, Leonard
See Bradbury, Ray (Douglas)

Douglas, Michael
See Crichton, (John) Michael

Douglas, (George) Norman
1868-1952 .... **TCLC 68**
See also BRW 6; CA 119; 157; DLB 34,
195; RGEL 2

Douglas, William
See Brown, George Douglas

Douglass, Frederick 1817(?)-1895 ..... **BLC 1;
NCLC 7, 55, 141; WLC**
See also AAYA 48; AFAW 1, 2; AMWC 1;
AMWS 3; CDALB 1640-1865; DA; DA3;
DAC; DAM MST, MULT; DLB 1, 43, 50,
79, 243; FW; LAIT 2; NCFS 2; RGAL 4;
SATA 29

Dourado, (Waldomiro Freitas) Autran
1926- .... **CLC 23, 60**
See also CA 25-28R; 179; CANR 34, 81;
DLB 145, 307; HW 2

Dourado, Waldomiro Freitas Autran
See Dourado, (Waldomiro Freitas) Autran

Dove, Rita (Frances) 1952- . **BLCS; CLC 50,
81; PC 6**
See also AAYA 46; AMWS 4; BW 2; CA
109; CAAS 19; CANR 27, 42, 68, 76, 97,
132; CDALBS; CP 7; CSW; CWP; DA3;
DAM MULT, POET; DLB 120; EWL 3;
EXPP; MTCW 1; PFS 1, 15; RGAL 4

Doveglion
See Villa, Jose Garcia

Dowell, Coleman 1925-1985 .... **CLC 60**
See also CA 25-28R; 117; CANR 10; DLB
130; GLL 2

Dowson, Ernest (Christopher)
1867-1900 .... **TCLC 4**
See also CA 105; 150; DLB 19, 135; RGEL
2

Doyle, A. Conan
See Doyle, Sir Arthur Conan

Doyle, Sir Arthur Conan
1859-1930 . **SSC 12, 83; TCLC 7; WLC**
See Conan Doyle, Arthur
See also AAYA 14; BRWS 2; CA 104; 122;
CANR 131; CDBLB 1890-1914; CMW
4; DA; DA3; DAB; DAC; DAM MST,
NOV; DLB 18, 70, 156, 178; EXPS;
HGG; LAIT 2; MSW; MTCW 1, 2; RGEL
2; RGSF 2; RHW; SATA 24; SCFW 2;
SFW 4; SSFS 2; TEA; WCH; WLIT 4;
WYA; YAW

Doyle, Conan
See Doyle, Sir Arthur Conan

Doyle, John
See Graves, Robert (von Ranke)

Doyle, Roddy 1958(?)- .... **CLC 81, 178**
See also AAYA 14; BRWS 5; CA 143;
CANR 73, 128; CN 7; DA3; DLB 194

Doyle, Sir A. Conan
See Doyle, Sir Arthur Conan

Dr. A
  See Asimov, Isaac; Silverstein, Alvin; Silverstein, Virginia B(arbara Opshelor)
Drabble, Margaret 1939- ...... CLC 2, 3, 5, 8, 10, 22, 53, 129
  See also BRWS 4; CA 13-16R; CANR 18, 35, 63, 112, 131; CDBLB 1960 to Present; CN 7; CPW; DA3; DAB; DAC; DAM MST, NOV, POP; DLB 14, 155, 231; EWL 3; FW; MTCW 1, 2; RGEL 2; SATA 48; TEA
Drakulic, Slavenka 1949- .... CLC 173
  See also CA 144; CANR 92
Drakulic-Ilic, Slavenka
  See Drakulic, Slavenka
Drapier, M. B.
  See Swift, Jonathan
Drayham, James
  See Mencken, H(enry) L(ouis)
Drayton, Michael 1563-1631 .... LC 8
  See also DAM POET; DLB 121; RGEL 2
Dreadstone, Carl
  See Campbell, (John) Ramsey
Dreiser, Theodore (Herman Albert) 1871-1945 .... SSC 30; TCLC 10, 18, 35, 83; WLC
  See also AMW; AMWC 2; AMWR 2; BYA 15, 16; CA 106; 132; CDALB 1865-1917; DA; DA3; DAC; DAM MST, NOV; DLB 9, 12, 102, 137; DLBD 1; EWL 3; LAIT 2; LMFS 2; MTCW 1, 2; NFS 8, 17; RGAL 4; TUS
Drexler, Rosalyn 1926- .... CLC 2, 6
  See also CA 81-84; CAD; CANR 68, 124; CD 5; CWD
Dreyer, Carl Theodor 1889-1968 ...... CLC 16
  See also CA 116
Drieu la Rochelle, Pierre(-Eugene) 1893-1945 .... TCLC 21
  See also CA 117; DLB 72; EWL 3; GFL 1789 to the Present
Drinkwater, John 1882-1937 .... TCLC 57
  See also CA 109; 149; DLB 10, 19, 149; RGEL 2
Drop Shot
  See Cable, George Washington
Droste-Hulshoff, Annette Freiin von 1797-1848 .... NCLC 3, 133
  See also CDWLB 2; DLB 133; RGSF 2; RGWL 2, 3
Drummond, Walter
  See Silverberg, Robert
Drummond, William Henry 1854-1907 .... TCLC 25
  See also CA 160; DLB 92
Drummond de Andrade, Carlos 1902-1987 .... CLC 18; TCLC 139
  See Andrade, Carlos Drummond de
  See also CA 132; 123; DLB 307; LAW
Drummond of Hawthornden, William 1585-1649 .... LC 83
  See also DLB 121, 213; RGEL 2
Drury, Allen (Stuart) 1918-1998 .... CLC 37
  See also CA 57-60; 170; CANR 18, 52; CN 7; INT CANR-18
Druse, Eleanor
  See King, Stephen (Edwin)
Dryden, John 1631-1700 ..... DC 3; LC 3, 21, 115; PC 25; WLC
  See also BRW 2; CDBLB 1660-1789; DA; DAB; DAC; DAM DRAM, MST, POET; DLB 80, 101, 131; EXPP; IDTP; LMFS 1; RGEL 2; TEA; WLIT 3
du Bellay, Joachim 1524-1560 .... LC 92
  See also GFL Beginnings to 1789; RGWL 2, 3
Duberman, Martin (Bauml) 1930- ..... CLC 8
  See also CA 1-4R; CAD; CANR 2, 63; CD 5

Dubie, Norman (Evans) 1945- .... CLC 36
  See also CA 69-72; CANR 12, 115; CP 7; DLB 120; PFS 12
Du Bois, W(illiam) E(dward) B(urghardt) 1868-1963 ..... BLC 1; CLC 1, 2, 13, 64, 96; HR 2; TCLC 169; WLC
  See also AAYA 40; AFAW 1, 2; AMWC 1; AMWS 2; BW 1, 3; CA 85-88; CANR 34, 82, 132; CDALB 1865-1917; DA; DA3; DAC; DAM MST, MULT, NOV; DLB 47, 50, 91, 246, 284; EWL 3; EXPP; LAIT 2; LMFS 2; MTCW 1, 2; NCFS 1; PFS 13; RGAL 4; SATA 42
Dubus, Andre 1936-1999 ..... CLC 13, 36, 97; SSC 15
  See also AMWS 7; CA 21-24R; 177; CANR 17; CN 7; CSW; DLB 130; INT CANR-17; RGAL 4; SSFS 10
Duca Minimo
  See D'Annunzio, Gabriele
Ducharme, Rejean 1941- .... CLC 74
  See also CA 165; DLB 60
du Chatelet, Emilie 1706-1749 .... LC 96
Duchen, Claire .... CLC 65
Duclos, Charles Pinot- 1704-1772 .... LC 1
  See also GFL Beginnings to 1789
Dudek, Louis 1918-2001 .... CLC 11, 19
  See also CA 45-48; 215; CAAS 14; CANR 1; CP 7; DLB 88
Duerrenmatt, Friedrich 1921-1990 ... CLC 1, 4, 8, 11, 15, 43, 102
  See Durrenmatt, Friedrich
  See also CA 17-20R; CANR 33; CMW 4; DAM DRAM; DLB 69, 124; MTCW 1, 2
Duffy, Bruce 1953(?)- .... CLC 50
  See also CA 172
Duffy, Maureen 1933- .... CLC 37
  See also CA 25-28R; CANR 33, 68; CBD; CN 7; CP 7; CWD; CWP; DFS 15; DLB 14; FW; MTCW 1
Du Fu
  See Tu Fu
  See also RGWL 2, 3
Dugan, Alan 1923-2003 .... CLC 2, 6
  See also CA 81-84; 220; CANR 119; CP 7; DLB 5; PFS 10
du Gard, Roger Martin
  See Martin du Gard, Roger
Duhamel, Georges 1884-1966 .... CLC 8
  See also CA 81-84; 25-28R; CANR 35; DLB 65; EWL 3; GFL 1789 to the Present; MTCW 1
Dujardin, Edouard (Emile Louis) 1861-1949 .... TCLC 13
  See also CA 109; DLB 123
Duke, Raoul
  See Thompson, Hunter S(tockton)
Dulles, John Foster 1888-1959 .... TCLC 72
  See also CA 115; 149
Dumas, Alexandre (pere) 1802-1870 .... NCLC 11, 71; WLC
  See also AAYA 22; BYA 3; DA; DA3; DAB; DAC; DAM MST, NOV; DLB 119, 192; EW 6; GFL 1789 to the Present; LAIT 1, 2; NFS 14, 19; RGWL 2, 3; SATA 18; TWA; WCH
Dumas, Alexandre (fils) 1824-1895 ...... DC 1; NCLC 9
  See also DLB 192; GFL 1789 to the Present; RGWL 2, 3
Dumas, Claudine
  See Malzberg, Barry N(athaniel)
Dumas, Henry L. 1934-1968 .... CLC 6, 62
  See also BW 1; CA 85-88; DLB 41; RGAL 4

du Maurier, Daphne 1907-1989 .. CLC 6, 11, 59; SSC 18
  See also AAYA 37; BPFB 1; BRWS 3; CA 5-8R; 128; CANR 6, 55; CMW 4; CPW; DA3; DAB; DAC; DAM MST, POP; DLB 191; LAIT 3; MSW; MTCW 1, 2; NFS 12; RGEL 2; RGSF 2; RHW; SATA 27; SATA-Obit 60; SSFS 14, 16; TEA
Du Maurier, George 1834-1896 ..... NCLC 86
  See also DLB 153, 178; RGEL 2
Dunbar, Paul Laurence 1872-1906 ... BLC 1; PC 5; SSC 8; TCLC 2, 12; WLC
  See also AFAW 1, 2; AMWS 2; BW 1, 3; CA 104; 124; CANR 79; CDALB 1865-1917; DA; DA3; DAC; DAM MST, MULT, POET; DLB 50, 54, 78; EXPP; RGAL 4; SATA 34
Dunbar, William 1460(?)-1520(?) .... LC 20; PC 67
  See also BRWS 8; DLB 132, 146; RGEL 2
Dunbar-Nelson, Alice .... HR 2
  See Nelson, Alice Ruth Moore Dunbar
Duncan, Dora Angela
  See Duncan, Isadora
Duncan, Isadora 1877(?)-1927 .... TCLC 68
  See also CA 118; 149
Duncan, Lois 1934- .... CLC 26
  See also AAYA 4, 34; BYA 6, 8; CA 1-4R; CANR 2, 23, 36, 111; CLR 29; JRDA; MAICYA 1, 2; MAICYAS 1; SAAS 2; SATA 1, 36, 75, 133, 141; SATA-Essay 141; WYA; YAW
Duncan, Robert (Edward) 1919-1988 .... CLC 1, 2, 4, 7, 15, 41, 55; PC 2
  See also BG 2; CA 9-12R; 124; CANR 28, 62; DAM POET; DLB 5, 16, 193; EWL 3; MTCW 1, 2; PFS 13; RGAL 4; WP
Duncan, Sara Jeannette 1861-1922 .... TCLC 60
  See also CA 157; DLB 92
Dunlap, William 1766-1839 .... NCLC 2
  See also DLB 30, 37, 59; RGAL 4
Dunn, Douglas (Eaglesham) 1942- .... CLC 6, 40
  See also BRWS 10; CA 45-48; CANR 2, 33, 126; CP 7; DLB 40; MTCW 1
Dunn, Katherine (Karen) 1945- .... CLC 71
  See also CA 33-36R; CANR 72; HGG; MTCW 1
Dunn, Stephen (Elliott) 1939- .. CLC 36, 206
  See also AMWS 11; CA 33-36R; CANR 12, 48, 53, 105; CP 7; DLB 105; PFS 21
Dunne, Finley Peter 1867-1936 ...... TCLC 28
  See also CA 108; 178; DLB 11, 23; RGAL 4
Dunne, John Gregory 1932-2003 ..... CLC 28
  See also CA 25-28R; 222; CANR 14, 50; CN 7; DLBY 1980
Dunsany, Lord .... TCLC 2, 59
  See Dunsany, Edward John Moreton Drax Plunkett
  See also DLB 77, 153, 156, 255; FANT; IDTP; RGEL 2; SFW 4; SUFW 1
Dunsany, Edward John Moreton Drax Plunkett 1878-1957
  See Dunsany, Lord
  See also CA 104; 148; DLB 10; MTCW 1
Duns Scotus, John 1266(?)-1308 ... CMLC 59
  See also DLB 115
du Perry, Jean
  See Simenon, Georges (Jacques Christian)
Durang, Christopher (Ferdinand) 1949- .... CLC 27, 38
  See also CA 105; CAD; CANR 50, 76, 130; CD 5; MTCW 1
Duras, Claire de 1777-1828 .... NCLC 154

Ekwensi, Cyprian (Odiatu Duaka)
1921- .... **BLC 1; CLC 4**
See also AFW; BW 2, 3; CA 29-32R; CANR 18, 42, 74, 125; CDWLB 3; CN 7; CWRI 5; DAM MULT; DLB 117; EWL 3; MTCW 1, 2; RGEL 2; SATA 66; WLIT 2

Elaine .... **TCLC 18**
See Leverson, Ada Esther

El Crummo
See Crumb, R(obert)

Elder, Lonne III 1931-1996 ..... **BLC 1; DC 8**
See also BW 1, 3; CA 81-84; 152; CAD; CANR 25; DAM MULT; DLB 7, 38, 44

Eleanor of Aquitaine 1122-1204 ... **CMLC 39**

Elia
See Lamb, Charles

Eliade, Mircea 1907-1986 .... **CLC 19**
See also CA 65-68; 119; CANR 30, 62; CDWLB 4; DLB 220; EWL 3; MTCW 1; RGWL 3; SFW 4

Eliot, A. D.
See Jewett, (Theodora) Sarah Orne

Eliot, Alice
See Jewett, (Theodora) Sarah Orne

Eliot, Dan
See Silverberg, Robert

Eliot, George 1819-1880 ...... **NCLC 4, 13, 23, 41, 49, 89, 118; PC 20; SSC 72; WLC**
See Evans, Mary Ann
See also BRW 5; BRWC 1, 2; BRWR 2; CDBLB 1832-1890; CN 7; CPW; DA; DA3; DAB; DAC; DAM MST, NOV; DLB 21, 35, 55; LATS 1:1; LMFS 1; NFS 17; RGEL 2; RGSF 2; SSFS 8; TEA; WLIT 3

Eliot, John 1604-1690 .... **LC 5**
See also DLB 24

Eliot, T(homas) S(tearns)
1888-1965 ...... **CLC 1, 2, 3, 6, 9, 10, 13, 15, 24, 34, 41, 55, 57, 113; PC 5, 31; WLC**
See also AAYA 28; AMW; AMWC 1; AMWR 1; BRW 7; BRWR 2; CA 5-8R; 25-28R; CANR 41; CDALB 1929-1941; DA; DA3; DAB; DAC; DAM DRAM, MST, POET; DFS 4, 13; DLB 7, 10, 45, 63, 245; DLBY 1988; EWL 3; EXPP; LAIT 3; LATS 1:1; LMFS 2; MTCW 1, 2; NCFS 5; PAB; PFS 1, 7, 20; RGAL 4; RGEL 2; TUS; WLIT 4; WP

Elizabeth 1866-1941 .... **TCLC 41**

Elizabeth I .... **LC 118**
See also DLB 136

Elkin, Stanley L(awrence)
1930-1995 .. **CLC 4, 6, 9, 14, 27, 51, 91; SSC 12**
See also AMWS 6; BPFB 1; CA 9-12R; 148; CANR 8, 46; CN 7; CPW; DAM NOV, POP; DLB 2, 28, 218, 278; DLBY 1980; EWL 3; INT CANR-8; MTCW 1, 2; RGAL 4

Elledge, Scott .... **CLC 34**

Elliott, Don
See Silverberg, Robert

Elliott, George P(aul) 1918-1980 .... **CLC 2**
See also CA 1-4R; 97-100; CANR 2; DLB 244

Elliott, Janice 1931-1995 .... **CLC 47**
See also CA 13-16R; CANR 8, 29, 84; CN 7; DLB 14; SATA 119

Elliott, Sumner Locke 1917-1991 ..... **CLC 38**
See also CA 5-8R; 134; CANR 2, 21; DLB 289

Elliott, William
See Bradbury, Ray (Douglas)

Ellis, A. E. .... **CLC 7**

Ellis, Alice Thomas .... **CLC 40**
See Haycraft, Anna (Margaret)
See also DLB 194; MTCW 1

Ellis, Bret Easton 1964- ...... **CLC 39, 71, 117**
See also AAYA 2, 43; CA 118; 123; CANR 51, 74, 126; CN 7; CPW; DA3; DAM POP; DLB 292; HGG; INT CA-123; MTCW 1; NFS 11

Ellis, (Henry) Havelock
1859-1939 .... **TCLC 14**
See also CA 109; 169; DLB 190

Ellis, Landon
See Ellison, Harlan (Jay)

Ellis, Trey 1962- .... **CLC 55**
See also CA 146; CANR 92

Ellison, Harlan (Jay) 1934- ... **CLC 1, 13, 42, 139; SSC 14**
See also AAYA 29; BPFB 1; BYA 14; CA 5-8R; CANR 5, 46, 115; CPW; DAM POP; DLB 8; HGG; INT CANR-5; MTCW 1, 2; SCFW 2; SFW 4; SSFS 13, 14, 15; SUFW 1, 2

Ellison, Ralph (Waldo) 1914-1994 .... **BLC 1; CLC 1, 3, 11, 54, 86, 114; SSC 26, 79; WLC**
See also AAYA 19; AFAW 1, 2; AMWC 2; AMWR 2; AMWS 2; BPFB 1; BW 1, 3; BYA 2; CA 9-12R; 145; CANR 24, 53; CDALB 1941-1968; CSW; DA; DA3; DAB; DAC; DAM MST, MULT, NOV; DLB 2, 76, 227; DLBY 1994; EWL 3; EXPN; EXPS; LAIT 4; MTCW 1, 2; NCFS 3; NFS 2; RGAL 4; RGSF 2; SSFS 1, 11; YAW

Ellmann, Lucy (Elizabeth) 1956- ..... **CLC 61**
See also CA 128

Ellmann, Richard (David)
1918-1987 .... **CLC 50**
See also BEST 89:2; CA 1-4R; 122; CANR 2, 28, 61; DLB 103; DLBY 1987; MTCW 1, 2

Elman, Richard (Martin)
1934-1997 .... **CLC 19**
See also CA 17-20R; 163; CAAS 3; CANR 47

Elron
See Hubbard, L(afayette) Ron(ald)

El Saadawi, Nawal 1931- .... **CLC 196**
See al'Sadaawi, Nawal; Sa'adawi, al-Nawal; Saadawi, Nawal El; Sa'dawi, Nawal al-
See also CA 118; CAAS 11; CANR 44, 92

Eluard, Paul .... **PC 38; TCLC 7, 41**
See Grindel, Eugene
See also EWL 3; GFL 1789 to the Present; RGWL 2, 3

Ensler, Eve 1953- .... **CLC 212**
See also CA 172; CANR 126

Elyot, Thomas 1490(?)-1546 .... **LC 11**
See also DLB 136; RGEL 2

Elytis, Odysseus 1911-1996 .... **CLC 15, 49, 100; PC 21**
See Alepoudelis, Odysseus
See also CA 102; 151; CANR 94; CWW 2; DAM POET; EW 13; EWL 3; MTCW 1, 2; RGWL 2, 3

Emecheta, (Florence Onye) Buchi
1944- .... **BLC 2; CLC 14, 48, 128**
See also AFW; BW 2, 3; CA 81-84; CANR 27, 81, 126; CDWLB 3; CN 7; CWRI 5; DA3; DAM MULT; DLB 117; EWL 3; FW; MTCW 1, 2; NFS 12, 14; SATA 66; WLIT 2

Emerson, Mary Moody
1774-1863 .... **NCLC 66**

Emerson, Ralph Waldo 1803-1882 . **NCLC 1, 38, 98; PC 18; WLC**
See also AAYA 60; AMW; ANW; CDALB 1640-1865; DA; DA3; DAB; DAC; DAM MST, POET; DLB 1, 59, 73, 183, 223, 270; EXPP; LAIT 2; LMFS 1; NCFS 3; PFS 4, 17; RGAL 4; TUS; WP

Eminescu, Mihail 1850-1889 .. **NCLC 33, 131**

Empedocles 5th cent. B.C.- .... **CMLC 50**
See also DLB 176

Empson, William 1906-1984 ... **CLC 3, 8, 19, 33, 34**
See also BRWS 2; CA 17-20R; 112; CANR 31, 61; DLB 20; EWL 3; MTCW 1, 2; RGEL 2

Enchi, Fumiko (Ueda) 1905-1986 ..... **CLC 31**
See Enchi Fumiko
See also CA 129; 121; FW; MJW

Enchi Fumiko
See Enchi, Fumiko (Ueda)
See also DLB 182; EWL 3

Ende, Michael (Andreas Helmuth)
1929-1995 .... **CLC 31**
See also BYA 5; CA 118; 124; 149; CANR 36, 110; CLR 14; DLB 75; MAICYA 1, 2; MAICYAS 1; SATA 61, 130; SATA-Brief 42; SATA-Obit 86

Endo, Shusaku 1923-1996 ..... **CLC 7, 14, 19, 54, 99; SSC 48; TCLC 152**
See Endo Shusaku
See also CA 29-32R; 153; CANR 21, 54, 131; DA3; DAM NOV; MTCW 1, 2; RGSF 2; RGWL 2, 3

Endo Shusaku
See Endo, Shusaku
See also CWW 2; DLB 182; EWL 3

Engel, Marian 1933-1985 .... **CLC 36; TCLC 137**
See also CA 25-28R; CANR 12; DLB 53; FW; INT CANR-12

Engelhardt, Frederick
See Hubbard, L(afayette) Ron(ald)

Engels, Friedrich 1820-1895 .. **NCLC 85, 114**
See also DLB 129; LATS 1:1

Enright, D(ennis) J(oseph)
1920-2002 .... **CLC 4, 8, 31**
See also CA 1-4R; 211; CANR 1, 42, 83; CP 7; DLB 27; EWL 3; SATA 25; SATA-Obit 140

Enzensberger, Hans Magnus
1929- .... **CLC 43; PC 28**
See also CA 116; 119; CANR 103; CWW 2; EWL 3

Ephron, Nora 1941- .... **CLC 17, 31**
See also AAYA 35; AITN 2; CA 65-68; CANR 12, 39, 83

Epicurus 341B.C.-270B.C. .... **CMLC 21**
See also DLB 176

Epsilon
See Betjeman, John

Epstein, Daniel Mark 1948- .... **CLC 7**
See also CA 49-52; CANR 2, 53, 90

Epstein, Jacob 1956- .... **CLC 19**
See also CA 114

Epstein, Jean 1897-1953 .... **TCLC 92**

Epstein, Joseph 1937- .... **CLC 39, 204**
See also AMWS 14; CA 112; 119; CANR 50, 65, 117

Epstein, Leslie 1938- .... **CLC 27**
See also AMWS 12; CA 73-76, 215; CAAE 215; CAAS 12; CANR 23, 69; DLB 299

Equiano, Olaudah 1745(?)-1797 . **BLC 2; LC 16**
See also AFAW 1, 2; CDWLB 3; DAM MULT; DLB 37, 50; WLIT 2

Erasmus, Desiderius 1469(?)-1536 ..... **LC 16, 93**
See also DLB 136; EW 2; LMFS 1; RGWL 2, 3; TWA

Erdman, Paul E(mil) 1932- .... **CLC 25**
See also AITN 1; CA 61-64; CANR 13, 43, 84

Fox, William Price (Jr.) 1926- .... **CLC 22**
See also CA 17-20R; CAAS 19; CANR 11;
CSW; DLB 2; DLBY 1981

Foxe, John 1517(?)-1587 .... **LC 14**
See also DLB 132

Frame, Janet .. **CLC 2, 3, 6, 22, 66, 96; SSC 29**
See Clutha, Janet Paterson Frame
See also CN 7; CWP; EWL 3; RGEL 2;
RGSF 2; TWA

France, Anatole .... **TCLC 9**
See Thibault, Jacques Anatole Francois
See also DLB 123; EWL 3; GFL 1789 to
the Present; MTCW 1; RGWL 2, 3;
SUFW 1

Francis, Claude .... **CLC 50**
See also CA 192

Francis, Richard Stanley 1920- ... **CLC 2, 22, 42, 102**
See also AAYA 5, 21; BEST 89:3; BPFB 1;
CA 5-8R; CANR 9, 42, 68, 100; CDBLB
1960 to Present; CMW 4; CN 7; DA3;
DAM POP; DLB 87; INT CANR-9;
MSW; MTCW 1, 2

Francis, Robert (Churchill)
1901-1987 .... **CLC 15; PC 34**
See also AMWS 9; CA 1-4R; 123; CANR
1; EXPP; PFS 12

Francis, Lord Jeffrey
See Jeffrey, Francis
See also DLB 107

Frank, Anne(lies Marie)
1929-1945 .... **TCLC 17; WLC**
See also AAYA 12; BYA 1; CA 113; 133;
CANR 68; CLR 101; DA; DA3; DAB;
DAC; DAM MST; LAIT 4; MAICYA 2;
MAICYAS 1; MTCW 1, 2; NCFS 2;
SATA 87; SATA-Brief 42; WYA; YAW

Frank, Bruno 1887-1945 .... **TCLC 81**
See also CA 189; DLB 118; EWL 3

Frank, Elizabeth 1945- .... **CLC 39**
See also CA 121; 126; CANR 78; INT CA-126

Frankl, Viktor E(mil) 1905-1997 ...... **CLC 93**
See also CA 65-68; 161

Franklin, Benjamin
See Hasek, Jaroslav (Matej Frantisek)

Franklin, Benjamin 1706-1790 .... **LC 25; WLCS**
See also AMW; CDALB 1640-1865; DA;
DA3; DAB; DAC; DAM MST; DLB 24,
43, 73, 183; LAIT 1; RGAL 4; TUS

Franklin, (Stella Maria Sarah) Miles (Lampe) 1879-1954 .... **TCLC 7**
See also CA 104; 164; DLB 230; FW;
MTCW 2; RGEL 2; TWA

Franzen, Jonathan 1959- .... **CLC 202**
See also CA 129; CANR 105

Fraser, Antonia (Pakenham) 1932- . **CLC 32, 107**
See also AAYA 57; CA 85-88; CANR 44,
65, 119; CMW; DLB 276; MTCW 1, 2;
SATA-Brief 32

Fraser, George MacDonald 1925- ...... **CLC 7**
See also AAYA 48; CA 45-48, 180; CAAE
180; CANR 2, 48, 74; MTCW 1; RHW

Fraser, Sylvia 1935- .... **CLC 64**
See also CA 45-48; CANR 1, 16, 60; CCA 1

Frayn, Michael 1933- . **CLC 3, 7, 31, 47, 176**
See also BRWC 2; BRWS 7; CA 5-8R;
CANR 30, 69, 114, 133; CBD; CD 5; CN
7; DAM DRAM, NOV; DLB 13, 14, 194,
245; FANT; MTCW 1, 2; SFW 4

Fraze, Candida (Merrill) 1945- .... **CLC 50**
See also CA 126

Frazer, Andrew
See Marlowe, Stephen

Frazer, J(ames) G(eorge)
1854-1941 .... **TCLC 32**
See also BRWS 3; CA 118; NCFS 5

Frazer, Robert Caine
See Creasey, John

Frazer, Sir James George
See Frazer, J(ames) G(eorge)

Frazier, Charles 1950- .... **CLC 109**
See also AAYA 34; CA 161; CANR 126;
CSW; DLB 292

Frazier, Ian 1951- .... **CLC 46**
See also CA 130; CANR 54, 93

Frederic, Harold 1856-1898 .... **NCLC 10**
See also AMW; DLB 12, 23; DLBD 13;
RGAL 4

Frederick, John
See Faust, Frederick (Schiller)
See also TCWW 2

Frederick the Great 1712-1786 .... **LC 14**

Fredro, Aleksander 1793-1876 .... **NCLC 8**

Freeling, Nicolas 1927-2003 .... **CLC 38**
See also CA 49-52; 218; CAAS 12; CANR
1, 17, 50, 84; CMW 4; CN 7; DLB 87

Freeman, Douglas Southall
1886-1953 .... **TCLC 11**
See also CA 109; 195; DLB 17; DLBD 17

Freeman, Judith 1946- .... **CLC 55**
See also CA 148; CANR 120; DLB 256

Freeman, Mary E(leanor) Wilkins
1852-1930 .... **SSC 1, 47; TCLC 9**
See also CA 106; 177; DLB 12, 78, 221;
EXPS; FW; HGG; MAWW; RGAL 4;
RGSF 2; SSFS 4, 8; SUFW 1; TUS

Freeman, R(ichard) Austin
1862-1943 .... **TCLC 21**
See also CA 113; CANR 84; CMW 4; DLB
70

French, Albert 1943- .... **CLC 86**
See also BW 3; CA 167

French, Antonia
See Kureishi, Hanif

French, Marilyn 1929- .. **CLC 10, 18, 60, 177**
See also BPFB 1; CA 69-72; CANR 3, 31,
134; CN 7; CPW; DAM DRAM, NOV,
POP; FW; INT CANR-31; MTCW 1, 2

French, Paul
See Asimov, Isaac

Freneau, Philip Morin 1752-1832 .. **NCLC 1, 111**
See also AMWS 2; DLB 37, 43; RGAL 4

Freud, Sigmund 1856-1939 .... **TCLC 52**
See also CA 115; 133; CANR 69; DLB 296;
EW 8; EWL 3; LATS 1:1; MTCW 1, 2;
NCFS 3; TWA

Freytag, Gustav 1816-1895 .... **NCLC 109**
See also DLB 129

Friedan, Betty (Naomi) 1921- .... **CLC 74**
See also CA 65-68; CANR 18, 45, 74; DLB
246; FW; MTCW 1, 2; NCFS 5

Friedlander, Saul 1932- .... **CLC 90**
See also CA 117; 130; CANR 72

Friedman, B(ernard) H(arper)
1926- .... **CLC 7**
See also CA 1-4R; CANR 3, 48

Friedman, Bruce Jay 1930- ...... **CLC 3, 5, 56**
See also CA 9-12R; CAD; CANR 25, 52,
101; CD 5; CN 7; DLB 2, 28, 244; INT
CANR-25; SSFS 18

Friel, Brian 1929- .... **CLC 5, 42, 59, 115; DC 8; SSC 76**
See also BRWS 5; CA 21-24R; CANR 33,
69, 131; CBD; CD 5; DFS 11; DLB 13;
EWL 3; MTCW 1; RGEL 2; TEA

Friis-Baastad, Babbis Ellinor
1921-1970 .... **CLC 12**
See also CA 17-20R; 134; SATA 7

Frisch, Max (Rudolf) 1911-1991 ... **CLC 3, 9, 14, 18, 32, 44; TCLC 121**
See also CA 85-88; 134; CANR 32, 74; CD-
WLB 2; DAM DRAM, NOV; DLB 69,
124; EW 13; EWL 3; MTCW 1, 2; RGWL
2, 3

Fromentin, Eugene (Samuel Auguste)
1820-1876 .... **NCLC 10, 125**
See also DLB 123; GFL 1789 to the Present

Frost, Frederick
See Faust, Frederick (Schiller)
See also TCWW 2

Frost, Robert (Lee) 1874-1963 .. **CLC 1, 3, 4, 9, 10, 13, 15, 26, 34, 44; PC 1, 39; WLC**
See also AAYA 21; AMW; AMWR 1; CA
89-92; CANR 33; CDALB 1917-1929;
CLR 67; DA; DA3; DAB; DAC; DAM
MST, POET; DLB 54, 284; DLBD 7;
EWL 3; EXPP; MTCW 1, 2; PAB; PFS 1,
2, 3, 4, 5, 6, 7, 10, 13; RGAL 4; SATA
14; TUS; WP; WYA

Froude, James Anthony
1818-1894 .... **NCLC 43**
See also DLB 18, 57, 144

Froy, Herald
See Waterhouse, Keith (Spencer)

Fry, Christopher 1907- .... **CLC 2, 10, 14**
See also BRWS 3; CA 17-20R; CAAS 23;
CANR 9, 30, 74, 132; CBD; CD 5; CP 7;
DAM DRAM; DLB 13; EWL 3; MTCW
1, 2; RGEL 2; SATA 66; TEA

Frye, (Herman) Northrop
1912-1991 .... **CLC 24, 70; TCLC 165**
See also CA 5-8R; 133; CANR 8, 37; DLB
67, 68, 246; EWL 3; MTCW 1, 2; RGAL
4; TWA

Fuchs, Daniel 1909-1993 .... **CLC 8, 22**
See also CA 81-84; 142; CAAS 5; CANR
40; DLB 9, 26, 28; DLBY 1993

Fuchs, Daniel 1934- .... **CLC 34**
See also CA 37-40R; CANR 14, 48

Fuentes, Carlos 1928- .. **CLC 3, 8, 10, 13, 22, 41, 60, 113; HLC 1; SSC 24; WLC**
See also AAYA 4, 45; AITN 2; BPFB 1;
CA 69-72; CANR 10, 32, 68, 104; CD-
WLB 3; CWW 2; DA; DA3; DAB; DAC;
DAM MST, MULT, NOV; DLB 113;
DNFS 2; EWL 3; HW 1, 2; LAIT 3; LATS
1:2; LAW; LAWS 1; LMFS 2; MTCW 1,
2; NFS 8; RGSF 2; RGWL 2, 3; TWA;
WLIT 1

Fuentes, Gregorio Lopez y
See Lopez y Fuentes, Gregorio

Fuertes, Gloria 1918-1998 .... **PC 27**
See also CA 178, 180; DLB 108; HW 2;
SATA 115

Fugard, (Harold) Athol 1932- . **CLC 5, 9, 14, 25, 40, 80, 211; DC 3**
See also AAYA 17; AFW; CA 85-88; CANR
32, 54, 118; CD 5; DAM DRAM; DFS 3,
6, 10; DLB 225; DNFS 1, 2; EWL 3;
LATS 1:2; MTCW 1; RGEL 2; WLIT 2

Fugard, Sheila 1932- .... **CLC 48**
See also CA 125

Fukuyama, Francis 1952- .... **CLC 131**
See also CA 140; CANR 72, 125

Fuller, Charles (H.), (Jr.) 1939- .... **BLC 2; CLC 25; DC 1**
See also BW 2; CA 108; 112; CAD; CANR
87; CD 5; DAM DRAM, MULT; DFS 8;
DLB 38, 266; EWL 3; INT CA-112;
MTCW 1

Fuller, Henry Blake 1857-1929 .... **TCLC 103**
See also CA 108; 177; DLB 12; RGAL 4

Fuller, John (Leopold) 1937- .... **CLC 62**
See also CA 21-24R; CANR 9, 44; CP 7;
DLB 40

Garrick, David 1717-1779 .... **LC 15**
 See also DAM DRAM; DLB 84, 213;
 RGEL 2
Garrigue, Jean 1914-1972 .... **CLC 2, 8**
 See also CA 5-8R; 37-40R; CANR 20
Garrison, Frederick
 See Sinclair, Upton (Beall)
Garrison, William Lloyd
 1805-1879 .... **NCLC 149**
 See also CDALB 1640-1865; DLB 1, 43,
 235
Garro, Elena 1920(?)-1998 .. **HLCS 1; TCLC 153**
 See also CA 131; 169; CWW 2; DLB 145;
 EWL 3; HW 1; LAWS 1; WLIT 1
Garth, Will
 See Hamilton, Edmond; Kuttner, Henry
Garvey, Marcus (Moziah, Jr.)
 1887-1940 .... **BLC 2; HR 2; TCLC 41**
 See also BW 1; CA 120; 124; CANR 79;
 DAM MULT
Gary, Romain .... **CLC 25**
 See Kacew, Romain
 See also DLB 83, 299
Gascar, Pierre .... **CLC 11**
 See Fournier, Pierre
 See also EWL 3
Gascoigne, George 1539-1577 .... **LC 108**
 See also DLB 136; RGEL 2
Gascoyne, David (Emery)
 1916-2001 .... **CLC 45**
 See also CA 65-68; 200; CANR 10, 28, 54;
 CP 7; DLB 20; MTCW 1; RGEL 2
Gaskell, Elizabeth Cleghorn
 1810-1865 .... **NCLC 5, 70, 97, 137; SSC 25**
 See also BRW 5; CDBLB 1832-1890; DAB;
 DAM MST; DLB 21, 144, 159; RGEL 2;
 RGSF 2; TEA
Gass, William H(oward) 1924- . **CLC 1, 2, 8, 11, 15, 39, 132; SSC 12**
 See also AMWS 6; CA 17-20R; CANR 30,
 71, 100; CN 7; DLB 2, 227; EWL 3;
 MTCW 1, 2; RGAL 4
Gassendi, Pierre 1592-1655 .... **LC 54**
 See also GFL Beginnings to 1789
Gasset, Jose Ortega y
 See Ortega y Gasset, Jose
Gates, Henry Louis, Jr. 1950- ... **BLCS; CLC 65**
 See also BW 2, 3; CA 109; CANR 25, 53,
 75, 125; CSW; DA3; DAM MULT; DLB
 67; EWL 3; MTCW 1; RGAL 4
Gautier, Theophile 1811-1872 .. **NCLC 1, 59; PC 18; SSC 20**
 See also DAM POET; DLB 119; EW 6;
 GFL 1789 to the Present; RGWL 2, 3;
 SUFW; TWA
Gawsworth, John
 See Bates, H(erbert) E(rnest)
Gay, John 1685-1732 .... **LC 49**
 See also BRW 3; DAM DRAM; DLB 84,
 95; RGEL 2; WLIT 3
Gay, Oliver
 See Gogarty, Oliver St. John
Gay, Peter (Jack) 1923- .... **CLC 158**
 See also CA 13-16R; CANR 18, 41, 77;
 INT CANR-18
Gaye, Marvin (Pentz, Jr.)
 1939-1984 .... **CLC 26**
 See also CA 195; 112
Gebler, Carlo (Ernest) 1954- .... **CLC 39**
 See also CA 119; 133; CANR 96; DLB 271
Gee, Maggie (Mary) 1948- .... **CLC 57**
 See also CA 130; CANR 125; CN 7; DLB
 207

Gee, Maurice (Gough) 1931- .... **CLC 29**
 See also AAYA 42; CA 97-100; CANR 67,
 123; CLR 56; CN 7; CWRI 5; EWL 3;
 MAICYA 2; RGSF 2; SATA 46, 101
Geiogamah, Hanay 1945- .... **NNAL**
 See also CA 153; DAM MULT; DLB 175
Gelbart, Larry (Simon) 1928- .... **CLC 21, 61**
 See Gelbart, Larry
 See also CA 73-76; CANR 45, 94
Gelbart, Larry 1928-
 See Gelbart, Larry (Simon)
 See also CAD; CD 5
Gelber, Jack 1932-2003 ...... **CLC 1, 6, 14, 79**
 See also CA 1-4R; 216; CAD; CANR 2;
 DLB 7, 228
Gellhorn, Martha (Ellis)
 1908-1998 .... **CLC 14, 60**
 See also CA 77-80; 164; CANR 44; CN 7;
 DLBY 1982, 1998
Genet, Jean 1910-1986 . **DC 25; CLC 1, 2, 5, 10, 14, 44, 46; TCLC 128**
 See also CA 13-16R; CANR 18; DA3;
 DAM DRAM; DFS 10; DLB 72; DLBY
 1986; EW 13; EWL 3; GFL 1789 to the
 Present; GLL 1; LMFS 2; MTCW 1, 2;
 RGWL 2, 3; TWA
Gent, Peter 1942- .... **CLC 29**
 See also AITN 1; CA 89-92; DLBY 1982
Gentile, Giovanni 1875-1944 .... **TCLC 96**
 See also CA 119
Gentlewoman in New England, A
 See Bradstreet, Anne
Gentlewoman in Those Parts, A
 See Bradstreet, Anne
Geoffrey of Monmouth c.
 1100-1155 .... **CMLC 44**
 See also DLB 146; TEA
George, Jean
 See George, Jean Craighead
George, Jean Craighead 1919- .... **CLC 35**
 See also AAYA 8; BYA 2, 4; CA 5-8R;
 CANR 25; CLR 1; 80; DLB 52; JRDA;
 MAICYA 1, 2; SATA 2, 68, 124; WYA;
 YAW
George, Stefan (Anton) 1868-1933 . **TCLC 2, 14**
 See also CA 104; 193; EW 8; EWL 3
Georges, Georges Martin
 See Simenon, Georges (Jacques Christian)
Gerald of Wales c. 1146-c. 1223 ... **CMLC 60**
Gerhardi, William Alexander
 See Gerhardie, William Alexander
Gerhardie, William Alexander
 1895-1977 .... **CLC 5**
 See also CA 25-28R; 73-76; CANR 18;
 DLB 36; RGEL 2
Gerson, Jean 1363-1429 .... **LC 77**
 See also DLB 208
Gersonides 1288-1344 .... **CMLC 49**
 See also DLB 115
Gerstler, Amy 1956- .... **CLC 70**
 See also CA 146; CANR 99
Gertler, T. .... **CLC 34**
 See also CA 116; 121
Gertsen, Aleksandr Ivanovich
 See Herzen, Aleksandr Ivanovich
Ghalib .... **NCLC 39, 78**
 See Ghalib, Asadullah Khan
Ghalib, Asadullah Khan 1797-1869
 See Ghalib
 See also DAM POET; RGWL 2, 3
Ghelderode, Michel de 1898-1962 ..... **CLC 6, 11; DC 15**
 See also CA 85-88; CANR 40, 77; DAM
 DRAM; EW 11; EWL 3; TWA
Ghiselin, Brewster 1903-2001 .... **CLC 23**
 See also CA 13-16R; CAAS 10; CANR 13;
 CP 7

Ghose, Aurabinda 1872-1950 .... **TCLC 63**
 See Ghose, Aurobindo
 See also CA 163
Ghose, Aurobindo
 See Ghose, Aurabinda
 See also EWL 3
Ghose, Zulfikar 1935- .... **CLC 42, 200**
 See also CA 65-68; CANR 67; CN 7; CP 7;
 EWL 3
Ghosh, Amitav 1956- .... **CLC 44, 153**
 See also CA 147; CANR 80; CN 7; WWE 1
Giacosa, Giuseppe 1847-1906 .... **TCLC 7**
 See also CA 104
Gibb, Lee
 See Waterhouse, Keith (Spencer)
Gibbon, Edward 1737-1794 .... **LC 97**
 See also BRW 3; DLB 104; RGEL 2
Gibbon, Lewis Grassic .... **TCLC 4**
 See Mitchell, James Leslie
 See also RGEL 2
Gibbons, Kaye 1960- .... **CLC 50, 88, 145**
 See also AAYA 34; AMWS 10; CA 151;
 CANR 75, 127; CSW; DA3; DAM POP;
 DLB 292; MTCW 1; NFS 3; RGAL 4;
 SATA 117
Gibran, Kahlil 1883-1931 . **PC 9; TCLC 1, 9**
 See also CA 104; 150; DA3; DAM POET,
 POP; EWL 3; MTCW 2
Gibran, Khalil
 See Gibran, Kahlil
Gibson, William 1914- .... **CLC 23**
 See also CA 9-12R; CAD 2; CANR 9, 42,
 75, 125; CD 5; DA; DAB; DAC; DAM
 DRAM, MST; DFS 2; DLB 7; LAIT 2;
 MTCW 2; SATA 66; YAW
Gibson, William (Ford) 1948- ... **CLC 39, 63, 186, 192; SSC 52**
 See also AAYA 12, 59; BPFB 2; CA 126;
 133; CANR 52, 90, 106; CN 7; CPW;
 DA3; DAM POP; DLB 251; MTCW 2;
 SCFW 2; SFW 4
Gide, Andre (Paul Guillaume)
 1869-1951 ..... **SSC 13; TCLC 5, 12, 36; WLC**
 See also CA 104; 124; DA; DA3; DAB;
 DAC; DAM MST, NOV; DLB 65; EW 8;
 EWL 3; GFL 1789 to the Present; MTCW
 1, 2; RGSF 2; RGWL 2, 3; TWA
Gifford, Barry (Colby) 1946- .... **CLC 34**
 See also CA 65-68; CANR 9, 30, 40, 90
Gilbert, Frank
 See De Voto, Bernard (Augustine)
Gilbert, W(illiam) S(chwenck)
 1836-1911 .... **TCLC 3**
 See also CA 104; 173; DAM DRAM, POET;
 RGEL 2; SATA 36
Gilbreth, Frank B(unker), Jr.
 1911-2001 .... **CLC 17**
 See also CA 9-12R; SATA 2
Gilchrist, Ellen (Louise) 1935- .. **CLC 34, 48, 143; SSC 14, 63**
 See also BPFB 2; CA 113; 116; CANR 41,
 61, 104; CN 7; CPW; CSW; DAM POP;
 DLB 130; EWL 3; EXPS; MTCW 1, 2;
 RGAL 4; RGSF 2; SSFS 9
Giles, Molly 1942- .... **CLC 39**
 See also CA 126; CANR 98
Gill, Eric 1882-1940 .... **TCLC 85**
 See Gill, (Arthur) Eric (Rowton Peter
 Joseph)
Gill, (Arthur) Eric (Rowton Peter Joseph)
 1882-1940
 See Gill, Eric
 See also CA 120; DLB 98
Gill, Patrick
 See Creasey, John
Gillette, Douglas .... **CLC 70**

Goldsmith, Oliver 1730-1774 .... **DC 8; LC 2, 48; WLC**
See also BRW 3; CDBLB 1660-1789; DA; DAB; DAC; DAM DRAM, MST, NOV, POET; DFS 1; DLB 39, 89, 104, 109, 142; IDTP; RGEL 2; SATA 26; TEA; WLIT 3

Goldsmith, Peter
See Priestley, J(ohn) B(oynton)

Gombrowicz, Witold 1904-1969 .... **CLC 4, 7, 11, 49**
See also CA 19-20; 25-28R; CANR 105; CAP 2; CDWLB 4; DAM DRAM; DLB 215; EW 12; EWL 3; RGWL 2, 3; TWA

Gomez de Avellaneda, Gertrudis
1814-1873 .... **NCLC 111**
See also LAW

Gomez de la Serna, Ramon
1888-1963 .... **CLC 9**
See also CA 153; 116; CANR 79; EWL 3; HW 1, 2

Goncharov, Ivan Alexandrovich
1812-1891 .... **NCLC 1, 63**
See also DLB 238; EW 6; RGWL 2, 3

Goncourt, Edmond (Louis Antoine Huot) de
1822-1896 .... **NCLC 7**
See also DLB 123; EW 7; GFL 1789 to the Present; RGWL 2, 3

Goncourt, Jules (Alfred Huot) de
1830-1870 .... **NCLC 7**
See also DLB 123; EW 7; GFL 1789 to the Present; RGWL 2, 3

Gongora (y Argote), Luis de
1561-1627 .... **LC 72**
See also RGWL 2, 3

Gontier, Fernande 19(?)- .... **CLC 50**

Gonzalez Martinez, Enrique
See Gonzalez Martinez, Enrique
See also DLB 290

Gonzalez Martinez, Enrique
1871-1952 .... **TCLC 72**
See Gonzalez Martinez, Enrique
See also CA 166; CANR 81; EWL 3; HW 1, 2

Goodison, Lorna 1947- .... **PC 36**
See also CA 142; CANR 88; CP 7; CWP; DLB 157; EWL 3

Goodman, Paul 1911-1972 ..... **CLC 1, 2, 4, 7**
See also CA 19-20; 37-40R; CAD; CANR 34; CAP 2; DLB 130, 246; MTCW 1; RGAL 4

GoodWeather, Harley
See King, Thomas

Googe, Barnabe 1540-1594 .... **LC 94**
See also DLB 132; RGEL 2

Gordimer, Nadine 1923- ...... **CLC 3, 5, 7, 10, 18, 33, 51, 70, 123, 160, 161; SSC 17, 80; WLCS**
See also AAYA 39; AFW; BRWS 2; CA 5-8R; CANR 3, 28, 56, 88, 131; CN 7; DA; DA3; DAB; DAC; DAM MST, NOV; DLB 225; EWL 3; EXPS; INT CANR-28; LATS 1:2; MTCW 1, 2; NFS 4; RGEL 2; RGSF 2; SSFS 2, 14, 19; TWA; WLIT 2; YAW

Gordon, Adam Lindsay
1833-1870 .... **NCLC 21**
See also DLB 230

Gordon, Caroline 1895-1981 . **CLC 6, 13, 29, 83; SSC 15**
See also AMW; CA 11-12; 103; CANR 36; CAP 1; DLB 4, 9, 102; DLBD 17; DLBY 1981; EWL 3; MTCW 1, 2; RGAL 4; RGSF 2

Gordon, Charles William 1860-1937
See Connor, Ralph
See also CA 109

Gordon, Mary (Catherine) 1949- .... **CLC 13, 22, 128; SSC 59**
See also AMWS 4; BPFB 2; CA 102; CANR 44, 92; CN 7; DLB 6; DLBY 1981; FW; INT CA-102; MTCW 1

Gordon, N. J.
See Bosman, Herman Charles

Gordon, Sol 1923- .... **CLC 26**
See also CA 53-56; CANR 4; SATA 11

Gordone, Charles 1925-1995 .. **CLC 1, 4; DC 8**
See also BW 1, 3; CA 93-96; 180; 150; CAAE 180; CAD; CANR 55; DAM DRAM; DLB 7; INT CA-93-96; MTCW 1

Gore, Catherine 1800-1861 .... **NCLC 65**
See also DLB 116; RGEL 2

Gorenko, Anna Andreevna
See Akhmatova, Anna

Gorky, Maxim .... **SSC 28; TCLC 8; WLC**
See Peshkov, Alexei Maximovich
See also DAB; DFS 9; DLB 295; EW 8; EWL 3; MTCW 2; TWA

Goryan, Sirak
See Saroyan, William

Gosse, Edmund (William)
1849-1928 .... **TCLC 28**
See also CA 117; DLB 57, 144, 184; RGEL 2

Gotlieb, Phyllis (Fay Bloom) 1926- .. **CLC 18**
See also CA 13-16R; CANR 7, 135; DLB 88, 251; SFW 4

Gottesman, S. D.
See Kornbluth, C(yril) M.; Pohl, Frederik

Gottfried von Strassburg fl. c.
1170-1215 .... **CMLC 10**
See also CDWLB 2; DLB 138; EW 1; RGWL 2, 3

Gotthelf, Jeremias 1797-1854 .... **NCLC 117**
See also DLB 133; RGWL 2, 3

Gottschalk, Laura Riding
See Jackson, Laura (Riding)

Gould, Lois 1932(?)-2002 .... **CLC 4, 10**
See also CA 77-80; 208; CANR 29; MTCW 1

Gould, Stephen Jay 1941-2002 .... **CLC 163**
See also AAYA 26; BEST 90:2; CA 77-80; 205; CANR 10, 27, 56, 75, 125; CPW; INT CANR-27; MTCW 1, 2

Gourmont, Remy(-Marie-Charles) de
1858-1915 .... **TCLC 17**
See also CA 109; 150; GFL 1789 to the Present; MTCW 2

Gournay, Marie le Jars de
See de Gournay, Marie le Jars

Govier, Katherine 1948- .... **CLC 51**
See also CA 101; CANR 18, 40, 128; CCA 1

Gower, John c. 1330-1408 .... **LC 76; PC 59**
See also BRW 1; DLB 146; RGEL 2

Goyen, (Charles) William
1915-1983 .... **CLC 5, 8, 14, 40**
See also AITN 2; CA 5-8R; 110; CANR 6, 71; DLB 2, 218; DLBY 1983; EWL 3; INT CANR-6

Goytisolo, Juan 1931- .... **CLC 5, 10, 23, 133; HLC 1**
See also CA 85-88; CANR 32, 61, 131; CWW 2; DAM MULT; EWL 3; GLL 2; HW 1, 2; MTCW 1, 2

Gozzano, Guido 1883-1916 .... **PC 10**
See also CA 154; DLB 114; EWL 3

Gozzi, (Conte) Carlo 1720-1806 .... **NCLC 23**

Grabbe, Christian Dietrich
1801-1836 .... **NCLC 2**
See also DLB 133; RGWL 2, 3

Grace, Patricia Frances 1937- .... **CLC 56**
See also CA 176; CANR 118; CN 7; EWL 3; RGSF 2

Gracian y Morales, Baltasar
1601-1658 .... **LC 15**

Gracq, Julien .... **CLC 11, 48**
See Poirier, Louis
See also CWW 2; DLB 83; GFL 1789 to the Present

Grade, Chaim 1910-1982 .... **CLC 10**
See also CA 93-96; 107; EWL 3

Graduate of Oxford, A
See Ruskin, John

Grafton, Garth
See Duncan, Sara Jeannette

Grafton, Sue 1940- .... **CLC 163**
See also AAYA 11, 49; BEST 90:3; CA 108; CANR 31, 55, 111, 134; CMW 4; CPW; CSW; DA3; DAM POP; DLB 226; FW; MSW

Graham, John
See Phillips, David Graham

Graham, Jorie 1951- .... **CLC 48, 118; PC 59**
See also CA 111; CANR 63, 118; CP 7; CWP; DLB 120; EWL 3; PFS 10, 17

Graham, R(obert) B(ontine) Cunninghame
See Cunninghame Graham, Robert (Gallnigad) Bontine
See also DLB 98, 135, 174; RGEL 2; RGSF 2

Graham, Robert
See Haldeman, Joe (William)

Graham, Tom
See Lewis, (Harry) Sinclair

Graham, W(illiam) S(idney)
1918-1986 .... **CLC 29**
See also BRWS 7; CA 73-76; 118; DLB 20; RGEL 2

Graham, Winston (Mawdsley)
1910-2003 .... **CLC 23**
See also CA 49-52; 218; CANR 2, 22, 45, 66; CMW 4; CN 7; DLB 77; RHW

Grahame, Kenneth 1859-1932 ...... **TCLC 64, 136**
See also BYA 5; CA 108; 136; CANR 80; CLR 5; CWRI 5; DA3; DAB; DLB 34, 141, 178; FANT; MAICYA 1, 2; MTCW 2; NFS 20; RGEL 2; SATA 100; TEA; WCH; YABC 1

Granger, Darius John
See Marlowe, Stephen

Granin, Daniil 1918- .... **CLC 59**
See also DLB 302

Granovsky, Timofei Nikolaevich
1813-1855 .... **NCLC 75**
See also DLB 198

Grant, Skeeter
See Spiegelman, Art

Granville-Barker, Harley
1877-1946 .... **TCLC 2**
See Barker, Harley Granville
See also CA 104; 204; DAM DRAM; RGEL 2

Granzotto, Gianni
See Granzotto, Giovanni Battista

Granzotto, Giovanni Battista
1914-1985 .... **CLC 70**
See also CA 166

Grass, Günter (Wilhelm) 1927- .... **CLC 1, 2, 4, 6, 11, 15, 22, 32, 49, 88, 207; WLC**
See Grass, Guenter (Wilhelm)
See also BPFB 2; CA 13-16R; CANR 20, 75, 93, 133; CDWLB 2; CWW 2; DA; DA3; DAB; DAC; DAM MST, NOV; DLB 75, 124; EW 13; EWL 3; MTCW 1, 2; RGWL 2, 3; TWA

Gratton, Thomas
See Hulme, T(homas) E(rnest)

Harper, Frances Ellen Watkins
1825-1911 ..... **BLC 2; PC 21; TCLC 14**
See also AFAW 1, 2; BW 1, 3; CA 111; 125;
CANR 79; DAM MULT, POET; DLB 50,
221; MAWW; RGAL 4

Harper, Michael S(teven) 1938- ... **CLC 7, 22**
See also AFAW 2; BW 1; CA 33-36R, 224;
CAAE 224; CANR 24, 108; CP 7; DLB
41; RGAL 4

Harper, Mrs. F. E. W.
See Harper, Frances Ellen Watkins

Harpur, Charles 1813-1868 .... **NCLC 114**
See also DLB 230; RGEL 2

Harris, Christie
See Harris, Christie (Lucy) Irwin

Harris, Christie (Lucy) Irwin
1907-2002 .... **CLC 12**
See also CA 5-8R; CANR 6, 83; CLR 47;
DLB 88; JRDA; MAICYA 1, 2; SAAS 10;
SATA 6, 74; SATA-Essay 116

Harris, Frank 1856-1931 .... **TCLC 24**
See also CA 109; 150; CANR 80; DLB 156,
197; RGEL 2

Harris, George Washington
1814-1869 .... **NCLC 23**
See also DLB 3, 11, 248; RGAL 4

Harris, Joel Chandler 1848-1908 ..... **SSC 19;**
TCLC 2
See also CA 104; 137; CANR 80; CLR 49;
DLB 11, 23, 42, 78, 91; LAIT 2; MAI-
CYA 1, 2; RGSF 2; SATA 100; WCH;
YABC 1

Harris, John (Wyndham Parkes Lucas)
Beynon 1903-1969
See Wyndham, John
See also CA 102; 89-92; CANR 84; SATA
118; SFW 4

Harris, MacDonald .... **CLC 9**
See Heiney, Donald (William)

Harris, Mark 1922- .... **CLC 19**
See also CA 5-8R; CAAS 3; CANR 2, 55,
83; CN 7; DLB 2; DLBY 1980

Harris, Norman .... **CLC 65**

Harris, (Theodore) Wilson 1921- .... **CLC 25,**
159
See also BRWS 5; BW 2, 3; CA 65-68;
CAAS 16; CANR 11, 27, 69, 114; CD-
WLB 3; CN 7; CP 7; DLB 117; EWL 3;
MTCW 1; RGEL 2

Harrison, Barbara Grizzuti
1934-2002 .... **CLC 144**
See also CA 77-80; 205; CANR 15, 48; INT
CANR-15

Harrison, Elizabeth (Allen) Cavanna
1909-2001
See Cavanna, Betty
See also CA 9-12R; 200; CANR 6, 27, 85,
104, 121; MAICYA 2; SATA 142; YAW

Harrison, Harry (Max) 1925- .... **CLC 42**
See also CA 1-4R; CANR 5, 21, 84; DLB
8; SATA 4; SCFW 2; SFW 4

Harrison, James (Thomas) 1937- ...... **CLC 6,**
14, 33, 66, 143; SSC 19
See Harrison, Jim
See also CA 13-16R; CANR 8, 51, 79; CN
7; CP 7; DLBY 1982; INT CANR-8

Harrison, Jim
See Harrison, James (Thomas)
See also AMWS 8; RGAL 4; TCWW 2;
TUS

Harrison, Kathryn 1961- .... **CLC 70, 151**
See also CA 144; CANR 68, 122

Harrison, Tony 1937- .... **CLC 43, 129**
See also BRWS 5; CA 65-68; CANR 44,
98; CBD; CD 5; CP 7; DLB 40, 245;
MTCW 1; RGEL 2

Harriss, Will(ard Irvin) 1922- .... **CLC 34**
See also CA 111

Hart, Ellis
See Ellison, Harlan (Jay)

Hart, Josephine 1942(?)- .... **CLC 70**
See also CA 138; CANR 70; CPW; DAM
POP

Hart, Moss 1904-1961 .... **CLC 66**
See also CA 109; 89-92; CANR 84; DAM
DRAM; DFS 1; DLB 7, 266; RGAL 4

Harte, (Francis) Bret(t)
1836(?)-1902 ... **SSC 8, 59; TCLC 1, 25;**
WLC
See also AMWS 2; CA 104; 140; CANR
80; CDALB 1865-1917; DA; DA3; DAC;
DAM MST; DLB 12, 64, 74, 79, 186;
EXPS; LAIT 2; RGAL 4; RGSF 2; SATA
26; SSFS 3; TUS

Hartley, L(eslie) P(oles) 1895-1972 ... **CLC 2,**
22
See also BRWS 7; CA 45-48; 37-40R;
CANR 33; DLB 15, 139; EWL 3; HGG;
MTCW 1, 2; RGEL 2; RGSF 2; SUFW 1

Hartman, Geoffrey H. 1929- .... **CLC 27**
See also CA 117; 125; CANR 79; DLB 67

Hartmann, Sadakichi 1869-1944 ... **TCLC 73**
See also CA 157; DLB 54

Hartmann von Aue c. 1170-c.
1210 .... **CMLC 15**
See also CDWLB 2; DLB 138; RGWL 2, 3

Hartog, Jan de
See de Hartog, Jan

Haruf, Kent 1943- .... **CLC 34**
See also AAYA 44; CA 149; CANR 91, 131

Harvey, Caroline
See Trollope, Joanna

Harvey, Gabriel 1550(?)-1631 .... **LC 88**
See also DLB 167, 213, 281

Harwood, Ronald 1934- .... **CLC 32**
See also CA 1-4R; CANR 4, 55; CBD; CD
5; DAM DRAM, MST; DLB 13

Hasegawa Tatsunosuke
See Futabatei, Shimei

Hasek, Jaroslav (Matej Frantisek)
1883-1923 .... **SSC 69; TCLC 4**
See also CA 104; 129; CDWLB 4; DLB
215; EW 9; EWL 3; MTCW 1, 2; RGSF
2; RGWL 2, 3

Hass, Robert 1941- ... **CLC 18, 39, 99; PC 16**
See also AMWS 6; CA 111; CANR 30, 50,
71; CP 7; DLB 105, 206; EWL 3; RGAL
4; SATA 94

Hastings, Hudson
See Kuttner, Henry

Hastings, Selina .... **CLC 44**

Hathorne, John 1641-1717 .... **LC 38**

Hatteras, Amelia
See Mencken, H(enry) L(ouis)

Hatteras, Owen .... **TCLC 18**
See Mencken, H(enry) L(ouis); Nathan,
George Jean

Hauptmann, Gerhart (Johann Robert)
1862-1946 .... **SSC 37; TCLC 4**
See also CA 104; 153; CDWLB 2; DAM
DRAM; DLB 66, 118; EW 8; EWL 3;
RGSF 2; RGWL 2, 3; TWA

Havel, Vaclav 1936- ..... **CLC 25, 58, 65, 123;**
DC 6
See also CA 104; CANR 36, 63, 124; CD-
WLB 4; CWW 2; DA3; DAM DRAM;
DFS 10; DLB 232; EWL 3; LMFS 2;
MTCW 1, 2; RGWL 3

Haviaras, Stratis .... **CLC 33**
See Chaviaras, Strates

Hawes, Stephen 1475(?)-1529(?) .... **LC 17**
See also DLB 132; RGEL 2

Hawkes, John (Clendennin Burne, Jr.)
1925-1998 .. **CLC 1, 2, 3, 4, 7, 9, 14, 15,**
27, 49
See also BPFB 2; CA 1-4R; 167; CANR 2,
47, 64; CN 7; DLB 2, 7, 227; DLBY
1980, 1998; EWL 3; MTCW 1, 2; RGAL
4

Hawking, S. W.
See Hawking, Stephen W(illiam)

Hawking, Stephen W(illiam) 1942- . **CLC 63,**
105
See also AAYA 13; BEST 89:1; CA 126;
129; CANR 48, 115; CPW; DA3; MTCW
2

Hawkins, Anthony Hope
See Hope, Anthony

Hawthorne, Julian 1846-1934 .... **TCLC 25**
See also CA 165; HGG

Hawthorne, Nathaniel 1804-1864 ... **NCLC 2,**
10, 17, 23, 39, 79, 95, 158; SSC 3, 29,
39; WLC
See also AAYA 18; AMW; AMWC 1;
AMWR 1; BPFB 2; BYA 3; CDALB
1640-1865; DA; DA3; DAB; DAC; DAM
MST, NOV; DLB 1, 74, 183, 223, 269;
EXPN; EXPS; HGG; LAIT 1; NFS 1, 20;
RGAL 4; RGSF 2; SSFS 1, 7, 11, 15;
SUFW 1; TUS; WCH; YABC 2

Hawthorne, Sophia Peabody
1809-1871 .... **NCLC 150**
See also DLB 183, 239

Haxton, Josephine Ayres 1921-
See Douglas, Ellen
See also CA 115; CANR 41, 83

Hayaseca y Eizaguirre, Jorge
See Echegaray (y Eizaguirre), Jose (Maria
Waldo)

Hayashi, Fumiko 1904-1951 .... **TCLC 27**
See Hayashi Fumiko
See also CA 161

Hayashi Fumiko
See Hayashi, Fumiko
See also DLB 180; EWL 3

Haycraft, Anna (Margaret) 1932-
See Ellis, Alice Thomas
See also CA 122; CANR 85, 90; MTCW 2

Hayden, Robert E(arl) 1913-1980 ..... **BLC 2;**
CLC 5, 9, 14, 37; PC 6
See also AFAW 1, 2; AMWS 2; BW 1, 3;
CA 69-72; 97-100; CABS 2; CANR 24,
75, 82; CDALB 1941-1968; DA; DAC;
DAM MST, MULT, POET; DLB 5, 76;
EWL 3; EXPP; MTCW 1, 2; PFS 1;
RGAL 4; SATA 19; SATA-Obit 26; WP

Haydon, Benjamin Robert
1786-1846 .... **NCLC 146**
See also DLB 110

Hayek, F(riedrich) A(ugust von)
1899-1992 .... **TCLC 109**
See also CA 93-96; 137; CANR 20; MTCW
1, 2

Hayford, J(oseph) E(phraim) Casely
See Casely-Hayford, J(oseph) E(phraim)

Hayman, Ronald 1932- .... **CLC 44**
See also CA 25-28R; CANR 18, 50, 88; CD
5; DLB 155

Hayne, Paul Hamilton 1830-1886 . **NCLC 94**
See also DLB 3, 64, 79, 248; RGAL 4

Hays, Mary 1760-1843 .... **NCLC 114**
See also DLB 142, 158; RGEL 2

Haywood, Eliza (Fowler)
1693(?)-1756 .... **LC 1, 44**
See also DLB 39; RGEL 2

Hazlitt, William 1778-1830 ...... **NCLC 29, 82**
See also BRW 4; DLB 110, 158; RGEL 2;
TEA

Hazzard, Shirley 1931- .... **CLC 18**
See also CA 9-12R; CANR 4, 70, 127; CN
7; DLB 289; DLBY 1982; MTCW 1

Head, Bessie 1937-1986 ...... BLC 2; CLC 25,
67; SSC 52
See also AFW; BW 2, 3; CA 29-32R; 119;
CANR 25, 82; CDWLB 3; DA3; DAM
MULT; DLB 117, 225; EWL 3; EXPS;
FW; MTCW 1, 2; RGSF 2; SSFS 5, 13;
WLIT 2; WWE 1

Headon, (Nicky) Topper 1956(?)- ..... CLC 30

Heaney, Seamus (Justin) 1939- ..... CLC 5, 7,
14, 25, 37, 74, 91, 171; PC 18; WLCS
See also BRWR 1; BRWS 2; CA 85-88;
CANR 25, 48, 75, 91, 128; CDBLB 1960
to Present; CP 7; DA3; DAB; DAM
POET; DLB 40; DLBY 1995; EWL 3;
EXPP; MTCW 1, 2; PAB; PFS 2, 5, 8,
17; RGEL 2; TEA; WLIT 4

Hearn, (Patricio) Lafcadio (Tessima Carlos)
1850-1904 .... TCLC 9
See also CA 105; 166; DLB 12, 78, 189;
HGG; RGAL 4

Hearne, Samuel 1745-1792 .... LC 95
See also DLB 99

Hearne, Vicki 1946-2001 .... CLC 56
See also CA 139; 201

Hearon, Shelby 1931- .... CLC 63
See also AITN 2; AMWS 8; CA 25-28R;
CANR 18, 48, 103; CSW

Heat-Moon, William Least .... CLC 29
See Trogdon, William (Lewis)
See also AAYA 9

Hebbel, Friedrich 1813-1863 . DC 21; NCLC
43
See also CDWLB 2; DAM DRAM; DLB
129; EW 6; RGWL 2, 3

Hebert, Anne 1916-2000 .... CLC 4, 13, 29
See also CA 85-88; 187; CANR 69, 126;
CCA 1; CWP; CWW 2; DA3; DAC;
DAM MST, POET; DLB 68; EWL 3; GFL
1789 to the Present; MTCW 1, 2; PFS 20

Hecht, Anthony (Evan) 1923-2004 .... CLC 8,
13, 19
See also AMWS 10; CA 9-12R; CANR 6,
108; CP 7; DAM POET; DLB 5, 169;
EWL 3; PFS 6; WP

Hecht, Ben 1894-1964 ..... CLC 8; TCLC 101
See also CA 85-88; DFS 9; DLB 7, 9, 25,
26, 28, 86; FANT; IDFW 3, 4; RGAL 4

Hedayat, Sadeq 1903-1951 .... TCLC 21
See also CA 120; EWL 3; RGSF 2

Hegel, Georg Wilhelm Friedrich
1770-1831 .... NCLC 46, 151
See also DLB 90; TWA

Heidegger, Martin 1889-1976 .... CLC 24
See also CA 81-84; 65-68; CANR 34; DLB
296; MTCW 1, 2

Heidenstam, (Carl Gustaf) Verner von
1859-1940 .... TCLC 5
See also CA 104

Heidi Louise
See Erdrich, Louise

Heifner, Jack 1946- .... CLC 11
See also CA 105; CANR 47

Heijermans, Herman 1864-1924 .... TCLC 24
See also CA 123; EWL 3

Heilbrun, Carolyn G(old)
1926-2003 .... CLC 25, 173
See Cross, Amanda
See also CA 45-48; 220; CANR 1, 28, 58,
94; FW

Hein, Christoph 1944- .... CLC 154
See also CA 158; CANR 108; CDWLB 2;
CWW 2; DLB 124

Heine, Heinrich 1797-1856 .... NCLC 4, 54,
147; PC 25
See also CDWLB 2; DLB 90; EW 5; RGWL
2, 3; TWA

Heinemann, Larry (Curtiss) 1944- .. CLC 50
See also CA 110; CAAS 21; CANR 31, 81;
DLBD 9; INT CANR-31

Heiney, Donald (William) 1921-1993
See Harris, MacDonald
See also CA 1-4R; 142; CANR 3, 58; FANT

Heinlein, Robert A(nson) 1907-1988 . CLC 1,
3, 8, 14, 26, 55; SSC 55
See also AAYA 17; BPFB 2; BYA 4, 13;
CA 1-4R; 125; CANR 1, 20, 53; CLR 75;
CPW; DA3; DAM POP; DLB 8; EXPS;
JRDA; LAIT 5; LMFS 2; MAICYA 1, 2;
MTCW 1, 2; RGAL 4; SATA 9, 69;
SATA-Obit 56; SCFW; SFW 4; SSFS 7;
YAW

Helforth, John
See Doolittle, Hilda

Heliodorus fl. 3rd cent. - .... CMLC 52

Hellenhofferu, Vojtech Kapristian z
See Hasek, Jaroslav (Matej Frantisek)

Heller, Joseph 1923-1999 . CLC 1, 3, 5, 8, 11,
36, 63; TCLC 131, 151; WLC
See also AAYA 24; AITN 1; AMWS 4;
BPFB 2; BYA 1; CA 5-8R; 187; CABS 1;
CANR 8, 42, 66, 126; CN 7; CPW; DA;
DA3; DAB; DAC; DAM MST, NOV,
POP; DLB 2, 28, 227; DLBY 1980, 2002;
EWL 3; EXPN; INT CANR-8; LAIT 4;
MTCW 1, 2; NFS 1; RGAL 4; TUS; YAW

Hellman, Lillian (Florence)
1906-1984 .. CLC 2, 4, 8, 14, 18, 34, 44,
52; DC 1; TCLC 119
See also AAYA 47; AITN 1, 2; AMWS 1;
CA 13-16R; 112; CAD; CANR 33; CWD;
DA3; DAM DRAM; DFS 1, 3, 14; DLB
7, 228; DLBY 1984; EWL 3; FW; LAIT
3; MAWW; MTCW 1, 2; RGAL 4; TUS

Helprin, Mark 1947- .... CLC 7, 10, 22, 32
See also CA 81-84; CANR 47, 64, 124;
CDALBS; CPW; DA3; DAM NOV, POP;
DLBY 1985; FANT; MTCW 1, 2; SUFW
2

Helvetius, Claude-Adrien 1715-1771 .. LC 26

Helyar, Jane Penelope Josephine 1933-
See Poole, Josephine
See also CA 21-24R; CANR 10, 26; CWRI
5; SATA 82, 138; SATA-Essay 138

Hemans, Felicia 1793-1835 ...... NCLC 29, 71
See also DLB 96; RGEL 2

Hemingway, Ernest (Miller)
1899-1961 .... CLC 1, 3, 6, 8, 10, 13, 19,
30, 34, 39, 41, 44, 50, 61, 80; SSC 1, 25,
36, 40, 63; TCLC 115; WLC
See also AAYA 19; AMW; AMWC 1;
AMWR 1; BPFB 2; BYA 2, 3, 13, 15; CA
77-80; CANR 34; CDALB 1917-1929;
DA; DA3; DAB; DAC; DAM MST, NOV;
DLB 4, 9, 102, 210, 308; DLBD 1, 15,
16; DLBY 1981, 1987, 1996, 1998; EWL
3; EXPN; EXPS; LAIT 3, 4; LATS 1:1;
MTCW 1, 2; NFS 1, 5, 6, 14; RGAL 4;
RGSF 2; SSFS 17; TUS; WYA

Hempel, Amy 1951- .... CLC 39
See also CA 118; 137; CANR 70; DA3;
DLB 218; EXPS; MTCW 2; SSFS 2

Henderson, F. C.
See Mencken, H(enry) L(ouis)

Henderson, Sylvia
See Ashton-Warner, Sylvia (Constance)

Henderson, Zenna (Chlarson)
1917-1983 .... SSC 29
See also CA 1-4R; 133; CANR 1, 84; DLB
8; SATA 5; SFW 4

Henkin, Joshua .... CLC 119
See also CA 161

Henley, Beth .... CLC 23; DC 6, 14
See Henley, Elizabeth Becker
See also CABS 3; CAD; CD 5; CSW;
CWD; DFS 2; DLBY 1986; FW

Henley, Elizabeth Becker 1952-
See Henley, Beth
See also CA 107; CANR 32, 73; DA3;
DAM DRAM, MST; MTCW 1, 2

Henley, William Ernest 1849-1903 .. TCLC 8
See also CA 105; DLB 19; RGEL 2

Hennissart, Martha 1929-
See Lathen, Emma
See also CA 85-88; CANR 64

Henry VIII 1491-1547 .... LC 10
See also DLB 132

Henry, O. ..... SSC 5, 49; TCLC 1, 19; WLC
See Porter, William Sydney
See also AAYA 41; AMWS 2; EXPS; RGAL
4; RGSF 2; SSFS 2, 18

Henry, Patrick 1736-1799 .... LC 25
See also LAIT 1

Henryson, Robert 1430(?)-1506(?) ..... LC 20,
110; PC 65
See also BRWS 7; DLB 146; RGEL 2

Henschke, Alfred
See Klabund

Henson, Lance 1944- .... NNAL
See also CA 146; DLB 175

Hentoff, Nat(han Irving) 1925- .... CLC 26
See also AAYA 4, 42; BYA 6; CA 1-4R;
CAAS 6; CANR 5, 25, 77, 114; CLR 1,
52; INT CANR-25; JRDA; MAICYA 1,
2; SATA 42, 69, 133; SATA-Brief 27;
WYA; YAW

Heppenstall, (John) Rayner
1911-1981 .... CLC 10
See also CA 1-4R; 103; CANR 29; EWL 3

Heraclitus c. 540B.C.-c. 450B.C. ... CMLC 22
See also DLB 176

Herbert, Frank (Patrick)
1920-1986 .... CLC 12, 23, 35, 44, 85
See also AAYA 21; BPFB 2; BYA 4, 14;
CA 53-56; 118; CANR 5, 43; CDALBS;
CPW; DAM POP; DLB 8; INT CANR-5;
LAIT 5; MTCW 1, 2; NFS 17; SATA 9,
37; SATA-Obit 47; SCFW 2; SFW 4;
YAW

Herbert, George 1593-1633 ...... LC 24; PC 4
See also BRW 2; BRWR 2; CDBLB Before
1660; DAB; DAM POET; DLB 126;
EXPP; RGEL 2; TEA; WP

Herbert, Zbigniew 1924-1998 ..... CLC 9, 43;
PC 50; TCLC 168
See also CA 89-92; 169; CANR 36, 74; CD-
WLB 4; CWW 2; DAM POET; DLB 232;
EWL 3; MTCW 1

Herbst, Josephine (Frey)
1897-1969 .... CLC 34
See also CA 5-8R; 25-28R; DLB 9

Herder, Johann Gottfried von
1744-1803 .... NCLC 8
See also DLB 97; EW 4; TWA

Heredia, Jose Maria 1803-1839 .... HLCS 2
See also LAW

Hergesheimer, Joseph 1880-1954 ... TCLC 11
See also CA 109; 194; DLB 102, 9; RGAL
4

Herlihy, James Leo 1927-1993 .... CLC 6
See also CA 1-4R; 143; CAD; CANR 2

Herman, William
See Bierce, Ambrose (Gwinett)

Hermogenes fl. c. 175- .... CMLC 6

Hernandez, Jose 1834-1886 .... NCLC 17
See also LAW; RGWL 2, 3; WLIT 1

Herodotus c. 484B.C.-c. 420B.C. .. CMLC 17
See also AW 1; CDWLB 1; DLB 176;
RGWL 2, 3; TWA

Herrick, Robert 1591-1674 .... LC 13; PC 9
See also BRW 2; BRWC 2; DA; DAB;
DAC; DAM MST, POP; DLB 126; EXPP;
PFS 13; RGAL 4; RGEL 2; TEA; WP

Herring, Guilles
See Somerville, Edith Oenone

Hospital, Janette Turner 1942- .... **CLC 42, 145**
 See also CA 108; CANR 48; CN 7; DLBY 2002; RGSF 2

Hostos, E. M. de
 See Hostos (y Bonilla), Eugenio Maria de

Hostos, Eugenio M. de
 See Hostos (y Bonilla), Eugenio Maria de

Hostos, Eugenio Maria
 See Hostos (y Bonilla), Eugenio Maria de

Hostos (y Bonilla), Eugenio Maria de
 1839-1903 .... **TCLC 24**
 See also CA 123; 131; HW 1

Houdini
 See Lovecraft, H(oward) P(hillips)

Houellebecq, Michel 1958- .... **CLC 179**
 See also CA 185

Hougan, Carolyn 1943- .... **CLC 34**
 See also CA 139

Household, Geoffrey (Edward West)
 1900-1988 .... **CLC 11**
 See also CA 77-80; 126; CANR 58; CMW 4; DLB 87; SATA 14; SATA-Obit 59

Housman, A(lfred) E(dward)
 1859-1936 .... **PC 2, 43; TCLC 1, 10; WLCS**
 See also BRW 6; CA 104; 125; DA; DA3; DAB; DAC; DAM MST, POET; DLB 19, 284; EWL 3; EXPP; MTCW 1, 2; PAB; PFS 4, 7; RGEL 2; TEA; WP

Housman, Laurence 1865-1959 .... **TCLC 7**
 See also CA 106; 155; DLB 10; FANT; RGEL 2; SATA 25

Houston, Jeanne (Toyo) Wakatsuki
 1934- .... **AAL**
 See also AAYA 49; CA 103; CAAS 16; CANR 29, 123; LAIT 4; SATA 78

Howard, Elizabeth Jane 1923- ..... **CLC 7, 29**
 See also CA 5-8R; CANR 8, 62; CN 7

Howard, Maureen 1930- .... **CLC 5, 14, 46, 151**
 See also CA 53-56; CANR 31, 75; CN 7; DLBY 1983; INT CANR-31; MTCW 1, 2

Howard, Richard 1929- .... **CLC 7, 10, 47**
 See also AITN 1; CA 85-88; CANR 25, 80; CP 7; DLB 5; INT CANR-25

Howard, Robert E(rvin)
 1906-1936 .... **TCLC 8**
 See also BPFB 2; BYA 5; CA 105; 157; FANT; SUFW 1

Howard, Warren F.
 See Pohl, Frederik

Howe, Fanny (Quincy) 1940- .... **CLC 47**
 See also CA 117; 187; CAAE 187; CAAS 27; CANR 70, 116; CP 7; CWP; SATA-Brief 52

Howe, Irving 1920-1993 .... **CLC 85**
 See also AMWS 6; CA 9-12R; 141; CANR 21, 50; DLB 67; EWL 3; MTCW 1, 2

Howe, Julia Ward 1819-1910 .... **TCLC 21**
 See also CA 117; 191; DLB 1, 189, 235; FW

Howe, Susan 1937- .... **CLC 72, 152; PC 54**
 See also AMWS 4; CA 160; CP 7; CWP; DLB 120; FW; RGAL 4

Howe, Tina 1937- .... **CLC 48**
 See also CA 109; CAD; CANR 125; CD 5; CWD

Howell, James 1594(?)-1666 .... **LC 13**
 See also DLB 151

Howells, W. D.
 See Howells, William Dean

Howells, William D.
 See Howells, William Dean

Howells, William Dean 1837-1920 ... **SSC 36; TCLC 7, 17, 41**
 See also AMW; CA 104; 134; CDALB 1865-1917; DLB 12, 64, 74, 79, 189; LMFS 1; MTCW 2; RGAL 4; TUS

Howes, Barbara 1914-1996 .... **CLC 15**
 See also CA 9-12R; 151; CAAS 3; CANR 53; CP 7; SATA 5

Hrabal, Bohumil 1914-1997 ...... **CLC 13, 67; TCLC 155**
 See also CA 106; 156; CAAS 12; CANR 57; CWW 2; DLB 232; EWL 3; RGSF 2

Hrabanus Maurus c. 776-856 .... **CMLC 78**
 See also DLB 148

Hrotsvit of Gandersheim c. 935-c.
 1000 .... **CMLC 29**
 See also DLB 148

Hsi, Chu 1130-1200 .... **CMLC 42**

Hsun, Lu
 See Lu Hsun

Hubbard, L(afayette) Ron(ald)
 1911-1986 .... **CLC 43**
 See also CA 77-80; 118; CANR 52; CPW; DA3; DAM POP; FANT; MTCW 2; SFW 4

Huch, Ricarda (Octavia)
 1864-1947 .... **TCLC 13**
 See also CA 111; 189; DLB 66; EWL 3

Huddle, David 1942- .... **CLC 49**
 See also CA 57-60; CAAS 20; CANR 89; DLB 130

Hudson, Jeffrey
 See Crichton, (John) Michael

Hudson, W(illiam) H(enry)
 1841-1922 .... **TCLC 29**
 See also CA 115; 190; DLB 98, 153, 174; RGEL 2; SATA 35

Hueffer, Ford Madox
 See Ford, Ford Madox

Hughart, Barry 1934- .... **CLC 39**
 See also CA 137; FANT; SFW 4; SUFW 2

Hughes, Colin
 See Creasey, John

Hughes, David (John) 1930- .... **CLC 48**
 See also CA 116; 129; CN 7; DLB 14

Hughes, Edward James
 See Hughes, Ted
 See also DA3; DAM MST, POET

Hughes, (James Mercer) Langston
 1902-1967 ..... **BLC 2; CLC 1, 5, 10, 15, 35, 44, 108; DC 3; HR 2; PC 1, 53; SSC 6; WLC**
 See also AAYA 12; AFAW 1, 2; AMWR 1; AMWS 1; BW 1, 3; CA 1-4R; 25-28R; CANR 1, 34, 82; CDALB 1929-1941; CLR 17; DA; DA3; DAB; DAC; DAM DRAM, MST, MULT, POET; DFS 6, 18; DLB 4, 7, 48, 51, 86, 228; EWL 3; EXPP; EXPS; JRDA; LAIT 3; LMFS 2; MAI-CYA 1, 2; MTCW 1, 2; PAB; PFS 1, 3, 6, 10, 15; RGAL 4; RGSF 2; SATA 4, 33; SSFS 4, 7; TUS; WCH; WP; YAW

Hughes, Richard (Arthur Warren)
 1900-1976 .... **CLC 1, 11**
 See also CA 5-8R; 65-68; CANR 4; DAM NOV; DLB 15, 161; EWL 3; MTCW 1; RGEL 2; SATA 8; SATA-Obit 25

Hughes, Ted 1930-1998 . **CLC 2, 4, 9, 14, 37, 119; PC 7**
 See Hughes, Edward James
 See also BRWC 2; BRWR 2; BRWS 1; CA 1-4R; 171; CANR 1, 33, 66, 108; CLR 3; CP 7; DAB; DAC; DLB 40, 161; EWL 3; EXPP; MAICYA 1, 2; MTCW 1, 2; PAB; PFS 4, 19; RGEL 2; SATA 49; SATA-Brief 27; SATA-Obit 107; TEA; YAW

Hugo, Richard
 See Huch, Ricarda (Octavia)

Hugo, Richard F(ranklin)
 1923-1982 .... **CLC 6, 18, 32**
 See also AMWS 6; CA 49-52; 108; CANR 3; DAM POET; DLB 5, 206; EWL 3; PFS 17; RGAL 4

Hugo, Victor (Marie) 1802-1885 .... **NCLC 3, 10, 21, 161; PC 17; WLC**
 See also AAYA 28; DA; DA3; DAB; DAC; DAM DRAM, MST, NOV, POET; DLB 119, 192, 217; EFS 2; EW 6; EXPN; GFL 1789 to the Present; LAIT 1, 2; NFS 5, 20; RGWL 2, 3; SATA 47; TWA

Huidobro, Vicente
 See Huidobro Fernandez, Vicente Garcia
 See also DLB 283; EWL 3; LAW

Huidobro Fernandez, Vicente Garcia
 1893-1948 .... **TCLC 31**
 See Huidobro, Vicente
 See also CA 131; HW 1

Hulme, Keri 1947- .... **CLC 39, 130**
 See also CA 125; CANR 69; CN 7; CP 7; CWP; EWL 3; FW; INT CA-125

Hulme, T(homas) E(rnest)
 1883-1917 .... **TCLC 21**
 See also BRWS 6; CA 117; 203; DLB 19

Humboldt, Wilhelm von
 1767-1835 .... **NCLC 134**
 See also DLB 90

Hume, David 1711-1776 .... **LC 7, 56**
 See also BRWS 3; DLB 104, 252; LMFS 1; TEA

Humphrey, William 1924-1997 .... **CLC 45**
 See also AMWS 9; CA 77-80; 160; CANR 68; CN 7; CSW; DLB 6, 212, 234, 278; TCWW 2

Humphreys, Emyr Owen 1919- .... **CLC 47**
 See also CA 5-8R; CANR 3, 24; CN 7; DLB 15

Humphreys, Josephine 1945- ..... **CLC 34, 57**
 See also CA 121; 127; CANR 97; CSW; DLB 292; INT CA-127

Huneker, James Gibbons
 1860-1921 .... **TCLC 65**
 See also CA 193; DLB 71; RGAL 4

Hungerford, Hesba Fay
 See Brinsmead, H(esba) F(ay)

Hungerford, Pixie
 See Brinsmead, H(esba) F(ay)

Hunt, E(verette) Howard, (Jr.)
 1918- .... **CLC 3**
 See also AITN 1; CA 45-48; CANR 2, 47, 103; CMW 4

Hunt, Francesca
 See Holland, Isabelle (Christian)

Hunt, Howard
 See Hunt, E(verette) Howard, (Jr.)

Hunt, Kyle
 See Creasey, John

Hunt, (James Henry) Leigh
 1784-1859 .... **NCLC 1, 70**
 See also DAM POET; DLB 96, 110, 144; RGEL 2; TEA

Hunt, Marsha 1946- .... **CLC 70**
 See also BW 2, 3; CA 143; CANR 79

Hunt, Violet 1866(?)-1942 .... **TCLC 53**
 See also CA 184; DLB 162, 197

Hunter, E. Waldo
 See Sturgeon, Theodore (Hamilton)

Hunter, Evan 1926- .... **CLC 11, 31**
 See McBain, Ed
 See also AAYA 39; BPFB 2; CA 5-8R; CANR 5, 38, 62, 97; CMW 4; CN 7; CPW; DAM POP; DLB 306; DLBY 1982; INT CANR-5; MSW; MTCW 1; SATA 25; SFW 4

Hunter, Kristin
 See Lattany, Kristin (Elaine Eggleston) Hunter

Hunter, Mary
 See Austin, Mary (Hunter)

Kim
See Simenon, Georges (Jacques Christian)

Kincaid, Jamaica 1949- ...... **BLC 2; CLC 43, 68, 137; SSC 72**
See also AAYA 13, 56; AFAW 2; AMWS 7; BRWS 7; BW 2, 3; CA 125; CANR 47, 59, 95, 133; CDALBS; CDWLB 3; CLR 63; CN 7; DA3; DAM MULT, NOV; DLB 157, 227; DNFS 1; EWL 3; EXPS; FW; LATS 1:2; LMFS 2; MTCW 2; NCFS 1; NFS 3; SSFS 5, 7; TUS; WWE 1; YAW

King, Francis (Henry) 1923- .... **CLC 8, 53, 145**
See also CA 1-4R; CANR 1, 33, 86; CN 7; DAM NOV; DLB 15, 139; MTCW 1

King, Kennedy
See Brown, George Douglas

King, Martin Luther, Jr. 1929-1968 . **BLC 2; CLC 83; WLCS**
See also BW 2, 3; CA 25-28; CANR 27, 44; CAP 2; DA; DA3; DAB; DAC; DAM MST, MULT; LAIT 5; LATS 1:2; MTCW 1, 2; SATA 14

King, Stephen (Edwin) 1947- .... **CLC 12, 26, 37, 61, 113; SSC 17, 55**
See also AAYA 1, 17; AMWS 5; BEST 90:1; BPFB 2; CA 61-64; CANR 1, 30, 52, 76, 119, 134; CPW; DA3; DAM NOV, POP; DLB 143; DLBY 1980; HGG; JRDA; LAIT 5; MTCW 1, 2; RGAL 4; SATA 9, 55; SUFW 1, 2; WYAS 1; YAW

King, Steve
See King, Stephen (Edwin)

King, Thomas 1943- .... **CLC 89, 171; NNAL**
See also CA 144; CANR 95; CCA 1; CN 7; DAC; DAM MULT; DLB 175; SATA 96

Kingman, Lee .... **CLC 17**
See Natti, (Mary) Lee
See also CWRI 5; SAAS 3; SATA 1, 67

Kingsley, Charles 1819-1875 .... **NCLC 35**
See also CLR 77; DLB 21, 32, 163, 178, 190; FANT; MAICYA 2; MAICYAS 1; RGEL 2; WCH; YABC 2

Kingsley, Henry 1830-1876 .... **NCLC 107**
See also DLB 21, 230; RGEL 2

Kingsley, Sidney 1906-1995 .... **CLC 44**
See also CA 85-88; 147; CAD; DFS 14, 19; DLB 7; RGAL 4

Kingsolver, Barbara 1955- . **CLC 55, 81, 130**
See also AAYA 15; AMWS 7; CA 129; 134; CANR 60, 96, 133; CDALBS; CPW; CSW; DA3; DAM POP; DLB 206; INT CA-134; LAIT 5; MTCW 2; NFS 5, 10, 12; RGAL 4

Kingston, Maxine (Ting Ting) Hong
1940- .... **AAL; CLC 12, 19, 58, 121; WLCS**
See also AAYA 8, 55; AMWS 5; BPFB 2; CA 69-72; CANR 13, 38, 74, 87, 128; CDALBS; CN 7; DA3; DAM MULT, NOV; DLB 173, 212; DLBY 1980; EWL 3; FW; INT CANR-13; LAIT 5; MAWW; MTCW 1, 2; NFS 6; RGAL 4; SATA 53; SSFS 3

Kinnell, Galway 1927- ..... **CLC 1, 2, 3, 5, 13, 29, 129; PC 26**
See also AMWS 3; CA 9-12R; CANR 10, 34, 66, 116; CP 7; DLB 5; DLBY 1987; EWL 3; INT CANR-34; MTCW 1, 2; PAB; PFS 9; RGAL 4; WP

Kinsella, Thomas 1928- .... **CLC 4, 19, 138**
See also BRWS 5; CA 17-20R; CANR 15, 122; CP 7; DLB 27; EWL 3; MTCW 1, 2; RGEL 2; TEA

Kinsella, W(illiam) P(atrick) 1935- . **CLC 27, 43, 166**
See also AAYA 7, 60; BPFB 2; CA 97-100, 222; CAAE 222; CAAS 7; CANR 21, 35, 66, 75, 129; CN 7; CPW; DAC; DAM NOV, POP; FANT; INT CANR-21; LAIT 5; MTCW 1, 2; NFS 15; RGSF 2

Kinsey, Alfred C(harles)
1894-1956 .... **TCLC 91**
See also CA 115; 170; MTCW 2

Kipling, (Joseph) Rudyard 1865-1936 . **PC 3; SSC 5, 54; TCLC 8, 17, 167; WLC**
See also AAYA 32; BRW 6; BRWC 1, 2; BYA 4; CA 105; 120; CANR 33; CDBLB 1890-1914; CLR 39, 65; CWRI 5; DA; DA3; DAB; DAC; DAM MST, POET; DLB 19, 34, 141, 156; EWL 3; EXPS; FANT; LAIT 3; LMFS 1; MAICYA 1, 2; MTCW 1, 2; RGEL 2; RGSF 2; SATA 100; SFW 4; SSFS 8; SUFW 1; TEA; WCH; WLIT 4; YABC 2

Kirk, Russell (Amos) 1918-1994 .. **TCLC 119**
See also AITN 1; CA 1-4R; 145; CAAS 9; CANR 1, 20, 60; HGG; INT CANR-20; MTCW 1, 2

Kirkham, Dinah
See Card, Orson Scott

Kirkland, Caroline M. 1801-1864 . **NCLC 85**
See also DLB 3, 73, 74, 250, 254; DLBD 13

Kirkup, James 1918- .... **CLC 1**
See also CA 1-4R; CAAS 4; CANR 2; CP 7; DLB 27; SATA 12

Kirkwood, James 1930(?)-1989 .... **CLC 9**
See also AITN 2; CA 1-4R; 128; CANR 6, 40; GLL 2

Kirsch, Sarah 1935- .... **CLC 176**
See also CA 178; CWW 2; DLB 75; EWL 3

Kirshner, Sidney
See Kingsley, Sidney

Kis, Danilo 1935-1989 .... **CLC 57**
See also CA 109; 118; 129; CANR 61; CD-WLB 4; DLB 181; EWL 3; MTCW 1; RGSF 2; RGWL 2, 3

Kissinger, Henry A(lfred) 1923- ..... **CLC 137**
See also CA 1-4R; CANR 2, 33, 66, 109; MTCW 1

Kivi, Aleksis 1834-1872 .... **NCLC 30**

Kizer, Carolyn (Ashley) 1925- ... **CLC 15, 39, 80; PC 66**
See also CA 65-68; CAAS 5; CANR 24, 70, 134; CP 7; CWP; DAM POET; DLB 5, 169; EWL 3; MTCW 1; PFS 18

Klabund 1890-1928 .... **TCLC 44**
See also CA 162; DLB 66

Klappert, Peter 1942- .... **CLC 57**
See also CA 33-36R; CSW; DLB 5

Klein, A(braham) M(oses)
1909-1972 .... **CLC 19**
See also CA 101; 37-40R; DAB; DAC; DAM MST; DLB 68; EWL 3; RGEL 2

Klein, Joe
See Klein, Joseph

Klein, Joseph 1946- .... **CLC 154**
See also CA 85-88; CANR 55

Klein, Norma 1938-1989 .... **CLC 30**
See also AAYA 2, 35; BPFB 2; BYA 6, 7, 8; CA 41-44R; 128; CANR 15, 37; CLR 2, 19; INT CANR-15; JRDA; MAICYA 1, 2; SAAS 1; SATA 7, 57; WYA; YAW

Klein, T(heodore) E(ibon) D(onald)
1947- .... **CLC 34**
See also CA 119; CANR 44, 75; HGG

Kleist, Heinrich von 1777-1811 ...... **NCLC 2, 37; SSC 22**
See also CDWLB 2; DAM DRAM; DLB 90; EW 5; RGSF 2; RGWL 2, 3

Klima, Ivan 1931- .... **CLC 56, 172**
See also CA 25-28R; CANR 17, 50, 91; CDWLB 4; CWW 2; DAM NOV; DLB 232; EWL 3; RGWL 3

Klimentev, Andrei Platonovich
See Klimentov, Andrei Platonovich

Klimentov, Andrei Platonovich
1899-1951 .... **SSC 42; TCLC 14**
See also Platonov, Andrei Platonovich; Platonov, Andrey Platonovich
See also CA 108

Klinger, Friedrich Maximilian von
1752-1831 .... **NCLC 1**
See also DLB 94

Klingsor the Magician
See Hartmann, Sadakichi

Klopstock, Friedrich Gottlieb
1724-1803 .... **NCLC 11**
See also DLB 97; EW 4; RGWL 2, 3

Kluge, Alexander 1932- .... **SSC 61**
See also CA 81-84; DLB 75

Knapp, Caroline 1959-2002 .... **CLC 99**
See also CA 154; 207

Knebel, Fletcher 1911-1993 .... **CLC 14**
See also AITN 1; CA 1-4R; 140; CAAS 3; CANR 1, 36; SATA 36; SATA-Obit 75

Knickerbocker, Diedrich
See Irving, Washington

Knight, Etheridge 1931-1991 ... **BLC 2; CLC 40; PC 14**
See also BW 1, 3; CA 21-24R; 133; CANR 23, 82; DAM POET; DLB 41; MTCW 2; RGAL 4

Knight, Sarah Kemble 1666-1727 .... **LC 7**
See also DLB 24, 200

Knister, Raymond 1899-1932 .... **TCLC 56**
See also CA 186; DLB 68; RGEL 2

Knowles, John 1926-2001 ... **CLC 1, 4, 10, 26**
See also AAYA 10; AMWS 12; BPFB 2; BYA 3; CA 17-20R; 203; CANR 40, 74, 76, 132; CDALB 1968-1988; CLR 98; CN 7; DA; DAC; DAM MST, NOV; DLB 6; EXPN; MTCW 1, 2; NFS 2; RGAL 4; SATA 8, 89; SATA-Obit 134; YAW

Knox, Calvin M.
See Silverberg, Robert

Knox, John c. 1505-1572 .... **LC 37**
See also DLB 132

Knye, Cassandra
See Disch, Thomas M(ichael)

Koch, C(hristopher) J(ohn) 1932- .... **CLC 42**
See also CA 127; CANR 84; CN 7; DLB 289

Koch, Christopher
See Koch, C(hristopher) J(ohn)

Koch, Kenneth (Jay) 1925-2002 .... **CLC 5, 8, 44**
See also CA 1-4R; 207; CAD; CANR 6, 36, 57, 97, 131; CD 5; CP 7; DAM POET; DLB 5; INT CANR-36; MTCW 2; PFS 20; SATA 65; WP

Kochanowski, Jan 1530-1584 .... **LC 10**
See also RGWL 2, 3

Kock, Charles Paul de 1794-1871 . **NCLC 16**

Koda Rohan
See Koda Shigeyuki

Koda Rohan
See Koda Shigeyuki
See also DLB 180

Koda Shigeyuki 1867-1947 .... **TCLC 22**
See Koda Rohan
See also CA 121; 183

Koestler, Arthur 1905-1983 ... **CLC 1, 3, 6, 8, 15, 33**
See also BRWS 1; CA 1-4R; 109; CANR 1, 33; CDBLB 1945-1960; DLBY 1983; EWL 3; MTCW 1, 2; NFS 19; RGEL 2

Kogawa, Joy Nozomi 1935- ...... **CLC 78, 129**
See also AAYA 47; CA 101; CANR 19, 62, 126; CN 7; CWP; DAC; DAM MST, MULT; FW; MTCW 2; NFS 3; SATA 99

Kohout, Pavel 1928- .... **CLC 13**
See also CA 45-48; CANR 3

Lacan, Jacques (Marie Emile)
1901-1981 .... **CLC 75**
See also CA 121; 104; DLB 296; EWL 3; TWA

Laclos, Pierre Ambroise Francois
1741-1803 .... **NCLC 4, 87**
See also EW 4; GFL Beginnings to 1789; RGWL 2, 3

Lacolere, Francois
See Aragon, Louis

La Colere, Francois
See Aragon, Louis

La Deshabilleuse
See Simenon, Georges (Jacques Christian)

Lady Gregory
See Gregory, Lady Isabella Augusta (Persse)

Lady of Quality, A
See Bagnold, Enid

La Fayette, Marie-(Madelaine Pioche de la Vergne) 1634-1693 .... **LC 2**
See Lafayette, Marie-Madeleine
See also GFL Beginnings to 1789; RGWL 2, 3

Lafayette, Marie-Madeleine
See La Fayette, Marie-(Madelaine Pioche de la Vergne)
See also DLB 268

Lafayette, Rene
See Hubbard, L(afayette) Ron(ald)

La Flesche, Francis 1857(?)-1932 ...... **NNAL**
See also CA 144; CANR 83; DLB 175

La Fontaine, Jean de 1621-1695 .... **LC 50**
See also DLB 268; EW 3; GFL Beginnings to 1789; MAICYA 1, 2; RGWL 2, 3; SATA 18

Laforgue, Jules 1860-1887 . **NCLC 5, 53; PC 14; SSC 20**
See also DLB 217; EW 7; GFL 1789 to the Present; RGWL 2, 3

Lagerkvist, Paer (Fabian)
1891-1974 ..... **CLC 7, 10, 13, 54; TCLC 144**
See Lagerkvist, Par
See also CA 85-88; 49-52; DA3; DAM DRAM, NOV; MTCW 1, 2; TWA

Lagerkvist, Par .... **SSC 12**
See Lagerkvist, Paer (Fabian)
See also DLB 259; EW 10; EWL 3; MTCW 2; RGSF 2; RGWL 2, 3

Lagerloef, Selma (Ottiliana Lovisa)
1858-1940 .... **TCLC 4, 36**
See Lagerlof, Selma (Ottiliana Lovisa)
See also CA 108; MTCW 2; SATA 15

Lagerlof, Selma (Ottiliana Lovisa)
See Lagerloef, Selma (Ottiliana Lovisa)
See also CLR 7; SATA 15

La Guma, (Justin) Alex(ander)
1925-1985 . **BLCS; CLC 19; TCLC 140**
See also AFW; BW 1, 3; CA 49-52; 118; CANR 25, 81; CDWLB 3; DAM NOV; DLB 117, 225; EWL 3; MTCW 1, 2; WLIT 2; WWE 1

Laidlaw, A. K.
See Grieve, C(hristopher) M(urray)

Lainez, Manuel Mujica
See Mujica Lainez, Manuel
See also HW 1

Laing, R(onald) D(avid) 1927-1989 . **CLC 95**
See also CA 107; 129; CANR 34; MTCW 1

Laishley, Alex
See Booth, Martin

Lamartine, Alphonse (Marie Louis Prat) de
1790-1869 .... **NCLC 11; PC 16**
See also DAM POET; DLB 217; GFL 1789 to the Present; RGWL 2, 3

Lamb, Charles 1775-1834 ..... **NCLC 10, 113; WLC**
See also BRW 4; CDBLB 1789-1832; DA; DAB; DAC; DAM MST; DLB 93, 107, 163; RGEL 2; SATA 17; TEA

Lamb, Lady Caroline 1785-1828 ... **NCLC 38**
See also DLB 116

Lamb, Mary Ann 1764-1847 .... **NCLC 125**
See also DLB 163; SATA 17

Lame Deer 1903(?)-1976 .... **NNAL**
See also CA 69-72

Lamming, George (William) 1927- ... **BLC 2; CLC 2, 4, 66, 144**
See also BW 2, 3; CA 85-88; CANR 26, 76; CDWLB 3; CN 7; DAM MULT; DLB 125; EWL 3; MTCW 1, 2; NFS 15; RGEL 2

L'Amour, Louis (Dearborn)
1908-1988 .... **CLC 25, 55**
See Burns, Tex; Mayo, Jim
See also AAYA 16; AITN 2; BEST 89:2; BPFB 2; CA 1-4R; 125; CANR 3, 25, 40; CPW; DA3; DAM NOV, POP; DLB 206; DLBY 1980; MTCW 1, 2; RGAL 4

Lampedusa, Giuseppe (Tomasi) di
.... **TCLC 13**
See Tomasi di Lampedusa, Giuseppe
See also CA 164; EW 11; MTCW 2; RGWL 2, 3

Lampman, Archibald 1861-1899 ... **NCLC 25**
See also DLB 92; RGEL 2; TWA

Lancaster, Bruce 1896-1963 .... **CLC 36**
See also CA 9-10; CANR 70; CAP 1; SATA 9

Lanchester, John 1962- .... **CLC 99**
See also CA 194; DLB 267

Landau, Mark Alexandrovich
See Aldanov, Mark (Alexandrovich)

Landau-Aldanov, Mark Alexandrovich
See Aldanov, Mark (Alexandrovich)

Landis, Jerry
See Simon, Paul (Frederick)

Landis, John 1950- .... **CLC 26**
See also CA 112; 122; CANR 128

Landolfi, Tommaso 1908-1979 .... **CLC 11, 49**
See also CA 127; 117; DLB 177; EWL 3

Landon, Letitia Elizabeth
1802-1838 .... **NCLC 15**
See also DLB 96

Landor, Walter Savage
1775-1864 .... **NCLC 14**
See also BRW 4; DLB 93, 107; RGEL 2

Landwirth, Heinz 1927-
See Lind, Jakov
See also CA 9-12R; CANR 7

Lane, Patrick 1939- .... **CLC 25**
See also CA 97-100; CANR 54; CP 7; DAM POET; DLB 53; INT CA-97-100

Lang, Andrew 1844-1912 .... **TCLC 16**
See also CA 114; 137; CANR 85; CLR 101; DLB 98, 141, 184; FANT; MAICYA 1, 2; RGEL 2; SATA 16; WCH

Lang, Fritz 1890-1976 .... **CLC 20, 103**
See also CA 77-80; 69-72; CANR 30

Lange, John
See Crichton, (John) Michael

Langer, Elinor 1939- .... **CLC 34**
See also CA 121

Langland, William 1332(?)-1400(?) ..... **LC 19**
See also BRW 1; DA; DAB; DAC; DAM MST, POET; DLB 146; RGEL 2; TEA; WLIT 3

Langstaff, Launcelot
See Irving, Washington

Lanier, Sidney 1842-1881 . **NCLC 6, 118; PC 50**
See also AMWS 1; DAM POET; DLB 64; DLBD 13; EXPP; MAICYA 1; PFS 14; RGAL 4; SATA 18

Lanyer, Aemilia 1569-1645 .... **LC 10, 30, 83; PC 60**
See also DLB 121

Lao-Tzu
See Lao Tzu

Lao Tzu c. 6th cent. B.C.-3rd cent. B.C. .... **CMLC 7**

Lapine, James (Elliot) 1949- .... **CLC 39**
See also CA 123; 130; CANR 54, 128; INT CA-130

Larbaud, Valery (Nicolas)
1881-1957 .... **TCLC 9**
See also CA 106; 152; EWL 3; GFL 1789 to the Present

Lardner, Ring
See Lardner, Ring(gold) W(ilmer)
See also BPFB 2; CDALB 1917-1929; DLB 11, 25, 86, 171; DLBD 16; RGAL 4; RGSF 2

Lardner, Ring W., Jr.
See Lardner, Ring(gold) W(ilmer)

Lardner, Ring(gold) W(ilmer)
1885-1933 .... **SSC 32; TCLC 2, 14**
See Lardner, Ring
See also AMW; CA 104; 131; MTCW 1, 2; TUS

Laredo, Betty
See Codrescu, Andrei

Larkin, Maia
See Wojciechowska, Maia (Teresa)

Larkin, Philip (Arthur) 1922-1985 ... **CLC 3, 5, 8, 9, 13, 18, 33, 39, 64; PC 21**
See also BRWS 1; CA 5-8R; 117; CANR 24, 62; CDBLB 1960 to Present; DA3; DAB; DAM MST, POET; DLB 27; EWL 3; MTCW 1, 2; PFS 3, 4, 12; RGEL 2

La Roche, Sophie von
1730-1807 .... **NCLC 121**
See also DLB 94

La Rochefoucauld, Francois
1613-1680 .... **LC 108**

Larra (y Sanchez de Castro), Mariano Jose de 1809-1837 .... **NCLC 17, 130**

Larsen, Eric 1941- .... **CLC 55**
See also CA 132

Larsen, Nella 1893(?)-1963 .... **BLC 2; CLC 37; HR 3**
See also AFAW 1, 2; BW 1; CA 125; CANR 83; DAM MULT; DLB 51; FW; LATS 1:1; LMFS 2

Larson, Charles R(aymond) 1938- ... **CLC 31**
See also CA 53-56; CANR 4, 121

Larson, Jonathan 1961-1996 .... **CLC 99**
See also AAYA 28; CA 156

La Sale, Antoine de c. 1386-1460(?) . **LC 104**
See also DLB 208

Las Casas, Bartolome de
1474-1566 .... **HLCS; LC 31**
See Casas, Bartolome de las
See also LAW

Lasch, Christopher 1932-1994 .... **CLC 102**
See also CA 73-76; 144; CANR 25, 118; DLB 246; MTCW 1, 2

Lasker-Schueler, Else 1869-1945 ... **TCLC 57**
See Lasker-Schuler, Else
See also CA 183; DLB 66, 124

Lasker-Schuler, Else
See Lasker-Schueler, Else
See also EWL 3

Laski, Harold J(oseph) 1893-1950 . **TCLC 79**
See also CA 188

Latham, Jean Lee 1902-1995 .... **CLC 12**
See also AITN 1; BYA 1; CA 5-8R; CANR 7, 84; CLR 50; MAICYA 1, 2; SATA 2, 68; YAW

Latham, Mavis
See Clark, Mavis Thorpe

Madison, James 1751-1836 .... **NCLC 126**
See also DLB 37
Maepenn, Hugh
See Kuttner, Henry
Maepenn, K. H.
See Kuttner, Henry
Maeterlinck, Maurice 1862-1949 ..... **TCLC 3**
See also CA 104; 136; CANR 80; DAM
DRAM; DLB 192; EW 8; EWL 3; GFL
1789 to the Present; LMFS 2; RGWL 2,
3; SATA 66; TWA
Maginn, William 1794-1842 .... **NCLC 8**
See also DLB 110, 159
Mahapatra, Jayanta 1928- .... **CLC 33**
See also CA 73-76; CAAS 9; CANR 15,
33, 66, 87; CP 7; DAM MULT
Mahfouz, Naguib (Abdel Aziz Al-Sabilgi)
1911(?)- .... **CLC 153; SSC 66**
See Mahfuz, Najib (Abdel Aziz al-Sabilgi)
See also AAYA 49; BEST 89:2; CA 128;
CANR 55, 101; DA3; DAM NOV;
MTCW 1, 2; RGWL 2, 3; SSFS 9
Mahfuz, Najib (Abdel Aziz al-Sabilgi)
.... **CLC 52, 55**
See Mahfouz, Naguib (Abdel Aziz Al-
Sabilgi)
See also AFW; CWW 2; DLBY 1988; EWL
3; RGSF 2; WLIT 2
Mahon, Derek 1941- .... **CLC 27; PC 60**
See also BRWS 6; CA 113; 128; CANR 88;
CP 7; DLB 40; EWL 3
Maiakovskii, Vladimir
See Mayakovski, Vladimir (Vladimirovich)
See also IDTP; RGWL 2, 3
Mailer, Norman (Kingsley) 1923- . **CLC 1, 2,**
3, 4, 5, 8, 11, 14, 28, 39, 74, 111
See also AAYA 31; AITN 2; AMW; AMWC
2; AMWR 2; BPFB 2; CA 9-12R; CABS
1; CANR 28, 74, 77, 130; CDALB 1968-
1988; CN 7; CPW; DA; DA3; DAB;
DAC; DAM MST, NOV, POP; DLB 2,
16, 28, 185, 278; DLBD 3; DLBY 1980,
1983; EWL 3; MTCW 1, 2; NFS 10;
RGAL 4; TUS
Maillet, Antonine 1929- .... **CLC 54, 118**
See also CA 115; 120; CANR 46, 74, 77,
134; CCA 1; CWW 2; DAC; DLB 60;
INT CA-120; MTCW 2
Maimonides 1135-1204 .... **CMLC 76**
See also DLB 115
Mais, Roger 1905-1955 .... **TCLC 8**
See also BW 1, 3; CA 105; 124; CANR 82;
CDWLB 3; DLB 125; EWL 3; MTCW 1;
RGEL 2
Maistre, Joseph 1753-1821 .... **NCLC 37**
See also GFL 1789 to the Present
Maitland, Frederic William
1850-1906 .... **TCLC 65**
Maitland, Sara (Louise) 1950- .... **CLC 49**
See also CA 69-72; CANR 13, 59; DLB
271; FW
Major, Clarence 1936- ... **BLC 2; CLC 3, 19,**
48
See also AFAW 2; BW 2, 3; CA 21-24R;
CAAS 6; CANR 13, 25, 53, 82; CN 7;
CP 7; CSW; DAM MULT; DLB 33; EWL
3; MSW
Major, Kevin (Gerald) 1949- .... **CLC 26**
See also AAYA 16; CA 97-100; CANR 21,
38, 112; CLR 11; DAC; DLB 60; INT
CANR-21; JRDA; MAICYA 1, 2; MAIC-
YAS 1; SATA 32, 82, 134; WYA; YAW
Maki, James
See Ozu, Yasujiro
Makine, Andrei 1957- .... **CLC 198**
See also CA 176; CANR 103
Malabaila, Damiano
See Levi, Primo

Malamud, Bernard 1914-1986 .. **CLC 1, 2, 3,**
5, 8, 9, 11, 18, 27, 44, 78, 85; SSC 15;
TCLC 129; WLC
See also AAYA 16; AMWS 1; BPFB 2;
BYA 15; CA 5-8R; 118; CABS 1; CANR
28, 62, 114; CDALB 1941-1968; CPW;
DA; DA3; DAB; DAC; DAM MST, NOV,
POP; DLB 2, 28, 152; DLBY 1980, 1986;
EWL 3; EXPS; LAIT 4; LATS 1:1;
MTCW 1, 2; NFS 4, 9; RGAL 4; RGSF
2; SSFS 8, 13, 16; TUS
Malan, Herman
See Bosman, Herman Charles; Bosman,
Herman Charles
Malaparte, Curzio 1898-1957 .... **TCLC 52**
See also DLB 264
Malcolm, Dan
See Silverberg, Robert
Malcolm, Janet 1934- .... **CLC 201**
See also CA 123; CANR 89; NCFS 1
Malcolm X .... **BLC 2; CLC 82, 117; WLCS**
See Little, Malcolm
See also LAIT 5; NCFS 3
Malherbe, Francois de 1555-1628 .... **LC 5**
See also GFL Beginnings to 1789
Mallarme, Stephane 1842-1898 ...... **NCLC 4,**
41; PC 4
See also DAM POET; DLB 217; EW 7;
GFL 1789 to the Present; LMFS 2; RGWL
2, 3; TWA
Mallet-Joris, Francoise 1930- .... **CLC 11**
See also CA 65-68; CANR 17; CWW 2;
DLB 83; EWL 3; GFL 1789 to the Present
Malley, Ern
See McAuley, James Phillip
Mallon, Thomas 1951- .... **CLC 172**
See also CA 110; CANR 29, 57, 92
Mallowan, Agatha Christie
See Christie, Agatha (Mary Clarissa)
Maloff, Saul 1922- .... **CLC 5**
See also CA 33-36R
Malone, Louis
See MacNeice, (Frederick) Louis
Malone, Michael (Christopher)
1942- .... **CLC 43**
See also CA 77-80; CANR 14, 32, 57, 114
Malory, Sir Thomas 1410(?)-1471(?) . **LC 11,**
88; WLCS
See also BRW 1; BRWR 2; CDBLB Before
1660; DA; DAB; DAC; DAM MST; DLB
146; EFS 2; RGEL 2; SATA 59; SATA-
Brief 33; TEA; WLIT 3
Malouf, (George Joseph) David
1934- .... **CLC 28, 86**
See also CA 124; CANR 50, 76; CN 7; CP
7; DLB 289; EWL 3; MTCW 2
Malraux, (Georges-)Andre
1901-1976 .... **CLC 1, 4, 9, 13, 15, 57**
See also BPFB 2; CA 21-22; 69-72; CANR
34, 58; CAP 2; DA3; DAM NOV; DLB
72; EW 12; EWL 3; GFL 1789 to the
Present; MTCW 1, 2; RGWL 2, 3; TWA
Malthus, Thomas Robert
1766-1834 .... **NCLC 145**
See also DLB 107, 158; RGEL 2
Malzberg, Barry N(athaniel) 1939- ... **CLC 7**
See also CA 61-64; CAAS 4; CANR 16;
CMW 4; DLB 8; SFW 4
Mamet, David (Alan) 1947- .. **CLC 9, 15, 34,**
46, 91, 166; DC 4, 24
See also AAYA 3, 60; AMWS 14; CA 81-
84; CABS 3; CANR 15, 41, 67, 72, 129;
CD 5; DA3; DAM DRAM; DFS 2, 3, 6,
12, 15; DLB 7; EWL 3; IDFW 4; MTCW
1, 2; RGAL 4
Mamoulian, Rouben (Zachary)
1897-1987 .... **CLC 16**
See also CA 25-28R; 124; CANR 85

Mandelshtam, Osip
See Mandelstam, Osip (Emilievich)
See also EW 10; EWL 3; RGWL 2, 3
Mandelstam, Osip (Emilievich)
1891(?)-1943(?) .... **PC 14; TCLC 2, 6**
See Mandelshtam, Osip
See also CA 104; 150; MTCW 2; TWA
Mander, (Mary) Jane 1877-1949 ... **TCLC 31**
See also CA 162; RGEL 2
Mandeville, Bernard 1670-1733 .... **LC 82**
See also DLB 101
Mandeville, Sir John fl. 1350- ...... **CMLC 19**
See also DLB 146
Mandiargues, Andre Pieyre de .... **CLC 41**
See Pieyre de Mandiargues, Andre
See also DLB 83
Mandrake, Ethel Belle
See Thurman, Wallace (Henry)
Mangan, James Clarence
1803-1849 .... **NCLC 27**
See also RGEL 2
Maniere, J.-E.
See Giraudoux, Jean(-Hippolyte)
Mankiewicz, Herman (Jacob)
1897-1953 .... **TCLC 85**
See also CA 120; 169; DLB 26; IDFW 3, 4
Manley, (Mary) Delariviere
1672(?)-1724 .... **LC 1, 42**
See also DLB 39, 80; RGEL 2
Mann, Abel
See Creasey, John
Mann, Emily 1952- .... **DC 7**
See also CA 130; CAD; CANR 55; CD 5;
CWD; DLB 266
Mann, (Luiz) Heinrich 1871-1950 ... **TCLC 9**
See also CA 106; 164, 181; DLB 66, 118;
EW 8; EWL 3; RGWL 2, 3
Mann, (Paul) Thomas 1875-1955 . **SSC 5, 80,**
82; TCLC 2, 8, 14, 21, 35, 44, 60, 168;
WLC
See also BPFB 2; CA 104; 128; CANR 133;
CDWLB 2; DA; DA3; DAB; DAC; DAM
MST, NOV; DLB 66; EW 9; EWL 3; GLL
1; LATS 1:1; LMFS 1; MTCW 1, 2; NFS
17; RGSF 2; RGWL 2, 3; SSFS 4, 9;
TWA
Mannheim, Karl 1893-1947 .... **TCLC 65**
See also CA 204
Manning, David
See Faust, Frederick (Schiller)
See also TCWW 2
Manning, Frederic 1882-1935 .... **TCLC 25**
See also CA 124; 216; DLB 260
Manning, Olivia 1915-1980 .... **CLC 5, 19**
See also CA 5-8R; 101; CANR 29; EWL 3;
FW; MTCW 1; RGEL 2
Mano, D. Keith 1942- .... **CLC 2, 10**
See also CA 25-28R; CAAS 6; CANR 26,
57; DLB 6
Mansfield, Katherine .... **SSC 9, 23, 38, 81;**
TCLC 2, 8, 39, 164; WLC
See Beauchamp, Kathleen Mansfield
See also BPFB 2; BRW 7; DAB; DLB 162;
EWL 3; EXPS; FW; GLL 1; RGEL 2;
RGSF 2; SSFS 2, 8, 10, 11; WWE 1
Manso, Peter 1940- .... **CLC 39**
See also CA 29-32R; CANR 44
Mantecon, Juan Jimenez
See Jimenez (Mantecon), Juan Ramon
Mantel, Hilary (Mary) 1952- .... **CLC 144**
See also CA 125; CANR 54, 101; CN 7;
DLB 271; RHW
Manton, Peter
See Creasey, John
Man Without a Spleen, A
See Chekhov, Anton (Pavlovich)
Manzano, Juan Francisco
1797(?)-1854 .... **NCLC 155**

Maso, Carole 19(?)- .... **CLC 44**
    See also CA 170; GLL 2; RGAL 4
Mason, Bobbie Ann 1940- ... **CLC 28, 43, 82, 154; SSC 4**
    See also AAYA 5, 42; AMWS 8; BPFB 2; CA 53-56; CANR 11, 31, 58, 83, 125; CDALBS; CN 7; CSW; DA3; DLB 173; DLBY 1987; EWL 3; EXPS; INT CANR-31; MTCW 1, 2; NFS 4; RGAL 4; RGSF 2; SSFS 3, 8, 20; YAW
Mason, Ernst
    See Pohl, Frederik
Mason, Hunni B.
    See Sternheim, (William Adolf) Carl
Mason, Lee W.
    See Malzberg, Barry N(athaniel)
Mason, Nick 1945- .... **CLC 35**
Mason, Tally
    See Derleth, August (William)
Mass, Anna .... **CLC 59**
Mass, William
    See Gibson, William
Massinger, Philip 1583-1640 .... **LC 70**
    See also DLB 58; RGEL 2
Master Lao
    See Lao Tzu
Masters, Edgar Lee 1868-1950 ...... **PC 1, 36; TCLC 2, 25; WLCS**
    See also AMWS 1; CA 104; 133; CDALB 1865-1917; DA; DAC; DAM MST, POET; DLB 54; EWL 3; EXPP; MTCW 1, 2; RGAL 4; TUS; WP
Masters, Hilary 1928- .... **CLC 48**
    See also CA 25-28R, 217; CAAE 217; CANR 13, 47, 97; CN 7; DLB 244
Mastrosimone, William 19(?)- .... **CLC 36**
    See also CA 186; CAD; CD 5
Mathe, Albert
    See Camus, Albert
Mather, Cotton 1663-1728 .... **LC 38**
    See also AMWS 2; CDALB 1640-1865; DLB 24, 30, 140; RGAL 4; TUS
Mather, Increase 1639-1723 .... **LC 38**
    See also DLB 24
Matheson, Richard (Burton) 1926- .. **CLC 37**
    See also AAYA 31; CA 97-100; CANR 88, 99; DLB 8, 44; HGG; INT CA-97-100; SCFW 2; SFW 4; SUFW 2
Mathews, Harry 1930- .... **CLC 6, 52**
    See also CA 21-24R; CAAS 6; CANR 18, 40, 98; CN 7
Mathews, John Joseph 1894-1979 .. **CLC 84; NNAL**
    See also CA 19-20; 142; CANR 45; CAP 2; DAM MULT; DLB 175
Mathias, Roland (Glyn) 1915- .... **CLC 45**
    See also CA 97-100; CANR 19, 41; CP 7; DLB 27
Matsuo Basho 1644-1694 .... **LC 62; PC 3**
    See Basho, Matsuo
    See also DAM POET; PFS 2, 7
Mattheson, Rodney
    See Creasey, John
Matthews, (James) Brander
    1852-1929 .... **TCLC 95**
    See also DLB 71, 78; DLBD 13
Matthews, (James) Brander
    1852-1929 .... **TCLC 95**
    See also CA 181; DLB 71, 78; DLBD 13
Matthews, Greg 1949- .... **CLC 45**
    See also CA 135
Matthews, William (Procter III)
    1942-1997 .... **CLC 40**
    See also AMWS 9; CA 29-32R; 162; CAAS 18; CANR 12, 57; CP 7; DLB 5
Matthias, John (Edward) 1941- .... **CLC 9**
    See also CA 33-36R; CANR 56; CP 7

Matthiessen, F(rancis) O(tto)
    1902-1950 .... **TCLC 100**
    See also CA 185; DLB 63
Matthiessen, Peter 1927- ... **CLC 5, 7, 11, 32, 64**
    See also AAYA 6, 40; AMWS 5; ANW; BEST 90:4; BPFB 2; CA 9-12R; CANR 21, 50, 73, 100; CN 7; DA3; DAM NOV; DLB 6, 173, 275; MTCW 1, 2; SATA 27
Maturin, Charles Robert
    1780(?)-1824 .... **NCLC 6**
    See also BRWS 8; DLB 178; HGG; LMFS 1; RGEL 2; SUFW
Matute (Ausejo), Ana Maria 1925- .. **CLC 11**
    See also CA 89-92; CANR 129; CWW 2; EWL 3; MTCW 1; RGSF 2
Maugham, W. S.
    See Maugham, W(illiam) Somerset
Maugham, W(illiam) Somerset
    1874-1965 .. **CLC 1, 11, 15, 67, 93; SSC 8; WLC**
    See also AAYA 55; BPFB 2; BRW 6; CA 5-8R; 25-28R; CANR 40, 127; CDBLB 1914-1945; CMW 4; DA; DA3; DAB; DAC; DAM DRAM, MST, NOV; DLB 10, 36, 77, 100, 162, 195; EWL 3; LAIT 3; MTCW 1, 2; RGEL 2; RGSF 2; SATA 54; SSFS 17
Maugham, William Somerset
    See Maugham, W(illiam) Somerset
Maupassant, (Henri Rene Albert) Guy de
    1850-1893 . **NCLC 1, 42, 83; SSC 1, 64; WLC**
    See also BYA 14; DA; DA3; DAB; DAC; DAM MST; DLB 123; EW 7; EXPS; GFL 1789 to the Present; LAIT 2; LMFS 1; RGSF 2; RGWL 2, 3; SSFS 4; SUFW; TWA
Maupin, Armistead (Jones, Jr.)
    1944- .... **CLC 95**
    See also CA 125; 130; CANR 58, 101; CPW; DA3; DAM POP; DLB 278; GLL 1; INT CA-130; MTCW 2
Maurhut, Richard
    See Traven, B.
Mauriac, Claude 1914-1996 .... **CLC 9**
    See also CA 89-92; 152; CWW 2; DLB 83; EWL 3; GFL 1789 to the Present
Mauriac, Francois (Charles)
    1885-1970 .... **CLC 4, 9, 56; SSC 24**
    See also CA 25-28; CAP 2; DLB 65; EW 10; EWL 3; GFL 1789 to the Present; MTCW 1, 2; RGWL 2, 3; TWA
Mavor, Osborne Henry 1888-1951
    See Bridie, James
    See also CA 104
Maxwell, William (Keepers, Jr.)
    1908-2000 .... **CLC 19**
    See also AMWS 8; CA 93-96; 189; CANR 54, 95; CN 7; DLB 218, 278; DLBY 1980; INT CA-93-96; SATA-Obit 128
May, Elaine 1932- .... **CLC 16**
    See also CA 124; 142; CAD; CWD; DLB 44
Mayakovski, Vladimir (Vladimirovich)
    1893-1930 .... **TCLC 4, 18**
    See Maiakovskii, Vladimir; Mayakovsky, Vladimir
    See also CA 104; 158; EWL 3; MTCW 2; SFW 4; TWA
Mayakovsky, Vladimir
    See Mayakovski, Vladimir (Vladimirovich)
    See also EW 11; WP
Mayhew, Henry 1812-1887 .... **NCLC 31**
    See also DLB 18, 55, 190
Mayle, Peter 1939(?)- .... **CLC 89**
    See also CA 139; CANR 64, 109
Maynard, Joyce 1953- .... **CLC 23**
    See also CA 111; 129; CANR 64

Mayne, William (James Carter)
    1928- .... **CLC 12**
    See also AAYA 20; CA 9-12R; CANR 37, 80, 100; CLR 25; FANT; JRDA; MAI-CYA 1, 2; MAICYAS 1; SAAS 11; SATA 6, 68, 122; SUFW 2; YAW
Mayo, Jim
    See L'Amour, Louis (Dearborn)
    See also TCWW 2
Maysles, Albert 1926- .... **CLC 16**
    See also CA 29-32R
Maysles, David 1932-1987 .... **CLC 16**
    See also CA 191
Mazer, Norma Fox 1931- .... **CLC 26**
    See also AAYA 5, 36; BYA 1, 8; CA 69-72; CANR 12, 32, 66, 129; CLR 23; JRDA; MAICYA 1, 2; SAAS 1; SATA 24, 67, 105; WYA; YAW
Mazzini, Guiseppe 1805-1872 .... **NCLC 34**
McAlmon, Robert (Menzies)
    1895-1956 .... **TCLC 97**
    See also CA 107; 168; DLB 4, 45; DLBD 15; GLL 1
McAuley, James Phillip 1917-1976 .. **CLC 45**
    See also CA 97-100; DLB 260; RGEL 2
McBain, Ed
    See Hunter, Evan
    See also MSW
McBrien, William (Augustine)
    1930- .... **CLC 44**
    See also CA 107; CANR 90
McCabe, Patrick 1955- .... **CLC 133**
    See also BRWS 9; CA 130; CANR 50, 90; CN 7; DLB 194
McCaffrey, Anne (Inez) 1926- .... **CLC 17**
    See also AAYA 6, 34; AITN 2; BEST 89:2; BPFB 2; BYA 5; CA 25-28R, 227; CAAE 227; CANR 15, 35, 55, 96; CLR 49; CPW; DA3; DAM NOV, POP; DLB 8; JRDA; MAICYA 1, 2; MTCW 1, 2; SAAS 11; SATA 8, 70, 116, 152; SATA-Essay 152; SFW 4; SUFW 2; WYA; YAW
McCall, Nathan 1955(?)- .... **CLC 86**
    See also AAYA 59; BW 3; CA 146; CANR 88
McCann, Arthur
    See Campbell, John W(ood, Jr.)
McCann, Edson
    See Pohl, Frederik
McCarthy, Charles, Jr. 1933-
    See McCarthy, Cormac
    See also CANR 42, 69, 101; CN 7; CPW; CSW; DA3; DAM POP; MTCW 2
McCarthy, Cormac ...... **CLC 4, 57, 101, 204**
    See McCarthy, Charles, Jr.
    See also AAYA 41; AMWS 8; BPFB 2; CA 13-16R; CANR 10; DLB 6, 143, 256; EWL 3; LATS 1:2; TCWW 2
McCarthy, Mary (Therese)
    1912-1989 .. **CLC 1, 3, 5, 14, 24, 39, 59; SSC 24**
    See also AMW; BPFB 2; CA 5-8R; 129; CANR 16, 50, 64; DA3; DLB 2; DLBY 1981; EWL 3; FW; INT CANR-16; MAWW; MTCW 1, 2; RGAL 4; TUS
McCartney, (James) Paul 1942- . **CLC 12, 35**
    See also CA 146; CANR 111
McCauley, Stephen (D.) 1955- .... **CLC 50**
    See also CA 141
McClaren, Peter .... **CLC 70**
McClure, Michael (Thomas) 1932- ... **CLC 6, 10**
    See also BG 3; CA 21-24R; CAD; CANR 17, 46, 77, 131; CD 5; CP 7; DLB 16; WP
McCorkle, Jill (Collins) 1958- .... **CLC 51**
    See also CA 121; CANR 113; CSW; DLB 234; DLBY 1987

O'Flaherty, Liam 1896-1984 .... **CLC 5, 34; SSC 6**
See also CA 101; 113; CANR 35; DLB 36, 162; DLBY 1984; MTCW 1, 2; RGEL 2; RGSF 2; SSFS 5, 20

Ogai
See Mori Ogai
See also MJW

Ogilvy, Gavin
See Barrie, J(ames) M(atthew)

O'Grady, Standish (James)
1846-1928 .... **TCLC 5**
See also CA 104; 157

O'Grady, Timothy 1951- .... **CLC 59**
See also CA 138

O'Hara, Frank 1926-1966 .... **CLC 2, 5, 13, 78; PC 45**
See also CA 9-12R; 25-28R; CANR 33; DA3; DAM POET; DLB 5, 16, 193; EWL 3; MTCW 1, 2; PFS 8; 12; RGAL 4; WP

O'Hara, John (Henry) 1905-1970 . **CLC 1, 2, 3, 6, 11, 42; SSC 15**
See also AMW; BPFB 3; CA 5-8R; 25-28R; CANR 31, 60; CDALB 1929-1941; DAM NOV; DLB 9, 86; DLBD 2; EWL 3; MTCW 1, 2; NFS 11; RGAL 4; RGSF 2

O Hehir, Diana 1922- .... **CLC 41**
See also CA 93-96

Ohiyesa
See Eastman, Charles A(lexander)

Okada, John 1923-1971 .... **AAL**
See also BYA 14; CA 212

Okigbo, Christopher (Ifenayichukwu)
1932-1967 .... **BLC 3; CLC 25, 84; PC 7**
See also AFW; BW 1, 3; CA 77-80; CANR 74; CDWLB 3; DAM MULT, POET; DLB 125; EWL 3; MTCW 1, 2; RGEL 2

Okri, Ben 1959- .... **CLC 87**
See also AFW; BRWS 5; BW 2, 3; CA 130; 138; CANR 65, 128; CN 7; DLB 157, 231; EWL 3; INT CA-138; MTCW 2; RGSF 2; SSFS 20; WLIT 2; WWE 1

Olds, Sharon 1942- .. **CLC 32, 39, 85; PC 22**
See also AMWS 10; CA 101; CANR 18, 41, 66, 98, 135; CP 7; CPW; CWP; DAM POET; DLB 120; MTCW 2; PFS 17

Oldstyle, Jonathan
See Irving, Washington

Olesha, Iurii
See Olesha, Yuri (Karlovich)
See also RGWL 2

Olesha, Iurii Karlovich
See Olesha, Yuri (Karlovich)
See also DLB 272

Olesha, Yuri (Karlovich) 1899-1960 . **CLC 8; SSC 69; TCLC 136**
See also Olesha, Iurii; Olesha, Iurii Karlovich; Olesha, Yury Karlovich
See also CA 85-88; EW 11; RGWL 3

Olesha, Yury Karlovich
See Olesha, Yuri (Karlovich)
See also EWL 3

Oliphant, Mrs.
See Oliphant, Margaret (Oliphant Wilson)
See also SUFW

Oliphant, Laurence 1829(?)-1888 .. **NCLC 47**
See also DLB 18, 166

Oliphant, Margaret (Oliphant Wilson)
1828-1897 .... **NCLC 11, 61; SSC 25**
See Oliphant, Mrs.
See also BRWS 10; DLB 18, 159, 190; HGG; RGEL 2; RGSF 2

Oliver, Mary 1935- .... **CLC 19, 34, 98**
See also AMWS 7; CA 21-24R; CANR 9, 43, 84, 92; CP 7; CWP; DLB 5, 193; EWL 3; PFS 15

Olivier, Laurence (Kerr) 1907-1989 . **CLC 20**
See also CA 111; 150; 129

Olsen, Tillie 1912- ... **CLC 4, 13, 114; SSC 11**
See also AAYA 51; AMWS 13; BYA 11; CA 1-4R; CANR 1, 43, 74, 132; CDALBS; CN 7; DA; DA3; DAB; DAC; DAM MST; DLB 28, 206; DLBY 1980; EWL 3; EXPS; FW; MTCW 1, 2; RGAL 4; RGSF 2; SSFS 1; TUS

Olson, Charles (John) 1910-1970 .. **CLC 1, 2, 5, 6, 9, 11, 29; PC 19**
See also AMWS 2; CA 13-16; 25-28R; CABS 2; CANR 35, 61; CAP 1; DAM POET; DLB 5, 16, 193; EWL 3; MTCW 1, 2; RGAL 4; WP

Olson, Toby 1937- .... **CLC 28**
See also CA 65-68; CANR 9, 31, 84; CP 7

Olyesha, Yuri
See Olesha, Yuri (Karlovich)

Olympiodorus of Thebes c. 375-c.
430 .... **CMLC 59**

Omar Khayyam
See Khayyam, Omar
See also RGWL 2, 3

Ondaatje, (Philip) Michael 1943- .... **CLC 14, 29, 51, 76, 180; PC 28**
See also CA 77-80; CANR 42, 74, 109, 133; CN 7; CP 7; DA3; DAB; DAC; DAM MST; DLB 60; EWL 3; LATS 1:2; LMFS 2; MTCW 2; PFS 8, 19; TWA; WWE 1

Oneal, Elizabeth 1934-
See Oneal, Zibby
See also CA 106; CANR 28, 84; MAICYA 1, 2; SATA 30, 82; YAW

Oneal, Zibby .... **CLC 30**
See Oneal, Elizabeth
See also AAYA 5, 41; BYA 13; CLR 13; JRDA; WYA

O'Neill, Eugene (Gladstone)
1888-1953 ... **DC 20; TCLC 1, 6, 27, 49; WLC**
See also AAYA 54; AITN 1; AMW; AMWC 1; CA 110; 132; CAD; CANR 131; CDALB 1929-1941; DA; DA3; DAB; DAC; DAM DRAM, MST; DFS 2, 4, 5, 6, 9, 11, 12, 16, 20; DLB 7; EWL 3; LAIT 3; LMFS 2; MTCW 1, 2; RGAL 4; TUS

Onetti, Juan Carlos 1909-1994 ... **CLC 7, 10; HLCS 2; SSC 23; TCLC 131**
See also CA 85-88; 145; CANR 32, 63; CDWLB 3; CWW 2; DAM MULT, NOV; DLB 113; EWL 3; HW 1, 2; LAW; MTCW 1, 2; RGSF 2

O Nuallain, Brian 1911-1966
See O'Brien, Flann
See also CA 21-22; 25-28R; CAP 2; DLB 231; FANT; TEA

Ophuls, Max 1902-1957 .... **TCLC 79**
See also CA 113

Opie, Amelia 1769-1853 .... **NCLC 65**
See also DLB 116, 159; RGEL 2

Oppen, George 1908-1984 ..... **CLC 7, 13, 34; PC 35; TCLC 107**
See also CA 13-16R; 113; CANR 8, 82; DLB 5, 165

Oppenheim, E(dward) Phillips
1866-1946 .... **TCLC 45**
See also CA 111; 202; CMW 4; DLB 70

Opuls, Max
See Ophuls, Max

Orage, A(lfred) R(ichard)
1873-1934 .... **TCLC 157**
See also CA 122

Origen c. 185-c. 254 .... **CMLC 19**

Orlovitz, Gil 1918-1973 .... **CLC 22**
See also CA 77-80; 45-48; DLB 2, 5

O'Rourke, P(atrick) J(ake) 1947- .. **CLC 209**
See also CA 77-80; CANR 13, 41, 67, 111; CPW; DLB 185; DAM POP

Orris
See Ingelow, Jean

Ortega y Gasset, Jose 1883-1955 .... **HLC 2; TCLC 9**
See also CA 106; 130; DAM MULT; EW 9; EWL 3; HW 1, 2; MTCW 1, 2

Ortese, Anna Maria 1914-1998 .... **CLC 89**
See also DLB 177; EWL 3

Ortiz, Simon J(oseph) 1941- ... **CLC 45, 208; NNAL; PC 17**
See also AMWS 4; CA 134; CANR 69, 118; CP 7; DAM MULT, POET; DLB 120, 175, 256; EXPP; PFS 4, 16; RGAL 4

Orton, Joe ...... **CLC 4, 13, 43; DC 3; TCLC 157**
See Orton, John Kingsley
See also BRWS 5; CBD; CDBLB 1960 to Present; DFS 3, 6; DLB 13; GLL 1; MTCW 2; RGEL 2; TEA; WLIT 4

Orton, John Kingsley 1933-1967
See Orton, Joe
See also CA 85-88; CANR 35, 66; DAM DRAM; MTCW 1, 2

Orwell, George ...... **SSC 68; TCLC 2, 6, 15, 31, 51, 128, 129; WLC**
See Blair, Eric (Arthur)
See also BPFB 3; BRW 7; BYA 5; CDBLB 1945-1960; CLR 68; DAB; DLB 15, 98, 195, 255; EWL 3; EXPN; LAIT 4, 5; LATS 1:1; NFS 3, 7; RGEL 2; SCFW 2; SFW 4; SSFS 4; TEA; WLIT 4; YAW

Osborne, David
See Silverberg, Robert

Osborne, George
See Silverberg, Robert

Osborne, John (James) 1929-1994 .... **CLC 1, 2, 5, 11, 45; TCLC 153; WLC**
See also BRWS 1; CA 13-16R; 147; CANR 21, 56; CDBLB 1945-1960; DA; DAB; DAC; DAM DRAM, MST; DFS 4, 19; DLB 13; EWL 3; MTCW 1, 2; RGEL 2

Osborne, Lawrence 1958- .... **CLC 50**
See also CA 189

Osbourne, Lloyd 1868-1947 .... **TCLC 93**

Osgood, Frances Sargent
1811-1850 .... **NCLC 141**
See also DLB 250

Oshima, Nagisa 1932- .... **CLC 20**
See also CA 116; 121; CANR 78

Oskison, John Milton
1874-1947 .... **NNAL; TCLC 35**
See also CA 144; CANR 84; DAM MULT; DLB 175

Ossian c. 3rd cent. - .... **CMLC 28**
See Macpherson, James

Ossoli, Sarah Margaret (Fuller)
1810-1850 .... **NCLC 5, 50**
See Fuller, Margaret; Fuller, Sarah Margaret
See also CDALB 1640-1865; FW; LMFS 1; SATA 25

Ostriker, Alicia (Suskin) 1937- .... **CLC 132**
See also CA 25-28R; CAAS 24; CANR 10, 30, 62, 99; CWP; DLB 120; EXPP; PFS 19

Ostrovsky, Aleksandr Nikolaevich
See Ostrovsky, Alexander
See also DLB 277

Ostrovsky, Alexander 1823-1886 .. **NCLC 30, 57**
See Ostrovsky, Aleksandr Nikolaevich

Otero, Blas de 1916-1979 .... **CLC 11**
See also CA 89-92; DLB 134; EWL 3

O'Trigger, Sir Lucius
See Horne, Richard Henry Hengist

Otto, Rudolf 1869-1937 .... **TCLC 85**

Otto, Whitney 1955- .... **CLC 70**
See also CA 140; CANR 120

Otway, Thomas 1652-1685 ... **DC 24; LC 106**
See also DAM DRAM; DLB 80; RGEL 2

Pascal, Blaise 1623-1662 .... **LC 35**
   See also DLB 268; EW 3; GFL Beginnings
     to 1789; RGWL 2, 3; TWA
Pascoli, Giovanni 1855-1912 .... **TCLC 45**
   See also CA 170; EW 7; EWL 3
Pasolini, Pier Paolo 1922-1975 .. **CLC 20, 37,**
   106; PC 17
   See also CA 93-96; 61-64; CANR 63; DLB
     128, 177; EWL 3; MTCW 1; RGWL 2, 3
Pasquini
   See Silone, Ignazio
Pastan, Linda (Olenik) 1932- .... **CLC 27**
   See also CA 61-64; CANR 18, 40, 61, 113;
     CP 7; CSW; CWP; DAM POET; DLB 5;
     PFS 8
Pasternak, Boris (Leonidovich)
   1890-1960 ...... **CLC 7, 10, 18, 63; PC 6;**
   SSC 31; WLC
   See also BPFB 3; CA 127; 116; DA; DA3;
     DAB; DAC; DAM MST, NOV, POET;
     DLB 302; EW 10; MTCW 1, 2; RGSF 2;
     RGWL 2, 3; TWA; WP
Patchen, Kenneth 1911-1972 .... **CLC 1, 2, 18**
   See also BG 3; CA 1-4R; 33-36R; CANR
     3, 35; DAM POET; DLB 16, 48; EWL 3;
     MTCW 1; RGAL 4
Pater, Walter (Horatio) 1839-1894 . **NCLC 7,**
   90, 159
   See also BRW 5; CDBLB 1832-1890; DLB
     57, 156; RGEL 2; TEA
Paterson, A(ndrew) B(arton)
   1864-1941 .... **TCLC 32**
   See also CA 155; DLB 230; RGEL 2; SATA
     97
Paterson, Banjo
   See Paterson, A(ndrew) B(arton)
Paterson, Katherine (Womeldorf)
   1932- .... **CLC 12, 30**
   See also AAYA 1, 31; BYA 1, 2, 7; CA 21-
     24R; CANR 28, 59, 111; CLR 7, 50;
     CWRI 5; DLB 52; JRDA; LAIT 4; MAI-
     CYA 1, 2; MAICYAS 1; MTCW 1; SATA
     13, 53, 92, 133; WYA; YAW
Patmore, Coventry Kersey Dighton
   1823-1896 .... **NCLC 9; PC 59**
   See also DLB 35, 98; RGEL 2; TEA
Paton, Alan (Stewart) 1903-1988 ...... **CLC 4,**
   10, 25, 55, 106; TCLC 165; WLC
   See also AAYA 26; AFW; BPFB 3; BRWS
     2; BYA 1; CA 13-16; 125; CANR 22;
     CAP 1; DA; DA3; DAB; DAC; DAM
     MST, NOV; DLB 225; DLBD 17; EWL
     3; EXPN; LAIT 4; MTCW 1, 2; NFS 3,
     12; RGEL 2; SATA 11; SATA-Obit 56;
     TWA; WLIT 2; WWE 1
Paton Walsh, Gillian 1937- .... **CLC 35**
   See Paton Walsh, Jill; Walsh, Jill Paton
   See also AAYA 11; CANR 38, 83; CLR 2,
     65; DLB 161; JRDA; MAICYA 1, 2;
     SAAS 3; SATA 4, 72, 109; YAW
Paton Walsh, Jill
   See Paton Walsh, Gillian
   See also AAYA 47; BYA 1, 8
Patterson, (Horace) Orlando (Lloyd)
   1940- .... **BLCS**
   See also BW 1; CA 65-68; CANR 27, 84;
     CN 7
Patton, George S(mith), Jr.
   1885-1945 .... **TCLC 79**
   See also CA 189
Paulding, James Kirke 1778-1860 ... **NCLC 2**
   See also DLB 3, 59, 74, 250; RGAL 4
Paulin, Thomas Neilson 1949-
   See Paulin, Tom
   See also CA 123; 128; CANR 98; CP 7
Paulin, Tom .... **CLC 37, 177**
   See Paulin, Thomas Neilson
   See also DLB 40
Pausanias c. 1st cent. - .... **CMLC 36**

Paustovsky, Konstantin (Georgievich)
   1892-1968 .... **CLC 40**
   See also CA 93-96; 25-28R; DLB 272;
     EWL 3
Pavese, Cesare 1908-1950 .... **PC 13; SSC 19;**
   TCLC 3
   See also CA 104; 169; DLB 128, 177; EW
     12; EWL 3; PFS 20; RGSF 2; RGWL 2,
     3; TWA
Pavic, Milorad 1929- .... **CLC 60**
   See also CA 136; CDWLB 4; CWW 2; DLB
     181; EWL 3; RGWL 3
Pavlov, Ivan Petrovich 1849-1936 . **TCLC 91**
   See also CA 118; 180
Pavlova, Karolina Karlovna
   1807-1893 .... **NCLC 138**
   See also DLB 205
Payne, Alan
   See Jakes, John (William)
Paz, Gil
   See Lugones, Leopoldo
Paz, Octavio 1914-1998 . **CLC 3, 4, 6, 10, 19,**
   51, 65, 119; HLC 2; PC 1, 48; WLC
   See also AAYA 50; CA 73-76; 165; CANR
     32, 65, 104; CWW 2; DA; DA3; DAB;
     DAC; DAM MST, MULT, POET; DLB
     290; DLBY 1990, 1998; DNFS 1; EWL
     3; HW 1, 2; LAW; LAWS 1; MTCW 1, 2;
     PFS 18; RGWL 2, 3; SSFS 13; TWA;
     WLIT 1
p'Bitek, Okot 1931-1982 .... **BLC 3; CLC 96;**
   TCLC 149
   See also AFW; BW 2, 3; CA 124; 107;
     CANR 82; DAM MULT; DLB 125; EWL
     3; MTCW 1, 2; RGEL 2; WLIT 2
Peacham, Henry 1578-c. 1644 .... **LC 119**
   See also DLB 151
Peacock, Molly 1947- .... **CLC 60**
   See also CA 103; CAAS 21; CANR 52, 84;
     CP 7; CWP; DLB 120, 282
Peacock, Thomas Love
   1785-1866 .... **NCLC 22**
   See also BRW 4; DLB 96, 116; RGEL 2;
     RGSF 2
Peake, Mervyn 1911-1968 .... **CLC 7, 54**
   See also CA 5-8R; 25-28R; CANR 3; DLB
     15, 160, 255; FANT; MTCW 1; RGEL 2;
     SATA 23; SFW 4
Pearce, Philippa
   See Christie, Philippa
   See also CA 5-8R; CANR 4, 109; CWRI 5;
     FANT; MAICYA 2
Pearl, Eric
   See Elman, Richard (Martin)
Pearson, T(homas) R(eid) 1956- .... **CLC 39**
   See also CA 120; 130; CANR 97; CSW;
     INT CA-130
Peck, Dale 1967- .... **CLC 81**
   See also CA 146; CANR 72, 127; GLL 2
Peck, John (Frederick) 1941- .... **CLC 3**
   See also CA 49-52; CANR 3, 100; CP 7
Peck, Richard (Wayne) 1934- .... **CLC 21**
   See also AAYA 1, 24; BYA 1, 6, 8, 11; CA
     85-88; CANR 19, 38, 129; CLR 15; INT
     CANR-19; JRDA; MAICYA 1, 2; SAAS
     2; SATA 18, 55, 97; SATA-Essay 110;
     WYA; YAW
Peck, Robert Newton 1928- .... **CLC 17**
   See also AAYA 3, 43; BYA 1, 6; CA 81-84,
     182; CAAE 182; CANR 31, 63, 127; CLR
     45; DA; DAC; DAM MST; JRDA; LAIT
     3; MAICYA 1, 2; SAAS 1; SATA 21, 62,
     111; SATA-Essay 108; WYA; YAW
Peckinpah, (David) Sam(uel)
   1925-1984 .... **CLC 20**
   See also CA 109; 114; CANR 82

Pedersen, Knut 1859-1952
   See Hamsun, Knut
   See also CA 104; 119; CANR 63; MTCW
     1, 2
Peele, George .... **LC 115**
   See also BW 1; DLB 62, 167; RGEL 2
Peeslake, Gaffer
   See Durrell, Lawrence (George)
Peguy, Charles (Pierre)
   1873-1914 .... **TCLC 10**
   See also CA 107; 193; DLB 258; EWL 3;
     GFL 1789 to the Present
Peirce, Charles Sanders
   1839-1914 .... **TCLC 81**
   See also CA 194; DLB 270
Pellicer, Carlos 1897(?)-1977 .... **HLCS 2**
   See also CA 153; 69-72; DLB 290; EWL 3;
     HW 1
Pena, Ramon del Valle y
   See Valle-Inclan, Ramon (Maria) del
Pendennis, Arthur Esquir
   See Thackeray, William Makepeace
Penn, Arthur
   See Matthews, (James) Brander
Penn, William 1644-1718 .... **LC 25**
   See also DLB 24
PEPECE
   See Prado (Calvo), Pedro
Pepys, Samuel 1633-1703 ... **LC 11, 58; WLC**
   See also BRW 2; CDBLB 1660-1789; DA;
     DA3; DAB; DAC; DAM MST; DLB 101,
     213; NCFS 4; RGEL 2; TEA; WLIT 3
Percy, Thomas 1729-1811 .... **NCLC 95**
   See also DLB 104
Percy, Walker 1916-1990 .... **CLC 2, 3, 6, 8,**
   14, 18, 47, 65
   See also AMWS 3; BPFB 3; CA 1-4R; 131;
     CANR 1, 23, 64; CPW; CSW; DA3;
     DAM NOV, POP; DLB 2; DLBY 1980,
     1990; EWL 3; MTCW 1, 2; RGAL 4;
     TUS
Percy, William Alexander
   1885-1942 .... **TCLC 84**
   See also CA 163; MTCW 2
Perec, Georges 1936-1982 .... **CLC 56, 116**
   See also CA 141; DLB 83, 299; EWL 3;
     GFL 1789 to the Present; RGWL 3
Pereda (y Sanchez de Porrua), Jose Maria
   de 1833-1906 .... **TCLC 16**
   See also CA 117
Pereda y Porrua, Jose Maria de
   See Pereda (y Sanchez de Porrua), Jose
     Maria de
Peregoy, George Weems
   See Mencken, H(enry) L(ouis)
Perelman, S(idney) J(oseph)
   1904-1979 .. **CLC 3, 5, 9, 15, 23, 44, 49;**
   SSC 32
   See also AITN 1, 2; BPFB 3; CA 73-76;
     89-92; CANR 18; DAM DRAM; DLB 11,
     44; MTCW 1, 2; RGAL 4
Peret, Benjamin 1899-1959 .... **PC 33; TCLC**
   20
   See also CA 117; 186; GFL 1789 to the
     Present
Peretz, Isaac Leib
   See Peretz, Isaac Loeb
   See also CA 201
Peretz, Isaac Loeb 1851(?)-1915 .... **SSC 26;**
   TCLC 16
   See Peretz, Isaac Leib
   See also CA 109
Peretz, Yitzkhok Leibush
   See Peretz, Isaac Loeb
Perez Galdos, Benito 1843-1920 ..... **HLCS 2;**
   TCLC 27
   See Galdos, Benito Perez
   See also CA 125; 153; EWL 3; HW 1;
     RGWL 2, 3

EWL 3; EXPN; EXPP; FW; LAIT 4;
MAWW; MTCW 1, 2; NFS 1; PAB; PFS
1, 15; RGAL 4; SATA 96; TUS; WP;
YAW

Plato c. 428B.C.-347B.C. .... **CMLC 8, 75;
WLCS**
See also AW 1; CDWLB 1; DA; DA3;
DAB; DAC; DAM MST; DLB 176; LAIT
1; LATS 1:1; RGWL 2, 3

Platonov, Andrei
See Klimentov, Andrei Platonovich

Platonov, Andrei Platonovich
See Klimentov, Andrei Platonovich
See also DLB 272

Platonov, Andrey Platonovich
See Klimentov, Andrei Platonovich
See also EWL 3

Platt, Kin 1911- .... **CLC 26**
See also AAYA 11; CA 17-20R; CANR 11;
JRDA; SAAS 17; SATA 21, 86; WYA

Plautus c. 254B.C.-c. 184B.C. ...... **CMLC 24;
DC 6**
See also AW 1; CDWLB 1; DLB 211;
RGWL 2, 3

Plick et Plock
See Simenon, Georges (Jacques Christian)

Plieksans, Janis
See Rainis, Janis

Plimpton, George (Ames)
1927-2003 .... **CLC 36**
See also AITN 1; CA 21-24R; 224; CANR
32, 70, 103, 133; DLB 185, 241; MTCW
1, 2; SATA 10; SATA-Obit 150

Pliny the Elder c. 23-79 .... **CMLC 23**
See also DLB 211

Pliny the Younger c. 61-c. 112 ...... **CMLC 62**
See also AW 2; DLB 211

Plomer, William Charles Franklin
1903-1973 .... **CLC 4, 8**
See also AFW; CA 21-22; CANR 34; CAP
2; DLB 20, 162, 191, 225; EWL 3;
MTCW 1; RGEL 2; RGSF 2; SATA 24

Plotinus 204-270 .... **CMLC 46**
See also CDWLB 1; DLB 176

Plowman, Piers
See Kavanagh, Patrick (Joseph)

Plum, J.
See Wodehouse, P(elham) G(renville)

Plumly, Stanley (Ross) 1939- .... **CLC 33**
See also CA 108; 110; CANR 97; CP 7;
DLB 5, 193; INT CA-110

Plumpe, Friedrich Wilhelm
1888-1931 .... **TCLC 53**
See also CA 112

Plutarch c. 46-c. 120 .... **CMLC 60**
See also AW 2; CDWLB 1; DLB 176;
RGWL 2, 3; TWA

Po Chu-i 772-846 .... **CMLC 24**

Podhoretz, Norman 1930- .... **CLC 189**
See also AMWS 8; CA 9-12R; CANR 7,
78, 135

Poe, Edgar Allan 1809-1849 ..... **NCLC 1, 16,
55, 78, 94, 97, 117; PC 1, 54; SSC 1,
22, 34, 35, 54; WLC**
See also AAYA 14; AMW; AMWC 1;
AMWR 2; BPFB 3; BYA 5, 11; CDALB
1640-1865; CMW 4; DA; DA3; DAB;
DAC; DAM MST, POET; DLB 3, 59, 73,
74, 248, 254; EXPP; EXPS; HGG; LAIT
2; LATS 1:1; LMFS 1; MSW; PAB; PFS
1, 3, 9; RGAL 4; RGSF 2; SATA 23;
SCFW 2; SFW 4; SSFS 2, 4, 7, 8, 16;
SUFW; TUS; WP; WYA

Poet of Titchfield Street, The
See Pound, Ezra (Weston Loomis)

Pohl, Frederik 1919- .... **CLC 18; SSC 25**
See also AAYA 24; CA 61-64, 188; CAAE
188; CAAS 1; CANR 11, 37, 81; CN 7;
DLB 8; INT CANR-11; MTCW 1, 2;
SATA 24; SCFW 2; SFW 4

Poirier, Louis 1910-
See Gracq, Julien
See also CA 122; 126

Poitier, Sidney 1927- .... **CLC 26**
See also AAYA 60; BW 1; CA 117; CANR
94

Pokagon, Simon 1830-1899 .... **NNAL**
See also DAM MULT

Polanski, Roman 1933- .... **CLC 16, 178**
See also CA 77-80

Poliakoff, Stephen 1952- .... **CLC 38**
See also CA 106; CANR 116; CBD; CD 5;
DLB 13

Police, The
See Copeland, Stewart (Armstrong); Sum-
mers, Andrew James

Polidori, John William 1795-1821 . **NCLC 51**
See also DLB 116; HGG

Pollitt, Katha 1949- .... **CLC 28, 122**
See also CA 120; 122; CANR 66, 108;
MTCW 1, 2

Pollock, (Mary) Sharon 1936- .... **CLC 50**
See also CA 141; CANR 132; CD 5; CWD;
DAC; DAM DRAM, MST; DFS 3; DLB
60; FW

Pollock, Sharon 1936- .... **DC 20**

Polo, Marco 1254-1324 .... **CMLC 15**

Polonsky, Abraham (Lincoln)
1910-1999 .... **CLC 92**
See also CA 104; 187; DLB 26; INT CA-
104

Polybius c. 200B.C.-c. 118B.C. ...... **CMLC 17**
See also AW 1; DLB 176; RGWL 2, 3

Pomerance, Bernard 1940- .... **CLC 13**
See also CA 101; CAD; CANR 49, 134;
CD 5; DAM DRAM; DFS 9; LAIT 2

Ponge, Francis 1899-1988 .... **CLC 6, 18**
See also CA 85-88; 126; CANR 40, 86;
DAM POET; DLBY 2002; EWL 3; GFL
1789 to the Present; RGWL 2, 3

Poniatowska, Elena 1933- . **CLC 140; HLC 2**
See also CA 101; CANR 32, 66, 107; CD-
WLB 3; CWW 2; DAM MULT; DLB 113;
EWL 3; HW 1, 2; LAWS 1; WLIT 1

Pontoppidan, Henrik 1857-1943 .... **TCLC 29**
See also CA 170; DLB 300

Ponty, Maurice Merleau
See Merleau-Ponty, Maurice

Poole, Josephine .... **CLC 17**
See Helyar, Jane Penelope Josephine
See also SAAS 2; SATA 5

Popa, Vasko 1922-1991 . **CLC 19; TCLC 167**
See also CA 112; 148; CDWLB 4; DLB
181; EWL 3; RGWL 2, 3

Pope, Alexander 1688-1744 ...... **LC 3, 58, 60,
64; PC 26; WLC**
See also BRW 3; BRWC 1; BRWR 1; CD-
BLB 1660-1789; DA; DA3; DAB; DAC;
DAM MST, POET; DLB 95, 101, 213;
EXPP; PAB; PFS 12; RGEL 2; WLIT 3;
WP

Popov, Evgenii Anatol'evich
See Popov, Yevgeny
See also DLB 285

Popov, Yevgeny .... **CLC 59**
See Popov, Evgenii Anatol'evich

Poquelin, Jean-Baptiste
See Moliere

Porete, Marguerite c. 1250-1310 .. **CMLC 73**
See also DLB 208

Porphyry c. 233-c. 305 .... **CMLC 71**

Porter, Connie (Rose) 1959(?)- .... **CLC 70**
See also BW 2, 3; CA 142; CANR 90, 109;
SATA 81, 129

Porter, Gene(va Grace) Stratton .. **TCLC 21**
See Stratton-Porter, Gene(va Grace)
See also BPFB 3; CA 112; CWRI 5; RHW

Porter, Katherine Anne 1890-1980 ... **CLC 1,
3, 7, 10, 13, 15, 27, 101; SSC 4, 31, 43**
See also AAYA 42; AITN 2; AMW; BPFB
3; CA 1-4R; 101; CANR 1, 65; CDALBS;
DA; DA3; DAB; DAC; DAM MST, NOV;
DLB 4, 9, 102; DLBD 12; DLBY 1980;
EWL 3; EXPS; LAIT 3; MAWW; MTCW
1, 2; NFS 14; RGAL 4; RGSF 2; SATA
39; SATA-Obit 23; SSFS 1, 8, 11, 16;
TUS

Porter, Peter (Neville Frederick)
1929- .... **CLC 5, 13, 33**
See also CA 85-88; CP 7; DLB 40, 289;
WWE 1

Porter, William Sydney 1862-1910
See Henry, O.
See also CA 104; 131; CDALB 1865-1917;
DA; DA3; DAB; DAC; DAM MST; DLB
12, 78, 79; MTCW 1, 2; TUS; YABC 2

Portillo (y Pacheco), Jose Lopez
See Lopez Portillo (y Pacheco), Jose

Portillo Trambley, Estela
1927-1998 .... **HLC 2; TCLC 163**
See Trambley, Estela Portillo
See also CANR 32; DAM MULT; DLB
209; HW 1

Posey, Alexander (Lawrence)
1873-1908 .... **NNAL**
See also CA 144; CANR 80; DAM MULT;
DLB 175

Posse, Abel .... **CLC 70**

Post, Melville Davisson
1869-1930 .... **TCLC 39**
See also CA 110; 202; CMW 4

Potok, Chaim 1929-2002 ... **CLC 2, 7, 14, 26,
112**
See also AAYA 15, 50; AITN 1, 2; BPFB 3;
BYA 1; CA 17-20R; 208; CANR 19, 35,
64, 98; CLR 92; CN 7; DA3; DAM NOV;
DLB 28, 152; EXPN; INT CANR-19;
LAIT 4; MTCW 1, 2; NFS 4; SATA 33,
106; SATA-Obit 134; TUS; YAW

Potok, Herbert Harold -2002
See Potok, Chaim

Potok, Herman Harold
See Potok, Chaim

Potter, Dennis (Christopher George)
1935-1994 .... **CLC 58, 86, 123**
See also BRWS 10; CA 107; 145; CANR
33, 61; CBD; DLB 233; MTCW 1

Pound, Ezra (Weston Loomis)
1885-1972 .. **CLC 1, 2, 3, 4, 5, 7, 10, 13,
18, 34, 48, 50, 112; PC 4; WLC**
See also AAYA 47; AMW; AMWR 1; CA
5-8R; 37-40R; CANR 40; CDALB 1917-
1929; DA; DA3; DAB; DAC; DAM MST,
POET; DLB 4, 45, 63; DLBD 15; EFS 2;
EWL 3; EXPP; LMFS 2; MTCW 1, 2;
PAB; PFS 2, 8, 16; RGAL 4; TUS; WP

Povod, Reinaldo 1959-1994 .... **CLC 44**
See also CA 136; 146; CANR 83

Powell, Adam Clayton, Jr.
1908-1972 .... **BLC 3; CLC 89**
See also BW 1, 3; CA 102; 33-36R; CANR
86; DAM MULT

Powell, Anthony (Dymoke)
1905-2000 .... **CLC 1, 3, 7, 9, 10, 31**
See also BRW 7; CA 1-4R; 189; CANR 1,
32, 62, 107; CDBLB 1945-1960; CN 7;
DLB 15; EWL 3; MTCW 1, 2; RGEL 2;
TEA

Powell, Dawn 1896(?)-1965 .... **CLC 66**
See also CA 5-8R; CANR 121; DLBY 1997

Powell, Padgett 1952- .... **CLC 34**
See also CA 126; CANR 63, 101; CSW;
DLB 234; DLBY 01

Powell, (Oval) Talmage 1920-2000
See Queen, Ellery
See also CA 5-8R; CANR 2, 80
Power, Susan 1961- .... **CLC 91**
See also BYA 14; CA 160; CANR 135; NFS 11
Powers, J(ames) F(arl) 1917-1999 ..... **CLC 1, 4, 8, 57; SSC 4**
See also CA 1-4R; 181; CANR 2, 61; CN 7; DLB 130; MTCW 1; RGAL 4; RGSF 2
Powers, John J(ames) 1945-
See Powers, John R.
See also CA 69-72
Powers, John R. .... **CLC 66**
See Powers, John J(ames)
Powers, Richard (S.) 1957- .... **CLC 93**
See also AMWS 9; BPFB 3; CA 148; CANR 80; CN 7
Pownall, David 1938- .... **CLC 10**
See also CA 89-92, 180; CAAS 18; CANR 49, 101; CBD; CD 5; CN 7; DLB 14
Powys, John Cowper 1872-1963 ... **CLC 7, 9, 15, 46, 125**
See also CA 85-88; CANR 106; DLB 15, 255; EWL 3; FANT; MTCW 1, 2; RGEL 2; SUFW
Powys, T(heodore) F(rancis) 1875-1953 .... **TCLC 9**
See also BRWS 8; CA 106; 189; DLB 36, 162; EWL 3; FANT; RGEL 2; SUFW
Prado (Calvo), Pedro 1886-1952 ... **TCLC 75**
See also CA 131; DLB 283; HW 1; LAW
Prager, Emily 1952- .... **CLC 56**
See also CA 204
Pratchett, Terry 1948- .... **CLC 197**
See also AAYA 19, 54; BPFB 3; CA 143; CANR 87, 126; CLR 64; CN 7; CPW; CWRI 5; FANT; SATA 82, 139; SFW 4; SUFW 2
Pratolini, Vasco 1913-1991 .... **TCLC 124**
See also CA 211; DLB 177; EWL 3; RGWL 2, 3
Pratt, E(dwin) J(ohn) 1883(?)-1964 . **CLC 19**
See also CA 141; 93-96; CANR 77; DAC; DAM POET; DLB 92; EWL 3; RGEL 2; TWA
Premchand .... **TCLC 21**
See Srivastava, Dhanpat Rai
See also EWL 3
Preseren, France 1800-1849 .... **NCLC 127**
See also CDWLB 4; DLB 147
Preussler, Otfried 1923- .... **CLC 17**
See also CA 77-80; SATA 24
Prevert, Jacques (Henri Marie) 1900-1977 .... **CLC 15**
See also CA 77-80; 69-72; CANR 29, 61; DLB 258; EWL 3; GFL 1789 to the Present; IDFW 3, 4; MTCW 1; RGWL 2, 3; SATA-Obit 30
Prevost, (Antoine Francois) 1697-1763 .... **LC 1**
See also EW 4; GFL Beginnings to 1789; RGWL 2, 3
Price, (Edward) Reynolds 1933- ... **CLC 3, 6, 13, 43, 50, 63, 212; SSC 22**
See also AMWS 6; CA 1-4R; CANR 1, 37, 57, 87, 128; CN 7; CSW; DAM NOV; DLB 2, 218, 278; EWL 3; INT CANR-37; NFS 18
Price, Richard 1949- .... **CLC 6, 12**
See also CA 49-52; CANR 3; DLBY 1981
Prichard, Katharine Susannah 1883-1969 .... **CLC 46**
See also CA 11-12; CANR 33; CAP 1; DLB 260; MTCW 1; RGEL 2; RGSF 2; SATA 66

Priestley, J(ohn) B(oynton) 1894-1984 .... **CLC 2, 5, 9, 34**
See also BRW 7; CA 9-12R; 113; CANR 33; CDBLB 1914-1945; DA3; DAM DRAM, NOV; DLB 10, 34, 77, 100, 139; DLBY 1984; EWL 3; MTCW 1, 2; RGEL 2; SFW 4
Prince 1958- .... **CLC 35**
See also CA 213
Prince, F(rank) T(empleton) 1912-2003 .... **CLC 22**
See also CA 101; 219; CANR 43, 79; CP 7; DLB 20
Prince Kropotkin
See Kropotkin, Peter (Aleksieevich)
Prior, Matthew 1664-1721 .... **LC 4**
See also DLB 95; RGEL 2
Prishvin, Mikhail 1873-1954 .... **TCLC 75**
See Prishvin, Mikhail Mikhailovich
Prishvin, Mikhail Mikhailovich
See Prishvin, Mikhail
See also DLB 272; EWL 3
Pritchard, William H(arrison) 1932- .... **CLC 34**
See also CA 65-68; CANR 23, 95; DLB 111
Pritchett, V(ictor) S(awdon) 1900-1997 ... **CLC 5, 13, 15, 41; SSC 14**
See also BPFB 3; BRWS 3; CA 61-64; 157; CANR 31, 63; CN 7; DA3; DAM NOV; DLB 15, 139; EWL 3; MTCW 1, 2; RGEL 2; RGSF 2; TEA
Private 19022
See Manning, Frederic
Probst, Mark 1925- .... **CLC 59**
See also CA 130
Prokosch, Frederic 1908-1989 ...... **CLC 4, 48**
See also CA 73-76; 128; CANR 82; DLB 48; MTCW 2
Propertius, Sextus c. 50B.C.-c. 16B.C. .... **CMLC 32**
See also AW 2; CDWLB 1; DLB 211; RGWL 2, 3
Prophet, The
See Dreiser, Theodore (Herman Albert)
Prose, Francine 1947- .... **CLC 45**
See also CA 109; 112; CANR 46, 95, 132; DLB 234; SATA 101, 149
Proudhon
See Cunha, Euclides (Rodrigues Pimenta) da
Proulx, Annie
See Proulx, E(dna) Annie
Proulx, E(dna) Annie 1935- ...... **CLC 81, 158**
See also AMWS 7; BPFB 3; CA 145; CANR 65, 110; CN 7; CPW 1; DA3; DAM POP; MTCW 2; SSFS 18
Proust, (Valentin-Louis-George-Eugene) Marcel 1871-1922 ..... **SSC 75; TCLC 7, 13, 33, 161; WLC**
See also AAYA 58; BPFB 3; CA 104; 120; CANR 110; DA; DA3; DAB; DAC; DAM MST, NOV; DLB 65; EW 8; EWL 3; GFL 1789 to the Present; MTCW 1, 2; RGWL 2, 3; TWA
Prowler, Harley
See Masters, Edgar Lee
Prudentius 348-c. 410-15 .... **CMLC 78**
See also EW 1; RGWL 2, 3
Prus, Boleslaw 1845-1912 .... **TCLC 48**
See also RGWL 2, 3
Pryor, Richard (Franklin Lenox Thomas) 1940- .... **CLC 26**
See also CA 122; 152
Przybyszewski, Stanislaw 1868-1927 .... **TCLC 36**
See also CA 160; DLB 66; EWL 3

Pteleon
See Grieve, C(hristopher) M(urray)
See also DAM POET
Puckett, Lute
See Masters, Edgar Lee
Puig, Manuel 1932-1990 .... **CLC 3, 5, 10, 28, 65, 133; HLC 2**
See also BPFB 3; CA 45-48; CANR 2, 32, 63; CDWLB 3; DA3; DAM MULT; DLB 113; DNFS 1; EWL 3; GLL 1; HW 1, 2; LAW; MTCW 1, 2; RGWL 2, 3; TWA; WLIT 1
Pulitzer, Joseph 1847-1911 .... **TCLC 76**
See also CA 114; DLB 23
Purchas, Samuel 1577(?)-1626 .... **LC 70**
See also DLB 151
Purdy, A(lfred) W(ellington) 1918-2000 .... **CLC 3, 6, 14, 50**
See also CA 81-84; 189; CAAS 17; CANR 42, 66; CP 7; DAC; DAM MST, POET; DLB 88; PFS 5; RGEL 2
Purdy, James (Amos) 1923- .... **CLC 2, 4, 10, 28, 52**
See also AMWS 7; CA 33-36R; CAAS 1; CANR 19, 51, 132; CN 7; DLB 2, 218; EWL 3; INT CANR-19; MTCW 1; RGAL 4
Pure, Simon
See Swinnerton, Frank Arthur
Pushkin, Aleksandr Sergeevich
See Pushkin, Alexander (Sergeyevich)
See also DLB 205
Pushkin, Alexander (Sergeyevich) 1799-1837 .... **NCLC 3, 27, 83; PC 10; SSC 27, 55; WLC**
See Pushkin, Aleksandr Sergeevich
See also DA; DA3; DAB; DAC; DAM DRAM, MST, POET; EW 5; EXPS; RGSF 2; RGWL 2, 3; SATA 61; SSFS 9; TWA
P'u Sung-ling 1640-1715 .... **LC 49; SSC 31**
Putnam, Arthur Lee
See Alger, Horatio, Jr.
Puttenham, George 1529-1590 .... **LC 116**
See also DLB 281
Puzo, Mario 1920-1999 .... **CLC 1, 2, 6, 36, 107**
See also BPFB 3; CA 65-68; 185; CANR 4, 42, 65, 99, 131; CN 7; CPW; DA3; DAM NOV, POP; DLB 6; MTCW 1, 2; NFS 16; RGAL 4
Pygge, Edward
See Barnes, Julian (Patrick)
Pyle, Ernest Taylor 1900-1945
See Pyle, Ernie
See also CA 115; 160
Pyle, Ernie .... **TCLC 75**
See Pyle, Ernest Taylor
See also DLB 29; MTCW 2
Pyle, Howard 1853-1911 .... **TCLC 81**
See also AAYA 57; BYA 2, 4; CA 109; 137; CLR 22; DLB 42, 188; DLBD 13; LAIT 1; MAICYA 1, 2; SATA 16, 100; WCH; YAW
Pym, Barbara (Mary Crampton) 1913-1980 .... **CLC 13, 19, 37, 111**
See also BPFB 3; BRWS 2; CA 13-14; 97-100; CANR 13, 34; CAP 1; DLB 14, 207; DLBY 1987; EWL 3; MTCW 1, 2; RGEL 2; TEA
Pynchon, Thomas (Ruggles, Jr.) 1937- ...... **CLC 2, 3, 6, 9, 11, 18, 33, 62, 72, 123, 192; SSC 14, 84; WLC**
See also AMWS 2; BEST 90:2; BPFB 3; CA 17-20R; CANR 22, 46, 73; CN 7; CPW 1; DA; DA3; DAB; DAC; DAM MST, NOV, POP; DLB 2, 173; EWL 3; MTCW 1, 2; RGAL 4; SFW 4; TUS
Pythagoras c. 582B.C.-c. 507B.C. . **CMLC 22**
See also DLB 176

Q
See Quiller-Couch, Sir Arthur (Thomas)

Qian, Chongzhu
See Ch'ien, Chung-shu

Qian, Sima 145B.C.-c. 89B.C. .... **CMLC 72**

Qian Zhongshu
See Ch'ien, Chung-shu
See also CWW 2

Qroll
See Dagerman, Stig (Halvard)

Quarles, Francis 1592-1644 .... **LC 117**
See also DLB 126; RGEL 2

Quarrington, Paul (Lewis) 1953- ..... **CLC 65**
See also CA 129; CANR 62, 95

Quasimodo, Salvatore 1901-1968 .... **CLC 10; PC 47**
See also CA 13-16; 25-28R; CAP 1; DLB 114; EW 12; EWL 3; MTCW 1; RGWL 2, 3

Quatermass, Martin
See Carpenter, John (Howard)

Quay, Stephen 1947- .... **CLC 95**
See also CA 189

Quay, Timothy 1947- .... **CLC 95**
See also CA 189

Queen, Ellery .... **CLC 3, 11**
See Dannay, Frederic; Davidson, Avram (James); Deming, Richard; Fairman, Paul W.; Flora, Fletcher; Hoch, Edward D(entinger); Kane, Henry; Lee, Manfred B(ennington); Marlowe, Stephen; Powell, (Oval) Talmage; Sheldon, Walter J(ames); Sturgeon, Theodore (Hamilton); Tracy, Don(ald Fiske); Vance, John Holbrook
See also BPFB 3; CMW 4; MSW; RGAL 4

Queen, Ellery, Jr.
See Dannay, Frederic; Lee, Manfred B(ennington)

Queneau, Raymond 1903-1976 ..... **CLC 2, 5, 10, 42**
See also CA 77-80; 69-72; CANR 32; DLB 72, 258; EW 12; EWL 3; GFL 1789 to the Present; MTCW 1, 2; RGWL 2, 3

Quevedo, Francisco de 1580-1645 .... **LC 23**

Quiller-Couch, Sir Arthur (Thomas)
1863-1944 .... **TCLC 53**
See also CA 118; 166; DLB 135, 153, 190; HGG; RGEL 2; SUFW 1

Quin, Ann (Marie) 1936-1973 .... **CLC 6**
See also CA 9-12R; 45-48; DLB 14, 231

Quincey, Thomas de
See De Quincey, Thomas

Quindlen, Anna 1953- .... **CLC 191**
See also AAYA 35; CA 138; CANR 73, 126; DA3; DLB 292; MTCW 2

Quinn, Martin
See Smith, Martin Cruz

Quinn, Peter 1947- .... **CLC 91**
See also CA 197

Quinn, Simon
See Smith, Martin Cruz

Quintana, Leroy V. 1944- ...... **HLC 2; PC 36**
See also CA 131; CANR 65; DAM MULT; DLB 82; HW 1, 2

Quintilian c. 35-40-c. 96. .... **CMLC 77**
See also AW 2; DLB 211; RGWL 2, 3

Quiroga, Horacio (Sylvestre)
1878-1937 .... **HLC 2; TCLC 20**
See also CA 117; 131; DAM MULT; EWL 3; HW 1; LAW; MTCW 1; RGSF 2; WLIT 1

Quoirez, Francoise 1935- .... **CLC 9**
See Sagan, Francoise
See also CA 49-52; CANR 6, 39, 73; MTCW 1, 2; TWA

Raabe, Wilhelm (Karl) 1831-1910 . **TCLC 45**
See also CA 167; DLB 129

Rabe, David (William) 1940- .. **CLC 4, 8, 33, 200; DC 16**
See also CA 85-88; CABS 3; CAD; CANR 59, 129; CD 5; DAM DRAM; DFS 3, 8, 13; DLB 7, 228; EWL 3

Rabelais, Francois 1494-1553 .... **LC 5, 60; WLC**
See also DA; DAB; DAC; DAM MST; EW 2; GFL Beginnings to 1789; LMFS 1; RGWL 2, 3; TWA

Rabinovitch, Sholem 1859-1916
See Aleichem, Sholom
See also CA 104

Rabinyan, Dorit 1972- .... **CLC 119**
See also CA 170

Rachilde
See Vallette, Marguerite Eymery; Vallette, Marguerite Eymery
See also EWL 3

Racine, Jean 1639-1699 .... **LC 28, 113**
See also DA3; DAB; DAM MST; DLB 268; EW 3; GFL Beginnings to 1789; LMFS 1; RGWL 2, 3; TWA

Radcliffe, Ann (Ward) 1764-1823 ... **NCLC 6, 55, 106**
See also DLB 39, 178; HGG; LMFS 1; RGEL 2; SUFW; WLIT 3

Radclyffe-Hall, Marguerite
See Hall, (Marguerite) Radclyffe

Radiguet, Raymond 1903-1923 ...... **TCLC 29**
See also CA 162; DLB 65; EWL 3; GFL 1789 to the Present; RGWL 2, 3

Radnoti, Miklos 1909-1944 .... **TCLC 16**
See also CA 118; 212; CDWLB 4; DLB 215; EWL 3; RGWL 2, 3

Rado, James 1939- .... **CLC 17**
See also CA 105

Radvanyi, Netty 1900-1983
See Seghers, Anna
See also CA 85-88; 110; CANR 82

Rae, Ben
See Griffiths, Trevor

Raeburn, John (Hay) 1941- .... **CLC 34**
See also CA 57-60

Ragni, Gerome 1942-1991 .... **CLC 17**
See also CA 105; 134

Rahv, Philip .... **CLC 24**
See Greenberg, Ivan
See also DLB 137

Raimund, Ferdinand Jakob
1790-1836 .... **NCLC 69**
See also DLB 90

Raine, Craig (Anthony) 1944- .. **CLC 32, 103**
See also CA 108; CANR 29, 51, 103; CP 7; DLB 40; PFS 7

Raine, Kathleen (Jessie) 1908-2003 .. **CLC 7, 45**
See also CA 85-88; 218; CANR 46, 109; CP 7; DLB 20; EWL 3; MTCW 1; RGEL 2

Rainis, Janis 1865-1929 .... **TCLC 29**
See also CA 170; CDWLB 4; DLB 220; EWL 3

Rakosi, Carl .... **CLC 47**
See Rawley, Callman
See also CA 228; CAAS 5; CP 7; DLB 193

Ralegh, Sir Walter
See Raleigh, Sir Walter
See also BRW 1; RGEL 2; WP

Raleigh, Richard
See Lovecraft, H(oward) P(hillips)

Raleigh, Sir Walter 1554(?)-1618 .... **LC 31, 39; PC 31**
See also Raleigh, Sir Walter
See also CDBLB Before 1660; DLB 172; EXPP; PFS 14; TEA

Rallentando, H. P.
See Sayers, Dorothy L(eigh)

Ramal, Walter
See de la Mare, Walter (John)

Ramana Maharshi 1879-1950 .... **TCLC 84**

Ramoacn y Cajal, Santiago
1852-1934 .... **TCLC 93**

Ramon, Juan
See Jimenez (Mantecon), Juan Ramon

Ramos, Graciliano 1892-1953 .... **TCLC 32**
See also CA 167; DLB 307; EWL 3; HW 2; LAW; WLIT 1

Rampersad, Arnold 1941- .... **CLC 44**
See also BW 2, 3; CA 127; 133; CANR 81; DLB 111; INT CA-133

Rampling, Anne
See Rice, Anne
See also GLL 2

Ramsay, Allan 1686(?)-1758 .... **LC 29**
See also DLB 95; RGEL 2

Ramsay, Jay
See Campbell, (John) Ramsey

Ramuz, Charles-Ferdinand
1878-1947 .... **TCLC 33**
See also CA 165; EWL 3

Rand, Ayn 1905-1982 ...... **CLC 3, 30, 44, 79; WLC**
See also AAYA 10; AMWS 4; BPFB 3; BYA 12; CA 13-16R; 105; CANR 27, 73; CDALBS; CPW; DA; DA3; DAC; DAM MST, NOV, POP; DLB 227, 279; MTCW 1, 2; NFS 10, 16; RGAL 4; SFW 4; TUS; YAW

Randall, Dudley (Felker) 1914-2000 . **BLC 3; CLC 1, 135**
See also BW 1, 3; CA 25-28R; 189; CANR 23, 82; DAM MULT; DLB 41; PFS 5

Randall, Robert
See Silverberg, Robert

Ranger, Ken
See Creasey, John

Rank, Otto 1884-1939 .... **TCLC 115**

Ransom, John Crowe 1888-1974 .. **CLC 2, 4, 5, 11, 24; PC 61**
See also AMW; CA 5-8R; 49-52; CANR 6, 34; CDALBS; DA3; DAM POET; DLB 45, 63; EWL 3; EXPP; MTCW 1, 2; RGAL 4; TUS

Rao, Raja 1909- .... **CLC 25, 56**
See also CA 73-76; CANR 51; CN 7; DAM NOV; EWL 3; MTCW 1, 2; RGEL 2; RGSF 2

Raphael, Frederic (Michael) 1931- ... **CLC 2, 14**
See also CA 1-4R; CANR 1, 86; CN 7; DLB 14

Ratcliffe, James P.
See Mencken, H(enry) L(ouis)

Rathbone, Julian 1935- .... **CLC 41**
See also CA 101; CANR 34, 73

Rattigan, Terence (Mervyn)
1911-1977 .... **CLC 7; DC 18**
See also BRWS 7; CA 85-88; 73-76; CBD; CDBLB 1945-1960; DAM DRAM; DFS 8; DLB 13; IDFW 3, 4; MTCW 1, 2; RGEL 2

Ratushinskaya, Irina 1954- .... **CLC 54**
See also CA 129; CANR 68; CWW 2

Raven, Simon (Arthur Noel)
1927-2001 .... **CLC 14**
See also CA 81-84; 197; CANR 86; CN 7; DLB 271

Ravenna, Michael
See Welty, Eudora (Alice)

Rawley, Callman 1903-2004
See Rakosi, Carl
See also CA 21-24R; CANR 12, 32, 91

Richardson, Henry Handel .... **TCLC 4**
See Richardson (Robertson), Ethel Florence
Lindesay
See also DLB 197; EWL 3; RGEL 2; RGSF
2

Richardson, John 1796-1852 .... **NCLC 55**
See also CCA 1; DAC; DLB 99

Richardson, Samuel 1689-1761 ...... **LC 1, 44;
WLC**
See also BRW 3; CDBLB 1660-1789; DA;
DAB; DAC; DAM MST, NOV; DLB 39;
RGEL 2; TEA; WLIT 3

Richardson, Willis 1889-1977 .... **HR 3**
See also BW 1; CA 124; DLB 51; SATA 60

Richler, Mordecai 1931-2001 .... **CLC 3, 5, 9,
13, 18, 46, 70, 185**
See also AITN 1; CA 65-68; 201; CANR
31, 62, 111; CCA 1; CLR 17; CWRI 5;
DAC; DAM MST, NOV; DLB 53; EWL
3; MAICYA 1, 2; MTCW 1, 2; RGEL 2;
SATA 44, 98; SATA-Brief 27; TWA

Richter, Conrad (Michael)
1890-1968 .... **CLC 30**
See also AAYA 21; BYA 2; CA 5-8R; 25-
28R; CANR 23; DLB 9, 212; LAIT 1;
MTCW 1, 2; RGAL 4; SATA 3; TCWW
2; TUS; YAW

Ricostranza, Tom
See Ellis, Trey

Riddell, Charlotte 1832-1906 .... **TCLC 40**
See Riddell, Mrs. J. H.
See also CA 165; DLB 156

Riddell, Mrs. J. H.
See Riddell, Charlotte
See also HGG; SUFW

Ridge, John Rollin 1827-1867 ...... **NCLC 82;
NNAL**
See also CA 144; DAM MULT; DLB 175

Ridgeway, Jason
See Marlowe, Stephen

Ridgway, Keith 1965- .... **CLC 119**
See also CA 172

Riding, Laura .... **CLC 3, 7**
See Jackson, Laura (Riding)
See also RGAL 4

Riefenstahl, Berta Helene Amalia 1902-2003
See Riefenstahl, Leni
See also CA 108; 220

Riefenstahl, Leni .... **CLC 16, 190**
See Riefenstahl, Berta Helene Amalia

Riffe, Ernest
See Bergman, (Ernst) Ingmar

Riggs, (Rolla) Lynn
1899-1954 .... **NNAL; TCLC 56**
See also CA 144; DAM MULT; DLB 175

Riis, Jacob A(ugust) 1849-1914 ..... **TCLC 80**
See also CA 113; 168; DLB 23

Riley, James Whitcomb 1849-1916 .... **PC 48;
TCLC 51**
See also CA 118; 137; DAM POET; MAI-
CYA 1, 2; RGAL 4; SATA 17

Riley, Tex
See Creasey, John

Rilke, Rainer Maria 1875-1926 .... **PC 2;
TCLC 1, 6, 19**
See also CA 104; 132; CANR 62, 99; CD-
WLB 2; DA3; DAM POET; DLB 81; EW
9; EWL 3; MTCW 1, 2; PFS 19; RGWL
2, 3; TWA; WP

Rimbaud, (Jean Nicolas) Arthur
1854-1891 ... **NCLC 4, 35, 82; PC 3, 57;
WLC**
See also DA; DA3; DAB; DAC; DAM
MST, POET; DLB 217; EW 7; GFL 1789
to the Present; LMFS 2; RGWL 2, 3;
TWA; WP

Rinehart, Mary Roberts
1876-1958 .... **TCLC 52**
See also BPFB 3; CA 108; 166; RGAL 4;
RHW

Ringmaster, The
See Mencken, H(enry) L(ouis)

Ringwood, Gwen(dolyn Margaret) Pharis
1910-1984 .... **CLC 48**
See also CA 148; 112; DLB 88

Rio, Michel 1945(?)- .... **CLC 43**
See also CA 201

Rios, Alberto (Alvaro) 1952- .... **PC 57**
See also AMWS 4; CA 113; CANR 34, 79;
CP 7; DLB 122; HW 2; PFS 11

Ritsos, Giannes
See Ritsos, Yannis

Ritsos, Yannis 1909-1990 .... **CLC 6, 13, 31**
See also CA 77-80; 133; CANR 39, 61; EW
12; EWL 3; MTCW 1; RGWL 2, 3

Ritter, Erika 1948(?)- .... **CLC 52**
See also CD 5; CWD

Rivera, Jose Eustasio 1889-1928 ... **TCLC 35**
See also CA 162; EWL 3; HW 1, 2; LAW

Rivera, Tomas 1935-1984 .... **HLCS 2**
See also CA 49-52; CANR 32; DLB 82;
HW 1; LLW 1; RGAL 4; SSFS 15;
TCWW 2; WLIT 1

Rivers, Conrad Kent 1933-1968 .... **CLC 1**
See also BW 1; CA 85-88; DLB 41

Rivers, Elfrida
See Bradley, Marion Zimmer
See also GLL 1

Riverside, John
See Heinlein, Robert A(nson)

Rizal, Jose 1861-1896 .... **NCLC 27**

Roa Bastos, Augusto (Antonio)
1917- .... **CLC 45; HLC 2**
See also CA 131; CWW 2; DAM MULT;
DLB 113; EWL 3; HW 1; LAW; RGSF 2;
WLIT 1

Robbe-Grillet, Alain 1922- .... **CLC 1, 2, 4, 6,
8, 10, 14, 43, 128**
See also BPFB 3; CA 9-12R; CANR 33,
65, 115; CWW 2; DLB 83; EW 13; EWL
3; GFL 1789 to the Present; IDFW 3, 4;
MTCW 1, 2; RGWL 2, 3; SSFS 15

Robbins, Harold 1916-1997 .... **CLC 5**
See also BPFB 3; CA 73-76; 162; CANR
26, 54, 112; DA3; DAM NOV; MTCW 1,
2

Robbins, Thomas Eugene 1936-
See Robbins, Tom
See also CA 81-84; CANR 29, 59, 95; CN
7; CPW; CSW; DA3; DAM NOV, POP;
MTCW 1, 2

Robbins, Tom .... **CLC 9, 32, 64**
See Robbins, Thomas Eugene
See also AAYA 32; AMWS 10; BEST 90:3;
BPFB 3; DLBY 1980; MTCW 2

Robbins, Trina 1938- .... **CLC 21**
See also CA 128

Roberts, Charles G(eorge) D(ouglas)
1860-1943 .... **TCLC 8**
See also CA 105; 188; CLR 33; CWRI 5;
DLB 92; RGEL 2; RGSF 2; SATA 88;
SATA-Brief 29

Roberts, Elizabeth Madox
1886-1941 .... **TCLC 68**
See also CA 111; 166; CLR 100; CWRI 5;
DLB 9, 54, 102; RGAL 4; RHW; SATA
33; SATA-Brief 27; WCH

Roberts, Kate 1891-1985 .... **CLC 15**
See also CA 107; 116

Roberts, Keith (John Kingston)
1935-2000 .... **CLC 14**
See also BRWS 10; CA 25-28R; CANR 46;
DLB 261; SFW 4

Roberts, Kenneth (Lewis)
1885-1957 .... **TCLC 23**
See also CA 109; 199; DLB 9; RGAL 4;
RHW

Roberts, Michele (Brigitte) 1949- .... **CLC 48,
178**
See also CA 115; CANR 58, 120; CN 7;
DLB 231; FW

Robertson, Ellis
See Ellison, Harlan (Jay); Silverberg, Robert

Robertson, Thomas William
1829-1871 .... **NCLC 35**
See Robertson, Tom
See also DAM DRAM

Robertson, Tom
See Robertson, Thomas William
See also RGEL 2

Robeson, Kenneth
See Dent, Lester

Robinson, Edwin Arlington
1869-1935 .... **PC 1, 35; TCLC 5, 101**
See also AMW; CA 104; 133; CDALB
1865-1917; DA; DAC; DAM MST,
POET; DLB 54; EWL 3; EXPP; MTCW
1, 2; PAB; PFS 4; RGAL 4; WP

Robinson, Henry Crabb
1775-1867 .... **NCLC 15**
See also DLB 107

Robinson, Jill 1936- .... **CLC 10**
See also CA 102; CANR 120; INT CA-102

Robinson, Kim Stanley 1952- .... **CLC 34**
See also AAYA 26; CA 126; CANR 113;
CN 7; SATA 109; SCFW 2; SFW 4

Robinson, Lloyd
See Silverberg, Robert

Robinson, Marilynne 1944- ...... **CLC 25, 180**
See also CA 116; CANR 80; CN 7; DLB
206

Robinson, Mary 1758-1800 .... **NCLC 142**
See also DLB 158; FW

Robinson, Smokey .... **CLC 21**
See Robinson, William, Jr.

Robinson, William, Jr. 1940-
See Robinson, Smokey
See also CA 116

Robison, Mary 1949- .... **CLC 42, 98**
See also CA 113; 116; CANR 87; CN 7;
DLB 130; INT CA-116; RGSF 2

Rochester
See Wilmot, John
See also RGEL 2

Rod, Edouard 1857-1910 .... **TCLC 52**

Roddenberry, Eugene Wesley 1921-1991
See Roddenberry, Gene
See also CA 110; 135; CANR 37; SATA 45;
SATA-Obit 69

Roddenberry, Gene .... **CLC 17**
See Roddenberry, Eugene Wesley
See also AAYA 5; SATA-Obit 69

Rodgers, Mary 1931- .... **CLC 12**
See also BYA 5; CA 49-52; CANR 8, 55,
90; CLR 20; CWRI 5; INT CANR-8;
JRDA; MAICYA 1, 2; SATA 8, 130

Rodgers, W(illiam) R(obert)
1909-1969 .... **CLC 7**
See also CA 85-88; DLB 20; RGEL 2

Rodman, Eric
See Silverberg, Robert

Rodman, Howard 1920(?)-1985 .... **CLC 65**
See also CA 118

Rodman, Maia
See Wojciechowska, Maia (Teresa)

Rodo, Jose Enrique 1871(?)-1917 .... **HLCS 2**
See also CA 178; EWL 3; HW 2; LAW

Rodolph, Utto
See Ouologuem, Yambo

Rodriguez, Claudio 1934-1999 .... **CLC 10**
See also CA 188; DLB 134

Smith, A(rthur) J(ames) M(arshall)
1902-1980 .... **CLC 15**
See also CA 1-4R; 102; CANR 4; DAC;
DLB 88; RGEL 2

Smith, Adam 1723(?)-1790 .... **LC 36**
See also DLB 104, 252; RGEL 2

Smith, Alexander 1829-1867 .... **NCLC 59**
See also DLB 32, 55

Smith, Anna Deavere 1950- .... **CLC 86**
See also CA 133; CANR 103; CD 5; DFS 2

Smith, Betty (Wehner) 1904-1972 ... **CLC 19**
See also BPFB 3; BYA 3; CA 5-8R; 33-
36R; DLBY 1982; LAIT 3; RGAL 4;
SATA 6

Smith, Charlotte (Turner)
1749-1806 .... **NCLC 23, 115**
See also DLB 39, 109; RGEL 2; TEA

Smith, Clark Ashton 1893-1961 .... **CLC 43**
See also CA 143; CANR 81; FANT; HGG;
MTCW 2; SCFW 2; SFW 4; SUFW

Smith, Dave .... **CLC 22, 42**
See Smith, David (Jeddie)
See also CAAS 7; DLB 5

Smith, David (Jeddie) 1942-
See Smith, Dave
See also CA 49-52; CANR 1, 59, 120; CP
7; CSW; DAM POET

Smith, Florence Margaret 1902-1971
See Smith, Stevie
See also CA 17-18; 29-32R; CANR 35;
CAP 2; DAM POET; MTCW 1, 2; TEA

Smith, Iain Crichton 1928-1998 .... **CLC 64**
See also BRWS 9; CA 21-24R; 171; CN 7;
CP 7; DLB 40, 139; RGSF 2

Smith, John 1580(?)-1631 .... **LC 9**
See also DLB 24, 30; TUS

Smith, Johnston
See Crane, Stephen (Townley)

Smith, Joseph, Jr. 1805-1844 .... **NCLC 53**

Smith, Lee 1944- .... **CLC 25, 73**
See also CA 114; 119; CANR 46, 118;
CSW; DLB 143; DLBY 1983; EWL 3;
INT CA-119; RGAL 4

Smith, Martin
See Smith, Martin Cruz

Smith, Martin Cruz 1942- .. **CLC 25; NNAL**
See also BEST 89:4; BPFB 3; CA 85-88;
CANR 6, 23, 43, 65, 119; CMW 4; CPW;
DAM MULT, POP; HGG; INT CANR-
23; MTCW 2; RGAL 4

Smith, Patti 1946- .... **CLC 12**
See also CA 93-96; CANR 63

Smith, Pauline (Urmson)
1882-1959 .... **TCLC 25**
See also DLB 225; EWL 3

Smith, Rosamond
See Oates, Joyce Carol

Smith, Sheila Kaye
See Kaye-Smith, Sheila

Smith, Stevie .... **CLC 3, 8, 25, 44; PC 12**
See Smith, Florence Margaret
See also BRWS 2; DLB 20; EWL 3; MTCW
2; PAB; PFS 3; RGEL 2

Smith, Wilbur (Addison) 1933- .... **CLC 33**
See also CA 13-16R; CANR 7, 46, 66, 134;
CPW; MTCW 1, 2

Smith, William Jay 1918- .... **CLC 6**
See also AMWS 13; CA 5-8R; CANR 44,
106; CP 7; CSW; CWRI 5; DLB 5; MAI-
CYA 1, 2; SAAS 22; SATA 2, 68, 154;
SATA-Essay 154

Smith, Woodrow Wilson
See Kuttner, Henry

Smith, Zadie 1976- .... **CLC 158**
See also AAYA 50; CA 193

Smolenskin, Peretz 1842-1885 .... **NCLC 30**

Smollett, Tobias (George) 1721-1771 ... **LC 2,
46**
See also BRW 3; CDBLB 1660-1789; DLB
39, 104; RGEL 2; TEA

Snodgrass, W(illiam) D(e Witt)
1926- .... **CLC 2, 6, 10, 18, 68**
See also AMWS 6; CA 1-4R; CANR 6, 36,
65, 85; CP 7; DAM POET; DLB 5;
MTCW 1, 2; RGAL 4

Snorri Sturluson 1179-1241 .... **CMLC 56**
See also RGWL 2, 3

Snow, C(harles) P(ercy) 1905-1980 ... **CLC 1,
4, 6, 9, 13, 19**
See also BRW 7; CA 5-8R; 101; CANR 28;
CDBLB 1945-1960; DAM NOV; DLB 15,
77; DLBD 17; EWL 3; MTCW 1, 2;
RGEL 2; TEA

Snow, Frances Compton
See Adams, Henry (Brooks)

Snyder, Gary (Sherman) 1930- . **CLC 1, 2, 5,
9, 32, 120; PC 21**
See also AMWS 8; ANW; BG 3; CA 17-
20R; CANR 30, 60, 125; CP 7; DA3;
DAM POET; DLB 5, 16, 165, 212, 237,
275; EWL 3; MTCW 2; PFS 9, 19; RGAL
4; WP

Snyder, Zilpha Keatley 1927- .... **CLC 17**
See also AAYA 15; BYA 1; CA 9-12R;
CANR 38; CLR 31; JRDA; MAICYA 1,
2; SAAS 2; SATA 1, 28, 75, 110; SATA-
Essay 112; YAW

Soares, Bernardo
See Pessoa, Fernando (Antonio Nogueira)

Sobh, A.
See Shamlu, Ahmad

Sobh, Alef
See Shamlu, Ahmad

Sobol, Joshua 1939- .... **CLC 60**
See Sobol, Yehoshua
See also CA 200

Sobol, Yehoshua 1939-
See Sobol, Joshua
See also CWW 2

Socrates 470B.C.-399B.C. .... **CMLC 27**

Soderberg, Hjalmar 1869-1941 ...... **TCLC 39**
See also DLB 259; EWL 3; RGSF 2

Soderbergh, Steven 1963- .... **CLC 154**
See also AAYA 43

Sodergran, Edith (Irene) 1892-1923
See Soedergran, Edith (Irene)
See also CA 202; DLB 259; EW 11; EWL
3; RGWL 2, 3

Soedergran, Edith (Irene)
1892-1923 .... **TCLC 31**
See Sodergran, Edith (Irene)

Softly, Edgar
See Lovecraft, H(oward) P(hillips)

Softly, Edward
See Lovecraft, H(oward) P(hillips)

Sokolov, Alexander V(sevolodovich) 1943-
See Sokolov, Sasha
See also CA 73-76

Sokolov, Raymond 1941- .... **CLC 7**
See also CA 85-88

Sokolov, Sasha .... **CLC 59**
See Sokolov, Alexander V(sevolodovich)
See also CWW 2; DLB 285; EWL 3; RGWL
2, 3

Solo, Jay
See Ellison, Harlan (Jay)

Sologub, Fyodor .... **TCLC 9**
See Teternikov, Fyodor Kuzmich
See also EWL 3

Solomons, Ikey Esquir
See Thackeray, William Makepeace

Solomos, Dionysios 1798-1857 .... **NCLC 15**

Solwoska, Mara
See French, Marilyn

Solzhenitsyn, Aleksandr I(sayevich)
1918- .. **CLC 1, 2, 4, 7, 9, 10, 18, 26, 34,
78, 134; SSC 32; WLC**
See Solzhenitsyn, Aleksandr Isaevich
See also AAYA 49; AITN 1; BPFB 3; CA
69-72; CANR 40, 65, 116; DA; DA3;
DAB; DAC; DAM MST, NOV; DLB 302;
EW 13; EXPS; LAIT 4; MTCW 1, 2; NFS
6; RGSF 2; RGWL 2, 3; SSFS 9; TWA

Solzhenitsyn, Aleksandr Isaevich
See Solzhenitsyn, Aleksandr I(sayevich)
See also CWW 2; EWL 3

Somers, Jane
See Lessing, Doris (May)

Somerville, Edith Oenone
1858-1949 .... **SSC 56; TCLC 51**
See also CA 196; DLB 135; RGEL 2; RGSF
2

Somerville & Ross
See Martin, Violet Florence; Somerville,
Edith Oenone

Sommer, Scott 1951- .... **CLC 25**
See also CA 106

Sommers, Christina Hoff 1950- ...... **CLC 197**
See also CA 153; CANR 95

Sondheim, Stephen (Joshua) 1930- . **CLC 30,
39, 147; DC 22**
See also AAYA 11; CA 103; CANR 47, 67,
125; DAM DRAM; LAIT 4

Sone, Monica 1919- .... **AAL**

Song, Cathy 1955- .... **AAL; PC 21**
See also CA 154; CANR 118; CWP; DLB
169; EXPP; FW; PFS 5

Sontag, Susan 1933- .... **CLC 1, 2, 10, 13, 31,
105, 195**
See also AMWS 3; CA 17-20R; CANR 25,
51, 74, 97; CN 7; CPW; DA3; DAM POP;
DLB 2, 67; EWL 3; MAWW; MTCW 1,
2; RGAL 4; RHW; SSFS 10

Sophocles 496(?)B.C.-406(?)B.C. .... **CMLC 2,
47, 51; DC 1; WLCS**
See also AW 1; CDWLB 1; DA; DA3;
DAB; DAC; DAM DRAM, MST; DFS 1,
4, 8; DLB 176; LAIT 1; LATS 1:1; LMFS
1; RGWL 2, 3; TWA

Sordello 1189-1269 .... **CMLC 15**

Sorel, Georges 1847-1922 .... **TCLC 91**
See also CA 118; 188

Sorel, Julia
See Drexler, Rosalyn

Sorokin, Vladimir .... **CLC 59**
See Sorokin, Vladimir Georgievich

Sorokin, Vladimir Georgievich
See Sorokin, Vladimir
See also DLB 285

Sorrentino, Gilbert 1929- .. **CLC 3, 7, 14, 22,
40**
See also CA 77-80; CANR 14, 33, 115; CN
7; CP 7; DLB 5, 173; DLBY 1980; INT
CANR-14

Soseki
See Natsume, Soseki
See also MJW

Soto, Gary 1952- ... **CLC 32, 80; HLC 2; PC
28**
See also AAYA 10, 37; BYA 11; CA 119;
125; CANR 50, 74, 107; CLR 38; CP 7;
DAM MULT; DLB 82; EWL 3; EXPP;
HW 1, 2; INT CA-125; JRDA; LLW 1;
MAICYA 2; MAICYAS 1; MTCW 2; PFS
7; RGAL 4; SATA 80, 120; WYA; YAW

Soupault, Philippe 1897-1990 .... **CLC 68**
See also CA 116; 147; 131; EWL 3; GFL
1789 to the Present; LMFS 2

Souster, (Holmes) Raymond 1921- .... **CLC 5,
14**
See also CA 13-16R; CAAS 14; CANR 13,
29, 53; CP 7; DA3; DAC; DAM POET;
DLB 88; RGEL 2; SATA 63

Synge, (Edmund) J(ohn) M(illington)
   1871-1909 .... **DC 2; TCLC 6, 37**
      See also BRW 6; BRWR 1; CA 104; 141;
      CDBLB 1890-1914; DAM DRAM; DFS
      18; DLB 10, 19; EWL 3; RGEL 2; TEA;
      WLIT 4
Syruc, J.
      See Milosz, Czeslaw
Szirtes, George 1948- .... **CLC 46; PC 51**
      See also CA 109; CANR 27, 61, 117; CP 7
Szymborska, Wislawa 1923- ... **CLC 99, 190;**
      PC 44
      See also CA 154; CANR 91, 133; CDWLB
      4; CWP; CWW 2; DA3; DLB 232; DLBY
      1996; EWL 3; MTCW 2; PFS 15; RGWL
      3
T. O., Nik
      See Annensky, Innokenty (Fyodorovich)
Tabori, George 1914- .... **CLC 19**
      See also CA 49-52; CANR 4, 69; CBD; CD
      5; DLB 245
Tacitus c. 55-c. 117 .... **CMLC 56**
      See also AW 2; CDWLB 1; DLB 211;
      RGWL 2, 3
Tagore, Rabindranath 1861-1941 .... **PC 8;**
      SSC 48; TCLC 3, 53
      See also CA 104; 120; DA3; DAM DRAM,
      POET; EWL 3; MTCW 1, 2; PFS 18;
      RGEL 2; RGSF 2; RGWL 2, 3; TWA
Taine, Hippolyte Adolphe
      1828-1893 .... **NCLC 15**
      See also EW 7; GFL 1789 to the Present
Talayesva, Don C. 1890-(?) .... **NNAL**
Talese, Gay 1932- .... **CLC 37**
      See also AITN 1; CA 1-4R; CANR 9, 58;
      DLB 185; INT CANR-9; MTCW 1, 2
Tallent, Elizabeth (Ann) 1954- .... **CLC 45**
      See also CA 117; CANR 72; DLB 130
Tallmountain, Mary 1918-1997 .... **NNAL**
      See also CA 146; 161; DLB 193
Tally, Ted 1952- .... **CLC 42**
      See also CA 120; 124; CAD; CANR 125;
      CD 5; INT CA-124
Talvik, Heiti 1904-1947 .... **TCLC 87**
      See also EWL 3
Tamayo y Baus, Manuel
      1829-1898 .... **NCLC 1**
Tammsaare, A(nton) H(ansen)
      1878-1940 .... **TCLC 27**
      See also CA 164; CDWLB 4; DLB 220;
      EWL 3
Tam'si, Tchicaya U
      See Tchicaya, Gerald Felix
Tan, Amy (Ruth) 1952- . **AAL; CLC 59, 120,**
      151
      See also AAYA 9, 48; AMWS 10; BEST
      89:3; BPFB 3; CA 136; CANR 54, 105,
      132; CDALBS; CN 7; CPW 1; DA3;
      DAM MULT, NOV, POP; DLB 173;
      EXPN; FW; LAIT 3, 5; MTCW 2; NFS
      1, 13, 16; RGAL 4; SATA 75; SSFS 9;
      YAW
Tandem, Felix
      See Spitteler, Carl (Friedrich Georg)
Tanizaki, Jun'ichiro 1886-1965 ... **CLC 8, 14,**
      28; SSC 21
      See Tanizaki Jun'ichiro
      See also CA 93-96; 25-28R; MJW; MTCW
      2; RGSF 2; RGWL 2
Tanizaki Jun'ichiro
      See Tanizaki, Jun'ichiro
      See also DLB 180; EWL 3
Tannen, Deborah F. 1945- .... **CLC 206**
      See also CA 118; CANR 95
Tanner, William
      See Amis, Kingsley (William)
Tao Lao
      See Storni, Alfonsina

Tapahonso, Luci 1953- .... **NNAL; PC 65**
      See also CA 145; CANR 72, 127; DLB 175
Tarantino, Quentin (Jerome)
      1963- .... **CLC 125**
      See also AAYA 58; CA 171; CANR 125
Tarassoff, Lev
      See Troyat, Henri
Tarbell, Ida M(inerva) 1857-1944 . **TCLC 40**
      See also CA 122; 181; DLB 47
Tarkington, (Newton) Booth
      1869-1946 .... **TCLC 9**
      See also BPFB 3; BYA 3; CA 110; 143;
      CWRI 5; DLB 9, 102; MTCW 2; RGAL
      4; SATA 17
Tarkovskii, Andrei Arsen'evich
      See Tarkovsky, Andrei (Arsenyevich)
Tarkovsky, Andrei (Arsenyevich)
      1932-1986 .... **CLC 75**
      See also CA 127
Tartt, Donna 1963- .... **CLC 76**
      See also AAYA 56; CA 142
Tasso, Torquato 1544-1595 .... **LC 5, 94**
      See also EFS 2; EW 2; RGWL 2, 3
Tate, (John Orley) Allen 1899-1979 .. **CLC 2,**
      4, 6, 9, 11, 14, 24; PC 50
      See also AMW; CA 5-8R; 85-88; CANR
      32, 108; DLB 4, 45, 63; DLBD 17; EWL
      3; MTCW 1, 2; RGAL 4; RHW
Tate, Ellalice
      See Hibbert, Eleanor Alice Burford
Tate, James (Vincent) 1943- ..... **CLC 2, 6, 25**
      See also CA 21-24R; CANR 29, 57, 114;
      CP 7; DLB 5, 169; EWL 3; PFS 10, 15;
      RGAL 4; WP
Tate, Nahum 1652(?)-1715 .... **LC 109**
      See also DLB 80; RGEL 2
Tauler, Johannes c. 1300-1361 ...... **CMLC 37**
      See also DLB 179; LMFS 1
Tavel, Ronald 1940- .... **CLC 6**
      See also CA 21-24R; CAD; CANR 33; CD
      5
Taviani, Paolo 1931- .... **CLC 70**
      See also CA 153
Taylor, Bayard 1825-1878 .... **NCLC 89**
      See also DLB 3, 189, 250, 254; RGAL 4
Taylor, C(ecil) P(hilip) 1929-1981 .... **CLC 27**
      See also CA 25-28R; 105; CANR 47; CBD
Taylor, Edward 1642(?)-1729 . **LC 11; PC 63**
      See also AMW; DA; DAB; DAC; DAM
      MST, POET; DLB 24; EXPP; RGAL 4;
      TUS
Taylor, Eleanor Ross 1920- .... **CLC 5**
      See also CA 81-84; CANR 70
Taylor, Elizabeth 1932-1975 ..... **CLC 2, 4, 29**
      See also CA 13-16R; CANR 9, 70; DLB
      139; MTCW 1; RGEL 2; SATA 13
Taylor, Frederick Winslow
      1856-1915 .... **TCLC 76**
      See also CA 188
Taylor, Henry (Splawn) 1942- .... **CLC 44**
      See also CA 33-36R; CAAS 7; CANR 31;
      CP 7; DLB 5; PFS 10
Taylor, Kamala (Purnaiya) 1924-2004
      See Markandaya, Kamala
      See also CA 77-80; 227; NFS 13
Taylor, Mildred D(elois) 1943- .... **CLC 21**
      See also AAYA 10, 47; BW 1; BYA 3, 8;
      CA 85-88; CANR 25, 115; CLR 9, 59,
      90; CSW; DLB 52; JRDA; LAIT 3; MAI-
      CYA 1, 2; SAAS 5; SATA 135; WYA;
      YAW
Taylor, Peter (Hillsman) 1917-1994 .. **CLC 1,**
      4, 18, 37, 44, 50, 71; SSC 10, 84
      See also AMWS 5; BPFB 3; CA 13-16R;
      147; CANR 9, 50; CSW; DLB 218, 278;
      DLBY 1981, 1994; EWL 3; EXPS; INT
      CANR-9; MTCW 1, 2; RGSF 2; SSFS 9;
      TUS

Taylor, Robert Lewis 1912-1998 .... **CLC 14**
      See also CA 1-4R; 170; CANR 3, 64; SATA
      10
Tchekhov, Anton
      See Chekhov, Anton (Pavlovich)
Tchicaya, Gerald Felix 1931-1988 .. **CLC 101**
      See Tchicaya U Tam'si
      See also CA 129; 125; CANR 81
Tchicaya U Tam'si
      See Tchicaya, Gerald Felix
      See also EWL 3
Teasdale, Sara 1884-1933 .... **PC 31; TCLC 4**
      See also CA 104; 163; DLB 45; GLL 1;
      PFS 14; RGAL 4; SATA 32; TUS
Tecumseh 1768-1813 .... **NNAL**
      See also DAM MULT
Tegner, Esaias 1782-1846 .... **NCLC 2**
Fujiwara no Teika 1162-1241 .... **CMLC 73**
      See also DLB 203
Teilhard de Chardin, (Marie Joseph) Pierre
      1881-1955 .... **TCLC 9**
      See also CA 105; 210; GFL 1789 to the
      Present
Temple, Ann
      See Mortimer, Penelope (Ruth)
Tennant, Emma (Christina) 1937- .. **CLC 13,**
      52
      See also BRWS 9; CA 65-68; CAAS 9;
      CANR 10, 38, 59, 88; CN 7; DLB 14;
      EWL 3; SFW 4
Tenneshaw, S. M.
      See Silverberg, Robert
Tenney, Tabitha Gilman
      1762-1837 .... **NCLC 122**
      See also DLB 37, 200
Tennyson, Alfred 1809-1892 ... **NCLC 30, 65,**
      115; PC 6; WLC
      See also AAYA 50; BRW 4; CDBLB 1832-
      1890; DA; DA3; DAB; DAC; DAM MST,
      POET; DLB 32; EXPP; PAB; PFS 1, 2, 4,
      11, 15, 19; RGEL 2; TEA; WLIT 4; WP
Teran, Lisa St. Aubin de .... **CLC 36**
      See St. Aubin de Teran, Lisa
Terence c. 184B.C.-c. 159B.C. ...... **CMLC 14;**
      DC 7
      See also AW 1; CDWLB 1; DLB 211;
      RGWL 2, 3; TWA
Teresa de Jesus, St. 1515-1582 .... **LC 18**
Terkel, Louis 1912-
      See Terkel, Studs
      See also CA 57-60; CANR 18, 45, 67, 132;
      DA3; MTCW 1, 2
Terkel, Studs .... **CLC 38**
      See Terkel, Louis
      See also AAYA 32; AITN 1; MTCW 2; TUS
Terry, C. V.
      See Slaughter, Frank G(ill)
Terry, Megan 1932- .... **CLC 19; DC 13**
      See also CA 77-80; CABS 3; CAD; CANR
      43; CD 5; CWD; DFS 18; DLB 7, 249;
      GLL 2
Tertullian c. 155-c. 245 .... **CMLC 29**
Tertz, Abram
      See Sinyavsky, Andrei (Donatevich)
      See also RGSF 2
Tesich, Steve 1943(?)-1996 .... **CLC 40, 69**
      See also CA 105; 152; CAD; DLBY 1983
Tesla, Nikola 1856-1943 .... **TCLC 88**
Teternikov, Fyodor Kuzmich 1863-1927
      See Sologub, Fyodor
      See also CA 104
Tevis, Walter 1928-1984 .... **CLC 42**
      See also CA 113; SFW 4
Tey, Josephine .... **TCLC 14**
      See Mackintosh, Elizabeth
      See also DLB 77; MSW

Thackeray, William Makepeace
1811-1863 .... **NCLC 5, 14, 22, 43; WLC**
See also BRW 5; BRWC 2; CDBLB 1832-
1890; DA; DA3; DAB; DAC; DAM MST,
NOV; DLB 21, 55, 159, 163; NFS 13;
RGEL 2; SATA 23; TEA; WLIT 3

Thakura, Ravindranatha
See Tagore, Rabindranath

Thames, C. H.
See Marlowe, Stephen

Tharoor, Shashi 1956- .... **CLC 70**
See also CA 141; CANR 91; CN 7

Thelwell, Michael Miles 1939- .... **CLC 22**
See also BW 2; CA 101

Theobald, Lewis, Jr.
See Lovecraft, H(oward) P(hillips)

Theocritus c. 310B.C.- .... **CMLC 45**
See also AW 1; DLB 176; RGWL 2, 3

Theodorescu, Ion N. 1880-1967
See Arghezi, Tudor
See also CA 116

Theriault, Yves 1915-1983 .... **CLC 79**
See also CA 102; CCA 1; DAC; DAM
MST; DLB 88; EWL 3

Theroux, Alexander (Louis) 1939- .... **CLC 2,
25**
See also CA 85-88; CANR 20, 63; CN 7

Theroux, Paul (Edward) 1941- ..... **CLC 5, 8,
11, 15, 28, 46**
See also AAYA 28; AMWS 8; BEST 89:4;
BPFB 3; CA 33-36R; CANR 20, 45, 74,
133; CDALBS; CN 7; CPW 1; DA3;
DAM POP; DLB 2, 218; EWL 3; HGG;
MTCW 1, 2; RGAL 4; SATA 44, 109;
TUS

Thesen, Sharon 1946- .... **CLC 56**
See also CA 163; CANR 125; CP 7; CWP

Thespis fl. 6th cent. B.C.- .... **CMLC 51**
See also LMFS 1

Thevenin, Denis
See Duhamel, Georges

Thibault, Jacques Anatole Francois
1844-1924
See France, Anatole
See also CA 106; 127; DA3; DAM NOV;
MTCW 1, 2; TWA

Thiele, Colin (Milton) 1920- .... **CLC 17**
See also CA 29-32R; CANR 12, 28, 53,
105; CLR 27; DLB 289; MAICYA 1, 2;
SAAS 2; SATA 14, 72, 125; YAW

Thistlethwaite, Bel
See Wetherald, Agnes Ethelwyn

Thomas, Audrey (Callahan) 1935- .... **CLC 7,
13, 37, 107; SSC 20**
See also AITN 2; CA 21-24R; CAAS 19;
CANR 36, 58; CN 7; DLB 60; MTCW 1;
RGSF 2

Thomas, Augustus 1857-1934 .... **TCLC 97**

Thomas, D(onald) M(ichael) 1935- . **CLC 13,
22, 31, 132**
See also BPFB 3; BRWS 4; CA 61-64;
CAAS 11; CANR 17, 45, 75; CDBLB
1960 to Present; CN 7; CP 7; DA3; DLB
40, 207, 299; HGG; INT CANR-17;
MTCW 1, 2; SFW 4

Thomas, Dylan (Marlais) 1914-1953 .... **PC 2,
52; SSC 3, 44; TCLC 1, 8, 45, 105;
WLC**
See also AAYA 45; BRWS 1; CA 104; 120;
CANR 65; CDBLB 1945-1960; DA; DA3;
DAB; DAC; DAM DRAM, MST, POET;
DLB 13, 20, 139; EWL 3; EXPP; LAIT
3; MTCW 1, 2; PAB; PFS 1, 3, 8; RGEL
2; RGSF 2; SATA 60; TEA; WLIT 4; WP

Thomas, (Philip) Edward 1878-1917 . **PC 53;
TCLC 10**
See also BRW 6; BRWS 3; CA 106; 153;
DAM POET; DLB 19, 98, 156, 216; EWL
3; PAB; RGEL 2

Thomas, Joyce Carol 1938- .... **CLC 35**
See also AAYA 12, 54; BW 2, 3; CA 113;
116; CANR 48, 114, 135; CLR 19; DLB
33; INT CA-116; JRDA; MAICYA 1, 2;
MTCW 1, 2; SAAS 7; SATA 40, 78, 123,
137; SATA-Essay 137; WYA; YAW

Thomas, Lewis 1913-1993 .... **CLC 35**
See also ANW; CA 85-88; 143; CANR 38,
60; DLB 275; MTCW 1, 2

Thomas, M. Carey 1857-1935 .... **TCLC 89**
See also FW

Thomas, Paul
See Mann, (Paul) Thomas

Thomas, Piri 1928- .... **CLC 17; HLCS 2**
See also CA 73-76; HW 1; LLW 1

Thomas, R(onald) S(tuart)
1913-2000 .... **CLC 6, 13, 48**
See also CA 89-92; 189; CAAS 4; CANR
30; CDBLB 1960 to Present; CP 7; DAB;
DAM POET; DLB 27; EWL 3; MTCW 1;
RGEL 2

Thomas, Ross (Elmore) 1926-1995 .. **CLC 39**
See also CA 33-36R; 150; CANR 22, 63;
CMW 4

Thompson, Francis (Joseph)
1859-1907 .... **TCLC 4**
See also BRW 5; CA 104; 189; CDBLB
1890-1914; DLB 19; RGEL 2; TEA

Thompson, Francis Clegg
See Mencken, H(enry) L(ouis)

Thompson, Hunter S(tockton)
1937(?)- .... **CLC 9, 17, 40, 104**
See also AAYA 45; BEST 89:1; BPFB 3;
CA 17-20R; CANR 23, 46, 74, 77, 111,
133; CPW; CSW; DA3; DAM POP; DLB
185; MTCW 1, 2; TUS

Thompson, James Myers
See Thompson, Jim (Myers)

Thompson, Jim (Myers)
1906-1977(?) .... **CLC 69**
See also BPFB 3; CA 140; CMW 4; CPW;
DLB 226; MSW

Thompson, Judith .... **CLC 39**
See also CWD

Thomson, James 1700-1748 .... **LC 16, 29, 40**
See also BRWS 3; DAM POET; DLB 95;
RGEL 2

Thomson, James 1834-1882 .... **NCLC 18**
See also DAM POET; DLB 35; RGEL 2

Thoreau, Henry David 1817-1862 .. **NCLC 7,
21, 61, 138; PC 30; WLC**
See also AAYA 42; AMW; ANW; BYA 3;
CDALB 1640-1865; DA; DA3; DAB;
DAC; DAM MST; DLB 1, 183, 223, 270,
298; LAIT 2; LMFS 1; NCFS 3; RGAL
4; TUS

Thorndike, E. L.
See Thorndike, Edward L(ee)

Thorndike, Edward L(ee)
1874-1949 .... **TCLC 107**
See also CA 121

Thornton, Hall
See Silverberg, Robert

Thorpe, Adam 1956- .... **CLC 176**
See also CA 129; CANR 92; DLB 231

Thubron, Colin (Gerald Dryden)
1939- .... **CLC 163**
See also CA 25-28R; CANR 12, 29, 59, 95;
CN 7; DLB 204, 231

Thucydides c. 455B.C.-c. 395B.C. .. **CMLC 17**
See also AW 1; DLB 176; RGWL 2, 3

Thumboo, Edwin Nadason 1933- .... **PC 30**
See also CA 194

Thurber, James (Grover)
1894-1961 .. **CLC 5, 11, 25, 125; SSC 1,
47**
See also AAYA 56; AMWS 1; BPFB 3;
BYA 5; CA 73-76; CANR 17, 39; CDALB
1929-1941; CWRI 5; DA; DA3; DAB;

DAC; DAM DRAM, MST, NOV; DLB 4,
11, 22, 102; EWL 3; EXPS; FANT; LAIT
3; MAICYA 1, 2; MTCW 1, 2; RGAL 4;
RGSF 2; SATA 13; SSFS 1, 10, 19;
SUFW; TUS

Thurman, Wallace (Henry)
1902-1934 .... **BLC 3; HR 3; TCLC 6**
See also BW 1, 3; CA 104; 124; CANR 81;
DAM MULT; DLB 51

Tibullus c. 54B.C.-c. 18B.C. .... **CMLC 36**
See also AW 2; DLB 211; RGWL 2, 3

Ticheburn, Cheviot
See Ainsworth, William Harrison

Tieck, (Johann) Ludwig
1773-1853 .... **NCLC 5, 46; SSC 31**
See also CDWLB 2; DLB 90; EW 5; IDTP;
RGSF 2; RGWL 2, 3; SUFW

Tiger, Derry
See Ellison, Harlan (Jay)

Tilghman, Christopher 1946- .... **CLC 65**
See also CA 159; CANR 135; CSW; DLB
244

Tillich, Paul (Johannes)
1886-1965 .... **CLC 131**
See also CA 5-8R; 25-28R; CANR 33;
MTCW 1, 2

Tillinghast, Richard (Williford)
1940- .... **CLC 29**
See also CA 29-32R; CAAS 23; CANR 26,
51, 96; CP 7; CSW

Timrod, Henry 1828-1867 .... **NCLC 25**
See also DLB 3, 248; RGAL 4

Tindall, Gillian (Elizabeth) 1938- ...... **CLC 7**
See also CA 21-24R; CANR 11, 65, 107;
CN 7

Tiptree, James, Jr. .... **CLC 48, 50**
See Sheldon, Alice Hastings Bradley
See also DLB 8; SCFW 2; SFW 4

Tirone Smith, Mary-Ann 1944- .... **CLC 39**
See also CA 118; 136; CANR 113; SATA
143

Tirso de Molina 1580(?)-1648 .... **DC 13;
HLCS 2; LC 73**
See also RGWL 2, 3

Titmarsh, Michael Angelo
See Thackeray, William Makepeace

**Tocqueville, Alexis (Charles Henri Maurice
Clerel Comte) de** 1805-1859 .. **NCLC 7,
63**
See also EW 6; GFL 1789 to the Present;
TWA

Toer, Pramoedya Ananta 1925- ...... **CLC 186**
See also CA 197; RGWL 3

Toffler, Alvin 1928- .... **CLC 168**
See also CA 13-16R; CANR 15, 46, 67;
CPW; DAM POP; MTCW 1, 2

Toibin, Colm
See Toibin, Colm
See also DLB 271

Toibin, Colm 1955- .... **CLC 162**
See Toibin, Colm
See also CA 142; CANR 81

Tolkien, J(ohn) R(onald) R(euel)
1892-1973 .... **CLC 1, 2, 3, 8, 12, 38;
TCLC 137; WLC**
See also AAYA 10; AITN 1; BPFB 3;
BRWC 2; BRWS 2; CA 17-18; 45-48;
CANR 36, 134; CAP 2; CDBLB 1914-
1945; CLR 56; CPW 1; CWRI 5; DA;
DA3; DAB; DAC; DAM MST, NOV,
POP; DLB 15, 160, 255; EFS 2; EWL 3;
FANT; JRDA; LAIT 1; LATS 1:2; LMFS
2; MAICYA 1, 2; MTCW 1, 2; NFS 8;
RGEL 2; SATA 2, 32, 100; SATA-Obit
24; SFW 4; SUFW; TEA; WCH; WYA;
YAW

Toller, Ernst 1893-1939 .... **TCLC 10**
See also CA 107; 186; DLB 124; EWL 3;
RGWL 2, 3

Walker, George F. 1947- .... **CLC 44, 61**
See also CA 103; CANR 21, 43, 59; CD 5; DAB; DAC; DAM MST; DLB 60

Walker, Joseph A. 1935- .... **CLC 19**
See also BW 1, 3; CA 89-92; CAD; CANR 26; CD 5; DAM DRAM, MST; DFS 12; DLB 38

Walker, Margaret (Abigail)
1915-1998 .... **BLC; CLC 1, 6; PC 20; TCLC 129**
See also AFAW 1, 2; BW 2, 3; CA 73-76; 172; CANR 26, 54, 76; CN 7; CP 7; CSW; DAM MULT; DLB 76, 152; EXPP; FW; MTCW 1, 2; RGAL 4; RHW

Walker, Ted .... **CLC 13**
See Walker, Edward Joseph
See also DLB 40

Wallace, David Foster 1962- ... **CLC 50, 114; SSC 68**
See also AAYA 50; AMWS 10; CA 132; CANR 59, 133; DA3; MTCW 2

Wallace, Dexter
See Masters, Edgar Lee

Wallace, (Richard Horatio) Edgar
1875-1932 .... **TCLC 57**
See also CA 115; 218; CMW 4; DLB 70; MSW; RGEL 2

Wallace, Irving 1916-1990 .... **CLC 7, 13**
See also AITN 1; BPFB 3; CA 1-4R; 132; CAAS 1; CANR 1, 27; CPW; DAM NOV, POP; INT CANR-27; MTCW 1, 2

Wallant, Edward Lewis 1926-1962 ... **CLC 5, 10**
See also CA 1-4R; CANR 22; DLB 2, 28, 143, 299; EWL 3; MTCW 1, 2; RGAL 4

Wallas, Graham 1858-1932 .... **TCLC 91**

Waller, Edmund 1606-1687 .... **LC 86**
See also BRW 2; DAM POET; DLB 126; PAB; RGEL 2

Walley, Byron
See Card, Orson Scott

Walpole, Horace 1717-1797 .... **LC 2, 49**
See also BRW 3; DLB 39, 104, 213; HGG; LMFS 1; RGEL 2; SUFW 1; TEA

Walpole, Hugh (Seymour)
1884-1941 .... **TCLC 5**
See also CA 104; 165; DLB 34; HGG; MTCW 2; RGEL 2; RHW

Walrond, Eric (Derwent) 1898-1966 .... **HR 3**
See also BW 1; CA 125; DLB 51

Walser, Martin 1927- .... **CLC 27, 183**
See also CA 57-60; CANR 8, 46; CWW 2; DLB 75, 124; EWL 3

Walser, Robert 1878-1956 ..... **SSC 20; TCLC 18**
See also CA 118; 165; CANR 100; DLB 66; EWL 3

Walsh, Gillian Paton
See Paton Walsh, Gillian

Walsh, Jill Paton .... **CLC 35**
See Paton Walsh, Gillian
See also CLR 2, 65; WYA

Walter, Villiam Christian
See Andersen, Hans Christian

Walters, Anna L(ee) 1946- .... **NNAL**
See also CA 73-76

Walther von der Vogelweide c.
1170-1228 .... **CMLC 56**

Walton, Izaak 1593-1683 .... **LC 72**
See also BRW 2; CDBLB Before 1660; DLB 151, 213; RGEL 2

Wambaugh, Joseph (Aloysius), Jr.
1937- .... **CLC 3, 18**
See also AITN 1; BEST 89:3; BPFB 3; CA 33-36R; CANR 42, 65, 115; CMW 4; CPW 1; DA3; DAM NOV, POP; DLB 6; DLBY 1983; MSW; MTCW 1, 2

Wang Wei 699(?)-761(?) .... **PC 18**
See also TWA

Warburton, William 1698-1779 .... **LC 97**
See also DLB 104

Ward, Arthur Henry Sarsfield 1883-1959
See Rohmer, Sax
See also CA 108; 173; CMW 4; HGG

Ward, Douglas Turner 1930- .... **CLC 19**
See also BW 1; CA 81-84; CAD; CANR 27; CD 5; DLB 7, 38

Ward, E. D.
See Lucas, E(dward) V(errall)

Ward, Mrs. Humphry 1851-1920
See Ward, Mary Augusta
See also RGEL 2

Ward, Mary Augusta 1851-1920 ... **TCLC 55**
See Ward, Mrs. Humphry
See also DLB 18

Ward, Nathaniel 1578(?)-1652 .... **LC 114**
See also DLB 24

Ward, Peter
See Faust, Frederick (Schiller)

Warhol, Andy 1928(?)-1987 .... **CLC 20**
See also AAYA 12; BEST 89:4; CA 89-92; 121; CANR 34

Warner, Francis (Robert le Plastrier)
1937- .... **CLC 14**
See also CA 53-56; CANR 11

Warner, Marina 1946- .... **CLC 59**
See also CA 65-68; CANR 21, 55, 118; CN 7; DLB 194

Warner, Rex (Ernest) 1905-1986 ...... **CLC 45**
See also CA 89-92; 119; DLB 15; RGEL 2; RHW

Warner, Susan (Bogert)
1819-1885 .... **NCLC 31, 146**
See also DLB 3, 42, 239, 250, 254

Warner, Sylvia (Constance) Ashton
See Ashton-Warner, Sylvia (Constance)

Warner, Sylvia Townsend
1893-1978 .. **CLC 7, 19; SSC 23; TCLC 131**
See also BRWS 7; CA 61-64; 77-80; CANR 16, 60, 104; DLB 34, 139; EWL 3; FANT; FW; MTCW 1, 2; RGEL 2; RGSF 2; RHW

Warren, Mercy Otis 1728-1814 ..... **NCLC 13**
See also DLB 31, 200; RGAL 4; TUS

Warren, Robert Penn 1905-1989 .. **CLC 1, 4, 6, 8, 10, 13, 18, 39, 53, 59; PC 37; SSC 4, 58; WLC**
See also AITN 1; AMW; AMWC 2; BPFB 3; BYA 1; CA 13-16R; 129; CANR 10, 47; CDALB 1968-1988; DA; DA3; DAB; DAC; DAM MST, NOV, POET; DLB 2, 48, 152; DLBY 1980, 1989; EWL 3; INT CANR-10; MTCW 1, 2; NFS 13; RGAL 4; RGSF 2; RHW; SATA 46; SATA-Obit 63; SSFS 8; TUS

Warrigal, Jack
See Furphy, Joseph

Warshofsky, Isaac
See Singer, Isaac Bashevis

Warton, Joseph 1722-1800 .... **NCLC 118**
See also DLB 104, 109; RGEL 2

Warton, Thomas 1728-1790 .... **LC 15, 82**
See also DAM POET; DLB 104, 109; RGEL 2

Waruk, Kona
See Harris, (Theodore) Wilson

Warung, Price .... **TCLC 45**
See Astley, William
See also DLB 230; RGEL 2

Warwick, Jarvis
See Garner, Hugh
See also CCA 1

Washington, Alex
See Harris, Mark

Washington, Booker T(aliaferro)
1856-1915 .... **BLC 3; TCLC 10**
See also BW 1; CA 114; 125; DA3; DAM MULT; LAIT 2; RGAL 4; SATA 28

Washington, George 1732-1799 .... **LC 25**
See also DLB 31

Wassermann, (Karl) Jakob
1873-1934 .... **TCLC 6**
See also CA 104; 163; DLB 66; EWL 3

Wasserstein, Wendy 1950- ... **CLC 32, 59, 90, 183; DC 4**
See also CA 121; 129; CABS 3; CAD; CANR 53, 75, 128; CD 5; CWD; DA3; DAM DRAM; DFS 5, 17; DLB 228; EWL 3; FW; INT CA-129; MTCW 1, 2; SATA 94

Waterhouse, Keith (Spencer) 1929- . **CLC 47**
See also CA 5-8R; CANR 38, 67, 109; CBD; CN 7; DLB 13, 15; MTCW 1, 2

Waters, Frank (Joseph) 1902-1995 .. **CLC 88**
See also CA 5-8R; 149; CAAS 13; CANR 3, 18, 63, 121; DLB 212; DLBY 1986; RGAL 4; TCWW 2

Waters, Mary C. .... **CLC 70**

Waters, Roger 1944- .... **CLC 35**

Watkins, Frances Ellen
See Harper, Frances Ellen Watkins

Watkins, Gerrold
See Malzberg, Barry N(athaniel)

Watkins, Gloria Jean 1952(?)- .... **CLC 94**
See also BW 2; CA 143; CANR 87, 126; DLB 246; MTCW 2; SATA 115

Watkins, Paul 1964- .... **CLC 55**
See also CA 132; CANR 62, 98

Watkins, Vernon Phillips
1906-1967 .... **CLC 43**
See also CA 9-10; 25-28R; CAP 1; DLB 20; EWL 3; RGEL 2

Watson, Irving S.
See Mencken, H(enry) L(ouis)

Watson, John H.
See Farmer, Philip Jose

Watson, Richard F.
See Silverberg, Robert

Watts, Ephraim
See Horne, Richard Henry Hengist

Watts, Isaac 1674-1748 .... **LC 98**
See also DLB 95; RGEL 2; SATA 52

Waugh, Auberon (Alexander)
1939-2001 .... **CLC 7**
See also CA 45-48; 192; CANR 6, 22, 92; DLB 14, 194

Waugh, Evelyn (Arthur St. John)
1903-1966 .. **CLC 1, 3, 8, 13, 19, 27, 44, 107; SSC 41; WLC**
See also BPFB 3; BRW 7; CA 85-88; 25-28R; CANR 22; CDBLB 1914-1945; DA; DA3; DAB; DAC; DAM MST, NOV, POP; DLB 15, 162, 195; EWL 3; MTCW 1, 2; NFS 13, 17; RGEL 2; RGSF 2; TEA; WLIT 4

Waugh, Harriet 1944- .... **CLC 6**
See also CA 85-88; CANR 22

Ways, C. R.
See Blount, Roy (Alton), Jr.

Waystaff, Simon
See Swift, Jonathan

Webb, Beatrice (Martha Potter)
1858-1943 .... **TCLC 22**
See also CA 117; 162; DLB 190; FW

Webb, Charles (Richard) 1939- .... **CLC 7**
See also CA 25-28R; CANR 114

Webb, Frank J. .... **NCLC 143**
See also DLB 50

Webb, James H(enry), Jr. 1946- ...... **CLC 22**
See also CA 81-84

Webb, Mary Gladys (Meredith)
1881-1927 .... **TCLC 24**
See also CA 182; 123; DLB 34; FW

Wharton, Edith (Newbold Jones)
    1862-1937 ... SSC 6, 84; TCLC 3, 9, 27, 53, 129, 149; WLC
    See also AAYA 25; AMW; AMWC 2; AMWR 1; BPFB 3; CA 104; 132; CDALB 1865-1917; DA; DA3; DAB; DAC; DAM MST, NOV; DLB 4, 9, 12, 78, 189; DLBD 13; EWL 3; EXPS; HGG; LAIT 2, 3; LATS 1:1; MAWW; MTCW 1, 2; NFS 5, 11, 15, 20; RGAL 4; RGSF 2; RHW; SSFS 6, 7; SUFW; TUS

Wharton, James
    See Mencken, H(enry) L(ouis)

Wharton, William (a pseudonym) . CLC 18, 37
    See also CA 93-96; DLBY 1980; INT CA-93-96

Wheatley (Peters), Phillis
    1753(?)-1784 ... BLC 3; LC 3, 50; PC 3; WLC
    See also AFAW 1, 2; CDALB 1640-1865; DA; DA3; DAC; DAM MST, MULT, POET; DLB 31, 50; EXPP; PFS 13; RGAL 4

Wheelock, John Hall 1886-1978 .... CLC 14
    See also CA 13-16R; 77-80; CANR 14; DLB 45

Whim-Wham
    See Curnow, (Thomas) Allen (Monro)

White, Babington
    See Braddon, Mary Elizabeth

White, E(lwyn) B(rooks)
    1899-1985 .... CLC 10, 34, 39
    See also AITN 2; AMWS 1; CA 13-16R; 116; CANR 16, 37; CDALBS; CLR 1, 21; CPW; DA3; DAM POP; DLB 11, 22; EWL 3; FANT; MAICYA 1, 2; MTCW 1, 2; NCFS 5; RGAL 4; SATA 2, 29, 100; SATA-Obit 44; TUS

White, Edmund (Valentine III)
    1940- .... CLC 27, 110
    See also AAYA 7; CA 45-48; CANR 3, 19, 36, 62, 107, 133; CN 7; DA3; DAM POP; DLB 227; MTCW 1, 2

White, Hayden V. 1928- .... CLC 148
    See also CA 128; CANR 135; DLB 246

White, Patrick (Victor Martindale)
    1912-1990 ...... CLC 3, 4, 5, 7, 9, 18, 65, 69; SSC 39
    See also BRWS 1; CA 81-84; 132; CANR 43; DLB 260; EWL 3; MTCW 1; RGEL 2; RGSF 2; RHW; TWA; WWE 1

White, Phyllis Dorothy James 1920-
    See James, P. D.
    See also CA 21-24R; CANR 17, 43, 65, 112; CMW 4; CN 7; CPW; DA3; DAM POP; MTCW 1, 2; TEA

White, T(erence) H(anbury)
    1906-1964 .... CLC 30
    See also AAYA 22; BPFB 3; BYA 4, 5; CA 73-76; CANR 37; DLB 160; FANT; JRDA; LAIT 1; MAICYA 1, 2; RGEL 2; SATA 12; SUFW 1; YAW

White, Terence de Vere 1912-1994 ... CLC 49
    See also CA 49-52; 145; CANR 3

White, Walter
    See White, Walter F(rancis)

White, Walter F(rancis) 1893-1955 ... BLC 3; HR 3; TCLC 15
    See also BW 1; CA 115; 124; DAM MULT; DLB 51

White, William Hale 1831-1913
    See Rutherford, Mark
    See also CA 121; 189

Whitehead, Alfred North
    1861-1947 .... TCLC 97
    See also CA 117; 165; DLB 100, 262

Whitehead, E(dward) A(nthony)
    1933- .... CLC 5
    See also CA 65-68; CANR 58, 118; CBD; CD 5

Whitehead, Ted
    See Whitehead, E(dward) A(nthony)

Whiteman, Roberta J. Hill 1947- ...... NNAL
    See also CA 146

Whitemore, Hugh (John) 1936- .... CLC 37
    See also CA 132; CANR 77; CBD; CD 5; INT CA-132

Whitman, Sarah Helen (Power)
    1803-1878 .... NCLC 19
    See also DLB 1, 243

Whitman, Walt(er) 1819-1892 .. NCLC 4, 31, 81; PC 3; WLC
    See also AAYA 42; AMW; AMWR 1; CDALB 1640-1865; DA; DA3; DAB; DAC; DAM MST, POET; DLB 3, 64, 224, 250; EXPP; LAIT 2; LMFS 1; PAB; PFS 2, 3, 13; RGAL 4; SATA 20; TUS; WP; WYAS 1

Whitney, Phyllis A(yame) 1903- .... CLC 42
    See also AAYA 36; AITN 2; BEST 90:3; CA 1-4R; CANR 3, 25, 38, 60; CLR 59; CMW 4; CPW; DA3; DAM POP; JRDA; MAICYA 1, 2; MTCW 2; RHW; SATA 1, 30; YAW

Whittemore, (Edward) Reed, Jr.
    1919- .... CLC 4
    See also CA 9-12R, 219; CAAE 219; CAAS 8; CANR 4, 119; CP 7; DLB 5

Whittier, John Greenleaf
    1807-1892 .... NCLC 8, 59
    See also AMWS 1; DLB 1, 243; RGAL 4

Whittlebot, Hernia
    See Coward, Noel (Peirce)

Wicker, Thomas Grey 1926-
    See Wicker, Tom
    See also CA 65-68; CANR 21, 46

Wicker, Tom .... CLC 7
    See Wicker, Thomas Grey

Wideman, John Edgar 1941- ... BLC 3; CLC 5, 34, 36, 67, 122; SSC 62
    See also AFAW 1, 2; AMWS 10; BPFB 3; BW 2, 3; CA 85-88; CANR 14, 42, 67, 109; CN 7; DAM MULT; DLB 33, 143; MTCW 2; RGAL 4; RGSF 2; SSFS 6, 12

Wiebe, Rudy (Henry) 1934- .. CLC 6, 11, 14, 138
    See also CA 37-40R; CANR 42, 67, 123; CN 7; DAC; DAM MST; DLB 60; RHW

Wieland, Christoph Martin
    1733-1813 .... NCLC 17
    See also DLB 97; EW 4; LMFS 1; RGWL 2, 3

Wiene, Robert 1881-1938 .... TCLC 56

Wieners, John 1934- .... CLC 7
    See also BG 3; CA 13-16R; CP 7; DLB 16; WP

Wiesel, Elie(zer) 1928- .... CLC 3, 5, 11, 37, 165; WLCS
    See also AAYA 7, 54; AITN 1; CA 5-8R; CAAS 4; CANR 8, 40, 65, 125; CDALBS; CWW 2; DA; DA3; DAB; DAC; DAM MST, NOV; DLB 83, 299; DLBY 1987; EWL 3; INT CANR-8; LAIT 4; MTCW 1, 2; NCFS 4; NFS 4; RGWL 3; SATA 56; YAW

Wiggins, Marianne 1947- .... CLC 57
    See also BEST 89:3; CA 130; CANR 60

Wigglesworth, Michael 1631-1705 .... LC 106
    See also DLB 24; RGAL 4

Wiggs, Susan .... CLC 70
    See also CA 201

Wight, James Alfred 1916-1995
    See Herriot, James
    See also CA 77-80; SATA 55; SATA-Brief 44

Wilbur, Richard (Purdy) 1921- ..... CLC 3, 6, 9, 14, 53, 110; PC 51
    See also AMWS 3; CA 1-4R; CABS 2; CANR 2, 29, 76, 93; CDALBS; CP 7; DA; DAB; DAC; DAM MST, POET; DLB 5, 169; EWL 3; EXPP; INT CANR-29; MTCW 1, 2; PAB; PFS 11, 12, 16; RGAL 4; SATA 9, 108; WP

Wild, Peter 1940- .... CLC 14
    See also CA 37-40R; CP 7; DLB 5

Wilde, Oscar (Fingal O'Flahertie Wills)
    1854(?)-1900 .... DC 17; SSC 11, 77; TCLC 1, 8, 23, 41; WLC
    See also AAYA 49; BRW 5; BRWC 1, 2; BRWR 2; BYA 15; CA 104; 119; CANR 112; CDBLB 1890-1914; DA; DA3; DAB; DAC; DAM DRAM, MST, NOV; DFS 4, 8, 9; DLB 10, 19, 34, 57, 141, 156, 190; EXPS; FANT; LATS 1:1; NFS 20; RGEL 2; RGSF 2; SATA 24; SSFS 7; SUFW; TEA; WCH; WLIT 4

Wilder, Billy .... CLC 20
    See Wilder, Samuel
    See also DLB 26

Wilder, Samuel 1906-2002
    See Wilder, Billy
    See also CA 89-92; 205

Wilder, Stephen
    See Marlowe, Stephen

Wilder, Thornton (Niven)
    1897-1975 .. CLC 1, 5, 6, 10, 15, 35, 82; DC 1, 24; WLC
    See also AAYA 29; AITN 2; AMW; CA 13-16R; 61-64; CAD; CANR 40, 132; CDALBS; DA; DA3; DAB; DAC; DAM DRAM, MST, NOV; DFS 1, 4, 16; DLB 4, 7, 9, 228; DLBY 1997; EWL 3; LAIT 3; MTCW 1, 2; RGAL 4; RHW; WYAS 1

Wilding, Michael 1942- ...... CLC 73; SSC 50
    See also CA 104; CANR 24, 49, 106; CN 7; RGSF 2

Wiley, Richard 1944- .... CLC 44
    See also CA 121; 129; CANR 71

Wilhelm, Kate .... CLC 7
    See Wilhelm, Katie (Gertrude)
    See also AAYA 20; BYA 16; CAAS 5; DLB 8; INT CANR-17; SCFW 2

Wilhelm, Katie (Gertrude) 1928-
    See Wilhelm, Kate
    See also CA 37-40R; CANR 17, 36, 60, 94; MTCW 1; SFW 4

Wilkins, Mary
    See Freeman, Mary E(leanor) Wilkins

Willard, Nancy 1936- .... CLC 7, 37
    See also BYA 5; CA 89-92; CANR 10, 39, 68, 107; CLR 5; CWP; CWRI 5; DLB 5, 52; FANT; MAICYA 1, 2; MTCW 1; SATA 37, 71, 127; SATA-Brief 30; SUFW 2

William of Malmesbury c. 1090B.C.-c. 1140B.C. .... CMLC 57

William of Ockham 1290-1349 ..... CMLC 32

Williams, Ben Ames 1889-1953 ..... TCLC 89
    See also CA 183; DLB 102

Williams, C(harles) K(enneth)
    1936- .... CLC 33, 56, 148
    See also CA 37-40R; CAAS 26; CANR 57, 106; CP 7; DAM POET; DLB 5

Williams, Charles
    See Collier, James Lincoln

Williams, Charles (Walter Stansby)
    1886-1945 .... TCLC 1, 11
    See also BRWS 9; CA 104; 163; DLB 100, 153, 255; FANT; RGEL 2; SUFW 1

Williams, Ella Gwendolen Rees
    See Rhys, Jean

Williams, (George) Emlyn
    1905-1987 .... CLC 15
    See also CA 104; 123; CANR 36; DAM DRAM; DLB 10, 77; IDTP; MTCW 1

Literary Criticism Series
Cumulative Topic Index

This index lists all topic entries in Gale's *Children's Literature Review* (CLR), *Classical and Medieval Literature Criticism* (CMLC), *Contemporary Literary Criticism* (CLC), *Drama Criticism* (DC), *Literature Criticism from 1400 to 1800* (LC), *Nineteenth-Century Literature Criticism* (NCLC), *Short Story Criticism* (SSC), and *Twentieth-Century Literary Criticism* (TCLC). The index also lists topic entries in the Gale Critical Companion Collection, which includes the following publications: *The Beat Generation* (BG), and *Harlem Renaissance* (HR).

Topic Index

Topic Index

NCLC Cumulative Nationality Index

NCLC-161 Title Index

ISBN 0-7876-8645-X

90000

9 780787 686451